# California

## THE ROUGH GUIDE

D0444366

There are more than seventy Rough Guide titles covering
destinations from Amsterdam to Zimbabwe

**Forthcoming titles include**
China • Jamaica • New Zealand • South Africa

**Rough Guide Reference Series**
Classical Music • The Internet • Jazz • World Music

**Rough Guide Phrasebooks**
Czech • French • German • Greek • Italian
Mexican Spanish • Portuguese • Spanish • Thai • Turkish

**Rough Guides on the Internet**
http://www.roughguides.com/
http://www.hotwired.com/rough

**Rough Guide Credits**

| | |
|---|---|
| Text Editor: | Annie Shaw |
| Series Editor: | Mark Ellingham |
| Editorial: | Martin Dunford, Jonathan Buckley, Jo Mead, Samantha Cook, Alison Cowan, Amanda Tomlin, Lemisse Al-Hafidh, Catherine McHale, Vivienne Heller, Paul Gray |
| Online editors: | Alan Spicer (UK), Andrew Rosenberg (US) |
| Production: | Susanne Hillen, Andy Hilliard, Melissa Flack, Judy Pang, Link Hall, Nicola Williamson, David Callier, Helen Ostick |
| Finance: | John Fisher, Celia Crowley, Catherine Gillespie |
| Marketing & Publicity: | Richard Trillo, Simon Carloss (UK), Jean-Marie Kelly, Jeff Kaye (US) |
| Administration: | Tania Hummel |

For this edition thanks must go to all those readers who have taken time to write in with comments, particularly: Kenneth Bradley; Carl Brady; Bergit Breid; Joachim Buscher; Mark Colby; Betty Dobson; Kirk Lalwani; Marc Lankhorst; Duncan Lissett; Ian Ogilvie; Edward Parry; Peter Quilter; Patrick Rawles; Judith Ravenscroft; Helen Williams; Geoff Winter and Angela Wolferts. Thanks also to Wendy Ferguson, co-author on the first two editions; Catherine Brindley and Bruce P Gerstman who contributed so fully to this edition; Huw Molseed at *Booktrust*, Susanne Hillen, Judy Pang, Nicola Williamson and Helen Ostick for production; Melissa Flack and David Callier for skilful cartography and a lot of patience; Julie Soller and Andrew Rosenberg for meticulous fact-checking; and Robin Sawers for proof-reading. Last but not least, continued thanks are due to Martin Dunford for editing the first edition, Greg Ward for the second, and Samantha Cook for the third.

**Paul Whitfield** would In addition, like to thank Toby Pyle at the Hostelling International head office, Judy Boyce at the Russian River Chamber of Commerce, and Annie for beavering away organizing his trip.

This fourth edition published June 1996 by Rough Guides Ltd, 1 Mercer Street, London WC2H 9QJ.

Distributed by The Penguin Group:
Penguin Books Ltd, 27 Wrights Lane, London W8 5TZ
Penguin Books USA Inc., 375 Hudson Street, New York 10014, USA
Penguin Books Australia Ltd, 487 Maroondah Highway, PO Box 257, Ringwood, Victoria 3134, Australia
Penguin Books Canada Ltd, 10 Alcorn Avenue, Toronto, Ontario, Canada M4V 1E4
Penguin Books (NZ) Ltd, 182–190 Wairau Road, Auckland 10, New Zealand

Typeset in Linotron Univers and Century Old Style to an original design by Andrew Oliver.
Printed in the UK by The Bath Press

**Illustrations** in Part One and Part Four by Edward Briant
Basics illustration by Cathie Felstead; Contexts illustration by Sally Davies.

A catalogue record for this book is available from the British Library
ISBN 1-85828-181-4

# California

## THE ROUGH GUIDE

Written and researched by
**Deborah Bosley, Jamie Jensen,
Mick Sinclair and Paul Whitfield**

With additional accounts by
Catherine Brindley and Bruce P Gertsman

THE ROUGH GUIDES

# LIST OF MAPS

---

## MAP SYMBOLS

| | | | |
|---|---|---|---|
| 〰70〰 | Interstate | ⌂ | Cave |
| ⬡1⬡ | U.S. Highway | ⋏ | Canyon |
| Hwy-64 | Highway | ⌆ | Mountain range |
| ▬▬▬ | Railway | ▲ | Mountain peak |
| — — — | Ferry route | ⇃ | Waterfall |
| ▬▪▬▪▬ | International border | ⸬ | Marshland |
| ▬·▬·▬ | State border | ⍦ | Oasis |
| ▬ ▬ ▬ | Chapter division boundary | (i) | Information office |
| ——— | Wall | ⊠ | Post office |
| ✕ | Airport | ▪ | Building |
| △ | Campsite | ✚ | Church |
| ⌂ | Historical house | ⁺₊⁺ | Cemetery |
| ♙ | Castle | ▨ | National Park |
| ⸸ | Church | ▨ | Park |
| ♦ | Museum | ⣿ | Beach |
| ⚒ | Golf course | | |

# CONTENTS

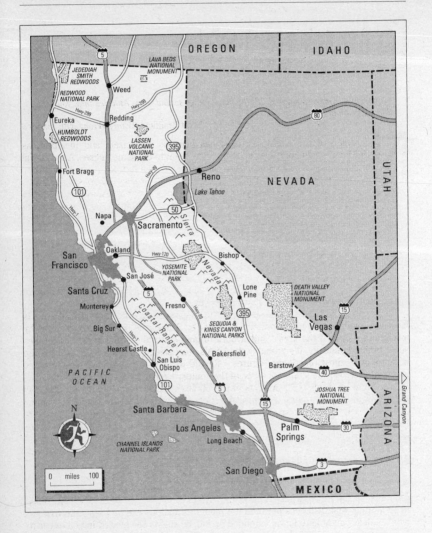

# INTRODUCTION

*California is America squared. It's the place you go to find more America than you ever thought possible.*

Scott Bradfield, *What's Wrong with America*

No region of the world, perhaps, has been as publicized, and idealized, as **California**, and none lives up to the hype to quite the same degree. A terrestrial paradise of sun, sand, surf and sea, it has a whole lot more besides: high mountain ranges, fast-paced glitzy cities, deep primeval forests, and hot dry deserts. Having zoomed from the Stone Age to Silicon Valley in little more than a couple of centuries, California doesn't dwell on the past. In some ways this part of America represents the ultimate "now" society, with all that that entails – life is lived very much in the fast lane, and conspicuous consumption is emphasized to the exclusion of almost everything else. But this is only one side of the coin; the deeper sense of age here often gets skimmed over. Provided you get out of the cities, it is readily apparent in the landscape: dense groves of ancient trees, primitive rock carvings left by the aboriginal Native American culture, and the eerie ghost towns of the Gold Rush pioneers. A land of superlatives, California really is full of the oldest, the tallest, the largest, the most spectacular, all of which goes far beyond local bravura.

It's important to bear in mind, too, that the supposed "superficiality" of California is largely a myth – an image promoted as much by Americans on the East coast as by foreigners – even if the area's endeavours to gain cultural credibility can sometimes seem brash. Politically, it's probably the USA's most schizophrenic region, home state of some of its most reactionary figures – Ronald Reagan and Richard Nixon to name just two – yet also the source of some of the country's most progressive political movements. Some of the fiercest protests of the Sixties emanated from here, and in many ways this is still the heart of liberal America. Consider the level of environmental awareness, which puts the smoky East to shame; and the fact that California has set *the* standard for the rest of US (and the world) regarding gay pride and social permissiveness. Economically, too, the region is crucial, whether it's in the traditionally dominant film industry, the recently ascendant music business, or in the increasingly important financial markets in which Los Angeles has come to set the pace.

## Where to go

California is the third largest state in the US, covering nearly 160,000 square miles: keep in mind that distances between the main destinations can be huge, and that you won't, unless you're here for an extended period, be able to see everything on one trip.

In an area so varied it's hard to pick out specific highlights. You may well start off in **Los Angeles**, far and away the biggest and most stimulating city: a maddening collection of freeways and beaches, seedy suburbs and high-gloss neighbourhoods and extreme lifestyles that you should at least once, even if you make a quick exit for more relaxed locales. From Los Angeles you have a number of choices. You can head south to **San Diego** – a smaller, up-and-coming city, with broad, welcoming beaches and a handy position close to the Mexican border; or you could push inland to the Californian **desert** areas, notably **Death Valley** – as its name suggests, a barren inhospitable landscape of volcanic craters and windswept sand dunes that in summer (when you can fry an egg on your car bonnet) becomes the hottest place on earth. It's a logical trip from here across to the **Grand Canyon** via **Las Vegas**: though not in

California, we've included these last two in Chapter Three of the *Guide*. An alternative is to make the steady journey up the **Central Coast**; a gorgeous run, by car especially, following the shoreline north through some of the state's most dramatic scenery, and taking in some of its liveliest small towns, notably Santa Barbara and Santa Cruz.

The Central Coast makes the transition from Southern to Northern California – a break that's more than just geographical. **San Francisco**, at the top end, is California's second city, and quite different from LA: the coast's oldest, most European-looking city, it's set compactly over a series of steep hills, with wooden houses tumbling down to water on both sides. San Francisco also gives access to some of the state's most extraordinary scenery, not least in the national parks to the east, especially **Yosemite**, where powerful waterfalls cascade into a sheer glacial valley that's been immortalized by Ansel Adams and countless others in search of the definitive landscape photograph.

**North** of San Francisco, the population thins and the physical look changes yet again. The climate is wetter up here, the valleys that much greener, flanked by a jagged coastline shadowed by mighty redwoods, the tallest trees in the world. Though many visitors choose to venture no further than the **Wine Country** and the Russian River valley on weekend forays from the city, it's well worth taking time out to explore the state's northernmost regions, a volcano-scarred desolation that's as different from the popular image of California as it's possible to be.

## When to go

California's climate comes close to its sub-tropical ideal. In **Southern California** in particular you can count on endless days of sunshine from May to October, and warm dry nights – though **LA**'s notorious smog is at its worst when the temperatures are highest, in August and September.

Right along the **coast** mornings can be hazily overcast, especially in May and June, though you can still get a suntan – or sunburn – even under greyish skies. In winter temperatures drop somewhat, but more importantly it can rain for weeks on end, causing massive mudslides that wipe out roads and hillside homes. Inland, the deserts are warm in winter and unbearably hot (120°F is not unusual) in summer; desert nights can be freezing in winter, when, strangely but beautifully, it can even snow. For serious **snow**, head to the mountains, where hiking trails at the higher elevations are blocked from November to June every year: skiers can take advantage of well-groomed slopes along the Sierra Nevada mountains and around Lake Tahoe.

The coast of Northern California is wetter and cooler than the south, its summers tempered by sea-breezes and fog, and its winters mild but wet. **San Francisco**, because of its exposed position at the tip of a peninsula, can be chilly all year, with summer fogs tending to roll in to ruin what may have started off as a pleasant sunny day. Head a mile inland, and you're back in the sun.

| DAYTIME TEMPERATURES (MAX & MIN°F) | | | | | | | |
|---|---|---|---|---|---|---|---|
| | Jan | | April | | July | | Oct |
| **San Diego** | 65 | 46 | 68 | 54 | 76 | 63 | 73 | 58 |
| **Los Angeles** | 65 | 47 | 71 | 53 | 83 | 63 | 77 | 57 |
| **Fresno** | 55 | 36 | 75 | 47 | 99 | 63 | 80 | 48 |
| **San Francisco** | 55 | 42 | 64 | 47 | 72 | 54 | 71 | 51 |
| **Death Valley** | 65 | 37 | 91 | 61 | 116 | 87 | 91 | 51 |

# PART ONE

# THE

# BASICS

# GETTING THERE FROM BRITAIN AND EUROPE

Though flying to California from Europe is pretty straightforward, choosing the best route can be more complicated than you might think, with prices fluctuating wildly according to how and when you go. Some airlines have non-stop services from Britain, but the majority of options are so-called "direct" flights, which can land several times, waiting an hour or so at each stop – a flight is called direct as long as it keeps the same *flight number* throughout its journey. The first place the plane lands is your point of entry into the US, which means you'll have to collect your bags and go through customs and immigration formalities there, even if you're continuing on to California on the same plane. This can be a real pain after a ten-hour journey, so it's worth finding out before you book a ticket.

## FARES, ROUTES AND AGENTS

Although you can fly to the US from any of the regional airports, the only **non-stop flights** from Britain to California are from London. Most of these land at LA, the hub of the region's air travel. Fewer travel non-stop to San Francisco, and you can't fly non-stop at all to San Diego. The non-stop **flight time** is around eleven hours from London to San Francisco or LA; add an hour at least for each intervening stop on direct flights, twice that if you have to change planes. Following winds ensure that return flights are always an hour or two shorter than outward journeys. Because of the time difference between Britain and the West Coast (eight hours almost all year), flights usually leave Britain in mid-morning, while flights back from the US tend to arrive in Britain early in the morning.

Britain remains one of the best places in Europe to obtain flight bargains, though **fares** vary widely according to season, availability and the current level of inter-airline competition. The comments that follow can only act as a general guide, so be sure to **shop around** carefully for the best offers by checking the travel ads in the weekend papers, on the holiday pages of ITV's *Teletext* and, in London, scouring *Time Out* and the *Evening Standard*. Giveaway magazines aimed at young travellers, like *TNT*, are also useful resources.

**Stand-by deals** (open-dated tickets which you pay for and then decide later when you want to fly – if there's room on the plane) are few and far between, and don't give great savings: in general you're better off with an **Apex** ticket.

The prices given below (in £ sterling) are a general indication of the (minimum) transatlantic air fares currently obtainable from specialist companies; remember to add between £25–35 airport tax to these figures. Each airline decides the exact dates of its seasons. Prices are for departures from London and Manchester.

| | LOW Nov 1–Dec 14, Dec 25–Mar 28, Apr 11–Apr 30 | | SHOULDER Mar 29–Apr 10, May 1–Jun 30, Sep 1–Oct 31 | | HIGH Jul 1–Aug 31, Dec 15–Dec 24 | |
|---|---|---|---|---|---|---|
| | one-way | return | one-way | return | one-way | return |
| Los Angeles | 195 | 289 | 195 | 332 | 235 | 475 |
| San Francisco | 195 | 289 | 195 | 332 | 235 | 475 |

One word of **warning**: it's not a good idea to buy a **one-way** ticket to the States. Not only are they rarely good value compared to a round-trip ticket, but US immigration officials usually take them as a sign that you aren't planning to go home, and may refuse you entry.

The conditions on these are pretty standard whoever you fly with – seats must be purchased seven days or more in advance, and you must stay for at least one Saturday night; tickets are normally valid for up to six months. Some airlines also do less expensive **Super-Apex** tickets, which fall into two categories: the first are approximately £150 cheaper than an ordinary Apex but must be bought 21 days in advance and require a minimum stay of seven days and a maximum stay of one month, the second are around £100 less than an Apex, must be purchased fourteen days in advance and entail a minimum stay of a week and a maximum stay of two months – such tickets are usually non-refundable or changeable. **"Open-jaw"** tickets can be a good idea, allowing you to fly into LA, for example, and back from San Francisco for little or no extra charge; fares are calculated by halving the return fares to each destination and adding the two figures together. This makes a convenient option for those who want a fly-drive holiday (see below).

Generally, the most expensive time to fly is **high season**, roughly between June and August and around Christmas. May and September are slightly less pricey, and the rest of the year is considered low season and cheaper still. Keep an eye out for slack season bargains, and, additionally, make sure to check the exact dates of the seasons with your operator or airline; you might be able to make major savings by shifting your departure date by a week – or even a day. **Weekend rates** for all return flights tend to be around £30 more expensive than those in the week.

For an overview of the various offers, and unofficially discounted tickets, go straight to an **agent** specializing in low-cost flights (we've listed some below). Especially if you're under 26 or a student, they may be able to knock up to thirty percent off the regular Apex fares when there are no special airline deals.

The same agents also offer cut-price seats on **charter flights**. These are particularly good value if you're travelling from a British city other than London, although they tend to be limited to the summer season, be restricted to so-called "holiday destinations" and have fixed departure and return dates. Brochures are available in most high street travel agents, or contact the specialists direct.

Finally, if you've got a bit more time, or want to see a bit more of the USA, it's often possible to stop over in **another city** – New York especially – and fly on from there for little more than the cost of a direct flight to California. Also, with increased competition on the **London–Los Angeles** route, thanks to *Virgin Atlantic* among others and price wars between US carriers, the cost of a connecting flight from LA to San Francisco has been brought down to as low as £40. Many airlines also offer **air passes**, which allow foreign travellers to fly between a given number of US cities for one discounted price. For more details on long-distance travel within the US see p.8.

## COURIER FLIGHTS

It's still possible, if not as common as it used to be, for those on a very tight budget to travel as **couriers**. Courier firms such as *Bridges Worldwide* (☎0181/759 5040) offer opportunities to travel at discounted rates (as low as £150–200 return to New York, or £200 return to the West Coast) in return for delivering a package. There'll be someone to check you in and to meet you at your destination, which minimizes any red-tape hassle. However, you'll have to travel light, with only a cabin-bag, and accept tight restrictions on travel dates. For other phone numbers, check the Yellow Pages, as these businesses come and go.

## PACKAGES

**Packages** – fly-drive, flight/accommodation deals and guided tours (or a combination of all three) – can work out cheaper than arranging the same trip yourself, especially for a short-term stay. The obvious drawbacks are the loss of flexibility and the fact that most schemes use hotels in the mid-range bracket, but there is a wide variety of options available.

High-street travel agents have plenty of brochures and information about the various combinations.

## FLY-DRIVE

**Fly-drive deals**, which give cut-rate (sometimes free) car rental when buying a transatlantic ticket, always work out cheaper than renting on the spot and give especially great value if you intend to do a lot of driving. On the other hand, you'll probably have to pay more for the flight than if you booked it through a discount agent. Competition between airlines (especially *Northwest* and *TWA*) and tour operators means that it's well worth phoning to check on current special promotions.

*Northwest Flydrive* offers excellent deals for not much more than an ordinary Apex fare; for example, a return flight to LA or San Francisco and a week's car rental costs around £350 per person in low season. Several of the other companies listed in the box offer similar, and sometimes cheaper, packages.

Watch out for hidden extras, such as local taxes, and "drop-off" charges, which can be as much as a week's rental, and Collision Damage

Waiver insurance (see p.27–8). Remember, too, that while you can drive in the States with a British licence, there can be problems renting vehicles if you're under 25. For complete car-rental and driveaway details, see "Getting Around" (p.26).

### FLIGHT AND ACCOMMODATION DEALS

There's really no end of combined **flight and accommodation deals** to California, and although you can often do things cheaper independently, you won't be able to do the *same* things cheaper – in fact, the equivalent room booked separately will normally be a lot more expensive – and you can leave the organizational hassles to someone else. Drawbacks include the loss of flexibility and the fact that you'll probably have to stay in hotels in the mid-range to expensive bracket, even though

---

### FLIGHTS FROM BRITAIN

The following carriers operate **non-stop flights** from London to California (all from Heathrow unless stated otherwise).

**Air New Zealand**, five times a week from Heathrow to Los Angeles.

**American Airlines**, daily to Los Angeles.

**British Airways**, daily to Los Angeles and San Francisco; daily to Los Angeles from Gatwick.

**TWA**, daily to Los Angeles and San Francisco.

**United Airlines,** daily to Los Angeles and San Francisco.

**Virgin Atlantic**, daily to Los Angeles and San Francisco.

The following carriers operate **one-stop direct flights** from London to California (all from Gatwick unless stated otherwise).

**American Airlines**, daily from Heathrow via Dallas to San Francisco.

**British Airways**, five a week from Heathrow in high season via Los Angeles to San Diego.

**Continental**, daily via Denver, Miami, Houston or Newark to Los Angeles, San Francisco and San Diego.

**Delta**, daily via Cincinatti or Atlanta to Los Angeles, San Francisco and San Diego.

**Northwest**, four a week via Minneapolis to Los Angeles and San Francisco.

**TWA**, daily from Gatwick via St Louis to Los Angeles and San Francisco.

The following carriers operate **direct flights from regional airports to the US**.

**American Airlines**, from Manchester to Chicago and New York, and from Glasgow to Chicago.

**British Airways**, from Manchester and Glasgow to New York.

**Delta**, from Manchester to Atlanta.

**Northwest**, from Glasgow to Boston.

### AIRLINES

| | | | |
|---|---|---|---|
| Air New Zealand | ☎0181/741 2299 | Northwest | ☎01293/561000 |
| American Airlines | ☎0181/572 5555 | TWA | ☎0171/439 0707 |
| British Airways | ☎0345/222111 | United | ☎0181/990 9900 |
| Continental | ☎0800/776464 | Virgin Atlantic | ☎01293/747747 |
| Delta | ☎0800/414767 | | |

Toll-free phone numbers for airlines **in the United States** are listed on p.8.

## LOW-COST FLIGHT AGENTS IN BRITAIN

**Bridge The World**
1–3 Ferdinand St, London NW1 ☎0171/916 0990

**Campus Travel**
52 Grosvenor Gardens, London SW1
*Branches nationwide* ☎0171/730 2101

**Council Travel**
28a Poland St, London W1V ☎0171/437 7767

**Destination Group**
41–45 Goswell Rd, London EC1 ☎0171/253 9000

**STA Travel**
86 Old Brompton Rd, London SW7
*Branches nationwide* ☎0171/361 6262

**Trailfinders**
42–50 Earls Court Rd, London W8
*Branches nationwide* ☎0171/938 3366

**Travel Bug**
597 Cheetham Hill Rd, Manchester M8 5EJ
☎0161/721 4000

**Travel Cuts**
295a Regent St, London W1 ☎0171/637 3161

**Union Travel**
93 Piccadilly, London W1 ☎0171/493 4343

less expensive accommodation is almost always available.

A handful of tour operators (see below) offer quite deluxe packages. Of these, *Virgin Holidays* are about the least expensive: for example, seven nights in San Francisco plus return flight costs around £629–849 per person. Discount agents can set up more basic packages for just over £500 each. Pre-booked accommodation schemes, under which you buy vouchers for use in a specific group of hotels, are not normally good value – see p.35.

## TOURING AND ADVENTURE PACKAGES

A simple and exciting way to see a chunk of California's extensive wilderness, without being hassled by too many practical considerations, is to take a specialist **touring and adventure package**, which includes transport, accommodation, food and a guide. Some of the more adventurous carry small groups around on minibuses and use a combination of budget hotels and camping (equipment, except a sleeping bag, is provided). Most also have a food kitty of maybe £25 per week, with many meals cooked and eaten communally, although there's plenty of time to leave the group and do your own thing.

*TrekAmerica* is one UK-based company to offer such deals; a typical package would be ten days in California and the "Wild West" for £400 or so excluding flights. Other operators are listed on p.7. If you're interested in **backcountry hiking**, the San Francisco-based *Sierra Club* (see p.45) offers a range of tours that take you into parts of the state that most

people never see. Again, see the list below for addresses.

## FLIGHTS FROM IRELAND

Both *Delta* and *Aer Lingus* fly to California **direct from Ireland**. The cheapest flights **from Ireland** – if you're under 26 or a student – are available from *USIT*. Student-only return fares to **San Francisco** or **Los Angeles** range from IR£389 to IR£569. Ordinary Apex fares are only marginally higher.

*USIT* can be contacted at Aston Quay, O'Connell Bridge, Dublin 2 (☎01/6778117), while *Aer Lingus* is at 40 O'Connell St, Dublin 1 (☎01/844 4777), and *Delta Airlines* is at 24 Merrion Square, Dublin 2 (☎01/676 8080; ☎1800/768080).

## FLIGHTS FROM EUROPE

It is generally far cheaper to fly non-stop to California from London than any other **European** city. However, for the best deals to New York from Brussels and Paris, contact **Nouvelles Frontières**, 87 boulevard de Grenelle, 75015 Paris (☎41.41.58.58) and 2 boulevard M Lemonnier, 1000 Brussels (☎02/547 4444). Its London branch is at 11 Blenheim St, W1 (☎0171/629 7772).

Other options are the cut-price charter flights occasionally offered from major European cities; ask at your nearest travel agent for details. In Germany, look for discount **youth fare** deals which *United* offers (to those under 26 booking 72 hours or less in advance) from Frankfurt, its continental hub (☎069/605020).

## SPECIALIST HOLIDAY OPERATORS

**Airtours**
Wavell House, Helmshore, Rossendale,
Lancs BB4 4NB ☎01706/240033

**AmeriCan Adventures**
45 High St, Tunbridge Wells,
Kent TN1 1XL ☎01892/511894

**Bon Voyage**
18 Bellevue Rd, Southampton,
Hants SO15 2AY ☎01703/330332

**British Airways Holidays**
Astral Towers, Bettsway, London Road,
Crawley, West Sussex RH10 2XA ☎01293/722727

**Contiki Travel**
Wells House, 15 Elmfield Rd,
Bromley, Kent BR1 1LS ☎0181/290 6422

**Destination USA**
41–45 Goswell Rd,
London EC1 ☎0171/253 2000

**Explore Worldwide**
I Frederick St, Aldershot,
Hants GU11 1LQ ☎01252/319448

**First Choice**
First Choice House, London Road, Crawley,
West Sussex RH10 2HB ☎01293/560777

**Greyhound International**
Sussex House, London Road,
East Grinstead,
West Sussex RH19 1LD ☎01342/317317

**Key to America**
1–3 Station Rd, Ashford,
Middlesex TW15 2UW ☎01784/248777

**North America Travel Service**
7 Albion St, Leeds LS1 5ER ☎0113/246 1466
*Also branches in Nottingham, Manchester and
Barnsley.*

**Northwest Flydrive**
PO Box 45, Bexhill-on-Sea,
East Sussex TN40 1PY ☎01424/224400

**Premier Holidays**
Westbrook, Milton Road,
Cambridge CB4 1YQ ☎01223/516516

**Top Deck**
131 Earls Court Rd,
London SW5 ☎0171/370 4555

**Trans Atlantic Vacations**
3A Gatwick Metro Centre, Balcombe Road,
Horley, Surrey RH6 9GA ☎01293/774441

**TrekAmerica**
Trek House, The Bullring,
Deddington, Oxford OX15 OTT ☎01869/338777

**Unijet**
"Sandrocks", Rocky Lane, Haywards Heath,
West Sussex RH16 4RH ☎01444/459191

**Virgin Holidays**
The Galleria, Station Road, Crawley,
West Sussex RH10 1WW ☎01293/617181

## GETTING THERE FROM NORTH AMERICA

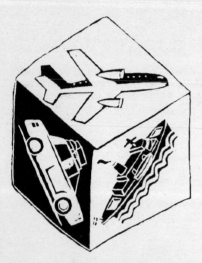

Getting to California from anywhere else in North America is never a problem; the region is well serviced by air, rail and road networks. All the main airlines operate daily scheduled flights to San Francisco and LA from across the country, and there are daily flights from Toronto and Vancouver as well. Flying remains the best but most expensive way to travel; taking a train comes a slow second. Travelling by bus is the least expensive method, but again is slow, and is much less comfortable than either train or plane.

### BY AIR

To Los Angeles, many domestic flights land at the city's international **LAX** airport, as well as the smaller airports at Burbank, Long Beach, Ontario and John Wayne in Orange County. For San Francisco, besides the main **San Francisco International Airport** (known as SFO), two others, both in the Bay Area, may be useful – particularly **Oakland International** (OAK), across the bay but easily accessible. The third Bay Area airport, **San Jose Municipal** (SJO), forty miles south, is a bit out of the way but has

### AIRLINES IN THE USA AND CANADA

**Aer Lingus** ☎1-800/223-6537 or ☎212/557-1110

**Aero California** ☎1-800/237-6225

**Aeromexico** ☎1-800/237-6639

**Air Canada** ☎1-800/776-3000; in Canada call directory inquiries for local toll-free number

**Air France** ☎1-800/237-2747; in Canada ☎1-800/667-2747

**American Airlines** ☎1-800/433-7300

**America West** ☎1-800/2FLYAWA

**British Airways** ☎1-800/247-9297; in Canada ☎1-800/668-1059

**Canadian** ☎1-800/426-7000; in Canada ☎1-800/665-1177

**Continental** ☎1-800/525-0280

**Delta Airlines** (☎1-800/221-1212; in Canada, call directory inquiries for local toll-free number

**Iberia** ☎1-800/772-4642; in Canada ☎1-800/423-7421

**Icelandair** ☎1-800/223-5500

**KLM** ☎1-800/374-7747; in Canada ☎1-800/361-5073

**Lufthansa** ☎1-800/645-3880; in Canada ☎1-800/563-5954

**Mesa** ☎1-800/933-6372

**Northwest** ☎1-800/225-2525

**SAS** ☎1-800/221-2350

**Southwest** ☎1-800/435-9792

**Tower Air** ☎1-800/221-2500

**Trans World Airlines** ☎1-800/221-2000

**United Airlines** ☎1-800/241-6522

**US Air** ☎1-800/428-4322

**Virgin Atlantic** ☎1-800/862-8621

Note that not all the above airlines fly domestic routes within the US. The **Canadian directory enquries** number is ☎-1-800/555-1212.

good connections with the western US, LA especially. Some carriers also fly to **San Diego**'s Lindburgh airport non-stop.

As airlines tend to match each other's prices, there's generally little difference in the quoted fares. Barring another fare war, round-trip prices start at around $350 from New York, slightly less from Midwest cities and slightly more from Toronto and Montréal. What makes more difference than your choice of carrier are the conditions governing the ticket – whether it's fully refundable, the time and day and most importantly the **time of year** you travel. Least expensive of all is a non-summer-season midweek flight, booked and paid for at least three weeks in advance. While it's good to call the airlines directly to get a sense of their official fares, it's also worth checking with a reputable **travel agent** (such as the ones listed above) to find out about any **special deals** or student/youth fares that may be available.

In addition to the big-name scheduled airlines, a few lesser-known carriers run no-frills flights, which can prove to be very good value, especially if you're only planning to buy a **one-way** ticket to California. *Tower Air*, the New York-based charter operator, has five flights a week from New York to Los Angeles for $162; an onward flight (usually on *Southwest* or *United*) to San Francisco adds another $59 or so. *Southwest* flies from a host of Midwestern and Western cities at rock-bottom prices; eight daily flights leave Salt Lake City for Oakland (it doesn't go directly to San Francisco) from between $49 and $109. Its lowest fare out of Seattle to Oakland is $39, while LA to Oakland can go as low as $19.

Travellers intending to fly from **Canada** are likely to find that, with less competition on these routes (*Canadian* flies to San Francisco only from Vancouver; most other routes are monopolized by *Air Canada*), fares are somewhat higher than they are for flights wholly within the US. You may well find that it's worth the effort to get to a US city first, and fly on to California from there.

### BY TRAIN

If you have a bit more money and hanker after a few more creature comforts (all the trains have private cabins and dining cars), or simply have the time and inclination to take in some of the rest of the US on your way to California, then an *Amtrak* **train** may be just the ticket for you. The most spectacular train journey of all has to be the

For all information on ***Amtrak* fares and schedules**, and to make reservations, use the toll-free number

☎**1-800/USA-RAIL**

Do not call individual stations.

*California Zephyr*, which runs all the way from Chicago to San Francisco and comes into its own during the ride through the Rockies west of Denver. After climbing alongside raging rivers through gorgeous mountain **scenery**, the route drops down the west flank of the Rockies and races across the Utah and Nevada deserts by night, stopping at Salt Lake City and Reno. The next day the train climbs up and over the mighty Sierra Nevada, following the route of the first transcontinental railroad on its way into Oakland, where you change to a bus for the ride into San Francisco.

The major southern route approaches California through New Mexico and Arizona – connecting buses from Flagstaff head to the Grand Canyon – and eventually arrives at Los Angeles.

*Amtrak* **fares** are often more expensive than flying, though off-peak discounts and special deals can make the train an economical as well as an aesthetic choice. One-way cross-country fares are around $250, though if you're travelling round-trip you can take advantage of what they call "**All-Aboard America**" fares, which are zone-based and allow three stopovers in between your origin and eventual return. Travel within the West (from Denver to the Pacific) costs $198 between September and May or $228 June to August; within the West and Midwest (west of Chicago) costs $258/318; and for the entire USA the cost is $318/378. While *Amtrak*'s basic fares are quite good value, if you want to travel in a bit more comfort the cost rises quickly. **Sleeping compartments**, which include small toilets and showers, start at around $100 per night for one or two people, including three meals a day.

### BY BUS

Bus travel is the most tedious and time-consuming way to get to California, and, for all the discomfort, won't really save you much money. **Greyhound** (☎1-800/231-2222) is the sole long-distance operator – a one-way APEX ticket from New York to San Francisco, bought 14 days in advance, costs $79.50; purchased on the day of travel it's $125.

The only reason to go *Greyhound* is if you're planning to visit a number of other places en route; *Greyhound*'s **Ameripass** is good for unlimited travel within a certain time, and costs $250 for 7 days, $350 for fifteen days and $450 for thirty days. **Foreign visitors** can buy Ameripasses before leaving home; see p.30 for details.

An alternative, in every sense, is the San Francisco-based *Green Tortoise* bus company; see p.31 for details.

## BY CAR

Driving your own car gives the greatest freedom and flexibility, but if you don't have one (or don't trust the one you do have), one option worth considering is a **driveaway**. Companies operate in most major cities, and are paid to find drivers to take a customer's car from one place to another – most commonly between California and New York. The company will normally pay for your insurance and your first tank of gas; after that, you'll be expected to drive along the most direct route and to average 400 miles a day. Most driveaway companies are keen to use foreign travellers (German tourists are ideal, it seems), but if you can convince them you are a safe bet they'll take something like a $200 deposit, which you get back after delivering the car in good condition. It makes obvious sense to get in touch in advance, to spare yourself a week's wait for a car to turn up. Look under "Driveaways" in the Yellow Pages and phone around for the latest offers; or try one of the ninety branches of *Auto Driveaway*, based at 310 S Michigan Ave in Chicago (☎312/341-1900).

**Renting a car** is the usual story of phoning your local branch of one of the majors (*Avis, Hertz, Budget, Thrifty*, etc – listed on p.27), of which *Thrifty* tends to be the cheapest. Most companies have offices at destination airports, and addresses and phone numbers are comprehensively documented in the Yellow Pages.

Also worth considering are **fly-drive deals**, which give cut-rate (and sometimes free) car rental when buying an air ticket. They usually work out cheaper than renting on the spot and are especially good value if you intend to do a lot of driving.

## PACKAGE TOURS

Many operators run all-inclusive **packages** which combine plane tickets and hotel accommodation with (for example) sightseeing, wining and dining, or excursions to tourist sites. Even if the "package" aspect doesn't thrill you to pieces, these deals can still be more convenient and sometimes even work out to be more economical than arranging the same thing yourself, providing you don't mind losing a little flexibility. With such a vast range of packages available, it's impossible to give an overview – major travel agents will have brochures detailing what's on offer.

# GETTING THERE FROM AUSTRALASIA

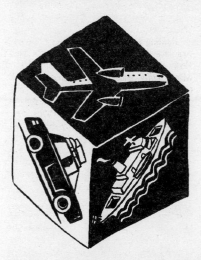

The **low** season for flights to the US from Australia and New Zealand is Feb–March and Oct 16–Nov 30; the **shoulder** season is Jan 16–31, April–May and July 1–Oct 15; the **high** season is Dec 1–Jan 15.

**Other than charter deals, seasonal bargains and all-in packages which may be on offer from high street travel agents, the cheapest flights from Australasia to the US are available from the specialists listed below.**

From Australia and New Zealand, Los Angeles and San Francisco are the main points of entry to the US. With any of the American carriers, you can continue on to **New York** for around US$170 on top of the fare to the West Coast. Most flights stop off in Honolulu, Hawaii; you can usually stay over for as long as you like

## SPECIALIST AGENTS AND OPERATORS

**Adventure Specialists**
69 Liverpool St, Sydney ☎02/9261 2927
*Arranges adventure treks, tours, rail and bus passes.*

**Adventure World**
73 Walker St, Sydney ☎02/956 7766
8 Victoria Ave, Perth ☎09/9221 2300
101 Great South Rd, Auckland ☎09/524 5118
*Individual and small group exploratory tours and treks in California and across the US.*

**American Travel Centre**
2nd Floor, 262 Adelaide St, Brisbane (☎07/3221 4788).

**CreativeTours**
Grafton St, Woollahra, Sydney ☎02/386 2111
*Escorted bus tours, air passes and accommodation packages.*

**Exodus Expeditions**
81a Glebe Point Rd, Sydney ☎1800/800 724
*Small group escorted adventure and wilderness tours.*

**Insight**
39–41 Chandos St, St Leonards, NSW ☎02/437 4660

*In conjunction with airlines, offers accommodation packages, car rental and bus tours. Agent for TrekAmerica, small group adventure specialist for 18–38s.*

**Peregrine**
258 Lonsdale St, Melbourne ☎03/663 8611
407 Great South Rd, Penrose, Auckland ☎09/525-3074
*Representatives for AmeriCan Adventure's camping holidays.*

**Sydney International Travel Centre**
75 King St, Sydney ☎02/9299 8000
*Travel arrangements, accommodation, bus and rail tours and ski packages. Agent for AmeriCan and Swingaway.*

**Triangle Vacations**
81 Brunswick St, Fortitude Valley, Brisbane ☎07/3216 0855
*Gay-oriented tours and accommodation packages in California and elsewhere in the US.*

**Wiltrans/Maupintour**
189 Kent St, Sydney ☎02/255 0899
*Rail journeys and escorted adventure tours in the US*

## AIRLINES AND AGENTS IN AUSTRALASIA

**Air New Zealand**
5 Elizabeth St, Sydney ☎02/9223 4666
Quay St, Auckland ☎09/357 3000

**Anywhere Travel**
345 Anzac Parade, Kingsford,
Sydney ☎02/663 0411

**Brisbane Discount Travel**
360 Queen St, Brisbane ☎07/3229 9211

**British Airways**
64 Castlereagh St, Sydney ☎02/9258 3300
154 Queen St, Auckland ☎09/356 8690

**Budget Travel**
69 Fort St, Auckland ☎09/309 4313

**Discount Travel Specialists**,
Shop 53,
Forrest Chase, Perth ☎09/221 1400;
☎08/9221 1400 from Sept 1997

**Flight Centres**
Circular Quay, Sydney ☎02/9241 2422
Bourke St, Melbourne ☎03/9650 2899
205–225 Queen St, Auckland ☎09/309 6171
152 Hereford St, Christchurch ☎03/379 7145
50–52 Willis St, Wellington ☎04/472 8101

**KLM**
5 Elizabeth St,
Sydney ☎02/9231 6333 or 1-800/505 747

**MAS Malaysian Airlines**
16 Spring St,
Sydney ☎02/364 3500; local-call rate 13 2627
Floor 12, Swanson Centre,
12–26 Swanson St, Auckland ☎09/373 2741

**Northwest**
309 Kent St, Level 13,
Sydney NSW ☎02/290 4455

**Passport Travel**
320b Glenferrie Rd, Malvern,
Melbourne ☎03/9824 7183

**Qantas**
Chifley Square,
cnr Hunter and Phillip streets,
Sydney ☎02/957 0111
Qantas House, 154 Queen St,
Auckland ☎09/357 8900

**Singapore Airlines**
17–19 Bridge St, Sydney ☎02/9236 0144
West Plaza Building,
corner of Customs and Albert streets,
Auckland ☎09/379 3209

**STA Travel**
732 Harris St, Ultimo,
Sydney ☎02/9212 1255 or 1-800/637 444
256 Flinders St, Melbourne ☎03/9347 4711
10 High St, Auckland ☎09/366 6673
233 Cuba St, Wellington ☎04/385 0561
223 High St, Christchurch ☎03/379 9098

**Topdeck Travel**
45 Grenfell St, Adelaide ☎08/8232 7222

**Trailfinders**
Hides Corner, Shield St, Cairns ☎07/041 1199

**Tymtro Travel**
Wallaceway Shopping Centre,
Chatswood, Sydney ☎02/413 1219

**United**
10 Barrack St, Sydney ☎02/237 8888
7 City Rd, Auckland ☎09/307 9500

for no extra charge. Various **coupon deals** which are valid in continental US are available with your main ticket, allowing you to fly to destinations across the States. A minimum purchase of three coupons usually applies, for example *American Airlines*' **Coupon Pass** costs $US319 for the first three, and between $50 and $100 for subsequent tickets (maximum of ten in total).

From **Australia**, there are direct flights to **Los Angeles** and **San Francisco** with *United Airlines* daily from Sydney (low season AU$1752/ high season $3007), *Air New Zealand* five times a week from Sydney (AU$1750/3005), and *Quantas* daily from Cairns, Brisbane, Sydney and Melbourne (AU$1878/3005), Darwin (AU$2360/2751) and Perth (AU$2618/3200).

From **New Zealand**, the best direct deals are out of **Auckland** (add about NZ$100 for Christchurch and Wellington departures) to Los Angeles with *Air New Zealand* (daily, NZ$1869/2819), *MAS* and *Qantas* (both several times weekly, NZ$1860/2805), or *United Airlines* to LA or **San Francisco** (daily NZ$1869/2809).

**Round-the-world** deals from Australasia, such as *Cathay Pacific/United Airlines'* "Globetrotter" and *Air New Zealand/KLM/Northwest's* "World Navigator" packages, both of which offer six stopovers worldwide and limited backtracking, start at AU$2349/2899 or NZ$2999/3449. The most US-oriented package, only available in Australia, is *Singapore/TWA's* "Easyworld", which allows unlimted stopovers worldwide with a maximum of eight within the US (flat rate AU$3023).

# ENTRY REQUIREMENTS FOR FOREIGN VISITORS

## VISAS

Under the **Visa Waiver Scheme,** designed to speed up lengthy immigration procedures, British citizens and citizens of Austria, Andorra, Belgium, Brunei, Denmark, Finland, France, Germany, Iceland, Ireland, Italy, Japan, Liechtenstein, Luxembourg, Monaco, the Netherlands, New Zealand, Norway, San Marino, Spain, Sweden and Switzerland visiting the United States for a period of less than ninety days only need a **full passport** (UK citizens should note that a British Visitor's Passport is *not* acceptable) and a **visa waiver form**. The latter will be provided either by your travel agency, or by the airline during check-in or on the plane, and must be presented to immigration on arrival. The same form covers entry across the land borders with Canada and Mexico as well as by air. However, those eligible for the scheme must apply for a visa if they

intend to work, study, or stay in the country for more than ninety days.

Prospective visitors from Australia and all other parts of the world not mentioned above require a valid passport and a **non-immigrant visitor's visa**. How you'll obtain a visa depends on what country you're in and your status on application, so telephone the nearest Embassy or Consulate listed on p.14.

In **Britain**, only British or EU citizens, and those from other countries eligible for the visa waiver scheme, can apply by post – fill in the application form available at most travel agents and send it with a full passport and a SAE to the nearest US Embassy or Consulate. Expect a wait of one to three weeks before your passport is returned. All others must apply in person, making an appointment in advance. Visa application fees in Britain are currently £13.75.

**Canadian citizens** are in a particularly privileged position when it comes to crossing the border into the US. Though it is possible to enter the States without your passport, you should really have it with you on any trip that brings you as far as California. Only if you plan to stay for more than ninety days do you need a visa.

Bear in mind that if you cross into the States in your car, trunks and passenger compartments are subject to spot searches by US Customs personnel, though this sort of surveillance is likely to decrease as remaining tariff barriers fall over the next few years. Remember, too, that Canadians are legally barred from seeking gainful employment in the US.

In **Australasia** application forms are available through travel agents; you need to include your passport and one signed passport photo, and either post it (include SAE) or personally lodge it at the American Consulate in Sydney or Auckland (see below) or Non-Immigrant Visas, Private Bag 92022, Auckland 1. Processing takes ten working days for postal applications, two for personal applications; there is no application fee. In Sydney, the **USA Tourist Service**, 75 King St (☎02/299-1222), can advise on visa issues.

Whatever your nationality, visas are not issued to convicted felons and anybody who owns up to being a communist, fascist or drug dealer.

### IMMIGRATION CONTROL

The standard immigration regulations apply to all visitors, whether or not they are using the Visa Waiver Scheme. During the flight, you'll be handed an **immigration form** (and a customs declaration; see below), which must be given up at immigration control once you land. The form requires details of where you are staying on your first night (if you don't know, write "touring") and the date you intend to **leave** the US. You should be able to prove that you have enough money to support yourself while in the US – $300–400 a week is usually considered sufficient – as anyone revealing the slightest intention of working while in the country is likely to be refused admission. You may also experience difficulties if you admit to being HIV

### US EMBASSY AND CONSULATES IN CANADA

**Embassy:**
100 Wellington St,
Ottawa, ON K1P 5T1     ☎613/238-5335

**Consulates:**
Suite 1050, 615 Macleod Trail,
**Calgary, AB** T2G 4T8     ☎403/266-8962
Suite 910, Cogswell Tower, Scotia Square,

**Halifax, NS** B3J 3K2     ☎902/429-2480
Complex Desjardins, South Tower,
**Montréal, PQ** H5B 1G1     ☎514/281-1468
2 Place Terrasse Dufferin,
**Québec City, PQ** G1R 4T9     ☎418/692-2095
360 University Ave,
**Toronto, ON** M5G 1S4     ☎416/595-1700
1095 W Pender St,
**Vancouver, BC** V6E 2M6     ☎604/685-4311

### US EMBASSIES AND CONSULATES ELSEWHERE

**UK**
5 Upper Grosvenor St,
**London** W1A 1AE     ☎0171/499 9000;
visa hotline ☎0891/200290

3 Regent Terrace,
**Edinburgh** EH7 5BW     ☎0131/556 8315

Queens House, 14 Queen St,
**Belfast** BT1 6EQ     ☎01232/328239

**Australia**
Moonah Place,
Canberra, ACT 2600     ☎06/270 5000
39 Castlereagh Street
Sydney     ☎1800/805 924

**Denmark**
Dag Hammerskjöld Allé 24,
2100 Copenhagen     ☎31/ 42 31 44

**Ireland**
42 Elgin Rd, Ballsbridge,
Dublin     ☎01/6687122

**Netherlands**
Museumplein 19,
1071 DJ Amsterdam     ☎020/575 5309

**New Zealand**
29 Fitzherbert Terrace, Thorndon,
Wellington     ☎4/472 2068
Corner of Shortland and
O'Connell Streets,
Auckland     ☎09/3032724

**Norway**
Drammensveien 18,
0244 Oslo     ☎47/22 44 85 50

**South Africa**
11th Floor, Kine Centre,
Commissioner and Kruis streets,
PO Box 2155, Johannesburg     ☎11/331 1681

**Sweden**
Strandvägen 101,
Stockholm     ☎08/783 5300

positive or having AIDS or TB. Part of the immigration form will be attached to your passport, where it must stay until you leave, when an immigration or airline official will detach it.

## CUSTOMS

Customs officers will relieve you of your customs declaration and check whether you're carrying any fresh foods. You'll also be asked if you've visited a farm in the last month: if you have, you may well have your shoes taken away for inspection. The **duty-free allowance** if you're over 17 is 200 cigarettes and fifty cigars (*not* Cuban) and, if you're over 21, a litre of spirits. As well as foods and anything agricultural, it's prohibited to carry into the country any articles from North Korea, Iran, Iraq, Libya, Serbia, Montenegro or Cuba, obscene publications, lottery tickets, chocolate liqueurs or pre-Columbian artefacts. Anyone caught carrying drugs into the country will not only face prosecution, but be entered in the records as an undesirable and probably denied entry for all time.

## EXTENSIONS AND LEAVING

The date stamped on your passport is the latest you're legally allowed to stay. Leaving a few days later may not matter, especially if you're heading home, but more than a week or so can result in a protracted, rather unpleasant, interrogation from officials, which may cause you to miss your flight and be denied entry to the US in future, and your American hosts and/or employers to face legal proceedings.

To get an **extension** before your time is up, apply at the nearest **US Immigration and Naturalization Service** (INS) office (the address will be under the Federal Government Offices listings at the front of the phone book). They will automatically assume that you're working illegally and it's up to you to convince them otherwise. Do this by providing evidence of ample finances, and, if you can, bring along an upstanding American citizen to vouch for you.

---

**BRITISH CONSULATES IN CALIFORNIA**

3701 Wilshire Blvd, # 312 Los Angeles
CA 90010 ☎213/385-7381

1 Sansome St, # 850 San Francisco
CA 94104 ☎415/981-3030

---

You'll also have to explain why you didn't plan for the extra time initially.

## STAYING ON

Anyone planning an extended legal stay in the United States should apply for a special **working visa** at any American Embassy *before* setting off. Different types of visas are issued, depending on your skills and length of stay, but unless you've got relatives (parents or children over 21) or a prospective employer to sponsor you, your chances are at best slim.

**Illegal work** is nothing like as easy to find as it used to be, now that the government has introduced fines as high as $10,000 for companies caught employing anyone without a **social security number** (which effectively proves you're part of the legal workforce). Even in the traditionally more casual establishments like restaurants and bars, things have really tightened up, and if you do find work it's likely to be of the less visible, poorly paid kind – washer-up instead of waiter. Making up a fictitious social security number, or borrowing one from somebody else, is of course completely illegal, as are **marriages of convenience**; usually inconvenient for all concerned and with a lower success rate than is claimed.

---

**Foreign students** have a slightly better chance of a prolonged stay in California, especially those who can arrange some sort of "year abroad" through their university at home. Otherwise you can apply directly to a university; if they'll have you (and you can afford the painfully expensive fees charged to overseas students), it can be a great way to get to know the country, and maybe even learn something useful. The US grants more or less unlimited visas to those enrolled in full-time further education. Another possibility for students is to get on to an Exchange Visitor Program, for which participants are given a J-1 visa that entitles them to accept paid summer employment and apply for a social security number. However, most of these visas are issued for jobs in American **summer camps**, which aren't everybody's idea of a good time; they fly you over, and after a summer's work you end up with around $500 and a month to six weeks to blow it in. If you live in Britain and are interested, contact *BUNAC* (16 Bowling Green Lane, London EC1; ☎0171/251 3472), or *Camp America* (37 Queens' Gate, London SW7; ☎0171/581 7373).

## INSURANCE, HEALTH AND PERSONAL SAFETY

### TRAVEL INSURANCE COMPANIES IN THE UK

**Columbus Travel Insurance**, 17 Devonshire Square, London EC2M 4SQ (☎0171/375 0011). *Also does an annual multi-trip policy which offers twelve months' cover for £125.*

**Endsleigh Insurance**, 97–107 Southampton Row, London WC1B 4AG (☎0171/436 4451). *Generally offers the cheapest deals at around £35 for three weeks to cover life, limb and luggage (with a 25 percent reduction if you choose to forgo luggage insurance).*

**Frizzell Insurance**, Frizzell House, County Gates, Bournemouth, Dorset BH1 2NF (☎01202/ 292 333).

### INSURANCE

Though not compulsory, **travel insurance** is *essential* for **foreign travellers**. The US has no national health system and you can lose an arm and a leg (so to speak) having even minor medical treatment. Bank and credit cards (particularly *American Express*) often have certain levels of medical or other insurance included, especially if you use them to pay for your trip.

If you plan to participate in water sports, or do some hiking or skiing, you'll probably have to pay an extra premium; check carefully that any insurance policy you are considering will cover you in case of an accident. Note also that very few insurers will arrange on-the-spot payments in the event of a major expense or loss; you will usually be reimbursed only after going home. In all case of loss or theft of goods, you will have to contact the local police to have a report made out so that your insurer can process the claim.

### BRITISH COVER

Most **travel agents** and tour operators will offer you insurance when you book your flight or holiday, and some will insist you take it. These policies are usually reasonable value, though as ever, you should check the small print. If you feel the cover is inadequate, or you want to compare prices, any travel agent, **insurance broker** or **bank** should be able to help. If you have a good "all risks" home insurance policy it may well cover your possessions against loss or theft even when overseas, and many private medical schemes also cover you when abroad – make

sure you know the procedure and the helpline number. On all policies, read the small print to ensure the cover includes a sensible amount for medical expenses – this should be at least £1,000,000, which will cover the cost of an air ambulance to fly you home in the event of serious injury or hospitalization.

### AUSTRALASIAN COVER

In **Australia**, *CIC Insurance*, offered by *Cover-More Insurance Services* (Level 9, 32 Walker St, North Sydney; ☎02/9202 8000; branches in Victoria and Queensland), has some of the widest cover available which can be arranged through most travel agents. It costs around AUS$190 for 32 days. Other major operators include *UTAG* (347 Kent St, Sydney; ☎1800/809 462), *AFTA* (144 Pacific Hwy, North Sydney; ☎02/956 4800) and *Ready Plan* (141–147 Walker St, Dandenong, Victoria; ☎1800/337 462; and 10th Floor, 63 Albert St, Auckland).

In **New Zealand**, a good range of policies is offered by *STA* and *Flight Centres* (see p.12).

### NORTH AMERICAN COVER

Before buying an insurance policy, **North American travellers** should check that they're not already covered for health charges or costs by their current **health insurance**. If you are unable to use a phone or if the practitioner requires immediate payment, save all the **forms** to support a claim for subsequent reimbursement. Remember also that time limits may apply when making claims after the fact, so promptness in contacting your insurer is highly advisable. Holders of official **student/teacher/youth cards** are entitled to accident coverage and hospital in-patient benefits. **Students** will often find that their student health coverage extends during the vacations and for one term beyond the date of last enrolment.

Not surprisingly, few if any American health insurance plans cover against **theft** while travelling, though **homeowners' or renters'** insurance often covers you for up to $500 while on the road, though conditions and maximum amounts vary from company to company.

After exhausting the possibilities above, you might want to contact a specialist **travel insurance** company; your travel agent can usually recommend one, or see the box below. Policies are comprehensive (accidents, illnesses, delayed or lost luggage, cancelled flights, etc), but maximum payouts tend to be meagre. Premiums vary, so shop around. The best deals are usually to be had through student/youth travel agencies – *ISIS* policies, for example. If you're planning to do any "dangerous sports" (skiing, mountaineering, etc), figure on a surcharge of twenty to fifty percent.

Most North American travel policies apply only to items lost, stolen or damaged while in the custody of an identifiable, responsible third party – hotel porter, airline, luggage consignment, etc. Even in these cases you will have to contact the local police within a certain time limit.

### HEALTH ADVICE FOR FOREIGN TRAVELLERS

If you have a serious **accident** while in the US, emergency medical services will get to you quickly and charge you later. For emergencies or ambulances, dial ☎**911**, the nationwide emergency number (or whatever variant may be on the information plate of the payphone).

Should you need to see a **doctor**, lists can be found in the Yellow Pages under "Clinics" or "Physicians and Surgeons". A basic consultation fee is $50–100, payable in advance. Medications aren't cheap either – keep all your receipts for later claims on your insurance policy.

Many **minor ailments** can be remedied using the fabulous array of potions and lotions available in **drugstores**. Foreign visitors should bear in mind that many pills available over the counter at home need a prescription in the US – most codeine-based painkillers, for example – and that

### TRAVEL INSURANCE COMPANIES IN NORTH AMERICA

**Access America**, PO Box 90310, Richmond, VA 23230 (☎1-800/284-8300).

**Carefree Travel Insurance**, PO Box 310, 120 Mineola Blvd, Mineola, NY 11501 (☎1-800/323-3149).

**International Student Insurance Service (ISIS)** – sold by *STA Travel*, which has several branches in the US (head office is 48 E 11th St, New York, NY 10003; ☎1-800/777-0112).

**Travel Assistance International**, 1133 15th St NW, Suite 400, Washington, DC 20005 (☎1-800/821-2828).

**Travel Guard**, 1145 Clark St, Stevens Point, WI 54481 (☎1-800/826-1300).

**Travel Insurance Services**, 2930 Camino Diablo, Suite 300, Walnut Creek, CA 94596 (☎1-800/937-1387).

local brand names can be confusing; ask for advice at the **pharmacy** in any drugstore.

Travellers from Europe do not require **inoculations** to enter the US.

### CRIME AND PERSONAL SAFETY

**No one could pretend that California is trouble-free, although away from the urban centres, crime is often remarkably low-key. Even the lawless reputation of Los Angeles is far in excess of the truth, and most of the city, by day at least, is fairly safe; at night, though, a few areas are completely off limits. Members of the notorious LA gangs are a rare sight outside their own territories (which are usually well away from where you're likely to be), and they tend to kill each other rather than tourists. By being careful, planning ahead, and taking care of your possessions, you should, generally speaking, have few real problems.**

#### MUGGING AND THEFT

The biggest problem for most travellers is the threat of **mugging**. It's impossible to give hard and fast rules about what to do if you're confronted by a mugger. Whether to run, scream or fight depends on the situation – but most locals would just hand over their money.

Of course, the best thing is simply to avoid being mugged, and a few basic rules are worth

## STOLEN TRAVELLERS' CHEQUES AND CREDIT CARDS

Keep a record of the numbers of your **travellers' cheques** separately from the actual cheques; if you lose them, ring the issuing company on the toll-free number below.

They'll ask you for the cheque numbers, the place you bought them, when and how you lost them and whether it's been reported to the police. All being well, you should get the missing cheques reissued within a couple of days – and perhaps an emergency advance to tide you over.

### EMERGENCY NUMBERS

| | | | |
|---|---|---|---|
| **Mastercard** (*Access*) | ☎1-800/999-0454 | **Diners Club** | ☎1-800/234-6377 |
| **American Express** | (TCs) ☎1-800/221-7282 | **Thomas Cook** | ☎1-800/223-7373 |
| | (credit cards) ☎1-800/528-4800 | **Visa** | ☎1-800/227-6811 |

remembering: *don't* flash money around; *don't* peer at your map (or this book) at every street corner, thereby announcing that you're a lost stranger; even if you're terrified or drunk (or both), try not to appear so; avoid dark streets, especially ones you can't see the end of; and in the early hours stick to the roadside edge of the pavement so it's easier to run into the road to attract attention. If you have to ask for directions, choose your target carefully. Another idea is to carry a wad of cash, perhaps $50 or so, separate from the bulk of your holdings so that if you do get confronted you can hand over something of value without it costing you everything.

If the worst happens and your assailant is toting a gun or (more likely) a knife, try to stay calm: remember that he (for this is generally a male pursuit) is probably scared too. Keep still, don't make any sudden movements – and hand over your money. When he's gone, you should, despite your shock, try to find a phone and dial ☎911, or hail a cab and ask the driver to take you to the nearest police station. Here, report the theft and get a reference number on the report to claim insurance and travellers' cheque refunds. If you're in a big city, ring the local *Travelers Aid* (their numbers are listed in the phone book) for sympathy and practical advice. For specific advice for women in case of mugging or attack, see p.46.

Another potential source of trouble is having your **hotel room burgled**. Always store valuables in the hotel safe when you go out; when inside keep your door locked and don't open it to anyone you are suspicious of, and if they claim to be hotel staff and you don't believe them, call reception on the room phone to check.

### CAR CRIME

Crimes committed against tourists driving **rental cars** in the US have garnered headlines around the world in recent years. In major urbanized areas, any car you rent should have nothing on it – such as a particular licence plate – that makes it easy to spot as a rental car. When driving, under no circumstances stop in any unlit or seem-

**Foreign visitors** tend to report that the police are helpful and obliging when things go wrong, although they'll be less sympathetic if they think you brought the trouble on yourself through carelessness. One way non-Americans might accidentally break the law is by **jaywalking**. If you cross the road on a red light or anywhere except an intersection, and are spotted by a cop, you're likely to get a stiff talking-to – and possibly a ticket, leading to a $20 fine. You might also fall foul of America's puritanical **drinking laws** which prohibit drinking in most public places – parks, beaches and the like.

Needless to say, having bags snatched that contain travel documents can be a big headache, none more so than **losing your passport**. If the worst happens, the only British Consulate in California which (very grudgingly) issues passports under normal circumstances is in LA, at 3701 Wilshire Blvd (☎213/385-7381). If you're in LA at the time, things will be reasonablly straightforward. If you're not, phone them, giving an address where they can send you an application form, enclosing a notarized (ie specially stamped at any major bank) photocopy of any ID you might still have plus a $30 reisssuing fee. The passport issuing process can take six weeks: to speed things up, for another $10 the Consulate can telex record departments back home.

ingly deserted urban area – and especially not if someone is waving you down and suggesting that there is something wrong with your car. Similarly, if you are "accidentally" rammed by the driver behind, do not stop immediately but drive on to the nearest well-lit, busy area and **phone ☏911 for assistance**. Keep your doors locked and windows never more than slightly open. Do not open your door or window if someone approaches your car on the pretext of asking directions. Hide any valuables out of sight, preferably locked in the boot or in the glove compartment (any valuables you don't need for your journey should be left in your hotel safe).

## COSTS, MONEY AND BANKS

To help with planning your vacation in California, this book contains detailed price information for lodging and eating. Unless otherwise stated, the hotel price codes given (explained on p.33) are for the cheapest double room throughout most of the year, exclusive of any local taxes which may apply, while meal prices include food only and not drinks or tip. For museums and similar attractions, the prices we quote are generally for adults; you can assume that children get in half-price. Naturally, costs will increase slightly overall during the life of this edition, but the relative comparisons should remain valid.

### COSTS

**Accommodation** is likely to be your biggest single expense. Few hotel or motel rooms cost under $30; it's more usual to pay between $40 and $80 for anything halfway decent in a city, and rates in rural areas are not much cheaper. Although hostels offering dorm beds – usually for $12–15 – are reasonably common, they are by no means everywhere, besides which they save little money for two or more people travelling together. Camping, of course, is cheap, ranging from free to about $18 per night, but is rarely practical in or around the big cities.

As for **food**, $15 a day is enough to get an adequate life-support diet, while for a daily total of around $30 you can dine pretty well. Beyond this, everything hinges on how much sightseeing, taxi-taking, drinking and socializing you do. Much of any of these – especially in the major cities – and you're likely to be getting through upwards of $50 a day. San Francisco in particular seems to invite spending and having fun; above all, it's a place to **shop**.

The rates for **travelling around**, especially on buses, and to a lesser extent on trains and even planes, may look inexpensive on paper, but the distances involved mean that costs soon mount up. For a group of two or more, **renting a car** can be a very good investment, not least because it enables you to stay in the ubiquitous budget motels along the interstate highways instead of relying on expensive downtown hotels.

Remember that a **sales tax** of 7.75 percent is added to virtually everything you buy in stores except for groceries, but isn't part of the marked price. In addition, a couple of the big cities apply a **hotel tax**; this can add as much as fourteen percent to the total bill.

### TRAVELLERS' CHEQUES AND BANKS

**US dollar travellers' cheques** are the best way to carry money, for both American and foreign visitors; they offer the great security of knowing that lost or stolen cheques will be replaced. You should have no problem using the better-known cheques, such as *American Express* and *Visa*, in the same way as cash in shops,

## MONEY: A NOTE FOR FOREIGN TRAVELLERS

Even when the exchange rate is at its least advantageous, most western European visitors find virtually everything – accommodation, food, gas, cameras, clothes and more – to be better value in the US than it is at home. However, if you're used to travelling in the less expensive countries of Europe, let alone in the rest of the world, you shouldn't expect to scrape by on the same minuscule budget once you're in the US.

Regular upheaval in the world money markets causes the relative value of the **US dollar** against the currencies of the rest of the world to vary considerably. Generally speaking, one **pound sterling** will buy between $1.40 and $1.80; one **Canadian dollar** is worth between 70¢ and $1; one **Australian dollar** is worth between 67¢ and 88¢; and one **New Zealand dollar** is worth between 55¢ and 72¢.

### BILLS AND COINS

**US currency** comes in **bills** worth $1, $5, $10, $20, $50 and $100, plus various larger (and rarer) denominations. Confusingly, all are the same size and same green colour, making it necessary to check each bill carefully. The dollar is made up of 100 cents with **coins** of 1 cent (known as a **penny**), 5 cents (a **nickel**), 10 cents (a **dime**) and 25 cents (a **quarter**). Very occasionally you might come across JFK **half-dollars** (50¢), **Susan B Anthony dollar coins**, or a **two-dollar bill**. Change (quarters are the most useful) is needed for buses, vending machines and telephones, so always carry plenty.

restaurants and gas stations (don't be put off by "no checks" signs, which only refer to personal cheques). Be sure to have plenty of the $10 and $20 denominations for everyday transactions.

**Banks** are generally open from 10am until 4pm Monday to Thursday, and 10am to 6pm on Friday. Most major banks change dollar travellers' cheques for their face value (not that there's much point in doing this – and some charge for the privilege, so ask before you do), and **change foreign travellers' cheques and currency**. Exchange bureaux, always found at airports, tend to charge less commission: *Thomas Cook* or *American Express* are the biggest names. Rarely, if ever, do hotels change foreign currency. **Emergency phone numbers** to call if your checks and/or credit cards are stolen are on p.18.

To find the nearest bank that sells a particular brand of travellers' cheque, or to buy cheques by phone, call the following numbers: *American Express* (☎1-800/673 3782), *Citicorp* (☎1-800/645 6556), *MasterCard International/Thomas Cook* (☎1-800/223 7373), *Visa* (☎1-800/227 6811).

### PLASTIC MONEY AND CASH MACHINES

If you don't already have a **credit card**, you should think seriously about getting one before you set off. For many services, it's simply taken for granted that you'll be paying with plastic. When renting a car (or even a bike) or checking into a hotel you may well be asked to show a credit card to establish your creditworthiness –

even if you intend to settle the bill in cash. **Visa**, **Mastercard** (known elsewhere as **Access**), **Diners Club**, **American Express** and **Discover** are the most widely used.

With *Mastercard* or *Visa* it is also possible to **withdraw cash** at any bank displaying relevant stickers, or from appropriate automatic teller machines (**ATMs**). *Diners Club* cards can be used to cash personal cheques at *Citibank* branches. *American Express* cards can only get cash, or buy travellers' cheques, at *American Express* offices (check the Yellow Pages) or from the travellers' cheque dispensers at most major airports. Most **Canadian** credit cards issued by hometown banks are honoured in the US.

ATM cards held by visitors from other states may well work in some Californian machines – check with your bank before you leave home. Not only is this method of financing safer, but at around only a dollar per transaction it's economical as well.

Most major credit cards issued by **foreign banks** are accepted in the US, as well as cash-dispensing cards linked to international networks such as *Cirrus* and *Plus* – once again, check before you set off, as otherwise the machine may simply gobble up your plastic friend. Overseas visitors should also bear in mind that fluctuating

Each of the two main networks operates a toll-free line to let customers know the location of their nearest ATM; *Plus System* is ☎1-800/THE-PLUS, *Cirrus* is ☎1-800/4CI-RRUS.

exchange rates may result in spending more (or less) than expected when the item eventually shows up on a statement.

## EMERGENCIES

Assuming you know someone who is prepared to send you money in a crisis, the quickest way is to have them take the cash to the nearest **Western Union** office (information on ☎1-800/325-6000 in the US, ☎0800-833833 in the UK; ☎02/953-5693 in Australia; and ☎0800-808040 in New Zealand) and have it instantaneously **wired** to the office nearest you, subject to the deduction of five to ten percent commission: the bigger the transaction the lower the percentage. **American Express Moneygram** (☎1-800/543-4080) offers a similar service.

It's also possible to have money wired directly from a bank in your home country to a bank in the US, although this is somewhat less reliable because it involves two separate institutions. If you go this route, the person wiring the funds to you will need to know the telex number of the bank the funds are being wired to. Having money wired from home is never convenient or cheap, and should be considered a last resort.

If you have a few days' leeway, sending a postal money order, exchangeable at any post office through the mail is a cheaper option. The equivalent for foreign travellers is the **international money order**, for which you need to allow up to seven days in the international air mail before arrival. An ordinary cheque sent from overseas takes two to three weeks to clear.

Foreign travellers in difficulties have the final option of throwing themselves on the mercy of their nearest national **Consulate** (see p.14), which will – in worst cases only – repatriate you, but will never, under any circumstances, lend you money. See p.15 for the addresses of consulates in LA and San Francisco.

# COMMUNICATIONS: PHONES AND THE MAIL

Visitors from overseas tend to be impressed by the speed and efficiency of communications in the US (with the exception of the US mail, which is incredibly slow and careless). California largely lives up to this high standard, partly at least because its major cities are important business hubs that depend upon reliable links to the East Coast, as well as being able to keep in touch with the many isolated settlements in the state itself. In rural areas you may find it frustrating just getting to the nearest public phone – which may be many miles away – but in general keeping in touch is easy.

## TELEPHONES

Californian **telephones** are run by a huge variety of companies, many of which were hived off from the previous *Bell System* monopoly – the successor to which is the nationwide *AT&T* network.

**Public telephones** invariably work, and in cities at any rate can be found everywhere – on street corners, in train and bus stations, hotels, bars and restaurants. They take 5¢, 10¢ and 25¢ coins. The cost of a **local call** from a public phone (generally one within the same area code)

### USEFUL NUMBERS

**Emergencies** ☎911; ask for the appropriate emergency service: fire, police or ambulance

**Long-distance directory information** ☎1 (Area Code)/555-1212

**Directory enquiries for toll-free numbers** ☎1-800/555-1212

varies from a minimum of 20¢, and is usually 25¢; when necessary, a voice on the line telling you to pay more.

Some numbers covered by the same area code are considered so far apart that calls between them count as **non-local** (*zone calls*). These cost much more and sometimes require you to dial 1 before the seven-digit number. Pricier still are **long-distance calls** (ie to a different area code, and always preceded by a 1), for which you'll need plenty of change. Non-local calls and long-distance calls are much less expensive if made between 6pm and 8am – the cheapest rates are after 11pm – and calls from **private phones** are always much cheaper than those from public phones. Detailed rates are listed at the front of the **telephone directory** (the White Pages, a copious source of information on many matters).

Making telephone calls from **hotel rooms** is usually more expensive than from a payphone,

though some budget hotels offer free local calls from rooms – ask when you check in. An increasing number of phones accept **credit cards**, while anyone who holds a credit card issued by an American bank can obtain an **AT & T charge card** (information on ☎1-800/874-4000 ext 359). Foreign visitors will have to make do with **phone cards** – in denominations of $5, $10 and $20 – bought from general stores, some hostels and relatively few *7-Elevens*. These provide you with a temporary account (just tap in the number printed on the card), and work out a lot cheaper than feeding coins into a payphone, especially if calling abroad.

Many government agencies, car rental firms, hotels and so on have **toll-free numbers**, which always have the prefix ☎1-800. Within the US, you can dial any number starting with those digits free of charge, though some numbers only operate inside California: it isn't apparent from

---

## INTERNATIONAL TELEPHONE CALLS

**International calls** can be dialled direct from private or (more expensively) public phones. You can get assistance from the **international operator (☎00)**, who may also interrupt every three minutes asking for more money, and call you back for any money still owed immediately after you hang up. The **lowest rates** for international calls to Europe are between 6pm and 7am, when a direct-dialled three-minute call will cost roughly $5.

In **Britain**, it's possible to obtain a free **BT Chargecard (☎0800/800 838)**, using which all calls from overseas can be charged to your quarterly domestic account. To use these cards in the US, or to make a **collect call** (to "reverse the charges"), contact the carrier: *AT&T* ☎1-800/445-5667; *MCI* ☎1-800/444-2162; or *Sprint* ☎1-800/800-0008.

British visitors who are going to be making a number of calls **to the US**, and who want to be able to call ☎1-800 numbers, otherwise inaccessible from outside the country, should take advantage of the **Swiftcall** telephone club. You need a touch-tone phone. Call your nearest office (see box; daily 8am–midnight); once you've paid by credit card for however many units you want, you are given a PIN. Any time you want to get an international line, simply dial ☎0171/488-0800, punch in your PIN, and then dial as you would were you in the US, putting a 1 before the area code, followed by the number. Calls to the USA – including ☎1-800 calls – cost about 16p per minute, a **saving** of over 50 percent.

**SWIFTCALL NUMBERS**

| | |
|---|---|
| London ☎0171/488-2001 | Manchester ☎0161/245-2001 |
| Glasgow ☎0141/616-2001 | Dublin ☎01/671-0457 |
| Belfast ☎01232/314-524 | |

**Australia**'s **Telstra Telecard** (application forms available from Telstra offices) and **New Zealand Telecom**'s **Calling Card** (contact ☎04/382 5818) can be used to make calls charged to a domestic account or credit card.

The telephone code to dial **TO THE US** from the outside world (excluding Canada) is 1.

To make international calls **FROM the US**, dial 011 followed by the country code:

| | | | |
|---|---|---|---|
| **Australia** 61 | **Denmark** 45 | **Germany** 49 | **Ireland** 353 |
| **Netherlands** 31 | **New Zealand** 64 | **Sweden** 46 | **United Kingdom** 44 |

## TELEPHONE AREA CODES IN CALIFORNIA

Los Angeles 213

West Los Angeles 310

Orange County 714

San Francisco 415

East Bay 510

Monterey & San Jose 408

Pasadena 818

Santa Barbara 805

San Bernardino & Riverside area 909

San Diego & eastern California 619

Wine Country & North Coast 707

Sacramento & northeastern California 916

the number until you try. Numbers with the prefix ☎1-900 are pay-per-call lines, generally quite expensive and almost always involving either sports or phone sex. Some numbers, particularly those of consumer services, employ letters as part of their number. The letters are on the button, thus for example, ☎1-800/TAXI becomes ☎1-800/8294.

California has numerous **area codes** – three-digit numbers which must precede the seven-figure number if you're calling from abroad or from a region with a different code. In this book, we've highlighted the local area codes at appropriate moments in the text. With any specific number we give, we've only included the area code if it's not clear from the text which one you should use, or if a given phone number lies outside the region currently being described.

### MAIL SERVICES

**Post offices** usually open Monday to Friday from 9am until 5pm, and Saturday from 9am to noon, and there are blue **mail boxes** on many street corners. Ordinary **mail within the US** costs 32¢ for letters weighing up to an ounce; addresses must include the **zip code**, and a return address must be written on the envelope. **Air mail** from California to Europe generally

takes about a week. Postcards, aerograms and letters weighing up to half an ounce (a single sheet) cost 60¢.

The last line of the address is made up of an abbreviation denoting the state (in California "CA") and a five-figure number – the **zip code** – denoting the local post office. (The additional four digits you will sometimes see appended to zip codes are not essential.) Letters which don't carry the zip code are liable to get lost or at least delayed; if you don't know it, phone books carry a list for their service area, and post offices – even in Britain – have directories.

Letters can be sent c/o **General Delivery** (what's known elsewhere as **poste restante**) to the one relevant post office in each city, but *must* include the zip code and will only be held for thirty days before being returned to sender – so make sure there's a return address on the envelope. If you're receiving mail at someone else's address, it should include "c/o" and the regular occupant's name; otherwise it, too, is likely to be returned.

Rules on sending **parcels** are very rigid: packages must be sealed according to the instructions given at the start of the Yellow Pages. To send anything out of the country, you'll need a green **customs declaration form**, available from a post office. **Postal rates** for sending a parcel weighing up to 1lb are $9.75 to Europe, $11.20 to Australasia.

### TELEGRAMS AND FAXES

To send a **telegram** (also known as a *wire*), don't go to a post office but to a *Western Union* office (listed in the Yellow Pages). Credit card holders can dictate messages over the phone. **International telegrams** cost slightly less than the cheapest international phone call: one sent in the morning from California should arrive at its destination the following day. For domestic telegrams ask for a **mailgram**, which will be delivered to any address in the country the next morning.

Public **fax** machines, which may require your credit card to be "swiped" through an attached device, are found at photocopy centres and, occasionally, bookstores.

## INFORMATION, MAPS AND THE MEDIA

Advance information for a trip to California can be obtained by post from the California Office of Tourism, 801 K St, Suite 1600, Sacramento, CA 95814-3520 (☎916/322-2881 or 1-800/862-2543). Once you've arrived, you'll find most towns have visitor centers of some description – often called the Convention and Visitors Bureau (CVB) or Chamber of Commerce, and all are listed in the *Guide*. These will give out detailed information on the local area and can often help with finding accommodation. Free newspapers in most places carry news of events and entertainment.

Most of the tourist offices we've mentioned can supply you with good **maps**, either free or for a small charge, and, supplemented with our own maps, these should be enough for general sightseeing and touring. *Rand McNally* produces a decent low-cost ($2.50) map of the state plus detailed **city plans**, and its *Road Atlas*, covering the whole country plus Mexico and Canada, is a worthwhile investment If you're travelling further afield. *Gousha's* state map ($2.25), however, is slightly better. For driving or cycling through rural areas, the *Atlas & Gazetteer: Northern California* and *Atlas & Gazetteer: Southern and Central California* (published by DeLorme; $16.95 each) are valuable companions, with detailed city plans, marked campsites and reams of national park and forest information. For something more detailed, say for **hiking** purposes, ranger stations in parks and wilderness areas all sell good-quality local hiking

maps for $1–3, and camping stores generally have a good selection too. The *American Automobile Association* ( ☎1-800/222-4357), based at 4100 E Arkansas Drive, Denver, CO 80222, provides free maps and assistance to its members, and to British members of the *AA* and *RAC*.

Most bookstores will have a range of local trail guides, the best of which we've listed under "Books" in *Contexts*.

### THE MEDIA

The only **newspaper** that's read all over California is the *Los Angeles Times*, which gives probably the best coverage of state, national and world events in the country. Otherwise newspapers tend to excel at reporting their own area but generally rely on agencies for their foreign – and even some national – reports. Major newspapers from other parts of the US such as the *New York Times*, and overseas newspapers, tend to be found only in vending machines in the bigger cities and specialist bookstores elsewhere.

Every community of any size has at least a few **free newspapers**, found in street distribution bins, in cafés, bars or just lying around in piles. It's a good idea to pick up a full assortment: some simply cover local goings-on, others provide specialist coverage of interests ranging from long-distance cycling to getting ahead in business – and the classified and personal ads can provide hours of entertainment. Many of them are also excellent sources for bar, restaurant and nightlife information, and we've mentioned the most useful titles in the *Guide*.

### TELEVISION

Californian **TV** is pretty much the standard network barrage of sitcoms and quiz shows. A number of Spanish-language cable channels serve the state's large Hispanic population; a smaller number are aimed at other, particularly Asian, ethnic groups.

There's hardly a motel room in the state that's not hooked up to **cable**, although the number of channels available to guests varies from place to place. Most cable stations are no better than the major networks (*ABC*, *CBS* and *NBC*), though some of the more specialized channels are consistently interesting. The *ARTS* channel broadcasts enjoyable, if po-faced, arts features, imported

## MAP AND TRAVEL BOOK SUPPLIERS

### UK

**London**

*Daunt Books*, 83 Marylebone High St, W1 (☎0171/224 2295).

*National Map Centre*, 22–24 Caxton St, SW1 (☎0171/222 4945).

*Stanfords*, 12–14 Long Acre, WC2 (☎0171/836 1321); 52 Grosvenor Gardens, London SW1W 0AG; 156 Regent St, London W1R 5TA.

*The Travel Bookshop*, 13–15 Blenheim Crescent, London W11 2EE (☎0171/229 5260).

*The Travellers Bookshop*, 25 Cecil Court, WC2 (☎0171/836 9132).

**Edinburgh**

*Thomas Nelson & Sons Ltd*, 51 York Place, Edinburgh EH1 3JD (☎0131/557-3011).

**Glasgow**

*John Smith and Sons*, 57–61 St Vincent St, G2 5TB (☎0141/221 7472).

Maps by **mail or phone order** are available from *Stanfords;* ☎0171/836 1321.

### IRELAND

**Dublin**

*Easons Bookshop*, 40 O'Connell St, Dublin1 (☎01/873 3811).

*Fred Hanna's Bookshop*, 27–29 Nassau St, Dublin 2 (☎01/677 1255).

*Hodges Figgis Bookshop*, 56–58 Dawson St, Dublin 2 (☎01/677 4754).

**Belfast**

*Waterstone's*, Queens Bldg, 8 Royal Ave, Belfast BT1 1DA (☎01232/247355).

### UNITED STATES

**The Complete Traveler Bookstore**, 199 Madison Ave, New York, NY 10016 (☎212/685-9007); 3207 Fillmore St, San Francisco, CA 92123 (☎415/923- 1511).

**Forsyth Travel Library**, 9154 W 57th St, Shawnee Mission, KS 66201 (☎1-800/367-7984).

**Map Link Inc**, 25 E Mason St, Santa Barbara, CA 93101 (☎805/965-4402).

**Phileas Fogg's Books & Maps**, #87 Stanford Shopping Center, Palo Alto, CA 94304 (☎1-800/233- FOGG in California; ☎1-800/533-FOGG elsewhere in US).

**Rand McNally**,* 444 N Michigan Ave, Chicago, IL 60611 (☎312/321-1751); 150 E 52nd St, New York, NY 10022 (☎212/758-7489); 595 Market St, San Francisco, CA 94105 (☎415/777-3131); 1201 Connecticut Ave NW, Washington, DC 2003 (☎202/223-6751).

**The Savvy Traveller**, 310 S Michigan Ave, Chicago, IL 60604 (☎312/913-9800).

**Sierra Club Bookstore**, 730 Polk St, San Francisco, CA 94109 (☎415/923-5500).

**Traveler's Bookstore**, 22 W 52nd St, New York, NY 10019 (☎212/664-0995).

**Note**: *Rand McNally* now has 24 stores across the US; call ☎1-800/333-0136 (ext 2111) for the location of your nearest store, or for **direct mail** maps.

### CANADA

**Open Air Books and Maps**, 25 Toronto St, Toronto, ON M5R 2C1 (☎416/363-0719).

**Ulysses Travel Bookshop**, 4176 St-Denis, Montréal (☎514/289-0993).

**World Wide Books and Maps**, 714 Granville St, Vancouver, BC V6Z 1E4 (☎604/687-3320).

### AUSTRALIA

**Adelaide**

*The Map Shop*, 16a Peel St, Adelaide, SA 5000 (☎08/8231 2033).

**Melbourne**

*Bowyangs*, 372 Little Bourke St, Melbourne, VIC 3000 (☎03/9670 4383).

**Sydney**

*Travel Bookshop*, 20 Bridge St, Sydney, NSW 2000 (☎02/9241 3554).

**Perth**

*Perth Map Centre*, 891 Hay St, Perth, WA 6000 (☎09/322 5733; ☎08/9322 5733 from Sep 1997).

### NEW ZEALAND

**Specialty Maps**, 58 Albert St, Auckland (☎09/307 2217).

TV plays and the like. *CNN (Cable Network News)* offers round-the-clock news, *HBO (Home Box Office)* shows recent big-bucks movies, *AMC (American Movie Company)* shows old black-and-white films, and *ESPN* exclusively covers sport. Finally, there's *MTV* (seemingly absent from the menu of most chain hotels), the thirty-something *VH-1* and a number of other music stations.

Many major sporting occasions are transmitted on a pay-per-view basis. To watch events like world heavyweight boxing bouts you may have to pay as much as $40, either to your motel or to a bar that's putting on a live screening. Virtually every hotel and motel now offers a choice of movies that have just finished their cinema run, for around $7 a movie.

### RADIO

**Radio** stations are even more abundant than TV channels, and the majority, again, stick to a bland commercial format. Except for news and chat, stations on the **AM** band are best avoided in favour of **FM**, in particular the nationally funded public and college stations, found between 88 and 92 FM. These provide diverse and listenable programming, be it bizarre underground rock or obscure theatre, and they're also good sources for local nightlife news.

Though the large cities boast good specialist **music** stations – contemporary, jazz and classical – for most of the time you'll probably have to resort to skipping up and down the frequencies, between re-run Eagles tracks, country and western tunes, fire-and-brimstone Bible thumpers and crazed phone-ins. Driving through rural areas can be frustrating; for hundreds of miles you might only be able to receive one or two (very dull) stations. Finally, **Mexican stations** – many broadcast using very powerful transmitters located south of the border – provide an enjoyable, alternative flavour of Southern California, even if you don't speak Spanish.

## GETTING AROUND CALIFORNIA

Although distances can be great, getting around California is seldom much of a problem. Certainly, things are always easier if you have a car, but between the major cities there are good bus links and a reasonable train service. The only regions where things are more difficult using public transport are the isolated rural areas, though even here, by adroit forward-planning, you can usuallly get to the main points of interest on local buses and charter services, details of which are in the relevant sections of the *Guide*.

### BY CAR

**Driving** is by far the best way to get around California. Los Angeles, for example, has grown up and assumed its present shape since cars were invented, sprawling for so many miles in all directions that your hotel may be fifteen or twenty miles from the sights you came to see, or perhaps simply on the other side of a freeway which there's no way of crossing on foot. Away from the cities, many places are almost impossible to reach without your own transport; most national and state parks are only served by public transport as far as the main visitor center, if that. What's more, if you are planning on doing a fair amount of camping, renting a car can save you money by allowing access to free campsites.

Drivers wishing to **rent** cars are supposed to have held their licences for at least one year

## ROAD CONDITIONS

The California Department of Transportation (aka CalTrans) operates a **toll-free 24-hour information line** (☎1-800/427-ROAD) giving up-to-the-minute details of road conditions throughout the state. On a touch-tone phone simply input the number of the road ("5" for I-5, "299" for Hwy-299, etc) and a recorded voice will tell you about any relevant weather conditions, delays, detours and snow closures, etc. From out of state, or without a touch-tone phone, similar information is available on ☎916/445-1534.

Nevada Highways has a similar system on ☎1-702/793-1313.

(though this is rarely checked); people under 25 years old may encounter problems, and will probably get lumbered with a higher than normal insurance premium. Car rental companies (listed below) will also expect you to have a credit card; if you don't they may let you leave a hefty **deposit** (at least $200), but don't count on it. The likeliest tactic for getting a good deal is to phone the major firms' toll-free numbers and ask for their best rate – most will try to beat the offers of their competitors, so it's worth haggling.

In general the lowest rates are available at the airport branches – $149 a week for a subcompact is a fairly standard budget rate. Always be sure to get free unlimited mileage, and be aware that leaving the car in a different state to the one in which you rent it will incur a **drop-off charge** that can be as much as $200 or more – however, many companies do not charge drop-off fees within California itself; check before you book if you plan a one-way drive. Also, don't automatically go for the cheapest rate, as there's a big difference in the quality of cars from company to company; industry leaders like *Hertz* and *Avis* tend to have newer, lower-mileage cars, often with air-conditioning and stereo cassette decks as standard equipment – no small consideration on a 2000-mile desert drive.

Alternatively, various **local** companies rent out new – and not so new (try *Rent-a-Heap* or *Rent-a-Wreck*) – vehicles. They are certainly cheaper than the big chains if you just want to spin around a city for a day, but you have to drop them back where you picked them up, and free mileage is seldom included, so they work out far more costly for long-distance travel. Addresses and phone numbers are listed in the Yellow Pages.

When you rent a car, read the small print carefully for details on **Collision Damage**

| CAR RENTAL COMPANIES | | | |
|---|---|---|---|
| **IN NORTH AMERICA** | | Avis | ☎0181/848 8733 |
| Alamo | ☎1-800/354-2322 | **Budget** | ☎0800/181181 |
| Avis | ☎1-800/331-1212 | **Dollar (Eurodollar)** | ☎01895/233300 |
| **Budget** | ☎1-800/527-0700 | **Hertz** | ☎0345/555888 |
| **Dollar** | ☎1-800/421-6868 | **Holiday Autos** | ☎0171/491 1111 |
| **Enterprise** | ☎1-800/325-8007 | | |
| **Hertz** | ☎1-800/654-3131; | **IN AUSTRALIA** | |
| | in Canada ☎1-800/263-0600 | Avis | ☎1-800/225 533 |
| **Holiday Autos** | ☎1-800/422-7737 | **Budget** | ☎13/2848 |
| **National** | ☎1-800/CAR-RENT | **Hertz** | ☎13/1918 |
| **Payless** | ☎1-800/729-5377 | | |
| **Rent-A-Wreck** | ☎1-800/535-1391 | **IN NEW ZEALAND** | |
| **Thrifty** | ☎1-800/367-2277 | Avis | ☎09/525 1982 |
| **Value** | ☎1-800/327-2501 | **Budget** | ☎09/275 2222 |
| | | **Fly and Drive Holidays** | ☎09/366 0759 |
| **IN THE UK** | | **Hertz** | ☎09/309 0989 |
| Alamo | ☎0800/272200 | | |

## DRIVING FOR FOREIGN VISITORS

UK nationals can **drive** in the US on a full UK driving licence (International Driving Permits are not always regarded as sufficient). Fly-drive deals are good value if you want to **rent** a car (see p.4–5), though you can save up to 60 percent simply by booking in advance with a major firm. If you choose not to pay until you arrive, be sure you take a written confirmation of the price with you. Remember that it's safer not to rent a car straight off a long transatlantic flight; and that standard rental cars have **automatic transmissions**.

It's also easier and cheaper to book **RVs** in advance from Britain. Most travel agents who specialize in the US can arrange RV rental, and usually do it cheaper if you book a flight through them as well. A price of £1000 for a five-berth van for two weeks is fairly typical. Once you have a vehicle, you'll find **petrol** (US "gasoline") is fairly cheap, a self-served US gallon (3.8 litres) of **unleaded** – which most cars use – ranging from $1.20 in selected urban stations to around $1.90 in remote areas where you've little choice but to pay their inflated prices. Occasionally higher rates are charged for paying by credit card. In California most petrol stations are self-service: when removing the nozzle from the pump, remember to lift or turn the lever to activate it.

American **miles** are the same as British miles but sometimes **distances** are given in **hours** – the length of time it should take to drive between any two places. There are obviously other differences between driving in the US and in Britain, not least the fact that rules and regulations aren't always nationally fixed. Many foreign travellers have problems at first adjusting to **driving on the right**. This can be remarkably easy to forget – some people draw a cross or tie a ribbon on their right hand to remind them.

There are several **types of road**. The best for covering long distances quickly are the wide, straight and fast **Interstate highways**, usually at least six-lane motorways and always prefixed by "I" (eg I-5) – marked on maps by a red, white and blue shield bearing the number. Even-numbered Interstates usually run east–west and those with odd numbers north–south. Driving on these roads is easier than it first appears, but you need to adapt quickly to the American habit of **changing lanes**: US drivers do this frequently, and overtake on both sides. In California you are also permitted to stay in the fast lane while being overtaken on the inside. All these roads are free: there are none of the turnpikes found in the east. Big overhead signs warn you if the road's about to split towards two different destinations (this happens quite often), or an exit's coming up. Sometimes a lane *must* exit, and if you lose concentration you're liable to leave the Interstate accidentally – no great calamity as it's easy enough to get back on again. **Missing an exit** is more annoying – U-turns are strictly illegal, and you have to continue to the next exit. In urban areas during busy periods, getting on the freeway can be time-consuming, **filter traffic lights** at certain on-ramps allowing only one vehicle at a time to pass.

---

**Waiver (CDW)**, sometimes called Liability Damage Waiver (LDW), a form of insurance which often isn't included in the initial rental charge but is well worth considering. This specifically covers the car that you are driving yourself, as you are in any case insured for damage to other vehicles. At $9–13 a day, it can add substantially to the total cost, but without it you're liable for every scratch to the car – even those that aren't your fault. Some credit card companies offer automatic CDW coverage to anyone using their card; read the fine print beforehand in any case.

You should also check your **third-party liability**. The standard policy often only covers you for the first $15,000 of the third party's claim against you, a paltry sum in litigation-conscious America. Companies strongly advise taking out third-party insurance, which costs a further $10–12 a day but indemnifies the driver for up to $2,000,000.

If you **break down** in a rented car, there'll be an emergency number pinned to the dashboard. You can summon the highway patrol on one of the new emergency phones stationed along freeways (usually at half-mile intervals) and many other remote highways (mostly every two miles) – although as the highway patrol and state police cruise by regularly, you can just sit tight and wait. Raising your car hood is recognized as a call for assistance, although women travelling alone should be wary of doing this.

Another tip, for women especially, is to rent a **mobile telephone** from the car rental agency – you often only have to pay a nominal amount until you actually use it, and in larger cities they increasingly come built in to the car; but having a phone can be reassuring at least, and a poten-

A grade down, and broadly similar to British dual carriageways and main roads, are the **State highways** (eg Hwy-1) and the **US highways** (eg US-395). Some major roads in cities are technically state highways but are better known by their local name. Hwy-2 in Los Angeles, for instance, is better known as Santa Monica Boulevard. In rural areas, you'll also find much smaller **County Roads**; their number is preceded by a letter denoting their county. In built-up areas **streets** are arranged on a grid system and labelled at each junction.

Although the law says that drivers must keep up with the flow of traffic, which is often hurtling along at 70mph, the official **speed limit** in California is 55mph (65mph on some stretches of I-5), with lower signposted limits – usually around 30–35mph – in built-up areas. There are no **spot fines** but if given a ticket for **speeding**, your case will come to court and the size of the fine will be at the discretion of the judge; $75 is a rough minimum. If **the police** do flag you down, don't get out of the car, and don't reach into the glove compartment as the cops may think you have a gun. Simply sit still with your hands on the wheel; when questioned, be polite and don't attempt to make jokes.

As for other possible violations, US law requires that any **alcohol** be carried unopened in the boot of the car, and it can't be stressed enough that **driving while intoxicated (DWI)** is a very serious offence. If a police officer smells alcohol on your breath, he/she is entitled to administer a breath, saliva or urine test. If you fail, you'll be locked up with other inebriates in the *drunk tank* of

later be heard by a judge, who can fine you $200, or in extreme (or repeat) cases, imprison you for thirty days. Less serious offences include making a **U-turn** on an Interstate or anywhere where a single unbroken line runs along the middle of the road; driving in **car pool lanes** with fewer than two people in the vehicle; **parking on a highway**; and front-seat passengers riding without fastened **seatbelts**. At **junctions**, one rule is crucially different from the UK: you can turn right on a red light if there is no traffic approaching from the left; otherwise red and amber mean sto1 Stopping is also compulsory, in both directions, when you come upon a school bus disgorging passsengers with its lights flashing.

Once at your destination, you'll find in cities at least that **parking meters** are commonplace. Charges for an hour range from 25¢–$1. **Car parks** (US *parking lots*) charge up to $10 a day. If you park in the wrong place (such as within 10ft of a fire hydrant) your car is likely to be towed away or **wheel-clamped**; a sticker on the windscreen tells you where to pay the $30 fine. Watch out for signs indicating the **street cleaning** schedule, as you mustn't park overnight before an early-morning clean. The violation is often waived for first-offenders but clearing your name is a hassle all the same. **Validated parking**, where your fee for parking in, say, a shopping mall's lot is waived on production of a receipt from one of the stores, is common, as is **valet parking** at even quite modest restaurants, for which a small tip is expected.

tial lifesaver should something go terribly wrong.

One variation on renting is a **driveaway**, whereby you drive a car from one place to another on behalf of the owner, paying only for the gas you use. The same rules as for renting apply, but look the car over before you take it, as you'll be lumbered with any repair costs, and a large fuel bill if the vehicle's a big drinker. The most common routes are between California and New York, although there's a fair chance you'll find something that needs shifting up the coast, from Los Angeles to San Francisco. See p.10 for further details.

## RENTING AN RV

Besides cars, Recreational Vehicles or **RVs** (camper vans) can be rented for around $400 a week, although outlets are surprisingly rare, as

people tend to own their RVs: in LA try *El Monte Rents*, 12061 E Valley Blvd, CA 91732 (☎818/443-6158). The *Recreational Vehicle Rental Association*, 3930 University Drive, Fairfax VA 22030 (☎703/591-7130 or 1-800/336-0355), publishes a newsletter and a directory of rental firms. Some of the larger companies offering RV rentals are *Cruise America* (☎1-800/327-7799, *Go! Vacations* (☎1-800/845-9888), and *Grand Travel Systems* (☎602/939-6909 or 1-800/849-9959).

On top of the rental fees, take into account the cost of gas (some RVs do 12 miles to the gallon or less) and any drop-off charges, in case you plan to do a one-way trip across the country. Also, it is rarely legal simply to pull up in an RV and spend the night at the roadside – you are expected to stay in designated parks that cost up to $20 per night.

## ADVANCED PLANNING FOR OVERSEAS TRAVELLERS

### *AMTRAK* RAIL PASSES

**Foreign travellers** have a choice of four **rail passes**; including the **Coastal Pass**, which permits unlimited train travel on the east and west coasts, but not between the two.

|  | **15-day** (June–Aug) | **15-day** (Sept–May) | **30-day** (June–Aug) | **30-day** (Sept–May) |
|---|---|---|---|---|
| **Far West** | $205 | $185 | $265 | $235 |
| **West** | $265 | $215 | $330 | $290 |
| **Coastal** | – | – | $230 | $205 |
| **National** | $355 | $245 | $440 | $350 |

On production of a passport issued outside the US or Canada, the passes can be bought at *Amtrak* stations in the US. In the **UK**, you can buy them from *Destination Marketing*, 2 Cinnamon Row, York Place, London SW11 3TW (☎0171/978 5212); in **Ireland**, contact *Campus Travel/Eurotrain* (☎01/874 1777); in **Australia**, *Walshes World* (☎02/232 7499); and in **New Zealand**, *Atlantic & Pacific* (☎071/ 978 5212).

In addition, **All Aboard America** fares – available to anyone within a 45 day period – allow up to three stops on a round-trip ticket. See p.9 for details.

### *GREYHOUND* AMERIPASSES

Foreign visitors can buy a *Greyhound* **Ameripass**, offering unlimited travel within a set time limit, before leaving home: most travel agents can oblige. In the UK, they cost £65 (4-day; Mon–Thurs only), £80 (5-day), £105 (7-day), £145 (15-day), £195 (30-day) or £325 (60-day). *Greyhound*'s office is at Sussex House, London Road, East Grinstead, West Sussex RH19 1LD (☎01342/317317). No daily extensions are available.

The first time you use your pass, it will be dated by the ticket clerk (which becomes the commencement date of the ticket), and your destination is written on a page which the driver will tear out and keep as you board the bus. Repeat this procedure for every subsequent journey.

### AIR PASSES

All the main American airlines (and *British Airways* in conjunction with *USAir*) offer **air passes** for visitors who plan to fly a lot within the US; these have to be bought in advance, and in the UK are usually sold with the proviso that you cross the Atlantic with the relevant airline. All the deals are broadly similar, involving the purchase of at least three **coupons** (for around £160 and around £55 for each additional coupon), each valid for a flight of any duration in the US.

The **Visit USA** scheme entitles foreign travellers to a 30 percent discount on any full-priced US domestic fare, provided you buy the ticket before you leave home. If you just plan to buy one flight, good low-season fares from New York, Washington and Boston to California are around $300–350 round-trip; LA is marginally less expensive than San Francisco.

## BY BUS

If you're travelling on your own, and making a lot of stops, **buses** are by far the cheapest way to get around. The main long-distance service is **Greyhound**, which links all major cities and many smaller towns. Out in the country, buses are fairly scarce, sometimes appearing only once a day, and here you'll need to plot your route with care. But along the main highways, buses run around the clock to a fairly full timetable, stopping only for meal breaks (almost always fast-food dives) and driver changeovers. *Greyhound* buses are slightly less uncomfortable than you might expect, too, and it's feasible to save on a

night's accommodation by travelling overnight and sleeping on the bus – though you may not feel up to much the next day.

To avoid possible hassle, lone female travellers in particular should take care to sit as near to the driver as possible, and to arrive during daylight hours, as many bus stations are in fairly dodgy areas. It used to be that any sizeable community would have a *Greyhound* station; in some places the post office or a gas station doubles as the bus stop and ticket office, and in many others the bus service has been cancelled altogether. Reservations, either in person at the station or on the toll-free number, are not essential but recommended – if a bus is full you may be forced to wait until the next one, sometimes overnight or longer.

**Fares** average 10¢ a mile, which can add up quickly; for example, $49 from Los Angeles to San Francisco one-way. For long-trip travel riding the bus costs about the same as the train; consider-ing the time (75 hours coast-to-coast, if you eat and sleep on the bus) it's not that much cheaper than flying. However, the bus is the best deal if you plan to visit a lot of places and *Greyhound*'s **Ameripasses** for domestic travellers are good for unlimited travel nationwide for seven days ($179), fifteen days ($289) and 30 days ($399); the reduced rates for foreign travellers are on p.30.

*Greyhound* produces a condensed **timetable** of major country-wide routes, but does not distribute it to travellers; to plan your route, pick up the free route-by-route timetables from larger stations.

Bear in mind that fair-sized distances can be covered for very little money (if also very slowly) using **local buses**, which connect neighbouring districts. It's possible, for example, to travel from San Diego to Los Angeles for $3.50, but it'll take all day and at least three changes of bus to do it.

### GREEN TORTOISE

One alternative to Long-Distance Bus Hell is the slightly countercultural *Green Tortoise*, whose buses, furnished with foam cushions, bunks, fridges and rock music, ply the major Californian cities, running between Los Angeles, San Francisco and on into the Pacific Northwest. In summer, they also cross the country to New York and Boston, transcontinental trips which amount to mini-tours of the nation, taking 10–14 days (at a current cost of $279–349, not includ-ing contributions to the food fund which amount to around $7 a day), and allowing plenty of stops for hiking, river-rafting and hot springs. Other *Green Tortoise* trips include excursions to the major national parks (in 16 days for $499), and north to Alaska.

**Main Office**: 494 Broadway, San Francisco, CA 94133; ☎415/956-7500 or 1-800/227-4766.

And of course, there's always the hippyish *Green Tortoise*, which runs between the major Californian cities (see box).

## BY TRAIN

Unlike elsewhere in the US, travelling on the *Amtrak* **rail** network is a viable way of getting about California, thanks in great measure to the growing number of *Amtrak Thruway* buses, which bring passengers from the many rail-less parts of the state to the trains. Travelling by train is more expensive than *Greyhound*, $75 one-way between Los Angeles and San Francisco, for example, but unlike on a bus, a smooth journey with few if any delays is a near certainty. All the major cities are connected and the carriages clean, comfortable, tidy and rarely crowded. Probably the prettiest route is the *Coast Starlight*, which winds along the coast between Santa Barbara and San Luis Obispo, a 100-mile coast-line ride during which it's not unusual to see seals, dolphins or even whales in the waters offshore. The other LA-to-SF *Amtrak* routes head inland, by bus to Bakersfield then by rail north through the dull San Joaquin Valley. Avoid these unless you are making for Yosemite National Park.

Americans can cut **fares** greatly by using one of three **All Aboard America rail passes**, each of which gives unlimited travel for 45 days; for details see p.9. The coastal pass available to foreign travellers (see p.30) is not sold to US citizens.

For all information on *Amtrak* **fares and schedules** in the US, use the toll-free number ☎1-800/USA-RAIL; do not phone individual stations. (8727245)

## BY PLANE

A **plane** is obviously the quickest way of getting around California, and much less expensive than you may think; by keeping up to date with the ever-changing deals being offered by airlines – check with your local travel agent or read the ads in local newspapers – you may be able to take advantage of heavily discounted fares.

Airlines with a strong route structure in the state include *American*, *Continental*, *Delta*, *Northwest*, *Southwest*, *TWA* and *United*. Phone the airlines for routes and schedules, then buy your ticket from a travel agent using the computerized Fare Assurance Program, which processes all the available ticket options and searches for the lowest fare, taking into account the special needs of individual travellers. One agent using the service is *Travel Avenue* (☎1-800/333-3335).

At off-peak times, flights between Los Angeles and San Francisco can cost as little as $80 one-way (only slightly more than the equivalent train fare), though may well require a booking to be made 21 days in advance.

## CYCLING

In general, **cycling** is a cheap and healthy method of getting around all the big **cities**, some of which have cycle lanes and local buses equipped to carry bikes – strapped to the outside. In **country areas**, certainly, there's much scenic, and largely level, land, especially around Sacramento and the Wine Country.

Bikes can be **rented** for $25 a day, $90–100 a week (more for a mountain or all-terrain bike), from outlets usually found close to beaches, university campuses, or simply in areas which are good for cycling; the local visitor center will have details. Apart from the coastal fog, which tends to clear by midday, you'll encounter few **weather** problems (except perhaps sunburn) but remember that the further north you go, the lower the temperatures become.

For **long-distance cycling** you'll need a good quality, multi-speed bike (but don't immediately plump for a mountain bike, unless you are planning a lot of off-road use – good road conditions and trail restrictions in national parks make a touring bike an equally good or better choice), also maps and a helmet (not a legal necessity, but a very

good idea). A route avoiding the Interstates (on which cycling is illegal) is essential, and it's also wise to cycle north to south, as the wind blows this way in the summer and can make all the difference between a pleasant trip and acute leg-ache. Of the **problems** you'll encounter, the main one is traffic: wide, cumbersome and slow recreational vehicles, and in Northern California enormous logging trucks whose slipstream will pull you towards the middle of the road. Be particularly careful if you're planning to cycle along Hwy-1 on the central coast, since besides heavy traffic, it has tight curves, dangerous precipices, and is prone to fog.

If you're camping as well as cycling, look out for **hiker/biker campgrounds** ($3 per person per night), which are free of cars and campervans, dotted across California's state parks and beaches. Many of them were set up in 1976 as part of the **Pacific Coast Bicentennial Bike Route** running 1000 miles from the Mexican to the Oregon border. Sites are allotted on a first-come-first-served basis, and all offer water and toilet facilities but seldom showers. For more information, write to *Hostelling International – USA* (see p.36); *Adventure Cycling Association* (formerly *Bikecentennial*), 150 E Pine St, Missoula, MT 59807 (☎406/721-1776); or the *Sierra Club* (address on p.45).

---

**HITCHING**

The usual advice given to **hitchhikers** is that they should use their common sense; in fact, of course, common sense should tell anyone that hitchhiking in the US is a **bad idea**. We do not recommend it under any circumstances.

# ACCOMMODATION

Accommodation standards in California – as in the rest of the US – are high, and costs inevitably form a significant proportion of the expenses for any trip to the state. It can be possible to haggle, however, especially in the chain motels, and if you're on your own, it's possible to pare costs by sleeping in dormitory-style hostels, where a bed can cost $12–15. However, groups of two or more will find it little more expensive to stay in the far more plentiful motels and hotels, where basic rooms away from the major cities typically cost anything upwards of $30 per night. Many hotels will set up a third single bed for around $5 to $10 on top of the regular price, reducing costs for three people sharing. By contrast, the lone traveller will have a hard time of it: "singles" are usually double rooms at an only slightly reduced rate. Prices quoted by hotels and motels are almost always for the actual room rather than for each person using it.

**Motels** are plentiful on the main approach roads to cities, around beaches and by the main road junctions in country areas. High-rise **hotels** predominate along the popular sections of the coast and are sometimes the only accommodation in city centres. In major cities **campgrounds** tend to be on the outskirts, if they exist at all.

Wherever you stay, you'll be expected to **pay in advance**, at least for the first night and perhaps for further nights too, particularly if it's high season and the hotel's expecting to be busy. Payment can be in cash or in dollar travellers' cheques, though it's more common to give your credit card number and sign for everything when you leave. **Reservations** are only held until 5pm or 6pm unless you've told them you'll be arriving late. Most of the larger chains have an advance booking form in their brochures and will make reservations at another of their premises for you.

Since cheap accommodation in the cities and on the popular sections of the coast is snapped up fast, always **book ahead** whenever possible, using the suggestions in this book.

## HOTELS AND MOTELS

**Hotels** and **motels** are essentially the same thing, although motels tend to be located beside the main roads away from city centres – and thus are much more accessible to drivers. The budget ones are pretty basic affairs, but in general there's a uniform standard of comfort everywhere – double rooms with bathroom, TV and phone – and you don't get a much better deal by paying,

## ACCOMMODATION PRICE CODES

Throughout this book, accommodation prices have been graded with the symbols below, according to the cost of the least expensive double room throughout most of the year. Expect prices in most places to jump into the next highest category on Friday and Saturday nights.

However, with the exception of the budget interstate motels, there's rarely such a thing as a set rate for a room. A basic motel in a seaside or mountain resort may double its prices according to the season, while a big-city hotel which charges $200 per room during the week will often slash its tariff at the weekend when all the business types have gone home. Particularly in scenic areas, prices might leap into the next higher category at weekends. As the high and low seasons for tourists vary widely across the state, astute planning can save a lot of money. Watch out also for local events, which can raise rates far above normal.

Only where we explicitly say so do these room rates include local taxes.

| | | | | |
|---|---|---|---|---|
| ① up to $30 | ② $30–45 | ③ $45–60 | ④ $60–80 | ⑤ $80–100 |
| ⑥ $100–130 | ⑦ $130–175 | ⑧ $175–250 | ⑨ $250+ | |

## NATIONAL HOTEL, HOSTEL AND MOTEL CHAINS

Most of the hotel and lodging chains listed below publish handy free directories (with maps and illustrations of their properties). Although we have indicated typical room rates (using the codes explained on p.33), bear in mind that the location of a particular hotel or motel has a huge impact on price.

| | | | |
|---|---|---|---|
| Best Western (③–⑥) | ☎1-800/528-1234 | ITT Sheraton (⑤ and up) | ☎1-800/325-3535 |
| Budgetel (③) | ☎1-800/428-3438 | La Quinta Inns (④) | ☎1-800/531-5900 |
| Comfort Inns (④–⑤) | ☎1-800/221-2222 | Marriott Hotels (⑥ and up) | ☎1-800/228-9290 |
| Courtyard by Marriott (⑤–⑥) | ☎1-800/321-2211 | Motel 6 (②–③)) | ☎505/891-6161 |
| Days Inn (④–⑤) | ☎1-800/325-2525 | Ramada Inns (④ and up) | ☎1-800/272-6232 |
| Econolodge (①–③) | ☎1-800/446-6900 | Red Carpet Inns (②) | ☎1-800/251-1962 |
| Embassy Suites Hotels (⑥) | ☎1-800/362-2779 | Red Roof Inns (③) | ☎1-800/848-7878 |
| Fairfield Inns (③) | ☎1-800/228-2800 | Scottish Inns (②) | ☎1-800/251-1962 |
| Friendship Inns (③) | ☎1-800/424-4777 | Select Inns (②) | ☎1-800/641-1000 |
| Hallmark Inns (③) | ☎1-800/251-3294 | Sleep Inns (③) | ☎1-800/221-2222 |
| Hampton Inns (④–⑤) | ☎1-800/426-7866 | Sonesta (⑤ and up) | ☎1-800/766-3782 |
| Hilton Hotels (⑤ and up) | ☎1-800/445-8667 | Stouffer Hotels (⑤ and up) | ☎1-800/468-3571 |
| Holiday Inns (⑤ and up) | ☎1-800/465-4329 | Susse Chalet (②–③) | ☎1-800/524-2538 |
| Hostelling International – | | Super 8 Motels (③–④) | ☎1-800/800-8000 |
| American Youth Hostels (①) | ☎1-800/444-6111 | Travelodge (②) | ☎1-800/255-3050 |
| Howard Johnson (②–⑤) | ☎1-800/654-2000 | YMCA (①–②) | ☎1-800/922-9622 |

say, $50 instead of $35. Over $50, the room and its fittings simply get bigger and more luxurious, and there'll probably be a swimming pool which guests can use for free. Paying over $100 brings you into the realms of the en-suite jacuzzi.

While inexpensive diners may be everywhere, a growing number of California hotels are providing a **complimentary breakfast**. Sometimes this will be no more than a cup of coffee and a sticky bun; increasingly, however, it is a sit-down affair likely to comprise fruit, cereals, muffins and toast. In the pricier places, you may also be offered made-to-order omelettes.

In most places you'll be able to find cheap one-off hotels and motels simply by keeping your eyes open – they're usually advertised by enormous roadside signs. Alternatively, there are a number of budget-priced **chains** whose rooms cost around $28–45, such as *Econolodge*, *Days Inn* and *Motel 6*. Mid-priced options include *Best Western*, *Howard Johnson*, *Travelodge* and *Ramada* – though if you can afford to pay this much ($50–100) there's normally somewhere nicer to stay. When it's worth blowing a hunk of cash on somewhere really atmospheric we've said as much in the *Guide*. Bear in mind the most upscale

establishments have all manner of services which may appear to be free but for which you'll be expected to **tip** in a style commensurate with the hotel's status – ie big. For more on tipping see p.39 and 56.

### DISCOUNTS AND RESERVATIONS

During **off-peak periods** many motels and hotels struggle to fill their rooms and it's worth **haggling** to get a few dollars off the asking price. Staying in the same place for more than one night will bring further reductions. Additionally, pick up the many **discount coupons** which fill tourist information offices and look out for the free *Traveler Discount Guide*. Read the small print, though: what appears to be an amazingly cheap room rate sometimes turns out to be a per-person charge for two people sharing, and limited to midweek.

### B&B INNS AND HOTELS

**Bed and breakfast** in California is a luxury – even the mattresses have to conform to a standard of comfort far higher than those in hotels. Typically, the bed-and-breakfast inns, as they're usually known, are restored buildings in

## HOTEL DISCOUNT VOUCHERS

For the benefit of overseas travellers, many of the higher-rung hotel chains offer **pre-paid discount vouchers**, which in theory save you money if you're prepared to pay in advance. To take advantage of such schemes, British travellers must purchase the vouchers in the UK, at a usual cost of £30–60 per night for a minimum of two people sharing. However, it's hard to think of a good reason to buy them; you may save a nominal amount on the fixed rates, but better-value accommodation is not exactly difficult to find in the US, and you may well regret the inflexibility imposed upon your travels. Most UK travel agents will have details of the various voucher schemes.

the smaller cities and more rural areas – although the big cities also have a few, especially San Francisco. Even the larger establishments – often distinguished by being called B&B Hotels – tend to have no more than ten rooms, without TV and phone but often with plentiful flowers, stuffed cushions and an over-contrived homey atmosphere; others may just be a couple of furnished rooms in someone's home, or an entire apartment where you won't even see your host. Victorian and Romantic are dominant themes; while selecting the best in that vein, we've also gone out of our way to seek out those which don't conform.

While always including a huge and wholesome breakfast (5 courses is not unheard of), prices vary greatly: anything from $55 to $200 depending on location and season. Most fall between $75 and $95 per night for a double, a little more for a whole apartment. Bear in mind, too, that they are often booked well in advance, and even if they're not full, the cheaper rooms which determine our price code may be already taken.

## Ys AND HOSTELS

At an average of $12 per night per person, **hostels** are clearly the cheapest accommodation option in California other than camping. There are three main kinds of hostel-type accommodation in the US: YMCA/YWCA hostels (known as "*Ys*") offering accommodation for both sexes, or in a few cases, women-only accommodation; official *HI–AYH* hostels; and the growing *AAIH* (*American Association of Independent Hostels*) organization.

Prices in **YMCAs** range from around $12 for a dormitory bed to $18 for a single or double room. Not all Ys offer accommodation many being basically health clubs. Those that do are often in older buildings in less than ideal neighbourhoods, but facilities can include a gymnasium, a swimming pool, and an inexpensive cafeteria.

You'll find *HI-AYH* hostels (the prefix is usually shortened to *HI* in listings) in major cities and popular hiking areas, including national and state parks, across California. Most urban hostels have 24-hour access, while rural ones may have a curfew and limited daytime hours. *HI* also operates a couple of small "home hostels" in the state; though similar to other hostels you need to reserve in advance or there may be no one there to receive you. Rates at *HI* hostels range from $7 to $18 for *HI* members; non-members generally pay an additional $3 per night.

Particularly if you're travelling in high season, it's advisable to **book ahead** through one of the specialist travel agents or international youth hostel offices: *HI-AYH* has a free booking service on ☎1-800/444-6111. Some *HI* hostels will allow you to use a **sleeping bag**, though officially they should (and many do) insist on a **sheet sleeping bag**, which can usually be rented at the hostel. The maximum stay at each hostel is technically three days, though this is again a rule which is often ignored if there's space. Few hostels provide meals but most have **cooking** facilities: alcohol, smoking and, of course, drugs are banned.

The **independent** hostels in the *AAIH* group are usually a little less expensive than their *HI* counterparts, and have fewer rules. The quality is not as consistent; some can be quite poor, others absolutely wonderful. In popular areas, especially

For a list of B&Bs throughout the state and in specific areas, contact one or more of the following:

**Bed and Breakfast International**, Box 282910, San Francisco CA 94128-2910 (☎415/696-1690).

**California Office of Tourism** (see p.24), asking for the brochure *Californian Bed and Breakfast Inns*.

**Colby International**, 139 Round Hey, Liverpool L28 1RG (☎0151/220 5848 or in the US ☎703/551-5005) for bed-and-breakfast rooms and apartments in the main cities and along the Central Coast.

LA, San Francisco and San Diego, they compete fiercely for your business with airport and train station pick-ups, free breakfasts and free bike hire. There is often no curfew and, at some, a party atmosphere is encouraged at barbeques and keg parties.Their independent status may be due to a failure to come up to the *HI*'s (fairly rigid) criteria, but often it's simply because the owners prefer not to be tied down by *HI* regulations. Standards range from downright unsafe to excellent; naturally, we've included the latter in this book.

All the information in this book was accurate at the time of going to press; however, youth hostels are often shoestring organizations, prone to changing address or closing down altogether. Similarly, new ones appear each year; check the noticeboards of other hostels for news.

## CAMPING

California campgrounds range from the primitive (a flat piece of ground that may or may not have a water tap) to others which are more like open-air hotels, with shops, restaurants and washing facilities. Naturally enough, prices vary accordingly, ranging from nothing for the most basic plots, up to $20 a night for something comparatively luxurious. There are plenty of campgrounds but often plenty of people intending to use them as well: take care over plotting your route if you're intending to camp in the national parks, or anywhere at all during public holidays or the high season, when many grounds will be either full or very crowded. Vacancies often exist in the grounds outside the parks – where often the facilities are marginally better – and by contrast, some of the more basic campgrounds in isolated areas will often be empty whatever time of year you're there, and if there's any charge at all you'll need to pay by leaving the money in the bin provided.

Look out too for **hiker/biker campgrounds**, at $3 per person per night, much cheaper than most sites but only available if you are travelling under your own steam (see p.32).

Much of California is in the public domain, and, if you're backpacking, you can **camp rough** pretty much anywhere you want in the gaping **wilderness areas** and **deserts**. However, you must first get a **wilderness permit** (either free or $1), and usually a **campfire permit**, from the nearest park rangers' office. You should also take the proper precautions: carry sufficient food and drink to cover emergencies, inform the park ranger of your travel plans, and watch out for the bears and rattlesnakes, and the effect *your* presence can have on *their* environment. See "Backcountry Camping, Hiking and Wildlife" on p.43. For more information on these undeveloped regions – which are often protected within either "national parks" or "national forests", again see p.43 – contact the *Western Regional Information Office*, National Park Service, Fort Mason, Bldg 201, San Francisco, CA 94123 (☎415/556-0560); or the *US Forest Service*, 630 Sansome St, San Francisco, CA 94111 (☎415/705-2874).

**Two private companies** oversee a multitude of campgrounds all over California, although these are almost exclusively for RVs. For their brochures and lists contact **California Travel Parks Association**, PO Box 5648, Auburn CA 95604 (☎916/885-1624); and **Kampgrounds of America (KOA)**, PO Box 30558, Billings, MT 59114 (☎406/248-7444). More tent-friendly sites can be found in the state parks (see p.45). These can be booked ahead (for a $6.75 fee) through a computerized system called **MISTIX**, part of the *Ticketron* ticket agency, which has offices in most towns or can be phoned on ☎1800/444-7275.

## LONG-TERM ACCOMMODATION

**Apartment-hunting** in California is not the nightmare it is in, say, New York: accommodation is plentiful and not always expensive, although the absence of housing associations and co-ops means that there is very little really cheap accommodation anywhere except in very isolated country areas. Accommodation is almost always rented unfurnished so you'll have to buy furniture; expect to pay $700 a month for a studio or one-bedroom apartment and upwards of $1000 per month for two to three bedrooms in Los Angeles or San Francisco. Most landlords will expect one month's rent as a deposit, plus one month in advance.

There is no statewide organization for accommodation so you'll have to check out the options in each place. By far the best way to find somewhere is to ask around – often short-term lets come up via word of mouth. Otherwise rooms for rent are often advertised in the windows of houses and local papers have "Apartments For Rent" sections. In **Los Angeles** the best source is the *LA Weekly*, although you should also scan the *LA Times* classifieds. In **San Francisco** check out the *Chronicle* and the free *Bay Area Guardian*, *East Bay Express* – and, for women, *Bay Area Women's News*.

# FOOD AND DRINK

**It's not too much of an exaggeration to say that in California – its cities, at least – you can eat whatever you want, whenever you want. On every main street, a mass of restaurants, fast-food places and coffee shops try to outdo one another with bargains and special offers.**

California's cornucopia stems largely from its being one of the most agriculturally rich parts of the country. Junk food is as common as anywhere else in the US, but the state also produces its own range of highly nutritious goodies: apples, dates, grapes, kiwi fruits, melons, oranges and peaches are everywhere, joined by abundant fish and seafood from the ocean and high-quality meat and dairy goods. You'll rarely find anything that's not fresh, be it a bagel or a spinach-in-Mornay-sauce croissant (California's mix'n'match food concoctions can be as anarchic as its architecture), and even fast food won't necessarily be rubbish.

California is also one of the most health-conscious states in the union, and the supermarket shelves are chock-full of products which if not fat-free, are low-fat, low-sodium, caffeine-free and dairy-free. Much the same ethic runs through the menu of most restaurants, though you needn't worry about going hungry: portions are as huge as elsewhere in the States, and what you don't eat can always be "boxed up" for later consumption.

## BREAKFAST

For the price, on average $4–7, breakfast is the best-value and most filling meal of the day. Go to a **diner**, or, slightly smarter, a **café** or **coffee shop**, all of which serve breakfast until at least 11am, with some diners serving them all day. There are often special deals at earlier times too, say 6–8am, when the price may be even lower.

The breakfasts themselves are pretty much what you'd find all over the country. **Eggs** are the staple ingredient, in a variety of styles: "sunny side up" (fried on one side, leaving a runny yolk), "over" (flipped over in the pan to stiffen the yolk), or "over easy" (flipped for a few seconds giving just a hint of solidity to the yolk). **Omelettes** are popular, usually made with three eggs and available with a range of exotic fillings (avocado, for instance). There is usually also some form of **meat** available: ham or bacon, streaky and fried to a crisp; or sausages, skinless and spicy, sometimes shaped as disc-like "sausage patties".

All breakfasts come with **toast**: rye, white or wholewheat bread generally, though white, dense and tangy **sourdough bread** is increasingly common. Alternatives are an **English muffin** (a toasted bread roll) or an **American muffin**, a fruitcake traditionally made with bran and sugar, often flavoured with blueberries, poppyseed or chocolate chip. If you wish, you can add **waffles** or **pancakes** to the combination, consumed swamped in butter with lashings of sickly-sweet corn syrup, flavoured to mimic the more delicate and expensive maple syrup. A concession to California's love of light food is the option of **fruit**: typically apple, banana, orange, pineapple or strawberry, wonderfully styled and served on their own or with pancakes, though costing as much as a full-blown fry-up.

Wherever you eat, a dollar or so will entitle you to wash the meal down with as much **coffee** as you can stomach; **tea** is less common, but isn't hard to find. Be warned, though, that anything called "English tea" will be a poor-quality brew made with weak tea bags or an inferior Earl Grey. Better to try the wide range of **herbal teas** (don't pronounce the "h"): apple and cinnamon, blackcurrant, emperors (a very spicy herb) and ginseng, peppermint and camomile, and a huge selection of others are available. A cup will cost from 30¢ to $1, and be served straight or with lemon rather than milk.

## LUNCH AND SNACKS

Most Californian workers take their lunch break between 11.30am and 2.30pm, and during these hours you should look for the low-cost **set menus** on offer – generally excellent value. Chinese restaurants, for example, frequently have help-yourself rice and noodles or dim sum feasts for $5–8, and many Japanese restaurants give you a chance to eat sushi much more cheaply ($7–10) than usual. Most Mexican restaurants are exceptionally well priced all the time, and you can get a good-sized lunch in one for $4–5. In Northern California, watch out for seafood restaurants selling **fish and chips**: the fish is breaded and then fried – a vast improvement on English batter – and the chips are real chipped potatoes rather than the American French fry matchsticks you normally find. A plateful is about $5. Look, too, for **clam chowder**, a thick, creamy shellfish soup served almost everywhere for $2 or $3, sometimes using a hollowed-out sourdough cottage loaf as a bowl.

As you'd expect, there's also **pizza**, available from chains like *Pizza Hut*, *Pizzaland* and *Shakey's*. All are dependable and offer broadly the same range; count on paying around $8–10 for a basic two-person pizza. If it's a warm day and you can't face hot food, look for a deli (see below) that has a **salad bar**, where you can help yourself for $3. Consider also California's favourite healthy fast food: **frozen yoghurt**, which is sold in most places by the tub for $2.

For **quick snacks**, you'll find many **delis** do ready-cooked meals for $3–4 as well as a range of **sandwiches** "to go", which can be meals in themselves, filled with a custom-built combination of meat, cheese, seafood, pasta and salad.

**Bagels**, also, are everywhere: thick, chewy rolls with a hole in the middle, filled with anything you fancy. **Street stands** sell hot dogs, burgers, tacos, or a slice of pizza for around $1.50 and most shopping malls have ethnic fast-food stalls, often pricier than their equivalent outside, but usually edible and filling. Be a little wary of the grottier **Mexican fast-food** stands if you're buying meat, although they're generally filling, very cheap and often more authentic than the Tex-Mex outlets. There are chains, too, like *El Pollo Loco* and *Taco Bell*, which sell swift tacos and burritos for around 50¢. And of course the inevitable **burger chains** are as ubiquitous here as anywhere in the US: *Wendy's*, *Burger King* and *McDonald's* are the familiar names, along with *Jack-in-the-Box* – a drive-through takeout where you place your order by talking to a plastic clown – and others, all of which now offer more adventurous menus than previously.

Finally, just about any of these places will serve **sodas**. Each brand is available in caffeine-free and sugar-free varieties (though there's even in reaction to this a brand called *Jolt*, which promises "all the sugar and twice the caffeine"). You can buy sodas from street-vending machines and in supermarkets for about 50¢ a can, or from a fast-food outlet in three sizes – large, larger and gargantuan – for between 50¢ and $1.50, each with ice added by the shovelful.

## RESTAURANTS

Even if it often seems swamped by the more fashionable regional and ethnic cuisines, traditional **American cooking** – juicy burgers, steaks, fries, salads (invariably served before the main dish) and baked potatoes – is found all over California. Cheapest of the food chains is the California-wide *Sizzler*, although you'll rarely need to spend more than $10 for a solid blowout anywhere.

By contrast, though, it's **California cuisine**, geared towards health and aesthetics, that's raved about by foodies on the West Coast – and rightly so. Basically a development of French *nouvelle cuisine*, utilizing the wide mix of fresh, locally available ingredients, California cuisine is based on physiological efficiency – eating only what you need to and what your body can process. Vegetables are harvested before maturity and steamed to preserve a high concentration of vitamins, with a strong flavour – and to look better on the plate. Seafood comes from

oyster farms and the catches of small-time fishermen, and what little meat there is on the menu tends to come from animals reared on organic farms. The result is small but beautifully presented portions, and high, high prices: it's not unusual to spend $50 a head (or much more) for a full dinner with wine; the minimum you'll need for a sample is $20 which will buy an entrée. To whet your appetite, starters include mussels in jalapeño and sesame vinaigrette, snails in puff pastry with mushroom purée, and, among main courses, roasted goat's cheese salad with walnuts, swordfish with herb butter and tuna with cactus ratatouille.

Restaurants serving California cuisine build their reputation by word of mouth; if you can, ask a local enthusiast for recommendations, or simply follow our suggestions in the *Guide*, especially in Berkeley, the recognized birthplace of California cuisine. Of other American regional cooking, **Cajun** remains in vogue. Also known as "creole", it originated in Louisiana as a way of saving money by cooking up leftovers. It's centred on black beans, rice and seafood, and is always highly spiced. There are a few relatively inexpensive places to find it (charging around $8), but its cachet has pushed prices up tremendously, and in most places it's not really a budget option.

Although technically ethnic, **Mexican** food is so common that it often seems like (and, historically, often is) an indigenous cuisine, especially in Southern California. What's more, day or night, it's the cheapest type of food to eat: even a full dinner with a few drinks will rarely be over $12 anywhere except in the most upmarket establishment. In the main, Mexican food here is

## AMERICAN FOOD TERMS FOR FOREIGN TRAVELLERS

| | | | |
|---|---|---|---|
| A la mode | With ice cream | Gyros | Small Greek kebabs |
| Au jus | Meat served with a gravy made from its own juices | Hash browns | Potato chunks or grated potato chips pan-fried in fat |
| Biscuit | Scone | Hero | French-bread sandwich |
| BLT | Bacon, lettuce and tomato toasted sandwich | Hoagie | Another French-bread sandwich |
| Broiled | Grilled | Home fries | Pan-fried, thick-cut and often greasy breakfast potatoes |
| Brownie | A fudgy, filling chocolate cake | Jello | Jelly |
| Buffalo wings | Type of barbequed chicken wings | Jelly | Jam |
| Chips | Potato crisps | Muffin | Small cake made with bran and/or blueberries |
| Cilantro | Coriander | | |
| Clam chowder | Thick soup made with clams and other seafood | Popsicle | Ice lolly |
| | | Potato chips | Crisps |
| Cookie | Biscuit | Pretzels | Savoury circles of glazed pastry |
| Corn dog | Hot dog dipped in corn batter, usually served on a stick | Seltzer | Fizzy/soda water |
| | | Sherbet | Sorbet |
| Eggplant | Aubergine | Shrimp | Prawns |
| English muffin | Toasted bread roll | Sub | Yet another French-bread sandwich |
| Entree | Main course | | |
| Frank | Frankfurter (hot dog) | Soda | Generic term for any soft drink |
| (French) fries | Chips | Surf 'n' Turf | Restaurant serving fish and meat |
| Gravy | White lard-like sauce poured over biscuits for breakfast | Teriyaki | Chicken or beef, marinated in soy sauce and grilled |
| Grits | Ground white corn, served hot with butter, often a breakfast side dish. | Zucchini | Courgettes |

### MEXICAN SPECIALITIES

| | | | |
|---|---|---|---|
| Burritos | Folded tortillas stuffed with refried beans or beef, and grated cheese | Chiles rellenos | Green chillies stuffed with cheese and fried in egg batter |

more use of fresh vegetables and fruit, but the essentials are the same: lots of rice and pinto beans, often served refried (ie boiled, mashed and fried), with variations on the **tortilla**, a thin maize dough pancake that comes in several forms. You can eat it as an accompaniment to your main dish; wrapped around the food and eaten by hand (a **burrito**); folded, fried and filled (a **taco**); rolled, filled and baked (an **enchilada**); or fried flat and topped with a stack of food (a **tostada**). One of the few options for vegetarians in this meat-oriented cuisine is the **chile relleno**, a green pepper stuffed with cheese, dipped in egg batter and fried.

Other ethnic cuisines are plentiful too. **Chinese** food is everywhere, and can often be as cheap as Mexican. **Japanese** is more expensive and fashionable – sushi is worshipped by some Californians. **Italian** food is popular, but can be expensive once you leave the simple pastas and explore the exotic pizza toppings or the specialist Italian regional cooking that's fast catching on. **French** food, too, is widely available, though always pricey, the cuisine of social climbers and power-lunchers and rarely found outside the larger cities. **Thai**, **Korean**, and **Indonesian** food is similarly city-based, though usually cheaper; **Indian** restaurants, on the other hand, are thin on the ground just about everywhere and often very expensive – although as Indian cuisine catches on the situation is gradually changing for the better, with a sprinkling of moderately priced Southern Indian food outlets.

## DRINKING

While typically American **bars** and **cocktail lounges** do exist in California – long dimly lit counters with a few punters perched on stools before a bartender-cum-guru, and tables and booths for those who don't want to join in the

| | | | |
|---|---|---|---|
| *Enchiladas* | Soft tortillas filled with meat and cheese or chilli and baked | *Quesadilla* | Folded soft tortilla containing melted cheese |
| *Fajitas* | Like tacos but a soft flour tortilla stuffed with shrimp, chicken or beef | *Salsa* | Chillies, tomato and onion and cilantro |
| | | *Tacos* | Folded, fried tortillas, stuffed with chicken, beef or (occasionally) cow's brains |
| *Frijoles* | Refried beans, ie mashed fried beans. | | |
| *Guacamole* | Thick sauce made from avocado, garlic, onion and chilli, used as a topping | *Tamales* | Corn meal dough with meat and chilli, wrapped in a corn husk and baked |
| | | *Tortillas* | Maize dough pancakes |
| *Mariscos* | Seafood | *Tostada* | Fried, flat tortillas, smothered with meat and vegetables |
| *Nachos* | Tortilla chips topped with melted cheese | | |

## AMERICAN SPIRITS

As for **drinking**; American beer is consumed to quench thirst rather than to get drunk, and it's with spirits, or **"hard liquor"** that the US really excels: the range, even in a run-of-the-mill bar is enough to put the best-stocked British pub to shame. Whatever you order you'll get it in a glass full of ice ("on the rocks"); to avoid this demand it "straight up". You need to be careful when ordering whiskey. Unless you ask for Scotch or Irish you'll be served the heavier-tasting *bourbon*, the more common brands of which are *Jim Beam*, *Old Grandad* and *Wild Turkey* (*Jack Daniels* is not technically a bourbon as it's made in Tennessee, not Kentucky). There are startling arrays of different gins and vodkas (*Stolychnaya* or "stoly" is the most popular), and always a good selection of rums from white to dark to every shade in between, including the explosive *Bacardi 151* – 75 percent pure alcohol. Remember that in America, a Martini is a cocktail made with gin and a dash of white vermouth; if you want the British kind use the generic term, pronouced "ver-mooth". Spirits generally cost $2–2.50 "a shot" – a slightly larger measure than the UK "single". By sacrificing your tastebuds, money can be saved ordering a **well drink**, essentially the low-cost brand of gin, vodka, bourbon, whisky or rum that is kept behind the bar for the impecunious.

drunken bar-side debates – in freeway-dominated Los Angeles, the traditional neighbourhood bar is as rare as the traditional neighbourhood. There are exceptions, but LA bars tend to be either extremely pretentious or extremely seedy, neither good for long bouts of social drinking. On the other hand, San Francisco is the consummate boozing town, still with a strong contingent of old-fashioned, get-drunk bars that are fun to spend an evening in even if you don't plan to get legless.

To **buy and consume alcohol** in California you need to be 21, and could well be asked for ID even if you look much older. **Licensing laws and drinking hours** are, however, among the most liberal in the country (though laws on drinking and driving are not; see p.29). Alcohol can be bought and drunk any time between 6am and 2am, seven days a week; and, as well as bars, nightclubs and restaurants are nearly always can

fully licensed. In addition, it is permitted by California law to take your own bottled wine into a restaurant, where the corkage fee will be $5–10. You can buy beer, wine or spirits more cheaply and easily in supermarkets, many delis, and, of course, liquor stores (closed on Sundays).

American **beers** fall into two diametrically opposite categories: wonderful and tasteless. You'll probably be familiar with the latter, which are found everywhere: light, fizzy brands such as *Budweiser*, *Miller*, *Schlitz* and *Michelob*, the only nationally sold variety likely to find fans among British beer drinkers. The alternative is a fabulous range of **"microbrewed"** beers, the product of a wave of backyard and in-house operations that swelled about ten years ago and has now matured to the point that many pump out over 150,000 barrels a year and are classed as "regional breweries". Head for one of the **brewpubs** (many are listed in the *Guide* along with breweries you can visit) and you'll find hand-crafted beers such as crisp pilseners, wheat beers and stouts on tap, at prices only marginally above those of the national brews. Bottled micro-brews, like Chico's hoppy *Sierra Nevada Pale Ale* and the full-bodied, San Francisco-brewed *Anchor Steam Beer* are sold throughout the state, while *Red Tail Ale* is found throughout Northern California.

Alternatively, do what most locals do and stick to **imported** beers, especially the Mexican brands *Bohemia, Corona, Dos Equis, Superior* and *Tecate*. Expect to fork out $2 for a glass of draught beer, slightly more for a bottle or an imported beer. Taste aside, imported beers gain advocates for their comparative alcoholic strength.

Don't forget that in all but the more preten-tious bars, several people can save money by buying a (quart or half-gallon) **"pitcher"** of beer for $4–6. If bar prices are a problem, you can stock up with **six-packs** from a supermarket ($3–5 for domestic, $5–8 for imported brews).

If you're partial to the internationally known Californian **wines**, like *Gallo* and *Paul Masson*, you may be surprised to learn that they are held in low regard on the West Coast, and produced in plants resembling oil refineries. Most people prefer the produce of California's innumerable, and invariably good, smaller wineries. The Napa and Sonoma Valleys – which produce predomi-nantly dry wines made from French-strain grapes – are widely, and rightly, regarded as the cradle of the Californian wine industry. Wines are cate-gorized by grape-type rather than place of origin: *Cabernet Sauvignon* is probably the most popular, a fruity and palatable red. Also widespread are the heavier reds – *Burgundy, Merlot* and *Pinot*

*Noir*. Among the whites, *Chardonnay* is very dry and flavourful, and generally preferred to *Sauvignon Blanc* or *Fumé Blanc*, though these have their devotees. The most unusual is the strongly flavoured *Zinfandel*, which comes in white (mocked by wine snobs, but popular none-theless), red or rosé.

You can learn a lot about Californian wine by taking a **winery tour**, mostly including free tast-ings (although some charge $4–5 for a full glass or two), a number of which we've mentioned in the *Guide*. Or, before leaving home, write to the Wine Institute, 165 Post St, San Francisco, CA 94108, for their informative booklet and winery directory. The best lesson of all, of course, is simply to buy the stuff. It's fairly inexpensive: a decent glass of wine in a bar or restaurant costs under $2, a bottle $7–10. Buying from a super-market is better still – just $5–8 a bottle.

**Cocktails** are extremely popular, especially during **happy hours** (usually any time between 5pm and 7pm) when drinks are half-price and there's often a buffet thrown in. Varieties are innumerable, sometimes specific to a single bar or cocktail lounge, and they cost anything between $3 and $6.

An increasing alternative to drinking dens, **coffee bars** (look out for any joint with "Java" in the title) play a vibrant part in California's social scene, and are havens of high-quality coffee far removed from the stuff served in diners. In larger towns and cities, cafés will boast of the quality of the roast, and offer specialities such as espresso with lemon peel (which accentuates the bitterness wonderfully) as well as a full array of cappuccinos, lattes and the like, served straight, iced, organic or flavoured with syrups. Herbal teas and light snacks are often also on the menu.

# BACKCOUNTRY CAMPING, HIKING AND WILDLIFE

**California has some fabulous backcountry and wilderness areas, coated by dense forests and capped by great mountains. Unfortunately, while still immensely rewarding – and it's one of *the* compelling reasons for coming to California – it isn't all as wild as it once was, thanks to the thousands who tramp through each year. If you're intending to do the same, you can help preserve the special qualities of the environment by observing a few simple rules. For practical information on travelling through the deserts, see the box on p.204.**

The US's protected backcountry areas fall into a number of potentially confusing categories. Most numerous are **state parks**, owned and operated by the individual states. Some 275 in all, they include state beaches, state historic parks and state recreational areas, often around sites of geological or historical importance and not necessarily in rural areas. Daily fees are usually $3–5, though a $75 **annual pass** gives free access to most sites for a year.

**National parks** – such as Yosemite and Death Valley – are large, federally controlled and preserved areas of great natural beauty comprising several different features or ecosystems; entry is usually $5. These are supplemented by the smaller **national monuments** ($3–4), like Devil's Postpile and Lava Beds, with just one major feature, and **national seashores**. If you plan to visit a few of these, invest in a **Golden Eagle Passport** ($25 cash from any national park entrance), which grants both driver and passengers (or if cycling or hiking, the holder's immediate family) access to all California's national parks for a calendar year. Excellent free **ranger programmes** – such as guided walks or slide shows – are held throughout the year. The federal government also operates **national recreation areas**, often huge hydro dams where you can jetski or windsurf free from the necessarily restrictive laws of the national parks. Campgrounds and equipment-rental outlets are always abundant.

California's eighteen **national forests** cover twenty percent of the state's surface area. Most of them border the national parks, and are also federally administered (by the US Forest Service), but with much less protection. More roads run through national forests, and often there is some limited logging and other land-based industry operated on a sustainable basis.

All the above forms of protected land can contain **wilderness areas**, which aim to protect natural resources in their most native state. In practice this means there's no commercial activity at all; buildings, motorized vehicles and bicycles are not permitted, nor are firearms and pets. Overnight camping is allowed, but **wilderness permits** (free to $1) must be obtained in advance from the land management agency responsible. In California, Lava Beds, Lassen, Death Valley, Sequoia-Kings Canyon, Joshua Tree, Pinnacles, Point Reyes and Yosemite all have large wilderness areas – 94 percent of Yosemite – with only the regions near roads, visitor centers and buildings designated as less stringently regulated "front country".

## CAMPING

When **camping rough**, check that fires are permitted before you start one; if they are, use a stove in preference to local materials – in some places firewood is scarce, although you may be

---

### ESSENTIAL EQUIPMENT

Choose your **tent** wisely. Many Sierra sites are on rock with only a thin covering of soil so driving pegs in can be a problem. Free-standing dome-style tents are therefore preferable. Go for one with a large area of mosquito netting and a removable fly sheet: tents designed for harsh European winters can get horribly sweaty once the sun gets up.

Most developed campgrounds are equipped with **fire rings** with some form of grill for cooking, but many people prefer a *Coleman* **stove,** powered by white gas, a kind of super-clean gasoline. Both stoves and white gas (also used for *MSR* backcountry stoves) are widely available in camping stores. Other camping stoves are less common. Equipment using butane and propane – *Camping Gaz* and, to a lesser extent, *EPI gas*, *Scorpion* and *Optimus* – is on the rise, though outside of major camping areas you'll be pushed to find supplies: stock up when you can. If you need methylated spirits for your *Trangia*, go to a hardware store and ask for **denatured alcohol**.

## BACKCOUNTRY DANGERS AND WILDLIFE

You're likely to meet many kinds of **wildlife** and come upon unexpected **hazards** on your travels through the wilderness, but only a few are likely to present problems. With due care, many potential difficulties can be avoided.

Hiking **in the foothills** should present few problems but you should check your clothes frequently for **ticks** – pesky blood-sucking insects which are known to carry Lyme disease. If you have been bitten, and especially if you get flu-like symptoms, get advice from a park ranger. Also annoying around water are **mosquitoes**; carry candles scented with citronella to keep them at bay.

Other than in a national park, you're highly unlikely to encounter a **bear**. Even there, it's rare to stumble across one in the wilderness. Reduce the likelihood by making noise (carrying bells in your pack isn't a bad idea) as you walk. If you meet one, keep calm, lie slowly down on the ground and stay there without moving. The bear will get bored and move away. If a bear visits your camp, scare it off by banging pots and pans – if it doesn't go, you should. Leave backpacks open and lying on the ground so a bear can examine the contents without tearing them apart. It will be after your food, which should be stored in airtight containers when camping. Some campgrounds are equipped with **bear lockers**, which you are obliged to use to store food when not preparing or eating it. Camp stores in Yosemite, Kings Canyon and Sequoia national parks rent hard plastic **bear-resistant canisters** ($3 a day) which can be carried on wilderness trips. Elsewhere, you should hang both food and garbage from a high branch (too weak to support the weight of a bear) some distance from your camp. **Never feed a bear**: it'll make the bear dependent on humans for food. Bears within state and national parks are protected, but if they spend too much time around people the park rangers are, depressingly, left with no option but to shoot them. Finally, never get between a mother and her cubs. Young animals are cute; irate mothers are not.

**Rattlesnakes** (only the female actually rattles), which live in the desert areas and drier foothills up to around 7000ft, seldom attack unless provoked: do not tease or try to handle them. Rattlesnake bites are rarely fatal but you might suffer severe tissue damage (see p.205 for advice on what to do if bitten).

**Mountain lions** (aka cougars, panthers or pumas) are being hard hit by increasing urban expansion. Former habitats (from deserts to coastal and sub-alpine forests) are being built on, and there have been attacks on joggers in newly suburbanized areas. Sightings are rare, but to reduce the chance of an unwanted encounter, avoid walking by yourself, especially after dark, when lions tend to hunt. Make noise as you walk, wield a stick and keep children close to you. If you encounter one, face the lion, try to appear larger by raising your arms or holding your coat above you and it will probably back away. If not, throw rocks and sticks in its vicinity.

**Campsite critters** – ground squirrels, chipmunks and racoons – are usually just a nuisance though they tend to carry diseases and you should avoid contact. Only the **marmot** is a real pest, as it likes to chew through radiator hoses and car electrics to reach a warm engine on a cold night. Before setting off in the morning, check the motor for gnawed components, otherwise you might find yourself with a seized engine and a cooked or, at best, terrified marmot as a passenger. Boots and rucksacks also come in for marmot scrutiny.

**Poison oak** is one thing that isn't going to come and get you, though you may come up against it. Recognized by its shiny configuration of three dark-green veined leaves (turning red or yellow in autumn) which secrete an oily juice, this twiggy shrub or climbing vine is found in open woods or along stream banks throughout much of California. It's highly allergenic, so avoid touching it. If you do, washing with strong soap, taking frequent dips in the sea and applying cortisone cream usually helps relieve the symptoms in mild cases; in extreme cases, see a doctor.

In the mountains, your biggest dangers have nothing to do with the flora or fauna. Late **snows** are common, giving rise to the possibility of avalanches and meltwaters, which make otherwise simple stream crossings hazardous. **Drowning** in fast-flowing meltwater rivers is the single biggest cause of death in the Kings Canyon and Sequoia National Parks. The riverbanks are strewn with large, slippery boulders – keep well clear unless you are specifically there for river activities.

With much of the High Sierra above 10,000ft **Acute Mountain Sickness** (aka altitude sickness) is always a possibility. Only those planning to bag one of the 14,000-foot peaks are likely to have to contend with much more than a slight headache, but it pays to be on the alert and to acclimatize slowly. Try to limit your exertions for the first day or so, drink plenty of fluids, eat little and often, and note any nausea, headaches or double vision. If you experience any of these symptoms, the only solution is to descend until they ease, then ascend more gradually.

For more on the hazards of snakes and spiders, see Chapter Three, *The Deserts, Las Vegas and the Grand Canyon*; and for more on Californian wildlife generally, see *Contexts*.

allowed to use deadwood. No open fires are allowed in wilderness areas, where you should also try to camp on previously used sites. Where there are no toilets, **bury human waste** at least four inches into the ground and a hundred feet from the nearest water supply and camp. **Burn rubbish**, and what you can't burn, carry away. A growing problem is *Giardia*, a water-borne protozoan causing an intestinal disease, symptoms of which are chronic diarrhoea, abdominal cramps, fatigue and loss of weight, that requires treatment. To avoid catching it, **never drink** from rivers and streams, however clear and inviting they may look (you never know what unspeakable acts people – or animals – further upstream have performed in them). Before you drink it, **water** that isn't from taps should be boiled for at least five minutes, or cleansed with an iodine-based purifier (such as *Potable Aqua*) or a *Giardia*-rated filter, available from camping or sports shops.

Finally, don't use ordinary soaps or detergents in lakes and streams; you can buy special ecological soap for such a purpose.

## HIKING

Wilderness areas start close to the main areas of national parks. There is normally no problem entering the wilderness for day walks, but overnight trips require **wilderness permits** (see above). In peak periods, a quota system operates for the most popular paths, so if there's a hike you specifically want to do, obtain your permit well ahead of time (at least two weeks, more for popular hikes). When completing the form for

In California, the **Sierra Club**, c/o Outings Dept, 730 Polk St, San Francisco CA 94110 (☎415/776-2211), offers a range of backcountry hikes into otherwise barely accessible parts of the High Sierra wilderness, with food and guide provided. The tours are summer-only, cost around $300 for a fortnight and are heavily subscribed, making it essential to book at least three months in advance. You'll also have to pay about $40 to join the club.

your permit, be sure to ask a park ranger for weather conditions and general information about the hike you're undertaking.

Hikes covered in the *Guide* (usually appearing in boxes) are given with length and estimated walking time for a healthy but not especially fit adult. **State parks** have graded trails designed for people who drive to the corner store, so anyone used to walking and with a moderate degree of fitness will find these ratings very conservative.

To reserve campgrounds in **national parks** – highly advisable during the summer – contact the booking agency *MISTIX* on ☎619/452-8787 and 1-800/367-2267 (367-CAMP).

Reserving sites in **state parks** means phoning a different *MISTIX* number, ☎1-800/444-7275. A charge of $6.75 per reservation is levied. Generally you can reserve up to eight weeks in advance but not less than two days before you arrive.

To reserve campsites in **national forests** contact *Biospherics* on ☎1-800/280-CAMP

## WOMEN TRAVELLERS

**Practically speaking, though a woman travelling alone is certainly not the attention-grabbing spectacle in California that she might be elsewhere in the world (or even elsewhere in the US), you're likely to come across some sort of harassment.** More serious than the odd offensive comment, rape statistics in the US are high, and it goes without saying that, even more than anyone else, women should *never* hitch alone – this is widely interpreted as an invitation for trouble, and there's no shortage of weirdos to give it. Similarly, if you have a car, be careful whom you pick up: just because you're in the driving seat doesn't mean you're safe. If you can, avoid travelling at night by public transport – deserted bus stations, while not necessarily threatening, will do little to make you feel secure, and where possible you should team up with another woman. On *Greyhound* buses, follow the example of other lone women and sit as near to the front – and the driver – as possible.

Californian **cities**, especially San Francisco, can feel surprisingly safe. But as with anywhere, particular care has to be taken at night. **Mugging** is nowhere near the problem it is in

New York, but you can't relax totally – though a modicum of common sense can often avert disasters. Walking through unlit, empty streets is never a good idea, and you should take cabs wherever possible. The advice that women who *look* confident tend not to encounter trouble is, like all home truths, grounded in fact but not written in stone; those who stand around looking lost and a bit scared are prime targets, but nobody is immune. Provided you listen to advice, though, and stick to the better parts of a town, going into **bars** and **clubs** alone should pose no problems, especially in San Francisco and LA, where there's generally a pretty healthy attitude towards women who choose to do so and whose privacy will be respected – only extremely unevolved specimens will assume you're available. If in doubt, gay and lesbian bars are usually a trouble-free alternative.

**Small towns** in rural areas are not blessed with the same liberal attitudes toward lone women travellers that you'll find in the cities. If your **vehicle breaks down** in a country area, walk to the nearest house or town for help; *don't* wait by the vehicle in the middle of nowhere hoping for somebody to stop – they will, but it may not be the kind of help you're looking for. Should disaster strike, all major towns have some kind of rape counselling service available; if not, the local sheriff's office will make adequate arrangements for you to get help, counselling, and, if necessary, get you home.

The **National Organization for Women** is a central women's issues group whose lobbying has done much to effect positive legislation. NOW branches, listed in local phone directories, can provide referrals for specific concerns such as rape crisis centres and counselling services, feminist bookstores and lesbian bars.

Further back-up material can be found in *Places of Interest to Women* ($8; Ferrari Publications, PO Box 37887, Phoenix AZ; ☎602/863-2408), an annual guide for women travelling in the US, Canada, the Caribbean and Mexico.

Specific **women's contacts** are listed in the city sections of the *Guide*.

# TRAVELLERS WITH DISABILITIES

**Travellers with mobility problems or other physical disabilities are likely to find California – as with the US in general – to be much more in tune with their needs than anywhere else in the world. All public buildings must be wheelchair-accessible and have suitable toilets; most city street corners have dropped kerbs; subways have elevators, and most city buses are able to kneel to make access easier and are built with space and handgrips for wheelchair users. Most hotels and restaurants (certainly any built in the last ten years or so) have excellent wheelchair access.**

## GETTING TO AND AROUND CALIFORNIA

Most **airlines**, transatlantic and within the US, do whatever they can to ease your journey, and will usually let attendants of people with serious disabilities accompany them at no extra charge. The Americans with Disabilities Act of 1990 obliged all air carriers to make the majority of their services accessible to travellers with disabilities within five to nine years.

Almost every **Amtrak train** includes one or more coaches with accommodation for disabled passengers. Guide dogs travel free, and *Amtrak* will provide wheelchair assistance at its train stations, adapted seating on board and a fifteen percent discount on the regular fare, all provided 24 hours' notice is given. Passengers with hearing impairment can get information on ☎1-800/523-6590.

Travelling by **Greyhound** and **Amtrak Thruway** buses, however, is not to be recommended. Buses are not equipped with lifts for wheelchairs, though staff will assist with boarding (intercity carriers are required by law to do this), and the "Helping Hand" scheme offers two-for-the-price-of-one tickets to passengers unable to travel alone (carry a doctor's certificate).

The major **car rental** firms can, given sufficient notice, provide vehicles with hand controls (though these are usually only available on the more expensive models, and you'll need to reserve well in advance). The *American Automobile Association* (see p.24 produces the *Handicapped Driver's Mobility Guide* for **drivers with disabilities** (available from *Quantum-*

*Precision Inc*, 225 Broadway, Suite 3404, New York, NY 10007). There are no longer differences in state **parking regulations for disabled motorists**; the Department of Transportation has decreed that all state licences issued to disabled persons must carry a three-inch square international access symbol, and each state must provide placards bearing this symbol to be hung from the rear-view mirror – the placards are blue for permanent disabilities, red for temporary (maximum of six months). More information can be obtained from your state motor vehicle office.

As in other parts of the world, the rise of the **self-service gas station** is unwelcome for many disabled drivers. The state of California has addressed this by changing its laws so that most service stations are required to provide full service to disabled drivers at self-service prices.

## INFORMATION

The California Office of Tourism's free 200-page *California Travel Planning Guide* lists "handicap facilities" at places of accommodation and attractions (though perhaps a bold capital **H** would have been easier to pick out than mentions in the text – and some attractions which do have facilities for disabled visitors, such as San Diego Zoo, are not listed as accessible). The *San Francisco Lodging Guide* (free from the San Francisco CVB, PO Box 6977, San Francisco, CA 94101) lists many "wheelchair-accessible" properties – hotels, motels, apartments, B&Bs, hostels, RV parks – in the city and surrounding counties; as always, travellers should call to confirm details. **In San Francisco**, the *Mayor's Council on Disabilities* puts out an annual guide for disabled visitors; write c/o Box 1595, San Francisco, CA, or call ☎415/554-8755. The *Center for Independent Living*, 2539 Telegraph Ave in Berkeley (☎415/284-1740) has long been one of the most effective disabled people's organizations in the world; it has a variety of counselling services.

**National organizations** facilitating travel for people with disabilities include **SATH**, the **Society for the Advancement of Travel for the Handicapped** (345 Fifth Ave, #347, New York, NY 10016; ☎212/447-7284), a nonprofit travel-industry grouping which includes travel agents, tour operators, hotel and airline management and people with disabilities. They will pass on any enquiry to the appropriate member; allow plenty of time for a response. **Mobility International USA** (PO Box 10767, Eugene, OR 97440; ☎503/343-1284) answers transport queries and operates an exchange programme for disabled people. This is the US branch of a British organization, whose main office is at 228 Borough High St, London SE1 1JX (☎0171/403 5688). **Travelin' Talk** (PO Box 3534, Clarksville, TN 37043-3534; ☎615/552-6670), the brainchild of Rick Crowder, energetic Disabled American of the Year 1991, is a network to assist travellers with disabilities, on the principle that the most reliable information and advice comes from another disabled person. Extensive listings of services for travellers with disabilities are disseminated in a quarterly newsletter (available in large print, or on cassette).

Other useful resources are *Travel for the Disabled*, *Wheelchair Vagabond* and *Directory for Travel Agencies for the Disabled*, all produced by **Twin Peaks Press**, PO Box 129, Vancouver, WA 98666 (☎206/694-2462 or 1-800/637-2256 ).

## ACCOMMODATION

The big motel and hotel chains are often the safest bet for accessible **accommodation**; there are plenty of excellent local alternatives, of course, but with a chain at least you'll know what to expect. At the higher end of the scale *Embassy Suites* (☎1-800/362-2779, voice; 1-800/458-4708, TDD) have been working to implement new standards of access which meet and exceed ADA requirements, involving both new construction and the retrofitting of all 100 existing hotels, and providing special training to all employees. Although the President of **Hyatt International Corporation** (☎1-800/233-1234) summed up the hotel industry's initial reaction to the ADA as "the end of the world as we know it," *Hyatt* has also committed itself to extensive redesign to improve accessibility.

## THE GREAT OUTDOORS

Citizens or permanent residents of the US who have been "medically determined to be blind or permanently disabled" can obtain the **Golden Access Passport**, a free lifetime entrance pass to those federally operated parks, monuments,

historic sites, recreation areas and wildlife refuges which charge entrance fees. The pass must be picked up in person, from the areas described, and it also provides a fifty percent discount on fees charged for facilities such as camping, boat launching and parking. The **Golden Bear Pass** (free to the disabled) offers similar concessions to state-run parks, beaches and historic sites.

For visitors to **national parks** the outstanding *Access America Guide: An Atlas of the National Parks* costs $44.95, from *Northern Cartographic* (Suite 131, 4050 Williston Rd, South Burlington, VT 05403; ☎802/860-2886). It's also available in four separate (and less comprehensive) volumes from *Grove Weidenfeld*, 841 Broadway, New York NY each volume costing $10–11. The *Guide* contains useful information for visitors with mobility impairments, or hearing, visual, or developmental disabilities, and is spiral-bound for ease of handling, with large-print text. Access evaluations are based on national and federal standards and cover campsites, lodging, transportation, visitor centers and adventure tours. Some accounts by visitors with disabilities are also included.

The **Disabled Outdoors Foundation** (2052 W 23rd St, Chicago, IL 60608; ☎312/927-6834 ) is a clearing house for information for the disabled person looking for recreational facilities and adaptive recreational gear. The *Disabled Outdoors Magazine* is the Foundation's quarterly magazine covering outdoor activities for sportspersons with disabilities (US $10, Can $16 yearly). Also useful is *Easy Access to National Parks*, by Wendy Roth and Michael Tompane ($15), a detailed guide to all US national parks for people with disabilities, senior citizens, and families with young children, published by the *Sierra Club* (730 Polk St, San Francisco, CA 94110; ☎415/776-2211, voice; ☎415/398-5384, TDD).

**Yosemite National Park** (PO Box 577, CA 95389; ☎209/372-0515, voice; 209/372-4726, TDD) can supply general information direct, but an invaluable guide is *Access Yosemite National Park* ($7.95), a one-park excerpt from its parent publication, above.

The **state parks** service also offers reduced rates for permanently disabled people who apply by mail for a *Disabled Discount Pass* ($3.50 once-only payment) to Department of Parks & Recreation, Disabled Discount Pass Program, PO Box 942806, Sacramento, CA

94296-0001. This gives a fifty percent discount on all parking and camping fees above $3 except at Hearst Castle.

## PACKAGES

Many US **tour companies** cater for disabled travellers or specialize in organizing disabled group tours. State tourist departments should be able to provide lists of such companies; failing that, ask the *National Tour Association*, 546 E Main St, PO Box 3071, Lexington, KY 40596 (☎606/226-4444 or 1-800/755-8687). They can put you in touch with operators whose tours match your needs.

## TRAVELLING WITH CHILDREN

**Travelling with kids in California is relatively problem-free; children are readily accepted – indeed welcomed – in public places everywhere. Hotels and motels are well used to them, most state and national parks organize children's activities, every town or city has clean and safe playgrounds – and of course LA's Disneyland is the ultimate in kids' entertainment. Restaurants make considerable efforts to encourage parents to bring their offspring. All the national chains offer bolster chairs and a special kids' menu, packed with huge, excellent-value (though not necessarily healthy) meals – cheeseburger and chips for 99¢, and so on.**

Local tourist offices (see p.24) can provide specific information on what California has to offer children, and various **guidebooks** have been written for parents travelling with children – as *California With Kids* ($18), in the Frommer's Family Guides list, and the very helpful *Trouble Free Travel with Children* ($6.95), available through Publishers Group West. John Muir Publications puts out a series of books for children, called *Kidding Around*, which tell about the history and describe the various sights of major US cities.

## GETTING AROUND

Most families choose to travel **by car**, and while this is the least problematic way to get around

it's worth planning ahead to assure a pleasant trip. Don't set yourself unrealistic targets if you're hoping to enjoy a driving vacation with your kids – those long, boring journeys on the Interstate can be disastrous. If you're on a fly-drive vacation, note that when **renting a car** the company is legally obliged to provide free car seats for kids. RVs are also a good option for family travel, combining the convenience of built-in kitchens and bedrooms with freedom of the road (see *Getting Around* on p.29 for details).

Children under two years old **fly** free on domestic routes, and for ten percent of the adult fare on international flights – though that doesn't mean they get a seat, let alone frequent-flier miles. When aged from two to twelve they are usually entitled to half-price tickets.

Travelling **by bus** may be the cheapest way to go, but it's also the most uncomfortable for kids. Under-twos travel (on your lap) for free; ages two to four are charged ten percent of the adult fare, as are any toddlers who take up a seat. Children under twelve years old are charged half the standard fare.

**Taking the train** is by far the best option for long journeys – not only does everyone get to enjoy the scenery, but you can get up and walk around, relieving pent-up energy. Most cross-country trains have sleeping compartments, which may be quite expensive but are likely to be seen as a great adventure. On *Amtrak*, two children aged between two and fifteen can travel at half fare with each adult passenger.

# SENIOR TRAVELLERS

For many senior citizens, retirement brings the opportunity to explore the world in a style and at a pace that is the envy of younger travellers. As well as the obvious advantages of being free to travel during the quieter, more congenial and less expensive seasons, and for longer periods, anyone over the age of 62 can enjoy the tremendous variety of discounts on offer to those who can produce suitable ID. Both *Amtrak* and *Greyhound*, for example, and many US airlines, offer (smallish) percentage reductions on fares to older passengers.

Any US citizen or permanent resident aged 62 or over is entitled to free admission for life to all National Parks, monuments and historic sites using a **Golden Age Passport**, for which a once-only $10 fee is charged; it can be issued at any such site. This free entry also applies to any accompanying car passengers in their car, or for those hiking or cycling, the passport-holder's immediate family. It also gives a fifty percent reduction on fees for camping, parking and boat launching.

The **Golden Bear Pass** (free to seniors) offers similar concessions to state-run parks, beaches and historic sites, subject to a means test. There is also a Senior Citizen Discount (based on proof of age only) giving $1 off parking and $2 off family camping except where the fee is less than $3.

**Museums**, art galleries and even **hotels** offer small discounts, and since the definition of Senior can drop as low as 55, it is always worth asking.

The **American Association of Retired Persons**, 601 E St NW, Washington DC 20049 (☎1-800/424-3410 or 202/434-2277), membership of which is open to US residents aged fifty or over for an annual fee of $8, organizes group travel for senior citizens and can provide discounts on accommodation and vehicle rental. The *National Council of Senior Citizens*, 1331 F St NW, Washington DC 20004 (☎202/347-8800), is a similar organization with a yearly membership fee of $12 per person or married couple, $30 for three years, or $150 for life.

# GAY AND LESBIAN CALIFORNIA

The gay scene in California is huge, albeit heavily concentrated in the major cities. San Francisco, where anything between a quarter and a third of the voting population is reckoned to be gay or lesbian, is the premier gay city of the world; Los Angeles comes a close second, and up and down the coast gay men and women enjoy the kind of visibility and influence those in other places can only dream about. Gay politicians, and even police officers, are more than a novelty here and representation at every level is for real. Resources, places, facilities and organizations are endless.

In Los Angeles, the gay population has been growing steadily since the earliest days of the movie industry – a job which gave considerably greater freedom of lifestyle than most others at the time. Later, during World War II, the

military purged suspected homosexuals at their point of embarkation. For those expecting to serve in the Pacific war zone, this meant they got off in San Francisco – where, unable to face the stigma of a return home, many remained, their ranks later swelled by gays who lost their government jobs during McCarthy's swipes of the 1950s.

In both these cities, the activism of the 1960s succeeded in highlighting gay issues, but they only developed into fully mainstream topics during the 1970s, when, particularly in San Francisco, gays organized themselves into the largest and most influential minority group in the city. Politicians realized that the gay vote was the difference between winning and losing and quickly got on the case. In 1977 San Francisco got its first city official on the Board of Supervisors, the openly gay Harvey Milk. Milk's hero status was assured forever when, in 1978, he was

## GAY AND LESBIAN PUBLICATIONS

Of national **publications** to look out for, most of which are available from any good bookstore, by far the best are the range produced by The Damron Company (PO Box 422458, San Francisco, CA 94142; ☎415/255-0404) or 1-800/462-6654. These include the Address Book, a pocket-sized yearbook full of listings of hotels, bars, clubs and resources for gay men, costing $15; the Women's Traveller, which provides similar listings for lesbians ($12); the Road Atlas, which shows lodgings and entertainment in major cities ($15); and The Damron Accommodations Guide with colour photos of gay-friendly places to stay in Canada and the US ($19). Gay Yellow Pages ($12; PO Box 533, Village Station, New York NY 10014; ☎212/674-0120) is also a valuable resource. Other works to look out for are the travel books published by **Ferrari**, PO Box 37887, Phoenix, Arizona 85069

(☎609/863-2408), though neither of them is specific to California: the Ferrari For Men ($16) and Ferrari For Women ($14) pocket guides both cover general travel and entertainment information for gay men and lesbians respectively.

The Advocate (Liberation Publications, Suite 1000, 6922 Hollywood Blvd, Los Angeles, CA 90028; $3.95) is a bimonthly national gay news magazine, with features, general info and classified ads (not to be confused with Advocate Men, which is a soft-porn magazine). Another useful lesbian publication is Gaia's Guide (132 W 24th St, New York, NY 10014; $6.95), a yearly international directory with a lot of US information. Specific to San Francisco is the hilariously frank Betty & Pansy's Severe Queer Review ($11 from local bookstores), which will tell you where and what in no uncertain terms. Not for the prim.

assassinated by another councillor, the conservative Dan White.

Since the heady Seventies, however, and in the face of the AIDS crisis, the energies of gay men and women have been directed to the protection of existing rights and helping victims of the disease. California has lost many to AIDS, but the state, perhaps more than anywhere else, has responded quickly and with compassion and intelligence: public health programmes have had hitherto unheard of sums of money pumped into them, and attitudes across the board are broad-minded and supportive.

Ghettoization, then, is no longer a problem for Californian gays, although there are sizeable, predominantly gay areas in almost all the major cities – San Diego's **Hillcrest**, Los Angeles' **West Hollywood**, San Francisco's **Castro** district – and both Guerneville and Palm Springs have earned gay resort status. However, although tolerance is high everywhere, the liberal attitudes of the major cities are not always reflected in the more isolated areas. For a complete rundown on local **resources**, **bars** and **clubs**, see the relevant city chapters of the Guide.

# SPORTS

Nowhere in the country do the various forms of athletic activity and competition have a higher profile than in California. The big cities generally have at least one team in each of the major professional sports – football (though LA is about to lose its last football team to Oakland), baseball and basketball (see sports boxes) – sometimes as well as supporting sides in the more unusual spectator sports of indoor soccer, volleyball, ice hockey, wrestling and even roller derby.

## AMERICAN SPORTS FOR OVERSEAS VISITORS

For foreign visitors, American sports can appear something of a mystery, not least the passion for **intercollegiate sports** – college and university teams, competing against one another in the Pacific-10 Conference, usually with an enthusiasm fuelled by passionate local rivalries. In Los Angeles, USC and UCLA have an intense and high-powered sporting enmity, with fans on each side as vociferous as any European soccer crowd, and in the San Francisco Bay Area, the rivalry between UC Berkeley and Stanford is akin to that of Britain's Oxford and Cambridge.

## FOOTBALL

**Football** in America attracts the most obsessive and devoted fans of any sport, perhaps because there are fewer games played – only sixteen in a season, which lasts throughout the fall. With many quick skirmishes and military-like movements up and down the field, it's ideal for television, and nowhere is this more apparent than during the **televised games** which are a feature of many bars on Monday nights – though most games are played on Sundays.

The game lasts for four fifteen-minute quarters, with a fifteen-minute break at half-time. But since time is only counted when play is in progress, matches can take up to three hours to complete, mainly due to interruptions for TV advertising. Commentators will discuss the game throughout to help your comprehension, though they use such a barrage of statistics to illustrate their remarks that you may feel hopelessly confused. Not that it matters – the spectacle of American football is fun to experience, even if you haven't a clue what's going on. Players tend to be huge, averaging about six foot five and weighing upwards of seventeen stone; they look even bigger when they're suited up for battle in shoulder pads and helmets. The best players become nationally known celebrities, raking in millions of dollars in fees for product endorsements on top of astronomical salaries.

### Teams and tickets

All major teams play in the **National Football League** (NFL), the sport's governing body, which divides the teams into two conferences of equal stature, the **National Football Conference** (NFC) and the **American Football Conference** (AFC). In turn, each conference is split into three divisions, East, Central and West. For the end of season playoffs, the best team in each of the six divisions plus a second-place wildcard from each conference fight it out for the title.

The Californian **teams** are the San Francisco **49ers**, the Oakland **Raiders** – both always near the top of the NFL – and the San Diego **Chargers**. There are no second division equivalents, though the **college teams**, particularly USC and UCLA, serve as a training ground for future NFL stars.

**Tickets** cost $15–35 for professional games, $5–10 for college games. Call on the following numbers:

| | |
|---|---|
| NFL | ☎212/758-1500 |
| San Diego Chargers | ☎619/280-2121 |
| San Francisco 49ers | ☎408/526-4949 |
| Oakland Raiders | ☎310/322-3451 |

### BASEBALL

**Baseball**, much like cricket in its relaxed, summertime pace and seemingly byzantine rules, is often called "America's pastime", though its image was tarnished by the bitter strike by players which shortened the 1994 and 1995 seasons and saw the unthinkable cancelling of the World Series in 1994.

Games are played – 162 each full season – all over the US almost every day from April to

## THE RULES OF FOOTBALL

The **rules of American football** are fairly simple: the **field** is 100 yards long by 40 yards wide, plus two **endzones** at each end; there are two teams of eleven men. The game begins with a **kickoff**, after which the team in possession of the ball tries to move downfield to score a **touchdown**, while the opposing team tries to stop them. The attacking team has four chances to move the ball forward ten yards and gain a **first down**; otherwise they forfeit possession to the opposition. After the kickoff the **quarterback**, the leader of the attack, either passes the ball to a **running back**, or throws the ball through the air downfield to a **receiver**. Play ends when the man with the ball is tackled to the ground, or if the pass attempt falls incomplete.

A **touchdown**, worth six points, is made when a player crosses into the defending team's endzone carrying the ball; unlike in rugby, no actual touching down is necessary, it is enough just to carry the ball over the line. A **field goal**, worth three points, is scored when the **place-kicker** — always the smallest man on the team and usually the lone foreigner — kicks the ball, as in rugby, through the **goalposts** that stand in the endzone. If the attacking team has failed to move the ball within scoring range, and seems unlikely to gain the required ten yards for another first down, they can elect to **punt** the ball, kicking it to the other team.

A change of possession can also occur if the opposition players manage to **intercept** an attempted pass.

### THE RULES OF BASEBALL

The setup for baseball looks like the English game of rounders, with four **bases** set at the corners of a 90-foot diamond. The base at the bottom corner is called **home plate**, and serves much the same purpose as do the stumps in cricket. Play begins when the **pitcher**, standing on a low **pitcher's mound** in the middle of the diamond, throws the ball at upwards of a hundred miles an hour, making it curve and bend as it travels towards the **catcher**, who crouches behind home plate; seven other defensive players take up **positions**, one at each base and the others spread out around the field of play.

A **batter** from the opposing team stands beside home plate and tries to hit the ball. If the batter swings and misses, or if the pitched ball crosses the plate above the batter's knees and below his chest, it counts as a **strike**; if he doesn't swing and the ball passes outside this **strike zone**, it counts as a **ball** — equivalent to a "no ball" in cricket. If the batter gets **three strikes** against him he is **out**; **four balls** and he gets a free **walk**, and takes his place as a runner on first base.

If he succeeds in hitting the pitched ball into **fair territory** (the wedge between the first and third bases), the batter runs toward first base; if the opposing players catch the ball before it hits the ground, the batter is **out**. Otherwise they field the ball and attempt to relay it to first base before the batter gets there; if they fail he is **safe** — and stays there, being moved along by subsequent batters until he makes a complete circuit and scores a **run**. The most exciting moment in baseball is the **home run**, when a batter hits the ball over the outfield fences, a boundary 400 feet away from home plate; he and any runners on base when he hits the ball each score a run. If there are runners on all three bases it's called a **grand slam**, and earns four runs.

The nine players per side bat in rotation; each side gets **three outs per inning**, and there are **nine innings per game** — the "top" of the innings is when the first team is batting, or is about to bat; the "bottom" of the innings is during the second team's turn. Games normally last two to three hours, and are never tied; if the scores are level after nine innings, extra innings are played until one side pulls ahead and wins.

September, with the league championships and the World Series, the final best-of-seven play-off, lasting through October. Watching a game, even if you don't understand what's going on, can be at the least a pleasant day out, drinking beer and eating hot dogs in the bleachers unshaded benches beyond the outfield offered at rock-bottom prices; tickets are cheap and the crowds usually friendly and sociable.

### Teams and tickets

All Major League baseball teams play in either the **National League** or the **American League**, each of equal stature and split into three divisions, East, Central and West. For the end of season playoffs and the World Series, the best team in each of the six divisions plus a second-place wildcard from each conference fight it out for the title.

California's Major League clubs are the **Oakland A's**, many times champions of the American League, **Los Angeles Dodgers**, **San Diego Padres**, **California Angels** and the **San Francisco Giants**. In addition, there are also numerous **minor league** clubs, known as **farm teams** because they supply the top clubs with talent. Details are included in relevant chapters of the *Guide*.

**Tickets** for games cost $5–15 per seat, and are generally available on the day of the game. Call on the following numbers:

| | |
|---|---|
| Major League | ☎212/339-7800 |
| National League | ☎212/339-7700 |
| American League | ☎212/339-7600 |
| Los Angeles Dodgers | ☎213/224-1500 |
| San Diego Padres | ☎619/283-4494 |
| San Francisco Giants | ☎415/468-3700 |
| California Angels | ☎714/937-7200 |
| Oakland Athletics (A's) | ☎510/638-4900 |

## BASKETBALL

**Basketball** is one of the few professional sports that is also actually played by many ordinary Americans, since all you need is a ball and a hoop. It's a particularly popular sport in low-income inner-city areas, where school playgrounds are packed with young hopefuls.

The professional game is played by athletes of phenomenal agility, seven-foot-tall giants who float through the air over a wall of equally tall defenders, seeming to change direction in mid-flight before slam-dunking the ball (smashing it through the hoop which such force that the backboard sometimes shatters) to score two points. Games last for an exhausting 48 minutes of playing time, around two hours total.

### Teams and tickets

California's basketball clubs, including the **Los Angeles Lakers**, who play in front of a crowd of celebrities (actor Jack Nicholson, for example, has a season-long front court seat), haven't met with much success in the 1990s. Other pro teams include the Golden State **Warriors** (who play in Oakland), the Sacramento **Kings** and the Los Angeles **Clippers**. LA's **UCLA** long dominated the college game, winning national championships throughout the 1960s, though now they struggle to keep up with the other university sides.

**Tickets** cost $10–30 for professional games, $4–10 for college games. Call on the following numbers:

| | |
|---|---|
| National Basketball Association (NBA) | ☎212/407-8000 |
| Golden State Warriors | ☎510/638-6300 |
| Los Angeles Clippers | ☎213/745-0400 |
| Los Angeles Lakers | ☎310/419-3100 |
| Sacramento Kings | ☎916/928-0000 |

## PARTICIPANT SPORTS

**Surfing** is probably the best-known Californian pastime, immortalized in the songs of the Beach Boys and Frankie Avalon. The Southern California coast up to San Francisco is dotted with excellent surfing beaches. Some of the finest places to catch a wave, with or without a board, are at **Tourmaline Beach** near San Diego, **Huntington Beach** and **Malibu** in Los Angeles, along the coast north of **Santa Barbara**, and at **Santa Cruz** – where there's a small but worthy surfing museum.

**Cycling** is an increasingly popular sport, with California home to some highly competitive, world-class road races, particularly around the Wine Country. The heavy-duty, all-terrain **mountain bike** was invented here, designed to tackle the slopes of Mount Tamalpais in Marin County. Special mountain bike parks, most of them operating in summer only, exploit the groomed snow-free runs of the Sierra ski bowls of Lake Tahoe and Mammoth. In such places, and throughout California, you can rent bikes for $20–30 a day; see "Getting Around", p.32, for more on general cycling.

**Skiing** is the biggest mass-market participant sport, with downhill resorts all over California – where, believe it or not, it snows heavily most winters. In fact, the Sierra Nevada mountains offer some of the best skiing in the US, particularly around Lake Tahoe, where the 1960 Winter Olympics were held. You can rent equipment for about $40 a weekend, plus another $35 to $50 a day for lift tickets.

A cheaper option is **cross-country skiing**, or ski-touring. A number of backcountry ski lodges in the Sierra Nevada offer a range of rustic accommodation, equipment rental and lessons, from as little as $20 a day for skis, boots and poles, up to about $200 for an all-inclusive weekend tour.

All these, and other sporting outlets and facilities, are detailed in the relevant chapters of the *Guide*.

# FESTIVALS AND PUBLIC HOLIDAYS

**Someone, somewhere is always celebrating something in California, although apart from national holidays, few festivities are shared throughout the entire state. Instead, there is a disparate multitude of local events: art and craft shows, county fairs, ethnic celebrations, music festivals, rodeos, sandcastle building competitions, and many others of every hue and shade.**

Among California's major annual events are the **gay and lesbian freedom** parades held in June in LA and, particularly, San Francisco; the **Academy Awards** in LA in March, and the world-class **Monterey Jazz Festival** in September. These and other local highlights are covered in the text. In addition, California tourist offices can provide full lists, or you can just phone the visitor center in a particular region ahead of your arrival and ask what's coming up.

## PUBLIC HOLIDAYS

The biggest and most all-American of the **national festivals and holidays** is **Independence Day** on the Fourth of July, when the entire country grinds to a standstill as people get drunk, salute the flag and partake of firework displays, marches, beauty pageants and more, all in commemoration of the signing of the Declaration of Independence in 1776. **Halloween** (October 31) lacks any such patriotic overtones, and is not a public holiday despite being one of the most popular yearly flings. Traditionally, kids run around the streets banging on doors demanding "trick or treat", and being given pieces of candy. These days that sort of activity is mostly confined to rural and suburban areas, while in bigger cities Halloween has grown into a massive gay celebration: in West Hollywood in LA and San Francisco's Castro district, the night is marked by mass cross-dressing, huge block parties and general licentiousness. More sedate is **Thanksgiving Day**, on the last Thursday in November. The third big event of the year is essentially a domestic affair, when relatives return to the familial nest to stuff themselves with roast turkey, and (supposedly) fondly recall the first harvest of the Pilgrims in Massachusetts – though in fact Thanksgiving was already a national holiday before anyone thought to make that connection.

On the national **public holidays** listed below, shops, banks and offices are liable to be closed all day. Many states also have their own additional holidays, and in some places Good Friday is a half-day holiday. The traditional **summer season** for tourism runs from **Memorial Day to Labor Day**; some tourist attractions are only open during that period.

January 1 **New Year's Day**
January 15 **Martin Luther King Jr's Birthday**
Third Monday in February **Presidents' Day**
**Easter Monday**
Last Monday in May **Memorial Day**
July 4 **Independence Day**
First Monday in September **Labor Day**
Second Monday in October **Columbus Day**
November 11 **Veterans' Day**
Last Thursday in November **Thanksgiving Day**
December 25 **Christmas Day**

# DIRECTORY FOR OVERSEAS VISITORS

**ADDRESSES** Though initially confusing for overseas visitors, American addresses are masterpieces of logical thinking. Generally speaking, roads in built-up areas are laid out to a grid system, creating "blocks" of buildings: addresses of buildings refer to the block, which will be numbered in sequence, from a central point usually downtown; for example, 620 S Cedar will be six blocks south of downtown. In small towns, and parts of larger cities, "streets" and "avenues" often run north–south and east–west respectively; streets are usually named (sometimes alphabetically), avenues generally numbered.

**CIGARETTES AND SMOKING** Smoking is a much-frowned-upon activity in the US, and especially so in California where some cities have banned smoking in all public places, including bars. It's quite possible to spend a month in the States without ever smelling tobacco; most cinemas have banned smoking, restaurants are either divided into non-smoking and smoking sections or, more commonly, are entirely non-smoking, and smoking is universally forbidden on public transport and in elevators. Cigarettes are sold in virtually any food shop, drugstore or bar, and also from vending machines on the outside walls of these establishments. A packet of twenty costs around $2 – much cheaper than in Britain – though most smokers buy cigarettes by the carton for around $17.

**DEPARTURE TAX** All airport, customs and security taxes are included in the price of your ticket.

**DRUGS** Possession of under an ounce of the widely consumed marijuana is a noncriminal offence in California, and the worst you'll get is a $200 fine. Being caught with more than an ounce, however, means facing a criminal charge for dealing, and a possible prison sentence – stiffer if caught anywhere near a school. Other drugs are, of course, completely illegal and it's a much more serious offence if you're caught with any.

**ELECTRICITY** 110V AC. The insubstantial two-pronged plugs have now largely been replaced by a more sturdy three-pronged affair. Some travel plug adapters don't fit American sockets.

**FLOORS** In the US, what would be the ground floor in Britain is the *first* floor, the first floor the *second* floor and so on.

**ID** Should be carried at all times. Two pieces should diffuse any suspicion, one of which should have a photo: driving licence, passport and credit card(s) are your best bets.

**MEASUREMENTS AND SIZES** The US has yet to go metric, so measurements are in inches, feet, yards and miles; weight in ounces, pounds and tons. American pints and gallons are about four-fifths of Imperial ones. Clothing sizes are always two figures less what they would be in Britain – a British women's size 12 is a US size 10 – while British shoe sizes are half a size below American ones for women, and one size below for men.

**TIME** California runs on Pacific Standard Time (PST), eight hours behind GMT in winter and three hours behind the East Coast. British Summer Time runs almost concurrent with US Daylight Saving Time – implemented from the last Sunday in April to the last Sunday in October – causing a seven-hour time difference for two weeks of the year.

**TIPPING** You really shouldn't leave a bar or restaurant without leaving a tip of *at least* fifteen percent (unless the service is utterly disgusting): it causes a lot of embarrassment and nasty looks, and a short paypacket for the waiter/waitress at the end of the week. About the same should be added to taxi fares, and rounded up to the nearest 50¢ or dollar. A hotel porter should get roughly $1 for each bag carried to your room. When paying by credit card you're expected to add the tip to the total bill before filling in the amount and signing.

**VIDEOS** The standard format used for video cassettes in the US is different from that used in Britain. You cannot buy videos in the US compatible with a video camera bought in Britain.

**WHALE-WATCHING** During November and December, Californian gray whales migrate from the Arctic to their breeding grounds off the coast of Baja California, making their return journey during February and March. Along the coast in these months you'll often find open-air whale-themed events, generally with a display or talk about the whales, and with food, drink and even music supplied, as people peer out to the ocean hoping for (and usually getting) a glimpse of the great creatures.

# THE

# GUIDE

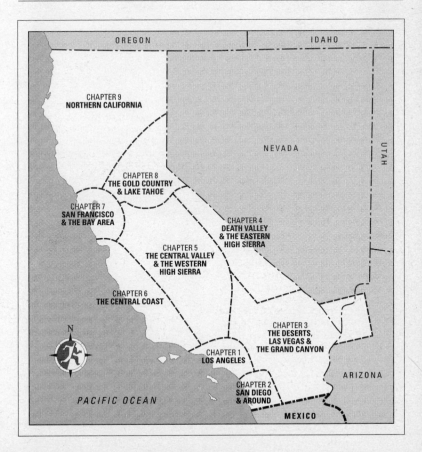

# CHAPTER ONE

# LOS ANGELES

The rambling metropolis of **LOS ANGELES** sprawls across the floor of a great desert basin in a colourful jangle of fast-food joints, shopping malls, palm trees and swimming pools, bounded by snowcapped mountains and the Pacific Ocean, and held together by an intricate network of high-speed freeways rising above a thousand square miles of architectural anarchy. It's an extremely visual, often voyeuristic, city, and famously hard to make sense of – understandable, in F Scott Fitzgerald's phrase, "only dimly, and in flashes".

For all that, LA can surprise you with a powerful sense of familiarity. The entertainment industry has been popularizing the city ever since film-makers arrived in the 1910s, attracted by a climate which allowed them to film outdoors year-round, plenty of cheap open land on which to build elaborate sets, and nearby landscapes varied enough to form an imaginary backdrop to just about anywhere in the world. Since then, the money and glamour of Hollywood have enticed countless thousands of would-be actors, writers, designers and, more recently, rock stars. The myth of overnight success is very much part of the LA mind-set, but so is the reality of sudden disaster: floods, fires and earthquakes are facts of life here, and the co-existence of both extremes lends an on-the-edge, almost unhinged personality to the city. LA, certainly, is like nowhere else on earth. Mud-wrestling venues and porn cinemas stand next door to quality bookstores and trendy restaurants, in a relentless but strangely addictive assault on the senses that can make everywhere else you go afterwards somehow tame and almost predictable.

LA is also a very young city. Just over a century ago, it was a bi-cultural community of white American immigrants and wealthy Mexican ranchers, with a population of under fifty thousand. Only on completion of the transcontinental railroad in the 1880s did the city really begin to grow, consistently doubling in population every ten years. Hundreds of thousands descended upon the basin, lured by the prospect of living in a subtropical paradise. Ranches were subdivided into innumerable suburban lots and scores of new towns, and land speculators marketed an enduring image of Los Angeles, epitomized by the family-sized suburban house (with swimming pool and two-car garage) set amid the orange groves in a glorious land of sunshine. The boom years came after World War II when many of the veterans who'd passed through on their way to the South Pacific came back to stay, buying government-subsidized houses and finding well-paid work in the mushrooming aeronautics industry.

In the late 1980s, though, Southern California was hit *very* hard by post-Cold War cutbacks. Unemployment reached a peak of ten percent, with crime rocketing as a result. Unemployment is now back down to 5.1 percent, but the conservative suburb of Orange County, also known as the Orange Curtain, is still in a state of shock nicknamed White Fright. Its residents have become so scared of LA's crime that they have retreated into "gated communities", housing estates with boundary fences and roads patrolled by private security forces. Safely locked in, they voted in 1994 for Proposition 187, a state law denying access to health and education services to illegal immigrants, particularly the Mexican "wetbacks" they perceive as responsible for the city's problems.

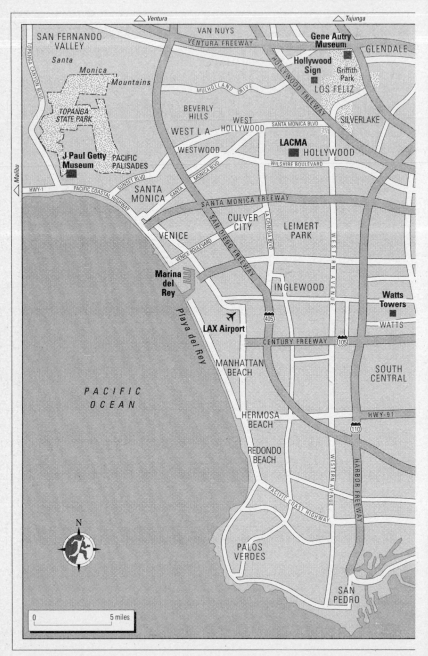

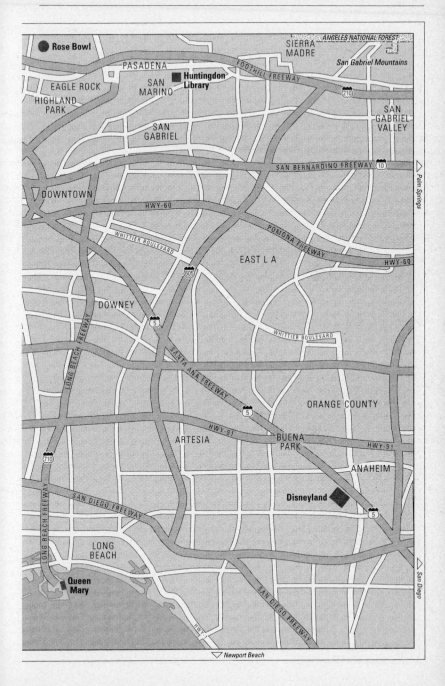

In LA proper, numerous glossy museums, built during the 1980s, mean that Los Angeles is still an international centre of visual art; and the forest of downtown skyscrapers is proof of its key position as the high-finance gateway between America and the Far East. But the extent of the contradictions involved in dwelling in – and visiting – a city that contains at least fifty thousand homeless alongside some of the highest standards of living in the world are never far away. Race rioting has been as much a part of LA history as film-making. Four years on in South Central, the *Rebuild LA* programme has yet to make much of a dent in the devastation caused by 1992's riots. Empty lots stand where there were supermarkets, and it's still easier to buy a quart of whisky than to buy groceries. The psychological scars go much deeper.

When he chose to play the so-called "race card" in the 1995 double murder trial of fallen football hero O J Simpson, lead defence attorney Johnnie Cochran tapped into questions and emotions that are at the core of the city and, some would say, of contemporary America. Dubbed "The Trial of the Century" by the numerous legal correspondents who became household names in the year-long made-for-TV court-room drama, the case epitomized LA's fascination with fame, money and sex. It also brought confirmation of long-standing racism and corruption within the LAPD to a world audience. Whether the gaze of the world will make any difference to a city that seems unable or unwilling to let go of historical prejudices, and its geographical, political, social and economic ghettos, remains to be seen.

Because Los Angeles has four telephone **area codes** – ☎213, ☎310, ☎818 and ☎714 – we have included the code in each number.

# Arrival and information

**Arriving** in LA is potentially one of the most nerve-wracking experiences you're ever likely to have. However you get to the city, and especially if you're not driving, you're faced with a sprawling urban monster that can be a source of bewilderment even for people who've lived in it for years. Provided you don't panic, however, the city is far from the savage beast it first appears.

## By plane

All European and many domestic **flights** use Los Angeles International Airport – always known as **LAX** – sixteen miles southwest of downtown LA (☎310/646-5252). If you're on a budget, and not planning to rent a car (in which case see "Driving and car rental"), the cheapest option is to take the free **"C" shuttle bus** (not "A" or "B", which serve the parking lots), running 24 hours a day from each terminal, to the LAX Transit Center at Vicksburg Avenue and 96th Street. From here, local **buses** (the *MTA* and others) leave for different parts of LA – see "City transport" on p.65 for more details.

The most convenient way into town is to ride a minibus service such as **Airport Shuttle** (☎1-800/545-7745) or **SuperShuttle** (☎1-800/554-3146), which run to downtown, Hollywood, West LA and Santa Monica (the *SuperShuttle* also goes to Long Beach and Disneyland) and deliver you to your door; most have flashing signs on their fronts, advertising their general destination. If you're heading for the Santa Monica area, or the South Bay, another possibility is the **Coast Shuttle** (☎310/417-3988). Fares vary depending on your destination, but are generally around $18. The shuttles run around the clock from outside the baggage reclaim areas, and you should never have to wait more than fifteen or twenty minutes; pay the fare when you board.

**Taxis** from the airport are always expensive: reckon on at least $25 to downtown, $30 to Hollywood and $85 to Disneyland. Unlicensed taxi operators may approach you and offer flat fares to your destination; it's not really a good idea to take them up on it, but if tempted, bargain fiercely, and agree the fare *before* you set off. Don't even consider using the **Metro** system to get to your destination from LAX, it involves three time-consuming transfers, very difficult with luggage, just to set foot in downtown Los Angeles.

The vast majority of flights into LA use LAX, but if you're arriving from elsewhere in the US, or Mexico, you may land at one of the **other airports** in the LA area – at Burbank, Long Beach, Ontario or Orange County's John Wayne Airport. These are similarly well served by car rental firms; or if you want to use public transport phone the *MTA Regional Information Network* (Mon–Fri 6am–8.30pm, Sat–Sun 8am-6pm; ☎213/626-4455 or 1-800-COMMUTE, outside LA ☎1-800/2LA-RIDE) on arrival and tell them where you are and where you want to go.

## By bus

The main **Greyhound** bus terminal, at 1716 E Seventh St, is in a seedy section of downtown – though access is restricted to ticket holders and it's safe enough inside. There are **other Greyhound terminals** elsewhere in LA, which handle fewer services: in Hollywood at 1409 Vine St; in Pasadena at 645 E Walnut St; in Santa Monica at 1433 Fifth St; and in Anaheim at 1711 S Manchester Blvd. Only the downtown terminal is open round-the-clock; all have toilets and left luggage lockers.

**Green Tortoise** also runs weekly services to LA from San Francisco ($30 one-way), stopping in Hollywood at *McDonald's* on Vine Street, a block south of Sunset Boulevard, and in Santa Monica at the *HI-LA/Santa Monica*, 1434 Second St at Santa Monica Boulevard.

## By train

Arriving in LA by **train**, you'll be greeted with the expansive architecture of Union Station, on the north side of downtown at 800 N Alameda St. *Amtrak* trains also stop at outlying stations in the LA area; for all listings call *Amtrak* (☎1-800/USA-RAIL).

## By car

The main routes by **car** into Los Angeles are the interstate highways, all of which pass through downtown. From the east, I-10, the San Bernardino Freeway, has replaced the more sonorous Route 66. Of the non-interstate routes into the city, US-101, the scenic route from San Francisco, cuts across the San Fernando Valley and Hollywood into downtown; Hwy-1, which follows the entire coast of California, takes surface streets through Malibu, Santa Monica, the South Bay and Orange County.

# Information

For free maps, accommodation suggestions and general information, the **CVB** operates two **visitor centers**: downtown at 695 S Figueroa St (Mon–Fri 8am–5pm, Sat 8.30am–5pm; ☎213/689-8822), and in Hollywood at the *Janes House*, 6541 Hollywood Blvd (Mon–Fri 9am–5pm; ☎213/689-8822). You can also call toll-free for information on ☎1-800/228-2452.

Other LA suburbs have their own bureaus: in Santa Monica at 1400 Ocean Ave (daily 10am–4pm; ☎310/393-7593); Anaheim opposite Disneyland at 800 W Katella Ave (daily 9am–5pm; ☎714/999-8999); Beverly Hills, 239 S Beverly Drive (☎310/271-8174 or 1-800/345-2210); Long Beach, 1 World Trade Center, Suite 300 (☎310/436-3645), and, less usefully, in West Hollywood, 9000 Sunset Blvd (☎310/274-7294).

All the centers offer free **maps** of their area, but you'd do better to spend $1.75 on *Gousha Publications'* fully indexed "Los Angeles and Hollywood Street Map", available from vending machines in visitor centers and most hotel lobbies. If you're in LA for a considerable period of time, the fully indexed *LA County Thomas Guide* is the definitive **road atlas**. It's no good if you're absolutely lost and have no idea of the city compass, (use a freeway map, local streetguides and ring ahead to your destination for directions instead), but for a meticulous, up-to-date guide of hard-to-find streets, every driver in this city should have one.

### Newspapers and magazines

LA has just one **daily newspaper** of consequence: the *Los Angeles Times,* available from street corner racks all over Southern California (50¢). The Sunday edition is huge, and its *Calendar* section contains the most complete listings of what's on and where, as well as reviews and gossip of the city's arts and entertainment worlds. Of the city's many **free papers**, much the fullest and most useful is the free *LA Weekly*, with over a hundred pages of trendier-than-thou news, features and listings. A more grown-up second is the smaller and harder-to-find *LA Reader*, with well-informed reviews and comment, and the less established *LA Village View* is also worth a look. Copies of the free papers are available all over LA, especially at cafés and record- and bookstores.

To get a sense of how style-conscious LA sees itself, thumb through a copy of the monthly *Los Angeles* magazine ($2.50) or the younger and less mainstream *Buzz* ($3). Both are packed with gossipy news and profiles of local movers and shakers, as well as reviews of what's hot (and what's not) in the city's restaurant and club scenes. There are also dozens of less glossy, more erratic 'zines – including *Spunk, Planet Homo* and *The Edge* – focusing on LA's diverse gay and lesbian culture and nightclubs.

# City transport

The only certainty when it comes to **getting around** LA is that wherever and however you're going, you should allow plenty of time to get there. Obviously, this is partly due to the sheer size of the city, but the confusing entwinements of freeways and the tailbacks common during rush hours can make car trips lengthy undertakings – and the fact that most local buses stop on every corner hardly makes bus travel a speedy alternative.

## Driving and car rental

The best way to get around LA – though by no means the only way – is to **drive**. Despite the traffic being bumper-to-bumper much of the day, the **freeways** are the only way to cover long distances quickly. The system, however, can be confusing, especially since each stretch can have two or three names (often derived from their eventual destination, however far away) as well as a number. Four major freeways fan

---

**MTA OFFICES AND INFORMATION**

For **MTA route and transfer information**, phone ☎1-800-COMMUTE or ☎213/626-4455 (Mon–Fri 6am—8.30pm, Sat–Sun 8am–6pm ); be prepared to wait, and be ready to give precise details of where you are and where you want to go. Otherwise, you can go in person to the Gateway Transit Center or the two other main offices: at 515 S Flower St, on level C of Arco Plaza (Mon–Fri 7.30am–3.30pm); or in Hollywood at 6249 Hollywood Blvd (Mon–Fri 10am–6pm).

## MTA BUS ROUTES

*MTA*'s buses fall into six categories, as outlined below. Some of the routes can be characterized by their passengers; the early morning east–west route along Wilshire Boulevard is full of Latin American service workers travelling to the homes of their Westside employers, whereas tourists dominate the route west along Venice Boulevard to the beach. The drivers add to the atmosphere too; some deliver a chirpy running commentary of the journey, others are woundingly abrupt. Whatever bus you're on, if travelling alone, especially at night, sit up front near the driver. Try and sit near a ventilation hatch, too, as the air conditioning can emit a rather sickly-sweet odour.

**#1–99** – local routes to and from downtown.

**#100–299** – local routes to other areas.

**#300–399** – limited-stop routes (usually rush hours only).

**#400–499** – express routes to and from downtown.

**#500–599** – express routes, other areas.

**#600–699** – special service routes (for sports events and the like).

### MAJOR LA BUS SERVICES

**From LAX to:**

Downtown #42, #439.

Long Beach (via Redondo Beach) #232.

West Hollywood #220 (for Hollywood change to #1 along Hollywood Boulevard or #4 along Santa Monica Boulevard).

**To and from downtown:**

Along Hollywood Blvd #1.

Along Sunset Blvd #2, #3.

Along Santa Monica Blvd #4.

Along Melrose Ave #10, #11.

Along Wilshire Blvd #20, #21, #22, #320.

**From downtown to:**

Santa Monica #22.

Venice #33, #333, #436.

Forest Lawn Cemetery #90, #91.

Exposition Park #38, #81.

Huntington Library #79.

Burbank Studios #96.

San Pedro #446; #142 for Catalina, #447 change to #147 for Ports O'Call Village.

Manhattan Beach/Hermosa Beach/ Redondo Beach #439.

Redondo Beach/Palos Verdes #443, #444.

Long Beach #60.

Disneyland #460.

out from downtown: the Hollywood Freeway (a section of US-101), heads northwest through Hollywood into the San Fernando Valley; the Santa Monica Freeway (I-10) crosses West LA to Santa Monica; the Harbor Freeway (I-110) runs south to San Pedro; and the Santa Ana Freeway (I-5) passes Disneyland and continues through Orange County. For **shorter journeys**, especially between downtown and the coast, the wide avenues and boulevards are a better option, not least because you get to see more of the city.

All the major **car rental** firms have branches all over the city (simply look in the phone book for the nearest office or call one of the toll-free numbers listed in *Basics* on p.27), and most have their main office close to LAX, linked to each terminal by a free shuttle bus. A number of smaller rental companies specialize in everything from old bangers to Batmobiles. *Rent-a-Wreck*, 12333 W Pico Blvd (☎310/478-0676), has mid-Sixties Mustang convertibles; *Dream Boats*, 8536 Wilshire Blvd (☎310/659-3277), deals in pink Cadillacs and '57 T-birds. Expect to pay in the region of $50 per day.

**Parking** is a particular problem downtown, along Melrose Avenue's trendy Westside shopping streets, and in Santa Monica. Anywhere else is less troublesome, but watch out for restrictions – some lampposts boast as many as four placards listing do's and don'ts. Sometimes it's better to shell out $5 for valet parking than get stuck with a $28 ticket for parking in a residental zone.

## Public transport

The bulk of LA's public transport is operated by the *LA County Metropolitan Transit Authority* (*MTA* or **"Metro"**), which is still sometimes abbreviated to its old name, the *RTD*. Its brand-new, massive, glass-domed **Union Station Gateway Intermodel Transit Center**, to the east of Union Station on Vignes Street, is the new heart of the system, expected to serve 100,000 commuters a day travelling by *Metrorail*, light rail, commuter rail, *Amtrak* and the regional bus systems.

### Metrorail

Hampered by a series of construction scandals and budget difficulties, LA's **Metrorail** system is beginning to come into at least partial use. A light rail network that will one day cover the whole of Los Angeles county, it is currently made up of three lines. The underground **Red Line** as yet reaches only about a mile from the Transit Center west to Wilshire Boulevard at MacArthur Park, but will eventually open up a route to Hollywood and into the San Fernando Valley, fully linking the east/west axis of the city into the next century. Of more use to residents than tourists, the **Green Line** runs between the commuter districts of El Segundo and Nowalk, along the middle of the Century Freeway. Tantalizingly close to LAX, but in practical terms absolutely useless if you are in a hurry, the placing of the line has attracted much criticism. Currently the most complete route, the **Blue Line** leaves downtown and heads overground through South Central to Long Beach. It's a safe journey through some of the most economically depressed areas of the city, and highlights the normality of everyday commuters' lives rather than the gangs and guns of media repute. A trolley line from downtown to Pasadena is also under construction, though *MTA* has yet to announce an estimated due date. **Fares** on all journeys are $1.35 one way. Peak-hour trains run at five- to six-minute intervals, at other times every ten to fifteeen minutes. Don't bring takeaway refreshments on the trains – the fine is $250.

### Buses

Car-less Angelenos are still most at ease with **buses**. Although initially bewildering, the gist of the *MTA* bus network is quite simple: the main routes run east–west (ie between downtown and the coast) and north–south (between downtown and the South Bay). Establishing the best transfer point if you need to change buses can be difficult, but with a bit of planning you should have few real problems – though you should always allow plenty of time.

Area brochures and maps are available free from *MTA* offices, and you can pick up diagrams and timetables for individual routes on the bus (maps of the entire network have not been printed for some time due to the route disruption caused by the *Metrorail* construction). Buses on the major arteries between downtown and the coast run roughly every fifteen minutes between 5am and 2am; other routes, and the **all-night services** along the major thoroughfares, are less frequent, usually every thirty minutes or hourly. At night be careful not to get stranded downtown, waiting for connecting buses.

The standard **single fare** is $1.35; **transfers**, which can be used in one direction within the time marked on the ticket (usually three hours), cost 25¢ more; **express buses** (a limited commuter service), and any others using a freeway, are usually $1.85 though sometimes more. Put the correct money (coins or notes) into the slot when getting on. If you're staying a while, you can save some money with a **monthly pass**, which costs around $49 (slightly more to include express buses) and also gives reductions at selected shops and travel agents.

## GUIDED TOURS OF LA

One quick and easy way to see something of LA is from the window of a **guided bus tour**. These vary greatly in cost and quality. The **mainstream tours** carrying large bus-loads around the major sights are only worth considering if you're very pushed for time – none covers anything that you couldn't see for yourself at less cost. **Specialist tours** tail-ored to suit particular interests, which usually carry smaller groups of people, are often better value. **Studio tours** of film and TV production areas are covered on day trips by most of the mainstream operators, though again you'll save money by turning up independently.

### MAINSTREAM TOURS
By far the most popular of the mainstream tours is the half-day **"stars' homes"** jaunt. Usually including the Farmer's Market, Sunset Strip, Rodeo Drive, the Hollywood Bowl and Chinese Theatre, as well as, of course, the "stars' homes", this is much less tempting than it sounds – frequently no more than a view of the gate at the end of the driveway of the house of some TV or celluloid celebrity. Other programmes include tours around the Westside at night, to the beach areas, the *Queen Mary*, day-long excursions to Disneyland and shopping trips to the Mexican border city of Tijuana.

Costs are $30 minimum per person; assorted leaflets are strewn over hotel lobbies and visitor centers. You can make reservations at (and be picked up from) most hotels. Otherwise contact one of the following booking offices:

**Casablanca Tours**, at the *Hollywood Roosevelt*, 7000 Hollywood Blvd (☎213/461-0156).

**Starline Tours**, at the *Janes House*, 6541 Hollywood Blvd (☎213/957-5520 or 5521).

**Hollywood Fantasy Tours**, 6731 Hollywood Blvd (☎213/469-8184).

### SPECIALIST TOURS
The typical specialist tours listed are also generally $30 plus per person. For more suggestions, pick up the free *LA Visitors Guide* from hotels and visitor centers.

**The California Native**, 6701 W 87th Place (☎310/642-1140). Sea kayaking and adventure hikes. Tour uninhabited islands off the coast of California for $99 and up.

**Grave Line Tours**, PO Box 931694, Hollywood (☎213/469-4149). Two-and-a-half hours in the back of a 1969 Cadillac hearse pausing at the scene of nigh-on every eventful death, scandal, perverted sex act and drugs orgy that ever tainted Hollywood and the surrounding area. Leaves daily at 9.30am from the corner of Hollywood Boulevard and Orchid Avenue with overflow cortege running at 12.30pm and 3.30pm.

**SPARCtours**; *the Murals of LA*, 685 Venice Blvd, Venice (☎310/822-9560). Public art in LA is alive and well in the tradition of Diego Rivera, and this is a thoroughly enlightening tour of the "mural capital of the world".

**Black LA Tours**, 3420 W 43rd St, STE 108 (☎213/750-9267). Black historical and entertainment tours.

**Googie Tours** (☎213/980-3480). Pilgrimages to Southern California's remaining space-age glass and formica diners. Choose between the six-hour "San Gabriel Valley" and "Behind the Orange Curtain" tours, the three hour "Coffee Shop Modern & More" jaunt, or the four-hour, night-time "Cocktails 'n' Coffee Shops" trip.

### STUDIO TOURS
For some small insight into how a film or TV show is made, or just to admire the special effects, there are guided tours costing $6–33 at *Warner Bros Studios*, *NBC Televison Studios*, *Universal Studios*, all in the San Fernando Valley; see p.132. If you want to be **part of the audience** in a TV show, the street just outside the Chinese Theatre is the major solicitation spot: TV company reps regularly appear handing out free tickets, and they'll bus you to the studio and back. All you have to do, once there, is laugh and clap on cue.

There are also the mini **DASH** buses, with a flat fare of 25¢. They ply a circuit around Hollywood, and five routes through the centre of downtown roughly every ten minutes between 6.30am and 6pm on weekdays, every fifteen minutes between 10am and 5pm on Saturday, but not at all on Sunday.

Other **local bus services** include: *Orange County (OCTD)* ☎714/636-7433; *Long Beach (LBTD)* ☎310/591-2301; *Culver City* ☎310/253-6500; *Santa Monica* ☎310/451-5444.

### Taxis

You can find **taxis** at most terminals and major hotels. Otherwise phone: among the more reliable companies are *Independent Cab Co* (☎1-800/521-8294), *LA Taxi* (☎627-7000) and *United Independent Taxi* (☎1-800/822-TAXI). The basic fare is $1.90, plus $1.60 for each mile: the driver won't know every street in LA but will know the major ones; ask for the nearest junction and give directions from there.

## Cycling

**Cycling** in LA may sound perverse, but in some areas it can be one of the better ways of getting around. There are beach bike paths between Santa Monica and Redondo Beach, and from Long Beach to Newport Beach, and many equally enjoyable inland routes, notably around Griffith Park, the grand mansions of Pasadena, and along the LA River. Contact the *AAA* (☎213/741-3111) or the *LA Department of Transportation* (☎213/485-3051) for maps and information.

The best place to **rent a bike** for the beaches is on Washington Street around Venice Pier, where numerous outlets include *Spokes'n'Stuff* (☎310/306-3332); in summer bike rental stands line the beach. For Griffith Park, use *Woody's Bicycle World*, 3157 Los Feliz Blvd (☎213/661-6665). Prices range from $8 a day for a clunker to $15 a day or more for a ten-speed.

For similar cost, the beachside stores also rent **roller skates and blades**. Try *House of Skates*, 4 Rose Ave at Ocean Front Walk, Venice (☎310/399-1728).

## Walking and hiking

Although some people are surprised to find sidewalks in LA, let alone pedestrians, **walking** is in fact the best way to see much of downtown and a number of other districts. You can structure your stroll by taking a **guided walking tour**, the best of which are organized by the *Los Angeles Conservancy* (☎213/623-CITY), whose treks around downtown's battered but still beating heart is full of heyday Art Deco movie palaces and architechtural gems like the Bradbury Building (see p.80). Among many alternatives, it runs downtown tours every Saturday, leaving the *Biltmore Hotel* on Olive Street at 10am (reservations essential; $5). See the box below for details of other tour operators. You can also take guided **hikes** through the wilds of the Santa Monica Mountains and Hollywood Hills free of charge every weekend with a variety of organizations, including the *Sierra Club* (☎213/387-4287), the *State Parks Department* (☎1-800/444-7275) and the *Santa Monica Mountains National Recreation Area* (☎818/597-1036).

# Accommodation

Since LA has 100,000-plus rooms, finding **accommodation** is easy. Whether you're looking for a budget place to rest your head, or a world-class hotel where you can hobnob with Hollywood stars and entertainment industry tycoons, LA has something for everyone – and the post-riot, post-recession downturn in tourism means that prices are often reasonable.

## ACCOMMODATION PRICES

All accommodation prices in this book have been coded using the symbols below. Note that prices are for the least expensive double rooms in each establishment. For a full explanation see p.33 in *Basics*. Bear in mind that in Los Angeles all quoted room rates are subject to a **room tax** – currently fourteen percent on top of your total bill.

① up to $30    ② $30–45    ③ $45–60    ④ $60–80    ⑤ $80–100

⑥ $100–130    ⑦ $130–175    ⑧ $175–250    ⑨ $250+

That said, however, finding somewhere that's low-priced and well-located is more difficult, though not impossible. If you're driving, of course, you needn't worry about staying in a less than ideal location – a freeway is never far away. Otherwise you'll need to be a sight more choosy about the district you plump for, as getting across town can be a time-consuming business.

**Motels** and the lower-range hotels start at around $40 for a double, but many are situated in unappealing or out-of-the-way areas and often you'll find you gain by paying a little more for a decent location in any of a number of other, non-chain mid-range hotels. **Bed and breakfast inns** are rare in LA, and tend to be expensive and frequently fully booked. For those on a budget, **hostels** are dotted all over the city, many in good locations, though at some stays are limited to a few nights. Camping, perhaps surprisingly, is also an option: there are a few **campgrounds** on the edge of the metropolitan area – along the beach north of Malibu, and in the San Gabriel mountains, for example – but you'll need a car to get to them. Hostels and campgrounds are listed at the end of this section. **College rooms** are also sometimes available for rent during student vacation time: contact **UCLA** Interfraternity Council (☎310/825-7878) or **USC**'s off-campus housing office (☎1-800/USC-4632) for information.

LA is so big that if you want to see it all without constantly having to cross huge expanses, it makes sense to divide your stay between several districts. Prices – and options – vary by area. Downtown and Hollywood both have a few cheap and many mid-range hotels, while more salubrious West LA, Santa Monica, Venice and Malibu are predominantly mid-to-upper-range territory. Among options further out, the South Bay and Harbor area, well connected with other parts of town, carries a good selection of low- to mid-range hotels (and a hostel) strung mostly along the Pacific Coast Highway (PCH). It's only worth staying in Orange County, thirty miles southeast of downtown, if you're aiming for Disneyland or are travelling along the coast: hotels under $70 a night are a rarity and you must book at least a week in advance, especially if a convention is in town. Unfortunately many of the plentiful rooms along Katella Avenue and Harbor Boulevard in Anaheim are run down and depressing, even though they charge up to $100 a night. By far a better alternative are the hostels and coastal campsites in easy reach.

Since there are no **booking agencies**, and visitor centers don't make accommodation reservations (though they will offer information and advice), you can only book a room through a travel agent or by phoning the hotel directly. Ask if there are special weekend or midweek rates. Especially at the lower end of the price scale, hotels are cheaper if booked by the week than the night, and don't be afraid to **haggle**: LA's tourism industry is struggling, and some places will offer lower rates if you ask.

Hotels are listed below by neighbourhood, with specific accommodation options for gay and lesbian travellers listed in a special section on p.155. In case you're arriving on a late flight, or leaving on an early one, we've also listed a few places to stay near the airport: hotels near LAX are blandly similar and generally in the $60–80 price range, but have complimentary limo service to and from the terminals.

## Downtown and around

**Biltmore Hotel**, 506 S Grand Ave at Fifth (☎213/24-1011 or 1-800/245-8673). Classical architecture combined with modern luxury to make your head swim. ⑦–⑨.

**City Center Motel**, 1135 W Seventh St at Lucas (☎213/628-7141). Bare but clean with Sixties-style decor, a 10–15-min walk to downtown. ②.

**Figueroa Hotel**, 939 S Figueroa St at Olympic (☎213/627-8971 or 1-800/421-9092). Mid-range hotel on the southern side of downtown, with a jacuzzi-equipped pool and 24-hour coffee shop. ④–⑤.

**Holiday Inn Downtown**, 750 Garland Ave at Eighth (☎213/628-5242 or 1-800/465-4329). On the western fringe of downtown beside the Harbor Freeway. ⑤.

**Hotel Inter-Continental**, 251 S Olive St at Fourth (☎213/617-3300 or 1-800/442-5251). Brand-new Bunker Hill hotel, home to financial kingpins and Academy Award attendees. Very plush, adjacent to MOCA and the Music Center. ⑦.

**Kawada Hotel**, 200 S Hill St at Second (☎213/621-4455 or 1-800/752-9232). Comfortable and clean if plain rooms in recently renovated, medium-sized hotel, near the Civic Center and popular with value-oriented business travellers. ④.

**Nutel Motel**, 1906 W Third St at Bonnie Brae (☎213/483-6681). A few blocks from MacArthur Park (sometimes dicey for pedestrians at night) about a mile from downtown. ③.

**Orchid Hotel**, 819 S Flower St at Eighth (☎213/624-5855). Easily the best deal in the heart of downtown, near the Seventh and Flower *Metrorail* station. Though there may be the odd drunk in the lobby, it's clean comfortable and safe. Weekly rates. ②.

**Park Plaza**, 607 S Park View St, between Sixth and Wilshire (☎213/384-5281). Facing MacArthur Park, this has a sumptuous lobby and marble floor, but ordinary rooms. ④.

**The Westin Bonaventure**, 404 S Figueroa St, between Fourth and Fifth (☎213/624-1000 or 1-800/228-3000). Luxury post-modern masterpiece or nightmare depending on your point of view. Five glass towers, six-storey lobby with a "lake". Breathtaking exterior elevator ride to a rotating cocktail lounge which averages seven proposals of marriage a week. ⑧–⑨.

## Hollywood

**Best Western Hollywood**, 6141 Franklin Ave, between Gower and Vine (☎213/464-5181). Part of the nationwide chain; with cable TV and heated pool, in the heart of Hollywood. ④.

**Dunes Sunset Motel**, 5625 Sunset Blvd (☎213/467-5171 or 1-800/452-3863). On the eastern side of Hollywood, far enough away from the weirdness of Hollywood Boulevard to feel safe; also good for reaching downtown. ③.

**Holiday Inn Hollywood**, 1755 N Highland Ave (☎1-800/465-4329). Massive, but perfectly placed. The price becomes reasonable with triple occupancy. ③–④.

**Hollywood Metropolitan Hotel**, 5825 Sunset Blvd (☎213/962-5800). The best at the price in central Hollywood. ④.

**Hollywood Towne House Hotel**, 6055 Sunset Blvd at Gower (☎213/462-3221). An odd mix of Seventies decor and Sixties fittings, though the phones, which connect to the front desk only, date back to the Twenties. The place itself is clean and comfortable enough. ②–③.

**Radisson Hollywood Roosevelt**, 7000 Hollywood Blvd, between Highland and La Brea (☎1-800/423-8262). The first hotel built for the movie greats. Though the rooms are plain, the place has been lately revamped and reeks with atmosphere. ⑥.

**Saharan Motor Hotel**, 7212 Sunset Blvd at Poinsetta (☎213/874-6700). Unexciting but functional, and comparatively good value, considering its useful location. ③.

**Sunset 8 Motel**, 6515 Sunset Blvd between Wilcox and Highland (☎213/461-2748). Many of the rooms on this strip rent by the hour, vibrating bed included. This place, though downtrodden, is a cut above. If you see a clean room grab it for a brief stay near Hollywood's traditional sights. Across from the former *Hollywood Athletic Club* and a coin-op laundromat. ②.

## West LA

**Beverly Hills Hotel**, 9641 Sunset Blvd (☎310/276-2251). Painted bold pink and green and surrounded by its own exotic gardens, this famous hotel to the stars, open again after a two-year refurbishment, is pretty hard to miss. Marilyn Monroe once stayed here, and one of the bungalows is decorated in her honour. ⑨.

**Beverly Laurel Motor Hotel**, 8018 Beverly Blvd at Laurel (☎213/651-2441). Pleasant hotel popular with Europeans, with a trendy, rather Warholian new coffee shop, *Swingers*, downstairs (see p.136). Full of people hoping for a peek at Madonna, whose record company, Matador, has offices next door. ④.

**Bevonshire Lodge Motel**, 7575 Beverly Blvd at Curson (☎213/936-6154). Well situated for both West LA and Hollywood. The pool is a bit murky, but all of the functionally decorated rooms come with a refrigerator, and for a few dollars more you can have a kitchenette. ③.

**Chateau Marmont**, 8221 Sunset Blvd at Crescent Heights (☎213/626-1010). Exclusive French-style hotel – one-time haunt of John and Yoko; earlier saw the likes of Boris Karloff, Greta Garbo, Errol Flynn, Jean Harlow et al. Mostly ⑨.

**Claremont Hotel**, 1044 Tiverton Ave (☎310/208-5957). Cheerful and inexpensive small hotel a block from UCLA and Westwood Village. ③.

**Hotel Bel Air**, 701 Stone Canyon Rd (☎310/472-1211 or 1-800/648-1097). LA's nicest hotel bar none, in a lushly overgrown canyon above Beverly Hills. Go for a beautiful brunch by the Swan pond if you can't afford the rooms which reach a dizzying $435 a night. ⑨.

**Hotel Del Flores**, 409 N Crescent Drive at Little Santa Monica (☎310/274-5115). Three blocks from Rodeo Drive, small, pleasant and excellent value. ③–④.

**Le Parc**, 733 N West Knoll (☎1-800/578-4837 or 310/855-8888). Apartment hotel with studios, one- and two-bedroomed suites, rooftop pool and Jacuzzi with view of the hills. A British rock star hangout. ⑦–⑧.

**Le Reve Hotel**, 8822 Cynthia St (☎310/854-1111 or 1-800/424-4443). Gay friendly place a few blocks north of Santa Monica Blvd, in the heart of West Hollywood. Elegant suites in the style of a French provincial inn. ⑥–⑧.

## Santa Monica, Venice and Malibu

**Bayside Motel**, 2001 Ocean Ave at Bay (☎310/396-6000). Just a block from Santa Monica beach and the Sixties-style café scene of Main Street, to which the original psychedelic bathroom tiles pay tribute. No phones in the room, but comfortable, with ocean views from the more expensive rooms. ③.

**Cadillac Hotel**, 8 Dudley Ave at Rose (☎310/399-8876). Stylishly restored Art Deco hotel/hostel bang on the Venice Boardwalk. Thirty of its rooms are private, but there are nine additional dorm rooms at a third of the price. Sundeck, pool, gym and sauna. ①/④.

**Channel Road Inn**, 219 W Channel Rd at PCH (☎310/459-1920). Romantic getaway nestled in lower Santa Monica Canyon, with ocean-view hot tub and free bike rental. Eat free grapes and sip champagne in one of 7 rooms, priced according to the "view". ⑤–⑧.

**Hotel Carmel**, 201 Broadway at Second (☎310/451-2469). The best budget bet in Santa Monica, two blocks from the beach. ④.

**Hotel Santa Monica**, 3102 Pico Blvd at 31st (☎310/450-5766 or 1-800/231-7679). In the heart of Santa Monica, a mile from the beach. ④.

**Loew's Santa Monica Beach Hotel**, 1700 Ocean Ave at Pico (☎310/458-6700). Santa Monica's newest hotel: a deluxe affair overlooking the ocean and the Santa Monica pier, often in demand as a film set. The best rooms top $400. ⑧–⑨.

### AIRPORT HOTELS

**Days Inn**, 901 W Manchester Blvd (☎310/649-0800 or 1-800/231-2508). Outdoor pool, free parking, free LAX shuttle. ④.

**The Cockatoo Inn**, 4334 Imperial Hwy (☎1-800/262-5286). Country-style motel in a faceless suburb, but just a stone's throw from LAX. Free shuttle and breakfast. ③.

**Howard Johnson**, 8620 Airport Blvd (☎310/645-7700). A mile northeast of LAX, with a swimming pool and complimentary airport shuttle. ④.

**Travelodge LAX South**, 1804 E Sycamore Ave (☎310/615-1073). Just five minutes south of LAX; convenient for the South Bay. Rates include use of the pool and free tea, coffee and breakfast. ④.

**Malibu Riviera Motel**, 28920 PCH (☎310/457-9503). Quiet place just outside town, less than a mile from the beach, with a sundeck and jacuzzi. Ideal if you're planning a drive up the coast. ④.

**Malibu Surfer Motel**, 22541 PCH (☎310/456-6169). Ghastly shag carpeting and Seventies decor, but located across from the beach and boasting a kingsize bed, refrigerator and TV in every room. Prices depend on the surf season. ④/⑤.

**Pacific Shore Hotel**, 1819 Ocean Ave at Pico, Santa Monica (☎310/451-8711). A popular stop for package-tour Europeans, with great bay views. ⑤.

**Santa Monica Travelodge**, 1525 Ocean Ave (☎310/451-0761 or 1-800/255-3050). One of the reliable nationwide chain. ⑤.

## The South Bay and Harbor Area

**East-West Motel**, 625 S PCH (☎310/316-1184). Doubles $10 cheaper than at other low-end options. Reasonably clean with TV, phone and laundry available. ②.

**Hotel Hermosa**, 2515 PCH (☎310/318-6000). Plush hotel at moderate prices, a short walk to the beach. ④–⑤.

**Palos Verdes Inn**, 1700 S PCH, Palos Verdes (☎310/316-4200 or 1-800/421-9241). Affordable luxury on the edge of Redondo Beach and at the foot of the Palos Verdes hills; three blocks from the beach. ④–⑤.

**The Road Way Inn**, 50 Atlantic Ave at Ocean (☎310/435-8369). Safe bet a block from the beach, a serviceable base for exploring Long Beach and vicinity. Free-in-room movies. ③.

**Seahorse Inn**, 233 N Sepulveda Blvd, Manhattan Beach (☎310/376-7951 or 1-800/233-8050). Faded pastel exterior but large, tastefully furnished rooms have movie channels. A little bit further from the beach than others, but there's a pool. ②.

**Sea Sprite Ocean Front Apartment Motel**, 1016 Strand (☎310/376-6933). Right next to the beach. Ask the manager what's available as there are several different room options with varying prices. ④–⑤.

## Around Disneyland

**Anaheim Inn**, 1630 South Harbor Blvd at Katella, Anaheim (☎714/774-1050). One of three good-value hotels in Anaheim, all owned by the Stovall family. The others are *Stozalls Inn*, 1110 W Katella Ave (☎714/778-1880), and *Pavillion*, 1176 W Katella Ave (☎714/776-0140). ④.

**Desert Palm Suites**, 631 W Katella Ave, Anaheim (☎1-800/521-6420). Very comfortable spacious rooms with refrigerators, microwaves, VCRs and continental breakfast. Price jumps when a convention is in town. ③.

**The Disneyland Hotel**, 1150 W Cerritos Ave at West St, Anaheim (☎714/778-6600). The place to go for a pricey Disney-themed wedding with Mickey in attendance. Though the substantial room rate does not include admission to the park, the Disneyland monorail does stop right outside. ⑦.

**Motel 6**, 921 S Beach Blvd, Anaheim (☎714/827-9450). Closer to Knotts Berry Farm than Disneyland but the cheapest option around. ①–②.

## The Orange County Coast

**Hotel Laguna**, 425 S Coast Hwy at Laguna (☎714/494-1151). In the centre of Laguna Beach. If you have the cash, this is the place to spend it. Atmospheric and comfortable, and nearly every room has a sea view. ⑤–⑦.

**Mission Inn**, 26891 Ortega Hwy at I-5 (☎714/493-1151). Rooms at this reasonably priced place come with use of Jacuzzi and pool. ③–④.

**Ocean View Motel**, 16196 PCH at Seal Beach, Sunset Beach (☎310/592-2700). Family-run establishment with clean rooms. Get a jacuzzi in your room for an extra $15. ②.

**The Road Way Inn**, 50 Atlantic Blvd, Long Beach (☎310/435-8369). Generic rooms with refrigerators. ②.

**Sail-Inn Motel**, 2627 Newport Blvd (☎714/675-1841). Fairly basic accommodation, but it's the least costly you're likely to find in the Newport area. Close to Balboa Peninsula. ③–④.

**Seacliff Motel**, 1661 S Coast Hwy (☎714/494-9717). A mile south of Laguna Beach, but right on the ocean. ③–④.

## The San Gabriel and San Fernando Valleys

**Belair-Bed & Breakfast**, 941 N Frederic Ave (☎818/848-9227). By far the best value in Burbank. ②.

**Ritz-Carlton Huntington Hotel**, 1401 S Knoll, Pasadena (☎818/568-3900). Utterly luxurious refurbished landmark 1906 hotel, discreetly tucked away in residential Pasadena. Suites start at $350. Rooms ⑦.

**Sheraton Universal**, 333 Universal Terrace, Burbank (☎818/980-1212 or 1-800/325-3535). Large and luxurious hotel on the Universal Studios lot, with health club and outdoor pool. ⑧.

**Vagabond Inn Hotel**, 1203 E Colorado Blvd at Michigan, Pasadena (☎818/449-3170). Friendly budget chain motel, usefully placed for exploring Pasadena. Other *Vagabond Inns* are at 2863 E Colorado Blvd (☎ 818/578-9791 or 1-800/468-2251) and 20157 Ventura Blvd, Woodland Hills (☎818/347-8080), the latter with a large heated pool. ②–③.

## Hostels

**Banana Bungalow-Hollywood Hotel**, 2775 Cahuenga Blvd at Highland (☎213/851-1129 or 1-800/446-7835). Popular large hostel in the Hollywood Hills, with free airport shuttles, city tours to Venice Beach and Universal and a relaxed atmosphere – despite being just 100 yards from the Hollywood Freeway. Outdoor pool, free parking, and as much beer as you can drink every second night for $3. Dorms $15–18, and more expensive private doubles. ①.

**HI-Anaheim/Fullerton**, 1700 N Harbor Blvd at Brea, Anaheim (☎714/738-3721). Convenient (for Disneyland at least) and comfortable, on the site of a former dairy farm. The hostel's excellent facilities include a grass volleyball court, golf driving range and picnic area. There are only 22 beds, so reservations are a must. Summer check-in 5–11pm, rest of year 4–10pm. Mornings open 7.10–10.30am. *Orange County Transport Authority* bus #43 stops outside. Members $14, others $17. ①.

**HI-LA/Santa Monica**, 1436 Second St at Broadway, Santa Monica (☎310/393-9913). A few strides from the sands, the building was LA's Town Hall from 1887 to 1889, and retains its charm, with a pleasant inner courtyard with ivy covered walls and a skylight. Members $15, others $17 – the price includes laundry machines and huge kitchens. Smoking and drinking are prohibited. Open 24hr. Reservations essential in summer. ①.

### LA AREA CAMPGROUNDS

A company called *Destinet* (☎1-800/444-7275) now processes reservations at many of the campgrounds listed below, and can look for an alternative if your chosen site is full. It charges a $6.75 fee per reservation per night up to a maximum of eight people per site, including one vehicle.

**Bolsa Chica Campground** (☎714/846-3460). Facing the ocean in Huntington Beach. $14 for campers with a self-contained vehicle. No tent camping.

**Chilao Flat**, on Hwy-2 twenty miles northeast of Pasadena (☎818/574-1613). The only campground in the San Gabriel Mountains reachable by car, though there are many others accessible on foot. For more details contact the Angeles National Forest Ranger Station at 701 N Santa Anita Ave, Arcadia (☎818/574-1613).

**Dockweiler Beach County Park** (☎310/305-9545 or via *Destinet*). On Vista del Mar, almost at the western end of the LAX runways. Mainly for RVs, tent sites cost $17–25.

**Doheny State Beach Campground**, Dana Point (☎714/496-6171 or via *Destinet)*. Often packed with families, especially at weekends. $16–21 per site.

**Leo Carrillo State Beach Park**, Malibu (☎818/706-1310 or via *Destinet*). Partly on the beach, 25 miles northwest of Santa Monica on Pacific Coast Hwy, and served twice an hour in summer by *MTA* bus #434. $16.

**Malibu Creek State Park** 1925 Las Vignes Rd, fifteen minutes from the centre of the San Fernando Valley (☎818/706-8809) A rustic campground in a park which can become crowded at times. Sixty sites in the shade of huge oak trees, almost all with fire pits, solar heated showers and flush toilets.

**San Clemente State Beach Campground**, two miles south of San Clemente (☎714/492-7146 or via *Destinet*). $20 hook-up sites, $16 others.

**HI-LA South Bay**, 3601 S Gaffey St, building #613, San Pedro (☎310/831-8109). Sixty beds in old US Army barracks, with friendly staff and a panoramic view of the Pacific. Ideal for seeing San Pedro, Palos Verdes and the whole Harbor area. Open 7–11am and 4pm–midnight. $14 members, $16 others; private rooms $27 per person. *MTA* bus #446 passes close by but it's a 2-hour journey from downtown, or take the *SuperShuttle* from LAX. ①.

**Hostel California**, 2221 Lincoln Blvd at Venice, Venice (☎310/305-0250). Built for the 1984 Olympics, this was LA's first hostel. Twelve six-bed dorms with kitchens, pool table, big-screen TV, linen and parking. Cheap shuttle bus to and from LAX. $14, or $84 a week. ①.

**Huntington Beach Colonial Hostel**, 421 Eighth St at Pecan, Huntington Beach (☎714/536-3315). Four blocks from the beach and mostly double rooms. Sleeping bags are allowed. Open 8am–11pm. Key rental after 1pm, $1 (plus a $20 deposit). Dorms $14.30, private rooms $16.50 per person. ①/②.

**Jim's at the Beach**, 17 Brooks Ave at Speedway, Venice (☎310/399-4018). Beachside dorm accommodation on production of a passport. $15 per night or $90 per week, including free breakfast. ①.

**Share Hotel**, 20 Brooks Ave at Speedway, Venice (☎310/392-0325). Apartments, each with 6-8 people sharing facilities and bedrooms. $18, including breakfast and dinner Mon–Fri. ①.

# Orientation

Spilling over a vast flat basin and often lacking well-defined divisions, LA is not a city in the usual sense. Instead, it's a massive conglomeration of interconnected districts, not all of which have that much in common. Travelling from one side to the other takes you through virtually every social extreme imaginable, from mind-boggling beachside luxury to the most severe inner-city poverty anywhere in the US – a result of the city's dizzying growth within such a confined area. With the basin bordered by desert to the east, mountains to the north and ocean to the west, the millions of new arrivals who have poured in have had to fill the spaces between what were once geographically quite isolated and small communities, creating a metropolis on the most mammoth scale.

If LA has a heart, however, it's **downtown**, in the centre of the basin, its towering office blocks punctuating what's for the most part a very low and level skyline. With everything from avant-garde art to the abject dereliction of Skid Row, downtown offers a taste of almost everything you'll find elsewhere around the city, compressed (unusually for LA) into an area of small, easily walkable blocks. It's a good place to get your initial bearings, and, usefully, the hub of the transport network. **Around downtown**, a serviceable label for a hotchpotch of areas with little in common except for being adjacent to or fanning out from downtown demonstrates still more of LA's diversity: from the elaborate Victorian relics of the turn-of-the-century suburbs, and the later Art Deco buildings that characterized the city in the Twenties, to the centre of LA's enormous Hispanic population, home to some rare sights of enjoyable street life, and the sprawl of dull and desperate neighbourhoods that make up South Central LA.

Away from downtown, you'll probably spend most of your time in the broad corridor that runs 25 miles west to the coast. Here are LA's best-known and most interesting districts, the first of which, **Hollywood**, has streets caked with movie legend – even if the genuine glamour is long gone. Tourists flock here, and it's also where some of LA's most eccentric street people choose to parade themselves. Neighbouring **West LA**, on the other hand, is home to the city's newest money, shown off in the incredibly expensive shops of Beverly Hills and the posey restaurants and nightspots of the Sunset Strip, and on its western edge merges into **Santa Monica** and **Venice** – the quintessential coastal LA of palm trees, white sands, and laid-back living. The coastline itself is perhaps the major draw, stretching north from here twenty miles to the northern edge of LA and **Malibu**, noted for its celebrity residences and their keenly guarded privacy.

## LA'S MUSEUMS

Aerospace Building p.85
Armand Hammer Museum p.106
Beit HaShoa Museum of Tolerance p.106
Burbank Studios p.132
Cabrillo Marine Museum p.116
California Afro-American Museum p.85
Children's Museum p.78
Forrest Ackerman's Sci-Fi and Monster
    Mansion p.93
George C Page Discovery Center p.101
Gene Autry Western Heritage Museum
    p.97
Hall of Economics and Finance p.85
Hollywood Wax Museum p.94
Huntington Library and Art Gallery p.130
J Paul Getty Museum p.112
La Brea Tar Pits p.101
LA County Museum of Art p.101

LA County Museum of Natural History p.85
Laguna Beach Museum of Art p.126
Long Beach Museum of Art p.117
Maritime Museum (San Pedro) p.116
Movieland Wax Museum p.121
Museum of Flying p.110
Municipal Art Gallery p.93
Museum of Contemporary Art (MOCA)
    p.78
Museum of Science and Industry p.85
Newport Harbor Art Museum p.125
Norton Simon Museum p.129
Pacific Asia Museum p.129
Peterson Automotive Museum p.101
Richard Nixon Library and Birthplace p.122
Skirball Museum p.84
Southwest Museum p.90
Universal Studios p.133
Will Rogers Museum p.112

South along the coast from Venice, the three **South Bay beach cities** are quieter, lived in by middle-class, family-oriented commuters, and a long way in spirit from the more bustling and fad-conscious portions of the city. The beaches are the sole focus of attention here, their bluffs and coves leading on to the **Harbor Area** – though, again, despite recent facelifts and some mildly enjoyable resort areas, there's nothing to detain you for more than half a day.

**Orange County**, directly east of the Harbor Area, is mainly lifeless suburban sprawl, and the only reason most people come here is to visit **Disneyland**, the city's biggest single tourist attraction and the granddaddy of all theme parks. If you're not keen on seeing "the happiest place on Earth" – as Disneyland calls itself – it's best to hug the coast and continue south, along the **Orange County Coast**, whose string of surprisingly individualistic communities is well positioned for a few days' exploration on the way to San Diego.

In the opposite direction, LA has also grown on the other side of the hills that make up the northern wall of the basin to the **San Gabriel and San Fernando Valleys**, which stretch east and west until LA fades into desert, mountains and ocean. The valleys are distanced from mainstream LA life socially as well as geographically, their inhabitants the butt of most Angeleno hick jokes, and on the whole there is no reason to venture here. The few honourable exceptions include a number of worthwhile art collections and a couple of working (and tourable) film studios, as well as the most famous of LA's cemeteries.

# Downtown LA

From the homeless families on the steps of City Hall to the phallic towers of multinational finance, nowhere else do the social, economic and ethnic divisions of LA clash quite as loudly and clearly as in the square mile that makes up **DOWNTOWN LA**. In

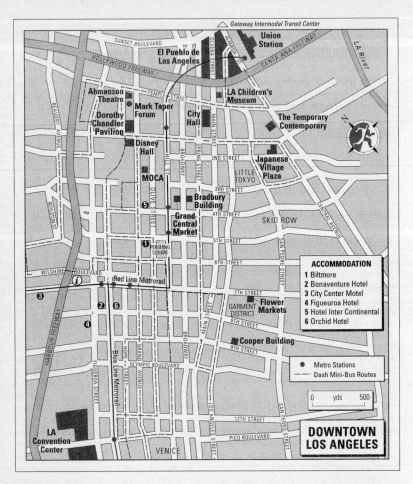

△ Gateway Intermodal Transit Center

Union Station

El Pueblo de Los Angeles

SUNSET BOULEVARD

HOLLYWOOD FREEWAY

SANTA ANA FREEWAY

LA River

Ahmanson Theatre

TEMPLE STREET

Mark Taper Forum

Dorothy Chandler Pavilion

City Hall

LA Children's Museum

The Temporary Contemporary

Disney Hall

2ND STREET

Japanese Village Plaza

MOCA

BROADWAY

SPRING STREET

LITTLE TOKYO

3RD STREET

Bradbury Building

OLIVE STREET

Grand Central Market

4TH STREET

SKID ROW

CENTRAL AVENUE

5TH STREET

PERSHING SQUARE

6TH STREET

SAN PEDRO STREET

WILSHIRE BOULEVARD

Red Line Metrorail

7TH STREET

Flower Markets

GARMENT DISTRICT

8TH STREET

Cooper Building

9TH STREET

Blue Line Metrorail

OLYMPIC BOULEVARD

GRAND AVENUE

HARBOR FREEWAY

FIGUEROA STREET

HOPE STREET

LOS ANGELES STREET

**ACCOMMODATION**

1 Biltmore
2 Bonaventure Hotel
3 City Center Motel
4 Figueroa Hotel
5 Hotel Inter Continental
6 Orchid Hotel

● Metro Stations
--- Dash Mini-Bus Routes

0   yds   500

**DOWNTOWN LOS ANGELES**

12TH STREET

PICO BOULEVARD

LA Convention Center

VENICE

the space of a few short blocks, adobe buildings and Mexican market stalls give way to Japanese-style shopping plazas and avant-garde art galleries, and you're as likely to rub shoulders with a high-flying yuppie as with a down-and-out drunk. Though it's long been the commercial focus of the city, and always the seat of local government, as businesses spread out across the basin in the postwar boom years, so the area became more dilapidated. Things picked up in the 1980s, when revitalization initiatives created museums, theatres and a rash of plush new condos for young professionals, but these have ultimately only served to intensify the extremes, and downtown remains the city's most changed – and changing – neighbourhood.

Each part of downtown has its own share of history, museums and architecture, and it makes most sense to divide the area into simple geographic segments and see it on foot, starting with the original LA settlement on the **Northside**, crossing into the brasher and more modern corporate-tower-dominated **Westside**, continuing through the chaotic streets and historic movie theatres of **Broadway**, and finally stepping into the strange combination of street people (an estimated 15,000 homeless live on downtown's streets), warehouses and occasionally expensively experimental art galleries which makes up the **Eastside**.

Downtown can easily be seen in a day, and if your feet get tired you can hop aboard the *DASH* **buses** which run every ten minutes on five loop systems through key areas (look for the silver-signed bus stops). Forget about bringing a **car**: not only is parking expensive (around $5 per hour), it's hard to come by; in any case downtown is the hub of the *MTA* networks and easily accessible by public transport.

## The Northside

To see downtown LA, start at the beginning. **El Pueblo de Los Angeles**, off Alameda Street, was the site of the original late-eighteenth-century Mexican settlement of Los Angeles and the few very early buildings that remain evoke a strong sense of LA's Spanish and Mexican origins. The **plaza church** is the city's oldest and has long served as a sanctuary for illegal Central American refugees (the right of immigration officers to enter the church to evict them is an ongoing controversy). Try and squeeze in during one of the Mariachi Masses (Sun 11.30am & 4.30pm), held completely in Spanish and accompanied by a six-piece Mariachi band.

You can also see the city's first **firehouse**, with a small but intriguing roomful of firefighting gear, and the exterior of the handsome mission-style **Pico House**, LA's most luxurious hotel when it opened in 1870, but now closed to the public. **Olvera Street**, which runs north from the plaza, is a less successful restoration, contrived in part as a pseudo-Mexican village market. Taken over for numerous festivals throughout the year, like November's Day of the Dead, when Mexicans traditionally honour the spirits of the departed (see p.148), the street is at its best on such familial occasions.

Olvera Street was the creation of one Christine Stirling, who, with other powerful citizens and help from the city government, tore down the slum she found here in 1926 and built much of what you see today, incorporating some of the salvageable historic structures. For the next twenty years she organized fiestas and worked to popularize the city's Mexican heritage while living in the early nineteenth-century **Avila Adobe** at 10 Olvera St – touted as the oldest structure in Los Angeles, although almost entirely rebuilt out of reinforced concrete following the 1971 earthquake. Inside the house are two **museums** (Tues–Sun 10am–3pm; free) – one an idealized view of pueblo-era domestic life; the other, across the landscaped courtyard, telling the cleaned-up official version of how the LA authorities connived to get a secure supply of water for the city (for the real story, see p.133).

Across the street, a **visitor center** (Mon–Sat 10am–3pm, closed on holidays;☎213/ 628-1274) offers the usual information, and shows an informative free film (Mon–Sat 11am & 2pm) on the history of Los Angeles. For a more detailed look at the pueblo area, there are also free **guided walking tours** leaving on the hour between 10am and 1pm, Tuesday to Saturday, from the building next to the firehouse.

**Union Station**, across Alameda Street from Olvera, echoes LA's roots in a rather different way: a magnificent example of monumental mission-style municipal architecture, finished in 1939. The running-down of the country's rail network means it's no longer the evocative point of arrival and departure it once was, but the building itself is in fine condition, with a spacious vaulted lobby, heavy wooden benches and intact Deco signs, surrounded by courtyards planted in informal combinations of fig trees and jacarandas. Once thronging with passengers, it now sees just a few trains each day, although the new **Union Station Gateway Intermodel Transit Center** (see p.65) has been built with the intention of bringing back the crowds.

Constructed on the site of LA's original Chinatown, Union Station wasn't welcomed by everyone. Many of the displaced families moved to an area just west and north of

Olvera Street, and by 1938, what's now **CHINATOWN** was established, along North Broadway and North Spring streets. It's not the bustling affair you'll find in a number of other US cities, however, and unless it's Chinese New Year, when there's a parade of dragons and firework celebrations, there's little point in turning up here except to eat in one of the restaurants.

Across the channel of the Santa Ana Freeway from Olvera Street, the **Civic Center** is a collection of plodding bureaucratic office buildings around a lifeless plaza. The exception to this, the Art Deco **City Hall**, known to the world through LA cop badges seen in TV shows ever since *Dragnet*, was until 1960 the city's tallest structure. Though its 28th-storey 360° observation deck is closed for seismic renovations, you can still get a good look at the inside of the building on the free tours (daily 10am & 11am; reserve on ☎213/485-4423).

Northeast of City Hall, at 310 N Main St, the **Children's Museum** (summer Tues–Fri 9.15am–1pm, Sat & Sun 10am–5pm; rest of year varied weekday hours, Sat & Sun 10am–5pm; $5, children $3, free for all weekdays in winter; ☎213/687-8801) is largely uninspired but a good place to dump the kids. More edifying, on the south side of the Civic Center plaza, are the free tours of the **Los Angeles Times** building (Mon–Fri 11.15am; ☎213/237-5757) which show how the West Coast's biggest newspaper is put together.

## The Westside: Bunker Hill

Up until a century ago the area south of the Civic Center, **BUNKER HILL**, was LA's most elegant neighbourhood, its elaborate mansions and houses connected by funicular railroad to the growing business district down below. As with all of downtown, though, the population soon moved to stylish new suburbs and many of the old homes were converted to rooming houses, later providing the seedy backdrop for noirish low-budget detective movies.

The *Angel's Flight* funicular, too, which ran above Third Street between Hill and Olive, was torn down in 1969 to make way for the massive office towers that now form the heart of the growing **FINANCIAL DISTRICT**. The funicular has been slated for reconstruction for the last seven years, with little visible progress, and except when something special is going on, this isn't the city's most fascinating neighbourhood. Most of the fifty-storey towers have a concourse of shops and restaurants at their base, high-style shopping malls designed to provide a synthetic street life for the brokers and traders, jaded from the day-to-day routine of setting up mega-buck deals.

### The Museum of Contemporary Art

The largest and most ambitious development in the district is the **California Plaza** on Grand Avenue, a billion-dollar complex of offices and luxury condos centring on the **Museum of Contemporary Art (MOCA)** (Tues–Wed & Fri–Sun 11am–5pm, Thurs–Fri 11am–8pm; $6, free Thurs 5–8pm). Funded by a one percent tax on the value of all new downtown construction, MOCA opened at the end of 1986 in an effort to raise the cultural stature of the area (and of the whole city). Designed by showman architect Arata Isozaki as a "small village in the valley of the skyscrapers", it justifies a visit for the building alone, its playful exterior a welcome splash of colour among the dour downtown skyscrapers.

A barrel-vaulted entrance pavilion on Grand Avenue opens on to an outdoor sculpture plaza, off which are the ticket booth, the museum store and the entrance to the administration wing, covered in diamond-shaped green aluminum panels with bright pink joints. Stairs lead down from the upper plaza to a smaller courtyard, between the café and, finally, the main entrance to the galleries.

The brainchild of the high-rollers of the LA art world, MOCA was put together as a gesture of goodwill – and, cynics say, to raise the value of the works they loan for display. Much of the gallery is used for cutting-edge temporary exhibitions, and the bulk of the permanent collection is from the Abstract Expressionist period, including work by Frank Kline, Mark Rothko and the impressive multi-media memorials of Antoni Tapies and Jean Fautrier. You'll also find plenty of Pop Art, espoused by Robert Rauschenberg's urban junk and Claes Oldenburg's papier-mâché representations of hamburgers and gaudy fast foods.

That said, there are few singularly great pieces among the established names, and most of the compelling ideas are expressed amid the paintings and sculpture of the rising stars in the stock bequeathed by collector Barry Lowen. Hard to categorize, these are something of a greatest hits collection of work by artists you're likely to come across in the trendier city galleries – Jennifer Bartlett, David Salle, Anselm Keifer, Eric Fisch and Ellsworth Kelly, to name a famous few. The museum is also strong on photography, and has recently aquired the two-thousand-print collection of New York dealer Robert Freidhaus, featuring the work of Dianne Arbus, Larry Clark, Robert Frank, Lee Freidlander, John Pfahl and Gerry Winograd, among others.

The theatre on the lower floor of MOCA hosts some bizarre multimedia shows and performances, as well as the more standard lectures and seminars (☎213/621-2766 for details). The best time to visit MOCA is on a Thursday evening in summer, when entry is free, and concerts, usually jazz or classical and also free, are laid on. At other times, a ticket to MOCA also entitles you to same-day entrance to the *Temporary Contemporary* (see p.81), the museum's open exhibition space on the Eastside of downtown.

## Around MOCA

If MOCA's highbrow tone gets too demanding, there's relief in the shallow but amusing **Wells Fargo Museum** (Mon–Fri 9am–4pm; free) at the base of the shiny red towers of the *Wells Fargo Center*. It tells the history of *Wells Fargo & Co*, the bank of Gold Rush California, with among other things a two-pound nugget of gold, some mining equipment and a simulated stagecoach journey from St Louis to San Francisco.

A block away, the shining glass tubes of the **Westin Bonaventure Hotel** (see "Accommodation", p.70) have become one of LA's most unusual landmarks. The disappointing interior doubles as a shopping mall and office complex – an M C Escher-style labyrinth of spiralling ramps and balconies that is disorientating enough to make it necessary to consult a colour-coded map every twenty yards or so. But brace yourself and step inside for a ride in the glass elevators that run up and down the outside of the building, giving views over much of downtown and beyond.

From the *Bonaventure*'s rotating skyline bar you'll get a bird's-eye view of one of LA's finest buildings, the Los Angeles **Central Library** across the street, restored after an arson attack many years back. The concrete walls and piers of the lower floors, enlivened by Lee Laurie's figurative sculptures symbolizing the "Virtues of Philosophy" and the "Arts", form a pedestal for the squat central tower, which is topped by a brilliantly coloured pyramid roof. The library, built in 1926, was the last work of architect Bertram Goodhue, and its pared-down, angular lines set the tone for many LA buildings, most obviously the City Hall.

In exchange for planning permission, the developers of the **First Interstate World Center** across Fifth Street – the tallest building west of Chicago – agreed to pay some fifty million dollars toward the restoration of the library. Around the base of the tower, a huge staircase, modelled after the Spanish Steps in Rome, curves up to Bunker Hill between a series of terraces with outdoor cafés and boutiques – not wildly thrilling, but as good a way to ascend the hill as any.

## Broadway and Pershing Square

Though it's hard to picture now, **Broadway** once formed the core of Los Angeles' most fashionable shopping and entertainment district, lively with movie palaces and department stores. Today it's largely taken over by the clothing and jewellery stores of a bustling Hispanic community, a cash-rich hustle and bustle where as many pesos change hands as dollars, all to a salsa soundtrack blaring from ghetto blasters nailed to the walls. The most vivid taste of the area is to be had amid the pickled pigs' feet, sheep's brains and other delicacies inside the **Grand Central Market**, on Broadway between Third and Fourth. It's a real scrum but without doubt the best place (at least for carnivores) to enter the spirit of things.

The **Bradbury Building** (Mon–Sat 9am–5pm; free) across the street makes for a break from the mayhem of the market, its magnificent sunlit atrium surrounded by wrought-iron balconies, and open-cage elevators alternating up and down on opposite sides of the narrow court, with elaborate open staircases at either end. The whole place is an art director's dream – not surprisingly, most of the income for this 1893 office building is generated by film shoots: *Bladerunner* and *Citizen Kane* were both filmed here. Tourists are now only permitted in the lobby, but it's a great view up.

Aside from the street life, the best things about Broadway are the great movie palaces of the **THEATER DISTRICT**, some of whose "enchanted realms" still function today. Two are especially noteworthy: next to the Grand Central Market, the opulent 1918 **Million Dollar Theater**, its whimsical terracotta facade mixing buffalo heads with bald eagles in typical Hollywood Spanish Baroque style, was built by theatre magnate Sid Grauman, who went on to build the Egyptian and Chinese Theatres in Hollywood (see p.94 & p.95). It's now a South American-style evangelical meeting hall and entry is of course, free to all. The **Los Angeles Theater**, at 615 S Broadway, is even more extravagant, built in ninety days for the world premiere of Charlie Chaplin's *City Lights* in 1931, and crowning what had become the largest concentration of movie palaces in the world. The plush lobby behind the triumphal arch facade is lined by marble columns supporting an intricate mosaic ceiling, while the 1800-seat auditorium is enveloped by *trompe l'oeil* murals and lighting effects.

With the advent of TV, the rise of the car and LA's drift to the suburbs, the movie palaces lost their customers and fell into decline. An underground parking lot was built in **Pershing Square** in an attempt to bring the punters back – a task in which it failed, and many of the movie houses are these days showing exploitation and Spanish-language films to sadly depleted numbers. Pershing Square itself, however, is nowadays an amenable place, benefiting greatly from a recent overhaul. Inspired by the work of Mexican architect Luis Barragan, brightly painted concrete elements – including a massive bell tower that chimes on the hour – provide a very attractive, clearly defined (and easy to clean) public area that's proving popular both with lunching office workers and leisurely layabouts.

Some of the buildings around the square have – albeit after years of neglect – emerged in fine form also. The most prominent of these, the **Biltmore Hotel**, stands over the west side of the square, its three brick towers rising from a Renaissance Revival arcade along Olive Street. Inside, the grand old lobby that was the original main entrance has an intricately painted Spanish beamed ceiling that you can admire over a pricey glass of wine. A block south, at 617 S Olive St, the Art Deco **Oviatt Building** is another sumptuous survivor. The ground floor housed LA's most elegant haberdashery, catering to dapper types such as Clark Gable and John Barrymore, and has since been converted into the exquisite (and outrageously expensive) *Rex Il Restaurante* (see p.141). If you can't afford a $100-a-head meal, the elevators, which open on to the street level exterior lobby, are still worth a look, featuring hand-carved oak panelling, designed and executed by Parisian craftsman René Lalique.

# The Eastside

A block east of Broadway, downtown takes a downturn in LA's **SKID ROW**: a shabby, downtrodden area around Los Angeles Street south from City Hall that has a more than slightly threatening air. A seedy neighbourhood for decades, Skid Row has the dubiously arty associations to match. The Doors posed here for the cover of their album, *Morrison Hotel*, and Charles Bukowski is just one luminary of the booze'n' broads school of writers who've used the bars and poolrooms as a source of inspiration. At the new **Union Rescue Mission**, 545 S San Pedro St (call ☎213/347-6300 to arrange a visit), a public art project, "The Voice of the Homeless" designed by R B Krivaneck, is the new face of the Skid Art movement. Consisting of two parts, "Orientation Rotunda" and "Electronic Statement", the piece was created around interviews with the local dispossessed. Their words in English and Spanish have been applied to the rotunda – nouns in the top tier, adjectives in the middle, verbs at the bottom – with negative and positive attributes placed at 180° angles from one another, allowing anyone standing in the middle to create a variety of sentences. An additional interactive element will shortly allow local people to create statements of their own through a computer connected to an electronic message board, 18ft above San Julian Street on the mission's west wall.

To the south of Skid Row, the lively **GARMENT DISTRICT**, with its Mexican food wagons and cut-rate shops, is a respite from the bleak streets. The **Cooper Building**, which takes up most of the Ninth Street block between Santee and Los Angeles streets, is famous for its infrequent (designer) sample sales. It also houses at least fifty stores where you'll find big markdowns on outfits that may normally be out of your price range. At the atmospheric early morning **Flower Market** (daily 5–11am) on Wall Street between Eighth and Ninth, you can mingle with the wholesalers and buy flowers for a fraction of the high street prices.

Over the last ten years the northern boundaries of Skid Row have been pushed back by the sanitized shopping precincts of **LITTLE TOKYO** – the clearest evidence of the Japanese money that accounted for most of the new construction in LA during the 1980s. If you feel like a quick taste of this, head for the **Japanese American Cultural and Community Center**, 244 S San Pedro St, whose **Doizaki Gallery** (Tues–Sun noon–5pm; free), shows traditional and contemporary Japanese art and calligraphy. The centre also includes the **Japan America Theater**, which regularly hosts Kabuki theatre groups. Improbably shoehorned between the two and easy to miss, the stunning **James Irvine Garden**, with a 170-foot stream running along its sloping hillside, is a real inner-city treasure. Though named after its biggest financial contributor, it really owes its existence to the efforts of two hundred Japanese-American volunteers who gave up their Sundays to carve the space out of a flat lot.

From the cultural centre, a zigzagging pathway takes you through the Shoji screens, sushi bars, shops and Zen rock gardens of **Village Plaza** and along to the new **Japanese American Museum** at First and Central (Tues–Sun 10am–5pm; $4), a converted Buddhist temple now housing exhibits on everything from origami to the internment of Japanese-Americans during World War II. A replica internment hut stands out front.

Across the street from Little Tokyo is the **Temporary Contemporary** at 152 N Central Ave (hours and prices as for MOCA, to which a ticket also entitles same-day entrance, see p.78) – an exhibition space in a converted police garage that shows works by contemporary artists other LA museums won't touch. Initially developed, as its name suggests, as the temporary home of the Museum of Contemporary Art, the success of the gallery was such that it was kept on as an alternative exhibition space to the more refined main building. A space-frame awning and steam-shrouded bamboo garden marks the entrance, otherwise hidden away amongst a multistorey parking garage and derelict buildings.

# Around downtown

The LA sprawl begins as soon as you leave downtown, whose diverse environs tend to be forgotten quarters, scythed by freeways, and with large distances separating their few points of interest. Added together, however, there's quite a bit worth seeing, in areas either on the perimeters of downtown or simply beginning here and continuing for many miles south or east. The districts immediately west of downtown, around **Angelino Heights** and **Echo Park**, are where the upper crust of LA society luxuriously relocated itself at the turn of the century in groupings of wooden Victorian houses, mostly in impressive states of preservation – vivid indicators of the prosperity of their time, just as the nondescript drabness surrounding them now evidences the blight which later befell the area. Much the same applies to the streets around **MacArthur Park**, though they still contain some of the impressive commercial architecture that set the stylistic tone for the city in the 1920s.

The other areas that surround downtown are too far apart for it to make sense to try to see them consecutively; each is a ten- to thirty-minute drive away from the next. Directly south of downtown, the long succession of unimaginative low-rent housing developments is interrupted only by the contrast of the **USC campus**, populated by conservative, well-off students, and the neighbouring **Exposition Park**, with acres of gardens and several museums, a couple of which merit going out of your way to see. Beyond here, the deprivation resumes, leading into LA's most depressed area – the vast urban nightmare of **South Central LA**. A chilling counterpoint to the commercial vibrancy of downtown, this forms the main route between downtown and the Harbor Area, and, while it's certainly a place to stop only with caution or with someone who knows the area, it does give a picture of the grim reality behind LA's glamorous myths. More appealing is the Hispanic-dominated **East LA**, the largest Mexican city outside Mexico, and a buzzing district of markets, shops and street-corner music that gives a tangible insight into the other, relatively unacknowledged, side of LA. It's less hectic north of downtown, where amid the preserved homes of the **Highland Park District**, the **Southwest Museum** holds a fine and extremely comprehensive collection of Native American artefacts.

## Angelino Heights and Echo Park

Long before there was a Malibu or a Beverly Hills, some of the most desirable addresses in Los Angeles were in **ANGELINO HEIGHTS**, LA's first suburb, laid out in the flush of a property boom at the end of the 1880s on a hilltop a little way west of downtown. Though the boom soon went bust, the elaborate houses that were built here, especially along **Carroll Avenue**, have survived and been recently restored as reminders of the optimism and energy of the city's early years. There's a dozen or so in all, and most repay a look for their catalogue of late-Victorian details – wraparound verandahs, turrets and pediments, set oddly against the downtown skyline; one, with a weird Great Pyramid roof, was used as the set for the haunted house in Michael Jackson's *Thriller* video. All the homes are private, and not generally open to visitors, though the Angelino Heights Community Organization (☎213/413-8756) sometimes offers tours.

At the foot of the hill, to the west of Angelino Heights, **Echo Park** is a tiny park of palm trees set around a lake. In the large, white, arcaded building on the northern edge of the lake, the evangelist **Aimee Semple McPherson** used to preach fire and brimstone sermons to five thousand people, with thousands more listening in on the radio. The first in a long line of network evangelists, "Sister Aimee" died in mysterious circumstances in 1944, but the building is still used for services by her Four Square

Gospel ministry, who dunk converts in the huge water tank during mass baptisms. A more typical reflection of life in Echo Park appears in Alison Anders' 1994 *Mi Vida Loca (My Crazy Life)*, a semi-fictional film based on the street life of local girl gangs, some scenes of which were shot here.

## MacArthur Park and around

**Wilshire Boulevard** leaves downtown between Sixth and Seventh as the main surface route across 25 miles of Los Angeles to the Santa Monica beaches. It was named by and for entrepreneur Gaylord Wilshire, who made a fortune selling an electrical device that claimed to restore greying hair to its original colour. Wilshire used the proceeds from this and other ventures to buy up a large plot of land west of Westlake Park, later renamed **MacArthur Park**, through the centre of which he ran the wide thoroughfare. When the property market collapsed in 1888, Gaylord discovered politics, ran for Congress (and lost), and later moved to England, where made friends with George Bernard Shaw and the Fabian Socialists. The park has since fallen into disrepair and, despite police efforts, remains a venue for drug deals after dark, but the new Red Line *Metrorail* connection has turned its patches of green and large lake into the nearest relief from the sidewalks of downtown.

Half a mile west, the **Bullocks Wilshire** department store is a seminal building of Art Deco Los Angeles, the most complete and unaltered example of late-1920s architecture in the city. Built in 1929, in what was then a beanfield in the suburbs, *Bullocks* was the first department store in LA to be built outside downtown, and the first to build its main entrance at the back of the structure adjacent to the parking lot – catering for the automobile in a way that was to become the norm in this car-obsessed city. Transportation was the spirit of the time, and throughout the building mural and mosaic images of planes and ocean liners glow with activity in a studied celebration of the (then) modern world. Sadly, the building was badly vandalized during the 1992 riots, and has since closed its doors.

The **Ambassador Hotel**, just past Vermont Avenue at 3400 Wilshire Blvd, is another landmark of the boulevard's golden age. From the early 1920s to the late 1940s, when the hotel was the winter home of transient Hollywood celebrities, its *Cocoanut Grove* club was a favourite LA nightspot. The large ballroom hosted some of the early Academy Award ceremonies, and was featured in the first two versions of *A Star is Born* – though the hotel's most notorious event occurred on June 5, 1968, when **Bobby Kennedy** was fatally shot in the hotel kitchen while trying to avoid the press after winning the California Presidential Primary. Converted into a film studio and closed to public view, billboards now advertise the ballroom to film location hunters.

From the *Ambassador* you can either continue west up the so-called "Miracle Mile" (see p.101) or, two blocks south of Wilshire, between Vermont and Western, look in on **KOREATOWN**, the largest concentration of Korean people outside Korea and five times bigger – and infinitely more genuine and lively – than Chinatown and Little Tokyo combined. If you want to eat Korean food there's simply no better place. However, it's by no means without its tensions; in 1991 an unarmed black girl was shot and killed by a Korean shopkeeper, and the area has its share of LA's inter-racial violence – TV images of heavily armed Koreans "defending" their property against rioters filled screens during the 1992 riots.

## The USC Campus

The **USC** (University of Southern California) **CAMPUS**, a few minutes south of downtown, is an enclave of wealth in one of the city's poorer neighbourhoods. USC or "University of Spoiled Children" is one of the most expensive universities in the country, its undergraduates thought of as more likely to have rich parents than fertile brains. Indeed, the stereotype is often borne out, both by their easy-going, suntanned, beach-bumming nature, and by the fact that USC is more famous for its sporting prowess than academic achievement. Alumni include O J Simpson who collected college football's highest honour, the Heiseman Trophy, when he played for USC. There have been attempts to integrate the campus population more closely with the local community, but for the moment at least USC is something of an elitist island, right down to its own fast-food outlet.

Though sizeable, the campus is reasonably easy to get around. If you do want to visit, however, you might find it easiest to take the free hour-long **walking tour** (Mon–Fri 10am–2pm by appointment; ☎213/743-2183). Without a guide, a good place to start is in the **Doheny Library** (during academic year Mon–Fri 8am–5pm, Sat 9am–5pm; free), where you can pick up a campus map and pass an hour or so investigating the large stock of overseas newspapers and magazines on the second floor, although they tend to be at least three weeks behind the times and UCLA (see p.107) has a better selection. Another place for general information is the **Students Union** building, just across from the library and straight out of *Beverly Hills 90210*. Food is priced to make the college money, and the **bar** is an under-used and claustrophobic room with mirrored walls and terrible beer.

Of things to see, USC's art collection is housed in the **Fisher Gallery** on Exposition Boulevard (during academic year Tues–Sat noon–5pm; free), which stages several major international exhibitions each year, and has a broad permanent stock. Elsewhere in the building, you can see smaller shows of students' creative efforts in the **Helen Lindhurst Architecture Gallery** (Mon–Fri noon–6pm, Sat noon–5pm; free) and **Helen Lindhurst Fine Arts Gallery** (Mon–Fri 9am–5pm; free).

The campus is also home to the **George Lucas Film School**, named after the producer who studied here, which is a decidedly mainstream rival to the UCLA film school in Westwood. Ironically, **Steven Spielberg**, one of the biggest box-office directors in the history of film, couldn't get in to USC when he applied as an aspiring director. Now, his name is hallowed here, and writ large on the wall of the large and expensive cinema-and-TV-school auditorium he later funded. A short walk away, the **Arnold Schoenberg Institute** (Mon–Fri 10am–4pm; free) is a study centre devoted to the pioneering composer whose wide influence on modern musical thought – largely through his experiments with atonal structures – is even more remarkable when you consider that he had no formal training. Schoenberg, born in Austria in 1871, came to the US to escape the Nazis, and spent the fourteen years before his death in 1951 in LA. The reception area holds a mock-up of his studio, while the small auditorium displays his personal mementoes. During the academic year, students often give free lunchtime concerts of the great man's music.

Just off the campus proper, on the other side of Figueroa Street, the Hebrew Union College's **Skirball Museum** (Tues–Fri 11am–4pm, Sun 10am–5pm; free) devotes several rooms to describing some of the history, beliefs and rituals of the Jewish religion. Inasmuch as it concentrates on more mystical elements of the faith it's fairly absorbing, although anything dealing with the more controversial political ramifications is conspicuously absent.

Between USC and Exposition Park, sports fans may want to stop at the **Coliseum** on Hoover Boulevard. The site of the 1932 and 1984 Olympic Games is currently under renovation and there's not much to see other than an imposing grand arch on the facade and muscular commemorative statues, but on a quiet day it's an atmospheric stop-off.

# Exposition Park

Across Exposition Boulevard from the campus, **EXPOSITION PARK** is, given the grim nature of the surrounding area, one of the most appreciated parks in LA, incorporating lush landscaped gardens, a major sports stadium and a number of decent museums.

It's large by any standards, but the park retains a sense of community – a feeling bolstered by its function as a favourite lunchtime picnic place for schoolkids. After eating, their number one spot tends to be the **California Museum of Science and Industry**, set among a cluster of **museums** off Figueroa Street (unless otherwise stated all daily 10am–5pm; free); though largely uncritical, it has scores of working models and thousands of pressable buttons. Just outside, the **Hall of Health** includes a replica "classic" American diner carrying displays on what not to eat if you want to stay healthy.

There's more fun and games at the neighbouring **Hall of Economics and Finance**, where with the aid of a few machines you can wreck the American economy – though all the simulations are, again, irritatingly lightweight. Next door, the **Aerospace Building** marked by the DC10 parked outside, is even blander: a few models and displays pertaining to space and weather prediction. Better instead to head for the stimulating **California Afro-American Museum**, which has diverse, temporary exhibitions on the history, art and culture of black people in the Americas.

The **Los Angeles County Museum of Natural History** (Tues–Sun 10am–5pm, $6) may also have greater appeal. Apart from housing the biggest collection, it's also the nicest building in the park – an explosion of Spanish Revival with echoing domes, travertine columns and a marble floor. Foremost among the exhibits is a tremendous stock of dinosaur bones and fossils, and some individually imposing skeletons (usually casts) including the crested "duck-billed" dinosaur, the skull of a Tyrannosaurus Rex, and the astonishing frame of a Diatryma – a huge bird incapable of flight. But there's a lot beyond strictly natural history in the museum, and you should allow several hours at least for a comprehensive look around. In the fascinating pre-Columbian Hall are Mayan pyramid murals and the complete contents of a Mexican tomb (albeit a reconstruction), while the Californian history sections usefully document the early (white) settlement of the region during the Gold Rush era and after, with some amazing photos of Los Angeles in the 1920s. Topping the whole place off is the gem collection: several breathtaking roomfuls of crystals, their qualities enhanced by special lighting.

On a sunny day, spare some time for walking through Exposition Park's **Rose Garden** (daily 9am–5pm; free). The flowers are at their most fragrant in April and May, when the bulk of the 45,000 annual visitors come by to admire the 16,000 rose bushes and the downright prettiness of their setting.

## South Central LA

Lacking the scenic splendour of the coast, the glamour of West LA and the history of downtown, **SOUTH CENTRAL LA** hardly ranks on the tourist circuit – especially since it burst onto the world's TV screens as the focal point of the April 1992 **riots** (see box on p.86). However much wealthy white LA would like to pretend South Central doesn't exist, it's an integral part of the city, if only in terms of size: a big, roughly circular chunk reaching from the southern edge of downtown to the northern fringe of the Harbor Area. The population is mostly black, with a few pockets of Hispanic and Asian, interspersed here and there by bottom-of-the-heap working-class whites. Oddly enough, it doesn't look so terribly run-down at first sight, mostly made up of detached bungalows enjoying their own patch of palm-shaded lawn. But this picture is deceptive, and doesn't conceal for long the fact that just about all the people around here are very poor, get an abysmal deal at school and at work, and have little chance of climbing the social ladder and escaping to the more affluent parts of the city – unless they become sportsmen or rap artists.

What will immediately strike you in South Central LA is the sheer monotony of the place: every block for twenty-odd miles looks much like the last, enlivened periodically

## THE LA RIOTS

The unexpected acquittal in 1992 of five white Los Angeles police officers, charged with using excessive force after they were videotaped kicking and beating black motorist Rodney King, could almost have been calculated to provoke a violent backlash in LA's poverty-stricken ghettos. What few predicted, however, was the sheer scale of the response to the verdict. The violence and anger far surpassed the Watts Riots of 1965 (see below), beginning in South Central LA with motorists being pulled from their cars and attacked, and quickly escalating into a chaos of arson, shooting and looting that spread across the city from Long Beach to Hollywood. Downtown police headquarters were surrounded by a mixed crowd of blacks, Hispanics and whites, chanting "No Justice, No Peace", as state governor Pete Wilson appealed for calm on live TV. It took the imposition of a four-day dusk-to-dawn curfew, and the presence on LA's streets of several thousand well-armed US National Guard troops, to restore calm – whereupon the full extent of the rioting became apparent. The worst urban violence seen in the US this century had left 58 dead, nearly 2000 injured, and caused an estimated $1 billion worth of damage. With much of the devastation in the city's poorest areas, a relief operation of Third World dimensions was mounted to feed and clothe those most severely affected by the carnage. A second trial, on charges that the officers violated Mr King's civil rights, resulted in a two-year prison sentence for one of the officers.

Though ignited by a single incident, the riots were a very real indication of the tensions in a city whose controllers (and its affluent inhabitants) have traditionally been all too ready to turn a blind eye to social problems. Prompted by the Rodney King case, the Warren Christopher Commission was set up to investigate racial prejudice within the LAPD. Sadly, its recommendations had all too blatantly not been implemented by the time of the O J Simpson trial in 1995, when the racial tensions and prejudices of the city's most under privileged areas resurfaced.

by fast-food outlets, dingy supermarkets and uninviting factory sites. You'll see a lot of this by driving past on the Harbor Freeway (Hwy-110), which links downtown to the Harbor Area, or by way of one of the more minor roads such as Central Avenue.

## Watts

The district of **WATTS**, on the southernmost fringe of downtown, achieved notoriety as the scene of the six-day **Watts Riot** of August 1965. The arrest of a 21-year-old unemployed black man, Marquette Frye, on suspicion of drunken driving, gave rise to charges of police brutality and led to bricks, bottles and slabs of concrete being hurled at police and passing motorists during the night. The situation had calmed by the next morning, but the following evening both young and old black people were on the streets, giving vent to an anger generated by years of what they felt to be less than even-handed treatment by the police and other white-dominated institutions. Weapons were looted from stores and many buildings set alight (though few residential buildings, black-owned businesses or community services, such as libraries and schools, were touched); street barricades were erected, and the events took a more serious turn. By the fifth day the insurgents were approaching downtown, which – along with the fear spreading through white LA – led to the call-out of the National Guard: 13,000 troops arrived, set up machine-gun placements and road blocks, and imposed an 8pm to dawn curfew, which caused the rebellion to subside.

In the aftermath of the uprising, which left 36 dead, one German reporter said of Watts, "it looks like Germany during the last months of World War II". Much of it still does – Watts is by far the ugliest part of South Central LA. The promises of investment made after 1965 never amounted to much; indeed any forward strides made during the

1970s have long since been wiped out by wider economic decline, and eclipsed by the events of 1992.

Watts hit the headlines again in 1975 when members of the revolutionary Symbionese Liberation Army (SLA), who had kidnapped publishing heiress Patti Hearst, fought a lengthy – and televised – gun battle with police until the house they were trapped in burned to the ground. The site of the battle, at 1466 E 54th St, is now a vacant lot, though the surrounding houses are still riddled with bullet holes.

The one valid reason to come here is to see the Gaudi-esque **Watts Towers**, sometimes called the Rodia Towers, at 1765 E 107th St. Constructed from iron, stainless steel, old bedsteads and cement, and decorated with fragments of bottles and around 70,000 crushed seashells, these striking pieces of street art are surrounded by more than a little mystery. Their maker Simon Rodia had no artistic background or training at all, but laboured over the towers' construction from 1921 to 1954, refusing offers of help and unable to explain either their meaning or why on earth he was building them. Once finished, Rodia left the area, refused to talk about the towers, and faded into complete obscurity. 1994's earthquake left the towers shrouded in scaffolding, but the bandages are due off soon; call the adjacent Watts Tower Arts Center (☎213/847-4646) to check on their condition.

The **Dunbar Hotel Black Historical Cultural Museum** at 4225 S Central Ave, marks the first US hotel built specifically for blacks and patronized by almost every prominent African-American during the 1930s, 1940s and 1950s. It's due to open shortly, but at the moment you can only see the hotel's restored lobby and facade; for information call ☎213/234-7882.

## Compton, Inglewood and Gardena

Between Watts and the Harbor Area, only a few districts are of passing interest. Despite its fame as the home of many of LA's rappers – NWA, for example, sang venomously of its ills on their album *Straight Outta Compton* – **COMPTON** is not a place where strangers should attempt to sniff out the local music scene. History buffs secure in their cars, however, might fancy a stop at the **Dominguez Ranch Adobe**, 18127 S Alameda St (Tues & Wed 1–4pm, 2nd & 3rd Sun of each month 1–4pm; free conducted tour ☎310/631-5981), now restored and chronicling the social ascent of its founder, Juan Jose Dominguez – one of the soldiers who left Mexico with Padre Serra's expedition to found the California missions and whose long military service was acknowledged in 1782 by the granting of these 75,000 acres of land. As the importance of the area grew, so did the influence of Dominguez's descendants, who became powerful in local politics.

On the other side of the Harbor Freeway, west of Watts, **INGLEWOOD**, unenticing in itself, is home to the **Hollywood Park Racecourse,** a landscaped racetrack with lagoons and tropical vegetation, and a state-of-the-art computer-operated screen to give punters a view of the otherwise obscured back straight. Next door are the white pillars which ring **The Forum**, the 17,000-seat stadium that is the headquarters of both the *LA Lakers* (basketball) and the *LA Kings* (hockey), and is also a major concert venue; see "Listings" on p.161 for more.

One of the safer segments of South Central LA, **GARDENA**, a few miles south, is best known for its large Japanese population and, more importantly, a city ordinance which permits gambling – rare in California. Along Vermont and Western avenues, half a dozen or so clubs devoted to poker are combined with restaurants and cocktail lounges, which charge a half-hourly rental on seats ($1–24). Food and drink is served round the clock, though the bars are separate from the tables. Slightly tacky perhaps, but if you're desperate for a flutter…

## Leimert Park

As a general rule its not a good idea to venture into South Central looking for entertainment, unless you are with a local. **Leimert Park**, on the district's western fringe, may be an exception. Nowadays it's hard to believe that during the years when an unwritten, LAPD-enforced code kept African-Americans south of Wilshire Boulevard, the many nightclubs on Central Avenue were the focus of a thriving big-name jazz scene. Here in the park at its centre – an oasis of vintage jazz records and live jazz venues, cafés serving Ethiopian coffee and arts centres like *The Black Gallery* – still fizzes something of the old energy.

## East LA

You can't visit LA without being made aware of the Hispanic input to the city's demography and character, whether it be through the thousands of Mexican restaurants, the innumerable Spanish street names – or, most obviously, through the sheer volume of Spanish spoken by people on the streets. None of this is surprising given LA's proximity to Mexico, but equally apparent are the clear distinctions between the Latino community and white LA. As a rule it's the former who do the menial jobs for the latter, and, although a great number live in the US lawfully, they're also the people who suffer most from the repeated drives against illegal immigration.

Of the many Hispanic neighbourhoods all over LA, the key one is **EAST LA**, a sizeable fist of the city that begins two miles east of downtown, across the concrete-clad dribble of the Los Angeles river. There was a Mexican population here long before the white settlers arrived, and from the late nineteenth century onwards millions more arrived, coming here chiefly to work on the land. As the white inhabitants gradually moved west towards the coast, the Mexicans stayed, creating a vast Spanish-speaking community that's more like a Hispanic barrio than part of a North American city.

### THE GANGS OF LOS ANGELES

South Central LA is the heartland of the city's infamous **gangs**, said to number over seventy thousand members between them. The gangs have existed for forty years and often encompass several generations of a family. Each new wave of immigration adds to the rosta of gangs which usually, though not always, organize themselves by ethnicity, but it's only recently, with the massive influx of drug money, that violence has escalated and automatic weaponry (not least Uzi machine guns) has become commonplace. Although most fatalities (there are about 500 a year) are a direct result of drug-trade rivalry, in recent years there's been an increase in "drive-by shootings", the vast majority of which take place in established gangland areas. It was indicative of LA's entrenched racial and social divisions that it wasn't until the death of a white professional woman during a shootout in West LA in 1987, that a gang-related death caused widespread publicity and led to major anti-gang initiatives on the part of the police. The resulting clampdowns have seen a thousand arrests made on a single night but on the whole have made little real headway in tackling the problem – and seem unlikely to do so until the outlook for people in LA's poorer sections improves. According to the *American Journal of Science*, gang murders accounted for a staggering 43 percent of all LA homicides in 1994.

Despite the violence, an outsider is unlikely to see much evidence of the gangs beyond the occasional blue or red scarf (the colours of the Crips and Bloods, the two largest gangs) tied around a street sign to denote "territory"; and you stand even less chance of witnessing inter-gang warfare. As for personal danger, driving through South Central LA by day is generally safe, but be wary of delays at traffic lights, and avoid the area at night unless you're with someone who knows their way around.

Activity in East LA (commonly abbreviated to "ELA" or "East Los") tends to be outdoors, in cluttered markets and busy shops. Non-Hispanic visitors are comparatively thin on the ground, but you are unlikely to meet any hostility on the streets during the day – though you should steer clear of the rough and very male-dominated bars, and avoid the whole area after dark.

**Guadalupe**, the Mexican image of the mother of god, appears in mural art all over East LA, nowhere better than at the junction of Mednick Ave and Cesar Chavez Blvd. When a housing project across the street was demolished in the early 1970s, one wall, bearing a particularly remarkable image of the Blessed Mother surrounded by a rich band of rainbow colours, was saved from the wrecking ball and reinstated across the street. Lined with blue tile, it now forms an unofficial shrine where worshippers place fresh flowers and candles.

Other than the street life and murals, there are few specific "sights" in East LA. The best plan is just to turn up on a Saturday afternoon (the liveliest part of the week) and stroll along **Brooklyn Avenue**, which begins at the northeast edge of Boyle Heights and features some wild pet shops, with free-roaming parrots and cases of boa constrictors, and a number of **botanicas shops**, which cater to practitioners of *Santeria* – a religion that is equal parts voodoo and Catholicism. Browse amid the shark's teeth, dried devil fish and plastic statuettes of Catholic saints and buy magical herbs, ointments or candles after consulting the shopkeeper and explaining (in Spanish) what ails you. Only slightly less exotic fare can be found in **El Mercado de Los Angeles**, 3425 E First St, an indoor market not unlike Olvera Street but much more authentic.

Afterwards go to the junction of **Soto and Brooklyn**, where at 5pm each afternoon *Norteños* combos (upright bass, accordion, guitar and banjo sexto) freely showcase their talents, hoping to be booked for weddings; failing that, listen to the mariachi bands that strike up at 6.30pm outside the *Olympic Donut Shop*, at First and Boyle, four blocks south of Brooklyn Avenue.

## The Highland Park District

North of downtown, the **Pasadena Freeway** curves its way along a dry riverbed towards the foothill community whose name it bears. The freeway, LA's first, was completed in 1940 as the Arroyo Seco Parkway. Highway engineers have since learned their lessons, but be aware that this antiquated roadway has "stop" signs on the on-ramps and exit curves so sharp that the speed limit is 5mph.

Beside the freeway, two miles from downtown, the **HIGHLAND PARK DISTRICT** has a number of exuberantly detailed Victorian houses brought together from around the city to form **Heritage Square**, a fenced-off ten-acre park at 3800 Homer St (Wed–Sun noon–4pm; $5). Just beyond the next freeway exit, at 200 E Ave 43, the **Lummis House** (Fri–Sun 12–4pm) is the well-preserved home of Charles F Lummis, a publicist who was at the heart of LA's nineteenth-century boom. Unlike many of the real-estate speculators and journalists who did little more than publicize and glorify aspects of the Southern Californian good life, Lummis did some genuinely good deeds: he was an early champion of civil rights for Native Americans, and worked to save and preserve many of the missions, which were then in ruin. His house was a cultural centre of turn-of-the-century Los Angeles, where the literati of the day would meet to discuss poetry and the art and architecture of the Southwest. Lummis built this house for himself in an ad-hoc mixture of mission and medieval styles, naming it *El Alisal* after the many large sycamore trees (*Alisal* in Spanish) that shade the gardens. He constructed the thick walls out of rounded granite boulders taken from the nearby riverbed, and the beams over the living room of old telephone poles. The solid wooden front doors are similarly built to last, reinforced with iron and weighing a literal ton, while the plaster-and-tile interior is rustically kitted out with hand-cut timber ceilings and home-made furniture.

## The Southwest Museum

Although people in LA scarcely know about it, the **Southwest Museum** (Tues–Sun 11am–5pm; $5), which rises castle-like below Mount Washington, was Charles F Lummis' most enduring achievement and is well worth an afternoon's visit. Half a mile north of the Lummis House (take a bus along Figueroa Street from downtown), the recently renovated museum is the oldest in Los Angeles, founded in 1907. Its name is a bit deceptive – there are displays of Native American artefacts from all over North America, with exhibits of pre-Columbian pottery, coastal Chumash rock art and a full-size Plains Indian Cheyenne tepee. The museum also hosts travelling exhibitions, and its educational programme of lectures, films and theatrical events have made it an international centre for indigenous American cultures. The Braun Research Library has an unmatched collection of recordings and photographs of Native Americans from the Bering Straits to Mexico, and the museum shop features Navajo rugs, kachina dolls and turquoise jewellery, as well as an extensive selection of books and specialist publications.

# Hollywood

*The violet hush of twilight was descending over Los Angeles as my hostess, Violet Hush, and I left its suburbs headed towards Hollywood. In the distance a glow of huge piles of burning motion-picture scripts lit up the sky. The crisp tang of frying writers and directors whetted my appetite. How good it was to be alive, I thought, inhaling deep lungfuls of carbon monoxide.*

S J Perelman

If a single place name epitomizes the LA dream of glamour, money and overnight success, it's **HOLLYWOOD**. Ever since American movies, and their stars, became the international symbols of the good life, Hollywood has been a magnet to millions of tourists on once-in-a-lifetime pilgrimages and an equally massive assortment of hopefuls drawn by the thought of riches and glory. Even if the real prospects of success were one in a million, enough people were taken in by the dream to make Hollywood what it is today – a weird combination of insatiable optimism and total despair. It may be a cliché, but Hollywood *does* blur the edges of fact and fiction, simply because so much *seems* possible here – and yet so little, for most people, actually is.

The truth is that Hollywood was more a centre of corruption and scandal than the city of dreams the studio-made legend suggested. Successful Hollywoodites actually spent little time here – they left as soon as they could afford to for the privacy of the hills or coast. Many of the big film companies, too, relocated long ago, leaving Hollywood in isolation, with prostitution, drug dealing and seedy adult bookstores becoming the reality behind the fantasy. Things have brightened up a little in the last few years, but the district can still be dangerous – though not to the extent that you should think twice about coming.

## Orientation

Approaching from downtown, **East Hollywood** is the first taste of the district, a ramshackle and grubby area of cheap housing where shop signs are often in Spanish. Things pick up in **Central Hollywood**, a compact area that's the real movie history territory, swarmed around by an eccentric street mix of social derelicts and star-struck tourists. Whether the memories have been hammered-up into bizarre shrines, or forgotten and turned into parking lots, Central Hollywood has them in quantity, and you'd have to be avidly uninterested in filmlore to find the place dull. Protecting Hollywood from the outside world, the rising slopes of the Santa Monica Mountains constitute a

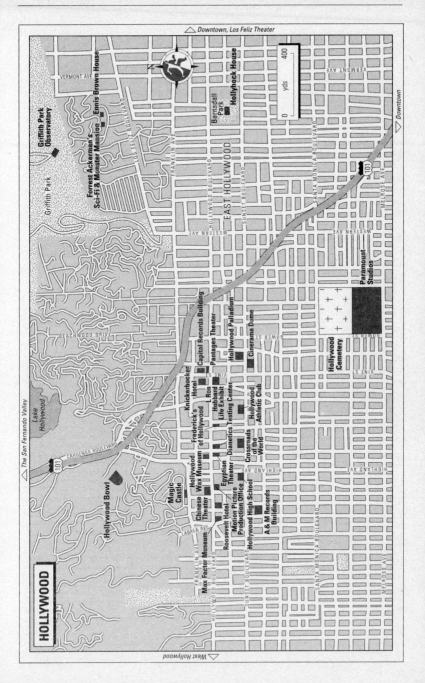

HOLLYWOOD

Downtown, Los Feliz Theater

West Hollywood

The San Fernando Valley

Downtown

VERMONT AVE

Griffith Park
Observatory

Forrest Ackerman's
Sci-Fi & Monster Mansion

Ennis Brown House

Griffith Park

Barnsdall
Park

Hollyhock House

EAST HOLLYWOOD

VERMONT AVE

FRANKLIN BOULEVARD

LOS FELIZ BOULEVARD

HOLLYWOOD BOULEVARD

SUNSET BOULEVARD

SANTA MONICA BOULEVARD

WESTERN AVE

WESTERN AVE

MELROSE AVE

Lake
Hollywood

BEACHWOOD DRIVE

CAHUENGA BOULEVARD

Paramount
Studios

Hollywood
Cemetery

Capital Records Building

Pantages Theater

Hollywood Palladium

Cinerama Dome

VINE ST

GOWER AVE

VINE ST

Knickerbocker
Hotel

Frederick's
of Hollywood

L. Ron
Hubbard
Life Exhibit

Hollywood
Athletic Club

Dianetics Testing Center

Crossroads
of the
World

Hollywood Bowl

Magic
Castle

Hollywood
Wax Museum

Chinese
Theater

Egyptian
Theater

A & M Records
Building

Roosevelt Hotel

Motion Picture
Production Office

Hollywood High School

Max Factor Museum

FRANKLIN AVE

LA BREA AVE

HOLLYWOOD BOULEVARD

SUNSET BOULEVARD

HIGHLAND AVE

HIGHLAND AVE

SANTA MONICA BOULEVARD

MELROSE AVE

0    yds    400

section of **Griffith Park** – several thousand acres of nature offering rugged hiking trails and busy sports and picnic grounds, which forms a scenic northern edge to the area. Beyond the park, the more westerly of the slopes form the high ground known as the **Hollywood Hills**: exclusive homes perched on snaking driveways that are the most tangible reminders of the wealth generated in the city – and the incredible roll call of household names which has sprung from it. A small intermediary area between the park and East Hollywood, **Los Feliz Village** has become a trendy place to live and socialize, so much so that pop stars (namely the Beastie Boys and Kim Deal of Sonic Youth) have opened small boutiques here.

## East Hollywood

By night extremely seedy, by day tattily vibrant, **EAST HOLLYWOOD** is mostly inhabited by Hispanic immigrants who have yet to fulfil the American dream. The area bordering Central Hollywood can be particularly unpleasant: this end of Sunset Boulevard is a notorious red-light strip, along whose length Hugh Grant famously encountered Divine Brown in 1995. But as ever in Los Angeles, where perimeter neighbourhoods bordering the hills are highly sought after, the streets around Beachwood Canyon, and at the foot of Griffith Park, have evolved into downbeat but popular places to live and hang out, and Mediterranean-style homes now litter the hillside.

### A HISTORY OF HOLLYWOOD

Given its racy character, it's odd to think that Hollywood started life as a temperance colony, intended to provide a sober God-fearing alternative to raunchy downtown LA, eight miles away by rough country road. Purchased and named by a pair of devout Methodists in 1887, the district remained autonomous until 1911, when they were forced, in return for a regular water supply, to affiliate their own city to LA as a suburb. The film industry, meanwhile, gathering momentum on the East Coast, needed somewhere with guaranteed sunshine and a diverse assortment of natural backdrops to enable pictures to be made quickly, and somewhere to dodge patent laws that had restricted film-making in the east. Southern California, with its climate, scenery and isolation, was the perfect spot. A few offices affiliated to eastern film companies were opened downtown from 1906, but independent hopefuls soon discovered the cheaper rents on offer in Hollywood. The first studio opened here in 1911, and within three years the place was packed with film-makers – many of them, like Cecil B DeMille who shared his barn-converted office space with a horse, destined to be the big names of the future.

The ramshackle industry expanded fast, bringing instant profits and instant fame, and the hopefuls who arrived eager for a slice of both soon swamped the original inhabitants, outraging them with their hedonistic lifestyles. Yet movie-making was far from being a financially secure business, and it wasn't until the release of D W Griffith's *The Birth of a Nation* in 1915 that the power of film was demonstrated. The film's right-wing account of the Civil War caused riots outside cinemas and months of critical debate in the newspapers – and for the first time drew the middle classes to the screens to see what all the fuss was about. It was also the movie which first experimented with the narrative style and production techniques that gradually became standard in classic Hollywood cinema.

Modern Hollywood took shape from the 1920s on, when film production grew more specialized and many small companies either went bust or were incorporated into one of the handful of bigger studios that came to dominate film-making. Hollywood's enduring success is in making slick, pleasurable movies that sell – from the hard-bitten *film noir* of the 1940s to the new creativity of film-makers such as Francis Ford Coppola, Martin Scorsese and Quentin Tarantino. Ultimately, though, it's been big names, big bucks and conservatism that have kept Hollywood alive. With its profits gnawed into by television and rock music, the film industry today rarely even thinks about taking risks.

Four blocks north of Sunset Boulevard, the **SILVERLAKE** neighbourhood was home to some of Hollywood's first studios, now largely converted into trendy restaurants and galleries. Walt Disney opened his first studio at 2719 Hyperion Ave in 1926 (it's now a grocery store); and the Keystone Kops were dreamt up in Mack Sennett's studio at 1712 Glendale Blvd, where just a single sound studio now remains.

Nearby **LOS FELIZ VILLAGE** is home to many different communities, with fair-sized Hispanic and gay contingents. On busy summer nights its bars are full of students from the local **American Film Institute Campus**, USC party animals, and slumming arty types from the Hollywood Hills. Johnny Depp's *Ed Wood* was partly shot, and premiered, at the architecturally impressive but a bit run-down **Vista** movie theatre, just off Hollywood Boulevard near Virgil.

**Hollyhock House**, on a small hill close to the junction of Hollywood Boulevard and Vermont Avenue (Tues–Sun noon–3pm; $2), was the first of architect Frank Lloyd Wright's contributions to LA, though it was largely designed, with minimal acknowledgement, by his student, Rudolph Schindler. Completed in 1921, covered with Mayan motifs and imbued with an Art Deco fervour, it's an intriguingly obsessive dwelling, whose original furniture (now replaced by detailed reconstructions) continued the conceptual flow. The bizarre quality of the building was obviously too much for its oil heiress owner, Aline Barnsdall, who lived here only for a short time before donating both the house and the surrounding land to the city authorities for use as a cultural centre. In keeping with this wish, the grounds of the house became known as **Barnsdall Park**, in which the **Municipal Art Gallery** (Wed–Sun 12.30–5pm, Friday 12.30–8.30pm; $1.50) was erected to give exposure to new Southern Californian artists. If you've no interest in art or architecture, the park is still worth a visit as one of the few quiet spots around here to enjoy a view: the Hollywood Hills in one direction, all of downtown and beyond in the other.

Another Wright building, the 1924 **Ennis Brown House** looms over Los Feliz on Glendower Avenue. One of four of his local structures to feature "textile" concrete block, its ominous, pre-Columbian appearance has added atmosphere to over sixty movies, from Vincent Price horror flicks to *Blade Runner*. Also on Glendower, **Forrest Ackerman's Sci-Fi and Monster Mansion** (visit by appointment only; ☎213/MOON-FAN) boasts a truly amazing hoard of more than 300,000 items of horror, fantasy and sci-fi memorabilia. Ackerman, former editor of *Famous Monsters of Filmland* magazine, has filled eighteen rooms of the "Ackermansion" with such delights as the fake breasts worn by Jane Fonda in *Barbarella*, the robot from *Metropolis* and the life masks of Boris Karloff, Bella Lugosi and Lon Chaney. Sixty-seven years in the making, this is a unique collection enhanced by the draw of the man himself: numerous personal anecdotes and odds and ends of gossip make his one-on-one tour a must.

## Central Hollywood

The myths, magic, fable and fantasy splattered throughout the few short blocks of **CENTRAL HOLLYWOOD** would put a medieval fairytale to shame. With the densest concentration of faded glamour and film mythology in the world, a pervasive sense of nostalgia makes the area deeply appealing in a way no measure of commercialism can diminish. Although you're much more likely to find a porno theatre than spot a star (no bona fide "somebody" would be seen dead here these days), the decline that blighted the area from the early 1960s is slowly receding in the face of prolonged efforts by local authorities - including repaving Hollywood Boulevard with a special tarmac that sparkles in the streetlights. Nevertheless the place still gets hairy after dark, when the effects of homelessness, drug addiction and prostitution are more evident, on-leave US marines strut along the sidewalks and Hispanic adolescents cruise Hollywood Boulevard in flashy customized cars.

## Along Hollywood Boulevard

Following Hollywood Boulevard west, you'll come to the junction of **Hollywood and Vine**, a juxtaposition of street names that still tingles the spines of dedicated Hollywoodphiles, some of whom can be spotted standing in respectful silence before crossing the road. During the golden years the rumour spread that any budding star had only to parade around this junction to be "spotted" by big-shot film directors (the major studios were in those days all concentrated nearby), who nursed coffees behind the windows of neighbouring restaurants. In typical Hollywood style the whole tale was blown wildly out of proportion, and while many real stars did pass by, it was only briefly on their way to and from work, and the crossing did nothing but earn a fabulous reputation. The only thing marking the legend today, apart from disappointed tourists, is a small plaque on the wall of the *New York Pizza Express*.

A block on, at Hollywood and Ivar, the frighteningly sanitized **L Ron Hubbard Life Exhibit** (9.30am–10pm, tours at 10am, 1.30pm, 3.30pm, 5.30pm and 8pm; $5) is the latest manifestation of the Hubbardization of Hollywood, home to the highest concentration of Scientologists in the world. It details Hubbard's early career as a teenage explorer and B-movie and comic book writer, lays out the tenets of Scientology, and culminates in a *Wizard of Oz*-style presentation in which a ten-foot image of Ron dispenses recorded advice at the push of a button. Further along Hollywood Boulevard at no. 6741, the Church's walk-in **Dianetics Testing Center** (read "recruitment office") gives personality tests to people who fear they have "occasional twitches of the muscles when there is no need for it".

The bulky **Knickerbocker Hotel**, 1714 Ivar Ave, is now an old people's retirement centre, but was also where the widow of legendary escapologist, Harry Houdini, conducted a rooftop seance in an attempt to assist her late spouse in his greatest escape of all. During the 1930s and 1940s, the hotel had a reputation for rooming some of Hollywood's more unstable characters and a number of lesser-name suicides plunged from its high windows. At 1825 Ivar St is the flea-bag rooming house where author and screenwriter **Nathanael West** lived during the late 1930s, after coming west to revive his flagging financial situation. Gazing over the street's parade of extras, hustlers and make-believe cowboys, he penned the classic satirical portrait of Hollywood, *The Day of the Locust*.

Back on Hollywood Boulevard, at no. 6608, the purple and pink **Frederick's of Hollywood** is a Hollywood landmark. Opened in 1947, it has been (under-)clothing Hollywood's sex goddesses ever since, and many more mortal bodies all over the world through its mail-order outlet. Inside, the **lingerie museum** (open when the shop is; free) displays some of the company's best corsets, bras and panties, donated by a host of happy big-name wearers, ranging from Lana Turner to Belinda Carlisle.

A little further on, at no. 6708, the very first Hollywood premiere (*Robin Hood*, an epic swashbuckler starring Douglas Fairbanks Sr), took place in 1922 at the **Egyptian Theatre**. Financed by impresario Sid Grauman, in its heyday the *Egyptian* was a glorious fantasy, modestly seeking to re-create the Temple of Thebes, its usherettes dressed as Cleopatra. This great old building was shattered in the 1994 earthquake, has been bought by the city, and is currently in the process of renovation to its former faux glory.

The **Hollywood Wax Museum**, 6767 Hollywood Blvd (Mon–Thurs & Sun 10am–midnight, Fri & Sat 10am–2am; $7.95), is a tawdry selection of dummies of the obvious people. Besides Spock's ears, Marilyn's backside and Dolly's breasts, there's a replica of da Vinci's painting *The Last Supper* – very peculiar, as are many of the people who stumble in during the small hours.

Much of the pavement along this stretch of Hollywood Boulevard is marked by the brass name plates that make up the **Walk of Fame** (officially beginning at Hollywood and Vine). The laying of the plates began in 1960, instigated by the local Chamber of

Commerce which thought that by enshrining the big names it could somehow restore the boulevard's faded glamour and boost tourism. Selected stars have to part with several thousand dollars for the privilege of being included: among them are Marlon Brando (1717 Vine St), Marlene Dietrich (6400 Hollywood Blvd), Michael Jackson (6927 Hollywood Blvd), Elvis Presley (6777 Hollywood Blvd) and Ronald Reagan (6374 Hollywood Blvd).

Nothing as vulgar as money can taint the appeal of the foot and hand prints embedded in the concrete concourse of **Mann's Chinese Theatre** at 6925 Hollywood Blvd, opened in 1927 as a lavish setting for premieres of swanky new productions. Through the halcyon decades, this was *the* spot for movie first-nights, and the public crowded behind the rope barriers in their thousands to watch the movie aristocrats arriving for the screenings. The foot-and-hand-prints-in-concrete idea came about when actress Norma Talmadge accidentally (though some say it was a deliberate publicity stunt) trod in wet cement while visiting the construction site with the owner Sid Grauman. The first formally to leave their marks were Mary Pickford and Douglas Fairbanks Sr, who ceremoniously dipped their digits when arriving for the opening of *King of Kings*, and the practice continued into the last decade or so – Steven Segal is just one of the latter-day big cheeses. It's certainly fun to work out the actual dimensions of your favourite film stars, and to discover if your hands are smaller than Julie Andrews' or your feet are bigger than Rock Hudson's (or both). As for the building, it's an odd version of a classical Chinese temple, replete with dodgy Chinese motifs and upturned dragon tail flanks. Try to take a peek at the Art Deco splendour of the lobby even if you're not going in for a movie.

To catch a movie in the making, cross the road to the **Motion Picture Production Office**, Room 602, 6922 Hollywood Blvd (Mon–Fri 8am–5pm), which issues a free "shoot sheet" every weekday from 10.30am, detailing exactly what's being filmed around town that day. Most film shoots hire a couple of off-duty LAPD officers for "security", but not all sets are impenetrable.

A few doors down, 7000 Hollywood Blvd, the **Roosevelt** was movieland's first luxury hotel. Opened in the same year as the Chinese Theatre, it fast became the meeting place of top actors and screenwriters, its *Cinegrill* restaurant feeding and watering the likes of W C Fields, Ernest Hemingway and F Scott Fitzgerald, not to mention legions of hangers-on. In 1929 the first Oscars were presented here, beginning the long tradition of Hollywood rewarding itself in the absence of honours from elsewhere. Look inside for a view of the splashing fountains and elegantly weighty wrought-iron chandeliers of its marble-floored lobby, and for the intelligently compiled pictorial **History of Hollywood** on the second floor. The place is thick with legend: on the staircase from the lobby to the mezzanine, Bill "Bojangles" Robinson taught Shirley Temple to dance; and the ghost of Montgomery Clift (who stayed here while filming *From Here to Eternity*) apparently haunts the place, announcing his presence by blowing a bugle. Surviving lounge divas like Eartha Kitt still put on the occasional show at the *Cinegrill*.

Around the corner at 1666 N Highland Ave, the **Max Factor Museum** (Mon–Sat 10am–4pm; free and free parking) is a testament to the days when women fell into three categories: redhead, brunette and blonde. The famous kissing machine used to test the endurance of Factor's potions and the calibration machine invented to determine which features needed equalizing, are both on show, as is a scroll of honour of the many ladies who took Max to their powdered bosom, and swore by him.

## Along Sunset Boulevard

There's more Hollywood nostalgia directly south of the central section of Hollywood Boulevard, on and around the less touristy **Sunset Boulevard**, which runs parallel. You might start your explorations at the corner of **Sunset Boulevard** and **Gower Street**. During the industry's formative years, when unemployed movie extras hopeful of a few days' work with one of the small local B-movie studios would hang around here, the junction earned the nicknames "Gower gulch" and "poverty row".

The delectable Spanish Revival-style building at 6525 Sunset Blvd was, from the 1920s until the 1950s, known as the **Hollywood Athletic Club**. Another of Hollywood's legendary watering holes, the likes of Charlie Chaplin, Clark Gable and Tarzan himself lounged beside its Olympic-sized pool, while Johns Barrymore and Wayne held drinking parties in the apartment levels above. After standing empty for 25 years, the building re-opened in 1990 as a billiards club, bar and restaurant.

The grouping of shops at the **Crossroads of the World**, 6672 Sunset Blvd, isn't much to look at now, but when finished in 1936 this was one of LA's major tourist attractions. The central plaza supposedly resembles a ship, surrounded by shops designed with Tudor, French, Italian and Spanish motifs – the idea being that the shops are the ports into which the shopper would sail. Oddly enough, time has been kind to this place, and considering the more recent and far brasher architecture found in LA, this has a definite, if muted, charm.

### The Hollywood Memorial Cemetery

Despite the beliefs of some of their loopiest fans, even the biggest Hollywood stars are mortal, and the many LA cemeteries that hold their tombs get at least as many visitors as the city's museums. One of the least heralded and least dramatically landscaped of them, though with more than its fair share of big names, is the **Hollywood Memorial Cemetery** (daily 8am–5pm; free), close to the junction of Santa Monica Boulevard and Gower Street and overlooked by the famous water tower of the neighbouring *Paramount Studios* (whose even more famous gates are just around the corner on Santa Monica Boulevard).

In the southeastern corner of the cemetery, the cathedral mausoleum sets the tone for the place, a solemn collection of tombs that includes, at no. 1205, the resting place of **Rudolph Valentino**. In 1926 10,000 people packed the cemetery when the celebrated screen lover died aged just 31, and to this day on each anniversary of his passing (23 August), at least one "Lady in Black" will likely be found mourning – a tradition that started as a publicity stunt in 1931 (the first weeping damsel claimed to be a former paramour of Valentino's but was exposed as a hired actress) and has continued ever since. While here, spare a thought for the more contemporary screen star, Peter Finch, who died in 1977. His crypt is opposite Valentino's and tourists often lean their rears unknowingly against it while photographing Rudolph's marker.

Fittingly, outside the mausoleum, the most pompous grave in the cemetery belongs to **Douglas Fairbanks Sr**, who with his wife Mary Pickford did much to introduce social snobbery to Hollywood. Even in death Fairbanks keeps a snooty distance from the pack, his ostentatious memorial, complete with sculptured pond, only reachable by a shrubbery-lined path from the mausoleum. In quite a different vein, one of the cemetery's more recent arrivals was **Mel Blanc**, "the man of a thousand voices" – among them Bugs Bunny, Porky Pig, Tweety Pie and Sylvester – whose epitaph simply reads "That's All, Folks".

## Griffith Park

Vast **GRIFFITH PARK**, between Hollywood and the San Fernando Valley (daily 5am–10.30pm, mountain roads close at dusk; free), is a combination of gentle greenery and rugged mountain slopes that makes a welcome escape from the mind-numbing hubbub almost everywhere else in the city. The largest municipal park in the country, it's also one of the few places where LA's multitude of racial and social groups at least go through the motions of mixing fairly happily. Above the landscaped flat sections, where the crowds assemble to picnic, play sports or visit the fixed attractions, the hillsides are rough and wild, marked only by foot and bridle paths, leading into desolate but appealingly unspoilt terrain that gives great views over the LA basin and out towards the ocean. Bear in mind, though, that while the park is safe by day, its reputation for after-dark violence is well founded.

## Around the park

There are four **main entrances** to Griffith Park. Western Canyon Road, north of Los Feliz Boulevard, enters the park through **the Ferndell** – as the name suggests, a lush glade of ferns, from which numerous trails run deeper into the park – continuing up to the **Observatory** (Tues–Fri 2–10pm, Sat–Sun 12.30–10pm; free), familiar from its use as a backdrop in *Rebel Without A Cause*, and with moderately interesting science displays and shows in the Planetarium (every 90min; $4) and Laserium (Tues–Thurs & Sun at 6pm & 8.45pm, Fri–Sat & various holidays at 6pm, 8.45pm & 9.45pm; $6.50). More enticingly, on clear nights there are brilliant views of the cosmos through the powerful **telescope** mounted on the roof (daily 7–10pm; free). One Saturday a month, the LA Astronomical Society gathers on the front lawn. Thirty or forty telescopes and their knowledgeable owners set up at 1pm to see the sun through filters and stay until the area closes, happy to discuss the planets and stars with passers-by.

Descending from the observatory by way of Vermont Canyon Road (effectively the continuation of Western Canyon Road) brings you to the small **bird sanctuary**, set within a modest-sized wooded canyon. Various species have been encouraged to nest here, but as the birds aren't in captivity you might not see them. Across the road is the **Greek Theatre**, an open-air amphitheatre that seats nearly five thousand beneath its Greek-style columns – though if you're not going in for a show (the *Greek* is a venue for big-name rock, jazz and country music concerts during summer) you'll see just the bland exterior.

Opposite the entrance to the park on the corner of Riverside Drive and Los Feliz Boulevard is the **William Mulholland Memorial Fountain**, whose cascades are a reminder of the man credited with building the aqueduct that gave the city its first reli-able supply of water in 1902, a feat that's part of a long saga laced with scandal and corruption (see p.133).

Crystal Springs Drive, off Riverside Drive, takes you to the Ranger Station; and the **northern end** of the park, over the hills in the San Fernando Valley, is best reached directly by car from the Golden State Freeway, although you can take the park roads (or explore the labyrinth of hiking trails) that climb the park's hilly core. At the end of the journey, don't bother with the cramped **LA Zoo** (summer daily 10am–6pm; rest of year daily 10am–5pm; $8.25) or the old locomotives of the **Travel Town Transportation Museum** (May–Oct Mon–Fri 10am–5pm, Sat– Sun 10am–6pm; Nov–April slightly reduced hours; free).

## The Gene Autry Western Heritage Museum

Sharing a parking lot with the zoo, the **Gene Autry Western Heritage Museum** (Tues–Sun 10am–5pm; $7.50), at the northeastern corner of Griffith Park near the junc-

---

### HIKING AND BIKING IN GRIFFITH PARK

The steeper parts of Griffith Park, which blend into the foothills of the Santa Monica Mountains, are the focus of a variety of **hikes**. You can get maps from the **ranger station**, at 4730 Crystal Springs Rd (☎213/655-5188) – also the starting point for **guided hikes** and atmospheric **evening hikes**, held whenever there's a full moon. The rangers also have maps for drivers that detail the best vantage points for views over the whole of Los Angeles, not least from the highest place in the park – the summit of Mount Hollywood. The park is also a great place for cycling; closest place to **rent a bike** is *Woody's Bicycle World*, 3157 Los Feliz Blvd (☎213/661-6665).

tion of the Ventura and Golden State freeways, bears the name of the "singing cowboy" who cut over six hundred discs from 1929, starred in blockbusting Hollywood Westerns during the 1930s and 1940s, and became even more of a household name through his TV show in the 1950s.

Autry fans hoping for a shrine to the man who pined the immortal *That Silver-Haired Daddy of Mine*, are in for a shock, however: the **collection** – from buckskin jackets and branding irons to Frederic Remington's emotive sculptures of turn-of-the-century Western life and the truth about the shoot-out at the OK Corral – is a serious and very credible attempt to explore the mind-set and concerns of those who participated in the US's colonization of the West.

# The Hollywood Hills

Quite apart from giving the chance to appreciate how flat the LA basin is, the views from the **Hollywood Hills** feature perhaps the oddest, most opulent, selection of properties to be found anywhere. Around these canyons and slopes, which run from Hollywood itself into Benedict Canyon above Beverly Hills, mansions are so commonplace that only the half-dozen fully blown castles (at least, Hollywood-style castles) really stand out.

**Mulholland Drive**, which runs along the crest, passes some of the most notorious abodes – Rudolph Valentino's extravagant **Falcon Lair**; Errol Flynn's **Mulholland House**; the former home of actress Sharon Tate, where some of the Manson family killings took place; and a number of run-of-the-mill million-dollar residences belonging to an assortment of luminaries, visionaries, former politicians and movie moguls, some of whom have helped forge LA's reputation for ostentatious and utterly decadent living.

Unfortunately, though, most of the houses are hidden away, and there's no real way to explore in depth without your own car and a knowledgeable friend to help pinpoint the sights, spread widely across every hillside. You could use one of the guided tours (see p.66), but for the most part you can't get close to the most elaborate dwellings anyway, and none are open to the public.

## Lake Hollywood

Hemmed in among the hills between Griffith Park and the Hollywood Freeway, **Lake Hollywood** feels like a piece of open country in the heart of the city. The clear, calm

---

### THE HOLLYWOOD SIGN

One thing you can see from more or less anywhere in Hollywood is the **Hollywood Sign**, erected to spell "Hollywoodland" in 1923 as a promotional device to sell property at the foot of the hills. The "land" part was removed in 1949, leaving the rest as a world-renowned symbol of the entertainment industry here. It has also (unjustifiably) gained a reputation as a suicide spot, ever since would-be movie star Peg Entwhistle terminated her career and life here in 1932, aged 24. It was no mean feat – the sign being as difficult to reach then as it is now: from the end of Beachwood Drive she picked a path slowly upward through the thick bush and climbed the fifty-foot-high "H," eventually leaping from it to her death. Stories that this act led to a line of failed starlets desperate to make their final exit from Tinseltown's best known marker are untrue however – though many troubled souls may have died of exhaustion while trying to get to it. There's no public road (Beachwood Drive comes nearest, but ends at a closed gate) and you'll incur minor cuts and bruises while scrambling to get anywhere near. In any case, infra-red cameras and radar-activated zoom lenses have been installed to catch graffitti writers, and innocent tourists who can't resist a close look are also liable for the $103 fine. It's simply not worth the bother.

waters, actually a reservoir intended to lubricate the whole of LA in times of drought, make a delightful spot, surrounded by clumps of pines in which squirrels, lizards and a few scurrying skunks and coyotes easily outnumber humans.You can't get too near the water, as metal fences protect it from the general public, but the footpaths that encircle it are pleasant for a stroll. There's no social kudos associated with being seen trotting around the footpath – which may explain why so few Angelenos deem it worthy of their presence. Their loss, nature's gain.

You can only reach the lake by car. The **lake access road** is open from 7am until noon and 2pm until 7pm on weekdays, and 7am till 7.30pm on weekends: to get to it, turn right onto Dix Street (a block north of Franklin Avenue), left into Holly Drive and climb to Deep Dell Place; from there it's a sharp right into Weidlake Drive and left past a "no through road" sign.

### The Hollywood Bowl

Where Highland Avenue hits the Hollywood Freeway, a twenty-minute walk from Hollywood Boulevard, the **Hollywood Bowl** is an open-air auditorium opened in 1921, which has since gained more fame than it deserves. The Beatles played here in the mid-1960s, but the Bowl's principal function is as home to the Los Angeles Philharmonic, who give evening concerts from July to September. These are far less highbrow than you might imagine. It's long been the done thing to eat a picnic in the grounds before making the climb to your seat, and nowadays the consumption tends to continue throughout the show, often rendering the music barely audible above the crunching of popcorn and fried chicken, and the clink of empty wine bottles rolling down the steps. It's probably not a choice spot for lovers of fine music, but can be fun nonetheless, and ticket prices start at $1. If you're really broke, come to the Bowl Tuesday through Friday between 9.30am and noon to listen to rehearsals for free.

More, but not much more, about the Bowl's history can be gleaned from the video show inside the small **Hollywood Bowl Museum**, near the entrance, where there's also a routine collection of musical instruments from around the world. Having undergone considerable refurbishment, the museum is due to reopen soon – call ☎213/850-2058 for details.

# West LA

LA's so-called "Westside" begins immediately beyond Hollywood in **WEST LA**, which contains some of the city's most expensive neighbourhoods. Bordered by the foothills of the Santa Monica Mountains to the north and the Santa Monica Freeway to the south, West LA is fashionable LA, and perhaps closer than anywhere else to embodying the stylish images that the city projects to the outside world. Actually, once you're there, the reality is often less dazzling: away from the showcase streets are the usual long, residential blocks, only marginally less drab than normal with their better tended lawns, swisher supermarkets, cleaner gas stations – and a higher class of fast-food stand.

The single best reason to come to West LA is the engrossing collection of the **LA County Museum of Art**, on the eastern perimeter of the area in the still firmly Jewish **Fairfax district**. It's not until you cross west of Fairfax Avenue that West LA truly reveals itself in **West Hollywood** – a major centre for art and design, clogged by posey restaurants and boutiques and, less chic, the clubs at the core of the city's music scene. **Beverly Hills**, a little way west, is less gregarious but more affluent: you may need an expense account to buy a sandwich but it's a matchless place to indulge in upscale window shopping on the way to the more roundly appealing **Westwood Village**. The main business in this low-rise, Spanish Revival, near-pedestrianized area has always

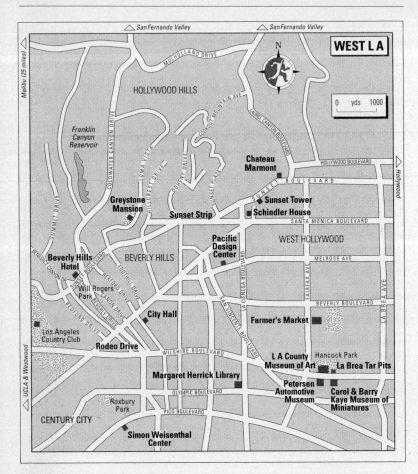

been movies – seeing them rather than making them. The original Deco palaces still remain, a short way from the **UCLA Campus** – the second of LA's university sites and home to a number of galleries and museums.

## The Fairfax District and the LA County Museum of Art

The West LA section of **Fairfax Avenue**, between Santa Monica and Wilshire, is the backbone of the city's Jewish community. Apart from countless temples, yeshivas, kosher butcher shops and delicatessens there's little actually to see here, but by local standards it's a refreshingly vibrant neighbourhood, and easily explored on foot. Fairfax continues down to the lacklustre wooden structures of **Farmer's Market**, at the junction with Third Street (June–Sept Mon–Sat 9am–8pm; Oct–May Mon–Sat 9am–6.30pm, Sun 10am–5pm; free), which, despite its stalls groaning under fresh fruit and veg, is overrated as a place to eat and drink. Further on, the *May Company* department store on Wilshire Boulevard was built in 1934 to announce the western entrance to the premier property development of the time, the **Miracle Mile**, as it was named, which stretched along Wilshire from here to the edge of downtown and is still lined with Art Deco monuments. The department stores have long since shut up shop, but an unprecedented number of museums, including LACMA, now create an impressive "Museum Mile" in their place. Although many of the office blocks are empty, look out for the **Wilshire Tower** at no. 5514, a Zigzag Moderne tower stepping up from a streamlined two-storey pedestal, and, just east of La Brea Avenue, the 1929 black-and-gold **Security Pacific Bank**.

### The LACMA, the La Brea Tar Pits and Peterson Automotive Museum

Oddly enough, the **LA County Museum of Art** or LACMA (Tues–Thurs 10am–5pm, Fri 10–9pm, Sat–Sun 10am–6pm; $6, free second Wed of month) is one of the least impressive of the buildings along the Miracle Mile, plopped down in 1965 in a fit of municipal-mindedness that has never really taken root. The buildings aside, though, some of the collections of applied art here are among the best in the world, and despite the loss of Armand Hammer's stock of paintings to his own museum in Westwood (see p.106), it justifies a lengthy visit. If you arrive on a Wednesday before 1pm, check out the schedule of films playing in the **Leo S Bing Theater**, where you can see anything from a Hitchcock classic to a screwball comedy for only $1.

The LACMA is enormous, and there's no way you could see the lot in one go; you're best off selecting a few periods you're interested in and sticking to them. Get a **map** of the complex from the information desk in the Anderson building, since the various collections are continually shifted around from one wing to another. Alongside many excellent collections of Southeast Asian sculpture and Middle Eastern decorative arts, the **Fearing Collection** consists of funeral masks and sculpted guardian figures from the ancient civilizations of pre-Columbian Mexico. There's also a broad selection of works by **contemporary Californian artists**, particularly Richard Diebenkorn. Where the museum really excels, however, is in its specializations, notably the prints and drawings in the **Robert Gore Rifkind Center for German Expressionist Studies**, which includes a library of magazines and tracts from Weimar Germany, and the **Pavilion for Japanese Art**. This is a recent addition to the museum, built to resemble the effects of traditional *shoji* screens, filtering varying levels and qualities of light through to the interior. Displays include painted screens and scrolls, ceramics, and lacquerware, rivalling the collection of the late Emperor Hirohito as the most extensive in the world.

The roof combs of the pavilion make a playful reference to the tusks of a model mastodon sinking slowly into the adjacent **La Brea Tar Pits**, a large pool of smelly tar ("*la brea*" is Spanish for tar) surrounded by full-size models of mastodons and sabretooth tigers. In prehistoric times, such creatures tried to drink from the thin layer of water covering the tar in the pits, only to become stuck fast. Millions of bones belonging to the animals (and one set of human bones) have been found here and reconstructed in the adjacent **George C Page Discovery Center** (Tues–Sun 10am–5pm; $6). Tar still seeps from the ground, and, during 1988, a by-product, methane gas, caught fire underground and spread flames through the Fairfax streets.

Across the street, at 6060 Wilshire Blvd, is the **Peterson Automotive Museum** (Tues–Sat 10am–6pm; closed Mon except holidays; $7). The baby of media mogul Robert Peterson, its three floors pay sumptuous if superficial homage to the automobile, with special exhibits of movie stars' cars, customized lowriders and vintage footage of land-speed record attempts in the desert. It fails to explain the reasons behind the collapse of LA's early public transport system and the city's subsequent obsession with what Tom Wolfe called the "Kandy-Kolored Dream Machine", but it has enough mint-condition classic models to render the car-crazy delirious with joy.

The next museum along the road is the less appetizing **Carol and Barry Kaye Museum of Miniatures**, 5900 Wilshire Blvd (Tues–Sat 10am–5pm; $7.50), housing the world's most comprehensive collection of miniatures. Exhibits include a Victorian mansion, medieval palace, Japanese garden and Hollywood Bowl, complete with pint-sized Ella, Satchmo and Dizzy.

## St Elmo's Village

Not far from the art works on display in the County Museum, **St Elmo's Village** at 4836 St Elmo Drive, a mile south of Wilshire (☎213/931-3409), is a popular version of community art-in-action. An arts project now more than twenty years old, the colourful murals and sculptures here grew out of efforts to foster a constructive and supportive environment for local youth. It's now also the site of the **Festival of the Art of Survival**, an annual celebration of hippy-flavoured folk and popular art and music held each Memorial Day.

# West Hollywood

Between Fairfax Avenue and Beverly Hills, **WEST HOLLYWOOD** is the newest of LA's constituent cities. Thanks to various legal technicalities, it was for many years a separate administrative entity from the rest of Los Angeles, notorious for its after-hours vice clubs and general debauchery. Things changed in 1983, however, when the autonomous city of West Hollywood was established, partly to clean up the place and partly to represent the interests of the predominantly gay community. There are still sleazy rent-boy areas around La Brea Avenue in the east, but much of the rest has smart-ened up considerably, from the new sculpture garden down the centre of **Santa Monica Boulevard**, the district's main drag, to the flashy dance clubs and designer clothes stores appearing over the rest of the neighbourhood. In front of the **Tomkat Theater**, beneath a marquee that has proclaimed everything from *Deep Throat* to *In Thrust We Trust*, the alternative **Porno Walk of Fame** is devoted entirely to X-rated film stars. The extremities of Seventies porn legends John Holmes, Marilyn Chambers and Harry Reems, as well as more recent inductees like gay superstar Ryan Idol, are preserved à la Mann's Chinese. Don't expect anything beyond a hand or footprint, though.

**Melrose Avenue**, LA's trendiest shopping street, runs parallel to Santa Monica Boulevard three blocks south, a streetscape that at times resembles nothing more than a low-budget 1950s sci-fi feature: neon and Art Deco abound among a fluorescent rash of designer and second-hand boutiques, exotic antique shops, avant-garde galleries and high-fashion restaurants. Record shops, too, are everywhere, all good places for checking what's going on locally. The west end of Melrose is more upmarket, with furniture shops and art galleries spread out around the hulking, bright blue glass mass of the **Pacific Design Center**, a wholesale furniture marketplace on Melrose at San Vicente Boulevard known locally as the "Blue Whale" because of the way it dwarfs its low-rise neighbours.

The stylistic extremes of Melrose Avenue are also reflected in the area's domestic architecture. Three blocks east of La Cienega Boulevard, the 1922 **Schindler House**, 835 N King's Rd (tours Sat & Sun 1–5pm, and by appointment ☎213/651-1510; $5 donation), was for years the blueprint of California modernist architecture, with sliding canvas panels designed to be removed in summer, exposed roof rafters, and open-plan rooms facing onto outdoor terraces – banal in replication but compel-ling in the original. The structure was first conceived as two houses: one for the architect R M Schindler and his wife, one for a second couple, sharing a central kitchen, and planned in an S-shape with each wing curling around a private garden. Coming from his native Austria via Frank Lloyd Wright's studio to work on the Hollyhock House (p.93), Schindler was so pleased with the California climate that he built this house without any bedrooms, romantically planning to sleep outdoors year-round in covered sleeping baskets on the roof; he misjudged the weather, however, and soon moved inside.

# WEST HOLLYWOOD

HOLLYWOOD BOULEVARD
SUNSET BOULEVARD
HOLLYWOOD HILLS
City Limit
FOUNTAIN AVENUE
CITY OF WEST HOLLYWOOD
SANTA MONICA BOULEVARD
HOLLOWAY DRIVE
Warner Hollywood
Pacific Design
MELROSE AVENUE
Fairfax High School
Beverly Hills
BEVERLY BOULEVARD
City Limit
Beverly Center
CBS Television City
3RD STREET
BURTON WAY
Farmers Market
3RD STREET
WILSHIRE BOULEVARD
6TH STREET
LACMA
La Brea Tar Pits
WILSHIRE BOULEVARD

0 yds 900

## WEST HOLLYWOOD RESTAURANTS, BARS AND NIGHTCLUBS

### Restaurants

1. Canter's Deli
2. Citrus
3. East India Grill
4. Eat A Pita
5. Ed Debevic's
6. Erewhon
7. French Market Place
8. Georgia
9. The Gumbo Pot
10. Hard Rock Café
11. India's Oven
12. Kate Mantillini
13. L'Orangerie
14. The Pearl
15. Ships
16. The Source
17. Spago
18. Swingers
19. Tail O' The Pup
20. Tommy Tang's
21. Trader Vics
22. Ziggy G's

### Bars and Nightclubs

23. Barney's Beanery
24. Café Largo
25. Coconut Teaszer
26. King's Road Espresso Bar
27. The Living Room
28. The Roxy
29. 7969
30. The Viper Room
31. Whisky-a-Go-Go
32. Club Lingerie
33. Doug Weston's Troubador
34. Molly Malone's
35. Rage

For reviews of all the above places, see "Eating", "Drinking: bars, pubs and cafés" and "Nightlife" listings starting on p.134.

Four blocks west, **La Cienega Boulevard** divides West Hollywood roughly down the middle, separating the next-wave trendies on the Hollywood side from the establishment couturiers on the Beverly Hills border. La Cienega ("the swamp" in Spanish) holds a mixture of LA's best and most expensive restaurants and art galleries, and continues south, passing the huge **Beverly Center** shopping mall at Beverly Boulevard – a seemingly impenetrable fortress of brown plaster that was thrown up in 1982 on top of the fun-but-faded **Beverlyland** amusement park. Another landmark structure, and one that managed to survive the wrecker's ball by some adroit repositioning, is the **Tail o' the Pup**, the world-famous hot-dog stand shaped like a (mostly bun) hot dog, which was moved a block away from La Cienega to 329 San Vicente Blvd to make way for the garish *Sofitel* hotel.

Further south, right on the Beverly Hills border at 333 S La Cienega, the **Margaret Herrick Library** of the Academy of Motion Picture Arts and Sciences (as in the Academy Awards) holds a huge hoard of film memorabilia and scripts inside a Moorish-style building that used to be a water treatment plant.

## Sunset Strip

Above western Hollywood, on either side of La Cienega Boulevard, the roughly two-mile long conglomeration of restaurants, plush hotels and nightclubs on Sunset Boulevard has long been known as **Sunset Strip**. These establishments first began to appear during the early 1920s, along what was then a dusty dirt road serving as the main route between the Hollywood movie studios and the West LA "homes of the stars". F Scott Fitzgerald and friends spent many leisurely afternoons over drinks here, around the swimming pool of the long-demolished *Garden of Allah* hotel, and the nearby *Ciro's* nightclub was *the* place to be seen in the swinging 1940s, surviving today as the original *Comedy Store*. With the rise of TV the Strip declined, only reviving in the 1960s when a scene developed around the landmark *Whisky-a-Go-Go* club, which featured seminal psychedelic rock bands such as Love and Buffalo Springfield during the heyday of West Coast flower power. Since the annexation of West Hollywood, the striptease clubs and "head shops" have been phased out, and this fashionable area now rivals Beverly Hills for entertainment-industry executives per square foot.

Some tourists come to the strip just to see the enormous **billboards**. The ruddy-faced and reassuring Marlboro Man is now a fixture, but there are many more along the strip that consistently re-invent the medium: fantastic commercial murals animated with eye-catching gimmicks and saturated colours to match the blue-blue of California summer skies.

Greta Garbo was only one of many stars and starlets to appreciate the quirky character of the huge Norman castle that is the **Chateau Marmont Hotel**, towering over the east end of the Sunset Strip at no. 8221. Built in 1927 as luxury apartments, this stodgy block of white concrete has long been a Hollywood favourite. Howard Hughes used to rent the entire penthouse so he could keep an eye on the bathing beauties around the pool below, and the hotel made the headlines in the 1980s when comedian John Belushi died of a heroin overdose in the hotel bungalow that he used as his LA home. Belushi's spirit lives on across the street at no. 8430: **The House of Blues**, in which his estate is a prime investor, is a bar in the *Hard Rock Café/Planet Hollywood* mould (see p.151), and plays much of the man's music.

## Beverly Hills and Century City

Probably the most famous small city in the world, **BEVERLY HILLS** has over the years sucked in more than its fair share of wealthy residents (the local pawnbrokers have an Oscar and a Ferrari for sale). It's not a particularly welcoming place, especially if your clothes don't match the elegant attire of the residents – the pets in Beverly Hills are better dressed and groomed than some of the people elsewhere in LA. It can be fun, though, to stroll the designer stores of Rodeo Drive and, if driving, take a spin by the mansions up in the canyons before the police (and Beverly Hills has more police per capita than anywhere else in the US) ask for your ID.

Beverly Hills divides into two distinct halves, separated by the old train line down Santa Monica Boulevard. **Below the tracks** are the flatlands of modest houses on rectangular blocks, set around the "Golden Triangle" business district that fills the wedge between Santa Monica and Wilshire Boulevards. **Rodeo Drive** cuts through the triangle in a two-block-long concentrated showcase of the most expensive names in international fashion. It's an intimidatingly stylish area, each boutique trying to outshine the rest: none as yet charges for admission, though some require an invitation. Presumably by virtue of their impeccable movie star credentials, the owners of **Planet Hollywood** have opened a massive food and merchandising operation right next to an exclusive shopping area adjacent to Rodeo on Wilshire – a coup beyond the dreams of *McDonald's* or *Burger King*.

**Above the tracks** is the upmarket part of residential Beverly Hills, its gently curving drives converging on the gorgeous and gauche pink plaster **Beverly Hills Hotel**, on Sunset and Rodeo. Built in 1913 to attract wealthy settlers to what was then a town of just five hundred people, and currently owned by the Sultan of Brunei, the hotel's social cachet makes its *Polo Lounge* a prime spot for movie execs to power-lunch.

In the verdant canyons and foothills above Sunset a number of palatial estates lie hidden away behind landscaped security gates. **Benedict Canyon Drive** climbs from the hotel up past many of them, beginning with the first and most famous: the lavish **PickFair** mansion, built for Mary Pickford and Douglas Fairbanks in 1919 and setting the tone for the exclusive community that has grown up around it; from the gate at 1143 Summit Drive you can just glimpse the house. Further up Benedict Canyon, Harold Lloyd's **Green Acres**, where he lived for forty years, with its secret passageways and large private screening room, survives intact, though the grounds, which contained a waterfall and a nine-hole golf course, have since been broken up into smaller lots.

The grounds of the biggest house in Beverly Hills, Greystone Mansion, are now maintained as a public park by the city, who use it to disguise a massive underground reservoir. Though the fifty-thousand-square-foot manor house is rarely open, you can visit the sixteen-acre **Greystone Park** at 905 Loma Vista, from 10am to 5pm daily. Up the hill are the fabulously expensive tract homes of **Trousdale Estates**, a late-Fifties exercise in ostentatious banality, with two sub-repro Greek columns per stucco shed – and, as a bonus, a panoramic view.

## Century City

The only tall buildings punctuating West LA's flat skyline are the gleaming spires of **CENTURY CITY**, just west of Beverly Hills, erected during the Sixties on the backlot of the 20th Century-Fox film studios. The plate-glass office towers aren't at all inviting, rising sharply and inhospitably skywards from sidewalks that have never been used – a perhaps typically Sixties disaster, planned at a time when sweeping gestures towards sweeping vistas were the order of the day. The massive **ABC Entertainment Center** complex, on Avenue of the Stars, might conceivably bring you here – its *Schubert Theater* is one of LA's leading live theatres, specializing in touring productions of the latest Andrew Lloyd Webber hit (see p.154).

Along the south edge of Century City, **Pico Boulevard** is quintessential LA: mile after mile of single-storey shop fronts, auto parts stores and delis, with a mini-mall on every other corner. To the west, look through the front gates of the still-working **20th Century-Fox** film and TV studios to catch a glimpse of the intact New York City street set used for the production of *Hello Dolly!*.

Less frivolously, just east of Century City, below Beverly Hills, an inauspicious white building houses the **Simon Wiesenthal Center for Holocaust Studies** at 9786 West Pico Blvd. The US headquarters of the organization devoted to tracking down ex-Nazis, the center has an extensive library of Holocaust-related documents, photographs and accounts – but the main draw for visitors is the affecting **Beit HaShoa Museum of Tolerance** (Mon–Thurs 10am–4pm, Fri 10-1pm, Sun 11am–4pm; $8), an extraordinary interactive resource centre aimed at exposing the lies of revisionist historians. The most technologically advanced institution of its kind, it uses videotaped interviews to provide LA's frankest examination of the 1992 riots, and leads the visitor through re-enactments outlining the rise of Nazism to a harrowing conclusion in a replica gas chamber.

## Westwood Village and the UCLA campus

Just west of Beverly Hills, on the north side of Wilshire Boulevard, **WESTWOOD VILLAGE** is one of LA's more user-friendly neighbourhoods, a grouping of low-slung redbrick buildings that went up in the late 1920s, along with the nearby campus of the nascent University of California at Los Angeles (UCLA). It's an area that's easily explored on foot, and one very much shaped by the proximity of the university campus, which is really the lifeblood of the area.

**Broxton Avenue**, the main strip of Westwood Village, was for many years the weekend cruising strip of choice for Westside teenagers. Following a gang- related shooting outside on Broxton in the late-1980s the popularity of the area waned, although it still attracts students making the circuit of record stores, video parlours and diners. It's also a big movie-going district, with thirty or so cinema screens within a quarter-mile radius.

Much of the original Spanish Revival design has survived the intervening years of more unimaginative construction, though the ordinary businesses of the old days have been replaced by fancy boutiques and designer novelty shops. The tower at the end of the street belongs to the 1931 **Fox Westwood Village**, which, together with the neon-signed *Bruin* across the street, is sometimes used by movie studios for "sneak" previews of films to gauge audience reaction. Check the "Calendar" section of the *LA Times* for showings.

South of the village, Westwood Boulevard has more cinemas, a few interesting shops and a number of specialist bookstores below Wilshire Boulevard. This section of Wilshire exploded in the 1970s with oil-rich high-rise developments, leading to a change of scale that would seem bizarre anywhere outside of LA. Modest detached houses sit next to twenty-storey condo towers in which penthouse apartments with private heliports sell for upwards of $12 million.

Inside one of the towers, on the corner with Westwood Boulevard, the **Armand Hammer Museum of Art and Culture Center** (Tues–Wed & Fri-Sat 11am–7pm, Thurs 11am-9pm, Sun 11am-5pm; $4.50, Thurs 6-9pm free) is one of the city's most debated art stashes, amassed over seven decades by the flamboyant and ultra-wealthy boss of the Occidental Petroleum Corporation. Art critic Robert Hughes called the paintings here "a mishmash of second or third-rate works by famous names", but while the Rembrandts and Rubens may be less than stunning, the nineteenth-century pieces like Van Gogh's intense and radiant *Hospital at Saint Remy* more than make amends. In a separate gallery, the museum's costliest acquisition is also the most disappointing: the *Codex Hammer* – which Hammer bought for $2 million and renamed after himself – comprises two dozen pages from the notebooks of the sixteenth-century visionary artist-engineer Leonardo da Vinci. Now suspended between plexiglass panels above an English summation of their contents, the pages are filled by hard-to-decipher ramblings on hydraulics.

Across Wilshire from the museum, at the end of the driveway behind the tiny *Avco* cinema, you'll find Hammer's speckled marble tomb, sharing the tiny cemetery of **Westwood Memorial Park** with the likes of movie stars Peter Lorre and Natalie Wood, wildman jazz drummer Buddy Rich, and, to the left of the entrance in the far northeast corner, the lipstick-covered plaque that marks the resting place of **Marilyn Monroe**.

### The UCLA campus

The **UCLA campus** is the dominant feature in Westwood, a grouping of Italianate buildings spread generously over well-landscaped grounds. It's worth a wander if you've time to kill, particularly for a couple of good exhibition spaces. The student union building, at the north end of Westwood Boulevard, half a mile north of the village, has a bowling alley, a good bookstore and a "rideboard" offering shared-expense car rides; and there's also a decent coffee house, in Kerckhoff Hall just behind.

Before embarking on your exploration, pick up a **map** from various information kiosks scattered around campus. Of things to see, the spacious rotunda of the **Powell Library**, on one side of the central quadrangle, was where Aldous Huxley put in long hours at the card catalogues in the late 1930s, researching his novel *After Many a Summer*, based on the life and legend of William Randolph Hearst. At the northern end of campus, fronted by the large Franklin D Murphy **Sculpture Garden** (always open; free), which contains work by Rodin, Maillol, Moore and other modern artists, all shaded under the June blooms of the jacaranda trees, the **Wight Art Gallery** holds a variety of top-quality visiting exhibitions (Tues–Fri 11am–5pm, Sat & Sun 1–5pm; free).

Nearby, UCLA's **film school**, famed for producing offbeat film-makers like Francis Ford Coppola, Alison Anders and Alex Cox, also has one of the most extensive collections of old films and TV programmes in the world, examples of which are shown daily, often for free, in the large auditorium in **Melnitz Hall**. Check the bulletin board in the lobby or phone ☎310/206-FILM for the current schedule.

# Santa Monica, Venice and Malibu

Set along an unbroken, twenty-mile strand of clean, white-sand beaches, and home to a diverse assortment of LA's finest stores, restaurants and art galleries, the small, self-contained communities that line the **Santa Monica Bay** feature some of the best of what Los Angeles has to offer, with none of the smog or searing heat that can make the rest of the metropolis unbearable. The entire area is well served by public transport, near (but not too near) the airport, and there's a wide selection of accommodation, making the area an ideal base for seeing the rest of LA.

**Santa Monica**, set on palm-tree-shaded bluffs above the blue Pacific, is the oldest, biggest and best-known of the resort areas. Once a wild beachfront playground, and the memorable location for many scenes from the underworld stories of Raymond Chandler, it's now a self-consciously healthy and liberal community, which has enticed a large expatriate British community of writers and rock stars, ranging from Rod Stewart to John Lydon. Thanks to relatively liberal Santa Monica Council there are also plenty of homeless people, who set up their camps in local parks.

Directly south, **Venice**'s once-expansive network of canals and the beachfront boardwalk bring together a lively mixture of street performers, roller skaters and casual voyeurs.

North from Santa Monica along the Pacific Coast Highway, **Pacific Palisades** is a gathering of hugely expensive suburban houses clinging to the lower foothills of the nearby mountains. Aside from some pioneering postwar architecture, however, there's

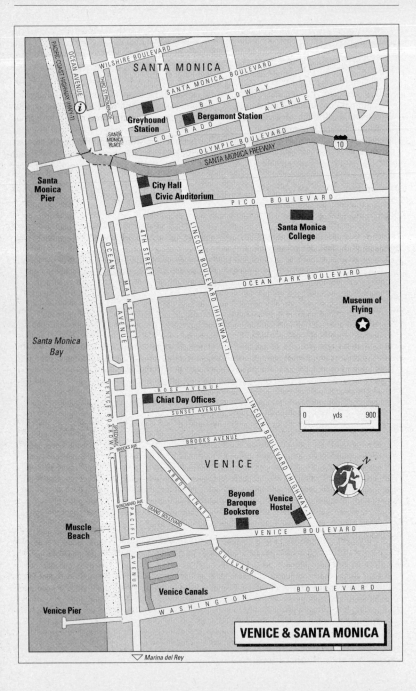

VENICE & SANTA MONICA

nothing much to see, though you could push a few miles inland to **Will Rogers State Park**, home and museum of one of the legends of the American West, and with some rewarding hiking paths leading into the neighbouring canyons.

A few miles further along the coastal road, the **J Paul Getty Museum** is rightly acknowledged as one of the world's finest collections of classical art, and reason enough alone for visiting the area. Close by, **Topanga Canyon** has more hiking, its reputation as haven of back-to-nature hippiedom gone, but still with a surprisingly wild set of trails leading into the the the deep, wooded canyons and sculptured rock outcrops of the Santa Monica Mountains.

**Malibu**, at the top of the bay, twenty miles from Santa Monica and the northernmost edge of LA, is a whole other world, studded with beach colony houses owned by those who are famous enough to need privacy and rich enough to afford it. For all that, you don't have to be a millionaire to enjoy its fine surfing beaches, or the birds, seals – and, in migrating season, whales – for which this part of the coast is noted.

# Santa Monica

As little as a century ago, most of the land between **SANTA MONICA** and what was then Los Angeles was covered by beanfields and citrus groves, interrupted by the occasional outposts of Hollywood and Beverly Hills. Like so much of the state, the land was owned by the Southern Pacific Railroad, who tried – and failed – to make Santa Monica into the port of Los Angeles, losing out to other interests who dredged the harbour at Wilmington, near Long Beach. The linking of the beachfront with the rest of Los Angeles by the suburban streetcar system meant the town instead grew into one of LA's premier resorts – a giant funfair city that was the inspiration for Raymond Chandler's anything-goes "Bay City", described in *Farewell My Lovely*. Today Chandler wouldn't recognize the place: changes in the gaming laws and the advent of the private swimming pool have led to the removal of the offshore gambling ships and many of the bathing clubs, and Santa Monica is among the city's more elegant seaside towns – a transformation hurried along by an influx of fashionable residents.

Santa Monica lies across 26th Street from West LA, and splits into three distinct portions. The town itself, holding a fair slab of Santa Monica's history and its day-to-day business, sits on the coastal bluffs; below there's the pier and beach; while Main Street, running south from close to the pier towards Venice, is a style-conscious quarter, with designer restaurants and fancy shops.

## The Town

Santa Monica reaches nearly three miles inland, but most things of interest are situated within a few blocks of the beach. Make your first stop the **Visitor Information Office** (daily 10am–4pm; ☎310/393-7593), in a kiosk just south of Santa Monica Boulevard along Ocean Boulevard in Palisades Park (the cypress-tree-lined strip which runs along the top of the bluffs). Its handy free map shows the whole of the town and the routes of the Santa Monica *Big Blue Bus* transit system, a useful Westside complement to the *MTA* network.

Two blocks east of Ocean Boulevard, between Wilshire and Broadway, the **Third Street Promenade** is the closest LA comes to energetic street life. A pedestrianized stretch long popular with buskers and itinerant evangelists, and lined by a variety of fashionable clothing outlets and restaurants, the promenade underwent a successful refurbishment several years ago and now attracts a lively crowd. It's fun simply to hang out in the cafés, pubs and nightclubs, play a game of pool, or browse through the many secondhand and fine-art book shops. The mall is anchored at its southern end by the expensive **Santa Monica Place**, a white stucco shopping precinct styled by noted LA architect Frank Gehry that has the usual assortment of upmarket chain stores, plus a food hall where you can sample fast food from around the world.

Santa Monica has a number of fine **galleries** selling works by emerging local and international artists. **Bergamont Stations**, a collection of former tramcar sheds at 2525 Michigan Ave near the intersection of 26th and Cloverfield, houses a multitude of small art galleries (most open Tues–Fri 11am–5.30pm). Many of LA's latest generation of artists – such as Mike Kelley, Lari Pittman and Erika Rothenberg – have shown here, and the construction of two small theatre stages in adjoining warehouses will no doubt draw comparably rising stars of the performing arts. The **Side Street Projects**, 1629 18th St (hours vary; information on ☎310/829-0779) is another of the town's ambitious young art spaces. It hosts international collaborative shows, runs a workshop and puts on the "Miracle on 18th Street" December sale of handcrafted ornaments; it also originated the "For The Time Being" project, in which poetry-reciting parking meters were set up around Los Angeles to provide grants for artists living with HIV or AIDS.

Further inland, it's less easy to stumble upon Santa Monica's worthwhile sights. On the northern border, **San Vicente Boulevard**'s grassy tree-lined strip is a joggers' freeway, and races through the plush houses of **Brentwood**, including the house where Marilyn Monroe was found dead in 1962, at 12305 5th Helena Drive. South of San Vicente, the flashy novelty and clothing shops of **Montana Avenue** reflect the upward mobility of the area.

At the southeast corner of Santa Monica Boulevard, Ocean Park Boulevard spears off to another place you'd be unlikely ever to stumble upon by chance, the **Museum of Flying** (Wed–Sun 10am–5pm; $7), at the Santa Monica Municipal Airport (now used only by private planes). The major employer in the early years of Santa Monica, the Donald Douglas Aircraft Company, had its main factory here – birthplace of the DC-3 and other planes which pioneered commercial aviation – and the old premises display a number of vintage aircraft.

## The pier and beach

Despite the many features on top of the bluffs, the real focal point of Santa Monica life is down below, on the **beach** and around **Santa Monica pier**, the only reminder that the city was ever anything but a quiet coastal suburb. Jutting out into the bay at the foot of Colorado Avenue, the pier is a great example of its kind, recently expanded after half of it was washed away by winter storms, with new rides, a giant helter-skelter and a restored 1922 wooden **carousel** (daily 9am–6pm; $1 a ride) – you might recognize it from the 1973 movie *The Sting*. The pier also has a cheerful array of shooting galleries and bumper cars, and is sometimes the site of free concerts and assorted celebrations.

The grand beach houses just north of the pier were known as the "Gold Coast", because of the many Hollywood personalities who lived in them. The largest, now the **Sand and Sea** beach club, was built as the servants' quarters of a massive 120-room house, now demolished, that belonged to William Randolph Hearst. MGM boss Louis B Mayer owned the adjacent Mediterranean-style villa, where the Kennedy brothers were later rumoured to have had their liaisons with Marilyn Monroe. If you're not intending to stretch out on the sands, you can follow the **bike path**, which begins at the pier, twenty miles south to Palos Verdes. Or, on foot, wander south along the beach to Pico Boulevard and head two blocks inland to Main Street.

## Main Street

Santa Monica underwent a major change following completion of the Santa Monica Freeway in 1965, which brought the beachfront homes within a fifteen-minute drive of downtown and isolated the bulk of the town from **Main Street**, five minutes' walk from the pier – where the collection of novelty shops, kite stores and classy restaurants is now one of the popular shopping districts on the Westside.

Beyond shopping, eating and drinking, though, there's not much to do or see. **California Heritage Museum** on Main Street at Ocean Park Boulevard (Thurs–Sun 11am–4pm; $3) is the city's effort to preserve some of its architectural past in the face of new money. Two houses were moved here to escape demolition. One hosts temporary displays on Californian cultural topics as the reign of the Dodgers, and has several rooms restored to variously evoke the years 1890–1930. The other is known as the *Victorian Restaurant* and serves tea on its patio at weekends (reserve on ☎310/392-8537). Not all of Santa Monica has been so lucky, however. Ocean Park Boulevard was one of the main routes to the coast via the old streetcars of the Pacific Electric, and the entire beachfront between here and the Venice border, now overshadowed by massive grey condominiums, used to be the site of the largest and wildest of the amusement piers, the fantastic **Pacific Ocean Park**. "P-O-P", as it was known, had a huge roller coaster, a giant funhouse and a boisterous midway arcade, described by architectural historian Reyner Banham as a "fantasy in stucco and every known style of architecture and human ecology". Sadly, not a trace remains.

# Venice

Immediately south of Santa Monica, **VENICE** was laid out in the marshlands of Ballona Creek in 1905 by developer Abbot Kinney as a romantic replica of the northern Italian city. Intended to attract artsy folk from Los Angeles to sample its sub-European Bohemian air, this twenty-mile network of canals, lined by sham palazzos and waterfront homes, never really caught on, and the coming of the automobile finished it off altogether. Many of the canals were filled in, and the area, now annexed by the city of Los Angeles, fell into disrepair, with most of the home sites being taken over by oil wells – an era that features in Orson Welles' film *A Touch of Evil*, in which derelict Venice stars as a seedy border town.

Kinney was, however, ahead of his time. A fair bit of the original plan survives, and the pseudo-European atmosphere has since proved just right for pulling in the artistic community he was aiming at, making Venice one of the coast's trendier spots. Main Street, for instance, is home to the experimental offices of advertising firm **Chiat Day**. Marked by a huge pair of binoculars at the entrance, the Frank Geary-designed offices have no assigned desks, leaving employees to roam free with laptops and mobile phones, through spartan rooms lined with original modern art. Elsewhere, a strong alternative arts scene centres around the **Beyond Baroque Literary Arts Center and Bookshop** in the old City Hall at 681 Venice Blvd (Tues–Fri 10am–5pm, Sat 12pm–5pm; ☎310/822-3006), which holds regular readings and workshops of poetry, prose and drama.

**Windward Avenue** is the town's main artery, running from the beach into what was the Grand Circle of the canal system, now paved over and ringed by a number of galleries and the Venice post office, inside which a mural depicts the early layout. Leading to the beach, the original Romanesque **arcade**, around the intersection with Pacific Avenue, is alive with health-food shops, used-record stores and roller skate rental stands. Here and there colourful and portentous giant **murals** cover the whitewashed walls of the original hotels, and of the Venice Pavilion on the beach. The few remaining **canals** are just a few blocks south, below Venice Boulevard and east of Pacific, where the original quaint little bridges survive, and you can sit and watch the ducks paddle around in the stagnant waters.

It's **Venice Beach** that draws most people to the town. Nowhere else does LA parade itself quite so openly and as sensuously as it does along the **Venice Boardwalk**, a wide pathway also known as Ocean Front Walk. Year-round at weekends and every day in summer it is packed with people and people-watchers, jugglers, fire-eaters, Hare Krishnas and roller-skating guitar players. You can buy anything you might need to look like a local without ever leaving the beach: cheap sunglasses, T-shirts, personal stereos and tennis shoes. South of Windward is **Muscle Beach**, a now legendary outdoor weightlifting centre where serious-looking hunks of muscle drive some serious iron, and high-flying gymnasts swing on the adjacent rings and bars.

Incidentally, be warned that **Venice Beach at night** is a dangerous place, taken over by street gangs, drug dealers and assorted psychos. Even walking on the beach after dark is illegal, and anywhere in the immediate vicinity you should take great care.

## Pacific Palisades and Will Rogers State Park

The town of **PACIFIC PALISADES**, which rises on the bluffs two miles north of Santa Monica pier, is slowly but very surely falling away into the bay, most noticeably on the point above Chautauqua Boulevard and Pacific Coast Highway, otherwise known as "PCH". With each winter's rains, a little bit more of the bluffs gets washed away in mud slides, blocking traffic on PCH, and gradually shrinking the back yards of the clifftop homes. There are few places of interest among the suburban ranch houses, although some of the most influential buildings of post-war LA were constructed here – **Charles Eames' house**, for example, at 203 Chautauqua St, fashioned out of prefabricated industrial parts in 1947.

In complete contrast, and a better place to spend a few hours, a mile east along Sunset Boulevard from the top of Chautauqua is the **Will Rogers State Historic Park** (summer daily 8am–7pm; rest of year daily 8am–6pm; free, parking $4), a steep climb from the MTA bus (#2) stop. This was the home and ranch of the Depression-era cowboy philosopher and journalist Will Rogers, one of America's most popular figures of the time – after his death in a plane crash in 1935, there was a nationwide thirty-minute silence. He was renowned for his downhome, common-sense thinking, and the saying that he "never met a man he didn't like". The overgrown ranch-style house serves as an informal **museum** (daily 10am–5pm; free), filled to overflowing with cowboy gear and Native American art; and the 200-acre park has miles of foot and bridle paths, one of which leads up to the top of Topanga Canyon.

## The J Paul Getty Museum

From Pacific Palisades, PCH follows the curve of the bay towards Malibu. Three miles or so on, a huge French chateau towers above the shore, coincidentally marking the otherwise easily missed entrance to the **J Paul Getty Museum** at 17985 PCH (Tues–Sun 10am–5pm; free; ☎310/458-2003), housed in a replica Pompeiian villa that holds the Getty collection of Greek and Roman antiquities. If driving, you must make parking reservations by phoning well in advance; otherwise park at the end of Sunset Boulevard and pay for a $5 taxi up the hill, or take MTA bus #434 from Santa Monica, and ask the bus driver for a free pass.

The Getty Museum displays the art collection of the colossally wealthy oil magnate, John Paul Getty, who began collecting art in the 1930s, at first showing it in his house. In 1976, two years after the museum opened, Getty died, leaving the unprecedented sum of $1.3 billion to continue the work he had started, and the place is now notorious in the art world for having more money than it knows what to do with. Under American tax laws, the Getty Trust must spend a portion of its endowment (in the order of $250 million) every year, which means in effect that the museum can outbid anyone in the world to get what it wants, thereby inflating international art prices beyond the reach of most institutions and encouraging shady behaviour among the museum's suppliers. It's said that a sizeable part of the collection was speedily acquired by a curator who bought overpriced works by the crateload on behalf of private individuals, who then bequeathed the art to the museum and claimed the cost as a (often gigantic) tax write-off.

Even so, you'd be crazy to miss the place while you're in LA. The fake Roman Villa, a copy of the Villa dei Papiri in Pompeii, is gorgeously sited high above the ocean, and – sour grapes aside – the quality of the exhibits means the Getty Museum ranks among the world's finest. As the collection is, not surprisingly, determined by the enthusiasms of Getty himself, there's a formidable array of his major interest, Greek and Roman statuary, including the only remaining work (an athlete) of Lysippos, sculptor to Alexander the Great. You'll also see a feast of ornate furniture and decorative arts, with clocks, chandeliers, tapestries and gilt-edged commodes, designed for the French nobility from the reign of Louis XIV, filling several overwhelmingly opulent rooms. Getty was much less interested in painting – although he did scoop up a very fine stash from the Renaissance and Baroque periods, including works by Rembrandt, Rubens, de la Tour and more – but a large collection has been amassed since his death, featuring all the major names from the thirteenth century to the present: drawings by Raphael and Bernini, paintings of the Dutch Golden Age and a handful of French Impressionists, to name just a few. By contrast, there's also an extensive and highly absorbing collection of photographs by Man Ray, Laszlo Moholy-Nagy and notable others.

## Topanga Canyon

A mile beyond the Getty Museum, a turning leads up into Topanga Canyon, a fermenting ground for West Coast rock music in the 1960s, when Neil Young, the Byrds and other artists moved here, holding all-night jam sessions in the sycamore groves along Topanga Creek. The canyon still has the wildness that attracted them, especially in winter and early spring, when mud slides threaten houses and waterfalls cascade down the cliffs, and the hillsides are covered in golden poppies and wildflowers. A hundred and fifty thousand acres of these mountains and the seashore have been protected as the Santa Monica Mountains National Recreation Area, but as yet very few people take advantage of the fine views and fresh air, thus missing out on the sight of the deer, coyotes and the odd mountain lion that still live here. Park rangers offer free guided hikes throughout the mountains most weekends (for information and reservations phone ☎818/597-9192), and there are self-guided trails through the canyon's Topanga State Park, off Old Topanga Canyon Road at the crest of the mountains, with spectacular views out over the Pacific.

Beyond Topanga Canyon, the beaches and ocean-views are blocked off by mile after mile of private homes all the way to Malibu. There are a few signposted beach-access points but most of the rock stars and others who can afford to live here treat the sands and seas as their own. Although any bit of land below the high-tide line is legally in the public domain, you're sure to feel like a trespasser.

## Malibu

Everyone has heard of **MALIBU**; the very name conjures up images of beautiful people sunbathing on a palm-fringed beach and lazily consuming cocktails. And the image is not so very far from the truth – even though you might not think so on arrival. As you enter the small town, the succession of ramshackle surf shops and fast-food stands scattered along both sides of PCH around the graceful Malibu Pier don't exactly reek of money; but the secluded estates just inland are as valuable as any in the entire US.

The south-facing beach next to the pier, Surfrider Beach, was the surfing capital of the world in the 1950s and early 1960s, popularized by the many Beach Blanket Bingo movies filmed here, starring the likes of Annette Funicello and Frankie Avalon. It's still a big surfing spot: the waves are best in late summer, when storms off Mexico cause them to reach upwards of eight feet. Just beyond is **Malibu Lagoon State Park**, a nature reserve and bird refuge; birdwatching walks around the lagoon are offered some weekends, and there's a small **museum** (Wed–Sat 11am–3pm; $2), detailing the history of the area.

Most Malibu residents live in the houses and small ranches that hide away in the narrow canyons on the edges of the town, together forming a well-off, insular community with a long-established dread of outsiders. Up until the 1920s all of Malibu was owned by one **May K Rindge**, who hired armed guards and dynamited roads to keep travellers from crossing her land on their way to and from Santa Monica. Rindge fought for years to prevent the state from building the Pacific Coast Highway across her property, but lost her legal battle in the State Supreme Court, and her money in the Depression. Her son took over the ranch and quickly sold much of the land, establishing the **Malibu Colony** at the mouth of Malibu Canyon as a haven for movie stars. There's very little to see here except the garage doors of the rich and famous; if you must, you can enter on foot or cycle a mile or so along PCH, on the other side of the hill. You'd do better, though, just visiting the **Trancas Market**, near the gated entrance to the colony – good both for star-spotting and stocking up on food and drink before a day on the sands.

Much of **Malibu Creek State Park**, at the crest of Malibu Canyon Road along Mulholland Drive, used to belong to 20th Century-Fox studios, who filmed many Tarzan pictures here and used the chaparral-covered hillsides to simulate South Korea for the TV show *MASH*. The 4000-acre park includes a large lake, some waterfalls, and nearly fifteen miles of hiking trails. Nearby **Paramount Ranch**, another old studio backlot, has an intact Western Town movie set, where you can play gunfighter, near Mulholland Drive on Cornell Road.

### The beaches

Five miles along the coast from Malibu Pier, **Zuma Beach** is the largest of the Los Angeles County beaches, popular with San Fernando Valley high-school kids, who drive over Kanan-Dume road to escape the sweltering inland summer heat. Adjacent **Point Dume State Beach**, below the bluffs, is a lot more relaxed, especially up and over the rocks at its southern tip, where **Pirate's Cove** is used by nudists. The rocks here are also a good place to look out for seals and migrating gray whales in winter, as the point juts out into the Pacific at the northern lip of Santa Monica Bay.

**El Matador State Beach**, about 25 miles up the coast from Santa Monica, is about as close as an ordinary Joe can get to the private-beach seclusion enjoyed by the stars. Thanks to its northern location and an easily missable turn off PCH, its rocky coved sands are a recluse's dream. Another five miles along PCH, where Mulholland Drive reaches the ocean, **Leo Carrillo State Beach Park** marks the northern border of LA County and the end of the *MTA* bus (#434) route. The mile-long sandy beach is divided by Sequit Point, a small bluff that has underwater caves and a tunnel you can pass through at low tide. Leo Carrillo is also the nearest and most accessible **campsite** for the rest of LA (see p.73). Five miles further on, at **Point Mugu State Park**, there are some very good walks through mountain canyons, and campsites right on the beach. Point Mugu is also the site of the US Navy's Pacific Missile Test Center, which takes up most of the five miles of coast south of Ventura (see p.308), at the southern edge of the Central Coast.

# The South Bay and Harbor Area

South of Venice and Marina del Rey, the coast is dominated by the runways of LAX, a huge Chevron Oil refinery, and LA's main sewage treatment plant. Beyond this industrial zone, however, is an eight-mile strip of beach towns – **Manhattan Beach**, **Hermosa Beach** and **Redondo Beach** – collectively known as the South Bay. These are more modest (though far from poor), quieter, more suburban and smaller than the

Westside beach communities. Along their shared beach-side bike path the joggers and roller skaters are more likely to be locals than poseurs from other parts of LA, and all three can make a refreshing break if you like your beaches without pretentious packaging. Each has a beckoning strip of white sand, and Manhattan and Hermosa especially are well equipped for surfing and beachsports. They're also well connected to the rest of the city – within easy reach of LAX and connected by regular buses to downtown LA.

Visible all along this stretch of the coast, the large vegetated peninsula of **Palos Verdes** looks more tempting than it really is, much of it an upmarket residential area, although the comparatively rough-hewn little city of **San Pedro** is a worthwhile destination around the far side (not least for the local youth hostel, the area's cheapest accommodation by a long way; see p.74) sited on the LA harbour, the busiest cargo port in the world and still growing. On the other side of the harbour, **Long Beach**, connected to downtown by express bus #456, is best known as the resting place of the *Queen Mary*.

Perhaps the most enticing, and certainly the strangest place in the area is **Catalina Island**, only twenty miles offshore and easily reached by ferry. It's almost completely conserved wildland, with many unique forms of plant and animal life and just one small, offbeat centre of population.

## Manhattan Beach, Hermosa Beach and Redondo Beach

Accessible along the bike path from Venice, or by car along Pacific Coast Highway, **MANHATTAN BEACH** is a likeable place with a healthy well-to-do air, home mainly to white-collar workers whose middle-class stucco homes tumble towards the beach, uncluttered by high-rise hotels. There's not much to see or do away from the beach (unless you want to seek out the video rental store where Quentin Tarantino once worked), but then that's the main reason for coming. Surfing is a major local pastime, there's a two-week international surf festival each August, and the city is a major centre for beach volleyball, evidenced by the profusion of nets across the sands. If you can, call at the **historical center** in the post office building at 425 15th St (Sat–Sun only noon–3pm; free), for its entertaining collection of photos and oddments from the city's earliest days. If these whet your appetite, you can purchase (for $1) a map that describes a history-flavoured **walking tour**.

**HERMOSA BEACH**, across Longfellow Boulevard, is more down-at-heel than Manhattan Beach, its houses less showy, with a younger, more effervescent mood. The centre, near the foot of the pier around Hermosa and Pier avenues, is an unlikely setting for one of the South Bay's best-known nightspots, *The Lighthouse* (see p.151). Again, there's little of note except the beach, though you should take a look in the well-stocked **Either/Or** bookshop, 124 Pier Ave (see p.159), once a haunt of writer Thomas Pynchon.

Despite some long family-oriented strips of sand, and fine views of Palos Verdes' stunning greenery, **REDONDO BEACH**, situated south of Hermosa, is less inviting. Scores of condos and large hotels line the beachfront, and the food and drink spots around the yacht-lined King's Harbor are off limits to impecunious visitors.

## Palos Verdes

A great green hump marking LA's southwest corner, **PALOS VERDES** isn't of special interest, but it can be enjoyable to explore the bluffs and coves along the protected coastline. **Malaga Beach**, by Torrance County Beach just south of Redondo, is a popular scuba-diving spot; **Abalone Cove**, reached from the parking lot on Berkentine Road, off Palos Verdes Drive, boasts rock and tide pools, and off-shore kelp beds alive with rock scallops, sea urchins and, of course, abalone. A couple of miles east at the end of a path off Peppertree Drive, Smugglers Cove is a renowned **nudist beach**.

While you're in the area, don't miss **Wayfarer's Chapel**, at 5755 Palos Verdes Drive Designed by Frank Lloyd Wright's son, Lloyd, it's a tribute to the eighteenth-century Swedish scientist and mystic Emanuel Swedenborg. The ultimate aim is for the redwood grove around the chapel to grow and entangle itself around the glass-framed structure – a fusing of human handiwork with the forces of nature of which Swedenborg would have been proud.

A few miles further on, just before the end of Palos Verdes Drive, **Point Fermin Park** is a small tip of land prodding into the ocean. In the park is a curious little wooden lighthouse dating from 1874 (no admittance), and a whale-watching station where you can read up on the winter migrations. Bottle-nosed dolphins can often be seen during their fall departure and spring return, and there's also the less seasonally dependent thrill of spotting hang-gliders swooping down off the cliffs.

From the park, it's an easy stroll along Bluff Place and down the 29th Street stairway to Cabrillo Beach and the excellent **Cabrillo Marine Museum**, at 3720 Stephen White Drive (Tues–Fri noon–5pm, Sat & Sun 10am–5pm; free). A diverse collection of marine life has been imaginatively and instructively assembled: everything from predator snails and the sarcastic fringehead (a rare fish whose outrageous name makes sense once you see it) to larger displays on otters, seals and whales.

## San Pedro and around

About three miles further on along Bluff Place, the scruffy harbour city of **SAN PEDRO** is in stark contrast to the affluence of the rest of Palos Verdes. It was a small fishing community until the late nineteenth century, when the construction of the LA harbour nearby brought a huge influx of labour, much of it drawn from the migrants who arrived on the ships, chiefly from Portugal, Greece and Yugoslavia. Many of these, and their descendants, never left the place, lending a striking racial mix to the town, manifest around the narrow sloping central streets in one of LA's densest groupings of ethnic groceries.

Some of this history is revealed in the **Maritime Museum**, on the harbour's edge at the foot of Sixth Street (Sun–Tues 10am–5pm; free), while the **Bloody Thursday Monument**, on the corner of Sixth and Beacon close to the City Hall, is another reminder of the city's gritty past. It marks the 1934 strike by local waterfront workers, commemorating the two who were killed when police and private guards opened fire. A fifteen-minute walk along the shore from the museum will bring you to the overrated **Ports O'Call Village** – a dismal batch of wooden and corrugated iron huts supposedly capturing the flavour of exotic seaports around the world. Don't bother to visit.

Between San Pedro and Long Beach (connected by *LBTD* bus #142, or *MTA* #146) soar two tall road bridges, giving aerial views of oil wells and docks, and the vast Naval Supplies Center (through which the buses sometimes pass to pick up civilian workers). Just inland, the community of **WILMINGTON** is home to the palatial Greek-style **Banning House** at 401 E Main St (guided tours Tues–Sun 12.30pm, 1.30pm & 2.30pm, and at 3.30pm at weekends; free). A mid-nineteenth-century entrepreneur, Phineas Banning made his fortune when the value of the land he purchased here increased astronomically as the harbour was developed. Through his promoting of the rail link between the harbour and central LA he also became known as "the father of Los Angeles transportation" – no mean accolade at a time when the local transport system was one of the best in the world.

## Long Beach

Not so long ago you would have given **LONG BEACH** a miss. Once the stamping ground of off-duty naval personnel, its porn shops and sleazy bars made the place just the wrong side of seedy. The last decade or so, however, saw a billion dollar cash injection into the town that has led – in the downtown area at least – to a spate of glossy office buildings, a convention centre, new hotels, a swanky shopping mall and a clean-up campaign that has restored some of the best turn-of-the-century buildings on the coast. Inland from downtown, however, it's a different story – grim, uninviting housing developments on the perimeter of the impoverished district of South Central LA (see p.85).

**Downtown** Long Beach is clearly the place to spend most of your time, with, especially along Pine Avenue, the best of Long Beach's rescued architecture and numerous thrift stores, antique/junk emporiums and bookshops. Nearby, on Third Street, is the succinctly named **"The Mural"**, whose depiction of the Long Beach population appears to be contemporary but was in fact painted in the 1930s under Roosevelt's New Deal, unwittingly predicting the racial mixture that Long Beach attained much later. From the mural, the pedestrianized Promenade leads towards the sea, passing the concrete open-air auditorium – often the site of free art and music events – and crosses the busy Ocean Beach Boulevard into **Shoreline Village**, a waterfront entertainment belt. It's a bit contrived but fine for a quick look, especially at weekends when Long Beach youth is on parade.

Ocean Boulevard leads away from Shoreline Village down to **Breakers Hotel**: twelve storeys of Spanish Revival pinkness topped by a green copper roof. A mile further on, 2300 Ocean Blvd was once owned by Fatty Arbuckle and now houses the **Long Beach Museum of Art** (Wed–Thurs & Sat–Sun noon–5pm, Fri 5–8pm; $2), neatly fringed by a sculpture garden. Inside you'll see a small but substantial collection of contemporary Southern Californian art, and some very experimental screenings from the **video annexe**. Another mile in this direction, the **Belmont Shores** area was built by old – and is maintained by new – money. Its main thoroughfare, Second Street, a collection of designer shops and yuppie-frequented cafés, sustains the affluent style of the surrounding avenues, where many of the wealthy Long Beachites of the 1920s had their homes.

Between November and March, more than fifteen thousand whales cruise the "Whale Freeway" past Long Beach on their annual migration to and return from winter breeding and berthing grounds in Baja California. *Shoreline Village Cruises* (☎310/495-5884) and *Star Party Cruises* (☎310/431-6833) operate good whale-watching trips for between $8 and $12.

## The Queen Mary

Long Beach's most famous attraction is not indigenous at all. The mighty ocean liner, the **Queen Mary**, was acquired by the local authorities with the specific aim of bolstering tourism, and has generally succeeded in doing so. The *Queen Mary* lies across the bay, opposite Shoreline Village, and is easily accessible either by a lengthy walk or free *Long Beach Transit* shuttle from downtown. Now kitted out as a luxury hotel, and open daily from 10am until 6pm for $7 guided tours (if you look around on your own it's free of charge), the ship is as tangible a testament to the hypocrisy of the British class system as you'll find. The suggestion is that all who sailed on the vessel – the flagship of the *Cunard Line* from the 1930s until the 1960s – enjoyed the extravagantly furnished lounges and the luxurious cabins, all carefully restored and kept sparkling. But a glance at the spartan third-class cabins reveals something of the real story, and the tough conditions experienced by the impoverished migrants who left Europe on the ship hoping to start a new life in the US. The red British telephone kiosks around the decks and the hammy theatrical displays in the engine room and wheelhouse – closer to *Star Trek* than anything nautical – don't help, but it's nonetheless a marvellous ship, well worth a look.

# Catalina Island

Though it's overlooked by many foreign visitors, **CATALINA ISLAND**, a mix of uncluttered beaches and wild hills twenty miles off the coast, is favoured by Californians in the know. Claimed by the Portuguese in 1542 as San Salvador, and renamed by the Spanish in 1602, it has somehow stayed firmly outside the historical mainstream. Since 1811, when the indigenous Gabrileño Indian population was forced to resettle on the mainland, the island has been in private ownership, and has over the years grown to be something of a resort – a process hastened by businessman William Wrigley Jr (part of the Chicago-based chewing gum dynasty), who financed the construction of the Art Deco Avalon Casino, still the island's major landmark, in the 1920s.

The island has become a popular destination for boaters and nature lovers, and its small marina overflows with luxury yachts and cruise ships in summer. Even so, tourism has been held largely at bay: the hotels are unobtrusive among the whimsical architecture and cars are a rarity, as there's a ten-year waiting list to bring one over from the mainland. Consequently most of the 3,000 islanders walk (the "city" of Avalon covers just one square mile), ride bikes or drive electrically powered golf carts or mokes.

### Arrival and accommodation

Depending on the season, a round **ferry trip** from San Pedro or Long Beach to Catalina Island's one town, **Avalon**, costs between $20 and $30. *Catalina Cruises* (☎1-800/228-2546) and *Catalina Express* (☎310/519-1212) run several services daily. From Newport Beach (see p.125) to Avalon, the *Catalina Passenger Service* (☎714/673-5245) runs a daily round trip, for about $30. You could, alternatively, take a catamaran day excursion from San Diego with *SeaJet*, which would set you back $69, (☎619/696-0088). If you get seasick or feel extravagant, **helicopter** services to Avalon, costing around $100 round-trip, are offered by *Island Express* (☎310/510-2525) from Long Beach and San Pedro.

Be warned that the price of hotel **accommodation** in Avalon hovers upwards of $85, and most beds are booked up throughout the summer and at weekends. The most interesting **hotel** is the *Zane Grey Pueblo Hotel* (☎310/510-0966; ③–⑤), detailed below, but the cheapest is usually the *Atwater*, on Sumner Avenue just back from the sea (☎1-800/4-AVALON; ③). The *Bayview Hotel*, on Whittley Avenue (☎310/510-7070; ③), is also reasonable. The only budget option is **camping** (around $7.50 per person). *Hermit Gulch* (☎310/510-8368) is the closest site to Avalon and consequently the busiest. Three other sites – *Black Jack*, *Little Harbor* and *Two Harbors* – in Catalina's interior, all bookable on ☎310/510-0303, are usually roomier. Of **places to eat**, *Catalina Cantina,* 311 Crescent Ave (☎310/510-0100), is the best, offering tasty and moderately priced Mexican staples washed down with fresh fruit margaritas, and live music at weekends.

### Transport and trips

*Catalina Safari Shuttle Bus* runs between Avalon and Two Harbors for $29 round trip. *Catalina Island Company* (☎310/510-2500 or 1-800/4-AVALON) offers **tours** of the island, ranging from whistle-stop town jaunts and short voyages in glass-bottomed boats ($6.75 each) to a fuller four-hour affair ($23) – the only way to see the interior of Catalina without hiking. **Mokes**, for which you need a driver's licence, and **bikes** (both of which are banned from the rough roads outside Avalon) can be rented (for $30 a day) from the stand opposite the *Busy Bee* restaurant on Bay Shore Drive.

The waters around the island are rich in yellowtail, calico bass, barracuda and sharks. *Catalina Mako* (☎310/510-2720) runs **charter fishing trips** for around $95 an hour (although you can fish for free from the pleasure pier), and snorkel and scuba gear is available for rent at **Catalina Divers Supply** (☎310/510-0330).

## Avalon

AVALON can be fully explored on foot in an hour, with maps issued by the **Chamber of Commerce** at the foot of the ferry pier (☎310/510-1520). The best place to begin is at the **Avalon Casino**, a sumptuous 1920s structure, with mermaid murals, gold-leaf ceiling motifs, an Art Deco ballroom, and a small **museum** (daily 10.30am–4pm; $1) displaying Native American artefacts from Catalina's past.

On the slopes above the casino, the **Zane Grey Pueblo Hotel** (see above) is the former home of the Western author, who visited Catalina with a film crew to shoot *The Vanishing American* and liked the place so much he never left, building for himself this pueblo-style house, complete with a beamed ceiling and thick wooden front door. It's now a hotel, with rooms themed after his books and a pool shaped like an arrowhead, and makes a handy place to rest after climbing the hill, both to admire the views over Avalon and the bay, and to examine the few items kept from Grey's time.

## The interior

If possible, venture into the **interior** of Catalina. You can take a tour (see above) if time is short; if it isn't, get a free **wilderness permit**, which allows you to hike and camp, from the Chamber of Commerce or the **Parks and Recreation office** (☎310/510-0688), both in Avalon. Mountain biking requires a $50 permit from the **Catalina Island Conservancy**, 125 Calressa Ave, Avalon (☎310/510-1421) or the *Two Harbors* campsite.

The carefully conserved wilderness of the interior holds a wide variety of flora and fauna, some of it unique. Keep an eye out for the Catalina Shrew, so rare it's only been sighted twice, and the Catalina Mouse, bigger and healthier than its mainland counterpart thanks to abundant food and lack of natural enemies. There are also buffalo, descended from a herd of fourteen left behind by a Hollywood film crew and now thinned out annually in an October round-up, deer, mountain goats, lizards and rattlesnakes.

# Anaheim: Disneyland and around

*Life in Anaheim, California, was a commercial for itself, endlessly replayed. Nothing changed; it just spread farther and farther in the form of neon ooze. What there was always more of had been congealed into permanence long ago, as if the automatic factory that cranked out these objects had jammed into the on position.*

Philip K Dick, *A Scanner Darkly*

In the early 1950s, illustrator/film-maker Walt Disney conceived a theme park where his cartoon characters – Mickey Mouse, Donald Duck, Goofy and the rest, already indelibly imprinted on the American mind – would come to life, and his fabulously successful company would rake in even more money from them.

**Disneyland** opened in 1955, in anticipation of the acres of orange groves thirty miles southeast of downtown – at **ANAHEIM** and, inland, in **Orange County** – becoming the nexus of population growth in Southern California. The theory proved correct, and the area around Anaheim is pure Eisenhower era – staunchly conservative suburbs made up of mile after mile of unvarying residential plots and still one of the US's fastest growing areas, though much of this could be put down to the presence of Disneyland itself, without which the local economy would be much the poorer.

Certainly the park, and the scores of hotels and restaurants that have opened up in its wake utterly dominate the Anaheim area, and the boom doesn't look like slowing. If you're not coming to see Disneyland, you may as well give the place a miss: it hasn't an ounce of interest in itself. But if you do come, or are staying in one of Anaheim's many hotels, the creakier rides at **Knotts Berry Farm** go some way to restoring wholesome notions of what amusement parks used to be like; the **Movieland Wax Museum** is mildly entertaining; and, on an entirely different note, the **Crystal Cathedral** is an architecturally imposing – and unflinching – reminder of the potency of the evangelical movement. If you're a sports fan, note also that both the *LA Rams* (football) and the *California Angels* (baseball), play at Anaheim Stadium; see p.161 for the facts.

# Disneyland

It's hard to think of anything that comes closer to demonstrating the wishful thinking of the modern US than **DISNEYLAND** (summer daily 8am–1am; rest of year Mon–Fri 10am–6pm, Sat 9am–midnight, Sun 9am–10pm; $33 adults, $26 kids, parking $6; ☎714/ 999-4565), the most famous, most carefully constructed, most award-winning theme park anywhere – and the blueprint for imitations worldwide. Disneyland is a phenome-non, the ultimate fantasy, with the emphasis strongly on family fun. While it has been known for people to cruise around Disneyland on LSD, it is not a good idea; the authori-ties take a dim view of anything remotely antisocial, and anyone acting out of order will be thrown out; in any case the place is surreal enough without the need for mind-expanding drugs.

Bear in mind, too, that Disneyland is not LA's only large-scale amusement park; the whirlwind rides at Magic Mountain, for example (see p.134), are consistently better.

## Practicalities

Disneyland is at 1313 Harbor Blvd, Anaheim, about 45 minutes by **car** from downtown using the Santa Ana Freeway. By **train** from downtown (there are 9 a day), make the thirty-minute journey to Fullerton, from where *OCTD* buses will drop you at Disneyland or Knotts Berry Farm. By **bus**, use *MTA* #460 from downtown, which takes about ninety minutes, or the quicker *Greyhound* service, which runs thirteen times a day, and takes 45 minutes to Anaheim, from where it's an easy walk to the park. From Long Beach, *MTA* bus #149 connects both Knotts Berry Farm and Disneyland, taking just over an hour.

As for **accommodation**, most people try to visit Disneyland just for the day and spend the night somewhere else, or at home. It's not a very appealing area, and anyway most of the hotels and motels close to Disneyland cost well in excess of $70 per night; still, the park is at its least crowded first thing after opening, so staying nearby can help avoid the crowds. If you must stay, the *HI-Anaheim/Fullerton* hostel is by far the best bet; see p.72 for further recommendations.

A massive central kitchen produces all the **food** that's eaten in the park (you're not permitted to bring your own), unloading popcorn, hot dogs, hamburgers and other all-American produce from the many stands by the ton. For anything healthier or more substantial, you'll need to leave the park and travel a fair way. The "Eating" listings on p.137 suggest some options.

## The park

The only way to enjoy Disneyland is to jump into it with both feet: don't think twice about anything and go on every ride you can. The admission price includes them all, although during peak periods you might have to wait in line for hours – lines are shortest when the park opens, so get there early.

From the front gates, **Main Street** leads through a scaled-down, camped-up replica of a turn-of-the-century Midwestern town, filled with small souvenir shops, food stands and penny arcades, to Sleeping Beauty's Castle, a pseudo-Rhineland palace at the heart of the park. **Adventureland**, nearby, contains two of the best rides in the park: the *Pirates of the Caribbean*, a boat trip through underground caverns, singing along with drunken pirates, and the *Haunted Mansion*, a riotous "doom buggy" tour in the company of the house spooks. While here, make a point of taking the *Jungle Cruise* through the audio-animatronic jungles of the Congo, with a live narration that's the only part of Disneyland taking the mickey out of Mickey Mouse.

Over four hundered "Imagineers" worked to create the **Indiana Jones Adventure**, Disney's biggest opening in years. Two hours of queuing are built into the ride, with an interactive archeological dig and 1930s-style newsreel show leading up to the main feature – a giddy journey along 2,500ft of skull-encrusted corridors in which you face fireballs, burning rubble, venomous snakes and inevitably, a rolling-boulder finale.

Less fun is **Frontierland**, the smallest and most all-American of the various theme-lands, taking its cues from the Wild West and the tales of Mark Twain, who grew up in the same town – Hannibal, Missouri – as Walt himself.

**Fantasyland**, across the drawbridge from Main Street, shows off the cleverest but also the most sentimental aspects of the Disney imagination: *Mr Toad's Wild Ride* through Victorian England, *Peter Pan* flying over London, and *It's a Small World*, a tour of the world's continents in which animated dolls warble the same cloying song over and over again.

There's only one spot in the park where you can actually see the outside world: by looking over the boundary walls when riding the *Skyway* cars that travel via a dangling cable from Fantasyland into **Tomorrowland.** This is Disney's vision of the future, where the *Space Mountain* roller coaster zips through the pitch-blackness of outer space, Michael Jackson dances in 3-D in the movie *Captain E-O*, and R2D2 pilots a runaway space cruiser through the *Star Wars* galaxy of Luke Skywalker and Darth Vader.

In addition to these fixed attractions, over-the-top **firework displays** explode every summer night at 9pm, and all manner of parades and special events celebrate important occasions – such as Mickey Mouse's birthday.

# Around Disneyland

It's hard to escape the clutches of Disneyland even when you leave: everything in the surrounding area seems to have been designed to service the needs of its visitors. A few places within easy reach offer a chance to forget, at least temporarily, its existence, but if Disneyland has given you a taste for distortions of reality, there's always the Richard Nixon Library and Birthplace to enjoy in Yorba Linda.

### Knott's Berry Farm and the Movieland Wax Museum

If you're a bit fazed by the excesses of Disneyland, you might prefer the more traditional **Knott's Berry Farm**, four miles northwest off the Santa Ana Freeway at 8039 Beach Blvd (summer Sun–Thurs 9am–11pm, Fri–Sat 9am–midnight; rest of year Mon–Fri 10am–6pm, Sat 10am–10pm, Sun 10am–7pm; $26.95). This relaxed, rough-at-the-edges park was born during the Depression when people began queuing up for the fried chicken dinners prepared by Mrs Knott, a local farmer's wife. To amuse the children while they waited for their food, Mr Knott reconstructed a Wild West ghost town and added amusements until the park had grown into the sprawling carnival of roller coasters and thrilling rides that stands today.

Across the street at 7662 Beach Blvd, the **Movieland Wax Museum** (summer daily 9am–7pm; $12.95), is a Madame Tussaud's for the Hollywood set, displaying a collection of wax dummies posed in scenes from favourite films and TV shows. The Marx Brothers, Captain Kirk and the crew from the *Starship Enterprise*, and Arnold

Schwarzenegger may not be essential viewing, but they're good for a laugh. Both attractions are on the *MTA* #460 route from downtown.

## The Crystal Cathedral

The impressive **Crystal Cathedral**, on the other side of Disneyland just off the Santa Ana Freeway on Chapman Avenue,(daily 9am–4pm; free), is a rather less frivolous attraction. A Philip Johnson design of tubular space frames and plate glass walls, it forms part of the vision of hard-sell evangelist Reverend Robert Schuller, who, not content with owning the world's first drive-in church (next door to the cathedral), commissioned this dramatic prop to boost the ratings of his televised Sunday sermons. These shows reach their climax with the special Christmas production, using live animals in biblical roles and people disguised as angels suspended on ropes. Schuller raised $1.5 million for the construction of the building during one Sunday service alone – a statistic worth pondering as you stroll around the echoey interior.

## Yorba Linda: the Richard Nixon Library and Birthplace

Mickey Mouse may be its most famous resident, but conservative Orange County's favourite son is former US president Richard Milhouse Nixon, born in 1913 in what is now the freeway-caged **YORBA LINDA**, about eight miles northeast of Disneyland. Here, the **Richard Nixon Library and Birthplace**, 18001 Yorba Linda Blvd (Mon–Sat 10am–5pm, Sun 11am–5pm; $4.95), is an unrelentingly hagiographical library (really a museum) that offers a chance to dwell on the fascinating rise to – and fall from – power of a man who forged a career from lies and secrecy, and finally resigned from the world's most powerful job in total disgrace.

Now his last resting place (both he and his wife are buried in the grounds), the museum and gardens are dedicated to preserving the sanitized image Nixon wanted the American public to swallow. Oversized gifts from world leaders, amusing campaign memorabilia, and a laugh-a-line collection of obsequious letters written by and to Nixon (including one he despatched to the boss of *McDonald's* proclaiming the fast-food chain's hamburgers to be "one of the finest food buys in America") form the core of the exhibition, but it's in the constantly running archive radio and TV recordings that the distinctive Nixon persona really shines through.

Although famously humiliated in 1960s live TV debates with John F Kennedy (refusing to wear make-up, and with a visible growth of beard, Nixon perspired freely under the TV lights and was seen as the embodiment of sleaze), Nixon had earlier used the medium to save his political life. In 1952, the discovery of undeclared income precipitated the "fund crisis", which cast doubts over Nixon's honesty. Incredibly, with the **"Checkers speech"**, he convinced 58 million viewers of his integrity with a broadcast to rival the worst soap opera. Exuding mock sincerity, he cast himself as an ordinary American struggling to raise a family, buy a house, and provide for the future – and climaxed his performance with the statement that, regardless of the damage it may do to his career, he would not be returning the cocker spaniel dog (Checkers) given to him as a gift and now a family pet.

Throughout the museum, Nixon's face leers down in Big Brother fashion from almost every wall, but only inside the **Presidential Auditorium** (at the end of the corridor packed with notes attesting to the president's innocence in the Watergate Affair) do you get the chance to ask him a question. Many possibilities spring to mind, but the choice is limited to those already programmed into a computer. Ten or so minutes after making your selection, Nixon's gaunt features will fill the overlarge screen and provide the stock reply – as endearingly and believably as ever.

## RICHARD M NIXON: A LIFE IN POLITICS

Qualified as a lawyer and fresh from wartime (non-combat) service in the US Navy, Richard Milhouse Nixon **entered politics** as a Republican Congressman in 1946, without so much as a civilian suit to his name. A journalist of the time observed that Nixon employed "the half-truth, the misleading quotation, the loose-joined logic" to cast doubts on his rival – traits he was to perfect in the years to come.

Shortly after arriving in Washington, the fresh-faced Nixon joined the **House Un-American Activities Committee** (HUAC), a group of reds-under-the-bed scaremongers led by the fanatical Joseph McCarthy (whose greatest achievement, perhaps, was to make Nixon look like a moderate). Through the now notorious anti-Communist "witch trials", McCarthy and Nixon wrecked the lives and careers of many Americans who had idealistically flirted with Communism in their youth.

Nixon's meteoric rise culminated in becoming Eisenhower's vice president in 1953, aged just 39. Seven years later, Nixon was defeated in his own bid for the nation's top job by the even younger John F Kennedy, a loss which led him into the **"wilderness years"**. Staying out of the public spotlight, he took a highly lucrative post with a Los Angeles law firm and wrote *Six Crises*, a book whose deep introspection came as a surprise – and convinced many of the author's paranoia.

Seeking a power base for the next presidential campaign, Nixon contested the governorship of California in 1961. His humiliating defeat prompted a short-lived "retirement" and did nothing to suggest that seven years later he would beat Ronald Reagan to the Republican nomination and be **elected president** in 1969.

Nixon had attained his dream, but the country he inherited was more divided than at any time since the Civil War. The **Vietnam conflict** was at its height, and his large-scale illegal bombing of Cambodia earned him worldwide opprobrium. He was however able to bask in the glory of a slight thaw in the Cold War: a change of direction by Mao Tse-tung improved relations with China, and the first strategic arms limitation talks (SALT) treaties were agreed with the USSR.

Recession and unemployment didn't prevent Nixon's decisive re-election in 1972, but his second term was ended prematurely by the cataclysmic **Watergate Affair**. In January 1973, seven men were tried for breaking into and bugging the headquarters of the Democratic Party in the Watergate building in Washington, an act that was discovered to have been financed with money allocated to the Campaign to Re-elect the President (CREEP). From their testimonies, a trail of deceit lead deep into the corridors of the White House – and eventually to the president himself.

Nixon may not have sanctioned the actual bugging operation, but there was ample evidence to suggest that he participated in the cover-up. Ironically, his insistence on taping all White House conversations in order to ease the writing of his future memoirs was to be the major stumbling block to his surviving the crisis. Facing the threat of impeachment, President Nixon **resigned** in 1974.

The full pardon granted to Nixon by his successor, Gerald Ford (appointed to the vice-presidency during Watergate – some allege, on the condition of such a pardon being given) did little to arrest a widespread public disillusionment with the country's political machine. The rose-tinted faith, long held by many Americans, in the unflinching goodness of the President *per se* seemed irredeemably shattered. Remarkably, however, the years since Richard Nixon's ignoble demise saw him quietly seek to establish elder-statesman credentials, opining on world and national affairs through books and newspaper columns. He died in 1994 and was buried at Yorba Linda.

# The Orange County Coast

As Disneyland grew, so did the rest of Orange County. Besides providing tourist services, the region become a major centre for light industry and home to many of the millions who poured into Southern California during the Sixties and Seventies –

its population density is even greater than that of neighbouring, more metropolitan, Los Angeles County. But it was expansion without style, and those who could afford to soon left the anonymous inland sprawl for the more characterful coast. As a result, the **ORANGE COUNTY COAST**, a string of towns stretching from the edge of the Harbor Area to the borders of San Diego County 35 miles south, is suburbia with a shoreline: swanky beachside houses line the sands, the general ambience is easy-going, conservative and affluent, and the population seemingly dominated by bronzed eighteen-year-olds.

As the names of the main towns suggest – **Huntington Beach**, **Newport Beach** and **Laguna Beach** – there's no real reason beyond sea and sand to go there. But they do provide something of a counterpart to LA's more cosmopolitan side, and, despite the destructive bushfires of 1993 they do form appealing stopovers on a leisurely journey south. You might even spy a bit of countryside: unlike most of the city's other districts, the communities here don't stand shoulder-to-shoulder but are a few miles apart, in many instances divided by an ugly power station but sometimes by a piece of undeveloped coast. The one place genuinely meriting a stop is just inland at **San Juan Capistrano**, site of the best kept of all the Californian missions. Further on, there's little to see before you reach adjoining San Diego County, but the campsite at **San Clemente** provides the only cheap accommodation along the southern part of the coast.

If you're in a rush to get from LA to San Diego, you can skip the coast by passing through Orange County on the inland San Diego Freeway. The coastal cities, though, are linked by the more adventurous Pacific Coast Highway (PCH), part of Hwy-1, which you can pick up from Long Beach (or from the end of Beach Boulevard, coming from Anaheim), though it's often heaving in summer.

*OCTD* bus #1 rumbles along PCH roughly hourly throughout the day. *Greyhound* connections aren't so good: San Clemente gets nine buses a day and two early morning buses go to San Juan Capistrano, but there are none to Huntington, Laguna or Newport Beach. Most *Greyhound* buses bound for San Diego use the freeway. *Amtrak* is a good way to get from downtown LA (or Disneyland) to San Juan Capistrano, but the only other coastal stop is at San Clemente. One point to remember is that you can travel all the way along the coast from LA to San Diego using local buses for about $4 – though you should allow a full day or more for the journey.

## Huntington Beach

**HUNTINGTON BEACH** is the first place of any interest on the Orange County coast, wildest of the beach communities and one that you don't need a fortune to enjoy. It's a compact little place composed of engagingly ramshackle single-storey cafés and beach stores grouped around the foot of a long pier. The beach is the sole focus: it was here that Californian **surfing** began – imported from Hawaii in 1907 to encourage curious day-trippers to visit on the *Pacific Electric Railway*. Top surfers still flock to Huntington Beach for the annual **OP Pro Surfing Championship**, a world-class televised event held each June. Year-round during the day massed ranks of mixed-ability surfers attempt to coax a ride from even the smallest wave; at night, everyone lays aside their boards and joins in the barbecues, cooked on the beach's own fire rings. On the Fourth of July, beach BBQs are supplemeneted by the inevitable fireworks display, and in October the largely blonde and suntanned locals celebrate a plausible **Oktoberfest**, with German food and music. Otherwise, once you've exhausted the beach and the local shops, there's not much else, although Huntington Beach is a good place to be based for a while, with Orange County's cheapest beds in the **youth hostel** at 421 Eighth St, three blocks from the pier (see p.74 for details).

## Newport Beach and Corona Del Mar

Ten miles south from Huntington, **NEWPORT BEACH** could hardly provide a greater contrast. With ten yacht clubs and ten thousand yachts, this is upmarket even by Orange County standards, a chic image-conscious town that people visit to acquire a tan they can show off on the long stretches of sand or in the bars alongside. You'll need a pocketful of credit cards and a presentable physique to join them, but the sheer exclusivity of the place may be an attraction in itself.

Newport Beach is spread around a natural bay that cuts several miles inland, but *the* place to hang out is on the thin **Balboa Peninsula**, along which runs the three-mile-long beach. The most youthful and boisterous section is about halfway along, around Newport Pier at the end of 20th Street. North of here, beachfront homes restrict access; to the south the wide sands are occupied by a sporty crowd and, further along, around the second of Newport's two piers, the **Balboa Pier**, by seasiding families. Balboa Pier is the most touristy part of Newport, but it does hold a marina from which you can escape to Catalina Island (see pp.115 & 119), or take a boat ride on the *Pavilion Queen* (summer daily 11am–5pm; rest of year daily 11am–3pm; $6–8) around Newport's own, much smaller, islands.

On the peninsula there's little in the way of conventional sights, but you might cast an eye over the exterior (there's no public access) of the constructivist-style **Lovell House** on 13th Street, designed by Rudolph Schindler and finished in 1926. Described by one contemporary critic as "epoch-making", it is raised on five concrete legs, with the living quarters jutting out towards the edge of the sidewalk, and formed the basis of the architect's international reputation.

Away from the peninsula, Newport Beach is home to the much-hyped **Newport Harbor Art Museum** at 850 San Clemente Drive (Tues–Sun 11am–5pm; $4, free Tues), another of Southern California's internationally important art museums, which stages occasionally brilliant exhibitions of contemporary work.

Just a few miles along PCH from Newport, **CORONA DEL MAR** is a much less ostentatious place, worth a short stop for its good beach and the **Sherman Foundation Center**, devoted to the horticulture of the American Southwest and raising many vivid blooms in its **botanical gardens**. Between here and Laguna Beach lies an invitingly unspoilt three-mile-long hunk of coastline, protected as **Crystal Coves State Park**. It's perfect to explore on foot, far from the crowds. *OCTD* bus #1 stops alongside.

---

### LAGUNA'S FESTIVALS

Laguna hosts a number of large summer **art festivals** over a six-week period during July and August. The best-known (and most bizarre) is the **Pageant of the Masters**, a kind of great paintings charade in which the participants pose in front of a painted backdrop to portray a famous work of art. It might sound ridiculous, but it's actually quite impressive, and takes a great deal of preparation – something reflected in the prices: $15 for the cheapest tickets for shows which sell out months in advance (though you may be able to pick up cancellations on the night). The idea for the pageant was hatched during the Depression as a way to raise money for local artists, and the action takes place at the Irving Bowl, close to where Broadway meets Laguna Canyon Road, a walkable distance from the Laguna Beach bus station. The pageant is combined with the **Festival of the Arts** held at the same venue during daylight hours.

The excitement of both festivals waned in the Sixties, when a group of hippies created the alternative **Sawdust Festival**, in which local artists and craftspeople set up makeshift studios to demonstrate their skills – now just as established but a lot cheaper and easier to get into than the other two. It takes place at 935 Laguna Canyon Rd, and admission is around $4.

# Laguna Beach

Nestling among the crags around a small sandy beach, **LAGUNA BEACH** grew up late in the nineteenth century as a community of artists, drawn by the beauty of the location. You need a few million dollars to live here nowadays, but there's a relaxed and tolerant feel among the inhabitants, who span everything from rich industrialists to left-overs from the 1960s when Laguna became a hippy haven – even Timothy Leary was known to hang out at the *Taco Bell* on PCH. The scenery is still the great attraction, and despite the massive growth in population Laguna remains relatively unspoilt, with a still flourishing minor arts scene manifest in the many craftshops and galleries crammed into the narrow streets.

PCH passes right through the centre of Laguna, a few steps from the small main **beach**. From the beach's north side, an elevated wooden walkway twists around the coastline above a conserved **ecological area**, enabling you to peer down on the ocean and, when the tide's out, scamper over the rocks to observe the tide-pool activity. From the end of the walkway, make your way through the legions of posh beachside homes (which often make beach access difficult) and head down the hill back to the centre. You'll pass the **Laguna Beach Museum of Art** (summer Tues–Sun 11am–5pm, $4), which has changing exhibitions from its stock of Southern Californian art from the 1900s to the present day. A few miles along is less-touristed **SOUTH LAGUNA**, where the wonderfully secluded Victoria and Aliso beaches are among several below the bluffs.

## Dana Point

From Laguna it's often possible to see **Dana Point**, a fat promontory jutting into the ocean about four miles south. It was named after sailor and author Richard Henry Dana Jr, whose *Two Years Before the Mast* – a novel of life on the high seas in the early days of California – described how cattle hides were flung over these cliffs to trading ships waiting below. He ended his voyaging career here in 1830, and there's a statue of him and a replica of his vessel, *The Pilgrim*, at the edge of the harbour – part of what's now a town spread over the entire headland. Both are fairly unremarkable, however, as indeed is the place as a whole, although you'll need to pass by on your way to San Juan Capistrano.

# San Juan Capistrano and San Clemente

Three miles inland from Dana Point along the I-5 freeway, most of the small town of **SAN JUAN CAPISTRANO** is built in a Spanish Colonial style derived from the **Mission San Juan Capistrano** on Camino Capistrano in the centre of town (daily 8.30am–5pm; $4), a short walk from the *Amtrak* stop. The seventh in California's chain of missions, this was founded by Junipero Serra in 1776; and within three years was so well populated that it outgrew the original chapel. Soon after, the **Stone Church** was erected, the ruins of which are the first thing you see as you walk in. The enormous structure had seven domes and a bell tower but was destroyed by an earthquake soon after its completion in 1812. For an idea of how it might have looked, visit the full-sized reconstruction – now a working church – just northwest of the mission.

The rest of the mission is in an above-average state of repair, due to an ongoing restoration programme. The **chapel** has most atmosphere: small and narrow, deco-rated with Indian drawings and Spanish artefacts from its earliest days, and set off by a sixteenth-century altar from Barcelona. In a side room is the chapel of St Peregrin; during the 1970s, a woman suffering from cancer prayed for six months to the saint asking to be cured, and afterwards her doctor declared that the cancer had indeed disappeared. Now the tiny room is kept warm by the heat from the dozens of candles lit by hopeful cancer sufferers who arrive here from all over the US and Mexico.

The other restored buildings reflect the mission's practical role during the Indian period: the kitchen, the smelter, and the workshops used for dyeing, weaving and candle-making. There's also a rather predictable **museum**, which gives a broad histori-cal outline of the Spanish progress through California and displays odds and ends from the mission's past.

The mission is also noted for its **swallows**, popularly thought to return here from their winter migration on March 19. They sometimes do arrive on this day – along with large numbers of tourists – but the birds are much more likely to show up as soon as the weather is warm enough, and when there are enough insects on the ground to provide a decent homecoming banquet.

### San Clemente

Five miles south of San Juan Capistrano down I-5, the town of **SAN CLEMENTE** is a pretty little place, its streets contoured around the hills, lending an almost Mediterranean air. Because of its proximity to one of the largest military bases in the state, **Camp Pendleton**, it's a popular weekend retreat for military personnnel. It's also predominantly a retirement town which had a brief moment of fame during the 1970s, when President Nixon convened his Western White House here. The 25-acre estate and house are visible from the beach, which is clean and virtually deserted, and there's a decent campground (see p.73), but otherwise there's very little here to detain you.

# The San Gabriel and San Fernando Valleys

The northern limit of LA is defined by two long, wide valleys lying beyond the hills from the central basin, starting close to one another a few miles north of downtown and spanning outwards in opposite directions – east to the deserts around Palm Springs, west to Ventura on the Central Coast.

The **San Gabriel Valley** was settled by farmers and cattle ranchers who set up small towns on the lands of the eighteenth-century Mission San Gabriel. The foothill communities grew into prime resort towns, luring many here around the turn of the century. **Pasadena**, the largest of the foothill communities, holds many elegant period houses, as well as the brilliant but underpublicized **Norton Simon Museum**, and has lately become an out-of-town focus for celebrity-owned restaurants, moviegoers and lowrider-cruising teenagers. Above Pasadena, the slopes of the San Gabriel Mountains are littered with explorable remains from the resort days, and make great spots for hiking and rough camping, although you'll nearly always need a car to get to the trail-heads. The areas around Pasadena are generally less absorbing, although, to the south, WASP-ish **San Marino** is dominated by the **Huntington Library**, a stash of art and literature ringed by botanical gardens that itself makes the journey into the valley worthwhile.

The **San Fernando Valley**, spreading west, is *the* valley to most Angelenos: a sprawl of tract homes, mini-malls, fast-food drive-ins and auto-parts stores. It has more of a middle-American feel than anywhere else in LA, inhabited – at least, in the popular LA imagination – by macho men and bimbo-esque "Valley Girls", who even have their own dialect. There are a few isolated sights, notably **Forest Lawn Cemetery** – an over-the-top statement in graveyard architecture that's hard to imagine anywhere except in LA – but otherwise, beyond a couple of minor historical sites, it's the **movies** that bring people out here. Rising land values in the 1930s pushed many studios out of Hollywood and over the hills to **Burbank**, an anodyne community now overpowered by several major film and TV companies, whose behind-the-scenes tours are the only chance in LA to see the basics of film-making.

At the far west end, the ultra-conservative suburb of **Simi Valley** is known for two things: finding five police officers "not guilty" of beating Rodney King in April 1992 (see

## EARTHQUAKE CITY: THE SAN FERNANDO VALLEY

The devastating 6.8 magnitude earthquake that shook LA on the morning of January 17, 1994 was one of the most destructive disasters in US history. Fifty-five people were killed, two hundred more suffered critical injuries, and the economic cost has been estimated at some $8 billion (by way of comparison, the construction of the Channel Tunnel between Britain and France cost around $4 billion). One can only guess how much higher these totals would have been had the quake hit during the day, when the many collapsed stores would have been crowded with shoppers and the roads and freeways full of commuters.

As it is, the tremor toppled chimneys and shattered windows all over Southern California, with the worst damage concentrated at the epicentre in the San Fernando Valley, where a dozen people were killed when a Northridge apartment building imploded. At the northern edge of the valley, the vital I-5/Hwy-14 interchange was destroyed, killing just one motorist but snarling traffic for at least a year, while in West LA, the Santa Monica Freeway overpass collapsed onto La Cienega Boulevard at one of LA's busiest intersections.

The northern San Fernando Valley was also the epicentre of LA's previous worst earthquake, the 6.5 magnitude tremor of February 9, 1971 – also in the early morning hours – which caused a similar toll of death and destruction.

Small earthquakes happen all the time in LA, usually doing no more than rattling supermarket shelves and making dogs howl. In theory, all the city's new buildings are "quake-safe", and, in the light of a 5.8 Richter-Scale earthquake on October 1, 1987 that killed only one person, seemed to be paying off. The extent of the crisis in January 1994, however, has given the city the chance to rebuild on a scale not previously imagined: quite to what extent the dreams of the architects, the local newspapers and the citizens themselves will be realized remains to be seen.

If a sizeable earthquake strikes when you're in LA, try to protect yourself under something sturdy, such as a heavy table or a door frame, and well away from windows or anything made of glass. Afterwards, don't use telephones or electricity unless you have to, as this may overload the systems. It's little comfort, for visitors or residents, to know that the widely feared "Big One", a quake above 7.5 on the Richter Scale, is due to hit sometime in the next thirty years.

p.86), and providing a home for the **Ronald Reagan Presidential Library** (Mon-Sat 10am-5pm, Sun noon-5pm; $4), a federal library containing all the papers pertaining to the Reagan administration.

# Pasadena

Marking the entrance to the San Gabriel Valley, **PASADENA** is as much the home of the *grandes dames* of Los Angeles society as it is to the "little old lady from Pasadena" of the Jan and Dean song. In the 1880s, wealthy East Coast tourists who came to California looking for the good life found it in this foothill resort ten miles north of Los Angeles, where luxury hotels were built and railways cut into the nearby San Gabriel mountains to lead up to taverns and astronomical observatories on the mile-high crest. Many of the early, well-to-do visitors stayed on, building the rustically sprawling houses that remain, but as LA grew so Pasadena suffered, mainly from the smog which the mountains collect. The downtown area underwent a major renovation in the 1980s, with modern shopping centres being slipped in behind Edward Hopperish 1920s facades, but the historic parts of town have not been forgotten. Maps and booklets detailing self-guided tours of Pasadena architecture and history are available from the **Pasadena CVB** at 171 S Los Robles Ave (Mon–Fri 9am–5pm, Sat 10am–4pm; ☎818/795-9311). If you're around at the right time, watch out also for the New Year's Day **Tournament of Roses**, which began in 1890 to celebrate and publicize the mild

Southern California winters, and now attracts over a million visitors every year to watch its marching bands and elaborate flower-emblazoned floats (see box on p.148).

A block north of Colorado Boulevard, a replica Chinese Imperial Palace houses the **Pacific Asia Museum** at 46 N Los Robles Ave (Wed–Sun 10–5pm; $3), which has a wide range of objects from Japan, China and Thailand – though if you have even the slightest interest in the art of South East Asia, your time would be better spent at the collection of the Norton Simon Museum, quarter of a mile away on the other side of downtown.

## The Norton Simon Museum

You may not have heard of the **Norton Simon Museum**, but its collections, housed in a modern building at 411 W Colorado Blvd (Thurs–Sun noon–6pm; $4), are in many ways broader in range and more consistently excellent than either the County or Getty museums. Established and overseen by the eponymous industrialist until his death in 1993, the museum (perhaps because of its unfashionable location) sidesteps the hype of the LA art world to concentrate on the quality of its presentation. You could easily spend a whole afternoon – or two – wandering through the spacious galleries.

The core of the collection is Western European painting from the Renaissance to the modern period. It's a massive collection, much of it rotated, but most of the major pieces are on view constantly. You'll see Dutch paintings of the seventeenth century – notably Rembrandt's vivacious *Titus, Portrait of a Boy* and Frans Hals' quietly aggressive *Portrait of a Man* – and Italian Renaissance work from Pietro Longhi and Guido Reni. Among more modern works, there's a good sprinkling of French Impressionists and post-Impressionists: Monet's *Mouth of the Seine at Honfleur*, Manet's *Ragpicker* and a Degas capturing the extended yawn of a washerwoman in *The Ironers*, plus works by Cézanne, Gauguin, and Van Gogh. Perhaps the most extraordinary painting in the entire collection is Picasso's *Woman with Book*, finished in 1932.

As a counterpoint to the Western art, the museum has a fine collection of **Asian sculpture**, including a very sexy twelfth-century *Loving Couple* that leaves nothing to the imagination, and many highly polished Buddhist and Hindu figures, a mix of the contemplative and the erotic, some inlaid with precious stones.

## The Gamble House

Behind the museum, across the freeway, Orange Grove Avenue leads into a hillside neighbourhood containing some of Pasadena's finest houses. The **Pasadena Historical Society** on Walnut and Orange Grove (Thurs–Sun 1–4pm; $4) occupies one of them, decorated with its original 1905 furnishings and paintings, and with displays on Pasadena's history. The building later became the Finnish Consulate, and much of the folk art on display comes from Pasadena's "twin town" of Jarvenpää in Finland.

But it's the **Gamble House**, 4 Westmoreland Place (hour-long tours Thurs–Sun noon–3pm; $4), which brings people out here. Built in 1908, and one of the masterpieces of (and greatest influence on) Southern Californian vernacular architecture, it's a style you'll see replicated all over the state, at once relaxed and refined, freely combining elements from Swiss chalets and Japanese temples in a romantic, sprawling shingled house. Broad eaves shelter outdoor sleeping porches, which in turn shade terraces on the ground floor, leading out to the spacious lawn. The interior was crafted with the same attention to detail, and all the carpets, cabinetry and lighting fixtures, designed specifically for the house, remain in excellent condition.

The area around the Gamble House is filled with at least eight other less lavish **houses** by the two brothers (the firm of "Greene & Greene") who designed it, including Charles Greene's own house at 368 Arroyo Terrace, which leads down into the Arroyo Seco via Holly Street. A quarter of a mile north of the Gamble House is a small, concrete block house by Frank Lloyd Wright, *La Miniatura*, which you can glimpse through the gate opposite 585 Rosemont Ave. All of these houses are private.

## Into the foothills

Below the Gamble House, the western edge of Pasadena is defined by the Arroyo Seco canyon. Arroyo Boulevard winds along here, under the slim and soaring **Colorado Boulevard Bridge**, a spot favoured by stunt flyers in the barnstorming 1920s. It continues up through Brookside Park to pass the 104,000-seat **Rose Bowl** (Mon–Fri 9am–4pm; $2), site of the 1994 World Cup Soccer Final; as well as a huge and very popular **flea market** on the second Sunday of each month. On the other side of the Foothill Freeway, **Descanso Gardens** (daily 9am–4.30pm; $5), in the La Canada district, concentrates all the plants you might see in the mountains into 155 acres of landscaped park. The gardens are especially brilliant during the spring, when all the wild flowers are in bloom.

From La Canada, the **Angeles Crest Highway** (Hwy-2) heads up into the mountains above Pasadena. This area was once dotted with resort hotels and wilderness camps, and today you can hike up any number of nearby canyons and come across the ruins of old lodges that either burned down or were washed away towards the end of the hiking era in the 1930s, when automobiles became popular. One of the most interesting of these trails, a five-mile round trip, follows the route of the Mount Lowe Railway, once one of LA's biggest tourist attractions, from the top of Lake Avenue up to the old railway and the foundations of **"White City"** – formerly a mountaintop resort of two hotels, a zoo and an observatory. Today a brass plaque embedded in concrete is the only reminder of the resort, and even this is slowly becoming overgrown with pine trees and incense cedars. The Crest Highway passes through the **Angeles National Forest**, where you can hike and camp most of the year and ski in winter to Mount Wilson, high enough to be the major siting spot for TV broadcast antennae, and with a small **museum** (daily 10am–3pm; $1) beside the 100-inch telescope of the 1904 Mount Wilson Observatory. Although on a clear day there are views out over the entire Los Angeles area, it's hard to believe you are only a few hours' drive from some of the most over-developed "attractions" in the world.

# The Huntington Library

South of Pasadena, **SAN MARINO** is a dull, upper-crust little suburb with few redeeming features beyond the **Huntington Library, Art Collections and Botanical Gardens**, off Huntington Drive at 1151 Oxford Rd (Tues–Fri 1–4.30pm, Sat–Sun 10am–4.30pm; suggested donation $7.50). Part of this is made up of the collections of Henry Edwards Huntington, the nephew of the childless multimillionaire Collis P Huntington, who owned and operated the Southern Pacific Railroad – which in the nineteenth century had a virtual monopoly on transportation in California. Henry, groomed to take over the company from his uncle, was dethroned by the board of directors and took his sizeable inheritance to Los Angeles, where he bought up the existing streetcar routes and combined them as the *Pacific Electric Railway Company*. It was a shrewd investment: the company's "Redcars" soon became the largest network in the world, and Huntington the largest landowner in the state, buying up farmlands and extending the streetcar system at a huge profit. He retired in 1910, moving to the manor house he had built in then-genteel San Marino, devoting himself full-time to buying rare books and manuscripts, and – in an ironic twist of fate – marrying his uncle's widow Arabella and acquiring her collection of English portraits.

You can pick up a self-guided walking tour of each of the three main sections from the bookstore and information desk in the covered pavilion. The **Library**, right off the main entrance, is a good first stop, its two-storey exhibition hall containing numerous manuscripts and rare books, among them a Gutenberg Bible, a folio edition of Shakespeare's plays, and – the highlight – the **Ellesmere Chaucer**, a c.1410 illuminated manuscript of *The Canterbury Tales*. Displays around the walls trace the history of printing and of the English language from medieval manuscripts to a King James Bible, through Milton's *Paradise Lost* and Blake's *Songs of Innocence and Experience*, to first editions of Swift, Coleridge, Dickens, Woolf and Joyce.

To decorate the **main house**, a grand mansion done out in Louis XIV carpets and later French tapestries, the Huntingtons travelled to England and returned laden with the finest art money could buy. Most of it still hangs on the walls. Unless you're a real fan of eighteenth-century English portraiture, head through to the back extension, added when the gallery opened in 1934, which displays, as well as works by Turner, van Dyck and Constable, the stars of the whole collection: Gainsborough's *Blue Boy* and Reynolds' *Mrs Siddons as the Tragic Muse*.

You'll find paintings by Edward Hopper and Mary Cassatt, and a range of Wild West drawings and sculpture, in the **Scott Gallery for American Art**. For all the art and literature, though, it's the grounds that make the Huntington really special, and the acres of beautiful themed **gardens** surrounding the buildings include a Zen Rock Garden, complete with authentically constructed Buddhist Temple and Tea House. The Desert Garden has the world's largest collection of desert plants, including twelve acres of cacti in an artful setting – a distillation of the natural landscape of Los Angeles. While strolling through these botanical splendours, you might also call in on the Huntingtons themselves, buried in a neo-Palladian mausoleum at the northwest corner of the estate, beyond the rows of an orange grove.

## East of Pasadena: Arcadia and Sierra Madre

Foothill Boulevard, parallel to the Foothill Freeway (I-210), is better known as part of the one and only **Route 66**, formerly the main route across the US, "from Chicago to LA, more than three thousand miles all the way". The freeway stole Route 66's traffic, and following Foothill Boulevard out of Pasadena nowadays leads to the adjacent town of **ARCADIA**, whose **State and County Arboretum** on Baldwin Avenue (daily 9am–5pm; $5) has forests of trees arranged according to their native continent. The site was once the 127-acre ranch home of "Lucky" Baldwin, who made his millions in the silver mines of the Comstock in the 1870s. He settled here in 1875, and built a fanciful white palace along a palm-treed lagoon, later used in the TV show *Fantasy Island*, on the site of the 1839 Rancho Santa Anita. He also bred horses, and raced them on a neighbouring track that has since grown into the **Santa Anita Racetrack** (racing Oct to early Nov, & late Dec to late April, Wed–Sun post time 12.30pm or 1pm; $3–$8), still the most beautiful and glamorous racetrack in California.

The district of **SIERRA MADRE**, on the northern edge of town, lies directly beneath Mount Wilson and is worth a visit if you're a hiker. A seven-mile round-trip trail up to the summit has recently been restored and is now one of the best hikes in the range. The trailhead is 150 yards up the private Mount Wilson Road.

South of Sierra Madre stands the valley's original settlement, the church and grounds of **Mission San Gabriel Arcangel** (daily 9am–4.30pm; $3). Still standing at the corner of Mission and Serra in the heart of the small town of **San Gabriel**, the mission was established here in 1771 by Junipero Serra. Though still partially covered in scaffolding following decades of damage by earthquakes and the elements, the church and grounds have recently been reopened, its grapevine-filled gardens giving some sense of mission-era life.

## Glendale and Forest Lawn Cemetery

**GLENDALE**, eight miles north of downtown and the gateway to the San Fernando Valley, was once a fashionable suburb of LA. Now it's a nondescript dormitory community hovering between the Valley and LA proper, and the only reason to come here is to visit the Glendale branch of **Forest Lawn Cemetery** at 1712 S Glendale Ave (daily 9am–5pm; free) – immortalized with biting satire by Evelyn Waugh in *The Loved One*, and at the vanguard of the American way of death for decades. Founded in 1917 by a Doctor Hubert Eaton, this fast became *the* place to be seen dead, its pompous landscaping and oversized artworks attracting celebrities by the dozen to buy their own little piece of heaven.

It's best to climb the hill and see the cemetery in reverse from the **Forest Lawn Museum**, whose hotchpotch of old artefacts from around the world includes coins from ancient Rome, Viking oddments, medieval armour, and a mysterious sculpted Easter Island figure, discovered being used as ballast in a fishing boat in the days when the statues could still be removed from the island. How it ended up here is another mystery, but it is the only one on view in the US. Next door to the museum, the grandiose **Resurrection and Crucifixion Hall** houses the largest piece of religious art in the world, *The Crucifixion* by Jan Styka – though you're only allowed to see it during the ceremonial unveiling every hour on the hour (and you'll be charged $1 for an eyeful). Besides this, Eaton owned a stained glass re-creation of da Vinci's *Last Supper* and, realizing that he only needed one piece to complete his set of "the three greatest moments in the life of Christ", he commissioned American artist Robert Clark to produce *The Resurrection* – an effort which is also only viewable when unveiled, though this happens on the half-hour. If you can't be bothered to stick around for the showings (with both, in any case, the size is the only aspect that's particularly impressive), you can get a good idea of what you're missing from the scaled-down replicas just inside the entrance.

From the museum, walk down through the terrace gardens – loaded with sculptures modelled on the greats of classical European art – to the **Freedom Mausoleum**, where you'll find a handful of the cemetery's better-known graves. Just outside the mausoleum's doors, Errol Flynn lies in an unspectacular plot (unmarked until 1979), rumoured to have been buried with six bottles of whisky at his side, while a few strides away is the grave of Walt Disney. Inside the mausoleum itself you'll find Clara Bow, Nat King Cole, Jeanette MacDonald and Alan Ladd handily placed close to each other on the first floor. Downstairs are Chico Marx, and his brother Gummo – originally an active member of the comedy team, who later spurned the limelight to become the Marx Brothers' agent and business manager. To the left, heading back down the hill, the **Great Mausoleum** is chiefly noted for the tombs of Clark Gable (next to Carole Lombard, who died in a plane crash just three years after marrying him), and Jean Harlow, in a marble-lined room which cost over $25,000, paid for by fiancé William Powell.

A number of **other Forest Lawn cemeteries** continue the style of the Glendale site, to a much less spectacular degree. There's a Hollywood Hills branch in Burbank (6300 Forest Hills Drive, close to Griffith Park) which has a formidable roll call of ex-stars – Buster Keaton, Stan Laurel, Liberace, Charles Laughton and Marvin Gaye – but little else to warrant a visit. The others, even less interesting, are at Covina Hills, Cypress Beach and Long Beach.

## Burbank and the studios

Although Hollywood is the name that's synonymous with the movie industry, in reality many of the studios – if they were ever there at all – moved out of Tinseltown long ago, and much of the nitty-gritty business of actually making films goes on over the hills in otherwise boring **BURBANK**, the perennial butt of smart LA jokes. Hot, smoggy and in some places downright ugly, Burbank nonetheless has a media district bustling with production activity, thanks to the explosion in demand from overseas markets, cable TV and broadcast networks. Disney recently constructed a gleaming new building to house over seven hundred animators, and Warner Brothers is planning an $800 million expansion to its premises over the next twenty years.

Near the junction of the Ventura and Hollywood freeways are a number of **film and television studios** offering "insider" tours. **NBC**, at 3000 W Alameda St (Mon–Fri 9am–3pm; $6; ☎818/840-3537), runs a frank and interesting ninety-minute tour of the largest production facility in the US, with the chance to be in the audience for the taping of a programme (phone ahead for free tickets). It's worth the price of admission just to see *Tonight Show* host and the West Coast answer to David Letterman, Jay Leno, in action.

The **Warner Bros Studios**, 4000 Warner Blvd at Hollywood Way (Mon–Fri 9am–4pm; $27; ☎818/954-1744), lays on an instructive, fairly technical behind-the-scenes look (called the "VIP tour") at how a movie is made, touring the backlot stage sets and passing an actual shoot whenever possible. Try to reserve a place a month in advance if possible – tours are limited to thirty people a day – and note that children under ten are not allowed.

The largest of the old backlots belongs to **Universal Studios**, whose tours (summer daily 8am–10pm; rest of year daily 9am–7pm; $33; ☎818/508-9600) are firmly tourist-oriented, four hours long and, with its high-tech interactive rides, more like a trip around an amusement park than a film studio. The first half consists of a narrated streetcar ride through a make-believe set where you can experience the fading magic of the parting of the Red Sea and a collapsing bridge; the second takes place inside the corny Entertainment Center, where unemployed actors and stuntmen engage in convincing Wild West shoot-outs and stunt shows based on the latest film releases. You never actually get to see any filming.

The **Universal Amphitheater**, which hosts pop concerts in summer, is also part of the complex, as is a twenty-screen movie theatre complex, with a lobby reminiscent of 1920s movie palaces; there's also the *Victoria Station* restaurant, which has the old departures board from London's Victoria Station hanging above the bar. **Universal CityWalk**, also on the same huge lot, is a few square blocks of neon-lit themed restaurants, free to all who pay the $5 parking (redeemable at the cinemas), where rock bands churn out MOR covers, street perfomers caper through slick set pieces, and giant TV screens run ads for the latest *Universal* release. After Thanksgiving each year, an open-air ice-rink adds to the merriment.

## Mission San Fernando and Magic Mountain

At the north end of the Valley the San Diego, Golden State and Foothill freeways join together at I-5, the quickest route north to San Francisco. Standing near the junction at 15151 San Fernando Mission Blvd, the church and many of the buildings of **Mission San Fernando Rey De España** (Mon, Thurs & Fri 1pm–3pm; $4) had to be completely rebuilt following the 1971 earthquake. It's hard to imagine now, walking

---

### THE LA AQUEDUCT

Just beyond the Mission San Fernando, I-5 runs past two of LA's main reservoirs, the water in which has been brought hundreds of miles through the **California Aqueduct** from the Sacramento Delta, and through the **LA Aqueduct** from the Owens Valley and Mono Lake on the eastern slopes of the Sierra Nevada mountains.

However, with all due respect to the engineering expertise involved, the legality of the arrangements by which the City of Los Angeles gained control of such a distant supply of water is still disputed. Agents of the city, masquerading as rich cattle-barons interested in establishing ranches in the Owens Valley, bought up most of the land along the Owens River before selling it on, at personal profit, to the City of Los Angeles. These sharp practices provided the inspiration for Roman Polanski's 1974 movie *Chinatown*.

For more on Mono Lake and the Owens Valley, see p.257 and p.266.

through the nicely landscaped courtyards and gardens, but eighty-odd years ago, the then-dilapidated mission was used as a backdrop for several films made by Hollywood pioneer D W Griffith, not least *Our Silent Paths*, his tale of the Gold Rush.

Another twenty miles north, past the cascading spillway of the LA Aqueduct, Hwy-14 splits off east across the Mojave desert, while I-5 continues north past Valencia and **Magic Mountain** (park opens summer daily 10am–10pm; rest of year Sat–Sun only 10am–8pm; $29, $5 parking), a three-hundred-acre complex that has some of the fastest and wildest roller coasters and rides in the world – a hundred times more thrilling than anything at Disneyland.

## Los Encinos State Historic Park and northwards

At the western end of the San Fernando Valley, the Ventura Freeway (US-101) passes below the increasingly expensive hillside homes of **Sherman Oaks** and **Encino**, close to which the **Los Encinos State Historic Park**, on Balboa Boulevard (Wed–Sun 10am–5pm, tours 1–4pm; grounds free, tours $2), is all that remains of the original Native American settlement and later Mexican hacienda that were here. The high-ceilinged rooms of the 1849 adobe house open out onto porches, shaded by oak trees (in Spanish, "encinos") and kept cool by the two-foot-thick walls.

West of Encino, Topanga Canyon Boulevard crosses the Ventura Freeway, leading south towards Malibu (p.113) or north to **Stony Point**, a bizarre outcrop of sandstone that has been used for countless budget Western shoot-outs, and in recent years as a popular venue for LA's contingent of lycra-clad rock climbers. The area, though crossed by both *Amtrak* and *Metrorail* coastal trains, certainly has a desolate spookiness about it, and it comes as little surprise to learn that during the late 1960s the Charles Manson "family" lived for a time at the **Spahn Ranch**, just west at 12000 Santa Susana Pass.

# Eating

LA's **restaurants** cover every extreme: whatever you want to eat and however much you want to spend, you're spoilt for choice. **Budget food** is as plentiful as in any other US city, ranging from good sit-down meals in street-corner coffee shops and cafés to big franchise burgers. Almost as common, and just as cheap, is **Mexican food**. This is the closest thing you'll get to an indigenous LA cuisine – most notably in the *burrito*, a filled tortilla that's rarely seen in Mexico and is available everywhere, both from street vendors and comfortable restaurants. If you simply want to load up quickly and cheaply, the options are almost endless, and include free food available for the price of a drink at **happy hours**.

However, you should also try to take at least a few meals in LA's **top-notch restaurants**, which serve superb food in consciously cultured surroundings – if only to watch the city's many self-appointed food snobs going through their paces. There are scores

---

**LA RESTAURANTS**

Budget: diners & delis p.135
Californian/American/Cajun p.139
Chinese/Japanese/Thai/Korean p.142
Indian/Sri Lankan/Middle Eastern/
   Ethiopian p.143

Italian/Spanish/Greek /Pizza p.140
Mexican/Latin American p.138
24-hour eats p.138
Vegetarian/Wholefood p.144

of restaurants that whack up their prices on the back of a good review, and get away with it because they know the place will be packed with first-timers trying to impress their cohorts by claiming that they've been eating there for years.

Catering appears to be the movie stars' sideline of choice these days, and LA is littered with **celebrity-owned** outfits – like Steven Spielberg's submarine-shaped sandwich store and the brand-new *Planet Hollywood* in Beverly Hills (where displays include Forrest Gump's box of chocolates) – but the food is usually so unremarkable we haven't listed them.

## Budget food: coffee shops, delis, diners and drive-ins

Budget food is everywhere in LA, at its best in the many small and stylish **coffee shops**, **delis** and **diners** that serve wholesome soups, omelettes, sandwiches and so forth; it's easy to exist entirely this way and never have to spend much more than $6 for a full meal.

There are of course the internationally franchised fast-food places on every street – *McDonald's, Burger King* et al – and locally based chains of **hamburger stands**, most open 24 hours a day; *Fatburger*, originally at San Vicente and La Cienega on the border of Beverly Hills has branches everywhere.

Sadly, but surely, the best of the 1950s **drive-ins**, such as *Tiny Naylors* in Hollywood, last seen in Wim Wenders' LA saga *The State of Things*, have been torn down to make room for mini-malls, although *In-n-Out Burgers* drive-ins are all over the San Gabriel and San Fernando Valleys.

### Downtown and around

**Clifton's Cafeteria**, 648 S Broadway (☎213/485-1726). Classic 1930s cafeteria complete with redwood trees, waterfall and mini-chapel; the food is traditional meat-and-potatoes American, and cheap too (macaroni and cheese for about $1).

**Grand Central Market**, 317 S Broadway (☎213/624-2378). Choose from dozens of market stalls selling $1.50 tacos, deli sandwiches and cheap Chinese food – and 24 fresh fruit and vegetable drinks from *Geraldine's* at the Hill Street entrance.

**Langer's Deli**, 704 S Alvarado St (☎213/483-8050). "When in doubt, eat hot pastrami" says the sign, though you still have to choose from over twenty ways of having it, and a huge deli selection. Half a block south of the MacArthur Park *Metrorail* station.

**Lindsey's**, 112 W Ninth St (☎213/624-6684). Lively and comfortable café that's a cut above the usual coffee shop standard, serving large, crisp salads, thick burgers and delicious pastries.

**Pantry**, 877 S Figueroa St (☎213/972-9279). There's always a queue for the hearty portions of very meaty American cooking – chops and steaks, mostly – in this 24-hr diner owned by Mayor Riordan.

**Philippe's Famous French Dip Sandwiches**, 1001 N Alameda St (☎213/628-3781). Spit-and-sawdust café, a block north of Union Station. Long communal tables and a decor unchanged since 1908.

**Shabbzz Restaurant and Bakery**, 3405 W 43rd St, Leimert Park, South Central (☎213/299-8688). Jazz greats waft out of the speakers, Malcolm X and Muhammed Ali grace the walls, and chilli ($2) and bean pie ($1.50) are among the delights on the menu.

**The Yorkshire Grill**, 610 W Sixth St (☎213/629-3020). Big sandwiches and friendly service for under $10. Popularity with the 9–5 crowd means a wait for a table between noon and 2pm.

### Hollywood

**Alex Donut**, 6211 Franklin Ave (☎213/464-6148). The classic American doughnuts served here are a real sugar rush. Try the foot-long cinanamon twist if you are up to it.

**Hampton's**, 1342 N Highland Ave (☎213/469-1090). Gourmet hamburgers with a choice of over fifty toppings, plus an excellent salad bar.

**Johnny Rockets**, 7507 Melrose Ave (☎213/651-3361). Chrome-and-glass, Fifties-derived hamburger joint, open until 2am at weekends.

**Maurice's Snack 'n' Chat**, 5549 W Pico Blvd (☎213/931-3877). Everything here is cooked to order: spoon bread or baked chicken requires a call two hours ahead, though you can just call in for fried chicken, pork chops, grits or salmon croquettes. Autographed pictures of celebrity diners – from Sammy Davis Jnr to Ted Kennedy – line the walls.

**Pinks Hot Dog Stand**, 711 N La Brea Ave (☎213/931-4223). Cheap, enormous and famous chilli-dogs and hot Polish sausages that put the "Dodger Dogs" served at the Dodgers baseball stadium to shame.

**Village Coffee Shop**, 2695 Beachwood Drive (☎213/467-5398). A classic laid-back coffee shop in the hills below the Hollywood sign, with a pleasant, out-of-town ambience.

**Yukon Mining Co**, 7328 Santa Monica Blvd (☎213/851-8833). Excellent 24-hr coffee shop that bears not a hint of schizophrenia, though it caters both to the local gay community and old-timers from the neighbouring senior citizens' home.

## West LA

**The Apple Pan**, 10801 W Pico Blvd (☎ 310/475-3585). Grab a spot at the counter and enjoy freshly baked apple pie and the best hamburgers in the world. Fans of *Beverly Hills 90210* take note, the *Peach Pit* was shamelessly copied from this landmark restaurant.

**Barney's Beanery**, 8447 Santa Monica Blvd (☎213/654-2287). Infinite variety of hot dogs, hamburgers and bowls of chili, and over 200 bottled beers, amid dimly lit pool tables.

**Canter's Deli**, 419 N Fairfax Ave (☎213/651-2030). Huge sandwiches for around $7, excellent kosher soups served round-the-clock by waitresses in pink uniforms and running shoes.

**Cassell's Hamburgers**, 3266 W Sixth St (☎213/387-5502). No-frills, lunch-only takeout hamburger stand that some swear by.

**Duke's**, 8909 Sunset Blvd (☎310/652-9411). A favourite haunt of rock stars staying at the *Tropicana*, this place attracts a motley crew of night owls. Open until 4am at the weekend.

**Ed Debevic's**, 134 N La Cienega Blvd (☎310/659-1952). Fifties-style diner with singing waitresses and pricey beer.

**Hard Rock Café**, in the *Beverly Center*, Beverly Blvd at San Vicente (☎310/276-7605). Long waits and loud music but the food's not half-bad.

**Johnny's**, next to *May's* department store on Fairfax and Wilshire (☎213/938-3521). Tasteless food and a drafty atmosphere but this landmark café has been home to many a film shoot, including *Reservoir Dogs*, allegedly.

**John O'Groats**, 10516 W Pico Blvd (☎310/204-0692). Excellent cheap breakfasts and lunches, though not a place to come if you're in a hurry.

**Kate Mantillini**, 9109 Wilshire Blvd (☎310/278-3699). Well-prepared versions of classic American diner food, served up in one of LA's most stylish interiors. Open late on weekends.

**Nate'n'Al's**, 414 N Beverly Drive (☎310/274-0101). The best-known deli in Beverly Hills, popular with movie people.

**Ships**, corner of La Cienega and Olympic Blvd (☎310/652-0401). The best food of any coffee shop in LA; try the *Ship Shape* hamburger, on sourdough bread, with a chocolate shake. Open 24hr.

**Tail o' the Pup**, 329 N San Vicente Blvd (☎310/652-4517). Worth a visit for the roadside pop architecture alone, though the dogs and burgers are good too.

**Swingers**, *Beverly Laurel Motor Lodge*, 8018 Beverly Blvd at Laurel (☎213/651-2441). Warhol-inspired wallpaper, Beastie Boys on the jukebox, and filling sandwiches for under $10, all enjoyed by LA's suntan grunge contingent.

**Ziggy G's**, 8730 Sunset Blvd (☎310/659-1225). Great pastrami sandwiches, lox, chicken soup and egg cream in a NYC-style deli with a bar open 24hr.

## Santa Monica, Venice and Malibu

**Bicycle Shop Café**, 12217 Wilshire Blvd, Santa Monica (☎310/826-7831). Pseudo-bistro serving light meals and salads that's also a good place to drink.

**Café 50s**, 838 Lincoln Blvd, Venice (☎310/399-1955). No doubts about this place: Ritchie Valens on the jukebox, burgers on the tables.

**Café Montana**, 1610 Montana Ave, Santa Monica (☎310/829-3990). Good breakfasts and excellent salads and grilled fish in this art-gallery-cum-café on the newest strip of upmarket Santa Monica.

**Gilliland's**, 2424 Main St, Santa Monica (☎310/392-3901). Highly eclectic menu of good and hearty foods, from tangy samosas to a thick Irish stew.

**Rae's Diner**, 2901 Pico Blvd, Santa Monica (☎310/828-7937). Classic 1950s diner behind a turquoise-blue facade, open 6am–10pm. Don't miss the fresh biscuits and gravy breakfasts.

**Reel Inn**, 18661 PCH, Malibu (☎310/456-8221). Low-key seafood diner by the beach, with appealing prices and a good atmosphere. Also at 1220 W Third St, Santa Monica (☎310/395-5538).

**The Sidewalk Café**, Venice Boardwalk, Venice (☎310/399-5547). Breakfast on the beach, and watch the daily parade of beach people. Live music most evenings.

## The South Bay and Harbor Area

**Café 50s**, 140 Pier Ave, Hermosa Beach (☎310/374-1955). Juicy hamburgers and bulging sandwiches in a Fifties Americana setting. Slightly pricey but fun.

**East Coast Bagel Company**, 5753 E PCH, Long Beach (☎310/985-0933) Excellent wide selection of bagels, ranging from New York staples to California hybrids like the jalapeno-cheddar bagel stuffed with cream cheese.

**Hofburger at Hof's Hut**, 4823 E Second St, Long Beach (☎310/439-4775). Cutesy "California Dreamin' " architecture, but one bite of a juicy Hofburger and you know you've found the real deal.

**Johnnie's Broiler**, 7447 Firestone Blvd, Downey (☎310/927-3383). The real McCoy complete with Jell-O, fries, coffee and cigarette smoke. On Wed nights, Fifties-car fanatics park outside in their Chevys and Fords and are waited upon by perky, roller-skating teens.

**Ocean View Café**, 229 13th St, Manhattan Beach, (☎310/545-6770). Light breakfasts and soup and baguettes for around $4.

**The Local Yolk**, 3414 Manhattan Ave, Manhattan Beach, (☎310/546-4407). As the name suggests, everything done with eggs, plus muffins and pancakes.

**Pier Bakery**, 100-M Fisherman's Wharf, Redondo Beach (☎310/376-9582). A small but satisfying menu featuring the likes of jalapeno cheese bread and cinammon rolls. Hot, doughy churros are made fresh before your eyes for $1.

**Russell's**, 5656 E Second St, Long Beach (☎310/434-0226). Worth a trip to sample the great burgers and fresh pies.

**Tony's Famous French Dip Sandwiches**, 701 Long Beach Blvd, Long Beach (☎310/435-6238). The name says it all, but alongside the dips is a beckoning array of soups and salads.

## Disneyland and around

**Angelo's**, 511 S State College Blvd, Anaheim (☎714/533-1401). Straight out of *Happy Days*, a drive-in complete with roller-skating car-hops, neon signs, vintage cars and, incidentally, good burgers. Open until 2am on weekends.

**Belisle**, 12001 Harbor Blvd, Garden Grove (☎714/750-6560). Open late for filling sandwiches, meat pies and a variety of things baked.

**Knott's Berry Farm**, 8039 Beach Blvd, Buena Park (☎714/827-1776). People flocked here for the delicious fried chicken dinners long before Disneyland was around, and they still do.

**Mimi's Café**, 18342 Imperial Highway (☎714/996-3650). Huge servings, low prices and a relaxing atmosphere just down the street from the Nixon Library.

## Orange County Coast

**C'est Si Bon**, 149 Riverside Ave off PCH, Newport Beach (☎714/645-0447) Small seaside café serving croissants, baguettes, and French cheese, paté and coffee.

**Ruby's**, Balboa Pier, Newport Beach (☎714/675-RUBY). The first, and one of the best, of the retro-streamline 1940s diners that have popped up all over LA.

## The San Gabriel and San Fernando Valleys

**Dr Hogly-Wogly's Tyler Texas Bar-B-Q**, 8136 Sepulveda Blvd, Van Nuys (☎818/780-6701). Long lines for some of the best chicken, sausages, ribs and beans in LA.

**Goldstein's Bagel Bakery**, 86 W Colorado Blvd, Pasadena (☎818/792-2435). If money's tight, feast here on day-old 15¢ bagels; otherwise enjoy fresh pastries, coffees and teas.

**Hidden Springs Café**, 23255 Angeles Forest Hwy, Angeles National Forest (☎818/792-9663). The only restaurant on the Angeles Forest Highway. Filling portions are served in open stone rooms with real fires and rustic decor as eclectic as the clientele, which includes Hell's Angels, fly-fishers, gold-miners and tourists.

**The Hat**, 491 N Lake Ave, San Gabriel (☎818/449-1844). Very popular roadside stand selling good burgers and French-dip sandwiches.

**Portos Bakery**, 315 Brand Blvd, Glendale (☎8818/956-5996). Popular and cheap café serving Cuban flaky pastries, cheesecakes soaked in rum, as well as more standard muffins, danishes, croissants and tort. The hot sandwiches are $3, meat pies are 70¢, and cappuccino is a rock-bottom $1.50.

**Pie'n'Burger**, 913 E California Blvd, Pasadena (☎818/795-1123). Classic coffee shop, with good burgers and excellent fresh pies.

**Rose Tree Cottage**, 824 E California Blvd, Pasadena (☎818/793-3337). Cream or high tea in a country home setting so thoroughly English that it's the West Coast HQ of the British Tourist Board. Reservations are essential.

**Soda Fountain at Fair Oaks Pharmacy**, 1526 Mission St, South Pasadena (☎818/799-1414). A run-of-the-mill corner store transformed into a fabulous old-fashioned soda fountain.

# Mexican and Latin American

LA's **Mexican** restaurants are the city's best – and most plentiful – eating standby, serving tasty, healthy and filling food for as little as $5 a head, including the requisite ice-cold bottle of *Bohemia* or *Corona* beer. They're at their finest and most authentic in East LA, on the borders of downtown, which is the centre of LA's huge Hispanic community, although there's a good selection of more sanitized examples all over the city. Aside from restaurants, there are far less enticing but even cheaper (though without the beer) Mexican fast-food outlets like *Taco Bell*, *Pollo Pollo*, *Pollo Rico* and *El Pollo Loco* (the best of the bunch) just about everywhere.

## Downtown and around

**El Cholo**, 1121 S Western Ave (☎213/734-2773). One of LA's first big Mexican restaurants and still one of the best, despite the drunken frat-rats from USC.

**El Tepayac**, 812 N Evergreen Ave, East LA (☎213/267-8668). Huge burritos and very hot salsa – be prepared to wait in line.

**King Taco Warehouse**, 4504 E Third St 4027, East LA (☎213/264-4067 or 4661). More like a mini-mall than a restaurant, with every kind of taco imaginable.

**Luminarias**, 3500 Ramona Blvd, Monterey Park (☎213/268-4177). Slightly sanitized and with some unusual views: two freeways and a women's prison. (Also live salsa music; see p.152)

**Ciro's Mexican Food**, 705 N Everery Ave, East LA (☎213/269-5104). A split-level cave of a dining room, serving enormous platters of shrimp and mole specials. The flautas bannered prominently across the menu are the main draw, and every meal comes with guacomole.

## Hollywood

**Burrito King**, 2109 W Sunset Blvd at Alvarado (☎213/413-9444). Excellent carnitas burritos and tasty tostadas from this small stand across the parking lot from a car wash; open until 2am.

**El Coyote**, 7312 Beverly Blvd (☎213/939-2255). Labyrinthine restaurant serving hearty Mexican food, and lots of it. Low-priced, lethal margaritas are the house speciality, served in a grungy bar with soccer on the screen.

**Mario's Peruvian Seafood Restaurant**, 5786 Melrose Ave (☎213/466-4181). The chefs look Asian but this is authentic Peruvian fare, the result of an influx of Japanese into Brazil and Peru in the1920s. Supremely tender squid, and a hint of soy sauce in some dishes.

**Mexico City**, 2121 N Hillhurst Ave (☎213/661-7227). Spinach enchiladas and other Californian versions of Mexican standards. Red booths, wall-length windows and a young crowd. You're allowed to smoke in the adjoining bar, a rarity in Los Angeles.

**Yuca's Hut**, 2056 N Hillhurst Ave (☎213/662-1214). Tasty al fresco burritos opposite *Mexico City*.

## West LA

**Casa Carnitas**, 4067 Beverly Blvd (☎213/667-9953). Tasty Mexican food from the Yucatán: the dishes are inspired by Cuban and Caribbean cooking – lots of seafood, too.

**El Mexicano Deli & Restaurant**, 1601 Sawtelle Blvd (☎310/473-8056). Cosy combo deli and restaurant, with a breakfast special of two eggs, fried beans, rice and salad at an unbeatable $2.95. The deli section is like an old-fashioned general store, selling fruit, vegetables and canned products from south of the border.

**La Salsa**, 11075 W Pico Blvd at Sepulveda (☎310/479-0919). A pilgrimage spot for Spike Jones fans (he immortalized the road junction in his hit, *Pico and Sepulveda*), and for lovers of soft tacos and dangerously hot salsa.

**Mi Ranchito Restaurant**, 8694 W Washington Blvd, Culver City (☎310/837-1461). Don't be put off by the ramshackle interior. The Veracruzean seafood dishes and the broad selection of Mexican fare are excellent. Bittersweet mole sauce and goat tacos a speciality.

## Santa Monica and Venice and Malibu

**La Cabana**, 738 Rose Ave, Venice (☎310/399-9841). Corn tortillas as thick as pancakes, and interesting stuffed quesadillas. Prepare to wait on Fri and Sat nights.

**Mariasol**, 401 Santa Monica Pier, Santa Monica (☎310/917-5050). *Cervezas* with a view, hidden away at the end of the pier. On weekend afternoons, the small rooftop deck affords a sweeping panorama from Malibu to Venice.

**Marix Tex-Mex Playa**, 118 Entrada Drive, Pacific Palisades (☎310/459-8596). Flavourful fajitas and massive margaritas in this rowdy but stylish beachfront cantina.

## The South Bay and Harbor Area

**Pancho's**, 3615 Highland Ave, Manhattan Beach (☎310/545-6670). Big portions, comparatively cheap for the area.

## The San Gabriel and San Fernando Valleys

**Don Cuco's**, 3911 Riverside Drive, Burbank (☎818/842-1123). Good local place, close to Burbank studios, which does a great Sunday brunch.

**Merida**, 20 E Colorado Blvd, Pasadena (☎818/792-7371). Unusual Mexican restaurant, featuring dishes from the Yucatán; try the spicy pork wrapped up and steamed in banana leaves.

**Senor Fish**, 4803 Eagle Rock Blvd, Eagle Rock (☎818/257-7167) The best fish tacos this side of Rosarita, with charbroiled halibut for under $8, in a converted house with patio. Don't be scared off by the occasional cockroach– that's the floorshow.

**Rudy's Bean Pot**, 6737 Foothill Blvd, Tujunga (☎818/352-8787). Fine burgers and Mexican food. The "Street Rods Welcome" has led to a traditional Wednesday night gathering of custom classics and hot rods in the parking lot outside.

**Woofle Burger**, 46 N Lake St, Pasadena (☎818/792-7292). Praised by the *LA Weekly* and *LA Times* for its chilli, tamales and burgers. Woofles with fresh fruit and *huevos rancheros* are served for breakfast.

# American, California cuisine and Cajun

Down-to-earth **American** cuisine, with its steaks, ribs, baked potatoes and mountainous salads, has a deceptively low profile in faddish LA, although it's available almost everywhere and usually won't cost more than $10 for a comparative blow-out. Much more prominent – and more expensive, at upwards of $15 – is **California cuisine**, based on fresh local ingredients, more likely grilled than fried, and stylishly presented. Another rage is for spicy, fish-based **Cajun** cooking, still available in authentic form and fairly cheaply, at around $8 for a stomach-full – though you'll pay twice as much at somewhere trendy.

### Downtown and around

**McCormick and Schmicks**, 633 W Fifth St (☎213/629-1929). Swank seafood joint for business types with a preposterously cheap weekend dinner special (4–8pm & 9.30–11.30pm) – $1.95 each for your choice of ten dinner plates including calamari, quesadilla and fish tacos with black beans.

**Bernard's**, 506 S Grand Ave in the *Biltmore Hotel* (☎213/612-1580). Beautifully preserved, lushly decorated dining room in this landmark hotel, serving contemporary versions of classic American meat and fish dishes.

**B 'n' Bar-B-Que**, 1958 W Florence Ave (☎213/671-8190) and 10303 Avalon Blvd in Watts (☎757-0221). Slabs of LA's best ribs, smothered in your choice of barbecue sauce, served with baked beans and a sweet potato tart.

**Checkers Restaurant**, 535 S Grand Ave in the *Checkers Kempinski Hotel* (☎213/624-0000). One of the most elegant downtown restaurants, serving top-rated California cuisine all day. For a special treat, try the "spa breakfast" served poolside on the rooftop patio.

**Engine Co 28**, 644 S Figueroa St (☎213/624-6996). All-American grilled steaks and seafood, served in a converted fire station. Great French fries and an excellent wine list.

**Pacific Dining Car**, 1310 W Sixth St (☎213/483-6000). Styled to look like an English supper club, and housed inside an old railroad carriage. Open 24hr for (very expensive) steaks. Breakfast is the best value.

### Hollywood

**Musso and Frank's Grill**, 6667 Hollywood Blvd (☎213/467-7788). Since it opened in 1919 anyone who's anyone in Hollywood has been seen in the dark-panelled dining room, though at $15 for bacon and eggs you pay for the atmosphere. Better stick to the bar (see p.146).

**Pinot Hollywood's Restaurant and Martini Bar**, 1448 Gower St (☎213/461-8800). Upmarket American food in a spacious environment, plus 24 types of martini and Polish potato vodka.

### West LA

**Citrus**, 6703 Melrose Ave (☎213/857-0034). The trendiest and best of the newer upmarket restaurants, serving California cuisine in an outdoor-style setting indoors. Reservations essential; lunch for two costs around $60.

**Georgia**, 7250 Melrose Ave (☎213/633-8420). Downhome Southern cooking served in a mahogany dining room for about $20 a plate. Part-owned and frequented by Denzel Washington, it draws basketball players, actors and wannabes.

**The Gumbo Pot**, 6333 W Third St in the Farmer's Market (☎213/933-0358). Delicious and dirt-cheap Cajun cooking; try the *gumbo yaya* of chicken, shrimp and sausage, and the fruit-and-potato salad.

**L'Orangerie**, 903 N La Cienega Blvd (☎310/652-9770). Nouvelle California-style French cuisine; "Very pretty, very romantic, very French and very expensive" is how *Gault-Millau* describes it: if you haven't got the $150 it takes to sit down, enjoy the view from the bar.

**Spago**, 1114 Horn Ave above Sunset Blvd (☎310/652-4025). Perhaps LA's most famous restaurant, both for its chef Wolfgang Puck, the inventor of "designer pizza", and for its star-studded clientele. The Hollywood galaxy is reshaped nightly, depending upon who gets sat where. Expensive – you're paying as much to be seen as for the great food. Reservations are absolutely essential.

## Italian, Spanish, Greek and pizza

After years of having nothing more exotic than the established takeout pizza chains – *Piece o' Pizza* and *Shakey's* are among the more widespread names – LA has woken up to the delights of regional **Italian** cuisine, and there is a growing number of specialist restaurants, especially around the Westside, serving more refined and varied Italian food. Another recent phenomenon is the **designer pizza**, invented at Hollywood's *Spago* restaurant (where it costs $10 a slice), and made to a traditional formula but topped with duck, shiitake mushrooms and other exotic ingredients. The problem with all this is that it doesn't come cheap: even a pasta dish in the average Italian restaurant can cost upwards of $8, and the least elaborate designer pizza will set you back around $15. **Spanish** food and tapas bars have similarly become a swish night out for LA's Westside thirtysomethings. In contrast, if you're looking for **Greek** food, you'll have to look hard – restaurants are thin on the ground but well worth tracking down.

## Downtown

**La Bella Cucina**, 949 S Figueroa St (☎213/623-0014). Fabulous pizzas and homemade pastas, with the accent on northern and rural Italian cuisine.

**California Pizza Kitchen**, 330 S Hope St (☎213/626-2616). Inventive pizzas; not cheap but worth the extravagance. Another branch in West LA.

**Rex il Restaurante**, 517 S Olive St (☎213/627-2300). Possibly the most expensive but definitely the most elegant restaurant in LA, housed in the René Lalique-crafted one-time haberdashery.

## Hollywood

**Campanille**, 624 S La Brea Ave (☎213/938-1447). Incredible but extremely expensive northern Italian dishes made by another of LA's famous chefs, Nancy Silverton. If you can't afford a full dinner, just try the dessert or pick up some of the best bread in Los Angeles.

**Palermo**, 1858 N Vermont Ave (☎213/663-1178). As old as Hollywood, and with as many devoted fans, who flock here for the stodgy pizzas and gallons of cheapish red wine.

## West LA

**California Pizza Kitchen**, 12 N La Cienega Blvd (☎310/854-6555). Slightly pricey, super-stylish designer-pizza joint, always packed and serving good salads and calzone. Another branch downtown.

**Cava**, 8384 W Third St (☎213/658-8898). Latin and Iberian dishes appear on the menu, but the main attraction is tapas accompanied by shots of primo sherry.

**La Masia**, 9077 Santa Monica Blvd (☎310/273-7066). Upscale Castilian dining, after which you can hit the dancefloor and enjoy a spot of salsa and merengue.

**Mario's**, 1001 Broxton Ave, Westwood Village (☎310/208-7077). Far and away the best pizza in West LA; try the house special pesto in place of tomato sauce for a real treat. Also serves a wide range of pasta dishes.

## Santa Monica, Venice and Malibu

**Abott's Pizza Company**, 1407 Abbot Kinney Blvd, Venice (☎310/396-7334). Owned by former New Yorkers, the rock and roll Shiffer brothers, this home of the bagel crust pizza tops them with your choice of seeds, tangy sweet citrus sauce or shiitake and wild mushroom sauce.

**Boston Wildflour Pizza**, 2616 Lincoln Blvd (☎310/392-8551) and 2807 Main St, Santa Monica (☎310/399-9990). A cheese slice is $2 in the *LA Times*-nominated "Best Thin Pizza" house.

**Wolfgang Puck Express**, 1315 Third Street Promenade, Santa Monica (☎310/576-4770). On the second floor of an anodyne food mall, but the cheap pizzas and Chinois chicken and Caesar salads are justly famous.

## The South Bay and Harbor Area

**Algeria Café & Tapas Bar**, 115 Pine Ave, Long Beach ( ☎310/436-3388). Tapas, gazpacho and a variety of *platos principales* served with sangria on the patio, and to the beat of live Flamenco at weekends. There's a pastry and sandwich deli on the premises too.

**Giovanni's Salerno Beach Restaurant**, 193 Culver Blvd, Playa Del Rey (☎310/821-0018). The tasty southern Italian food takes second place to the decor: this 31-year-old eatery is a riot of Christmas decorations, inflatable toys, live birds and fish, maps of Italy and framed photos. It all began when the owners didn't get around to taking the Christmas decorations down one year . . .

**Mangiano**, 128 Manhattan Beach Blvd, Manhattan Beach (☎310/318-3434). Fairly pricey but worth it for the specialist northern Italian seafood.

**Santorini Restaurant**, 2529 PCH, Torrance, South Bay (☎310/534-8898). As good as Greek food gets in the South Bay. Rough retsina, tzatziki and good fresh bread add to the authenticity.

### The San Gabriel and San Fernando Valleys

**La Scala Presto**, 3821 Riverside Drive, Burbank (☎818/846-6800). Stylish and tasty antipasti, pizza and fresh pasta.

## Chinese, Japanese, Thai and Korean

LA's most fashionable districts offer high-style sushi bars and dim sum restaurants, favoured by Far East businessmen and fast-lane yuppies alike, in which you can easily eat your way through more than $20. Lower priced and much less pretentious outlets tend, not surprisingly, to be downtown, in **Little Tokyo** and **Chinatown**, where you can get a fair-sized meal for under $10. Thai and Korean food – for which you can expect to pay $10 to $15 per meal – are popular, although the latter has as yet to spread beyond the confines of **Koreatown**.

### Downtown and around

**Dong Il Jang**, 3455 W Eighth St, Koreatown (☎213/383-5757). A cosy Korean restaurant where the meat is grilled at your table.

**Grand Star Restaurant**, 934 Sun Mun Way, Chinatown (☎213/626-2285). Go late as there's video karaoke from 8pm–1am at this Chinese place on Sunday, Tuesday and Wednesday.

**Mandarin Deli**, 727 N Broadway (☎213/623-6054). Very edible and very cheap noodles, dumplings, and other hearty staples.

**Mitsuru Café**, 117 Japanese Village Blvd, Little Tokyo (☎213/613-1028). On a hot day nothing beats the snow cones at *Mitsuru*, in such exotic flavours as *kintoki* (azuki-bean paste) or *milk kintoki* (sweet custard). On a cold day, try the *imagawayaki* – azuki beans baked in a bun.

**Monkee's**, 679 N Spring St, Chinatown (☎213/628-6717). Long-standing favourite for fresh fish.

**Ocean Seafood**, 750 N Broadway (☎213/687-3088). Cavernous but often crowded restaurant serving cheap and excellent food that's well worth the wait.

**Restaurant Horikawa**, 111 S San Pedro St, Little Tokyo (☎213/680-9355). Upmarket Japanese restaurant, popular with Japanese business people.

**Shibucho**, 333 S Alameda St, Little Tokyo (☎213/626-1184). Excellent sushi bar in the heart of Little Tokyo; go with someone who knows what to order, as the waiters don't speak English.

**Vermont House**, 154 S Vermont Ave, Koreatown (☎213/383-7593). Housed in a grubby mini-mall and with a partially translated menu, but serving steaming $10 bowls of stew and soup right up until 3.30am.

**VIP Palace**, 3014 Olympic Blvd, Koreatown (☎213/388-9292). Korean restaurant, especially strong on spicy barbecued beef.

### Hollywood

**Katsu**, 1972 N Hillhurst Ave (☎213/665-1891). Minimalist sushi bar for the cyberpunk brigade; the only splash of colour is in the artfully presented bits of fish on your plate.

**Thai Beer**, 7513 Sunset Blvd (☎213/883-8434). Plainer-looking than its rivals along Sunset and Hollywood, but the cheap, spicy Chinese and Thai soups, noodles and stir-fries are excellent.

### West LA

**A Taste Of Tibet**, 11110 W Olympic Blvd (☎310/473-7311). In the absence of a ready supply of yak meat the sausages are stuffed with beef, but the *thupka* and *momos* are just like mama used to make.

**Chung King**, 11538 W Pico Blvd (☎310/477-4917). The best neighbourhood Chinese restaurant in LA, serving spicy Szechuan food: don't miss out on the *bum-bum* chicken and other house specialties.

**Mishima #2**, 8474 W Third St (☎213/782-0181). *Udon* and *soba* are quickly replacing sushi as the Japanese dish of choice in west LA. *Mishima* is the reason: bright and spacious, it serves bowls of hot and cold noodles for about what you'd pay at your local burger chain drive-thru.

**The Sushi House**, 12013 W Pico Blvd (☎310/479-1507). Reggae and sushi coalesce in a hole in the wall bar with only four tables and 14 chairs that fill up fast. Try the "Superman", a rainbow-coloured roll of salmon, yellowtail, whitefish and avocado.

**Tommy Tang's**, 7473 Melrose Ave (☎213/651-1810). Excellent, very popular Thai food in a medium-sized restaurant. It's also the incongruous setting for occasional full drag nights.

## Santa Monica, Venice and Malibu

**Chin Chin**, 11740 San Vicente Blvd, Brentwood (☎310/826-2525). Flashy but not overpriced dim sum café, open till midnight.

**Chaya**, 110 Navy St, Venice (☎310/396-1179). Coolly elegant cultural crossroads serving Japanese and Mediterranean foods to a smart clientele.

**Chinois on Main**, 2709 Main St, Santa Monica (☎310/392-9025). The man who created designer pizza at *Spago* (see p.140) afterwards turned his sights across the Pacific to China and opened this enduringly popular restaurant, a melding of nouvelle French and Chinese cuisine serving sizzling dishes such as fresh fish in garlic and ginger, all designed to go with the green-and-black decor. Very expensive, but worth it for a splurge.

**Flower of Siam**, 2553 Lincoln Blvd, Venice (☎310/827-9986). Thai food guaranteed to set your tastebuds on fire.

**Lighthouse Buffet**, 201 Arizona Ave, Santa Monica (☎310/451-2076). All-you-can-eat sushi; indulge to your heart's content for under $9 at lunchtime or $17 in the evening.

## The San Gabriel and San Fernando Valleys

**Genmai-Sushi**, 4454 Van Nuys Blvd, Sherman Oaks (☎818/986-7060). *Genmai* is Japanese for brown rice, but you can still get soft shell crabs in ponzu sauce along with the sushi and seasonal macrobiotic dishes and the eponymous staple.

**Saladang**, 363 S Fair Oaks Ave, Pasadena (☎818/793-8123). A warehouse space whose snaking air conditioner ducts contrast with handmade tablecloths and ancestral photographs. The *pad thai* and Saladang spicy noodles would pass muster anywhere.

**Sea Star**, 2000 W Main St, Alhambra (☎818/282-8833). Dim sum at its best: pork *baos*, potstickers and dumplings, and delicious sweets.

# Indian, Sri Lankan, Middle Eastern and Ethiopian

**Indian** restaurants are thin on the ground in LA, but Indian food is enjoying an upsurge in popularity, and the number is growing – with menus often embracing uniquely Californian dishes. **Artesia** is home to a recognizable community of Indian shops and food stores along Pioneer Boulevard. **Middle Eastern** places in LA are few, and tend to be fairly basic, as do the city's even fewer **Ethiopian** food outlets. Most of the Indian and Middle Eastern restaurants in Hollywood or West LA fall into a fairly mid-range price bracket – between $8 and $12 for a full meal, less for a vegetarian Indian dish.

## Hollywood

**Addis Ababa**, 6263 Leland Way, a block south of Sunset Blvd (☎213/463-9788). Unpretentious Ethiopian food, served with fresh *injera* bread.

**Chamika Catering**, 1717 N Wilcox Ave (☎213/466-8960). Inexpensive papadums, *rotis* (garlic and coconut stuffed pancakes) and chicken, beef or lamb curries, marinated in special Sri Lankan sauces. Strawberry or mango delight wash the food down.

**India Inn**, 1638 N Cahuenga Blvd (☎213/461-3774). Good, low-cost Indian restaurant.

**India's Oven**, 7231 Beverly Blvd (☎213/936-1000). Bring your own bottle to this friendly, award-winning Indian restaurant.

**Shamshiry**, 5229 Hollywood Blvd (☎213/469-8434). The best of West LA's Iranian restaurants, offering kebabs, pilafs and exotic sauces.

**Eat A Pita**, 465 N Fairfax Ave (☎213/651-0188). Open-air stand serving cheap, cheerful and filling falafel, humus and vegetable juice drinks popular with locals from the nearby TV-and film-workers bedsitland.

## West LA

**East India Grill**, 345 N La Brea Ave (☎213/936-8844). Southern Indian cuisine given the California treatment: specialities include spinach curry and curried pasta.

**Noura Cafe**, 8479 Melrose Ave (☎213/651-4581). Moderately priced Middle Eastern specialities. At night the leafy crowded patio is lit by a central circular sandpit. For beginners, the "taster's delight" plate – hummus, baba ganoush, tabouli, falafel, fried eggplant, zucchini and stuffed grape leaf – is a good, filling bet.

# Vegetarian and wholefood

It's small wonder that mind- and body-fixated LA has a wide variety of **wholefood** and **vegetarian** restaurants, and even less of a shock that the bulk of them are found on the consciousness-raised Westside. Some vegetarian places can be very good value ($4 or so), but watch out for the ones that flaunt themselves as a New Age experience and include music – these can be three times as dear. Otherwise for a picnic try the local right-on but not bad *Trader Joe's* – which started as a liquor store with a sideline in unusual food, but now supplies imported cheeses, breads and canned foods to the Europeans who crave them most – or the frequent **Farmer's Markets**, heaving with organic produce, advertised in the press. Healthfood stores are listed in "Shopping".

## Hollywood

**Inaka**, 131 S La Brea Ave (☎213/936-9353). Vegetarian and macrobiotic food with a strong Japanese theme. Live music at weekends.

**The Bodhi Garden Restaurant**, 1498 Sunset Blvd (☎213/250-9023). Vegetarian Vietnamese food, including fancy dishes like sweet and sour walnuts, bean curd and black moss, though a $3.50 lunch will fill you up and cleanse you from the inside out. The crowd is eclectic, and the decor features chubby Buddhas resting alongside offerings of fruit. Closed Tues.

## West LA

**Nowhere Café**, 8009 Beverly Blvd (☎213/655-8895). Slightly costly but extremely good-for-you wholefood meals.

**The Source**, 8301 Sunset Blvd (☎213/656-6388). Started as a hippy hangout and still serves the healthiest veggie food on the Strip. It's where Woody found Diane Keaton in *Annie Hall*.

## Santa Monica, Venice and Malibu

**Figtree's Café**, 429 Ocean Front Walk, Venice (☎310/392-4937). Tasty veggie food and grilled fresh fish on a sunny patio just off the Boardwalk.

**Inn of the Seventh Ray**, 128 Old Topanga Rd, Topanga Canyon (☎310/455-1311). The ultimate New Age restaurant, serving vegetarian and other wholefood meals in a gorgeous mountains setting. Excellent desserts, too.

**Shambala Café**, 607 Colorado Ave (☎310/395-2160). Apart from organic chicken, the menu is meat-free, with shrimp, pasta, tofu, eggplant and some interesting seaweed dishes.

---

### HAPPY HOURS

Many bars and some restaurants have **happy hours**, usually from 5pm until 7pm, when drinks are cheap, maybe half-price, and there'll be a selection of help-yourself snacks: taco dips, chips or popcorn. A few offer piles of free food that you can attack once you've bought a drink – and thereby save you the cost of dinner later on.

### The South Bay and Harbor Area

**The Spot**, 110 Second St, Hermosa Beach (☎310/376-2355). A staggering array of vegetarian dishes, based on Mexican and other international cuisines and free of refined sugar or any animal products. All the water is purified, too.

# Drinking: bars, pubs and coffee bars

Social **drinking** in LA is far less popular than it is up the coast in San Francisco. Many bars are simply places to pose while waiting to meet friends, before heading off to pose again somewhere more exotic. However, it is possible to have a good time. You should be able to get a drink – at least a beer or a glass of wine – almost anywhere, and for serious, uninterrupted drinking there are bars and cocktail lounges on every other corner – just look for the neon signs. In fickle Los Angeles, bar styles go in and out of fashion like nobody's business, often according to music and showbiz trends. Currently the craze is for lounge music, dodgy Hawaiian motifs and stripping, but it'll probably be something else by the time you read this.

The recommendations below have a little more character than most: enjoyable places either for an entire evening's socializing or a quick splash on the way to somewhere else. As you'd expect, they reflect their locality: a clash of beatniky artists and financial whizz kids downtown; the legacy of the movies and the subsequent arrival of leather-clad rock fans in Hollywood; the cleaner-cut trendiness of West LA; a batch of jukebox and dartboard-furnished bars in Santa Monica evidence of the British contingent in the area, and the less fashionable, more hedonistic beachside bars of the South Bay. A few hard-bitten bars are open the legal maximum hours (from 6am until 2am daily), though you're liable to be drinking alone if you arrive for an early liquid breakfast; busiest hours are between 9pm and midnight.

If you want something of the bar atmosphere without the alcohol, present yourself at one of the fast-growing band of gregarious **coffee bars**; lately they've become the places to be seen, not least because they won't leave a hardened socialite too drunk to drive home – a crime that carries harsh penalties in LA.

### Downtown

**Al's Bar**, 305 S Hewitt St (☎213/687-3558). At the heart of the trendy Loft District art scene; drink cans of cheap beer in post-apocalyptic-looking, smoke-filled rooms, with a pool table and occasional live acts. Just a few blocks from downtown's ever expanding tent city, so be prepared for homeless people to offer to watch your car for $1.

**Bona Vista at the Westin Bonaventure**, 404 S Figueroa St (☎213/624-1000). Thirty five floors up this constantly rotating cocktail lounge spins faster after a few of the expensive drinks, and offers an unparalleled view of the sun setting over the city.

**Casey's Bar**, 613 S Grand Ave (☎213/629-2353). White floors, dark wood-panelled walls and nightly piano music; a regular drop-in spot for office workers on their way home.

### Hollywood

**Bar Deluxe**, 1710 N Las Palmas St (☎213/469-1991). Enjoy sake, beer and rockabilly in a bare-bones crimson-lit bar, prettified by a suspended 125 gallon aquarium.

**Barragan Café**, 1538 W Sunset Blvd (☎213/250-4256). Actually a Mexican restaurant, but reputedly producing the most alcoholic margarita in LA.

**Boardners**, 1652 N Cherokee Ave (☎213/462-9621). A likeably unkempt neighbourhood bar – a welcome rarity in the heart of Hollywood.

**Cat N' Fiddle**, 6530 Sunset Blvd (☎213/468-3800). A boisterous but comfortable pub with expensive English beers on draught and live jazz on Saturdays. See also "Nightlife".

**The Dresden Room**, 1760 N Vermont Ave (☎213/665-4298). Wed night is open mike, otherwise the resident husband-and-wife lounge act takes requests from the crowd of old-timers and goatee-wearing hipsters.

**Formosa Café**, 7156 Santa Monica Blvd (☎213/850-9050). Tiny ex-silent-era film studio done out in pillar-box red Chinese style (à la *Mann's Chinese Theatre*), with a fair amount of weekend traffic.

**Mugi**, 5221 Hollywood Blvd (☎213/462-2039). The ultimate drag bar outside of Saigon; a huge double-sided bar and postage-stamp stage, home to club kids, Asian businessmen, street types no-holds barred drag queens. You may even be shown the back room full of costumes.

**Musso and Frank's**, 6667 Hollywood Blvd (☎213/467-7788). If you haven't had a drink in this 1940s landmark bar, you haven't been to Hollywood. It also serves food (see p.140).

**Pinot Hollywood's Restaurant and Martini Bar**, 1448 Gower St (☎213/461-8800). Twenty-four types of martini and Polish potato vodka, served in airy surroundings. See also "Eating".

**The Power House**, 1714 N Highland Ave (☎213/463-9438). Enjoyable heavy rockers' watering hole just off Hollywood Boulevard; few people get here much before midnight.

**Three of Clubs**, 1123 Vine St (no phone). Unmarked entrance next to a gas station past Hollywood. A Sixties-style club atmosphere with low lighting, couches and a cigarette girl. Plenty to look at weekends, but a bit quiet in the week.

**Tikki Ti**, 4427 W Sunset Blvd (☎213/669-9381). Tiny grass-skirted cocktail bar straight out of *Hawaii-Five-O*. The Filipino owners mix deadly coconut-based concoctions at about $5 a hit.

## West LA

**Barney's Beanery**, 8447 Santa Monica Blvd (☎310/654-2287). Well-worn poolroom bar, stocking over 200 beers. It also serves food.

**Molly Malone's Irish Pub**, 575 S Fairfax Ave (☎213/935-1577). Self-consciously authentic Irish bar, from the music to the shamrocks in the foaming Guinness (see also p.151).

**Tom Bergin's**, 840 S Fairfax Ave (☎213/936-7151). Great place for Irish Coffee, less rough and ready than *Molly Malone's* down the road.

**Trader Vics**, 9876 Wilshire Blvd (☎310/276-6345). The home of the original mai tai, this kitsch Polynesian fantasy has been around since 1955. A staggering 200 cocktails are available. The strongest, the Queens's Park Swizzle, isn't on the menu – ask for it if you dare.

## Santa Monica, Venice and Malibu

**Crown and Anchor Pub**, Santa Monica Pier (☎310/394-6385). English-style pub with imported British brews.

**McGinty's Irish Pub**, 2615 Wilshire Blvd, Santa Monica (☎310/828-9839). Friendly, often raucous small pub with dartboards and frequent live music.

**The Oarhouse**, 2941 Main St, Venice (☎310/396-4725). Studenty bar which gets suitably rowdy on a Friday.

**Ye Olde King's Head**, 116 Santa Monica Blvd (☎310/451-1402). Jukebox, dartboards and signed photos of all your favourite rock dinosaurs.

## San Gabriel Valley

**The Colorado**, 2640 E Colorado Blvd (☎818/449-3485). Salty bartenders, cheap drinks and a couple of pool tables amid a decor based around hunting.

# Coffee bars

**All-Star Theatre Café**, 1714 North Ivar Ave, Hollywood (☎213/962-8898). Antiques store-cum-café-cum-pool hall with a 1920s feel and comfortably overstuffed armchairs. Never opens until 7pm.

**Betelgeuse**, 7160 Melrose Ave, Hollywood (☎213/243-8229). Mispronounced as in the film. Attracts an underground crowd who often screen their 8 and 16mm films to an audience of their peers.

**Big and Tall**, 7311 Beverly Blvd, West Hollywood (☎213/939-1403). Coffee and pastries in a bookstore environment, with much of the literature aimed at the gay community. A good place for information.

**Bourgeois Pig**, 5931 Franklin Ave, Hollywood (☎213/962-6366). Hip environment and outrageously overpriced cappuccinos, though fun for people-watching.

**The Expresso Bar**, 1039 E Green St, Pasadena (☎818/356-9095). Open mike nights and a fine array of strong coffees.

**Highland Grounds**, 742 N Highland Ave, Hollywood (☎213/466-1507). The poshest and posiest of LA's coffee bars, serving iced latte and whole pancakes. At night it's a club, with poetry readings and anonymous bands.

**Iguana Café**, 10934 Camirillo St, N Hollywood (☎818/763-7735). The most popular of the Valley cafés frequented by artists and those who perform in variable open mike sessions.

**Java Man**, 157 Pier Ave, Hermosa Beach (☎310/379-7209). Tables lit by halogen lamps, and a rotating display of work from local artists. The espresso ($1–3) is your best bet.

**King's Road Espresso House**, 8361 Beverly Blvd, West Hollywood (☎213/655-9044). Sidewalk café with the usual beautiful staff. Popular day and night with the *nuovo* beatnik crowd.

**The Living Room**, 112 S La Brea Ave, West Hollywood (☎213/933-2933). Imaginatively decorated, spacious and welcoming café with good food and drink, open till the wee hours.

**The Novel Café**, 212 Pier Ave, Santa Monica (☎310/396-8566). Used books and high-backed wooden chairs set the tone, but this is a surprisingly unpretentious place, with good coffees, teas and pastries.

**The World Café**, 2820 Main St, Santa Monica (☎310/392-1661; www. worldcafe.la.com). Surf the Net with other technophiles on the patio, or drag yourself away and drink in the dark café/bar.

# Nightlife: clubs and discos

Like most things in LA, **nightlife** here is very style-conscious, and LA's clubs are probably the wildest in the country. Ranging from absurdly faddish hangouts to industrial noise cellars, even the more image-conscious joints are often more like singles bars, with plenty of dressing-up, eyeing-up and picking-up (and sometimes not much else) going on, and everybody claiming to be either a rock star or in the movies. If you don't fall for the make-believe, the city's nightlife jungle can be great fun to explore, if only to eavesdrop on the vapid chat. Nowadays, many of the more interesting and unusual clubs are homeless, run by a couple of DJs specializing in a musical/fashion theme and operating wherever and whatever night of the week they can in a borrowed space. As a result, the trendier side of the club scene is hard to pin down, and you should always check the *LA Weekly* before setting out.

Not surprisingly, Friday and Saturday are the busiest nights, but during the week things are often cheaper, and though less crowded, rarely any less enjoyable. Everywhere, between 11pm and midnight is the best time to turn up, things usually hitting their peak from midnight to 2am. There's nearly always a cover charge, usually from $5 to $10, and a minumum age of 21 (it's normal for ID to be checked, so bring your passport or other photo ID), and you should obviously dress with some sensitivity to the club's style – there's no point in turning up at a hip-hop club in stilettos. That said, prohibitive dress codes are a rarity, and although you may be more welcome if you look completely outrageous, you won't be excluded from anywhere purely on account of your clothes.

## Downtown

**Glam Slam**, 333 S Boylston St (☎213/482-6626). Very glam but not posey club, owned and inspired by the artist formerly known as Prince – hence the purple dance floor. It's best to dress nice, though no one over 21 gets turned away.

**Mayan**, 1038 S Hill St (☎213/746-4287). Convince the doorman that you deserve to be allowed in and your reward is a place among the cool and most fashionable of LA, eager to shake a leg in gorgeous surrounds. Fri and Sat; $12, no sneakers.

## Hollywood

**Arena**, 6655 Santa Monica Blvd (☎213/462-1291). Work up a sweat to funk, hip-hop and house sounds on a massive dance floor inside a former ice factory; $4-7.

**Club Lingerie**, 6507 Sunset Blvd (☎213/466-8557). Long-established, stylish modern dance club with intimate bar and music varying from rockabilly to jazz to post-industrial thrash; $5–10. See also "Live Music".

## LA'S FESTIVALS

**January**

**1** Tournament of Roses in Pasadena. A parade of floral floats and marching bands along a five-mile stretch of Colorado Boulevard.

**February**

**First full moon after 21** Chinese New Year. Three days of dragon-float street parades and cultural programmes, based in Chinatown.

**March**

**17** St Patrick's Day. No parade but freely flowing green beer in the "Irish" bars along Fairfax Avenue.

**End** The Academy Awards are presented at the Shrine Auditorium or Dorothy Chandler Pavilion. Bleacher seats are available to watch the limousines draw up and the stars emerge for the ceremony, but the exclusive industry parties are off limits, though the live TV coverage of the winners sweating their way around every bash in town is an enlightening glimpse of the stars as the mascara runs.

**April**

**Early** The Blessing of the Animals. A long-established Mexican-originated ceremony held to thank animals for the services they provide to humankind. Locals arrive in Olvera Street to have their pets blessed, then watch the attendant parade.

**May**

**5** Cinco de Mayo. A day-long party to commemorate the Mexican victory at the Battle of Puebla (and not Mexican Independence Day as some Californians think). Besides a spirited parade in Olvera Street, several blocks of downtown are blocked off for perfomances by renowned Chicano and Hispanic musicians. There are also celebrations with Mexican food, drink and music in most LA parks.

**June**

**Late** Gay Pride. Parade on Santa Monica Boulevard in West Hollywood. Carnival atmosphere and an all-male drag football cheer team.

**August**

**First two weeks** Culmination of the South Bay's International Surf Festival, where globally famed surfers compete.

**10–14** Nisei Week in Little Tokyo. A celebration of Japanese America, with martial arts demonstrations, karaoke, Japanese brush painting, baby shows and performance.

**September**

**4** LA's birthday. A civic ceremony and assorted street entertainment around El Pueblo de Los Angeles to mark the founding of the original pueblo in 1781.

**Last two weeks** Los Angeles County Fair in Pomona, in the San Gabriel Valley. The biggest County Fair in the country, with livestock shows, eating contests and fairground rides.

**October**

**Second weekend** LA Street Scene. Free rock music, fringe theatre and comedy on the streets of downtown. Usually running at the same time is the West Hollywood Street Festival, a display of handmade arts and crafts and a general slap-on-the-back for LA's newest constituent city.

**Middle** Watts Jazz Festival. Two days of free music with the Watts Towers as a backdrop.

**31** Halloween Parade. More West Hollywood frolicking

**November**

**3** Dia de Los Muertos (Day of the Dead) is celebrated throughout East Los Angeles and for the tourists on Olvera Street. Mexican traditions, such as picnicking on the family burial spot are upheld.

**First week** Citicorp Plaza dedicates its downtown Christmas tree. Tree-lighting events also take place in Griffith Park.

**End** Hollywood Christmas Parade. The first and best of the many Yuletide events, with a cavalcade of mind-boggling floats.

**Continental Club**, 1743 N Cahuenga Blvd (☎213/463-SOUL). Looks like an old bus depot, and has an inside *Crush Bar* playing Motown hits; $5–8.

**The Derby**, 4500 Los Feliz Blvd (☎213/663-8979). Restored supper club with gorgeous high wooden ceilings and round bar, that has become the epicentre of LA's swingdancing craze. Classes in retro-jazz, rockabilly and be-bop dance are available to get you up to speed.

**Dragonfly**, 6510 Santa Monica Blvd (☎213/466-6111). Unusual decor, two large dance rooms, an "eye-contact" bar and club nights that are continually buzzing.

**Florentine Gardens**, 5951 Hollywood Blvd (☎213/464-0706). Stuck between the Salvation Army and a porno theatre, but very popular with the faddish LA crowd. Cover $5–10, dress code varies.

**Probe**, 836 N Highland Ave (☎213/461-8301). Ultra-trendy but friendly club that hosts top DJs: Sun for 1970s hits (and mostly gay). One of LA's more enjoyable clubs; cover $4–6.

## West LA

**Coconut Teaszer**, 8117 Sunset Blvd (☎213/654-4773). Poseurs, rockers and voyeurs mix uneventfully on the two dance floors. No cover before 9pm, otherwise $5. See also "Live Music".

**7969**, 7969 Santa Monica Blvd (☎213/654-0280). West Hollywood's longest running gay and lesbian disco has drag shows on Mon, women-only on Tues and English Acid on Wed. It's also the place to go if you're into LA's latest fad, stripping. Call for details; cover varies. Over 18s only. See also "Gay and lesbian bars and clubs".

**Union**, 8210 Sunset Blvd (☎213/654-1001). Relaxed supper club with funk, soul and r'n'b groove room. Frequented by the young actor crowd on Tues.

**Viper Room**, 8852 Sunset Blvd (☎310/358-1881). Stellar live acts, a famous owner and a headline-hitting past. Nights include *Mr Phat's Royal Martini Club* on Thurs. See also "Live Music".

# Live Music

LA has a near-overwhelming choice if you're looking for **live music**. The fact that new bands haven't broken through until they've won over an LA crowd means there's seldom an evening without something exciting going on. Ever since the nihilistic punk bands of a decade or so ago – Circle-Jerks, X, Black Flag – drew the city away from its cocaine-sozzled laid-back West Coast image, LA's **rock music** scene has been second to none in the States, to the extent that it has replaced the film industry as the quick route to riches and fame. There's a proto-rock star at every corner, and the guitar case is in some districts (notably Hollywood) an almost *de rigueur* accessory. The punk phenomenon has, of course, long since been overtaken, and nowadays the trend is for various heavy-metal hybrids, ranging from 100mph thrash metal and its wild, teenage devotees to, more recently, glam metal, which mates classic heavy rock poses with more acceptably mainstream music, and grunge, born up the coast in Seattle. Conversely, the influence and popularity of South Central's **hip-hop and rap** music is barely in evidence elsewhere in LA, though a number of DJs play one-off club nights – track them down via radio and print. Don't, however, go hunting down the local rappers in their home territory – see "South Central LA" on p.85 for why you should stay clear.

In addition to local talent there are always plenty of British and European names in town, from major artists to independents. There's an enormous choice of **venues**, and inevitably it's a constantly changing scene, but the clubs we've listed are pretty well established. Most open at 8pm or 9pm; headline bands are usually onstage between 11pm and 1am. Admission ranges from $8 up to $15 and you should phone ahead to check set times and whether the gig is likely to sell out (if it is you can have tickets held at the door up to showtime). As with discos, you'll need to be 21 and will almost certainly be asked for ID. As ever, *LA Weekly* is the best source of **listings.**

Although you can satisfy most musical tastes, these are not what the city does best, probably because they're just not fashionable enough. However, **country music** is fairly prevalent, at least away from trendy Hollywood, and the Valleys are hotbeds of hillbilly and swing. There's **jazz**, too, played in a few genuinely authentic downbeat dives, though more commonly found being used to improve the atmosphere of a restaurant. You're not obliged to eat in these places, however, and entry will often be free, although in most cases it does help to be fairly tidily dressed.

The lively Latin dance music of **salsa**, immensely popular among LA's Hispanic population, was promoted heavily by record companies in the city during the mid-1970s. At the time it failed to cross over into the mainstream, though this is now changing. Even so, it's still found, mostly in the bars of East LA, though it's worth saying that (aside from the places we've listed) these are very male-oriented gathering places and visitors may well feel out of place – though they're rarely dangerous. Finally there's a small live **reggae** scene, occasionally featuring biggish names but more often sticking to the increasingly numerous local bands.

## The big performance venues.

**Greek Theater**, in Griffith Park (☎213/460-6488). An outdoor, summer-only venue with a broad range of big-name musical acts.

**Hollywood Palladium**, 6215 Sunset Blvd, Hollywood (☎213/466-4311). Once a big-band dance hall, with an authentic 1940s interior.

**LA Sports Arena**, 3939 S Figueroa St, downtown (☎213/480-3232). Cavernous with no atmosphere at all, perfect for mega metal bands.

**Pantages Theater**, 6233 Hollywood Blvd, Hollywood (☎213/462-3104). An atmospheric Art Deco theater, in the heart of historic Hollywood.

**Universal Amphitheater**, Universal Studios, Burbank (☎818/980-9421). A huge but acoustically excellent auditorium with regular rock shows.

### WHAT'S ON AND TICKETS

Apart from the radio stations listed below, which carry details, previews and sometimes free tickets for forthcoming events, the best sources of **what's on information** are the *LA Weekly* and *LA Reader*, and the "Calendar" section of the Sunday *Los Angeles Times*. You can buy seats for concerts or sports events from **Ticketmaster**, which has branches in *Tower Records* and *Music Plus* stores, and charge-by-phone numbers (☎213/680-3232 or 714/740-2000). A quick way through the maze of LA's **theatres** is to phone **Theatrix** (☎213/466-1767), which handles reservations and provides details on what's playing at several of the smaller venues.

### RADIO STATIONS

**KCRW** 89.8 FM The best new music and transatlantic imports, and one of the few good sources of world news. A news link-up is being set up with the British BBC, whose radio dramas currently run at weekends.

**KCSN** 85.9 FM Latino classics and salsa.

**KFWB** 980 AM The best local news, plus talk shows.

**KLSX** 97.1 FM Carries the morning show of outrageous NY shock-jock, Howard Stern.

**KMAX** 107.1 FM Surf reports and frivolous surf news from 5–7am at weekends.

**KNX** 1070 Sports reports at 15 and 45 minutes past the hour.

**KPCC** 89.3 FM Jazz and blues concerts knowledgeably presented, plus arty talk radio.

**KPFK** 90.7 FM Up-to-the minute-opinions, politics, news and music, from sceptics with a left-of-centre perspective.

**KROQ** 106.7 FM Laddishly presented non-stop grunge, and a teen sex advice clinic run by qualified doctor and an ex-junkie DJ.

**KUSC** 91.5 FM Classical, jazz, world music.

**KXLU** 88.9 FM Underground hip-hop and performer interviews on Saturday night.

## Rock venues

**anti-club**, 4658 Melrose Ave, Hollywood (☎213/661-3913). Occasionally great, but far fewer worthwhile bands play here now than used to.

**Café Largo**, 432 N Fairfax Ave, West LA (☎213/852-1073). Intimate cabaret venue that often features LA's more unusual live bands. Free–$10.

**Club Lingerie**, 6507 Sunset Blvd, West LA (☎213/466-8557). Wide-ranging venue that's always at the forefront of what's new; $3–8. See also "Nightlife: clubs and discos".

**Doug Weston's Troubadour**, 9081 Santa Monica Blvd, West Hollywood (☎310/276-6168). The best-known club for the heaviest riffs and shaggiest manes.

**The Lighthouse**, 30 Pier Ave, Hermosa Beach (☎310/372-6911). A broad booking policy which spans rock, jazz, reggae and more; cover varies.

**The Roxy**, 9009 Sunset Blvd, West LA (☎310/276-2222). The showcase of the music industry's new signings, intimate and with a great sound system; cover varies.

**The Viper Room**, 8852 Sunset Blvd, West LA (☎310/358-1880). Less painfully trendy than many clubs, though it has gained a certain notoriety since River Phoenix OD'd here in late 1993. Tues jam nights have cheap drinks. Cover $3–6. See also "Nightlife: clubs and discos".

**Whisky-a-Go-Go**, 8901 Sunset Blvd, West LA (☎310/652-4202). Courtesy of The Doors, this was for many years LA's most famous rock-and-roll club, now it's mainly hard rock; $5–10.

## Country and folk venues

**The Foothill Club**, 1922 Cherry Ave, Signal Hill (☎310/494-5196). A glorious dance hall from the days when hillbilly was cool, complete with mural showing life-on-the-range. Punk, roots and surf-rock Thurs–Sat $8.

**Longhorn Saloon**, 21211 Sherman Way, Canoga Park (☎818/340-4788). Live country and blues-ish bands nightly except Mon. Frequent star-studded jam sessions; $3.

**McCabe's**, 3103 W Pico Blvd, Santa Monica (☎310/828-4403). The back room of LA's premier acoustic guitar shop; long the scene of some excellent and unusual shows; $5–10.

**Molly Malone's Irish Pub**, 575 S Fairfax Ave, West LA (☎213/935-1577). Traditional Irish music and American folk; see also "Drinking: bars, pubs and coffee bars". $5.

**The Palomino**, 6907 Lankershim Blvd, North Hollywood (☎818/764-4010). Long the best place to catch visiting country singers, also good for r'n'b and the odd goth gig; $5–10.

**The Silver Bullet**, 3321 South St, Long Beach. A riotous Country and Western talent competition is held here every Tues, and dance lessons most other nights; free–$3.

## Jazz venues

**The Baked Potato**, 3738 Cahuenga Blvd, North Hollywood (☎818/980-1615). A small but near-legendary contemporary jazz spot, where many reputations have been forged; $8 or $5 on Thurs.

**BB Kings Blues Club**, 1000 Universal Center Drive, Burbank (☎818/6-BBKING). Once past the garish CityWalk exterior, it's all catfish, deep-fried pickle and Southern hospitality. *Lucilles,* the club room, features acoustic blues at the weekends. Full bar, no age limit, low cover.

**Cat N' Fiddle Pub**, 6530 Sunset Blvd (☎213/468-3800). This pseudo-English pub has jazz, usually a dual-sax quintet, on Sun 7–11pm; no cover. See also "Drinking: bars, pubs and coffee bars".

**House of Blues**, 8430 Sunset Blvd (☎213/650-1451). Over-commercialized mock sugar shack, with good but pricey live acts. The *Gospel Blues Lunch*, at two-hourly intervals between noon and 6pm on Sun is an all-you-can-eat buffet ($24) with a live local gospel choir. Heavily influenced by the life and legend of John Belushi, whose estate has a business interest.

**Jazz Bakery**, 3233 Helms Ave, Culver City (☎310/271-9039). More performance space than club, the brainchild of singer Ruth Price. The best local musicians play alongside big-name visitors.

**World Stage**, 4344 Degnan Blvd (☎213/293-2451). Very informal, bare-bones rehearsal space that attracts top-name players like drummers Billy Higgins and Max Roach. Jam sessions on Thurs, gigs Fri and Sat.

## Salsa venues

**La Cita**, 336 S Hill St, downtown (☎213/972-9785). Traditional Hispanic music played nightly at 9pm in totally authentic, as-yet-untouristed downtown bar at the foot of Bunker Hill. Cheap drinks, no cover.

**Luminarias**, 3500 Ramona Blvd, Monterey Park, East LA (☎213/268-4177). Hilltop restaurant (see p.138) with live salsa reckoned to be as good as its Mexican food; no cover.

**Zabumba**, 10717 Venice Blvd (☎310/841-6525). More bossa nova Brazilian than straight salsa, but still great.

## Reggae venues

**Golden Sails Hotel**, 6285 E PCH (☎310/498-0091). Some of the best reggae bands from LA and beyond on Fri and Sat; $8.

**Kingston 12**, 814 Broadway, Santa Monica (☎310/451-4423). LA's only 7-nights-a-week venue for reggae music. Small and comfortable; $10–12.

# Classical music, opera and dance

Considering its size and stature in the other arts, LA has very few outlets for **classical music**. The Los Angeles Philharmonic (☎213/972-7300), the only major name in the city, performs regularly during the year, and the Los Angeles Chamber Orchestra (☎213/622-7001) appears sporadically at different venues; also, during the semester, students of the Schoenberg Institute give **free lunchtime concerts** on the USC campus. But otherwise attractions are thin, and you may have to rely on what is at least a fairly regular influx of internationally known performers throughout the year. Watch the press, especially the *LA Times*, for details, and expect to pay from $8 to $30 for most concerts, much more for really big names.

For **opera** you're far better off going to San Francisco, although the Music Center Opera (☎213/972-7211) stages productions between September and June, as does Orange County's Opera Pacific (☎213/480-3232 or 714/740-2000), which performs both grand opera and operettas. Prices can be anything from $10 to $120.

The last fifteen years or so have seen an increase in **dance** activity in LA. The big event of the year is the **Dance Kaleidoscope**, held over two weeks in July at the John Anson Ford Theater and organized by the Los Angeles Area Dance Alliance (LAADA; ☎213/343-5120) – a co-operative supported by all LA's smaller dance companies that provides a central source of information on events. Otherwise check for performances at the **universities**, where some of the most exciting new names in dance have residencies.

## Major venues

**The Dorothy Chandler Pavilion**, in the *Music Center*, 1365 N Grand Ave, downtown (☎213/972-7211 or 7460). From Oct until May home to the LA Philharmonic, which performs at 8pm on weeknights and 2.30pm on Sun. Also used by the Music Center Opera and other top names. Every other year, it also hosts the Oscars.

**The Hollywood Bowl**, 2301 N Highland Ave, Hollywood (☎213/850-2000). The LA Philharmonic gives open-air concerts here Tues–Sat evenings from July to Sept (see p.99 for more on the Bowl).

**Japan America Theater**, 244 S San Pedro St (☎213/680-3700). Dance and performance works drawn from Japan and the Far East.

**John Anson Ford Theater**, 2850 Cahuenga Blvd (☎213/972-7200). Besides the summer Dance Kaleidoscope, this open-air venue also has one-off productions by local groups.

**Orange County Performing Arts Center**, 600 Town Center Drive, Costa Mesa (☎714/556-ARTS). Home of the Pacific Symphony Orchestra and Opera Pacific.

**The Pacific Amphitheater**, 100 Fair Drive, Costa Mesa (☎310/410-1062). A big open-air venue, Orange County's answer to the Hollywood Bowl.

**Royce Hall**, on the UCLA campus (☎310/825-9261 or 2101). Classical concerts often involving big names throughout the college year.

**The Shrine Auditorium**, 3228 Royal St (☎213/748-5116), box office at 655 S Hill St (☎213/749-5123). Distinctive looking building that hosts regular performances by choral gospel groups and alternate Academy Awards ceremonies.

**UCLA Center for the Performing Arts**, 10920 Wilshire Blvd (☎310/825-9261). Hosts a wide range of touring companies, and also runs an "Art of Dance" series between Sept and June, which usually has an experimental emphasis.

# Comedy

Gags are cracked every night all over LA at a range of **comedy clubs** across the city. Although rising stars and utterly-without-hope beginners can be spotted on the "underground", open-mike scene, the vast majority of famous and soon-to-be-famous comedians, both stand-up and improvisational, appear at the more established clubs, most of them in Hollywood or West LA. These venues usually have a bar, charge a cover of $8–12, and put on two shows each evening, generally starting at 8pm and 10.30pm – the later one is generally more popular. The better-known places are open every night, but are often solidly booked on Friday and weekends; other venues have comedy only on certain nights.

## Comedy venues

**The After-Dark Theater**, 49 S Pine Ave, Long Beach (☎310/437-5326). A mixed range of hopeful stand-up comics.

**Comedy & Magic Club**, 1018 Hermosa Beach (☎310/372-1193). Strange couplings of naff magic acts and good-quality comedians.

**The Comedy Store**, 8433 W Sunset Blvd, West LA (☎213/656-6225). LA's comedy showcase and popular enough to be spread over three rooms – which means there's usually space, even at weekends. Always a good line-up too.

**Groundling Theater**, 7307 Melrose Ave, West LA (☎213/934-9700). Another pioneering improvisational venue where only the gifted survive.

**The Ice House**, 24 N Mentor Ave, Pasadena (☎818/577-1894). The comedy mainstay of the Valley, very established and fairly safe.

**Igby's Cabaret**, 11637 W Pico Blvd at Tennessee Place (☎310/477-3553). Newish venue, boasting some surprise big-name turns alongside entertaining hopefuls.

**The Improvisation**, 8162 Melrose Ave, West LA (☎213/651-2583). Known for hosting some of the best acts working in the area, so book ahead and join the schmoozefest.

**LA Cabaret Comedy Club**, 17271 Ventura Blvd, Encino (☎818/501-3737). Stand-up comics of mixed worth.

**LA Connection**, 13442 Ventura Blvd, Sherman Oaks (☎818/784-1868). An improvisation showcase for highly rated obnoxiousness specialists. Seldom less than memorable.

**The Laugh Factory**, 8001 Sunset Blvd, West Hollywood (☎213/656-8860). Stand-ups of varying standards and reputations, with the odd big name.

**Uncabaret**, *Luna Park*, 655 N Robertson Blvd, West Hollywood (☎310/652-0611). A fortnightly (every other Friday) improvisational stand-up gig which has recently featured some semi-famous names.

**Upfront Comedy Showcase**, 123 Broadway Ave, Santa Monica (☎310/319-3477). Nightly improvisational comedy based on audience suggestions.

# Theatre

LA has a very active **theatre** scene. While the bigger venues host a predictable array of clapped-out old musicals and classics starring a crowd-pulling line-up of big film names, there are over a hundred "Equity waiver" theatres with fewer than a hundred seats, enabling non-Equity-cardholders to perform; and a vast – and somewhat incestuous – network of fringe writers, actors and directors. A number of alternative theatres have sprung up in Hollywood west of Cahuenga Boulevard, revolving around **The Complex**, a group of six small theatres at 6470/6 Santa Monica Blvd (☎213/466-1767). Tickets are

You can get **information** and book theatre **tickets** through *Theatrix* (☎213/466-1767).

less expensive than you might expect: a big show will set you back upwards of $25 (matinees are cheaper), smaller shows around $8 to $20, and you should always book ahead.

### Fringe theatres
**Cast-At-The-Circle**, 804 N El Centro Ave, Hollywood (☎213/462-0265). Small Hollywood theatre hosting a variety of smaller productions.
**Gene Dynarski Theater**, 5600 Sunset Blvd, Hollywood (☎213/660-8587). Small-time character actor Dynarski built this likeable little theatre himself to rent out to small companies.
**Odyssey Theater Ensemble**, 2055 S Sepulveda Blvd (310/477-2055). Well-respected Westside theatre company, relocated in new home.
**Powerhouse Theater**, 3116 Second St, Santa Monica (☎310/392-6529). Adventurous and risk-taking experimental shows.

### Major theatres
**Coronet Theater**, 366 N La Cienega Blvd, West Hollywood (☎310/657-7377). Home of the LA Public Theater, whose productions include the odd famous name, and whose lively bar is patronized by excessively theatrical types.
**Geffen Playhouse**, 10886 Le Conte Ave, Westwood (☎310/208-5454). One of the smaller of the major theatres, often with one-person shows. Hollywood connection.
**Mark Taper Forum**, 135 N Grand Ave, downtown (☎213/972-7690). Theatre in the three-quarter round, frequently innovative new plays.
**Schubert Theater**, ABC Entertainment Center, Century City (☎310/553-9000). The only "good" thing about Century City is that you can come here to ogle the razzamatazz Andrew Lloyd Webber musicals.

# Film

It's no shock to find that many major feature **films** are released in LA months (sometimes years) before they play anywhere else in the world, and a huge number of cinemas show both the new releases and the classic favourites – though there are comparatively few places screening independent and foreign movies. Depending on where you go and what you see, a ticket will be around $7.50.

For **mainstream cinema**, though less popular than it used to be, Westwood still has a high concentration of movie houses, as does Santa Monica promenade. Of the multi-screen facilities, the eighteen-screen *Cineplex Odeon*, at Universal Studios (☎818/508-0588), is a plush complex that includes a pair of pseudo-Parisian cafés. Another, more enterprisingly programmed, is the *Beverly Cineplex* (☎310/652-7760) in the Beverly Center mall (see p.157), which has fourteen tiny screens featuring artsy independent film programmes and first-run blockbusters.

For **cheap and free films**, the places to hit are the *Bing Theater* at the County Art Museum, 5905 Wilshire Blvd (☎213/857-6010), which has afternoon screenings of many neglected Hollywood classics and charges just $1; the USC and UCLA campuses also often have interesting free screenings aimed at film students, announced on campus notice boards. Otherwise, the best places to find **art-house and cult films** are the *New Beverly Cinema*, 7165 Beverly Blvd (☎213/938-4038), especially strong on imaginative double bills, and the *Nuart Theater*, 11272 Santa Monica Blvd (☎310/478-6379), which runs rarely seen classics, documentaries and foreign-language films. Unlike other movie houses in the area, the *Los Feliz Theater*, 1822 N Vermont Ave, resisted a descent into the porn movie market in the 1960s; its three small screens still show international and low-budget American independent movies.

If you're looking for a golden-age-of-film **atmosphere**, you'll need either to take in an action triple bill in one of the historic downtown movie palaces (described on p.80, where the delirious furnishings may captivate your attention longer than the all-action triple-bills, or visit one of the Hollywood landmarks. *The Chinese Theatre*, 6925 Hollywood Blvd (☎213/468-8111), with its large screen, six-track stereo sound and fabulously tacky Art Deco interior, shows relentlessly mainstream films, but the first-night audience's loud participation is entertainment in itself. If this doesn't appeal, you could always indulge in the near-wraparound screen of the *Cinerama Dome*, 6360 Sunset Blvd (☎213/466-3401).

# Gay and lesbian LA

Although nowhere near as big as that of San Francisco, the **gay scene** in LA is far from invisible, and gay people are out and prominent in workplaces and environments right across the city. Of a number of specific areas where gay people tend to locate, the best known is the autonomous city of **West Hollywood**, which has a gay-led council and has become synonomous with the (affluent, white) gay lifestyle, not just in LA but all over California. The section of West Hollywood on Santa Monica Boulevard east of Doheny Drive has restaurants, shops and bars primarily aimed at gay men. Another out-and-proud community is **Silverlake**, at its most evident in the gay-oriented bars and restaurants along Hyperion Boulevard.

Gay couples will find themselves readily accepted at just about any LA **hotel**, but there are a few that cater especially for gay travellers and can also be useful sources of information on the LA gay scene generally. We've also listed below a few restaurants that cater specifically to gay men and lesbians. For up-to-date (if ad-packed), gay-oriented publications, see "Information" on p.64.

### Gay resources
**AIDS Project Los Angeles**, 1313 Vine St (☎213/993-1600). Sponsors fund-raisers throughout the year and an annual walkathon.
**A Different Light**, 8853 Santa Monica Blvd (☎213/668-0629). The city's best known gay and lesbian bookshop, with monthly art shows, readings, women's music events and comfortable chairs for lounging.
**Gay and Lesbian Community Services Center**, 1625 N Schrader Blvd (☎213/993-7400). Counselling, health-testing and information. It also publishes*The Center News*, a useful bi-monthly magazine.
**Gay Community Yellow Pages**, 1604 Vista Del Mar Ave, LA, CA 90028 (☎213/469-4454). Gay businesses, publications, services and gathering places listed yearly; available all over LA.

### Gay hotels
**Coral Sands Hotel**, 1730 N Western Ave, West Hollywood (☎1-800/367-7263). Exclusively geared towards gay men. All rooms face the inner courtyard pool. Basically very cruisy. ④.
**Holloway Motel,** 8465 Santa Monica Blvd, West Hollywood (☎213/654-2454).Typical clean roadside motel. ③.
**Ramada** 8585 Santa Monica Blvd, West Hollywood (☎310/652-6400 or 1-800/845-8585). Very gay-friendly, modern Art Deco-styled place with brand-new rooms. ④.

### Gay and lesbian restaurants
**Figs,** 7929 Santa Monica Blvd, West Hollywood (☎213/654-0780). Highly recommended all-American downhome cooking.
**French Market Place**, 7985 Santa Monica Blvd, West Hollywood (☎310/654-0898). Theme restaurant that's at least as much fun as Disneyland. Almost 100 percent gay clientele.

**Gloria's Café**, 3603 W Sunset Blvd (☎213/664-5732). Popular local hangout that's a great spot for dinner, especially Cajun.

**Mark's Restaurant**, 861 N La Cienega, West Hollywood (☎310/652-5252). High-end, gay-owned place serving California cuisine.

**Paradise Bar**, 8745 Santa Monica Blvd (☎310/659-6785). Gay-owned restaurant serving mostly California cuisine.

## Gay and lesbian bars and clubs

**Arena**, 6655 Santa Monica Blvd (☎213/462-1291). Many clubs under one huge roof, large dance floors throbbing to funk, Latin and hi-NRG grooves – and sometimes live bands – on Wed, Sat and Sun. Also called **Circus**, when it hosts the mostly-male *Pink Feather* club on Tues and a mixed gay night on Fri.

**Detour**, 1087 Manzanita, Silverlake (☎213/664-1189). A friendly and quite cheap denim and leather bar.

**Girl Bar**, 657 N Robertson Blvd, West Hollywood (☎310/659-0471). Madonna's been here and Chastity Bono once worked behind the bar. The cavernous dance floor warms up eventually with the help of girl go-go dancers.

**Jewel's Catch One**, 4067 W Pico Blvd (☎213/734-8849). Sweaty dance barn, packed with gay men on Wed, women on Thurs and a mixed crowd the rest of the week; $3–7.

**Klub Banshee**, location varies (☎310/288-1601). Weekend dance club for women, held at various locations around LA.

**Le Bar**, 2375 Glendale Blvd, Silverlake (☎213/660-7595). Quiet and welcoming bar, with a pool table.

**The Palms**, 8572 Santa Monica Blvd, West Hollywood (☎310/652-6188). Mostly house and dance nights at West Hollywood's most established lesbian bar.

**Probe**, 836 N Highland Ave (☎213/461-8301). LA's longest-running gay men's disco, playing all the Euro Pop dance hits.

**Rage**, 8911 Santa Monica Blvd, West Hollywood (☎310/652-7055). Very flash gay men's club playing the latest hi-NRG. Drinks are cheap, the cover varies.

**7969**, 7969 Santa Monica Blvd, West Hollywood (☎213/654-0280). Formerly called *Peanuts*, West Hollywood's oldest mixed gay and lesbian disco has drag shows on Mon, women-only on Tues for topless girl dancers, and *Fetish* and *Fuck!* on Sat. Call for details; cover varies.

# Women's LA

It's hardly surprising that a city as big as LA should have such an organized **women's** network, with many resource centres, bookstores, publications and clubs. Women travellers are unlikely to encounter any problems which aren't applicable to all the West Coast (for more on which see *Basics*, p.46), but the resources here are much more developed.

Any of the following are good sources of general and detailed information on the local women's movement, though there's an inevitable crossover with the city's sizeable lesbian community – see "Gay and Lesbian LA", above. *LA Woman*, Los Angeles' largest women's magazine, profiling local personalities and providing a calendar of events, is available from most newsstands and bookstores.

**Bread and Roses**, 13812 Ventura Blvd, Sherman Oaks (☎818/986-5376). In the heart of the San Fernando Valley, this store caters to women of all social, racial, ethnic and sociological backgrounds.

**Sisterhood Bookstore**, 1351 Westwood Blvd (☎310/477-7300). Westside landmark, just south of Westwood Village, selling books, music, cards, jewellery and a comprehensive selection of literature pertaining to the women's movement both nationally and internationally.

**Women's Yellow Pages**, 13601 Ventura Blvd, No. 374, Sherman Oaks, CA 91423 (☎310/398-5761). A yearly published listing of over 1400 women-owned businesses and services. Call or write for a copy.

# Shopping

**Shopping** in LA is an art. The level of disposable income in the wealthy parts of the city is astronomical, and touring the more outrageous stores can be a great insight into LA life – revealing who's got the money and what they're capable of wasting it on. Whether you want to pop out for a new light bulb or pair of socks, lay waste to a wad or simply be a voyeur in the orgy of acquisition, there are, besides the run-of-the-mill retailers you'll find anywhere, big **department stores**, mega-sized **malls** – where most of the serious shopping goes on – and **Rodeo Drive**, three blocks of the world's most exclusive and expensive shopping. The trendiest shops line **Melrose Avenue**, between La Brea and Fairfax in West Hollywood. **Old Town Pasadena** boasts a few of the more upmarket chains, while the few blocks above Prospect on N Vermont Avenue in Los Feliz Village are home to some of the underground's trendier boutiques.

The city also has a good assortment of specialist stores, sporting extensive selections of **books and records**. There's an equally diverse assortment of **food stores**, from corner delis and supermarkets to fancy cake stores and gourmet markets. You'll also find several **miscellaneous** stores selling perfect LA souvenirs.

## Department stores and malls

Each of LA's neighbourhoods has a collection of ordinary stores and mini-malls. You'll find much the best sources of cheap toiletries and staples at places such as *K-Mart* and *Pic'n'Save*, the latter specializing in dirt-cheap discontinued goods. A step up from these in price and quality, though still good for general shopping, are the city's **department stores**, which more often than not are included within massive **malls**, often resembling self-contained city suburbs as much as shopping precincts, around which Angelenos do the bulk of their serious buying.

### The malls

**Beverly Center**, Beverly and La Cienega Blvd, West Hollywood. Chic shopping at its best: seven acres of boutiques, a *Bullocks* department store, a multiplex cinema – and a *Hard Rock Café* – all under one roof.
**Century City Marketplace**, 10250 Santa Monica Blvd, Century City. Outdoor mall with 100 upscale shops, including a branch of New York's Metropolitan Museum gift shop. The place to come to see stars do their shopping
**Santa Monica Place**, Broadway and Second St, Santa Monica. Sunny, skylit mall with three tiers of stylish shops. The outdoor Third Street Promenade, which runs north from the mall, is one of the most popular shopping and nightlife precincts in all of LA.

### RODEO DRIVE

The black hole for expense accounts is **Rodeo Drive** in Beverly Hills, a solid line of exclusive stores to which you might be drawn by sheer curiosity. One store worth looking into is *Fred Hayman*, at 273 N, one of the first stores on Rodeo Drive and housing the autographed photos of a number of Hollywood celebs alongside its mostly Italian designer-menswear. Another is *Polo Ralph Lauren*, 444 N, which caters to well-heeled WASPS who fancy themselves as canine-fixated English gentry. Besides thousand-dollar suits and monogrammed Wellingtons, there are exquisitely carved walking sticks and mounted game heads, and a huge assortment of wooden dogs, bronze dogs and paintings of dogs. At the foot of Rodeo Drive are LA's premier department stores, including *Barney's* and, most famously, *Neiman-Marcus*, 9700 Wilshire Blvd, who sell everything from $5 Swiss truffles to his'n'hers leopard skins.

**Seventh Street Marketplace**, Seventh and Figueroa streets, downtown. Anchored by *Robinson-May* and *Bullock's* department stores, at the foot of the Citicorp office towers.

**Westside Pavillion**, Pico and Westwood Blvd, West LA. Postmodern shopping complex centered on *Nordstrom's* and *Robinson-May* department stores. The former is a typically LA clothes, shoes, jewellery and cosmetics store that provides regular customers with a personal "shopper" (ie an employee who does all the legwork around the store and comes back with a choice of goods).

# Food and drink

Since eating out in LA is so common, you may never have to shop for **food** at all. But if you're preparing a picnic, or want to indulge in a spot of home cooking, there are plenty of places to stock up. **Delis**, many open round the clock, are found on more or less every corner in LA; **supermarkets** are almost as common, some open 24 hours, or at least until 10pm – *Lucky's, Alpha-Beta, Pavilion, Ralph's* and *Trader Joe's* are the names to look out for. There are also **ethnic groceries and markets**, and – although much more expensive – the **gourmet markets and stores**, not to mention a bizarre collection of one-off outlets for all kinds of food oddities, mainly clustered in fashionable West LA. To buy **drink** you need go no further than the nearest supermarket – *Trader Joe's* is the cheapest and best.

## Pastries and cakes

**Mousse Fantasy**, 2130 Sawtelle Blvd, West LA (☎310/479-6665). A Japanese version of a French patisserie. The Green Tea Mousse cake is a taste of heaven.

**The Cheese Store**, 419 N Beverly Drive, Beverly Hills (☎310/278-2855). Over 400 types of cheese from all over the world, including every kind produced in the US.

**Mrs Field's Cookies**, 907 Westwood Blvd, Westwood (☎310/208-0096). Chewy, sweet cookies, made to a "secret recipe" that has plenty of devoted fans – and branches all over the US.

**Viktor Benes Continental Pastries**, 8718 W Third St, West LA (☎310/276-0488). The place for freshly baked bread, coffee cakes and Danish pastries.

## Delis and groceries

**Bay Cities Importing**, 1517 Lincoln Blvd, Santa Monica (☎310/395-8279). Like a gigantic deli, with piles of fresh pasta, spices, meats, sauces and many French and Middle Eastern imports.

**La Canasta in El Mercado**, 3425 E First St, East LA (☎213/269-2953). Three floors of authentic Mexican food and Central American food: chillis, chayotes and mouthwatering desserts.

**Claro's Italian Market**, 1003 E Valley Blvd, San Gabriel (☎818/288-2026). A compact but well-stocked haven of Italian wines, chocolate, crackers and own-brand frozen meals. A second room houses a hot and cold deli and a bakery with at least 40 varieties of cookie.

**Erewhon**, 7660 Beverly Blvd, West LA (☎213/937-0777). Next door to the *CBS* studios, selling pricey health food staples and all the wheat grass you can drink. The epitome of self/health-obsessed Los Angeles.

**Full O' Life**, 2525 W Magnolia Blvd, Burbank (☎818/845-8343). This mother of all health food stores dates back to 1959. It now offers a complete market, deli, dairy, restaurant and book department, and there are two nutritionists and a neuropathic doctor on the premises daily. The menu is organic and can be specially ordered.

**Gianfranco**, 11363 Santa Monica Blvd (☎310/477-7777). All Italian: pastas, cheeses, stuffed shells and meatballs.

**Living Planet**, 340 E Fourth St, Long Beach (☎310/495-0276). Finches, an indoor brook and a mini-Japanese rock garden characterize this pillow-strewn haven for New Agers. The vegetarian deli sells pasta and burritos and is one of the few places you can buy a soy latte.

**Standard Sweets and Snacks**, 18600 Pioneer Blvd, Artesia (☎310/860-6364). A good Indian finger food joint selling vegetarian dosas (pancakes) and delicious sweets.

**Wild Oats Community Market**, 603 S Lake Ave, Pasadena (☎818/792-1778). The best selection of organic wine in LA in a pleasantly European market atmosphere. There are wine-tasting festivities in October.

# Books

There are almost as many bookstores in LA as there are people. Of the ubiquitous **discount chains** that have spread across the US in the last few years, *Crown* offer the latest hardbacks and blockbusters plus many more (and magazines) at knock-down prices.

The city is also exceptionally well served by a wide range of **specialist bookstores** and many **secondhand bookstores**, worthy of several hours' browsing along the miles of dusty shelves.

## Specialist bookstores

**A Different Light**, 8853 Santa Monica Blvd, West Hollywood (☎310/854-6601). The city's best known gay and lesbian bookstore, with monthly art shows, readings, women's music events and comfortable chairs for lounging.

**Amok Books**, 1764 N Vermont Ave, Los Feliz (☎213/655-0956). Mayhem, true crimes, fanzines and neuropolitics; the extremes of information in print. A small shop with a large mail order clientele favoured by tabloid TV researchers. Now publishing its own authors.

**Bodhi Tree**, 8585 Melrose Ave, Hollywood (☎310/659-1733). New Age, occult and Philip K Dick.

**Book Soup**, 8818 W Sunset Blvd, West LA (☎310/659-3110). Great selection, right on Sunset Strip, open daily until midnight.

**Either/Or**, 124 Pier Ave, Hermosa Beach (☎310/374-2060). Thomas Pynchon's favourite LA bookstore, with a voluminous fiction selection and a wide variety of New Age tomes, and free publications littering the floor. Open till 11pm every night.

**Hennessey and Ingalls**, 1254 Third St Promenade, Santa Monica (☎310/458-9074). An impressive range of art and architecture books that may otherwise be hard to find; also rare posters and catalogues.

**Larry Edmunds Book Shop**, 6658 Hollywood Blvd, Hollywood (☎213/463-3273). Stacks of books on every aspect of film and theatre, with movie stills and posters.

**Midnight Special**, 1318 Third St Promenade, Santa Monica (☎310/393-2923). A large general bookstore, with eccentrically filled shelves and a broad focus on politics and social sciences.

**Norton Simon Museum Bookstore**, 411 W Colorado Blvd, Pasadena. Prices in this museum-attached store are lower than in any other art bookstore in LA, and the stock is superb.

**Scene of the Crime**, 13636 Ventura Blvd, Sherman Oaks (☎818/981-2583). New and used collection spanning everything criminal from hard-boiled private dicks to whodunnits, housed in a small room done up in the manner of the study of a country mansion.

## Secondhand books

**Acres of Books**, 240 Long Beach Blvd, Long Beach (☎310/437-6980). Worth a trip down the Blue Line *Metrorail* just to wallow in LA's largest secondhand collection.

**Book City**, 6627 Hollywood Blvd (☎213/466-2525). Tightly packed from floor to ceiling with eclectic titles.

# Music

If anything, **record stores** are even more plentiful than bookstores in LA. However, with the rise of the CD, these days only secondhand specialists like the ones we've listed below bother to stock significant numbers of vinyl records.

**Aron's Records**, 1150 N Highland Ave (☎213/469-4700). Secondhand discs – all styles, all prices, huge stock.

**House of Records**, 2314 Pico Blvd, Santa Monica (☎310/450-1222). Singles from 1949 to the present.

**Moby Disc**, 14410 Ventura Blvd, Sherman Oaks (☎818/990-2920). Secondhand and deletion stockist.

**Music and Memories**, 5057 Lankershim, N Hollywood (☎818/761-9827). 300 Sinatra LP's, and others that sound like he should be on them.

**Poo-Bah Records**, 1101 E Walnut Ave, Pasadena (☎818/449-3359). American and imported New Wave.

**Rhino Records**, 1720 Westwood Blvd (☎310/474-8685). The biggest selection of international independent releases. Also at 328 Santa Monica Blvd, Santa Monica (☎310/394-0842).

**Vinyl Fetish**, 7305 Melrose Ave (☎213/935-1300). Besides the punk and post-punk merchandise, a good place to discover what's new on the LA music scene.

## Miscellaneous

As you might imagine, creative juices flow freely in Los Angeles and its stores are no exception. There's no limit to what you can buy in LA's **miscellaneous stores**, and some of the outlets beggar belief. If it's gimmicks you're after, you won't go home empty-handed.

**LA County Coroner Gift Shop**, 1104 N Mission Rd (☎213/343-0760). Probably LA's weirdest shopping experience, with everything from beach towels to T-shirts and toe-tag key chains – all essential only-in-LA souvenirs.

**Beverly Hills Firefighters and Police Officers Association Department Store**, 421 N Rodeo Drive (☎310/278-1565). Soft toys, clothing and all sorts of paraphernalia adorned with LAPD and emergency services logos. A best-seller is the sweatshirt emblazoned with a barred jail cell and the words "Beverly Hills Bed and Breakfast".

# Listings

**Airport Information** *Hollywood/Burbank* ☎213/840-8847; *John Wayne/Orange County* ☎714/834-2400; *LAX* ☎310/646-5252; *Long Beach* ☎310/421-8293; *Ontario* ☎714/785-8838.

**Automobile Club of Southern California**, 2601 S Figueroa St (☎213/741-3111). For maps and other motoring information.

**Beach Information** Weather conditions ☎310/457-9701; surfers' weather ☎213/379-8471.

**Coastguard Search and Rescue** ☎310/4980-4444.

**Consulates** *UK*, 11766 Wilshire Blvd (☎310/477-3322); *Australia*, 11895 Wilshire Blvd (☎310/444-9310); *New Zealand*, 10960 Wilshire Blvd (☎310/207-1605).

**Currency Exchange** Outside of banking hours daily at LAX until 11.30pm. On Sat also at *Deak-International*, main office at 677 S Figueroa St, 10am–4pm.

**Dental Treatment** The cheapest place is the *USC School of Dentistry* (☎213/743-2800), on the USC Campus, costing $20–200. Turn up and be prepared to wait all day.

**Directory Enquiries** Local ☎411; Long distance 1, then area code, then 555-1212.

**Emergencies** ☎911. For less urgent needs: ambulance ☎213/483-6721; fire ☎213/384-3131 or 213/262-2111; paramedics ☎213/262-2111; police ☎213/625-3311.

**Hospitals** The following have 24hr emergency departments: Cedars-Sinai Medical Center, 8700 Beverly Blvd (☎310/855-6517); Good Samaritan Hospital, 616 Witmer St (☎213/397-2121); UCLA Medical Center, Tiverton (☎310/825-8611); Le Conte in Westwood Village (☎310/825-2111).

**International Newspapers** Both the USC and UCLA campuses have libraries holding recent overseas newspapers for browsing. Day-old English and European papers are on sale at *Universal News Agency*, 1655 N Las Palmas (daily 7am–midnight), and *World Book and News*, 1652 N Cahuenga Blvd (24hr).

**Left Luggage** At *Greyhound* stations and LAX for $1 a day ($2 for larger lockers).

**Mexican Tourist Office**, Suite 224, 10100 Santa Monica Blvd (☎310/203-8151). Call in for general information and to pick up a tourist card – necessary if you're heading over the border. Open Mon–Fri 9am–5pm.

**Pharmacies** 24-hr pharmacy at *Kaiser Permanente* in the LA Medical Center, 4867 Sunset Blvd, Hollywood (☎213/667-8301)and various *Thrifty* drugstores downtown.

**Post Office** The main downtown post office is at 900 N Alameda St (☎213/617-4543), next to Union Station. Zip Code is 90086; pick up letters Mon–Fri 8am–3pm.

**Smog** Like many other things in the city, LA's smog is more hype than reality. However, the city's basin has always been hazy, and, now exacerbated by car fumes, the air quality *is* often very poor and, especially in the Valleys in late summer, can sometimes be quite dangerous. An air-quality index is published daily, and if the air is really bad, warnings are issued on TV, press.

**Sports** Baseball: the *LA Dodgers* (☎213/224-1500) play at Dodger Stadium near downto.. 15; *California Angels* (☎714/937-7200) at Anaheim Stadium in Orange County, sea Basketball: the *LA Lakers* (☎310/419-3100) are at the Forum, in Inglewood, seats (often imj to get) $15–35. Football: the *LA Rams* (☎714/937-6767) also play at Anaheim Stadium, seats $1 Pasadena's 102,000-capacity Rose Bowl, seven miles northeast of downtown LA, is used for t annual New Year's Day Rose Bowl football game, and was the venue for several games in soccer's 1994 World Cup final. Hockey: *LA Kings* are also based at the Forum (☎310/419-3182), seats $10–25.

## travel details

### Trains

**Los Angeles** to: Anaheim (6–8 daily; 44min); Fullerton (for Disneyland) (6–8 daily; 35min); Las Vegas (1 daily; 6hr 55min); Pasadena (1 daily; 24min); San Bernardino (2 daily; 1hr 32min); San Clemente (1 daily; 1hr 30min); San Francisco (1 daily; 11hr 5min); San Juan Capistrano (6–8 daily; 1hr 15min). Also one train and four connecting buses daily to Glendale (15min); Van Nuys (30 min); Oxnard (1hr 30min); Ventura (1hr 57min).

### Buses

**Los Angeles** to: Las Vegas (13 daily; 6hr 15min); San Diego (7 daily; 3hr); San Francisco (9 daily; 11hr).

TWO

radio and in the
n, seats $6-
rs, $6-15.
ossible
-40.
sible

# GO AND AROUND

ree from smog, jungle-like entwinements of freeways, and shocking extremes of wealth and poverty, **San Diego** and much of its surrounding county represent the acceptable face of Southern California. Pipped by Los Angeles in the race to become *the* Southern Californian city, San Diego was for a long time considered an insignificant spot between Los Angeles and Mexico, but is now exacting revenge on its overgrown rival 125 miles to the north. Built on a gracefully curving bay, San Diego is not only scenically inviting, it also boasts a range of museums that is among the nation's most impressive, an evocative and nowadays well-tended history, several major tourist attractions, and much to discover away from the usual visitors' points of call.

Not surprisingly, the city is very much the social and commercial hub of San Diego County, and things change as you travel out from the metropolis. The **North County** divides into two quite different sections: the small and often enticing beach communities strung along the coast from the northern edge of San Diego itself to the rugged chaparral of the Camp Pendleton marine base; and, inland, the vineyards and avocado groves of a large agricultural area that reaches east towards much wilder and more mountainous land. Most settlements away from the coast are tiny and insular, and some have barely changed since the Gold Rush: a number of deep forests and several state parks are ideal for exploration by hiking and taking obscure back roads.

South from San Diego, there's little between the city and Mexico. **Tijuana**, just 25 miles from downtown, is an obvious jumping-off point for explorations of the whole country, and while it may not be the most appealing destination in Mexico, it's an entertaining enough place to spend a few hours – as thousands of Californians do each weekend. And since most of the border formalities are waived for anyone travelling less than twenty miles or so into Mexico, day trips to the party-time beach town of Rosarito and the more enticing Ensenada are perfectly viable.

Of course, there is also heavy traffic in the other direction, as hordes of Mexicans, both legal and "wetback", flood into Southern California. Most are hotel and restaurant workers, but first- and especially second-generation migrants are gradually becoming integrated into less menial levels of the workforce. However, Mexicans in San Diego County are largely ghettoized, their presence resented by those born-and-bred Californians who can't see beyond the evident strain on the social welfare and the healthcare system. Such prejudices eased the passage, in 1994, of "Proposition 187", which denies illegals access to all manner of social services.

---

### ACCOMMODATION PRICES

All accommodation prices in this book have been coded using the symbols below. Note that prices are for the least expensive double rooms in each establishment. For a full explanation see p.33 in *Basics*.

| | | | | |
|---|---|---|---|---|
| ① up to $30 | ② $30–45 | ③ $45–60 | ④ $60–80 | ⑤ $80–100 |
| ⑥ $100–130 | ⑦ $130–175 | ⑧ $175–250 | ⑨ $250+ | |

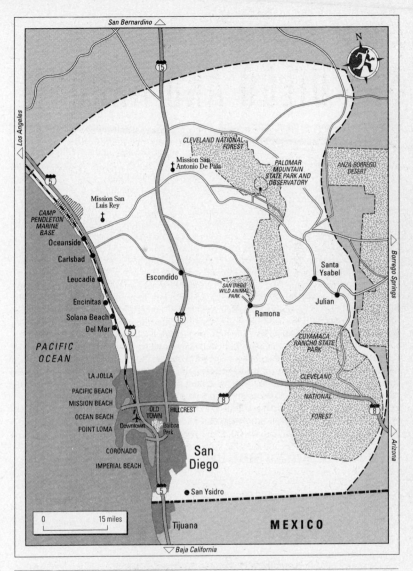

San Bernardino

Los Angeles

CLEVELAND NATIONAL FOREST

Mission San Antonio De Pala

PALOMAR MOUNTAIN STATE PARK AND OBSERVATORY

ANZA-BORREGO DESERT

Mission San Luis Rey

CAMP PENDLETON MARINE BASE

Oceanside

Carlsbad

Leucadia

Escondido

SAN DIEGO WILD ANIMAL PARK

Santa Ysabel

Borrego Springs

Encinitas

Solana Beach

Del Mar

Ramona

Julian

PACIFIC OCEAN

CUYAMACA RANCHO STATE PARK

LA JOLLA

PACIFIC BEACH

MISSION BEACH

OCEAN BEACH

POINT LOMA

OLD TOWN

HILLCREST

Downtown

Balboa Park

CLEVELAND

NATIONAL

FOREST

Arizona

San Diego

CORONADO

IMPERIAL BEACH

San Ysidro

0    15 miles

Tijuana

**MEXICO**

Baja California

# SAN DIEGO

Basking in almost constant sunshine and with its humidity tempered by the proximity of the ocean, **SAN DIEGO**, the second largest city in the state, is a near-perfect holiday resort. Anyone can enjoy idling on its varied beaches and viewing the obvious sights: San Diego Zoo, Sea World and the museums and sculptured greenery of Balboa

The telephone **area code** for San Diego and the surrounding area is ☎619.

Park. But at least as important as these is the recent expensive facelift given to the downtown area, restoring a sense of the city's real history and character.

The national image of San Diegans as healthy, affluent and conservative is true to a large extent — San Diego is certainly cleaner, and cleaner-cut, than Los Angeles or San Francisco. Yet it's also an extremely amiable and easy-going place. Increasing numbers of aspirant young professionals – the embodiment of the comfortable Southern Californian lifestyle – have swept away the reputation for dull smugness that San Diego acquired through the Sixties and Seventies and given the city quite a different face. The presence of two college campuses (SDSU and UCSD) also keeps the cobwebs away – and helps sustain the image of a city that's on the up-and-up.

The first European to land on Californian soil, the Portuguese adventurer Juan Rodríguez Cabrillo (in the employ of the Spanish), put ashore at Point Loma, a spot about ten miles from the centre of present-day San Diego, in 1542. White settlement didn't begin until two centuries later, however, with the building of a mission – the first in California – and a garrison, on a site overlooking San Diego Bay. Conflict between *Californios* and the fresh waves of settlers from the Midwest led to the raising of the Stars and Stripes over San Diego in 1847, an event closely followed by the transference of the Mexican provinces to the US. But San Diego missed out on the new mail route to the west and was plagued by a series of droughts through the 1860s, causing many bankruptcies. The arrival of the transcontinental Santa Fe railroad, soon followed by the building of the *Hotel del Coronado*, resulted in an economic boom through the 1880s, and a few decades later came the first of two international expositions in Balboa Park, which were to establish San Diego (and the park itself) nationwide.

In terms of major trade and significance the city has long played second fiddle to Los Angeles, although it has benefited to a large extent from a military presence. During World War II, the US Navy took advantage of the numerous sheltered bays and made San Diego its Pacific Command Center – a function it retains to the present day. The military dominates the local economy, along increasingly with tourism, not least in the hundreds of families who arrive in the city each week to watch their offspring participate in the Marine Academy's graduation ceremony.

# Arrival and information

**Drivers** will find it simple to reach the city centre from any of the three interstate highways: I-5 is the main link from Los Angeles and passes through the northern parts of the central city; from the east, I-8 runs through Hotel Circle before concluding in Ocean Beach; and I-15, the main route from inland San Diego County, cuts through the city's eastern suburbs. **Parking lots** are scattered around downtown, and there's plenty of metered parking – free overnight, but not allowed on evenings when the streets are being cleaned.

All forms of **public transport** drop you in the heart of downtown San Diego: **trains** use the Santa Fe Depot, close to the western end of Broadway, while the **Greyhound** terminal is even more central at Broadway and First Avenue. Lindbergh Field **airport** is only two miles from downtown, so low-flying jets are a feature of the city. There are two terminals, East and West, connected with downtown by bus #2 ($1.50), the service starting around 6am and finishing just after midnight. Obviously, given the distance, **taxis** into town aren't expensive, and quite a few hotels – even some of the budget ones

– offer guests a free **airport limo** service. All the main **car rental** firms have desks at the airport (see "Listings" on p.192).

## Information

A good first stop in the city is the **International Visitor Information Center**, 11 Horton Plaza, downtown at F Street and First Avenue (daily 8.30am–5pm; ☎236-1212), which has maps, the useful *Official Visitors Guide*, and all kinds of information on the area, including accommodation. Another useful source is the *HI-AYH* office inside the hostel foyer at 500 W Broadway (☎232-1133); outside business hours a recorded message gives local hostel information. For eating and entertainment information, scan the free weekly *San Diego Reader* and *Metropolitan*, which can be found in many shops, bars and clubs; you could also try the tourist-aimed *In San Diego Today* and Thursday's *San Diego Union-Tribune*.

# City transport

Despite its size, **getting around** San Diego without a car is easy, whether using buses, the tram-like Trolley or a rented bike. Taxis are also an option: the average fare is $2 for the first mile and $1.40 for each mile thereafter. Travelling can be harder at night, with most public transport routes closing down around 11pm or midnight. The transport system won't break anyone's budget, but a number of cut-rate tickets and passes can reduce costs over a few days or weeks.

## Buses

Of the seven companies that operate **buses** in the San Diego area, by far the most common is *San Diego Transit* (☎233-3004), which covers much of the city. There's a flat-rate fare of $1.75 (or $2 on the few express routes), transfers are free, and you should pay the exact fare when boarding (dollar bills are accepted). In general, the service is reliable and swift, with even comparatively far-flung spots connected to downtown – known on route maps and timetables as "Center City" and very much the hub of the network – at least twice an hour.

If you have any **queries** about San Diego's local buses, call into **The Transit Store**, 449 Broadway (Mon–Sat 8.30am–5.30pm; ☎234-1060) for detailed timetables, the free *Regional Transit Guide*, the Day Tripper Transit Pass, and monthly passes.

## The Trolley

Complementing bus travel around the city is the **San Diego Trolley** (often called the "Tijuana Trolley"), a tram that runs on the sixteen miles of track from the Santa Fe Depot (departures from C Street) to the US-Mexico border at San Ysidro. Within San Diego, fares are $1–1.50, to the border, $1.75. Tickets should be bought from the machines at Trolley stops, and occasionally an inspector may appear and demand proof of payment. Apart from being a cheap way to reach Mexico, the Trolley is a link to the southern San Diego communities of National City, Chula Vista and Palm City, and from the "transfer station" at Imperial and 12th its Euclid Avenue line makes much of south-

---

### USEFUL SAN DIEGO BUS ROUTES

The following buses connect **downtown San Diego** with the surrounding area:

| | | |
|---|---|---|
| **Balboa Park** #7, #16, #25. | **Hillcrest** #3, #11, #25. | **Mission Beach** #34. |
| **Coronado** #19, #903, #904. | **Imperial Beach** #901. | **Ocean Beach** #35. |
| **East San Diego** #1, #15. | **La Jolla** #34. | **Pacific Beach** #30, #34 |

---

### OLD TOWN TROLLEY TOURS

Not to be confused with the San Diego Trolley, the **Old Town Trolley Tour** is a two-hour narrated trip around San Diego's most interesting areas, including downtown, Balboa Park, the Old Town and Coronado, aboard an open-sided motor-driven carriage. A single ticket ($16) lasts all day and you can board and reboard the trolley at any of its stops. If you're short of time in San Diego, the tour is an excellent way to cover a lot of ground quickly, and the driver's anecdote-packed commentary is never boring. Leaflets detailing the route are found in hotel lobbies and at tourist information offices; alternatively call ☎298-8687.

---

eastern San Diego easily accessible. A new section of the network, due to open in 1996, runs to Old Town San Diego. Trolleys leave every fifteen minutes during the day; the last service back from San Ysidro leaves at 1am (and there's one an hour through Saturday night), so an evening of south-of-the-border revelry and a return to San Diego the same night is quite possible.

#### Cut-rate tickets and passes

If you intend to use public transport a lot, buy the **Day Tripper Transit Pass**, which lasts one or four consecutive days ($5 or $15 respectively) and is valid on any San Diego Transit bus, as well as the Trolley and the San Diego Bay ferry (which sails between Broadway Pier downtown and Coronado; $2 each way, 50¢ for bicycles – see p.181 for more details). If you're around for a few weeks and using buses regularly, get a **Monthly Pass**, giving unlimited rides throughout one calendar month for $48; or the half-price, two-week version which goes on sale midway through each month.

#### Cycling

A good city for **cycling**, San Diego has many miles of bike paths as well as some fine park and coastal rides. Rental shops are easy to find, especially prevalent around bike-friendly areas: three reliable outlets are *Bikes & Beyond*, at the Ferry Landing, 1201 First St, Coronado (☎435-7180), *Hillcrest Bike Shop*, 141 W Washington St, Hillcrest (☎296-0618), and *Hamel's Action Sport Center*, 704 Ventura Place, Mission Beach (☎488-5050); such outlets also rent out roller blades and surf boards. You can carry bikes on several city bus routes; board at any bus stop displaying a bike sign and tack your machine securely (they're known to fall off) to the back of the bus. The Transit Store has copies of an explanatory leaflet entitled *How To Take Your Bike For A Ride*, and hands out free passes that allow you to take your bike on the Trolley.

# Accommodation

**Accommodation** is plentiful throughout San Diego, at prices to suit all pockets. Hotels and motels are abundant, and there's also a decent selection of hostels and B&Bs – only travellers with tents are likely to feel restricted, with just a couple of inconveniently located and comparatively expensive campgrounds to choose between.

The restoration of downtown – the best base if you're without a car and want to do more than idle by the ocean – has given rise to three hostels and a batch of surprisingly inexpensive hotels in renovated buildings. Sleeping is marginally more expensive at the many beach motels, though both Ocean Beach and Mission Beach have hostels and Coronado has a couple of excellent upmarket hotels. There's another group of motels close to the Old Town, useful if you're driving or just staying for a night while seeing the immediate area, and budget motels line the approach roads to the city.

**Bed and breakfast** accommodation is in ever increasing supply, especially in the Hillcrest district. Contact the downtown visitor center (see p.165), or send $3.95 for the *Bed & Breakfast Directory for San Diego*, PO Box 3292, San Diego, CA 92163 (☎1-800/ 619-7666).

Wherever you're staying, especially if you're arriving in summer, it's wise to **book in advance** – where this is essential, we've said as much below – though again, the downtown visitor center has a large stock of accommodation leaflets (many of which carry discount vouchers) and will phone around hotels, motels or hostels on your behalf for free. **Gay** travellers are unlikely to encounter hostility wherever they choose to stay in San Diego, and several hotels and bed and breakfast inns are particularly noted for their friendliness to gay guests (see p.191).

## Hostels

**Banana Bungalow**, 707 Reed Ave, Pacific Beach (☎273-3060 or 1-800/5-HOSTEL). Who cares about poky, scruffy rooms when you can party all night and sleep all day on the beach immediately outside? A free simple breakfast, keg nights, barbeques, a communal kitchen and a good rides board flesh out the package. Doubles for $35, six-person dorms for $15, twelve-person dorms for $11 and floor space, when there's nothing else, for $7. Turn off Mission Boulevard at no. 4250, or take bus #34. ①/②.

**Grand Pacific Hostel**, 437 J St at Fifth, downtown (☎232-3100 or 1-800/438-8622). Well placed hostel in a gracious Victorian house on the edge of the Gaslamp District. Beds in 6–8 bed rooms, with sheets and continental breakfast, for $12–16 depending on season; doubles available for $30. Free bike use, organized tours to Tijuana, and a handy shuttle to LA make this the best of the city hostels. ①/②.

**HI-Downtown**, 500 W Broadway at India, downtown (☎232-1133). Well-equipped hostel between the *Greyhound* and train stations. Combined with the *YMCA* and as popular with military personnel as with travellers. Dorms $10 for *HI* members, $13 for others, and more expensive private doubles. No curfew. ①/②.

**HI-Elliott Hostel**, 3790 Udal St, Ocean Beach (☎223-4778). Well-run, friendly and minus the relentless party-time atmosphere that prevails at the other hostels. However, it's a couple of miles back from the beach and, at six miles from downtown (on bus #35), awkward for getting about the rest of San Diego. Eight-bed (or smaller) dorms ($12) and double rooms ($15); non-members $3 extra. ①.

**Jim's San Diego**, 1425 C St (☎235-0234). Small, shared rooms at good rates in this friendly hostel close to downtown, just off the C Street Trolley route. First night $13 ($1 off for *IYHA* and students), subsequent nights $12, and weekly rates available; breakfast is included and there are barbeques every Wed and Sun. ①.

**Ocean Beach International Backpackers Hostel**, 4961 Newport Ave, Ocean Beach (☎223-7873 or 1-800/339-7263). New, predominantly fun-oriented place a block from the beach. Bikes and boards available for rent, and videos playing every night. Space in a 4-bed dorm $12, double rooms $15 each, all with sheets, showers and continental breakfast. Reserve in advance and get picked up, free, from your bus, train or plane. ①.

**YWCA**, 1012 C St, downtown (☎239-0355). Atmospheric 1920s structure with women-only accommodation, in small dorms or tidy private rooms. On the C Street Trolley route. ②.

## Downtown

**Corinthian Suites**, 1840 Fourth Ave at Elm (☎236-1600). Nicely furnished rooms with cooking facilities. ②.

**Downtown Inn**, 600 G St at Seventh (☎238-4100). Pleasant, modern hotel, with cable TV, cooking facilities and fridges in each room. ②.

**Horton Grand**, 311 Island Ave at Third (☎232-3861 or 1-800/542-1886). Classy, modernized century-old hostelry with fireplaces in most rooms, and staff dressed in Victorian-era costumes. ⑥.

**Hotel St James**, 830 Sixth Ave (☎234-0155). Gracious old building tastefully refurbished, though the comfortable rooms are slightly poky. ④.

**La Pensione**, 1700 India St, Little Italy (☎236-8000). Great value small hotel in a quiet area within walking distance of the city centre. The rooms, around a central court, are smallish but tastefully done out and equipped with microwave and fridge. ②–③.

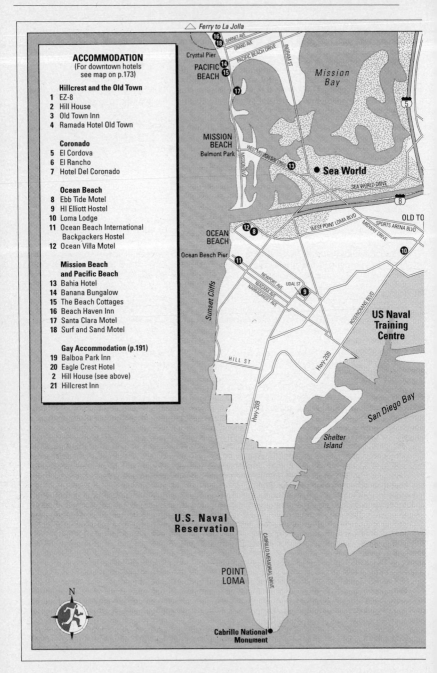

△ Ferry to La Jolla

**ACCOMMODATION**
(For downtown hotels
see map on p.173)

**Hillcrest and the Old Town**
1  EZ-8
2  Hill House
3  Old Town Inn
4  Ramada Hotel Old Town

**Coronado**
5  El Cordova
6  El Rancho
7  Hotel Del Coronado

**Ocean Beach**
8  Ebb Tide Motel
9  HI Elliott Hostel
10 Loma Lodge
11 Ocean Beach International
   Backpackers Hostel
12 Ocean Villa Motel

**Mission Beach
and Pacific Beach**
13 Bahia Hotel
14 Banana Bungalow
15 The Beach Cottages
16 Beach Haven Inn
17 Santa Clara Motel
18 Surf and Sand Motel

**Gay Accommodation (p.191)**
19 Balboa Park Inn
20 Eagle Crest Hotel
2  Hill House (see above)
21 Hillcrest Inn

Crystal Pier

PACIFIC
BEACH

Mission
Bay

MISSION
BEACH
Belmont Park

● Sea World

SEA WORLD DRIVE

OCEAN
BEACH
Ocean Beach Pier

WEST POINT LOMA BLVD

SPORTS ARENA BLVD

OLD TO

MIDWAY DRIVE

Sunset Cliffs

NEWPORT AVE

UDAL ST

NIAGARA AVE

NARRAGANSETT AVE

ROSECRANS BLVD

**US Naval
Training
Centre**

HILL ST

Hwy 209

San Diego Bay

Shelter
Island

**U.S. Naval
Reservation**

CABRILLO MEMORIAL DRIVE

POINT
LOMA

N

**Cabrillo National ●
Monument**

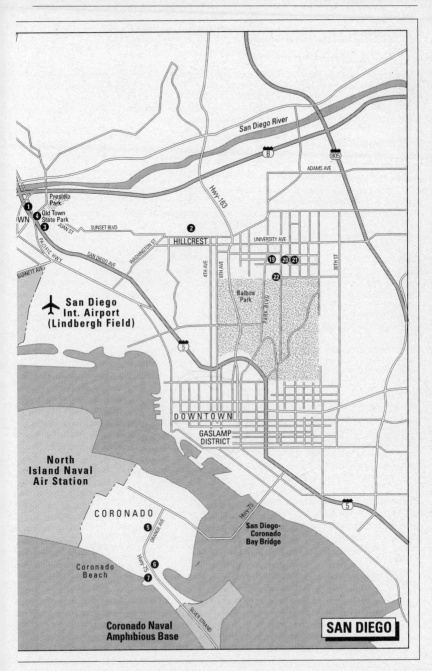

**Marriott Suites**, 701 A St at Seventh (☎696-9800 or 1-800/962-1367). Swish high-rise; quiet periods can bring big reductions on the regular rates. ⑦.

**The Maryland Hotel**, 630 F St (☎239-9243). Amenable restored hotel, if somewhat lacking in frills, in a good downtown location. ②.

**Pickwick Hotel**, 132 W Broadway at First (☎234-9200 or 1-800/675-7122). Though large and characterless, this shares a building with the *Greyhound* station, making it a convenient, inexpensive place to flop down after a long bus journey. ②.

**7 & 1 Mototel**, 1919 Pacific Hwy (☎1-800/624-9338). Located in a quiet section of downtown close to Seaport Village; all rooms have fridges and coffee-makers. ②.

## Hillcrest and the Old Town

**EZ-8**, 4747 Pacific Hwy, Old Town (☎295-2512). Unexceptional motel with the area's lowest rates. ②

**Hill House**, 2504 A St, Hillcrest (☎239-4738). Mixed gay and straight B&B. See p.191. ④

**Old Town Inn**, 4444 Pacific Hwy, Old Town (☎1-800/225-9610). Serviceable base within a few strides of the Old Town's liveliest areas. ③.

**Ramada Hotel Old Town**, 2435 Jefferson St, Old Town (☎1-800/260-8500). An attractive exterior conceals average rooms and facilities; nonetheless, it does offer a great location, free evening cocktails and a complimentary, albeit skimpy, breakfast. ⑥.

## Coronado

**El Cordova**, 1351 Orange Ave (☎435-4131 or 1-800/229-2032). The best deal in Coronado, but no secret so you'll need to reserve at least six months ahead. Lovely rooms in hacienda-style buildings ranged around lovely gardens. There's the obligatory pool, and some rooms have kitchenettes. ④/⑤.

**El Rancho**, 370 Orange Ave (☎435-2251). Tiny but attractive motel with relaxing decor, ranking as the cheapest on this side of the water. Rooms come equipped with microwave ovens and fridges, and there's a Jacuzzi for guests' use. ③.

**Hotel Del Coronado**, 1500 Orange Ave (☎522-8000 or 1-800/468-3533). The place that put Coronado on the map and which is still the area's major tourist sight (see p.181) – it's been pampering wealthy guests for over a century. ⑦.

## Ocean Beach

**Ebb Tide Motel**, 5082 W Point Loma Blvd (☎224-9339). Modestly sized motel that's handy for the beach and has kitchenettes and cable in rooms. ②.

**Loma Lodge**, 3202 Rosecrans St (☎222-0511 or 1-800/266-0511). Among the best value in the district, with a beckoning pool and complimentary breakfast; good for exploring the peninsula though not close to the beach. ②–③.

**Ocean Villa Motel**, 5142 W Point Loma Blvd (☎224-3481 or 1-800/759-0012). Usefully placed for the sands, with kitchenette-equipped ocean-view rooms and a pool. ③.

## Mission Beach and Pacific Beach

**Bahia Hotel**, 998 W Mission Bay Drive, Mission Beach (☎488-0551 or 1-800/288-0770). Sprawling pleasure complex curling around the waters of Mission Bay – a watersports fan's delight. ⑥.

**The Beach Cottages**, 4255 Ocean Blvd, Mission Beach (☎483-7440). Beside the beach and *Banana Bungalow*, three blocks south of the pier, but away from the crush – a relaxing place for a few days of quiet tanning. ④.

**Beach Haven Inn**, 4740 Mission Blvd, Pacific Beach (☎272-3812 or 1-800/831-6323). Comfortable, tastefully decorated rooms around heated pool; continental breakfast included. One of the nicest places to unwind at the beach. Sept–May ④; July & Aug ⑤.

**Santa Clara Motel**, 839 Santa Clara Place, Mission Beach (☎488-1193). No-frills rooms with kitchenettes an easy walk from the hectic Mission Beach sands, and a good half-mile north of Belmont Park. Winter ②, summer ④.

**Surf & Sand Motel**, 4666 Mission Blvd, Pacific Beach (☎483-7420). Cosy motel close to the beach. ③.

## MISSION BEACH APARTMENTS

Apartments rented by the week make up the bulk of the accommodation in Mission Beach – a great place to be if your primary concerns are sea, sun and surf. Typically sleeping between four and six people, they cost from $250–300 a week, and can be a good deal for several people who are sharing, although it's essential to book at least six months ahead. A number of agents offer deals; try *Beach & Bayside Vacations*, 7657 Wellington Ave (☎565-7986), or *Penny Realty Beach & Bay Rentals*, 3803 Mission Blvd (☎1-800/748-6704).

## La Jolla

**Colonial Inn**, 910 Prospect St (☎454-2181 or 1-800/832-5525). A Twenties landmark sited in the heart of La Jolla and a short walk from the cove; various package deals, especially in winter, bring significant savings on the regular rate. ⑧.

**La Jolla Cove Suites**, 1155 Coast Blvd (☎459-2621 or 1-800/248-2683). Kitchen-equipped rooms and suites right by the sea – better value for 3 or 4 people sharing the $160 two-bedroom suites. ⑨/⑥.

**La Valencia Hotel**, 1132 Prospect St (☎454-0771 or 1-800/451-0772). Within these radiant pink walls Hollywood celebs enjoyed themselves in the 1920s; today the place is less glamorous but no less plush, with beautiful public areas and sea views. No reductions. ⑦.

**Prospect Park Inn**, 1110 Prospect St (☎454-0133 or 1-800/433-1609). Well priced for the area, with views over the ocean and complimentary breakfast and afternoon tea. Studios and a range of rooms. ⑤–⑥.

## Campgrounds

Of the city's half-dozen **campgrounds**, only two accept tents. The best-placed of these is *Campland on the Bay*, 2211 Pacific Beach Drive (☎1-800/BAY FUN), linked to downtown by bus #30; the alternative, *San Diego Metro KOA*, 111 N Second Ave (☎1-800/762-CAMP), is fifteen miles south in Chula Vista – from downtown, take bus #29 or the Trolley to 24th Street. Both charge over $20 for the most basic sites, making **Silver Strand State Park** (☎435-5184; $14), a couple of miles south of Coronado on bus #901 (see p.182), a reasonable option, if inconvenient for the city.

# The City

You never feel under pressure in San Diego to do anything other than enjoy yourself. Though the work-hard play-hard ethic is as prevalent here as anywhere else in Southern California, the accent is very strongly on the second part of the equation. Indeed, the city, with its easily managed central area, scenic bay, lively beaches, plentiful parks and commendable museums, is hard not to like from the moment you arrive – even New York street people are known to migrate to San Diego for the winter.

The city divides into several fairly easily defined sections. You'll probably spend at least some of your time **downtown**, where anonymous high-rise bank buildings stand shoulder-to-shoulder with more personable structures from San Diego's earlier boom days, in what's now the café- and bar-choked **Gaslamp District**, bestowing a mood more welcoming than is usual in American city centres. Besides being the nucleus of the public transport network, downtown contains a fair chunk of the city's nightlife, and has much inexpensive accommodation. A few miles northeast, the well-maintained parkland of massive **Balboa Park** not only contains San Diego's major museums and the highly rated San Diego Zoo, but is perfectly suited for strolls and picnics beside the walkways that cut around the many acres of carefully nurtured plant life. A similar distance northwest of downtown is where the city really got started: the first white settlement growing up beneath the hill that was site of the original San Diego mission, an area now fastidiously sanitized as **Old Town San Diego**. The sense of history here is often powerfully evoked and quite believable, despite the inevitable Mexican-themed shops and restaurants which strain credibility – though not to the extent that you should be put off visiting. A couple of other districts close to downtown don't have any points of interest as such, but can be worth a call for different reasons. You might find yourself in **East San Diego**, whose large college campus livens up what is an otherwise featureless sprawl; while **Hillcrest**'s eclectic mix of trendy young professionals, gays, solvent bohemians and would-be artists make it one of the city's best areas for ethnic eating and intellectually slanted nightlife.

More appealing for pure relaxation are the **beach** communities – all within easy reach of downtown and good for a half-day trip out, or longer, if bronzing beside the ocean is your main reason for being in San Diego (see pp.180–186 for details).

# Downtown San Diego

Always vibrant and active, **DOWNTOWN** contains the real pulse of San Diego and is much the best place to start a tour of the city. Improvement initiatives begun in the late 1970s have restored many of the city's older buildings, resulting in several blocks of stylishly renovated 1920s architecture, while the more recent, sleek bank buildings symbolize the city's growing economic importance on the Pacific Rim. Though downtown is largely safe by day, at night it can be unwelcoming place, and you should confine your after-dark visits to the restaurants and clubs of the comparatively well-lit and well-policed Gaslamp District.

## Along Broadway

One of the most memorable first impressions of San Diego is that received by travellers arriving by train at the **Santa Fe Railroad Depot**, whose tall Moorish archways, built to welcome visitors to the 1915 Panama-California Exposition in Balboa Park, still evoke a sense of grandeur. The architecture of the Depot provides a dramatic contrast to the post-modern contours of the neighbouring **American Plaza**, a combination of high-rise offices and glass-roofed public areas, which began as a symbol of San Diego's pre-eminence in international finance in the mid-1980s but found its development stunted by the economic slump of the early 1990s. Nonetheless, the plaza succeeds in throwing a sheltering canopy over the main terminal of the San Diego Trolley, and over the entrance to the downtown branch of La Jolla's **Museum of Contemporary Art** (Tues–Thurs & Sat 10am–5pm, Fri 10am–8pm, Sun noon–5pm; $4, free first Tues of month), which frequently stages temporary shows of compelling contemporary work.

American Plaza marks the western end of **Broadway**, a busy main drag which slices through the centre of downtown. The most hectic portion of Broadway is the block between Fourth and Fifth Avenues, where the pedestrian traffic is a broad mix: shoppers, sailors, yuppies, homeless people and others, some lingering around the fountains on the square outside **Horton Plaza** (Mon–Fri 10am–9pm, Sat 10am–8pm, Sun 11am–6pm), San Diego's major upmarket shopping place and a posing platform for the city's spoilt young things. Though in essence a typical American shopping mall, Horton Plaza differs in that it has no roof, making the most of the region's sunny climate: a deliberate attempt to resemble a Mediterranean plaza, albeit one with pseudo Art Deco features and the odd dollop of Victoriana. Completed in 1985 for a cool $140 million, Horton Plaza became the centrepiece of the new-look downtown, and gave the signal for prices to soar in the nearby condo developments. The top level, with its open-air eating places, is the one to make for. Although the food is more expensive here than in the streets, it's fun to sit over a coffee or snack and watch the parade go by – especially on Saturday when the suburban mall rats show off their latest T-shirts and $100 wraparound shades. Few of

**DOWNTOWN SAN DIEGO**

△ Little Italy (1 block)    △ Hillcrest (25 blocks)

CEDAR ST
BEECH ST
ASH ST
A ST
B ST
C ST
BROADWAY
E ST
F ST
G ST
MARKET ST
ISLAND AVE
J ST
K ST

**ACCOMMODATION**
1 Downtown Inn
2 Grand Pacific Hostel
3 HI-Downtown Hostel
4 Horton Grand
5 Marriott Suites
6 Maryland Hotel
7 Pickwick Hotel
8 Hotel St. James

Firehouse Museum
San Diego County Administration Center
Maritime Museum
San Diego Bay Ferry Docking Stage
Santa Fe Railroad Depot & American Plaza
Greyhound Station
Tramline
Transit Store
Horton Plaza
Library
Newtown Park
GAS LAMP DISTRICT
William Heath Davis House
Seaport Village
San Diego Convention Center
Embarcadero Marina Park

Coronado
PACIFIC HIGHWAY
NORTH HARBOR DRIVE
KETTNER BOULEVARD
COLUMBIA ST
INDIA ST
STATE ST
UNION ST
FRONT ST
FIRST AVE
SECOND AVE
THIRD AVE
FOURTH AVE
FIFTH AVE
SIXTH AVE
SEVENTH AVE
EIGHTH AVE
Balboa Park
YWCA & Jim's Hostel

N
EMBARCADERO
HARBOR DRIVE
Tramline

0    200 yds

East San Diego & Coronado ▽

the stores are worth much more than a browse, but don't miss the 21-foot-tall **Jessop Clock**, on level one, made for the California State Fair of 1907.

Further along Broadway things begin to get tatty and dull, but walk a couple of blocks or so for the secondhand bookstores (such as *Wahrenbrock's Book House*, 726 Broadway) and the **library**, 820 E St (Mon–Thurs 10am–9pm, Fri & Sat 9.30am–5.30pm), which has book sales on Friday and Saturday and an extensive reference section where you can pore over Californian magazines and newspapers. Tucked away on an upper floor of the library, the **Wangenheim Room** (Mon–Sat 1.30–4.30pm) holds the obsessive collection of local turn-of-the-century bigwig Julius Wangenheim, including Babylonian clay tablets, palm-leaf books from India, silk scrolls from China and many more trans-global curios documenting the history of the printed word – worth a stop for its oddity value.

Less quirky, but a useful time-passer, the **Firehouse Museum**, six blocks north of Broadway at 1572 Columbia St (Wed–Fri 10am–2pm, Sat & Sun 10am–4pm; $2, first Sun free), dutifully maintains firefighting appliances and outfits and has photographs vividly recalling some of San Diego's most horrific fires – and the men, horses and equipment who tackled them.

## The Gaslamp District
South of Broadway, the **Gaslamp District** occupies a sixteen-block area running south to K Street, bordered by Fourth and Seventh Avenues. This was the heart of San Diego when it was still a frontier town, and was, according to local opinion, full of "whore-

houses, opium dens and guys getting rolled". The area remained at the core of local carnality for years: street prostitution, though illegal from 1916, flourished here until the late 1970s, when the revitalization operation cleaned things up – and the city's flesh-for-sale moved to the erotic-dancer bars near the Sports Arena, a couple of miles northwest.

The few remaining adult emporia are incongruities on the smart streets lined with cafés, antique stores, art galleries – and ersatz "gaslamps", powered by electricity. This is now the heart of the city's nightlife, its Friday and Saturday night bustle unimaginable just a few years ago. There's also a relatively high police profile designed to keep the area clean and safe. A tad artificial it may be, but the Gaslamp District is intriguing to explore, not least for the scores of late nineteenth-century buildings in various stages of renovation. They're best discovered – and the area's general history gleaned – during the two-hour **walking tour** (Sat 11am; $5, includes admission to the William Heath Davis House) which begins from the small cobbled square at the corner of Fourth and Island Avenues. The square is within the grounds of the **William Heath Davis House** (Mon–Fri 1.30–4.30pm, Sat 11am–2pm; $3), included in the walking tour, though also visitable on your own. It was William Davis who founded "New Town" San Diego in 1850, believing that a waterfront location (the fledgling city had previously been located a few miles inland and to the north – the site of Old Town San Diego; see p.178) would stimulate growth. It didn't, at least not for some time, and Davis left the city before long, eventually dying penniless. He, and the more influential Alonzo Horton, are remembered in the house through photos, while the fittings and furnishings recreate something of the mood of their times.

Even without the walking tour, there's a lot to be enjoyed around this area simply by keeping your eyes open. One of the finest interiors in the whole city is in *Johnny M's 801*, a seafood restaurant at 801 Fourth Ave, restored in the style of the tavern which opened here in 1907 (see also p.186). Diners stuff themselves with crabs' legs beneath an epic stained-glass dome and on a tiled floor once described as "the handsomest floor in the state" – even if you're not hungry, drop in for a look. Also worth a peek is the **Horton Grand**, a hotel opposite the William Davis House, painstakingly rebuilt in Victorian style with original artefacts from what was one of the raunchiest hotels in the country; the management claim that it was the site of the "Canary Cottage", one of the West's more notorious brothels. If you fancy staying here, see "Accommodation".

## The Embarcadero, Seaport Village and around

Over the last few years, the once-shabby streets south of the Gaslamp District have been transformed by the arrival of elegant, expensive condos – providing a fitting setting for the San Diego Convention Center, a $165-million boost to civic pride that opened in 1989 and is booked solidly into the twenty-first century. For non-convention-going visitors, the most interesting facet of the building is the sail-like roof imitating the yachts tethered in the marina, just beyond, which also indicates the beginning of the **Embarcadero**, a pathway that continues for a mile or so along the bayside, curling around to the western end of downtown.

The path is favoured by San Diegan strollers, joggers and kite-flyers, and most out-of-towners get no further along than **Seaport Village**, a twee but mildly enjoyable collection of souvenir shops and restaurants, often with free clown and puppet shows laid on for kids. You should, however, make a point of strolling the full length of the Embarcadero, as it makes an enjoyable route to the trio of historic ships moored beside Harbor Drive, which is also the departure point for the ferry to Coronado (see p.181).

The three vintage sailing craft, just north of the B Street Pier, make up the **Maritime Museum** (daily 9am–8pm; $6). The most interesting of them is the *Star of India*, built in 1863 and now the world's oldest still-afloat merchant ship. Alongside, the

*Berkeley*, which served for sixty years as a ferry on San Francisco Bay, and the *Medea*, a small steam-powered yacht, are of very minor appeal.

Landlubbers nonplussed by the Maritime Museum should explore the **San Diego County Administration Center** (Mon–Fri 8.30am–5pm; free), one of the most distinctive public buildings in California: a rich burst of Spanish colonial with a beaux-arts arrangement of gold and azure tiles. It's one of the unsung beauties of San Diego, and from Harbour Drive you can walk right through the foyer to the main entrance, on the way viewing the *Guardian of Water* statue (on the Harbor Drive side) and the three interior murals.

# Balboa Park and San Diego Zoo

The thousand sumptuous acres of green **BALBOA PARK** contains one of the largest groupings of museums in the US. Yet its real charm is simply itself: its trees, gardens, traffic-free promenades – and a thumping concentration of Spanish colonial-style buildings.

Balboa Park was a wasteland inhabited by cacti, rattlesnakes and lizards until 1898, when a local woman, Kate Sessions, began cultivating nurseries and planting trees there in lieu of rent. The first buildings were erected for the 1915 Panama-California Exposition, held to celebrate the opening of the canal. The memories of its success lingered well into the Depression, and in 1935 another building programme was undertaken for the California-Pacific Exposition.

## Along El Prado: the major museums

The major museums flank **El Prado**, the park's pedestrianized east–west axis which bulges out to form a plaza at the heart of the park. Here you'll find the **Timkin Art Gallery** (Oct–Aug Tues–Sat 10am–4.30pm, Sun 1.30–4.30pm; closed Sept; free), filled with high quality art that makes the stiflingly formal atmosphere and the evangelical zeal of the attendants worth enduring. Inside, fine works from the early Renaissance to the nineteenth century include impressive pieces by Rembrandt and El Greco, and a stirring collection of Russian icons.

By contrast, the **San Diego Museum of Art** (Tues–Sun 10am–4.30pm; $6) has few individually striking items: many of the major names are represented, but not by their most acclaimed work. There's a solid stock of European paintings from the Renaissance and succeeding styles through to the nineteenth-century "Europe in Transition" canvases, matched by a fairly uninspiring US selection from the same century, and finally some welcome bright rooms of moderns. The biggest surprises,

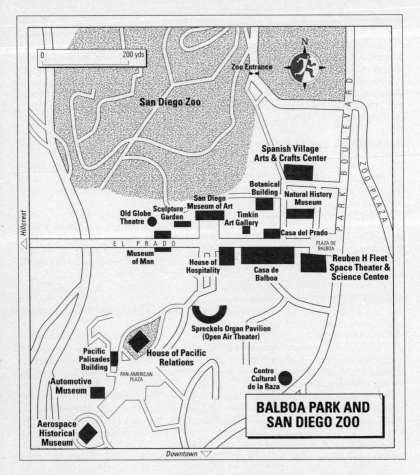

perhaps, are amid the exquisitely crafted pieces within the Asian section, mainly from China and Japan but with smaller representations from India and Korea. Outside, don't miss the **Sculpture Court and Garden**, which you can walk into free at any time, with a number of formidable works, most notably those by Henry Moore and Alexander Calder.

The contents of the **Museum of Man** (daily 10am–4.30pm; $4), which straddles El Prado, veer from the banal to the excellent – and into the truly bizarre. The demonstrations of tortilla-making and Mexican loom-weaving are laboured, while the large number of replicas – particularly the huge "Mayan" stones that dominate the ground level – would have more impact simply as photos. But there's much to be seen and be fascinated by, not least the Native American displays; the temporary shows, too, can be absorbing.

The structure between the House of Hospitality and the Space Theater (see below) replicates the *Casa de Balboa* – built for the 1915 Expo to display the latest gadgetry – and houses four small museums. Of these, just two will occupy you for more than a few minutes: the **Museum of Photographic Arts** (daily 10am–5pm; $3), mounting challenging temporary shows, and the **Museum of San Diego History** (Wed–Sun 10am–4.30pm; $4), virtually next door, cleverly charting the booms and busts that have turned San Diego from uninviting scrubland into the fifth biggest city in the US within 150 years. Of the building's other collections, the **Hall of Champions** (daily 10am–4.30pm; $3) is dull unless you're knowledgeable on American sports in general, and San Diegan athletic achievers in particular; and only the craftsmanship put into creating scaled-down versions of large chunks of the US, and the tracks crossing them, make the **San Diego Railroad Museum** (Wed–Fri 11am–4pm, Sat & Sun 11am–5pm; $3) viewable.

The **Reuben H Fleet Space Theater and Science Center** (daily 9.30am–9.30pm; Theater $3.50, Science Center $2.50), close to the Park Boulevard end of El Prado, is one of the most recent and most hyped features of Balboa Park, with a "gee whiz" attitude out of step with everything around it. The Science Center has a lame batch of child-oriented exhibits, although impressive sensations can be induced by the Space Theater's dome-shaped tilting screen and 152 loudspeakers, which will take you on stomach-churning trips into volcanoes, over waterfalls and through outer space.

Across the plaza, the worthy **Natural History Museum** (daily 10am–4.30pm; $5), has a great collection of fossils, a comprehensive if somewhat unappetizing array of stuffed creatures, an entertaining hands-on mineral section, and an affecting section called "On The Edge", dealing with a few of the numerous species of wildlife whose existence is threatened and pulling no punches when explaining why. A short walk behind the Natural History building, the **Spanish Village Arts and Crafts Center** (daily 11am–4pm; free) dates from the 1935 Expo and was designed in the style of a Spanish village. Some 42 craftspeople now have their workshops here and you can watch them practise their skills: painting, sculpture, photography, pottery and glass-working. It's fun to walk through, though you'd have to be pretty loaded to buy any of the original works.

### The rest of the park

The fifteen-minute walk to the Aerospace Historical Museum, the major collection away from El Prado, takes you past several spots of varying interest. There's a **puppet theatre** (shows at 11am, 1pm & also 3.30pm at weekends; $1.50, children $1), in the Pacific Palisades building; the **Spreckels Organ Pavilion** (free Sunday concerts) is home to the world's largest pipe organ; and the series of cottages comprising the **House of Pacific Relations** (Sun 1.30–4pm; free) contains extremely kitsch collections from countries all over the world – enjoy the proffered tea, coffee and cakes but don't expect any multicultural education.

All but the most technically minded could find a better place to pass an hour than in the **Aerospace Museum** (daily 10am–4.30pm; $5); if you're really keen to see a replica of *The Spirit of St Louis* (aviator Charles Lindbergh began the journey that was to make him the first solo pilot to cross the Atlantic in San Diego), you can do so quickly and for nothing because it's in the entrance hall. Otherwise, on the paying side of the turnstiles, there's a numbing mass of portraits of anyone who was ever anyone in aviation, and fairly tedious collections of model planes, real planes and plane-related artefacts charting the ages of manned flight from the Wright brothers to the Space Shuttle.

Next to the Aerospace building, the **Automotive Museum** (May–Aug daily 9am–5pm; Sept–April daily 10.30am–4.30pm; $5) continues the technological theme, with a host of cars, bikes and other internal-combustion contraptions. The most curious item, however, is the *Lincoln Continental* which carried President Reagan to a would-be assassin's bullet in 1981.

### San Diego Zoo

The **San Diego Zoo** (mid-June to early Sept daily 9am–10pm, early Sept to mid-June daily 9am–6pm, last entry an hour before closing; $13), immediately north of the main museums, is one of the city's biggest and best-known attractions. As zoos go, it's undoubtedly one of the world's best, with a wide selection of animals – among them very rare Chinese pheasants, Mhorr gazelles and a freak-of-nature two-headed corn snake – as well as some pioneering techniques of keeping them in captivity: animals are restrained in "psychological cages", with moats or ridges rather than bars. It's an enormous place, and you can easily spend a full day here; take a bus tour early on to get a general idea of the layout, or survey the scene on the vertiginous *Skyfari* overhead tramway. Bear in mind, though, that many of the creatures get sleepy in the midday heat and retire behind bushes to take a nap. There's a children's zoo as well, with walk-through bird cages and an animal nursery.

The $13 **admission** only covers entry to the main zoo; to include the children's zoo, a 35-minute bus tour and unlimited rides on the *Skyfari* you'll need the $16 *Deluxe Ticket Package*. A $27 ticket also admits you to the San Diego Wild Animal Park (near Escondido; see p.196) within a five-day period.

### Centro Cultural de la Raza

Visiting all the museums in Balboa Park, or spending hours threading through the crowds at the zoo, could well leave you too jaded even to notice the unassuming round building on the edge of the park beside Park Boulevard. This, the **Centro Cultural de la Raza** (Wed–Sun noon–5pm; free), mounts strong temporary exhibits on Native American and Hispanic life in an atmosphere altogether less stuffy than the showpiece museums of the park – make time for it.

# Old Town San Diego

In 1769, Spanish settlers chose what's now Presidio Hill as the site of the first of California's missions. As the soldiers began to leave the mission and the presidio, they settled at the foot of the hill. This was the birthplace of San Diego, later to be dominated by Mexican officials and afterwards the early arrivals from the eastern US, and the area is now preserved as **OLD TOWN SAN DIEGO** (locally referred to as "the Old Town"), a state historical park that holds a number of original adobe dwellings, together with the inevitable souvenir shops. It is undoubtedly a tourist trap, but one of the best in its class.

### Old Town Practicalities

To **get to the Old Town**, take bus #4 or #5 from downtown; by car, take I-5 and exit on Old Town Avenue, following the signs. Alternatively, from I-8 turn off onto Taylor Street and head left on Juan Street. Without a good map, trying to weave here through the streets from Balboa Park is doomed to failure.

Most things in the park which aren't historical – the shops and restaurants – open around 10am and close at 10pm (though a number of the restaurants are doing business until about midnight or later), but the **best time** to be around is during the afternoon, when you can learn something of the general history of the area and enter the more interesting of the adobes (including several which are otherwise kept locked) with the excellent **free walking tour**, which leaves at 2pm from outside the Machado y Silvas Adobe by the plaza. You can get details on this, and other aspects of the park, at the **visitor center** inside the park on San Diego Avenue (daily 10am–5pm; ☎219-1019).

### Exploring the Old Town

Many of the old structures are thoughtfully preserved and contain a lot of their original furnishings, giving a good indication of early San Diegan life. Of the places not covered on the walking tour, one of the more significant is the **Casa de Estudillo** on Mason Street (summer 10am–6pm; rest of year daily 10am–5pm; $2), built by the commander of the presidio, José Mariá de Estudillo, in 1827. Next door, the **Casa de Bandini** was the home of the politican and writer Juan Bandini and the social centre of San Diego during the mid-nineteenth century. Following the switch of ownership of California, the house became the *Cosmopolitan Hotel*, considered among the finest in the state, and some of the elegant features of that period can still be seen in the dining room. You can wander through the rest of the building freely, and reward yourself with a lavish Mexican lunch in the courtyard restaurant (see "Eating").

Most of the other buildings in and around the park need little more than a passing glance, with the exception of the **Whaley House**, just beyond the park gates on San Diego Avenue (Wed–Sun 10am–4.30pm; $4). The first brick house in California – once the home of Thomas Whaley, an early San Diego luminary – displays furniture and photos from his time, and a reconstruction of the courtroom held here from 1869. A few strides south of the Whaley House, a faintly spooky **cemetery**, once the site of public executions, holds tombs whose inscriptions read like a *Who's Who* of late nineteenth-century San Diego.

Modest though it is, the cemetery makes a better stop than the **San Diego Union Building**, where the city's newspaper began in 1868; the Old West memorabilia inside the **Seeley Stables** (times as Casa de Estudillo; admission with the same ticket); or the **Heritage Park**, just north on Juan Street, where several Victorian buildings have been gathered from around the country – to be inhabited at weekends by period-attired history fanatics.

It's more productive to walk along Conde Street and peer into the atmospheric, sculpture-filled interior of the **Old Adobe Chapel**, dating from the 1850s and used as a place of worship until 1917. The lack of markers to the chapel means that visitors often unknowingly pass it by. On the other hand, many deliberately choose to avoid one of the park's more curious places: the **Mormon Battalion visitor center** (daily 9am–9pm; free) which, provided you're not spiritually suggestible (Mormons are always eager to recruit) and can tolerate the sentimental accounts, adds up to an absorbing hour. The center commemorates a crucial and heroic episode in Mormon history: the two-thousand-mile march of the Mormons after the assassination of the religion's founder, Joseph Smith, in Carthage, Illinois, in 1844. Travelling west in search of religious freedom, Smith's followers volunteered to fight in the Mexican-American War, reinforcing the US army in the West, and built a wagon road from Santa Fe to California, an arduous undertaking that involved carving through Box Canyon (see p.223) in the Anza Borrego Desert. After a spell of occupation in San Diego, most of the Mormons headed up to what became Salt Lake City, establishing a community too remote to suffer further persecution – and now too big and powerful to be threatened by non-believers.

## Bazaar del Mundo

An idealized recreation of an eighteenth-century Mexican street market, **Bazaar del Mundo** fills a corner of the Old Town. Though ringed by gift shops, it's enjoyable enough on a Sunday afternoon, when there's free music and folk dancing in its tree-shaded courtyard. It's also a fair place to **eat**: stands serve fresh tortillas, *La Panaderia* sells Mexican pastries for a dollar, and the *Casa de Pico* (see "Eating", p.187) is worth a longer meal break.

## Presidio Hill: the Serra Museum – and the San Diego Mission

The Spanish-style building that now sits atop Presidio Hill is only a rough approximation of the original mission – moved in 1774 – but contains the intriguing **Junípero Serra Museum** (Tues–Sat 10am–4.30pm, Sun noon–4.30pm; $3): a gathering of Spanish furniture, diaries and historical documents pertaining to the man who led the Spanish colonization of California, and an acerbic commentary on the struggles of a few devoted historians to preserve anything of San Diego's Spanish past against the wishes of dollar-crazed developers.

Outside the museum, pause awhile by the Serra Cross, a modern marker on the site of the original mission. To find the actual mission, you'll need to travel six miles north to 10818 San Diego Mission Rd, where the **Mission Basilica San Diego de Alcalá** (daily 9am–5pm; $1), was relocated to be near a water source and fertile soils – and to be further from the likelihood of attack by rebellious Indians. The present building (take bus #43 from downtown) is still a working parish church (mass daily at 7am and 5pm), and is one of the least visited of all the California missions, a peaceful complex that gives welcome respite from the nearby freeways – a mood perhaps enhanced by the decay that seriously affects parts of the building, despite a thorough renovation programme begun in the 1930s. Walk through the dark and echoey church to the garden, where two small crosses mark the graves of Native American neophytes – making this California's oldest cemetery – and to the chapel's fourteenth-century stalls and altar, imported from Spain. A small **museum** holds a collection of Native American craft objects and historical articles from the mission, including the crucifix held by Junípero Serra at his death in 1834. Despite accusations that the missionary campaign was one of kidnapping, forced baptisms, and treatment of natives as virtual slaves, Serra was beatified during 1988 in a ceremony at the Vatican, the Pope declaring him a "shining example of Christian virtue and the missionary spirit".

## East San Diego and Hillcrest

Scruffy **EAST SAN DIEGO** is largely suburban sprawl, only really of interest if you want to venture into its western fringes as far as 1925 K St, the site of **Villa Montezuma** (Fri–Sun noon–4.30pm; $3). Ignored by the majority of visitors to San Diego, possibly due to its location, the villa is a florid show of Victoriana, with a rich variety of domes and all manner of loopy eccentricities. Local kids know the villa simply as the "haunted house", a nickname that doesn't seem unreasonable when you see the place. It was built for Jesse Shepard – English-born but noted in the US as composer, pianist, author and all-round aesthete – and paid for by a group of culturally aspirant San Diegans in the 1880s, and the glorious stock of furniture remains, as do many ornaments and oddments and the dramatic stained-glass windows. It's a house that well reflects Shepard's introspective nature and interest in spiritualism, both of which must have been entirely out of step with brash San Diego through the boom years. To **get to the villa** without a car, you can either make the long walk (about 45min) from downtown, take buses #3, #5 or #16, each stopping within about five blocks, or use the Trolley, transferring to the Euclid Avenue line and getting off near 20th Street.

North of downtown and on the northwest edge of Balboa Park, **Hillcrest** is an increasingly lively and artsy area, thanks to the wealthy liberals who've moved into the district in recent years. It's also the centre of the city's **gay community** and home to a couple of gay hotels (see "Accommodation"). The streets around University and Fifth, easily reached from downtown on buses #3 or #11, hold a selection of interesting cafés and restaurants (detailed under "Eating") and a fine gathering of Victorian homes.

# The beaches

San Diego undeniably excels with its fine array of museums and historic sites, but thousands are happy to trade the time spent in Balboa Park (or indeed their whole time in the city) for a few days on the city's **beaches**. They're not strong on scenic beauty or seclusion, but they're fine for sunbathing and swimming, and opportunities abound to rent roller blades or a boogie board and enter into the Southern Californian spirit of it all.

Directly south of downtown across the bay, **Coronado** is a plush and well-manicured settlement, reflecting the wholesome nature of the large naval base to which it's home. Traditionally, Coronado's visitors have been wealthy health-seekers, here for its sea breezes, palm trees and famous (and expensive) hotel. Just beyond, and much less upscale, **Imperial Beach**'s chief draw is simply the quiet of a seldom crowded stretch of sand, and, if you're into such things, the horse-riding trails nearby.

Across the bay to the north, the rugged **Point Loma** peninsula forms the western wall of San Diego Bay, with trees along its spine and a craggy shoreline often marked by explorable tidepools – though no fun at all for sunbathing. **Ocean Beach**, at the base of the peninsula, is extremely lively on its sands but the exclusive and wealthy community that's developed a little way inland is tempering its reputation for all-out partying. These days much of Ocean Beach's former youthful vitality has moved to **Mission Beach**, eight miles northwest of downtown, and the adjoining, and slightly more salubrious, **Pacific Beach**, ("PB" to its friends), linked by a beachside walkway which, on any weekend, is where you'll find San Diego at its most exuberant. The city is at its most chic, however, a few miles further north up the coast in stunning **La Jolla**, whose coastline of almost too-perfect caves and coves is matched on land by short, litter-free streets lined by small coffee bars and art galleries, and a tantalizingly designed modern art museum.

## Coronado and Imperial Beach

Across San Diego Bay from downtown, the bulbous blob of **CORONADO** is a well-scrubbed resort community with a major naval station occupying its western end. It's of very limited interest, save for an historic hotel and the engagingly long and thin streak of sands – a natural breakwater for the bay – that runs south. The simplest way to get here is on the **San Diego Bay ferry** ($2 each way) which leaves Broadway Pier daily on the hour between 9am and 9pm (10pm Fri & Sat), returning on the half-hour. From the ferry landing on First Street, shuttle bus #904 (Mon & Tues hourly, Wed–Sun half-hourly) runs the mile up Coronado's main street, Orange Avenue, to the *Hotel del Coronado*. Alternatively use bus #901 (or #19, though this only goes as far as the naval station) from downtown.

By road, you cross the **Coronado Bridge** (southbound drivers without passengers have to pay a $1 toll), its struts decorated with enormous murals depicting daily Hispanic life, best seen from the community park beneath the bridge in the district of Barrio Logan.

The town of Coronado grew up around the **Hotel del Coronado**, a whirl of turrets and towers erected as a health resort in 1888. Using Chinese labourers who worked in round-the-clock shifts, the aim was to lure the ailing rich from all parts of the US – a plan in which it succeeds to this day, although the hotel and its elaborate architecture have lost much of their charm, dwarfed by newer high-rises. Nevertheless, if you're passing, the place is certainly worth dropping into, if only for its glamour-soaked history. Through the lobby and courtyard a small basement **museum** records the hotel's past. It was at the "del", as it's locally known, in 1920 that Edward VIII (then Prince of Wales) first met Mrs Simpson (then a Coronado housewife) – a contact which eventually led to their marriage and his abdication from the British throne, and is remembered here by an unintentionally hilarious cardboard head stuffed on top of a dinner suit. More thrilling is the tablecloth signed by Marilyn Monroe and the rest of the cast who filmed *Some Like It Hot* at the hotel in 1958. Outside, past the tennis courts occasionally graced by world champions but more commonly by moneyed guests, are the sands and palms on and around which much of the movie's action took place. More recently, an episode of *Baywatch* was shot on those same sands. A guided, hour-long **historical tour** ($10) wends its way around the hotel, beginning in the lobby at 10am and 11am on Thursday, Friday and Saturday.

A less grandiose place to explore Coronado's past is at the **Coronado Beach Historical Museum**, 1126 Loma Ave (Wed–Sun 10am–4pm; free), where photos and knick-knacks remember the community's early pioneers and also some of its first naval aviators. Nearby, the **Coronado Visitor Information Center**, 1111 Orange Ave (Mon–Sat 9am–5pm, Sun 10am–4pm; ☎437-8788 or 1-800/622-8300) carries reams of practical information on the area.

### Silver Strand and Imperial Beach

For a little isolation, follow Silver Strand Boulevard along the glistening sands south of the *Hotel del Coronado* (bus #901). Here you'll find plenty of good spots to stretch out and relax – though no food and drink facilities at all – foremost among them **Silver Strand State Beach** (daily 8am–dusk; $4 per vehicle) where you can camp (see p.171). At the end of Silver Strand Boulevard, down-at-heel **IMPERIAL BEACH** is a contrast to smart Coronado, but does have a pleasant and fairly quiet beach, disturbed only by the helicopters periodically buzzing in and out of the naval air station. Also peaceful is nearby **Border Field State Park**, a flat area noted for its horse trails, right by the Mexican border and reached by car along Tia Juana Street from San Ysidro.

To return directly to San Diego from Imperial Beach, take bus #934 to the Trolley and head north through dreary Chula Vista and National City.

## Ocean Beach and Point Loma

Once ruled by a drug-running chapter of Hell's Angels, **OCEAN BEACH**, six miles northwest of downtown and accessible from there on bus #35, is now one of the more sought-after addresses in San Diego. Vacant plots with a sea view regularly change hands for half a million dollars, and the single-storey adobe dwellings that have been home to several generations of Portugese fishing families and characterized the area as recently as a decade ago, have virtually disappeared – the few that remain look like dinky-sized outhouses beside the opulent newer structures. The new money is less in evidence at the main beach, half a mile south by the pier; **Newport Street** here, rife with the trappings of beach culture, is where most young backpackers spend their time, amid rows of cheap snack bars, T-shirt stalls and surf and skate rental shops. The beach itself can be enjoyable for those with the right inclination – especially at weekends, when you really shouldn't bother coming unless you're in the mood to party.

Further south from the pier – and the best of the beaches – rise the dramatic **Sunset Cliffs**, a great vantage point for watching the sun go down, and the grandstand of choice during the San Diego Yacht Club's defence of the America's Cup title in 1995. Be warned, though, that the cliffs are notoriously unstable and more than a few people have tumbled over the edge after an afternoon of excess on the beach.

Beyond here, you're into the hilly and very green peninsula of **POINT LOMA** – most of it owned by the navy, which has been beneficial in keeping some of the more attractive parts of the coastline unspoilt and accessible to the public. You can get here direct from downtown by taking bus #2 and transferring to #6 at Rosecrans Street and Thirtieth Avenue, but there's little to see until you get past the naval base to the southern extremity, and the **Cabrillo National Monument** (daily 9am–5.15pm; 7-day pass $4 per vehicle, $2 per pedestrian or cyclist). It was here that Cabrillo and crew became the first Europeans to land in California, though that's as far as the historical interest goes, for they quickly reboarded their vessel and sailed away. The startling views from this high spot, however, across San Diego Bay to the downtown skyline and right along the coast to Mexico, easily repay the journey here, and there's ample discovering the marine life in the numerous tidepools around the shoreli a clearly marked **nature walk** beginning close to the monument.

Also nearby, a **visitor center** informs on what creatures you might the tides are most willing to reveal them (obviously the pools are flooded at high tide). If your timing is wrong, climb the hill to the **Old San Diego Lighthouse** and take a quick tour of the interior (usually daily 11am–3pm). As it happens, the structure led an unfulfilled life: soon after it was built it was realized that the beacon would be obscured by fog, and another lighthouse was erected at a lower elevation.

Facing the Pacific, a mile or two from the monument, a platform makes it easy to view the November to March **whale migration**, when scores of gray whales pass by on their journey between the Arctic Ocean and their breeding grounds off Baja California.

## Mission Bay and Sea World

Heading northwest from downtown towards the coast, you pass through the unre-deemed area surrounding the Sports Arena – frequented by military personnel for its topless bars and by unfussy tourists for its low-priced, spartan hotels – before reaching **MISSION BAY**, whose mud flats quickly become a landscaped expanse of lagoons and grassy flatlands usually crowded with watersports fanatics. From Ocean Beach, only a couple of miles away, you need to cross the San Diego River on Sunset Cliffs Boulevard.

Mission Bay is also the setting for San Diego's most popular tourist attraction, **Sea World** (daily 9am–dusk; $28.95, children $20.95, parking $5) – take Sea World Drive off I-5, or bus #9 from downtown. It's a good place to bring kids, though the high price dictates that you allow a whole day if you do come. Highly organized and cleverly run, Sea World has a large number of exhibits and timetabled events (get the day's schedule as you enter), ranging from "performances" by killer whales and dolphins, designed to demonstrate the creatures' intelligence and skills, to the eerie sight of the heads of hundreds of moray eels protruding from the hollow rocks of the Forbidden Reef display. Of the rest, two features in particular draw the crowds: the Shark House, where all manner of sharks circle menacingly, although none of them is as violent or as demon-strative as the infamous Great White, an eat-anything monster that Sea World hopes one day to raise and keep in captivity; and the Penguin Exhibit – a mock Antarctica behind glass, where hundreds of the birds noisily jump around on ice and dive into the water.

## Mission Beach and Pacific Beach

Anyone of a nervous disposition, or lacking a tanned, toned physique, might well find **MISSION BEACH**, the peninsula that separates Mission Bay from the Pacific Ocean, too hot to handle. On the other hand, the raver-packed sands, scantily clad torsos and surfboard-clutching hunks might be precisely what you've come to California for.

In summer bumper-to-bumper traffic fills Mission Boulevard, the sole through-road; at such times the fastest way to get about is on bike or blade along Ocean Front Walk, the concrete boardwalk running the length of the beach (see "City Transport" for rental outlets).

First impressions may suggest otherwise, but the city authorities have made major endeavours to limit the anarchic hedonism long associated with this classic example of Southern California beachlife, including approving the opening of the squeaky-clean **Belmont Park**, by the southern end of Ocean Front Walk. This funfair, with its collec-tion of swimwear stores, pricy fitness centre and seaside snack stalls, has encouraged more families to use the area but, so far, has made little impact on the beach's free-wheeling character.

,y following Mission Boulevard north you cross from the social inferno of Mission ,each into the more sedate **PACIFIC BEACH**. Here, expensive oceanside homes with tidy lawns set a refined tone, although there's still plenty to enjoy: a more than serviceable beach around Crystal Pier, and Garnet Avenue running inland from the pier, lined by funky eating places and nightspots. Adept surfers are no strangers to Pacific Beach either; a mile north of the pier, **Tourmaline City Surf Park**, regularly pounded by promising waves, is reserved exclusively for their use.

# La Jolla and around

"A nice place – for old people and their parents", wrote Raymond Chandler of **LA JOLLA** (pronounced *La HOYA*) in the 1950s, though that didn't stop him moving here (his former house is at 6005 Camino de la Costa) and setting much of his final novel *Playback* in the town, renaming it "Esmeralda". Since Philip Marlowe concluded his last case, La Jolla has been infused by new money and fresh vitality, and its opulence is now less stuffy and more welcoming. The main section, around Prospect Street and Girard Avenue, has spotless sidewalks flanked by tidy grassy verges, and numerous chic art galleries sit side-by-side with equally chic cafés.

This means it's pretty expensive, too, but it's worth coming at least to savour the town's unique (if clearly contrived) elegance and the newly expanded La Jolla site of the **Museum of Contemporary Art**, 700 Prospect St (Tues & Thurs–Sat Sun 10am–5pm, Wed 10am–8pm, Sun noon–5pm; $4, free first Tues of month), which has a huge – and regularly changing – stock of paintings and sculptures from 1955 onwards. Minimal, Pop and California schools are in evidence, bolstered by a strong range of temporary shows – and fabulous views of the Pacific surf crashing against the rocks immediately below the building's huge windows. The museum also has exhibition space downtown; see p.172.

The museum was once the home of Ellen Scripps, a prominent local philanthropist whose seemingly endless reserves of wealth were injected into La Jolla through the first half of the century. It was she who commissioned architect Irving Gill (who raised several distinctive public buildings in La Jolla) to design her house, and even today the Scripps name is almost everywhere, not least in the small, neat and exquisitely tasteful **Ellen Scripps Browning Park**, on the seaward side of the museum. Where the park meets the coast is the start of **La Jolla Cove**, much of it an ecological reserve, with an underwater park whose clear waters make it perfect for snorkelling.

### Further along the coast

North of the cove, upmarket residential neighbourhoods stretch from the clifftops to the main route, Torrey Pines Road. Following this thoroughfare and then La Jolla Shores Drive, which soon branches left, you'll find nothing of interest for several miles until you reach the **Stephen Birch Aquarium-Museum** (daily 9am–5pm; $6.50, parking $2.50), part of the Scripps Institute of Oceanography, which provides entertaining up-close views of captive marine life, informative displays on the earth's ecology, and exhibits detailing the marine exploration work carried out by the Institute.

On a hillside setting above the museum and also reached from Torrey Pines Road, the **University of California at San Diego (UCSD)** campus is a bland affair, only meriting a call if you fancy trekking around to locate the various specially commissioned works, scattered around the 1200-acre grounds, which constitute the **Stuart Collection of Sculpture**. The first acquisition, in 1983, has yet to be bettered: Niki de Saint Phalle's *Sun God*, a large colourful bird whose outstretched wings welcome visitors to the parking lot opposite Peterson Hall. To find the rest, pick up a leaflet from the office in the Visual Arts Building.

Without the benefit of a car, you can reach the campus on bus #34 from downtown, which ends its route a mile or two away at a spick-and-span shopping mall called

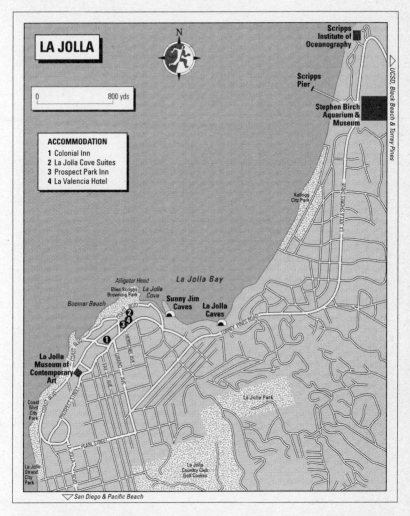

**LA JOLLA**

N

0          800 yds

**ACCOMMODATION**
1 Colonial Inn
2 La Jolla Cove Suites
3 Prospect Park Inn
4 La Valencia Hotel

Scripps
Institute of
Oceanography

Scripps
Pier

Stephen Birch
Aquarium &
Museum

UCSD Black Beach & Torrey Pines

LA JOLLA SHORES DRIVE

Kellogg
City Park

Alligator Head    *La Jolla Bay*

Ellen Scripps   *La Jolla*
Browning Park   *Cove*

Boomar Beach

Sunny Jim
Caves

La Jolla
Caves

TORREY PINES ROAD

COAST BLVD

HERSCHEL AVE

FAY AVE

GIRARD AVE

La Jolla
Museum of
Contemporary
Art

Coast
Blvd
City
Park

PROSPECT STREET

COAST BLVD

PEARL STREET

La Jolla
Strand
City
Park

La Jolla Park

La Jolla
Country Club
Golf Course

▽ *San Diego & Pacific Beach*

*University Towne Square*. Come here for the commendable shows of indigenous arts and crafts from around the globe staged at the **Mingei International Museum of World Art**, 4405 La Jolla Village Drive (Tues–Sat 11am–5pm, Sun 2–5pm; $3), delightfully incongrous among the upmarket stores.

## Beyond La Jolla: Torrey Pines State Preserve

As it leaves the campus area, La Jolla Shores Drive meets North Torrey Pines Road. A mile north of the junction, Torrey Pines Scenic Drive, branching left, provides the only access (via a steep path) to **Blacks Beach**, the region's premier, clothing optional, gay beach. This lies within the southern confines of the **Torrey Pines State Preserve** (daily 9am–sunset; parking $4), best entered a few miles further north, which preserves the country's rarest species of pine, the Torrey Pine – one of two surviving stands. Despite their scarcity, the pines are not especially distinctive, although thanks to salty conditions and stiff ocean breezes, they do manage to contort their ten-foot frames into a variety of tortured, twisted shapes best viewed at close quarters from the half-mile **Guy Fleming trail**, which starts near the beachside parking lot. The small **museum and interpretive center** (daily 9am–5pm; free) will tell you more than you need to know about Torrey Pines, especially if your visit coincides with a **guided nature tour** (Sat & Sun 11.30am & 1.30pm). The less scenic **beach trail** (0.8 miles) leads from the interpretive center down to Flat Rock and a popular beach. Beyond the preserve you're into the North County community of Del Mar (see p.193).

# Eating

Wherever you are in San Diego, you'll have few problems finding somewhere to **eat** good food at good value. Everything from crusty coffeeshops to stylish ethnic restaurants are in copious supply, and unsurprisingly, Mexican food is much in evidence, especially in the **Old Town**.The **Gaslamp District**, which has the greatest concentration of restaurants and bars, explodes on Friday and Saturday nights. The ascendant **Little Italy**, on the northern fringes of downtown, is still too small a quarter to challenge the bohemian hegemony of **Hillcrest**, the most appealing area to simply hang out and eat.

## Downtown and Little Italy

**Anthony's Fish Grotto**, 1360 Harbor Drive (☎232-5103). Cut-rate offshoot of a local seafood institution, justly famed for its freshly caught main courses. Right by the Maritime Museum.

**Athens Market Taverna**, 109 W F St (☎234-1955). Popular Greek restaurant with fine food at affordable prices – and belly dancers gyrating between the tables at weekends.

**Caffe Italia**, 1704 India St at Date St, Little Italy (☎234-6767). Sandwiches, salads, cakes, gelati and coffee served in a sleek modern interior or out on the sidewalk.

**Café Lulu**, 419 F St (☎238-0144). Taking orders until 4am, this is downtown's latest-opening food spot, offering delicate quiches and lasagne, plus a large selection of coffees to help you stay awake.

**Café 222**, 222 Island Ave at Second Ave (☎236-9902). Industrial-looking café serving some of the city's best breakfasts and lunches, with inventive twists on traditional sandwiches and burgers (including vegetarian), at reasonable prices. Open 7am–2pm.

**California Café**, Top Floor, Horton Plaza (☎238-5440). A good place to sample California cuisine without breaking your budget. It's not cheap, but lunch dishes can be had for $8–11.

**Croce's Restaurant & Jazz Bar**, 802 Fifth Ave (☎233-4355). Pricey but excellent range of pastas and salads; the Sunday jazz brunch is the talk of the town. See also "Nightlife".

**Dick's Last Resort**, 345 Fourth Ave (☎231-9100). Regular American food served by the bucket in a brash frat-house setting, with flea-market furniture and loud-mouthed waiters. Fun if you're in a convivial mood.

**Filippi's Pizza Grotto**, 1747 India St at Date St, Little Italy (☎232-5094). Thick, chewy pizzas and a handful of pasta dishes served in an entertaining small room at the back of an Italian grocery. A winner.

**Fio's Cucina Italiana**, 801 Fifth St at F St (☎234-3467). Very classy, fairly expensive Italian place serving the likes of lobster ravioli and gnocchi in rabbit sauce. Invent a special occasion.

**Galaxy Grill**, 522 Horton Plaza (☎234-7211). A Fifties-style diner that's the prime location in this upscale shopping mall to sit and munch a burger and watch the well-groomed crowds glide by.

**Grand Central Café**, 500 Broadway (☎234-2233). Shares a building with the *HI-Downtown* (see "Accommodation"), and serves wholesome, inexpensive dishes throughout the day. Closed Sun.

**Johnny M's 801**, 801 Fourth Ave (☎233-1131). Quantity takes precedence over quality, though the piles of seafood are still very edible inside what's one of downtown's most impressive historic interiors (see p.174).

**Karl Strauss Old Columbia Brewery**, 1157 Columbia St (☎234-2739). Solid American lunches best eaten while gazing at the workings of the in-house brewery, which produces several ales worth sampling. See also "Nightlife".

**Olé Madrid Café**, 755 Fifth St (☎557-0146). Enjoyable mid-priced Spanish restaurant, with an informal ambience aided by flamenco dancers midweek. After dinner at weekends, it becomes a very popular funk and dance venue – see "Nightlife".

**Pacifically Fish**, 624 E St (☎696-0855). Fresh fish and a good choice of chowders and seafood cocktails, all at fair prices.

**Super Taco Loco**, 1153 Sixth Ave at B St (☎231-6676). Tremendous stock of takeaway taco, with every imaginable filling at bargain prices.

## Hillcrest

**The French Side of the West**, 2202 Fourth St (☎234-5540). A fixed price (around $20) buys a slap-up French dinner with a choice of main courses.

**The Good Egg**, 7947 Balboa Ave (☎565-4244). Until 9am, as much coffee as you can drink for 5¢, provided you buy a breakfast: the gigantic pancakes created from various mouthwatering ingredients are a wise choice. On the northern edge of Hillcrest.

**Ichiban**, 1449 University Ave (☎299-7203). There are few better places in which to enjoy quality Japanese cuisine than this unpretentious and simple restaurant. The combination platters are extremely well priced, and you can get your fill for under $10.

**Kung Food**, 2949 Fifth Ave (☎298-7302). Decent though unspectacular homespun vegetarian cuisine, in a non-smoking environment. Mains $8–10.

**Monsoon**, 3975 Fifth Ave (☎298-3155). Hillcrest's newer vegetarian place, with a modern feel and a menu dominated by soups, sandwiches and burgers for around $6.

**Stefano's**, 3671 Fifth Ave (☎296-0975). Finely prepared meals, a relaxing atmosphere and decent prices make this the top place in the area for Italian food. Jazz played on Sunday.

**Thai Chada**, 142 University Ave (☎297-9548). Exquisite gourmet Thai dishes at modest cost, with heaps of care lavished on both food and service. One of the best restaurants in town.

## Old Town

**Aztec Dining Room**, 2811 San Diego Ave (☎295-2965). Reliable Mexican outlet just north of the Old Town, and very popular with locals.

**The Brigantine**, San Diego Ave (☎298-9840). Sumptuous seafood in inventive styles in this award-winning but not too expensive fish restaurant.

**Café Coyote**, Old Town Esplanade, 2461 San Diego Ave (☎291-HOWL). Good Southwestern-influenced menu in the synthetic surrounds of a shopping mall; popular with cruising late-teens.

**Casa de Pico**, Bazaar del Mundo (☎297-3267). Impressive selection of quality Mexican food, but the incessant crowds can be off-putting.

**Garden House**, 2480 San Diego Ave (☎220-0723). Tea, coffee and muffins beside a shady lawn, an oasis in bustling Old Town.

**Old Town Mexican Café y Cantina**, 2489 San Diego Ave (☎297-4330). Lively and informal Mexican diner; only at breakfast are you unlikely to have to wait in line for a table.

**Old Town Thai Restaurant**, 2540 Congress St (☎291-6720). Simply decorated place a block away from most of the restaurants and serving an extensive array of Thai, Vietnamese and Chinese dishes. Excellent lunches for $5 and plenty of vegetarian dishes. Closed Mon.

**Village Kitchen**, 2497 San Diego Ave (☎294-4180). Good-sized portions of Mexican and American food cooked and presented in a wholesome, unpretentious style.

## Coronado

**Kensington Coffee Company**, 1106 First St (☎437-8506). Aromatic coffees, imported teas and pastries that make for a tasty snack close to the landing stage.

**McP's Pub**, 1107 Orange Ave (☎435-4280). Down-to-earth ersatz-Irish bar that does a neat line in lunchtime sandwiches and stews. See also "Nightlife".

**Mexican Village Restaurant**, 120 Orange Ave (☎435-1822). Long-standing Mexican diner of ballroom dimensions, patronized as much for its margaritas and music as for its food.

**Miguel's Cocina**, 1351 Orange Ave (☎437-4237). Brilliant fish tacos and a full range of other Mexican choices. Worth seeking out.

**Stretch's**, 943 Orange Ave (☎435-8886). For the health-conscious, extremely good-for-you meals using only the freshest natural ingredients.

## Ocean Beach

**The Old Ocean Beach Café**, 4967 Newport Ave (☎223-2521). Casual beachside diner by the pier, favoured by locals.

**Qwiig's Bar & Grill**, 5091 Santa Monica Ave (☎221-1101). Crisp salads and ultra-fresh seafood are the trademarks at this place just north of the pier. Perfect for oceanfront oyster-eating.

**The Venetian**, 3663 Voltaire St (☎223-8197). Excellently priced pizzas and pasta, very welcome after a hard day on the beach.

## Mission Beach and Pacific Beach

**The Eggery**, 4130 Mission Blvd, Mission Beach (☎274-3122). A coffee shop with imagination, serving breakfast – omelette, pancakes etc – until 2pm.

**Giulio's**, 809 Thomas Ave, Pacific Beach (☎483-7726). Dependable Italian food at more-than-fair prices.

**Luigi's Italian Restaurant**, 3210 Mission Blvd, Mission Beach (☎488-2818). Enormous pizzas and a rowdy beachside atmosphere, bolstered by competing TV sets.

**Red Onion**, 3125 Ocean Front Walk, Mission Beach (☎488-9040). Beside the beachside boardwalk, with a riotous atmosphere as huge helpings of Mexican food are washed down with killer margaritas. See also "Nightlife".

**Saska's**, 3768 Mission Blvd, Pacific Beach (☎488-5754). Laid-back dining place where substantial breakfasts are served all day and (nearly) all night, alongside the usual selection of main meals.

## La Jolla

**Ashoka**, 8008 Girard Ave (☎454-6263). Slightly pretentious Indian restaurant, but the combination lunchtime deals for under $10 are unmatched.

**John's Waffle Shop**, 7906 Girard Ave (☎454-7331). This hole-in-the-wall place surrounded by designer clothing stores has been perfecting the art of the waffle since the 1950s – the long lines outside (especially on Sun) are proof of its success. Other diner favourites fill out the menu.

**Star of India**, 1025 Prospect St (☎459-3355). Mostly northern Indian cuisine, with good vegetarian and tandoori choices. Most mains $13–15.

**Sushi on the Rock**, 1277 Prospect St (☎456-1138). Tempting array of inexpensive sushi combination plates served to a soundtrack of rock and reggae.

# Nightlife

San Diego's arch-conservatism is apparent even in the city's **nightlife**: money is lavished on pursuits such as classical music and opera, but the crowds flock to a large batch of much-of-a-muchness beachside discos and boozy live music venues – or spend the evening in a coffee bar. It may be narrow in scope, but at least there's plenty going on. For full listings, pick up the free *San Diego Reader*, buy the Thursday edition of the *San Diego Union-Tribune*, or seek out the youth-lifestyle-oriented *Slamm* at some of the places listed below. **Cover** charges at live music venues range from $2 to $8, unless someone big is playing.

## Bars

**The Daily Planet**, 1200 Garnet Ave, Pacific Beach (☎272-6066). Sizeable sports bar with a 3–6pm happy hour, and cut-rate drinks offered through the evening. Dancing at weekends, Karaoke Sunday and Monday night football in season.

**La Jolla Brewing Company**, 7536 Fay Ave, La Jolla (☎456-2739). Currently the liveliest evening rendezvous in La Jolla, where a youngish crowd quaffs the home-brewed beers and makes merry beneath vintage surfboards and photos of historic San Diego.

**Karl Strauss Old Columbia Brewery**, 1157 Columbia St at B, downtown (☎234-2739). Where discerning beer hunters enjoy ales and lagers brewed on the premises. See also "Eating".

**Olé Madrid Café**, 755 Fifth St, downtown (☎557-0146). Spanish restaurant that on weekends becomes a very popular funk and dance club. Arrive before 11pm if you want to get in. See also "Eating".

## MAJOR VENUES

Any big name in contemporary music visiting San Diego is likely to appear at one of the following **major venues**:

**Belly Up Tavern**, 143 S Cedros Ave, Solana Beach (☎481-9022; see p.193).

**Copley Symphony Hall**, 750 B St, downtown (☎699-4205).

**The New Bacchanal**, 8022 Claremont Mesa Blvd (☎277-7326).

**Humphrey's**, 2241 Shelter Island Drive (☎523-1010).

**San Diego Convention Center**, 111 W Harbor Drive, downtown (☎525-5000).

**San Diego Sports Arena**, 3500 Sports Arena Blvd (☎220-TIXS).

### TICKETS

Assuming they're available, **half-price tickets** for theatre and classical music events for that evening can be bought at *Times Arts Tix*, between Horton Plaza and Broadway (Tues–Sat 10am–7pm; ☎497-5000), which also handles full-price advance sales. On Saturday, half-price tickets are available for Sunday performances.

Otherwise, tickets for all major shows can be had from the venue or through *Ticketmaster* (☎278-TIXS); there's also a **Concert Hotline** on ☎563-0024.

**Red Onion**, 3125 Ocean Front Walk, Mission Beach (☎488-9040). Beachside Mexican restaurant whose bar is the social hotspot of Mission Beach. See also "Eating".

**RJ's Riptide Brewery**, 310 Fifth Ave at K St, downtown (☎231-7700). One of a growing number of micro-breweries in San Diego, with a choice of 14 homemade beers and plenty more from around the world. Happy hour (4–7pm) and moderately priced food.

## Coffee bars

**Gas Haus**, 640 F St, downtown (☎232-5866). Alcohol-free, eclectically decorated café where roller-blading teenagers, students and ageing hippies co-exist on deep couches, and take each other on at pool.

**Java**, 837 G St, downtown (☎235-4012). The antidote to surfer-dominated beach clubs, where the intellectually inclined peruse current-affairs magazines and sip fine coffees and teas.

**Mekka Java**, 412 K St, downtown (☎235-8843). Late-night café along the lines of the *Gas Haus*. Every conceivable coffee combination and good music to boot.

**Mission Coffeehouse**, 3795 Mission Blvd, Mission Beach (☎488-9060). Late-opening café where you can sink into the soft furnishings while enjoying good coffee and light meals.

**Quel Fromage**, 523 University Ave, Hillcrest (☎295-1600). Linger over a coffee while reading overseas newspapers or viewing the small-scale art exhibitions. A good place to seek out listings and gay-interest free papers.

**Upstart Crow**, Seaport Village, downtown (☎232-4855). Coffee bar fused with a bookstore which makes for a lively cross section of customers – and a surfeit of reading material.

**Zanzibar**, 976 Garnet Ave, Pacific Beach (☎272-4762). Relatively serene retreat from the brash bars along this strip. Coffees, sandwiches and muffins served until 2am, or 4am at weekends. There's another branch at 904 Pearl St, La Jolla (☎456-1152), with acoustic sets on Fri, jazz on Sat.

## Live music venues

**B St Restaurant & Sports Bar**, 425 W B St, downtown (☎236-1707). Upmarket New Orleans-style jazz haunt for slinky sophisticates.

**Blind Melons**, 710 Garnet Ave, Pacific Beach (☎483-7844). Earthy, live blues croaked out nightly from 9pm, in a spot right by the pier.

**Bodie's**, 528 F St, downtown (☎236-8988). Rowdy bar with rock, blues and r'n'b combos nightly. Usually no cover.

**The Casbah**, 2501 Kettner Blvd, downtown (☎232-4355). Varying roster of blues, rock and indie bands.

**Casey's Pub**, 714 Garnet Ave, Pacific Beach (☎274-5523). The nightly band can be anything from young hopefuls to fading Californian rock legends making their last stand.

**Croce's Top Hat**, 805 Fifth Ave, downtown (☎233-4355). Classy jazz in the back room of a pricey restaurant; has a jazz brunch on Sun. See also "Eating".

**Island Saloon**, 104 Orange Ave, Coronado (☎435-3456). Standard bar which rocks to local r'n'b groups on Fri and Sat.

**McP's Pub**, 1107 Orange Ave, Coronado (☎435-0528). Rock and blues, with folk music early in the week. See also "Eating".

**Patrick's II**, 428 F St, downtown (☎233-3077). No-frills bar with matching r'n'b bands most nights. Occasional jazz and blues. $3 cover at weekends.

**Spirit**, 1130 Buenos Ave, Mission Bay (☎276-3993). Glam, metal, goth and grunge bands all get a look-in at this long-running alternative venue open every night .

**Winston's Beach Club**, 1921 Bacon St, Ocean Beach (☎222-6822). Rock bands most nights, reggae on Thurs. Close to the pier.

## Clubs and discos

**Club 5th Avenue**, 835 Fifth Ave (☎238-7191). Upmarket nightspot in the basement of a nine-teenth-century building, mostly used by expensively dressed San Diegans shaking an after-dinner leg.

**Emerald City**, 945 Garnet Ave, Pacific Beach (☎483-9920). Lively disco with drink specials at week-ends, and the *Underworld* industrial and Gothic night on Sunday.

**Marrakesh**, 756 Fifth Ave, downtown (☎231-8353). Moroccan restaurant that transforms itself into a club later on, with DJ-led dance grooves at the weekend, jazz on Wednesday and reggae on Thursday, often with cheap drinks early on.

## Theatre

There's a thriving **theatre** scene in San Diego, with several mid-sized venues and many smaller fringe venues putting on quality shows. Tickets are $20–25 for a major produc-tion, $10–15 for a night on the fringe. The *San Diego Reader* carries full listings. The main **venues** are the Old Globe Theater, part of the Simon Edison Complex for the Performing Arts in Balboa Park (☎239-2255), the Civic Theater at Third and B streets (☎236-6510), and the La Jolla Playhouse at the Mandell Weiss Center on the UCSD campus (☎551-1010).

## Comedy

A couple of clubs regularly host **comedy** acts bound for the more glamorous venues of LA or New York. The cheapest shows, around $8, are midweek; expect to pay $10 on Friday or Saturday. The main **venues** are Comedy Store, 916 Pearl St, La Jolla (☎454-9176), and Comedy Isle, 998 W Mission Bay Drive, Mission Beach (☎448-6872).

## Film

San Diego has many **cinemas**, most of them offering the latest Hollywood blockbust-ers. Scan the newspapers for full listings; admission is usually $5–8, a few dollars less for most matinée shows. For more adventurous programmes – foreign-language films, monochrome classics or cult favourites – look for the afternoon screenings (daily except Sun) at the San Diego Public Library, 820 E St, downtown (☎236-5489).

## Classical music and opera

From October to May, the well-respected **San Diego Symphony Orchestra** appears at the Copley Symphony Hall, 750 B St (☎699-4205); tickets are $10–35. During the summer, the orchestra plays outdoors at the Summer Pops series in Embarcadero Marina Park by Seaport Village. The **San Diego Opera**, frequently boasting top inter-national guest performers during its January to May season, is based at the Civic Theater (see above); cheapest seats are $12, but reduced-rate standing tickets are usually on sale thirty minutes before curtain-up.

# Gay and Lesbian San Diego

Mostly centred on the Hillcrest area, San Diego's **gay and lesbian** population makes its presence felt through a number of publications and resource centres, and a network of gay bars and clubs. Also, several hotels and bed and breakfast inns are noted for their friendliness towards gay and lesbian travellers – several being all but exclusively gay. For sun worshippers, the place to go is Blacks Beach (see p.185) north of La Jolla.

### Publications and resource centres

The primary source of gay and lesbian news, views and upcoming events is the free *Gay & Lesbian Times*, appearing weekly and distributed through gay bars and clubs, many of the city's coffee bars, and most gay-run businesses. Look out, too, for the newsy *Update* with its *Etcetera* insert full of personals, classifieds and a "what's on" bulletin board. The LA-based *Edge* also makes its way down here. You can learn more by calling at the **Lesbian and Gay Men's Community Center**, 3780 Fifth Ave, Suite 2 (☎692-2077), or the **Women's Resource Center**, 3355 Mission Ave, Suite 111, Oceanside (☎757-3500).

### Bars and clubs

**Caliph**, 3102 Fifth Ave, downtown (☎298-9495). Piano bar with live music aimed mainly at an older gay clientele.

**Club West Coast**, 2028 Hancock St, Old Town (☎295-3724). A three-floor disco very popular with a gay and straight crowd. Mainly under-25s.

**The Flame**, 3780 Park Blvd, Hillcrest (☎295-4163). The city's premier lesbian club, open for dancing, pool and occasional live acts from early evening to early morning. Tues is a no-holds-barred "Boys Night".

**Number One Fifth Avenue**, 3845 Fifth Ave, Hillcrest (☎299-1911). Smartly dressed gay men sip cocktails on the patio. DJs play requests on Wed and Sat, mainly Fifties through Seventies.

**Rich's**, 1051 University Ave, Hillcrest (☎295-0750). Popular club with heavy dance grooves Fri & Sat, and *Hedonism* night on Thurs when the hat-check even accepts T-shirts and jeans, so you can dance in your Calvin Kleins. $5 cover at weekends.

### Gay accommodation

**Balboa Park Inn**, 3402 Park Blvd, Hillcrest (☎298-0823). Sizeable B&B in a Spanish colonial-style building, within walking distance of Balboa Park and its museums and popular with gay, lesbian and straight guests. Some rooms have kitchenettes and there's a Jacuzzi. ④.

**Eagle Crest Hotel**, 3942 Eighth Ave, Hillcrest (☎298-9898). One of the least expensive hotels in the area, but still with TVs and refrigerators in rooms. Mostly gay and lesbian. ②.

**Hillcrest Inn**, 3754 Fifth Ave, Hillcrest (☎293-7078 or 1-800/258-2280). Predominantly gay hotel right in the heart of Hillcrest. Newly refurbished, mostly non-smoking, rooms all have bath, refrigerator and microwave. It's a little characterless but has a friendly atmosphere. ③.

**Hill House**, 2504 A St, Hillcrest (☎239-4738). Affordable near-luxury in a bed and breakfast inn, filled with fireplaces and rocking chairs, close to Balboa Park. ④.

# Listings

**American Express** Main branches are at 258 Broadway (☎234-4455) and 1020 Prospect St in La Jolla (☎459-4161). Both open Mon–Fri 9am–5pm.

**Amtrak recorded schedule information** ☎239-9021.

**Arts and entertainment hotline** For a recorded run-through of events, phone ☎234-ARTS.

**Beach and surf conditions** ☎221-8884.

**Car Rental** *Alamo*, 2942 Kettner Blvd (☎297-0311); *Avis* 3875 N Harbor Drive (☎1-800/331-1212); *Budget*, 2535 Pacific Highway (☎1-800/283-4382); *Hertz* 3871 N Harbor Drive (☎1-800/654-3131); *Rent-a-Wreck*, 1904 Hotel Circle North (☎1-800/228-8235); *Thrifty* 1120 W Laurel (☎239-2281).

**Disabled assistance** *Accessible San Diego*, PO Box 124526, San Diego 92119-4256 (☎279-0704).

**Flea Market** The huge *Kobey's Swap Meet* takes place at the Sports Arena, 3500 Sports Arena Blvd; Thurs–Sun 7am–3pm.

**Hospitals** For non-urgent treatment, the cheapest place is the Beach Area Family Health Center, 3705 Mission Blvd, Mission Beach (☎488-0644).

**Left Luggage** At the *Greyhound* terminal ($2 for 6hr, $4 for 24hr) and, for ticketed travellers, at the Santa Fe Depot ($1.50 for 24hr).

**Pharmacy** 24-hour pharmacy at Sharp Cabrillo Hospital, 3457 Kenyon St, between downtown and Ocean Beach (☎221-3400).

**Post Offices** The downtown post office is at 815 E St (Mon–Fri 8.30am–5pm, Sat 8.30am–noon), but for *poste restante* (general delivery) use the main office at 2535 Midway Drive, between downtown and Mission Beach (Mon–Fri 8.30am–5pm, Sat 8.30am–4.40pm; zip code 92138; ☎293-5410).

**Rape Crisis Center/Hotline** 2467 E St (☎233-3088).

**Sport** Football: the *San Diego Chargers* play in the Jack Murphy Stadium in Mission Valley (☎563-8281). Baseball: the *San Diego Padres* play in the same stadium as the Chargers, tickets from the stadium office or *Ticketron* (☎283-4494).

**Thomas Cook** 177 Horton Plaza, downtown (☎235-0900), and Suite 170, La Jolla Gateway, 9191 Towne Center Drive, La Jolla (☎457-0841).

**Ticketron** Call ☎565-9947 for the nearest branch, or look in the phone book.

**Traveler's Aid** At the airport, daily 9am–10pm (☎231-7361), and at Santa Fe Depot (☎234-5191).

**Weather** Recorded information ☎289-1212.

**Victims of Crime Resource Center** ☎1-800/842-8467.

**Western Union** ☎1-800/325-6000.

**What's On** A recorded rundown of what's on and what's open: ☎239-9696.

# AROUND SAN DIEGO

San Diego County lies largely north of the city, and it veers from small, sleepy suburban communities to completely open – and rugged – country. Passing through at least some of it is unavoidable, though how much time you actually spend in the region depends on whether you want to allow several days to camp out and follow forest and desert hikes, or simply to dash along the coast as fast as possible to Los Angeles.

To the south there's Mexico, or more accurately the Mexican border city of **Tijuana**. To be honest this isn't up to much, giving the merest hint of how Mexico really is and a much stronger taste of the US's comparative affluence – most visitors are shoppers and it's hard to avoid the tensions that arise from that. However, it is at least a different country, and is extremely easy to reach from San Diego. Visit if only to say you've been there.

## Getting around San Diego County

**Transport** around the region is straightforward. By car, I-5, skirting along the coast, and I-15, a little deeper inland, are the main links with the north, while I-8 heads east from San Diego towards the southern part of the Anza-Borrego Desert (see p.221). The area east of I-15, around the scattered rural communities, is covered by a simple network of smaller roads. Public transport is no problem between San Diego and the North County coast, with frequent *Greyhound* buses and *Amtrak* trains between LA and San Diego calling at most communities, though only a skeletal bus service penetrates inland. In contrast, you're spoilt for choice on ways of getting to the Mexican border.

The telephone **area code** for San Diego County is ☎619.

# The North County Coast

The towns of the **North County Coast** stretch forty miles north from San Diego in a pretty much unbroken line as far as the Camp Pendleton marine base, which divides the county from the outskirts of Los Angeles. There's often little to distinguish one community from another, all chiefly populated by a strange mix of slick San Diego commuters and beach bums, and the main attraction is the coast itself: miles of fine sandy beaches and great opportunities for swimming and surfing. Otherwise there's little to take up your time.

## Del Mar

The tall bluff that marks the northern edge of the city of San Diego and holds Torrey Pines State Preserve (see p.185) forms the southern boundary of **DEL MAR**, a smart and pleasant little town whose **racetrack** is famous throughout the West for its meetings between late June and early September ($3). If you're around between late June and early July, head for the **Southern California State Exposition**, held at the Del Mar Fairgrounds, with barbecues and livestock, and a fair amount of contemporary arts and music events. The same venue also stages the **Jumping Frog Jamboree** during the last week of April, a peculiar – and cruel – event to which you can either bring your own frog or rent one for the day. There's little else to delay you in Del Mar, however, although the train station is just a pebble's throw from an inviting beach.

## Solana Beach

**SOLANA BEACH**, the next town north from Del Mar, makes a better place for an overnight stop. Motels line the coast road, there's some decent nightlife – the *Belly Up Tavern*, 143 S Cedros Ave (☎481-9022), is one of the major mid-sized music venues in the area (see the box on p.189 for details) – and striking views over the ocean from the Solana Beach County Park. If you're driving, take a quick detour inland along Hwy-8, passing the rolling Fairbanks Ranch (built by the film star, Douglas Jr) to **Rancho Santa Fe**, a small but extremely rich community shaded by trees and given its distinctive Spanish architectural flavour through the 1920s and 1930s.

## Encinitas and Leucadia

**ENCINITAS** is a major flower-growing centre, its abundant blooms at their best during the spring, when soft waves of colour from the flowers cast a calm and collected air over the whole place. It's no surprise that an Indian guru chose the town as the HQ of the *Self-Realization Fellowship*, beside the coast road at the south end of town. The Fellowship's serene **Meditation Gardens**, around the corner at 216 K St (Tues–Sat 9am–5pm, Sun 11am–5pm; free), are open to all, and there's further flower power nearby at the **Quail Botanical Gardens**, 230 Quail Gardens Drive (daily 8am–5pm; $2; free tours Sat 10am). For more local information call at the **visitor center**, 345 First St (☎753-6041). Encinitas, and the adjoining community of **LEUCADIA** three miles to the north, both offer reasonably priced **accommodation**, such as the *Moonlight Beach Motel*, 233 Second St, Encinitas (☎753-0623 or 1-800/323-1259; ③), nicely located for the beach with kitchenettes in all rooms. Otherwise, there's the landscaped **campground** at San Elijo Beach State Park ($16; ☎753-5091 or *MISTIX*), near **Cardiff-by-the-Sea** just to the south, whose name (the whim of its founder's English wife, which also explains the presence of Manchester and Birmingham avenues) is its only interesting feature.

## Carlsbad

Surfers constitute the major element of **South Carlsbad State Beach** (with a busy $16 cliff-top campground; ☎438-3143 or *MISTIX*), marking the edge of **CARLSBAD**, one of the few coastal communities with a past worth shouting about. During the early 1880s, water from a local spring was deemed to have the same invigorating qualities as the waters of Karlsbad, a European spa town in what was then Bohemia (now part of the Czech Republic). Carlsbad thus acquired its name and a money-spinning reputation as a health Resort, ably promoted by pioneer-settler turned entrepreneur John Frazier, whose image in bronze now overlooks the (now dry) original springs.

The springs and most things you'll need are close to the junction of Carlsbad Boulevard (the coast road) and Carlsbad Village Drive; along the latter, inside the train station, the **visitor center** (Mon–Fri 9am–5pm, Sat 10am–4pm, Sun 10am–2pm; ☎434-6093 or 1-800/227-5722) will give you a sense of the town's history.

Other than the campground, the best **place to stay** is the *Ocean Manor Beach Motel*, 2950 Ocean St (☎729-2493 or 1-800/624-SAND; ④), overlooking the water but with its own pool and rooms with kitchenettes. Two well-priced places to **eat** are *Pollos Maria*, 3055 Harding St (☎729-4858), for fast, tasty Mexican food, and, out from the centre but easy to find thanks to its "Danish windmill", a branch of *Pea Soup Andersen's*, 850 Palomar Airport Rd (☎931-1400), with an all-American menu of sandwiches and salads, and a chunky pea soup famous since the 1920s.

## Oceanside, Mission San Luis Rey and around

The most northerly town on the San Diego county coast, **OCEANSIDE** is dominated by the huge **Camp Pendleton marine base** and has little to redeem itself. But, for those without a car, it's a major transport centre (*Amtrak, Greyhound* and local bus services all pass through) and the easiest place from which to reach Mission San Luis Rey (see below).

If you find yourself having to **stay** here, the *Beechwood Motel*, 210 Sixth St (☎722-3866; ②), is tolerable and cheap. For **eating**, *The Hill Street Coffee House*, 524 S Hill St (☎966-0985), is a real find in Oceanside's fast food wasteland. It's an old house with bohemian leanings, with great coffee, cakes, sandwiches and salads, and live music on Saturday nights. For a surfeit of entertainment, you could take a look at the **California Surf Museum** (Mon–Fri noon–4pm, Sat & Sun 10am–4pm; free), nearby at 308 North Pacific St, or the lagoon-centred **Buena Vista Audubon Nature Centre**, 2202 S Hill St (Tues–Sat 10am–4pm, Sun 1–4pm; free).

Four miles inland from Oceanside along Hwy-76 and accessible on local bus #313, **Mission San Luis Rey**, 4050 Mission Ave (Mon–Sat 10am–4.30pm, Sun noon–4.30pm; $3), is the largest of the Californian missions, founded in 1798 by Padre Laséun and once home to three thousand Native Americans. Franciscan monks keep the impressively restored mission's spiritual function alive while the **museum** and serene candle-lit **chapel** evoke earlier times. Even if you don't go inside, look around the foundations of the guards barracks immediately outside the main building, and, across the road, the remains of the mission's ornate sunken gardens (daily 9am–4.30pm; free), once *Lavanderías*, where the mission's inhabitants did their washing.

The strong sense of history at the mission is fast being diluted by new property developments all around, the commercial spillover from Oceanside that is creeping into the community of **San Luis Rey** itself. To escape, push on another four miles beyond San Luis Rey to the **Rancho Guajome Regional Park** (9.30am to an hour before dusk; $1 per vehicle) with its centrepiece, the ranch, a twenty-room adobe building erected in the mid-eighteenth century as home for the newly married Cave Cortes and Ysidora Bandini, who turned the place into a major social gathering place. Among the many celebrities entertained at the ranch were Ulysses S Wright and Helen Hunt Jackson, who, according to legend, based the central character of *Ramona*, her sentimental tale of Indian life during the mission era, on Ysidora's maid. After Cortes' death in 1874, Ysidora fought to maintain the upkeep of the place but over the years it fell into a dilapidation that was halted only when the building was bought by the county authorities. There are **free guided tours** of the house each weekend at 2pm, but at any other time just walk into the courtyard – whose still fountains and ragged greenery make a spooky suggestion of glamorous times past.

Highway 76 continues inland to Mission Asistencia San Antonio de Pala, and to the Palomar Observatory, both described below. Along the coast beyond Oceanside, the **military** has kept its territory in a raw state, creating a vivid impression of how stark the land was before industrialization took hold. When manoeuvres aren't in progress, it's possible to pitch a tent in the lower parts of the camp area, close to the uncluttered **beach**. The northern part of the camp, around the San Onofre Nuclear Plant, is popular with surfers because the plant's by-products apparently keep the water warm – though you might prefer to stay clear.

# The North County inland

**Inland**, the North County is quite different from the coastal strip, given over to farming as far as the terrain allows and with no sizeable towns, the outlook one of thick forests, deep valleys and mile-high mountain ranges. Besides a few reminders of the ancient indigenous cultures, remnants from the mission era, and a few tiny settlements – some of which can comfortably consume an hour or two of your time – it's best to make for the area's state parks and enjoy some leisurely countryside walks, or venture east to the dramatic Anza-Borrego desert (see p.221).

## Escondido

About forty miles north of San Diego on I-15, the unhurried dormitory town of **ESCONDIDO** sits in a quiet valley. The town is accessible on buses #20, #810 or #820 from downtown San Diego; you're dropped seven miles out at the North County Fair shopping mall, but bus #381 will get you into town. The extremely well-informed **CVB**, 720 N Broadway (Mon–Fri 8.30am–5pm, Sat 10am–4pm; ☎745-4741 or 1-800/848-3336) provides information for the entire north San Diego County area.

In Escondido itself, the main focus of visitor attention is **Heritage Walk** in Grape Day Park, which leads into and around several restored Victorian buildings (Thurs–Sat 1–4pm; free) and to a 1925 railroad car that holds an elaborate scale model of the railroad which once linked Escondido to Oceanside. A couple of commendable wineries lie on Escondido's outskirts. The **Orfila Winery**, set in stunning scenery at 13455 San Pasqual Rd (daily 10am–6pm), offers tastings of wines produced by a former Napa Valley vintner, while the **Deer Park Winery**, 29013 Champagne Blvd (daily 9am–5pm), also shows off a sizeable collection of vintage cars to anyone who turns up to sample the produce of its vines.

To most Americans over 65, however, Escondido is best known for the **Lawrence Welk Resort**, a thousand-acre vacation complex of golf courses, guest villas and the *Welk Dinner Theater*, eight miles north of the town off I-15 (no public transport). Welk himself rose from accordion-playing obscurity to become an adored band leader, TV celebrity and inventor of an anodyne sound known as "champagne music". Even if you don't consider Welk a role model for aspiring composers, there's something to be said for taking a look at the hagiographical account of his life displayed around the lobby of the theatre, and for gorging yourself on the $10 lunch buffet laid out in the nearby restaurant.

## North from Escondido

Hwy-S6 leads out from Escondido fifteen miles to **Mission Asistencia San Antonio de Pala** (daily 6am–6pm; $2), close to the junction with Hwy-76 from Oceanside. Built as an outpost of Mission San Luis Rey, this lay in ruins until the Cupeno Indians were ousted from their tribal home (to make room for the building of Warner Hot Springs) and moved to this area, where the mission was revived to serve as their church. The buildings here now are rarely used and are all reconstructions of the originals, but they're not without atmosphere, supplemented by the breeze whispering through the gaping windows and the eerie silence hanging over the cemetery. There's a small basic **campground** opposite the mission.

Continuing east, Hwy-76 runs into **Cleveland National Forest** and a good sprinkling of **campgrounds** (both state- and federal-run). The enormous forest stretches south from here almost to the Mexican border, although less-than-hardcore backpackers tend to prefer the **Palomar Mountain State Park** (info: ☎742-3462), on Hwy-S7, for its cooler, higher altitude (some parts rise above 5000ft) and enjoyable, fairly unarduous hiking trails. **Camping** at the Doane Valley site costs $14 (reserve through *MISTIX*) and supplies are available at the well-stocked *Palomar Mountain General Store* at the junction of routes S6 and S7.

Capable of seeing a billion light years into the cosmos, the two-hundred-inch telescope of the **Palomar Observatory** on Hwy-S6 (daily 9am–4pm; free) is something of a legend in astronomy circles. As a visitor, it's not possible to view the distant galaxies directly, but look in on the observatory's impressive collection of deep-space photographs taken using the powerful telescope.

## East from Escondido

Ten miles east from Escondido on Hwy-78 (bus #307, not Sun) and thirty miles north of San Diego (bus #878 or #879 from the *Grossmont Center*, Tues–Sat), the **San Diego Wild Animal Park** on San Pasqual Valley Road (mid-June to Sept Mon–Wed 9am–5pm, Thurs–Sun 9am–8pm; rest of year daily 9am–4pm; $18.95, combined ticket with San Diego Zoo $27) is the major tourist target in the area: a 2100-acre enclosure that's about as enjoyable as any safari park, a place to spend the day rather than a brief stop-off. It's obviously a place for kids, and attractions include a sizeable aviary, noisy with the massed squawks of tropical birds, a mock-African Bush, a Kilimanjaro hiking trail, not to mention elephant rides and various films and exhibitions. Admission includes a fifty-minute ride on the *Wgasa Bush Line Monorail*, which skirts through the outer reaches of the park, where the animals – among them lions, tigers, cheetahs, deer and monkeys – roam in relative freedom.

---

### THE NORTH EAST RURAL BUS SYSTEM

The only **bus service** through the sparsely populated northeastern section of the county is the reliable but infrequent *North East Rural Bus System* (☎765-0145; calls answered Mon–Sat 7am–noon & 2–5pm) that links San Diego with Escondido, Ramona, Santa Ysabel and Julian and runs Monday to Saturday, continuing on selected days into the Anza-Borrego desert (see p.221).

The departure point in San Diego is the *Grossmont Center* near El Cajon, roughly ten miles east of downtown (get there with city bus #15). It's strongly advisable to phone at least a day in advance to check schedules – and you must phone ahead if you want to be collected from Cuyamaca State Park. Board the buses either at marked stops or, where there are none, simply flag the vehicle down. A consolation for the scarcity of buses are the low **fares**: just $2.50 from San Diego to Julian, for example. Bicycles are carried free of charge but, again, you need to reserve in advance.

In contrast to the crowded coast, the population – and the landscapes – become increasingly sparse as you press further east along Hwy-78, into a region that's a near-impossible nut to crack without personal transport (see the box opposite). If you're coming this way by car directly from San Diego, use Hwy-67 and join Hwy-78 at **Ramona**, eighteen miles from Escondido, and continue east for sixteen miles to **SANTA YSABEL**, a tiny crossroads community enlivened by two things. Right on Hwy-78 just before its junction with Hwy-79 you can't miss *Dudley's Bakery*, famous far and wide for its homebaked breads and pastries at giveaway prices – the date, nut and raisin loaf is justly a popular line. A mile and a half north of town on Hwy-79, the tiny **Santa Ysabel Mission** (daily 7am–dusk; $1 donation), a 1924 replacement of an 1818 original, sits in moody isolation. There's a small chapel and, around the side, a one-room **museum** (same hours and another $1 donation) detailing the history of the mission.

# Julian

A different atmosphere prevails in **JULIAN**, seven miles southeast of Santa Ysabel on Hwy-78, and surrounded by pines – a sure sign that you're entering the foothills of the mountains that divide the coastal side of the county from the desert. Indeed, you're some 4000ft up and even in summer it can get a bit brisk. Hard as it may be to believe today, the discovery of gold here in 1869 turned Julian into the second-biggest town in the San Diego area. Since then, the local population has stayed constant at around 1500, and has earned more from harvesting apples than from precious metal: the cider and apple pies made and produced here bring thousands of weekend visitors. You might also consider using Julian as a temperate base from which to make forays into the Anza-Borrego desert (see p.221) less than ten miles to the east.

With its little buildings and carefully nurtured downhome charms, Julian is immediately appealing, but a short stroll reveals little of consequence beyond the shops, realty stores and restaurants grouped along Main Street. The *Julian Café*, 2612 Main St (☎765-2712), has the best atmosphere and good-value, basic **food**; *Kendal's Korner*, 2603 B St (☎765-1560) is its chief competitor, though only until 5pm (8pm at weekends). The **Chamber of Commerce**, 2129 Main St (Mon & Wed–Fri 10am–4pm; ☎765-1857), has details of the town's many **B&Bs**. Among these, the *Julian Hotel*, at the junction of Main and B (☎765-0201 or 1-800/734-5854; ④–⑤), is the oldest still-functioning hotel in the state. For something cheaper, try *Julian B* (☎765-2200; ③), where you can also rent bikes, or **camp** in the Cuyamaca Rancho State Park (see below).

If you find yourself with a few spare hours in Julian, take a look at the absorbing clutter inside the **Pioneer Museum** on Hwy-78 just off Main Street (April–Nov Tues–Sun 10am–4pm; Dec–March Sat & Sun 10am–4pm; $1). Alternatively, wander half a mile up C Street to the **Eagle Gold Mine Museum** (daily 10am–3pm; $7), where you can get an inkling of the subterranean perils faced by the town's early settlers.

## Cuyamaca Rancho State Park

You could spend at least a few hours among the oaks, willows, sycamores and Ponderosa and Jeffrey pines that fill the **Cuyamaca Rancho State Park** (unrestricted entry), which starts nine miles south of Julian along Hwy-79. Even if you stay for days, you won't see everything: from lush sub-alpine meadows to stark mountain peaks, the park spans 25,000 acres, much of it designated wilderness area and only crisscrossed by a hundred miles of hiking trails (see box below), many of them hugging the 5000-foot contour.

Pick up information and maps, from the **park headquarters** (Mon–Fri 8am–5pm; ☎765-0755), sixteen miles south of Julian beside Hwy-79 in the heart of the park. At the same place, check the latest on the park's **campgrounds** strung along Hwy-79, (reservation through *MISTIX* recommended on summer weekends; $12–14), chiefly *Paso*

## HIKES IN THE CUYAMACA MOUNTAINS

Widely condsidered a four-season hiking area, the trails in the Cuyamaca Mountains seldom fall below 4500ft. Outside the summer months snow is always a possibility, and even in summer, nights are cool and thunderstorms common.

**Cuyamaca Peak Trail** (6 miles; 4hr; 1600ft ascent). Despite following the vehicle-free, paved Cuyamaca Peak Fire Road, this is the most rewarding of all the park's trails; a steep climb from either the *Paso Picacho* campsite (day-use fee) to a 6512-foot summit giving views east to the desert and west to the Pacific Ocean.

**Harvey Moore Trail** (12 miles; 7–8hr; 1000ft ascent). This well signposted loop trail is relatively flat and winds through several ecological zones – prairie, oak woodland, meadowland and chaparral – all perfect territory for a cowboy such as Harvey Moore, the park's first superintendent in the 1930s. Start a mile south of the park HQ.

**Middle Peak** (6 miles; 4hr; 1000ft ascent). There are several routes to Middle Peak, all easier than the Cuyamaca Peak Trail. The most direct is Sugar Pine Trail, named after the tall pines which bear the world's longest cones. The trail starts at the *Boy Scout* camp, ten miles south of Julian where the road turns sharply east at the end of the dammed Cuyamaca Lake.

*Picacho*, twelve miles south of Julian, and *Green Valley*, five miles further south. These sites (where a $5 day-use fee is charged) are the only accommodation on offer unless you are prepared to hike into the $3 backcountry sites: *Arroyo Seco* is a mile and a half northwest of *Green Valley*, and *Granite Spring* is almost five miles east.

For some historical back-up to the scenery, drop into the excellent **Indian Museum** (Mon–Fri 8.30am–4.30pm, Sat & Sun 10am–2pm; free), right by the park HQ, which details the formidable resistance of the local Native Americans to Spanish attempts to cut down the area's forests; this group also strongly resisted the arrival of settlers from the eastern US and was one of the last to be forced onto reservations. For more on the native peoples, take a stroll along the nature trails at Paso Picacho and at the park headquarters.

# Tijuana and northern Baja California

**TIJUANA** has the odd distinction of being both one of the least interesting places in Mexico and one of the most visited cities in the world. Twenty million people a year cross the border here, most of them Californians on day-long shopping expeditions seeking somewhere cheaper and more colourful to spend money than their local mall. And they find it: blankets, pottery, cigarettes, tequila, dentistry or car repair – everything is lower-priced in Tijuana than in the US (though more expensive than in the rest of Mexico), and all of it is hawked with enthusiasm.

What's most dramatic about Tijuana for first-time arrivals is the abrupt realization of the vast economic gulf separating the two countries. Crossing the frontier area takes you past beggars crouched in corners and dirty children scuffling for change thrown by tourists. It's both a depressing and revealing experience. For regular visitors, however, it's a shock that soon fades; it's also unrepresentative of Tijuana itself which is, in fact, one of the wealthiest Mexican cities, thanks to its duty-free status and the large number of Southern Californian manufacturing companies who are relocating south of the border to exploit the cheaper workforce here.

Whatever its faults, Tijuana is, at least, quite unique, and you could hardly find a more intriguing day trip out from San Diego. However, it's not typically Mexico, and if you want a proper taste of the country you'd do well to hurry on through. Things are also much safer these days than was the case a decade or so ago when Tijuana lived up to a rough border town image. Then prostitution was rife and the streets extremely creepy after dark; these days the red-light area is limited to the easily avoided blocks around the junction of Avenida Artícula and Mutualismo. Provided you take the usual amount of care there's little danger in most parts of town.

The main streets and shopping areas are a mile or so from the border in **downtown**, where the major thoroughfare is Avenida Revolución, lined with street vendors and people trying to hassle you into the shopping emporia. Stroll up and down for a while to get the mood and then retire to one of the plentiful bars and watch the throng in the company of a sizeable margarita (in the bigger bars expect to pay $1.50 for a large one, $1 for a tequila and about 75¢ for a beer). At night, the action mostly consists of inebriated North American youths dancing themselves silly in flashy discos – not hard to find around the main streets.

As a break from shopping or drinking, visit the **Centro Cultural** rising like a huge golf ball from the ramshackle city skyline, on the corner of Paseo de los Héroes and Mina. Multimedia shows in the **Cine Planetario** (Mon–Fri 3–9pm, Sat & Sun 11am–

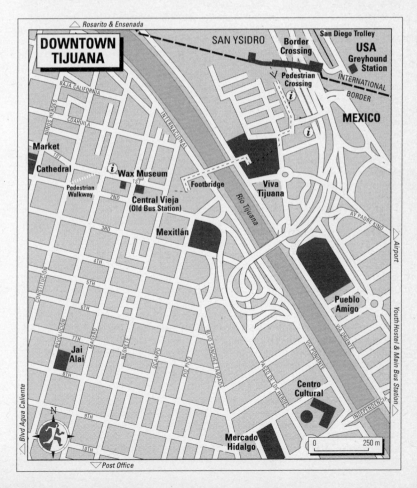

9pm; $5) and the **museum** (daily 11am–8pm; $1, free with movie) give strong accounts of regional Mexican cultures.

Lesser attractions include **Mexitlán** (summer daily 10am–10pm; rest of year Wed–Fri 10am–6pm, Sat & Sun 9am–9pm; $3), a miniature Mexican theme park with models of famous Mexican buildings, folklore performances and more resturants and shops; a new and very tacky **wax museum** at Madero and First (don't waste your money); and various modern shopping malls.

## Practicalities

Getting to Tijuana from San Diego could hardly be easier. The San Diego Trolley (see p.165) ends its route close to the elevated concrete walkway which leads over the border, as does bus #932 from the Santa Fe Depot in downtown San Diego. If you arrive by *Greyhound*, you'll have to walk across the border and reboard for the ride into Tijuana proper – hardly worthwhile since it is just as quick to continue by foot into downtown Tijuana from the border crossing.

Crossing into Mexico, **border formalities** are mínimal: simply negotiate a turnstile and you're there. Customs and immigration checks are only carried out twenty miles or so inside the country, so you only need to be carrying a Mexican Tourist Card if you're continuing on from Tijuana. These are available free from any Mexican consulate in the US – see the phone book for the one nearest you – and also, somewhat unofficially, at the border. Returning to the US, however, the formalities are as stringent as anywhere (see *Basics*, p.13). Even if you've just travelled down for the day, you will need to satisfy the usual entry requirements. Dollars are accepted as readily as pesos everywhere in Tijuana, but although you can **change money** at any of the banks along Avenida Revolución, it's only worth doing so if you're travelling further into Mexico. That said, you'll get marginally better prices if you do pay in pesos. Only *Bánamex* will change travellers' cheques.

If you do want to sample Tijuana's discos into the small hours and stay overnight, the **accommodation** options are fairly good, if basic. You'll spend much less here for a **hotel** room than you would north of the border, and many passable lodgings can be found close to the central streets. At the lowest end of the price scale are *Catalina*, Fifth at Madero (☎85-97-48; ②) and *St Francis*, Second between Revolución and Madero (☎85-49-03; ②). Slightly more upmarket, the *Hotel Nelson*, Avenida Revolución 503 (☎85-43-03; ②), has rooms with cable.

# Into Mexico

As for **travelling further into Mexico**, on the whole the northwest of the country has little to tempt visitors, and many people head straight for Mexico City and the regions beyond. A closer option, though, is the peninsula of Baja California, which has miles of unspoilt coast and a few moderately sized cities. The only sensible destinations within easy reach of Tijuana are **Rosarito**, *the* south-of-the-border party beach, and the sizeable town of **Ensenada**, your best introduction to more typical Mexican life. Both are briefly described below, and for full details, pick up the *Rough Guide to Mexico*, most easily available in San Diego from *Le Travel Store*, 745 Fourth Ave (☎544-0005).

## Rosarito

Forty-five minutes south of Tijuana, on buses from *Central Vieja* bus terminal at First and Madero, the old coast road hits the sea at **ROSARITO** which boasts much the best beach in these parts. It is much more restful here than in Tijuana, but at weekends it too has all-pervasive frat-house atmosphere. The town's landmark is the smart and once elegant *Rosarito Beach Hotel* (☎661/2-01-44; ④), to which Hollywood's Prohibition refugees fled for a little of the hard stuff in the Thirties. For a cheaper **place to stay**, try *Hotel California*

## GETTING TO, AND AROUND, NORTHERN BAJA

Personal formalities present no problems for a quick trip to northern Baja: visitors to Tijuana, Rosarito and Ensenada staying for up to 72 hours need only their passports and are not required to obtain tourist cards. **Vehicle permits** are not required in Baja but most US rental agencies don't allow their vehicles into Mexico, so you'll need to approach companies such as *Fuller Auto Rentals*, 560 Auto Park Drive, Chula Vista (☎656-3370) who do. With your own vehicle ensure you get **Mexican insurance**, easily obtainable from numerous companies whose fliers are all over San Ysidro: try *Oscar Padilla's Drive-Thru*, 110 Calle Primero (☎428-2221), or *"Instant" Mexico*, 223 Via de San Ysidro (☎428-4717 or 1-800/345-4701). All things considered, it's probably easier to get the bus.

(☎661/2-25-50; ②), towards the southern end of the main drag. There's no shortage of reasonable taco **restaurants**, many specializing in fish dishes: just wander along and gauge which seems currently the most popular. The weekend bonhomie is particularly frenzied at the beachside *Papas and Beer*, a *Bohemia*-and-beach-volleyball bar.

## Ensenada

Venturing to **ENSENADA**, two hours south from Tijuana's *Central Vieja*, brings a taste of the real Mexico. Cruise ships from San Diego dock here, and at weekends the bars are thronged with Americans, but otherwise Ensenada ticks by, gently milking dollars from *norteños* who have wised up to the town's superiority over Tijuana.

On Avenida Mateos you'll find the majority of the bars, restaurants, souvenir shops and places organizing sport-fishing trips. Drag yourself away for a little while to tour and taste the produce of the *Bodegas de Santo Tomás* **winery** (tours daily 11am, 1pm & 3pm; $2; ☎617/8-33-33) at Miramar 666 between Calle 6 and Calle 7. Sadly, most vintages aren't a patch on even run-of-the-mill offerings from north of the border. The only other local attraction is **La Bufadora**, a natural blowhole six miles south of Ensenada, which occasionally spouts up to eighty feet, though thirty is more common. Buses leave roughly hourly from the Tres Cabezas park on the coast road at the bottom of Avenida Riveroll.

The pick of the **accommodation** (book at weekends) is the *Best Western Cortez Motor Hotel*, Mateos 1089 at Castillo (☎667/8-23-07; ④); though *Motel America*, Mateos at Espinoza (☎667/6-13-33; ①) is decent and has a lot more local flavour. Famous throughout Southern California, *Hussongs Cantina*, Ruiz 113, has managed to maintain its rumbustious reputation and heaves at weekends. Soak up the beer with fish tacos from the **fish market** by the harbour, or the straightforward Mexican dishes at *El Charro*, Mateos 486.

## travel details

### Trains

**San Diego to**: Anaheim (9 daily; 2hr); Del Mar (10 daily; 34min); Los Angeles downtown (10 daily; 2hr 47min); Oceanside (10 daily; 1hr); San Clemente (1 daily; 1hr 8min); San Juan Capistrano (10 daily; 1hr 23min).

### Buses

**San Diego, downtown to**: Anaheim (12 daily; 2hr 15min); Long Beach (5 daily; 2hr 15min); Los Angeles downtown (14 daily; 2hr); Oceanside (12 daily; 1hr); San Clemente (4 daily; 1hr 30min).

**San Diego, Grossmont Center to**: Cumacaca (5 a month; 2hr 10min); Julian (2 a week; 1hr 30min); Ramona (4 a week; 1hr 10min); Santa Ysabel (4 a week; 1hr 35min).

### International buses

**San Diego to**: Tijuana (14 daily; 50min).

# CHAPTER THREE

# THE DESERTS, LAS VEGAS AND THE GRAND CANYON

T he **deserts** of Southern California represent only a fraction of the half a million square miles of North American Desert that stretch away eastwards into another four states and cross the border into Mexico in the south. Contrary to the monotonous landscape you might expect, California's deserts are a varied and ever-changing kaleidoscope, dotted with occasional harsh little settlements. The one thing you can rely on is that it will be uniformly hot, inhospitable and dry – though desert rainfall is highly irregular, and a whole year's average of three or four inches may fall in a single storm. After being in drought for six years, the heavy rainfall of the 1992–93 winter transformed the desert hillsides into lush hulks, some say the greenest in living memory.

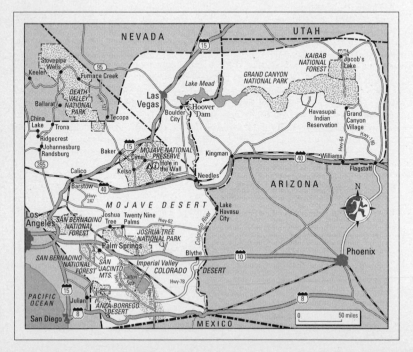

Unless otherwise specified, all desert telephone numbers have the **area code** ☎619.

Most of the 25 million acres that make up the desert are protected in state and national parks, but not all are entirely unspoiled. Three million acres are used by the US Government as military bases for training and weapons testing, and when underground nuclear explosions aren't shaking up the desert's fragile ecosystem, the region's many fans flock here to do their damage.

In spite of this, most of the desert remains a wilderness, and with a little foresight can be the undisputed highlight of your trip. Occupying a quarter of the state, California's desert divides into two distinct regions: the **Colorado** or **Low Desert** in the south, stretching down to the Mexican border and east into Arizona, and the **Mojave** or **High Desert**, which covers the south-central part of the state. The Low Desert is the most easily reached from LA, with the extravagantly wealthy **Palm Springs** serving as an access point – though pulling in the likes of Donald Trump for events like the Bob Hope Classic Golf Tournament, it's the kind of town you'll need a bankroll to really enjoy. The hiking trails around **Joshua Tree** are the big attraction for serious desert people, bridging the divide between Low and High Desert in a vast silent area of craggy trees. In contrast, **Imperial Valley** to the south – agricultural land, though you could pass through without realizing anyone lived there – and the **Salton Sea** beyond, are undiluted Low Desert. The heat is searing, and unless you're headed for states beyond there's no point making this part of your itinerary. However, the vast expanse of the **Anza-Borrego Desert**, the largest state park in the country, boasts multifarious varieties of vegetation and geological quirks and, with a little effort, can be as rewarding as the better-known deserts to the north.

Interstate 10 crosses the Low Desert from east to west and carries a considerable flow of traffic. Not unusually, this includes packs of bikers heading out for a long weekend ride and some high jinks in the popular gambling resorts, like **Lake Havasu City**, that dot the stunning **Colorado River** region on the California/Arizona border. I-15 cuts north from I-10 at **Barstow**, often a first stop for those heading into the High Desert. From here it's possible (and popular) to make the long and tiring trip to the neon oasis of **Las Vegas**, just across the border in Nevada, for some legalized gambling; once you've got that far, a day's drive east (or a thirty-minute flight) takes you to the magnificent **Grand Canyon** in Arizona. Afterwards you can loop back into California by way of Death Valley, part of the desert region but covered in Chapter Four.

## Getting around and accommodation

**Public transport** in the desert is poor to non-existent: Los Angeles connects easily with the major points – Palm Springs, Barstow, Las Vegas – and the Anza-Borrego is an easy trip from San Diego, but on arrival you're stuck without your own vehicle. If you do have a car, it will need to be in very good working order – don't rely on the

## DESERT SURVIVAL

To survive the rigours of the desert you have to be cool in more ways than one. Don't let adventure get the better of you and go charging off into the wilderness without heeding the warnings. The desert is rarely conquered by a pioneering spirit alone and every year people die here. Hikers are particularly vulnerable, especially those who venture beyond the designated areas of the national parks, but drivers too should not be blasé and take considerable precautions whatever their destination. On the highways, extra water and as full a tank of gas as possible should be all the precautions you need, but anything more adventurous requires planning. Above all, *think*. Tell somebody where you are going, and your expected time of return. Carry an extra two days' food and water and never go anywhere without a map. Only the well-prepared can enjoy the desert with any sense of security.

### CLIMATE AND WATER

First and most obviously you're up against a pretty formidable **climate**. This varies from region to region, but the basic safety procedures remain the same: not only are you doing battle with incredible heat, but at high elevations at night you should be prepared for below-freezing temperatures too. Between May and September, when daytime temperatures regularly exceed 120°F, you really shouldn't come at all (although, of course, people do).

Outside of the summer months, the daytime temperature is more manageable, ranging between the mid-sixties and low nineties. At any time of year, you'll stay cooler during the day if you wear full-length sleeves and trousers, though you'll look incongruous amongst the bare legs and torsos. Also, a wide-brimmed hat and a pair of *good* sunglasses will spare you the blinding headaches that can result from the desert light.

You can never drink enough **liquid** in the desert: the body loses up to a gallon each day and even when you're not thirsty you are continually dehydrating and should keep drinking. Before setting off on any expedition, whether on foot or in a car, *two* gallons of water per person should be prepared; one is an absolute minimum, and don't save it for the walk back, drink it as you need it. Waiting for thirst, dizziness, nausea or other signs of dehydration before doing anything can be dangerous. If you notice any of these symptoms, or feel weak and have stopped sweating, it's time to get to the doctor. Watch your alcohol intake too: if you must booze during the day, compensate heavily with pints of water between each drink. Any activity in this heat can be exhausting so you also need to **eat** well, packing in the carbohydrates.

**Campers** need to take particular heed of these warnings especially if you are backpacking away from the main roads. In summer, ventures of more than one night are all but impossible as you end up having to carry more water than is comfortable. In the valleys, you may also have to contend with **flash floods**, which can appear from nowhere: an innocent-looking dark cloud can turn a dry wash into a raging river. Never camp in a dry wash and don't attempt to cross flooded areas until the water has receded.

### ROADS: ON WHEELS AND ON FOOT

**Roads and highways** across much of the desert are not maintained, and in an area where it's often a challenge to make it across existing dirt roads, trailblazing your own path through the desert is insanity. Of course you'll be tempted – if you must, rent a dune buggy or four-wheel drive and tear about one of the off-road driving areas specifically designated for this purpose.

Even sticking to the main highways, you stand a good chance of getting an **overheated engine**. If your car's temperature needle rises alarmingly, most likely when

Thunderbird you picked up in LA for $250 to get you through the worst of the desert. Three major interstate highways cross the desert from east to west. I-15 cuts directly through the middle of the Mojave on its way from Los Angeles to Las Vegas, joined at negotiating steep gradients, turn the air conditioning off and the heater on full-blast to cool the engine quickly. If this fails and the engine blows, stop with the car facing into the wind and the engine running, pour water over the radiator grille and top up the water reservoir. In an **emergency**, never leave the car: you'll be harder to find wandering around alone.

Among **other things you might consider taking along**, an emergency pack with flares, a first aid and snakebite kit (see below), matches and a compass, a shovel, a tyre pump and extra gas are always a good idea. A few white towels to drape over the dashboard, steering wheel and back ledge will save you a lot of discomfort when you get back in your car after leaving it parked for a few hours.

When **hiking**, try and cover most of your ground in the early morning: the midday heat is too debilitating, and you shouldn't even think about it when the mercury goes over 90°F. Almost all parks will require you to register with them – this is very wise, especially for those who are hiking alone. If you get lost, find some shade and wait. So long as you've registered, the rangers will eventually come and fetch you. However, they'll have a lot of trouble if you've fallen down an old mine shaft, so watch your footing and keep your eyes peeled for unexploded artillery.

### DESERT WILDLIFE

Most people's biggest fear of the desert is of encountering **poisonous creatures**. If you do, you'll be far better served by strong boots and long trousers than sports sandals and shorts. Not only do they offer some protection in case of attack, but firm footfalls send vibrations through the ground giving ample warning of your approach. Walk heavily and you're unlikely to see anything you don't want to.

Of all the **snakes** in the California desert, only the rattlesnake is poisonous. Of course you might not be able to tell a rattler from any other kind of snake; in fact many rattlers don't rattle at all. If in doubt, assume it is one. When it's hot, snakes lurk in shaded areas under bushes, around wood debris, old mining shafts and piles of rocks. When it's cooler, they sun themselves out in the open, but they won't be expecting you and if disturbed will attack. While **black widow spiders** and **scorpions** are non-aggressive, they are extremely venomous and easily disturbed. A bite from any of the above is initially like a sharp pin-prick, but within hours the pain becomes severe, usually accompanied by swelling and acute nausea. Forget any misconceptions you may harbour about sucking the poison out; it doesn't work and even tends to hasten the spread of venom. Since this travels mainly through the lymph system just under the skin, the best way of inhibiting the diffusion is to wrap the whole limb firmly, but not in a tourniquet, then contact a ranger or doctor as soon as possible. Do all you can to keep calm – a slower pulse rate limits the spread of the venom. It's a wise precaution to carry a **snakebite kit**, available for a couple of dollars from most sports and camping stores.

**Tarantulas** are not at all dangerous. A leg span of up to seven inches means they're pretty easy to spot, but if you're unlucky and get bitten don't panic – cleansing with antiseptic is usually sufficient treatment once you've got over the initial pain.

Nasty critters aren't the only things to avoid. Most **cacti** present few problems, but you should keep an eye out for the eight-foot *cholla* (pronounced *Choya*), or *jumping cholla* as they're called because of the way segments seem to jump off and attach themselves to you if you brush past. Don't use your hands to get them off, you'll just spear all your fingers; instead use a stick or comb to flick it off and remove the remaining spines with tweezers. The large pancake pads of prickly pear cactus are also worth avoiding: as well as the larger spines they have thousands of tiny, hair-like stickers that are almost impossible to remove. You should expect a good day of painful irritation before they begin to wear away. For more on the delights of desert flora and fauna, see *Contexts*.

Barstow by I-40, which then heads eastwards to the Grand Canyon. I-10 takes you from LA through the Palm Springs and Joshua Tree area, heading into Arizona. Some fast, empty, secondary roads can get you safely to all but the most remote areas of the desert; but be wary of using the lower-grade roads in between, which are likely to be unmaintained and often only passable by four-wheel drive. Other than at Palm Springs, **motels** in the California deserts are low in price, and you can generally budget for under $40 per night. However, even if cost is no object, you'll get a greatly heightened sense of the desert experience by spending some time **camping** out.

# THE LOW DESERT

Despite the **Low Desert's** hundreds of miles of beauty and empty highways, most visitors to the region have no intention of getting away from it all. They're heading for where it's at, **Palm Springs**, a few square miles overrun with the famous, the star-struck, the ageing and the aspirational. It is said, not completely in jest, that the average age and average temperature of Palm Springs are about the same – a steady 88. This is a town that sprays its olive trees to ensure that they won't grow olives (they're too "messy"), and fines home owners who don't maintain their property to what local officials deem to be a suitable standard. Despite its shortcomings, you'll find it hard to avoid: it's the first stopping point east from LA on I-10, and hub of a resort area – the **Coachella Valley** – that stretches out for miles around, along Hwy-111. The valley's farming communities have the distinction of forming part of the most productive irrigated agricultural centre in the world, growing dates, oranges, lemons and grapefruit in vast quantities, though sadly they're steadily giving way to the condos and complexes that comprise the ever-growing Palm Springs industry.

Fortunately you don't have to travel impossible distances to see the desert at its natural best. **Joshua Tree**, one of the most startling of California's national parks, lies one hour's drive east of Palm Springs, three and a half from LA. A day trip in a fast car would give you a taster, but you really need a couple of days to get to grips with Joshua Tree's sublime landscape, taking in the sunsets and the howl of coyotes at twilight. For all but the extra-bold, this is usually enough. The desert east of the park, to the Colorado River and Nevada, and south to the Mexican border, is arid and uncomfortable, with only the highly saline **Salton Sea** to break the monotony. Nature comes in more extreme forms in the **Anza-Borrego desert**, southwest of Joshua Tree, whose severe vistas are pacified by several oases and stacks of unusual vegetation.

## Palm Springs and around

*The delightful informality of the area makes it possible for you to observe the likes of Frank Sinatra at a nearby table in a popular restaurant, or Red Skelton strolling down the street, or former President Ford swinging a golf club on the fairway.*
California Office of Tourism

With its manicured golf courses, condominium complexes and some seven hundred millionaires in residence, **PALM SPRINGS** does not conform to any typical image of the desert. Purpose-built for luxury and leisure, it's a town of high prices, uniformly boring architecture (apart from the fabulous homes of the stars) and, for those not into pro-celebrity golf or expensive restaurants, an appalling lack of anything to see or do.

Palm Springs and its attendant resort suburbs sit in the lushest agricultural area of the Colorado Desert, with the massive bulk of Mount San Jacinto glowering over its low-level buildings, casting an instantaneous and welcome shadow over the town in the late afternoon. Since Hollywood stars were spotted enjoying a bit of mineral rejuvenation out here in the 1930s, it has taken on a celebrity status all its own, a symbol of good LA living away from the amorphous, smoggy city. In recent years it has also

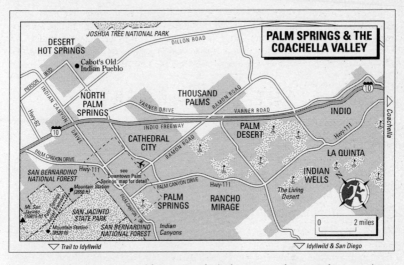

Within the map:

**PALM SPRINGS & THE COACHELLA VALLEY**

JOSHUA TREE NATIONAL PARK

DILLON ROAD

DESERT HOT SPRINGS

Cabot's Old Indian Pueblo

PIERSON BLVD

INDIAN CANYON DRIVE

Hwy 62

NORTH PALM SPRINGS

THOUSAND PALMS

VARNER DRIVE

RAMON ROAD

VARNER ROAD

INDIO

Coachella

10

INDIO FREEWAY

PALM DESERT

Hwy 111

CATHEDRAL CITY

RAMON ROAD

PALM CANYON DRIVE

Hwy 111

LA QUINTA

SAN BERNARDINO NATIONAL FOREST

Mountain Station (2650 ft)

see Downtown Palm Springs map for detail

PALM CANYON DRIVE

INDIAN WELLS

The Living Desert

Mt San Jacinto (10815 ft)

SAN JACINTO STATE PARK

PALM SPRINGS

RANCHO MIRAGE

Hwy 111

Mountain Station (8520 ft)

SAN BERNARDINO NATIONAL FOREST

Indian Canyons

0    2 miles

▽ Trail to Idyllwild                                                     ▽ Idyllwild & San Diego

become a major **gay** resort, with many exclusively gay – and extremely expensive – hotels, bars and restaurants. Every Easter weekend twenty thousand gay men flock here for the "White Party", four days of hedonism centred on the *Wyndham* and *Marquis* hotels in downtown Palm Springs. **Lesbians** get their turn a couple of weeks earlier during the Dinah Shaw Women's Golf Tournament.

For years, high-school kids arrived in their thousands, too, for the drunken revelry of Spring Break (around the end of March and beginning of April). Local antipathy finally persuaded the city council, under the leadership of one Sonny Bono, to ban the annual invasion in 1993, and the inebriated youth promptly decamped east to Lake Havasu City (see p.228). The alcoholically inclined still flock to Palm Springs, but *not* to get drunk: the *Betty Ford Center*, smack in the middle of the valley at Rancho Mirage, draws a star-studded patient list to its booze- and drug-free environment, attempting to undo a lifetime's behavioural disorders in a $20,000 two-week stay.

Despite there being little in the way of specific attractions, the town's siting is superb, surrounded by the beautiful Indian Canyons with the snowcapped mountains behind. Meteorologists have noted changes in the humidity of the desert climate around Palm Springs which they attribute to the moisture absorbed from the hundreds of swimming pools – the consummate condo accoutrement, and the only place you're likely to want to be during the day. When scarce water supplies aren't being used to fill the pools or nourish the nearby orchards, each of Palm Springs' vast golf-course complexes receives around a million gallons daily to maintain its rolling green pastures.

Palm Springs wasn't always like this. Before the wealthy settlers moved in it was the domain of the **Cahuilla**, who lived and hunted around the San Jacinto Mountains, to escape the heat of the desert floor. They still own much of the town, and via an odd checkerboard system of land allotment, every other square mile of Palm Springs is theirs and forms part of the **Agua Caliente Indian Reservation** – a Spanish name which means "hot water", referring to the ancient mineral springs on which the city rests. The land was allocated to the tribe in the 1890s, but exact zoning was never settled until the 1940s, by which time the development of hotels and leisure complexes was well under way. The Cahuilla, finding their land built upon, were left with no option but to charge rent, a system that has made them the richest native peoples in America. Today it is estimated that there are one hundred members of the Cahuilla with individual

## THE WINDMILLS OF PALM SPRINGS

After trawling through the dull eastern suburbs of Los Angeles, I-10 throws you a surprise at the San Gorgonio Pass just before Palm Springs. Over four thousand wind turbines choke the valley, their glinting steel arms sending shimmering patterns across the desert floor. This is the largest concentration of windmills in the country, generating enough electricity to service a small city, and the conditions are perfect. The sun beating down on the desert creates a low pressure zone which sucks air up from the cooler coastal valleys, funnelling it through the San Gorgonio Pass, the only break between two 10,000-foot-plus ranges of mountains. Strong winds often howl for days in spring and early summer, reaching an average speed of between fourteen and twenty miles per hour.

land-holdings worth $2 million or more. If anything, it looks like their purses will be growing fatter still: Palm Springs' first casino recently opened on reservation land.

## Arrival, information and getting around

Palm Springs lies 110 miles east of Los Angeles along the Hwy-111 turn-off from I-10. Arriving by **car**, you drive into town on N Palm Canyon Drive (Hwy-111), the main thoroughfare. Coming by **bus**, you'll arrive at the *Greyhound* terminus at 311 N Indian Canyon Drive, linked with LA ten times daily – a three-hour journey. **Trains** from LA only go as far as San Bernardino, about fifty miles away, from where a *Thruway* bus connects with Palm Springs. You can also **fly**, but this can be expensive – you'll land at the *Palm Springs Regional Airport*, 3400 E Tahquitz-McCallum Way (☎323-8161), from where you take bus #21 downtown.

The very helpful **visitor center**, 2781 N Palm Canyon Drive (daily 9am–5pm; ☎778-8418), can offer accommodation deals and has an exhaustive selection of maps – including one that details the homes of the famous ($5) – and brochures, plus various "what's on" guides (see p.214).

Travel to the resorts around Palm Springs – **Cathedral City**, **Rancho Mirage**, **Palm Desert**, **Indio**, **Indian Wells**, **La Quinta** – is possible with the *Sun Bus* (☎343-3451), which operates daily from 6am to 8pm (until 11pm on some routes) and charges 75¢ to get around town, plus 25¢ for each additional zone beyond; a day pass costs $3. It's unlikely that you'll need to use the bus to get around Palm Springs itself: downtown is no more than several blocks long and wide, and provided you don't mind the sun, walking is easy. For a **taxi**, call *Checker Cabs* (☎327-8979). To get the absolute best out of Palm Springs and the surrounding towns, though, you should think about **car rental**. *Aztec Rent-A-Car*, 450 N Indian Canyon Drive (☎325-2294) has cars for as little as $30 per day ($150 a week), while *Foxy Wheels*, 440 S El Cielo Rd (☎321-1234), also has good deals.

## Accommodation

Palm Springs was designed for the rich, and big luxury **hotels** far outnumber the affordable variety. One way of getting round this is to visit in summer when temperatures rise and prices drop dramatically. Many of the bigger hotels slash their prices by up to seventy percent, and even the smaller concerns give twenty to thirty percent off. The visitor center (see above) also offers special deals.

The north end of town along Hwy-111 holds the most affordable places, in the main perfectly acceptable and all with pools. **Bed and breakfast** inns are becoming more common, and with double room rates at around $80 per night are the best bargains. If you're travelling in a group, it may work out cheaper to **rent an apartment**: many of the homes in Palm Springs are used only for a brief spell and let out for the rest of the year. Again summer is the best time to look, but there is generally a good supply throughout the year. Palm Springs' daily paper, the *Desert Sun*, has rental information in its classified pages, and many rental agencies operate around town – the visitor center will be able to point you to the more affordable ones. **Camping** is not really a viable option, unless you have a camper van; the only tent site is *Lake Cahuilla* (☎564-4712 or 1-800/234-PARK) in La Quinta some six miles east of central Palm Springs. Otherwise, tent-carriers will have a better time exploring Joshua Tree.

Listed below are some of the more reasonable options, with **summer rates** quoted; in the popular October to April period, when you should also book in advance, you can expect the rates to be hiked up into the next price bracket. Some historical quirk of snobbery on the part of the city council dictates that accommodation can't be referred to as a motel, though some of the places listed obviously are.

Palm Springs now claims to have taken over from Key West as America's largest gay resort and has around 35 exclusively **gay hotels**, most of them in the Warm Sands district, half a mile southwest of downtown. However, such is the power of the pink dollar in Palm Springs that virtually *all* hotels here are gay-friendly.

## Hotels, motels and B&Bs

**Budget Host Inn**, 1277 S Palm Canyon Drive (☎325-5574 or1-800/829-8099). The cheapest place in town but still with clean, pleasant rooms, cable and a pool. ②.

**Casa Cody**, 175 S Cahuilla Rd, downtown (☎320-9346). Built in the 1920s by glamorous Hollywood pioneer Harriet Cody, this is the town's second oldest hotel, offering tastefully furnished Southwestern-style rooms, a shady garden, great pool and wonderful breakfasts in a good location two blocks from downtown. Large kitchen suites also available. ⑤/⑥.

**Desert Ho**, 120 West Vereda Sur (☎325-5159). Small, value-for-money hotel facing Mount San Jacinto. The nine large rooms are set around a beautiful pool and gardens. ④.

**Desert Lodge**, 1177 S Palm Canyon Drive (☎325-1356 or 1-800/385-6343). Spacious motel-style place with free continental breakfast and in-room movies. ③.

**Ingleside Inn**, 200 W Ramon Rd, downtown (☎325-0046). Another expensive hotel, but one with real class, having attracted such guests as Garbo, Dali and Brando over the years. Built on a private estate, each room has a personal steam bath and individual whirlpool. ⑥.

**Mira Loma**, 1420 N Indian Canyon Drive (☎320-1178 or 1-800/916-2668). Small, welcoming hotel with well-appointed rooms around a central pool by which breakfast is served at weekends. In 1949 Marilyn Monroe stayed in Room 3 while awaiting her big break. ②

**Motel 6**, 660 S Palm Canyon Drive (☎327-4200). Most central of the budget motels, with a good pool. ②.

**Quality Inn**, 1269 E Palm Canyon Drive (☎323-2775 or 1-800/288-5151). Modern motel with spacious grounds and restaurant. ②

**Super 8 Lodge**, 1900 N Palm Canyon Drive (☎322-3757). Decent motel on the approach into town from I-10, with good mountain views. ③.

**Travelodge**, 333 E Palm Canyon Drive (☎323-2775). Good, central quality chain that regularly has weekend offers. ④.

**Villa Royale**, 1620 S Indian Trail (☎327-2314 or 1-800/245-2314). Beautiful inn with individually designed and exquisitely furnished rooms and suites, most with Jacuzzi, ranged around a pool. In the winter season meals and drinks are served from the bougainvillea-draped restaurant. One room ④–⑦.

## Exclusively gay accommodation

**Avanti Resort**, 7115 San Lorenzo Rd (☎325-9723 or 1-800/572-2779). One of the least costly of the Warm Springs hotels, with an emphasis on fun. ③.

**Bee Charmer Inn**, 1600 E Palm Canyon Drive (☎778-5883). Lesbian motel a mile or so south of downtown, offering continental breakfast and pool. ④.

**Casa Rosa**, 589 Grenfall Rd (☎1-800/322-4151). Luxurious suites ranged around the pool where "natural sunbathing" is encouraged. Breakfast served poolside or in your room. ④.

**Smoke Tree Villa**, 1586 E Palm Canyon Drive (☎323-2231). Long-established lesbian motel with pool and spa, next door to the *Bee Charmer*. Rooms with a kitchen are available, and free continental breakfast and poolside drinks are added attractions. ④.

## Downtown Palm Springs

**Downtown Palm Springs** stretches for about half a mile along Palm Canyon Drive, a wide, bright and modern strip full of expensive boutiques and restaurants. By day, people wear visors and swoon in air-conditioned shopping malls; by night, the youth take over and cruise the main drag in their four-wheel drives with their stereos blaring.

Should your budget not run to the conventional extravagance of a luxury stay in Palm Springs, there are a handful of things to do that won't break the bank. The recently renovated **Palm Springs Desert Museum**, 101 Museum Drive (Tues–Thurs & Sat–Sun 10am–4pm, Fri 1–8pm; $5), is a part-art, part-natural history collection, funded by the locals in pursuit of some kind of prestige and cultural heritage. Whatever the motives, it's a fine museum, luxuriously housed and with strong collections of Native American and Southwestern art – so large, that despite the enormous exhibition space, only a small part can be shown at any given time. The only permanent display is the late actor William Holden's collection of Asian and African art. The natural science exhibits are surprisingly interesting and focus on the variety of animal and plant life in the desert, proving that it's not all sandstorms and rattlesnakes. Also inside the museum, the *Annenberg Theater* has a daily programme of shows, films and classical concerts (10am–4pm; ☎325-4490).

Rich people love to buy art, and the concentration of wealth in Palm Springs has fostered a disproportionate number of **art galleries**, not all of them good, along and around Palm Canyon Drive. The *B Lewin Galleries*, 210 S Palm Canyon Drive, is most impressive, with the world's largest collection of Mexican paintings, including works by Diego Rivera, Gustavo Montoya, Rufino Tamayo and Carlos Merida. The *Gallery at the Courtyard*, 777 E Tahquitz Way (☎320-9554), has an equally highbrow collection, and by appointment you can rub shoulders with connoisseurs looking for premium investments.

Downtown's most anarchic piece of landscape gardening can be seen at **Moorten's Botanical Gardens**, 1701 S Palm Canyon Drive (Mon–Sat 9am–4.30pm, Sun 10am–4pm; $2), a bizarre cornucopia of every desert plant and cactus, lumped together in no particular order but interesting for those who won't be venturing beyond town to see them in their natural habitat.

Knowing that they're in the thick of a megastar refugee camp, few can resist the opportunity to see the homes and country clubs of the international elite on a **celebrity tour**. As tacky as they are, these tours have some voyeuristic appeal, allowing you to spy on places like Bob Hope's enormous home, and the star-studded area known as **Little Tuscany** – Palm Spring's prettiest quarter, where the famous keep their weekend homes. The best part of the tour is not the houses, but the fascinating trivia about the lives of those who live in them. The much-married Zsa Zsa Gabor comes in for a lot of stick, particularly over her history of stripping ex-husbands of their assets (one of the oldest jokes in town says she's launching a new perfume – it's called *Citation*, just slap it on). Several companies offer tours, the best of them being *Palm Springs Celebrity Tours*, 4751 E Palm Canyon Drive (☎770-2700), which conducts one-hour jaunts for $11 and longer excursions around the country clubs and the Sinatra estate (where Frank used to bring Ava Gardner) for $16. Of course if you've got a car, you can do it yourself with a $5 map of the stars' homes from the visitor center (see p.210), but you'll miss the sharp anecdotal commentary that makes it such fun.

One reason people come here is to enjoy the Californian obsession with all things physical and get fit. The **mineral spring** that the Cahuilla discovered on the desert floor over a century ago has grown into the elaborate *Spa Hotel and Mineral Springs*

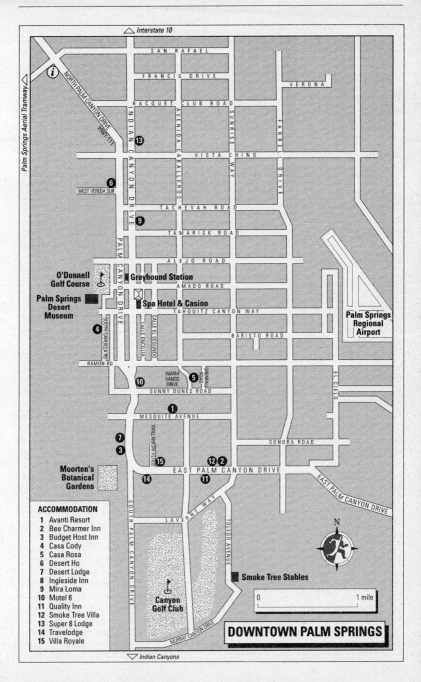

**DOWNTOWN PALM SPRINGS**

Interstate 10

Palm Springs Aerial Tramway

NORTH PALM CANYON DRIVE

HWY 111

SAN RAFAEL

FRANCIS DRIVE

VERONA

RACQUET CLUB ROAD

INDIAN CANYON DRIVE

AVENIDA CABALLEROS

SUNRISE WAY

FARRELL DRIVE

13

VISTA CHINO

6

WEST VEREDA SUR

TACHEVAH ROAD

9

TAMARISK ROAD

ALEJO ROAD

O'Donnell Golf Course

PALM CANYON DRIVE

Greyhound Station

AMADO ROAD

Palm Springs Desert Museum

Spa Hotel & Casino

TAHQUITZ CANYON WAY

Palm Springs Regional Airport

CALLE EL SEGUNDO

BARISTO ROAD

4

SOUTH CAHUILLA RD

RAMON RD

CALLE ENCILIA

10

WARM SANDS DRIVE

5

GRANVIA VALMONTE

EL CIELO

SUNNY DUNES ROAD

1

MESQUITE AVENUE

7

SOUTH PALM CANYON DRIVE

3

SONORA ROAD

15

12  2

EAST PALM CANYON DRIVE

Moorten's Botanical Gardens

14

11

EAST PALM CANYON DRIVE

LA VERNE WAY

TOLEDO AVENUE

N

**ACCOMMODATION**

1  Avanti Resort
2  Bee Charmer Inn
3  Budget Host Inn
4  Casa Cody
5  Casa Rosa
6  Desert Ho
7  Desert Lodge
8  Ingleside Inn
9  Mira Loma
10  Motel 6
11  Quality Inn
12  Smoke Tree Villa
13  Super 8 Lodge
14  Travelodge
15  Villa Royale

Smoke Tree Stables

Canyon Golf Club

MURRAY CANYON DRIVE

0          1 mile

Indian Canyons

complex, 100 N Indian Ave (daily 8am–7pm; ☎325-1461 or 1-800/854-1279). The "basic spa experience" is $15, although you're encouraged to spend a lot more at the on-site casino (where instead of the enervating clatter of coins winners receive a printout to cash later). Just as therapeutic is a swim in the **Olympic-sized pool** in the *Palm Springs Leisure Center*, Sunrise Way at Ramon Road (daily 11am–5pm; $3; ☎323-8278), a good alternative to the often crowded, and invariably small, hotel pools. Best of all is the 22-acre playground **Palm Springs Oasis Waterpark**, at 1500 Gene Autry Trail between Ramon Road and E Palm Canyon Drive (☎325-7873), where, for $17, you can surf on its one-acre pool and mess around on its seven waterslides. Heaps of fun.

# Around Palm Springs

Most visitors to Palm Springs never leave the poolside, but those who venture further afield will find that there is enough to keep them entertained for a day or two. The **Indian Canyons** are the most accessible piece of the outdoors, explorable on foot or horseback. Further afield, a couple of attractions in the surrounding **Coachella Valley** cities offer a glimpse of desert life before the Palm Springs boom, while one resort, **Cathedral City**, boasts some of the region's raunchiest nightlife. Seek refuge from the heat of the day by driving to the cool alpine town of **Idyllwild**, or take the **Aerial Tramway** and walk there, though you'll need a full day for the round trip.

### The Indian Canyons

A hardcore of desert enthusiasts visit Palm Springs for the **hiking** and **riding** opportunities in the **Indian Canyons**, on part of the **Agua Caliente Reservation** that lies to the east of downtown. Centuries ago, ancestors of the Cahuilla tribe settled in the canyons and developed extensive communities, made possible by the good water supply and animal stock. Crops of melons, squash, beans and corn were grown, animals hunted and plants and seeds gathered for food and medicines. Evidence of this remains, and despite the near extinction of some breeds, mountain sheep and wild ponies still roam the remoter areas. To reach the best of them, follow S Palm Canyon Drive about three miles southeast to the clearly signposted entrance. Of the three canyons here, **Palm Canyon** and **Andreas Canyon** (fall & winter daily 8am–5pm; spring & summer daily 8am–6pm; $5) are very beautiful and have the easiest hiking trails. About fifteen miles long, they're surprisingly lush oases of waterfalls, rocky gorges and palm trees, easily toured by car, although to appreciate them at their best, you should get out and walk for at least a few miles. A tiny trading post sells hiking maps, refreshments, and even raccoon hats, though to indulge in real Wild West fantasy you should see things on **horseback**. The *Smoke Tree Stables*, 2500 Toledo Ave (☎327-1372), offer one-, two- and four-hour riding tours of the Canyons, from $25 per hour – well worth it, especially if you go early morning (tours start from 7am) to escape the truly uncomfortable midday heat.

Sections of the canyons and surrounding land are set aside for the specific lunacy of **trailblazing** in jeeps and four-wheel drives. If you're a good, experienced driver with nerves of steel (or know one), you should rent your own from *Dune Off-Road Rentals*, 59755 Hwy-111 (Sept–May only; ☎325-0376), about four miles north of town, for around $50 for half a day. If, on the other hand, you're inexperienced but want a go, the same company offers one hour's instruction for $30, then an additonal hour for $30. For those who can't face the driving and want to learn something about the area while zooming through it, the **guided jeep adventure** is probably nearer the mark: *Desert Adventures* (☎324-3378), based at the entrance to Indian Canyons, offer excellent half-day tours of the Santa Rosa mountains for around $25 per hour, or $70 for half a day. One of its most popular tours takes you across the desert floor and two thousand feet up through Big Horn Sheep preserves, spectacular cliffs and steep-walled canyons. It's a bit expensive, but brilliant fun for the fearless.

## The Coachella Valley cities

The most visited of the resorts surrounding Palm Springs is **CATHEDRAL CITY** ("Cat City"), about five miles east along Hwy-111. Just another sprawling Coachella Valley community by day, by night it's a party town. Plenty of restaurants and some great, raucous **bars**, most part of a thriving **gay scene**, make for the best laugh you'll have in the desert, whether you're gay or not (see "Eating, drinking and nightlife"). Cathedral City is ten minutes by car or twenty on the #111 bus (until 11pm) from Palm Springs.

About eight miles north of Palm Springs, the now condo-crowded city of **DESERT HOT SPRINGS** was the site chosen for its isolation by Cabot Yerxa, the drop-out son of a high-tone East Coast family, who preferred a life of hardship in the desert to his Ivy-League life back home. **Cabot's Old Indian Pueblo**, 67-616 E Desert View Ave (daily except Tues 10am–4pm; $2.50) was his life's labour: a four-storey house made from bits and pieces he found in the desert and which took over twenty years to complete.

Finally **PALM DESERT**, a resort twelve miles southwest of Palm Springs along Hwy-111, is the safest place to witness the animal life that flourishes despite the inhospitable climate. Here, the **Living Desert**, 47-900 Portola Ave (Sept to mid-June daily 9am–5pm; $7), is home to coyotes, foxes, Big Horn sheep, snakes, gazelles and eagles, on view around a series of trails that cover the 1200-acre park. There's also a **botanical garden**, but this is only worth a look in spring when the desert is in bloom; at other times it's just a load of indistinguishable cacti.

## Idyllwild

Fifty miles from Palm Springs and five thousand feet up the opposite side of Mount San Jacinto, **IDYLLWILD** is the perfect antidote to in-your-face success. Fresh, cool and snow-covered in winter, this small alpine town of about two thousand inhabitants has only a few chalet-style restaurants and hotels, but it's a great place to slow up the cash drain that inevitably occurs on a visit to Palm Springs. It is accessible by heading twenty miles west along I-10 to Banning, then taking the exit for Hwy-243 which sweeps you up the mountain on a sharply curved road.

Idyllwild attracts visitors who want to walk on magnificent trails away from the searing heat of the desert basin below. **Mount San Jacinto State Park** surrounds the town and has numerous trails, ranging from a gentle meander along beautiful **Strawberry Creek** to a more strenuous trek along **Deer Springs Trail** to the stunning Suicide Rock and San Jacinto Peak, and the moderately difficult **Devil's Slide** to the Aerial Tramway (see below).

The **Forest Service Ranger Station**, 54270 Pine Crest Ave (daily 8am–4.30pm; ☎909/659-2117), has stacks of information about hiking and camping in the area and

### THE AERIAL TRAMWAY

When the desert heat becomes simply too much to bear, you can travel through five climatic zones from the arid desert floor to snow-covered alpine hiking trails on top of Mount San Jacinto on the **Palm Springs Aerial Tramway** on Tramway Drive, just off Hwy-111 north of Palm Springs (Mon–Fri 10am–9pm, Sat & Sun 8am–9pm; closed first two weeks in Aug; $17; ☎325-1391). Every thirty minutes large cable cars grind and sway over eight thousand feet to the Mountain Station near the 10,815ft summit. Literally breathtaking, it's well worth the nerve-wracking ascent for both the view, some 75 miles all the way to the Salton Sea, and the welcome change from the blistering heat to temperatures that drop by as much as 50°F. Cinder trails stretch for a couple of miles around, leading into a wilderness area through which, in a few hours, you can reach Idyllwild (on the Devil's Slide, see below). There's a **bar** and **restaurant** at the Mountain Station where, for a $4 voucher, you can eat as much as you want.

hands out the free **permits** required for all wilderness sites. You can set up **camp** anywhere over two hundred feet away from trails and streams, or in designated *Yellow Post Sites* (free) with fire rings but no water. There are also drive-in campsites run by the Forest Service ($7–9; ☎1-800/280-CAMP), the state park ($9–14; ☎*MISTIX*) and the county park ($12–14; ☎1-800/234-PARK).

Otherwise, you can **stay** in chalets and log cabins, most of which cost from $60–90 and usually sleep four or more people. The cheapest rooms are the little red-and-white chalets of *Singing Wood Motel* (☎909/659-2201; ②), 25525 Hwy-243, half a mile north of the ranger station; while *The Fireside Inn* (☎909/659-2966; ④) at 54540 North Circle Drive, about half a mile east is considerably more appealing with cosy wood-panelled rooms; and *The Strawberry Creek Inn*, 26370 Hwy-243 (☎909/659-3202 or 1-800/262-8969; ⑤), a few hundred yards south, is a B&B-style place for those craving real luxury.

# Eating, drinking and nightlife

Palm Springs has a pretty disappointing selection of reasonable **restaurants**, and it doesn't have the **nightlife** you'd imagine either. It's not unknown for people to choose to get drunk in their hotel room – or to go into LA for the night. Much closer at hand, however, is **Cathedral City**, ten miles down the road (see p.213), which offers a good range of bars and restaurants. The visitor center (see p.208) has details of **what's on** around town, and stocks the seasonal *Palm Springs Visitors Guide* and the gay bi-monthly *The Bottom Line*.

## Restaurants

The desert heat is stifling enough to suppress the healthiest of appetites, and most people go all day on nothing and suddenly find themselves ravenous at dusk. Sadly, few of the **restaurants** in Palm Springs merit their high prices, and supermarket shopping is a better bet for the budget-conscious: *Von's*, in the Palm Springs shopping mall, is open from early morning until around 11pm for basics.

**Eveleene's**, 664 N Palm Canyon Drive (☎325-4766). The affordable version of *Le Vallauris* (see below). Good French food for around $30 per head, but not a celebrity in sight.

**El Gallito**, 68820 Grove St, Cathedral City (☎328-7794). A busy Mexican cantina that has the best food for miles and lines to prove it – get there around 6pm to avoid the crowds.

**John Henry's Café**, 1785 Tahquitz Canyon Way at Sunrise Way (☎327-7667). Large portions of eclectic American fare, from rack of lamb to imaginative fish, perfectly served and at half the price you'd expect. Dinner is around $15; reserve after 2pm. Closed June–Sept.

**Louise's Pantry**, 124 S Palm Canyon Drive (☎325-5124). Original 1950s diner with low(ish) prices and huge servings. Especially good for breakfast. Closes 2.30pm.

**Nates**, 100 S Indian Canyon Drive. Good, large portions of fair-priced deli food right in the centre of town. An enormous variety of burgers and sandwiches through the day and full meals in the evening.

**Peabody's Coffee Bar & Jazz Studio**, 134 S Palm Canyon Drive (☎322-1877). The best place in town to sip an espresso, snack on sandwiches and salads, and settle down with a slightly off-beat publication. Poetry readings on Tues and jazz on Fri.

**Red Pepper**, 36-650 Sun Air Plaza, Cathedral City (☎770-7007). Moderately priced Mexican with excellent lamb specialities and a few Balkan and Albanian dishes for good measure. Relaxed atmosphere and good margaritas.

**Shame on the Moon**, 69-950 Frank Sinatra Drive at Hwy-111, Cathedral City (☎324-5515). Long-standing bistro with California cuisine and an intimate bar, attracting a loyal gay crowd.

**Thai Smile**, 653 N Palm Canyon Drive (☎320-5503). Few points for decor or ambience but great, authentic Thai green curries and the odd Szechuan dish for around $10.

**Le Vallauris**, 385 Tahquitz Canyon Way (☎325-5059 – reservations only). Palm Springs' best restaurant does not exactly hide its light under a bushel, describing itself as "*the* restaurant where the Stars entertain their friends"; and you are indeed likely to run into one or two once-renowned artistes. Even if star-gazing is not your style, the Californian/French/Italian cuisine is excellent, and the service impeccable. The price, however, is around $80 per head.

**Wheel-Inn Eat**, 16 miles west on I-10 at the Cabazon exit (marked by two fifty-foot concrete dinosaurs). Humble, 24-hour desert truck stop with a burly clientele and enormous portions – so unpretentious you'd think they'd never heard of Palm Springs. One of the dinosaurs houses a wonderfully kitsch gift shop

**The Wild Goose**, 67-938 Hwy-111, Cathedral City (☎328-5775). An antique-crammed award-winning restaurant serving great food for around $40 per head.

## Bars and clubs

If you're determined to spend your evening in Palm Springs, and you're not a member of one of the exclusive country clubs, you'd better be disco-crazy or you'll have to content yourself with dinner and an early night. On Thursdays (Sept–May 7–10pm) a tame **street carnival** takes place along N Palm Canyon Drive, downtown, with a few venues laying on live music.

**C C Construction Co**, 68–449 Perez Rd, Cathedral City (☎324-4241). The desert's largest gay club with "jig with a pig" evenings: shimmy with a gay cop and mix with a good-natured drag-queen crowd. Mostly disco and retro with country-and-western at weekends.

**Cecil's**, 1775 E Palm Canyon Drive (☎320-4202). Disco that's slightly more bearable than *Zelda's*, its music and customers rather easier to cope with.

**Chillers**, 262 S Palm Canyon Drive (☎325-3215). Live music for a rich, preppy crowd.

**Harley's Café**, 168 N Palm Canyon Drive (☎325-5350). Café and smart-beer-bar populated by twenty-somethings here for the occasional live jazz and blues. Decent meals by day.

**Zelda's**, 169 N Indian Canyon Drive (☎325-2375). Pick-up joint for a crowd that should really be in bed; Sun–Thurs only.

## Listings

**Bookstore** *Crown Books*, 332 S Palm Canyon Drive (☎325-1265). Travel guides, paperback fiction, maps etc.

**Cinema** *Courtyard 10*, 777 Taquitz Canyon Way (☎322-3456).

**Dry Cleaning** *American Cleaners and Laundry*, 364 S Indian Ave (☎320-8414).

**Hospital** *Desert Hospital*, 1150 N Indian Canyon Drive (☎323-6511).

**Left Luggage** at *Greyhound* station.

**Pharmacy** *Thrifty Drug and Discount Store*, 366 S Palm Canyon Drive.

**Police** ☎323-8116 in Palm Springs, ☎321-0111 in Cathedral City.

**Post Office** 333 E Amado Rd (Mon–Fri 8.30am–5pm; ☎325-9631).

**Travel Agency** *Las Palmas Travel*, 403 N Palm Canyon Drive (☎325-6311).

# Joshua Tree National Park

In a unique transitional area where the high Mojave meets the lower Colorado desert, 850 square miles of freaky trees, their branches ragged and gnarled, flourish in an otherwise sparsely vegetated landscape, making **JOSHUA TREE NATIONAL PARK** the most unusual, and fascinating, of California's national parks. With neither the sweeping sand dunes of Death Valley nor the ubiquitous wealth of Palm Springs, it conforms to no other image of the California desert. In recognition of its uniqueness, and the need for its preservation, the national park system took the area under its jurisdiction as a national monument in 1936 and has vigilantly maintained its beauty ever since. It lost some of the original area to mining interests in the 1950s, but that was more than compensated for in 1994 when it was promoted to a national park, with the addition of 234,000 acres. If you're staying in Palm Springs, there's no excuse not to visit; if you've further to come, make the effort anyway.

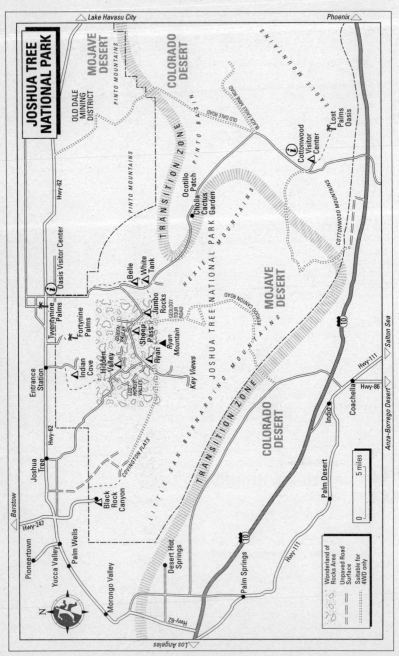

The grotesque trees, which can reach up to forty feet in height, have to contend with extreme aridity and rocky soil, and with the exception of springtime, when creamy white blossom clusters on the tips of the branches, the strain of their struggle to survive is evident. Complementary to the trees are great rockpiles, heaps of boulders pushed up from the earth by the movements of the Pinto Mountain fault, which runs directly below. Often as high as a hundred feet, their edges are rounded and smooth from thousands of years of flash floods and winds.

In all it's a mystical, even unearthly, landscape, best appreciated at sunrise or sunset when the whole desert floor is bathed in red light; at noon it can feel like an alien and threatening furnace, with temperatures often reaching 125°F in summer, though dropping to a more bearable 70°F in winter. If you're visiting between May and October you must stick to the higher elevations to enjoy Joshua Tree with any semblance of comfort. In the low desert part of the park, the Joshua trees thin out and the temperature rises as you descend below three thousand feet. Over eighty percent of the park is designated wilderness – get out of the car at least once or twice and note the silence.

## Some history

"Joshua Tree" may be a familiar name nowadays, thanks to U2, but previously it was almost unknown. Unlike the vast bulk of the state, no man, save a few Native Americans, prospectors and cowboys, has had the chance to spoil it. Despite receiving less than four inches of annual rainfall, the area is surprisingly lush, and although craggy trees and rockpiles are what define Joshua Tree today, it was grass that attracted the first significant pioneers. Early cattlemen heard rumours of good pastures from the forty-niners who hurried through on their way to the Sierra Nevada gold fields. The natural corrals made perfect sites for cattle rustlers to brand their illegitimate herds before moving them out to the coast for sale. Ambushes and gunfights were common. Seeking refuge in the mountains, rustlers, by chance, discovered small traces of gold and sparked vigorous mining operations that continued until the 1940s. To the Mormons who travelled through here in the 1850s, the area signified something entirely different; they saw the craggy branches of the trees as the arms of Joshua leading them to the promised land – hence the name.

# Practicalities

About an hour's drive northeast from Palm Springs, Joshua Tree National Park (always open; $5 per vehicle for 7 days, $3 per cyclist or hiker) is best approached from Hwy-62, which branches off I-10. You can enter the park via the west entrance at the town of **Joshua Tree**, or the northern entrance at **Twentynine Palms**, where you'll also find the **Oasis Visitor Center** (Feb–Sept daily 8am-5pm; Oct–Jan daily 8am–4.30pm; ☎367-7511) and several good **motels**. Alternatively, if you're coming from the south, there is an entrance and the **Cottonwood Visitor Center** (Mon–Thurs & Sun 8am–4pm, Fri–Sat 9am–5pm) seven miles north of I-10 on the Cottonwood Spring Road exit. It's worth stopping at one of the visitor centers to collect **maps** and the free *Joshua Tree Journal*.

Visiting the park using **public transport** is not really an option. *Morongo Basin Transit Authority* (☎367-7433 or 1-800/794-6282) and *Desert Stage Lines* (☎1-800/227-7758) each run a weekday service (1 daily; $9 one-way) from Palm Springs to the towns of Joshua Tree and Twentynine Palms, but not into the park itself. At best, you're looking at a ten-mile desert walk to get to anything very interesting. **Cyclists** are restricted to roads open to motor vehicles, so don't expect any off-road action: the nearest you'll get are the dirt surfaces of Geology Tour Road and the Covington Flats road. There is no bike rental anywhere near the park.

## Twentynine Palms and Joshua Tree

The appealing desert settlement of **TWENTYNINE PALMS** is neither a gloating leisure spot nor a totally useless hellhole, but a small, serviceable place that enjoys good weather and low-key living. It is also home to the world's largest marine base and 20,000 marines, whose numbers may swell with budget defence cuts and the closure of other, smaller bases. It is also a town of abandoned wives, who move here when their husbands' military postings come up and get left behind when they move on. Apart from that sad fact and the boom of gunfire that can be heard for miles around, Twentynine Palms is a wonderful place to visit. Just two minutes' drive from the park, and an all-important water source for local people, it's a fairly busy town by desert standards, stretching for about a mile along Hwy-62 with a fair selection of places to eat, drink and bed down. The climate has been considered perfect for convalescents ever since physicians sent World War I poison gas victims here for treatment of their respiratory illnesses, and development of health spas and real estate offices has been considerable.

Unquestionably, the best place in town to **stay** is the *Twentynine Palms Inn*, 73950 Inn Ave off National Monument Drive (☎367-3505; ③), where twelve adobe cabins are set around attractively arid grounds and gardens, and a central pool area contains a restaurant and bar. Owned by the same large family since 1928, this is not your average American accommodation. Built on the Oasis of Mara, the only privately owned oasis in the High Desert, the inn has several fault lines – including the Pinto Mountain fault – running beneath it. As the owner puts it, "We don't get the safe travellers". Healers and psychics gather around an energy spot in the grounds to get centred, cleanse their chakras and generally do the business. Physical cleansing (there's a spa) and massage are also available.

Among the cheaper options nearby are the *29 Palms Motel*, 71487 Twentynine Palms Hwy (☎367-2833; ②), and the *El Rancho Dolores Motel*, along the road at no. 73352 (☎367-3528; ①). Both have perfectly acceptable pools and good rooms, but are nowhere near as much fun as the *Inn*, which is also the best place to **eat**, with excellent $10–13 meals with soup and salad. Otherwise there's a serviceable selection of Mexican, Chinese and Italian places in town. Alternatively, head fifteen miles west to

---

### CAMPING IN JOSHUA TREE

Joshua Tree National Park has nine **campgrounds**, all concentrated in the northwest except for one at Cottonwood by the southern entrance. All have wooden tables, places for fires (bring your own wood) and pit toilets, but only two (*Black Rock Canyon* and *Cottonwood*) have water supplies and flush toilets. These cost $10 and $8 respectively, while all the rest are free, on a first-come-first-served basis with no facility for reservations, unless you are travelling as part of an educational or study group, in which case you should call ☎*MISTIX*, and pay a small fee ($10–30).

Each campground has its merits, but for relative solitude and a great, central location, the *Belle* (often closed in summer) and *White Tank* sites are perfect. The much larger *Jumbo Rocks* site is one of the highest, at 4400ft, and therefore a little cooler, while for the winter months you may prefer the lower altitude of *Cottonwood* in the south. *Black Rock Canyon* and *Indian Cove* can only be reached from within the park if you have a four-wheel-drive vehicle; otherwise you have to retrace your steps to the entrances on Hwy-62. The lack of showers, electrical and sewage hook-ups at any of the sites keeps the majority of RVers at bay, but in the popular winter months the place fills up quickly, especially at weekends. Each campsite is good for up to six people and two vehicles.

**Backcountry camping** is permitted provided you register before you head out. Twelve backcountry boards are dotted through the park at the start of most trails. Here you can self-register, leave your vehicle and gen up on the regulations which include prohibition of camping within a mile of a road, five hundred feet of a trail and 440 yards of a water source.

**JOSHUA TREE** town, and sink into a worn-out sofa at *Jeremy's Cappuccino Bar and Beer Haus*, 61597 Twentynine Palms Hwy (☎336-9799), enjoying great coffee, snacks, beer and breakfast, and occasional live music at weekends.

## Exploring the park

The best way to enjoy the park is to be selective. As with any desert area, you'll find the heat punishing and an ambitious schedule impossible. Casual observers will find a day trip plenty, though it's a nice idea to camp out for a couple of nights, and serious rock-climbers and experienced hikers may want to take advantage of the park's excellent if strenuous trails. The rangers and staff at the visitor centers will be able to recommend the most enjoyable itineraries, tailored to your requirements and abilities.

Never venture anywhere without a **map**: either the *Topographic Trail Map* ($8) or the *Recreation Map* ($7), both available at the visitor centers. Many of the roads are unmarked, hard to negotiate and restricted to four-wheel-drive use. If a road is marked as such, don't think about taking a normal car – you'll soon come to a grinding halt, and it could be quite a few panic-stricken hours before anybody finds you. Of course, maps are even more essential if you are planning to explore the park's **hiking trails** (see box on p.220).

Starting in the north of the park, quartz boulders tower around the *Indian Cove* camping area, and a trail from the eastern branch of the campground road leads to **Rattlesnake Canyon** – its streams and waterfalls (depending on rainfall) breaking an otherwise eerie silence among the monoliths. The **Fortynine Palms Oasis** to the east can only be visited on foot.

Moving south into the main section of the park, you drive through the **Wonderland of Rocks** area comprising giant, rounded granite boulders that draw **rock-climbers** from all over the world. The various clusters flank the road for about ten miles giving plenty of opportunity to stop for a little "bouldering" or, for those suitably equipped and skilled, to try more adventurous routes. Pick up a *Climber Ethics* leaflet from the visitor centers. Well signposted nature trails lead to **Hidden Valley** (1 mile), where cattle rustlers used to hide out, and to the rain-fed **Barker Dam** (1 mile) to the east: this is Joshua Tree's crucial water supply, built around the turn of the century by cattlemen (and rustlers) to prevent the poor beasts expiring halfway across the park. The route back passes a number of petroglyphs.

If you're **driving**, you can reach **Key's View** from here. This 5185-foot-high spot was named after Bill Keys, an eccentric trigger-happy miner who raised his family in this inhospitable landscape until he was locked away in the 1920s for shooting one of his neighbours over a right-of-way argument. He was revered for being a tough desert rat and indefatigable miner, who dug on long after less hardy men had abandoned the arid wasteland. The best views in the whole park can be had from up here, on a good day as far as the Salton Sea and beyond to Mexico – a brilliant desert panorama of badlands and mountains.

The road then passes the start of the Ryan Mountain hike and the turn-off for Geology Tour Road, which leads down through the best of Joshua Tree's **rock formations**. A little further on, the Jumbo Rocks campground is the start of a loop (1.7 miles) through boulders and desert washes to **Skull Rock**.

Almost at the transition zone between the Colorado and Mojave deserts and on the fringes of the Pinto Basin, the **Cholla Cactus Garden** is a quarter-mile loop through creosote bushes, jojoba and several cactus species, not least of them the "jumping" cholla (see box on p.205). Come at dusk or dawn for the best chance of seeing the mainly nocturnal desert wood rat.

## Around Joshua Tree

Directly **north** of the Joshua Tree National Park, the only real settlement is the huge *Marine Corps Air Ground Combat Center,* home to war games and other nefarious mili-

## HIKING IN THE JOSHUA TREE NATIONAL PARK

To get a real feel for the majesty of the desert you'll need to leave the main roads behind and hike. But **stick to the trails**: Joshua Tree is full of abandoned gold mines and although the rangers are fencing them as quickly as possible, there are hundreds they don't even know about. Watch for loose gravel around openings, undercut edges, never trust ladders or timber, and bear in mind that the rangers rarely check mines for casualties. Some of the shafts contain water and poisonous fumes, and even if you survive a fall, you'll still have to contend with snakes, scorpions and spiders.

Most of the trails listed below are all in the slightly cooler and higher Mojave Desert. There's tougher stuff on the eastern side of the park around **Pinto Basin**, a notorious danger zone when the flash floods strike. To cover it on foot, it's essential that you **register** at one of the visitor centers first and check the trail conditions with the rangers. You'll need to be well armed with maps and water supplies, and on the whole it's unwise even to attempt it unless you're a very experienced hiker or are travelling as part of a group. If you do reach here, you'll find no Joshua trees and few other signs of life. Even on the easier trails allow around an hour per mile: there's very little shade and you'll tire quickly.

**HIKES** – *listed northwest to southeast through the park.*

**Fortynine Palms Oasis** (3 miles; 2hr). One of the easiest trails, though still moderately strenuous. It leaves the badly signposted Canyon Road six miles west of the visitor center at Twentynine Palms. A barren rocky trail leads to this densely clustered and partly fire-blackened oasis which, since it was named, seems to have flourished on the seepage down the canyon. There's not enough water to swim in, nor are you allowed to camp (the oasis is officially closed 8pm–7am), but a late afternoon or evening visit presents the best wildlife rewards.

**Lost Horse Mine** (4 miles; 3hr). Another moderately strenuous trail climbs 450ft to the mine which in the 1890s made an average of $20,000 a week. The hike takes you through abandoned mining sites, with building foundations and equipment still intact, to the top of Lost Horse Mountain. The trail starts a mile east of Keys View Road.

**Ryan Mountain** (3 miles; 2hr). Some of the best views in the park are from the top of Ryan Mountain (5461ft), seven hundred strenuous feet above the desert floor. Start at the parking area near the *Sheep Pass* campground and follow the trail past the Indian Cave, which contains bedrock mortars once used by the Cahuilla and Serrano.

**Mastodon Peak** (3 miles; 2hr). Another peak climb, less strenuous but with great views, especially south to the Salton Sea. Start from the *Cottonwood* campground.

**Lost Palms Oasis** (7.5 miles; 5hr). This moderate trail leads across desert washes, past palo verde, cottonwood and ironwood trees to the largest stand of palms in the park, and presents possible scrambling side trips to Victory Palms and Munsen Canyon. There's little surface water, but often enough to lure Bighorn sheep. Start from the *Cottonwood* campground.

tary activities. More comfortingly, there are several sights northwest in **YUCCA VALLEY**. The **Hi-Desert Nature Museum**, 57117 Twentynine Palms Hwy (Tues–Sun 1–5pm; free), holds a largely poor collection of paintings and tacky souvenirs, but some commendable catches of snakes and scorpions; the **Desert Christ Park**, at no. 57090 (dawn–dusk; free), has 37 of local sculptor Antone Martin's massive fifteen-foot concrete figures depicting tales from the Bible – a fittingly bizarre addition to the region. Finally, **Pioneertown** is an old West town built in the 1940s by Gene Autry and Roy Rogers for the filming of movies and TV serials; it has full eating amenities and is a nice bit of synthetic cowboy country when the real thing gets too much.

If you've got a good car that can handle bad roads and mountain passes, then **back road driving** on the road between Palm Springs and LA is a fun way to get a sense of the Wild West. Arm yourself with a San Bernardino County map and explore the Lucerne Valley and the small towns of **Big Bear City** or **Fawnskin**.

# The Imperial Valley and Salton Sea

The patch of the Colorado desert **south** of Joshua Tree and Palm Springs is the least friendly of all the Californian desert regions and has little to encourage exploration. In any case, intense heat makes journeys in the winter uncomfortable and in the summer near impossible.

Sandwiched between Hwy-111 and Hwy-86, which branch off I-10 soon after Palm Springs and the Coachella Valley, the area from the **Salton Sea** down to the furnace-like migrant-worker towns of the agricultural **Imperial Valley** lies in the two-thousand-square-mile Salton Basin: aside from a small spot in Death Valley (see p.253), the largest area of dry land below sea level in the western hemisphere – and probably one of its least appealing. Hwy-86, for what it's worth, is California's most notorious two-lane highway, with a staggering record of deaths and accidents. There's not a lot to come here for unless you're heading for the Anza-Borrego desert or the Mexican border, and even then there are better routes you could take.

In the 1960s, there was a (failed) attempt to make the Salton Sea into a resort, and the RV parks and retirement homes around its rim remain, though they're sadly shorn of very much life. Some resorts were swamped by unusually high water levels, but blame for the failure of these ventures lies partially with the Salton Sea itself which, without a natural outlet (it is two hundred feet below sea level) is rapidly becoming grossly polluted – plagued by agricultural runoff and toxic wastes carried in by the New River from Mexico – and excessively saline. Fish carry a consumption warning, but people still swim and waterski on the sea.

The Salton Sea remains an important wintering area for shore birds and waterfowl. Brown pelicans come by in summer and terns and cormorants nest here. The best place to see them is the **National Wildlife Refuge** (daily dawn–dusk; free) at the sea's southern tip. By the informative **visitor center** (April–Sept Mon–Fri 7am–3.30pm; Oct–Mar daily 7am–3.30pm) there's a viewing platform, or you can take the twenty-minute Rock Hill Trail to the water's edge for a closer look. To get to the Refuge, take the poorly signposted backroads off Hwy-111 south of **Niland** or off Hwy-86 at **Westmorland**; both run past fields of alfalfa, cantaloupe, tomatoes and other crops – proof that just about anything will grow in this fertile land provided it is suitably irrigated.

The only other reasons you might stop are to **camp** at one of several lakeside sites on the eastern side of the Salton Sea ($7–8) or to eat some authentic **Mexican food**. Agricultural work brings thousands of Mexicans north of the border, and the restaurants generally cater to them: practise your Spanish.

# The Anza-Borrego desert

Southwest of the Salton Sea, though usually approached from San Diego (see Chapter Two), the **ANZA-BORREGO DESERT** is the largest state park in the country, covering 600,000 acres and, in contrast to the Imperial Valley, offering a diverse variety of plant and animal life as well as a legend-strewn history spanning Native American tribes, the first white trailfinders and Gold Rush times. It takes its double-barrelled name from Juan Baptista de Anza, a Spanish explorer who crossed the region in 1774, and the Spanish for the native bighorn sheep, *borrego cimarron*, which eats the brittle-brush and agave found here. Some of Anza-Borrego can be covered by car (confidence on gravel roads is handy), although you'll need four-wheel drive for the more obscure –

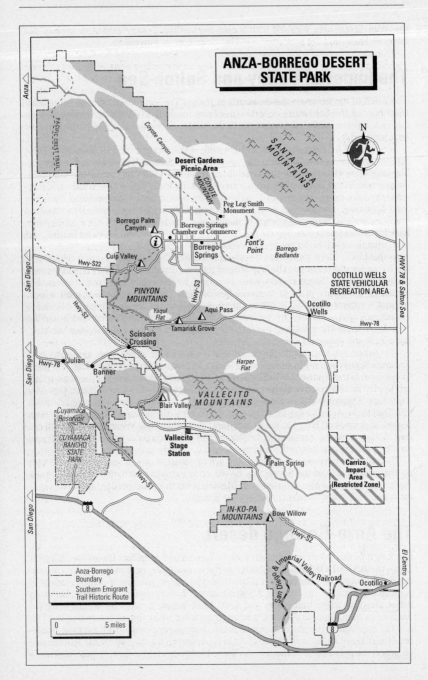

**ANZA-BORREGO DESERT STATE PARK**

N

Anza

PACIFIC CREST TRAIL

Coyote Canyon

SANTA ROSA MOUNTAINS

Desert Gardens Picnic Area

COYOTE MOUNTAIN

Peg Leg Smith Monument

Borrego Palm Canyon

Borrego Springs Chamber of Commerce

Font's Point

Borrego Springs

Borrego Badlands

Culp Valley

Hwy-S22

San Diego

PINYON MOUNTAINS

Hwy-S3

OCOTILLO WELLS STATE VEHICULAR RECREATION AREA

HWY 78 & Salton Sea

Hwy-S2

Yaqui Flat

Aqui Pass

Ocotillo Wells

Tamarisk Grove

Hwy-78

Scissors Crossing

San Diego

Hwy-78   Julian

Banner

Harper Flat

VALLECITO MOUNTAINS

Blair Valley

Cuyamaca Reservoir

CUYAMACA RANCHO STATE PARK

Vallecito Stage Station

Palm Spring

Carrizo Impact Area (Restricted Zone)

Hwy-S1

IN-KO-PA MOUNTAINS

Bow Willow

Hwy-S2

8

San Diego

San Diego & Imperial Valley Railroad

Ocotillo

8

El Centro

Anza-Borrego Boundary

Southern Emigrant Trail Historic Route

0        5 miles

and most interesting – routes, and there are over five hundred miles of hiking trails where vehicles are not permitted at all.

During the fiercely hot summer months the place is best left to the lizards, although most campgrounds stay open all year. The desert **blooming season**, between March and May, is popular, when scarlet octillo, orange poppies, white lilies and purple verbena, and other peacock-like wildflowers are a memorable – and fragrant – sight.

As well as taking the usual desert precautions (see box on pp.204-205), you should read the comments in *Basics* on p.44 – this is mountain lion territory.

## Practicalities

The Anza-Borrego Desert (always open; $5 per car, $3 per hiker, biker or bus passenger) is served by **public transport**; from San Diego, the *Northeast Rural Bus System* (see p.196) makes four trips a week to **BORREGO SPRINGS**, the park's one sizeable settlement, at the northern end of Hwy-S3. There's no reason to linger in Borrego Springs – it's only a place to gather (expensive) supplies and to use the **Chamber of Commerce**, 622 Palm Canyon Drive (June–Sept daily 10am–2pm; Oct–May daily 10am–4pm; ☎767-5555), for details of motels and restaurants. For information on desert hiking, camping, flora and fauna, you're far better off 3.5 miles west at the excellent **Visitor Information Center**, 200 Palm Canyon Drive (June–Sept Sat, Sun & holidays 9am–5pm; Oct–May daily 9am–5pm; ☎767-5311), where you can also pick up an informative free newspaper and a detailed map of the park. The center is landscaped into the desert floor so you barely notice it as you wander through the short **Desert Plant Trail**. When the center is closed, the administration office (Mon–Fri 9am–5pm) fills in.

If you're not feeling adventurous enough to camp (see below), there are a handful of **motels** in Borrego Springs, though only *Oasis*, at 366 W Palm Drive (☎767-5409; ③), and *Hacienda del Sol* (☎767-5442; ③), near the Chamber of Commerce, are at all afford-able. For plain but decent diner **meals**, make for *Kendall's Café* (☎767-3491), almost opposite the Chamber of Commerce. Just outside the eastern park boundary, **OCOTILLO WELLS** has basic facilities and the attractively located *Desert Ironwoods Motel*, 4875 Hwy-78 (☎767-5670; ③).

Recreational opportunities in the park are strictly controlled to preserve the fragile ecosystem. The main exception to this rule is the **Ocotillo Wells State Vehicular Recreational Area**, to the east of the park, a region mapped out for dune buggies and the like. Owners drive like demons in a maelstrom of tossed sand and engine noise; if you're tempted to join them, call Recreation Headquarters (daily 8am–5pm; ☎767-5391) for information or contact *Desert Rat Tours* (☎767-3755) in Borrego Springs ($40 for an hour-long accompanied spin); otherwise stay well clear. **Mountain biking** is permitted but only on paved and dirt roads; the hiking trails are off limits. Bikes can be rented ($30 a day), or you can negotiate guided tours ($15–20 an hour) from *Dan's Hike and Bike*, 648 Palm Canyon Drive (☎767-3872), behind the Chamber of Commerce.

## The park

Coming from the San Diego area through Julian (see p.197), you'll first hit the western section of the park which contains some of the more interesting historical debris. At Scissors Crossing, Hwy-78 intersects Hwy-S2 which follows the line of the old **Butterfield Stage Route**, the first regular line of communication between the eastern states and the newly settled West, which began service from 1857.

From Scissors Crossing, Hwy-S2 heads towards the park's southeast corner, travers-ing **Blair Valley**, with a primitive campground, and **Box Canyon**, where the Mormon Battalion of 1847 (see p.179), following what is now known as the **Southern Emigrant**

### CAMPING IN ANZA-BORREGO

Two developed and nine primitive campsites exist within the Anza-Borrego State Park, but this is one of the few parks which allows **open camping**, giving you the freedom to pitch a tent pretty much anywhere without a permit, although it's advisable to let a park ranger know your plans. The few provisos are that you don't drive off-road; don't camp near water holes; camp away from developed campsites; light fires only in fire rings or metal containers; collect no firewood; and leave the place as you found it, or cleaner. The only area where you must register is Borrego Palm Canyon.

The largest site, and the only one with RV hook-ups, is the *Borrego Palm Canyon* campground ($14 per tent site, $10 in summer) a mile from the visitor center. *Tamarisk Grove* (tent sites $14/$10), thirteen miles south on Hwy-S3, is the only other developed site. Both have hiker/biker sites for $3 each and charge $5 for day use of the facilities. Both also organize **guided hikes** and have regular discussion and activity evenings led by a park ranger. Places can be reserved through *MISTIX* (essential for holidays and weekends, and in the March–May blooming season). The other, primitive, campgrounds fill on a first-come-first-served basis; those in the backcountry always have space. All are accessible by road vehicles and are free, except for *Bow Willow* which charges $9/$7 and is the only one with drinking water. Most sites are below 1500ft which is fine in winter, but in the hotter months you might try *Culp Valley*, ten miles southwest of Borrego Springs, at a blissfully cool 3400ft. There is spring water here but you're better off bringing your own.

**Trail Historic Route**, forced a passage along the desert wash. It isn't especially spectacular, but makes for some safe desert walking, never more than a couple of hundred yards from the road. Nine miles further on, the **Vallecito Stage Station** is an old adobe stage rest stop that gives a good indication of the comforts – or lack of them – of early desert travel. To the south lies the least-visited portion of Anza-Borrego, good for isolated exploration and undisturbed views around Imperial Valley, where there's a vivid and spectacular clash as grey rock rises from the edges of the red desert floor, and a cool oasis at Palm Spring.

Northwest of Scissors Crossing, Hwy-S2 meets Hwy-22, which tortuously descends through fields of popcorn-shaped rock formations to Borrego Springs. Six miles further east is a memorial marker to Peg Leg Smith, an infamous local spinner of yarns from the Gold Rush days who is further celebrated by a festival of tall stories – the **Peg Leg Liars Contest** – which takes place at this spot on the first Saturday in April; anybody can get up before the judges and fib their hearts out, the most outrageous tales earning a modest prize. Roughly four miles further on, a fairly tough dirt road leads to **Font's Point** and a view over the **Borrego Badlands** – a long sweeping plain devoid of vegetation whose strange, stark charms are oddly inspiring. Sunset is the best time to fully appreciate the layered alluvial banding.

In the north of the park, the campsite at Borrego Palm Canyon marks the start of the **Borrego Palm Canyon Trail** (3 miles; 2hr; 350ft ascent), one of the most popular paths in the park. It follows a detailed nature trail to a dense concentration of desert palms – the only palms native to California.

# THE HIGH DESERT

Desolate, lifeless and silent, the **Mojave Desert**, mythic badland of the west, has no equal when it comes to hardship. Called the High Desert because it averages a height of around two thousand feet above sea level, the Mojave is very dry and for the most part deadly flat, dotted here and there by the prickly bulbs of a Joshua tree and an occasional abandoned miner's shed. For most, it's the barrier between LA and Las Vegas, an obstacle to get over before they reach either city; and, short on attractions as it is, you may want to follow their example. But you should linger a little just to see – and smell – what a desert is really like: a vast, impersonal, extreme environment, sharp with its own peculiar fragrance, and in spring alive with acres of fiery orange poppies – the state flower of California – and other brightly coloured wildflowers.

You will at least have relatively little company. If LA is the home of the sports car, the Mojave is the land of the dust-covered flat-bed truck, driven by the few who manage not to perish out here. The only other sign of life is the grim military subculture marooned on huge weapons-testing sites. There is a hard-core group of desert fans: backdrop for the legion of road movies spawned by the underground film culture in the late 1960s and early 1970s, the Mojave is a favourite with bikers and hippies drawn by the barren panorama of sand dunes and mountain ranges. But otherwise visitors are thin on the ground, and for most of the year you can rely on being almost entirely alone.

I-15 cuts through the heart of the Mojave, dividing it into two distinct regions. To the north is **Death Valley** (which, because of its unique character and proximity to the Owens Valley, is covered in Chapter Four), and to the south **Barstow**, the lacklustre capital of the Mojave, redeemed only by its location halfway between LA and **Las Vegas** on I-15, which makes it both a potential stopover between the two points and a good base for the surrounding attractions, explorable by dune buggy, on horseback or even on foot.

The area between Barstow and Vegas is known for its eerie isolation, and apart from some spectacular sand dunes and rock formations in the **Mojave National Preserve**, you might as well push on through – the amenities are rather random, catering mostly for the odd geologist or desert specialist, and Death Valley is that much more dramatic. South and east of here, close to the Nevada and Arizona borders, the desert is at its most demanding, utterly empty, inhospitable and potentially miserable, and the only reason you might find yourself in the region is if you're driving through on the way to the **Grand Canyon**.

# Barstow

Just a few hours from LA along the thundering, seemingly endless I-15, **BARSTOW** looms up out of the desert, providing a welcome opportunity to get out of the car. Though capital of the Mojave, it's a small town, consisting of just one main road lined with a selection of motels and restaurants that at least make an overnight stop possible. There, however, its appeal ends. A relentless sun manages to keep people in their air-conditioned homes for a good part of the day, and during the hottest part of the year Barstow can seem more like a ghost town.

## Practicalities

Near the junction of Barstow Road and I-15, the **California Desert Information Center** (daily 9am–5pm; ☎255-8760) has a good selection of maps of the surrounding area, lodging and restaurant guides and various flyers on local attractions.

If you're arriving by bus or train, you'll be dropped at the combined *Greyhound* and *Amtrak* station on First Street. A few blocks away, Main Street is the best place to look for a **motel**. All are of a similar standard and price, generally only distinguished by the condition of the neon sign outside. Cruise up and down until you find the best deal, but among those you might try are: *Desert Inn Motel*, 1100 E Main St (☎256-2146; ②), and the *Hillcrest Motel*, 1111 E Main St (☎256-1063; ③). For a little more comfort, try the corporate-style *Holiday Inn*, 1511 E Main St (☎256-5673; ④). You can **camp** eight miles north of Barstow in the simple *Owl Canyon Campground* ($4) at Rainbow Basin (see below), or if you need more facilities, at **CALICO**, a re-created ghost town (also detailed below) with shaded canyons where you can pitch a tent ($15) or hook-up campers for $19 per night including showers.

**Food** in Barstow, though far from exotic, is plentiful and cheap. Restaurants sit snugly between the many hotels on Main Street and are usually of the rib and steak variety, although you can get good Mexican food at *Rosita's*, 540 W Main St, or a reasonable Chinese meal at the *Golden Dragon*, 1231 E Main St. The best breakfasts in town are dished up at the coffeeshop next door to the *Holiday Inn*. Evening **entertainment** comes in the form of a few grubby bars frequented by bike gangs, the least threatening of which is the *Katz*, 127 W Main Street at First, open from 6am to 2am.

## Around Barstow

Most people who stop in Barstow are not here to enjoy the desert, but to visit the hideously contrived **Calico Ghost Town** (daily 9am–5pm; $5), ten miles east along I-15. In the late nineteenth century Calico produced millions of dollars worth of silver and borax and supported a population of almost four thousand. Attractively set in the colour-streaked Calico Hills, but subject to the extreme heat of the Mojave, the town was quickly deserted when the silver ran out. It's since been rather cynically – and insensitively – restored, with souvenir shops and hot-dog stands, and a main thoroughfare lined with ersatz saloons, an old school house, a vaudeville playhouse, and shops kitted out in period styles. However, should you so desire, there are miles of mining shafts and tunnels open to crawl around in – until claustrophobia forces you up for air.

Calico is brightened by its festivals, held throughout the year. The best of these is the end of March Spring Festival, which features the **World Tobacco Spitting Championships**. Huge beast-like men gather to chew the wad and direct streams of saliva and tobacco juice at an iron post, cheered on by rowdy crowds who take their sport seriously and their drink in large quantities. As the men (women are most definitely not allowed to compete) battle for the titles of best distance and most accurate spitter, the celebrations are jollied along by gallons of beer and some good bluegrass bands.

Primitive males also feature five miles northeast of Calico along I-15. The **Calico Early Man Site** (visit by guided tour only Wed 1.30 & 3.30pm, Thurs–Sun 9.30am–4pm; $1 donation), more popularly known as the "Calico Dig", has become one of the most important archeological sites in North America since it was excavated in 1964, its findings of old tools and primitive shelter (which some have suggested are around 200,000 years old) having dated mankind's presence to far earlier than was previously thought. Pick up details of the tour from the small caravan that serves as an information office.

Of equal prehistoric importance, but far more vivid, the **Rainbow Basin** (unrestricted access), eight miles north of town along Fort Irwin Road, is a rock formation that after thirty million years of wind erosion has been exposed as a myriad of almost electric colours. You'll see plenty of fossilized animal and insect remains, but most visitors will probably be content to weave the car through the tricky four-mile loop road around the canyon and marvel at the prettiness of it all. You can camp here (see "Practicalities" above) at basically equipped sites.

Heading some eight miles east on the other main highway out of Barstow, I-40, just past Dagget, the original Department of Energy's Solar One Power Plant has been replaced by the **SEGS II Solar Power Plant**, which, marked by a hundred-acre field of mirrors, is a surreal example of how California is putting its deserts to use. Anyone who has seen the film *Bagdad Café* will remember the light reflections the mirrors give off for miles around.

Finally, if you're sick of being cooped up in a car, consider trekking around on **horseback**, particularly at sunrise or sunset when the temperatures are more manageable and the colours at their richest. The *Pan McCue Ranch* (☎254-2184) in **YERMO**, eight miles east of Barstow along I-15, has daily riding tours across high desert terrain and through canyons. Long tours are available, but an hour or two – costing around $30 – is probably enough. If the plodding horses of *Pan McCue* aren't quick or scary enough for you, you could always try finding an all-terrain vehicle to go **dune-buggying** in. After wrecking much of the desert's fragile ecosystem, dune-buggying and biking have been confined by law to the dunes south of Barstow – though, ridiculously, the town has no facilities for hiring the vehicles. Try asking around in the town, or travel out to the dunes themselves and get friendly with one of the riders there.

## Baker and the Eastern Mojave

Unless you're completely at a loss for something to do, you'll miss little by skipping the **Eastern Mojave**. There's nothing much to see, few tourist facilities and an emptiness unmatched by anything else in the state. The region does have its advocates, though, as evidenced in the 1994 Desert Protection Act's transformation of 1.4 million acres of land between I-15 and I-40 into the **Mojave National Preserve**. If you're heading for Las Vegas and have time on your hands, a couple of sights here make a reasonable stop-off.

Stock up in **BAKER**, the main supply source for the immediate region and visit the spectacular **Kelso Dunes**, or "Devil's Playground", 45 miles or so southeast along Kelbaker Road. The five-mile stretch of sand dunes reaches up as high as seven hundred feet, making for an unbeatable photo opportunity if nothing else. The faint booming sound you might hear is caused by dry sand cascading down the steep upper slopes. Nearby the **Kelso depot** was built in 1924 for workers on the Union Pacific Railroad. The former canteen, built in classic Mexican style, is known as *The Beanery* and is now maintained as an historic park.

Turn north at Kelso to get to the small town of **CIMA** and the adjacent **Cima Dome**, a perfectly formed batholith rising some 1500ft above the desert floor. Cloaked in Joshua trees, parts of it can be visited on foot. Seventeen miles southeast of Cima you come to **Hole-in-the-Wall**, a volcanic rock field with a campsite ($8) and visitor center (Nov–April daily, hours vary; ☎928-2572), and a couple of hiking trails. Finally, a further ten miles south then six miles west along a spur are the limestone **Mitchell Caverns** (mid-Sept to mid-June tours Mon–Fri 1.30pm, Sat & Sun 1.30pm and 3pm; $4); ninety-minute tours lead you through the stalactites and stalagmites.

# The Colorado River area

Whilst you'd be well advised to steer clear of the Eastern Mojave, the eastern portion of the **Colorado Desert** is not so bleak. In recent years small resorts have sprung up along the **Colorado River**. The strength of the river, over a thousand miles long, has by this southern stage of its course been sapped by a succession of dams (though even in the Grand Canyon there are white-water rapids), until here it proceeds towards the Gulf of California in a stately flow, marking its western border as it goes.

If you're not heading east to the Grand Canyon itself – or if you're looking for an overnight stop en route – the stretch between Needles, the small border town on I-40, and Blythe a hundred miles south where I-10 meets Hwy-95, and especially **Lake Havasu City** in between the two, is the area to concern yourself with. Small waterfront settlements dot its course, some more interesting than others, but most dependent on the desire (or means) for watersports. In times of economic boom these small towns flourish, crammed with weekend boating parties, windsurfers, skiers etc, but in the last few years the average weekenders have had to tighten their belts and some of the towns are struggling. To get round this, places such as **Laughlin** in Nevada, right on the border with California and Arizona, have taken advantage of Arizona's restrictions on gambling and turned themselves into mini-Vegases, enjoying considerable popularity with packs of bikers who make a weekend of driving across the desert, spending all their money on gambling and drink and then riding back again.

## Lake Havasu City

The Colorado River's busiest resort, **LAKE HAVASU CITY** – which you'll have heard of, if not by name, as home to the displaced British landmark, **London Bridge** – is a strange mix of modern American mediocrity and mock-traditional British pomposity. For all that, it's not intolerable, especially at night, when the bridge is lit up. By day, the bridge makes an incongruous sight, but without question it looks a hell of a lot better in the middle of the desert with the Chemehuevi mountains behind it than it ever did between South London and the City. The resort's developer, millionaire Robert P McCulloch, bought the bridge (thinking it was Tower Bridge – or so the story goes) for 2.4 million dollars in the late 1960s, and painstakingly shipped it across the Atlantic Ocean and much of the continental US chunk by chunk before reassembling it over a channel dug to divert water from Lake Havasu, creating an island on the other side of the bridge known as Pittsburgh Point. Despite a glorious climate and development aimed squarely at the visitor, Lake Havasu doesn't really pull it off as a holiday destination, but as a stopover for a day or two it's pretty damned good.

Lake Havasu is best used as a place to rest, but should you want to get out and explore, head for the **Colorado River Indian Reservation** (daily 8am–sundown; $3), clearly signposted from Hwy-95, about twenty miles south of town. The attraction here is the reservation's collection of prehistoric giant rock figures or *intaglios*, originally made by "carving" the desert floor to shape, shedding the darker top layer of rock to reveal the lighter layers of sand beneath. The figures are so huge (up to 160 feet high) that it's hard to tell what you're looking at, but gaze long enough and you can discern a four-legged animal, and a human and spiral design – whether for artistic or religious purposes it's unclear.

The **Parker Dam**, near the small village of Parker, just before the entrance to the reservation, is worth a drive across only in passing to admire the modern engineering that halts the flow of the mightly Colorado River on its path to the Gulf of California.

## Practicalities

Lake Havasu City is adequately endowed with affordable accommodation, a surfeit of inexpensive restaurants and even a *Greyhound* bus that stops daily on its way to Las Vegas; the buses leave from *McDonald's*, 100 Swanson Ave, a block from London Bridge. Fortunately for those without cars, anything you'll need is within walking distance of the bridge.

**Motels** are abundant. Those closest to the centre include the *Windsor Inn Motel,* 451 London Bridge Rd (☎602/855-4135; ②), which boasts especially low rates, and the *Pioneer Hotel of Lake Havasu,* 271 S Lake Havasu Ave (☎1-800/528-5169; ⑤), which offers its own casino.

Lake Havasu's **restaurants** can't boast exotic cuisine, but almost all are good value for money and offer large, wholesome portions. Finding places is easy enough, but to get you started you might try: *Shrugrue's*, in the Island Fashion Mall at the end of London Bridge, which offers fresh fish, salads, pasta and traditional American food; *Max & Ma's*, 90 Swanson Ave, is a diner-style place that serves great breakfasts, sandwiches and steaks, or *New Peking Chinese Restaurant* at 2010 McCulloch Blvd, which specializes in excellent, low-priced Mandarin and Szechuan cooking.

# Las Vegas

When the bronzed visage of Engelbert Humperdinck leers out from a Nevada bill-board, and the laser beam from the *Luxor* pyramid shoots straight into the heavens, you know you're approaching **LAS VEGAS**, a flat, sprawling, hot city that's almost entirely devoted to game-playing. The first hours in Las Vegas are like entering another world: one where the religion is luck, the language is money, and time is measured by revolutions of a roulette wheel. Once you're acclimatized – and it can take quite a while – the whole spectacle can be absolutely exhilarating, assuming you haven't pinned your hopes, and your savings, on the pursuit of a fortune. Las Vegas is an unmissable destination, but one, admittedly, that palls for most visitors after a couple of (hectic) days.

Ironically, Nevada was the first state to outlaw **gambling**. Though it was made legal again in 1931, ostensibly to raise taxes to build schools, gaming remained fairly small-scale until 1946, when mobster Bugsy Siegel opened the *Flamingo*, the first major combined casino and hotel on what's now **the Strip**. Its instant success cemented Las Vegas' links with organized crime and instigated the system of attracting people to the gaming tables with the bribe of bargain-priced beds, food, drink and entertainment, a policy that still holds today – Las Vegas is one of the **least expensive** places to sleep and eat in the US. Yet, despite the full-frontal glamor that assaults you from all corners, the enduring image is not of high-spending playboys (seldom seen away from their complimentary hotel suites and secluded tables on the Strip), but of ordinary people standing for hours at a stretch feeding quarters from buckets into slot machines.

If, like most arrivals, you're in Las Vegas solely to gamble, there's not much to say beyond the fact that all the casinos are free, and open 24 hours per day, with acres of floor space packed full of ways to lose money: **one-armed bandits**, **video poker**, **blackjack** (21) with lightning-fast dealers, and loads of **craps**, **roulette wheels** and much much more. The casinos will just love it if you've come to play a **system**: with the odds stacked against you, your best hope of a large win is to bet your entire stake on one single play, and then stop, win or lose.

In the last few years, Las Vegas has started to wean itself from an exclusive dependency on gambling, and compete head on with Orlando for the family market. Colossal amounts of money have been spent on creating a new breed of resort hotels, such as the pseudo-Egyptian *Luxor*, and the 5000-room *MGM*, which may still feature casinos, but also serve as stupendous theme parks in their own right.

The other major reason to visit Las Vegas is to **get married**. Around eighty thousand weddings are performed here each year, many so informal that bride and groom just wind down the window of their car during the ceremony, and the concept of a Vegas wedding has become almost a byword for tongue-in-cheek chic. And once the honeymoon's over, the city is fast bypassing Reno as the country's quickie **divorce** capital, too.

Away from the Strip, and possibly downtown, the **rest of Las Vegas** needn't concern you at all. It's either given over to ordinary residential districts or to the business community – mining is the biggest industry after the gigantic tourist trade.

## Arrival, information and city transport

**Trains** arrive in downtown Las Vegas (westbound in the morning, eastbound in the evening); the station's platform leads directly into the *Union Plaza Hotel*, 1 Main St.

> The telephone **area code** for Las Vegas is ☎702.

The *Greyhound* terminal is at 200 S Main St downtown, though arriving buses also stop on the Strip, outside the *Stardust Hotel*, 3000 N Las Vegas Blvd. **Flights** land at **McCarran Airport**, a mile from the Strip and four from downtown. Many hotels have free buses to collect their guests, otherwise frequent minibuses run to the Strip ($3) and downtown ($4.50); a cab will cost around $10.

It's unlikely that you'll be straying far from the Strip, but should you need them, **local buses** (*Citizens' Area Transit*; ☎228–7433) run 24 hours per day between the Strip and downtown. The standard single fare on all buses is $1.25, or you can buy ten rides for $8. Given the comparatively small area and lack of places to go beyond the two main districts, you're even less likely to need a **taxi**. On Friday and Saturday nights especially, the Strip is so clogged with traffic that it's quicker to use I-15 to drive around.

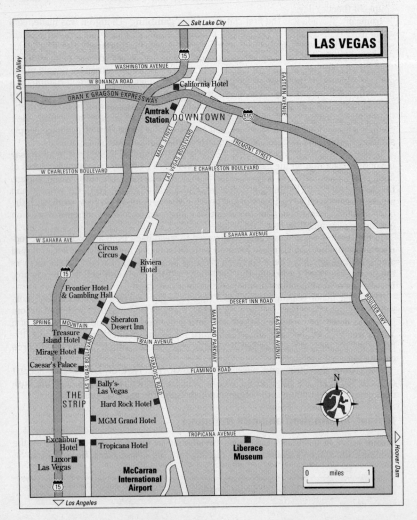

For **information**, pick up the free *Las Vegas Advisor*, which carries details of accommodation, mega-buffets, the latest shows, and assorted discount vouchers. There's also a **visitor center** is at 3150 Paradise Rd (Mon–Fri 8am–5pm; ☎892-7576), next to the vast Convention Center near the Strip. Unsurprisingly, there can be no easier city in which to **change money**: the casinos gladly convert almost any currency, and their walls are festooned with every conceivable ATM machine.

## Accommodation

Although Las Vegas has some 85,000 motel and hotel rooms (most of them hitched to casinos so you never have to go outside), it's best to book **accommodation** ahead if you're on a tight budget, or arriving on Friday or Saturday – upwards of 200,000 people descend upon the city every weekend. The visitor center has a reservation service on ☎1-800/332-5333.

If you're coming from anywhere else in the US, check local newspapers for advertisements outlining the latest Vegas accommodation bargains, as virtually all hotels and motels offer discounts and food vouchers. Rooms are very inexpensive, but be sure to get the rate confirmed for the duration of your stay – that $25 room you found on Thursday may cost $100 on Friday.

**Caesar's Palace**, 3570 S Las Vegas Blvd (☎731-7110 or 1-800/634-6661). Still the showcase of the Strip hotels; see the description below. Doubles can cost well over $1000. ⑦.

**California Hotel**, 12 Ogden Ave (☎385-1222 or 1-800/634-6255). One of the most popular mid-range hotels in downtown Vegas – anywhere else in the world it would be considered gigantic – with a small casino and a couple of great restaurants. ②.

**Circus Circus**, 2880 S Las Vegas Blvd (☎734-0410 or 1-800/634-3450). Strip hotel especially popular with families, with circus acts performing live above the casino floor. ②.

**Sheraton Desert Inn**, 3145 Las Vegas Blvd (☎733-4444 or 1-800/634-6906). Complete resort in the heart of the Strip, with one of the most prestigious entertainment line-ups. ⑤.

**El Cortez Hotel**, 600 E Fremont St (☎385-5200 or 1-800/634-6703). Older and smaller than most, this recently modernized downtown hotel is one of the better bargains. ①.

**Excalibur**, 3850 S Las Vegas Blvd (☎597-7777 or 1-800/937-7777). Arthurian legend built much larger than life. Four thousand rooms plus assorted drawbridges, turrets and nightly jousting matches; staff have to call guests *M'Lord* and *M'Lady*. ③.

**Hard Rock Hotel**, 4455 Paradise Rd (☎693-5000 or 1-800/473-7625). Claims to be the world's only rock 'n' roll casino, with "Sex Pistols" slot machines and the usual array of memorabilia. ③.

**Las Vegas Independent Hostel**, 1208 S Las Vegas Blvd (☎385-9955). Cheap and cheerful hostel with bare-bones accommodation. It also organizes tours of the region's national parks. $10 dorms, some private rooms. ①.

**Luxor**, 3900 S Las Vegas Blvd (☎262-4000 or 1-800/288-1000). This vast, black-glass pyramid is one of the newest and slickest of Vegas' latest family-entertainment style hotels. You can take an ersatz Nile barge to the elevators, then ride up the corners of the pyramid to your room overlooking the deserts. All that plus seven restaurants and assorted virtual reality experiences, plus the obligatory casino. ④.

**MGM Grand**, 3799 S Las Vegas Blvd (☎891-1111 or 1-800/929-1111). Boasting 5005 rooms, this is the world's largest hotel, home to the world's largest casino. It also houses a vast events arena, an amusement park (complete with roller coaster) and a *Wizard of Oz*–inspired theme park. ④.

**Motel 6**, 195 E Tropicana Ave (☎798-0728). The largest (880 rooms) and most expensive branch of this nationwide chain; just off the south end of the Strip. ③.

**Nevada Palace**, 5255 Boulder Hwy (☎455-8810 or 1-800/634-6283). Small quiet place east of the Strip. ②.

**Riviera**, 2901 S Las Vegas Blvd (☎734-5110 or 1-800/634-6753). Among the older and larger Strip hotels, with a colossal casino and lots of restaurants. ④.

**Tropicana**, 3801 S Las Vegas Blvd (☎739-2222 or 1-800/634-4000). The best of the Strip hotels, at least as far as non-gambling activities go, with swim-up gaming tables around the world's largest indoor–outdoor swimming pool. ③.

# The City

The **Strip** (centred around the 3000 blocks of Las Vegas Blvd south of downtown) provides the most familiar image of Las Vegas, all flashing neon and spectacle. Here you'll find the largest and most glamorous **casino-hotels** – complete self-contained fantasy lands of high camp and genuine excitement. Huge moving walkways sweep you into the casinos, but once you're inside it can be almost impossible to find your way out; the action keeps going day and night, and in this sealed and windowless environment you rapidly lose track of real time and real life. Even if you do manage to get back onto the streets during the day, the scorching heat is liable to drive you straight back indoors; night is the best time to venture out, when the Strip's at its brightest and gaudiest.

The best-known casino still encapsulates what Las Vegas is all about, and makes an ideal first port of call. At **Caesar's Palace**, the moving walkway swishes you past a full-sized replica of Caravaggio's *David* into a vast labyrinth of slots and green baize, where half-naked male employees strut around dressed as Roman centurions and the waitresses are all dead ringers for Cleopatra. In the extraordinary *Forum* of top-class restaurants and stores, the domed roof is lit to provide the illusion of a natural sky, which rapidly shifts through the cycles from dawn to dusk. North of *Caesar's Palace*, the sidewalk is thronged for the hourly eruptions of the volcano outside the *Mirage*, not to mention the flaming galleons of *Treasure Island*. The family-oriented **Circus Circus** a little further north has long attempted to pull in the punters by having live circus acts – a trapeze artist here, a fire-eater there, usually performing above dense crowds – and has now added its own water theme park, *Grand Slam Canyon*, vaguely modelled on the Grand Canyon with added roller coasters and river rides.

In the last few years, construction work on a scale unparalleled anywhere in the world has transformed the former desertscape at the far southern end of the Strip. **Excalibur**, with its vast drawbridge, crenellated towers, and relentless "medieval pageantry", opened in 1990, across the road from the ersatz Polynesia of the **Tropicana**, which may not be exactly convincing, but makes a great setting for some good-quality food and drink. 1993 saw the completion on the third corner of the junction of Las Vegas Blvd and Tropicana Ave of the **MGM Grand Hotel and Theme Park**, entered through the roaring mouth of MGM's trademark lion and equipped with a 33-acre movie-lot theme park filled with such rides as a *Journey to the Center of the Earth*.

Just south of *Excalibur* stands the extraordinary 30-storey bronze and glass pyramid of the *Luxor*, also opened in 1993 with a world-wide publicity fanfare. Like *Excalibur*, it belongs to Circus Circus Enterprises, who were able to finance its construction in the space of eighteen months from their free cash flow. The whole place plays endless variations upon the theme of Egyptian archeology, from the Sphinx that guards its main approach, regularly "boiling" the lagoon where it stands with lasers from its eyes, to the exact reconstruction of Tutankhamun's tomb inside. The most powerful artificial light beam ever created shines up from the apex of the pyramid; visible from planes circling over LA, 250 miles west, it supposedly pays tribute to the ancient Egyptian belief that the soul of a dead Pharaoh would rise directly into the skies.

The three miles of **Las Vegas Boulevard** between the Strip and **downtown Las Vegas** are lined by gas stations, fast-food drive-ins, and wedding chapels – getting married being simpler in Nevada than in any other state (see box). Downtown itself is a more compact few blocks of less spectacular casinos grouped around so-called "Glitter Gulch", the neon-illuminated junction of Main and Fremont. For the moment it's surprisingly low-key, and visitors who see Las Vegas for the first time from the downtown *Amtrak* or *Greyhound* terminals might well wonder what all the fuss is about. However, plans have been approved to turn the entire area into the "Fremont Street

Experience", by such means as roofing it with a hundred-foot steel air-conditioned Celestial Vault.

One haven of comparative serenity away from the casinos lies two miles east of the Strip: the **Liberace Museum** at 1775 E Tropicana Ave (Mon–Sat 10am–5pm, Sun 1–5pm; $6.50). Popularly remembered as a beaming buffoon who knocked out torpid toe-tappers, the earlier days of Liberace (he died in 1987) make for interesting study. He began his career playing piano in the rough bars of his native Milwaukee; a decade later, in the 1950s, he was being mobbed by adolescents and ruthlessly hounded by the scandal-hungry press. All this is remembered by a yellowing collection of cuttings and family photos, along with the odd candelabra, bejewelled quails' eggs with inlaid pianos, rhinestone-covered fur coats, glittering cars and more. The music, piped into the scented toilets, may not have improved with age, but the museum is a satisfying attempt to answer one of the seminal questions of our time – "how *does* a great performer top himself on stage?".

## Eating, drinking and entertainment

**Eating** is a real treat in Vegas. All the casinos are so keen to entice visitors onto their premises – and keep them there – that they offer superb-value round-the-clock **buffets**. The process starts off with a low-priced **breakfast**, normally served from 7am until 11am, and costing as little as 99¢ – or even free with a voucher – followed by a $5 **buffet lunch**, served until about 5pm, when it mutates into **dinner** and the price rises by a couple of dollars. If possible, try to avoid eating between 6pm and 9pm, when the lines at the bigger casinos can be endless. Watch out also for special or weekly events, such as the Friday evening *Seafood Extravaganza* at *Frontier's*, 3120 S Las Vegas Blvd.

Each casino has in addition at least one top-quality conventional restaurant, and though there are plenty of places to eat away from the Strip, or out in the suburbs, only

### GETTING MARRIED IN LAS VEGAS

Las Vegas deals with the sacrament of marriage much as it does everything else: in a brashly over-the-top manner that brings new meaning to the word "kitsch". There are four-teen pages of **wedding chapels** in Las Vegas' Yellow Pages, and the range of trappings is nearly unimaginable. Prices start at around $100 for the basic service, and the sky is literally the limit – you can get wed while floating in a hot-air balloon, or parachuting out of a plane.

You don't have to be a resident to get wed here, and you don't need a blood test, either – however, you must be at least eighteen years old and not already married, and purchase a $35 licence from the Clark County Marriage License Bureau at 200 Third St (Mon–Thurs 8am–midnight, Fri–Sun & holidays 24hr; ☎455-3156) before the ceremony (immediately before if you like – there's no waiting period).

The following is a shortlist of the more popular – and our favourite – chapels, most of which are congregated in the somewhat seedy part of Las Vegas between downtown and The Strip. All the casino hotels also have their own facilities.

**A Little White Chapel**, 1301 S Las Vegas Blvd (☎382-5943 or 1-800/545-8111). As featured on *Lifestyles of the Rich and Famous*, this is the place where Michael Jordan and Joan Collins, among others, got married. Open all day every day, with the "World's Only Drive-Up Wedding Window", if you're really in a hurry.

**Graceland Wedding Chapel**, 619 S Las Vegas Blvd (☎474-66545 or 1-800/824-5732). Home of the King – an Elvis impersonator will act as best man, give the bride away or serenade you, though unfortunately he can't legally perform the service.

**Little Church of the West**, 3692 S Las Vegas Blvd (☎739-7971 or 1-800/821-2452). On the National Register of Historic Places, this fifty-year-old chapel is one of the more peaceful and quiet places in which to exchange your Vegas vows.

an eccentric minority of visitors bother to venture off in search of them. **Drinks** – beer, wine, spirits and cocktails – are freely available in all the casinos to anyone gambling, and very cheap for anyone else.

Besides gambling, or just watching, Las Vegas **entertainment** includes credibility-straining "spectaculars" featuring golden-throated warblers and bad comedians, topped off with spangly dancing girls and thumping music. Show seats are $10 on average, but expect to pay (a lot) more if the likes of Frank Sinatra or Dean Martin are topping the bill. Tickets are available from the venues, or you can book by phone. Full details of what's coming up are in the tourist magazines.

**Bally's Big Kitchen**, *Bally's Casino*, 3645 S Las Vegas Blvd (☎739-4930). Popularly acknowledged as the best of the buffets; a quite phenomenal spread of fresh seafood, meats and salads, for around $5. The champagne Sterling Brunch, Sun 9am–2.30pm, is magnificent.

**Lombardi's**, *Caesar's Palace*, 3570 S Las Vegas Blvd (☎735-4663). Patio dining in the Forum at *Caesar's Palace* – or in a secluded interior dining room. Superb, well-priced rural Italian specialties.

**Marrakech**, 4632 S Maryland Pkwy (☎736-7655). Moroccan delicacies, eaten with the hands while seated on pillows in an enormous mock tent, engulfed by live belly dancers. Set menu only, costing around $25.

**Pasta Pirate**, *California Hotel*, 12 Ogden Ave (☎385-1222). Excellent seafood and pasta, moderately priced, amid nautical bric-a-brac. The *Redwood Bar and Grill* in the same hotel is equally good for seafood, this time in a traditional English setting.

**Sam's Town Uptown Buffet**, 5111 Boulder Hwy (☎456-7777). One of the lesser casinos, twenty minutes east of the Strip, but definitely one of the better buffets, plus live country music and dancing with no cover charge.

## Lake Mead and the Hoover Dam

Almost as many people as go to Las Vegas visit **LAKE MEAD**, an artificial expanse of water about thirty miles southeast of the city. It makes a bizarre spectacle, the blue waters a vivid counterpoint to the surrounding desert, but it gets excruciatingly crowded all year round. You can sail, scuba-dive, water-ski or fish at various points along the five-hundred-mile shoreline; get the details and make bookings through any travel agent before arriving, and bear in mind that accommodation is limited to RV-dominated campgrounds.

Fifteen miles beyond Boulder City on US-93, through the rocky ridges of the Black Mountains, is the **Hoover Dam**, responsible for creating the lake in 1935. Designed to block the Colorado River and provide low-cost electricity for the cities of the Southwest, it's one of the tallest dams ever built (760ft high), composed of sufficient concrete to build a two-lane highway from the West Coast to New York. Informative half-hour **guided tours** (summer daily 8am–6.45pm; rest of day daily 9am–4.15pm; $1) descend by lift to view the dam's insides. Without your own vehicle, the only way to get to Lake Mead and the dam from Las Vegas is on one of the many daily bus tours; *Gray Line* (☎384-1234) has an express tour (five hours) to the dam for $22.95, and an eight-hour tour to the dam and the lake for $36.60.

### MOVING ON FROM LAS VEGAS

You can get to Flagstaff in Arizona on *Greyhound*, and from there visit the **Grand Canyon** in Arizona year-round courtesy of the *Nava-Hopi* line (☎1-800/892-8687). However, the three-hundred mile journey takes virtually the entire day, in searing desert heat, so you might consider **flying**, which offers the added bonus of aerial views of Lake Mead and the Canyon itself – for details of airlines, see p.237. Las Vegas is also the closest city to **Death Valley**; see p.250 for details of how to get there.

# The Grand Canyon

The **GRAND CANYON OF THE COLORADO**, in Arizona three hundred long and featureless driving miles from Las Vegas, is one of those sights that you really *have* to see once in your life, and once you've ventured east of the California state line it would be a real shame to exclude it from your itinerary.

Although three million people come to see the Grand Canyon every year, it remains beyond the grasp of the human imagination. No photograph, no set of statistics, can prepare you for such vastness. At more than one mile deep, it's an inconceivable abyss; at from four to eighteen miles wide it's an endless expanse of bewildering shapes and colors, glaring desert brightness and impenetrable shadow, stark promontories and soaring never-to-be-climbed sandstone pinnacles. Somehow it's so impassive, so remote – you could never call it a disappointment, but at the same time many visitors are left feeling peculiarly flat. In a sense, none of the available activities can quite live up to that first stunning sight of the chasm. The **overlooks** along the rim all offer views that shift and change unceasingly from dawn to dusk; you can **hike** down into the depths on foot or by mule, hover above in a **helicopter** or raft through the **white-water rapids** of the river itself; you can spend a night at **Phantom Ranch** on the canyon floor, or swim in the waterfalls of the idyllic **Havasupai Reservation**; and yet that distance always remains – the Grand Canyon stands apart.

The vast majority of visitors come to the **South Rim**, which you'll find described in full on the next few pages – it's the most accessible part of the canyon, there are far more facilities (mainly at the Fred Harvey-owned **Grand Canyon Village**), and it's open year-round. There's another lodge and campground on the **North Rim**, which by virtue of its isolation can be a whole lot more evocative, but at one thousand feet higher this is usually closed by snow from mid-October until May. An even less eventful drive from Las Vegas brings you here via St George in southern Utah; for **accommodation** reservations (essential), contact *TWA Services*, Box 400, Cedar City, Utah 84721 (☎801/586-7686). Few people visit both rims; to get from one to the other demands either a two-day hike down one side of the canyon and up the other, or a 215-mile drive by road. Until the 1920s, the average visitor would stay for two or three weeks. These days it's more like two or three hours – of which forty minutes are spent actually looking at the canyon.

Finally, there's a definite risk that on the day you come the Grand Canyon will be invisible beneath a layer of **fog**; many people blame the 250 tons of sulfurous emissions pumped out every day by the Navajo Generating Station, seventy miles upriver at Page.

**Admission prices** to the park, valid for seven days on either rim, are $10 per vehicle, or $4 per pedestrian or cyclist.

## Getting to and from the Canyon

The most usual approach to the south rim of the Grand Canyon is by **road**, turning north off I-17 at **Williams** to drive the last 56 miles on Hwy-64, or detouring further east via the larger town of **Flagstaff** and then following Hwy-180 past the San Francisco mountains. The two roads join twenty miles before the canyon to pass through thick ponderosa pine forest.

The canyon itself is not visible from any distance – often not even from the rim road – so the restored **steam trains** which take 2hr 45min to run the 64 miles up from Williams offer few scenic delights. They pull in at the picturesque village station (daily, departing Williams 9.30am, and the canyon 3.15pm; round-trip fare $50 adults, $25 children under 12; ☎1-800/THE-TRAIN).

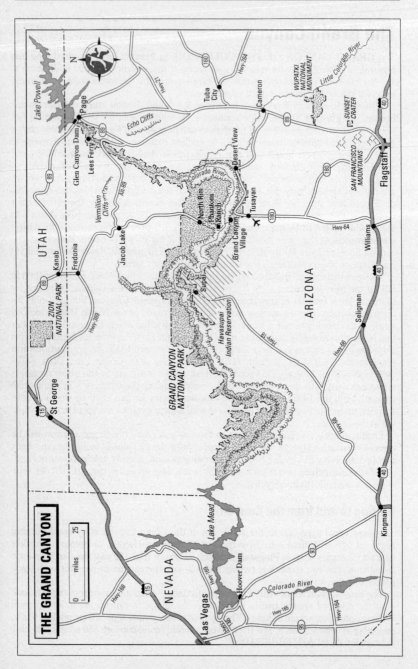

**THE GRAND CANYON**

0 miles 25

N

Lake Powell

Page

Glen Canyon Dam

Lees Ferry

Echo Cliffs

Hwy 21

Hwy 180

Hwy 264

Tuba City

Cameron

Little Colorado River

WUPATKI NATIONAL MONUMENT

SUNSET CRATER

UTAH

Hwy 89

Vermillion Cliffs

Alt-89

Colorado River

Desert View

North Rim

Phantom Ranch

Tusayan

SAN FRANCISCO MOUNTAINS

Flagstaff

Hwy 180

Jacob Lake

Grand Canyon Village

Kanab

Fredonia

Hwy 64

Williams

Supai

Hwy 389

ZION NATIONAL PARK

GRAND CANYON NATIONAL PARK

Havasupai Indian Reservation

Hwy 18

ARIZONA

Hwy 66

Seligman

St George

Hwy 89

Lake Mead

NEVADA

Las Vegas

Hwy 168

Hwy 169

Hoover Dam

Colorado River

Kingman

Hwy 93

Hwy 95

Hwy 164

Hwy 165

The Grand Canyon is simply the best known of the many extraordinary desert national parks of the American Southwest, and one that many visitors to California choose to include on their itineraries. There isn't scope in this book to extend our coverage to include **Zion** and **Bryce** in southern Utah, for example, but you'll find a full account of the region in the *Rough Guide: USA*.

The **airport** is just outside the park at Tusayan; hourly shuttle buses run the seven miles to the village, and *Budget* and *Dollar* rent cars. *Scenic Airlines* (☎1-800/634-6801) operates services to and from Las Vegas, Phoenix, Sedona, Flagstaff and elsewhere. Planes no longer fly directly above the canyon, but the Las Vegas flights give a good view and, with a bottom-rate one-way fare of around $30 (only available on the last flight of the day), save an awful lot of time.

During high season (roughly May–Sept) free **shuttle buses** operate every fifteen minutes within the village itself, and along the West Rim Drive (which at those times is barred to motorists), stopping at the main overlooks.

## Grand Canyon accommodation

The Fred Harvey company's monopoly on **accommodation** means that all the "lodges" in the village charge similar prices, with no budget alternative. To see the canyon, it makes little difference where in the village you stay. Even in the "rim-edge" places – *El Tovar Hotel* (⑥), and *Bright Angel* (③), *Thunderbird* and *Kachina* lodges (both ⑤) – few rooms offer much of a view, and in any case it's always dark by 8pm. Further back are the *Maswik Lodge* (③; cabins can be shared between groups), *Yavapai Lodge* near the visitor center (④) and *Moqui Lodge* at the park entrance (④).

**Camping** facilities (and a laundromat) are available at the *Mather* campground and RV park ($10; ☎638-7888) near the visitor center, at least one section of which is open year-round. If you arrive on foot, you don't need a reservation; all vehicles should, however, check in well in advance (you can book through *MISTIX* on ☎1-800/365-2267). The summer-only *Desert View* campground 26 miles east is first-come first-served, and has no hook-ups. It's also possible to camp inside the canyon itself, if you first obtain a free permit from the **Backcountry Reservations Office** at the *Mather* campground; indeed you can camp anywhere in Kaibab National Forest that is more than six hundred feet from a roadway.

If all the park accommodation is full, the nearest alternative is the underwhelming service village of **TUSAYAN**, just over a mile south of the park entrance. *Seven Mile Lodge* (☎638-2291; ③/⑤), usually offers the least expensive rooms; *Red Feather Lodge* (☎638-2414; ③/⑥), is a little more comfortable – prices at both soar in season. Much the most popular of the commercial **campgrounds** outside the park– with families, at least – is *Flintstone's Bedrock City* (☎635-2600; ⑤), 22 miles south at the junction of Hwys 64 and 180, which has its own prehistoric theme park.

## Grand Canyon eating

Thanks to the canyon's remoteness and lack of water, **food prices** tend to be well above average; if you're on a tight budget, bring your own. However, *Yavapai* and *Maswik* lodges have reasonable basic cafeterias, open until 10pm. *Bright Angel Lodge* has its own restaurant as well as the *Arizona Steakhouse*, both also open until 10pm, and

All in-park **accommodation reservations** are handled by *Grand Canyon National Park Lodges*, PO Box 699, Grand Canyon, AZ 86023 (same-day ☎638-2631, advance ☎638-2401).

The telephone **area code** for the Grand Canyon is ☎602.

both costing $15 to $30. At *El Tovar*, where the dining room looks right out over the canyon, the sumptuous menu is, however, enormously expensive. Breakfast is the most affordable; lunch and dinner can easily cost upwards of $40. In **Tusayan**,*We Cook Pizza and Pasta* (☎638-2278) is good but very pricey.

## Grand Canyon Village

**GRAND CANYON VILLAGE** is not a very stimulating place to spend any time. However, in the absence of significantly cheaper accommodation within fifty miles (for example, in **Tusayan** at the park entrance), there's little option but to stay here. The centrepiece is the magnificent **terrace**, in front of *Bright Angel Lodge* (usually the liveliest spot in town) and the black-beamed 1905 *El Tovar Hotel*, that gives many visitors their only look at the canyon – though the Colorado itself is too deep in the Inner Gorge to be seen from here. Further back are more lodges and gift shops, and employee housing, while about a mile east through the woods are the informative **visitor center** (8am–dusk; ☎638-7888), the **post office**, the **general store** and the **campground**.

## Along the South Rim

It's possible to walk along the South Rim for several miles in either direction from the village, the first few of them on railed and concreted pathways. The most obvious short

### GEOLOGY AND HISTORY OF THE CANYON

Layer upon layer of different rocks, readily distinguished by colour, and each with its own fossil record, recedes down into the Grand Canyon and back through time, until the strata at the river bed are among the oldest exposed rocks on earth. And yet how the canyon was **formed** is a mystery. Satellite photos show that the Colorado actually runs through the heart of an enormous hill (what the Indians called the *Kaibab*, the mountain with no peak); experts cannot agree on how this could happen. Studies show that the canyon still deepens, at the slow rate of 50ft per million years. Its fantastic sandstone and limestone formations were not literally carved by the river, however; they're the result of erosion by wind and extreme cycles of heat and cold. These features were named – **Brahma Temple**, **Vishnu Temple**, and so on – by Clarence Dutton, a student of comparative religion who wrote the first Geological Survey report on the canyon in 1881.

It may look forbidding, but the Grand Canyon is not a dead place. All sorts of desert **wildlife** survive here – sheep and rabbits, eagles and vultures, mountain lions, and, of course, spiders, scorpions, and snakes. The **human** presence has never been on any great scale, but signs have been found of habitation as early as 2000 BC, and the **Anasazi** were certainly here later on. A party of **Spaniards** passed through in 1540 – less than twenty years after Cortes conquered the Aztecs – searching for cities of gold, and one Father Garcés spent some time with the Havasupai in 1776. **John Wesley Powell**'s expeditions along the fearsome and uncharted waters of the Colorado in 1869 and 1871–72 were what really brought the canyon to public attention. A few abortive attempts were made to mine different areas, but facilities for tourism were swiftly realized to be a far more lucrative investment. With the exception of the Indian reservations, the Grand Canyon is now run exclusively for the benefit of visitors; although even as recently as 1963 there were proposals to dam the Colorado and flood 150 miles of the Canyon, and the Glen Canyon dam has seriously affected the ecology downstream.

excursions are to see the sun rise and set. At or near the village, the giant wall that reaches out in the west overshadows much of the evening view. If, however, you walk right out to Hopi Point at its end, looking down as you go onto the Bright Angel Trail as it winds across the Tonto Plateau, you may well see a magical **sunset**, with the Colorado – 350 feet wide at this point – visible way below.

The best place within walking distance to watch the **dawn** is **Mather Point**, a mile east of the visitor center. Nearby, if you can tear your eyes away from its panoramic bay windows, the **Yavapai Geologic Museum** (summer daily 9am–7pm) has illuminating displays on how the canyon may have been formed.

Further dramatic views are available along the **East Rim Drive** – although unless you take an excursion you'll need your own vehicle to see them. **Desert View**, 23 miles out from the village, is at 7500 feet the highest point on the South Rim. Visible to the east are the vast flatlands of the **Navajo Nation**; to the northeast, **Vermillion and Echo Cliffs**, and the grey bulk of **Navajo Mountain** ninety miles away; to the west, the gigantic peaks of **Vishnu** and **Buddha Temples**. Through the plains comes the narrow gorge of the **Little Colorado**; somewhere in the depths, before it meets the Colorado itself, is the *sipapu*, the hole through which the Hopi believe that men first entered this, the Third World. The odd-looking construction on the very lip of the canyon is **Desert View Watchtower**, built by Fred Harvey in 1932 in a conglomeration of Native American styles (though a steel frame props it all up) and decorated with Hopi pictographs. It contains a gift shop, as does the general store a few yards away. Groups of tarantulas are often seen in the evenings at Desert View, scuttling back into the warmth of the canyon for the night.

**Tusayan Ruin**, three miles west of Desert View (and not to be confused with modern Tusayan) is a genuine Anasazi pueblo, though not comparable in scale to the relics elsewhere in this region.

Finally, one of the most popular attractions, in Tusayan at the south entrance to the park, is the **Grand Canyon IMAX Theater** (March–Oct daily 8.30am–8.30pm; Nov–Feb daily 10.30am–6.30pm; $7 adults, $4 kids; ☎638-2203), a 34-minute giant-screen film show of death-defying feats in and above the canyon.

## Into the Canyon

A descent into the Grand Canyon offers something more than just another view of the same thing. Instead you pass through a sequence of utterly different landscapes, each with its own distinct climate, wildlife, and topography. It's a hostile environment, and one to be treated with respect. The basic rules are, first, that whatever time you spend hiking down, you should allow twice that to get back up again, and second, carry (and drink) at least one litre of water per person.

The temperature at river level is on average 20° higher than on the South Rim, and there's far less rain. The **ecology** down here is changing fast since Glen Canyon Dam was completed in the mid-1960s. Previously, up to a million tons of earth and rock hurtled past Phantom Ranch each day. Now it's more like 80,000; trees are establishing themselves that would previously have been swept away, and fish are becoming extinct.

There's only space here to detail the most popular **hiking trail**, the **Bright Angel**. Many of the others, such as the **Hermit**, date from the days prior to 1928, when the obstreperous Ralph Cameron controlled access to the Bright Angel and many other rim-edge sites by means of spurious mining claims, and the Fred Harvey company had to find other ways to get its customers down to the Colorado. These other trails tend to be overgrown now, or partially blocked by landslides; check before setting out. Aside from the trails, the **Havasupai Reservation**, a secluded and beautiful Native American settlement, is of particular note.

### GRAND TOURS

**Fred Harvey** does at least two short daily **coach tours** along the **rim** to the west and east of the village, a **sunset trip** to Yavapai point, and **mule** rides to Phantom Ranch. It also runs a five-hour **Smooth Water River Raft Excursion** through Glen Canyon ($80; ☎303/297-2757); whitewater rafting trips in the canyon proper – such as the 3–12-day **Wilderness River Adventures** to Glen Canyon (Box 717, Page, AZ 86040; ☎1-800/528-6154 or 645-3279) – are booked up literally years in advance, so this is probably your only chance of a trip along the river at short notice. Details from lodge transportation desks or on ☎638-2401.

**Aircraft tours** cost from around $55 for 30min ($30 child) up to as long as you like for as much as you've got. Operators include *Air Grand Canyon* (☎1-800/AIR-GRAND or 638-2686), *Grand Canyon Airlines* (☎1-800/528-2413 or 638-2407) and *Windrock Aviation* (☎1-800/24ROCKY or 638-9591). **Helicopter tours**, from $90 for 30min, are offered by *AirStar Helicopters* (☎638-2622), *Papillon Helicopters* (☎638-2419) and *Kenai Helicopters* (☎638-2412). Unless otherwise specified, all the companies are in **Tusayan**, at or near the airport.

## Bright Angel Trail

The **Bright Angel Trail**, followed on foot or mule by thousands of visitors each year, starts from the wooden shack in the village which was once the Kolb photographic studio. Allowing four or five hours to hike the 9.6 miles down to **Phantom Ranch**, and another eight or nine to get back up again, you should think carefully before attempting the round trip in one day. Many hikers choose instead to go as far as **Plateau Point** on the edge of the arid Tonto Plateau, an overlook above the Inner Gorge from which it is not possible to descend any further. In summer, you can obtain water along the trail, and only need to carry one litre of water per person; in winter, when there is none, you should carry two.

The first section of the trail was laid out by miners a century ago, along an old Havasupai route. There are two short tunnels in its first mile. After another mile, the **wildlife** starts to increase (deer, rodents and the ubiquitous ravens), and there are a few **pictographs** which have been all but obscured by graffiti.

At **Indian Gardens**, almost five miles down, there's a ranger station and campground with water. Here the trails split, to Plateau Point or down to the river via the **Devil's Corkscrew**, constructed by the WPA in the 1930s. It leads through sand dunes scattered with cacti and down beside **Garden Creek** to the Colorado, which you then follow for more than a mile to get to Phantom Ranch.

## Phantom Ranch

It's a real thrill to spend a night at the very bottom of the canyon, at the 1922 **Phantom Ranch**. The cabins are reserved exclusively for the use of excursionists on Fred Harvey two-day mule trips ($252 per person for one night, $353 for the winter-only two-night trips). There may, however, be $22 dorm beds (reservations must be made on ☎303/297-2757). Hikers must register with the *Bright Angel* transport desk the day prior to their reservation, by 4pm, or on that day call ☎638-2631 ext 6576 to confirm. Do not hike down without a reservation. All supplies reach Phantom Ranch the same way you do (an all-day hike on foot or mule), so **meals** are expensive, a minimum of $10.50 for breakfast and $17 for dinner.

The **suspension bridge** here was set in place in 1928 (hanging from twin cables carried down on the shoulders of 42 Havasupai). The delta of **Bright Angel Creek**, named by Powell to contrast with the muddy **Dirty Devil** upriver in Utah, is several hundred feet wide here, and strewn with boulders. All the water used on the South Rim now comes by pipeline from the North Rim, and crosses the river on the 1960s Silver

Bridge nearby. (Do not drink the water from any streams you pass, as it's swarming with illness-inducing bacteria.)

## Havasupai Reservation

The **Havasupai Reservation** really is another world. A 1930s anthropologist called it "the only spot in the United States where native culture has remained in anything like its pristine condition"; things have changed a little since then, but the sheer magic of its turquoise waterfalls and canyon scenery make this a very special place. Traditionally, the Native American Havasupai lifestyle was to spend summer on the canyon floor and winter on the plateau above. When the reservation was created in 1882, they were only granted land at the bottom of the canyon, and not until 1975 did the concession of another 251,000 acres up above make it possible to resume their ancient pattern.

Havasu Canyon is a side canyon of the Grand Canyon, about 35 miles as the raven flies from Grand Canyon village, but almost two hundred miles by road. Turn off the interstate at Seligman or Kingman onto AZ-66 which curves north between the two, stock up with food, water and gas, and then turn on to Arrowhead Hwy-18. The road ends at **Hualapai Hilltop**, an eight-mile hike from the village of **SUPAI**, where all visitors must pay a $15 entry fee.

Plans to build a road – or even a tramway – down into the canyon have always been rejected, in part because much of the income of the five or six hundred Havasupai comes from guiding visitors on foot, mule or horseback. Beyond Supai the trail becomes more difficult, but leads to a succession of spectacular waterfalls, including **Havasu Falls**, one of the best for swimming, and **Mooney Falls**, which was named after an unfortunate prospector who dangled here for three days in the 1890s, at the end of a snagged rope, before falling to his death.

A **campground** (☎448-2141) stretches between Havasu and Mooney Falls, and Supai itself holds *Havasupai Lodge* (☎448-2111; ⑤), along with a café, a general store, and the only post office in the US still to receive its mail by pack train. From time to time Supai is hit by freak floods which can result in the temporary closure of the campground and hotel.

# Flagstaff

As the nearest town of any size to the canyon, seventy miles northwest, **FLAGSTAFF** remains the major junction for road and rail passengers heading for the Grand Canyon. Although some of its old streets are still redolent with Wild West charm – its main thoroughfare, Santa Fe Avenue, was once part of Route 66, and before that, the pioneer trail west – there's not all that much of interest in the town itself. However, the exceptional **Museum of Northern Arizona** (daily 9am–5pm; $5), three miles northwest on Hwy-180 (and not on a local bus route), provides a good introduction to Arizona's native American cultures, past and present. At all times there are pots, rugs and kachina dolls on display, but *the* time to come is for the Indian Craftsmen Exhibitions each summer. The **Zuni** show lasts for five days around Memorial Day weekend in late May; the **Hopi** one is on the weekend closest to July 4, and the nine-day **Navajo** event is at the end of July and the start of August, with every item for sale.

## Practicalities

*Amtrak* trains still pull in at the wooden station house right in the heart of town, a minute's walk from the helpful **visitor center** at 101 W Santa Fe Ave (Mon–Sat 8am–9pm, Sun 8am–5pm; ☎1-800/842-7293 or 774-9541). Though the historic Santa Fe Railroad is busy with freight, the only passenger **trains** to stop here each day are the 7.15am to Albuquerque and the 9.10pm to Los Angeles. *Greyhound* and *Nava-Hopi*

(☎774-5003 or 1-800/892-8687) **buses** pull up at 399 S Malpais Lane, south of the tracks a few minutes' walk away.

Three buses run to the **Grand Canyon** each day in summer; the once-daily *Amtrak* connection, and *Nava-Hopi Tours*, whose three daily buses leave their office downtown at 114 W Route 66 ($2 round trip; 774-5003 or 1/800/892-8687). Both *Nava-Hopi* and the slightly more energetic *Northern Arizona Wilderness Tours* run (hurried) daily **excursions** of the Canyon, as well as to Navajo and Hopi country and beyond.

The least expensive **car rental**, which shared between a group should cost less than the bus, is *Budget Rent-a-Car* at 100 N Humphreys St (☎774-2763). To rent a **mountain bike**, try *Cosmic Cycles*, 113 S San Francisco St (☎779-1092).

Two basic central **hostels** offer dorm beds for around $11 and private rooms for $30: the HI-AYH-approved *Weatherford Hotel*, 23 N Leroux St (☎774-2731; ①), and the summer-only *Downtowner*, 19 S San Francisco St (☎774-8461; ①). The *Monte Vista* at 100 N San Francisco St (☎779-6971; ③) is a very pleasant little hotel with more comfortable rooms, each named after a movie star, while budget **motels** abound along the interstate in the Butler Avenue area. The best **campground** is three miles south on US-89A, at *Fort Tuthill County Park* (☎774-5139).

For **food**, *Charley's Pub and Restaurant* in the *Weatherford Hotel* makes a classy if unlikely contrast with the hostel rooms upstairs, serving good cheap food accompanied by live music (cocktail piano at lunch, bands at night). The area around San Francisco Street, south of the tracks and near the university, has largely been taken over by the alternative student crowd. The *Mad Italian* at no. 101 (☎779-1820) is a highly sociable **bar** with several pool tables, while *Hassib's* at no. 211 (☎774-1037) does a variety of mid-Eastern and European dishes, but closes early.

# The Western Mojave

The **western expanse of the Mojave Desert** spreads out on the north side of the San Gabriel Mountains, fifty miles from Los Angeles via Hwy-14, a barren plain that drivers have to cross to reach the alpine peaks of the eastern Sierra Nevada mountains or Death Valley, at the Mojave's northern edge. The few towns that have grown up in this stretch of desert over the past couple of decades are populated in the main by two sorts of people: retired couples who value the dry, clean air; and aerospace workers, employed in one of the many military bases or aircraft factories. **Lancaster**, near Edwards Air Force Base, is the largest town and one of the few places to pick up supplies; **Mojave**, thirty miles north, is a main desert crossroads and the last place to fill up your tank after dark for the next hundred miles. Hwy-14 joins up with US-395 another forty miles north, just west of the huge naval air base at **China Lake** and the faceless town of **Ridgecrest**, worth a look for its museum of Native American petroglyphs.

## Lancaster and the Antelope Valley

From the north end of LA's San Fernando Valley, Hwy-14 cuts off from I-5 and heads east around the foothills of the San Gabriel Mountains, passing **Placerita Canyon**, site of an early gold discovery that's been preserved as a nature reserve (daily 9am–5pm; free). Ten miles further on stands the massive sandstone outcrop of the **Vasquez Rocks**, once a hiding place for frontier bandits and bank robbers, and later used by Hollywood movie studios as the backdrop for low-budget Westerns. Beyond here Hwy-138 cuts off east,

Unless otherwise specified, all desert telephone numbers have the **area code** ☎619.

heading up to the ski resorts and lakes along the crest of the San Gabriel Mountains, while Hwy-14 continues across the sparsely settled flatlands of the Mojave Desert.

The biggest place for miles is the twin town of **LANCASTER**, a sprawling community of retirees and RV parks whose economy is wholly based on designing, building and testing aeroplanes, from B-1 bombers for the military to the record-setting *Voyager*, which flew non-stop around the globe in 1987. The **Blackbird Airpark**, at 25th Street, three miles west along Avenue P (Fri–Sun 10am–5pm; free; information on ☎277-8050), comprises just two sinister-looking black planes standing by the roadside. These are in fact the fastest and highest-flying planes ever created. The A-12 was designed in the 1950s as prototype for the SR-71 – the *Blackbird* – a reconnaissance plane which could reach 2,100 miles per hour at 85,000ft. Unless you strike one of the infrequent "open cockpit" days (call for details), all you can do is circle the planes admiring the sleek lines and astonishing statistics.

Otherwise, Lancaster's a dull place, but may be worth an overnight stop if you want to get an early start to see the desert before the sun heats everything to an unbearable degree. The **Chamber of Commerce** at 44335 Lowtree Ave (Mon–Fri 9am–5pm; ☎948-4518), just off the main drag, Avenue J, has information on places of interest in the desert, and on **accommodation** – at motels such as the *Tropic* (☎948-4912; ②) at 43145 Sierra Highway, on the east side of town, and the *All-Star Inn* (☎948-0435; ②) at 43540 W 17th St, just off Hwy-14.

Unlikely as it may seem at first glance, there are some things to see in the surrounding area, known as the **Antelope Valley** where, in the spring, the **California Poppy Reserve**, fifteen miles west of Hwy-14 on Lancaster Road, is in full bloom with the state flower, the Golden Poppy. Depending upon the amount and timing of the winter rains, the flowers peak between March and May, when the reserve is covered in bright orange blossom; in season, the **visitor center** (Mon–Fri 9am–4pm, Sat & Sun 9am–5pm; ☎924-0662) has interpretive displays of desert flora and fauna. The building itself is proof that passive-solar, underground architecture works: built into the side of a hill, it keeps cool naturally and is powered entirely by an adjacent windmill generator.

**Saddleback Butte State Park**, seventeen miles east of Lancaster at the junction of Avenue J and 170th St (daily dawn–dusk; $5 per vehicle), centres on a smallish hill whose slopes are home to a splendid collection of Joshua trees. It's also a likely spot to catch a glimpse of the Desert Tortoise, for whom the park provides a refuge from the motorcyclists and dune buggy enthusiasts who tear around the region. There's a **visitor center** (Feb–May & Oct–Nov only), a half-mile nature trail and under-used **campsites** ($10). The visitor center runs a campfire programme on Saturday evenings and nature hikes the following morning. Three miles southwest, the **Antelope Valley Indian Museum** on Avenue M (mid-Sept to mid-June Sat & Sun 10am–4pm; $3), housed in a mock Swiss chalet painted with Native American motifs, contains an extensive collection of ethnographic material from all over the state.

The desert and dry lake beds north of Lancaster make up **Edwards Air Force Base**, the US military testing ground for experimental, high-speed and high-altitude aircraft (such as the *Blackbird*, detailed above). Ninety-minute **tours** of NASA's Dryden Flight Research Facility (Mon–Fri 10.15am & 1.15pm; free; reserve at least a day in advance on ☎258-3446) include a short film (a jingoistic cross between *The Right Stuff* and *Top Gun*) and a look at hangars full of unique aeroplanes, including the missile-like *X-15*. The base is also one of the landing spots for the Space Shuttle, and thousands of people make the journey out here to welcome the astronauts home.

## Mojave and Tehachapi

**MOJAVE**, strung out along the highway thirty miles north of Lancaster, is a major junction on the interstate train network, though it's used solely by goods trains. The town itself – mostly a mile-long highway strip of gas stations, $25-a-night motels and franchised fast-food restaurants, open around the clock – is the last place to fill up on food and gas before continuing north into the Owens Valley or Death Valley.

About twenty miles west from Mojave, Hwy-58 reaches **TEHACHAPI**, another gas, food and lodging town, but with two minor claims to fame. Some 5100 **wind generators** – both familiar three-bladed windmills and more unusual egg-beater-style Darreius turbines – make the Tehachapi Wind Resource Area, ranked along Cameron Ridge to the east, one of the world's most productive renewable energy stations. Train enthusiasts, meanwhile, cross states to see groaning *Santa Fe* diesels hauling their mile-long string of boxcars around the **Tehachapi Loop**, eight miles west of town. Built in the 1870s as the only means of scaling the steep slopes of the region, the tracks cleave to the rockface, doubling back on themselves to make a complete 360° loop. The sight of a train twisting around a mountain, its front end 77ft above its tail, is awesome. You can't see it properly from Hwy-58, so follow the signs three miles from the Keene exit to a roadside plaque commemorating the loop's engineers.

# Randsberg and Ridgecrest

Northeast from Mojave, along Hwy-14, the desert is virtually uninhabited, the landscape only marked by the bald ridges of the foothills of the Sierra Nevada mountains that rise to the west, though you might see the odd ghostly sign of the prospectors who once roamed the region in search of gold and less precious minerals. Twenty miles north of Mojave, Hwy-14 passes through **Red Rock Canyon**, where brilliantly coloured rock formations have been eroded into a miniature version of Utah's Bryce Canyon; the highway passes right through the centre of the most impressive section, though if you walk just a hundred yards from the road you're more likely to see an eagle or coyote than another visitor. There's a **state park** (day use $5 per vehicle) with a **visitor center** (open spring & fall Fri–Sun) and a fairly primitive but beautifully sited **campground** ($7).

Continuing north of Red Rock Canyon, Hwy-14 merges into US-395 for the run into the Owens Valley (see Chapter Four). But a worthwhile detour cuts fifteen miles east to **RANDSBERG**, a near ghost town of two bars and four shops, its lifeblood provided by the Rand gold deposit of the Yellow Aster and Baltic mines, the last to be worked commercially in California. The **Desert Museum**, 161 Butte Ave (Sat & Sun 10am–5pm; free), has displays on the glory days of the 1890s, when upwards of three thousand people lived in the town, mining gold, silver and tungsten out of the arid, rocky hills. Stop in for a beer at the *White House Saloon* across the street, which also has bed and breakfast packages (☎374-2464; ③).

Twenty miles north of Randsberg Hwy-178 cuts east towards Death Valley to the sprawling desert community of **RIDGECREST**, dominated by the huge China Lake Naval Weapons Center. Jet fighters scream past overhead, taking target practice on land that's chock-full of ancient **petroglyphs**. Though access to the sites is strictly controlled, you can get some idea of the native culture of the Mojave Desert by visiting the **Maturango Museum**, off China Lake Blvd at 100 E Las Flores Ave (Wed–Sun 10am–5pm; $2), which as well as acting as regional **visitor center**, has exhibits on both the natural and cultural history of the region, including examples of the rock-cut figures. To get out and see the figures and designs in their natural surroundings, plan ahead and join one of the volunteer-led five-hour **tours** ($20) either by calling ☎375-6900, faxing ☎375-0479, or writing to the museum (Ridgecrest, CA 93555) well in advance.

Twenty miles east along Hwy-178 from Ridgecrest, an eight-mile dirt road (passable except after rain) leads to the **Trona Pinnacles**, five hundred tufa spires which stretch up to 140ft, and were considered extra-terrestrial enough to form a backdrop for parts of *Star Trek V*. Visit them on a half-mile nature trail near a primitive, free **campground**.

## travel details

**Trains**

**LA to**: Barstow (2 daily; 4hr); Flagstaff (1 daily; 11hr); San Bernadino, for Palm Springs (3 weekly; 3hr); Las Vegas (1 daily; 7hr).

**Buses**

*All buses are Greyhound unless otherwise stated*

**Grand Canyon to**: Flagstaff (3 *Nava-Hopi*, 1 *Amtrak Thruway* daily; 2hr); Las Vegas (1 *Nava-Hopi* daily; 6hr).

**Las Vegas to**: Barstow (7 daily & 2 *Amtrak Thruway* daily; 3hr); Flagstaff (1 daily; 5hr).

**LA to**: Barstow (11 daily & 2 *Amtrak Thruway* daily; 3hr); Las Vegas (13 daily & 2 *Amtrak Thruway* daily; 6hr 15min); Palm Springs (10 daily; 3hr).

**Palm Springs to**: Bakersfield (1 *Amtrak Thruway* daily; 5hr 40min); Joshua Tree (4 *Desert Stage Lines* daily; 1hr 30min); SanBernardino (1 *Amtrak Thruway* daily; 1hr 30min)

**San Diego to**: Borrego Springs (2 *North East Rural Bus System* a week; 2hr 50min); Butterfield Ranch (3 *North East Rural Bus System* a month; 2hr 50min); Scissors Crossing (3 *North East Rural Bus System* a month; 2hr 35min).

# CHAPTER FOUR

# DEATH VALLEY AND THE EASTERN HIGH SIERRA

The far eastern edge of California, rising up from the Mojave and cleaving to the border with Nevada, is a long narrow strip as scenically dramatic as anywhere else in the state, veering from blistering desert to ski country, much of it in the lee of the mighty High Sierra. It's a region devoid of Interstates, scarcely populated and, but for the scant reminders of gold-hungry pioneers, developed in only the most tentative way.

At the region's base, technically forming the Mojave's northern reach but more usually visited along with the Owens Valley, is **Death Valley**. The hottest place on earth and so remote that it's almost a region unto itself, this vast national park, is a distillation of the classic desert landscape: an arid, otherworldly terrain of brilliantly coloured, bizarrely eroded rocks, mountains and sand dunes, 150 miles from the nearest town.

The towering **eastern** peaks of the High Sierra drop abruptly to the largely desert – and deserted – landscape of the Owens Valley far below. Seen from the eastern side, the mountains are perfectly described by their Spanish name, *Sierra Nevada*, which literally translates as "snowcapped saw". Virtually the entire range is preserved as wilderness, and hikers and mountaineers can get higher much more quickly here than almost anywhere else in California: well-maintained roads lead to trailheads at over ten thousand feet, providing quick access to spires, glaciers and clear mountain lakes. **Mount Whitney**, at almost 14,500ft the highest point in the continental US, marks the southernmost point of the chain, which continues north for an uninterrupted 150 miles to the backcountry of Yosemite National Park.

The five-mile-wide **Owens Valley** starts at the foot of Mount Whitney, hemmed in to the east by the **White Mountains**, nearly as high but drier and less hospitable than the High Sierra, and home to the gnarled **bristlecone pines**, the oldest living things on earth. In between, US-395 runs the length of the valley, which has few signs of settlement at all beyond the sporadic roadside towns and the larger **Bishop**. Just a few miles further on, **Mammoth Lakes** is the region's liveliest resort, thick with skiers in winter and fishing enthusiasts in summer. Finally, at the far northern tip of the valley, the placid blue waters of ancient **Mono Lake** are set in a bizarre desert basin of volcanoes and steaming hot pools and the subject of an ongoing battle between environmentalists and the City of Los Angeles. Beyond, and far enough out of most people's way to deter the crowds, is the wonderful ghost town of **Bodie** which preserves a palpable sense of gold-town life eight thousand feet up in a parched, windswept valley.

### Getting around

US-395 is the lifeline of the Owens Valley and pretty much the only access to the area from within California. Once north of Mojave, where Hwy-58 branches west to

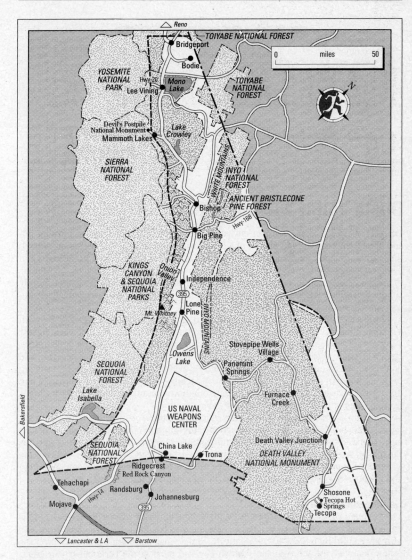

Bakersfield, no road crosses the Sierra Nevada until Hwy-120, a spur over the 10,000-foot Tioga Pass into Yosemite. To the east Hwy-190 cuts through the Panamint Range into Death Valley.

US-395 is travelled once daily by *Greyhound* between LA and Reno in Nevada (note that this bus is best used when travelling from north to south; otherwise most arrivals and departures are in the early hours of the morning) and has plenty of cheap motels along its length and campgrounds in the nearby foothills. Access to Death Valley without your own wheels is all but impossible: no public transport whatsoever runs into the park.

---

### ACCOMMODATION PRICES

All accommodation prices in this book have been coded using the symbols below. Note that prices are for the least expensive double rooms in each establishment. For a full explanation see p.33 in *Basics*.

| ① up to $30 | ② $30–45 | ③ $45–60 | ④ $60–80 | ⑤ $80–100 |
|---|---|---|---|---|
| ⑥ $100–130 | ⑦ $130–175 | ⑧ $175–250 | ⑨ $250+ | |

---

*Dial-a-Ride Shuttle Service* ($10 per person; ☎876-5518) runs minivans to the main High Sierra slopes and trails, picking up passengers from *Greyhound* stations and other points in the Owens Valley; make arrangements well in advance. A similar service is run by *Inyo Mono Dial-a-Ride* (☎872-1901).

# Death Valley National Park

**DEATH VALLEY** is an inhuman environment: barren and monotonous, burning hot and almost entirely without shade, much less water. At first sight it seems impossible that the landscape could support any kind of life; yet it's home to a great variety of living creatures, from snakes and giant eagles to tiny fishes and bighorn sheep. But it's the rocks that you come to see: deeply shadowed, eroded crevices at the foot of sharply silhouetted hills, whose exotic mineral content turns million-year-old mud flats into rainbows of sunlit phosphorescence.

Throughout the summer, the air temperature in Death Valley averages 120°F – with a recorded high of 135°F – and the ground can reach near boiling point; it's best to stay away at this time unless you're a real glutton for sweaty, potentially fatal punishment. Better to come during the spring, especially March and early April, when the wild flowers are in bloom and daytime temperatures average a manageable 65°F, dropping to the mid-forties at night. Any time between October and May it's generally mild and dry, with occasional rainfall on the surrounding mountains causing flash floods through otherwise bone-dry gulleys and washes.

The central north–south valley, after which the park is named, holds its two main outposts for provisions and accommodation: **Stovepipe Wells** and **Furnace Creek**. It is surrounded by many more, equally inhospitable desert valleys, punctuated with the remains of mine workings. High above stand the less-visited but far cooler peaks of the Panamint Range – from where you can see at once both the highest (Mount Whitney) and the lowest (near Badwater) points in the continental United States.

### Geology and history

The sculpted rock layers exposed in Death Valley, tinted by oxidized traces of various mineral deposits, comprise a nearly complete record of the earth's past, from 500 million-year-old mountains to the relatively young fossils of marine animals left on the valley floors by the Ice Age lakes which covered most of the park's low-lying areas. There's also dramatic evidence of volcanic activity, as at the massive Ubehebe Crater on the north side of the park.

Humans have lived in and around Death Valley for thousands of years, beginning about ten thousand years ago when the valley was still filled by a massive lake; the

---

The telephone **area code** for Death Valley and Owens Valley is ☎619.

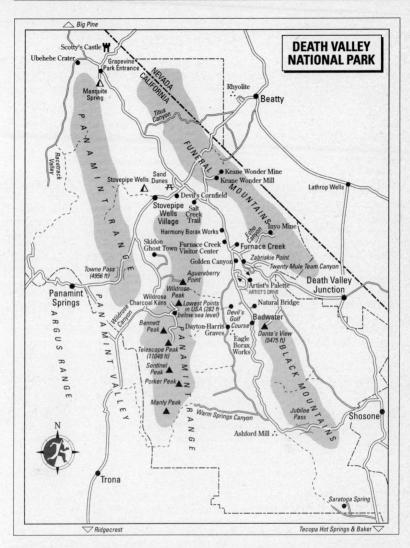

climate was then quite mild and wild game was plentiful. Later, wandering tribes of Desert Shoshone wintered near perennial freshwater springs in the warm valley, spending the long, hot summers at cooler, higher elevations in the surrounding mountains; there is still a small, inhabited Shoshone village near the *Furnace Creek Inn*.

The first whites passed through in 1849, looking for a short cut to the Gold Rush towns on the other side of the Sierra Nevada; they ran out of food and water but managed to survive, and gave Death Valley its name. For the next 75 years the only people willing to brave the hardships of the desert were miners, who searched for and found deposits of gold, silver and copper. The most successful mining endeavours

> For advice on **desert survival**, see the box on pp.204-205.

were centred on **borates**, a harsh alkaline used in detergent soaps. In the late nineteenth century borate miners developed twenty-mule-team wagons to haul the powders across the deserts to the railroad line at Mojave. In the 1920s the first tourist facilities were developed, and in 1927 the mining camp at Furnace Creek was converted into the *Furnace Creek Inn*. Six years later the two million acres of Death Valley and around were purchased by the US government, to be preserved as a national monument. In 1994, as part of the California Desert Protection Bill, Congress accorded it national park status and added a further 1.3 million acres to its area, making Death Valley the largest national park in the country outside Alaska.

# Getting to Death Valley

Death Valley is a long way from anywhere, and there's **no scheduled public transport** into the park. The nearest places served by buses are **BEATTY**, just inside Nevada and 35 miles from Furnace Creek, and Lone Pine in the Owens Valley (see p.257); neither is much use unless you have a bicycle. **Las Vegas**, in Nevada, is the nearest **city** to Death Valley; take US-95 past Nellis Air Force Base and the US nuclear weapons test range, turning south at Armagossa Valley for Death Valley Junction, or continuing to uninteresting Beatty, and heading in on Hwy-374.

**Driving** to Death Valley from **within California**, you should follow one of the routes below. Fill up your vehicle before you enter the park, as gas inside is pricy.

### The western approaches

From the west, there are two routes towards Death Valley, of equal length and running along either side of the China Lake Naval Weapons Base. Five miles west of Ridgecrest (see p.244), US-395 runs north along the west side of China Lake up to the dry bed of what used to be Owens Lake; the water that would naturally flow in to the lake has been diverted to Los Angeles, and is carried south by the aqueduct that parallels US-395. Just south of here, Hwy-190 cuts off due east to Hwy-136, the Lone Pine to Death Valley road – perhaps the prettiest drive into the park. Fifteen miles west of this junction a loop peels southeast to **Darwin**, and shortly after another road cuts north to **Lee Flat** and the **Saline Valley** – see p.256. At nearby **PANAMINT SPRINGS** are an expensive gas station and a motel (see below).

The less-travelled route loops sixty miles around the eastern side of China Lake and allows the quickest access into the more mountainous backcountry of Death Valley, an area once home to Charles Manson and his "Family". Wildrose Road, the continuation of Hwy-178 beyond Ridgecrest, curves through the chemical plants of **Trona** past the gold-mining town of **BALLARAT** – whose eroded adobe ruins still stand in the foothills three miles east of the highway – before joining Hwy-190 for the final fifteen miles east to the entrance to Death Valley. What makes this route worthwhile is the possibility of following the steep Mahogany Flat Road, which cuts off Wildrose Road thirteen miles south of Hwy-190, up the Panamint Mountains to **Telescope Peak** (see above), the highest and coolest part of the park. The road is well maintained, but although there is excellent free **camping** (see box on p.252), the nearest food, drinking water or gas are 25 miles away at Stovepipe Wells Village. Another potential side trip is to the **Skidoo Ghost Town** (see p.255) a few miles to the north.

### The southern approaches

Hwy-127 branches off I-15 at Baker (see p.227) – the last stop for supplies on the southern route into Death Valley – and cuts across fifty miles of desolate Mojave landscape before reaching any civilization. A couple of miles east of Hwy-127 two dilapidated settlements of scrappy trailer homes make unexpectedly decent places to stop off. The settlement of **TECOPA HOT SPRINGS** has become a popular winter retreat, thanks to its natural hot springs always open to the public and bequeathed in perpetuity by a local chief provided they remain free. Many people stay across the road at the bleak campsite ($6.50), though the hostel in nearby **TECOPA** is a better bet (see below).

The hamlet of **SHOSHONE**, eight miles north of Tecopa, wouldn't really rate a mention but for a decent motel (see below) within striking distance of the park. **DEATH VALLEY JUNCTION**, a further thirty miles north, offers no fuel, but its *Amargosa Hotel* (see below) houses the **Amargosa Opera House**, the creation of Marta Becket, a New York dancer and artist who settled here in the late 1960s. The inside of the theatre is painted with *trompe l'oeil* balconies peopled by sixteenth century Spanish nobles and revellers. Operas, in which Ms Becket takes almost all the parts herself, are staged here between October and May ($8; ☎852-4441).

## Entrance and information

**Entrance** to the park is $5 per vehicle, or $3 if you are walking or cycling. For that you get unrestricted entry for seven days, an excellent map and a copy of the biannual *Death Valley National Park* newspaper with up-to-date details on campsites and visitor services.

Most visitor facilities are concentrated in two settlements, both comprised solely of gas stations, motels and grocery stores. The busiest of the two, **FURNACE WELLS**, is right in the centre of the valley and has an excellent **visitor center** (winter daily 8am–7pm; ☎786-2331) with a small but interesting **museum** (same hours; free). **STOVEPIPE WELLS**, 25 miles to the northwest, is slightly smaller. More information is available from the **ranger stations** close to the park boundaries. The main ones are on the west side at *Wildrose Campground* on Hwy-178; at *Emigrant Campground* near Stovepipe Wells on Hwy-190; and on the northern edge of the park at Scotty's Castle.

## Accommodation and eating

To get the full impact of a desert visit you really need to **camp** out. For most of the year you don't even need a tent – it isn't going to rain – though a sleeping bag is a good idea. Camping is also much the cheapest way to stay in Death Valley: all the camp-grounds are operated by the National Park Service and most cost $6 a night, while sites without a water supply are free. If camping isn't an option you are limited to fairly expensive **hotels** and **motels** inside the park, or lower-cost possibilities on the fringes. Reservations should be made as early as possible, especially during peak holiday peri-ods. The following listing covers all the rooms in the park and the settlements nearby, but also see Lone Pine (p.257) for accommodation slightly further afield.

### Hotels, motels and hostels

**Amargosa Hotel**, Death Valley Junction (☎852-4441). Pleasantly run-down adobe hotel built by the Pacific Coast Borax Company in 1924. It has no TVs or phones, but boasts an attached opera house (see above). Ask to see a few rooms before choosing as they vary enormously – there's a *trompe l'oeil* wardrobe in the *Jezabel* room and cherubs in the *Baroque* . ③.

**El Portal Motel**, Beatty, Nevada (☎702/553-2912). Decent motel on the west side of town with reduced prices in summer. ②.

**Furnace Creek Inn**, Furnace Creek (☎786-2345). *The* place to stay if you're in the Valley with money to burn. Beautifully sited amid palms, with great views and plush rooms at a price. Closed from mid-May to mid-October. ⑨.

**Furnace Creek Ranch**, Furnace Creek (☎786-2345). Cheaper than the *Inn* , but redolent of a holi-day camp and with no sense of being in a desert. Open all year but overpriced for what are comfort-able but ordinary motel rooms – especially in summer when the cheaper rooms are closed. ④–⑤.

---

**CAMPING IN DEATH VALLEY**

Most sites cannot be reserved and stays are limited to thirty days (so that people don't move in for the winter). Take note of the altitude listed for each, as this indicates the kind of temperatures you can expect.

The main sites are at **Furnace Creek** ($10; open all year; – 196ft; reservable Oct–April through *MISTIX*) which fills up very early each day in winter; the enormous **Sunset** ($6; Oct–April; –190ft) and the designated "quiet" **Texas Spring** ($6; Oct–April; -190ft), both close to Furnace Creek; and at **Stovepipe Wells** ($6; Oct–April; sea level) – though the smaller and relatively shady site at **Mesquite Spring** ($6; all year; 1800ft), near Scotty's Castle on the north side of the park, is much more pleasant. There is one free site with water, **Emigrant** (Oct–April; 2100ft), eight miles west of Stovepipe Wells. This is on the way to the only place with guaranteed shade, the canyons on the forested slopes of Telescope Peak, on the western edge of the park. Here there are three free sites, **Wildrose** (all year, water available April–Nov; 4100ft), **Thorndike** (open March–Nov; 7500ft) and **Mahogany Flat** (March–Nov; 8200ft), just off the mostly paved Wildrose Road. The upper two are (just) accessible in ordinary cars, but high clearance or four-wheel-drive vehicles are better.

**Fires** are allowed in all sites except *Sunset, Stovepipe Wells* and *Emigrant*, but designated fireplaces must be used and no collecting of firewood is allowed.

Free **backcountry camping** is allowed in most areas of the park provided you keep a mile away from any roads (paved or otherwise) and a quarter of a mile from water sources. No permits are required, but voluntary backcountry **registration** is recommended.

---

**HI-Desertaire Home Hostel**, Old Spanish Trail, Tecopa (☎852-4580). A relaxed hostel an hour south of Furnace Creek. There are only six beds, but you can sleep outside in the warm desert air in a wooden tower with commanding views of the surrounding desert. Book the first night by phone or by writing to PO Box 306, Tecopa, CA 92389. ①.

**Panamint Springs Motel**, Panamint Springs (no phone). Basic motel 35 miles west of Stovepipe Wells. No pool, though one is planned. ③.

**Shoshone Inn**, Shoshone (☎852-4335). Reasonable motel with pool an hour south of Furnace Creek on Hwy-127 and near Tecopa Hot Springs. ③.

**Stagecoach Motel**, Beatty, Nevada (☎702/553-2419). Pleasant motel on the east side of town. ②.

**Stovepipe Wells Motel**, Stovepipe Wells (☎786-2387). Motel with comfortable rooms and a pool. ③–④.

## Eating

There's not a great variety of **places to eat** in Death Valley – you're limited to the hotel dining rooms and restaurants at Furnace Creek and Stovepipe Wells, all of which are fairly pricey. *Furnace Creek Ranch* is the only place with any choice: *Señor Coyote's International Restaurant*, which does good-value meals until 10pm, and *Tino's* Italian restaurant. To quench a **thirst** after a day in the sun, do as the few locals do and head to the *Corkscrew Saloon*, also at *Furnace Creek Ranch* and open until 1am. There's also an expensive grocery store here, and another at Stovepipe Wells.

# Exploring Death Valley

You can get an unforgettable feel for Death Valley just by passing through, and you could quite easily see almost everything in a day. If you have the time, though, aim to spend at least a night here, if possible camped out somewhere far from the main centres of activity. Even if you've got your own car, the best way to experience the huge and empty spaces and the unique landforms of Death Valley is to leave the roads and crowds behind and wander off – taking care to remember the way back. Sunrise and sunset are the best times to experience the colour that's bleached out by the midday sun, and they're also the most likely times for seeing the wildlife, mostly lizards, snakes and small rodents, which hide out through the heat of the day.

## Along the Badwater road

Many of the park's most unusual sights are located south of Furnace Creek along to the road to Badwater, which forks off Hwy-190 by the *Furnace Creek Inn*. Pick up a self-guided tour booklet (50¢) from a box at the junction. A good first stop, two miles along, is **Golden Canyon**. Periodic rainstorms over the centuries have washed a slot-shaped gully through the clay and silt here, revealing golden-hued walls that are particularly vibrant in the early evening. A three-quarter-mile-long interpretive trail winds into the U-shaped upper canyon, and a hike to Zabriskie Point (see box on p.256) continues from there.

Five miles further on, signs point to **Artist's Drive**, a tortuous one-way loop road, perhaps best left until the drive back, especially if this means catching the afternoon sun on the **Artist's Palette**, an evocatively eroded hillside covered in an intensely coloured mosaic of reds, golds, blacks and greens.

A couple of miles further south, a dirt road leads a mile to the **Devil's Golf Course**, a weird field of salt pinnacles and hummocks protruding a couple of feet from the desert floor. Capillary action draws saline solutions from below the surface where alternate layers of salt and alluvial deposits from ancient lakes have been laid down over the millennia. As the occasional rainfall evaporates, the salt accretes to form a landscape as little like a golf course as you could imagine.

It is another four miles south to **Badwater**, an unpalatable but non-poisonous thirty-foot-wide pool of water, loaded with chloride and sulphates, that's also the only home of the endangered, soft-bodied Death Valley snail and a species of tiny fish. Notice how much hotter it feels in the humid air beside the water. From the pool two rather uninteresting hikes, both around four miles long, lead across the hot, flat valley floor to the two **lowest points in the western hemisphere**, both at 282ft below sea level.

## Zabriskie Point and Dante's View

The badlands around **Zabriskie Point**, overlooking Badwater and the Artist's Palette off Hwy-190, four miles south of Furnace Creek, were the inspiration for Antonioni's eponymous 1970 movie. Even so, its sculpted spires of banded rock are less interesting than **Dante's View**, a further 21 miles south off Hwy-190 and then ten miles on a very steep (and very hot) road. At a point almost six thousand feet above the blinding white saltpan of Badwater, the valley floor does indeed look infernal. The view is best during

---

### PARK ACTIVITIES

Besides hiking and sightseeing, Death Valley offers ample opportunities for **mountain biking**. Only roads open to road vehicles are accessible to cyclists (hiking trails are off limits) but this still leaves plenty to go at for those who bring their machine along: there are no rentals available. The map provided with your entry ticket shows the major four-wheel-drive routes: Echo Canyon into the Funeral Mountains and the Inyo Mine, Cottonwood Canyon from Stovepipe Wells, and the Warm Springs Canyon/Butte Valley road in the south of the park are all worthwhile. Topographical maps are available at Furnace Creek visitor center.

**Horse-riding** is laid on by the *Furnace Creek Ranch* for $20 an hour, $30 for two and, when the phase of the moon is right, $25 for an hour-long evening ride.

After a day in the desert, **swimming** in a tepid pool is an ideal way to enjoy a balmy evening. The pools at the *Furnace Creek Ranch* and the *Stovepipe Wells Motel* are open to the public for a $2 fee.

the early morning, when the pink and gold Panamint Mountains across the valley are highlighted by the rising sun.

### North from Furnace Creek

In the township of Furnace Creek you could spend a few minutes in the **Borax Museum** (Mon–Fri 9am–4.30pm; free), which rather ploddingly tells the story of the mineral and its excavation, but you are better advised to head two miles north to the old **Harmony Borax Works** (unrestricted entry) where a quarter-mile interpretive trail tells of the mine and processing plant.

Twelve miles to the north, the **Keane Wonder Mine** and **Keane Wonder Mill** (unrestricted entry to both) were indeed wonderful during their heyday between 1904, when the mine was discovered by Jack Keane, and 1916. $1.1 million worth of gold and silver was extracted at the mountainside mine and worked at in the valley-floor mill, where it was carried down a three-quarter-mile-long aerial tramway which is still more or less intact. From the car park by the remains of the mill, a very steep path climbs alongside the thirteen tramway towers to the lowest of the mineshafts. It is only a mile but seems a lot more in the noonday heat. Don't be tempted to seek shelter in the adits and shafts leading off the path; all are dangerous and most unfenced.

Near Stovepipe Wells on the western side of the park spread the most extensive of the valley's **sand dunes**, some fifteen rippled and contoured square miles of ever changing dunes, just north of Hwy-190 to the east of the campground and ranger station. On the opposite side of Hwy-190 stands the **Devil's Cornfield**, an expanse of tufted grasses quite out of character with its surroundings.

West of the campground, at the end of a ten-mile dirt road, stand the sheer black walls of **Marble Canyon**, on which are scratched ancient and mysterious petroglyph figures.

## Outside the Valley

Some of the best places in the park are well outside the actual valley, notably **Telescope Peak**, on the western side of the park, the ghost town of **Rhyolite** to the east, and **Ubehebe Crater** to the north, an old volcanic crater whose ashen walls have mellowed to an earthy orange tinge. None of these see many tourists: they're well out of the way. **Scotty's Castle**, in contrast, is the most popular single stop in the park, and hordes of overheated tourists brave impending sunstroke waiting in long lines for the chance to wander through the surreal attraction of this unfinished but still luxurious mansion.

### Rhyolite

As ghost towns go, **RHYOLITE**, up a side road three miles west of Beatty, Nevada, is one of the more appealing. Rhyolite was a mining town whose mines were prematurely closed after just four boom years by 1908, due to a combination of mismanagement and thin pickings. By then the town had spread over the hillside (made of the rock which gave the town its name) and had its own train station. The station is still the town's dominant structure, but the remains of other buildings, including a jail, schoolhouse and bank, still stand, as does a **bottle house** built of some fifty thousand beer and spirit bottles in 1906. A more recent attraction is the distinctly off-beam roadside **sculpture garden** (unrestricted access), complete with structures built from car parts and a series of white fibreglass figures arranged in imitation of *The Last Supper*.

Visiting Rhyolite before Scotty's Castle gives you the opportunity to explore the one-way Titus Canyon road which winds past several crumbling lead mines. High-clearance vehicles are recommended.

## Scotty's Castle

On the north edge of the park, 45 miles from the visitor center, **Scotty's Castle** (hourly tours daily 9am–5pm; $8) is an extravagant Spanish Revival castle built during the 1920s as the desert retreat of wealthy Chicago insurance broker Albert Johnson, but known and named after the cowboy, prospector and publicity hound, "Death Valley" Scotty, who managed the construction, and claimed the house was his own, financed by his hidden gold mine. The million-dollar house features intricately carved wooden ceilings, waterfalls in the living room and, most entertaining of all, a remote-controlled player piano; plans for swimming pools and elaborate gardens were shelved when Johnson lost a fortune in the Wall Street Crash of 1929. In winter, you may have to wait as long as three hours for a place on one of the fifty-minute-long **tours** of the opulently furnished house, left pretty much as it was when Johnson died in 1948. Scotty himself lived here until 1954, and is buried on the hill just behind the house: a good place to wander while waiting for your tour.

## Ubehebe Crater, Racetrack Valley and the Eureka Sand Dunes

Five miles west of Scotty's Castle – though it might as well be five hundred miles for all the people who venture a look – gapes the half-mile wide **Ubehebe Crater**, the rust-coloured result of a massive volcanic explosion; a half-mile south sits its thousand-year-old younger brother, **Little Hebe**. Beyond the craters the road (high clearance vehicles recommended) continues west for another 27 dusty miles to **Racetrack Valley**, a two-and-a-half-mile-long mud flat across which giant boulders seem slowly to be racing, leaving faint trails in their wake. Scientists believe that the boulders are pushed along the sometimes icy surface by very high winds; sit and watch (but don't hold your breath) from the rock outcrop at the northern end, known as the **Grandstand**.

The extension of Death Valley into a national park claimed several features formerly outside its boundaries. The **Eureka Sand Dunes**, forty miles northwest of Scotty's Castle, are the most exciting. Far more extensive than those around Stovepipe Wells, these stand up to seven hundred feet above the surrounding land, making them the highest in California and a dramatic place to witness sunrise or sunset. While here, keep your eyes open for the Eureka Dunes Grass and Eureka Dunes Evening Primrose, both endemic to the area and federally protected.

## Skidoo Ghost Town, Wildrose Charcoal Kilns and Telescope Peak

To escape the heat and dust of the desert floor, head up Emigrant Canyon Road, off Hwy-190 in the west, into the Panamint Mountains. Ten miles up the canyon, a nine-mile dirt track turns off to the east toward **Skidoo Ghost Town**. Only a few ruins – and a number of roaming wild mules – remain of what in 1915 was a gold-mining camp of seven hundred people watered by snowmelt from Telescope Peak, 23 miles away, and kept informed by telegraph from Rhyolite. Well above the valley floor, it is tolerably cool but otherwise there's not much going for it.

The main road leads for another, very steep, fifteen miles over Emigrant Pass and down to the Wildrose ranger station and campground. To the right the road leads to Trona and Ridgecrest (see p.244), while a left turn carries you steeply up into the Panamint range, initially on tarmac then on gravel. Five miles beyond the ranger station the **Wildrose Charcoal Kilns** loom into view. This series of ten massive, beehive-shaped stone kilns some 25 feet high was used in the 1880s to make charcoal for use in the smelters of local silver mines. The road continues through juniper and pine forests past the free Thorndike campsite to its end at Mahogany Flat, where there's another free campground and the trailhead for the strenuous hike up **Telescope Peak**, which, at 11,049ft, is the highest – and coolest – point in the park (see box overleaf).

## HIKES IN AND AROUND DEATH VALLEY

Anything more than a short stroll in the desert heat can become an ordeal. This is less true of the Telescope Peak and Wildrose Peak walks in the Panamint Range, but you still need to carry all your water with you. Always register your intended route at the visitor center or any of the ranger stations and for anything a little more adventurous than the walks listed here, get yourself a topographic map from the visitor center. All listed distances and times are for the round trip.

**Golden Canyon to Zabriskie Point** (5 miles; 3hr; 500ft ascent). Start at Golden Canyon and follow the interpretive trail, continuing on an unmaintained, moderately strenuous trail to Zabriskie Point. Done in reverse it is all downhill.

**Mosaic Canyon** (4 miles; 2hr; 300ft ascent). A rough three-mile access road just west of Stovepipe Wells leads to the trailhead for a relatively easy hike through this water-smoothed canyon. There's some scrambling at the upper end.

**Telescope Peak** (14 miles; 8hr; 3000ft ascent). The easy-to-follow but moderately strenuous trail climbs from the trailhead by Mahogany Flat campsite, skirting a pair of 10,000-foot peaks, through bristlecone pines to the summit and its grand panorama of Death Valley and across to Mount Whitney and the eastern face of the Sierra Nevada mountains. Sign the summit register while you admire the view. There's no water en route except for snowmelt (often well into June) which should be treated. Crampons and ice axes may be required in harsh winters, and at all times you should self-register in the book a short way along the trail.

**Wildrose Peak** (8 miles; 5hr; 2000ft ascent). If winter conditions or your own level of fitness rule out Telescope Peak, this hike makes a perfect, easier alternative. Start by the Charcoal Kilns on Wildrose Canyon Road and wind up through piñon pines and juniper to a stunning summit panorama.

## Darwin Falls, Lee Flat and Saline Valley

A mile west of Panamint Springs along Hwy-190, a dirt road leads south to the tumbledown wooden ruins of **DARWIN**, a ghost of a mining town (though forty people still live here) that was built in the 1870s by prospectors searching for seams of silver, inspired by tales of an Indian who repaired an explorer's rifle by fashioning a gunsight out of solid silver. Nearby, and more interesting, are the thirty-foot, spring-fed **Darwin Falls**, reached by following a quarter-mile creekside trail up a small canyon.

You might not expect to see Joshua trees in Death Valley, but **Lee Flat**, a dozen miles west of Panamint Springs, has a whole forest of them on its higher slopes. At this point a dirt road leads north to Saline Valley. The main forest starts eight miles along at lower Lee Flat; a side road branches left to the densest section.

In **Saline Valley** in the far northwest corner of the park, old mine workings and the remains of a dilapidated salt tramway can be seen on your way to the generally clothing-free **hot springs** at Lower Warm Spring and Palm Spring. It's about a fifty-mile trek out here, so be prepared to camp out at the primitive site nearby, mercifully equipped with showers and toilets.

# Mount Whitney

Rising out of the northern reaches of the Mojave Desert, the Sierra Nevada Mountains announce themselves with a bang two hundred miles north of Los Angeles at **Mount Whitney**, the highest point on a silver-grey knifelike ridge of pinnacles that forms a nearly sheer wall of granite, eleven thousand feet above the valley below.

Mount Whitney lies on the eastern border of Sequoia National Park, and its sharply pointed peaks dominate the small roadside town of **Lone Pine** at its feet. The view of the High Sierra summits from the town is fantastic, captured by photographer Ansel Adams in a much-reproduced shot of the full moon suspended above the stark cliffs.

## Lone Pine and around

The town of **LONE PINE** itself is not all that impressive, little more than a string of motels and gas stations straggling along US-395. But it makes a good base for exploring the area, particularly if you're not prepared to camp out, and is also a final supply post for eastbound travellers approaching Death Valley (see p.246-247).

For information on hiking or camping, stop by the **Eastern Sierra Interagency Visitor Center** (June–Aug daily 7am–6.50pm; Sept–May daily 8am–4.50pm; ☎876-6222), a mile south of town on US-395 at the junction of Hwy-136, the Death Valley road. The center has practical and historical information on the whole of eastern California, including the High Sierra, Owens Valley, White Mountains, Death Valley and the latest on mountain and high pass conditions. Most of the region is protected within the massive **Inyo National Forest**, and if you're planning to spend any amount of time in the area, pick up the very helpful **map** ($3), which covers everything between Mount Whitney and Yosemite National Park, including all hiking routes and campgrounds. Interestingly, this is the only map that makes clear the extent of the City of Los Angeles' holdings in the Owens Valley – basically the entire valley floor.

Many early Westerns, and the epic *Gunga Din*, were filmed in the **Alabama Hills** immediately west of Lone Pine, a rugged expanse of sedimentary rock that's been sculpted into bizarre shapes by 160 million years of erosive winds and rains. Some of the oddest formations are linked by the **Picture Rocks Circle**, a paved road that loops around from Whitney Portal Road, passing by rocks shaped like bullfrogs, walruses and baboons; the 100-foot rock faces make it a popular place for rock-climbers to hone their skills. In celebration of its movie heritage, the town now hosts the **Lone Pine Film Festival**, usually in late September or early October, showing only films made here. Contact the Chamber of Commerce for details (see below).

### Practicalities

*Greyhound* buses stop at 107 S Main St. If you're looking for a **motel**, try *Trails Motel* (☎876-5555 or 1-800/524-9999; ②) at 633 S Main St, or the *Frontier Best Western* (☎876-5571 or 1-800/528-1234; ③). Decent **restaurants** along the highway include the *Pizza Factory*, 305 S Main St (☎876-4707), and the *Sierra Cantina*, 123 N Main St (☎876-5740). For hamburgers or a milkshake head for the *Frosty Stop*, 701 S Main St. In summer, the **swimming pool** at the high school opposite is open daily ($2); after a week in the mountains, you can get **cleaned up** at *Kirk's Sierra Barber Shop*, 104 N Main St, where you can take a hot shower for $3. For more **information** on local services, contact the **Chamber of Commerce** at 126 S Main St (Mon–Sat 9am–5pm; ☎876-4444).

# Into the Owens Valley

The **OWENS VALLEY** – stretching from Lone Pine north beyond Bishop – is hot, dry and numinously thrilling: a desolate desert landscape, bordered by parallel ridges of 14,000-foot peaks. It is almost entirely unpopulated outside of the few towns along the highway, though a few solitary souls live in old sheds and caravans off the many dirt roads and tracks that cross the floor of the valley. Years ago the area was a prime spot for growing apples and pears, but since 1913 its plentiful natural water supply, fed by the many streams which run down from the Sierra Nevada, has been drained away to fill the swimming pools of Los Angeles.

## Manzanar Relocation Camp and Independence

Just west of US-395, ten miles north of Lone Pine, on the site of the most productive of the Owens Valley orchards, stand the concrete foundations of the **Manzanar Relocation Camp**, where more than ten thousand Americans of Japanese descent were corralled during World War II. Considering them a threat to national security, the US government uprooted whole familes and confiscated all their property; they were released at the end of the war, though no apology was ever officially offered, and claims for compensation were only settled in 1988, when the government agreed to pay damages amounting to millions of dollars. The camp was once ringed by barbed wire and filled with row upon row of wooden bunkhouses; now only a couple of guard-houses and a small cemetery remain. As the bronze plaque on the guardhouse says: "May the injustices and humiliation suffered here as a result of hysteria, racism and economic exploitation never emerge again".The remains of the camp have now been designated a national historic site (daytime access only; free). Some of the former inmates return each year, on the last Saturday in April, in a kind of pilgrimage.

An evocative and affecting exhibit about Manzanar, detailing the experiences of many of the young children who were held there, is on display inside the **Eastern California Museum** (Wed–Mon 10am–4pm; donation) at 155 N Grant St, three blocks west of the porticoed County Courthouse in the town of **INDEPENDENCE**, six miles further north. The cinder-block museum also has displays on the natural environment of the Owens Valley, including the bighorn sheep that live in the mountains west of town, and exhibits on the region's history, from native Paiute basketry to old mining

---

### CLIMBING MOUNT WHITNEY

Climbing up to the 14,494-foot **summit** of Mount Whitney is a real challenge: it's a very strenuous, 21-mile round trip, made especially difficult by the lack of oxygen in the rare-fied air of what is the highest point in the lower 48 states. Vigorous hikers starting before dawn from the 8000-foot trailhead can be up and back before dark, but a couple of days spent acclimatizing up here is advisable. The trail gains over a mile in elevation, cutting up past alpine lakes to boulder-strewn Trail Crest Pass – the southern end of the 220-mile John Muir Trail that heads north to Yosemite. From the pass it climbs along the clifftops, finally reaching the rounded hump of the summit itself, where a stone cabin serves as an emergency shelter.

Between Memorial Day and mid-October – the only time the trail is normally free of snow – you have to do the whole trip in a day, unless you've booked one of the strictly limited **wilderness permits** which entitle you to spend the night camped out along the route. Apply well in advance to the Mount Whitney Ranger Station, PO Box 8, Lone Pine, CA 93545 (☎876-6200) or Wilderness Reservation Office, Sequoia and King's Canyon National Parks, Three Rivers, CA 93271 (☎209/565-3766). However, a few permits are also handed out on a first-come-first-served basis at the Lone Pine visitor center (see p.257) and no-shows are sometimes available, so it might be worth turning up early on the day – weekdays outside July and August are your best bets. Out of season, self-issue permits are available at the trailhead.

If a full-on slog to the summit doesn't appeal, make the relatively easy six-mile hike to the free, primitive *Trail Camp* at 12,000ft, from where a more manageable pitch for the summit can be made the following day.

Most people **camp** near the trailhead at the easily accesible *Whitney Portal* camp-ground (mid-May to mid-Oct; $10; reserve on ☎1-800/280-2267), thirteen miles west of Lone Pine and served by the *Backpacker Shuttle Service* (contact well in advance on ☎876-5518), which has a combined restaurant and camping-cum-general store, plus showers; or at the nearby *Whitney Trailhead Walk-in* (mid-May to mid-Oct; $5), which has water and toilets.

and farming equipment. There's also a reconstructed pioneer village behind the museum, made up of old buildings from all over the Owens Valley that have been brought together and restored here.

Independence takes its heroic name not from any great libertarian tradition but from a Civil War fort that was founded north of the town on the fourth of July, 1862; every year on that day there's a parade down Main Street followed by a mass barbecue and fireworks show in **Dehy Park**, along tree-shaded Independence Creek on the north side of town. The park is marked by a large and unexciting old steam locomotive, which once ran from here to Nevada on narrow gauge tracks.

### Practicalities

To **stay** here, try the inexpensive *Independence Courthouse Motel* at 157 N Edwards St (☎878-2732 or 1-800/801-0703; ②), or the much more atmospheric 1920s *Winnedumah Hotel*, 211 N Edwards St (☎878-2040; ③). There's a small **campground** ($5) half a mile west of town, reached by following Market Street beside the creek. For **food** stop by *Austin's General Store* at 130 S Edwards St, or (before 9pm), enjoy sandwiches, salads or main meals at the *Whistle Stop* opposite.

## Onwards from Independence

The minor Onion Valley Road leads beyond Independence's campground, twisting up the mountains to **Onion Valley**, ten miles west, where there's the *Onion Valley* **campground** (June to mid-Sept; $7; ☎876-6200) and the trailhead for **hiking** across the Sierra Nevada into Kings Canyon National Park, sixteen miles over Kearsarge Pass to Cedar Grove (see p.290). This is the easiest and shortest route across the Sierra; you can get the required, free wilderness permit from the Lone Pine visitor center (see p.257).

The slopes of Mount Williamson, south of Onion Valley, and of Mount Baxter to the north are the protected home of the rarely seen **California bighorn sheep**: nimble-footed creatures that roam around the steep, rocky slopes and sport massive, curling horns, which can be as large as a car tyre. The **Paiute Monument**, a giant boulder standing on the flat ridge of the Inyo Mountains, six miles east of Independence and clearly visible from US-395, resembles nothing so much as the monolith from the movie *2001*. Local legends tell of how members of the Paiute tribe would hide behind the smaller boulders at its base and ambush wild game that had been chased up from the hills below. There are lots of abandoned mineshafts and poorly marked tunnels at the foot of the mountains, so watch your step.

Ten miles north of Independence is the actual start of the **LA Aqueduct**. Follow any of the dirt tracks that head east from US-395 and you can't fail to spot the abandoned railroad stations built to haul in the material needed to construct the great ditch – which Space Shuttle astronauts claim to have seen while orbiting the globe.

Two-thirds of the way to Big Pine (see below), the **Tinnemaha Wildlife Viewpoint** warrants a brief pause to see if you can spot any of the 500-strong herd of Tule Elk, now-protected California natives which were nearly wiped out by the end of the nineteenth century.

## Big Pine and the White Mountains

The town of **BIG PINE**, thirty miles north, is slightly larger than Independence but has no greater appeal. There are a few gas stations; *Greyhound* buses stop once a day in each direction; and there are a couple of serviceable **motels** along US-395 – the *Big Pine Motel*, 370 S Main St (☎938-2282; ②), and the *Starlight Motel*, 511 S Main St (☎938-2011; ②). There is also the *Triangle* **campground** ($5) half a mile north of town at the junction of Hwy-168, several more up Glacier Lodge Road (see below), and reasonable diner **eating** at the *Country Kitchen*, 181 S Main St. Big Pine is, however, the gateway to two of the most unusual natural phenomena in California: the Palisade Glacier in the Sierra Nevada, west of the town, and the ancient Bristlecone Pine Forest in the barren White Mountains to the east. It is also a jumping off point for the northern section of Death Valley, in particular the Eureka Sand Dunes (see p.256) and the hot springs of the Saline Valley (see p.255).

## The Palisade Glacier

The southernmost glacier in the US, the **Palisade Glacier** sits at the foot of the impressive Palisade Crest, centre of one of the greatest concentrations of enjoyably climbable (though only for the experienced) peaks in the Eastern Sierra. To the south is Norman Clyde Peak, named after California's most prolific early mountaineer; Thunderbolt Peak and Mount Agassiz are highlights of the Inconsolable Range to the north of the glacier, itself an excellent introduction to snow and ice-climbing; while in the centre the immense bulk of Temple Crag offers a range of routes unparalleled outside of Yosemite Valley. The trailhead for all of these climbs, and the many local hikes, is ten miles west of Big Pine, at the end of Glacier Lodge Road, along which there are three, three-season, $9-a-night **campgrounds** – *Sage Flat, Upper Sage Flat* and *Big Creek* – all above 7000ft and with water and toilets; and a free site at 8300ft, a mile from the trailhead. *Glacier Lodge* (☎938-2837; ④), right at the end of the road, is a more luxurious alternative, with a restaurant and general store.

Before heading off into the wilderness, get a backcountry camping **permit** from the small ranger station at *Upper Sage Flat* camp. The icy-white glacier is nine miles from the end of the road on a well-marked trail along the north fork of Big Pine Creek, past a number of alpine lakes.

## The White Mountains

Big Pine is also the gateway to the intimidating **White Mountains**, a bald, dry, unwelcoming range, made up of some of the oldest, fossil-filled rock in California (hundreds of millions of years older than the Sierra), which acts as the eastern wall of the Owens Valley. The mountains are accessible only by car (or bike) via Hwy-168. Be sure to fill up on gas and **drinking water**, both of which are unavailable east of US-395. The highest point in the range, White Mountain, rises to a height of 14,246ft. Near the summit, a strenuous fifteen-mile hike from the end of a long dusty road, a research station (closed to the public) studies the physiology of high-altitude plant and animal life, which is in many ways similar to that of the arctic regions.

The gnarled trees that are the prime reason for coming here stand on the lower slopes in the ancient **Bristlecone Pine Forest**, but snow renders them inaccessible for all but three or four months in the summer. **Schulman Grove**, named after Dr Edmund Schulman who discovered and dated the trees in the mid-1950s, is the most accessible collection, at the end of the paved road that twists up from Hwy-168. The grove is split up into two self-guided nature trails. One, the mile-long Discovery Trail, passes by a number of splendid examples; the other, longer Methuselah Trail loops around past the oldest tree, the 4700-year-old Methuselah, and a small visitor center. **Patriarch Grove**, eleven miles further on, along a dusty dirt road that gives spectacular views of the Sierra Nevada to the west and the Great Basin ranges of the deserts to the east, contains the Patriarch Tree, the largest bristlecone pine.

Three miles beyond here, a gate prevents unauthorized vehicles from getting to the research station on the summit, though hikers and all-terrain **mountain bikes** are permitted to continue. In fact, the steep canyons running down from the ridge are tailor-made for thrill-seekers, who race down the steep washes at incredibly high speed. **Silver Canyon**, descending from just beyond Schulman Grove, is the route

## BRISTLECONE PINES

Bristlecone pines (*pinus longaeva*) are the oldest known living things on earth. Some of them have been alive for over four and a half thousand years (1500 years more than any sequoia), earning them a place in the *Guinness Book of Records*. The oldest examples cling to thin alkaline soils (predominantly dolomite) between 10,000 and 11,000 feet, where the low precipitation keeps the growing season to only 45 days a year. But such conditions, which limit the trees' girth expansion to an inch every hundred years, promotes the dense resin-rich and rot resistant wood that lasts for millennia. Battered and beaten by the harsh environment into bizarrely beautiful shapes and forms, they look like nothing so much as twenty-foot lumps of driftwood. The most photogenic examples comprise mostly dead wood, the live section often sustained by a thin ribbon of bark. Even when dead the wind-scoured trunks and twisted limbs hang on without decaying for upwards of another thousand-odd years, slowly being eroded by wind-driven ice and sand.

Bristlecones thrive at lower altitudes and in richer soils, but more rapid growth exhausts them much sooner. The fat and tall trees are barely recognizable as bristlecones to the untrained eye, though the five-needle bundles and the egg-shaped, barbed cone which lends the tree its name give the game away.

taken by the **Plumline Outback** – a rigorous mountain bike race – held each July; cyclists begin in Bishop, race up to the ridge and career back down again.

There is **camping** available, but no water; the only campground is 8600ft up at *Grandview* (May–Oct; free), two miles south of Schulman Grove. Backcountry camping is not permitted in the ancient Bristlecone Pine Forest, but elsewhere backpackers will need to obtain a free wilderness permit from the ranger station in Bishop, which can also tell you which springs and small creeks (if any) are flowing.

## Bishop

**BISHOP**, to a Californian, means outdoor pursuits. The largest town (population 3500) in the Owens Valley, it's an excellent base from which to explore the mountains that surround it; and if you want to try rock-climbing, hang-gliding, cross-country skiing or fly-fishing, there's no better place to be, with some of the world's best mountaineers offering their services through lessons and guided trips.

Bishop's best feature is its proximity to the wilderness, but there's also a laid-back ambience to the town which is worth hanging around to enjoy. It's an easy place to get to, with *Greyhound* calling at the station at 201 S Warren St (☎872-2721) and a *Dial-a-ride* service (☎872-1901 or 1-800/922-1930) to get you out to the trailheads.

Finding a **place to stay** is no problem either. The **visitor center** at 690 N Main St (Mon–Fri 9am–5pm, Sat & Sun 10am–4pm; ☎873-8405) on the north side of town has a visitor guide listing accommodation, most of it within a block of US-395 (Main Street through the town). The best budget options are the *El Rancho Motel*, 274 W Lagoon St on the south side of town (☎872-9251; ②), and the *Thunderbird Motel*, 190 W Pine St (☎1-800/82-TBIRD; ②); the *Creekside Inn*, 725 N Main St (☎872-3044; ③) offers large rooms and a complimentary breakfast.

With a 24-hour *Vons* store at 174 S Main St, and a number of cafés and diners, Bishop is a good spot to buy **food and supplies**. *Jack's Waffle Shop*, 437 N Main St, is open seven fluorescent-lit days a week for breakfasts and burgers. For good espresso and pastries, head to the pseudo-Dutch *Erick Schat's Bakkerij*, 736 N Main St (☎873-7156); and for lunch and dinner try *Bar-B-Q Bill's* at 187 S Main St (☎872-5535), *Pucchetti's Italian Café*, 772 N Main St, or the excellent *Whiskey Creek*, 524 N Main St (☎873-7174), which also has a lively **bar** open till 2am.

For information on **hiking** and **camping** in the area, contact the *White Mountain Ranger Station* at 798 N Main St (July to mid-Sept 7am–5pm; rest of year Mon–Fri 8am–4.30pm; ☎873-2500), which also issues the obligatory free wilderness permits. Another place worth a stop is *Wilson's East Side Sports*, an excellent mountaineering and sporting goods supply shop at 206 N Main St (☎873-7520). Hikers and backcountry campers in need of a **shower** can get one at the *Bishop City Pool* (Mon–Sat 7am–8pm; $1).

## Around Bishop

US-6 heads north and east from Bishop into Nevada, passing by the **Laws Railroad Museum** (daily 10am–4pm; donation), a restoration of the old town of **Laws**, five miles off US-395, with some old buildings and a slender black narrow-gauge train that used to run along the eastern edge of the Owens Valley. It's worth a quick look on your way to see the **Red Rock Canyon Petroglyphs**, four miles west of US-6; the rock carvings have been terribly vandalized, but enough remains of the spacey figures to justify a trip. Obtain a free permit from the Bureau of Lands Management, Suite E, 785 N Main St in Bishop (☎872-4881).

There are petroglyphs all over the Owens Valley – about the only sign of the Paiute peoples that once roamed the area, hunting and gathering and living off the land. Their descendants have been gathered in reservations outside each of the valley towns, the largest just west of Bishop along Hwy-168, where they've established the **Paiute Shoshone Indian Cultural Center** at 2300 W Line St, (Mon–Fri 9am–5pm, Sat & Sun 9am–4pm; donation). Here they put on displays of basketry and weaving, food gathering and processing, and of traditional ways of building; they also run a good bookstore.

Further west along this road, which runs up into the foothills of the Sierra Nevada, there are a number of **campgrounds** between 7500 and 9000 feet up – almost all with water and costing $10–11 a night. The shady *Sabrina* site, right by the lake of the same name, is perhaps the best.

A number of **hiking routes** set off up into the High Sierra wilderness from the end of the road. The trail from South Lake over Bishop Pass heads into Dusy Basin, where you can see the effects of centuries of glaciation in the bowl-like cirques and giant "erratic" boulders, left by receding glaciers. Another path follows the northern fork of Bishop Creek under the rusty cliffs of the Paiute Crags, before climbing over Paiute Pass into the Desolation Lakes area of the John Muir Wilderness.

## North towards Mammoth

**North of Bishop** US-395 climbs out of the Owens Valley up Sherwin Grade onto the 6500-foot-high Mono Basin. Eighteen miles north of Bishop, at the foot of the climb, Gorge Road leas west into the thousand foot deep **Owens River Gorge**, one of the best climbing spots on this side of the Sierra.

Much more of the money that flows into Bishop comes from the brigades of fishing enthusiasts, who spend their summer vacations angling for rainbow trout placed in the streams and lakes by the state government. The largest assembly of fisherfolk gather on the last Saturday in April around **Lake Crowley**, an artificial reservoir built to hold water diverted from Mono Lake, thirty miles north of town.

Just east of US-395, a mile south of the exit for Mammoth Lakes, is one of the more pleasurable and easily accessible examples of the region's volcanic activity in the hot springs that bubble up at **Hot Creek** (daily dawn–dusk; free). Jets of boiling water mix with the otherwise chilly, snow-melt water to form pools ranging from tepid to scalding; you have to search to find a happy medium, and it's a bit of a challenge since the flows are ever-changing (note, too, that the US Forest Service discourages bathing, as chemicals are sometimes produced in the springs not that anyone takes any notice). Paths and wooden steps lead down to the most likely spots, but wear shoes, because idiots have shattered bottles under the water. This is one of the best, and best known springs in the region; details of others appear in George William's *Hot Springs of the Eastern Sierra*, found in the area's bookshops and visitor centers.

# Mammoth Lakes and around

During winter, masses of weekend skiers speed through the Owens Valley from LA on their way to the slopes of Mammoth Mountain, forty miles north along US-395 from Bishop then five miles west on Hwy-203, above the resort town of **MAMMOTH LAKES**. Outside the Lake Tahoe basin this is the state's premier ski mountain, and it is for this and the summer fishing that Mammoth is traditionally known, although it now also hosts an increasing number of on- and off-road bike races. In short, Mammoth is an unbeatable spot for outdoor activities and is scenically as dramatic as just about anywhere in the Sierra.

With one of the longest Californian seasons (often stretching well into June), 2200 vertical feet of skiing and more than its fair share of deep powder, **Mammoth Mountain** is justly popular. Pick up **lift tickets** ($43 per day) from the Main Lodge on Minaret Road, where you can also rent **equipment** ($25 for basic skis, boots and poles), and book **lessons** ($25 per half-day). Without a ski pass, a cable car ride to the 11,053-foot summit will set you back $10.

In summer, fifty miles of snow-free ski slopes transform themselves into the 3500-acre **Mammoth Mountain Bike Park** ($12 a day for trail access, $20 for trails and the cable car, $35 a day for bike rental), likely to give avid mountain bikers the thrill of their lives. The season's highlight is the massive *World Cup* event held over the Fourth of July weekend, which features the *kamikaze*, the ultimate downhill race with speeds hitting sixty miles per hour. August sees the family-oriented *Adventure Week* (☎934-3068 or 1-800/367-6572 for information) with guided tours, night rides and special children's events. There's also 32-foot-high artificial **climbing rock** in town; details of this and further sporting activities appear in the box below. On a less energetic but equally lively note, the annual *Jazz Jubilee*, held in the second week in July (details on ☎934-2478), also packs the town out with trad-jazz types.

The daily *Greyhound* stops in the *McDonald's* parking lot on Hwy-203. During the ski season, get around on the four-line *Mammoth Shuttle* (☎934-0687). In summer, **rent a bike** (see box).

The best source of practical information for the area is the combined US Forest Service and Mammoth Lakes **visitor center** (summer daily 6am–5pm; rest of year daily 8am–4.30pm; ☎924-5500) on the main highway half a mile east of the town centre.

### Devil's Postpile National Monument

The evocatively named **Devil's Postpile National Monument** (free), ten miles west of town, is accessible in summer only, via a *Mammoth Shuttle* bus ($7) leaving every half-hour from *Mammoth Mountain Inn*, or by car along Minaret Road. A collection of slender, blue-grey basalt columns, some as tall as sixty feet, the Postpile was formed as lava from the eruption of Mammoth Mountain (really a volcano) cooled and fractured into multi-sided forms. The highlight of the monument is **Rainbow Falls**, reached by a two-mile hike through Red's Meadow and along the Middle Fork of the San Joaquin River, which drops over a hundred feet into a deep pool, the spray reflecting and refracting, especially at midday, to earn its name. The adjacent **Minarets Wilderness** is named after the spiky volcanic ridge just south of pointed Mount Ritter – one of the Sierra's most enticing high peaks.

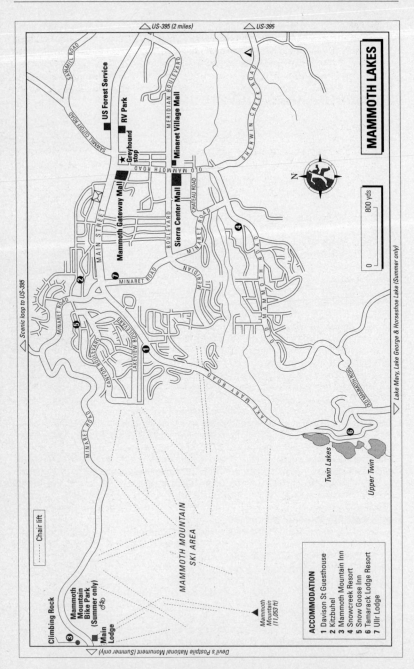

MAMMOTH LAKES

ACCOMMODATION
1 Davison St Guesthouse
2 Kitzbuhel
3 Mammoth Mountain Inn
4 Snowcreek Resort
5 Snow Goose Inn
6 Tamarack Lodge Resort
7 Ullr Lodge

## June Lake

The bustle of Mammoth Lakes sends a select group of skiers and summer visitors a few miles further north to the relative solitude of **June Lake** and its neighbours, Grant, Silver and Gull lakes. Reached by way of the seventeen-mile **June Lake Loop** road, which branches off US-395 thirteen miles north of the Mammoth turning, this region of high-altitude lakes is some of the most striking in these parts, and offers Mammoth's attractions on a more manageable scale.

## Accommodation

Mammoth offers so many **accommodation** opportunities, including three hostels, that beds are at a premium only during peak-season weekends. Winter prices are highest, summer rates (quoted here) come next, and in between some real bargains can be found. Campers should head for any of a number of the **campgrounds** close to the Devil's Postpile National Monument or in the Red's Meadow area. All have water and cost from $8 to $11. There's also excellent camping and backpacking in the Minarets Wilderness.

**Davison St Guesthouse**, Davison St, off Main Street (☎544-9093). Wooden A-frame chalet with mountain views. Four-bed rooms and dorm space from $15, with a kitchen available for guests' use. ①–③.

**Kitzbuhel**, Berner Sreet, off Minaret Rd (☎934-2352). Marginally the cheapest and probably the best of Mammoth's hostels with dorm beds from $10. There's a cooking area, Jacuzzi and large sitting room. Usually closed midweek in spring and fall. ①/②.

**Mammoth Mountain Inn**, Mammoth Mountain (☎934-2581 or 1-800/228-4947). *The* place to stay – right where the action is at the foot of the ski tows, adjacent to the bike park and overlooking the climbing rock. It's a touch sterile but you'll be well looked after. ⑤.

### ADVENTURE TRAVEL SPECIALISTS IN BISHOP, MAMMOTH LAKES AND AROUND

**Cross-country Ski Lodges** A number of backcountry lodges offer accommodation, skiing trips, instruction and rentals. Try *Rock Creek Winter Lodge*, PO Box 5, Mammoth Lakes 93546 (☎935-4452), or the *Tioga Pass Winter Resort*, PO Box 330, Lee Vining 93521 (☎209/379-2420).

**Ballooning** *Mammoth Balloon Adventures* (☎934-2060).

**Hang-gliding** Lessons and tandem flights offered by *Owens Valley Soaring*, 520 S Westridge, Bishop (☎387-2673).

**Kayaking** *Caldera Kayaks* (☎935-4942) based at Crowley Lake Marina runs guided kayak trips on Mono and Crowley lakes ($55) and rents out gear for $25–40 a day.

**Mountain Bike Tours and Rental** *Mammoth Adventure Connection* (☎934-0606) and *Cindy Whitehead Bike Services* (☎924-2955) both lead guided off-road treks and run instruction clinics for about $20 each per hour for two or more people.

**Mountaineering and Rock-climbing Guides** For expert instruction or guided trips in the High Sierra backcountry contact Tim Villanueva (☎872-4413), John Fischer (☎873-5037), or Todd Vogel (☎873-8526), all in Bishop, or Robert Parker (☎935-4921) in Mammoth. All cover rock climbing, alpine climbing and ski mountaineering and rates start from around $100 a day for one person, dropping rapidly as the size of the group increases. *Adventure Associates Inc* (☎924-5683) operates Mammoth's **climbing rock** ($12 per hour, $20 per day, group discounts) and rents sticky boots for $3. The rock is first-come-first-served, but reservations are recommended for ropes and orienteering courses.

**Pack Mules** If you want to enjoy the wilderness without the burden of a heavy backpack, for around $60 per day you join a mule train carrying your load from a number of outfits on both sides of the Sierra. Try *Pine Creek Pack Trains* (☎387-2797) and at Mammoth *Red's Meadow Pack Station* (☎934-2345 or 1-800/292-7758).

---

### SIERRA PASS CLOSURES

After coming through the Mojave or Death Valley it seems hard to imagine that many of the passes across the Sierra Nevada can remain closed well into June. Traditionally Memorial Day is the date for the **Tioga Pass** (into Yosemite) just below Mono Lake, to open, but harsh winters leave it closed until early July. Passes to the north of here, Hwy-108 and Hwy-4, tend to open a couple of weeks earlier, in mid-May; Hwy-88, yet further north, stays open all year. All close again with the first heavy snowfall, perhaps around mid-October. For information on the state of the highways call *CalTrans* on ☎1-800/427-ROAD (see box on p.27).

---

**Snowcreek Resort**, Old Mammoth Road, by the golf course (☎934-3333 or 1-800/544-6007). Well-appointed condos with a two-night minimum stay, spring and fall discounts (3 nights for 2), and use of the pool, spa and tennis club. Especially good value for groups. ⑥.

**Snow Goose Inn**, 57 Forest Trail (☎934-2660 or 1-800/874-7368). The pick of the bed and break-fast places. ④.

**Tamarack Lodge Resort**, Lake Mary Road (☎934-2442 or 1-800/237-6879). Rustic cabins with fully-equippped kitchens, beautifully situated beside Twin Lake right on the edge of a cross-country ski area. ④.

**ULLR Lodge**, 5920 Minaret Rd (☎934-2454). Private rooms from $20 midweek in summer, and popular 4-bed dorms with lockers. Showers are available to non-residents for $4. ①–③.

### Eating, drinking and nightlife

**Restaurants** are plentiful here, and for a ski resort, they're reasonably priced too, though the snack bars actually on the mountain are less competitive. To stock up on **groceries**, head for *Vons*, in the Minaret Village Mall. A couple of good **bars**, some with live **music**, provide entertainment after a day's activity.

**Giovanni's**, Vons Shopping Center, Old Mammoth Road (☎934-7563). The first stop for main-stream pasta and pizza at reasonable prices.

**Kegs and Cues**, Mammoth Gateway Mall (☎934-CUES). Eleven full-size pool tables to keep you away from the serious drinking. Open until 2am.

**Looney Bean Coffee Roasting Co.**, Main Street (☎934-1345). Great speciality teas and coffee – try the *Java Jerk* pick-me-up. Open until 11pm at weekends, later in the ski season.

**Moostachio Pete's**, Sierra Center Mall, Second Floor (☎934-6090). Classy northern Italian cuisine in this restaurant/bar co-owned by jazz supremo Joe Sample. Live jazz and blues to follow, Tues–Sun in ski season, Thurs–Sat in summer. Moderate to expensive.

**O'Kelly and Dunn**, Minaret Village Mall (☎934-9316). The world's cuisines are plundered for imaginative, moderately priced combinations of the best ingredients. Try the Louisiana bread pudding in bourbon. Also open for great breakfasts.

**Schat's Bakery & Café**, 3305 Main St (☎934-6055). Easily the best baked goods in town.

**The Stove**, 644 Old Mammoth Rd, opposite the Sherwin Plaza (☎934-2821). Long-standing Mammoth favourite, serving egg, waffle and pancake breakfasts, sandwiches and full meals later on – all served in massive portions.

**Whiskey Creek**, Main St and Minaret Rd (☎934-2555). One of the town's liveliest bars and restau-rants, with a new micro-brewery and bands Wed–Sun in winter, Thurs–Sat in summer.

---

# Mono Lake

The blue expanse of **Mono Lake** sits in the midst of a volcanic, desert tableland, its sixty square miles reflecting the statuesque, snowcapped mass of the eastern Sierra Nevada. At close on a million years old, it's an ancient lake, one of the oldest in North America, with two large volcanic islands, the light-coloured **Pahoa** and the shiny black **Negit**, surrounded by salty, alkaline water. It resembles nothing more than a science-fiction landscape, with great towers and spires formed by mineral deposits ringing the shores; hot springs surround the lake, and all around the basin are signs of lava flows and volcanic activity, especially in the cones of the Mono Craters, just to the south.

The lake's most distinctive feature, the strange, sandcastle-like **tufa** formations, have been exposed over the past fifty years or so since the City of Los Angeles began draining away the waters that flow into the lake (see box). The towers of tufa were formed underwater, where calcium-bearing freshwater springs well up through the carbonate-rich lake water; the calcium and carbonate combine and sink to the bottom as limestone, slowly growing into the weird formations you can see today. Before striking out for a close look at the lake and its tufa, call in at the excellent **Mono Basin Scenic Area Visitor Center**, a mile north of Lee Vining beside US-395 (May–Oct daily 9am–5pm; Nov–April Sat & Sun 9.30am–4.30pm; ☎647-3044). Here exhibits and a good short film detail the lake's geology, and rangers give talks on various aspects of its ecology. The center is also the place to check the free **guided walks** (July to early Sept daily 10am & 1pm) which leave from the **South Tufa Reserve**, one of the best places to look at the tufa spires, four miles east of US-395 via Hwy-120. Also here is **Navy Beach**, where you can float in salty water three times as buoyant as sea water. Adjacent to the south shore of the lake stands the **Panum Crater**, a 700-year-old

---

## THE BATTLE FOR MONO LAKE

At around a million years old, Mono Lake is one of the oldest bodies of water on the continent. It has survived several ice ages and all the volcanic activity that the area can throw at it, but the lake's biggest threat is the City of Los Angeles, which owns the riparian rights to Mono Lake's catchment. In 1941, the Los Angeles Department of Water and Power diverted four of the six streams that fed the lake into its Owens Valley Aqueduct, which drains the Mono Basin through an eleven-mile tunnel. This was an engineering marvel, dug through the volcanically active Mono Craters, but it's been overshadowed by the legal battle surrounding the depletion of the lake itself, still one of the biggest environmental controversies raging in California.

The **water level** in Mono Lake has dropped over forty feet since 1941, a disaster not only because of the lake's unique beauty, but also because Mono Lake is the primary nesting ground for California Gulls and a prime stopover point for thousands of migratory geese, ducks and swans. Mono Lake is now roughly half its natural size, and as the levels drop, the islands in the middle of the lake where the gulls lay their eggs become peninsulas, and the colonies fall prey to coyotes and other mainland predators. Also, as less fresh water reaches the lake, the landlocked water becomes increasingly alkaline, threatening the unique local ecosystem. Brine shrimp and alkali flies are about all that will thrive in the harsh conditions, but these are critical to the birdlife. Humans are not immune to the harmful effects: winds blowing across the salt pans left behind by the receding lake create clouds containing selenium and arsenic, both contributors to lung disease.

Seemingly oblivious to the plight of the lake, the City of Los Angeles built a second aqueduct in 1970 and the water level dropped even faster, sometimes falling eighteen inches. Prompted by scientific reports of an impending ecological disaster, a small group of activists set up the Mono Lake Committee in 1978, fighting for the preservation of this unique ecosystem partly through publicity campaigns – "Save Mono Lake" bumper stickers were once *de rigueur* for concerned citizens – and partly through the courts. Though the California Supreme Court declared in 1983 that Mono Lake must be saved, it wasn't until 1991 that emergency action was taken. A target water height of 6377ft above sea level (later raised to 6392ft) was grudgingly agreed to make Negit Island once again safe for nesting birds. Streams dry for decades are now flowing again, but it will be several years before the target levels are reached .

volcano riddled with deep fissures and fifty-foot towers of lava, visited on two short and fairly easy trials, the **Plug Trail** and **Rim Trail**.

On the north shore of the lake, three miles along US-395, stands **Mono Lake Country Park**, where a guided boardwalk trail ($2 donation) leads down to the lakefront and the best examples of mushroom-shaped tufa towers. Accessible by trail from the country park, or by a two-mile dirt road off Hwy-167, **Black Point** is the result of a massive eruption of molten lava some thirteen thousand years ago. As the lava cooled and contracted, cracks and fissures formed on the top, some only a few feet wide but as much as fifty feet deep.

Regular **canoe trips** (mid-June to mid-Sept Sat & Sun at 8am, 9.30am & 11am; $12; reservations recommended ☎647-6595) give a closer look at what the lake has to offer.

### Lee Vining

Within easy walking distance of Mono Lake, the small town of **LEE VINING** offers the usual range of visitor services along either side of US-395, and not a great deal more. *Greyhound* buses from the south stop daily in Lee Vining at 2.30am (there's no terminal in town, so simply flag the bus down from outside the *Lee Vining Supermarket*). It's better to arrive from the north on the bus from Reno, which comes in at the more reasonable 11am. The town's **Mono Lake Committee Information Center** (July to early Sept daily 9am–9pm; early Sept to June 9am–5pm; ☎647-6595) is primarily the shop window for the Committee's battle for Mono Lake, but also has helpful staff and many books on the Eastern Sierra.There are a couple of **motels** along US-395: *El Mono Motel* (☎647-6310; ②) and *Murphey's* (☎647-6316; ②). A number of **campgrounds** lie along Lee Vining Creek off Tioga Pass Road, Hwy-120, while the *Mono Vista RV Park* (☎647-6401; $12) is on US-395 just north of town. Stop by the **ranger station** (June–Aug daily 8am–4.30pm; Sept–May Mon–Fri 8am–4.30pm; ☎647-3000) a mile west of town to pick up wilderness permits for backcountry camping. **Eat** at *Nicely's Restaurant* on US-395 (☎647-6477), a great Fifties vinyl palace that opens at 6am.

# Bodie Ghost Town and Bridgeport

In the 1870s the gold-mining town of **BODIE** boasted three breweries, some sixty saloons and dance halls and a population of ten thousand, with a well-earned reputation as the raunchiest and most lawless mining camp in the West. Contemporary accounts describe a town that ended each day with a shootout on Main Street, and church bells, rung once for every year of a murdered man's life, that seemed never to stop sounding. The town boomed for less than ten years, from 1877 when a fairly poor existing mine collapsed exposing an enormously rich vein. Within four years this was the second largest town in the state after San Francisco, even supporting its own Chinatown. By 1885, the population was down to three thousand, and the gold and silver – a total now valued at over $750 million – was all but mined out. A series of fires progressively destroyed the town, and it was evacuated and closed down in 1942. What remains has been turned into the **Bodie Ghost Town and State Park** ($5 per car and $1 for a good self-guided tour booklet; ☎647-6445), thirteen miles (three of them dirt) along Hwy-270, which branches off US-395 eighteen miles north of Lee Vining. The park is open throughout the year (usually June–Aug 8am–7pm, Sept–May 10am–4pm), but phone for the current hours and road conditions, as snow often prevents easy access between December and April.

There are over 150 wooden buildings – about six percent of the original town – surviving in a state of arrested decay around the intact town centre. Some buildings have been re-roofed and others supported in some way, but it is by and large a faithful preservation: even the dirty dishes are much as they were in the 1940s, little damaged by fifty years of weathering. The **Miner's Union Building** on Main Street was the centre of the town's social life: founded in 1877, the union was one of the first in California, organized by workers at the Standard and Midnight mines. The building now houses a small **museum** (free), which paints a graphic picture of mining life. Occasional free **tours** depart from here in the summer, calling at the Methodist church with its surprisingly intact pipe organ, the general store with its beautiful pressed-steel ceiling, and the saloon.

Bodie is far enough out of the way for its evocatively derelict structures to be relatively free of other tourists (although August can be busy), giving the place an authentically eerie atmosphere absent from other US ghost towns. The place should keep you entertained for a few hours, so remember to bring all you need; there's no food available out here and the drinking fountains often fail.

The nearest facilities to Bodie are back on US-395, a mile beyond the Hwy-270 turn-off, at **Virginia Creek Settlement**, essentially just a campground (tent sites $10), a decent motel (☎932-7780; April–Oct only; ③) and an inexpensive Italian restaurant.

## Bridgeport

Six miles further on is the mountain hamlet of **BRIDGEPORT** – an isolated village that provided the new start in life for fugitive Robert Mitchum in the *film noir* masterpiece *Out of the Past*. The gas station he owned in the film is long gone, though the place is otherwise little changed, a pretty little community of ranchers and fishermen, worth stopping at for a look at the dainty white 1880 **County Courthouse** and the small local history **museum** (May–Sept daily 10am–5pm; $1), nearby in a restored old schoolhouse. Bridgeport **accommodation** ranges from a comfortable B&B, *The Cain House*, 340 Main St (☎932-7040 or 1-800/433-CAIN; ⑤), through decent motels such as the *Silver Maple Inn*, 310 Main St (☎932-7383 or 1-800/688-3351; ③) to the decidedly decrepit *Victoria House*, Main St (☎932-7020; ②), a building, which like several places in Bridgeport, is said to have been transported here from Bodie. For **eating**, *Hays Street Café*, on the southern approach to town, does the best breakfasts and lunches.

From Bridgeport, US-395 continues north into Nevada, through the capital Carson City and the gambling city of Reno, both described fully in Chapter Eight.

## travel details

### Buses

**Los Angeles to**: Bishop (1 daily; 7hr 30min); Bridgeport (1 daily; 10hr 50min); Lee Vining (1 daily; 10hr); Lone Pine (1 daily; 6hr); Mammoth Lakes (1 daily; 8hr 30min); Reno (1 daily; 13hr 30min). Note that this one bus leaves LA in the early evening and arrives at most of these destinations in the middle of the night.

**Reno to**: Bishop (1 daily; 6hr); Bridgeport (1 daily; 2hr 40min); Lee Vining (1 daily; 3hr 30min); Lone Pine (1 daily; 7hr 30min); Los Angeles (1 daily; 13hr 30min); Mammoth Lakes (1 daily; 5hr). This bus leaves Reno in the morning.

# CHAPTER FIVE

# THE CENTRAL VALLEY AND THE WESTERN HIGH SIERRA

The vast **interior** of California – stretching three hundred miles from the edges of the Mojave Desert in the south right up to the Gold Country and northern California – comprises the wide floor of the agricultural Central Valley (also known as the San Joaquin Valley) flanked on the east by the massive Sierra Nevada mountains. It's a region of unparalleled beauty, yet the ninety percent of Californians who live on the coast are barely aware of the area, encountering it only while driving between LA and San Francisco on the admittedly tedious I-5, and consider it the height of hicksville.

The **Central Valley** is radically different from anywhere else in the state. During the 1940s, this arid land was made super-fertile by a massive programme of aqueduct building, using water flowing from the mountains to irrigate the area. The valley, as flat as a pancake, is now almost totally comprised of farmland, periodically enlivened by scattered cities that offer a taste of ordinary Californian life away from the glitz of LA and San Francisco.

The reason most coastal Californians head through the Central Valley is to reach the **national parks** that cover the foothills and upper reaches of the Sierra Nevada Mountains. From the valley, a gentle ascent through rolling, grassy foothills takes you into dense forests of huge pine and fir trees, interspersed with tranquil lakes and cut by deep rocky canyons. The most impressive sections are protected within three national parks. **Sequoia** is home to the last few stands of prehistorically huge trees, giant sequoias which form the centrepiece of a rich natural landscape. **Kings Canyon** shares a common border with Sequoia – together they make up one huge park – and presents a similar, though even wilder, array of Sierra wonders, not least of them the miles of backcountry hiking trails. **Yosemite**, with its towering walls of silvery granite artfully sculpted by Ice Age glaciers, is the most famous of the parks and one of the few absolute must-sees in California. Only a few narrow, twisting roads penetrate the hundred miles of wilderness in between the parks, but the entire region is crisscrossed by hiking trails leading up into the pristine alpine backcountry of the western **High Sierra**, which contains the glistening summits of some of the highest mountains in the country.

### Getting around

**Drivers** who aren't particularly interested in exploring the wilds can simply barrel through on I-5, an arrow-straight interstate through the western edge of the Central

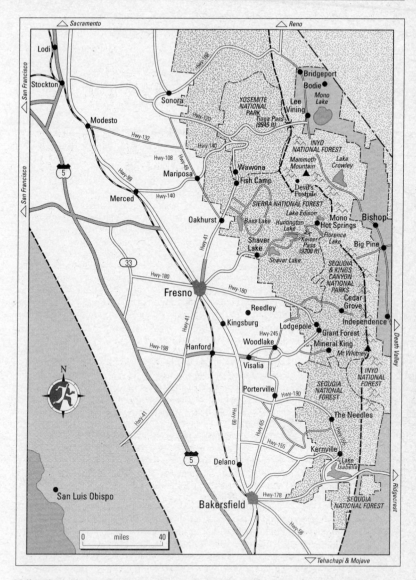

Valley that's the quickest route between LA and San Francisco. Four daily **trains** and frequent *Greyhound* **buses** run through the the the valley, stopping at the larger cities and towns along Hwy-99 – two of which, Merced and Fresno, have bus connections to Yosemite. Otherwise, getting to the mountains is all but impossible without a car, though with a bit of advance planning, you might be able to join one of the many camping trips organized by the *Sierra Club*, the California-based environmentalist group (see p.45).

# THE CENTRAL VALLEY

The **Central Valley** grows more fruit and vegetables than any other agricultural region of its size – a fact that touches the lives, in one way or another, of its every inhabitant. The area is much more conservative and midwestern in feel than the rest of California, but even if the nightlife begins and ends with the local ice-cream parlour, after the big cities of the coast it can all be refreshingly small-scale and enjoyable. Admittedly, nowhere has the energy to detain you long and, between the settlements, the drab hundred-mile vistas of almond groves and vineyards can be sheer torture; as can the weather – summers in the Central Valley are frequently scorching.

**Bakersfield**, the first town you come to across the rocky peaks north of Los Angeles, is hardly the valley's most prepossessing destination, but in recent years its **country music** scene has burgeoned into the best in the state. It also offers a museum recording the beginnings of the local population, and the chance to mess about on the Kern River. Greater rewards lie further on: **Visalia** is a likeable community, near which are two well-restored turn-of-the-century towns, **Hanford** and **Reedley**, plus the bizarre would-be Swedish village of **Kingsburg**.

In many ways the region's linchpin, **Fresno** is the closest thing to a bustling urban centre the valley has – and it's just about impossible to avoid. Though economically thriving, it's frequently voted the least desirable place to live in the US, and on arrival it's easy to see why – its redeeming features, such as they are, take a bit of time to discover. Beyond Fresno, in the northern reaches of the valley, lie sedate **Merced** and slightly more boisterous **Modesto** – where the highlight of the calendar is the annual celebration of the town's role as the inspiration for George Lucas' movie *American Graffiti*. At the top end of the valley **Stockton** is scenically improved by the delta that connects the city to the sea, but is otherwise a place of few pleasures, though you may have to pass through on your way from San Francisco to the Gold Country or the national parks.

## Bakersfield and around

An unappealing vision behind a forest of oil derricks, **BAKERSFIELD**'s flat and featureless look does nothing to suggest that this is one of the nation's liveliest country music communities, with a batch of venues where local musicians will blow your socks off. Other than music, however, there's little reason to be here: the town owes its existence to the fertile soil around the Kern River – once the longest river in the state but now dammed to form Lake Isabella (see p.274) – which stimulated agriculture, and to the discovery of local oil and gas deposits. The **Kern County Museum & Pioneer**

## COUNTRY MUSIC IN BAKERSFIELD

The main – and quite possibly only – reason to dally for more than a few hours in Bakersfield is to hear **country music**; on any weekend the town's numerous honky-tonks reverberate to the sounds of the best country musicians in the US, many of them local residents.

The **roots** of Bakersfield's country music scene are with the midwestern farmers who arrived in the Central Valley during the Depression, bringing their hillbilly instruments and campfire songs with them. This rustic entertainment quickly broadened into more contemporary styles, developed in the bars and clubs that began to appear in the town, where future legends such as Merle Haggard and Buck Owens (who now owns the local country radio station, KUZZ 107.9 FM) cut their teeth. A failed attempt to turn Bakersfield into "Nashville West" during the 1960s, and bring the major country music record labels here from their traditional base, has left the town eager to promote the distinctive "Bakersfield Sound": a far less slick and commercial affair than its Tennessee counterpart.

If you don't get to hear any live music, you can gain an inkling of the Bakersfield Sound from the 1988 hit *Streets of Bakersfield*, a duet by Buck Owens and Dwight Yoakam, and visit the *Buck Owens Music Centre*, a country music museum due to open in mid-1996, charting the rise and rise of Bakersfield's music, in the grounds of the Pioneer Village.

**Venues**

To find out **what's on**, read the Friday edition of the *Bakersfield Californian*, check the flyers at the tourist offices mentioned below, or phone one of the venues we've listed. Fridays and Saturdays are the liveliest nights, although there's often something to enjoy during the week, even if it's only the free **country dancing lessons** offered at many of the town's bars. There's never a cover charge, and live sets usually entail one band playing for four or five hours from around 8pm and taking a fifteen-minute break every hour. Stetson hats and flouncy skirts are the sartorial order of the day, and audiences span generations.

Most **venues** are hotel lounges or restaurant backrooms, though one not to be missed is *Trouts*, 805 N Chester Ave (☎805/399-6700), a country music bar a couple of miles north of downtown that's been in business nearly forty years. Closer to town, you might also try *Junction Lounge*, 2620 Pierce Rd (☎805/327-9651), or the *Sutter Street Bar & Grill*, at the *Ramada Inn*, 3535 Rosedale Hwy (☎805/327-8536). Another group of worthwhile venues are a thirty-minute drive across town: *Brandy's Tavern*, 2700 S Union Ave (☎805/831-9853); *Little Bit Country*, 3317 State Rd (☎805/393-8044), and *Porter's House*, 10701 Hwy-178 (☎805/366-6000).

**Village**, a couple of miles north of downtown at 3801 Chester Ave (Mon–Fri 8am–5pm, Sat 10am–5pm, Sun noon–5pm; $5), documents Bakersfield's development with an impressive collection of over fifty (mostly) restored buildings, many of them dating from the late-nineteenth or early twentieth century. Presumably unintentionally, the cumulative effect is to emphasize how boring the place is today.

## Practicalities

Bakersfield is an important public transport hub: it's the southern terminus of *Amtrak*'s San Joaquin route from San Francisco (connections to LA via *Thruway* bus). Travelling by *Greyhound* (1820 18th St) you may need to change routes here – although overnight stops are rarely necessary. The **Visitor Information Center**, 2101 Oak St (Mon–Fri 8am–5pm; ☎805/861-2367 or 1-800/500-KERN), and the **Chamber of Commerce**, 1033 Truxtun St (Mon–Thurs 8.30am–5pm, Fri 8.30am–4pm; ☎805/327-4421), supply local information.

Bakersfield is full of cheap **motels**, grouped together in two main clusters: at the junction of Pierce and 24th streets, and a couple of miles north around the Olive Drive exit off Hwy-99. At the former, the pool-equipped *EZ-8*, 2604 Pierce Rd (☎805/322-1901 or 1-800/326-6835; ②) marginally edges out the *Roadrunner Motel*, 2619 Pierce Rd (☎805/323-3727; ②), though the latter is cheaper if you are travelling alone. Around Olive Avenue the *Economy Inn*, 6100 Knudsen Drive (☎805/392-1800; ②), and *Motel 6*, 5241 Olive Tree Crescent (☎805/392-9700; ②), both have pools and are quite adequate.

Stay in tune with Bakersfield's country-music persona by **eating** at *Zingo's*, 2625 Pierce Rd, a truck stop whose frilly-aproned waitresses deliver plates of diner staples. *24th Street Café*, 1415 24th St, does top-rate breakfasts; *Joseph's*, hidden back off the road at 3013 F St, serves huge, very impressive calzone to a band of dedicated regulars; while *Noriega Hotel*, 525 Summer St (☎805/322-8419) offers Basque food, for which Bakersfield has gained something of a reputation.

## Lake Isabella and the Kern River

After a night spent in Bakersfield's smoky honky-tonks, you might like to clear your head by driving seventy miles east to the mile-wide **Lake Isabella**, typically alive with windsurfers, jet skiers and anglers. Mountain-biking and rock-climbing are also popular activities here, and the place is heaving in the summer. Information on activities and rental outlets are available from the lakeside **visitor center** (daily 8am–5pm; ☎805/379-5646) half a mile north of Hwy-178 along Hwy-155. Developed though barely shaded **campsites** ring the dry, scrubby lakeside, almost all costing $14 a pitch: there are always first-come-first-served sites or you can reserve at least a week in advance on ☎1-800/280-2267. The region is actually part of the Sequoia National Forest; further information on camping is available from the **Greenhorn Ranger District Office**, 15701 Hwy-178 (Mon–Fri 8am–4.30pm; ☎805/871-2223) on the outskirts of Bakersfield.

Lake Isabella is fed by the **Kern River** which churns down from the slopes of Mount Whitney and spills into the lake at **KERNVILLE** on its northern shore, the sort of town where anyone without aquatic paraphernalia looks out of place. Most people come to ride the Kern which ranks as one of the steepest rivers in the United States,

---

### RIDING THE KERN – RAFTING AND KAYAKING FROM KERNVILLE

Three main sections of the Kern River are regularly rafted: the **Lower Kern**, downstream of Lake Isabella and classed III–IV (fairly rugged); the **Upper Kern**, immediately upstream of Kernville and classed II–IV; and **The Forks**, fifteen miles upstream of Kernville, which is Class V (wild). By far the most popular section is the Upper Kern, the site for the **Lickety-Split** rafting trip – one for the first-timer with some long, rough rapids.

A one-hour Lickety-Split excursion to the Upper Kern (including the bus ride to the put-in) costs $18. Half-day runs cost around $50, day trips run close to the $100 mark, and three-day trips on The Forks can range up to $600. Wetsuits (essential early in the season and for the longer trips) are extra. Within this basic framework there are any number of permutations involving kayaking, eskimo rolling, river rescue and even rock-climbing on the nearby Kernville Slab. Generally there is little need to reserve ahead – the Lickety-Split is run throughout the day – except for the longer expeditions.

Of the many competitive operators in Kernville, two of the biggest are *Sierra South*, 11300 Kernville Rd (☎619/376-3745), and *Chuck Richards' Whitewater*, right next door at no. 11200 (☎619/379-4444 or 1-800/624-5950 for reservations only). If you have the equipment for private rafting or kayaking expeditions, you'll still need a free **permit** from any of the area's Forest Service offices.

dropping over 12,000ft along 150 miles, and producing some of the world's most exhilarating whitewater opportunities. The tougher stuff is generally left to the experts, but during the season, which usually runs from May until mid-August (longer if there has been a heavy winter), commercial rafting operators vie for custom (see box).

Only campers will find cheap **accommodation** in Kernville. Motels start at around $60 with *The Kernville Inn*, 11042 Kernville Rd (☎619/376-2206; ③), right in the centre and with a pool; and range up through the *Kern River Inn B&B*, 119 Kern River Drive (☎1-800/986-4382; ④) to the luxurious *Whispering Pines Lodge*, 13745 Sierra Way (☎619/376-3733; ⑤), a mile north of town by the river.

## The Sequoia National Forest

Bordering its national park namesake, the **Sequoia National Forest** is a vast canopy of pine trees punctuated by gleaming granite, reached on Hwy-155 from Lake Isabella or on the twisting and narrow **Western Divide Highway** (closed in winter during bad weather) from Kernville. Aside from numerous trailheads and more countless backcountry routes, specific points to aim for include **Dome Rock**, which tops out at over 7200ft but is only a short stroll from the highway some thirty miles north of Kernville, and **The Needles**, a series of tall pinnacles with some of America's finest and toughest crack climbs, a couple of miles to the south. Hikers can reach the top of The Needles by following the **Needles Lookout Trail** (5 miles round trip ; 4hr) from the trailhead half a mile south of the *Quaking Aspen* campsite (mid-May to mid-Nov; $10). This is one of several $10 **campsites** in the area, all offering basic facilities. South of The Needles, the interpretive **Trail of a Hundred Giants**, along Hot Springs Drive, ambles into a forest of giant sequoias. Not surprisingly, this same road leads to the **California Hot Springs** (☎805/548-6582), where $6 buys you a long soak.

The **forest headquarters** (☎784-1500) at 900 W Grand Ave, Bakersfield, has information on trails across the Inyo mountains and into the national parks.

# Visalia and Tulare County

As you leave Bakersfield heading north on Hwy-99, the oil wells fade into full-blown agricultural territory. You can turn east onto Hwy-190 at Tipton for the Sequoia National Forest (see above). Otherwise, nowhere merits a stop until you reach Tulare County, some seventy miles north of Bakersfield, where several small communities repay quick visits.

## Visalia

The first and largest of the towns north of Bakersfield is **VISALIA**, just west of Hwy-99 on Hwy-198. Due to a large oak forest that offered both shade and timber for home-building, Visalia was the first place in the Central Valley to be settled. Although the forest is gone, large numbers of oaks and eucalpytus are still planted around the city and local people put an extraordinary amount of care into the upkeep of parks and gardens. In short, it's a pretty place, with a calm and restful air – if you're seeking anything more active you'll be disappointed.

Visalia is best seen on foot: self-guided walking tours of its older parts can be obtained free from the **Chamber of Commerce**, 720 W Mineral King Ave (Mon–Fri 8.30am–5pm; ☎734-5876); or you could visit the **Tulare County Mooney Grove Park and Museum**, about two miles from the city centre at the end of South Mooney Boulevard. The museum (Mon & Wed–Fri 10am–4pm, Sat & Sun noon–6pm; $5) has a hotchpotch of local historical curios, and in the park you'll find the *End of the Trail* statue, originally made for the 1915 Panama Pacific Exhibition in San Francisco, which portrays the defeat of the Indians at the hands of advancing white settlers. Intentionally gloomy, the statue became well known throughout the West, and still inspires a host of copies and numerous snap-happy tourists.

### Practicalities

Visalia has a wide choice of places to **eat**: try the under-$5 Chinese lunch buffet at *Mooney's*, 2332 S Mooney Blvd (☎734-1688), *Merle's* Fifties-style drive-in diner down the street at no. 604, or the inexpensive American-style breakfasts and lunches at *Kay's Kafé*, 215 N Giddings Ave (☎732-9036). South Mooney Boulevard also has the densest concentration of **motels**: *Mooney Motel* at no. 2120 (☎733-2666; ②) is very reasonable with a pool, while *Econolodge* at no. 1400 (☎732-6641; ②) is a good standby for a few bucks more.

When it's time to **move on**, you're well placed for both the Sequoia National Park (46 miles away on Hwy-198; see below) and the northern end of the Sequoia National Forest – seventeen miles from Visalia on Hwy-245, which branches off Hwy-198. On the way to the national park, **Lake Kaweah** provides an opportunity to water-ski and catch fish, and is the best **camping** option in the area: either at *Horse Creek* (☎597-2301) beside Hwy-198 or, more expensively, at the *Kaweah Park Resort* (☎561-4424), a little further east.

# Hanford

Twenty-four miles west of Visalia on Hwy-198, **HANFORD** was named after James Hanford, a paymaster on the Southern Pacific Railroad who became popular with his employees when he took to paying them in gold. The town formed part of a spur on the railroad and became a major stopover on the route between Los Angeles and San Francisco, which it remains.

### The Town

The Visitor Agency (see below) can give you a map of the centre of town detailing the now spotless and spruced-up buildings around Courthouse Square which were the core of local life at the turn of the century. The honey-coloured **Courthouse** (Mon–Sat 10am–6pm, Sun 10am–5pm; closed Aug; free) retains many of its Neoclassical features – not least a magnificent staircase – and has, more recently, been occupied by shops and galleries. As you'd expect, the old Hanford **jail**, rather pretentiously modelled on the Paris Bastille, is only a ball-and-chain's throw away, now restored as a restaurant (*La Bastille*), although you can wander through to see the old cells – now and again used for secluded dining.

Much less ostentatiously, rows of two-storey porched dwellings, a few blocks east of the square, mark the district that was home to most of the eight hundred or so Chinese families who came to Hanford to work on the railroad. At the centre of the community was the **Taoist Temple** on China Alley (groups of 6–20 only and by appointment; $2.50 per person; more details from the Visitor Agency). Built in 1893, the temple served a social as well as a spiritual function, providing free lodging to work-seeking Chinese travellers, and was used as a Chinese school during the early 1920s. Everything inside is original, from the teak burl figurines to the marble chairs, and it's a shame that entry is so restricted. You can, however, take a look at another institution of Hanford's Chinese community: the **Imperial Dynasty Restaurant**, two doors along from the temple, still run by the family who opened it fifty years ago. The interior is simple and modest, but the fame of the cooking has spread far and wide and prices have risen as a result.

Mildly absorbing oddments from Hanford's past are gathered at the **Carnegie Museum**, 109 E Eighth St (Tues–Fri noon–3pm, Sat noon–4pm; free), filling part of the interior of the town's elegant 1905 library – one of many small-town libraries financed by altruistic millionaire industrialist Andrew Carnegie. The only other item of possible interest is the **Kings Art Center**, 605 N Douty St (Tues–Sun noon–3pm; free), with its temporary displays of contemporary painting, sculpture and photography.

## Practicalities

*Orange Belt Stages* (☎1-800/266-7433) provide twice-daily **bus** links to Visalia and the *Greyhound* station at Goshen Junction (for connections to Los Angeles and San Francisco), and also run a service across to San Luis Obispo on the coast. The town's **Visitor Agency** (Mon–Fri 9am–noon & 1–5pm; ☎582-05024 or 1-800/722-1114) is conveniently located inside the handsomely restored *Amtrak* depot at 200 Santa Fe Ave. If you decide to **stay** in Hanford your choice is limited to the *Irwin St Inn*, 522 N Irwin (☎583-8000; ④) and a couple of motels, the cheapest and most central being the *Downtown Motel*, 101 N Reddington (☎582-9036; ②).

## Kingsburg and Reedley

Over half the inhabitants of **KINGSBURG**, twenty miles north of Visalia on Hwy-99, are of Swedish descent, but it's only in the last twenty-five years that they've sought to exploit their roots, converting the town's buildings to Swedish-style architecture and plastering their windows and walls with tributes to the Swedish royal family and the Dana Horse (an object traditionally carved by woodcutters from the Dalarna district of Sweden). Save for such peculiarities, it hardly warrants a call, except perhaps on the third Saturday in May when it stages – predictably – a Swedish festival. Compared to Kingsburg, **REEDLEY**, five miles east, is a metropolis, though beyond its main thoroughfare – G Street – it's just as quiet, and the high point of local entertainment is watching the patient weavers at the **Mennonite Quilting Center**, 1010 G St (usually Mon–Fri 8.30am–5pm; free).

# Fresno

Almost classic in its ugliness, **FRESNO** is very much the hub of business in the Central Valley. Caught between being a farming town and a fully blown commercial city, Fresno seems to have missed out on the restoration programmes that have improved similar communities elsewhere in California, while its solution to traffic congestion has been to insert a freeway plumb through its centre. It's probably significant, too, that the indoor shopping mall was first seen here. For all that, Fresno does have its good points (not least a daily bus service to Yosemite) and, since the town can't easily be avoided, it's handy to know about them.

## The Town

**Downtown Fresno** is the business heart, with not much to view except the **Metropolitan Museum**, 1555 Van Ness Ave (daily 11am–5pm; $4, $1 on the first Wed of the month), which covers a bit of (almost) everything, mainly with temporary exhibitions. The best features are the re-creations of earthquakes, tornadoes and floods. The **Fresno Art Museum**, 2233 N First St at Clinton (Tues–Fri 10am–5pm, Sat & Sun noon–5pm; $2, Tues free), has a worthy but slightly desperate selection of paintings, sculpture and lithographs; there's more compelling stuff in the **Meux Home Museum** (guided tours Fri–Sun noon–3.30pm; free) at the corner of Tulare and R streets, just behind the *Amtrak* station. Built for what in the late nineteenth century was the staggering sum of $12,000, this was the home of a doctor who arrived from the Deep South, bringing with him the novelty of a two-storey house and a plethora of trendy Victorian

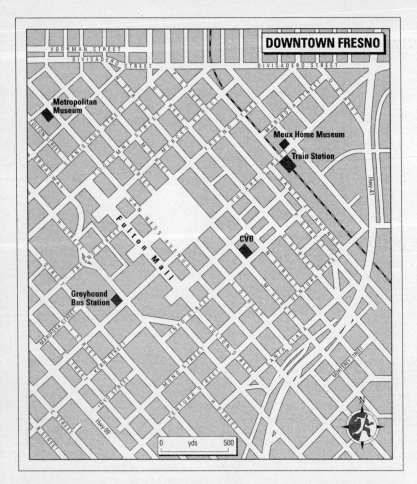

features. What isn't original is a convincing reconstruction, and the turrets, arches, and octagonal master bedroom help make the place stylish and absorbing – quite out of synch with the Fresno that has sprawled up around it.

In a town with a tradition of almond-growing and cattle-rustling, Fresno's so-called **Tower District**, three miles north of downtown at the junction of Wishon and Olive avenues, comes as a pleasant surprise. Proximity to the City College campus made the area something of a hippy hangout during the Sixties; today it has a well-scrubbed liberal bent, plus several blocks of antique shops and bookstores, ethnic restaurants and coffee bars to fill a few hours of idle browsing.

Over the rail tracks at the end of Olive Avenue on the Tower District's western edge, the tree-filled **Roeding Park** boasts the Fresno **zoo** (daily 10am–5pm; $3), a couple of amusement parks and a lake. This is where Fresnoites come to convince themselves that the city is a nice place to live, and strolling here on a sunny day you could almost start to believe them.

## Around Fresno

Seven miles west of the city, close to Hwy-99, Kearney Boulevard is a long, straight and exotically planted thoroughfare that was once the private driveway of Martin Kearney, an English-born turn-of-the-century agricultural pioneer and raisin mogul who had the road built to reach his home, the **Kearney Mansion** (Fri–Sun 1–3pm; $3) – maintained in the opulent French Renaissance style to which Kearney seemed addicted. He had even grander plans to grace Fresno with a French chateau, the mind-boggling designs for which are displayed here. Regarded locally as something of a mystery man, Kearney apparently led a pacey social life on both sides of the Atlantic, which may explain why he died following a heart attack during an ocean crossing.

Twenty minutes' drive north of Fresno are the **Forestiere Underground Gardens**, 5021 W Shaw Ave (tours on the hour June to early Sept Wed–Sun 10m–4pm; early Sept to Nov Sat & Sun noon–3pm; $5), newly opened to the public. A subterannean labyrinth of over fifty rooms, the gardens were constructed by Sicilian emigré and former Boston and New York subway tunneller Baldasare Forestiere, who came to Fresno in 1905. In a fanatical attempt to stay cool and protect his crops, Forestiere put his digging know-how to work, building underground living quarters and skylit orchards. His goal of a subterranean hotel was scuppered by his death in 1946, but wandering around what he achieved is a fascinating way to pass an hour out of the heat of the day.

## Practicalities

You can check details on everything in and around the city (and transport to and from the national parks) at the **CVB**, 808 M St (Mon–Fri 8am–5pm; ☎233-0836). The **bus** and **train** terminals are both downtown: *Greyhound* at 1033 H St and *Amtrak* at Tulare and Q. **Travelling onwards**, Fresno has in Hwy-41 a direct road link to Yosemite National Park (see p.294), and to Kings Canyon National Park (see p.288) in Hwy-180. To get to **Yosemite by bus**, catch the *VIA The Yosemite Connection* service ($20 each way; 4hr; ☎384-1315 or 1-800/369-7275) from the Fresno Air Terminal. To get to the air terminal, use the *Fresno Area Express* (☎498-1122) route #26, which runs hourly from downtown.

For those who want to enjoy the Tower District's nightlife, scores of inexpensive **motels**, all with pools, are clustered together near the junction of Olive Avenue (the district's main drag) and Hwy-99. Best deals here are the *Ramada*, 1804 W Olive Ave (☎442-1082; ③), and *Economy Inns*, 2570 S East St (☎486-1188; ②). You might save a few dollars, however, by using *Thrifty Lodge* at 777 N Parkway Drive (☎237-2175; ②), or the *Motel 6*, along the road at no. 933 (☎233-3913; ②).

To pick up fresh, good **food**, head for the **outdoor produce market**, at Merced and N (Tues, Thurs & Sat 7am–3pm). Otherwise, the Tower District is very much the place to eat and drink. You'll get good-value lunches and dinners, and excellent home-brewed beers, at the *Butterfield Brewing Company Bar & Grill*, 777 E Olive Ave (☎264-5521); the *Java Coffee Company*, 803 E Olive Ave (☎237-5282), presents soups and salads and mugs of very fine coffee, and the *Daily Planet*, 1211 W Wishon Ave (☎266-4259), displays gourmet aspirations with its fixed-price four-course dinner (usually $15).

The free monthly *Talk of the Tower District* lists upcoming events, gigs and the Tuesday night outdoor movies shown on the back wall of Olive Avenue's Tower Theater.

# Continuing north: Merced and Modesto

The best thing about sluggish **MERCED**, fifty miles north of Fresno, is its courthouse, a gem of a building in the main square that's maintained as the **County Courthouse Museum** (Wed–Sun 1–4pm; free). The striking Italian Renaissance-style structure, with columns, elaborately sculptured window frames and a cupola topped by a statue of the Goddess of Justice (minus her customary blindfold), was raised in 1875, dominating the town then as it still does now. Impressively restored in period style, the courtroom retained a legal function until 1951, while the equally sumptuous offices were vacated in the 1970s, leaving the place to serve as storage space for local memorabilia – most exotic among which is a Taoist shrine, found by chance in the back room of a Chinese restaurant.

Six miles out of Merced, close to the dormitory community of **ATWOOD**, the **Castle Air Museum** (daily 10am–4pm; free), adjoining an airforce base, displays thirty-odd military aircraft – mostly bulky bombers with a few fighters thrown in – and a slightly less militaristic collection of aviation paraphernalia.

## Practicalities

Neither of the sights are much of a reason to visit, though the convenient **bus links to Yosemite** are. *Greyhound* buses from Bakersfield, Sacramento and San Francisco stop at the station on W 16th St at N St where you'll find the **Chamber of Commerce**, 690 W 16th St (Mon–Fri 8.30am–5pm; ☎384-3333). The *Amtrak* station is at 24th and K streets, about ten blocks away on the opposite side of the town centre. Both stations are stops for the *VIA The Yosemite Connection* ($30 round trip, $17 one-way; 2hr 30min; ☎384-1315 or 1-800/369-7275) which makes the trip to Yosemite Village, via Mariposa, three times daily (currently departing 6.10am, 10am & 3pm).

The Mariposa exit from Hwy-99 leaves you right by two good **places to stay**: the *Holiday Inn Express*, 730 Motel Drive (☎283-0333 or 1-800/337-0333; ④), and the bargain *PS Happy Inn*, 740 Motel Drive (☎722-6291; ①/②), both with pool and continental breakfast. A third option are the two reservations-only *HI–Merced Home Hostels* (☎725-0407; ①), both of which organize bargain car rental (around $20 a day) through a local agency.

# Modesto

Forty miles further along Hwy-99, **MODESTO**, the childhood home of movie director George Lucas, became the inspiration (though not the location) for his movie *American Graffiti*, the classic portrayal of growing up in small-town America during the late 1950s. The movie contains a number of references to local people, particularly the teachers who rubbed Lucas up the wrong way in his formative years.

### The Town

Modesto has a less than action-packed nightlife, but the fine art of **cruising** still lives on along McHenry Avenue, which has replaced the favoured strip of Lucas's time, the four blocks on Tenth Street between G and K. Nearby, at 1404 G St, the *A&W Root Beer Drive-In* has roller-skating waitresses in celebration of the celluloid connection. Better still is the **Graffiti USA Festival & Cruise** – an annual commemoration of the late 1950s to early 1960s teen rituals which takes place on the second or third Saturday in June, with classic cars dusted off and cruised through the city. The event is so popular that regular traffic becomes severely disrupted, and the police have to limit the number of circuits.

It may seem hard to believe, but as a fairly typical Valley town, Modesto does have a history stretching back beyond duck-tail haircuts and bobby-sox. Its (comparatively) distant past is encapsulated by the shabbily grand **Modesto Arch** – erected in 1912 over Ninth and I to attract attention to the city's expanding economy – and, more imposingly, the Victorian **McHenry Mansion** at 906 15th St (Tues–Thurs & Sun 1–4pm; free), which is jam-packed with fixtures, fittings and the personal features of a family whose fate was linked with Modesto's for years. Robert McHenry was a successful wheat-rancher who did much to bring about a general uplift in the agricultural wellbeing of the area. Surprisingly, his luxurious dwelling was still being rented out as apartments, at quite low rates, as recently as the early 1970s.

A few minutes' walk from the mansion, the **McHenry Museum**, 1402 I St (Tues–Sun noon–4pm; free), originally financed by the McHenry family, sports mock-ups of a doctor's office, blacksmith's shop, dentist's surgery and gathering of cattle brands, revealing something of bygone days, although lacking the period atmosphere of the mansion. Adjoining the museum, the **Central California Art League Gallery** (Tues–Sat 11am–4pm; free) displays a show of regional painting and sculpture that should consume no more than a few minutes.

To find out more about the Graffiti festival, and to pick up maps and general information, contact Modesto's **CVB**, 1114 J St (Mon–Fri 8.30am–5pm; ☎577-5757). The *Greyhound* station is at J St and Ninth.

# Stockton and around

Perched at the far northern limit of the Central Valley, the immediately striking thing about **STOCKTON** is the sight of ocean-going freighters so far inland. The San Joaquin and Sacramento rivers converge here, creating a vast delta with thousands of inlets and bays, and a man-made deep-water channel enables vessels to carry the produce of the valley's farms past San Francisco and directly out to sea. But the geography that aided commerce also saddled Stockton with the image of being a grim place to live and a tough city to work in. During the Gold Rush it was a supply stop on the route to the gold mines, and it became a gigantic flophouse for broken and dispirited ex-miners who gave up their dreams of fortune and returned here to toil on the waterfront. Though valiant efforts have been made to shed this reputation and beautify the less attractive quarters, it's still primarily a hard-working, sleeves-rolled-up city.

A scattering of buildings downtown evoke the early decades of the century, thanks to which Stockton is often in demand as a film set. John Huston's downbeat boxing picture, *Fat City*, for example, was shot here. The walkway along the side of the channel offers views of pleasure craft and takes you through the moderately interesting **Warehouse**, a mix of shops, design companies and pricey snack stops inside a converted storehouse. In a similar vein, though marginally more appealing, the blocks bordered by Harding Way and Park Street, and El Dorado and California, a short way north of the centre, have been preserved as the **Magnolia Historical District**, with sixteen intriguing specimens of domestic architecture spanning seven decades from the 1860s. To find them all, pick up the free leaflet from the **San Joaquin CVB**, downtown at 46 W Fremont St (Mon–Fri 8am–5pm; ☎1-800/888-8016).

Roughly a mile west of the Magnolia district, in Pershing Park alongside Victory Avenue, Stockton gathers totems of its past in the varied and large stock of the **Haggin Museum**, 1201 N Pershing Ave (Tues–Sun 1.30–5pm; $2 donation). Not surprisingly, much is given over to agriculture, including the city's finest moment: the invention by local farmers of a caterpillar tread to enable tractors to travel over muddy ground, adapted by the British for use on tanks and standard use since for the military everywhere. In tremendous contrast, the museum also contains a batch of nineteenth-century French paintings, including works by Renoir and Gauguin, as well as Bouguereau's monumental *Nymphs Bathing*.

## Practicalities

Stockton's *Greyhound* station is at 121 S Center St; *Amtrak* at 735 S San Joaquin St. Even travelling by public transport doesn't mean you have to stay overnight in Stockton – connections both onwards to San Francisco and south down the valley are plentiful – but it can be worth stopping here to **eat**, ethnic restaurants being in good supply. For genuine, inexpensive Mexican food try *Chili's Bar & Grill*, 5756 Pacific Ave (☎474-9004), or *Arroyo's*, 324 S Center St (closed Mon; ☎462-1661). For Chinese there's *On Lock Sam*, 333 S Sutter St (☎466-4561), in Stockton since the last century; or *Dave Wong's*, 5602 N Pershing Ave (☎951-4152). A little more expensive, the *Catfish Café*, 1560 W Fremont St (☎466-2622), dishes out standard, but highly rated, American steaks and seafood.

There's a **campground** eight miles south of Stockton – *Dos Reis Park* (☎953-8800), just off I-5 – or you can stay in the city in one of the plentiful mid-range chain **hotels**. The pick of these are *Days Inn*, 33 N Center St (☎948-6151; ③) close to the *Greyhound* station; and *The Plaza*, 111 E March Lane (☎474-3301 or 1-800/633-3737; ⑤) about three miles north of downtown. There are budget **motels** near the Waterloo Road exit off Hwy-99.

## Micke Grove Park and Lodi

If Stockton begins to pall, or it's simply too nice a day to spend in a city, venture five miles north to the Armstrong Road exit off Hwy-99 for the pastoral relief – at least outside weekends and holidays – of the **Micke Grove Park** (daily 8am–dusk; parking $4 at weekends, $2 midweek), an oak grove which holds a Rose Garden, a Japanese Garden and a zoo. It also features the **San Joaquin Historical Museum** (Wed–Sun 1–4.45pm; $1), recording the evolution of the local agricultural industry and, more revealingly, the social history that accompanied it. Don't miss the Stockton clamshell dredge bucket, a tool used in the reclamation of the delta and restored and displayed like a major work of art.

Beyond the park, on the way north to Sacramento, the state capital (see p.465), sits **LODI**, a small country town immortalized in song by Creedence Clearwater Revival ("oh Lord, stuck in Lodi again"), though these days it's best known for its mass-market **wineries**, several of which offer daily tours and tastings. You can get a full list from the **Chamber of Commerce**, 215 W Oak St (Mon–Fri 8.30am–4.30pm; ☎334-4773), or the San Joaquin CVBVisitors' Bureau in Stockton.

# SEQUOIA AND KINGS CANYON NATIONAL PARKS

Separate parks but jointly run and with a long common border, the **SEQUOIA AND KINGS CANYON NATIONAL PARKS** contain an immense variety of geology, flora and fauna. **Sequoia National Park**, as you might expect from its name, contains the thickest concentration – and the biggest individual specimens – of giant sequoia trees to be found anywhere. These ancient trees tend to outshine (and certainly outgrow) the other features of the park – an assortment of meadows, peaks, canyons and caves. Notwithstanding a few notable exceptions, **Kings Canyon National Park** doesn't have the big trees but compensates with a gaping canyon gored out of the rock by the Kings River, which cascades in torrents down from the High Sierra during the snow-melt period. The few established sights (like the drive-on Auto Log) of both parks are near the main roads and concentrate the crowds. But this leaves the vast majority of the landscape untrammelled and unspoilt, but well within reach for willing hikers.

The **best time to come** is in late summer and fall, when the days are still warm, the nights are getting chilly at altitude, the roads remain free of snow and most visitors have left. Bear in mind that although most roads are kept open through the winter, snow blocks Hwy-180 into Kings Canyon and the road into Mineral King. From the first snowfall in, say, November through to early May you won't get to either of these places, and elsewhere facilities are cut back and camping is restricted to snow-free lowland sites. Of course, this is the time to visit for some superb cross-country skiing. For recorded weather and road information, call ☎565-3351.

## Arrival and information

Although easy to reach by **car** – a fifty mile drive along Hwy-198 from Visalia or a slightly longer journey from Fresno on Hwy-180 – Sequoia and Kings Canyon are not served by **public transport**. Once in Sequoia, reduce traffic congestion and your own parking problems by using the **shuttle bus** (late June to early Sept daily 8am–5pm; every 40min; $1 a ride, $4 all day) which runs between Lodgepole, the Sherman Tree, Giant Forest Village, Mono Rock and Crescent Meadow. Drivers should fill up with cheaper **gas** outside the park but some is available at Mineral King, Lodgepole, Grant Grove Village and Cedar Grove Village.

A **fee** of $5 per car, or $3 per hiker or biker, valid for seven days will be collected at the entrance stations; here you'll be given an excellent map and a copy of the free newspaper, *Sequoia Bark*, which has details and timetables for the numerous **guided hikes** and other interpretive activities, as well as general information on the parks.

Further information is available at the Park Headquarters at Foothills, a mile north of the southern (Hwy-198) entrance to the park (daily 8am–5pm; ☎565-3134); a booth at Giant Forest Village (daily noon–4pm; no phone); and **visitor centers** at Lodgepole, Grant Grove Village and Cedar Grove Village (see the relevant accounts for details). There are also useful **ranger stations** at Mineral King and in Kings Canyon.

## Accommodation

Outside the parks, the most reasonably priced **places to stay** are the motels lining the approach roads, a few miles from the entrances. The best selection is in the south at Three Rivers where you'll find *Buckeye Tree Lodge*, 46000 Hwy-198 (☎561-5900; ③) and the slightly pricier *Gateway Lodge*, 45978 Hwy-198 (☎561-4133; ③) which has a decent restaurant with a wonderful deck right over the Kaweah River. On Hwy-180, *Snowline Lodge* at no. 44138 (☎336-2300; ③) has fairly basic rooms and a great, rustic bar and restaurant, while *The Kings Canyon Lodge* (☎335-2405;③) has reasonable rooms and a good bar serving lunches. The family-oriented *Montecito-Sequoia Lodge* (☎565-3388 or 1-800/227-9900), on the Generals Highway (Hwy-198) between Grant Grove Village and Giant Forest Village, has rustic cabins and lodge rooms with private bath.

**Inside the parks**, all facilities, including accommodation, are managed by *Guest Services* (☎561-3314). Space is at a premium during the summer, although you can often pick up cancellations on the day. **Giant Forest Village** has by far the widest selection of ways of sleeping under a roof, most options accommodating up to four people. The most basic are the kerosene lamp-lit **rustic cabins** (②), which are too cold for winter use, rising through **standard cabins** (④) and **motel units** (④–⑤) to relatively luxurious **fireplace cabins** (⑥). **Grant Grove** offers standard and rustic cabins at similar prices, while **Cedar Grove** and **Stony Creek** (just outside the park boundary) only have motel units.

Those on a budget might want to try the basic hiker's cabins at **Bearpaw Meadow Camp** (mid-June to mid-Sept; ☎561-3341), eleven miles east of Giant Forest Village on the High Sierra Trail. The cost is $26 and for that you get bedding, towels and the option of meals and showers.

## Eating

There are **food** markets and cafeterias at Giant Forest Village, Lodgepole, Stony Creek and Cedar Grove Village, though none is spectacular and prices will be higher than

## CAMPING IN KINGS CANYON AND SEQUOIA

Except during public holidays, there is always plenty of **camping space** in the parks and the surrounding national forest. Unless otherwise stated, all sites operate on a first-come-first-served basis. Collecting firewood is prohibited. For **backcountry** camping get a free **wilderness permit** from the booth by the visitor center in Lodgepole (daily 7am–4pm; ☎565-3775) or a ranger station. There are public showers at Lodgepole, Grant Grove Village and Cedar Grove Village.

Campsites are listed south to north. Take note of the altitude listed for each, as this indicates the kind of temperatures you can expect.

**South Fork** (all year; $6 mid-May to Oct, free rest of year; 3600ft). Trailer-free site thirteen miles east of Lake Kaweah on the very southwestern tip of the park. Water available during fee period.

**Cold Springs**, Mineral King (April to mid-Nov; $5 late May to Sept, free rest of year; 7500ft). Excellent shaded riverside site 25 miles west of Hwy-198, with some very quiet walk-in sites. Gathering of dead wood permitted. Water available during fee period.

**Atwell Mill**, Mineral King (April to mid-Nov; $5 late May to Sept, free rest of year; 6650ft). Slightly less appealing than *Cold Springs*, but still quiet and pleasant, and five miles closer to the highway. Some tent-only sites. Water available during fee period.

**Potwisha** (all year; $10; 2100ft). Smallish, RV-dominated site close to Hwy-198 three miles northeast of the park's southern entrance. Water available.

**Buckeye Flat** (mid-April to mid-Oct; $10; 2800ft). Peaceful, trailer-free site six miles east of Hwy-198 close to the park's southern entrance. Water available.

**Lodgepole** (all year; $12 mid-May to Sept, $10 rest of year, free after heavy snow; 6700ft). Largest and busiest of the sites, four miles north of Giant Forest Village and close to the highway. Reservable through *MISTIX* in the high season, when there are pay showers and a camp store as well as the year-round water and flush toilets.

**Dorst** (late May to Sept; $10; 6800ft). Another large site, with flush toilets, twelve miles north of Giant Forest Village.

**Buck Rock** (all year; free; 6300ft). Excellent and under-utilised national forest site four miles west of the highway, midway between Lodgepole and Grant Grove Village. No water.

**Big Meadows** (all year; free; 6500ft). Similar site to *Buck Rock*, two miles further west.

**Princess** (all year; $6; 6000ft). National forest campground handily sited on the way into Kings Canyon.

**Sunset, Azalea** & **Crystal Spring**, Grant Grove Village. (*Azalea* year-round, others late May to mid-Sept; $10; 6500ft). Comparable large sites all within a few hundred yards of the Grant Grove visitor center.

**Sheep Creek, Sentinel, Canyon View** & **Moraine**, Cedar Grove Village (mid-May to Sept; $10; 4600ft). A series of all-but contiguous forest sites around the Cedar Grove visitor center. *Canyon View* is tents-only.

outside the park. The only fully fledged **restaurant** in either park is *Giant Forest Lodge Dining Room* at Giant Forest Village, which can offer fitting culinary rewards for a hard day's hiking, at an average cost of around $20. Dinner is served daily (5–9pm) and at weekends you can get breakfast (7–10am).

# Sequoia National Park

The two main centres in **SEQUOIA NATIONAL PARK** are **Giant Forest** and **Lodgepole** – the accommodation bases and starting points for most of the hiking trails. To the south there's also the more isolated Mineral King area. While trees are seldom scarce – patches where the giant sequoias can't grow are thickly swathed with pine and fir – the scenery varies throughout the park: sometimes subtly, sometimes

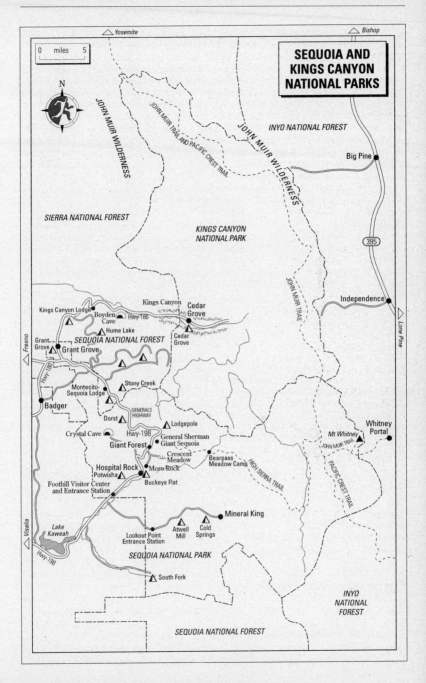

SEQUOIA AND
KINGS CANYON
NATIONAL PARKS

abruptly. Everywhere paths lead through deep forests and around meadows; longer treks rise above the tree line to reveal the barren peaks and gorgeous sights of the High Sierras.

The history of the park is laced with political intrigue. In the 1880s the Giant Forest area was bought by the *Co-Operative Land Purchase and Colonization Association*, a group of individuals known as the **Kaweah Colony** that had the idea of forming a workers' colony here. They began what became the four-year task of building a road from the Central Valley up to Giant Forest, intending to start commercial logging of the huge trees there. Due to legal technicalities, however, their rights to the area were disputed, and in 1890 a bill (probably instigated by a combination of agricultural and railroad interests) was passed by the Senate which effected the preservation of all sequoia groves. The colony lost everything, and received no compensation for the road, which remained in use for thirty years – although decades later the ex-leader of the colony acknowledged that the eventual outcome was of far greater benefit to society as a whole than his own scheme would have been.

# Mineral King

Lying in the southern section of the park, **Mineral King**, at 7800ft, can only be reached from June to September (sometimes longer) by the century-old twisting Mineral King Road, which branches from Hwy-198 near **Three Rivers**. Eager prospectors built the thoroughfare hoping the area would yield silver. It didn't, the mines were abandoned and the region – the only part of the high country accessible by car – was left to a couple of basic campgrounds and near-complete tranquility. Having negotiated the seven-hundred-odd twists and turns from the highway, you can relax by the river before hiking up over steep Sawtooth Pass and into the alpine bowls of the glaciated basins beyond. There's also a gentler introduction to the flora and fauna of Mineral King by way of a short **nature trail** from the *Cold Springs* campground.

Pick up practical information and wilderness permits from the **ranger station** (late May to Sept daily 7am–3.30pm and sometimes until 5pm; ☎565-3768) opposite the *Cold Springs* campground. Permits are required until late September and are in great demand. Reservations can be made in advance from March 1 and some permits are offered on a first-come-first-served basis. **Silver City**, near the *Atwell* campsite, is the only place you'll find food: limited provisions and a café/restaurant.

# Giant Forest and around

Entering the park on **Hwy-180 from Visalia**, you pass **Hospital Rock**, easily spotted by the side of the road and decorated with rock drawings and grain grinding holes from a Monache settlement first established here in 1350. The rock got its name from a trapper who accidentally shot himself in the leg and was treated by the local tribe – who are further remembered by a small outdoor exhibition telling something of their evolution and culture. The road opposite leads to the small and appealing *Buckeye Flat* campground.

From Hospital Rock, the road soon becomes the **Generals Highway** and climbs swiftly into the densely forested section of the park, the aptly labelled **Giant Forest**. GIANT FOREST VILLAGE, near the junction with Crescent Meadow Road, offers food, a reasonable bar and accommodation (see p.283), and makes a good base for exploring the features of the area. It is quite feasible to do an easy day walk taking in Moro Rock, Crescent Meadow, Tharp's Log and the General Sherman Tree (see all below).

### Along Crescent Meadow Road

A spur off the main highway, **Crescent Meadow Road**, provides easy access to a host of photo opportunities. The first attraction is the **Auto Log**, a fallen trunk chiselled flat enough to enable motorists to nose up onto it. Beyond here, a side loop leads to the dramatic **Moro Rock** (also accessible on a three-mile trail from the village), a granite monolith streaking wildly upward from the green hillside. Views from its remarkably level top can stretch 150 miles across the Central Valley and, in the other direction, to the towering Sierras (incidentally, the top is also reputed to make a good platform for feeling vibrations of distant earthquakes). Thanks to a concrete staircase, it's a comparatively easy climb up the rock, although at nearly 7000ft the altitude can be a strain.

Back on the road, you pass under the **Tunnel Log**: a tree that fell across the road in 1937 and has since had a vehicle-sized hole cut through its lower half. Further on, **Crescent Meadow** is, like other grassy fields in the area, more accurately a marsh, and too wet for the sequoias that form an impressive boundary around. Looking across the meadow gives the best opportunity to appreciate the changing shape of the ageing sequoia. The trail circling its perimeter (1.5 miles; 1hr; mainly flat) leads to **Log Meadow**, to which a farmer, Hale Tharp, searching for a summer grazing ground for his sheep, was led by local Native Americans in 1856. He became not only the first white man to see the giant sequoias, but also the first person actually to live in one – a hollowed-out specimen which still exists, remembered as **Tharp's Log**. Climb inside to appreciate the hewn-out shelves. From here the loop presses on to the still living **Chimney Tree**, its centre completely burnt out so that the sky is visible from its hollow base. Hardy backpackers can pick up the John Muir Trail here and hike the 74 miles to Mount Whitney (the tallest mountain in the continental US; see p.258); several less demanding trails cover the couple of miles back to Giant Forest Village.

### The big trees and Crystal Cave

Just north of Giant Forest on the Generals Highway (and reachable on foot by various connecting trails) is the biggest sequoia of them all. The three-thousand-year-old **General Sherman Tree** is 275ft high, with a base diameter of 36ft (and was, for a time, renamed the Karl Marx Tree by the Kaweah Colony). While it's certainly a thrill to be face-to-bark with what is widely held to be the largest living thing on earth, its extraordinary dimensions are hard to grasp alongside the almost equally monstrous sequoias around – and the other tremendous batch that can be seen on the **Congress Trail** (2 miles; 1–2hr; negligible ascent), which starts from here

When you've had your fill of the magnificent trees, consider a trip nine miles from Giant Forest Village along a minor road to **Crystal Cave** (50min guided tours May to late Sept daily 10am–3pm;$4) which has a mildly diverting batch of stalagmites and stalactites. Tickets can only be purchased at the Lodgepole and Foothill visitor centers at least a couple of hours beforehand. The early morning tours are not usually full. Remember to take a jacket.

## Lodgepole and around

Whatever your plans, you should stop at **LODGEPOLE VILLAGE** – four miles along the Generals Highway from Giant Forest Village – for the geological displays, film shows and general information at the **visitor center** (mid-May to Aug daily 8am–6pm, rest of year daily 8am–5pm; ☎565-3782). Lodgepole is at one end of the Tokopah Valley, a glacially formed canyon (not unlike the much larger Yosemite Valley) that's a piece of cake to explore on a number of hiking trails (see "Hikes" box). Foremost amongst them is the **Tokopah Valley Trail** – leading from Lodgepole through the valley to the base of Tokopah Falls, beneath the 1600-foot **Watchtower** cliff. The top of the Watchtower, and its great view of the valley, are accessible by way of the **Lakes Trail**, or try the sharpest ascent of all the Lodgepole hikes, the **Alta Peak and Alta Meadows Trail**, which rises four thousand feet over seven miles.

# Kings Canyon National Park

**KINGS CANYON NATIONAL PARK** is wilder and less visited than Sequoia, with just one real road, skirting the colossal canyon and ending close to the settlement of Cedar Grove, the starting point for most of the marked hikes and, along with Grant Grove close to the Big Stump entrance, site of the park's visitor facilities. Away from these two places, you're on your own. The vast untamed park has a maze-like collection of canyons and a sprinkling of isolated lakes – the perfect environment for careful self-guided exploration.

## Grant Grove, the Big Stump Area and Hume Lake

Confusingly, **Grant Grove** is an enclave of Kings Canyon National Park within the Sequoia National Forest, but unless you're planning a major backcountry hike across the parks' boundaries you'll have to pass through here before reaching Kings Canyon proper.

This concentrated stand of sequoias, sugar pines, incense cedar, black oak and mountain dogwood is named after the **General Grant** tree, which along with the **Robert E Lee** tree (also here), rivals the General Sherman for bulk. A half-mile trail (guides $1) wends its way amongst these and other giants, calling in at the **Fallen Monarch**, which you can walk through, and the **Gamlin Cabin**, where Israel and Thomas Gamlin lived while exploiting their timber claim until 1878. A useful **visitor center** (daily 8am–6pm; ☎335-2856) has all the background information you'll need.

---

### HIKING IN SEQUOIA AND KINGS CANYON

The trails in Kings Canyon and Sequoia see far less traffic than those in Yosemite, but can still get busy in high summer. A quota system applies, but if you're fairly flexible you should be able to land something by turning up early. For information and to reserve **permits**, call ☎565-3708 (Mon–Fri 8am–4.30pm). The visitor centers sell a series of trail guides ($1.50 each) with route descriptions of most of the short trails. Remember that this is **bear country**: read the box on p.44. Bear canisters can be rented ($3 a day and $75 deposit) from the ranger station in Mineral King and camp stores at Cedar Grove, Grant Grove and Lodgepole.

FROM MINERAL KING, SEQUOIA

**Eagle Lake Trail** (7 miles; 6–8hr; 2200ft ascent). Starting from the parking area a mile beyond the ranger station, this trail starts gently but gets tougher towards Eagle Lake. Highlights include the Eagle Sink Hole (where the river vanishes) and some fantastic views.

**Groundhog Meadow Trail** (2 miles; 1–2hr; 900ft ascent). Starting a quarter of a mile back from the road beyond the ranger station. A short but demanding trail which switchbacks up to Groundhog Meadow, from where there's a great view of Sawtooth Ridge.

**Mosquito Lakes No. 1 Trail** (7 miles; 6hr; 1150ft ascent). Follows the first half of the Eagle Lake Trail, then branches left to the lowest of the Mosquito Lakes at 9000ft.

**Mosquito Lakes No. 5 Trail** (10 miles; 8hr; 2300ft ascent). As above plus a bit, bringing you to the uppermost lake at over 10,000ft. Typically stupendous views.

**Paradise Peak via Paradise Ridge Trail** (9 miles; 9hr; 2800ft ascent). Superb walk starting opposite the *Atwell Mill* campground and climbing steeply to Paradise Ridge, which affords views of Moro Rock. From there it is a fairly flat stroll to the 9300-foot Paradise Peak.

FROM GIANT FOREST AND LODGEPOLE, SEQUOIA

**Alta Peak and Alta Meadows Trail** (14 miles; 8–10hr; 4000ft ascent). Starting a mile or so south of Lodgepole, this strenuous but rewarding trail rises four thousand feet over

Two miles south of Grant Grove, the **Big Stump Area** is named after the big stumps that litter the place – remnants from the first logging of sequoias carried out during the 1880s. Among these is the massive stump of a sequoia which was cut down to be taken to the 1875 World's Fair in Philadelphia – an attempt to convince cynical easterners that such enormous trees really existed. A mile-long nature trail leads through this scene of devastation. It's hardly an enjoyable experience, even if you can spot the ageing remains of flumes used to transport logs to the valley.

## Hume Lake and around

About eight miles north of Grant Grove, a minor road spurs off three miles to **HUME LAKE**, built as an artificial lake to provide water for logging flumes, and now forming the heart of an underpopulated area that's a good place to **spend a night**. Beside the lake, the comparatively large *Princess* campground (see p.284) is handily placed for the local hiking trails. If you want to walk through the area and into either park, stop at **Clingan's Junction** and the **Hume Lake Ranger District Office**, some seventeen miles before the park entrance (Mon–Fri 8am–5pm, Sat 8am–4.30pm; ☎338-2251), which has full details on the local campgrounds and trails.

## Kings Canyon Highway

Kings Canyon Highway, Hwy-180, runs from Grant Grove through the Sequoia National Forest and Hume Lake, before descending sharply into the steep-sided Kings

seven miles. The trail splits after three miles: there's an easy, level walk to Alta Meadow and its fine views of the surrounding peaks (and a four-mile trail to the desolate Moose Lake), or the daunting near-vertical hike to the stunning Alta Peak.

**Lakes Trail** (13 miles; 6–8hr; 2300ft ascent). Starting a mile or so south of Lodgepole, this popular if fatiguing trail leads past three lakes. The two furthest lakes, Emerald Lake and Pear Lake, have campgrounds and, for the really adventurous (and experienced), make good starting points for self-guided trekking into the mountains.

**Little Baldy Trail** (3 miles; 2–3hr; 700ft ascent). Starting from Little Baldy Saddle, six miles north of Lodgepole, this loop trail leads to the rocky summit of Little Baldy.

**Moro Rock via Soldiers Trail** (4.5 miles; 3–4hr; 300ft ascent). Starting at Giant Forest (just west of the cafeteria), this fairly easy self-guided trail leads through meadow and forest, calling at Hanging Rock, Moro Rock and Tunnel Log.

**Tokopah Trail** (3 miles; 2–3hr; negligible ascent). Starting from the Lodgepole visitor center, this is a valley walk beside the Marble Fork of the Kaweah River, leading to impressive granite cliffs and the Tokopah Falls.

FROM KINGS CANYON

**Cedar Grove Overlook Trail** (5 miles; 3–4hr; 1200ft ascent). Starting half a mile north of Cedar Grove Village on Pack Station Road, this switchback trail rises through forest and chaparral to a viewpoint overlooking Kings Canyon.

**Don Cecil Trail to Lookout Peak** (13 miles; 6–8hr; 4000ft ascent). Starting 400 yards east of Cedar Grove Village, a strenuous trail which largely follows the pre-highway road route. After two miles you reach the shady glen of Sheep Creek Cascade before pressing on up the canyon to the wonderfully panoramic summit.

**Hotel Creek–Lewis Creek Loop Trail** (8 miles; 5hr; 1200ft ascent). Follows the first two miles of the Cedar Grove Overlook trail, before branching downhill and returning to Cedar Grove through some extensively fire-damaged forest.

**Mist Falls Trail** (8 miles; 4–5hr; 600ft ascent). An easy sandy trail starts from Road's End, eventually climbing steeply to Mist Falls, one of the largest waterfalls in the twin parks.

Some measurements make this the deepest canyon in the US, at some 7900ft. Whatever the facts, its wall sections of granite and gleaming blue marble and the yellow pockmarks of yucca plants are visually outstanding: this is especially true from Junction View as the road winds its way down to the riverside. It's extremely perilous to wade into the river: people have been swept away even when paddling close to the bank in a seemingly placid section.

Near the foot of the canyon, the road passes **Boyden Cave** (summer daily 10am–5pm, 45min tours on the hour; $6), whose interior has a number of bizarre formations grown out of the forty-thousand-year-old rock, their impact intensified by the stillness and coolness inside. The cave stays at a constant 55°F, causing the numerous snakes and small animals who tumble in through the hole in the roof to enter instant hibernation.

### Cedar Grove

Once properly into the national park, the canyon sheds its V-shape and gains a floor, where **Cedar Grove** is named after the incense cedars which grow in proliferation around it. With a smattering of log cabins, a food store and snack bar, several campgrounds and, across the river, a **ranger station** (Mon–Thurs 7am–3pm, Fri & Sat 7am–5pm; ☎565-3793), this is as close to a built-up area as the park gets.

Three miles east are the **Roaring River Falls** which, when in spate, undoubtedly merit their name. Apart from the obvious appeal of the scenery, the main things to see around here are the **flowers** – leopard lilies, shooting stars, violets, Indian paintbrush, lupines and others – and a variety of bird life. The longer hikes through the creeks, many of them seven or eight miles long (see box on p.289), are fairly stiff challenges and you should carry drinking water. An easy alternative, however, is to potter along the **nature trail** (1.5 miles; 1–2hr; flat) around the edge of **Zumwalt Meadow**, a beckoning green carpet a mile beyond the falls and a short walk from the road, beneath the forbidding grey walls of Grand Sentinel and North Dome mountains. The meadow boasts a collection of big-leaf maple, cat's-tails and creek dogwood, and there's often a chance of an eyeful of animal life.

Just a mile further, Kings Canyon Road comes to an end at **Copper Creek**. Thirty years ago it was sensibly decided not to allow vehicles to penetrate further. Instead the multitude of canyons and peaks that constitute the Kings River Sierra are networked by **hiking paths**, all accessible from here and almost all best enjoyed armed with a tent and some provisions. To obtain **wilderness permits** in this area, call at the Road's End Wilderness Permit Station (daily 7am–2.45pm) at the end of Hwy-180. The less ambitious only need to venture a hundred yards riverward to **Muir Rock**, to see where John Muir (see box on p.296) conducted early meetings of the Sierra Club. On the way back down the valley, cut right and follow the **Motor Nature Trail** (westbound only) along the north side of the river back to Cedar Grove.

# The Sierra National Forest

Consuming the entire gaping tract of land between Kings Canyon and Yosemite, the **SIERRA NATIONAL FOREST** boasts some of the Californian interior's most beautiful mountain scenery, though it's less well known – and less visited – than either of its national park neighbours. A federally run area that lacks the environmental protection given to the parks, many of the rivers here have been dammed and much of the forest developed into resort areas that are better for fishing and boating than hiking. Central Valley residents stream up here at weekends through the summer. That said, there are far fewer people and any number of remote corners to explore, not least the rugged, unspoilt terrain of the vast **John Muir Wilderness** and the neighbouring **Ansel**

**Adams Wilderness** which contain some of the starkest peaks and lushest alpine meadows of the High Sierra. If you want to discover complete solitude and hike and camp in isolation, this is the place to do it – the sheer challenge of the environment can make the national parks look like holiday camps. But don't try any lone exploration without thorough planning and accurate maps, and don't expect buses to pick you up if you're tired – public transport is virtually nonexistent. We haven't highlighted walks in this area; there are hundreds of them, and any of the **ranger stations** can suggest suitable hikes, supply permits (neccessary for any overnight hikes into most of the forest) and sell you the detailed *Sierra National Forest Map* ($3.25), useful even if you are driving. As usual, overnight hikes require wilderness permits. **Dispersed camping** is allowed in most areas of the forest, provided you keep a hundred feet away from any stream; a free campfire permit is needed even for a portable stove.

The paltry network of roads effectively divides the forest into three main areas: the more southerly **Pineridge** district, accessible by way of Hwy-168; and the **Bass Lake** and the Mariposa district in the north, just off Hwy-41 between Fresno and Yosemite. The **Minarets Loop** reaches out into the Sierra to the southeast of Yosemite. Call ☎855-5360 for road information.

## The Pineridge District and the John Muir Wilderness

The best place for adventurous hiking is the **Pineridge** district, forty miles east from Fresno using Hwy-168. Around the **Kaiser Pass**, which scrapes 9200ft, you'll find isolated alpine landscapes, served by decent campsites, a couple of hotels and even some hot springs. The western section of the district is dominated by the weekend playgrounds of Huntington and Shaver lakes, while the east, up and over the Kaiser Pass, is hiking territory.

Hwy-168 – aka The Sierra Heritage National Scenic Byway – penetrates seventy miles into the forest among the snow-capped peaks of the **John Muir Wilderness**. It's a drive of at least four hours even in good weather – and this is an area prone to bad weather and road closure, although you can always get to the lakes. The **Pineridge District Office** (daily 8am–4.30pm; ☎841-3311) is located along Hwy-168 at Prather, five miles west of the forest entrance.

### Shaver and Huntington lakes

From the ranger station, Hwy-168 climbs eighteen miles to **Shaver Lake**, a mile-high community amongst the pines. If you fancy an afternoon dodging the jetskiers out on the lake, drop in at *Shaver LakeWatersports*, Shaver Lake Lodge Marina (☎841-8222) to rent windsurfers ($45 a day), kayaks ($7 an hour) and canoes ($15 an hour). Otherwise, there's little reason to stop except for groceries, gas, meals at one of the half-dozen restaurants, or perhaps to stay at either *Musick Creek Inn & Chalets* (☎841-3323; ③), which has motel units and A-frames; or *Shaver Lake Village* (☎841-7183 or 1-800/695-7368; ④/⑤), which has hotel rooms and studio cabins. There are a couple of decent **campsites** hereabouts: *Dorabelle*, near the lake on Dorabelle Road ($12; June to mid-Sept; reserve with *Biospherics*), which has water; and *Swanson Meadow*, two miles east on Dinkey Creek Road ($8), both at around 5500ft.

Beyond Shaver Lake, Hwy-168 climbs the 7500-foot Tamarack Ridge that effectively separates **Huntington Lake**, twenty miles east, from the Central Valley. This lake is more isolated than its neighbour over the hill but is almost equally popular; again watersports and angling are the pastimes of choice. There's a restaurant, a bar, a gas station, post office and general store all a few yards from the lake, while *Lakeside Resort* (☎893-3193; ③) provides shelted shorefront accommodation, with rustic knotty pine cabins sleeping four (bedlinen extra). From here on, the lakeshore is almost entirely taken up by campsites, all costing $14, bookable through *Biospherics* and with piped water. The useful **Eastwood ranger station** beside Huntington Lake (late May to early Sept daily 8am–5pm; ☎893-6611) has details. East off Hwy-168, just before the lake, the mile-long **Rancheria Falls Trail** (350ft ascent; 1hr round trip) is a woodland route to the 150-foot Rancheria Falls.

If you're craving solitude, head to the lake's western end, where a winding, forty-mile, partly-gravel road skirts the whole of the **Kaiser Wilderness**, passing a couple of free, primitive campsites, before rejoining Kaiser Pass Road on the east side. It's a trek, but once here you'll feel a million miles from anywhere.

## The Kings River District

Deep in the forest to the southeast of Shaver Lake and reachable along thirteen miles of the mountainous Dinkey Creek Road lies **Dinkey Creek**, from where several trails lead through alpine forest to a dozen or so small lakes. It is in this area that the north fork of the Kings River churns its way down fearsome Class III and IV rapids, an unsurpassed spot for **white-water river rafting**, at its swiftest and most exciting during the summer meltwater period. *Kings River Expeditions* (☎233-4881), *Spirit Whitewater* (☎373-3275) and *Zephyr River Expeditions* (☎532-6249) all run day-long trips costing around $100. Primitive free **campsites** are plentiful in this region. For more detailed information, consult the **Kings River Ranger District Office** (Mon–Fri 8am–4.30pm; ☎855-8321) at the southern edge of the district, near the Pine Flats Reservoir on Trimmer Springs Road.

## Beyond Kaiser Pass: Mono Hot Springs and around

A much quicker way to the wild country beyond Kaiser Pass starts at the Eastwood ranger station (see above) and climbs on a rapidly deteriorating road up to 9200 feet, passing the *Badger Flat* campsite ($8; no water) along the way. Eight miles from Eastwood, a side road leads to **White Bark Vista** with one of the best mountain views in these parts. Over the pass is a vast basin, draining the south fork of the San Joacqin River. The road drops past the *Portal Forebay* campsite ($8; no water) one of the best in the region, before reaching the **High Sierra Ranger Station** (late May to early Sept daily 7.30am–5pm; ☎877-3138). A mile east the road splits into two narrow and winding seven-mile routes: north to Lake Edison, its approach marred by a huge earth dam, and west to the more appealing Florence Lake. Both boast splendid scenery and hiking, fishing and camping opportunies, but don't hold enough to make a prolonged stay worthwhile.

**Mono Hot Springs**, two miles north of the junction on the road to Lake Edison, is the best thing about the region; a place to relax or clean up after hikes. For the full experience head for the modest *Mono Hot Springs Resort*, right on the banks of the San Joacqin River (mid-May to mid-Oct; ☎449-9054; ①/③), which offers individual mineral baths ($4) and showers ($3), and massages for $30 per half hour. Outside there's a chlorinated spa filled with spring water, costing $4 for an all-day pass. Accommodation ranges from simple cabins with communal ablutions and no linen to attractive modern suites with kitchen; reserve at weekends. The resort also has a small restaurant, an understocked general store, gas, and a large but decent campground ($10; water). Better still, across the river there's a five-foot-deep **natural pool** (unrestricted access), perfect for soaking your bones while stargazing. This is just one of many such pools (mostly more secluded) on this side of the river; ask around.

# Bass Lake and the Mariposa district

Without a car, the closest you can get to the wilderness is **OAKHURST** (reached on the *VIA* buses to Yosemite – see p.279 or p.280), the centre of the Mariposa district and just seven miles west of much the biggest tourist attraction in the area – the pine-fringed **BASS LAKE**. A stamping ground of Hell's Angels in the 1960s – the leather and licentiousness memorably described in Hunter S Thompson's book *Hell's Angels* – Bass Lake is nowadays a family resort, crowded with boaters and anglers in summer, but a good spot to rest for a day or two. The combined **Mariposa Ranger District Office** and **Southern Yosemite Visitor Bureau** (daily 9am–5pm; ☎683-4636) at the corner of Hwy-41 and Route 426 in Oakhurst stocks the misleadingly titled *Southern Yosemite Visitor's Guide*, full of information on the lake and district.

Road 222 runs right around the lake, though not always within sight of it. At the main settlement, also known as Bass Lake, you can buy groceries, eat moderately well and **spend the night** at *The Pines* (☎642-3121 or 1-800/350-7463; ⑦/⑧) in luxurious two-storey chalets with kitchens or even more palatial lakeside suites. By the south-western tip of the lake, *Miller's Landing Resort*, 37976 Road 222 (☎642-3633), offers cabins without bathrooms for $30 right up to fancy chalets and suites (②–⑥). *Miller's Landing* is also the best place to **rent aquatic equipment** – canoes and fishing boats are $25 and $50 a day respectively, while jetskis are $50 an hour.

Bass Lake is completely surrounded by $15-a-night family **campsites**, most oriented towards long stays beside your camper. In summer, book well in advance (call *Biospherics*), though no-shows are sometimes available at the California Land Management Office, 39900 Road 222 on the southwest side (late May to early Sept Mon–Fri 8am–8pm Sat & Sun 8am–9pm; ☎642-3212). For tent campers, the best site is *Lupine*, just north of *Miller's Landing*.

# The Minarets Loop

If Bass Lake is too commercial and overcrowded for you, the antidote starts immediately to the north. The Sierra Vista Scenic Byway, more succinctly known as the **Minarets Loop**, makes a ninety-mile circuit west of Hwy-41 topping out at the Clover Meadow Station (7000ft), trailhead for much of the magnificent **Ansel Adams Wilderness**. Apart from a lot of trailheads and campsites, there's not a great deal to it, though the views are fantastic and the people scarce. A straight circuit takes five hours. Stock up on supplies before you start: there are a few stores and gas stations dotted along the loop but, as ever, they're not cheap and the range is limited. Accommodation is largely restricted to campsites all (except two free sites) costing $10–15.

## The north side

Immediately north of Bass Lake is Beasore Road, but a better start for the circuit is Sky Ranch Road which cuts east four miles north of Oakhurst. First stop, after seven miles, is the **Nelder Grove Historical Area** (unrestricted entry), a couple of miles north along a dirt road. Over a hundred giant sequoias are scattered through the forest here, though the overall impression is of devastation evidenced by enormous stumps amongst the second-growth sugar pine, white fir and cedar. The mile-long "Shadow of the Giants" interpretive walk explains the logging activities which took place here in the 1880s and early 1890s and, with its low visitor count, offers a more serene communion with these majestic trees than do any of the national parks. A second interpretive trail leads from the attractive but mosquito-ridden *Nelder Campsite* (free; 5500ft; stream water) to **Bull Buck Tree**, once a serious contender for the world's largest tree. Several $10 campsites, most without running water are dotted either side of the road. The *Fresno Dome* site is particularly pleasant and acts as a base for a moderately strenuous walk to the top of the exfoliated granite namesake.

Sky Ranch Road joins Beasore Road at Cold Springs Meadow and continues to **Beasore Meadow**, where the summer-only *Jones Store* has supplied groceries, gas and meals for the best part of a century. The large **Globe Rock** heralds the end of asphalt for the next five miles, making *Minarets Pack Station* (June–Oct; ☎868-3405; ①), the return to tarmac, all the more welcome. As well as a general store and reasonable meals, the station offers simple lodging and horseback trips from $45 a day. It's a great base for wilderness trips, many of which start by the Clover Meadow Ranger Station, a couple of miles up a spur road (June–Oct daily 9am–5pm). Nearby are two free and wonderfully sited campsites, *Clover Meadow* and *Granite Creek*, the former with potable water.

## The south side

From *Minarets Pack Station*, the loop starts to descend, passing a small ranger outpost (daily 8am–4.30pm; ☎877-2218) en route to the rather disappointing **Arch Rock**, where the earth under a slab of granite has been undermined to leave a kind of bridge. Better to push on to the eight-mile side road to the dammed **Mammoth Pool**, where summer anglers boat on the lake and smoke their catch at one of four campsites. The quietest of them are *Sweetwater* ($10; 3800ft) and *Placer* ($10; 4100ft), away from the pool but by streams.

Back on the loop road, continue to **Mile High Vista** for endless views of mountain ranges and bursting granite domes stretching back to Mammoth Mountain (see p.263). There's little to stop for on the last 25 miles back to civilization, except for the mildly diverting **Sierra Mono Indian Museum** (Mon–Sat 9am–4pm; $2) at the junction of roads 25 and 22.

# YOSEMITE NATIONAL PARK

> *No temple made with hands can compare with the Yosemite. Every rock in its walls seems to glow with life. Some lean back in majestic repose; others, absolutely sheer or nearly so for thousands of feet, advance beyond their companions in thoughtful attitudes, giving welcome to storms and calms alike, seemingly aware, yet heedless, of everything going on about them.*
>
> John Muir, *The Yosemite*

More gushing adjectives have been thrown at **YOSEMITE NATIONAL PARK** than at any other part of California. But however excessive the hyperbole may seem, once you enter the park and turn the corner which reveals Yosemite Valley – only a small part of the park but the one at which most of the verbiage is aimed – you realize it's actually an understatement. For many, **Yosemite Valley** is, very simply, the single most dramatic piece of geology to be found anywhere in the world. Just seven miles long and one mile across at its widest point, it's walled by near-vertical, mile-high cliffs whose sides are streaked by cascading waterfalls and whose tops, a variety of domes and pinnacles, form a jagged silhouette against the sky. At ground level, too, the sights can be staggeringly impressive. Grassy meadows are framed by oak, cedar and fir trees, with a variety of wild flowers and wildlife – deer, coyotes and even black bears are not uncommon.

Perhaps understandably, tourists are even more common. Each year Yosemite has to cope with four million visitors, and if you're looking for a little peace it's advisable to avoid the Valley on weekends and holidays. That said, the whole park is diverse and massive enough to endure the crowds: you can visit at any time of year, even in winter when the waterfalls turn to ice and the trails are blocked by snow, and out of high summer even the valley itself resists getting crammed. Further-flung reaches of the park, especially around the crisp alpine Tuolumne Meadows, and the completely wild backcountry accessible beyond them, are much less busy all year round – nature in just about the most peaceful and elemental setting you could imagine. Everywhere you go, it is, of course, essential to be careful not to cause ecological damage or upset the wildlife population (see pp.43-45 of *Basics* for advice).

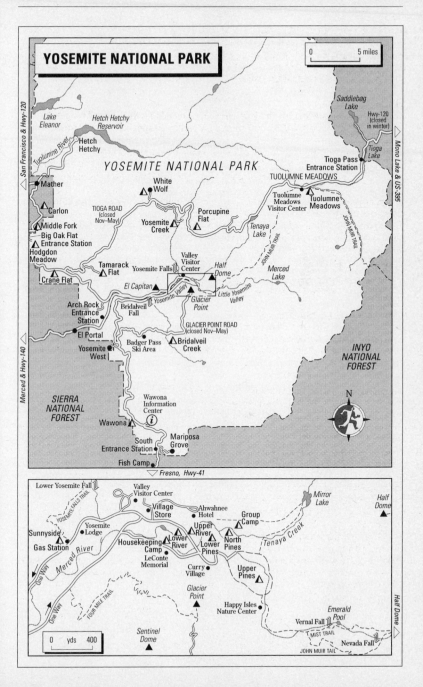

## JOHN MUIR AND THE SIERRA CLUB

Scottish immigrant **John Muir** worked as a mechanical inventor in Wisconsin until he nearly lost an eye in an accident. Discouraged, he set off in search of adventure and walked, via the Gulf of Mexico, to San Francisco. Arriving in 1868, he immediately asked directions for "anywhere that's wild" and began months of camping and exploration, reputedly carrying no more than a notebook, a tin cup and a supply of tea. His diary was published a year later as *My First Summer in the Sierra* and was an instant hit, becoming a classic of American geographical writing.

Muir was so taken by the Sierra, and Yosemite in particular, that he made it his home. Over the years, appalled by the destruction he saw taking place around him, he campaigned for the preservation of the Sierra Nevada range, and is credited with having prompted Congress to create Yosemite National Park in 1890. In 1892, he set up the **Sierra Club**, an organization whose motto "take only photographs; leave only footprints" has become a model for like-minded groups around the world.

In 1913, the construction of a dam in the northern reaches of Yosemite to provide water for San Francisco was a setback in the struggle to keep Yosemite free of development (many think the struggle to prevent it led to John Muir's death the following year), but the publicity actually aided the formation of the present National Park Service in 1916, which promised – and has since provided – greater protection. Muir's name crops up throughout California as a memorial to this inspirational figure, not least in the 212-mile John Muir Trail which twists through his favourite scenery from Yosemite Valley south to Mount Whitney.

### Some history

Yosemite Valley was created over thousands of years by glaciers gouging through and enlarging the canyon of the Merced River; the ice scraped away much of the softer portions of granite but only scarred the harder sections, which became the present cliffs. As the glaciers melted a lake formed, filling the valley, and eventually silting up to create the present valley floor.

Native American tribes occupied the area quite peaceably until the mid-nineteenth century, when the increasingly threatening presence of white Gold Rush settlers in the Central Valley led the tribes here to launch raiding parties to the nearest encampments. In 1851 Major James Savage led a force, the Mariposa Battalion, in pursuit of the Native Americans, trailing them into the foothills and beyond, and becoming the first white men to set foot in Yosemite Valley. It wasn't long before the two groups clashed properly, and the original population was moved out to white settlements to make way for farmers, foresters and, soon after, tourists (the first group of sightseers arriving in 1855). Moves were quickly afoot to conserve the natural beauty of the area: in 1864 Yosemite Valley and Mariposa Grove were preserved as the Yosemite Land Grant, the nation's first region specifically set aside to protect the wilderness. In 1890 it became America's third national park, thanks in great part to the campaigning work of Scottish naturalist John Muir (see box).

## Arrival and information

**Getting to Yosemite** by car is straightforward. Three roads enter the park from the west: Hwy-41 from Fresno, Hwy-140 from Merced and Hwy-120 from Stockton and the San Francisco Bay area. All are kept open throughout the year as far as the Valley. The only road into the eastern side of the park is Hwy-120, the 10,000-foot Tioga Pass Road, which branches off US-395 close to Lee Vining – though this is closed during winter and in bad weather. **Gas** can be hard to come by, especially after 6pm, and is expensive in the park, so fill up before heading into the mountains.

**Public transport into the park** is less easy, but possible, all services running through Wawona to Yosemite Village. From the Central Valley, *VIA The Yosemite Connection* (☎384-1315 or 1-800/369-7275) has a once daily service from Fresno (see p.279), and runs three times daily from **Merced** (see p.280). There is no longer any public transport over the Tioga Pass from Lee Vining and Hwy-395, but buses do connect the Valley with Tuolumne Meadows (see below).

Generally speaking, anything called a **sightseeing tour** which begins outside the park will involve you in an unsatisfying race through the Valley. You might, however, want to consider *Green Tortoise*'s three-day (two days in winter) packages (including camping near Tuolumne Meadows; see p.301) from San Francisco, costing $99 per person ($59 in winter), plus $20 for the food fund.

Yosemite is always open: **park entry** costs $5 per vehicle including passengers, $3 for each cyclist, hiker or bus passenger and is valid for seven days. Pay at the ranger stations when you enter, or if they're closed, at the visitor center in the Valley, or when you leave.

## Information

The park's most useful **visitor center** is at **Yosemite Village** (mid-June to early Sept daily 8am–8pm; April to mid-June & early Sept to late Nov daily 8am–6pm; late Nov to March daily 9am–5pm; ☎372-0299), where you can pick up information and maps, including a topographic map ($6) essential for any adventurous walks. For **free** hiking permits and all the route planning help you could ask for, pop next door to the **Wilderness Center** (mid-June to early Sept Sun–Fri 7.30am–7.30pm, Sat 6.30am–7.30pm; early Sept to mid–June daily 8am–5pm). There are other visitor centers at **Tuolumne Meadows** (summer only daily 8am–7.30pm; ☎372-0263); **Big Oak Flat** (summer only daily 8am–6pm); and **Wawona** (all year daily 8am–5pm). A couple of free **publications** are worth picking up at park entrances or visitor centers: the pertinent, quarterly *Yosemite Guide* and *Keep it Wild*, a guide to planning wilderness trips.

For a recording of **general information** on Yosemite and **weather and road conditions** phone ☎372-0200.

## Getting around

The three roads from the Central Valley end up at **Yosemite Valley**, roughly in the centre of the park's 1200 square miles, and home to its most dramatic scenery. At the

---

### WINTER IN YOSEMITE

From December to April, those prepared to cope with blocked roads and below-freezing temperatures are amply rewarded at Yosemite – thick snow, frozen waterfalls and far fewer people make for almost unimaginable beauty and silence. **Accommodation** is cheaper at these times too, and much easier to obtain, though weekends can still get pretty full. Many low-country **campsites** are open, and restrictions on backcountry camping are eased – you'll want a good sleeping bag and tent.

Much of Yosemite is fabulous **skiing** country. Lessons and equipment rental are available at the **Badger Pass Ski Area**, on the road to Glacier Point, accessible via shuttle ($18 round-trip) from the Valley. All-day lift tickets cost $28 at weekends and $22 midweek. Daily equipment rental will set you back $18 for downhill, $15 for cross-country and $30 for snowboards. Lessons start from $40. There are also various special deals offered from time to time; one of the best being the **free ski pass** if you stay at *Yosemite Lodge* or *The Ahwahnee* Sunday through Thursday between January and March. This deal also gives you free entry to the open-air Curry Village **ice skating** rink (normally $5, plus $2 skate rental).

southern edge of the park Hwy-41 passes the **Mariposa Grove** and **Wawona**; from here it's 27 miles further to the valley. **Tuolumne Meadows** is in the high country, sixty-odd miles northeast of the Valley, close to the Tioga Pass entrance (Hwy-120) on the eastern side of the park.

Free and frequent **shuttle buses** operate on the Valley floor, running anticlockwise on a loop that passes through, or close to, all the main points of interest, trailheads and accommodation areas. In high season they run between 7am and 10pm to most sections of the valley, with slightly reduced hours at other times. The summer-only **Tuolumne Bus** makes the two-and-a-half hour run to Tuolumne Meadows ($10 one way), leaving Yosemite at roughly 8am and departing Tuolumne at 1.30pm. There's also a **hikers' bus** running up to Glacier Point three times daily through the summer (☎372-1240).

**Cars** spoil everybody's fun on the valley floor; if you're driving in just for the day, leave your vehicle in the day-use parking lot at Curry Village. In any case, **cycling** is the best way to get around: a number of good bicycle paths cross the valley floor, but bike rental is limited to the outlets at *Yosemite Lodge* and *Curry Village* (April–Nov only) which charge $5 per hour or $16 per day. Bikes are poor-quality one-speeds but since cycling is only allowed on asphalt surfaces, that's all you need: leave your mountain bike at home.

Failing that, there are always **guided tours** (☎372-1240), which range from the rather dull two-hour valley floor spin, costing $14.25, to the all-day Mariposa and Glacier Point Grand Tour (June–Nov) at $40. These are bookable from accommodation reception areas, along with a variety of guided **horseback trips**, most of which loop around the base of Half Dome: expect to pay $31 for a couple of hours, $44 for half a day. A number of **guided hikes** are offered, too; you can get details in the *Yosemite Guide*.

## Accommodation

Once in the park, **accommodation** can be a problem; it's almost essential to book well in advance and anything other than camping can be surprisingly expensive. Even canvas tents cost what you would pay for a reasonable motel elsewhere. All accommodation in the national park – the majority of it right in the Valley – is operated by

### ROCK CLIMBING

Rock climbers the world over flock to Yosemite, drawn by the challenge of inching up. mile-high walls of sheer granite in the California sun. The **best season** for climbs in the Yosemite Valley is April and May before it gets too hot, and September before it gets too cold. Some areas, notably the southeast face of El Capitan, are occasionally off limits to protect the nesting sites of peregrine falcons.

Many climbers base themselves at the *Sunnyside Walk-In* campground, near *Yosemite Lodge*; a good place to pick up climbing tips and find out why the regulars have bestowed somewhat psychedelic names to certain routes, "Separate Reality" and "Ecstasy" among them.

A more organized introduction to the climber's craft is offered by the *Yosemite Mountaineering School*, which runs beginners' classes and lessons for the more advanced (at Tuolumne Meadows from June to August and in the Valley from September to May) starting at $6. Details are available from any of the visitor centers or by phoning ☎372-8444. The school is also the source of the "Go Climb a Rock" T-shirts that are Yosemite's best-selling souvenir.

Whatever type of climbing you do, follow the guidelines for "minimum impact climbing" – don't chip holds, use chalk that blends with the rock and take all litter, including human waste, away with you.

*Yosemite Concession Services* and must be reserved on ☎252-4848. Most places **reduce their charges** in winter, though weekend prices remain close to high season levels.

One solution to the problem is to stay just outside the park and commute into it daily. **FISH CAMP**, strung out along Hwy-41 south of the park, has a number of reasonably priced accommodation options just five miles from Wawona and the Mariposa Grove.

### In the Valley

**Ahwahnee Hotel**, a short distance from Yosemite Village at shuttle stop 4 (☎252-4848). Unless you strike lucky, you'll need to book months in advance to stay in this wonderfully grand hotel (see p.301) though you could come for a meal. ⑦.

**Curry Village**, a mile from Yosemite Village at shuttle stops 1 & 14 (☎252-4848). A large area dotted with canvas tent cabins, solid-walled cabins and motel-style rooms. ②–⑤.

**Housekeeping Tents**, half a mile from Yosemite Village at shuttle stop 12 (☎252-4848). Ranks of very simple canvas tents with sleeping platforms on which to place your bedpack ($2 extra). Blankets, showers and a stove are also extra, though the tents sleep up to four and only cost $39. Mid-March to late Oct only. ②.

**Yosemite Lodge**, half a mile west of Yosemite Village (☎252-4848). Sprawling site, its proximity to half-decent restaurants and grocery shops making it perhaps the most convenient accommodation in the Valley. It has reasonable wooden huts with and without bath, and much nicer regular rooms. ③–⑤.

### Outside the Valley

**Apple Tree Inn**, Hwy-41, Fish Camp (☎683-5111). Well-equipped, well-appointed cottages tucked away in the woods, some with kitchenettes. Bookings essential June–Aug. ⑤

**Owl's Nest**, 1235 Hwy–41, Fish Camp (☎683-3484). About the best deal on the southern side of the park, with guest rooms for two and self-contained cabins which will sleep up to eight ($15 per extra person). Nicely decorated, friendly and right by a stream. ④/⑤.

**Tuolumne Meadows Lodge**, Tuolumne (☎252-4848). Canvas tent cabins at nearly 9000ft. Only available late April to Oct. ②.

**Wawona Hotel**, Wawona (☎252-4848). An elegant hotel, parts of which date from 1879, with a distinctive wooden verandah. The nice rooms have baths, and there's a pool, tennis courts and a 9-hole golf course in the grounds.Worth a splurge if you can afford it. ④/⑤.

**White Chief Mountain Lodge**, 7776 White Chief Mountain Rd, Fish Camp (☎683-5444). Basic and functional motel units for two and nicer cabins for up to four. Just 300yd off Hwy-41. ④/⑥.

**White Wolf Lodge**, about halfway from the Valley to Tuolumne Meadows (☎252-4848). Cabins with attatched bathroom, and considerably more primitive tent cabins. ②/③.

## Eating and drinking

With one notable exception, **eating** in Yosemite is a function rather than a pleasure. Food, whether in restaurants or in the grocery stores around Yosemite Village (where there's a well-stocked supermarket), Curry Village, Wawona and Tuolumne Meadows, is more expensive inside the park than out. In Yosemite Village, there's the good if pricey *Mountain Room Broiler* (daily 5–9pm) at *Yosemite Lodge,* a downbeat cafeteria and a range of diners and snack bars, the best of which is *Degnan's Deli* (daily 7am–10pm), where massive sandwiches cost around $4. One of the most beautiful restaurants in the US, the baronial *Ahwahnee Dining Room* (☎372-1489 for reservations), has the best food in Yosemite – especially in winter when it brings in top chefs for weekend gourmandizing. Dinner is around $50 for three courses with wine; jacket and tie preferred. Breakfast and lunch are more casual and appreciably cheaper.

**Outside the valley** the choice is even more limited, though in the south of the park there's the relatively formal *Wawona Hotel Dining Room* at the *Wawona Hotel* (☎375-6556). Expect to fork out $40 for a full meal. Just off Hwy-120 on the way to Tuolumne, the *White Wolf Lodge* (☎252-4848) offers large portions of good value American food , and *the Tuolumne Meadows Lodge* (☎372-1313) serves family-style breakfasts and dinners. Just outside the park at Fish Camp, try the *White Chief Mountain Lodge* (☎683-5444) for steaks, fish and sandwiches at reasonable prices.

Yosemite Village is the centre of the park's **evening entertainment**, in the form of talks, photographic shows and even theatrical productions. The *Yosemite Guide* has the full programme. *Yosemite Lodge* has the valley's liveliest **bar**.

## Yosemite Valley

Even the most evocative photography can only hint at the pleasure to be found in simply gazing at **Yosemite Valley**. From massive hunks of granite rising five thousand feet up from the four-thousand-foot valley floor to the subtle colourings of wild flowers, the variations in the valley can be both enormous and discreet. Aside from just looking, there are many easy walks around the lush fields to waterfalls and lakes, and much tougher treks up the enormous cliffs (see "Hiking" box, p.304). Whichever way you decide to see it, the valley's concentration of natural grandeur is quite memorable. If there is any drawback, it's that this part of Yosemite is the busiest, and you're rarely far from other visitors or the park's commercial trappings: a couple of days exploring the valley leaves you more than ready to press on to the park's less populated regions.

---

### CAMPING

As with any national park, **camping** is the best way to really feel part of your surroundings, though this is less true in Yosemite Valley where the campsites are large and crowded. You can, and should, book up to twelve weeks beforehand (☎1-800/436-7275; from outside the US or Canada ☎619/452-8787). Otherwise you'll need to show up at the Curry Village Reservations Office very early in the morning and hope for cancellations. Other than the *Sunnyside Walk-In*, all sites cost $14. None has showers, but there are $2 **public showers** at the *Housekeeping Camp* – where you'll also find a **laundromat** (daily 7am–2.30pm & 3.30–10pm) – and at *Curry Village*, which has a public **swimming pool** (see "Accommodation" for details of both) .

In addition to the main campsites there are **backpacker campgrounds** in Yosemite Valley, Tuolumne Meadows and Hetch Hetchy, designed for hikers and cyclists and costing $2 per night. People with vehicles who are planning a wilderness trip can stay at these sites for one night at the beginning and end of the trip. In the valley, camping outside recognized sites in the valley is strictly forbidden.

Finally, with enough time you really should get out to one of the many **primitive campgrounds** in the backcountry. Designed specifically for hikers, these have fire rings and some form of water source, which must be treated. To use them, or to camp elsewhere in the backcountry, you must get a **wilderness permit** (see "Hiking" box, p.304) – as ever, you must camp a mile from any road, four miles from a populated area, and at least a hundred yards from water sources and trails.

IN THE VALLEY
**North Pines**, **Upper Pines**, **Lower Pines**, **Lower River** (April–Oct, Upper Pines April–Nov; $14; 4000ft). Largely indistinguishable, pine-shrouded sites, all with toilets, water and fire rings. Popular with RV users. Reservations essential.
**Sunnyside Walk-In** (all year; $3 per person; 4000ft). West of and away from the other valley sites, and very popular with rock climbers. Each plot is just a few yards from the inadequate parking spaces. The campground is non-reservable and often full by 9am in summer, so join the line early.
**Upper River** (April–Oct; $14; 4000ft). Similar to the other valley sites, but RVs are prohibited.

## Yosemite Village

Very much the heart of things in the valley, **YOSEMITE VILLAGE** has shops, banking facilities (with an ATM), restaurants, a post office (Mon–Fri 8.30am–5pm) and one of the park's **visitor centers** (see p.297). Beside the visitor center, the small but interesting **Indian Cultural Museum** (daily 8am–5.30pm; free), comprises a roomful of artefacts from the local Native Americans and, outside, a self-guided trail around a reconstructed group of their buildings. There's something of the more recent past to be found in the nearby **cemetery**, which holds the unkempt graves of some of the early white settlers who attempted to farm the valley, and often perished in its isolation. By contrast, and worth a quick look even if you don't intend to stay or eat there (if you do, see p.299), is the **Ahwahnee Hotel**, a short signposted walk from Yosemite Village. Built in 1927 from local rock, it was intended to blend into its surroundings and attract the richer type of tourist. It still does both fairly effortlessly, and has a viewable collection of paintings of Yosemite around the lobby and dining room.

## The Valley floor

There's little around the village to divert attention from Yosemite's beckoning natural features for long. It's true that you'll never be alone on the valley floor, but most of the

OUTSIDE THE VALLEY

**Bridalveil Creek** (June–Sept; $10; 7200ft). High country site off Glacier Point Road with good access to wilderness trails.

**Carlon** (April–Nov; free; 4400ft). Just outside the park boundary in the surrounding Stanislaus National Forest. Spacious sites with vault toilets but no water. Take Evergreen Road north for a mile and a half.

**Crane Flat** (June–Oct; $12; 6200ft). Northwest of the Valley, at the start of Hwy-120 and close to a stand of sequoias. Reservations required.

**Hodgdon Meadow** (April–Dec; $12; 4900ft). Relatively quiet site right on the park's western boundary just off Hwy-120. Take Old Big Oak Flat Road for half a mile. Reservations required May–Oct.

**Middle Fork** (all year; free; 4300ft). Half a mile south of and similar to the *Carlon* site.

**Porcupine Flat** (June–early Sept; $6; 8100ft). Small RV-free site near the road to Tuolumne Meadows, nearly forty miles from the valley . Stream water.

**Tamarack Flat** (June–early Sept; $6; 6300ft). Small RV-free site two miles off the Hwy-120 Tioga road, 23 miles from the Valley. Stream water.

**Tuolumne Meadows** (mid-May to Sept; $12; 8600ft). A streamside site in a sub-alpine meadow. It's popular with backpackers and car-campers alike, but you'll probably find a place. Several walk-in sites are reserved for hikers who wish to camp away from vehicles. Showers ($2) are available nearby.

**Wawona** (all year; $10; 4000ft). The only site in the southern sector of the park, approximately a mile or so north of the *Wawona Hotel*. Some walk-in sites are reserved for car-free campers.

**White Wolf** (June–early Sept; $10; 8000ft). Tent and RV site a mile north of Hwy-120 midway between the Valley and Tuolumne Meadows.

**Yosemite Creek** (June to early Sept; $6; 7600ft). A tent-only site ideal for escaping the crowds, though it can fill up very quickly in the summer. Inconveniently sited five miles off Hwy-120, but almost equidistant between the Valley and Tuolumne Meadows. Stream water.

crowds can be left behind by taking any path which contains much of a slope. The more strenuous hikes are detailed in the box on p.304.

One of the more popular easy strolls is to **Lower Yosemite Falls** (shuttle bus stop 7) just a few minutes' walk from *Yosemite Lodge*, at the western end of the valley. Come towards the end of summer and the falls are disappointing and barely worth even the minimal effort required to get there, but in spring ice-cold meltwater thunders down three hundred feet drenching onlookers in spray. If this inspires you, consider the walk to the far more impressive **Upper Yosemite Falls**, which crash down almost 1500ft in a single cascade. Together with the cataracts in between, the two drop the Yosemite River 2500ft, constituting the highest fall in North America.

Three other waterfalls can be easily reached from the valley. One of the more sensual is the 600-foot **Bridalveil Falls**, a slender ribbon at the valley's western end which in Ahwahneechee goes by the name of *Pohono*, "spirit of the puffing wind". The base of the falls is at the end of a quarter-mile trail from a parking lot four miles west of the village and is not on the shuttle route. More rugged routes head up Little Yosemite Valley to the 300-foot **Vernal Falls** and the 600-foot **Nevada Falls** beyond.

The **LeConte Memorial Lodge** (April–Sept Wed–Sun 10am–4pm; free; shuttle stop 12) was built by the Sierra Club to commemorate one of its original members, Joseph LeConte, an eminent scholar who died in Yosemite but whose wishes to be buried here were ignored. The granite block structure contains a library and displays on the Sierra Club, but is mainly of interest for its free programme of nature walks (Thurs–Sun 10am–noon) and educational lectures and slide shows (Fri–Sun 8pm).

Perhaps one of the most rewarding of the easy trails leads from shuttle stop 17 around the edge of the valley floor to **Mirror Lake** (2 miles; 1hr; 100ft ascent). This compellingly calm lake lies beneath the great bulk of Half Dome (see below), the rising cliff reflected on the lake's surface, and is best seen in the early morning, before too many others arrive. The lake is a microcosm of the whole Yosemite Valley, its meditative stillness due in part to the fact that it's slowly silting up as the valley floor has done since the last Ice Age. From Mirror Lake, trails continue around the lake (1 mile), to Tenaya Lake (11 miles) and to Tuolumne Meadows (21 miles). Most visitors to Mirror Lake follow the traffic-free paved road from the shuttle stop, but several easily found diversions steer you clear of the asphalt and the crowds.

### The big cliffs: El Capitan and Half Dome

Of the two major peaks that you can see from the valley, **El Capitan**, rising some 3500ft above the floor, is the biggest piece of exposed granite in the world. A sense of its dimensions can be gleaned by the fact that rock-climbers fast become invisible to the naked eye from ground level. Much the same applies to **Half Dome**, the sheerest cliff in North America, only seven degrees off the vertical. You can hike to its top by way of a steel staircase hooked on to its curving back from the far end of Little Yosemite Valley.

### Views of the valley: Glacier Point

The most spectacular views of Yosemite Valley are from **Glacier Point**, the top of a 3200-foot almost sheer cliff, 32 miles by road (usually open mid-May to late Oct) from the valley. It's possible to get there on foot using the very steep four-mile track (see "Hiking" box) which begins at the western end of the valley, beside Hwy-41, though the lazy person's method is to use the bus (see p.298) to go up and to take the trail down. The valley floor lies directly beneath the viewing point, and there are tremendous views across to Half Dome (easy from here to see how it got its name) and to the distant snowcapped summits of the High Sierra. In winter, one of the best **cross-country ski** trips is the eight miles here from the Badger Pass ski area.

# Outside the valley

However crowded the valley might be, the rest of the park sees very few tourists. Even places you can get to by car, like **Wawona** and **Mariposa Grove** on the park's southern edge, remain peaceful most of the time, and if you're willing to hike a few miles and camp out overnight, the 99 percent of Yosemite that's untouched by road contains acres of pristine scenery, especially around **Tuolumne Meadows** on the park's eastern border.

## Tuolumne Meadows

On the eastern edge of the park, the alpine **Tuolumne Meadows** have an atmosphere quite different from the valley; here, at 8500ft, you almost seem to be level with the tops of the surrounding snow-covered mountains and the air always has a fresh, crisp bite. That said, there can still be good-sized blasts of carbon monoxide at peak times in the vicinity of the campground – the only accommodation base in the area and within easy reach of the park's eastern entrance at Tioga Pass (Hwy-120). But it's a better starting point than the valley for backcountry hiking into the High Sierra, where seven hundred-odd miles of trails, both long and short, crisscross their way along the Sierra Nevada ridge. Also, because the growing season is short so high up, early summer in Tuolumne reveals a plethora of colourful wild blossoms. If you haven't the time for a long hike from here, at least stroll the half-mile trail to the naturally carbonated **Soda Springs**.

Between July and mid-August, a bus links Tuolumne and Yosemite Valley, and a free shuttle service also links Tuolumne to Tenaya Lake (July to early Sept 7am–6pm). Alternatively, it's possible to hike between the two settlements using part of the **John Muir Trail**, a distance of roughly twenty miles from the Happy Isles trailhead. The Pacific Crest Trail, stretching from Mexico right up to Canada, also passes through Tuolumne, and there are innumerable other paths into the canyons and valleys in the area. One of the best hikes leads north and west through the Grand Canyon of the Tuolumne River; get the full details from the **visitor center** at the Tuolumne campground.

## Wawona and the Mariposa Grove

Driving to Yosemite from Fresno, you'll probably pass through **WAWONA**, 27 miles west of the valley on Hwy-41, whose landmark is the *Wawona Hotel* (see p.299), surrounded by tennis courts and a golf course ($18 for 18 holes). Close by, the **Pioneer Yosemite History Center** (mid-June to early Sept daily 9am–5pm) is a collection of buildings culled from the early times of white habitation. The jail, homesteads, covered bridge and the like are good for a scoot around, and, once you're away from the main road, the area makes a quiet spot for a picnic. Stables here offer horseback rides ($31 for two hours up to $65 for a day; ☎375-6502).

**Mariposa Grove**, three miles east of Hwy-41 on a small road which cuts off just past the park's southern entrance, is the biggest and best of Yosemite's groves of giant sequoia trees. To get to the towering growths, walk the two-and-a-half mile loop trail from the parking lot at the end of the road, which is also served by a tram from the entrance (9am–6pm; $7).

Trails around sequoia groves call first at the **Fallen Monarch**, familiar from the 1899 photo, widely reproduced on postcards, in which cavalry officers and their horses stand atop the prostrate tree. The most renowned of the grouping, well marked along the route, is the **Grizzly Giant**, thought to be 2700 years old and with a lower branch thicker than the trunk of any non-sequoia in the grove. Other highlights include the now-fallen **Wawona Tunnel Tree** through which people drove their cars until it fell in

1969, the similarly bored **California Tunnel Tree**, which you can walk through, and all manner of trees which have grown together, split apart, been struck by lightning, or are simply staggeringly large. It's also worth dropping into the **Mariposa Grove Museum** (daily 9am–5.30pm; free), towards the top end of the trail, which has modest displays and photos of the mighty trees. For more on the life of the sequoia, see p.563 of *Contexts*.

## HIKING IN YOSEMITE NATIONAL PARK

To camp out overnight in most of Yosemite's designated wilderness you need a free **wilderness permit**. Between May and October a quota system is in operation, but with flexibility you should be able to get one, even in high summer. Popular trails – Merced River Trail up to Little Yosemite or Tuolumne Meadows to Lyle Fort – fill up quickly. You can **reserve in advance** for a $3 per person fee, up to six months and at least two days ahead of your planned trip; contact *Wilderness Reservations*, PO Box 545, Yosemite, CA 95389 (☎372-0740), stating your requirements and your desired itinerary with alterna- tives. Fortunately for the casual visitor, at least half the quota is offered on a first-come- first-served basis, so line up at one of the park's **ranger stations** early the day before you wish to start. Don't despair if you have trouble landing the trail you want: paths are so numerous that you may start at a less popular trailhead but end up doing largely the same hike.

Camping gear can be rented quite reasonably from *Yosemite Mountaineering School* (see p.298), as can bear-resistant canisters ($3 a day plus $75 deposit), which you'll also find in Yosemite's stores.

**Four-mile Trail** (10 miles; 5–6hr; 3200ft ascent). The asphalt path from the Valley floor to Glacier Point doesn't give much of a sense of being in the wilderness, but the magnifi- cent views make this one of the Valley's more popular day walks. Closed in winter.

**Half Dome** (17 miles; 10–12hr; 4800ft ascent). The route starts by following the Vernal and Nevada Falls Trail (below) and continues around the back of Half Dome. The final ascent is over the huge, smooth, humped back aided by a pair of steel ropes and wooden steps. Even with a head for heights, the near vertical 5000-foot drop from the top can induce vertigo. If you plan a one-day assault, you'll need to start at the crack of dawn.The final cabled section to the top is usually closed from November to May when the steps are taken away and the cables loosened

**Tuolumne Meadows to Yosemite Valley** (20 miles; 2 days; strenuous in parts; 10,000ft ascent). Several routes, all quite popular, leave from Yosemite to Tuolumne. All can be done fairly easily in two days if you're in reasonably good shape, less if done in reverse using the Tuolumne Shuttle. One of the best routes (reserve your permits early) follows the **John Muir Trail** up Little Yosemite Valley past Vernal and Nevada Falls and the base of the final climb up Half Dome.

**Upper Yosemite Falls** (7 miles; 4hr; 2700ft ascent). A fairly strenuous walk, the almost continuous ascent sapping on the leg muscles, but with fine views and, during the melt- water period at least, a chance to appreciate the power and volume of the water at the end. Start just by the *Sunnyside* campground (shuttle stop 7).

**Vernal and Nevada Falls** (7 miles; 6hr; 1900ft ascent) The trail begins at the southeast- ern side of the valley (shuttle bus stop 16).The route is steep and can be wet and slippery – it's not referred to as the "mist trail" for nothing – but otherwise is not especially tough, and the visual rewards of reaching either or both falls are tremendous.

## travel details

### Trains

The 4-times-daily *San Joaquin* service runs between Bakersfield and Oakland, the terminus for San Francisco. *Amtrak Thruway* bus connections from **Los Angeles** (Union Station, LAX, UCLA, Santa Monica, Long Beach and Glendale) link with the train at Bakersfield.

**Bakersfield to**: Fresno (2hr); Hanford (1hr 20min); Merced (2hr 50min); Oakland (6hr); Stockton (4hr).

### Buses

Buses are either *Greyhound* or *Amtrak Thruway*.

**Bakersfield to**: Merced (12 daily; 4–5hr).

**Fresno to**: Merced (15 daily; 1hr 10min); Modesto (17 daily; 2hr 10min); Stockton (9 daily; 3hr); Yosemite (1 daily; 3hr 30min).

**Hanford to**: San Luis Obispo (1 daily; 3hr).

**Los Angeles to**: Bakersfield (18 daily; 1hr 25min); Fresno (16 daily; 6hr 45min); Merced (9 daily; 6–8hr); Modesto (12 daily; 8hr 25min); Stockton (11 daily; 6hr 45min); Visalia (6 daily; 6hr 15min).

**Merced to**: Los Angeles (13 daily; 6–8hr); Modesto (6 daily; 1hr); Sacramento (8 daily; 3hr); San Francisco (6–7 daily; 4–5hr); Yosemite (3–5 daily; 2hr 45min).

**San Francisco to**: Bakersfield (7 daily; 7hr 20min); Fresno (9 daily; 4hr 40min); Merced (8 daily; 3hr 30min–5hr); Modesto (8 daily; 2hr 10min); Stockton (3 daily; 1hr 30min); Visalia (2 daily; 5hr).

**Stockton to**: Lodi (5 daily; 30min); Merced (6–7 daily; 2hr); Sacramento (11 daily; 1hr).

**Visalia to**: Hanford (2 daily; 1hr 30min); Reedley (1 daily; 40min).

# CHAPTER SIX

# THE CENTRAL COAST

After the hustle of LA and San Francisco, the four hundred miles of coastline in between – the **Central Coast** – can seem like the land that time forgot: sparsely populated outside the few medium-sized towns, and lined by clean, sandy beaches that are often little disturbed by modern life. Indeed, first-time visitors, and those who rarely set foot out of the cities, may be surprised to find just how much of the region survives in its natural state. The mountain ranges that separate the shore from the farmlands of the inland valleys are for the most part pristine wilderness, sometimes covered in thick forests of tall and slender redwood trees, while, in winter especially, fast-flowing rivers and streams course down valleys to the sea. All along the shore, sea otters and seals play in the waves, and endangered gray whales pass close by on their annual migration from Alaska to Mexico.

**Big Sur**, where the brooding Santa Lucia mountains rise steeply out of the thundering Pacific surf, is the heart of the region, and the best place to experience this untouched environment at its most dramatic. Nature aside, though, the Central Coast also marks the gradual transition from Southern to Northern California. The two largest towns here, **Santa Barbara** and **Santa Cruz**, are poles apart: Santa Barbara, a hundred miles north of Los Angeles, is a conservative, wealthy resort; Santa Cruz, 75 miles south of San Francisco, is a throwback to the 1960s, where long hair and tie-dye are still the order of the day. What they have in common is miles of broad clean **beaches**, with often chilly but always clean water and excellent surf, and a branch of the University of California energizing the local nightlife. In between, the small town of **San Luis Obispo** provides a languorous contrast to them both, and is a feasible base for the Central Coast's biggest tourist attraction, **Hearst Castle**, the opulent hilltop palace of publishing magnate William Randolph "Citizen Kane" Hearst.

The Central Coast is also one of the most historic parts of the state, and contains the bulk and the best of the late-eighteenth-century Spanish colonial **missions** – the first European settlements on the West Coast, set up to convert the natives to Christianity while co-opting their labour. Almost all of the towns that exist today grew up around the adobe walls and red-tiled roofs of these Catholic colonies, strung out along the Pacific, each deliberately sited a long day's walk from the next and typically composed of a church and a cloistered monastery, enclosed within thick walls to prevent attacks by Indian tribes. **Monterey**, a hundred miles south of San Francisco, was the capital of California under Spain, and later, Mexico, and today retains more of its early nineteenth-century architecture than any other city in the state; it's also a good base for one of the most beautiful of the missions, which stands three miles south in the uppercrust seaside resort of **Carmel**.

### Getting around the Central Coast

Getting around is easy by Californian standards: some of the best views in the state can be had from *Amtrak*'s Coast Starlight train, which runs bang along the coast up to San Luis Obispo before cutting inland north to San Francisco. *Greyhound* buses stop at most of the towns, particularly those along the main highway, US-101 – though a better route, if you've got a car, is the smaller Hwy-1, which follows the coast all the way but takes twice as long.

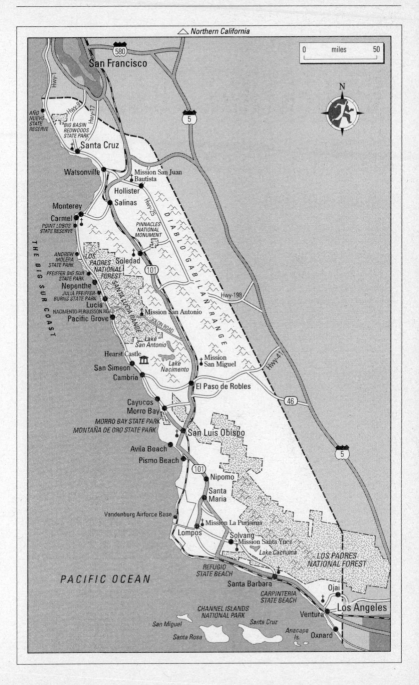

△ *Northern California*

580
**San Francisco**

5

0    miles    50

N

AÑo
NUEVO
STATE
RESERVE
BIG BASIN
REDWOODS
STATE PARK

**Santa Cruz**

**Watsonville**

Mission San Juan
Bautista

**Hollister**
**Salinas**

**Monterey**
**Carmel**
POINT LOBOS
STATE RESERVE

PINNACLES
NATIONAL
MONUMENT

ANDREW
MOLERA STATE PARK
PFEIFFER BIG SUR
STATE PARK

**Soledad**

101

**Nepenthe**
JULIA PFEIFFER
BURNS STATE PARK

**Lucia**
NACIMENTO-FERGUSSON ROAD

**Pacific Grove**

Mission San Antonio

JOLON ROAD

Lake
San Antonio

Hearst Castle

**San Simeon**
**Cambria**

Lake
Nacimiento

Mission
San Miguel

**El Paso de Robles**

46

**Cayucos**
**Morro Bay**
MORRO BAY STATE PARK
MONTAÑA DE ORO STATE PARK

**San Luis Obispo**

**Avila Beach**
**Pismo Beach**

101

**Nipomo**

**Santa
Maria**

Vandenburg Airforce Base

Mission La Purisima

**Lompos**

**Solvang**
Mission Santa Ynez

Lake Cachuma

LOS PADRES
NATIONAL FOREST

REFUGIO
STATE BEACH

*PACIFIC OCEAN*

**Santa Barbara**

CARPINTERIA
STATE BEACH

**Ojai**

CHANNEL ISLANDS
NATIONAL PARK

*San Miguel*

*Santa Cruz*

*Santa Rosa*

*Anacapa
Is.*

**Ventura**

**Los Angeles**

**Oxnard**

5

THE BIG SUR COAST

SANTA LUCIA RANGE

DIABLO GABILAN RANGE

Hwy 1
Hwy 17
Hwy 9
Hwy 25
Hwy 198
Hwy 41

LOS
PADRES
NATIONAL
FOREST

**Places to stay** are easy to find, at least outside summer weekends when otherwise quiet towns and beaches are packed solid with vacationing families. Opportunities for **camping** are plentiful, too, in a string of state parks, beaches and forests.

# Ventura and Ojai

The valleys of suburban Los Angeles meet the Pacific coast at **VENTURA**, a long-standing farming and fishing community that's slowly being submerged beneath an overlay of fast-food restaurants and mini-malls. The only real reason to stop, besides buying fresh strawberries or other seasonal produce from the many roadside stalls, is to catch a boat out to the offshore Channel Islands (see below) from the harbour four miles southwest of town. If you've got more time to spare, look in on the seemingly time-warped town centre, just north of the intersection of US-101 and Hwy-1, around the restored church of **Mission San Buenaventura** at 225 Main St (daily 10am–5pm; 50¢), founded in 1782. Also on Main Street are two small but reasonably engaging museums: the **Albinger Archaeological Museum**, at no. 113 (Wed–Sun 10am–4pm; free), has exhibits explaining 3500 years of local history, from ancient Native American cultures to the mission era; while across the street the **Ventura County Museum of History and Art** (Tues–Sun 10am–5pm; $2, free on Tues) takes up where the former leaves off, with exhibits on local pioneer families and their farming equipment.

*Amtrak* trains pull in near Harbor Boulevard and Figueroa Street, three blocks from the *Greyhound* stop at Thomson Boulevard and California Street. The **CVB** at 89 California St (Mon–Fri 8.30am–5pm, Sat 9am–4pm, Sun 10am–4pm; ☎648-2075) can help with accommodation and has local bus maps. As Ventura is a springboard for visiting the Channel Islands there is a **Channel Islands National Park visitor center** (daily 8am–5.30pm; ☎658-5730), next to the ferry landing in Ventura Harbor, which has well-presented displays on the geology and the native plant and animal life of the islands, including seals, sea lions, pelican rookeries and giant kelp forests. It also has up-to-date information on arranging trips, and a tower from which, on fine days, you can view the islands.

Nestled in the hills above Ventura, the small town of **OJAI** (pronounced *O-hi*) is a wealthy resort community, and centre for the exclusive health spas and tennis clubs that dot the surrounding countryside. It's also headquarters of the Krishnamurti Society, which spreads the word of the theosophist who lived and lectured here during the 1920s, considering the Ojai Valley "a vessel of comprehension, intelligence and truth". The **Krishnamurti Library**, several miles northeast of town at 1130 McAndrew Rd (Wed 1–9pm, Thurs–Sun 1–5pm; ☎646-4948), has details on his teachings. Otherwise, about the only place in town worth stopping at is *Bart's Books*, an outdoor bookstore at Cañada and Matilija, with an excellent selection of secondhand books.

The telephone **area code** for the southern Central Coast is ☎805.

The **Chamber of Commerce**, 338 E Ojai Ave (Mon–Fri 9.30am–4.30pm, Sat & Sun 10am–4pm; ☎646-8126), has information on the town's numerous B&B inns.

Six miles north of town, off scenic Hwy-33, are the *Wheeler Hot Springs*, 16825 Maricopa Hwy (Mon–Thurs 9am–9pm, Fri–Sun 9am–10pm; ☎646-8131), where you can soak in 105°F water for $10 per half-hour. Nearby is the **Los Padres National Forest**, and a decent **campground**.

# The Channel Islands National Park

Stretching north from Catalina Island off the coast of Los Angeles (see p.118), a chain of little-known desert islands has been protected in its natural state as the **CHANNEL ISLANDS NATIONAL PARK** (free entry), offering excellent hiking and close-up views of sea lions, as well as fishing and skin-diving through the many shipwrecks in the crystal-clear Pacific waters. All five of the main islands are accessible, though it is the closest, Anacapa, some 14 miles south of Ventura, which sees the most traffic.

Tiny **Anacapa** is actually two islets. West Anacapa is mostly a refuge for nesting brown pelicans, although Frenchy's Cove is a great beach and base for scuba or snorkelling expeditions. More happens on East Anacapa where there's a small visitor center and a mile-and-a-half-long nature trail. There are no beaches, but there's swimming in the cove where the boats dock.

West of Anacapa, **Santa Cruz** is the largest and highest of the islands, and the only one with some private ownership, at its eastern end. **Santa Rosa**, with its grasslands, is less rugged but still has its share of steep ravines. Hiking inland requires a permit.

The most distant island, windswept **San Miguel** – fifty miles offshore – is thought to be the burial place of sixteenth-century Spanish explorer Juan Cabrillo. No grave has been found but a monument has been erected at Cuyler Harbor on the eastern end. For many years San Miguel was used by the military as a bombing and missile range, so sticking to trails and keeping your eyes skinned for unexploded bombs is especially important.

South of the main group lies **Santa Barbara** Island, named by Sebastian Vizcaino who dropped by on Saint Barbara's Day (December 4) in 1602. The island's appeal these days is largely ornithological, as kestrels, larks and meadowlarks can all be seen on land gradually recovering its native flora after years of destruction by now extinct rabbits.

## Practicalities

Anacapa Island is served by several tours run by *Island Packers*, 1867 Spinnaker Drive in Ventura Harbor, three miles west of US-101 and a mile south of town (☎642-7688 for 24hr recorded information; ☎642-1393 for reservations 9am–5pm). Trips range from half-day non-landing excursions ($21), through full-day trips to East or West Anacapa ($37), to overnight stays ($48). The fifteen-mile trip takes an hour and a half each way, and there's a free, very basic **campground** a half-mile walk from the landing cove. Bring plenty of **food** and especially **water**, as none is available on the boat or on the island. Permits are required for camping. Boats don't run every day and often fill up, so call at least a couple of days ahead.

The **other islands** are more difficult to visit, though *Island Packers* run boats, less frequently, to them all. Day trips to the western end of Santa Cruz (3hr each way) are $49, overnight excursions to the eastern end are $80 or $110 (including camping or dorm accommodation) – book through *Island Packers*. Visits to Santa Rosa (5hr one way; $52 for the day, $80 including camping) are often combined with a stop (or camp) on San Miguel for the same price. Santa Barbara trips are a fraction cheaper.

An alternative way to reach Santa Cruz and Santa Rosa islands is to **fly** with *Channel Islands Aviation* (☎987-1301) which runs day trips and weekend excursions ($85 &

$150 respectively) from Camarillo Airport off Hwy-101, twenty miles south of Ventura. Santa Cruz is also the venue for **kayak** trips from Santa Barbara (see p.313).

Perhaps the best time of all to visit any of the islands is between Christmas and March when there's the chance of **whale-watching**. During these months, three trips daily from Santa Barbara Harbor are organized by *Condor* (☎963-3564) – these cost $24, and take about three hours.

The **Channel Islands National Park visitor center** in Ventura (see p.308) can help with trips, and has lots of information on the islands' flora and fauna.

# Santa Barbara

The six-lane freeway that races past the oil wells and offshore drilling platforms along the coast beyond Ventura slows to a more leisurely pace a hundred miles north of Los Angeles at **SANTA BARBARA**, a moneyed seaside resort that for years has been known as the "home of the newly wed and the nearly dead" – a not entirely inaccurate summary. The recent completion of the US-101 freeway, and the replacement of much of downtown with the vast modern *El Paseo* shopping mall, are taken by some as signs that this once quaint and quiet refuge is slowly but surely turning into yet another iden-tikit suburb, but for the time being it's a lively, fun place to visit – what Southern California is meant to be.

Home to Ronald Reagan, and weekend escape for much of the old money of Los Angeles, it's a conservative town, but undeniably beautifully sited. Rising on gently sloping hills above the Pacific, the insistent red-tiled roofs and white stucco walls of the low-rise buildings form a quickly familiar background to some fine examples of Spanish Revival architecture, while the golden beaches are wide and clean, lined by palm trees along a gently curving bay. Locals look tanned and healthy, playing volley-ball, surfing, or cycling along the shore.

## Arrival, information and transport

Getting to Santa Barbara is easy. *Greyhound* **buses** arrive from LA and San Francisco every couple of hours stopping downtown at 34 W Cabrillo St; *Amtrak* **trains** stop at the old Southern Pacific station at 209 State St, a block west of US-101. Santa Barbara **airport** (☎683-4011), eight miles from the town centre near the University of California at Santa Barbara at 515 Marxmiller Drive in Goleta, has a limited and very expensive scheduled service to other Californian cities. Carriers include *American Eagle* (☎1-800/433-7300) and *United*.

For more **information** on Santa Barbara, or for help with finding a place to stay, contact either the **Visitor Information Office** on East Beach at 1 Santa Barbara St (Mon–Sat 9am–5pm, Sun 10am–5pm; ☎965-3021) or *Hot Spots*, 36 State St (Mon–Sat 9am–9pm, Sun noon–4pm; ☎564-1637), tucked in behind the café of the same name and very helpful. The **US Forest Service** office in Goleta, near UCSB at 6144 Calle Real (☎683-6711), has information on **hiking** in the vicinity of Santa Barbara (and the many good trails easily accessible from downtown).

**Getting around** Santa Barbara is simple: your feet can take you most places and there's a quarter-a-ride shuttle bus which loops between downtown and the beach on a 10–15 minute schedule, and along the waterfront to the zoo every half-hour until 5.30pm, 8pm on Friday and Saturday. The outlying areas are covered by *Santa Barbara Metropolitan Transit District* buses (☎683-3702). If you want to **rent a car**, the best value is *U-Save Auto Rental*, 510 Anacapa St (☎963-3499), which rents late-model cars for as little as $24 a day including one hundred free miles. The chain offices are *Budget* (☎963-6651) and *Hertz* (☎967-0411), both at the airport.

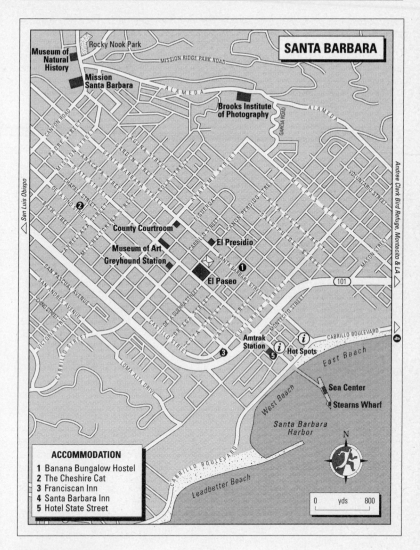

ACCOMMODATION

1 Banana Bungalow Hostel
2 The Cheshire Cat
3 Franciscan Inn
4 Santa Barbara Inn
5 Hotel State Street

## Accommodation

Holding some of the West Coast's most deluxe resorts – it's the sort of place movie stars go to get married, or to honeymoon – Santa Barbara is among the priciest places to **stay**, with rooms averaging over $110 a night. However, there is a hostel, and with a bit of advance planning finding somewhere good shouldn't take too big a bite out of your budget. The least expensive as well as most of the more moderate places are booked solid throughout the summer, but if you get stuck, enlist the assistance of *Hot*

*Spots* (see above) or the *Accommodations Santa Barbara* (☎687-9191) booking bureau. Also, while there's no **camping** in Santa Barbara proper, there are lots of grounds along the coast to the north and in the mountains of the Santa Ynez Valley.

**Banana Bungalow Hostel**, 210 E Ortega St (☎963-0154). Newly converted from commercial premises and catering to raucous backpackers. A party atmosphere pervades, engendered as much by the 2.30am curfew as the occasional keg parties. $13 a night. ①.

**The Cheshire Cat**, 36 W Valerio St (☎569-1610). Tastefully decorated B&B with hot tub and bikes for guests' use. Complimentary wine on arrival and breakfast under a palm tree. Ten minutes' walk from the restaurant zone. ⑥.

**Franciscan Inn**, 109 Bath St (☎963-8845). Comfortable, quiet and very clean motel, just a block from the beach with a pool, spa and complimentary breakfast. ④.

**Hotel State Street**, 121 State St (☎966-6586). Near the wharf and beach in a characterful old mission-style building, with free morning tea and coffee. Communal bathrooms. ②.

**Miramar Hotel Resort**, 1555 S Jameson Lane (☎969-2203). Slightly faded, once elegant beach resort with seaview rooms, and the only place in town with a private strand. ④.

**Motel 6**, 443 Corona del Mar (☎564-1392). Inexpensive but extremely popular beachfront lodging in no-frills chain motel. There's another north of the town centre at 3505 State St (☎687-5400). Both ③.

**San Ysidro Ranch**, 900 San Ysidro Lane (☎969-5046). Gorgeous, ultra-posh resort with private cottages in lovely gardens (Jackie and JFK spent their honeymoon here), in the hills ten minutes' drive south of town. ⑧.

**Santa Barbara Inn**, 901 E Cabrillo Blvd (☎966-2285 or 1-800/231-0431). Upscale oceanfront motel with large pool and lovely views. ⑦.

# The Town

The mission-era feel of Santa Barbara is no accident. Following a devastating earthquake in 1925, the city authorities decided to rebuild virtually the entire town in the image of an apocryphal Spanish Colonial past – even the massive *El Paseo* shopping mall is covered in pseudo-whitewashed adobe plaster – with numerous arcades linking shops, cafés and restaurants. It's surprisingly successful, and the square-mile town centre, squeezing between the south-facing beaches and the foothills of the Santa Ynez mountains, attracts one of the state's liveliest pedestrian scenes. **State Street** is the main drag, home to a friendly assortment of diners, bookstores, coffee bars and nightclubs catering to the needs of the locals – and the twenty thousand students at the nearby UCSB (see below) – as much as to visitors.

The town's few remaining, genuine mission-era structures are preserved as the **Presidio de Santa Barbara** (daily 10.30am–4.30pm; donations), in the centre of which are the two-hundred-year-old barracks of the old fortress, **El Cuartel**, standing two blocks east of State Street on Canon Perdido Street. The second-oldest building in California, this now houses historical exhibits and a scale model of the small Spanish colony. The more recent past is recounted in the Historical Society **museum**, a block away at 136 E de la Guerra St (Tues–Sat 10am-5pm, Sun noon–5pm; donations).

On the corner of State and Anapamu streets, the **Santa Barbara Museum of Art** (Tues–Wed & Fri–Sat 11am–5pm, Thurs 11am–9pm, Sun noon–5pm; $3) is of more interest, a refreshingly accessible small museum with some fine classical Greek and Egyptian statuary and a fairly comprehensive collection of American painting, as well as some French Impressionists. Just east of here, on Anapamu Street, the **Santa Barbara County Courthouse** is the one first-rate piece of Spanish Revival architecture in Santa Barbara, an idiosyncratic variation on the mission theme that has been widely praised as one of the finest public buildings in the US. Take a break in the sunken gardens, explore the quirky staircases, or climb the seventy-foot-high **clocktower** (daily 9am–5pm; free) for a view out over the town. Two blocks up State Street the landmark **Arlington Theater** is an intact and still-functioning 1930s movie palace and performance venue, whose *trompe l'oeil* interior simulates a Mexican village plaza.

## The beaches and around

Half a mile down State Street from the town centre, Cabrillo Street runs along the south-facing shore, a long, clean strand stretching from the yacht and fishing harbor beyond palm-lined **West Beach** to the volleyball courts and golden sands of **East Beach**, which hosts an outdoor arts and crafts market every Sunday. At the foot of State Street take a stroll among the pelicans on **Stearns Wharf**, the oldest wooden pier in the state, built in 1872 and recently restored, with seafood restaurants, ice cream stalls and a fish market at the far end. Also on the wharf is the **Sea Center** (daily 10am–5pm; $2), an educational centre that's an annexe of the natural history museum in the foothills above town. Just west of the pier world-class athletes keep in shape in the *Los Baños* open-air fifty-metre swimming pool ($2), while **windsurfers** can be rented from beachfront stalls. **Kayaks** are available from *Paddle Sports*, 100 State St ($20 for two hours, $40 a day; ☎899-4925),which also conducts lessons and runs all-inclusive paddling and snorkelling trips out to Santa Cruz Island ($295). *Beach Rentals*, 8 W Cabrillo St (☎963-5337), offers **bicycles** for around $30 a day, and provides a map of Santa Barbara's extensive system of bike paths; the longest and most satisfying leads west along the bluffs all the way to Isla Vista and UCSB, and passes a mile or so back from the rarely crowded, creekside **Arroyo Burro Beach** (locally known as "Hendry's"), four miles west of the wharf at the end of Las Positas Road. Alternatively head along the beachfront bike path two miles east past the Santa Barbara **zoo** (daily 10am–5pm; $5), and cycle around the **Andree Clark Bird Refuge** (unrestricted access) just beyond, an enclosed saltwater marsh where you can see a variety of seabirds, including egrets, herons and cormorants.

## The foothills: the Mission and the museums

One sight that's worth leaving the beach for is in the hills above the town: **Mission Santa Barbara** (daily 9am–5pm; $2), the so-called "Queen of the Missions", whose colourful twin-towered front makes it the most beautiful and impressive of all the California missions, sitting majestically in well-landscaped gardens overlooking the city and the ocean. The present structure was finished and dedicated in 1820, built of local sandstone to replace a series of three adobe churches that had been destroyed by earthquakes; a small **museum** displays historical artefacts from the mission archives. Get there by *SBMTD* bus, or walk or ride the half-mile from State Street up Mission Street and Mission Canyon.

Just beyond the mission at 2559 Puesta del Sol Rd, the **Natural History Museum** (Mon–Sat 9am–5pm, Sun 10am–5pm; $3) has intriguing and informative displays on the plants and animals of the ecosystems of Southern California, and an entrance constructed out of the skeleton of a Blue Whale. Across the road, **Rocky Nook Park** is a great place to picnic or wander among the trees; and, half a mile east of the mission, the **Brooks Institute of Photography**, at 1321 Alameda Padre Serra (daily 10am–4pm; free), displays over a thousand antique cameras and, more interestingly, mounts changing exhibitions of works by some of the world's best contemporary photographers.

# Eating

Because of its status as a prime resort area, Santa Barbara has a number of very good and very expensive **restaurants**, but it also has numerous more affordable options that offer a range of good food. Since it's right on the Pacific, you'll find a lot of seafood (and sushi); Mexican places are also numerous and of a very high standard.

**Enterprise Fish Company**, 225 State St (☎962-3313). Lively, moderately priced fish spot popular with locals and tourists alike.

**Esau's Coffee Shop**, 403 State St (☎965-4416). Ancient-looking café serving Santa Barbara's most popular greasy-spoon breakfasts. Open until 1pm.

**Joe's Café**, 536 State St (☎966-4638). Long-established bar and grill. A great place to stop off for a burger and a beer, more or less midway between the beach and the downtown museums.

**La Super-Rica Taquaeria**, 622 N Milpas St (☎962-2318). Some of the finest Yucatan cuisine to be found in these parts. Casual outdoor dining at a price.

**Palazzio Trattoria Italiana**, 1151 Coast Village Rd, Montecito (☎969-8565). Trattoria of choice for the region's smart set, though by no means intimidating. The portions are large, the prices moderate, and the tiramisu divine. Ten minutes' drive south of town.

**Paradise Café**, 702 Anacapa St (☎962-4416). Stylish, slightly upmarket 1940s era indoor/outdoor grill, with good steaks and ultra-fresh seafood.

**RG's Giant Hamburgers**, 922 State St (☎963-1654). The burgers here, meatless ones included, are regularly voted the biggest and best in Santa Barbara. Good salads too, and breakfast daily from 7am.

**World Café**, 1208 State St (☎962-5352). A wide range of affordable salads, sandwiches and healthy international food served in sunny, smoke-free surroundings.

**Zia's**, 532 State St (☎962-5391). Upscale but not expensive Santa Fe-style Mexican restaurant, with subtle variations on the tacos-and-burritos theme: try the fried chillis stuffed with pine nuts and melted cheese, or the Hopi blue-corn tortillas.

## Drinking and nightlife

There are quite a few **cafés**, **bars** and **clubs** along the entire length of State Street, especially in the downtown strip. You'll find good jazz at *Joseppi's* (see below), while the *Society for Jazz and World Music* (☎962-3575) puts on a variety of interesting new music all over town.

For the most up-to-date nightlife listings, check out a copy of the free weekly *Santa Barbara Independent*, available at area bookstores, record stores and convenience stores.

**Earthling Books**, 1137 State St (☎965-0926). Late-night café in Santa Barbara's biggest and best bookstore, with signings, talks and films at 7pm most evenings.

**Espresso Roma**, 728 State St (☎962-7241). Excellent coffee, and lively from early morning until late every night.

**Joseppi's**, 434 State St (☎962-5516). The town's best jazz in a non-smoking environment with a small cover charge.

**Sojourner Coffee House**, 134 E Cañon Perdido (☎965-7922). Coffee, beer, wine, and a range of vegetarian food, in a friendly, hippyish setting, with live music some nights.

**Zelo**, 630 State St (☎966-5792). One of Santa Barbara's more fashionable bars and restaurants, which evolves into a dance club as the night wears on, offering alternative dance, latin, retro and such throughout the week. Closed Mon.

# On from Santa Barbara

Continuing north from Santa Barbara you can either cut inland through the wine region of the Santa Ynez valley (see below) or continue along the coast where, a few miles along from Santa Barbara, you'll pass the thirty-year-old campus of the University of California at Santa Barbara – **UCSB** for short – which is better-known for its volleyball teams than academics. The characterless town of **Isla Vista** borders the campus on the west, and staircases lead down the bluffs to a sandy **beach** that has some good tidepools and, at the west end, a popular surfing area at Coal Oil Point; the estuary nearby has been preserved as a botanic study centre and nature refuge.

All along this part of the coast the **beaches** face almost due south, so the surf is very lively, and in winter the sun both rises and sets over the Pacific. About twenty miles out from Santa Barbara, **El Capitan State Beach** is a popular surfing beach, while **Refugio State Beach**, another three miles along, is one of the prettiest beaches in California, with stands of palm trees dotting the sands at the mouth of a small creek.

Inland on Refugio Road, up the canyon high in the hills, stands Rancho El Cielo, the one-time Western White House of retired President **Ronald Reagan**. Ten miles west, **Gaviota State Beach** is not as pretty, but there's a fishing pier and a large wooden railway viaduct that bridges the mouth of the canyon. All the state beaches have **campgrounds** at $16 a site, $3 for a hiker/biker site (reserve through *MISTIX*); and parking is $5.

Just beyond Gaviota the highways split, US-101 heading inland and the more spectacular Hwy-1 branching off nearer the coast. Half a mile off the highway, but a world away from the speeding traffic, is the small **Las Cruces hot spring** (daylight hours; parking $2), a pool of 95°F mineral water set in a shady, peaceful ravine. Take the turn-off for Hwy-1, but stay on the east side of the freeway and double back onto a small road a quarter of a mile to the parking lot at the end. Walk half a mile or so up the trail until you smell the sulphur.

## The Santa Ynez Valley

An alternative to the coastal route out of Santa Barbara is to take Hwy-154 up and over the very steep **San Marcos Pass** through the **Santa Ynez Valley**, a pleasant route through a prime wine-growing region that's popular with leather-clad bikers and masochistic cyclists.

Three miles out of Santa Barbara, the walls of the **Chumash Painted Cave**, on Painted Caves Road, are daubed with pre-conquest Native American art, but are only just visible as you can't actually enter the cave. On the other side of the San Marcos Pass the *Cold Springs Tavern*, under the massive concrete arch bridge at 5995 Stagecoach Rd, is a good place to stop for a beer and a bite to eat.

Two miles beyond the San Marcos Pass, Paradise Road follows the Santa Ynez River up to **Red Rocks**, an excellent swimming area amidst the stoney outcrops. **Lake Cachuma**, six miles further along Hwy-154, is a popular recreation area with a large **campground** charging $10 a night; it's not actually a lake but a massive reservoir that holds the overstretched water supply for Santa Barbara.

Beyond the lake, Hwy-246 cuts off to Solvang, while Hwy-154 continues on through the vineyards around **LOS OLIVOS**, where wineries like *Firestone*, 5017 Zaca Station Rd, offer free tours and tastings (daily 11am–4pm; ☎688-3940).

## Solvang and around

It is difficult to imagine anyone falling for the sham windmills and plastic storks that fill the town of **SOLVANG**, but people come by the coachload to see the community, which was established in 1911 by a group of Danes looking for a place to found a Danish folk school. Nowadays the town, three miles off US-101 on Hwy-246, lives off tourism, and locals dress up in "traditional" costume to entertain visitors. Of the plethora of all things Danish sold just about everywhere, the only things that make the town worth a stop are the fresh coffee and pastries.

There's marginal interest in the **Mission Santa Ines** (June–Sept daily 9am–7pm; Oct–May daily 9am–4.30pm; donations, tours $3) on the eastern edge of town, founded by Spanish friars a century before the Danes arrived. The mission itself is unremarkable, but worth a look for its curious plaques thanking the Franciscan fathers for improving the lives of the native Chumash, and a gift shop with an obsessive assortment of crucifixes and devotional items. If this doesn't grab you either, you'd really do better to give it all a miss and stop by **Nojoqui Falls County Park**, six miles from Solvang off US-101, where a gentle ten-minute walk brings you to a 75-foot waterfall. The route to the park is in any case gorgeous, winding along Alisal Road under thick garlands of Spanish moss that dangle from a canopy of oak trees.

# Lompoc

Hwy-1 splits off US-101 near Gaviota on a marvellous route through the inland valleys of the Santa Ynez mountains. **LOMPOC**, the only town for miles, calls itself the "flower seed-growing capital of the world", and claims to produce as much as three-quarters of the flower seeds sold on earth, the products of which during summer form a thick carpet of colour over the gently rolling landscape of the surrounding countryside. For a leaflet detailing where particular species have been planted this season, contact the **Lompoc Valley Chamber of Commerce**, 111 South I St (Mon–Fri 9am–5pm; ☎736-4567), where you can also find out about the **murals** which, in recent years, have sprung up to beautify an otherwise faceless downtown.

**Lompoc Museum**, 200 South H St (Tues–Fri 1–5pm, Sat & Sun 1–4pm; $2 donation), is strong on Chumash and other Native American artefacts, and also has material on the town's **original mission site**, the scant remains of which can be found three blocks to the south on F Street off Locust Avenue.

Lompoc is also the home of **Vandenburg Air Force Base**, sprawled along the western side of town, where various new missiles and guidance systems get put through their paces over the Pacific Ocean. Their vapour trails are visible for miles, particularly at sunset, though the only way to see any of it up close is by the *Amtrak* Coast Starlight **train**, which runs along the coast (see p.31). The route was writer **Jack Kerouac's** favourite rail journey: he worked for a while as a brakeman on the train and subsequently used the "Midnight Ghost" for a free ride between LA and the Bay area. Aerospace enthusiasts who plan at least a week ahead can visit the air base on four-hour **tours** ($13–17 depending on group size; ☎736-6381) which visit launch pads and a missile silo.

The **beaches** along this section of coast are secluded and undeveloped, and nearly inaccessible much of the year, either because of bad weather or impending missile launches. **Jalama Beach**, at the end of a twisting fourteen-mile road off Hwy-1, spreads beneath coastal bluffs where you can camp overnight; the large sand dunes of **Ocean Beach**, a broad strand at the mouth of the Santa Ynez River, ten miles west of Lompoc, are the nesting grounds of many seabirds.

## La Purisima Mission

Four miles east of Lompoc and signposted off Hwy-246, **La Purisima Mission State Park** (June–Aug daily 8am–6pm; Sept–May daily 9am–5pm; $5 per car) is the most complete and authentic reconstruction of any of the 21 Spanish missions in California, and one of the best places to get an idea of what life might have been like in these early colonial settlements. *La Mision la Purisima Concepcion de Maria Santisima*, as it's called, was founded in 1787 on a site three miles north of here, and by 1804 had converted around 1500 Chumash, five hundred of whom died in a smallpox epidemic over the next two years. In 1812 an earthquake destroyed all the buildings, and the fathers decided to move to the present site. The complex did not last long, however, after the missions were secularized in 1834, and over the next hundred years they were all but abandoned, pillaged by treasure-hunters and used as stables.

The buildings that stand here today were rebuilt on the ruins of the mission as part of a Depression-era project for the unemployed. From 1933 to 1940 over two hundred men lived and worked on the site, studying the remaining ruins and rebuilding the church and outbuildings using period tools and methods. Workers cavorted in puddles of mud to mix in the straw to make the adobe bricks, roof timbers were shaped with handtools, and even the colours of the paints were made from native plants.

The focus of the mission is a narrow church, furnished as it would have been in the 1820s; nearby, at the entrance, small but engaging displays of documents and artefacts from the mission era and photographs of the reconstruction are housed in the old wagon house that serves as a **museum** and gift shop. On summer weekends you might catch a "living history day", when volunteers dress up as padres and Indians, and hold a traditional Mass, along with craft demonstrations – fun if you like that kind of thing.

# Pismo Beach and Avila Beach

Most of the land along the Santa Maria River, 75 miles north of Santa Barbara, is given over to farming, and both Hwy-1 and US-101 pass through a number of small agriculture-based towns and villages. Some seem hardly to have changed since the 1930s, when thousands of Okies, as they were known, fled to the region from the Dustbowl of the Midwest – an era portrayed in John Steinbeck's novel and John Ford's movie, *The Grapes of Wrath*. They were notoriously poor: just off US-101, the little town of **NIPOMO** was the site of **Dorothea Lange**'s very famous 1936 photograph of a migrant mother who had just been forced to sell the tyres off her truck. Twenty-five miles north of Lompoc, Hwy-1 passes through the centre of **GUADALUPE**, a small farming village where Spanish signs and advertisements far outnumber those in English, and ramshackle saloons, cafés and vegetable stalls line the dusty streets. At the mouth of the river, five miles west of the highway at the end of Main Street, large **sand dunes** surround wetlands that are an essential habitat for endangered seabirds.

## Pismo Beach

The dunes stretch ten miles up the coast, reaching as far as two miles inland and ending just south of the loud and characterless holiday town of **PISMO BEACH**, where the two highways merge. The southern portion of the dunes, three miles south of the town, is open to off-road vehicle enthusiasts, who excite themselves flying up and over the sandpiles of the **Pismo Dunes State Vehicle Recreation Area** in dune buggies and four-wheel drives, motoring along the beach to reach them. Inland from the grey beach, the northern quarter of the dunes is protected as a **nature reserve**, a good place to hike around and play Lawrence of Arabia.

North from the nature reserve, between the town and the dune buggy area, a number of beachfront **campgrounds** line Hwy-1; mostly RV-packed, they all charge around $16 a site. The **Pismo Beach State Park** has hot showers and beach camping for $6, and is a good place to see the black and orange Monarch butterflies that winter in the eucalyptus trees here and leave before the summer crowds. The once-plentiful **Pismo clams** that gave the town its name, however (from the local Indian word *pismu*, or "blobs of tar" that the shells resemble), have been so depleted that any you might dig up nowadays are probably under the four-and-a-half inch legal minimum size.

Most of the town's commercial activity happens at the junction where Pomeroy Avenue crosses Hwy-1. The **Chamber of Commerce**, 581 Dolliver St (Mon–Fri 9am–5pm, Sat 10am–4pm, Sun noon–4pm; ☎773-4382 or 1-800/443-7778), is near the junction, as are a number of **motels** (②) and the shambolic but charming *El Pismo Inn*, 230 Pomeroy Ave (☎773-4529; ③), a faded former bolthole for movie stars on location. For something a little classier try the beachfront *Edgewater*, 280 Wadsworth Ave (☎773-4811 or 1-800/634-5858; ⑤), with heated pool, hot tubs and some rooms with kitchens. The only **public transport** is *Greyhound*, which stops downtown five times a day in each direction.

## Avila Beach

North of Pismo Beach the coastline becomes more rugged and interesting, with caves and tidepools below ever-eroding bluffs, and sea lions in the many coves. The three-mile-long strand in front of the summer resort town of **AVILA BEACH** is the last outpost of Southern California beach life, with a high concentration of tumbledown burger stands and one good budget **motel**, the *Surfside Resort*, 256 Front St (☎595-2300; ③). On the road into town, *Sycamore*, at 1215 Avila Beach Drive (☎593-7302 or 1-800/234-5831; ⑤), boasts rooms with their own private mineral baths.

Teenagers on the loose from their families cruise the Avila Beach boardwalk, while anyone old enough takes refuge in **bars** like *Mr Rick's*, at 480 Front St. The party atmosphere continues all summer long, and no one seems to mind the presence of nearby oil refineries and the **Diablo Canyon Nuclear Plant**, which straddles an earthquake fault six miles up the coast. (For what it's worth, three long bursts of a loud siren indicate catastrophe.) The scenic route north from here to San Luis Obispo, **See Canyon Road**, cuts off north a mile from US-101, climbing gradually up the narrow, overgrown canyon between sharply profiled volcanic cones, with great views out over the Pacific.

# San Luis Obispo

**SAN LUIS OBISPO**, ten miles northeast of Avila Beach and almost exactly halfway between LA and San Francisco, is a main stop-off for both *Amtrak* and *Greyhound*, and, although a few miles inland, makes the best base for exploring the nearby coast. It's still primarily an agricultural town, and a market centre for the farmers and ranchers of the surrounding countryside, something which contributes to its Middle American feeling – though the 16,000 students at the adjacent Cal Poly campus help keep things reasonably active. On the whole it is an appealing place to pass a night or two, with a town centre boasting some of the Central Coast's best architecture, from turreted Victorian residences along Buchon Street south of the town centre to some fine commercial buildings, not to mention any number of good places to eat, a couple of pubs, and – outside summer holiday weekends – places to stay for the asking.

## Arrival and information

The *Greyhound* terminal is at 150 South St, half a mile down Higuera Street from the centre of town near US-101, and there are regular bus connections with both LA and San Francisco. *Amtrak* trains stop once a day in each direction at the end of Santa Rosa Street, half a mile south of the business district; and a daily *Amtrak Thruway* bus arrives from Hanford in the Central Valley (see p.276). You can pick up a free walking-tour map highlighting much of the town's best architecture from the **Chamber of Commerce** at 1039 Chorro St (Tues–Fri 8am–5pm, Sat–Mon 10am–5pm; ☎781-2777), which will also help with finding a **place to stay**. To find out **what's on** and where, check out the free weekly *New Times* newspaper or tune to the excellent noncommercial community radio station KOTR 94.9 FM (☎927-5021), which has telephone events hotlines and is happy to play requests.

## Accommodation

Monterey Street was the site of the world's first **motel** – the *Milestone Mo-tel* – still standing and due to open again soon after a long hiatus. Meanwhile, its spirit lives on in the other motels that line the street up to its junction with US-101. Rates and availability fluctuate greatly depending on the time of year, but are generally quite inexpensive; there's also a **bed-and-breakfast** reservation service, *Megan's Friends* (☎544-4406), which can help you find a room in a local home or nearby inn. The best **camping** nearby is south of town beyond Pismo Beach, or north off Hwy-1 in Morro Bay.

**Adobe Inn**, 1473 Monterey St (☎549-0321 or 1-800/676-1588). Newly redecorated, English-owned motel with nice rooms; rates include breakfast. ③.

**Budget Motel**, 345 Marsh St (☎543-6443 or 1-800/458-8848). Simple motel but excellent value for the price. ②.

**Garden Street Inn**, 1212 Garden St (☎545-9802). Very central B&B in a restored 1880s house with comfortable rooms, complimentary wine on arrival and tasty breakfasts. ⑥.

**HI-San Luis Obispo Coast Hostel**, 1292 Foothill Blvd (☎544-4678). Comfortable hostel with dorm beds at $13 for members, $16 for others. It's a 20-min walk from the centre following Santa Rosa Street north. ①.

**La Cuesta Motor Inn**, 2074 Monterey St (☎543-2777 or 1-800/543-2777). As popular with business-people as vacationers, with spacious modern rooms and a good-sized swimming pool and spa. ④.

**Lamplighter**, 1604 Monterey St (☎543-3709 or 1-800/843-6882). Older but comfortable motel with a pool. Popular with families. ③.

**Madonna Inn**, 100 Madonna Road (☎543-3000). Local landmark (see below) set in over 2000 acres, offering over 100 theme-decorated rooms in a stupendously kitsch setting. ⑤.

# The Town

San Luis is eminently walkable, with a compact core centered around the late eight-eenth-century **Mission San Luis Obispo de Tolosa** (summer daily 7am–5pm; rest of year daily 7am–4pm; donations), a fairly dark and unremarkable church that was the prototype for the now ubiquitous red-tiled roof, developed as a replacement for the original, flammable thatch in response to arson attacks by Native American tribes. Between the mission and the tourist office, **Mission Plaza**'s terraces step down along San Luis creek, along which footpaths meander, crisscrossed by bridges every hundred feet and overlooked by a number of stores and outdoor restaurants on the south bank. Downstream, across a small park, the San Luis Obispo County **Historical Museum** (Wed–Sun 10am–4pm; free) holds a low-key collection of local artefacts tend-ing toward the domestic, housed in the richly detailed 1904 Carnegie Library building. The main drag, **Higuera Street** (pronounced *Hi-GEAR-a*), a block south of Mission Plaza, springs to life every Thursday afternoon and evening for the **Farmer's Market**, when the street is closed to cars and filled with vegetable stalls, mobile barbeques and street-corner musicians. All of San Luis comes out to sample the foods and entertain-ment of this weekly county fair.

Monterey Street, which leads up the hill from Mission Plaza, holds some of the best of the town's commercial buildings, notably the 1884 **Sinsheimer Building** at no. 849, which has California's only surviving cast-iron facade; the **J P Andrews Building**, a block or so up, with its elaborately detailed frontage of granite and terracotta; and, a block further on, the Art Deco **Fremont Theater**. Many other distinguished buildings lie south of the business district, some of which – along Marsh Street above Santa Rosa Street – were built for railroad workers and their families, a reminder of the days when San Luis was a bustling railroad town.

Standing out from the many turn-of-the-century houses, built for middle-class fami-lies in a variety of exuberant late-Victorian styles, with turrets and towers and other exotic touches, is a doctor's surgery on the corner of Santa Rosa and Pacific streets designed by **Frank Lloyd Wright** in 1955, at the end of his career. Wright's confident experimentation with forms and materials is as bold here as ever, most visibly in the abstracted images of the local volcanic landscape, cut out of plywood to form a frieze of windows and the clerestory above the waiting room – complete with signature hearth. The building isn't open for visits but during work hours you can pop in for a quick look.

If you have neither the time nor the inclination to sample the small-town charms of San Luis, at least stop to look at the now famous **Madonna Inn**, a shocking-pink behe-moth along the highway just south of town that is the ultimate in kitsch, with a laser-activated waterfall to flush the gents' urinals (which look like whale mouths) and

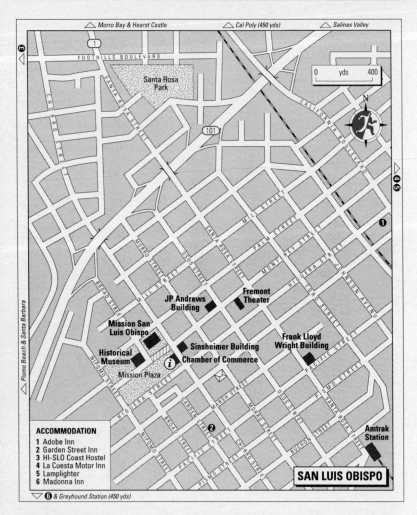

rooms decorated on a variety of themes from fairy-tale princesses to Stone Age cave-men. A very different sort of place is the **Shakespeare Press Museum** on the Cal Poly campus (Mon–Fri by appointment; ☎756-1108) – nothing to do with the Bard, but a great collection of old printing presses and lead typefaces, collected mainly from the frontier newspapers of California's Gold Rush towns.

## Eating and drinking

Higuera Street is the place to head to **eat**, especially during the Thursday afternoon Farmer's Market, when barbecues and food stalls set up amidst the jostling crowds. You'll also find a couple of popular **bars** and **cafés** on and just off Higuera, around the Mission Plaza area.

**Big Sky Café**, 1121 Broad St (☎545-5401). An airy, modern place with an emphasis on Cajun and Creole food. $7 dishes and an assortment of coffees.

**Buona Tavola**, 1037 Monterey St (☎545-8000). Small and stylish bistro with good range of moderately priced northern Italian food and wine.

**Chinatown Café**, 861 Palm St (☎543-1818). Since the 1930s this family-run place has been putting out the Central Coast's best Chinese food at good prices.

**The Graduate**, 990 Industrial Way (☎541-0969). A mile east of the centre but worth a trip for the low-priced beer and huge piles of food (all-you-can-eat specials before 9pm). Dancing nightly until 2am, popular with Cal Poly students.

**Hudson's Grill**, 1005 Monterey St (☎541-5999). Lively collegiate beer-and-burger bar that's open until midnight.

**Linnaea's Café**, 1110 Garden St, off Higuera (☎541-5888). A very successful small café, serving up good espresso and top-notch breakfasts, sandwiches, pastries, pies and cakes. There's usually live music at night, too.

**Rhythm Creekside Café**, across the river from the Historical Museum. Good, healthy, inexpensive food served on a waterfront terrace.

**Spike's**, 570 Higuera St (☎544-7157). This place has one of the best beer selections on the California Coast. Join its "Drink your way around the world" club and get a free beer for every dozen you sample – nobody minds if the burgers aren't that special.

**Thai Classic**, 1011 Higuera St (☎541-2025). Ignore the decor, the food's great – lots of traditional Thai cuisine at reasonable prices, with $4 weekday lunch specials. Closed Mon.

**Tortilla Flats**, 1051 Nipomo St at Higuera (☎544-7575). Raucous, neon-lit Mexican restaurant, better known for copious margaritas than great food, but with free happy hour nachos and dancing from 9pm.

# Morro Bay and the coast to Cambria

North of San Luis Obispo the highways diverge again, US-101 – and the trains and buses – speeding up through the Salinas Valley (see p.325), while Hwy-1 takes the scenic route along the coast. The first dozen miles of Hwy-1 follow the line of a ridgeback string of hills, a series of plugs from extinct volcanoes the most prominent of which have been dubbed the **Seven Sisters**. Two more continue the chain; the last is invisible under the sea, while the eighth is the coastal **Morro Rock** which, according to local lore, was named by the sixteenth-century explorer Vizcaino, who thought it looked like the Moorish domes of southern Spain. Nowadays it's off limits to the public in order to protect the nesting areas of the endangered peregrine falcons; in any case it's most impressive from a distance, dominating the fine harbour at **MORRO BAY**, where the local fishing boats unload their catches to sell in the many fish markets along the waterfront. The adjacent easy-paced resort town is accessible from San Luis Obispo via *CCAT* **bus** #7 (6 times daily; ☎541-CCAT), though apart from the many seafood restaurants the only places worth coming here for are spread out around the bay, miles from public transport. You get one of the best views of the rock and surrounding coastline from the top of **Cerro Alto**, eight miles east of Morro Bay off Hwy-41, a 2620-foot volcanic cone with good hiking and camping.

Closer in, on a point above the bay a mile south of town at the end of Main Street but providing a good view of Morro Rock, there's a small **Museum of Natural History** (daily 10am–5pm; $2); the **campground** across the street in Morro Bay State Park (reservable through *MISTIX*) costs $16 a night ($3 for hiker/biker sites) and has hot showers. Across the bay, the thin sandy peninsula that protects the harbour is hard to reach except by boat – it's entirely undeveloped and about the only place where you stand a chance of finding any Pismo clams. You can rent **kayaks**, which cost $6 per hour, from the likes of *Kayaks of Morro Bay*, 699 Embarcadero #9 (☎772-1119), or hike the two miles out there from Los Osos Valley Road.

**Montaña de Oro State Park** (free), four miles south at the end of Los Osos Valley Road, is much more primitive than the Morro Bay park, and has some excellent tide-

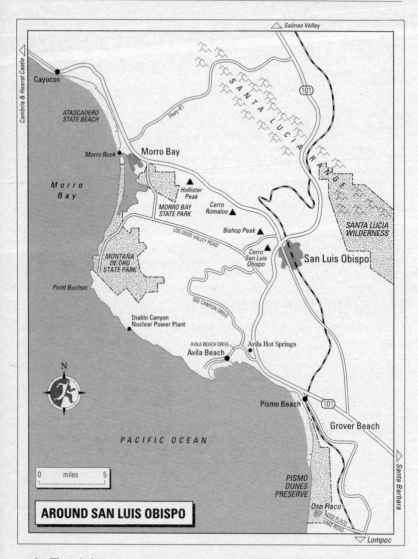

**AROUND SAN LUIS OBISPO**

pools. The windswept promontory stands solidly against the crashing sea, offering excellent hiking along the shore and through the sagebrush and eucalyptus trees of the upland hillsides, which in the spring are covered in golden poppies.

There are $9 **campsites** in the park, and numerous reasonably priced **motels** in town, including a recently improved *Motel 6*, 298 Atascadero Rd (☎772-5641; ②), close to the beach. For **eating** try *Hofbrau Der Albatross*, 571 Embarcadero (☎772-2411), essentially a classy burger and sandwich joint but with added bratwurst and sauerkraut. The **Chamber of Commerce** is at 161 Island St (Mon–Fri 9am–5pm; ☎772-4467).

The next town north is **CAYUCOS**, four miles along Hwy-1, originally a small port built by Englishman James Cass in the 1870s, and now a sleepy place ranged along sandy beaches with a nice pier. Surprisingly, it has some of the area's best **nightlife** in the *Cayucos Tavern*, 130 N Ocean St (☎995-3209), in the heart of the two-block-long ramshackle centre, with live bands at weekends and late-night poker games for gamblers.

## Cambria

**CAMBRIA**, ten miles to the north, is a touch pricey and more than a little pretentious, but about the best place to base yourself if you're visiting Hearst Castle, another seven miles further on. Hidden away in a wooded valley half a mile off Hwy-1, Cambria was an established town serving the local ranchers and fishermen long before Hearst Castle became the region's prime tourist attraction, and to some extent these days trades on its past, with a synthetic Olde English quarter along the highway. Skip this and head directly to the older and much nicer section half a mile east on Main Street, where the stores, restaurants and art galleries cater as much for locals as visitors.

There's not a lot to see or do in Cambria, but for **food and drink** the town excels. For details of the town's bed-and-breakfast inns, many of them on the seafront Moonstone Beach Drive and starting at around $70, contact the **Chamber of Commerce**, 767 Main St (daily 9am–5pm; ☎927-3624). Otherwise, the best **places to stay** are the *Cambria Palms Motel*, 2662 Main St (☎927-4485; ②), the *Bluebird Motel* at 1880 Main St (☎927-4634 or 1-800/552-5434; ③), or the *Cambria Pines Lodge* (☎927-4200 or 1-800/445-6868; ④) on Burton Drive on the hill above the town, which caters mostly to conferences, but also has very large rooms, and sometimes live music in its rustic, comfortable main bar. **Camping** is available in the **San Simeon State Park** two miles north along the coast: sites with and without showers for $16 or $9, and hiker/biker sites for $3 per person. The first two are reservable through *MISTIX*.

One of the best **breakfasts** this side of anywhere can be had at the *Redwood Café*, 2094 Main St. *Lombardi's Pasta Familia*, 4158 Bridge St (☎927-0777), lays on plentiful pasta, while *Camozzi's Saloon*, 2262 Main St (☎927-8941), is a rumbustious cowboy bar with occasional live bands.

# Hearst Castle and San Simeon

Forty-five miles northwest of San Luis Obispo, **HEARST CASTLE** sits on a hilltop overlooking rolling ranchlands and the Pacific Ocean. Far and away the biggest single attraction for miles, bringing in over a million visitors a year, the former holiday home of publishing magnate **William Randolph Hearst** is one of the most opulent and extravagant houses in the world. Its interior combines walls, floors and ceilings stolen from European churches and castles with Gothic fireplaces and Moorish tiles, and is filled to overflowing with Greek vases and medieval tapestries. It's actually more of a complex of buildings than a "castle". Three guesthouses circle the hundred-room main *Casa Grande* – the whole thing surrounded originally by a free-roaming zoo of lions, tigers, bears and zebras – in which Hearst held court over the most famous politicians and movie stars of the 1920s and 1930s. Winston Churchill, Charlie Chaplin, George Bernard Shaw and Charles Lindbergh were just a few who accepted Hearst's invitation to come and stay for as long as they liked.

Hearst Castle, which Hearst himself referred to as "the ranch" (the official name is now "Hearst San Simeon State Historic Monument"), manifests all the subtlety and lightness of touch one would expect from the man whose domination of the national media inspired Orson Welles' classic film *Citizen Kane*. Construction began after his mother's death in 1919, on the southern edge of the 250,000-acre ranch he inherited. The work, managed by architect Julia Morgan, was never actually completed: rooms would often be torn out as soon as they were finished in order to accommodate some bits and pieces of old buildings Hearst had just acquired, and much of the structure's rough reinforced concrete is still exposed. The main facade, a twin-towered copy of a Mudejar cathedral, stands at the top of steps that curve up from an expansive swimming pool of pure spring water, lined by a Greek colonnade and repro statues. Inside the house, ketchup and mustard bottles complete the place-settings of fine crystal and china on the long dark oak table of the baronial dining hall, festooned with banners from Siena's *Palio*.

## Practicalities

To see Hearst Castle you must take one of the guided **tours** (summer daily 8am–5pm; winter daily 8am–3pm; $14). Tour One, comprising a short film, an introductory spin around a guesthouse and the main rooms of the *Casa Grande*, is best for the first visit. If you're coming back, or are simply fascinated (and rich) enough to stay for a whole day, there are three other tours: Tour Two takes in the upper floors of the main house, including Hearst's library and bedroom suite, which occupies an entire floor; Tour Three concentrates on one of the guesthouses; Tour Four (summer only) emphasizes the grounds and gardens. Special evening tours ($25) visit the house and grounds at sunset. For more information, or to arrange for a wheelchair – there are lots of stairs – phone ☎927-2020.

All tours take about two hours, including the fifteen-minute-each-way bus ride up and down the hill, and leave from the parking lot and visitor center on Hwy-1 where you buy tickets. **Reservations**, always a good idea and necessary in summer when

---

### W R HEARST – *CITIZEN KANE*

It would be quite easy to portray William Randolph Hearst (or "W R") as a power-mad monster, but in retrospect he seems more like a very rich, over-indulged little boy. Born in 1863 as the only son of a multi-millionaire mining engineer, he was avidly devoted to his mother, Phoebe Apperson Hearst, one of California's most sincere and generous philanthropists, a founder of the University of California and the *Traveler's Aid* society.

Hearst learned his trade in New York City working for the inventor of inflammatory "Yellow Journalism", Joseph Pulitzer, who had four rules for how to sell newspapers: one – emphasize the sensational; two – elaborate on the facts; three – manufacture the news; four – use games and contests. When he published his own newspaper, Hearst took this advice to heart, his *Morning Journal* fanning the flames of American imperialism to ignite the Spanish-American War of 1898. As he told his correspondents in Cuba: "You provide the pictures, and I'll provide the war". Hearst eventually controlled an empire that at its peak during the 1930s sold 25 percent of the newspapers in the entire country, including two other New York papers, the *Washington Times*, and the *Detroit News* – as well as *Cosmopolitan* and *Good Housekeeping* magazines. In California Hearst's power was even more pronounced, with his San Francisco and Los Angeles papers controlling over sixty percent of the total market.

Somewhat surprisingly, considering his warmongering and extreme nationalism, Hearst was fairly middle-of-the-road politically, a lifelong Democrat who served two terms in the House of Representatives but failed in bids to be elected Mayor of New York and President of the US. Besides his many newspapers, Hearst owned eleven radio stations and two movie studios, in which he made his mistress Marion Davies a star. He was forced to sell off most of his holdings by the end of the Depression, but continued to exert power and influence until his death in 1951 aged 88.

tours sell out hours in advance, can be made through *MISTIX*. While waiting for the tour bus, find out more about Hearst and his castle from the excellent **museum** (daily 9am–5pm; free) in the rear half of the visitor center, beyond the point where you board the buses.

## San Simeon and north

The boarded-up pier of **SAN SIMEON**, an all-but-abandoned harbour town along the coast just north of Hearst Castle, is where all of Hearst's treasures were unloaded, as were the many tons of concrete and steel that went into the building of the house. Before the Hearsts bought up the land, San Simeon was a whaling and shipping port of which all that remains is a one-room schoolhouse and the 1852 *Sebastian's Store*, a combination post office, café and souvenir shop. The beach south of the pier is protected by San Simeon Point, which hooks out into the Pacific, making the beach safe for swimming. Along the highway three miles south there's a concentrated blot of gas stations, fast-food restaurants and **motels**, mostly overpriced but for a *Motel 6* (☎927-8691; ②/③). There's **camping** four miles south along the beach at San Simeon State Park (see p.323).

**North of Hearst Castle** the coastline is mostly rolling grasslands and cattle ranches, still owned and run by the Hearst family, with few buildings on the distant hills. Beyond here the highway seems to drop off in mid-air, marking the southern edge of Big Sur (see p.329), probably the most dramatic stretch of coastline in America.

# The Salinas Valley and Steinbeck Country

If you're in a hurry, US-101 through the **Salinas Valley** takes four hours to cover the 220 miles between San Luis Obispo and San Francisco, compared to the full day it takes to drive the more scenic coast along Hwy-1 through Big Sur. In any case, as both *Greyhound* and *Amtrak* take the inland route, you may not have the choice; of the two, *Greyhound* is for once the better option, as its local buses stop at all the small rural towns. The four-lane freeway closely follows the path of *El Camino Real*, the trail that linked the 21 Spanish **missions** – each a day's travel from its neighbour – through the miles of farmland along the Salinas River that are some of the most fertile in the nation.

This region is also popularly known as **Steinbeck Country** for having nurtured the Nobel Prize-winning imagination of writer **John Steinbeck**, whose naturalistic stories and novels, including the epic *East of Eden*, were set in and around the valley.

## The Salinas Valley

North of San Luis Obispo over the steep Cuesta Pass, US-101 drops down into the **Salinas Valley**, and, before long, **ATASCADERO**: a small town laid out to a curiously grand plan in 1914 that centres on its Palladian **City Hall**, a huge red-brick edifice whose domed rotunda now houses a small **museum** (Mon–Sat 1–4pm; free) describing the area's history.

**PASO ROBLES**, eight miles north, is a thriving little town surrounded by horse ranches, nut farms and a number of small, family-operated **wineries** that are among the finest in the state. Take a free and friendly tour (daily 10am–4pm) of the *Arciero* or *Meridian* wineries, five miles east of town on Hwy-46. Another ten miles east, at the junction of Hwy-41 near Cholame, pay your respects at the stainless steel monument near the site where **James Dean** met his maker in a silver Porsche Speedster on September 30, 1955.

> The telephone **area code** for the Salinas Valley, Big Sur
> and the northern Central Coast is ☎408.

Even if you're racing up US-101, it's worth taking a break from your journey to have a look at the most intact and authentic of California's Spanish missions, **Mission San Miguel Arcangel** (daily 9.30am–4.30pm; 50¢), just off the freeway in the small town of **SAN MIGUEL**. Built in 1816, it's the only mission in the chain not to have suffered the revisionist tendencies of a restoration. It was actually used for a while as a saloon and dance hall, though the chapel has been left pretty much unscathed, with colourful painted decoration and a marvellous sunburst reredos, complete with a striking Eye of God. The other buildings are interesting too, in their rough imprecision, with irregularly arched openings and unplastered walls forming a courtyard around a cactus garden.

There's a second mission, accessible only by car, twenty miles west of US-101 along the Jolon Road (G-18), which splits off the highway twelve miles north of San Miguel. The **Mission San Antonio de Padua** (Mon–Sat 9.30am–4.30pm, Sun 11am–5pm; donations) is a rarely visited restoration of the 1771 settlement, less sanitized than some of the missions and giving a very good idea of what life might have been like for the missionaries and their converts. This mission was among the most prosperous of the entire chain, and around the extensive grounds, in a wide valley of oak trees and tall grasses, a number of scattered exhibits describe the work that went on in the long-abandoned vineyard, tannery and gristmill. There's a monastic peace to Mission San Antonio these days, and the brown-robed Franciscan friars who live here are rarely disturbed, despite being in the middle of the Hunter Liggett Army Base; indeed the only sign of the military is at the gates of the base, five miles east of the mission, where you'll have to show your passport or some other form of ID. The large house across the valley from the mission used to belong to W R Hearst, who sold it and most of the land between here and Hearst Castle to the government in 1940 to help clear his $120 million debt. The **Nacimiento-Fergusson Road** leads from the mission on a tortuous but picturesque journey over the mountains, past a couple of enticing $10 national forest **campgrounds**, to Big Sur (see p.329).

Nearby **JOLON** has a market and gas station, and the washed-out ruins of an 1840s stagecoach stop at the **Old Dutton Hotel**. The San Antonio Reservoir, five miles southeast, has swimming, **camping** and showers along the west shore, as does the Nacimiento Reservoir further south.

The Jolon Road loops back to US-101 at **KING CITY**: "the most metropolitan cow town in the West", as it likes to be known. On the town's western edge, just off US-101, San Lorenzo Park is the site of the **Agricultural and Rural Life Museum** (daily 9am–5pm; free, parking $3, Sat & Sun $5), a collection of old barns, farmhouses and a one-room schoolhouse, all gathered here from various sites in Monterey county. The park also has a **campground** ($13) with hot showers, along the Salinas River. Backpacking permits for the **Ventana Wilderness** in the Santa Lucia Mountains, which divide the Salinas Valley from the Big Sur coast, are handled by the **US Forest Service** office, off the freeway at 406 S Mildred Ave (Mon–Fri 8am–5pm; ☎385-5434).

## The Pinnacles National Monument and around

From King City, you have a choice of approaches to the bizarre rock formations of the **Pinnacles National Monument** ($4 per vehicle); either follow G13 and Hwy-25 to the eastern entrance and the **visitor center** (daily 8am–5pm; ☎389-4485), or continue up Hwy-101 to Soledad (see below) and turn onto Hwy-146 to the more spectacular western side. Contrary to what appears on some maps, no road goes right through the monument, but the place is small and it is quite possible to hike from one side to the other and back in a day.

This region of grotesque volcanic spires, brilliant reds and golds against the blue sky, is best visited in the spring, when the air is still cool and the chaparral hillsides are covered in wild flowers, in particular the crimson California poppy and deep-lilac Owl's Clover. Its many **trails** include a four mile loop around the high peaks on the **Juniper Canyon Trail**, and the two-mile **Balconies Trail** to the multicoloured, 600-foot face of the **Balconies** outcrop – good for **rock-climbing** (register at the visitor center and use only brown chalk) – and a nearby series of talus **caves** (take a flashlight), formed by huge boulders that have become wedged between the walls of the narrow canyons. These pitch-black caves were popular with bandits who would hide out here after robbing stagecoaches.

The trails are exposed so, in summer, avoid hiking in the middle of the day and remember to carry plenty of **water**. There are nineteen walk-in **campgrounds** ($10), each of which only accommodates six people, and the commercial, swimming pool-equipped *Pinnacles Campground Inc* ($6 per person), just outside the park. All are first-come-first-served.

### Soledad, Mission Soledad and Paraiso hot springs

The nearest town to the Pinnacles is **SOLEDAD**, a quiet farming community twelve miles west of the western entrance. It has a definite Mexican flavour, its *panaderias* selling cakes and fresh tortillas – a good place to stock up on food and drink for a trip to the monument. The only other reason to stop is for a visit to **Mission Nuestra Señora de la Soledad** (daily except Tues 10am–4pm; donations), three miles west of US-101 on the south side of town, which lay neglected for over a hundred years until there was little left but a pile of mud. The mission was never a great success (perhaps because of its full name, which translates as the "most sorrowful mystery of the solitude"), suffering through a history of epidemics, floods and crop failures. Parts have been dutifully restored and now contain a museum on mission life; despite this, the **ruins** adjacent to the rebuilt church are the most evocative section.

More hedonistially you could head out to **Paraiso Hot Springs** (☎678-2882), seven miles further west, high above Soledad in the foothills of the Santa Lucia Mountains: a palm-treed oasis looking out across the Salinas Valley to the Gabilan Mountains and the Pinnacles National Monument. The natural hot springs were popular with the local Native Americans for their healing properties, and have been operated as a commercial venture since 1895. The series of pools costs $20 a day to enter, and you can **camp** here overnight for a further $5.

While you pamper yourself in the steamy water, it's worth remembering that most Californians know Soledad for one thing only: as site of the **Soledad State Penitentiary** – a grim building looming alongside US-101 two miles north of town where black militant "Soledad Brother" George Jackson was imprisoned for many years.

# Salinas

The second-largest city between LA and San Francisco and the seat of Monterey County, **SALINAS**, twenty miles north, is a sprawling agricultural town of 85,000 people. It's best known as the birthplace of Nobel Prize-winning writer John Steinbeck, and for the **California Rodeo**, the biggest in the state, held here during the third week in July. These attractions aside, you may well find yourself here anyway: Salinas is a main stop for *Greyhound* buses and the Coast Starlight train, and makes an excellent and inexpensive base for exploring the perhaps more obvious attractions of the **Monterey Peninsula**, twenty miles away over the Santa Lucia mountains, with the

*MST* bus #21 making the 55-minute trip every hour (see p.335) from the Transit Center on Salinas Street.

## The town ... and Steinbeck Country

Salinas and the agricultural valley to the south are often bracketed together as Steinbeck Country. The writer **John Steinbeck** was born and raised in Salinas, though there's not a lot left to remind you of his presence: he left the town in his mid-twenties to live in Monterey and later in New York City. His childhood home at 132 Central Ave has been turned into an English-style tearoom; head instead for the **Steinbeck Room** of the public library two blocks away at 110 W San Luis St (daily 10am–6pm; free), which displays a variety of manuscripts and memorabilia.

In Steinbeck's day as much as today, Salinas is a hotbed of labour disputes, with the gap between the wealthy owners and agribusiness empires that run the giant farms and the low-paid manual labourers who pick the produce still unbridged. In the 1960s and early 1970s the United Farm Workers union, under the leadership of Cesar Chavez and Dolores Huerta, had great success in organizing and demanding better pay and conditions for the almost exclusively Latino workforce, most notably masterminding a very effective boycott of the valley's main product, lettuce. But in the mid-1990s, workers are once again under siege, with wages less than half of what they were fifteen years ago amidst increasing worries about the dangers of exposure to pesticides and agricultural chemicals.

Knowing this, Salinas is not the sort of place where you'd expect to find a large public sculpture by a major avant-garde artist, but **Claes Oldenburg's** *Hat in Three Stages of Landing* is just that: a triad of giant yellow steel cowboy hats floating above the grass between the Salinas Community Art Gallery and the Rodeo Grounds, at 940 N Main St. On the outskirts of town, at the end of West Laurel Drive a mile west of US-101, the **Boronda Adobe** lies in the middle of rich farmland, virtually unaltered since its construction in 1848, alongside other historic structures that have been brought to the site as part of an expanding regional history centre.

Between Salinas and the Monterey Peninsula, twenty miles distant via Hwy-68, are a couple of other places of divergent interest. **SPRECKELS**, five miles southwest, is a small factory town with an arts-and-crafts feel, built in 1898 for employees of the Spreckels sugar factory, at the time the largest in the world: the small torchlike wooden objects on the gable ends of the many workers' cottages are supposed to represent sugar beets. Parts of the movie *East of Eden* were filmed here, including the famous scene when James Dean – playing Cal – hurls blocks of ice down a chute to get his father's attention.

---

### THE NOVELS OF JOHN STEINBECK

John Steinbeck's novels and stories are as valuable and interesting for their historical content as for their narratives. *The Grapes of Wrath*, his best-known work, was made into a film starring Henry Fonda while still at the top of the bestseller lists, having captured the popular imagination for its portrayal of the miseries of the Joad family on their migration to California from the Dust Bowl. *Cannery Row* followed in 1945, a nostalgic portrait of the Monterey fisheries, which ironically went into steep decline the year the book was published. Steinbeck spent the next four years writing *East of Eden*, an allegorical retelling of the biblical story of Cain and Abel against the landscape of the Salinas Valley, in which he expresses many of the values that underlie the rest of his work. Much of Steinbeck's writing is concerned with the dignity of labour, and with the inequalities of an economic system that "allows children to go hungry in the midst of rotting plenty". Although he was circumspect about his own political stance, when *The Grapes of Wrath* became a bestseller in 1939 there was a violent backlash against Steinbeck in Salinas for what were seen as his Communist sympathies.

Along Hwy-68 halfway to Monterey you'll come to **Laguna Seca Raceway** (☎373-1811), where race driver and part-time actor Paul Newman keeps in practice on the two-mile road course; races are held throughout the summer, and there's also **camping**.

## Salinas practicalities

Hourly *Greyhound* buses between LA and San Francisco stop in the centre of town at 19 W Gabilan St near Salinas St, while *Amtrak* trains leave once a day in each direction, two blocks away at 40 Railroad Ave. For a handy **place to stay** try the *Traveller's Hotel* at 16 E Gabilan St (☎758-1198; ①), which is convenient, if seedy; if you're driving choose from the many $45-a-night **motels** along Main Street on either side of US-101. For help with finding a place to stay, and for a free **map** and guide to the places that Steinbeck wrote about, contact the **Chamber of Commerce** at 119 E Alisal St (Mon–Fri 8.30am–noon & 1–5pm; ☎424-7611). There are quite a few good **Mexican restaurants** around the city, the best, oldest and most central being *Rosita's Armory Café*, 231 Salinas St, open daily from 9am until 3am for fine food and stiff margaritas.

# The Big Sur Coast

The California coastline is at its most spectacular along the ninety miles of rocky cliffs and crashing sea known as **BIG SUR**. This is not the lazy beachfront of Southern California, but a sublime landscape at the edge of a continent, where redwood groves line river canyons and the Santa Lucia mountains rise straight out of the blue Pacific. Named by the Spanish *El Pais Grande del Sur*, the "big country to the south" (of their colony at Monterey), it's still a wild and undeveloped region except for occasional outposts along the narrow **Hwy-1**, the dramatic coast road that follows a tortuous, exhilarating route carved out of bedrock cliffs five hundred feet above the Pacific Ocean, passing by mile after mile of rocky coves and steep, narrow canyons.

Before the highway was completed in 1937, the few inhabitants of Big Sur had to be almost entirely self-sufficient, farming, raising cattle and trapping sea otters for their furs. The only connections with the rest of the world were by infrequent steamship to Monterey, or by a nearly impassable trail over the mountains to the Salinas Valley. Perhaps surprisingly, even fewer people live in the area today than did a hundred years ago, and most of the land is still owned by a handful of families, many of whom are descendants of Big Sur's original pioneers. Locals have banded together to fight US government plans to allow offshore oil-drilling, and to protect the land from obtrusive development. If you'd like to know more about Big Sur's history and the contentious present, an excellent free **guide** to the area, *El Sur Grande*, is available at ranger stations and the Big Sur post office.

The coast is also the protected habitat of the sea otter, and gray whales pass by close to the shore on their annual winter migration. Visit in April or May to see the vibrant wildflowers and lilac-coloured ceanothus bushes, though the sun shines longest, without the morning coastal fog, in early autumn through until November. Hardly anyone braves the turbulent winters, when violent storms drop most of the eighty inches of rain that fall each year, often taking sections of the highway with it into the sea. Summer weekends, however, see the roads and campgrounds packed to overflowing – though even in peak season, if you're willing to walk a mile or two, it's still easy to get away from it all.

The best way to see Big Sur is slowly, leaving the car behind to wander through the many parks and wilderness preserves, where a ten-minute walk can put miles between you and any sign of the rest of the world. The only **public transport** is by the summer-only *MST* bus #22 from Monterey (see p.335) running as far south as Nepenthe, four times a day in each direction, though the narrow Hwy-1 is a perennial favourite with cyclists.

Much the most interesting, and most developed, stretch of Big Sur is the northern end, ranged along the wide and clear Big Sur River, 25 miles south of Monterey and focusing on **Pfeiffer Big Sur State Park**, where you can swim among giant boulders, hike up redwood canyons to a waterfall or sunbathe on a fine sandy beach. There is no Big Sur village as such, just a ten-mile string of grocery stores, gas stations and places to eat and drink dotted at roughly one-mile intervals either side of the Park. The main concentrations are by the post office two miles south of the Pfeiffer Big Sur State Park, at Fernwood a mile north of the park entrance and, confusingly, at The Village a further mile and a half north. Almost everything you may need to know is in the free *El Sur Grande* newspaper, but you could also call the **Chamber of Commerce** (☎667-2100).

We've gathered all our **accommodation**, **camping** and **eating** recommendations for the Big Sur area into comprehensive listings starting on p.332.

# Southern Big Sur

The southern coastline of Big Sur is the region at its most gentle – not unlike Portugal's Algarve, with sandy beaches hidden away below eroding yellow-ochre cliffs. The landscape grows more extreme the further north you go. Twenty miles north of Hearst Castle, a steep trail leads down along Salmon Creek to a coastal waterfall, while the chaparral-covered hills above were booming during the 1880s with the gold mines of the **Los Burros Mining District**.

Another ten miles north, the cliffs get steeper and the road more perilous around the vista point at **Willow Creek**, where you can watch the surfers and the sea otters playing in the waves. **Jade Cove**, a mile north, takes its name from the translucent California jade stones that are sometimes found here, mainly by scuba divers offshore. The rocky cove is a ten-minute walk from the highway, along a trail marked by a wooden stile in the cattle fence.

Just beyond the Plaskett Creek **campground**, half a mile north, **Sand Dollar Beach** is a good place to enjoy the surf or watch for **hang-gliders**, who launch themselves from sites in the mountains off the one-lane Plaskett Ridge Road. This steep road is good fun on a mountain bike, and passes by a number of free primitive campgrounds along the ridge, ending at the paved Nacimiento-Fergusson Road. Check at the **Pacific Valley ranger station** (☎927-4211; irregular hours) for up-to-date information on backcountry camping, since some areas may be closed in summer during the peak of the fire season. The station also handles the 25 permits a day allowed to people wanting to hang-glide, ten of which are given out on a first-come first-served basis on the day. **Pacific Valley Center**, a mile north, has an expensive gas station, a grocery store and a good coffee shop, open from 8am until dark.

## Kirk Creek to Julia Pfeiffer Burns State Park

The coastal **campsite** at **Kirk Creek** (see p.333) sits at the foot of the **Nacimiento-Fergusson Road**, which twists over the Santa Lucia mountains to the Salinas Valley. The road passes the excellent Mission San Antonio de Padua (see p.326), but it would be a shame to break the continuity of the drive up the coast, and in any case the views are better coming over the hills in the other direction. Two miles north of here, **Limekiln Creek** is named after the hundred-year-old lime kilns that survive in good condition along the creek behind the privately owned **campground**. In the 1880s local limestone was burned in these kilns to extract lime powder for use as cement, then carried on a complex aerial tramway to be loaded onto ships at Rocklands Landing. The ships that carried the lime to Monterey brought in most of the supplies to this isolated area.

**ESALEN**, ten miles further north, is named after the local Native Americans, the first tribe in California to be made culturally extinct. Before they were wiped out, they frequented the healing waters of the natural **hot spring** here (nightly 1–3.30am; $10; must reserve on ☎667-3047), at the top of a cliff two hundred feet above the raging Pacific surf – now owned and operated by the *Esalen Institute*. Since the 1960s, when all sorts of people came to Big Sur to smoke dope and get back to nature, Esalen has been at the forefront of the "New Age" human potential movement. Today's devotees tend to arrive in BMWs on Friday nights for the expensive, reservation-only massage treatments, yoga workshops and seminars on Eastern religion and philosophy; phone ☎667-3000 for information on classes and workshops.

**Julia Pfeiffer Burns State Park** (daily dawn–dusk; $6 parking), three miles north of Esalen along McWay Creek, has some of the best day hikes in the Big Sur area: a ten-minute walk from the parking area leads under the highway along the edge of the cliff to an overlook of a waterfall that crashes into a cove below Saddle Rock. A less-travelled path leads down from Hwy-1 two miles north of the waterfall (at milepost 37.85) through a two-hundred-foot-long tunnel to the wave-washed remains of a small wharf at **Partington Cove**, one of the few places in Big Sur where you can get to the sea.

## Nepenthe and Pfeiffer Beach

Big Sur's commercial development starts in earnest with **NEPENTHE**, a complex of restaurants and stores named after the mythical drug that induces forgetfulness of grief. It stands atop the hilltop site where star-crossed lovers Orson Welles and Rita Hayworth once shared a cabin. The excellent restaurant here has been run since the 1960s by the family of master knitter and painter Kaffe Fassett, who grew up in Big Sur – though *Café Kevah*, on a rooftop terrace just down the hill, is more affordable and has arguably more impressive views. Downstairs there's an outdoor sculpture gallery and a decent bookstore, including works by, among others, Henry Miller, who lived in the area on and off until the 1960s. The **Henry Miller Memorial Library** across Hwy-1 (daily, hours vary; $1 donation; ☎667-2574) displays an informal collection of first-edition books and mementoes of the writer's life in the house of Miller's old friend Emil White.

Two miles north, a barely marked road leads west from Hwy-1 a mile down Sycamore Canyon to Big Sur's best beach, **Pfeiffer Beach** (open until dusk), a sometimes windy, white-sand stretch dominated by a charismatic hump of rock whose colour varies from brown to red to orange in the changing light. Park where you can at the end of the road, and walk through an archway of cypress trees along the lagoon to the sands.

## The Big Sur River Valley

Two miles north of Pfeiffer Beach, and 65 miles north of Hearst Castle, Hwy-1 drops down behind a coastal ridge into the valley of the Big Sur River, where most of the accommodation and eating options are located.

The first stop should be he US Forest Service **ranger station** (daily 8am–6pm; ☎667-2423) which handles the camping permits for the Ventana Wilderness in the mountains above. A popular hike leads steeply up from the Pine Ridge trailhead behind the station six miles into the mountains to **Sykes Hot Springs** (unrestricted entry), just downstream from the free **campground** at Sykes Camp along the Big Sur River, continuing fifteen miles over the Santa Lucia mountains to the **Tassajara Zen Buddhist Center**, where you can reward yourself with a dip in the natural hot springs ($12; reservations required ☎659-2229).

Plumb in the middle of the valley, the **Pfeiffer Big Sur State Park** ($6 per vehicle) is one of the most beautiful and enjoyable parks in California, with miles of hiking trails and excellent swimming along the Big Sur River – which in late spring and summer has deep swimming holes among the large boulders in the bottom of the narrow steep-walled gorge. The water is clean and clear, nude sunbathing is tolerated (except on national holidays, when the park tends to be overrun with swarms of screaming children) and, since it's sheltered a mile or so inland, the weather is warmer and sunnier than elsewhere along the coast. This is also the centre for information on all the other parks in the area, and the main **campground** in the entire Big Sur region.

The most popular hiking trail in the park leads to the sixty-foot **Pfeiffer Falls**, half a mile up a narrow canyon shaded by redwood trees from a trailhead opposite the entrance. The thoroughly functional bridges over the river have an understated grace, as does the nearby amphitheatre – built by the Civilian Conservation Corps during the Depression – where rangers give excellent campfire talks and slide shows about Big Sur.

## Big Sur accommodation

In keeping with Big Sur's backwoodsy qualities, most of the available **accommodation** is in rustic (but rarely inexpensive) mountain lodges, and the very few rooms on offer are full most nights throughout the summer, especially on weekends. Mid-range accommodation is limited to a few cabins and motels, usually adjoining a privately operated campground or right along the highway, and not really ideal for getting the total Big Sur experience.

**Big Sur Campground**, a mile north of Pfeiffer Big Sur State Park (☎667-2322). Campground with the best of the cabins: wooden tent affairs sleeping up to three for $40 and fancier places from $65. ②–⑥.

**Big Sur Lodge**, in Pfeiffer Big Sur State Park (☎667-2171). Good-sized modern cabins arranged around a large swimming pool; popular with families. ④–⑥.

**Deetjen's Big Sur Inn**, on Hwy-1 7 miles north of Julia Pfeiffer Burns State Park (☎667-2377). The southernmost, oldest and perhaps nicest of the Big Sur lodges, with 20 very different rooms hand-crafted from thick redwood planks, all with fireplaces. ④–⑥.

**Glen Oaks Motel**, just over a mile north of Pfeiffer Big Sur State Park (☎667-2105). Tidy simple rooms with baths, close to the highway. ④.

**River Inn Resort**, two and a half miles north of Pfeiffer Big Sur State Park (☎667-2700 or 1-800/548-3610). Woodsy lodge with a handful of very nice (if pricey) rooms overlooking the river, and more basic motel-style rooms across Hwy-1. ④–⑦.

## Big Sur eating and drinking

Most of the places to **eat and drink** in Big Sur are attached to the inns and resorts listed above. Many of these are fairly basic burger-and-beer bars right along the highway, but there are a few special ones worth searching out, some for their good food and others for their views of the Pacific. Because of its isolation, prices anywhere in Big Sur are around 25 percent higher than you'd pay in town.

**Café Kevah**, Nepenthe (☎667-2660). Subtly prepared wholefood concoctions served up on a sunny, outdoor terrace. Big Sur's best views and a dozen healthy and flavoursome variations on Eggs Benedict, plus a range of coffees and ice-cold bottles of Red Tail Ale.

**Deetjen's Big Sur Inn**, on Hwy-1 7 miles north of Julia Pfeiffer Burns State Park (☎667-2377). Excellent, unhurried breakfasts ($8) and a variety of top-quality fish and vegetarian dinners ($13–25) in a snug, redwood-panelled room.

**Fernwood Burgers**, Hwy-1 a mile north of Pfeiffer Big Sur State Park (☎667-2422). For burgers or fish-and-chips, this budget diner is the place. There's a small grocery store/deli in the same building if you want to pick up supplies for a picnic.

**Glen Oaks Restaurant**, Hwy-1 in The Village (☎667-2264). Gourmet California cuisine – mostly fresh fish and pasta dishes, with some vegetarian options – in a cosy, flower-filled cottage. $12–16.

## CAMPING IN BIG SUR

**Public campgrounds** are dotted all along the Big Sur coast, in additon to a few less developed ones in the Santa Lucia mountains above, where you can also see deer, bobcats and (rarely) mountain lions. Sites along the coast are popular year-round, and all, unless otherwise stated, are available for around $15 a night (some with $3 per person hiker/biker sites) on a first-come, first-served basis, so get there early in the day to ensure a space. Reservations are, however, taken at Pfeiffer Big Sur State Park, through *MISTIX*. For further **information** on camping in Big Sur phone the State Parks (☎667-2315) or the Los Padres National Forest office in King City (☎385-5434).

The following campgrounds are listed south to north.

**Plaskett Creek**. Thirty miles north of Hearst Castle and a mile south of Pacific Valley. Across the highway from the ocean with some hiker/biker sites.

**Kirk Creek**. Three miles north of Pacific Valley and more exposed, but right on the ocean and with hiker/biker sites.

**Nacimiento**. Shaded, streamside site in the Santa Lucia mountains, 11 miles inland along the Nacimiento-Fergusson Road. Currently no water and no fee.

**Ponderosa**. Two miles further inland from the Nacimiento site and equally appealing. Currently no water and no fee.

**Pfeiffer Big Sur State Park**. This is the main campground in the area, with spacious and well shaded sites, many among the redwoods. Hot showers, a well-stocked store, a laundromat and some (officially) biker-only sites. $16.

**Andrew Molera State Park**. The only walk-in site around. A vast meadow, half a mile from the beach, with water and latrines. Since there are no designated sites, it is never full. Camping payment waives day-use fee. $3.

**Botcher's Gap**. Eight miles inland from Hwy-1 on Palo Colorado Road, eighteen miles north of Pfeiffer Big Sur State Park. A good base for exploring the Ventana Wilderness. No water and no fee.

There are also four commercially operated **campgrounds** in the Big Sur Valley: *Ventana* (☎667-2331), *Fernwood* (☎667-2422), *Riverside* (☎667-2414) and *Big Sur* (☎667-2322). All charge about $22 a night for two people, offer deluxe facilities, and accept reservations; they also rent out **cabins** (see "Big Sur accommodation", above). By Californian standards, all are fairly crowded, and all but *Riverside* mix tents with RVs.

**Nepenthe**, Nepenthe (☎667-2345). Up the hill from the *Café Kevah*, this steak-and-seafood place has a raging fireplace and a James Bond-ish après ski atmosphere.

**River Inn Resort**, at the north end of The Village (☎625-5255 or 1-800/548-3610). Tasty range of sautéed and grilled seafood starters and hearty main dishes, served in a spacious, redwood-log dining room. In summer you can linger over lunch or an evening drink in the lovely riverside garden, or on the sunny terrace; in winter, the fireplace attracts locals and visitors in about equal numbers. Also offers accommodation (see p.332) and lays on some kind of entertainment at the weekend.

## North to Monterey

Though it's rarely visited, **Andrew Molera State Park** (daily dawn–dusk; parking $4), five miles north of Pfeiffer Big Sur State Park is the largest park in Big Sur with two and a half miles of rocky oceanfront reached by a mile-long trail. It occupies the site of what was the El Sur Ranch, one of the earliest and most successful Big Sur cattle ranches, initially run by Juan Bautista Alvarado, who later became California governor, and later by English sea captain Roger Cooper, whose cabin is preserved here. You can reach it on some of the 15 miles of hiking trails also used for guided two-hour **horse-back rides** from the stables ($40–50; ☎625-8664 or 1-800/3030-8664). There is also walk-in **camping** (see box above).

From the north end of the park the Old Coast Road takes off inland from Hwy-1 up over the steep hills, affording panoramic views out over miles of coastline. The part-paved, roughly ten-mile road winds over wide-open ranch lands and through deep, slender canyons until it rejoins the main highway at **Bixby Creek Bridge**, fifteen miles south of Carmel. When constructed in 1932 this was the longest single-span concrete bridge in the world, and is the most impressive (and photogenic) engineering feat of the Coast Road project.

A mile and a half north, beyond the **Point Sur Light Station** (tours Sat 10am & 2pm, Sun 10am $5; ☎625-4419), a paved road turns off up **Palo Colorado Canyon**, past a number of houses and the remains of an old lumber mill obscured behind the redwood trees, finishing up eventually at Botcher's Gap campground on the edge of the Ventana Wilderness. On the coast at the foot of the road, the derelict buildings at **Notley's Landing** were once part of a bustling port community. The northernmost stop on the wild Big Sur coast is at **Garrapata State Park** (daily dawn–dusk), three miles south of Point Lobos and the Monterey Peninsula. A mile-long trail leads from Hwy-1 out to the tip of **Soberanes Point** – a good place to watch for sea otters and gray whales.

# The Monterey Peninsula

*Waves which lap quietly about the jetties of Monterey grow louder and larger in the distance . . . and from all around, even in quiet weather, the low, distant, thrilling roar of the Pacific hangs over the coast and the adjacent country like smoke from a battle.*

Robert Louis Stevenson, *The Old Pacific Capital.*

The dramatic headlands of the **Monterey Peninsula** mark the northern edge of the spectacular Big Sur coast, a rocky promontory where gnarled cypress trees amplify the collision between the cliffs and the thundering sea. The towns here thrive on the tourist trade, though each has a character very much its own. **Monterey**, largest of the three and a lively harbour town, was the capital of California under the Spanish and Mexicans, and retains many old adobe houses and places of genuine historic appeal alongside some overstated attractions. **Carmel-by-the-Sea**, on the other hand, three miles to the south, is a contrivedly quaint village of million-dollar holiday homes, best known for the many golf courses that line the coast nearby. Smallest of the trio, **Pacific Grove**, at the very tip of the peninsula amid its most arresting scenery, is far enough off the beaten track to preserve its Victorian seaside character reasonably intact.

## Arrival, information and getting around

The Monterey Peninsula juts out into the Pacific to form the Monterey Bay, a hundred miles south of San Francisco; coastal Hwy-1 cuts across its neck, and Hwy-68 links up with US-101 at Salinas, twenty miles east. *Greyhound* **buses** (three daily in each direction between LA and San Francisco) stop at the *Exxon* station, 1042 Del Monte Ave, along the Monterey waterfront. *Amtrak* **trains** stop in Salinas, connecting with local bus #21 for the 55-minute trip (every hour) to Monterey.

The Monterey Chamber of Commerce **tourist office** at 380 Alvarado St (Mon–Fri 9am–5pm; ☎649-1770) has fairly comprehensive accommodation listings but you might find it easier to call at the town's **visitor center**, 401 Camino El Estero (Mon–Sat 9am–6pm, Sun 9am–5pm; no phone): park outside for free and walk the six blocks into town. In Carmel, the **Carmel Business Association** (June–Aug daily 9am–6pm; Sept–May Mon–Fri 9am–5pm, Sat 11am–5pm; ☎624-2522), hidden away upstairs on San Carlos Street, midway between Fifth and Sixth, is another possible source of rooms but has

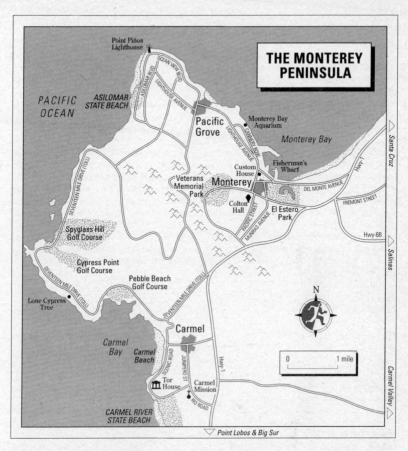

THE MONTEREY PENINSULA

Point Piños
Lighthouse

PACIFIC
OCEAN

ASILOMAR
STATE BEACH

Pacific
Grove

Monterey Bay
Aquarium

Monterey Bay

Custom
House

Fisherman's
Wharf

Veterans
Memorial
Park

Monterey

DEL MONTE AVENUE

Colton
Hall

El Estero
Park

FREMONT STREET

Spyglass Hill
Golf Course

Hwy-68

Cypress Point
Golf Course

Pebble Beach
Golf Course

Lone Cypress
Tree

N

Carmel

Carmel
Bay

Carmel
Beach

0        1 mile

Tor
House

Carmel
Mission

CARMEL RIVER
STATE BEACH

Santa Cruz
Salinas
Carmel Valley

Point Lobos & Big Sur

little other information, while the Pacific Grove **Chamber of Commerce** (Mon–Fri 9.30am–5pm; ☎373-3304), across from the Natural History Museum at Forest and Central, has walking tour maps of the town's historic buildings and can help find a room in the many local bed and breakfast inns. The best guides to **what's on** in the area are the widely available freebies *Go!*, *The Coast Weekly* and *Peninsula*, all with listings of movies, music and art galleries.

**Getting around** is surprisingly easy: *Monterey–Salinas Transit (MST)* buses (☎899-2555) run between 7am and 6pm (11pm on some routes), radiating out from Transit Plaza in the historic core of Monterey, and covering the entire region from Nepenthe on the Big Sur coast north to Watsonville near Santa Cruz and inland to the agricultural heartland of the Salinas Valley. The region is divided into four zones: the peninsula, Salinas, Big Sur and the north coast; fares are $1.25 per zone, and an all-day, single zone pass costs $3.75. The most useful routes are buses #4 and #5, which link Monterey with Carmel; #21, which runs between Monterey and Salinas; and #1, which runs along Lighthouse Avenue out to Pacific Grove; there's also the *WAVE* shuttle bus which runs every ten minutes from downtown to the Monterey Bay Aquarium on Cannery Row, and from Cannery Row to Pacific Grove, costing $1.25 but free if you can present an *MST* receipt for that day. The only way to get to the Big Sur coast on public transport is on bus #22, which leaves four times a day, in summer only.

Another option is to **rent a bike** for $20 a day: in Monterey, try *Adventures by the Sea*, 201 Alvarado Mall (☎372-1807) outside the Maritime Museum, or *Bay Sports*, 640 Wave St (☎646-9090) on Cannery Row; there's also a branch in Carmel (☎625-BIKE) on Lincoln between Fifth and Sixth. For more leisurely riding, *Moped Adventures* (☎373-2696) at 1250 Del Monte north of the Wharf has a range of bikes including tandems, plus mopeds at $50 for a three-hour session.

# Monterey Peninsula accommodation

What Santa Barbara is to southern California, the Monterey Peninsula is to the north, making it among the most exclusive and expensive resort areas in California, with **hotel** and **bed and breakfast** room rates averaging $120 a night. This may tempt you to stay elsewhere – in Santa Cruz, or in agricultural Salinas – and come here on day trips; the other budget option is to avail yourself of one of the many **motels** along Fremont Street, two miles north of the centre of Monterey via *MST* bus #9 (last bus back at 11.45pm) or #10.

The only **camping** within walking distance is in Veteran's Memorial Park, site of Steinbeck's fictional Tortilla Flat, at the top of Jefferson Street in the hills above town; it's only $3 a night if you're on foot or bike, or $15 per car, and is operated on a first-come-first-served basis.

## Motels

**Bayside Inn**, 2055 N Fremont St, Monterey (☎372-8071). Rooms with breakfast and use of a pool for $40. ②.

**Bide-a-Wee Motel**, 221 Asilomar Blvd, Pacific Grove (☎372-2330). Excellent value, no-frills rooms, including a few with kitchenettes. A two-minute walk to the ocean. ③.

**Carmel River Inn**, Rio Road at Hwy-1, Carmel (☎624-1575). Clean, pleasant and functional motel that was the model for Brian Moore's novel *The Great Victorian Collection*. Right on the banks of the Carmel River, near the beach and Carmel Mission. ③–④.

**Driftwood Motel**, 2362 N Fremont St, Monterey (☎372-5059). Among the best-value places on northern Monterey's motel row. ③.

**Motel 6**, 2124 N Fremont St, Monterey (☎646-8585). Basic motel, but you'll have to reserve a room months in advance. ③.

**Pacific Grove Motel**, Lighthouse Ave at Grove Acre, Pacific Grove (☎372-3218 or 1-800/858-8997). Simple, small motel in marvellous setting, 100 yards from the sea. Rates rise in summer and at weekends. ③.

## Hotels and B&B Inns

**Del Monte Beach**, 1110 Del Monte Ave, Monterey (☎649-4410). A bargain B&B close to the centre of Monterey. All the usual trappings for half the normal cost. ③–④.

**Green Gables Inn**, 104 Fifth St, Pacific Grove (☎375-2095). Plush doubles in one of the prettiest houses in a town of fine homes, on the waterfront just a few blocks from the Monterey Bay Aquarium. ⑤.

**Homestead**, Eighth & Lincoln, Carmel (☎624-4119). The least expensive accommodation in Carmel. Centrally placed, with rooms and cottages in attractive gardens. ③–④.

**Horizon Inn**, Third & Junipero, Carmel (☎624-5327 or 1-800/350-7723). Very reasonably priced bed and breakfast place with a pool. ⑤.

**Monterey Marriott**, 350 Calle Principal, Monterey (☎649-4234). Luxurious modern hotel right at the heart of historic Monterey, with views out over the bay and peninsula. Pricey, but in winter and spring the good-value "Aquarium Package" includes two tickets to the Monterey Bay Aquarium. ⑥–⑦.

**Pacific Grove Inn**, 581 Pine Ave at Forest, Pacific Grove (☎375-2825). Thoughtfully modernized 1904 mansion with spacious rooms, five blocks from the shore. ④.

**Seven Gables Inn**, 555 Ocean View Blvd, Pacific Grove (☎372-4341). Great views out over the beautiful coast from this immaculately restored, antique-filled Victorian mansion. Rates include full breakfast and afternoon tea and scones. ⑥.

# Monterey

The town of **MONTEREY** rests in a quiet niche along the bay formed by the forested Monterey Peninsula, proudly proclaiming itself the most historic city in California, a boast which, for once, may be true. Its compact town centre features some of the best vernacular **buildings** of California's Spanish and Mexican colonial past, most of which stand unassumingly within a few blocks of the tourist-thronged waterfront. The single best stop, though, not to be missed if you've got an afternoon to spare, is the **Monterey Bay Aquarium**, a mile west of town, at the end of the Steinbeck-memorializing Cannery Row.

Monterey was named by the Spanish merchant and explorer Vizcaino, who landed in 1602 to find an abundant supply of fresh water and wild game after a seven-month voyage from Mexico. Despite Vizcaino's enthusiasm for the site, the area was not colonized until 1770, although it played a pre-eminent role in the development of California thereafter. Under the Spanish the *Presidio de Monterey* was the military headquarters for the whole of Alta California, and thereafter Monterey continued to be the leading administrative and commercial centre of a territory that extended east to the Rocky Mountains and north to Canada, but had a total population, excluding Native Americans, of less than seven thousand.

American interest in Monterey was at first purely commercial, until 1842 when an American naval commodore received a false report that the US and Mexico were at war, and that the English were poised to take California. Commodore Catesby Jones anchored at Monterey and demanded the peaceful surrender of the port. Two days later the American flag was raised, though the armed but cordial US occupation lasted only until Jones examined the official documents closely, and realized he'd got it all wrong. When the Mexican-American War began in earnest in 1846 the United States took possession of Monterey without resistance. The discovery of gold in the Sierra Nevada foothills soon focused attention upon San Francisco, and Monterey became something of a backwater, hardly affected by the waves of immigration which followed.

## Old Monterey

Many of Monterey's wonderful old buildings have survived in pristine condition, and can be found, now preserved as the **Monterey State Historic Park**, scattered throughout the quarter-mile square of the modern city. A loosely organized, roughly mile-and-a-half-long **Path of History** connects the 37 sites, which tend to be open daily from 10am until 5pm. Many can't be entered or are free; others cost $2. A **Five for $5 ticket**, valid for two days, gives entry to four of the houses – Larkin House, Cooper-Molera Complex, Stevenson House and Casa Sobranes (otherwise $2 each) – and entitles you to go on one of the **walking tours** (daily 10.15am, 12.30pm & 2.30pm; ☎649-2836), leaving from the Maritime Museum, near the waterfront at the foot of the main drag, Alvarado Street.

The best place to get a feel for life in old Monterey is at the **Larkin House** (tours Fri–Wed 10am, 11am &, in summer, noon; $2), on Jefferson Street a block south of Alvarado, home of the first and only American Consul to California and successful entrepreneur, Thomas Larkin. New England-born Larkin, the wealthy owner of a general store and redwood lumber business, was one of the most important and influential figures in early California. He was actively involved in efforts to attract American settlers to California, and lobbied the Californians to turn towards the United States and away from the erratic government of Mexico. Through his designs for his own house, and the Customs House near Fisherman's Wharf, Larkin is credited with developing the now-familiar Monterey style of architecture, combining local adobe walls and the balconies of a Southern plantation home with a puritan Yankee's taste in ornament. The house, the first two-storey adobe in California, is filled with many millions of dollars' worth of antiques and is surrounded by gorgeous gardens which are open all day.

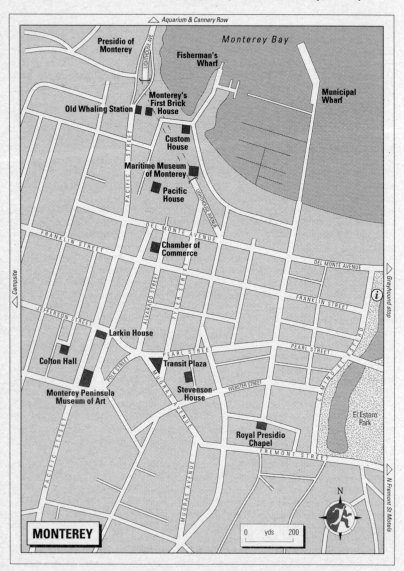

△ *Aquarium & Cannery Row*

*Monterey Bay*

**Presidio of Monterey**

**Fisherman's Wharf**

**Municipal Wharf**

**Monterey's First Brick House**

**Old Whaling Station**

**Custom House**

**Maritime Museum of Monterey**

**Pacific House**

DEL MONTE AVENUE

**Chamber of Commerce**

FRANKLIN STREET

DEL MONTE AVENUE

△ *Campsite*

FRANKLIN STREET

JEFFERSON STREET

ⓘ

▷ *Greyhound stop*

**Larkin House**

PEARL STREET

PEARL STREET

**Colton Hall**

**Transit Plaza**

WEBSTER STREET

**Stevenson House**

El Estero Park

**Monterey Peninsula Museum of Art**

**Royal Presidio Chapel**

FREMONT STREET

▷ *N Fremont St Motels*

N

**MONTEREY**

0    yds    200

## ROBERT LOUIS STEVENSON AND MONTEREY

The Gold Rush of 1849 bypassed Monterey for San Francisco, leaving the community little more than a somnolent Mexican fishing village – which was pretty much how the town looked when a 29-year-old, feverishly ill Scotsman arrived by stagecoach, flat broke and desperately in love with a married woman. **Robert Louis Stevenson** came to Monterey in the fall of 1879 looking for Fanny Osbourne, whom he had met while travelling in France two years before. He stayed here for three months, writing occasional articles for the local newspaper and telling stories in exchange for his meals at Jules Simoneau's restaurant behind what is now the **Stevenson House**, halfway between the Larkin House and the Royal Presidio Chapel (see below).

Stevenson witnessed Monterey – no longer politically important but not yet a tourist attraction – in transition, something he wrote about in his essay *The Old and New Pacific Capitals*. He foresaw that the lifestyle that had endured since the Mexican era was no match for the "Yankee craft" of the "millionaire vulgarians of the Big Bonanza", such as Charles Crocker whose lavish *Hotel Del Monte*, which opened a year later (the site is now the Naval Postgraduate School, east of downtown), turned the sleepy town into a seaside resort of international renown almost overnight.

Larkin, as unhappy with the American military government as he had been with the Mexicans, helped to organize the Constitutional Convention that convened in Monterey in 1849 to draft the terms by which California could be admitted to the US as the 31st state – which happened in 1850. The meetings were held in the grand white stone building across the street from his house, the then newly completed **Colton Hall**, now an engaging **museum** (free) furnished as it was during the convention, with quill pens on the tables and an early map of the West Coast, used to draw up the boundaries of the nascent state.

**Stevenson House**, at 530 Houston St (daily except Wed 10am–4pm; $2), is an old rooming house now filled with memorabilia of Robert Louis Stevenson and the time in which he lived (see box), much of it collected by the writer on his travels around the South Sea Islands. The oldest building in Monterey, the **Royal Presidio Chapel** (daily 8.30am–6pm; free), stands on Church Street at the top of Figueroa Street, half a mile east. This small and much-restored Spanish colonial church was built in 1795 as part of a mission founded here by Junipero Serra in 1770, the rest of which was soon removed to a better site along the Carmel River.

### The waterfront

Nowadays, catering to visitors is Monterey's main livelihood. A good deal of the trade is concentrated along the waterfront, around the tacky **Fisherman's Wharf**, where the catch-of-the-day is more likely to be families from San Jose than the formerly abundant sardines. Most of the commercial fishermen moved out long ago, leaving the old wharves and canneries as relics of a once-prosperous industry, and the source of scraps of fish which you can buy to throw at the fat sea lions floating in the dirty water under the piers.

The most prominent building near the wharf, at the foot of Pacific Street, is the modern **Maritime Museum of Monterey** (daily 10am–5pm; $5) with well-displayed but essentially mundane collections of ships in glass cases enlivened by interesting background on the town's defunct sardine industry. If none of this appeals, you should still pop in for the free, fourteen-minute film on Monterey history in preparation for the **Pacific House** (summer daily 10am–5pm; rest of year daily 10am–4pm; free), across the plaza, which since its construction in 1847 has been a courthouse, a rooming house and a dance hall. It is now the best of the local **museums**, with displays on Monterey history and a fair collection of Native American artefacts. While in the area, wander by the **Customs House** (summer daily 10am–5pm; rest of year daily 10am–4pm; free); this is the oldest governmental building on the West Coast, portions of which were built by Spain in 1814, Mexico in 1827 and the US in 1846. The balconied building has been restored and now displays 150-year-old crates of confiscated coffee and liquor in a small museum inside. A block west, look out for the unusual whalebone pavement in front of the period-furnished **Old Whaling Station** (Fri only 10am–2pm; free) and, next door, Monterey's **First Brick House** (summer daily 10am–5pm; rest of year daily 10am–4pm; free), the first house in the state constructed of brick, built in 1847 and now decked out as a restaurant, one of its previous incarnations.

## Cannery Row and the Monterey Bay Aquarium

A waterfront **bike path** runs from the wharf along the disused railroad two miles out to Pacific Grove, following the one-time Ocean View Avenue, renamed **Cannery Row** after John Steinbeck's evocative portrait of the rough-and-ready men and women who worked in and around the thirty-odd fish canneries here. During World War II Monterey was the sardine capital of the Western world, catching and canning some 200,000 tons of the fish each year. However, overfishing meant that by 1945 the fish were more or less all gone, and the canneries were abandoned, falling into disrepair until the 1970s, when they were rebuilt, redecorated and converted into shopping malls and flashy restaurants. Many have adopted names from Steinbeck's tales, and now pack in the tourists as profitably as they once packed sardines. It's all rather phoney, best visited in the early evening to take advantage of the low-priced food and drinks on offer during the many Happy Hours.

Ride, walk or take the *WAVE* shuttle from Fisherman's Wharf to the end of Cannery Row to visit its one (very) worthwhile feature: the engaging **Monterey Bay Aquarium** (daily 10am–6pm; $11.75; ☎648-4888 or 1-800/756-3737). Arrive early to avoid the summer lines or call to reserve ($3 fee for any number of tickets). Built upon the foundations of an old sardine cannery, and housed in modernist buildings that blend a sense of adventure with pleasant promenades along Monterey Bay, the acclaimed aquarium and study centre exhibits over five thousand marine creatures in innovative replicas of their natural habitats. Sharks and octopi roam around behind two-foot-thick sheets of transparent acrylic, there's a 300,000 gallon Kelp Forest tank, and a touch pool where you can pet your favourite bat rays. Try also to catch the sea otters at feeding time, usually 11am, 2pm, and 4.30pm: playful critters that were hunted nearly to extinction for their furs – said, with some two million hairs per square inch, to be the softest in the world.

# Pacific Grove

**PACIFIC GROVE** stands curiously apart from the rest of the peninsula, less known but more impressively sited than its two famous neighbours. The town began as a campground and Methodist retreat in 1875, a summertime tent city for revivalist Christians in which strong drink, naked flesh and reading the Sunday papers were firmly prohibited. The Methodists have long since gone, but otherwise the town is little changed. Its quiet streets, lined by pine trees and grand old Victorian wooden houses, are enlivened each year by hundreds of thousands of golden **monarch butterflies**, which come here from all over the western US and Canada to escape the winter chill. Forming soft orange and black blankets on the trees near the lighthouse at the very tip of the peninsula, the butterflies are the town's main tourist attraction, protected by local law.

Downtown Pacific Grove centres upon the intersection of Forest Street and Lighthouse Avenue, two miles northwest of central Monterey. Two blocks north at 667 Lighthouse Ave, the **Bookworks** bookstore and café (daily 9am–10pm; ☎372-2242), is the place to pick up more detailed guides to the local area, or just stop for a cup of coffee and a pastry. A block down Forest Street, on the corner of Central Avenue, the **Pacific Grove Museum of Natural History** (Tues–Sun 10am–5pm; free) has an interesting collection of local wildlife, including lots of butterflies, over four hundred stuffed birds, a relief model of the undersea topography and exhibits on the ways of life of the aboriginal Costanoan and Salinan Indians. Across the park, the **Chautauqua Hall** was for a time in the 1880s the focus of town life, as the West Coast headquarters of the instructional and populist Chautauqua Movement, a left-leaning, travelling university which reached thousands of Americans long before there was any accessible form of higher education. Nowadays the plain white building is used as a dance hall, with a three-piece band playing favourites from the Thirties and Forties every Saturday night, and square dancing on Thursday.

About the only reminder of the fundamentalist camp meetings are the intricately detailed, tiny wooden **cottages**, along 16th and 17th streets, which date from the revival days; in some cases wooden boards were simply nailed over the frames of canvas tents to make them habitable year-round. Down Central Avenue at 12th, at the top of a small wooded park overlooking the ocean, stands the deep-red Gothic wooden church of **Saint Mary's By-The-Sea**, Pacific Grove's first substantial church, built in 1887, with a simple interior of redwood beams polished to a shimmering glow, and an authentic signed Tiffany stained-glass window, nearest the altar on the left.

**Ocean View Boulevard**, which runs between the church and the ocean, circles along the coast around the town, passing the headland of **Lovers Point** – originally called Lovers of Jesus Point – where preachers used to hold sunrise services. Surrounded in early summer by the colourful red and purple blankets of blooming ice plant, it's one of the peninsula's best **beaches**, where you can lounge around and swim from the intimate, protected strand, or rent a glass-bottomed boat and explore the sheltered cove. Ocean View Boulevard runs another mile along the coast out to the tip of the peninsula, where the 150-year-old **Point Piños Lighthouse** (Sat, Sun & holidays 1–4pm; free), is the oldest operating lighthouse on the California coast.

Around the point, the name of the coastal road changes to Sunset Drive – which will make obvious sense if you're here at that time of day – and leads on to **Asilomar State Beach**, a wilder stretch with more dramatic surf, too dangerous for swimming, though the rocky shore provides homes for all sorts of tidepool life. The **Butterfly Trees**, where the monarchs congregate, are on Ridge Road, a quarter of a mile inland along Lighthouse Avenue. Hwy-68 from the end of Sunset Drive takes the inland route over the hills, joining Hwy-1 just north of Carmel, while the **Seventeen Mile Drive** ($6.50 per car), a privately owned, scenic toll road, loops from Pacific Grove along the coast south to Carmel and back again, passing by the golf courses and country clubs of Pebble Beach. Halfway along stands the trussed-up figure of the **Lone Cypress**, subject of many a postcard, and there are enough beautiful vistas of the rugged coastline to make it almost worth braving the hordes who pack the road on holiday weekends.

## Carmel

Set on gently rising headlands above a sculpted, rocky shore, **CARMEL**'s reputation as a rich resort belies its origins. There was nothing much here until the San Francisco earthquake and fire of 1906 led a number of artists and writers from the city to take refuge in the area, forming a bohemian colony on the wild and uninhabited slopes that soon became notorious throughout the state. Figurehead of the group was the poet George Stirling, and part-time members included Jack London, Mary Austin and the young Sinclair Lewis. But it was a short-lived alliance, and by the 1920s the group had broken up and an influx of wealthy San Franciscans had put Carmel well on its way to becoming the exclusive corner it is today.

Certainly, there's little about the town to welcome travellers of modest means and low credit-rating, and Carmel instead often seems the very epitome of parochial snobbishness. Local laws, enacted to preserve the rustic character of the town, prohibit parking meters, street addresses and postal deliveries (all mail is picked up in person from the post office); planning permission is required to cut down any tree, so they sprout everywhere, even in the middle of streets; and franchise stores or restaurants are banned outright within the city limits. For these aspects alone Carmel is probably worth a look at least, and the chance to catch a rare glimpse of ex-mayor Clint Eastwood may make the sterile shopping-mall atmosphere worth bearing for an hour or so; but without a doubt the town's best feature is the largely untouched nearby coastline, among the most beautiful in California.

Carmel's centre, fifteen minutes south of Monterey on *MST* bus #4 or #5, doesn't have much to recommend it – largely designer-shopping territory, in which Armani and Ralph Lauren rub shoulders with mock-Tudor tearooms and a number of **art galleries**, concentrated along Dolores Street between Fifth and Sixth, filled with uninspired watercolour renderings of golf scenes and local seascapes. The *Weston Gallery* on Sixth Street is worth a look, however, hosting regular shows of the best contemporary photographers and with a permanent display of works by Fox Talbot, Ansel Adams and Edward Weston – who lived in Carmel for most of his life. To get the lowdown on the other galleries, check out the free, widely available *Carmel Gallery Guide*.

Fortunately, the contrivedness of the town centre doesn't extend to the gorgeous, unspoilt coastline. **Carmel Beach**, down the hill at the end of Ocean Avenue, is a tranquil cove of emerald blue water bordered by soft white sand and cypress-covered cliffs, though the tides here are deceptively strong and dangerous – be careful if you chance a swim. A mile south from Carmel Beach along Carmel Bay, **Tor House** was, when built in 1919, the only building on a then treeless headland. The poet Robinson Jeffers (whose very long, starkly tragic narrative poems were far more popular in his time than they are today) built the small cottage and adjacent tower by hand, out of granite boulders he carried up from the cove below. Hourly guided **tours** of the house and gardens (Fri & Sat 10am–4pm; $5; under-12s prohibited; reservations essential on ☎624-1813) include a rather obsequious account of the writer's life and work.

Another quarter of a mile along Scenic Road, around the tip of Carmel Point, the mile-long **Carmel River State Beach** is less visited than the city beach, and includes a bird sanctuary on a freshwater lagoon that offers safe and sometimes warm swimming. Again, if you brave the waves, beware of the strong tides and currents, especially at the south end of the beach, where the sand falls away at a very steep angle, causing big and potentially hazardous surf.

## Carmel Mission

Half a mile or so up the Carmel River from the beach, also reachable by following Junipero Avenue from downtown, **Carmel Mission** (daily 10.30am–4.30pm; donations) – *La Misión San Carlos Borromeo del Rio Carmelo* – was founded in 1770 by Junipero Serra as the second of the California missions and the headquarters of the chain. Father Serra never got to see the finished church – he died before its completion and is buried under the floor in front of the altar. Finally completed by Father Lasuén in 1797, the sandstone church has since been well restored. The facade is unexpectedly exotic and whimsical; flourishes on the central pediment resemble cattle horns, and the interior walls curve gently into a vaulted ceiling to interesting effect. Some three thousand local Native Americans are buried in the adjacent **cemetery**, and three small **museums** in the mission compound recount the history of the missionary effort alongside ornate silver candle-holders, decorated vestments and relics of the life of Father Serra.

## Point Lobos State Reserve

Two miles south of the mission along Hwy-1, accessible in summer on *MST* bus #22, the **Point Lobos State Reserve** (summer daily 9am–7pm; spring & fall daily 9am–6pm; winter daily 9am–5pm; $6 parking) gives some of the best undisturbed views of the ocean and a chance to see everybody's favourite furry creature, the sea otter, in its natural habitat. The park, named after the *lobos marinos* – the noisy, barking sea lions that group on the rocks off the reserve's tip – protects some of the few remaining Monterey cypress trees on its knife-edged headland, despite being buffeted by relentless winds. Craggy granite pinnacles, landforms which inspired Robert Louis Stevenson's *Treasure Island*, reach out of jagged blue coves below, close to which sea lions and otters play in the crashing surf.

A number of **hiking trails** loop around the reserve, giving good views down into deep coves. The sea here is one of the richest underwater habitats in the state, and California gray whales are often seen offshore, migrating south in January and returning with young calves in April and early May. Because the point juts so far out into the ocean, you have a good chance of seeing them from surprisingly close, often as little as a hundred yards away.

Except for a small parking lot, the reserve is closed to cars, so lines sometimes form along the highway to wait for a parking space. You can get a worthwhile **guide** and **map** (50¢) at the entrance.

# Monterey Peninsula eating and drinking

There are many excellent **places to eat** all over the peninsula, though because it's a holiday resort, be prepared to spend a bit more than you'd have to elsewhere. By and large the offerings are pretty standard, mostly steaks and seafood, with pricey Mexican places playing off the Hispanic heritage. For a full list of the hundreds of eating options in the area, check out a copy of the free, weekly and widely available *Coast Weekly* or *Peninsula*. If you're on anything like a tight budget, the best eats are on the north side of Monterey along Fremont Street, and in the shopping malls along Hwy-1 south of Carmel.

## Budget food

**Chutney's Gourmet Café**, 230 Crossroads Blvd, Crossroads Mall, Hwy-1, Carmel (☎624-4785). Soups, salads, sandwiches and burgers in eccentric combinations in a lively, unpretentious café setting.

**Mediterranean Market**, Ocean Ave and Mission St, Carmel (☎624-2022). Perfect for packing a picnic basket for a day on the sands; full of fine cheeses, deli meats, bread and wine.

**Mom's Home Cookin'**, 1988 Fremont St, Seaside, Monterey (☎394-9191). Great BBQ ribs and chicken, plus cornbread, collard greens and all the trimmings.

**Old Monterey Café**, 489 Alvarado St, Monterey (☎646-1021). More-than-you-can-eat breakfasts, with great omelettes and buckwheat pancakes, plus tasty sandwiches; daily except Tues 7am–2.30pm.

**Power Juice and Food Co.**, 470 Alvarado St, Monterey (☎373-5635). A vegetarian and organic juice and snack place with baked potatoes, stacked bagels and healthy drinks at reasonable prices.

## Moderate to expensive

**La Boheme**, Dolores Street between Ocean and Seventh, Carmel (☎624-7500). Fine dining the Carmel way – in a scaled-down replica of a French country hotel courtyard, complete with whitewashed walls and hanging laundry. Multi-course, *prix-fixe* meals for less than $20 plus wine and service.

**Café Fina**, middle of Fisherman's Wharf, Monterey (☎372-5200). Pastas, wood-oven pizzas, and, of course, grilled fresh fish in the Wharf's most style-conscious setting.

**Fishwife Restaurant**, 1996 Sunset Drive at Asilomar, Pacific Grove (☎375-7107). Long-standing local favuorite, serving great food at reasonable prices – king prawns sautéed in red peppers and lime juice with rice and steamed vegetables for $10 – in cosy, unpretentious surroundings.

**Pepper's Mexicali Café**, 170 Forest Ave, Pacific Grove (☎373-6892). Gourmet Mexican seafood Californified into healthy, high-style dishes at reasonable prices.

**Toot's Lagoon**, on Dolores Street below Seventh, Carmel (☎625-1915). Good-sized portions on a wide-ranging menu – pizzas, salads, steaks, burgers, fresh fish and famous BBQ ribs – popular with families and for birthday outings.

**Triples**, 220 Oliver St, Monterey (☎372-4744). Light and healthy California cuisine, fresh fish and great salads, on a sunny outdoor patio or inside historic *Duarte's Store*. Behind the Pacific House in the Monterey State Historic Park.

**Tuck Box Tearoom**, Dolores Street between Ocean and Seventh, Carmel (☎624-6365). Breakfast, lunch and afternoon tea in half-timbered mock-Tudor Olde Englande setting; costly and kitsch but fun.

## Drinking and nightlife

A number of clubs on the Monterey Peninsula feature a fairly sedate range of live and canned music, though things do pick up a bit in September, when it hosts the world-class **Monterey Jazz Festival** at the County Fairgrounds east of town; phone ☎373-3366 for more information. Besides the places listed below, most restaurants have a bar or cocktail lounge, generally filled with golfers.

**After Dark**, 214 Lighthouse Ave, Monterey (☎373-7828). Mainly gay dance club with a more mixed clientele on Thursdays.

**Bay Books**, 316 Alvarado St, Monterey (☎375-1855). Sip coffee until 10pm (11pm at weekends) while browsing in one of Monterey's better book shops.

**The Club of Monterey**, Alvarado and Del Monte (☎646-9244). DJ-dance club with a fairly young, upscale crowd; darts and pool tables downstairs. Cover $1–8, with the odd live act.

**Doc Ricket's Lab**, 95 Prescott St, Cannery Row (☎649-4241). Popular drinking venue with occasional live acts, and disco most evenings.

**Planet Gemini**, 625 Cannery Row (☎373-1449). Mixed music and comedy venue usually with a $5 cover. Closed Mon.

# North from Monterey

The landscape around the **Monterey Bay**, between the peninsula and the beach town of Santa Cruz, 45 miles north, is almost entirely given over to agriculture. **CASTROVILLE**, ten miles north along Hwy-1, is surrounded by farmland which grows more than 85 percent of the nation's artichokes (try them deep-fried in one of the local cafés), while the wide **Pajaro Valley**, five miles further north, is covered with apple orchards, blossoming white in the spring. The marshlands that ring the bay at the mouths of the Salinas and Pajaro rivers are habitats for many of California's endangered species of coastal wildlife and migratory birds. At **Elkhorn Slough Estuarine Sanctuary** (Wed–Sun 9am–5pm; $3 donation) near the lively fishing port of **Moss Landing** – a good place to stop for seafood – you may spot a falcon or an eagle among the many pelicans that call it home. The **beaches** along the bay are often windy and not very exciting, though they're lined by sand dunes into which you can disappear for hours on end.

**Sunset State Beach**, fifteen miles south of Santa Cruz, has $14-a-night **campgrounds** (book through *MISTIX*; information only ☎688-3241) along a seven-mile strand. Four miles inland, east of Hwy-1, the earthquake-devastated town of **WATSONVILLE** was more or less the epicentre of the October 1989 Loma Prieta tremor that rattled San Francisco. Its once-quaint downtown of ornate Victorian houses and 1930s brick structures was virtually flattened, and more recently the area economy has been hard-hit by closure of its *Green Giant* vegetable-packing plant, once one of the largest in the country. Though there isn't a lot of interest for travellers, Watsonville is still the main transfer point between the Monterey and Santa Cruz bus systems, so you may well have to pass through.

### San Juan Bautista

Inland from the Monterey Bay area, on US-101 between Salinas and San Francisco, **SAN JUAN BAUTISTA** is about the only place worth making for: an old Mexican town that, but for a modest scattering of craft shops, has hardly changed since it was bypassed by the railroad in 1876. The early nineteenth-century **Mission San Juan Bautista** (daily 9.30am–4.30pm; $1 donation), largest of the Californian mission churches – and still the parish church of San Juan Bautista – stands on the north side of the town's central plaza, its original bells still ringing out from the bell tower; the arcaded monastery wing that stretches out to the left of the church contains relics and historical exhibits. If it all looks a bit familiar, you may have seen it before – the climactic stairway chase scene in Alfred Hitchcock's *Vertigo* was filmed here. In front of the church are explanatory panels on the **San Andreas Fault** which runs just a few yards away.

Most of the town that grew up around the mission has been preserved as a **state park** (daily 9am–5pm; $2), with sporadic exhibits interpreting the restored buildings. On the west side of the plaza, the two-storey, balconied adobe **Plaza Hotel** was a popular stopping place on the stagecoach route between San Francisco and Los Angeles; next door, the 1840 **Castro-Breen Adobe**, administrative headquarters of Mexican California, later belonged to the Breen family – survivors of the ill-fated Donner Party (see p.495) – who made a small fortune in the Gold Rush.

Across from the mission, the large **Plaza Hall** was built to serve as the seat of the emergent county government, but when the county seat was awarded instead to Hollister (a small farming community eight miles east, and scene of a motorcycle gang's rampage that inspired the movie *The Wild One*), the building was turned into a dance hall and saloon. The adjacent stables display a range of old stagecoaches and wagons, and explain how to decipher an array of cattle brands, from "lazy H" to "rockin double B". The commercial centre of San Juan Bautista, a block south of the plaza, lines Third Street in a row of evocatively decaying facades. If you're hungry, the best of the half-dozen **places to eat** is the *Mission Café*, on the corner of Mariposa Street: for more information contact the **Chamber of Commerce**, 402a Third St (☎623-2454).

# Santa Cruz

> *Santa Cruz is part of the post-orgy world, the world left behind after the great social and sexual convulsions. The refugees from the orgy – the orgy of sex, political violence, the Vietnam War, the Woodstock crusade – are all there, jogging along in their tribalism.*
>
> Jean Baudrillard, *America*

Seventy-five miles south of San Francisco, **SANTA CRUZ** is a hard place to pin down. In many ways it's the ideal Californian coastal town, a heady mix of intellect and pure pleasure that's perfect for a few days' stopover on your way north or south. And there are any number of things to occupy you, from surfing or sunning along the many miles of beaches, or hiking around the surrounding mountaintop forests, or riding the Big Dipper – the largest and wildest wooden roller coaster on the West Coast. But there's another side to Santa Cruz: the town has grown unwieldy over the last couple of decades fuelled largely by its role as a dormitory suburb for San Jose and Silicon

Valley. In spite of a reputation for Sixties liberalism, there's a long-term town-versus-gown split between the locals and the students from UCSC, and the town's suburbs have a redneck feel more akin to the Central Valley than the laid-back languid coast. Only rarely do you get the impression of a resort totally at ease with itself, and the underlying conflicts are one of the many reasons why the town has been so slow to rebuild following the destruction wreaked by the 1989 earthquake.

This tension adds spice to a visit to Santa Cruz. The town has an enduring reputation as a holdout from the 1960s, which is only fitting since this is where it all began. Ken Kesey and his Merry Pranksters turned the local youth on to the wonders of LSD years before it defined a generation, a mission recorded by Tom Wolfe in *The Electric Koolaid Acid Test*, and the area is still considered among the most politically and socially progressive in California. One upshot of this is that Santa Cruz has, in recent years, become to lesbians what San Francisco is to gay men, although the scene is, as yet, small.

The town is also surprisingly untouristed: no hotels spoil the miles of wave-beaten coastline – in fact, most of the surrounding land is used for growing fruit and vegetables, and roadside stalls are more likely to be selling apples or sprouts than postcards and souvenirs. Places to stay are for once good value and easy to find, and the town sports a range of bookstores and coffee houses, as well as some lively bars and nightclubs where the music varies from hardcore surf-punk to longtime local Neil Young and friends.

## Arrival, information and city transport

By **car**, Santa Cruz is on Hwy-1, 45 miles north of Monterey; Hwy-17 runs over the mountains, 33 miles from San Jose and US-101. **Greyhound buses** on the San Francisco–LA run stop three times a day in each direction at 425 Front St in the centre of town; *Peerless Stages* (☎423-1800) from Oakland and San Jose in the San Francisco Bay Area stop here four times a day, as do *Amtrak* Thruway buses, and there's a weekly *Green Tortoise*. Coming from the Monterey peninsula, local *MST* and *SCMTD* buses link up in Watsonville.

The **Santa Cruz Visitors' Council** at 701 Front St (Mon–Sat 9am–5pm, Sun 10am–4pm; ☎425-1234 or 1-800/833-3494) has lots of handy information on restaurants and places to stay, and sells a map of Santa Cruz's historic districts for $1.50. To find out **what's on** in the area, check out the free magazine rack at the **Bookshop Santa Cruz**, 1520 Pacific Ave (☎423-0900), where you'll find generally useful weeklies like the *Good Times* and the *Santa Cruz Metro*.

Santa Cruz has an excellent **public transport** system, based around the Metro Center wedged between Front Street and Pacific Ave, and operated by the *Santa Cruz Metropolitan Transit District* or *SCMTD* (daily 7am–6pm; ☎425-8600), which publishes *Headways*, a free bilingual guide to getting around the area. The basic fare is $1, an all-day pass is $3, and a five-day pass costs $15. Some of the most useful routes are: #1, which runs up the hill to UCSC; #71 to Watsonville; #67 along the eastern beaches; and #3 to the western beaches. Route #35, which runs up into the mountains to Big Basin Redwoods State Park, is equipped with bike racks.

Though there are buses to most of the beaches, you might find it easier to get around by **bicycle**: *Surf City Cycles*, 1121 Mission St (☎426-7299), or *The Dutchman*, 3961 Portola Ave at 46th Ave (☎476-9555), rent bikes from $25 a day, while the waterfront *Go-Skate*, 601 Beach St (☎425-8578) also rents out roller skates and surfboards. If you feel particularly daring, you can even get ocean-going **kayaks** for $10 an hour or $25 a day from *Venture Quest* on the wharf and at 125 Beach St (April–Oct Wed–Fri 9am–6pm, Sat & Sun 8am–7pm; ☎427-2267).

# Accommodation

Compared to most California beach resorts, **places to stay** in Santa Cruz are inexpensive and easy to come by, especially during the week or outside of summer. Most of the establishments we've listed offer good-value weekly rates. **Camping opportunities** in and around Santa Cruz are abundant and varied, from beaches to forests and points in between; **reservations** for all state park campgrounds are handled through *MISTIX*.

## Hotels, motels and B&Bs

**Capitola Venetian Hotel**, 1500 Wharf Rd, Capitola (☎476-6471 or 1-800/332-2780). Quirky, ageing beachfront hotel just across the bridge from Capitola's lively esplanade. All rooms have kitchens, some are two-bedroom suites; rates increase at weekends when there's a two-night minimum. Weekly rental begins at $250. Low season ③, peak season ⑥.

**Capri Motel**, 337 Riverside Ave (☎426-4611). The cheapest of a dozen or so budget motels near the beach and the boardwalk. Others include *Aladdin's*, 50 Front St (☎426-3575), and the *Mardi Gras*, 338 Riverside Ave (☎426-3707). All ②.

**Cliff Crest Inn**, 407 Cliff St (☎427-2609). Nicely furnished 1887 Queen Anne-style Victorian home set in lovely gardens at the top of Beach Hill. Rates include a full breakfast and afternoon sherry. ⑤.

**Econolodge**, 550 Second St (☎426-3626). The most salubrious of the beachfront motels, with a heated pool and continental breakfast. On Beach Hill: take Front Street from the boardwalk and then first right. ③.

**Inn Cal**, 370 Ocean St (☎458-9220 & 1-800/550-0055). Across the river from the centre of town, with clean, no-frills double rooms. A winter bargain and very popular in summer. ②/③.

**Motel Continental**, 414 Ocean St (☎429-1221). Top value for an off-the-bottom-rung motel. Comfortable, tastefully decorated rooms an easy walk to everything. ③.

**Sea and Sand Inn**, 201 West Cliff Drive (☎427-2400). Small and well-placed hotel with great views over the bay, beaches and Steamer Lane surfers. Complimentary breakfast. ④/⑤.

## Hostels

**HI–Pigeon Point Lighthouse Hostel**, Pescadero (☎415/879-0633). Located some 25 miles north of town, near Año Nuevo State Park, but well worth the effort for a chance to bunk down in the old lighthouse keeper's quarters right on the point. Dorm beds $12 per person, plus $3 for non-HI members; more expensive private doubles, and there's an excellent hot tub ($6 per half-hour) hanging out over the thundering surf. ①/②.

**HI–Santa Cruz Hostel**, 321 Main St (☎423-8304). Well-sited hostel in a set of cottages just a couple of blocks from the beach. The atmosphere is informal but the place is closed during the day and is often booked up in advance. Members $12. ①.

## Campgrounds

**Big Basin Redwoods State Park**, Hwy-236, Boulder Creek (☎338-6132). High up in the hills; sites with showers for $16, and numerous backcountry sites for hikers and mountain bikers. Also tent cabins from $36.

**Henry Cowell Redwoods State Park**, Hwy-9 (☎335-4598). In the hills above town and UC Santa Cruz, in a redwood grove along the San Lorenzo River. Bus # 35 serves the park, and sites cost $16 a night.

**New Brighton State Beach**, 1500 Park Avenue, Capitola (☎475-485). Three miles south of Santa Cruz on the edge of the beachfront village of Capitola, set on bluffs above a lengthy strand. Sites cost $16 a night, including hot showers.

# The Town

After the overcharged tourism of the Monterey Peninsula across the bay, Santa Cruz – a quiet, easy-going community of 45,000 residents plus some 10,000 students – comes as a welcome surprise, spread out at the foot of thickly wooded mountains along a

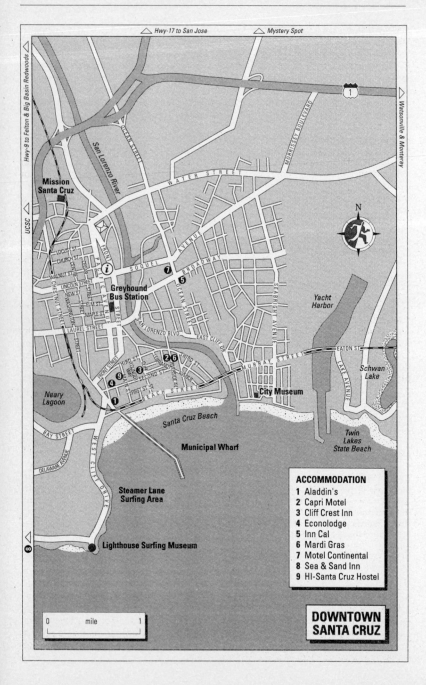

Hwy-17 to San Jose

Mystery Spot

Hwy-9 to Felton & Big Basin Redwoods

Watsonville & Monterey

UCSC

San Lorenzo River

OCEAN STREET

WATER STREET

MORRISSEY BOULEVARD

Mission
Santa Cruz

SOQUEL AVENUE

BROADWAY

N

LOCUST ST.
CHURCH ST.
WALNUT STREET
LINCOLN STREET
NEW ST.
ELM ST.
MAPLE ST.
LAUREL STREET
CHESTNUT STREET
COOPER ST.
FRONT AVENUE
PACIFIC AVENUE
CEDAR STREET
WASHINGTON ST.

*i*

Greyhound
Bus Station

FRONT STREET

OCEAN STREET

SEABRIGHT AVENUE

Yacht
Harbor

SAN LORENZO BLVD

EAST CLIFF DR

MURRAY STREET

EATON ST.

LAKE AVENUE

Schwan
Lake

THIRD ST.
THIRD ST.
SECOND ST.
FIRST ST.

City Museum

Neary
Lagoon

BEACH STREET

Santa Cruz Beach

Twin
Lakes
State Beach

BAY STREET

DELAWARE AVENUE

WEST CLIFF DRIVE

Municipal Wharf

Steamer Lane
Surfing Area

8

Lighthouse Surfing Museum

## ACCOMMODATION

1 Aladdin's
2 Capri Motel
3 Cliff Crest Inn
4 Econolodge
5 Inn Cal
6 Mardi Gras
7 Motel Continental
8 Sea & Sand Inn
9 HI-Santa Cruz Hostel

0     mile     1

## DOWNTOWN
## SANTA CRUZ

clean, sandy shore. There's not a lot to see in the town, almost all of which is within a ten-minute walk of the beach, apart from the many blocks of Victorian wooden houses – but the feel of the place is a treat.

The sluggish San Lorenzo river wraps around the town centre, two blocks east of **Pacific Garden Mall**, a landscaped, prettified and pedestrianized stretch of Pacific Avenue that has recovered from the devastation of the earthquake and is once again Santa Cruz's main street, lined with bookstores, record stores, beachwear shops and cafés, and home to some of the town's chic denizens as well as the fossilized fallout from the 1960s.

One place that survived the tremor is the ornate brick-and-stone **Octagon Building**, 118 Cooper St, at the north end of Pacific Avenue. Completed in 1882 as the Santa Cruz Hall of Records, it now houses a **museum** of local history (Tues–Sun 11am–4pm; free), with exhibits that dwell on the Victorian era. Three blocks away, at 126 High St, fragments dating from the region's earlier Spanish colonial days are shown off in a restored army barracks, next to a scaled-down copy of **Mission Santa Cruz** (daily 9am–5pm; donations). The original adobe church was destroyed by an earthquake in the mid-nineteenth century; the replica that stands on its site today is dwarfed by a large Gothic Revival church next door.

Between the town centre and the beach, **Beach Hill** rises at the foot of Pacific Avenue, its slopes lined with some of Santa Cruz's finest turn-of-the-century homes, such as the striking Queen Anne-style house at 417 Cliff St, and the slightly odd structure around the corner at 912 Third St, constructed out of the remains of a shipwreck.

## The boardwalk and around

Standing out at the foot of the low-rise town, the **Santa Cruz Boardwalk** (summer daily 11am–10pm; rest of year Sat & Sun only; free admission, rides $1.50–$3 each, unlimited rides $17.95) stretches half a mile along the sands, one of the last surviving beachfront amusement parks on the West Coast. Packed solid at the weekend with teenagers on the prowl, most of the time it's a friendly funfair where barefoot hippies mix with mushroom farmers and their families. First opened in 1907 as a gambling casino, the elegant *Cocoanut Grove* at the west end has recently been restored, and the grand ballroom now hosts 1940s swing bands and salsa and r'n'b combos which offer a change of pace from the raucous string of bumper cars, shooting galleries, log flume rides and ferris wheels that line up beside the wide beach, filled in with every sort of arcade game and test of skill. The star attraction is the **Giant Dipper**, a wild and wooden roller coaster that's listed on the National Register of Historic Places and often doubles for a Coney Island attraction in the movies.

Half a mile west of the boardwalk, the hundred-year-old wooden **Municipal Pier** juts out into the bay, crammed with fresh fish shops, burger joints and seafood restaurants, at the end of which people fish for crabs – you don't need a licence, and can rent tackle from one of the many bait shops. Just east of the boardwalk, across the river, the small **Santa Cruz City Museum of Natural History**, 1305 East Cliff Drive (Tues–Fri 10am–5pm, Sat & Sun 11am–4pm; $2), marked by a concrete whale, has concise displays describing local animals and sea creatures, and a brief description of the local Native American culture.

## The beaches

The **beach** closest to town, along the boardwalk, is wide and sandy, with lots of volleyball courts and water that, in August and September at least, is easily warm enough for swimming. However, not surprisingly it can get crowded and somewhat rowdy, so for a bit more peace and quiet, or to catch the largest waves, simply follow the coastline east or west of town to one of the smaller beaches hidden away at the foot of the cliffs: most are undeveloped and easily accessible.

From the City Museum, **East Cliff Drive** winds along the top of the bluffs, past many coves and estuaries. The nearest of the two coastal lagoons that border the volleyball courts of **Twin Lakes State Beach**, half a mile east, was dredged and converted into a marina in the 1960s; the other, **Schwan Lake** is still intact, its marshy wetlands serving as a refuge for sea birds and migrating waterfowl. Beyond Twin Lakes there's another long strand of beach, with good tidepools at Corcoran Lagoon, a half mile on.

East Cliff Drive continues past popular surfing spots off rocky **Pleasure Point**, to the small beachfront resort of **CAPITOLA**. The small town, three miles east of central Santa Cruz, began as a fishing village, living off the many giant tuna that populated the Monterey Bay, but soon became popular as a holiday spot, with its own railway line. The large wooden trestle of the now-disused railroad still dominates what is now a moneyed town, rising over the soft sands of **Hooper Beach**, west of the small fishing pier.

Capitola is especially attractive in late summer, when the hundreds of begonias – the town's main produce – are in bloom. Any time of year, stop by *Mr Toots*, upstairs from 221 Esplanade (see "Drinking and Nightlife", p.352), a café and bakery with great views out over the bay and live music most nights.

The beaches west of the Santa Cruz Boardwalk, along **West Cliff Drive**, see some of the biggest waves in California, not least at **Steamer Lane**, off the tip of Lighthouse Point beyond the Municipal Pier. The ghosts of surfers past, and the risks of shark attack, are animated at the **Surfing Museum** (daily except Tues noon–4pm; $1.50), housed in the old lighthouse on the point, which holds surfboards ranging from twelve-foot redwood planks used by the early pioneers to modern, high-tech, multi-finned cutters. A clifftop bicycle path runs two miles out from here to **Natural Bridges State Park** (8am–dusk; $6 per car), where waves have cut holes through the coastal cliffs, forming delicate arches in the remaining stone; three of the four bridges after which the park was named have since collapsed, leaving large stacks of stone sticking out of the surf. The park is also famous – like Pacific Grove further south – for its annual gathering of **monarch butterflies**, thousands of whom return each winter.

## Above Santa Cruz: UCSC and the mountains

The **University of California, Santa Cruz**, on the hills above the town (served by *SCMTD* bus #1), is very much a product of the 1960s: students don't take exams or get grades, and the academic programme stresses individual exploration of topics rather than rote learning. Architecturally, too, it's deliberately different, its 2000-acre park-like campus divided into small, autonomous colleges, where deer stroll among the redwood trees overlooking Monterey Bay – a decentralized plan, drawn up under the then-Governor Ronald Reagan, that cynics claim was intended as much to diffuse protests as to provide a peaceful backdrop for study. You can judge for yourself by taking one of the guided tours that start from the **visitor center** at the foot of campus (☎459-0111); be sure to keep an eye out for signs of the major expansion that's in the works, which will enable UCSC to absorb the overflow from overcrowded UC campuses elsewhere.

On the south side of the San Lorenzo River, three miles up Branciforte Drive from the centre of town, there's a point within the woods where normal laws of gravity no longer apply: trees grow at odd angles, balls roll uphill and bright yellow stickers appear on the bumpers of cars that pass too close to the **Mystery Spot** (frequent 35-min tours; summer daily 9.30am–8pm; rest of year daily 9.30am–4.30pm; $4). Many explanations are offered – including its being an extraterrrestrial signalling device that's wreaking havoc with local physics – but most of the disorientation is caused by the not-quite-square corners and perspective tricks used in the various exhibits, spread out around the cool forest.

High up in the mountains that separate Santa Cruz from Silicon Valley and the San Francisco Bay Area, *SCMTD* bus #35 runs to the village of **FELTON**, six miles north of

Santa Cruz on Hwy-9, where the hundred-year-old **Roaring Camp and Big Trees Narrow Gauge Railroad** (summer daily 11am–4pm; rest of year most weekdays at 11am, Sat & Sun noon–2.45pm, departing approximately every 90 mins; $12.50; ☎335-4484), steams on a six-mile loop amongst the massive trees that cover the slopes of the **Henry Cowell Redwoods State Park** (9am–dusk; $5 per car; ☎335-4598) along the San Lorenzo River gorge. From the same station the 1920s-era **Santa Cruz Big Trees and Pacific Railway Company** (early June to early Sept daily; late May to early June & early Sept to Oct weekends only; $14 round trip; ☎335-4484) powers down to the boardwalk and back (or you can board there and ride up) in around two and a half hours. **Felton Covered Bridge** out on the same road a mile east of town is also worth a look, if you've got a car; it spans the river between heavily wooded slopes.

Buses continue further up the mountains to the **Big Basin Redwoods State Park** ($5 per vehicle; ☎338-6132), an hour's ride from Santa Cruz, where acres of three-hundred-foot-tall redwood trees cover some 25 square miles of untouched wilderness, with excellent hiking and camping. A popular "Skyline-to-the-Sea" backpacking **trail** steps down through cool, moist canyons ten miles to the coast at **Waddell Creek Beach** – fifteen miles north of Santa Cruz and a favourite spot for watching world-class windsurfers negotiate the waves – from where *SCMTD* bus #40 (twice daily) will take you back to town.

# Eating

**Restaurants** in Santa Cruz run to two extremes: health-conscious, tofu-fired vegetarian places, and all-American burger-and-beer bars. In between there are bakeries and sandwich shops, and good seafood from a number of establishments on the wharf. The Wednesday afternoon **Farmer's Market** downtown, popular with local hippies, is a good place to pick up fresh produce.

## Budget food

**The Bagelry**, 320-A Cedar St (☎429-8049). Spacious, but usually packed, bakery selling coffees and cakes and an infinite range of filled bagels, open early until late.

**Dharma's Natural Foods**, 4250 Capitola (☎462-1717). A little way south of central Santa Cruz. Low-priced, healthy fast food; used to be called *McDharma's* before they got sued (guess who by?) for breach of trademark. Claims to be the oldest completely vegetarian restaurant in the country.

**El Paisano**, 605 Beach St at Riverside (☎426-2382). Very good and inexpensive Mexican place with great tamales a specialty. Two blocks from the boardwalk and beach.

**Taqueria Vallarta**, 608 Soquel Ave at Ocean (☎457-8226). Don't be put off by the fast-food ambience, the food is authentically Mexican (more burro than burrito) and abundant, and can be washed down with rice or tamarind drinks.

**Zoccoli's Deli**, 1534 Pacific Ave at Water St (☎423-1711). Great old Italian deli, displaced by the earthquake but still serving up great food, including a minestrone that's a meal in itself.

## Moderate to expensive

**Emi Restaurant**, 1001 Cedar St (☎423-7502). Housed in the old *Santa Cruz Hotel,* with top-rate Korean food; before or after, head to the upstairs cocktail and jazz lounge.

**Gabriella Café**, 910 Cedar St (☎457-1677). Elegant without being snooty, this place is gaining quite a reputation for its California cuisine.

**Margaritaville**, 221 Esplanade, Capitola (☎476-2263). One of many good restaurants lined up along the beach, offering sunset cocktails and huge plates of Mexican food.

**Miramar**, 45 Municipal Wharf (☎423-4441). Long-established, family-owned seafood restaurant, with gorgeous views – especially at sunset – of the Pacific and seafront homes. Modern menu and reasonable prices.

**Shadowbrook**, 1750 Wharf Rd, Capitola (☎475-1511). Very romantic steak and seafood place, stepping down along the banks of a creek.

## Drinking and nightlife

Santa Cruz has the Central Coast's best nightlife, with a number of unpretentious and unthreatening **bars and nightclubs** where the music varies from heavy-duty surf-thrash through lilting reggae to the rowdy rock of local resident Neil Young. For drinking, your best bet is the range of **espresso bars and coffee houses** that rival those in any big city. For details of the lesbian and gay scene, contact the *Santa Cruz Lesbian, Gay, Bisexual & Transgendered Community Center*, 1332 Commerce St (☎425-5422).

**The Catalyst**, 1011 Pacific Ave (☎423-1336). The main venue for big-name touring artists and up-and-coming locals, this medium-sized club has something happening nearly every night. Usually 21 and over only; cover varies.

**Herland**, 902 Centre St (☎429-6636). Women-only café with light food and an attached feminist and lesbian bookstore.

**Kuumbwa Jazz Center**, 320 Cedar St (☎427-2227). The Santa Cruz showcase for trad and modern jazz, friendly and intimate with cover ranging from $1–15.

**Palookaville**, 1133 Pacific Ave (☎454-0600). Touring bands and local talent play here. Cover varies widely.

**Caffe Pergolesi**, 418A Cedar St (☎426-1775). Great coffee house in an old wooden house with a garden. Open until around midnight.

**Mr Toots Coffee House**, 221A Esplanade (upstairs), Capitola (☎475-3679). Bustling tea-and-coffee café overlooking the beach and wharf, with live music most nights; open 8am until midnight (at least) every day.

**Santa Cruz Café and Roasting Co**, 1330 Pacific Ave (☎459-0100). Just the place to start the day, with an excellent range of coffees, by the bean or by the cup.

# The coast north to San Francisco

The **Año Nuevo State Reserve** (8am–sunset; parking $4), twenty-five miles north of Santa Cruz, was named by the explorer Vizcaino, who sailed past on New Year's Day 1603. It's a beautiful spot to visit at any time of year, and in winter you shouldn't miss the chance to see one of nature's most bizarre spectacles – the mating rituals of the Northern Elephant Seal. These massive, ungainly creatures, fifteen feet long and weighing up to three tons, gather on the rocks and sand dunes to fight for a mate. The male's distinctive, pendulous nostrils aid him in his noisy honking, which is how he attracts the females; their blubbery forms are capable of diving deeper than any other mammal, to depths of over 4500ft. Obligatory three-hour **tours** ($2; reserve through *MISTIX*) are organized during the breeding season; throughout the year you're likely to see at least a few, dozing in the sands. See *Contexts* for more on the elephant seal's mating habits, and on other coastal creatures.

Five miles north of Año Nuevo, Gazos Creek Road heads inland three miles to **Butano State Park** ($5 per car; ☎879-2040), which has five square miles of redwood trees, views out over the Pacific and **camping** amongst the redwoods for $14 ($3 for hiker/biker sites). Another two miles north along Hwy-1, and fifty miles south of the Golden Gate Bridge, the beginning of the San Francisco Peninsula is marked by the **Pigeon Point Lighthouse** and the adjacent **hostel** (see p.347), where you can spend the night in the old lighthouse keeper's quarters and relax in a hot tub, cantilevered out over the rocks. Pigeon Point took its name from the clipper ship, *Carrier Pigeon*, that broke up on the rocks off the point, one of many shipwrecks that led to the construction of the lighthouse in the late nineteenth century.

The cargo of one of these wrecked ships inspired residents of the nearby fishing village of **PESCADERO**, a mile inland on Pescadero Road, literally to "paint the town", using the hundreds of pots of white paint that were washed up on the shore. The two streets of the small village are still lined with white wooden buildings, and the descendants of the Portuguese whalers who founded the town keep up another, more enticing tradition, celebrating the **Festival of the Holy Ghost** every year, six weeks after Easter, with a lively and highly ritualized parade. Pescadero is also well known as one of the better places to **eat** on the entire coast, with an excellent restaurant, *Duarte's*, 202 Stage Rd (☎879-0464), serving moderately priced fish dinners and fresh fruit pies; the sporadically open *Tony's*, 1956 Pescadero Creek Rd (☎879-0106), with tasty fried artichoke hearts amongst the Greek, Chinese and American food, and *Los Amigos*, a celebrated fast-food Mexican in the gas station on the corner.

Half Moon Bay is the next place of note north along the coast, and is covered in the *San Francisco and the Bay Area* chapter on p.448.

## travel details

### Trains

**LA to**: *Amtrak's Coast Starlight* leaves at 9.50am for Oakland (1 daily; 10hr 30min; a shuttle bus connects to San Francisco); Salinas (1 daily; 8hr 10min); San Jose (1 daily; 9hr 40min); San Luis Obispo (1 daily; 5hr 20min); Santa Barbara (1 daily; 2hr 30min); and continues on through Sacramento, Chico, Redding, through Oregon to Seattle.

One train a day leaves Oakland at 7.30am on the return route.

### Long-distance buses

*All buses are Greyhound unless otherwise stated*

**LA to**: Salinas (9 daily; 9hr); San Francisco (9 daily; 13hr; also one *Green Tortoise* per week in each direction along the coast); San Luis Obispo (8 daily; 5hr 30min); Santa Barbara (8 daily; 2hr 30min), Santa Cruz (3 daily; 10hr 30min).

**Oakland to**: Santa Cruz (4 *Peerless Stages* daily; 2 hr 30min).

**San Francisco to**: LA (8 daily; 12hr); Monterey (3 daily; 4hr); Salinas (9 daily; 2 hr 45min); San Luis Obispo (5 daily; 6hr); Santa Barbara (5 daily; 9hr 30min); Santa Cruz (3 daily; 2hr 40min).

**San Jose to**: Santa Cruz (4 *Peerless Stages* daily; 1hr).

# CHAPTER SEVEN

# SAN FRANCISCO AND THE BAY AREA

*The Bay Area is so beautiful, I hesitate to preach about heaven while I'm here.*

Billy Graham

America's favourite city sits at the edge of the Western world, a position which lends even greater romantic currency to its legend. Arguably the most beautiful, certainly the most liberal city in the US, and one which has had more platitudes heaped upon it than any other, **SAN FRANCISCO** is in serious danger of being clichéd to death. But in the last twenty years the city has undergone a steady transition away from – or maybe out of – the iconoclasm which made it famous, to become a swanky, high-end town with a palpable air of widespread affluence. One by one the central neighbourhoods have been smartened up, with poorer families edged out into the suburbs, leaving only a couple of areas that could still be considered transitional. Interestingly, this gentrification is a by-product of the city's willingness to embrace all comers – the now wealthy and influential gay and singles communities, and the peculiarly eccentric entrepreneurism that has flourished here, are at the root of the city's steady growth.

For all the change, though, San Francisco remains a funky, individualistic, surprisingly small city whose people pride themselves on being the cultured counterparts to their cousins in LA – the last bastion of civilization on the lunatic fringe of America. A steadfast rivalry exists between the two cities. San Franciscans like to think of themselves as less obsessed with money, less riddled with status than those in the south – a rare kind of inverted snobbery that you'll come across almost immediately. But San Francisco has its own element of narcissism, rooted in the sheer physical aspect of the place. Downtown streets lean upwards on impossible gradients to reveal stunning views of the city, the bay and beyond. It has a romantic weather pattern, blanket fogs roll in unexpectedly to envelop the city in mist, adding a surreal quality to an already unique appearance. It's a compact and approachable place, one of the few US centres in which you can comfortably survive without a car. This is not, however, the California of monotonous blue skies and slothful warmth – the temperatures rarely exceed the seventies, and even during summer can drop much lower when consistent and heavy fogs muscle in on the city and the area as a whole.

**San Francisco** proper occupies just 48 hilly square miles at the tip of a slender peninsula, almost perfectly centred along the California Coast. But its metropolitan area sprawls out far beyond these narrow confines, east and north across to the far sides of the bay, and south back down the coastal strip. This is the **Bay Area**, one of the most rapidly growing regions in the US: only 750,000 people live in the city, but there are six million in the Bay Area as a whole. It's something of a mixed bag. In the **East Bay**, across one of the two great bridges that connect San Francisco with its

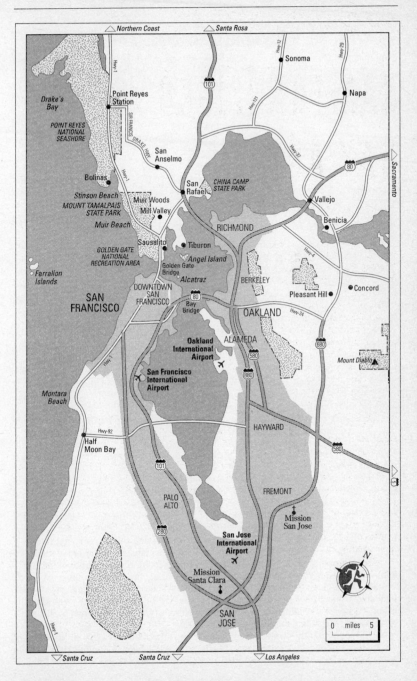

hinterland, are industrial Oakland and the radical locus of Berkeley, while to the south lies the gloating new wealth of the **Peninsula**, which its multi-billion dollar computer industries have earned the tag of "Silicon Valley", wiping out the agriculture which was predominant as recently as twenty years ago. Across the Golden Gate Bridge to the north, **Marin County** is the Bay Area's wealthiest suburb, its woody, leafy landscape and rugged coastline a bucolic – though in places *very* chic – harbinger of the delights of California's earthy northern coast. Specific practical information on the different Bay Area locales is given within the various regional accounts, which begin on p.420.

# SAN FRANCISCO

The original inhabitants of San Francisco were the **Ohlone**, who lived in some 35 villages spread out around the bay. Within a very few years of contact with the Spanish colonists, they were all but wiped out – some five thousand Ohlone, over half the estimated pre-contact population, are buried in mass graves on the grounds of **Mission Dolores**. The mission, which still stands, and a small military *presidio*, were established in 1776 by Juan Bautista de Anza as the sixth in the colonial Spanish chain of Catholic missions that ran the length of the state. Mexicans took over from the Spanish in the early 1820s, but their hold was a tenuous one and the area finally came under American rule in 1846. Two years later the discovery of gold in the Sierra foothills precipitated the rip-roaring **Gold Rush**, and the city was born. Within a year fifty thousand pioneers had travelled west, turning San Francisco from a muddy village into a thriving supply centre and transit town for the goldfields to the north and east. By the time the **transcontinental railroad** was completed in 1869 San Francisco was a lawless, rowdy boomtown of bordellos and drinking holes – a period brought to a swift conclusion in 1906 when a massive earthquake, followed by three days of fire, wiped out most of the city.

The city was quickly rebuilt, and in many ways saw its glory days in the first half of the twentieth century – writers like Dashiell Hammett and Jack London lived and worked here, as did Diego Rivera and other WPA-sponsored artists, and many of the city's landmark structures, including Coit Tower and both the Golden Gate and Bay bridges, were built in the 1920s and 1930s. By World War II San Francisco had been eclipsed by Los Angeles as the main West Coast city, and things remained relatively quiet until the emergence of the Beats in the 1950s, and later the hippy era of the 1960s – which brought international media attention to the counterculture antics of the inhabitants of the Haight-Ashbury district, especially during the 1967 "Summer of Love", whose fusion of music, protest, rebellion, and of course a lot of drugs, were soon emulated around the world. Traces of drop-out values linger some thirty years after the event – despite its comfortable wealth, this is still a city with a libertarian streak and a tradition of giving a stiff middle finger to authority.

San Francisco is the heart of one of the largest metropolitan areas in the country, but it retains a parochial air, and chooses its heroes with care. When the Pope came to visit in 1987, the city's traffic was rerouted to cope with an expected crowd of one and a half million. Only a very sorry-looking fifty thousand turned out. That same year the fiftieth anniversary of the Golden Gate Bridge, supposedly a small civil affair, brought five times that number of partying Bay Area residents onto the bridge in celebration of their cherished city – only a gay pride march could have matched the numbers. Similarly, the earthquake of October 1989 that literally rocked the city brought the best out of San Francisco: once the casualties had been taken care of and before electricity was restored, a party atmosphere took hold as people barbecued, stuck beers in ice boxes and rounded up neighbours in a show of community spirit and indifference to disaster.

The city's reputation as a politically liberal oasis was dented in the early 1990s when the then mayor, Frank Jordan, displayed a bully-boy approach to its growing homelessness problem. Nonetheless, the entire Bay Area is a firm Democrat stronghold, now back on course with a new, more progressive city mayor, Willie Brown. The significant **gay** community is influential, too, with clever politicians and businessmen well aware of the power of the pink dollar. Freedom is still the key word, and for all its failings, San Francisco remains one of the least prejudiced and most proudly distinct cities on earth.

# Arrival and information

All international and most domestic flights arrive at **San Francisco International Airport** (SFO; ☎721-0800), about fifteen miles south of the city. There are several ways of getting into town from here, each of which is clearly signed from the baggage reclaim areas. The least expensive is to take a *San Mateo County Transit* (*SamTrans*) **bus**, leaving from the airport's lower level. The #7F express takes around forty minutes to reach downtown (every 30min; $2), the slower #7B stops everywhere and takes over an hour (every 30min; $1), and a shuttle runs to the Daly City *BART* station (every 20min; $1). Bear in mind, though, that you're only allowed as much luggage as you can carry on your lap on the express route. The San Francisco **Airporter** bus ($8) picks up from outside each baggage claim area every fifteen minutes (5am–11pm) and travels to the downtown areas of Union Square and the Financial District. The blue **Supershuttle** and the **Yellow Airport Shuttle** minibuses cost a little more and are much quicker; they pick up every five minutes from outside the baggage claim area and will take you and up to five other passengers to any city-centre destination for around $15 per head. Be ruthless, though – competition for these is fierce.

**Taxis** from the airport cost $25–35 (plus tip) for any city location, more for East Bay and Marin County, and are good value if you're in a group or too tired to care. If you're planning to drive, there's the usual clutch of **car rental** agencies at the airport, all of which operate shuttle buses that circle the top departure level of the airport road and take you to their depot free of charge. Drive into town on either US-101 or the prettier I-280, a journey of about half an hour.

A number of domestic airlines (*Southwest* and *Continental* are two) fly into **Oakland International Airport** (OAK; see p.422 for details), across the bay. This airport is actually closer to downtown San Francisco than SFO, and efficiently connected with the city by the $2 *AirBART* shuttle bus from the Coliseum *BART* station. The third Bay Area airport, **San Jose Municipal** (SJO), also serves domestic arrivals, but is only worth considering if flights into the other two are booked up, or if you're going to be spending much time in the Silicon Valley.

The telephone **area code** for San Francisco is ☎415.

## Buses, trains and driving

All San Francisco's **Greyhound** services use the **Transbay Terminal** at 425 Mission St, near the Embarcadero *BART* station in the SoMa district. **Green Tortoise** buses disembark behind the Transbay Terminal on First and Natoma. **Amtrak** trains stop across the bay in **Richmond** (with easy *BART* transfers) and continue to Oakland, from where free shuttle buses run across the Bay Bridge to the Transbay Terminal.

The main route **by car** from the east is I-80, which runs via Sacramento all the way from Chicago. The main north–south route through California, I-5, passes by fifty miles east, and is linked to the Bay Area by I-580. US-101 and Hwy-1, the more scenic north–south routes, pass right through downtown San Francisco.

## Information

The main **San Francisco Visitor Information Center**, in Hallidie Plaza on the concourse of the Powell Street *BART/Muni* station (Mon–Fri 9am–5.30pm, Sat 9am–3pm, Sun 10am–2pm; ☎974-6900), makes a good benchmark for getting your bearings, as it's centrally located and at the hub of city transport systems. It has a good range of free maps, and staff will help with accommodation and travel information. Its useful free booklet, known as the "San Francisco Book", gives extensive listings on accommodation, sightseeing, exhibitions, restaurants and entertainment, as well as a useful shopping guide.

San Francisco's major **daily papers** are the *San Francisco Chronicle* in the morning, and in the afternoon the revamped *San Francisco Examiner*, which is making great efforts to capture the liberal market with in-depth reporting and syndicated (and in the case of Hunter S Thompson, controversial) columnists. On Sundays the two papers combine into a very large edition, most of which can be discarded apart from the *Datebook* section (also called the "Pink Pages"), which gives detailed listings of arts, clubs, films and events. There's an abundance of **free publications**, led by the *San Francisco Bay Guardian* and *SF Weekly*, and in the East Bay by the *East Bay Express*, all of which have lively reporting and invaluable listings.

# City transport

Getting around San Francisco is simple. In spite of the literally breathtaking hills, the city centre is small enough to make walking a feasible way to see the sights and get the feel of things. In addition, the excellent public transport system is cheap, efficient and easy to use, both in the city and the more urbanized parts of the surrounding Bay Area. We've detailed public transport options in the relevant Bay Area sections towards the end of this chapter, but to go any further afield you'd do well to rent a car. Cycling is a good option too, though you'll need stout legs to tackle those hills.

## Muni

The city's public transport is run by the **San Francisco Municipal Railway**, or *Muni* (☎673-6864), and is made up of a comprehensive network of **buses**, **trolley buses** and **cable cars**, which run up and over the city's hills, and underground **trains** which become **streetcars** when they emerge from the downtown metro system to split off and serve the suburbs. *Muni* trains run **throughout the night** on a limited service, except on the M-Ocean View line, which stops around midnight; buses, too, run all night, again at greatly reduced levels.

On buses and trains there's a flat **fare** of $1; on cable cars $2. With trains, you must purchase tickets to get through the barriers before descending to the platforms; on the buses, correct change is required on boarding. **Muni Passports**, available from the

Visitor Information Center (above), cost $6 for a one-day pass, $10 for three days and $15 for seven and are valid on all *Muni* services. If you're staying more than a week or so and need to rely heavily on public transport, get a **Fast Pass**, which costs $35 and is valid for unlimited travel on the *Muni* and *BART* systems within the city limits for a full calendar month. Note that Fast Passes are not available from *Muni* or *BART* stations; you can buy them at most supermarkets and newsagents.

For **more detailed information** pick up the handy *Muni* map ($2) from the Visitor Information Center or bookstores, though it's unlikely that you'll need to be familiar with more than a few of the major bus routes, the most important of which are listed below.

## Other public transport

A number of **other public transport networks** run into San Francisco, though these are most useful to connect with the rest of the Bay Area. Along Market Street downtown, *Muni* shares the station concourses with *BART*, the ultra-modern Bay Area Rapid Transit system, linking major points in San Francisco with the East Bay and outer suburbs. The **CalTrain** commuter railroad (its depot is at Fourth and Townsend, South of Market) connects San Francisco with points along the peninsula south to San Jose. **Golden Gate Ferry** boats leave from the Ferry Building on the Embarcadero, crossing the bay past Alcatraz to Marin County. For more details see the various Bay Area accounts later in this chapter.

---

### ■ USEFUL BUS ROUTES ■

**#38** From Geary Street via Civic Center, west to the ocean along Geary Blvd.

**#5** From the Transbay Terminal, west along the north side of Golden Gate Park to the ocean.

**#7** From the Ferry Terminal (Market Street) along Haight Street to the ocean.

**#24** From Castro Street north along Divisadero Street to Pacific Heights and Marina.

**#37** From Market Street to Twin Peaks.

**#30** From the CalTrain depot in SoMa, north to Fisherman's Wharf via North Beach and the Financial District.

**#22** From the Mission along Fillmore Street north to Pacific Heights.

**#15** From Third Street (SoMa) to Pier 39, Fisherman's Wharf, via the Financial District and North Beach.

**#20 (Golden Gate Transit)** From Civic Center to the Golden Gate Bridge.

### ■ *MUNI* TRAIN LINES ■

**Muni N-JUDAH LINE** From downtown west to Ocean Beach, via the Haight.

**Muni J-CHURCH LINE** From downtown to Mission and East Castro.

**Muni L-TARAVAL LINE** From downtown west to the zoo and Ocean Beach.

**Muni K-INGLESIDE LINE** From downtown to Balboa Park.

**Muni M-OCEAN VIEW** From downtown west to Ocean Beach.

### ■ CABLE CAR ROUTES ■

**Powell–Hyde** From Powell Street along Hyde through Russian Hill to Fisherman's Wharf.

**Powell–Mason** From Powell Street along Mason via Chinatown and North Beach to Fisherman's Wharf.

**California St** From the foot of California Street in the Financial District through Nob Hill to Polk Street.

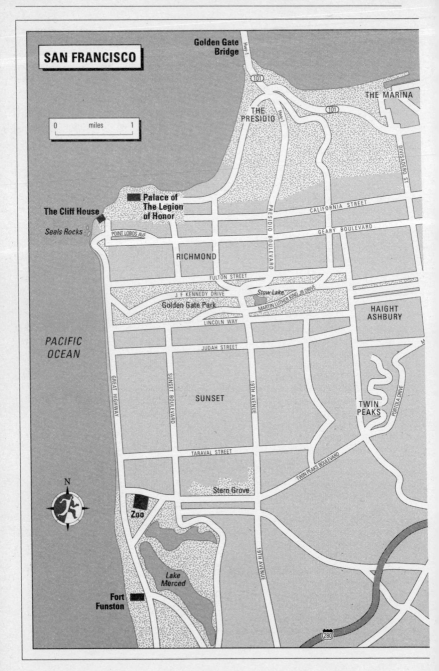

SAN FRANCISCO

Golden Gate Bridge

Hwy 1

101

THE MARINA

THE PRESIDIO

101

DIVISADERO ST

0   miles   1

Palace of The Legion of Honor

CALIFORNIA STREET

The Cliff House

GEARY BOULEVARD

Seals Rocks

POINT LOBOS AVE

PRESIDIO BOULEVARD

RICHMOND

FULTON STREET

J F KENNEDY DRIVE

Stow Lake

MARTIN LUTHER KING JR DRIVE

Golden Gate Park

HAIGHT ASHBURY

LINCOLN WAY

JUDAH STREET

PACIFIC OCEAN

GREAT HIGHWAY

SUNSET BOULEVARD

SUNSET

19TH AVENUE

TWIN PEAKS

PORTOLA DRIVE

TARAVAL STREET

TWIN PEAKS BOULEVARD

Stern Grove

N

Zoo

Lake Merced

19TH AVENUE

Fort Funston

280

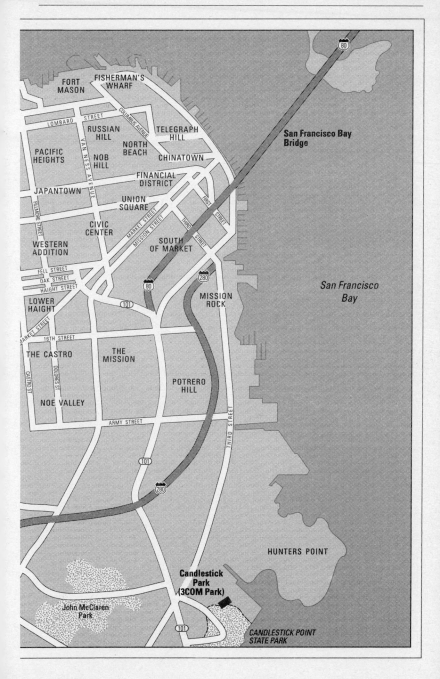

## Driving: taxis and cars

**Taxis**, as in most American cities, don't trawl the streets in San Francisco the way they do in some cities. Reputedly there are three thousand licensed taxis in the city, but if you want one and you're not in a busy part of town or near a big hotel you'll probably have to phone: try *Veterans* (☎552-1300) or *Yellowcab* (☎626-2345). Fares work out at approximately $1.90 for the first mile, $1.50 a mile thereafter.

You don't need a **car** to get around San Francisco, but if you're staying some way out from the centre, it can make life easier – especially if you want to see something of the Bay Area while you're here. Special rules for **driving** in the city are designed to contend with its often very steep gradients: you are obliged to turn your wheels to the kerb when parking on hills. It can be maddeningly difficult to find a place to leave the car, but don't lose your cool: **parking** restrictions in San Francisco are strictly enforced, and traffic officers will cheerfully ticket you – or tow your car away – in a matter of seconds. A number of **parking lots** in the South of Market industrial area charge $5 per day; more central garages charge that much per hour. Of these, the best deals are to be had in the multistorey garage at Sutter and Stockton, and the parking lots under Union Square downtown, under Portsmouth Square in Chinatown, and at Ghirardelli Square near Fisherman's Wharf.

## Cycling

In general, **cycling** is an economical and healthy method of getting around San Francisco and the Bay Area, some parts of which have cycle lanes; and local buses are often equipped to carry bikes strapped to the outside. Good-value city **rental shops** include *Park Cyclery,* 1749 Waller St (☎221-3777), which offers mountain bikes for $5 per hour or $120 a week. Golden Gate Park has some wonderful routes, as does Angel Island (see p.456).

---

### WALKING TOURS

There are some excellent personalized **walking tours** available in San Francisco. The better ones usually permit no more than five people to a group and can often make an informative and efficient way to get to know a particular area of town. The Visitor Information Center can give you a full list, but among those you might like to try are:

**All About Chinatown**, 812 Clay St (☎982-8839). Three-hour, $35 tour conducted by Chinatown native Linda Lee, including all the sights, history and anecdotes you can absorb and a *dim sum* lunch.

**City Guides** (☎557-4266). The most extensive range of guided walks, sponsored by the San Francisco Public Library and all free.

**Cruisin' the Castro**, 375 Lexington St (☎550-8110). The Supreme Champion of the walking tour circuit in San Francisco, Trevor Hailey, a resident of San Francisco's premier gay district for twenty years, takes you on a fascinating tour of this small area. Her knowledge includes everything from politics to the best parties and she embellishes her three-and-a-half-hour tour with funny stories. A tour costs $25 per person includes breakfast – worth every cent.

**Flower Power Haight-Ashbury Walking Tour** (☎221-8442). As well as reliving the Summer of Love and learning about important hippies, this two-hour tour will show you the Haight's past as a Victorian resort destination.

**Friends of Recreation and Parks**, MacLaren Lodge, Stanyan and Fell (☎221-1311). Tour Golden Gate Park with trained guides pointing out the park's flora, fauna and history. Free tours every weekend (call for times).

**Helen's Walk Tour** (☎510/524-4544). Helen Rendon, a four-foot-ten-inch dynamo, leads you around an area of your choice with her personal brand of commentary and historical perspective. $20 per person includes a stop for coffee and pastries.

## Organized tours

If you've just arrived, you may want to orientate yourself by taking an **organized tour**. *Gray Line Tours* (☎558-9400) will whip you around the city in three fairly tedious hours, stopping at Twin Peaks and Cliff House, for around $26 a head. Skip it unless you're really pushed for time and want to get a general idea of the city's layout with minimal effort.

Excruciatingly expensive but spectacular **aerial tours** of the city and Bay Area in light aircraft are available from several operators: *San Francisco Helicopter Tours* (☎1-800/400-2404) and *Scenic Air Tours* (☎1-800/957-2364) will fly you over the predictable sights for around $100. Meanwhile, *Mile High Airlines* (☎510/713-2359) specializes in fantasy flights for couples keen to enjoy each other as well as the sights. The bashful might prefer one of the more leisurely two-hour **bay cruises** operated by the *Blue & Gold Fleet* (☎781-7877) from piers 39 and 40 – though at $17 a throw these don't come cheap either, and in any case everything may be shrouded in fog.

# Accommodation

With over 30,000 hotel rooms, San Francisco isn't short on **accommodation**. Visitors are the city's number one business, and even during the peak summer months failure to phone ahead needn't find you stuck for a place to sleep. Since room rates average around $100 per night, accommodation may prove to be the major expense of your stay, but fortunately there are enough options in all price ranges – from youth hostels to five-star luxury hotels – to be able to find something to suit both your taste and your bank balance.

**Hotels** in the slightly seedy SoMa and Tenderloin areas start at around $30 per night, $120 per week – though they tend to be of the welfare variety and you shouldn't expect a private bath or even a toilet for that amount – while in the glitzier areas around Union Square or atop Nob Hill it's hard to find anything at all for under $120 a night. Try Hwy-101 coming in from the bridge for pleasant, if rather bland, **motels**. Wherever you stay, during the off season rates can drop considerably, and special deals are often available for guests who stay for longer periods. Always ask about reductions, as hoteliers generally won't volunteer the information if they think they can sell you a room at full price.

The city's **bed and breakfast** inns can be pricey, usually not less than $80 a night, but are usually cosier than a hotel and offer sumptuous breakfasts to boot. A dorm bed in a **hostel** is as cheap as you can get in San Francisco; **camping** is not really an option, as there are no sites within an hour's drive of the city.

If you do have trouble finding a place to stay, try contacting the ultra-efficient and friendly *San Francisco Reservations* (☎1-800/677-1550), which will find you a place without fail, though you should expect to spend upwards of $80 per night. It also has its own website – http:www.hotelres.com – which allows you to browse through pictures of hotels and check their locations on a map before you make reservations.

Hotels and B&Bs are listed below by neighbourhood, with hostels listed separately. In case you're arriving on a late flight, or leaving on an early one, we've also listed a few places to stay near the airport. Specifically **gay and women-only** accommodation options listed in special sections on pp.411 and 414.

## Downtown

**Beresford Arms Hotel**, 701 Post St at Jones (☎673-2600). Luxury B&B in the heart of town, well worth the few extra dollars. ⑤.
**Campton Place Hotel**, 340 Stockton St at Sutter (☎781-5555). Smallish Union Square hotel that draws in a quietly moneyed crowd. Luxurious but not showy, with a first class restaurant. ⑨.

**Cartwright Hotel**, 524 Sutter St at Mason (☎421-2865 or 1-800/227-3844). Distinguishes itself from its rivals with little touches such as fresh flowers, afternoon tea and bend-over-backwards courtesy. Good location one block north of Union Square. ⑥.

**Commodore International Hotel**, 825 Sutter St at Jones (☎923-6800). Classic San Francisco Deco structure a couple of blocks from Union Square with spacious, affordable rooms and a great atmosphere. ④–⑤.

**Dakota Hotel**, 606 Post St at Taylor (☎931-7475). Recently converted 1920s hotel near Union Square. Low rates, thanks to the lack of luxury trimmings or fancy service, but all rooms have antique baths. ④.

**Fairmont Hotel**, 950 Mason St at Sacramento (☎772-5000). Most famous of San Francisco's top-notch hotels, the *Fairmont* is an excessively decorated palace with seven restaurants, ten lounges all in need of a facelift, and fantastic views from the rooms. ⑦.

**Gates Hotel** 140 Ellis St at Powell (☎781-0430). Super-cheap downtown location, with rooms of a predictable standard. ①–②.

**Grant Plaza Hotel**, 465 Grant Ave at Pine (☎434-3883). Newly renovated hotel with clean rooms in the middle of Chinatown. ③.

**Harbor Court Hotel**, 165 Steuart St at Howard (☎882-1300 or 1-800/346-0555). Plush rooms, offering the best bay views of any hotel in the city, and guests have free use of the excellent YMCA health club next door. Next door to the fashionable *Harry Denton's* in the up-and-coming Embarcadero district. ⑦.

**Hotel Bedford**, 761 Post St at Leavenworth (☎673-6040). Excellent-value hotel with a high degree of personalized service. When you want to be looked after but don't have a top dollar budget, alight here. ⑥.

**Hotel David**, 480 Geary St (☎771-1600 or 1-800/524-1888). By no means the least expensive place in town, but a great Theater District location above San Francisco's largest and best Jewish deli. You get an all-you-can-eat breakfast, and free transport to the airport if you stay two nights or more. ④.

**Hotel Monaco**, 501 Geary St at Taylor (☎292-0100 or 1-800/214-4220). Best of the new wave of San Francisco hotels, offering great style and decor at affordable prices. Next door to the sumptuous but reasonable *Grand Café* . Highly recommended. ⑦.

**Hotel Triton**, 342 Grant Ave at Bush (☎394-0500 or 1-800/433-6611). Very stylish, very comfortable and very central hotel, catering to design professionals and weekend shoppers. Across the street from the Chinatown Gateway, two blocks from Union Square. ⑥.

**Huntington Hotel**, 1075 California St at Taylor (☎474-5400). Understated and quietly elegant compared to its Nob Hill compatriots, this is the hotel for the wealthy who don't need to flash it about. The only large hotel in town that is still family-run, its bars are neither rooftop, nor revolving, but instead opt for simple dark-wood furnishing, a piano player and a very intimate atmosphere. There are fax machines in all the rooms and a limousine service. ⑧.

**Hyde Plaza Hotel**, 835 Hyde St at Bush (☎885-2987). On the Tenderloin/Nob Hill border, this hotel offers unbelievably cheap accommodation. Small, clean and comfortable rooms with shared bath. ②.

**Mandarin Oriental San Francisco**, 222 Sansome St at California (☎885-0999). You'll need silly amounts of money if you want to stay in what are reputedly San Francisco's most luxurious hotel rooms but the views from said rooms, which start on the 47th floor of this impressive building, across the Financial District are pretty cool. Amenities include valet, concierge and 24-hr room service. ⑧–⑨.

**Petite Auberge**, 863 Bush St at Taylor (☎928-6000). One of two opulent B&Bs, next to one another on Bush Street. This one offers complimentary afternoon tea, wine and hors d'oeuvres as well as full breakfast. ⑥–⑦.

**Prescott Hotel**, 545 Post St at Mason (☎563-0303 or 1-800/283-7322). The flagship of hotelier Bill Kimpton's San Francisco properties, this small Union Square hotel offers understated luxury, four-star comfort – and preferred seating at the city's most popular restaurant, *Postrio*, with which it shares space. ⑧–⑨.

**Sir Francis Drake**, 450 Powell St at Post (☎227-5480). Don't be put off by the Beefeaters outside, this is a colonial California hotel whose greatest attraction is *Harry Denton's Starlight Roof* (see "Drinking: bars and cafés") on the 21st floor. ⑦.

**Ritz-Carlton**, 600 Stockton St at California (☎296-7465 or 1-800/241-3333). The most luxurious hotel in San Francisco perched on the stylish slope of Nob Hill with gorgeously appointed rooms, a swimming pool, multi-million dollar art collection and one of the city's best hotel restaurants, the *Dining Room*. ⑧–⑨.

**Westin St Francis**, 335 Powell St at Post (☎397-7000 or 1-800/228-3000). Truly grand hotel with a sumptuous lobby, five restaurants, an elegant bar and disappointingly plain rooms. Its reputation far outstrips the reality of a stay here, but as long as you don't mind the throngs of tourists who pour in to gape at the lobby, you'll be happy. ⑧.

**White Swan Inn**, 845 Bush St at Taylor (☎775-1775). The other Bush Street B&B, this one with a convincing English manor-house theme: raging fireplaces, oak-panelled rooms and afternoon tea. ⑨.

**York Hotel**, 940 Sutter St at Hyde (☎885-6800 or 1-800/808-YORK). Quiet, older hotel on the western edge of downtown. An essential stop for Hitchcock fans, this is where the dramatic stairway scenes in *Vertigo* were filmed. ⑥.

## North Beach and the Northern Waterfront

**Art Center Bed and Breakfast**, 1902 Filbert St at Laguna (☎567-1526). Quirky little inn that's a real home away from home. ⑤–⑥.

**Bed and Breakfast Inn**, 4 Charlton Court off Union Street (☎921-9784). One of the first B&Bs to be established in the city, this lovely, sun-drenched Victorian house, tucked away down a quiet side street, offers some of San Francisco's most pleasant accommodation. ④–⑧ depending on choice of room.

**Bel Aire Travelodge**, 3201 Steiner St at Lombard (☎921-5162). Good-value motel, one block from Lombard Street. ④–⑤.

**Edward II**, 3155 Scott St at Francisco (☎922-3000). Large and comfortable inn-style accommodation with free breakfast and afternoon sherry. ④–⑤.

**Holiday Lodge**, 1901 Van Ness Ave at Washington (☎1-800/367-8504). Good family hotel with pool and free parking close to Pacific Heights and Fisherman's Wharf. Landscaped grounds and bungalows give it a resort feel. Comfortable and secure. ⑤.

**Marina Inn**, 3110 Octavia St at Chestnut (☎928-1000). Comfortable, homely set-up, right off Lombard Street. ⑤.

**San Remo Hotel**, 2237 Mason St at Francisco (☎776-8688 or 1-800/352-7366). Pleasant, old-fashioned rooms (ie you'll have to share a bathroom) in nicely preserved North Beach house. Friendly staff and the best bargain in the area. ②–③.

**Tuscan Inn**, 425 North Point at Taylor (☎561-1100 or 1-800/648-4626). The most upmarket hotel on the waterfront, with afternoon wine tastings and free limo downtown. ⑥–⑦.

**Washington Square Inn**, 1660 Stockton St at Filbert (☎981-4220). Cosy B&B bang on North Beach's lovely main square. Non-smokers only. ⑥.

## Civic Center, South of Market and the Mission

**Abigail Hotel** 246 McAllister at Larkin (☎861-9728). Comfortable, stylish and affordable, this Civic Center hotel caters mainly to revellers performing at the nearby arts centres and sports an excellent vegan restaurant (believe it or not), *Millennium*, in its basement. Weekly and monthly rates available. Perfect for the hip but skint. ④.

**Albion House Inn**, 135 Gough St at Oak (☎621-0896). Small and comfortable B&B above a fine restaurant. ⑤.

**Amsterdam Hotel**, 749 Taylor St at Bush (☎1-800/637-3444). On Nob Hill, but actually closer to the Tenderloin, with good-value clean and pleasant rooms. ③–④.

**Atherton**, 685 Ellis St (☎474-5720). Cosy, clean, good-value hotel in the Civic Center. ④.

**Bay Bridge Inn**, 966 Harrison St at Sixth (☎397-0657). Basic and somewhat noisy but perfectly sited for late nights in SoMa's clubland. ④.

**Golden City Inn**, 1554 Howard St at 12th (☎255-1110). Best of the inexpensive SoMa hotels, smack in the middle of the district's nightlife scene. Unbelievably good value. ①–②.

**Inn at the Opera**, 333 Fulton St at Van Ness (☎863-8400). Deluxe B&B with 24-hr room service and morning limo downtown on weekdays. Stay here if you want to bump into visiting divas. ⑥–⑦.

**Pensione San Francisco**, 1668 Market St at Franklin (☎864-1271). A good base near the Civic Center, within walking distance of SoMa and the Castro. Doesn't offer breakfast but discounts lunch and dinner at the Japanese restaurant in the building. ③.

**Phoenix Hotel**, 601 Eddy St at Polk (☎776-1380.) Marginal neighbourhood on the edge of the Tenderloin but the hip music-biz crowd who lounge around the pool drinking cocktails don't seem to mind. ⑤.

**Sherman House**, 2160 Green St at Fillmore (☎563-3600). Rated the best in San Francisco by *Zagat* readers' guide, this small Cow Hollow hotel is one of the city's lesser-known jewels. ⑨.

**UN Plaza Hotel**, 45 McAllister St at Market (☎626-5200). Convenient location, three blocks from the Civic Center and Union Square. Classic Victorian lobby and large, comfy rooms. Great deals to be had in winter, always ask about special offers. ③–⑥.

## The Central Neighbourhoods

**Alamo Square Inn**, 719 Scott St at Grove (☎922-2055). A beautifully restored Victorian building. The rates aren't low, but guests get the use of a handsome dwelling, some rooms complete with fireplace and one with Jacuzzi. ⑤–⑥.

**Archbishops Mansion**, 1000 Fulton St at Steiner (☎563-7872). Deluxe, grandly-camp mansion that has been everything from its namesake to a school for wayward Catholic boys, and now a really quirky bed and breakfast. Attentive personal service and a variety of packages offering everything from getting fit to getting decked out by a professional image consultant. Home to Noel Coward's piano, this place is a riot. ⑦.

**Best Western Miyako**, 1800 Sutter St at Buchanan (☎921-4000 or 1-800/528-1234). Immaculate Japan Center hotel, with quiet rooms, some with steambaths. ⑤–⑥.

**Grove Inn**, 890 Grove St at Fillmore (☎929-0780). Nothing fancy, but good value and a fine location on Alamo Square. ④.

**Jackson Court**, 2198 Jackson Street (☎992-7670). Pacific Heights converted mansion, offering luxury B&B service. Very nice indeed. ⑦.

**The Mansion**, 2220 Sacramento St at Laguna (☎929-9444). Luxury-swaddled Victorian mansion, perched high up in the fancy reaches of Pacific Heights. ⑦–⑨.

**Red Victorian Bed and Breakfast (aka the Peace Center)**, 1665 Haight St at Cole (☎864-1978). Bang in the middle of the Haight-Ashbury, a time-warped B&B with hippy art gallery and rooms with New Agey themes, courtesy of owner Sami Sunchild. ④–⑥.

## Golden Gate Park, the Beaches and Outlying Areas

**Beach Motel**, 4211 Judah St (☎681-6618). Very average motel in a good spot by the edge of the park and Ocean beach. ③.

**Ocean Park Motel**, 2690 46th Ave (☎566-7020). A fair way from downtown (25 min by *Muni*), this is nonetheless a great Art Deco motel (San Francisco's first) opposite the zoo and the beach. Outdoor hot tub and Jacuzzi and play area for children. ③.

**Stanyan Park Hotel**, 750 Stanyan St at Waller (☎751-1000). Gorgeous, small Victorian hotel in a great setting across from Golden Gate Park, with friendly staff and free continental breakfast. ⑤.

---

### ■ AIRPORT HOTELS

**Best Western Grosvenor Hotel**, 380 South Airport Blvd (☎873-3200). Large comfortable hotel with pool and free shuttle service to the airport. ⑤.

**Goose Turets Bed and Breakfast**, 835 George Street, Montara (☎728-5451). Twenty minutes south of the airport, this is a more restful and intimate B&B alternative to the other airport accommodations. Close to the beaches and hiking trails, this is a perfect place to unwind either before or after a long trip. Sadly, no smoking. ⑤.

**Hilton at San Francisco Airport**, San Francisco Airport (☎589-0770). Actually on top of the airport, this is both easy to find and a guarantee that you won't miss your flight. Basic, business-class accommodation. ⑦.

**Motel 6**, 1101 Shoreway Road, Belmont (☎591-1471). When the money runs out, come to this no frills motel. Good preparation for a long and uncomfortable journey. ②.

**Radisson Hotel San Francisco Airport**, 1177 Airport Blvd (☎342-9200). Great facilities include restaurant, pool, jacuzzi, live music and a free shuttle to the airport. ⑤.

**Super 8 Lodge**, 111 Mitchell Ave (☎877-0770). Plain, motel-style accommodations with free airport shuttle between 6–11am. ③.

**Sunset Motel**, 821 Taraval St (☎681-3306). One of the finest little motels in San Francisco – clean, friendly and safe. ④.

## Hostels

**A Green Tortoise Guest House**, 494 Broadway at Kearny (☎834-1000). Funky Chinatown hostel with complimentary breakfast. From $19 per night single, $29 double, dorm $10. ①.

**HI-San Francisco at Union Square**, 312 Mason St at O'Farrell (☎788-5604). Large new downtown hostel with dorm beds for $13 a night. No curfew. HI members only; day memberships cost $3.

**HI-San Francisco International**, Building 240, Fort Mason (☎771-7277). On the waterfront between the Golden Gate Bridge and Fisherman's Wharf. One of the most comfortable and convenient hostels around. 150 beds, free parking. $13 per person and no day membership necessary because it's built on federal land. No curfew either. ①.

**Interclub/Globe Hostel**, 10 Hallam Place, between Seventh and Eighth off Folsom (☎431-0540). Lively, recently redecorated SoMa hostel with no curfew. $15 per person, per night; doubles $25.

**San Francisco International Guest House**, 2976 23rd St at Douglass (☎641-1411). Very popular with European travellers. Four-to-a-room dorms in the Mission plus a few private rooms. $14 per person, five-day minimum stay, after which price goes down to $11. No curfew. ①.

**YMCA Central Branch**, 220 Golden Gate Ave (☎885-0460). Well equipped and centrally located, two blocks from the Civic Center. Singles $28, doubles $38, price includes a free continental breakfast and use of the gym, swimming pool, squash courts and sauna. ①–②.

# The City

The first and most obvious thing that strikes the visitor is that San Francisco is a city of hills. Becoming familiar with these forty-odd hills is not just a good way to get your bearings; it will also give you a real insight into the city's class distinctions. As a general rule, geographical elevation is a stout indicator of wealth – the higher you live, the better off you are. Commercial square-footage is surprisingly small and mostly confined to the downtown area, and the rest of the city is made up of distinct, primarily residential neighbourhoods, most of which are very easily explored on foot. Armed with a good map you could plough through three a day, but frankly, the best way to get to know San Francisco is to dawdle, unbound by itineraries: the most interesting districts, certainly, merit at least half a day each of just hanging about.

The top right-hand corner of the peninsula, bordered by I-80 to the south, US-101 to the west, and the water, makes up the part of the city known as **downtown**, though really the neighbourhoods themselves make the best orientation points. The core of downtown, mainly north of the city's main artery, **Market Street** – the wide thoroughfare, lined with stores and office buildings, that bisects the city centre and is a main reference point for your wanderings – is signalled by the bay-front buildings of the **Embarcadero** and the corporate high-rises of the **Financial District**. Just beyond are the department stores and hotels that make up the city's busiest shopping district around **Union Square**, while above the lot, swanky **Nob Hill**, with its mansions and grand hotels, sits snootily on its quiet hilltop perch. A few blocks away, Nob Hill's borders merge with the neon intensity of **Chinatown**, easily the densest part of town and a good bet for great food.

At the northernmost tip of the city, **Fisherman's Wharf** and the waterfront has been carefully crafted with the visitor in mind – and pulls them in by the tour-bus-load. At night the area improves, but it's generally best to glimpse it in passing and make a beeline for the livelier old Italian enclave of **North Beach**, which, though chi chi in places, still harbours a vaguely literary bohemian population that's a hangover from the days of the Beats in the Fifties. Above here, the very desirable neighbourhoods of **Russian Hill** and **Telegraph Hill** flank North Beach on either side, affording fabulous views of the shimmering bay; just west, the truly rich enjoy similar vistas from the sumptuous homes of **Pacific Heights.**

Not a million miles from this rampant affluence, the slums of the **Tenderloin** form an often alarming quarter that begins a few blocks west of Union Square and runs south for a six-block stretch of dilapidated urban sleaze all the way to Market Street, home to a good many of the city's dispossessed. Crossing over Market Street, **South of Market** (or **SoMa**) used to be one of the city centre's few industrial enclaves, until the arty, nightclubbing crowd discovered it. However, the area is now caught up in the wave of unstoppable gentrification, and is beginning to host some smart buildings – foremost among them the new San Francisco Museum of Art – so it's only a matter of time before more bulldozers move in and the artists move out. **Civic Center**, a little way west, is San Francisco's municipal – and arts – nucleus and site of some of the city's more grandiose architecture, rather awkward among the stagnating slums that surround it.

Walk much further south or west from Civic Center and you're out of downtown and in the more staunchly residential neighbourhoods that enclose the city centre. A lengthy stroll or short bus ride southwest, the garrulous Hispanic district of **The Mission**, San Francisco's largest neighbourhood, is a good first choice for a trip further afield, filled with cheap restaurants, bars and clubs, and with a street life that's about as nonstop as San Francisco gets. **The Castro**, just beyond, has long been the city's primary gay district and makes no bones about it: refurbished for and by the gay community, and although to some extent tempered by the post-AIDS years, there's still an emphasis on cute shops and vigorous nightlife. West of downtown, the **Haight-Ashbury** district was once San Francisco's radical focus and tries hard to hold on to its countercultural traditions, with a caucus of left-wing bookstores, some tastefully tatty café-society and a smattering of residents still flying a slightly limp freak flag. At the end of Haight Street, **Golden Gate Park** is the antidote to all this: San Francisco's main city park and a sublime piece of landscape design, stretching west to the Pacific Shore and city beaches.

## Downtown: The Financial District

With its plate-glass-and-steel skyscrapers soaring dramatically into the sky to form San Francisco's only real high-rise district, casting long shadows where twenty years ago there were none, the **FINANCIAL DISTRICT** is the city's most dynamic neighbour-hood – a Manhattan in miniature that's a symbol of San Francisco's enduring wealth and prosperity. Sharp-suited workers clog the streets in well-mannered rush-hour droves, racing between their offices and the Montgomery *BART/Muni* station on Market Street. Originally, the centre of the city's financial dealings was entirely to the north of Market Street, where the old low-rise banking halls are now flanked by newer, larger structures of corporate power. But to avert the complete demolition of the area for more profitable towers, the city is nowadays directing new development to South of Market (see p.382).

The area comprises a veritable hotchpotch of architectural styles and periods, from Palladian piles to postmodern redoubts. Scattered between the banks and bars are the copy centres and computer boutiques that serve the offices above, with an occasional restaurant of note; the people are as dressed up as they come in this casual town, though they're still largely a testament to comfort before style. San Francisco's movers and shakers distinguish themselves from the rest of the American financial community on the last business day of the year, when local custom dictates that office workers throw their desk calendar pages out of the window. Standing on the street and looking skywards, the scene is reminiscent of a ticker-tape parade – not to be missed if you're in town for Christmas and New Year. Otherwise, there's not a lot to come for here, although on Friday evenings the bars buzz with relieved workers. Weekends are deserted, save for the odd tourist.

Still, there are gems to be discovered in the Financial District, best reached by a dramatic plunge downhill on the California Street cable car. Once cut off from the rest of San Francisco by the double-decker Embarcadero Freeway – which was damaged in the 1989 Earthquake, and finally torn down in 1992 – the **Ferry Building**, at the foot of Market Street, was modelled on the cathedral tower in Seville, Spain, and before the bridges were built in the 1930s, was the main point of arrival for fifty thousand cross-bay commuters daily. A few ferry boats still arrive here, but the characterless office units inside do little to suggest its former importance. Opposite, facing downtown, is

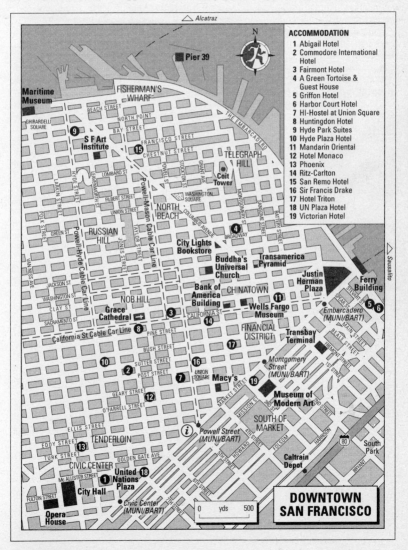

ACCOMMODATION

1 Abigail Hotel
2 Commodore International Hotel
3 Fairmont Hotel
4 A Green Tortoise & Guest House
5 Griffon Hotel
6 Harbor Court Hotel
7 HI-Hostel at Union Square
8 Huntingdon Hotel
9 Hyde Park Suites
10 Hyde Plaza Hotel
11 Mandarin Oriental
12 Hotel Monaco
13 Phoenix
14 Ritz-Carlton
15 San Remo Hotel
16 Sir Francis Drake
17 Hotel Triton
18 UN Plaza Hotel
19 Victorian Hotel

**DOWNTOWN SAN FRANCISCO**

the **Embarcadero** or **City Front District**, which has experienced quite a renaissance since the freeway was pulled down. Although dominated by the vast **Embarcadero Center** – a modern and rather unimaginative complex of offices, stores and cafés which stretches for several blocks west from **Justin Herman Plaza** – this little pocket of the city is nonetheless developing charm. Some very stylish hotels and the city's smartest new restaurants now sit along its bayview streets, and smart new residential blocks are springing up in unexpected corners. Tucked discreetly into a nondescript building at 121 Steuart St is the little-known **Jewish Museum** (Mon–Fri 10am–5pm; donation), which, far from being the sombre trudge through history its name suggests, has an impressive collection of contemporary work by Jewish artists.

From the Embarcadero, it's a few blocks down Market to **Montgomery Street** and the Financial District proper, where the grand pillared entrances and banking halls of the post-1906-earthquake construction era jostle for attention with the mixed bag of modern towers that is gradually moving in. For a real hands-on grasp of the dynamics of modern finance, the **World of Economics Gallery** in the **Federal Reserve Bank Building**, 101 Market St (Mon–Fri 10am–4pm), is unbeatable: computer games allow you to engineer your own stock-market disasters, while gallery exhibits detail recent scandals and triumphs in the financial world. The **Wells Fargo History Room**, 420 Montgomery St (Mon–Fri 10am–5pm), details the origins of San Francisco's banking and financial boom with exhibits from the days of the Gold Rush. Mining equipment, gold nuggets, photographs and even an old wagon show the far-from-slick roots of San Francisco's big money. You'll find similar illustrations of the era in the **Museum of American Money from the West** in the **Bank of California**, a Corinthian-columned temple at 400 California St (Mon–Fri 9am–5pm).

The city's second tallest tower, the **Bank of America** building on Kearny and California, is a plate-glass and marble beast that the bank had to sell off after some overzealous lending to developing countries. The great lump of black marble in the entryway is known by locals as the "banker's heart", and the prices in the *Carnelian Room* roof-top restaurant are equally uncharitable. Skip the food and simply take the elevator up for cocktails and an unforgettable view.

## Jackson Square and the Barbary Coast

A century or so ago, the northern flank of what is now the Financial District was part of the so-called **Barbary Coast**, a rough-and-tumble waterfront district packed with saloons and brothels where hapless young male visitors were given "Mickey Finns" and "Shanghaied" into involuntary servitude on merchant ships. Its wicked reputation made it off limits for military personnel up until World War II, and many of the old dives died an inevitable death. During the 1930s, the Barbary Coast became a low-rent district that attracted writers and artists including Diego Rivera, who had a studio on Gold Street at the height of his fame as the "communist painter sought after by the world's biggest capitalists". Most of these old structures have since been done up and preserved as the **Jackson Square Historic District** – not in fact a square, but a rectangle formed by Jackson, Montgomery, Gold and Sansome streets, making up a dense few blocks of low-rise, mostly brick buildings that now house the offices of advertising agencies and design firms, as well as the requisite cafés and watering holes.

The **Transamerica Pyramid**, at the foot of diagonal Columbus Avenue, is San Francisco's most unmistakable (some would say unfortunate) landmark and the city's tallest building, marking the edge of the Financial District and the beginning of North Beach. There was something of a rumpus when this went up, and it earned the name "Pereira's Prick" after its LA-based architect William Pereira, but since then it's become institutionalized as almost a symbol of San Francisco and figures on a great deal of the city's tourist and promotional literature. The original building on this site was the Montgomery Block, the city's first office building of any significance, but known more for the important names that moved in when the businesses moved off to alternative premises. Rudyard Kipling, Bret Harte, Robert Louis Stevenson, Mark Twain and William Randolph Hearst all rented office space in the building and regularly hung around the notorious "Bank Exchange" bar within. Legend also has it that Sun Yat-Sen – whose statue is in Chinatown, three blocks away (see p.374) – wrote the Chinese constitution and devised the successful overthrow of the Manchu Dynasty from his second-floor office here.

## Union Square

West of Kearny Street, around **Union Square**, the skyscrapers thin out and are replaced by the bright lights and window displays of San Francisco's **shopping district**: a collection of boutiques, specialty stores and department stores which stretches for several blocks in all directions. Limousines are bumper-to-bumper here, as the well-heeled pop in and out of their favourite emporia; by contrast, bums and winos sprawl across the green lawns of Union Square, having drifted in from the Tenderloin to do a brisker trade from passing shoppers. The square takes it name from the mass meetings held here on the eve of the Civil War by Northerners demonstrating their loyalty to the Union, but these days it's remembered more for the attempted assassination of President Gerald Ford outside the *St Francis Hotel* in 1975. It was also the location of Francis Ford Coppola's most paranoid film, *The Conversation*, where eavesdropper Gene Hackman spied on strolling lovers. The hotel played a similar role in many of **Dashiell Hammett**'s detective stories, as well as in his own life – in the 1920s he worked there as an operative for the Pinkerton detective agency, investigating the notorious rape and murder case against the silent movie star Fatty Arbuckle.

On Geary Street, west of the square, the optimistically named **Theater District** is a pint-sized Broadway of restaurants, tourist hotels, serious and "adult" theatres – as in New York's Broadway or London's Soho, the Theater District of San Francisco shares space with less rarefied institutions. Also part of this district, just north of the Square along Post and Sutter are downtown's least visible landmarks: some fourteen private clubs hidden behind discreet facades. Money isn't the only criteria for membership to these highly esteemed institutions, though being *somebody* usually is. Most notorious is the **Bohemian Club** at Post and Taylor. Better known for its *Bohemian Grove* retreat at the Russian River, where ex-Presidents and corporate giants get together for masonic rituals and schoolboy larks, the San Francisco chapter is housed in a Lewis Hobart Moderne-style building. Organized in the late 1880s by newspaper men and artists, it evolved into a businessmen's club with an arty slant, including Frank Norris, Ambrose Bierce and Jack London among its members.

On the eastern side of the square you'll find still more stores and **Maiden Lane**, a chic little urban walkway that before the 1906 earthquake and fire was one of the city's roughest areas, where prostitutes solicited openly and homicides averaged around ten a month. Nowadays, aside from some prohibitively expensive boutiques, its main feature is San Francisco's only **Frank Lloyd Wright** building, the pricey little **Circle Gallery** that was a tryout for the Guggenheim in New York. Inside, a gently curving ramp rises toward the skylit ceiling, taking you past some of the city's most expensive artwork.

If you're heading back up to the waterfront, **cable cars** run along Powell Street but are usually too packed to board at their Market Street origin. Move a few blocks up the hill where there are fewer people trying to get on, and climb to palatial Nob Hill before descending once more to the water's edge.

## Nob Hill

*Nob Hill, the hill of palaces, must certainly be counted the best part of San Francisco. It is there that the millionaires gather together, vying with each other in display. From thence, looking down upon the business wards of the city, we can decry a building with a little belfry, and that is the stock exchange, the heart of San Francisco; a great pump we might call it, continually pumping up the savings of the lower quarter to the pockets of the millionaires on the hill.*

Robert Louis Stevenson

If the Financial District is representative of new money in the city, the posh hotels and masonic institutions of **NOB HILL**, just above it, exemplify San Francisco's old wealth; it is, as Joan Didion wrote, "the symbolic nexus of all old California money and power". Perhaps San Francisco's most revered address, it's worth the stiff climb (though the wise will take the cable car) to view the mansions, hotels and elitist restaurants that serve those who come closest to being San Francisco gentry. There are very few sights as such, but nosing around is pleasant enough, taking in the aura of luxury that distinguishes the neighbourhood, and enjoying the views over the city and beyond.

Originally called the California Street Hill, the area became known as Nob Hill after robber-baron industrialists such as Leland Stanford and Charles Crocker came to the area to construct the Central Pacific Railroad, and built their mansions here. Only one of these ostentatious piles survived the 1906 fire – the brownstone mansion of James C Flood, which cost a cool $1 million in 1886 and is now the *Pacific Union Club*, a private retreat for the ultra-rich. Other, later residences have given way to hotels, the most elaborate of which is the **Fairmont Hotel** on California and Mason, until recently San Francisco's classiest joint and setting for the television soap opera *Hotel*. One block west on California stands one of the biggest hunks of sham-Gothic architecture in the US, **Grace Cathedral**. Construction began soon after the 1906 earthquake, though most of it was built, of faintly disguised reinforced concrete, in the early 1960s. One part that's worth a look is the entrance, adorned with faithful replicas of the fifteenth-century Ghiberti doors of the Florence Baptistry.

But the invention that made high-society life on the hills possible and practical – the **cable car** (the sort that runs along the ground, not swings precipitously from mountainsides) – is Nob Hill's dominant feature. Since 1873 when Scotsman Andrew Hallidie piloted the first of these little trolleys up the Clay Street hill to Portsmouth Square, they have been an integral part of San Francisco life. At their peak, just before the earthquake, over six hundred cable cars travelled 110 miles of track throughout the city, though by 1955 their usage had dwindled to such an extent that nostalgic citizens voted to preserve the remaining seventeen miles of track as a moving historic landmark. Today two of the three lines run from Powell Street to Fisherman's Wharf, while the steepest and best climbs Nob Hill along California Street from the Embarcadero. To make the ascent, they have to fasten onto a moving two-inch cable that runs beneath the streets, gripping on the slope then releasing at the top and gliding down the other side. These cables are powered by huge motors, which you can see in the **Cable Car Barn**, at Washington and Mason, recently renovated as a working museum (daily 10am–5pm; free) with exhibits of cars and trolleys. During some summers, trolley cars from all over the world (including an English one from Blackpool) are hauled out of storage and run along otherwise disused routes around the city.

## Chinatown

Completely distinct from any other neighbourhood in the city, **CHINATOWN** comprises 24 square blocks of seeming chaos smack in the middle of town, its main thoroughfare running from the ornamental Chinese gate on Bush along Grant to

## CHINESE NEW YEAR

If you're visiting at the end of January or early February, make an effort to catch the celebration of **Chinese New Year**, when the streets almost self-combust with energy and noise. Floats and papier-mâché monsters shimmy past as people hang off balconies, out of windows and shin up lampposts until there isn't an inch of space left.

Broadway. Dense, noisy, smelly, colourful and overcrowded, the second largest Chinese community outside Asia manages to be almost entirely autonomous, with its own schools, banks and newspapers. In among the brightly lit streets of restaurants, groceries and souvenir stores, however, the occasional dark and gloomy alleyway reminds you that commercial enterprise has not brought prosperity to all of the city's Chinese population.

The first Chinese arrived in Northern California in the late 1840s, many of them fleeing famine and the opium wars at home and seeking the easy fortunes of the Gold Rush. Later, in the 1860s, thousands more were shipped across to build the Transcontinental Railroad. At first the Chinese, or "coolies" as they were called (taken from the words *ku li*, meaning "bitter toil"), were accepted as hard-working labourers, but as the railroad neared completion and unemployment rose, many moved to San Francisco, to join what was already a sizeable community. The city didn't extend much of a welcome: jingoistic sentiment turned quickly into a tide of racial hatred, manifest in sometimes vicious attacks that bound the Chinese defensively into a solid, tight-knit community. The population stagnated until the 1960s, when the lifting of anti-Chinese immigration restrictions swelled the area's numbers to close on 160,000. Nowadays, the Chinese families that do well tend to move out to the more spacious districts of the Sunset and Richmond (see p.390), coming back on Sundays to shop and eat; however, the population is still massive, and now includes Vietnamese, Koreans, Thais and Laotians. By day the area seethes with activity and congestion, by night the traffic moves a little easier, but the blaze of neon and marauding diners gives you the feeling that it just never lets up. Overcrowding is compounded by a brisk tourist trade and sadly, though fish can still be found hanging from washing lines, Chinatown boasts some of the most egregiously tacky stores and facades in the city. Genuine snatches of ethnicity are sullied by pseudo-Chinese Americana at every turn.

You can approach Chinatown from many directions: as well as Nob and Russian Hills, North Beach blends into its northern edges, and if you're coming from the south, Union Square is just a few blocks away. It is from this direction that you'll encounter the large dragon-clad archway (a gift from the Government of Taiwan, and, judging by the look of it, not one that broke the bank) that crosses the intersection of Bush Street and **Grant Avenue**, a long, narrow street, crowded with gold-ornamented portals and brightly painted balconies perched above the souvenir stores and restaurants. Plastic Buddhas, floppy hats and chopsticks assault the eye from every doorway. Before the days of all-consuming tourism, Grant Avenue was known as Dupont Street, a wicked ensemble of opium dens, bordellos and gambling huts policed and frequently terrorized by Tong hatchet men – gangs who took it upon themselves to police and protect their district in any (usually extremely violent) way they saw fit. Their original purpose was to retaliate against the racial hooliganism, but they developed quickly into Mafia-style family feuding – as bloody as any of the Chicago gangster wars. These days there isn't much trace of them on the streets, but the mob continues to operate, battling for a slice of the lucrative West Coast drug trade.

Parallel to Grant, **Stockton Street** is closer to the real thing – Chinatown's main street, crammed with exotic fish and fruit and veg markets, bakeries and spice shops. Your dollar will go further here than anywhere else in the neighbourhood, and your search for the authentic face of Chinatown will be better rewarded. Two blocks down, **St Mary's Square** holds a sculpture of Sun Yat-Sen, founder of the Chinese Republic, its little old ladies and pastoral ambience a far cry from the days when this was the area's red light district.

Chinatown's history is well documented in the **Chinese Historical Society of America** at 650 Commercial St (Tues–Sat, noon–4pm; donations), which traces the beginnings of the Chinese community in the US and has a small but worthy collection of photographs, paintings and artefacts from the pioneering days of the last century. But to really get the measure of Chinatown, you should wander its alleys with their hidden temples and family clubs and organizations. Waverly Place is particularly good; in the late nineteenth century it was lined with brothels, but the earthquake helped clean up the area. There are three opulently decorated but skilfully hidden temples (nos. 109, 125 and 146), their interiors a riot of black, gold and vermillion. They're still in use and open to visitors, but the erratic opening times mean you'll have to take pot luck to get in. More accessible is **Buddha's Universal Church** at 720 Washington St, where America's largest Zen sect give tours on the second and fourth Sunday of each month. This five-storey building was painstakingly built by the sect's members from an exotic collection of polished woods, adorned everywhere by the mosaic images of Buddha. Not as rich with history, the **Chinese Cultural Center**, inside the *Holiday Inn* at 750 Kearny St (Tues–Sat 10am–4pm), does nonetheless host a regular programme of art shows, mostly contemporary, that go some way to dispelling the popular myth that Chinese art is all pastel colours and oblique images.

The best of Chinatown's very few **bars** is **Li Po's**, at 916 Grant Ave, a dimly lit retreat from the confusion of the surrounding streets, named after the Chinese poet, and something of a hangout for the small contingent of Chinese writers in the city. However, you are more likely to have come here to **eat** in one of over a hundred restaurants (see p.395). Some are historical landmarks in themselves, none less so than **Sam Woh's**, 813 Washington St, cheap and churlish ex-haunt of the Beats where Gary Snyder taught Jack Kerouac to eat with chopsticks, and had them both thrown out for his loud and passionate interpretation of Zen poetry.

Half a block east, **Portsmouth Square**, now best known as the roof of a multistorey garage, was the original centre of the city, and the place where Sam Brannan announced the discovery of gold – an event which transformed San Francisco from a sleepy Spanish pueblo into a rowdy frontier city. Though not the most attractive of parks these days, it's nonetheless an oasis in a very cramped part of town. Old men come to play chess, while younger ones fly past on skateboards; in the northwest corner there's a monument to Robert Louis Stevenson, who, it's claimed, used to come here to write. More recently, sculptor Thomas Marsh's bronze, *The Goddess of Democracy*, was erected here after an unsuccessful stay in Tianamen Square, Beijing in the spring of 1989.

## North Beach

Resting in the hollow between Russian and Telegraph Hills, and split down the middle by Columbus Avenue, **NORTH BEACH** likes to think of itself as the happening district of San Francisco. While not cutting-edge contemporary, North Beach's charm has endured several incarnations and fashion waves to remain one of the most consistently interesting areas of town. Originally the city's Italian quarter, since the 1950s – when the more prominent figures of the Beat movement gathered here – it has been among the sought-after neighbourhoods for anyone vaguely alternative. The place still has an Italian flavour, somehow resisting the encroaching neon of the strip joints and sex clubs on Broadway, and is home to some of the most loyally patronized bars and restaurants in the city. Rocketing real estate prices levelled off in the 1980s, and the die-hard freethinkers have just about managed to maintain their territory amid the sharp-suited young professionals slumming it in North Beach's traditionally scruffy cafés. Consequently, it is still a most likeable neighbourhood, inhabited by a solid core of people who remember what bohemia was really like. The anecdotes connected with North Beach are legion – get chatting to any barfly over fifty, they seem to know them all.

San Francisco's most visible landmark, the **Transamerica Pyramid** on Montgomery and Columbus, marks the southern edge of North Beach and the beginning of the more corporate identity of the Financial District. A little further up Columbus Avenue, the green flatiron **Columbus Tower** looks somewhat surreal against the backdrop of the downtown skyline. Developers have been trying to knock it down for years, but the efforts of its owner, film-maker Francis Ford Coppola, have so far ensured its survival. Across Columbus, the now defunct *Purple Onion* nightclub and the *Hungry i* down Jackson Street hosted some of the biggest names of the Fifties San Francisco scene. Politically conscious comedians such as Lenny Bruce (who made himself a name in the area for regular doped-out attempts to throw himself from the upper windows) and Mort

## THE BEATS IN NORTH BEACH

North Beach has always been something of a literary hangout: it was home to Mark Twain and Jack London for a while, among other boomtown writers. But it was the **Beat Generation** in the late 1950s that really put the place on the map, focusing media attention on the area – and the *City Lights* bookstore (see overleaf) – as literary capital of California. The first Beat writings had emerged a decade earlier in New York's Lower East Side from Jack Kerouac, Allen Ginsberg and William Burroughs, who like many writers of the time were frustrated by the conservative political climate, and whose lifestyle and values emphasized libertarian beliefs that America wasn't perhaps ready for. Nothing really crystallized, however, until a number of the writers moved out West, most of them settling in North Beach and forming an esoteric cluster of writers, poets, musicians and inevitable hangers-on around the *City Lights*. It wasn't long before the Beats were making news. In 1957 a storm of controversy rose up when police moved in to prevent the sale of Ginsberg's poem *Howl* under charges of obscenity – an episode the press latched onto immediately, inadvertently hyping the Beats to national notoriety, as much for their hedonistic antics as for the literary merits of their work. Within six months, Jack Kerouac's *On the Road*, inspired by his friend Neal Cassady's benzedrine monologues and recorded in a marathon two-week session in New York six years earlier – previously rejected by all the publishers he had taken it to – shot to the top of the bestseller lists.

As well as developing a new, more personal style of fiction and poetry, the Beats eschewed most social conventions of the time, and North Beach soon became almost a symbol across the nation of a wild and subversive lifestyle. The road trips and riotous partying, the drug-taking and embrace of Eastern spiritualism were revered and emulated nationwide. Whether the Beat message was an important one is a moot point; in any case, the Beats became more of an industry than a literary movement, and tourists poured into North Beach for "Beatnik Tours" and the like. The more enterprising fringes of bohemia responded in kind with "The Squaresville Tour" of the Financial District, dressed in Bermuda shorts and carrying plaques that read "Hi, Squares". The legend has yet to die, not least in North Beach itself, where Ferlinghetti has had his wish granted by City Hall and many of the city's streets have been renamed as a tribute to the famous figures who have graced the neighbourhood; indeed the small alley which runs down the side of the *City Lights* store has been called "Jack Kerouac Lane".

Sahl performed here, and even though these places have now closed or changed beyond recognition, the district continues to trade on a reputation earned decades ago.

Further along Columbus at Broadway, amid the flashing neon and sleazy clubs, the **City Lights Bookstore** was the first paperback bookstore in the US, established in 1953, and still owned by poet and novelist Lawrence Ferlinghetti. The vast collection of avant-garde, contemporary and Beat works is open for business and browsing until midnight, seven days a week. Next to the bookstore, across the narrow Kerouac Alley, **Vesuvio's** is an old North Beach bar where most of the local writers hung out at some point. The likes of Dylan Thomas and Jack Kerouac regularly got loaded here, and while times have changed considerably since then it remains a haven for the lesser-known to get ploughed with impunity and pontificate on the state of the arts. Assuming you leave *Vesuvio's* with your brain intact, you'll find yourself at the crossroads of **Columbus and Broadway**, where poetry meets porn in a raucous assembly of strip joints, rock venues and drag bars. The most famous, the now derelict *Condor Club*, is where Carol Doda's infamous revelation of her silicone-implanted breasts started the topless waitress phenomenon. Her nipples are no longer immortalized in neon above the door in tribute to the years of mammary fascination in the clubs around here, and nowadays business seems a bit slack along the strip as the doormen try to lure you through their darkened doorways. The **Finocchio Club** at 506 Broadway, now home to polished drag-acts (see p.409), was a famous speakeasy during prohibition.

As you continue north on Columbus, the bright lights fade and you enter the heart of the old **Italian neighbourhood**, an enclave of restaurants, cafés, delicatessens and off-beat stores set against a background of narrow streets and leafy enclosures. A quick diversion along any of the side streets will lead you to small landmarks such as the **Café Trieste**, at 601 Vallejo, a literary waking-up spot since the days of the Beats and still a reminder of more romantic times: the jukebox blasts out opera classics to a heavy-duty art crowd toying with their cappuccinos and browsing slim volumes of poetry.

A couple of hundred yards further along Columbus Avenue, **Washington Square Park** isn't, with five sides, much of a square; neither, due to urban overcrowding, is it much of a park. However, it's big and green enough for the elder Italians to rest on the benches and the neighbouring Chinese to do their Tai Chi routines on a Sunday morning, and is lined with stylish restaurants, where serious media people and politicos come to power-lunch. On the Columbus Avenue side of the park is one of old San Francisco pioneer Lily Coit's many tributes to her fascination with firemen; a big, bronze macho monument with men holding hoses. On the north side of the park the lacy spires of the **Church of St Peter and Paul**, where local baseball hero Joe DiMaggio married Marilyn Monroe, dominate the centre of the neighbourhood. Inside this stately Romanesque testament to local Italian pride (it also has a school built around it) is *La Madre del Lume*, a wonderful painting of a Madonna, child on hip, reaching into the inferno to pull out a sinner by his arm. Not quite so holy is the art at the **Tattoo Museum**, 841 Columbus Ave – actually a working tattoo parlour – where you can wonder at Lyle Tuttle's bizarre recordings of the flesh canvases who have submitted to his needle.

Two steep hills dwarf the area. To the east of Columbus Avenue, **TELEGRAPH HILL** is a neighbourhood of small alleys and houses perched on 45-degree inclines. It was once an extension of the wilder North Beach territory, but is now firmly rich country, its elegant homes dangling precipitously on the steep hills below **Coit Tower** (daily 10am–6pm; $3) – a monument to the firefighters who doused the flames of 1906, decorated with WPA murals depicting muscle-bound Californians working the land. Built with $100,000 bequeathed by Lily Coit in 1929, the 210-foot, simple concrete column is an attractive component of the city's skyline, but the greatest reward for the trudge uphill is to take the elevator up to the tower's observation deck – the swooping panorama takes in the bay and the famous Golden Gate Bridge in the north, to the more seductively simple Bay Bridge in the east.

To the west of Columbus, **RUSSIAN HILL** is an elegant neighbourhood named after the Russian sailors who died on an expedition here in the early 1800s and were buried on its southeastern tip. The neighbourhood today draws a steady stream of visitors, who come to drive down **Lombard Street**: a narrow, tightly curving street with a 5mph speed limit and a tailback of cars waiting to get onto it. Surrounded by palatial dwellings and herbaceous borders, Lombard is featured as often as the Golden Gate Bridge in San Francisco publicity shots, and at night when the tourists leave and the city lights twinkle below, it makes for a thrilling drive. But even without a car it's worth the journey up here for a visit to the **San Francisco Art Institute**, 800 Chestnut St (Tues–Sat 10am–5pm; free). The oldest art school in the West, the Institute has been central in the development of the arts in the Bay Area, and has four excellent galleries, three dedicated to painting and one to surrealist photography. The remarkably high standard of work puts some of San Francisco's galleries proper in a very shady second place. But the highlight of the institute is unquestionably the **Diego Rivera Gallery**, which has an outstanding mural executed by the painter in 1931 at the height of his fame. A small **cafeteria** at the back of the building offers cheap refreshments and great views of North Beach, Telegraph Hill and the bay.

From the western edge of Russian Hill along Union Street all the way to the Presidio, runs an area known as **COW HOLLOW**. Originally a small valley of pastures and dairies in the post-Gold Rush years, Cow Hollow languished until the 1950s when enterprising merchants decided its old clapboard dwellings had possibilities. Gorgeous old Victorian houses have had their faces lifted, and the stretch of Union between Van Ness and Divisadero now holds some very cutesy boutiques and cafés. Best seen on foot because of all the little alleyways and tucked-away basements, it's an excellent place to use up any excess dollars.

## Fisherman's Wharf, Alcatraz and the Northern Waterfront

San Francisco doesn't go dramatically out of its way to please the tourist on the whole, but with **Fisherman's Wharf** and the nearby waterfront district, it makes a rare exception. An inventive use of statistics allows the area to proclaim itself the most visited tourist attraction in the entire country; in fact this crowded and hideous ensemble of waterfront kitsch and fast-food stands make for a sad and rather misleading introduction to the city. Hard to believe now, but this was originally a serious fishing port, trawling in real crabs and not the frozen sort now masquerading as fresh on the stalls; the few fishermen that can afford the exorbitant mooring charges are usually finished by early morning and get out before the tourists arrive. The shops and bars here are among the most overpriced in the city and crowd-weary families do little to add to the ambience. It's pretty enough and has a handful of good seafood restaurants, but the best thing to do at the Wharf is leave.

Almost directly opposite, the **Cannery**, on Leavenworth Street, is a one-time fruit-packing factory that has experienced similar refurbishment. And at the far end of the Wharf, about half a mile away, **Pier 39** is another shopping complex, contrived to look like San Francisco of old, but failing rather miserably and charging heavily for the privilege. In between the two a cluster of exorbitantly priced museums and exhibitions are designed to relieve you of more money; not one is worth expending time on, unless you're with restless children. Further east, **Ghirardelli Square** at 900 N Point St is perhaps a fitting conclusion to this part of the waterfront, a former chocolate factory whose major parts have been transformed into pricey stores and restaurants – although some small-scale production does continue.

Two-hour **bay cruises** depart from piers 39 & 40 several times a day. Provided the fogs aren't too heavy, they give good city views (see p.363 for details).

## West from the Wharf

A little way west of the Wharf, beyond Ghirardelli Square, the **Golden Gate National Recreation Area** was established in 1972 to protect much-needed central park space for the city, and now encompasses almost seventy square miles of waterfront property, from the beaches to the south right up to the cliffs of Marin County across the Golden Gate Bridge. Closest to the Wharf, the **Aquatic Park** complex of buildings groups around the foot of Hyde Street, at its centre the "bathhouse" – a bold, Art Deco piece of architecture now home to the **National Maritime Museum** (summer daily 10am–6pm; rest of year Wed–Sun 10am–6pm; museum building free). It's worth dropping by just to see Hilaire Hiler's mural, symbolizing the lost continent of Atlantis in 37 hallucinogenic panels that dominate the main room. The rest of the complex includes a maritime library, and a forgettable collection of ocean-going memorabilia. At the adjacent **Hyde Street Pier**, the museum has restored a number of old wooden ships, including a transbay ferry ($3) filled with 1930s-era cars and trucks. Another, the *Balclutha* ($3), is the sole survivor of the great sailing ships that journeyed around Cape Horn in the 1800s, and later had bit parts in movies like *Mutiny on the Bounty*.

**Fort Mason**, half a mile west along the waterfront, sits behind a park at the end of *Muni* bus line #30. Originally a Civil War defence installation, now turned over to public use, the site includes a **youth hostel** (see p.367), the acclaimed **Magic Theater**

THE NORTHERN WATERFRONT

(see p.408) and two museums. Displays at the **Museo Italo-Americano** (Wed–Sun noon–5pm; free first Wed of the month) relate to the culture and history of the Italian community in the US; the rather better **Mexican Museum** which once stood here has now moved to SoMa (see p.383).

San Francisco's most theatrical piece of architecture lies at Marina Boulevard and Baker Street. **The Palace of Fine Arts** is not the museum its name suggests, but a huge, freely interpreted classical ruin originally built of wood and plaster for the Pan Pacific Exhibition in 1915 – held to celebrate the rebirth of the city after the 1906 catastrophe. Sentimental San Franciscans saved it from immediate demolition after the exhibition, and it crumbled with dignity until a wealthy resident put up the money for its reconstruction in 1958, making it the sole survivor of the Pan Pacific pageant, surrounded by a swan-filled lagoon and other touches of urban civility. Next door, over five hundred hands-on exhibits in the unsightly, shed-like **Exploratorium** (Tues & Thurs 1–5pm, Wed 1–9pm, Sat & Sun 10am–5pm; $8, $4 on Wed), demonstrate scientific principles of electricity, sound, lasers and more. From here the waterfront stretches west through the Presidio Army Base to the Golden Gate Bridge and beach area close to the park (see p.390).

The area around the Palace of Fine Arts has been tagged the **Marina** district by the young, image-conscious, money-no-object sort of professionals who live there. One of

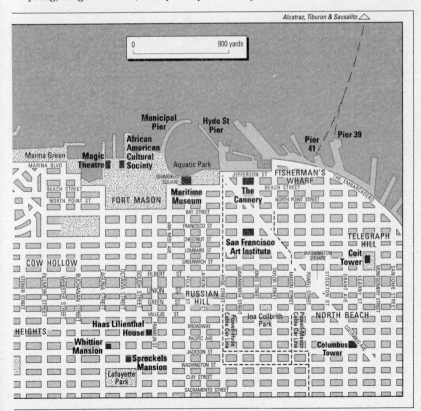

## ALCATRAZ

The rocky little islet of **Alcatraz**, rising out of San Francisco Bay, was originally home to nothing more than the odd pelican (*alcatraz* in Spanish). In the late nineteenth century, the island became a military fortress, and in 1934 it was converted into America's most dreaded **high-security prison**. Surrounded by freezing, impassable water, it was an ideal place for a jail, and safely kept some of America's most wanted criminals behind bars – Al Capone and Machine Gun Kelly were just two of the villains imprisoned here. The conditions were about as inhuman as you'd expect: inmates were kept in solitary confinement, in cells no larger than five by nine feet, most without light; they were not allowed to eat together, read newspapers, have a game of cards or even talk; relatives were permitted to visit them for only two hours each month. Escape really was impossible. In all, nine men managed to get off the rock, but there is no evidence that they made it to the mainland.

For all its usefulness as a jail, the island turned out to be a fiscal disaster. After years of generating massive running costs, not to mention whipping up a storm of public protest for its role as a prison for petty criminals, it closed in 1963. The remaining prisoners were distributed among decidedly less horrific detention centres, and the island remained abandoned until 1969, when a group of Native Americans staged an occupation as part of a peaceful attempt to claim the island for their people – citing treaties which designated all federal land not in use as automatically reverting to their ownership. Using all the bureaucratic trickery it could muster, the government finally ousted them in 1971, claiming the operative lighthouse qualified it as active.

Nowadays the only people to set foot on the island are the annual 750,000 tourists who participate in the excellent hour-long, self-guided audio tours ($5) of the abandoned rows of cells, which include some sharp anecdotal commentary .

Boats across to Alcatraz leave hourly from pier 41, beginning at 8.15am, with the last boat back at around 6pm (cost $8 per person).

the city's greenest districts, the Marina enjoys a prime waterfront location, open spaces and lots of trees. Ironically, though it was built specifically to celebrate the rebirth of the city after the massive earthquake of 1906, the Marina was the worst casualty of the earthquake in 1989 – tremors tore through fragile landfill and a good number of homes collapsed into a smouldering heap. The neighbourhood's commercial centre runs along **Chestnut Street** between Broderick and Fillmore. As a neighbourhood, it has a reputation for being something of a haven for swinging singles; the local watering holes are known as "high intensity breeder bars" and even the local *Safeway* has been dubbed "The Body Shop" because of the inordinate amount of cruising that goes on in the aisles.

Looming above, wealthy **PACIFIC HEIGHTS** is home to some of the city's most monumental Victorian piles. Among these, the wooden turrets of the **Haas-Lilienthal House** at 2007 Franklin St (Wed noon–4pm, Sun 11am–4.30pm; $3), with its Tiffany art glass and stencilled leather panelling, will give you some idea of what to expect at the neighbourhood's grand hotels and mansions that symbolize Old California wealth. The **Octagon House**, 2645 Gough at Union (call for visiting times; ☎441-7512), is, as the name suggests, a unique octagonal building, built in 1861 and purchased by the National Society of Colonial Dames of America, who have crammed it full of colonial and federal period antiques.

## The Tenderloin, Civic Center and South of Market

While much of San Francisco tends to be depicted as an urban utopia – and in some cases, almost lives up to the promise – the adjoining districts of the **Tenderloin**, **Civic Center** and **South of Market** reveal a city of harsh realities. Pretty tree-lined streets, hills and stunning views are conspicuously absent, and for the most part these areas are a gritty blue-collar reminder that not everybody here has it so good. The homeless and disaffected are very much in evidence – the flipside of Californian prosperity is alive and unwell. Sporadic attempts to improve the areas (like the removal of over three hundred homeless people who set up camp outside the offices of the former mayor), are at best well-meaning hit-and-misses or, at worst, patently cosmetic gestures that are bound to fail. Yet these districts are not uninteresting and neither are they as menacing as their LA equivalents, though you shouldn't expect to walk along this section of Market Street without being hassled for money.

## The Tenderloin

West of Union Square on the north side of Market, the **TENDERLOIN**, sandwiched between Civic Center and downtown, provides bold contrast with the rest of San Francisco: a small, uninviting area no more than four blocks by five, it remains the poorest and shabbiest spot in the city. Despite a recent wave of Vietnamese and Laotian immigrants, soup kitchens and flophouses remain the area's major industry, though it is here you'll find San Francisco's best budget accommodation and you may well find yourself staying in one of the numerous low-priced hotels and lodgings. The Tenderloin is at least smack in the middle of town, and you'll be safe as long as you keep your wits about you and don't mind vagrants asking you for money. With common sense you shouldn't find it threatening, though areas you might take care to avoid are those along **Taylor Street** and around the lower part of **Eddy** and **Turk** near Market. Gangs have made this their territory and nonchalantly mooching around is not recommended.

Partly as an attempt to spruce the area up, the city has gone to great lengths to design a "tramp-proof" **park** on Jones and Eddy, replete with every imaginable barrier to dissuade the locals from establishing residence. On a good day, and with heavy patrolling by local police, it can claim to be a success. In addition, the appearance of trendy nightspots and stupefyingly hip restaurants is doing more to make the area safe than any public programme has managed so far.

Attempts to dignify **Polk Street** to the west have been less successful. Even the police find this wild stretch hard to control, with cars kerb-crawling the strip of dodgy-looking bars for rent boys and prostitutes. Refreshingly sleazy after the sometimes tedious charm of other areas in San Francisco, Polk Street is a neon haven of gay bars, affordable small stores, movie theatres and, further up towards Russian Hill, some pretty good restaurants.

## Civic Center

Born out of a grand, celebratory architectural scheme, **CIVIC CENTER,** squashed between the quasi-slums of the Tenderloin and industrial SoMa, is an impressive layout of majestic federal and municipal buildings that can't help but look strangely out of synch, both with its immediate neighbours and with San Francisco as a whole. Its grand Beaux Arts structures, flags and fountains are at odds with the quirky wooden architecture that characterizes the rest of the city. It's the city's centre for the performing arts, and by night can look quite impressive – beautifully lit, and swarming with dinner suits heading in and out of the ballet, opera and symphony hall. But by day it's much less appealing, populated either by office workers from the various local government departments situated here, or by the homeless who loiter on the grass verges of the elegant central quadrangle.

Emerging from the *BART/Muni* station, the first thing you see is the **United Nations Plaza**, a memorial to the founding of the UN here in 1949 – though the only sign of life is on Wednesdays when it's the site of San Francisco's largest and cheapest **fruit and vegetable market**. Most other days it's a rather dismal location for the dispossessed to beg for small change around the fountains in front of the **City Hall**, at the northern edge of the quadrangle. Modelled on St Peter's in Rome, this huge, green-domed Baroque building of granite and marble is the city's most grandiose structure and forms the nucleus of Civic Center. It was here in 1978 that conservative councillor Dan White got past security and assassinated Mayor George Moscone and gay Supervisor Harvey Milk; later, when White was found guilty of manslaughter (not murder), it was the scene of violent demonstrations as gay protesters set fire to police vehicles and stormed the doors of the building.

Opposite City Hall, at Larkin and McAllister, the **San Francisco Public Library** is housed in an attractive, if crumbling, Beaux Arts building on four floors. On the third, the **San Francisco History Room** contains an extensive collection of books and photographs which, with the help of maps, details the city's evolution. To get a handle on the area's cultural venues, the **San Francisco Performing Arts Library and Museum**, 399 Grove St (Tues–Sat noon–5pm; free) has exhibitions related to performings arts not just in Civic Center, but the Bay Area as a whole. In addition, a number of galleries and smart shops are beginning to group themselves around the district: the **Vorpal Gallery**, 393 Grove St, has earned a reputation for consistently high-class contemporary paintings, while the **Arts Commission Gallery**, 155 Grove St, has both indoor and outdoor exhibitions by emerging Bay Area artists. There are no plans afoot for the beautiful **Veteran's Building** at Van Ness and McAllister, since the Museum of Modern Art found a new home South of Market (see below), but places like this don't stay empty for long – watch out for upcoming events in local listings.

Directly behind City Hall are San Francisco's cultural mainstays. The ritzy **War Memorial Opera House**, on Van Ness, is the pride and joy of the city's performing arts institutions – currently closed for essential earthquake-proofing, this is ornate Beaux-Arts architecture at its finest. In thoroughly modern contrast, the giant aquarium-like **Louise M Davies Symphony Hall** is home to the highly rated San Francisco Symphony Orchestra whose season runs from September to May (see p.407). Less rarified (but nonetheless well-known) entertainment can be found in the **Mitchell Brothers O'Farrell Theater**, 895 O'Farrell St. This San Francisco institution is notorious for its "sexual entertainment" and entered into legend several years ago when one of the Mitchell brothers murdered the other.

## South of Market

Although traditionally among San Francisco's least desirable (and most notorious) neighbourhoods, the district South of Market, aka **SOMA**, enjoyed a bit of a renaissance in the 1980s and entered the 1990s with an altered reputation. The recent arrival of the new **San Francisco Museum of Modern Art** completed its transformation. It's reminiscent in a way of New York's SoHo, and while by day it can seem little more than a bleak expanse of largely deserted warehouse spaces, by night it can fairly claim to be the epicentre of San Franciscan nightlife. The decline of San Francisco's shipping and rail freight industry in the 1950s and 1960s left much of the area desolate, but since the city planners put a stop to all new development in the Financial District there's been a boom in new construction here, highlighted by major projects such as the **Moscone Convention Center**, named after the Mayor who was assassinated along with Harvey Milk. Many of SoMa's abandoned warehouses have been converted into studio space and small art galleries, and the neighbourhood is now home to artists, musicians, hepcat entertainers and a number of trendy restaurants.

Of all the recent buildings, the most talked about has been the new home of the **Museum of Modern Art** (MoMa), 151 Third St (Tues–Sun 11am–6pm, Thurs 11am–9pm; $7, Thurs after 5pm $3.50, free first Tues of the month) designed by Swiss architect Mario Botta, which has more than doubled the exhibition space the museum had in the Veteran's Building, Civic Center, and – optimists predict – will make San Francisco the foremost centre for contemporary art on the West Coast. Major works include paintings by Jackson Pollock, Mark Rothko, Frida Kahlo and Diego Rivera. Georgia O'Keefe, Dali, Matisse and Picasso are also represented, if not at their peak. There is an excellent selection of photography, but the museum's strongest suit is its calendar of temporary exhibitions. Despite these many treasures, the building is arguably far more beautiful than anything inside – flooded with natural light from a soaring, truncated, cylindrical skylight, it's a sight to behold.

Opposite the museum is the other totem of civic pride, the **Yerba Buena Center**, bounded by Third and Fourth streets, Mission and Folsom. A spectacular $87 million project to house the arts, featuring a theatre and visual arts centre, its premise is to provide a forum for the work of San Francisco's diverse artistic and ethnic communities. Much of the work is provincial (naturally) compared to the stuff in the MoMa, although the **Mexican Museum** here (Tues–Sun 10am–5pm), recently moved from Fort Mason, displays a small but important collection of pre-Hispanic, colonial and folk art. The centre's best feature, however, is its setting – five and half acres of lovely gardens with a fifty-foot Sierra granite waterfall memorial to Martin Luther King Jr.

Above all, SoMa is the nucleus of **clubland**, the only place any self-respecting San Franciscan night owl will be seen after dark, and it's a chance to see the city's wildlife at its best. Folsom Street was once a major gay strip, the centre for much lewder goings-on than the now-respectable Castro, but recently the mix has become pretty diverse and you should expect to find anything but the very tame. The kernel of activity is around 11th and Folsom, where the largest grouping of clubs and bars draws crowds who don't mind waiting in line at weekends. Comparatively little traffic uses this intersection during the day, and it comes as a surprise to see the bumper-to-bumper and double-parked vehicles after midnight. If you want to check out the area during the day, head for the block of Folsom Avenue between Seventh and Ninth. *Brainwash* at 1122 Folsom Ave is the epitome of SoMa, a café where you can also do your laundry.

Nestled between Brannan and Bryant and Second and Third about half a mile away, **South Park** is the sole survivor of what in the 1870s was the city's most upscale district, a small square designed by an English architect to mirror London's fashionable Georgian squares. The construction of the Bay Bridge – which has its western foot just a block away – spelt the end of this as a residential neighbourhood, and the smart-set hightailed it to Pacific Heights. Long an industrial district, South Park has recently been rediscovered and increasingly houses the offices of architects and designers, who can be seen lunching at the chic French cafés on the square. Around the corner, where Third Street meets Brannan, a **plaque** marks the birthplace of *Call of the Wild* writer Jack London, though he soon escaped what were then pretty mean streets, enjoying his better days in Oakland and the valleys of Sonoma.

With all the new development, it can be hard to imagine what SoMa looked like before, but the real spirit of blue-collar, industrial San Francisco still exists around the abandoned docks and old shipyards known as **China Basin** and **Mission Rock**. Not much goes on here now, but the site has an isolated, romantic quality suited to desolate walks, stopping off for drinks at the few places that dot the shoreline. The easiest way to reach the area is to follow Third Street south from Market as it curves round to meet the docks at the **switchyards** where the drawbridge crosses China Basin Channel. It was here that **Jack Kerouac** worked as a brakeman in the Fifties, at the same time writing the material that was later to appear in *Lonesome Traveller*, detailing scenes of SoMa's skid row hotels, drunks and whores. A short walk south takes you to the heart of the China Basin, the old water inlet, and Mission Rock – the old Pier 50 that juts out into the bay. This was the focus of the old port where freight ships used to dock from Asia. Occasionally the odd ship will sail by, but today it's more likely to be the military ships from the Oakland Naval Base cruising the bay than the freight liners that used to jam the waterways. A few small boat clubs have sprung up along the waterfront, but most people come to visit the *Mission Rock Resort* or *The Ramp* – two creaky wooden structures that are local landmarks. *The Ramp* is quite the place to be on Sunday when people gather to hear live jazz on the small pier (see also p.401).

# The Mission

Low-rent, hip, colourful, occasionally dangerous and solidly Hispanic working-class, the **MISSION** is the one San Francisco neighbourhood that defiantly resists improvement. Positioned way south of downtown, it is the city's warmest area, avoiding the fogs that blanket most of the peninsula during the summer. Stretching from SoMa at its northern end down to Army Street in the south, the Mission is a large district, although with *BART* stations at each end, getting here isn't a problem.

As a first stop for immigrants to the city, the Mission is something of a microcosm of the history of San Francisco. It was first inhabited by Scandinavians and Germans, later the Irish, then the Italians, and now San Francisco's Hispanic population. It is from this that the area gets its marked political edge: this is perhaps the only truly radical pocket left in the city, with its left-wing, feminist and lesbian bookshops, Hispanic labour associations and the requisite bohemian bars and cafés. For the rest, it's a noisy melange of garages, furniture and junk stores, old movie houses and parking lots. Some cheap but chic new restaurants and bars have opened recently along one street – earning it the name "The Valencia Corridor" – and are beginning to pull in a more than local crowd. Add to this the fair concentration of lively nightspots, and the Mission is a good base if you're staying in the city for any length of time.

The district takes its name from the old **Mission Dolores**, 16th and Dolores (daily 10am–4pm; $2), the most ancient building to survive the 1906 earthquake and fire. Founded in 1776, it was the sixth in a series of missions built as Spain staked its claim to California, trying to "civilize" the natives with Christianity while utilizing their (cheap) labour. Cruel treatment and neglect, however, led to disease and many natives died; their graves, and those of white pioneers, can be seen in the cemetery next door. During the day tour buses are double parked outside, and if you really want to get the feel for this lovely old Mission, the 7.30am daily mass or the noon service in Spanish is a better bet. **Dolores Park**, a few blocks along at Dolores and 18th, high on a hill at the edge of the neighbourhood, is a pretty, quiet space to rest and take in the good views of the city, plagued though it is with defecating dogs and children on BMX bikes. Its southern bank is nicknamed "Dolores Beach" because of the crowds of semi-naked gay men who gather on warm days to work on their tans and eye each other up – it's quite a scene. Avoid it by night, however, when it becomes the local meeting place for the area's crack-dealers.

Most of the Mission's action goes on between 16th and 24th, and the *BART* stations along Mission, Valencia and Dolores. The one sight here is the **Levi Strauss & Co** factory at 250 Valencia St (free tours Wed 10am & 1pm; reserve on ☎565-9159), where you can see how the world's most famous jeans are made. Tours of the plant include the cutting and sewing operations and how to "stonewash" a pair of jeans and make your new pair look old.

What really sets the Mission apart from other neighbourhoods, however, are its **murals** – though with so many splashed about (there are over 200 in all) it's hard to know what to look at first. If you can't stomach taking yourself on an unexpurgated tour, you should at least go and see the brilliant tribute to local hero **Carlos Santana** adorning three buildings where 22nd Street meets South Van Ness. For more controversial subject matter take a walk down **Balmy Alley** between Folsom and Harrison off 24th Street (unquestionably the axis of Latino shopping, with Nicaraguan, Salvadorean, Costa Rican, Mexican and other Latin American stores and restaurants), where every possible surface is covered with murals depicting the political agonies of Central America. Started in 1973 by a group of artists and community workers, they have become the most quietly admired public art in San Francisco. For details of walking tours of the Mission see "City transport", p.362.

## The Castro

Arguably San Francisco's most progressive, if no longer most celebratory neighbourhood, **THE CASTRO** is the city's avowed queer-capital and as such, the best barometer for the state of the gay scene. As a district, the Castro occupies a large area that stretches south from Market Street as far as Noe Valley (see overleaf), but in terms of visible street life the few blocks from Market to 20th Street contain about all there is to see. People say many things about the changing face of the neighbourhood – some insist that it's still the wildest place in town, others reckon that post-AIDS it's a shadow of its former self – but all agree that things are not the same. It is claimed that over 10,000 men in this area alone have been lost to the virus. A walk down the Castro ten, or even five, years ago would have you gaping at the revelry, and while most of the same bars and hangouts still stand, these days they're host to an altogether different, younger and more conservative breed. But while there are no "sights" as such, it is the stories and the history connected with the district that make this area so interesting and give you an idea of just how progressive San Francisco really is. For an insider's view, Trevor Hailey's *Cruisin' The Castro* walking tour is just about unbeatable (see "City Transport" p .362).

**Harvey Milk Plaza**, by the Castro *Muni* station, is as good a place as any to start your wanderings, dedicated to the gay Supervisor (or councillor) who before his assassination in 1978 owned a camera store and was a popular figure in the Castro. Milk and Mayor George Moscone's assailant, Dan White, was a disgruntled ex-Supervisor who resigned when the liberal policies of Moscone and Milk didn't coincide with his conservative views. He later tried to get his post back but was refused by Moscone, and soon after sauntered into City Hall and shot them both. At the trial, White pleaded temporary insanity caused by harmful additives in his diet of fast food – a plea which came to be known as the "twinkie defence" (twinkies are synthetic-cream cakes) – and was sentenced to five years' imprisonment for manslaughter. The gay community reacted angrily to the brevity of White's sentence, and the riots that followed were among the most violent San Francisco has ever witnessed, protesters marching into City Hall turning over and burning police cars as they went. White was released in 1985 and moved to Los Angeles, where he committed suicide shortly after.

Before heading down the hill into the heart of the Castro, take a short walk across Market Street to the headquarters of the **Names Project** at no. 2362 (daily 10am–7pm). The organization was founded in the wake of the AIDS crisis and sponsored the creation of "The Quilt" – a gargantuan blanket composed of panels, each 6ft x 3ft (the size of a gravesite) and bearing the name of a man lost to the disease. Made by their lovers, friends and families, the panels are stitched together and regularly toured around the country; it has been spread a number of times on the Mall in Washington DC to dramatize the epidemic to seemingly indifferent governments. Sections of the quilt, too large to be exhibited in any one place in its entirety, continue to tour the world to raise people's awareness of the tragedy and keep the care programmes alive. Inside the showroom, you can see the thousands of panels stored on shelves; some are hung up for display and machinists tackle the endless task of stitching the whole thing together. Next door, **Under One Roof** is another organization raising money for various AIDS welfare agencies, by selling books, T-shirts and gifts.

Back on Castro Street, one of the first things you see is the **Castro Theater**, self-described as "San Francisco's landmark movie palace". It's undeniably one of San Francisco's better movie houses, as popular for its pseudo-Spanish baroque interior as it is for its billing, which includes revivals, twenty-minute performances on a Wurlitzer and some plush velvet surroundings. A little further down the hill, the junction of **Castro and 18th Street,** known as the "gayest four corners of the earth", marks the Castro's centre, cluttered with bookshops, clothing stores, cafés and bars. The side streets offer a slightly more exclusive range of exotic delicatessens, fine wine shops and fancy florists, and enticingly leafy residential territory that keeps a neat distance from the bright lights and noise of the main drag.

Before leaving the Castro, make an effort to go to **Twin Peaks**, about a mile and a half along Market from the Harvey Milk Plaza. (Travel west until you hit Twin Peaks Boulevard; the #37 Corbett bus will take you to Parkridge.) The highest point in the city, this gives a 360-degree view of the peninsula. Real-estate prices in the city are gauged in part by the quality of the views, so it's no surprise that the curving streets that wind around the slopes of Twin Peaks hold some of the city's most outrageously unaffordable homes. During the day, busloads of tourists arrive to point their Pentaxes, and often, during the summer crowds build up while waiting for the fog to lift. Better to go at night picking out landmarks from either side of the shimmering artery of Market Street. If you want to avoid the crowds (and pickpockets), Tank Hill, a small promontory just beneath Twin Peaks (you'll need a map to find your way through the maze of small streets) is perfect.

You might also consider a quick visit to **NOE VALLEY**, on the far side of the hill. Until a couple of years ago it was remarkable only for its insignificant status in the pantheon of San Francisco neighbourhoods; in fact, so good was it at failing to capture imaginations that it was fondly tagged "Noewhere Valley" by those who had any notion of where it is and what it's like. Sitting snugly in a sunny valley, the main vein of which runs along 24th Street, crammed with delicatessens, coffee shops, small boutiques and some excellent lunch venues, it has an air of rugged unfashionableness manifest in clean streets, blue-collar sports bars and a noticeable lack of street crime and vagrancy – all of which can be refreshing, after the sleaze of the Mission and SoMa. Needless to say, discerning professional San Franciscans have found it and it is fast becoming one of the city's most desirable neighbourhoods.

## Haight-Ashbury

Two miles west of downtown San Francisco, **HAIGHT-ASHBURY** is a neighbourhood that lent its name to an era, giving it a fame that far outstrips its size. A small area, spanning no more than eight blocks in length, centred around the junction of Haight and Ashbury Street and bordered by Golden Gate Park at its western edge, "The Haight", as it's known, was a respectable Victorian neighbourhood-turned-slum that emerged in the 1960s as the epicentre of the countercultural scene. Since then it's become slightly smartened up, but still retains a collection of radical bookstores, laid-back cafés, record shops and thrift stores that recall its era of international celebrity – when to some it was the scene of one the most significant of Sixties protest movements, to others simply the best acid party in history.

The Haight today has few real sights as such, relying instead on the constant turn-over of hip shopping spots to sustain its legend. Two blocks east of the Haight-Ashbury junction, **Buena Vista Park** is a mountainous forest of Monterey pines and California redwoods, used by dogwalkers in the daylight hours, but come nightfall the locale of much sex-in-the-shrubbery. Walk here accompanied by day and not at all at night, unless you're male and looking for some action. The **"Haight-Ashbury Free Clinic"**, at 558 Clayton St, is a venerable Sixties hangover: an unusual phenomenon, certainly, by American standards, which first began providing free health care when drugs-related illnesses became a big problem in the Haight. It now survives – barely – on contributions, continuing to treat local drug casualties and the poor, both dispropor-tionately large groups in this area of the city. Otherwise, stroll along the Haight and take advantage of what is still one of the best areas in town to **shop**. It shouldn't take more than a couple of hours to update your record collection, dress yourself up and blow money on good books and cold beers. Things get livelier as you move west, the increasing number of street musicians merging eventually into the hardcore hippy guitarists along what is known as the **Panhandle**, a finger-slim strip of greenery that eventually leads into Golden Gate Park.

### HIPPIES

The first **hippies** were an offshoot of the Beats, many of whom had moved out of their increasingly expensive North Beach homes to take advantage of the low rents and large spaces in the Victorian houses of the Haight. The post-Beat bohemia that subsequently began to develop here in the early 1960s was initially a small affair, involving drug use and the embrace of Eastern religion and philosophy, together with a marked anti-American political stance and a desire for world peace. Where Beat philosophy had emphasized self-indulgence, the hippies, on the face of it at least, attempted to be more embracing, focusing on self-coined concepts such as "universal truth" and "cosmic aware-ness". Naturally it took a few big names to get the ball rolling, and characters like Ken Kesey and his Merry Pranksters soon set a precedent of wild living, challenging author-ity and dropping (as they saw it) out of the established norms of society. Drugs were particularly important, and seen as an integral – and positive – part of the movement. LSD, especially, the effects of which were just being discovered and which at the time was not actually illegal, was claimed as an avant-garde art form, pumped out in private laboratories and distributed by Timothy Leary and his network of supporters with a prescription ("Turn on, tune in, drop out") that galvanized a generation into inactivity. An important group in the Haight at the time was The Diggers, who, famed for their parties and antics, truly believed LSD could be used to increase creativity. Before long life in the Haight began to take on a theatrical quality: Pop Art found mass appeal, light shows became legion, dress flamboyant, and the Grateful Dead, Jefferson Airplane and Janis Joplin made names for themselves. Backed by the business weight of promoter Bill Graham, the psychedelic music scene became a genuine force nationwide, and it wasn't long before kids from all over America started turning up in Haight-Ashbury for the free food, free drugs and free love. Money became a dirty word, the hip became "heads", and the rest of the world were "straights".

Other illustrious tenants of the Haight at this time include Kenneth Rexroth, who hosted a popular radio show and wrote for the *San Francisco Examiner*. Hunter S Thompson, too, spent time here researching and writing his book *Hell's Angels*, and was notorious for inviting Angels round to his apartment on Parnassus Street for noisy, long and occasionally dangerous drinking and drug-taking sessions.

Things inevitably turned sour towards the end of the decade, but during the heady days of the massive "be-in" in Golden Gate Park in 1966 and the so-called "Summer of Love" the following year, this busy little intersection became home to no less than 75,000 transitory pilgrims who saw it as the mecca of alternative culture.

The funkiest corner of the district lies at the eastern end of Haight Street, around the crossing with Fillmore Street. Known as the **Lower Haight**, and the centre of black San Francisco for decades, it briefly emerged a few years ago – thanks to low rents – as the major stomping ground for young hipsters. It flourished for a while with some of the city's grooviest bars, ethnic restaurants and meeting places, but the truth is there just isn't enough money or traffic in the neighbourhood to support such trendiness for long. However, given its proximity to downtown it's a fine place to get a cheap breakfast, browse the bookstores, rake through vintage clothing emporia and drink yourself silly. See "Eating and drinking" for a few good suggestions.

Ten blocks north of here, up Geary Street, **WESTERN ADDITION** is also firmly black, one of the city's most relentlessly poor neighbourhoods – dangerous in parts and certainly not tourist territory. Its boundaries reach to **JAPANTOWN**, something of a misnomer for what is basically a shopping mall with an eastern flavour – the Japan Center – around which only a small percentage of San Francisco's Japanese Americans actually live. Visit only to check out the **Kabuki Hot Springs**, 1750 Geary Blvd (Mon–Sat 10am–10pm; ☎922-6000): community baths with shiatsu massage, steam baths and other luxuriating facilities for around $20 per hour. If you're in the area, jump over a few blocks to where Geary Boulevard meets Gough and look at the monumentally elaborate **St Mary's Cathedral**.

# Golden Gate Park

Unlike most American cities, San Francisco is not short on green space, and **Golden Gate Park** is its largest, providing a wonderfully bucolic antidote to the centre of town. Despite the throngs of joggers, polo players, roller-skaters, cyclists and strollers it never gets overcrowded, and you can always find a spot to be alone. Designed by Frederick Olmsted (who also created Central Park in New York) in the late nineteenth century, this is one of the most beautiful, and safest, corners of the city, with none of the menace of its New York counterpart. Spreading three miles or so west from the Haight as far as the Pacific shore, it was constructed on what was then an area of wild sand dunes buffeted by the spray from the nearby ocean, with the help of a dyke to protect the western side from the sea. John McLaren, park superintendent for fifty-odd years, planted around a million trees here, and nowadays it's a peaceful and skilfully crafted spot to relax, with over a thousand acres of gardens, forests, lakes, waterfalls and museums.

Exploration of the whole place could take days of footwork. Among its more mainstream attractions, there's a Japanese Tea Garden, a horticultural museum (modelled on the Palm House at Kew Gardens), a Shakespeare Garden with every flower or plant mentioned in the writer's plays, not to mention the usual contingent of serious joggers, cyclists and roller-skaters. If you're feeling energetic, activities are many and quite cheap: **boat rental** is available on Stow Lake (parallel with 19th Ave) for around $9 per hour, and **horse-riding** for around $25 per hour from the *Golden Gate Stables* on J F Kennedy Drive and 34th Ave. But most people come here to do nothing whatsoever.

Of the park's numerous museums, the **M H de Young Museum** (Wed–Sun 10am–5pm; $5, free first Wed of each month and Sat mornings) is the largest, with San Francisco's most diverse range of painting and sculpture, ranging from the ancient art of Greece and Rome to an outstanding twentieth-century collection in the American Wing – a hundred or so paintings bequeathed by John D Rockefeller III. Rubens, Rembrandt and seventeenth-century European painters are also well represented; you can get an exhaustive commentary on all with a free "Directors Tour", actually a personal headset that you wear for about an hour. Next door, in the West Wing, the **Asian Art Museum** (same hours) has a rather less impressive, in fact drearily exhaustive, collection of ten thousand paintings, sculptures, ceramics and textiles from all over Asia. Donated by Avery Brundage in 1966, the collection receives much attention for its sheer vastness, but it's only worth seeing if you're an enthusiast.

You'll find another group of museums opposite, in the **California Academy of Sciences** (daily 10am–5pm; $6) – the perfect place to amuse restless children. There's a natural history museum with a thirty-foot skeleton of a 130 million-year-old dinosaur, and life-size replicas of humans throughout the ages. But the show-stealer is the collection of 14,500 specimens of aquatic life in the **Steinhart Aquarium** (daily 10am–5pm; $3), the best of which are the alligators and other reptiles lurking in a simulated swamp. Also, if you catch it at the right time, the **Morrison Planetarium** (schedule varies; ☎387-6300) can be a great experience. Laser shows and rock music draw often acid-crazed crowds for evening performances.

Slightly west of the museums is the usually crowded **Japanese Tea Garden** (daily 8am–6pm; $3, free 8–9am & 5–6pm). Built in 1894 for the California Midwinter Exposition, the garden was beautifully landscaped by the Japanese Hagiwara family, who were also responsible for the invention of the fortune cookie (despite the prevalent belief that fortune cookies are Chinese). The Hagiwaras looked after the garden until World War II, when along with other Japanese Americans they were sent to internment camps. A massive bronze Buddha dominates the garden, and bridges, footpaths, pools filled with shiny oversized carp, plus bonsai and cherry trees lend the place a peaceful feel – but for the busloads of tourists that pour in regularly throughout the day. The best way to enjoy the garden is to get there around 8am when it first opens and have a breakfast of tea and fortune cookies in the tea house.

During the summer, the park offers a $10 *Golden Gate Pass* which admits you to all the museums and tea garden, but probably the best things to do at the park are outdoors and free. On Sundays, in the central space near the museums, you can hear free concerts at the **Music Pavilion** bandstand; to enjoy the quieter corners of the park head west through the many flower gardens and eucalyptus groves towards the ocean. Perhaps the most unusual thing about Golden Gate Park is its substantial herd of bison, roaming around the **Buffalo Paddock** off JFK Drive near 38th Avenue; you can get closest to these noble giants at their feeding area at the far west end. Moving towards the edge of the park at Ocean Beach, passing a tulip garden and large windmill, you'll come to the **Beach Chalet** facing the Great Highway. This two-storey, white-pillared structure, designed by Willis Polk, is home to some of San Francisco's lesser-known public art. A series of frescoes painted in the 1930s depicts the growth of San Francisco as a city and the creation of Golden Gate Park.

## The Golden Gate Bridge

The orange towers of the **Golden Gate Bridge** – probably the most beautiful, certainly the most photographed bridge in the world – are visible from almost every point of elevation in San Francisco. As much an architectural as an engineering feat, the bridge took only 52 months to design and build and was opened in 1937. Designed by Joseph Strauss, it was the first really massive suspension bridge with a span of 4,200ft, and until 1959 ranked as the world's longest. Over 5000 gallons of paint are anually to keep the bridge in good condition. It connnects the city at its northwesterly point on the peninsula to Marin County and Northern California, rendering the hitherto essential ferry crossing redundant, and was designed to stand winds of up to a hundred miles an hour. Handsome on a clear day, the bridge takes on an eerie quality when the thick white fogs pour in and hide it almost completely. Perhaps the best-loved symbol of San Francisco, in 1987 the Golden Gate proved an auspicious place for a sunrise party when crowds gathered to celebrate its fiftieth anniversary. Some quarter of a million people turned up (a third of the city's population); the winds were strong and the huge numbers caused the bridge to buckle, but fortunately not to break.

You can either drive or walk across the bridge. The drive is probably the more thrilling of the two options as you race under the bridge's towers, but the thirty-minute walk across gives you time to take in its enormity and absorb the views of the city behind you and the headlands of Northern California straight ahead. Pause at the midway point and consider the seven or so suicides a month who choose this spot, 260ft up, for jumping off – apparently always facing the city as they do so. In 1995, when the suicide toll had reached almost one thousand, police kept the figures quiet to avoid a rush of would-be-suicides going for the dubious distinction of being the thousandth person to leap.

Standing beneath the bridge is almost as memorable as travelling over it. The **Fort Point National Historic Site**, a brick fortress built in the 1850s to guard the bay, gives a good sense of the place as the westernmost outpost of the nation. Formerly part of the now decommissioned Presidio army base, it was to have been demolished to make way for the bridge above, but the redesign of the southern approach – note the additional arch which spans it overhead – left it intact. It's a dramatic site, the surf pounding away beneath the great span of the bridge high above – a view made famous by Kim Novak's suicide attempt in Alfred Hitchcock's *Vertigo*. It is alleged by some that the water here makes for one of the best (if most foolhardy) surfing spots in the area. A small **museum** (daily 9am–4pm; free) inside the fort shows some rusty old cannons and firearms, although a far superior military collection can be seen in the **Presidio Army Museum** (Tues–Sun 10am–4pm; free) at Lincoln Blvd and Funston Ave in the Presidio proper, with uniforms, photographs and some detailed documentation of San Francisco's military history.

## Beaches and outlying areas

Filling up the western half of the city, and divided by Golden Gate Park, two residential districts – **Richmond** to the north, the **Sunset** to the south – have more in common with typical American suburbs than they do with the rest of San Francisco. Built almost entirely in the years following World War II and populated mainly by families, these neat, clean and terrifically dull neighbourhoods are well off the tourist map. Unless you're attracted by the thriving Asian neighbourhoods along Clement Street in Richmond, or the many Irish bars along Geary Boulevard and throughout the Sunset, you're most likely to visit the area in passing, en route to the breathtaking (but often fog-bound) coastline at its edge.

Partly due to the weather and partly due to the coldness of the ocean water, beach culture doesn't exist in San Francisco the way it does in Southern California, and people here tend to watch the surf rather than ride it. Powerful currents and crashing waves dissuade all but the most fearless swimmers, and as a result the city's beaches remain blissfully uncrowded. Stretching south a mile from the Golden Gate Bridge, **Baker Beach** is San Francisco's prettiest and most popular, drawing a mixed crowd of fishermen and *au naturel* sunbathers, and giving some great views of the soaring red bridge. It's also easy to reach: stairways drop down from Lincoln Avenue, and *Muni* bus #29 stops at the main parking lot every thirty minutes. A half-mile further southwest at the foot of the ritzy Sea Cliff district, **China Beach** is more protected and better for swimming, and also offers free showers and changing rooms.

Above the beaches, paths stretch south around the peninsula to **Lands End**: it takes about half an hour to get round the cliffs, tricky to negotiate but worth it for the brilliant views of the ocean. A small beach in a rocky cove beneath the cliffside walk is a favourite spot for gay sunbathers. Inland lies **Lincoln Park**, primarily a golf course, but as part of the Point Lobos Headlands it has some striking trails.

The isolated **California Palace of the Legion of Honor** (call ☎750-3600 for opening hours and prices) – best reached by taking the #38 bus from Geary Boulevard and alighting at the Lincoln Park Golf Course – is arguably San Francisco's best museum, housing a remarkable collection of fine art. It is probably also its most beautifully located, the romantic setting, graceful architecture and colonnaded courtyard combining to lend a truly elegant impression: a white-pillared twin of the more famous Legion d'Honneur in Paris. Built from a donation from the wealthy San Franciscan Spreckels family, it was erected in 1920 and dedicated on Abraham Lincoln's birthday in 1921. The museum was re-opened in 1995 after several years extensive seismic engineering and a grand face-lift, and it now displays the permanent collection to even greater advantage. The **Renaissance** is represented with the works of Titian, El Greco and sculpture from Giambologna, while some great canvases by Rembrandt and Hals, as well as Rubens' magnificent *Tribute Money*, are highlights of the seventeenth-century Dutch and Flemish collection. Among the **Impressionist** and **post-Impressionist** paintings are works by Courbet, Manet, Monet, Renoir, Degas and Cézanne, but the section dedicated to the sculpture of **Rodin** steals the show. One of the world's finest Rodin collections features bronze, porcelain and stone pieces including *The Athlete, Fugit Amor, The Severed Head of John the Baptist* and a small cast of *The Kiss*.

A rather bigger stop for the tour buses is the **Cliff House**, dangerously balanced on the western tip of the peninsula above the head of Ocean Beach. There's a **visitor center** here (Mon, Tues, Thurs & Fri 11am–5pm, Sat & Sun 10am–5pm), with information on the surrounding area and an exhibit on the original Cliff House built by Prussian immigrant Adolf Sutro in the late-nineteenth-century as an exclusive resort for the leisured classes, which burned down long ago. There's also a **museum** (daily 10.30am–7pm; free) which claims to have the largest collection of fruit machines and one-armed bandits in the world. The *Cliff House Restaurant* is where most visitors end up, though avoid it unless you want to pay through the nose to sit in a bar with an ocean view (no big deal in a city flanked on three sides by water).

Down by the water you'll find more picturesque ruins – what remains of the **Sutro Baths**. This collection of opulent recreational pools, gardens and elegant sculptures was another of Sutro's creations, sadly destroyed by fire in the 1960s. From here you can explore the ramparts and tunnels of the fortified coastline – a bit frightening at night, when the surf really starts crashing, but there's a certain romance too, and on a rare warm evening it becomes one of the city's favourite snogging spots.

Finally, you might want to visit San Francisco's small but expertly designed **zoo** (daily 10am–5pm; $6, free for under-12s): not bad as zoos go, thoughtfully crafted to resemble the natural habitat as much as possible. It's closer to the beaches than the city though, and unless you've got a car you'll have to go back downtown and board the L Taraval *Muni* to get here.

# Eating

With over four thousand restaurants of every possible ethnicity and style crammed onto the small peninsula, and scores of bars and cafés that are open all day (and some all night), **eating** is *the* culture in this town. San Franciscans gourmandize expertly around the city and most people will have at least four restaurant recommendations up their sleeves. It doesn't have to be expensive either, with **budget places** ranging from the usual array of pizza and burger joints to the **Chinese** restaurants in Chinatown and the **Mexican** places of the Mission – indeed, these are the two cuisines that San Francisco does best, or at least most widely. A little more expensively, **Italian** restaurants are common in North Beach and around much of the rest of downtown; **French** food is a perennial favourite, at least with the power-broking crowd, although *nouvelle cuisine* is finally beginning to loosen its grip on San Franciscan menus. **California cuisine** nowadays has grown away from its minimalist roots, but still features the freshest food, beautifully presented. **Japanese** food, notably sushi, is also still massively popular though not always affordable. **Thai**, **Korean** and **Indonesian** food is similarly in vogue, though usually cheaper. Not surprisingly, health-conscious San Francisco also has a wide range of **vegetarian** and **wholefood** restaurants, and it's rare to find anywhere that doesn't have at least one meat-free item on the menu. With the vineyards of Napa and Sonoma Valley on the city's doorstep, quality **wines** are a high-profile feature in most San Francisco restaurants.

Be warned: **San Francisco closes up early** and you'll be struggling to find places that will serve you much after 10 or 11pm, unless they're of the 24-hour diner variety. And thanks to recent statewide legislation you now cannot **smoke** in any restaurant in the city.

In the listings that follow, the **restaurants** are arranged by cuisine, together with a roundup of where to eat around the clock. However, San Francisco chefs being the innovators that they are, the latest craze is for combining styles – Chinese/French for example – and it can be difficult to categorize restaurants, so don't take the breakdowns below as set in stone: there's no such thing as a straight anything in this town.

## Budget food: breakfasts, burgers and diners

**Bagdad Café**, 2295 Market St at Noe (☎621-4434). Good, hearty breakfasts and burgers served 24 hours per day.

**Brain Wash Laundromat/Café**, 1122 Folsom St at Seventh, SoMa (☎861-3663). If you don't mind watching people pile their dirties into the machines, this is a surprisingly good venue for well-prepared, simple sandwiches, pizzas and salad. A boisterous SoMa hangout, providing a good opportunity to check out the locals.

**Courtyard Café**, 3913 24th St (☎282-0344). Where Noe Valley goes to wake up. Great breakfasts and affordable lunches and dinners. A deli and international periodicals section make this great for browsing over breakfast.

**The Grubstake**, 1525 Pine St at Van Ness (☎673-8268). Converted 1920s railroad dining car, with some of the city's best late-night burgers.

**Hamburger Mary's**, 1582 Folsom St at 12th, SoMa (☎626-1985). Raucous SoMa burger bar, with punky waiting staff and good range of vegetarian options. Inexpensive, and open late for the club-going crowds.

**Mel's Drive-In**, 3355 Geary Blvd at Stanyan (☎387-2244) and 2165 Lombard St at Fillmore (☎921-3039). Straight out of *American Graffiti*, with burgers, fries, milkshakes and a lot of rock & roll on the jukebox. No longer a drive-in, but open late – after midnight every night, till 3am at weekends.

**Mission Rock Resort**, 817 China Basin at Mission Rock (☎621-5538). Good bargain breakfasts and lunches, which you can eat on the wharf when the weather's good. Great location overlooking the old shipyards.

**Orphan Andy's**, 3991 17th St at Castro (☎864-9795). Favourite Castro hangout, serving burgers, omelettes and breakfast 24 hours a day.

**The Pine Crest**, 401 Geary St (☎885-6407). Every inch the greasy diner, but ideal for getting rid of your spare change and hunger at the same time.

**Spaghetti Western**, 576 Haight St at Fillmore (☎864-8461). Best breakfasts for miles and a lively Lower Haight crowd to look at while you chow down.

**Sparky's Diner**, 240 Church St at Market (☎621-6001). 24-hour Castro diner cooking up burgers, pastas and pizzas plus breakfasts including a very good Eggs Florentine. Beer and wine too.

## American and California cuisine

**Aqua**, 253 California St at Battery (☎956-9662). Gorgeously decorated, mainly seafood restaurant that pulls in a discerning Financial District crowd.

**Biscuit and Blues**, 401 Mason St at Geary (☎292-2583). Sounds too good to be true, but you can eat great Creole food for around $10 a head and listen to live blues.

**Bix**, 56 Gold St off Montgomery near Jackson Square (☎433-6300). Jackson Square restaurant kitted out like a majestic ocean liner, with torch singer, sax player and pianist – even if the food was rubbish you'd be enchanted with the place. Actually, the food is great: straightforward, classic dishes. Not surprisingly, a hot spot, where you'd be well advised to reserve in advance. Dinner for two should probably set you back around $80 with drinks, but if you're into elegant dining experiences you should definitely go.

**Cypress Club**, 500 Jackson St at Columbus (☎296-8555). Jackson Square hot spot famed for its delicately presented, inventive California cuisine, served up in one of the most stylish dining rooms to be found in San Francisco – a cross between the *Ritz Carlton* and a Bedouin tent.

**The Dining Room**, *Ritz Carlton Hotel,* 600 Stockton at California (☎296-7465). The hotel's signature restaurant, run by celebrity chef Gary Danko, this is the perfect place for a special occasion. You'll be lucky to escape for under $80 a head with wine, but sometimes such extravagance is really worth it.

**Firefly**, 4288 24th St (☎821-7652). Noe Valley restaurant with wide-ranging, innovative menu and a knowing crowd. Very much a neighbourhood joint.

**Flying Saucer**, 1000 Guerrero St at 22nd, Mission (☎641-9955). A new neighbourhood hot spot offering exquisitely put-together, adventurous cuisine that mixes fruit with meat and every wacky combination you can think of.

**42 Degrees**, 235 16th St at Third (☎777-5558). At the time of press this was the last word in San Franciscan dining for the fashionable without trust funds. Great location down on the old dockyards with a stark modern interior and well-made simple Californian cuisine. For the time being at least, it's a very cool place.

**Grand Café**, 501 Geary St at Jones (☎292-0101). European dishes with a Californian twist served in a converted turn of the century ballroom next door to the stylish *Hotel Monaco*. The food is superb, but the art nouveau decor is even better. Best of all, eating here won't break the bank. Highly recommended.

**Hard Rock Café**, 1699 Van Ness Ave at Clay (☎885-1699). Standard *Hard Rock* clone, downtown. Loud music, rock'n'roll decor and the sort of crowd who don't mind waiting in line for hours for the above-average burgers.

**Johnny Love's**, 1500 Broadway at Polk (☎931-6053). Mainly a singles bar, this raunchy joint also has a large eating area where the food is probably too good to be wasted on the lurching drunks therein. If you like your dinner accompanied by booming rock music, look no further.

**Julie's Supper Club**, 1123 Folsom St at Seventh (☎861-0707). The cuisine, both at the bar and in the back room restaurant, can only be described as eclectic. The decor however, is straight out of a B-52's/Jetsons dream. Worth a look, especially if you can get there before 9pm and escape the $5 cover for the live jazz in the evenings. See also "Drinking: bars and cafés".

**Liberty Café**, 410 Cortland Ave (☎695-8777). Excellent food, beautifully prepared in this Bernal Heights favourite. Best of all, you get dinner for under $20.

**Lou's Pier 47**, 300 Jefferson St at Taylor (☎771-0377). Incongruously placed among the pricey seafood joints on Fisherman's Wharf. Not just one of the best places to hear live r'n'b in the city, it also serves fresh, inexpensive seafood. A must for dinner, a few beers and great music. See also "Live music".

**LuLu's**, 816 Folsom St at Fourth (☎495-5775). The latest in chic mastication, *LuLu's* has an international/Californian menu and the chefs cook in open kitchens wearing headphones. Such obviously studied ambience should not put you off the food, however, which is excellent. A small café adjoining the main restaurant is ideal for a quick, inexpensive meal.

**Maye's Original Oyster House**, 1233 Polk St at Sutter (☎474-7674). In business since the 1860s, this is one of the city's oldest restaurants, turning out reasonably priced, well-cooked fish dishes. Oysters by the half-dozen with a beer at the bar for the budget conscious or less hungry.

**Miss Pearl's Jam House**, 601 Eddy St at Polk (☎775-5267). The cooking may be Caribbean but the experience in this Tenderloin joint is definitely Californian. Run in conjunction with the *Phoenix* hotel that shares the site (see p.365), *Miss Pearl's* is full of muso types who enjoy the nightly live reggae and downhome atmosphere. Seated at the tables surrounding the pool, you feel as though you're having a resort holiday in the middle of town. The menu, particularly the fish, is outstanding and not bank-breaking. Highly recommended. See also "Live music".

**Moose's**, 1652 Stockton St at Filbert (☎987-7800). Run by the former proprietors of the *Washington Square Bar & Grill*, who have taken many of their old clients and become the latest word in power lunching for the media-politico crowd. Headphone-clad chefs (another gimmick) cook great food from the open kitchen. See also "Drinking: bars and cafés".

**Original Joe's**, 144 Taylor St at Eddy (☎775-4877). Inexpensive American/Italian restaurant, good for steaks, ribs, salads and the like.

**Patio Café**, 531 Castro St at 18th (☎621-4640). Casual terrace restaurant serving wholesome grills and pastas, and good-value weekend brunches where you can sling back inexpensive cocktails.

**Plump Jack**, 3127 Fillmore St at Filbert (☎563-4755). Good American grill-type food and great drinks, but the main reason to come here is to watch the sleek Pacific Heights matrons eyeing up the wealthy youngsters from the Marina.

**Postrio**, 545 Post St at Mason (☎776-7825). Everybody's favourite top-notch San Francisco restaurant – come for breakfast if you can't score a dinner reservation – thanks to the high-style ambience and five-star reputation of chef Wolfgang Puck serving up Californian dishes with Asian and Mediterranean influences.

**Slow Club**, 2501 Mariposa St, Potrero Hill (☎241-9390). Good, reasonably priced imaginative cooking and a very artsy crowd who come to listen to the live jazz at this venerable SoMa hangout.

**Stars**, 555 Golden Gate Ave at Van Ness (☎861-7827). See and be seen home of the rich and powerful, the food is indisputably good but not within the price range of most mortals. Best to sit at the bar with a martini and some oysters watching San Francisco society glide by.

**Swan's Oyster Depot**, 1517 Polk St at California (☎673-1101). You wouldn't know it by the simple decor, but this is one of the city's best and oldest seafood places – take a seat at the bar (there are no tables) for half a dozen fresh-shucked West Coast oysters, washed down with a glass of ice-cold *Anchor Steam* beer. Open 8.30am–5.30pm.

**Tadich's**, 240 California St at Battery (☎391-2373). The oldest restaurant in California, wood panelling and very much a San Francisco institution. Grilled fresh seafood and excellent desserts.

**Vertigo**, 600 Montgomery St at Washington (☎433-7520). The food is Italian/French/Asian (very Californian) and the service is uppity. Built in the base of the Transamerica Pyramid, the interior of the restaurant is more exciting than the expensive grub. Good place to spy smug Financial District types from the safe distance of the excellent bar.

**Washington Square Bar and Grill**, 1707 Powell St at Union (☎982-8123). It may have lost a little of its cachet since the owners sold it and opened *Moose's* across the square (see above), but this is still the place to sip smart cocktails at the bar and sample the food, cooked to rich and heavy perfection. If you want to catch the corner of San Francisco society that still smokes and drinks, this is your scene. See also "Drinking: bars and cafés".

**Zuni Café**, 1658 Market St at Gough (☎552-2522). Despite the often snotty servicee and unprepossessing location on Market Street, Zuni has remained a chic place to be seen for the last five years, simply because the food is so damned good. Californian *nouvelle cuisine* for around $30 a head with a glass of wine.

## Italian

**Calzone's**, 430 Columbus Ave at Broadway (☎397-3600). Busy bar and restaurant right at the heart of North Beach, serving lush pizzas and calzone.

**Capp's Corner**, 1600 Powell St at Union (☎989-2589). Funky, family-style restaurant, where fashionable clients line up for the big portions.

**Enoteca Lanzone**, Opera Plaza, 601 Van Ness St, Civic Center (☎928-0400). A favourite with opera-goers, where the menu may be priced beyond most budgets, but the "Grappa Room" offers 140 different varieties of the stuff.

**Fior d'Italia**, 601 Union St at Powell (☎986-1886). This is the place to go when you're fed up with fancy new-age Italian cooking and posturing and you just want the real thing. Great old-timer scene going on at the bar.

**Frascati**, 1901 Hyde St at Green (☎928-1406). Attractive Russian Hill venue for delicious pastas and seafood.

**Golden Boy**, 542 Grant Ave at Columbus (☎982-9738). Good venue to sample exotic pizza by the slice. Mix'n'match your flavours.

**Gold Spike**, 527 Columbus Ave at Vallejo (☎986-9747). More like a museum than a restaurant with enough photographs, mooseheads and war souvenirs to keep you occupied during what can be a long wait for the excellent-value $15 six-course dinner.

**Green Valley Restaurant**, 510 Green St (☎788-9384). Good, hearty meals in a basic but busy place full of North Beach families and birthday celebrants. Eat till you drop for around $12.

**Il Pollaio**, 555 Columbus Ave at Green (☎362-7727). You'd be hard pushed to spend more than $15 for a blow-out meal in this postage stamp restaurant, where sheer value for money more than makes up for the lack of elbow room.

**Kuleto's**, 221 Powell St at O'Farrell (☎397-7720). Action packed downtown hangout with modern Italian cuisine and a very inviting bar. The interior design of this restaurant has won awards. If you're into that kind of thing.

**Little Joe's**, 523 Broadway at Montgomery (☎433-4343). There's always a line, but the inexpensive, enormous portions of well-cooked food in this North Beach institution are well worth waiting for.

**Noe Valley Pizza**, 3898 24th St at Sanchez (☎647-1664). If you love garlic, this is your place – every pizza is loaded with it.

**North Beach Pizza**, 1499 Grant Ave at Union (☎433-2444). Good location in the middle of one of the best bar-hopping areas in the city. Tasty and low priced, it's just the ticket for a drink-induced munchie.

**Ristorante Ecco**, 101 South Park, between Second and Third, Bryant and Brannan (☎495-3291). Robust, imaginative modern cuisine served in this modern SoMa trattoria. Very nice.

**The Stinking Rose**, 325 Columbus Ave at Broadway (☎781-7673). Subtitled "A Garlic Restaurant", and they're not kidding: *everything* they serve is steeped in the stuff.

**Vicolo Pizza**, 20 Ivy off Franklin at Market (☎863-2382). You have probably never eaten pizza as good as this and are unlikely to want to have any other kind afterwards. Popular Hayes Valley venue.

## French

**Boulevard**, 1 Mission St at Steuart (☎543-6084). When you want great French food without the attitude, look no further than this beautiful new brasserie-style restaurant that currently has a waiting list for tables in the happening Embarcadero district. Book in advance.

**Café Claude**, 7 Claude Lane, between Grant and Kearny (☎981-5565). More than any of the other imitations in town, this one feels like Paris with its great old furnishings. Go in the evening to find a young, loose crowd listening to jazz and getting dinner for around $20.

**Ernie's**, 847 Montgomery St (☎397-5969). Downtown favourite that's far from inexpensive, but has a *haute cuisine* menu and a lovely Victorian interior made famous by its role in Hitchcock's *Vertigo*. Dinner for two costs around $100, but the $15 *prix-fixe* three-course lunches are the city's best budget gourmet treat.

**Julius' Castle**, 1541 Montgomery St at Telegraph Hill (☎392-2222). A San Francisco institution for lovers, or just lovers of the romantic, this Telegraph Hill restaurant serves pretty pricey, if delicious food, but hopefully the incredible view of the San Francisco Bay will keep your eyes off the bill.

**Le Charm**, 315 Fifth St at Molsom (☎546-6128). This is more like it.. Good, unpretentious French food in this SoMa bistro ideally placed for the new museums and arts centres. You can park, too.

**South Park Café**, 108 South Park (☎495-7275). Chic SoMa gathering place for aficionados of all things French, especially pastries and good brandy. See also "Drinking: bars and cafés".

## Chinese, Thai and Indonesian

**Bangkok 16**, 3214 16th St (☎431-5838). Moderately priced Thai restaurant down in the Mission, with a great selection for vegetarians. For meat eaters they do a mean lamb satay.

**Brandy Ho's Original Hunan**, 217 Columbus Ave at Jackson (☎788-7527). Excellent, long-established Hunan restaurant. There's another newer branch at 450 Broadway.

**Basil Restaurant and Bar**, 1175 Folsom St (☎546-9711). When you want ethnic food with a white atmosphere, this is the place. Simple, exquisite Thai dishes served in this quiet, classy SoMa restaurant.

**Borobudor**, 700 Post St at Jones (☎775-1512). A little pocket of authentic Indonesia just a couple of blocks from Union Square. Eat early if you want to avoid the karaoke.

**Cloisonne**, 601 Van Ness Ave, downtown (☎441-2232). First-class Cantonese food, moderately priced and served in luxurious surroundings. Most customers are off to the opera, so it tends to be quite formal. You won't be refused if you turn up in jeans, but you might feel out of place.

**Eliza's**, 205 Oak (☎621-4819). Not your average Chinese dive, this place is all stained glass and fresh flowers, serving excellent Chinese food to a knowing Hayes Valley crowd.

**Empress of China**, 838 Grant Ave at Clay (☎434-1345). Without doubt, the poshest place in town to get to grips with Chinese cooking, with an incredible selection of dishes and amazing views over neighbouring North Beach. You'll be lucky to pay less than $20 for a main course.

**House of Nanking**, 919 Kearny St (☎421-1429). Arguably the best Chinese restaurant in the city, you will have to wait ages for a table and not mind being cramped when you get one. Don't expect decor, just good food – a classic Chinatown dive.

**Harbor Village**, 4 Embarcadero Center at Battery ☎781-8833). Downtown's best dim sum, especially popular for Sunday lunch, with standard Cantonese dishes for dinner.

**Manora's Thai Cuisine**, 1600 Folsom St at 12th (☎861-6224). Massively popular SoMa hangout, you may have to wait, but it's worth it for the light, spicy and fragrant dishes at around $6–10 each. Also a branch in the Mission at 3226 Mission (☎550-0856)

**New Asia**, 722 Pacific Ave at Grant (☎391-6666). Considering Chinatown is so pressed for space, it's amazing that a place this big survives. It serves some of the most authentic dim sum in town, with waitresses pushing carts down the aisles, shouting out their wares as they pass.

**The Pot Sticker**, 150 Waverly Place, off Clay St between Stockton & Grant (☎397-9985). Extensive menu offering Szechuan and Hunan dishes in this inexpensive and often crowded Chinatown favourite.

**Sam Woh's**, 813 Washington St at Grant (☎982-0596). Basic late-night (until 3am) restaurant that attracts the North Beach crowds when the bars turn out. You have to climb dodgy old steps through the kitchen to reach the eating area.

**Taiwan Restaurant,** 445 Clement St (☎387-1789). Stellar Chinese grub in this quick, efficient and inexpensive Richmond favourite.

**Thai Stick,** 698 Post St at Jones (☎928-7730). Popular downtown Thai hangout that offers a wide selection of vegetarian dishes and promises that everything is made without MSG.

**Thep Phanom Restaurant**, 400 Waller St at Fillmore (☎431-2526). Simple, delicate decor and beautifully prepared Thai dishes make this Lower Haight restaurant seem more expensive than it really is. You'll pay no more than $8 for main course dishes, but you'll have to wait in line.

**Tommy Toy's Cuisine Chinoise**, 655 Montgomery St at Columbus (☎397-4888). Without rival the most elegant Chinese restaurant in San Francisco. Exotic variations on Cantonese favourites, prepared with a *nouvelle* emphasis on ultra-fresh ingredients and served in a spacious candle-lit room, make for an enchanting dining experience.

## Japanese and Korean

**Benkay**, *Hotel Nikko,* 222 Mason St (☎394-1111). Hi-tech, minimal and ultra-modern, *Benkay* is the Jean-Paul Gaultier of the restaurant biz, in a plush location downtown. The theme is *Kaiseki*, a succession of many exquisite courses served by kimono-clad waitresses. If you've got around $100 to blow on dinner for two, you'll love it.

**Ebisu**, 1283 Ninth Ave at Irving (☎566-1770). Rated as one of the top sushi bars in town, the fish is fresh and the queue for a seat at the 18-seat sushi bar can be long. Go early to this favourite Richmond restaurant.

**Ma Tante Sumi**, 4243 18th St at Douglass (☎552-6663). Interesting one this: Japanese with a French twist, producing innovative combinations of dishes ranging from the very light to the incredibly rich. A popular Castro dining spot.

**Mifune**, 1737 Post St at Webster (☎922-0337). Moderately priced Japanese specialities to take away.

**Moshi Moshi**, 2092 Third St (☎861-8285). Obscure SoMa restaurant full of people who pride themselves on finding such an out-of-the-way gem. Excellent Japanese, sushi and seafood, moderately priced.

**Silver Moon**, 2301 Clement St (☎386-7852). Light seafood and vegetarian Japanese dishes.

**Sushi Bar**, 1800 Divisadero at Bush (no phone). Bright, inexpensive and quick.

**Sushi Boat Restaurant**, 389 Geary Blvd (☎781-5111). Perfect for those who can't resist a gimmick, this place will make your sushi and then float it over to you on a little boat. Hours of fun for the kids, if you can find any that'll eat sushi.

**Yoshida Ya**, 2909 Webster St at California (☎346-3431). San Francisco has countless sushi bars, but few where you can actually kick off your shoes and eat at low tables on futoned floors. This is just such a place; expect to pay around $25 per head for a good selection of sushi and a few drinks.

## Indian

**Appam**, 1261 Folsom St at Ninth (☎626-2798). Indian food with a mild, modern slant in this stylish SoMa restaurant. Great atmosphere, and the old Indian method of "Dum Pukht" cooking is employed. Dishes are prepared in large clay pots in an open kitchen where you can watch as nan breads and kulchas bake in the tandoori oven.

**Gaylord**, Ghirardelli Square, 900 North Point at Larkin, Fisherman's Wharf (☎771-8822). One of the very few Indian restaurants in San Francisco and probably the best, though you should expect to pay around $20 for a main course. Still, it's worth it if you're dying for a curry.

**Maharani**, 1122 Post St at Van Ness (☎775-1988). Voted one of the top ten restaurants in the US by the Academy of Restaurant Sciences (whoever the hell they are), this is indeed an intimate place to eat delicious food from traditional low-seated alcoves. For the romantic curry lover.

**Scenic India**, 532 Valencia St at 16th (☎621-7226). Spartan Mission restaurant that serves inexpensive Indian food. Part of the new wave of Valencia Corridor restaurants that is doing so much for the area.

**Sirtaj India Cuisine**, 48 Fifth St (☎957-0140). Quiet retreat from the madness of the surrounding SoMa area, this is a lovely place to stop for the bargain 13-course buffet lunch for only $6.99.

**Zante's**, 3489 Mission (☎821-3949). This is a weird one, an Indian restaurant that serves pizza – surprisingly tasty.

## Vegetarian

**Amazing Grace**, 216 Church St at Market (☎626-6411). Rated highly by local vegetarians, with a standard menu starting at around $5 a dish.

**Green's**, Building A, Fort Mason Center, Fort Mason (☎771-6222). A converted army supply warehouse that's now San Francisco's only Zen Buddhist restaurant, serving unusual and delicious macrobiotic and vegetarian food to an eager clientele. Always busy, despite average cost of $40 per head.

**Millennium**, 246 McAllister St at Larkin (☎487-9800). You'd swear it couldn't be done, but this restaurant has managed to make delicious meals for vegans – sugar, dairy, cholesterol and everything else you can think of-free. Stylish un-vegetarian decor. Meat-eaters go and be amazed.

**Now and Zen**, 1826 Buchanan St at Sutter (☎922-9696). Cosy vegan restaurant in Japantown that serves excellent food, but steer clear of the organic wine.

**Real Good Karma**, 501 Dolores St at 18th (☎621-4112). Hearty and nutritious portions of vegetarian and wholefood dishes in informal surroundings.

**Val 21**, 995 Valencia St at 21st (☎821-6622). Vegetarian and wholefood finally becomes trendy in this modern Mission hotspot. New York atmosphere with high ceilings and an avant-garde crowd.

## Greek and Middle Eastern

**The Golden Turtle**, 2211 Van Ness Ave at Vallejo (☎441-4419). Though primarily a Vietnamese restaurant, this Russian Hill venue serves up an extensive selection of kebabs and other Middle Eastern dishes, all of which cost under $10.

**Helmand**, 430 Broadway at Montgomery (☎362-0641). Excellent, inexpensive Afghani food. Exotic, unique and very popular.

**Mamounia**, 441 Balboa St at Fifth (☎752-6565). Eat Moroccan food with your fingers and pay through the nose for the privilege. Tastes good though.

**Marraketch**, 419 O'Farrell St at Taylor (☎776-6717). Aromatic Moroccan cuisine and belly dancers to entertain you while you pile it in.

## 24-HOUR EATS

This is just a brief checklist of some of the places that serve food around the clock; for full details of the following, see the appropriate reviews in our listings.

**Bagdad Café**, 2295 Market St (☎621-4434).

**The Brasserie**, *Fairmont Hotel*, 950 Mason St (☎772-5000).

**Orphan Andy's**, 3991 17th St (☎864-9795).

**The Pine Crest**, 401 Geary St (☎885-6407).

**Sparky's Diner**, 240 Church St (☎621-6001).

**Pasha's**, 1516 Broadway at Polk (☎885-4477). An extraordinary dining experience. Moroccan and Middle Eastern dishes served while you sit on the floor watching belly dancers gyrate past your table, proffering their cleavage for you to insert dollar bills. Go with a group of rowdy drunks, or not at all.

**Steve the Greek**, 1431 Polk St (no phone). Authentic Greek (including plastic tablecloths) and ultra-low-priced spot close to Civic Center.

**Socca Restaurant**, 5800 Geary Blvd (☎379-6720). Inspired Mediterranean and Middle-Eastern cooking in this smart Richmond restaurant that has comfortable booths and fine bar.

**Yaya Cuisine,** 1220 Ninth Ave at Lincoln (☎566-6966). Romantic, candle-lit Middle-Eastern restaurant near Golden Gate Park, with a Californian twist. Good vegetarian selection and overall excellent value.

## Mexican and South American

**Café do Brasil**, 104 Seventh St at Mission (☎626-6432). Great Brazilian tapas and international cuisine.

**Cadillac Bar,** One Holland Court, off Howard St between Fourth & Fifth (☎543-8226). By the standards of most Mexican restaurants, this one is fairly upmarket, and offers live guitar music to help your burritos go down.

**Café Marimba**, 2317 Chestnut St (☎776-1506). More a scene than a restaurant, though good food is available. This popular Marina hangout has twenty-something varieties of tequila for twentysomethings.

**Cha Cha Cha**, 1801 Haight St at Shrader (☎386-5758). First-rate Carribean/Cuban cuisine served in loud, brightly painted surroundings. Great place for swilling oversized margaritas. Open late and always packed.

**Chava's Mexican Restaurant**, 3248 18th St (☎552-9387). Packed-out Mission favourite that serves good, honest grub. Their huevos rancheros are the perfect hangover cure for Sunday Brunch.

**El Balazo**, 1654 Haight St (☎864-8608). Mexican food, healthy style. Have your burrito filled with prawns, vegetables, tofu and any other unlikely ingredients. Very popular with the Haight-Ashbury crowd who come to listen to the Spanish guitar music and slug back beers.

**Ensenada Restaurant**, 2976 Mission St (☎826-4160). One of the more cheerful looking of the Mission's inexpensive restaurants with Mexican art on the walls and a standard menu with full meals for around $5. Open late with a full gang of guitar-clad men to serenade you.

**Las Guitarras**, 3200 24th St (☎285-2684). Noisy Mexican favoured by the locals. Don't expect a fine dining experience, but you can count on a good hearty dinner.

**La Taqueria**, 2889 Mission St at 25th (☎285-7117). Always busy with locals, which is as good a recommendation as any for its fairly standard Mexican menu. Service is slow, but the food is fresh and delicious.

**Mom's Cooking**, 1192 Geneva St (☎585-7000). Small, crowded place on the fringes of the Mission district. You may have to wait for a table, but it's well worth it for the super-inexpensive fresh Mexican food.

**Roosevelt Tamale Parlor**, 2817 24th St (☎550-9213). For a couple of dollars you couldn't find a better meal in town. Tamales, rice and a beer should set you up for around $6.

**Sweet Heat,** 3324 Steiner (☎474-9191). Healthy Mexican food for a squeamish Marina crowd who are worried about fat and cholesterol.

# Drinking: bars and cafés

Since its lawless, boomtown days, San Francisco has long been thought of as a **drinking** town. However, the city's attitude to alcohol is increasingly going the way of the rest of California, and it is no longer fashionable (or in some circles even acceptable) to drink. Nowadays a faint whiff of sanctimony hovers over the social scene, and San Franciscans are leaving their traditional watering holes in favour of the singles bars of the Nineties, **cafés**. The city is dotted with excellent cafés serving first-rate coffees, teas and soft drinks in addition to beer and wine. More social than utilitarian, people hang out in these generally lively venues to pass time as much as refresh themselves. Other non-drinkers looking for social alternatives to bars are opting for the old English tradition of **afternoon tea** (see p.401). So far it has only taken root in the big hotels, but neighbourhood cafés are catching on fast.

If you do want to drink alcohol, however, it's still true that the city's huge array of **bars**, from seedy late-night dives to rooftop piano lounges with glittering views, can be one of its real pleasures. Though spread fairly evenly over the city, they are particularly numerous in North Beach, the Haight, SoMa and the Mission, with the former – where they literally line up one after the other – being your best bet for serious bar-hopping. As for style, on the whole San Francisco bars are rough-hewn, informal affairs, with the slicker places concentrated around the downtown area and in the Financial District. Most of them are open mid-morning and close around 2am, with after-hours drinking (once a standard feature of the small neighbourhood bar) becoming increasingly uncommon.

Unsurprisingly, the city has many specifically **gay bars** (see below), most plentifully in the Castro – although few bars are at all threatening for either gay men or lesbians, or women on their own.

### Downtown bars

**The Big Four**, *Huntington Hotel*, 1075 California St at Taylor. Classy hotel bar, aimed squarely at the sedate set who want a well-made drink in civilized surroundings.

**Gordon Biersch Brewery**, 2 Harrison St at Embarcadero. Bayfront microbrewery housed in converted Hills Brothers coffee warehouse. Good bar food and some of the best beers in San Francisco bring out downtown's overpaid twentysomethings.

**Harry Denton's**, 161 Steuart St at Howard. For the after-work Financial District crowd, this is San Francisco's prime place to cruise and be cruised. Fortunately, the fully stocked bar has enough rare

---

### ROOFTOP BARS

**Carnelian Room**, 555 California St at Kearny. The best of the rooftop cocktail lounges, 52 floors up in the Bank of America Building. A truly elegant spot for some smart cocktails; bring smart money.

**Equinox**, *Hyatt Regency*, The Embarcadero. Good for the novelty value only, this rooftop cocktail lounge attracts crowds of tourists who ascend its dizzy spires just to look at the views. The whole thing revolves, so you get a 360° view of the city without ever leaving your seat. Serious drinkers wouldn't be caught dead in here – have a drink, revolve and leave.

**Harry Denton's Starlight Roof**, *Sir Francis Drake Hotel*, 450 Powell St at Sutter. Dress up and drink martinis. This is a sophisticated grown-up scene with a moneyed crowd who come for the live jazz.

**Top of the Mark**, *Mark Hopkins Hotel*, California St at Mason. The most famous of the rooftop bars, its reputation surpasses the actual experience of drinking up here, and generally it only attracts tourists and hotel guests who can't be bothered to find anywhere else.

bourbons and West Coast microbrews to make whiling away an evening very pleasant indeed, even if you're not on the prowl. Great interior.

**Li Po's Bar**, 916 Grant Ave at Jackson. Named after the Chinese poet, *Li Po's* is something of a literary hang-out among the Chinatown regulars. Enter through the false cavern front and sit at the very dimly lit bar where Wayne Wang filmed *Chang is Missing*.

**The London Wine Bar**, 415 Sansome St at Sacramento. Dubiously tagged as "America's first wine bar", this place is a suitably pretentious and expensive locale for the Financial District clones that flock here after work. Open Mon–Fri until 9pm.

**Pied Piper Bar at Maxfields**, *Sheraton Palace Hotel*, 639 Market St. Part of a glamorous old-world hotel, this bar is famous for Maxfield Parish's *Pied Piper* painting that hangs over the bar.

**Royal Exchange**, 301 Sacramento St (☎956-1710). The consummate Financial District after-work hangout for the pretty people.

**Tonga Room**, *Fairmont Hotel*, Powell and Mason streets. Outrageously lavish Polynesian theme bar with waitresses in grass skirts, a native-laden raft floating around the room, and expensive cocktails. Fun if you like the joke and are in the mood for camp hilarity. See also "Live music".

## North Beach and the Northern Waterfront bars

**Balboa Café**, 3199 Fillmore St at Greenwich. A favourite with the young upmarket singles of the Marina. Very good food, too.

**Curtain Call**, 1980 Union St. Quiet, relaxed piano bar. Not the place for rowdy partying.

**Harry's**, 2020 Fillmore St. A bona fide saloon, this elegantly decorated hangout serves a mixed, unpretentious crowd and makes for a great night's drinking.

**Lost & Found Saloon**, 1353 Grant Ave. North Beach's most enticing dive, where your outfit doesn't matter. Live music usually means the place starts rocking around midnight.

**Paragon**, 3251 Scott St at Francisco. Slick Marina supper club that's more about the music and drinking than eating, though that too is tasty and inexpensive. Nightly jazz and a smooth crowd. Recommended.

**Perry's**, 1944 Union St at Buchanan. Sophisticated meat market, featured in Armistead Maupin's *Tales of the City* as the quintessential breeder bar.

**The Saloon**, 1232 Grant Ave at Vallejo. This bar has stood for over a hundred years and seen use as a whorehouse and Prohibition speakeasy. Today the old structure creaks nightly as blues bands and crowds of enthusiastic dancers do their thing.

**San Francisco Brewing Co**, 155 Columbus Ave at Pacific. A must for beer fans who tire quickly of the insipid American variety, this North Beach hang-out makes its own full-flavoured brews on the premises.

**Savoy Tivoli**, 1434 Grant Ave at Green. Without a doubt, this place is North Beach's most attractively decorated and populated bar, also serving good, reasonably priced food – although the emphasis is definitely on liquid enjoyment.

**Spec's**, 12 Adler St. Long-standing North Beach bar where a jocular drinking crowd enjoy their cocktails by the shaker. Particularly handy for women drinking alone: the barman will hand a card which reads "Sir, the lady is not interested in your company" to anyone who hassles you. A most civilized place to get ploughed.

**Tosca Café**, 242 Columbus Ave at Broadway. The theme here is opera, in time-worn but still stylish surroundings. Mingle with media people at the bar or slump into a comfy red leather booth and try to talk above the sound-level of the arias.

**Vesuvio's**, 255 Columbus Ave at Broadway. Legendary North Beach Beat haunt in the 1950s, and still catering to an arty but friendly crowd who prop up the bar, into the small hours. Next to *City Lights Bookstore*, it's a good place to peruse your new purchases over a drink.

**Washington Square Bar & Grill**, 1707 Powell St at Union. Primarily a restaurant, but worth checking out for the great bar and the chance to spy on the media and literary crowd who have made this their second home. Some of the thunder has been stolen by *Moose's* across the square, but regulars still flock.

## Bars in Civic Center, SoMa and the Mission

**Brain Wash Laundromat/Café**, 1122 Folsom St at Seventh. Great idea – a café/bar and laundromat where you can have breakfast or a beer while you do your washing. Needless to say it's popular with the young and novelty-conscious. See also "Eating".

**Café Babar**, 994 Guerrero St at 22nd. Hip hang-out in the Mission with pool tables and a young, alternative crowd.

**Café du Nord**, 2170 Market St. A quiet neighbourhood restaurant for years, this has recently become hyper-hip since it started its programme of nightly cabaret and jazz on Wed, reviving the old tradition of supper clubs. Quite the place for dinner and drinks, though it's OK just to have a beer at the bar if the budget won't stretch. See also "Live music".

**The Dovre Club**, 3541 18th St at Guerrero. Solid Irish bar, full of Gaelic charmers.

**El Rio**, 3158 Mission St at Army. When it isn't staging one of its specials (salsa on Sun, funk on Wed and world music on Fri), this is a great place for a quiet drink and a game on one of San Francisco's most handsome pool tables.

**Julie's Supper Club**, 1123 Folsom St at Seventh. A popular restaurant, but best for sitting at the bar munching good-value Cajun snacks and listening to the free live jazz – if you get in before 9pm, after that it's $5.

**Mission Rock Resort**, 817 China Basin at Mission Rock. Scruffy, blue-collar bar down the old dockyards, great for a cheap beer and views of the bay.

**Paradise Lounge**, 1501 Folsom St. Cleverly constructed on two floors, you can suit your mood with a game of pool and a quiet drink upstairs or dance to live music downstairs. See also "Live music".

**The Ramp**, 855 China Basin (☎621-2378). Way out on the old docks, this is well worth the half-mile trek from downtown (you'll need a car unless you're a seasoned walker) to sit out on the patio and sip beers overlooking the abandoned piers and new boatyards. Free jazz on Sun afternoons.

**Slow Club**, 2501 Mariposa, Protrero Hill. Cool bar and jazz club with an informal neighbourhood feel. Perfect for low-key socializing.

**The Up & Down Club**, 1151 Folsom St at Eighth. One of the city's best jazz venues, this small club split across two floors serves great drinks and draws a lively attractive crowd out for a good time. The fact that it's owned by supermodel Christy Turlington doesn't do it any harm.

**The Uptown**, 200 Capp St at 17th & Mission. Best of the Mission's neighbourhood bars, embracing an eclectic clientele who shoot pool, drink like fiends and fall all over the scruffy leatherette

---

### AFTERNOON TEA

One of the nicest ways to finish an afternoon of intense consuming in the downtown stores is to partake in the latest SF social custom – **afternoon tea** in one of the plush Union Square hotels. In true California style, the food is exquisite, and you'll be offered the gamut from cucumber and watercress sandwiches to fresh fruit sorbets and scones with cream.

**Campton Place**, 340 Stockton St (☎781-5555). Tea served daily in the hotel bar, 2.30–4.30pm. Haunt of the weary shopper.

**Four Seasons Clift Hotel**, 495 Geary St (☎775-4700). A good post-matinee venue in the Theater District. Daily 3–5pm.

**Garden Court** In the *Sheraton Palace*, 2 New Montgomery St at Market (☎392-8600). The best thing about the recent renovation of this landmark hotel was the restoration of its exquisite lobby, where you can sip fine teas while enjoying the soothing live harp music. Make reservations, it fills up. Tues–Sat 2–4.30pm.

**King George Hotel**, 334 Mason St (☎781-5050). A Laura Ashley nightmare, where customers nibble at finger sandwiches in mock-British cottage surroundings. Only for Anglophiles and homesick Brits. Mon–Sat 3–6.30pm.

**Mandarin Oriental**, 222 Sansome St (☎885-0999). This is more like it; cakes galore, under millions of dollars worth of Austrian crystal chandeliers, with soft piano music.

**Mark Hopkins**, 999 California St (☎392-3434). Standard teas served on lovely Wedgwood china. Daily 2.30–5pm.

**Neiman Marcus**, 150 Stockton St (☎362-3900). A personal favourite; tea is served in the glorious *Rotunda* restaurant at the top of the store. Watch the rich social X-rays nibble fearfully at the calorie-laden food. Daily 2.30–5pm

**Ritz-Carlton**, 600 Stockton St (☎296-7465). The fanciest of them all, this is the place to slurp tea to the accompaniment of tinkling harp.

upholstery. Some simply go to watch the ball game on TV. A more bizarre collection of characters would be hard to find. Don't miss it.

## Bars in the Central Neighbourhoods

**Harry's On Fillmore**, 2020 Fillmore St at Clay. Nightly jazz and blues in this laid-back neighbourhood bar where the Western Addition becomes Pacific Heights.

**Hayes & Vine**, 377 Hayes St. Well-decorated, affordable wine bar in the up & coming Hayes Valley district.

**Jack's Bailey Bar**, 26th St at Church. Comfy neighbourhood bar with proper armchairs, where you can really recline into a pint.

**The Mad Dog in the Fog**, 530 Haight St at Steiner. Aptly named by the two lads from Birmingham, England, who own the joint, this is one of the Lower Haight's most loyally patronized bars, with darts, English beer, copies of *The Sun* newspaper and a typical pub menu that includes bangers and mash, hearty ploughman's and the like. Amazingly, it is not the ex-pat English, but the trend-conscious young blades of the Lower Haight who find it so groovy.

**Noc Noc**, 557 Haight St at Steiner. Decorated like an Egyptian tomb. Draws a fashionable but informal young crowd for new wave music and flasks of hot sake.

**The Rat and the Raven**, 4054 24th St at Noe. Friendly, hard-drinking neighbourhood bar with pool, darts and, if you're into country music, a superb jukebox.

## Bars in Golden Gate Park, the beaches and outlying areas

**Blue Danube Coffee House**, 306 Clement St at Third. Café society alive and well in the suburbs? Not quite, but about as alternative as you'll get in the Richmond.

**Boathouse**, 1 Harding Park Avenue (on Lake Merced). Popular sports bar, with a superb view of Lake Merced and occasional live music.

**Last Day Saloon**, 406 Clement St at Fourth. Very lively bar in the Richmond with regular live music including rock, surfer rock, blues and soul. $5 cover.

**Pig & Whistle Pub**, 2801 Geary Blvd at Collins. Good range of English and California microbrews, and the cheapest happy hour in SF – $2 pints of beer 4–7pm daily. Pool table and dartboards, plus very good pub food.

**The Plough and Stars**, 116 Clement St at First. Irish ex-pat bar with live music on alternate evenings.

## Cafés

**Bohemian Cigar Store**, 566 Columbus Ave at Union. Small informal North Beach hangout for sipping coffee or slinging beers.

**Buena Vista Café**, 2765 Hyde St at Beach, Fisherman's Wharf. If you like your coffee with a kick, this is the place for you. Claims to be the home of the world's first Irish coffee, which isn't hard to believe – it's certainly the best in town and the crowds who pack the place are testimony to the generously laced coffee. Good, inexpensive food too, making it a decent stop-off for a sightseeing lunch.

**Café Flor**, 2298 Market St at Noe. Lively, mostly gay café near the Castro serving great breakfasts and lunch till 3pm. A popular cruising spot for the locals who come to string a coffee out for hours and be seen reading the latest in hip gay literature. Drown in a sea of newspapers and pretty faces. See also "Gay and lesbian bars".

**Café La Boheme**, 3138 24th St at Mission. As the name suggests, a badly dressed crowd, but a staggering range of coffees keeps the Mission's caffeine addicts coming from sunrise until late at night.

**Café Picaro**, 3120 16th St at Mission. Very popular, no-frills spot where you can get cheap lunches and browse through the hundreds of books that line the walls. Opposite the *Roxie* movie theater in the Mission.

**Café Roma**, 414 Columbus Ave at Green. Not big on atmosphere, but a quiet spot to read the paper over a coffee, while checking out the classical, cherub-adorned murals and ornate decor.

**Café Trieste**, 601 Vallejo St at Grant. Noisy North Beach Italian café, popular with a serious literary crowd who hang out and listen to the opera classics that boom from the jukebox. Saturday lunchtimes are a treat – the family who run it get up and sing. Get there by noon to get a seat.

**Community Blend Café**, 233 Fillmore St at Haight. Enjoy an excellent breakfast (served all day) or glass of wine in the contrived shabbiness of this Lower Haight gallery-cum-café, where groovy people come to write in their journals.

**Muddy Waters**, 3913 24th St at Valencia and 521 Valencia at 16th. The Mission's young and funky come here to wake up or waste an afternoon. Fashionably scruffy and festooned with newsprint.

**South Park Café**, 108 South Park. Chic SoMa rendezvous, where architects and other creative professionals meet their peers to drink in tasteful surroundings. See also "Eating".

**Steps of Rome,** Columbus at Vallejo. Venerable North Beach late night café where the taxi drivers congregate. If you're looking for caffeine action after midnight, this is your place.

# Nightlife

Compared to Los Angeles, where you need money and attitude in equal amounts, San Francisco's nightlife demands little of either. This is no 24-hour city, and the approach to socializing is often surprisingly low-key, with little of the pandering to fads and fashions that goes on elsewhere. The casualness is contagious, and manifest in a **club scene** that, far as it is from the cutting edge of hip, is encouragingly inexpensive compared to other cities. Thirty dollars can buy you a decent night out, including cover charge, a few drinks and maybe even a taxi home. The **live music** scene is similarly economical – and, frankly, what the city does best: San Franciscans may be relatively unconcerned with fashion, but there are some excellent rock, jazz and folk venues all over town, many entertaining you for no more than the price of a drink.

San Francisco has a great reputation for **opera** and **classical music**. Its orchestra and opera company are among the most highly regarded in the country. **Theatre** is accessible and much less costly, with discount tickets available, but most of the mainstream downtown venues – barring a couple of exceptions – are mediocre, forever staging Broadway reruns, and you'd do better to take some time to explore the infinitely more interesting fringe circuit.

**Cabaret and comedy** are also lively, and **film**, too, is almost as big an obsession as eating in San Francisco, and you may well be surprised by the sheer number of movie theaters – repertory and current release – that flourish in this city.

## Clubbing

Still trading on a reputation for hedonism earned decades ago, San Francisco's **nightclubs** in fact trail light years behind those of other large American cities. That said, the compensations are manifold – no waiting for hours, high cover charges, ridiculously priced drinks or feverish posing. Instead you'll find a diverse range of small to medium-sized, affordable clubs in which leather-clad goths rub shoulders with the bearded and beaded, alongside a number of gay hangouts (listed on p.413) still rocking to the

---

### LISTINGS AND TICKET INFORMATION

Apart from the flyers posted up around town, the *Sunday Chronicle*'s "Pink Pages" supplement is about the best source of **listings** and **what's on information**; you might also check the free weekly *Bay Guardian*, the *San Francisco Weekly*, and a host of other more specific publications listed below under the relevant sections.

For **tickets**, the *Bay Area Seating Service* (*BASS*, ☎776-1999 or 510/762-2277) is the major Bay Area booking agency. You can either reserve with a credit card on these numbers, or in person at one of their many branches in record stores such as *Tower Records* or *Wherehouse*. **Theatre tickets** are also on sale at the *Tix* ticket booth on Union Square; see "Theatre" below for details.

## THREE BABES AND A BUS

One excellent way to get the flavour of San Francisco's clubs when you first arrive is to experience the *Three Babes and a Bus* tour (☎552-2582) of various hot spots around town. For $30, the three women who organize the tours will drag you around on their bus for an evening, visiting clubs and throwing in the odd drink. In between visits there is much carousing and game-playing on board.

sounds of high-energy funk and Motown. You'll find the occasional place which is up to the minute, playing acid jazz, jungle and the like, but what San Francisco does best is all the old favourites – songs you know the words to; clubbing is more of a party than a pose in this city and much the better for it. The greatest concentration of clubs is in **SoMa**, especially the area around 11th Street and Folsom, though the **Mission** is similarly well provided with bars and small live music venues – not to mention a couple of outrageous drag bars – of almost exclusively Latin origin. There are a few places in **North Beach** too, so just pick a neighbourhood and explore.

Unlike most other cities, where the action never gets going until after midnight, many San Francisco clubs have to **close** at 2am during the week, so you can usually be sure of finding things well under way by 11.30pm. At weekends, most places stay open until 3 or 4am. Very few venues operate any kind of restrictive **admission** policy, and only on very busy nights are you likely to have to wait. It's usually entirely acceptable to wander in and out of any club, so long as you have the regulation hand stamp.

### The clubs

**Casanova**, 527 Valencia St at 16th (☎863-9328). Laid-back neighbourhood bar until the sun goes down and the music gets turned up, drawing a fashion-conscious body-pierced Mission crowd. Get in early for Happy Hour, make a night of it and avoid the cover charge.

**Cat's Grill and Alley Club**, 1190 Folsom St at Eighth (☎431-3332). Perfect for the mature clubber, the *Cat's Grill* puts on a bit of entertainment – anything from belly-dancing snake-charmers to women's open mike – to get everybody warmed up, serves a few tapas and then turns the music up for a right good dance.

**Club 181**, 181 Eddy St (☎673-8181). Dreadful location, smack in the vortex of the Tenderloin, but take a cab or valet park and check out one of San Francisco's coolest nightspots, serving food till around 11pm and dancing to acid-jazz, house, funk and soul bands with a very good-time crowd. Highly recommended.

**Club Oz**, *Westin St Francis Hotel*, 335 Powell St (☎956-7777). Sky-line dance room on the 32nd floor of the hotel draws a young dance-crazy crowd. Worth going just for the view.

**Covered Wagon Saloon**, 917 Folsom St (☎974-5906). Definitely one of the better SoMa places – they serve up a very varied menu of different one-nighters, offering everything from hip-hop to Sixties pop.

**DNA Lounge**, 375 11th St at Harrison (☎626-1409). Club which changes its music style nightly but draws the same young hipsters. Large dance floor downstairs and when the dancing gets too much you can lounge around in comfy sofas on the mezzanine. Tues–Sun 9pm–4am; cover $7.

**DV8**, 55 Natoma St between First and Second, Mission and Howard (☎777-1419). Huge, ornate Travolta-style Seventies survivor, this is the closest San Francisco comes to rivalling the big clubs of New York and Los Angeles, decorated by Keith Haring pop-art and playing high-energy funk and house music. It also has a nice members-only bar that's worth bluffing your way into if you can. About the only club in town worth dressing up for. Cover $10. Wed–Sat.

**El Rio**, 3158 Mission St at Army (☎ 282-3325). Latin, jazz and samba are the speciality here, with live salsa bands on Sunday, dancing to modern funk on Friday, in a friendly, anything-goes atmosphere. Open 3pm–2am during the week, and 3pm–6am at weekends.

**The End Up**, or Sixth St at Harrison (☎495-9550). A mostly gay crowd, but recently discovered by the weekend clubbers, and a good place for the hardcore party animal. Open continuously from 6am on Sat morning until 2am Mon. Small cover. See also "Gay and lesbian San Francisco".

**Holy Cow**, 1531 Folsom St at 12th (☎621-6087). Young club fiends try hard to be cool, but a good rave once it warms up. A huge plastic cow hangs outside, you can't miss it. Usually no cover. Tues–Sun.

**Leopard Lounge**, 2125 Lombard St at Fillmore (☎771-2583). Seventies funk and acid jazz djs help the Marina professionals remember the importance of going out and having a good time.

**Nickie's**, 460 Haight St at Fillmore (☎621-6058). Varied menu of music styles keeps this small Lower-Haight joint rocking.

**Palladium**, 1031 Kearny St at Columbus (☎434-1308). Three dance floors, MTV screens and a crowd that can't be persuaded to quit before 6am Fri & Sat. Good old disco-fun.

**Release**, 1015 Folsom St at Sixth (☎337-7457). Another dance club pumping out Seventies nostalgia which seems to have a limitless supply of punters – there's a nice barbeque on the outside patio for when the dancing gets too much.

**Townsend**, 177 Townsend St at Third (☎974-6020). A must for house fans, this place really cranks up the bass and keeps it blaring. Thurs–Sat. Cover $6.

# Live music: rock, jazz and folk

San Francisco's **music scene** reflects the character of the city as a whole: laid back, eclectic, and not a little nostalgic. The options for catching **live music** are wide and the scene is consistently progressive, characterized by the frequent emergence of good young bands. However, San Francisco has never recaptured its crucial Sixties role, and these days is principally renowned as a venue for good r'n'b, psychedelia, folk and rock standards, as well as country and western and Latin American bands. **Jazz** is very good and not just confined to the city proper: the East Bay in particular is very strong on jazz/funk/blues bands.

**Bands** are extremely easy to catch. Many restaurants offer live music, so you can eat, drink and dance all at once and often with no cover charge; ordinary neighbourhood bars regularly host groups, often for free, and there are any number of good and inexpensive small venues, spread out across the city. Few fall into any particular camp, with most varying their bill throughout the week, and it can be hard to specify which of them cater to a certain music style. Many also double as clubs, hosting some kind of disco after the live music has stopped.

What follows is a pretty comprehensive list of established venues, but be sure to check the music press, the best of which is the free *BAM* (*Bay Area Music*). Available in most record stores, it carries exhaustive listings of events in the city and Bay Area as a whole.

## The large performance venues

Although San Francisco has a couple of major-league concert halls, bear in mind that some of the Bay Area's best large-scale venues, where the big names tend to play, are actually across the bay in Oakland and Berkeley. See the relevant listings later in this chapter.

**Great American Music Hall**, 859 O'Farrell St at Polk (☎885-0750). Civic Center venue, too small for major names but too large for local yokels, and hosting a range of musical styles from balladeers to thrash bands. The lovely interior – it used to be a burlesque house and upscale bordello – makes for a great night out.

**The Warfield**, 982 Market St at Sixth (☎775-7722). *The Warfield* can usually be relied upon to stage major rock crowd-pullers. Chart bands, big-name indie groups and popular old-timers keep the place packed.

## Rock, folk and country

**Albion**, 3139 16th St at Valencia (☎552-8558). Primarily just a simple Mission neighbourhood bar, which occasionally hosts local bands on its tiny stage. Small, inexpensive and intimate, it's ideal for a night out on the cheap. No cover.

**Hotel Utah**, 500 Fourth St at Bryant (☎421-8308). Good selection of mainly country bands which you can usually see for free or a very small cover.

**Lost and Found Saloon**, 1353 Grant Ave at Columbus (☎397-3751). Informal North Beach hangout with a catch-all selection of music styles.

**Lou's**, 300 Jefferson St at Taylor (☎771-0377). Country/rock and blues bar on Fisherman's Wharf that hosts good local bands. Weekend lunchtimes are a good time to check out the lesser-knowns in relative peace. Come nightfall it's madness. No cover before 9pm. See also "Eating".

**Nightbreak**, 1821 Haight St at Shrader (☎221-9008). Slightly shabby, small Haight venue where new wave and Goth bands play to a matching crowd. Very dark, very loud, and very crowded.

**Paradise Lounge**, 1501 Folsom St at 11th (☎861-6906). Good SoMa venue to see up-and-coming rock bands (usually three per night), or take a break for a game of pool upstairs.

**Plough and Stars**, 116 Clement St (☎751-1122). In Richmond, this is quite a way from downtown but worth the trip if you're into Irish folk music. Very much the haunt of the Irish ex-pat community.

**Purple Onion**, 140 Columbus Ave at Broadway (☎398-8415). Established North Beach venue for hearing a good selection of rock and country

**Saloon**, 1232 Grant St at Columbus (☎397-3751). Always packed to the gills, this is undeniably North Beach's best spot for some rowdy R&B.

## Jazz and Latin American

**Bahia Cabana**, 1600 Market St at Franklin (☎861-8657). Lively bar and supper club with good Brazilian and samba bands – attracts a skilled dancing crowd who can shake it with a vengeance. 21 and over only. Live music and dj dancing seven nights a week.

**Bimbo's 365 Club**, 1025 Columbus Ave at Chestnut (☎474-0365). Varied menu of music styles from jazz to ska, always something worth seeing on the weekly bill.

**Blondie's Bar & No Grill**, 540 Valencia St at 16th (☎864-2419). One of the reasons the Mission is such an up-and-coming nightlife area. The varied menu of music and entertainment pulls a fashionable, good-time crowd.

**Bajone's**, 3140 Mission St (☎648-6641). Unusual – and refreshing – age-mix for San Francisco, ranging from 25 to 65. Excellent Latin jazz nightly. Casual, unpretentious and genuine. $6 cover at weekends.

**Café du Nord**, 2170 Market St at Church (☎861-5016). Excellent, friendly and affordable venue to catch nightly live music while you sample the food on offer or just drink at the bar. Mostly jazz with some mambo and salsa thrown in. Recommended. See also "Drinking: bars and cafés".

**Jack's Bar**, 1601 Fillmore St at Geary (☎567-3227). Small, intimate bar with jazz and blues three nights a week. Open mike comedy night Tues.

**Miss Pearl's Jam House**, 601 Eddy St at Polk (☎775-JAMS). Attached to the super-hip *Phoenix* hotel, this Caribbean restaurant features some great reggae. See also "Eating".

**Paragon**, 3251 Scott St at Francisco (☎922-2456). Smart, cool new Marina venue for a fashion-conscious crowd who come to enjoy the nightly jazz, jazz fusion, funk and soul. Recommended.

**Pasand Lounge**, 1875 Union St at Laguna (☎922-4498). Unusual club where you can come to eat Indian food and listen to very mellow jazz in the comfortable lounge.

**The Plush Room**, *York Hotel*, 940 Sutter St at Hyde (☎885-2800). Newly revived San Francisco institution, which has successfully recreated its former glory and on a good night attracts a very glamorous crowd. Tickets around $20; 21 and over only.

**The Rite Spot Café**, 2099 Folsom St (☎552-6066). Informal, café-style club with jazz and R&B bands. Open Mon–Sat, serving snacks, drinks and coffee until 1am. Small cover at weekends.

**Slim's**, 333 11th St at Folsom (☎621-3330). Slick but reliable showcase for internationally known bands. Not cheap, but a better class of jazz act and a grown-up crowd.

**The Tonga Room**, *Fairmont Hotel*, 950 Mason St at Powell (☎772-5000). An absolute must for fans of the ludicrous, or just the very drunk. The whole place is decked out as a Polynesian village, complete with pond and simulated rainstorms, and a grass-skirted band play terrible jazz and pop covers on a raft in the middle of the water. See also "Drinking: bars and cafés".

# Classical music, opera and dance

Though the San Francisco arts scene has to fight against a reputation for provincialism, this is the only city on the West Coast to boast its own professional **symphony** orchestra, **ballet** and **opera** companies, each of which has a thriving upper-crust social suppor scene, wining and dining its way through fund-raisers and the like. During the summer months, look out for the **free concerts in Stern Grove** (at 19th Avenue and Sloat Boulevard) where the symphony orchestra, opera and ballet give open-air performances for ten successive Sundays (starting in June). Both the ballet and the opera venues are closed for essential engineering work until the beginning of the 1997 season and will be performing at temporary venues around the city. Call for details or check the newspaper listings for where and when.

## Concert halls

**Louise M Davies Symphony Hall**, 201 Van Ness Ave at Hayes (☎431-5400). The permanent home of the San Francisco Symphony Orchestra, which offers a year-round season of classical music and sometimes performances by other, often offbeat musical and touring groups. Established in 1909 as a small musical group, the orchestra rose to international prominence in the 1950s when it started touring and recording. Although not quite on par with the New York Philharmonic or Chicago Symphony, they're not far behind and certainly among the top half-dozen US orchestras. Recently they have spent much time in the recording studio with their Danish maestro, Herbert Blomstedt, receiving acclaim for many of their performances, such as the award-winning cycle of Nielsen symphonies. Prices obviously depend on the performance, but are marginally lower than either the opera or ballet, with the least expensive seats going for around $20.

**War Memorial Opera House**, 301 Van Ness Ave at Grove (ticket and schedule information ☎864-3330). A night at the opera in San Francisco is no small-time affair. The Opera House, designed by architect Arthur Brown Jr, the creator of City Hall and Coit Tower, makes a very opulent venue for the San Francisco Opera Association which has been performing here since the building opened in 1932 By far the strongest of San Francisco's cultural trio, the Opera Association has won critical acclaim for its performances of the classics as well as lesser known Russian works that other companies prefer not to tackle. The SF Opera carries considerable international weight and pulls in big names like Placido Domingo and Kiri Te Kanawa on a regular basis. Its main season runs from the end of September for 13 weeks, and its opening night is one of the principal social events on the West Coast. Sporadically, they also have a summer season during June and July. Tickets cost upwards of $40 – for which you do at least get supertitles with the foreign-language operas. **Standing room** costs a bargain $8, and 300 tickets are available (one per person) at 10.30am on the day of performance.

**The San Francisco Ballet**, 455 Franklin at Fulton (☎861-5600). The city's ballet company, the oldest and third largest in the US, puts on an ambitious annual six-month (Jan–June) programme of both classical and contemporary dance. Founded in 1933, the ballet was the first American company to stage full-length productions of *Swan Lake* and *Nutcracker*. They've won Emmys, broadcast, toured and generally earned themselves a reputation for ambition: overreaching themselves drove them toward bankruptcy in the 1970s and they seemed to be sliding until 1985, when the Icelandic Helgi Tomasson, "premier danseur" of the New York City Ballet, stepped in as artistic director. Since his appointment, the company can seem to do no wrong and some proud San Franciscans consider it "America's premier ballet company". Critical opinion hasn't quite concurred as yet, but the tickets (which cost upwards of $30) are by no means overpriced.

# Theatre

The majority of the city's **theatres** congregate downtown around the Theater District. Most aren't especially innovative (although a handful of more inventive fringe places are scattered in other parts of town, notably SoMa), but tickets are reasonably inexpensive – up to $30 a seat – and there's usually good availability.

Tickets can be bought direct from the theatre box offices, or, using a credit card, through *BASS* (☎776-1999 or 510/762-2277). The *Tix Bay Area* ticket booth on the Stockton Street side of Union Square regularly has last-minute tickets for as much as half off the marked price (Mon–Sat 11am–6pm; ☎433-7717).

## Downtown

**American Conservatory Theater**, 415 Geary St (☎749-2ACT). San Francisco's flagship theatre company, whose building recently re-opened after earthquake damage. The company performs a season of eight classic and contemporary plays, with a lot of Shakespeare.

**Golden Gate Theater**, 1 Taylor St at Market (☎474-3800). Originally constructed during the 1920s and recently restored to its former splendour, the *Golden Gate* is San Francisco's most elegant theatre, with marble flooring, rococo ceilings and gilt trimmings. It's a pity that the programmes don't live up to the surroundings – generally a mainstream diet of Broadway musicals on their latest rerun, although they occasionally manage to pull a big name out of the bag for a one-man Vegas-type show.

**Lorraine Hansberry Theater**, 620 Sutter St at Mason (☎474-8800). Radical young group of black performers whose work covers traditional theatre as well as more contemporary political pieces and jazz/blues musical reviews. Impressive.

**The Orpheum**, 1192 Market St at Eighth (☎474-3800). Showtime, song and dance performances and "light" cabaret-style theatre.

**Stage Door Theater**, 420 Mason St at Post (☎749-2228). Attractive, medium-sized turn-of-the-century theatre, run by the *American Conservatory Theater* group.

**Theatre On The Square**, 450 Post St at Mason (☎433-9500). Converted Gothic theatre with drama, musicals, comedy and mainstream theatre pieces.

### Elsewhere

**Beach Blanket Babylon Series**, *Club Fugazi Cabaret*, 678 Green St at Powell (☎421-4222). One of the few musts for theatregoers in the city, its formality smacks of a Royal Command Performance, but the shows themselves are zany and fast-paced cabarets of jazz singers, dance routines and comedy, very slickly put together.

**Climate Theater**, 252 Ninth St at Folsom (☎626-9196). Small, reputable SoMa theatre, specializing in fringe/alternative productions. Cheaper and probably a lot more stimulating than some of the downtown efforts.

**Intersection for the Arts**, 446 Valencia St at 16th (☎626-3311). Well-meaning, community-based group that tackles interesting productions in inadequate facilities.

**The Magic Theater**, Fort Mason Center, Building D (☎441-8822). The busiest and largest company after the *ACT*, and probably the most exciting, the *Magic Theater* specializes in the works of contemporary playwrights and emerging new talent; Sam Shepard traditionally premieres his work here.

**Mission Cultural Center**, 2868 Mission St at 24th (☎821-1155). An organization dedicated to preserving and developing Latin culture, staging small but worthy productions using the wealth of talented but underrated performers in San Francisco's Latin community.

**Phoenix Theater**, 301 Eighth St (☎621-4423). Small SoMa playhouse that specializes in readings, one-act plays and sketches.

**Theater Artaud**, 450 Florida St (☎621-7797). Very modern theatre in a converted warehouse that tackles the obscure and abstract; visiting performers, both dance and theatrical. Always something interesting.

**Theater Rhinoceros**, 2926 16th St (☎861-5079). San Francisco's only uniquely gay theatre group, this company, not surprisingly, tackles productions that confront gay issues, as well as lighter, humorous productions.

## Comedy

Comedians have always found a welcoming audience in San Francisco, but in the last few years the alternative **comedy and cabaret scene** has been reborn. Some new, excellent venues have opened, and while many may be smartening up beyond the tastes of some, they will undoubtedly be able to draw bigger names to the city.

Few of the comedians are likely to be familiar: as with any cabaret you take your chances, and whether you consider a particular club to be good will depend on who happens to be playing the week you go. You can expect to pay roughly the same kind of cover in most of the clubs ($7–15), and two-drink minimums are common. There are usually two shows per night, the first kicking off around 8pm and a late show starting at around 11pm. For bargains, check the press for "Open Mike" nights when unknowns and members of the audience get up and have a go; there's rarely a cover charge for these evenings and, even if the acts are diabolical, it can be a fun night out.

## Comedy venues

**Cobbs Comedy Club**, *The Cannery*, 2801 Leavenworth St at Beach (☎563-5157). Small venue, popular on the cabaret circuit, where new performers often get the chance of their first live appearance.

**Coconut Grove**, 1415 Van Ness Ave at Bush (☎776-1616). The cover is a little higher than usual at this venue, but worth it for the plush, spacious interior, grown-up vibe and excellent acts that this classy joint manages to pull in.

**Finocchio's**, 506 Broadway at Kearny (☎982-9388). A San Francisco institution and former Prohibition speakeasy, *Finocchio's* presents a small cast of female impersonators who run through textbook routines, heavy on the sauciness. At one time it was considered outrageous; these days it's more than a little tame, good for cheap laughs and expensive drinks.

**The Improv**, 401 Mason St (☎441-7787). The chain store of the comedy world, with a string of venues in different cities, *The Improv* draws some good established talent and also has an eye for up-and-coming acts. Mon is the least expensive and best night, when guest company *Theater of the Deranged* presents a completely improvised night's entertainment.

**Josie's Cabaret and Juice Joint**, 3583 16th St at Noe (☎861-7933). A good all-rounder offering a mixed menu of cabaret, comedy, live music and dancing.

**Morty's**, 1024 Kearny St (☎986-6678). Old North Beach club that evokes the Lenny Bruce era of comedy. None of the acts are quite up to that standard, but the club itself has a genuine feel that makes it worth the trip.

**The Punch Line**, 444 Battery St at Washington (☎397-7553). Frontrunner of the city's "polished" cabaret venues, this place has an intimate, smoky feel that's ideal for downing expensive cocktails and laughing your head off. The club usually hosts the bigger names in the world of stand-up and is always packed.

## Film

After eating, watching **films** is the next favourite San Francisco pastime. For one thing it's inexpensive (rarely more than $8, sometimes as little as $4), and secondly there's a staggering assortment of current-release and repertory film houses, with programmes that range from the latest general-release films to Hollywood classics, iconoclastic Sixties pieces, and a selection of foreign and art films that's usually as good as (if not better than) most European centres. Film-going in San Francisco is a pleasure: there are rarely lines, and the cinemas are often beautiful Spanish-revival and Art Deco buildings that are in themselves a delight to behold.

### Cinemas

**The Alhambra**, Polk St and Union (☎775-2137). One of the city's grandest movie theatres; a gorgeous, plush, Moorish interior. Shows a mix of current releases and reruns.

**ATA-Artists Television Access**, 992 Valencia St at 21st (☎824-3890). Nonprofit media center that puts on the city's most challenging barrage of film and TV productions, often with a political or psychosexual bent.

**The Castro Theater**, 429 Castro St at Market (☎621-6120). Perhaps San Francisco's most beautiful movie house, offering a steady stream of reruns, Hollywood classics and (best of all) a Wurlitzer organ played between films by a man who rises up from below the stage.

### FILM FESTIVALS

**The San Francisco Film Festival**, specializing in political and short films you wouldn't normally see, is held at various cinemas around the city, but usually centres on the *Kabuki* eight-screen theatre (see below), in the first couple of weeks in May. Tickets sell extremely fast and you'll need to book around four days in advance for all but the most obscure movies. Just as popular is the **Gay and Lesbian Film Festival**, held in June at the *Castro Theater*. If you know you're going to be in town for either, call ahead for programmes by contacting the theatres.

**Kabuki Cinemas**, Post St and Fillmore (☎931-9800). Attractive, modern building in the Japan Center complex, where eight screens show mainly current-release movies.

**The Lumiere**, 1572 California St at Polk (☎885-3200). Another opulent Spanish-revival art house, a bit run-down but often with an interesting programme of obscure art films as well as a select choice of current-release films.

**Pacific Film Archive**, at the *University Art Museum*, Durant Ave, Berkeley (☎510/642-1412). For the serious film fan, this is perhaps the best movie theatre in California, with seasons of contemporary works from around the world plus revivals of otherwise forgotten classics. The cinema is not strictly in San Francisco proper, but across the bay in Berkeley (see p.429).

**The Red Vic**, 1727 Haight St at Cole (☎282-0318). Friendly collective, formerly housed in a room full of ancient couches where you could put your feet up, and now moved to smarter premises up the street. Same idea, though, showing popular reruns and cult films.

**The Roxie**, 3117 16th St at Valencia (☎863-1087). San Francisco's trendiest, independent rep house situated in the heart of the Mission, showing a steady diet of punk, new wave and political movies.

**The Royal**, 1529 Polk St at Sacramento (☎474-0353). Once elegant, now a decaying old theatre looking about a week away from demolition. Varied, innovative programming, though.

**The Strand**, 1127 Market St (☎621-2227). Dark, appropriately scruffy surroundings for cult films and B-movies.

# Gay and lesbian San Francisco

San Francisco's reputation as a city for gay celebration is not new – in fact it could even be outdated. This is still the undoubted gay capital of the world, but despite a high profile, the gay scene hasn't had much to celebrate in the last few years and there's been a definite move from the outrageous to the mainstream. It's unlikely that even AIDS will wipe out the increasing number of gay activists in public office, but it has made them more conservative in approach, if not in policy. The exuberant energy that went into the posturing and parading of the 1970s has taken on a much more sober, down-to-business attitude, and these days you'll find more political activists organizing conferences than drag queens throwing parties.

Certainly, post-AIDS, San Francisco's gay scene is a different way of life altogether. The Seventies were notorious for the bar-and-bathhouse culture and the busy and often anonymous promiscuity which went with it, but this toned down abruptly when AIDS first became a problem in the latter part of the decade. This wasn't a foregone conclusion by any means. Many men saw the closure of the bathhouses as an infringement on their civil liberties, rooted in homophobia – and the rumour that AIDS is germ warfare by the US government has been slow to die.

**Socially**, San Francisco's gay scene has also mellowed, though in what is an increasingly conservative climate in the city generally, gay parties, parades and street fairs still swing better than most. Like any well-organized section of society, the gay scene definitely has its social season, and if you're here in June, you'll coincide with the Gay and Lesbian Film Festival, Gay Pride Week, the Gay Freedom Day Parade and numbers of conferences. Come October, the street fairs are in full swing and Halloween still sees some of the most outrageous carryings-on. **Lesbian culture** flowered in the 1980s, but today, though women's club nights do exist, the scene is more in evidence in bookstores than bars. Details of gay accommodation, bars and clubs appear below; mention of gay bookshops and theatre and film ventures are under the relevant headings earlier in this chapter.

## Neighbourhoods

Traditionally, the area for gay men has been the **Castro**, together with a few bars and clubs in the **SoMa** area – though gay life these days is much less ghettoized and there are bars and clubs all over town. Rent boys and pimps prowl **Polk Street**, not the safest

## CONTACTS AND RESOURCES

**AIDS Hotline** (☎863-2437). 24-hour information and counselling.

**Bay Area Bisexual Network**, 2404 California St (☎654-2226). Referral service for support groups, social connections and counselling.

**Dignity**, 133 Golden Gate Ave (☎584-1714). Catholic worship and services.

**Gay Legal Referral Services**, Box 1983 SF (☎621-3900). Enquiries regarding legal problems and legal representation.

**Gay Men's Group**, 450 Stanyan St (☎750-5661). Support group and advice on places to go, contacts, etc.

**Gay Men's Therapy Center** (☎673-1160). How to cope with AIDS issues and fears, grief counselling, etc.

**Gay Therapy Center**, 3393 Market St (☎558-8828). Counselling and help with coming out.

**Lesbian/Gay Switchboard** (☎841-6224). 24-hour counselling and advice. Contacts and activities referral service.

**SF AIDS Foundation**, 25 Van Ness Ave (☎864-4376). Referral service providing advice, testing, support groups.

**SOL (Slightly Older Lesbians)**, Pacific Center, 2712 Telegraph Ave, Berkeley 94705 (☎841-6224). A gathering place and referral service for women over 30.

**Woman to Woman** (☎939-6626). Confidential introductions.

### PUBLICATIONS

New clubs and groups spring up all the time, and you should keep an ear to the ground as well as referring to the many free gay publications: *The Sentinel, Coming Up, The Bay Area Reporter* and *Gay Times* all give listings of events, services, clubs and bars in the city and Bay Area. Women should also keep an eye out in bookstores for *On Our Backs* and *Bad Attitude*, two magazines that often have pointers to lesbian organizations in town. Also useful for men and women is *The Gay Book*, a telephone-cum-resource book available in gay bookstores. Alternatively, if you don't mind forking out $7, a must-have for every visiting gay man with a sense of humour is *Betty & Pansy's Severe Queer Review*, listing everything from the best place to eat upscale food to the best cruising alleys – in unashamedly explicit detail.

area at 2am, but neither is it a danger zone if you use common sense. Lesbian interests are more concentrated in the East Bay than the city, although women's activities thrive in the **Mission**.

## Gay accommodation

Not surprisingly, San Francisco has several **accommodation** options that cater specifically to gay travellers. Most are geared towards men, although it's unlikely that lesbians would be turned away; see "Women's San Francisco", for women-only alternatives. All of the places we've listed below are in San Francisco. In the rest of the Bay Area, gay travellers (including couples) rarely raise eyebrows, and your sexual orientation shouldn't be an issue.

**Anna's Three Bears**, 114 Divisadero at Haight (☎255-3167). Deluxe accommodation including full breakfast if you want to be near the Castro but not in it. Pricey but worth it. ⑧.

**Beck's Motor Lodge**, 2222 Market St at Church (☎621-8212). Standard motel close to the Castro. ③.

**Casa Loma Hotel**, 600 Fillmore St (☎552-7100). Mid-sized, friendly hotel with sauna, jacuzzi, sun deck and a lively bar. ②.

**Gough Hayes Hotel**, 417 Gough St at Hayes (☎431-9131). Bit of a flophouse, but popular with a rowdy crowd. ③.

**Inn on Castro**, 321 Castro St at Market (☎861-0321). A long-standing favourite with visiting gays, this luxury bed and breakfast doesn't come cheap, but is worth the price for the large rooms and good breakfasts. About two minutes' walk from the Castro. ⑤–⑥.

**Leland Hotel**, 1315 Polk St at Bush (☎441-5141). Attractively decorated Polk Gulch hotel. Weekly rates available. ③–④.

**Queen Anne Hotel**, 1590 Sutter St at Post (☎262-2663). Very much a gay hotel with overdone decor, full valet service and complimentary afternoon tea and sherry. ⑥–⑦.

**24 Henry**, 24 Henry St (☎864-5686). Intimate guest house in a quiet street just off the heart of the Castro. ④.

**Twin Peaks Hotel**, 2160 Market St at Dolores (☎621-9467). Set in the hills above, this is a quieter and prettier location not far from the Castro, even if the rooms are small and short on luxury. ②–③.

# Bars

San Francisco's **gay bars** are many and varied, ranging from cosy cocktail bars to no-holds-barred leather and chain hangouts. In the last few years every single lesbian bar (never more than a couple anyway) has disappeared, and if you want exclusively female company you'll have to check out clubs that have lesbian nights, or venture over to the East Bay, which has traditionally catered rather better to gay women. Bear in mind, too, that the increasingly integrated nature of the gay scene means that formerly exclusively male bars now have a sizeable lesbian contingent; indeed, most are perfectly welcoming for straights. Take note that places we've listed as bars may switch on some music later on and transform into a club; we've listed the better ones that do this under "Clubs".

**Alta Plaza**, 2301 Fillmore at Clay. Catering to the Pacific Heights junior executive crowd. Boys in suits looking for similar.

**Badlands**, 4121 18th St at Noe. Not quite as cruisy as the *Midnight Sun* (following), but the lively thirtysomething crowd are not exactly here to read the papers either.

**Café Flor**, 2298 Market St at Noe. Very much the in spot before dark. Attractive café, with matching clientele and leafy outdoor area, and no shortage of people eyeing each other up. Very mixed, lots of women. See also "Drinking: bars and cafés".

**Café San Marcos**, 2367 Market St at Castro. A Castro institution always referred to as "the café", this place has gone from being a gay bar to a lesbian bar and is now mixed. Restaurant downstairs and bar and pool tables upstairs. A bit couply, though it gets cruisier at weekends.

**The Castro Station**, 456 Castro St at 18th. Noisy disco bar that manages to pack 'em in even in the middle of the day. Very much the die-hard scene of the 1970s, with a fair number in their leather trousers.

**El Rio**, 3158 Mission St at Army. Mixed crowds gather for cabaret on Wed, but on most nights this is an exclusively gay bar popular with Hispanics from the local Mission district. Live Samba on a Sun afternoon draws a mostly female gay crowd.

**Empress Lily**, 4 Valencia at Market. Formerly an old, little-frequented dive known as the *Travel Lounge*, this bar has had a big revival of its fortunes since the gay community got hold of it and turned it into one of the liveliest venues for drag shows for miles. Draws a good, mixed crowd.

**La India Bonita**, 3089 16th St at Valencia. Family-run, light-hearted drag-queen bar. Mostly for Hispanics; there were no English speakers at the last visit. Highly recommended.

**Midnight Sun**, 4067 18th St at Castro. Young white boys dressed to the nines and cruising like maniacs in this noisy Castro video bar.

**The Mint**, 1942 Market St at Guerrero. Gay karaoke bar where a mixed crowd goes to live out its fantasies of being Diana Ross, or at least a Supreme.

**Moby Dick**, 4049 18th St at Noe. Civilized-looking neighbourhood bar by day, gets rowdier by night. Pool tables and TV screens for the shy.

**The Phoenix**, 482 Castro St at 18th. Being only one of Castro's two dance bars, it not surprisingly draws a large, exuberant crowd.

**Rawhide**, 280 Seventh St at Folsom. If men in chaps are your scene, go no further than this dimly lit SoMa landmark that plays country and western and bluegrass music to a jovial mixed crowd. Definitely recommended.

**SF Eagle**, 12th and Harrison St. Easily the best known leather bar in San Francisco. Large outdoor area with stage. Best time for a visit is for the $8 Sunday brunch when they have a 'beer bust' 3–6pm to raise money for AIDS.

**The Stud**, 399 Ninth St at Harrison. A favourite dancing spot with a mixed but mostly gay crowd. Variable cover charge depending on the night, and some raucous times and shameless freaking out on the dance floor. A San Francisco institution, highly recommended.

**The Swallow**, 1750 Polk Street at Clay. This sophisticated piano bar pulls in a well-behaved middle-aged crowd who just want a good drink and some conversation. Not for randy party animals.

**Twin Peaks**, 17th and Castro. The Castro's first blatantly gay bar, with large see-through windows to make the point. Draws a low-key older crowd who gather for quiet drinks and conversation.

**Uncle Bert's Place**, 4086 18th St at Castro. Lives up to its name – a cosy neighbourhood bar.

# Clubs

Many **gay clubs** are simply bars that host various club nights at least once a week. Pleasingly unpretentious, they rank among the city's best, and although a number are purely male affairs, with women-only discos few and far between, the majority, particularly those listed below under the heading "Mixed", welcome gay people of both sexes. Because in recent years all the **lesbian bars** seem to have disappeared, the women now usually share space with gay bars and host one-night affairs from various venues. The nature of these club nights mean that they change all the time – check for details in the local press.

## Mixed

**Baby Judy's Discoteque**, 527 Valencia St. Goodness, what a group gathers here on a Wed. Most of the crowd seem to be body-pierced, tatooed, arty and flamboyant.

**The Box**, 715 Harrison St at Third. Very popular dance club that plays a good selection of funk and house music. Currently the hot favourite for dance-serious men and women. Thurs.

**Breathe Deep**, 1015 Folsom St at Sixth (☎998-9515). Set in a small room of a large SoMa nightspot on Tuesdays, this is the club for people that want to get stoned and talk. Not just for dancing.

**Club Universe**, 177 Townsend at Third (☎985-5241). San Francisco's hottest Sat night club, this large, cavernous space draws people of all ages, orientation and gender for dancing to progressive house music until 7am. One for the tireless or very high. $10.

**The End Up**, Sixth St at Harrison (☎495-9550). Changes its bill weekly, but most nights are gay or mixed – always a safe bet when you're stuck for a place to go.

## Mainly for men

**Esta Noche**, 3079 16th St at Valencia (☎861-5757). Discomania Latin-style. Young men and their pursuers dance to a hi-NRG disco beat reminiscent of the 1970s.

**Futura**, 174 King St at Third behind *Townsend* club (☎974-6020). On Thursday nights, San Francisco's gay Latin contingent gathers to dance to high energy Spanish house music. Quite a scene.

**La India Bonita**, 3089 16th at Valencia (☎621-9294). Family-run drag queen bar. Latin high-jinx and revelry.

**Lily's**, 4 Valencia at Market (☎864-7028). Bar with separate room for drag shows. Draws a very mixed crowd.

**Rawhide**, 280 Seventh St at Folsom (☎621-1197). Country and western dance hall. Hysterical good fun if you're into square dancing and the like.

**The Stud**, 399 Ninth St at Harrison (☎863-6623). An oldie but a goodie. Has been popular for years for its energetic, uninhibited dancing and good times.

## Mainly for women

**Café San Marcos**, 2367 Market St at Castro. On Fri nights this popular Castro venue becomes the local lesbian lounge.

**Comme Nous** (at the *CoCo Club*), 139 Eighth St at Mission (☎553-8719). Slightly precious lesbian gatherings happen every Sat night. If you take your sexuality very seriously and want others to do the same, join the other navel-gazers here.

**Club Q** (at the *Kennel Club*), 628 Divisadero St (☎931-9858). Fri disco patronized by a young, ethnically mixed group of women. Always packed.

**Faster Pussycat**, 911 Folsom St at Fifth (☎561-9771). Wednesday night dance club for a twenty/thirty-something lipstick lesbian crowd.

**Girl Spot** (at *The Stud*), 399 Ninth St at Harrison (☎337-4962). The city's most friendly women-only evening where everyone from the toughest dyke to the most fey femme just wants to have a good time. No politics, no posturing, just fun.

**Muff Dive - A Dive for Dykes**, at *The CW Saloon*, 911 Folsom St at Fifth (☎974-1585). Sun evening club night for a mixed bag of women of all ages and styles.

**Junk** (at *The Stud*), 399 Ninth St at Harrison (☎863-6623). Leather and flannel night for wimmin on Thurs.

# Women's San Francisco

The flip side of San Francisco's gay revolution has in some **women's** circles led to a separatist culture, and women's resources and services are sometimes lumped together under the lesbian category. While this may be no bad thing, it can be hard to tell which organizations exist irrespective of sexuality. Don't let this stop you from checking out anything that sounds interesting; nobody is going to refuse you either entry or help if you're not a lesbian – support is given to anybody who needs it. Similarly women's health care is very well provided for in San Francisco and there are numerous clinics you can go to for routine gynaecological and contraceptive services: payment is on a sliding scale according to income, but even if you're flat broke, you won't be refused treatment.

## Women's accommodation

**Campton Place**, 340 Stockton St at Post (☎781-5555). Not specifically a women's hotel, but favoured by female executives who like the discreet profile and safe, quiet floors. ⑦–⑨.

**House o' Chicks**, 2162 15th St at Sanchez (☎861-9849). Catering to "low-maintenance lesbians" who are looking for a communal, homestay-type environment. ③–④.

**The Langtry**, 637 Steiner St at Hayes, Alamo Square (☎863-0538). Each room in this nineteenth-century mansion is dedicated to a famous woman in history. There's also a hot tub, sundeck and views of the city. Fabulous but not cheap. ⑥–⑦.

**Mary Elizabeth Inn**, 1040 Bush St at Jones (☎673-6768). Run by the United Methodist Church, so don't expect a swinging dyke scene. However, you can rely on a safe place to stay. ③–④.

**642 Jones**, 642 Jones St at Post (☎775-1711). Comfortable, secure building that is quite safe despite being situated in the unpleasant Tenderloin district. Weekly rates are among the city's best deals: singles $120 per week, doubles $170. Men are allowed, though outnumbered 40 to 1. ①–②.

### CONTACTS AND RESOURCES

**Bay Area Resource Center**, 318 Leavenworth St (☎474-2400). Services, information and clothing.

**Radical Women**, 523A Valencia St (☎864-1278). Socialist feminist organization dedicated to building women's leadership and achieving full equality. Meetings held on the second and fourth Tues of each month.

**Rape Crisis Line** (☎647-7273). 24-hour switchboard.

**Women's Building**, 3543 18th St (☎431-1180). Central stop in the Mission for women's art and political events. A very good place to get information also – the women who staff the building are happy to deal with the most obscure of enquiries.

**Women's Health Center No 1**, 3850 17th St (☎558-3908). Free contraception, AIDS testing, pregnancy testing and a well-women's clinic.

**Women's Needs Center**, 1825 Haight St (☎221-7371). Low-cost health care and referral service.

**Women's Yellow Pages**, 270 Napoleon St (☎821-1357). Call for a copy of this invaluable directory, with everything from where to stay to where to get your legs waxed.

# Shopping Malls

San Francisco is a good place for **shopping**; all the international names are displayed in downtown storefronts, but where the city really excels is in its range of smaller-scale outlets, great for picking up odd and unusual things you wouldn't find at home. The great majority of places are low-key and unpretentious. Not only does this mean slightly lower prices, but it also makes shopping a more pleasant, stress-free activity all round.

If you want to run the gauntlet of designer labels, or just watch the style brigades in all their consumer fury, **Union Square** is the place to aim for. Heart of the city's shopping territory, it has a good selection of big-name and chic stores – expense account stuff admittedly, but good for browsing.

For things that you can actually afford, you'll have a less disheartening and more interesting time in neighbourhoods such as **Haight-Ashbury** and the **Mission**, where the secondhand, quirky and plain bizarre are in abundance, fascinating to pick through if you're at a loose end or on the lookout for some good American kitsch and unique souvenirs; the Mission, especially, has some marvellous secondhand **clothing** stores. The city in general is home to a small but excellent array of **bookstores**, and its one-off, independent **record stores** are unbeatable for rare birds to add to your collection.

## Department stores and shopping malls

If you want to pick up a variety of things in a hurry, without having to roam all over town, it's hard to beat the one-stop convenience of **department stores** or, increasingly, **shopping malls**. Though even San Francisco's most opulent stores aren't in the same league as *Harrods* or *Bloomingdales*, and the few urban shopping malls still feel as though they'd be happier in the suburbs, they are useful and can even be quite lively.

**Emporium**, 835 Market St (☎764-2222). Best value of all the department stores, *Emporium* seems to have a never ending sale which is good for picking up American staples – jeans, cottons, etc.

**Macy's**, Stockton and O'Farrell (☎397-3333). Probably the city's best-stocked store, and as such a good place for general shopping, even if it's not a patch on its New York counterpart. Nonetheless, brimming with trinkets, and a dangerous place to go with a full wallet. Beautifully presented merchandise hawked noisily from all sides.

**Nieman Marcus**, 150 Stockton St at O'Farrell (☎362-3900). The sheer cheek of the pricing department has earned this store the nickname "Needless Mark-up". Undoubtedly Union Square's most beautiful department store, however, with its classic rotunda, and good for browsing.

**Nordstrum**, 865 Market St at Powell (☎243-8500). Shoppers flock here for the high-quality fashions, as well as a chance to ride on the spiral escalators that climb the four-storey atrium.

**Sak's Fifth Avenue**, 384 Post St at Powell(☎986-4300). Since *I Magnin* closed its doors in 1995, SAKS has become *the* high-end speciality shopping store. A scaled-down version of its New York sister store, geared largely to the middle-aged shopaholic.

### Shopping malls

**Crocker Galeria**, 50 Post St at Kearny (☎392-5522). The most recent in the new wave of shopping malls, this has been built to a modern and attractive design, and features some very pricey showcase boutiques. It's all very nice for a wander, but expensive.

**Embarcadero Center**, at Embarcadero *BART/Muni* station at the foot of California St (☎772-0500). Ugly, four-plaza shopping complex with almost 200 stores, distinguished from other anodyne shopping malls only by the occasional work of art and a quite carefully planned layout.

**Ghirardelli Square**, 900 North Point at Larkin (☎775-5500). This attractive turn-of-the-century building used to be a chocolate factory, but is now home to 70 stores and some great restaurants – the nicest way to drop dollars at the Wharf.

**Japan Center**, Post St at Buchanan (☎922-6776). Surprisingly characterless five-acre complex of stores, movie theatres and restaurants with a Japanese theme.

**San Francisco Shopping Centre**, Fifth and Market Streets (☎495-5656). A good-looking mall; glass, Italian marble, polished green granite and spiral escalators up and down its nine storeys all add to the seductive appeal of spending money with California-style panache.

# Food and drink

Food faddists will have a field day in San Francisco's many **gourmet stores**, which are on a par with the city's restaurants for culinary quality and diversity. The simplest neighbourhood deli will get your taste buds jumping, while the most sophisticated places are enough to make you swoon.

Be sure to try such **local specialities** as *Boudin*'s sourdough bread, *Gallo* salami and *Anchor Steam* beer. Bear in mind, too, that however overwhelming the food on offer in San Francisco itself may seem, some of the very best places are to be found across the bay in Berkeley. For more basic stocking up there are, of course, **supermarkets** all over the city (*Safeway* is probably the most widespread name), some of them open 24 hours per day.

**Auntie Pasta**, 3101 Fillmore St at Filbert (☎921-7576). Fresh pasta and sauces to heat and eat. Great if you don't want to dine out or cook.

**Boudin**, 156 Jefferson St, Fisherman's Wharf (☎928-1849). They only make one thing – sourdough bread – but it's the best around.

**California Wine Merchant**, 3237 Pierce St at Chestnut (☎567-0646). Before you set off for the Wine Country (see p.504), pick up a sample selection at this Marina wine emporium so you know what to look out for.

**Canton Market**, 1135 Stockton St at Jackson (☎982-8600). One of the more exotic Chinatown delis. The decor may be a bit stark, and the store unbearably crowded, but the selection (and prices) make it worth the effort.

**Casa Lucas**, 2934 24th St at Guerrero (☎826-4334). Mission store with an astonishing array of exotic fruits and vegetables that includes a dozen varieties of banana.

**David's**, 474 Geary St at Taylor (☎771-1600). The consummate Jewish deli, open until 1am. A downtown haven for the after-theatre crowd and night owls.

**Graffeo Coffee**, 733 Columbus Ave at Filbert (☎986-2420). Huge sacks of coffee are piled up all around this North Beach store – you can smell the place from half a block away.

**Harvest Ranch Market**, 2285 Market St at Church (☎626-0805). Health-nut heaven. Organic everything.

**Liguria Bakery**, 1700 Stockton St at Filbert, North Beach (☎421-3786). Marvellous old-world Italian bakery, with deliciously fresh *focaccia*.

**Molinari's**, 373 Columbus Ave (☎421-2337). Bustling North Beach Italian deli, jammed to the rafters with goodies.

**Rainbow Grocery**, 1899 Mission St at 15th (☎863-0620). Progressive politics and organic food in this Mission wholefood store.

**Sunrise Deli and Café**, 2115 Irving St at 25th (☎664-8210). Speciality Middle Eastern foodstuffs – stuffed vine leaves, egg plant and hummus.

**Tokyo Fish Market**, 1908 Fillmore St at Haight (☎931-4561). Every type of fish. It's fun to look, even if you don't want to buy.

**Urban Cellars**, 3821 24th St at Church (☎824-2300). The dipsomaniac's dream – hundreds of wines and exotic spirits taking booze shopping to its zenith.

# Bookstores

Although San Francisco does boast some truly excellent **bookstores,** the range of reading material on offer is surprisingly small for a city with such a literary reputation.

The established focus for literature has long been in North Beach, in the area around the legendary *City Lights* bookstore, but increasingly the best spots, particularly for contemporary creative writing, are to be found in the lower-rent Mission district, which is home to some of the city's more energized – and politicized –

bookstores. There are a few **secondhand booksellers** in the city itself, but these can't compare with the diverse bunch across the bay in Oakland and Berkeley. Most bookstores tend to open every day, roughly 10am–8pm, though *City Lights* is open daily until midnight.

## General bookstores

**The Booksmith**, 1644 Haight St at Belvedere (☎863-8688). Good general Haight-Ashbury bookstore with an excellent stock of political and foreign periodicals.

**Border's**, 400 Post St at Powell (☎399-1633). San Francisco's newest and best bookstore with over 160,000 books to chose from as well as CD's videos and software.

**City Lights Bookstore**, 261 Columbus Ave at Broadway (☎362-8193). America's first paperback bookstore, and still the city's best, with a range of titles including *City Lights'* own publications.

**Crown Books**, 1245 Sutter S at Polk (☎441-7479) and 518 Castro St at 18th (☎552-5213). San Francisco branches of the nationwide chain, selling new general books at discounted prices.

**Tillman Place Bookstore**, 8 Tillman Place, off Grant Ave, near Union Square (☎392-4668). Downtown's premier general bookstore and certainly one of the oldest, with a beautifully elegant feel.

## Specialist and secondhand bookstores

**About Music**, 375 Grove St at Gough (☎647-3343). Tiny, hole-in-the-wall place crammed with books on classical and contemporary music.

**A Different Light**, 489 Castro St at 18th (☎431-0891). Well-stocked gay bookshop, diverse and popular.

**Around the World**, 1346 Polk St at Pine (☎474-5568). Musty, dusty and a bit of a mess, this is a great place to spend hours poring over first editions, rare books and records.

**Books Etc**, 538 Castro St at 18th (☎621-8631). Stocks the gamut of gay publishing, from psychology to soft-core porn.

**Bound Together Anarchist Collective Bookstore**, 1369 Haight St (☎431-8355). Haight-Ashbury store specializing in radical and progressive publications.

**China Books**, 2929 24th St (☎282-2994). Mission bookstore with books and periodicals from China, and a good number of publications on the history and politics of the Third World.

**Columbus Books**, 540 Broadway at Union (☎986-3872). North Beach store with a good selection of new and used books, and a large guide and travel books section.

**Fanning's Bookstore**, Second Floor, Ghirardelli Square. Speciality bookstore that only offers works of Northern Californian writers – including Hammett, London, Twain and Steinbeck.

**Great Expectations**, 1512 Haight St at Ashbury (☎863-5515). Radical liberal bookstore with hundreds of T-shirts bearing political slogans; some funnier than others.

**Maelstrom Books**, 572 Valencia St at 17th (☎863-9933). One of the Mission's many secondhand bookstores; they trade almost anything.

**Modern Times**, 968 Valencia St at 21st (☎282-9246). Good selection of gay and lesbian literature, many radical feminist publications, and a hefty stock of Latin American literature and progressive political publications. Stages regular readings of authors' works.

**Old Wives' Tales**, 1009 Valencia St at 22nd (☎821-4675). A women's bookshop in ithe Mission, where *Shameless Hussy* and the *Women's Press Collective* publish a large number of titles.

**Rand McNally**, 595 Market St at Second (☎777-3131). Brand-new store selling travel guides, maps and paraphernalia for the person on the move.

**Sierra Club Bookstore,** 730 Polk St at Eddy (☎923-5600). Indispensable for the camper or hiker, check in here before you wander off to explore the great wide yonder.

**Small Press Traffic**, 3599 24th St (☎285-8394). Down in the Mission. Don't be misled by the unprepossessing storefront: this is San Francisco's prime outlet for independent, contemporary fiction and poetry, with an astounding range of books and literary magazines (and postcards too). It's also the best place, along with *City Lights*, to find out about readings and writing workshops.

**William Stout Architectural Books**, 804 Montgomery St at Jackson (☎391-6757). One of San Francisco's world-class booksellers, with an excellent range of books on architecture, building, and urban studies.

## Record stores

San Francisco's **record stores** are of two types: massive, anodyne warehouses pushing all the latest releases, and impossibly small specialist stores crammed to the rafters with obscure discs.

The big places like *Tower Records* are more or less identical to those throughout the world, though foreign visitors tend to find the prices marginally cheaper than back home. More exciting is the large number of **independent** retailers and **secondhand and collectors' stores**, where you can track down anything you've ever wanted, especially in West Coast jazz or psychedelic rock.

**Aquarius Music**, 3961 24th St at Noe (☎647-2272). Small neighbourhood store with friendly, knowledgeable staff. Emphasis on indie rock, jazz and blues.

**Butch Wax Records**, 4077 18th St at Castro (☎431-0904). A hangover from 1970s gay discomania, this Castro shop is the best place in town for hard to find 12" singles, rare grooves and Euro-beat.

**Discolandia**, 2964 24th St at Mission (☎826-9446). Join the snake-hipped groovers looking for the latest in salsa and Central American sounds in this Mission outlet.

**Discoteca Habana**, 24th and Harrison (no phone). Caribbean and samba recordings.

**Embarcadero Discs and Tapes**, 2 Embarcadero Center (☎956-2204). Up-to-the-minute CDs and tapes.

**Groove Merchant Records**, 776 Haight St at Scott (☎252-5766). Very groovy Lower Haight soul and jazz shop.

**Jack's Record Cellar**, 254 Scott St at page (☎431-3047). The city's best source for American secondhand records –r'n'b, jazz, country and rock & roll. They'll track down rare discs and offer you the chance to listen before you buy.

**Musica Latina/American Music Store**, 2388 Mission St at 19th (☎647-2098). Mission store selling music from all over the continent, including South America.

**Reckless Records**, 1401 Haight St at Masonic (☎431-3434). If you can't complete your Sixties collection here, you never will.

**Record Finder**, Noe St at Market (☎431-4443). One of the best independents, with a range as broad as it's absorbing. Take a wad and keep spending.

**Record House**, 1550 California St (☎474-0259). Nob Hill archive library of over 25,000 Broadway and Hollywood soundtracks. Great record-finding service.

**Record Rack**, 3987 18th St (☎552-4990). Castro emporium focusing mainly on 12" singles. The accent is definitely on stuff you can dance to.

**Recycled Records**, 1377 Haight St at Masonic (☎626-4075). Good all-round store, with a decent selection of music publications, American and imported.

**Rocky Ricardo's**, 448 Haight St at Fillmore (☎864-7526). Formerly an exclusive purveyor of 45s, it has recently introduced a few albums, but the theme remains the same: 1960s and 1970s soul and funk. Brilliant.

**Rough Trade**, 1529 Haight St at Townsend (☎621-4395). Because of its London connections, this is the first place in town to get British imports. Good reggae and indie rock selection.

**Star Alley**, 322 Linden Alley between Fell and Hayes (☎552-3017). Rap, soul, jazz, gospel and reggae specialist, out in Western Addition. Any track ever cut by a black artist you'll find here.

## Drugs, beauty products and toiletries

**Body Time**, 2072 Union St (☎922-4076). Though they sold the original name to the UK-based *Body Shop*, they still put out a full range of aromatic natural bath oils, shampoos and skin creams.

**Common Scents**, 3920 24th St (☎826-1019). Natural oils, cures, remedies and bath salts.

**Embarcadero Center Pharmacy**, 1 Embarcadero Center (☎788-4511). Prescription drugs and general medical and toiletry supplies.

**Fairmont Pharmacy**, 801 Powell St (☎362-3000). Huge pharmacy, perfumery and toiletry supply store that also has a good selection of maps and books on San Francisco.

**Mandarin Pharmacy**, 895 Washington St (☎989-9292). This amiable, well-stocked drugstore is a sanctuary in the bustle of Chinatown.

**Skin Zone,** 575 Castro St (☎626-7933). Every unguent imaginable at very reasonable prices. Look for *Skin Zone*'s own brand for real bargains.

**Thrifty JR**, 2030 Market St (☎626-7387). Also at 2664 Mission St (☎282-8600) and 1449 Webster St (☎928-1856). General prescription and non-prescription drug and medical needs.

## Miscellaneous
In among the designer clothes stores and art galleries of the Union Square area, a handful of stores sell **treasurable objects**; though prohibitively expensive, many repay a look-in at least. Check out also the countless **secondhand clothes** stores specializing in period costume, from Twenties gear to leftover hippy garb. Better still, explore the myriad of charitable **thrift stores**, where you can pick up high-quality cast-offs for next to nothing. We've also pulled together in this section some of the city's **miscellaneous** shops specializing in things you often need desperately but never know where to find.

**American Rag Co**, 1305 Van Ness Ave at Bush (☎474-5214). As secondhand clothing stores go, this one is expensive, but it's probably also superior to most others in San Francisco.

**Brooks Cameras**, 125 Kearny St at Post (☎362-4708). High-quality camera store with full repair department.

**Community Thrift**, 625 Valencia St at 18th (☎861-4910). Gay thrift store in the Mission with clothing, furniture and general junk. All proceeds are ploughed back into local gay groups.

**FAO Schwarz**, 48 Stockton St at Market (☎394-8700). Mega-toystore on three floors designed to turn children into monsters.

**Good Vibrations**,1210 Valencia St at 23rd (☎974-8980). Hard to describe with any delicacy. Dildo store, sex toy emporium and a great selection of smutty books – everything for the sexually aware.

**Gump's**, 135 Post St at Kearny (☎982-1616). Famous for its jade, oriental rugs and objects cast in crystal, silver and china. More fuel for fantasies than genuine consumption.

**Headlines**, 838 Market St (☎989-8240) and 557 Castro St (☎626-8061). Good, cheap clothes and huge range of novelty gift items. Fun to browse, even if you don't want to spend any money.

**San Francisco Symphony Thrift Store**, 2223 Fillmore St (☎563-3123). Top-rate vintage clothing store in Pacific Heights, with flamboyant and original pieces going for top dollar.

**St Vincent de Paul**, 1519 Haight St (☎863-3615). Also at 425 Fourth St in the Mission. Queen of the junk stores, *St Vinnie's* will keep you amused for hours. You could spend money all day and still have change from $50.

**Worn Out West**, 1850 Castro St at 19th (☎431-6020). Gay secondhand cowboy gear – a trip for browsing, and if you're serious about getting some Wild West kit, this is the least expensive place in town to pick out a good pair of boots, stylish Western shirts and chaps.

# Listings

**American Express**, 237 Post St (☎981-5533). Mon–Fri 9am–5.30pm, Sat 9.30am–4.30pm.

**Babysitting** *Bay Area Babysitting Agency* (☎991-7474).

**Car Rental** All the major firms have branches in the airport; here we've listed their offices in town: *Alamo*, 687 Folsom St (☎882-9440), from $24.95 per day; *Avis*, 675 Post St (☎885-5011), week-long deals from $175; *Dollar*, 364 O'Farrell St (☎771-5300), from $26.95 per day; *Enterprise;* 1133 Van Ness Ave (☎441-3369), small cars available from $23 per day; *Hertz*, 433 Mason St (☎771-2200), good weekly deals from $185; *Reliable*, 349 Mason St (☎928-4414), $22 per day; *Thrifty*, 299 Ellis St (☎673-6675), from $24 per day, or $130 per week.

**Children** San Francisco is very much a place for adults – more so than, say, LA, where Disneyland and Universal Studios are major attractions – and there aren't many things to occupy young ones. Of the few places that exist, the *Exploratorium* in the Marina District is excellent, as is the *Steinhart Aquarium* in Golden Gate Park; and the *Lawrence Hall of Science* in Berkeley will captivate any young mind. For more organized distractions, try the *Great America* amusement park in San Jose, or the animal-themed *Marine World/Africa USA* in Vallejo, accessible by transbay ferry.

**Churches**. Grace Cathedral on Nob Hill at 1051 Taylor St caters to an Episocpalian (Anglican) congregation, and Catholics can worship at St Mary's Cathedral, 600 California St.

**Consulates** *UK*, 1 Sansome St (☎981-3030); *Ireland*, 655 Montgomery St (☎392-4212); *Australia* (for *New Zealand* as well), 360 Post St (☎362-6160); *Netherlands*, 601 California St (☎981-6454).

**Dental Treatment** San Francisco Dental Office, 132 The Embarcadero (☎777-5115). 24-hr emergency service and comprehensive dental care.

**Disabled Visitors** Steep hills aside, the Bay Area is generally considered to be one of the most barrier-free cities around, and physically challenged travellers are well catered for. Most public buildings have been modified for disabled access, all *BART* stations are wheelchair-accessible, and most buses have lowering platforms for wheelchairs – and, usually, understanding drivers. In San Francisco, the *Mayor's Council on Disabilities* puts out an annual guide for disabled visitors; write c/o Box 1595, San Francisco, CA, or phone (☎554-6141). The *Center for Independent Living*, 2539 Telegraph Ave in Berkeley (☎841-4776), has long been one of the most effective disabled people's organizations in the world; they have a variety of counselling services and are generally a useful resource.

**Ferries** *Golden Gate Ferries* to Marin County, The Ferry Building, east end of Market St (☎332-6600); *Red & White Fleet* ferries to Alcatraz from Pier 41, Fisherman's Wharf (☎546-2805).

**Hospitals** The *San Francisco General Hospital*, 1001 Protrero Drive (☎821-8111), has a 24-hour emergency walk-in service. *Health Center No. 1*, 3850 18th St (☎558-3905), offers a drop-in medical service with charges on a sliding scale depending on income, and free contraception and pregnancy testing. *Davies Medical Center,* Castro and Duboce Streets has 24hr emergency care and a doctors' referral service. The *Haight-Ashbury Free Clinic*, 558 Clayton St (Mon–Fri noon–9pm; ☎431-1714), provides a general health care service with special services for women and detoxification.

**Left Luggage** *Greyhound*, 50 Seventh St (☎433-1500); open daily 5.30am–12.30am.

**Legal Advice** *Lawyer Referral Service* (☎764-1616).

**Passport and Visa Office** US Dept of Immigration, 525 Market St (☎974-9941).

**Post Office** You can collect general delivery mail from the main post office, 101 Hyde St, in the Civic Center (Mon–Fri 9am–5.30pm, Sat 9am–3pm; ☎441-8329), but letters will only be held for 30 days before being returned to sender, so make sure there's a return address on the envelope. If you're receiving mail at someone else's address, it should include "c/o" and the regular occupant's name; otherwise it too is likely to be returned.

**Public Library** Civic Center, between Market St and Van Ness Ave (☎558-3191). Mon–Sat 9am–6pm, until 9pm Tues and Thurs.

**Sports** Baseball: the San Francisco *Giants* play at often cold and foggy Candlestick (now 3COM) Park, south of the city (☎467-8000), while Oakland's *A's* play at the usually sunny Oakland Coliseum (☎510/638-0500). Ticket prices vary from $7 for standing room in the gods to $100 for a field-side box. Basketball: the *Golden State Warriors* play at Oakland Arena (☎638-6000). Football: the fabulous San Francisco *49ers*, many-time Super Bowl champions, also appear at 3COM Park (☎468-2249). It can be really hard to get hold of a ticket for their games; you may be lucky and get in for around $25, but you have to be prepared to fork out as much as $100 for a good seat. Ice hockey: the Bay Area's newest sports team is the San Jose *Sharks* (☎408/287-4275), based at their own brand-new arena in the South Bay. Advance tickets for all Bay Area sports events are available through the *BASS* charge-by-phone ticket service (☎510/762-*BASS*), as well as from the teams themselves.

**Tax** In San Francisco and the Bay Area the sales tax is 7.5 percent, plus a 0.5 percent "earthquake" tax. Hotel tax will add 5–11 percent onto your bill.

**Telegrams** *Western Union*, 697 Howard St (☎495-7301). Open daily 7am–midnight.

**Travel Agents** *Council Travel*, 312 Sutter St (☎421-3473); *STA Travel*, 166 Geary St, Suite 702 (☎391-8407).

**Whale-watching** The nonprofit *Oceanic Society* , Building E, Fort Mason Center(☎441-1104), runs seven-hour boat trips from the Marina to observe the gray whales on their migration from Alaska to Baja. Incredible, but even the strongest constitutions will need travel sickness pills to survive the choppy seas in the small boat. Trips cost $35 and should be booked in advance.

# THE BAY AREA

Of the six million people who make their home in the San Francisco Bay Area, only a lucky one in eight lives in the actual city of San Francisco. Everyone else is spread around one of the many smaller cities and suburbs that ring the bay, either down the peninsula or across one of the two impressively engineered bridges that span the chilly waters of the world's most exquisite natural harbour. There's no doubt about the supporting role these places play in relation to San Francisco – always "The City" – but each has a distinctive character, and contributes to the range of people and landscapes that makes the Bay Area one of the most desirable places in the US to live or to visit.

Across the grey steel Bay Bridge, eight miles from downtown San Francisco, the East Bay is home to the lively, left-leaning cities of Oakland and Berkeley, which together have some of the best bookstores and restaurants, and most of the live music venues in the greater Bay Area. The weather's generally much sunnier and warmer here too, and it's easy to reach by way of the space-age BART trains that race under the bay. The remainder of the East Bay is filled out by Contra Costa County, which includes the short-lived early state capital of California – the near-ghost town of Benicia – as well as the former homes of writers John Muir and Eugene O'Neill.

South of the city, the Peninsula holds some of San Francisco's oldest and most upscale suburbs, reaching down along the bay into the computer belt of the Silicon Valley around San Jose – California's fastest-growing city – though apart from some fancy houses there's not a lot to see. The beaches down here are excellent, though – sandy, clean and uncrowded – and there's a couple of youth hostels in old lighthouses hard on the edge of the Pacific.

For some of the most beautiful land- and seascapes in California, cross the Golden Gate Bridge or ride a ferry boat across the bay to Marin County, a mountainous peninsula that's one-half wealthy suburbia and one-half unspoilt hiking country, with redwood forests rising sheer out of the thundering Pacific Ocean. A range of 2500-foot peaks divides the county down the middle, separating the yacht clubs and plush bay-view houses of Sausalito and Tiburon from the nearly untouched wilderness that runs along the Pacific coast, through Muir Woods and the Point Reyes National Seashore. North of Marin County, at the top of the bay, and still within an hour's drive of San Francisco, the Wine Country regions of the Sonoma and Napa Valleys make an excellent day trip; they're detailed in "Northern California", beginning on p.504.

# The East Bay

The largest and most-travelled bridge in California, the Bay Bridge heads east from downtown San Francisco, part graceful suspension bridge and part heavy-duty steel truss. Built in 1933 as an economic booster during the Depression, the bridge is made from enough steel cable to wrap around the earth three times. Completed just seven months before the more famous (and better-loved) Golden Gate, it works a lot harder for a lot less respect: a hundred million vehicles cross the bridge each year, though you'd have to search hard to find a postcard of it. Indeed, its only claim to fame – apart from the much-broadcast videotape of its partial collapse during the 1989 earthquake – is that Treasure Island, where the two halves of the bridge meet, hosted the 1939 World's Fair. During World War II the island became a Navy base, which, pending post-Cold War closures, it remains; just inside the gates there's a small museum (daily 10am–3pm; free) with pictures of the Fair amid maritime memorabilia. The island also offers great views of San Francisco and the Golden Gate.

The Bay Bridge – and the BART trains that run under the bay – finish up in the heart of the East Bay in Oakland, a hard-working, blue-collar city that earns its livelihood from shipping and transportation services, evidenced by the massive Port of Oakland whose huge cranes dominate the place, lit up at night like futuristic dinosaurs. Oakland spreads north along wooded foothills to Berkeley, an image-conscious university town that looks out across to the Golden Gate and collects a mixed bag of pinstriped Young Republicans, ageing 1960s radicals, and Nobel prize-winning nuclear physicists in its cafés and bookstores.

Unless otherwise specified, the telephone **area code** for the East Bay is ☎510.

Berkeley and Oakland blend together so much as to be virtually the same city, and the hills above them are topped by a twenty-mile string of forested **regional parks**, providing much needed fresh air and quick relief from the concrete grids below. The rest of the East Bay is filled out by Contra Costa County, a huge area that contains some intriguing, historically important waterfront towns – well worth a detour if you're passing through on the way to the Wine Country region of the Napa and Sonoma valleys – as well as some of the Bay Area's most inward-looking suburban sprawl. Curving around the **North Bay** from the heavy-industrial landscape of Richmond, and facing each other across the narrow **Carquinez Straits**, both Benicia and Port Costa were vitally important during California's first twenty years of existence after the 1849 Gold Rush; they're now strikingly sited but little-visited ghost towns. In contrast, standing out from the soulless dormitory communities that fill up the often baking hot **inland valleys**, are the preserved homes of an unlikely pair of influential writers: the naturalist John Muir, who, when not out hiking around Yosemite and the High Sierra, lived most of his life near **Martinez**, and playwright Eugene O'Neill, who wrote many of his angst-ridden works at the foot of **Mount Diablo**, the Bay Area's most impressive peak.

## Arrival

You're most likely to be staying in San Francisco when you visit the East Bay, though it is possible and sometimes better value to fly direct to **Oakland Airport**, particularly if you're coming from elsewhere in the US. Domestic airlines which serve the airport include *American*, *Southwest*, *AmericaWest* and *Delta*. It's an easy trip from the airport into town: take the Air*BART* Shuttle van (every 15 min; $2) from outside the terminal direct to the Coliseum *BART* station, from where you can reach Oakland, Berkeley, or San Francisco. In addition, various privately operated shuttle buses cost from $10.

Oakland's *Greyhound* **bus station** is in a dubious part of town, alongside the I-980 freeway on San Pablo Avenue at 21st. *Amtrak* **trains** terminate at Second Street near Jack London Square in Oakland, though it's a better option to get off at Richmond and change there onto *BART*.

The most enjoyable way to arrive in the East Bay is to take the commuter **ferry** ($3.75 each way; ☎522-3300) that sails every hour from San Francisco's Ferry Building and Pier 39 to Oakland's Jack London Square.

## Getting around

The East Bay is linked to San Francisco via the underground *BART* transbay subway (Mon–Sat 6am–midnight, Sun 9am–midnight). Three lines run from Daly City through San Francisco and on to downtown Oakland, before diverging to service East Oakland out to **Fremont**, Berkeley, north to **Richmond**, and east into Contra Costa County as far as **Concord**. Fares range from 85¢ to $3, and the cost of each ride is deducted from the total value of the ticket, purchased from machines on the station concourse. If you're relying on *BART* to get around a lot, buy a **high-value ticket** ($5 or $10) to avoid having to stand in line to buy a new ticket each time you ride. To phone *BART* from San Francisco dial ☎788-*BART*; from the East Bay it's ☎465-*BART*.

From East Bay *BART* stations, pick up a free transfer saving you 25¢ on the $1.10 fares of *AC Transit* (☎839-2882), which provides a good bus service around the entire East Bay area, especially Oakland and Berkeley. *AC Transit* also runs buses on a number of routes to Oakland and Berkeley from the Transbay Terminal in San Francisco. These operate all night, and are the only way of getting across the bay by public transit once *BART* has shut down. You can pick up excellent free maps of both *BART* and the bus system from any station. A smaller-scale bus company that can also prove useful, the *Contra Costa County Connection* (☎676-7500), runs buses to most of the inland areas, including the John Muir and Eugene O'Neill historic houses.

One of the best ways to get around is **by bike**; a fine cycle route follows Skyline and Grizzly Peak Boulevards along the wooded crest of the hills between Berkeley and Lake Chabot. If you haven't got one, rent touring bikes or mountain bikes from *Carl's Bikes* (☎835-8763), 2416 Telegraph Ave in Oakland, and from *Cal Adventures* (☎642-4000), 2301 Bancroft Way on the UC Berkeley campus. For those interested in **walking tours**, the city of Oakland sponsors free "discovery tours" (☎238-3050) of various neighbourhoods.

If you're **driving**, allow yourself plenty of time to get there: the East Bay has some of California's worst traffic, with I-80 in particular jam-packed 16 hours a day.

## Information

The downtown **Oakland CVB** at 550 Tenth St, near the 12th Street *BART* station (Mon–Fri 8.30am–5pm; ☎839-9000), offers free maps and information, as does the **Berkeley CVB**, 1834 University Ave (Mon–Fri 9am–5pm; ☎549-7040). If you're spending any time at all in the Berkeley area, pick up a copy of *Berkeley Inside/Out* by Don Pitcher (Heyday Books, $12.95), an informative guide that'll tell you everything you ever wanted to know about the town and its inhabitants. For information on hiking or horse-riding in the many parks that top the Oakland and Berkeley hills, contact the **East Bay Regional Parks District**, 11500 Skyline Blvd (☎562-7275). The widely available (and free) *East Bay Express* has the most comprehensive listings of what's on in the vibrant East Bay music and arts scene. The troubled daily *Oakland Tribune* (50¢) is also worth a look for its coverage of local politics and sporting events.

## East Bay accommodation

Surprisingly, it's not a great deal cheaper to **stay** in the East Bay than in San Francisco, and, in truth, there's little to choose from anyway. **Motels and hotels**, at around $40–60 a night, are slightly better value for money than their San Francisco equivalents, and there are a couple of **dorm-bed** places for those on a budget. **Bed and breakfast** is a more pleasant option, and there are also a couple of **campgrounds**, though these are hard to reach without a car.

### Hotels, motels and B&Bs

**Claremont Hotel**, 41 Tunnel Rd at Ashby Ave on the Oakland/Berkeley border (☎843-3000). At the top end of the scale, this grand Victorian palace has panoramic bay view rooms and all-inclusive "weekend breaks". ⑧.

**Dean's Bed & Breakfast**, 156 Pedestrian Way, Oakland (☎652-5024). A hidden and inexpensive room with pool, hot tub, private entrance and Japanese garden tucked away in Rockridge. Personable owner who stays out of your way needs a reservation in advance. ④.

**East Brother Light Station**, 117 Park Place, San Pablo Bay (☎233-2385). A handful of rooms in a converted lighthouse, on an island in the middle of the bay. Not a handy base for seeing the sights, this is a retreat and adventure for an evening. Prices include highly rated gourmet dinners as well as breakfast. ⑨.

**Elmwood House**, 2609 College Ave, Berkeley (☎540-5123). Attractive, turn-of-the-century house with B&B rooms not far from UC Berkeley. ④.

**French Hotel**, 1538 Shattuck Ave, North Berkeley (☎548-9930). Small and comfortable, in the heart of Berkeley's Gourmet Ghetto. ⑤.

**Golden Bear Motel**, 1620 San Pablo Ave, West Berkeley (☎525-6770). The most pleasant of the many motels in the "flatlands" of West Berkeley, though somewhat out of the way. ③.

**Gramma's**, 2740 Telegraph Ave, Berkeley (☎549-2145). Pleasant, if slightly dull, rooms with fireplaces in a pretty mock-Tudor mansion half a mile south of UC Berkeley. ⑤–⑥.

**Holiday Inn Bay Bridge**, 1800 Powell St, Emeryville (☎658-9300). Not outrageously pricey considering the great views to be had from the upper floors. Free parking. ⑤.

**Hotel Durant**, 2600 Durant Ave, Berkeley (☎845-8981). Fairly plain but well worn and comfortable, and very handy for the UC Berkeley campus. ⑤.

**Hotel Mac**, 10 Cottage Ave, Point Richmond (☎787-0100). Built in 1907, the recently refurbished *Mac* boasts luxurious rooms with unbeatable prices. This was supposedly John Rockefeller's favourite place to stay when visiting his *Standard Oil* enterprise. ⑤.

**Marriot Hotel**, 200 Marina Bvld, Berkeley (☎548-7920). Comfortable hotel verging on the upscale. Some rooms have a view of the bay. ⑥.

**Ramada Inn**, 920 University Ave, Berkeley (☎849-1121). Bargain rooms with live music nightly, mostly blues. Near Berkeley Marina. ③.

**Travelodge**, 423 Seventh St, downtown Oakland (☎451-6316). Spacious rooms, some of which have kitchens, make this a good option for families or groups. ④.

**Shattuck Hotel**, 2086 Allston Way, Berkeley (☎845-7300). Very central and newly refurbished, near Berkeley *BART*. ⑤.

**Union Hotel and Gardens**, 401 First St, Benicia (☎707/746-0100). Bordello from 1882 until 1950, since converted into a comfortable bed and breakfast with twelve rooms. ④.

**Waterfront Plaza Hotel**, 10 Washington St, Oakland (☎836-3800). Newly redecorated hotel moored on the best stretch of the Oakland waterfront. ⑥.

## Hostels

**Berkeley YMCA**, 2001 Allston Way, Berkeley (☎848-6800). Ideal East Bay mixed-sex accommodation a block from the Berkeley *BART*, with single rooms for $25, including use of gym and swimming pool. ①.

**Haste-Channing Summer Visitor Housing**, 2424 Channing Ave, Berkeley (☎642-5925 or 642-4444). Summer-only dorm rooms for $50. ③.

## Campgrounds

**Chabot Regional Park**, off I-580 in East Oakland (☎562-2267). Walk-in, tent-only places, with hot showers and lots of good hiking nearby; reserve through *MISTIX* in summer.

**Mount Diablo State Park**, 20 miles east of Oakland off I-680 in Contra Costa County (☎837-2525). RV and tent places; likewise, book through *MISTIX* in summer.

# Oakland

A quick trip across the Bay Bridge or on *BART* brings you to **OAKLAND**, a solidly working-class counterbalance to upwardly mobile San Francisco: the workhorse of the Bay Area, one of the busiest ports on the West Coast, and the western terminal of the rail network. It's not all hard slog, though: the climate is rated the best in the US, often sunny and mild when San Francisco is cold and dreary, and, despite the 1991 fire that ravaged the area, there's great hiking around the redwood- and eucalyptus-covered hills above the city – and views right over the entire Bay Area.

Oakland has more historical and literary associations than important sights. **Gertrude Stein** and **Jack London** both grew up in the city, at about the same time though in entirely different circumstances – Stein was a stockbroker's daughter, London an orphaned delinquent. The macho and adventurous London is far better remembered – most of the waterfront, where he used to steal oysters and lobsters, is now named in his memory – while Stein is all but ignored. Perhaps this is due to her book, *Everybody's Autobiography*, in which she wrote: "What was the use of me having come from Oakland, it was not natural for me to have come from there yes write about it if I like or anything if I like but not there, *there is no there there*" – a quote which has haunted Oakland ever since. The city's businesses have a history of deserting their hometown when the going gets good, and even its football team, the Raiders, defected to Los Angeles for thirteen years. Nonetheless, the majority of Oaklanders stick with the city, and would argue that there is indeed a there there, notably in the small and trendy communities of Rockridge, Piedmont Avenue and the lively Grant Avenue.

Jack London's mildly socialist leanings set a style for the city, and Oakland has been the breeding ground for some of America's most unabashedly revolutionary **political movements** ever since. The 1960s saw the city's fifty-percent black population find a voice through the militant Black Panther movement, and in the 1970s Oakland was again on the nation's front pages, when the Symbionese Liberation Army's ransom for kidnapped heiress Patty Hearst was a demand for free food distribution to the city's poor.

Oakland is still very much its own city, and it's worth taking the time to get a feel for its diversity and dynamism.

## Downtown Oakland

Coming by *BART* from San Francisco, get off at the 12th Street–Civic Center station and you're in **downtown Oakland**, a compact district of spruced-up Victorian store-fronts overlooked by modern hotels and office buildings that has been in the midst of an ambitious programme of restoration and redevelopment for over a decade. Fraught with allegations of illegal dealings and incompetent planning, so far the programme has been less than a complete success. To make way for the moat-like I-980 freeway – the main route through Oakland since the collapse of the Cypress Freeway in the 1989 earthquake – entire blocks were cleared of houses, some of which were saved and moved to **Preservation Park** at 12th Street and Martin Luther King Jr Way. The late nineteenth-century commercial centre along Ninth Street west of Broadway, now tagged **Victorian Row**, underwent a major restoration some years ago, but many of the buildings are still waiting for tenants. By way of contrast stroll a block east of Broadway, between Seventh and Ninth, to Oakland's **Chinatown**, whose bakeries and restaurants are as lively and bustling – if not as picturesque – as those of its more famous cousin across the Bay.

Luckily, not all of downtown Oakland has the look of a permanent building site. The city experienced its greatest period of growth in the early twentieth century, and many of the grand buildings of this era survive a few blocks north along Broadway, centred on the awkwardly imposing 1914 **City Hall** on 14th Street. Two blocks away at 13th and Franklin stands Oakland's most unmistakable landmark, the chateau-esque lantern of the **Tribune Tower**, the 1920s-era home of the *Oakland Tribune* newspaper.

Further north, around the 19th Street *BART* station, are some of the Bay Area's finest early twentieth-century buildings, highlighted by the outstanding Art Deco interior of the 1931 **Paramount Theater** at 2025 Broadway (tours Sat 10am; $5; ☎465-4600), which shows Hollywood classics on selected Friday nights. Nearby buildings are equally flamboyant, ranging from the wafer-thin Gothic "flatiron" office tower of the **Cathedral Building** at Broadway and Telegraph, to the Hindu temple-like facade of the magnificent 3500-seat **Fox Oakland** (now closed) on Telegraph at 19th – the largest movie house west of Chicago at the time it was built in 1928 – and, across the street, the 1931 **Floral Depot**, a group of small Moderne storefronts faced in black-and-blue terracotta tiles with shiny silver highlights.

West of Broadway, the area around the *Greyhound* bus station on San Pablo Avenue is fairly seedy. San Pablo used to be the main route in and out of Oakland before the freeways were built, but many of the roadside businesses are now derelict, especially around the industrial districts of **Emeryville**. Some of the old warehouses have been converted into artists' lofts and studios, though any gentrification there might be is diffused by the scenes on the street, where prostitutes and drug-dealers hang out

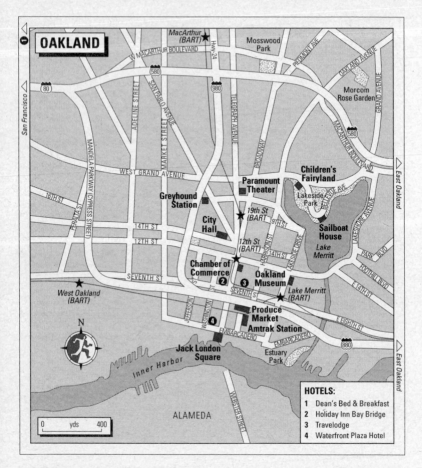

under the neon signs of the dingy bars and gambling halls such as the *Oaks Card Club*, where the father of "Oaktown" (the local name for Oakland) rapper M C Hammer, used to work.

## Lake Merritt and the Oakland Museum

Five blocks east of Broadway, the eastern third of downtown Oakland comprises **Lake Merritt**, a three-mile-circumference tidal lagoon that was bridged and dammed in the 1860s to become the centrepiece of Oakland's most desirable neighbourhood. All that remains of the many fine houses that once circled the lake is the elegant **Camron-Stanford House**, on the southwest shore at 1418 Lakeside Drive, a graceful Italianate mansion whose sumptuous interior is open for visits (Wed 11am–4pm, Sun 1–5pm; $2). The lake is also the nation's oldest wildlife refuge, and migrating flocks of ducks, geese, and herons break their journeys here. **Lakeside Park** lines the north shore, where you can rent canoes and rowing boats ($4 per hour), and a range of sailing boats and catamarans ($4–10 per hour) from the Sailboat House (summer daily 10am–5pm;

winter Sat & Sun only; ☎444-3807) – provided you can convince the staff you know how to sail. A miniature Mississippi riverboat makes thirty-minute lake **cruises** ($1) on weekend afternoons, and kids will like the puppet shows and pony rides at the Children's Fairyland (summer daily 10am–5.30pm; winter Sat & Sun only; $1.50), along Grand Avenue on the northwest edge of the park. Every year, on the first weekend in June, the park comes to life during the **Festival at the Lake**, when all of Oakland gets together to enjoy nonstop music and performances from local bands and entertainers.

Two blocks south of the lake, or a block up Oak Street from the Lake Merritt *BART* station, the **Oakland Museum** (Wed–Sat 10am–5pm, Sun noon–7pm; $5 donation) is perhaps Oakland's most worthwhile stop, not only for the exhibits but also for the superb modern building in which it's housed, topped by a terraced rooftop sculpture garden that gives great views out over the water and the city. The museum covers many diverse areas: displays on the **ecology** of California, including a simulated walk from the seaside through various natural habitats up to the 14,000-foot summits of the Sierra Nevada mountains; state history, ranging from old mining equipment to the guitar that Berkeley-born Country Joe MacDonald played at the Woodstock festival in 1969; and a broad survey of works by California artists and craftspeople, some highlights of which are pieces of turn-of-the-century **arts and crafts furniture**. You'll also see excellent **photography** by Edward Muybridge, Dorothea Lange, Imogen Cunningham and many others. The museum has a collector's gallery that rents and sells works by California artists.

## The waterfront, Alameda, and West Oakland

Half a mile down from Downtown Oakland on *AC Transit* bus #51A, at the foot of Broadway on the Waterfront, **Jack London Square** is Oakland's sole concession to the tourist trade. Also accessible by direct ferry from San Francisco (see "Arrival"; p.422), this somewhat anaesthetic complex of harbourfront boutiques and restaurants was named after the self-taught writer who grew up pirating shellfish around here, but is about as distant from the spirit of the man as it's possible to get. Jack London's best story, *The Call of the Wild*, was written about his adventures in the Alaskan Yukon, where he carved his initials in a small cabin that has been reconstructed here; another survivor is *Heinhold's First and Last Chance Saloon*, a seedy bar where London spent much of his wayward youth.

If you're not a keen fan of London (and if you are, you'd be better off visiting his Sonoma Valley ranch – see p.512), there are still a few worthwhile things to do here. **The Ebony Museum of Arts** at 30 Alice St (Tues–Sat 11am–6pm, Sun noon–6pm; free) is worth a visit for its African art and pop American counterculture collectables. Otherwise, walk a few short blocks inland to the **Produce Market**, along Third and Fourth streets, where a couple of good places to eat and drink lurk among the rail tracks (see "Eating" on p.438). This bustling warehouse district has fruit and vegetables by the forklift load, and is at its most lively early in the morning, from about 5am.

*AC Transit* bus #51A continues from Broadway under the inner harbour to **Alameda**, a quiet and conservative island of middle America dominated by a large, empty naval air station, one of the first to be closed by President Bill Clinton in 1995 – although massive nuclear-powered aircraft carriers still dock here occasionally. Alameda, which has been hit very hard by post-Cold War military cutbacks, was severed from the Oakland mainland as part of a harbour improvement programme in 1902. The fine houses along the original shoreline on Clinton Street were part of the summer resort colony that flocked here to the *contra costa* or "opposite shore" from San Francisco, near the now demolished Neptune Beach amusement park. The island has since been much enlarged by dredging and landfill, and 1960s apartment buildings now line the long, narrow shore of **Robert Crown Memorial Beach** along the bay – a quiet, attractive spot.

**West Oakland** – an industrial district of warehouses, rail tracks, 1960s housing projects and decaying Victorian houses – may be the nearest East Bay *BART* stop to San Francisco, but it's light years away from that city's prosperity. Despite the obvious poverty, it's quite a safe and settled place, but the only time anyone pays any attention to it is when something dramatic happens; in the double-whammy year of 1989, for example, when Black Panther Huey Newton was gunned down here in a drugs-related revenge attack, and the double-decker I-880 freeway that divided the neighbourhood from the rest of the city collapsed in on itself during the earthquake, killing dozens of commuters.

Local people have successfully resisted government plans to rebuild the old concrete eyesore (current plans call for it to be rerouted closer to the harbour); where the freeway used to run through is now the broad and potentially very attractive **Nelson Mandela Parkway**. But otherwise this remains one of the Bay Area's poorest and most neglected neighbourhoods, and apart from a marvellous stock of turn-of-the-century houses there's little here to tempt tourists.

## East Oakland

The bulk of Oakland spreads along foothills and flatlands to the east of downtown, in neighbourhoods obviously stratified along the main thoroughfares of Foothill and MacArthur boulevards. Gertrude Stein grew up here, though when she returned years later in search of her childhood home it had been torn down and replaced by a dozen Craftsman-style bungalows – the simple 1920s wooden houses that cover most of **East Oakland**, each fronted by a patch of lawn and divided from its neighbour by a narrow concrete driveway.

A quick way out from the gridded streets and sidewalks of the city is to take *AC Transit* bus #15A from downtown east up into the hills to Joaquin Miller Park, the most easily accessible of Oakland's hilltop parks. It stands on the former grounds of the home of the "Poet of the Sierras," Joaquin Miller, who made his name playing the eccentric frontier American in the literary salons of 1870s London. His poems weren't exactly acclaimed (his greatest poetic achievement was rhyming "teeth" with "Goethe"), although his prose account; *Life Amongst the Modocs*, documenting time spent with the Modoc people near Mount Shasta, does stand the test of time. It was more for his outrageous behaviour that he became famous, wearing bizarre clothes and biting debutantes on the ankle.

Perched in the hills at the foot of the park, the pointed towers of the **Mormon Temple** look like missile-launchers designed by the Wizard of Oz – unmissable by day or floodlit night. In December, speakers hidden in the landscaping make it seem as if the plants are singing Christmas carols. Though you can't go inside (unless you're a confirmed Mormon), there are great views out over the entire Bay Area, and a small museum explains the tenets of the faith (daily 9am–9pm; free).

Along the bay south to San Jose stretch some twenty miles of tract house suburbs, and the only vaguely interesting area is around the end of the *BART* line in **FREMONT**, where the short-lived *Essanay* movie studios were based. *Essanay*, the first studios on the West Coast, made over 700 films in three years, including Charlie Chaplin's *The Tramp* in 1914. Not much remains from these pre-Hollywood days, however, and the only real sight is the **Mission San Jose de Guadalupe** on Mission Boulevard south of the I-680 freeway (daily 10am–5pm; donation), which in the best traditions of Hollywood set design was completely rebuilt in Mission style only a few years ago.

## North Oakland and Rockridge

The horrific October 1991 **Oakland fire**, which destroyed 3000 homes and killed 26 people, did most of its damage in the high-priced hills of North Oakland. It took the better part of two years, but most of the half-million dollar houses have been rebuilt, and though the lush vegetation that made the area so attractive will never be allowed to grow back, things are pretty much back to normal. Which is to say that these bay-view homes, some of the Bay Area's most valuable real estate, look out across some of its poorest – the neglected flatlands below that in the 1960s were the proving grounds of Black Panthers Bobby Seale and Huey Newton.

Broadway is the dividing line between the two halves of North Oakland, and also gives access (via the handy *AC Transit* #51 bus) to most of what there is to see and do. The **Oakland Rose Garden**, on Oakland Avenue three blocks east of Broadway (April–Oct daily dawn–dusk; free), repays a look if you come during the day. One of Oakland's most neighbourly streets, **Piedmont Avenue**, runs in between, lined by a number of small bookstores and cafés. At the north end of Piedmont Avenue, the **Mountain View Cemetery** was laid out in 1863 by Frederick Law Olmsted (designer of New York's Central Park) and holds the elaborate dynastic tombs of San Francisco's most powerful families – the Crockers, the Bechtels and the Ghirardellis. You can jog or ride a bike around the well-tended grounds, or just wonder at the enormous turtles in the pond.

Back on Broadway, just past College Avenue (see below), Broadway Terrace climbs up along the edge of the fire area to **Lake Temescal** – where you can swim in summer – and continues on up to the forested ridge at the **Robert Sibley Regional Preserve**. This includes the 1761-foot volcanic cone of Round Top Peak and offers panoramas of the entire Bay Area. Skyline Boulevard runs through the park and is popular with cyclists, who ride the twelve miles south to Lake Chabot or follow Grizzly Peak Boulevard five miles north to Tilden Park through the Berkeley Hills.

Most of the Broadway traffic, and the *AC Transit* #51 bus, cuts off onto College Avenue through Oakland's most upscale shopping district, **Rockridge**. Spreading for half a mile on either side of the Rockridge *BART* station, the quirky stores and restaurants here, despite their undeniably yuppie overtones, are some of the best around and make for a pleasant afternoon's wander.

# Berkeley

*This Berkeley was like no somnolent Siwash out of her own past at all, but more akin to those Far Eastern or Latin American universities you read about, those autonomous culture media where the most beloved of folklores may be brought into doubt, cataclysmic of dissents voiced, suicidal of commitments chosen – the sort that bring governments down.*

Thomas Pynchon, *The Crying of Lot 49*

More than any other American town, **BERKELEY** conjures up an image of 1960s student dissent. During that era, when university campuses were protesting against the Vietnam War, it was the students of the University of California, Berkeley, who led the charge, gaining a name for themselves as the vanguard of what was increasingly seen as a challenge to the very authority of the state. Full-scale battles were fought almost daily here at one point, on the campus and on the streets of the surrounding town, and there were times when Berkeley looked almost on the brink of revolution itself: students (and others) throwing stones and gas bombs were met with tear-gas volleys and truncheons by National Guard troops under the nominal command of the then-Governor Ronald Reagan. It was, of course, inspired by the mood of the time, and in an increasingly conservative America, Berkeley politics are nowadays decidedly middle-of-the-road. But despite an influx of non-rebellious students, a thriving bedrock of exclusive California cuisine restaurants, and the recent dismantling of the city's rent control program, something of the progressive legacy does still linger in the many

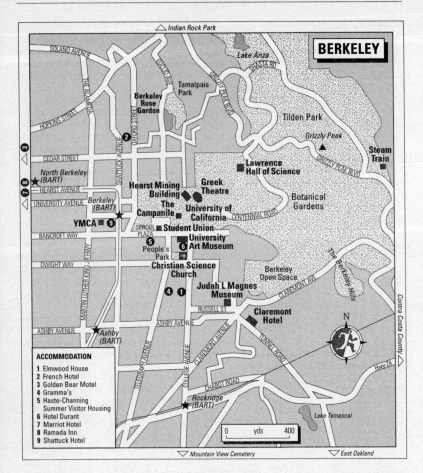

△ Indian Rock Park

**BERKELEY**

Lake Anza

SOLANO AVENUE

THE ALAMEDA

HOPKINS STREET

Tamalpais Park

Berkeley Rose Garden

SHASTA RD

GRIZZLY PEAK BLVD

Tilden Park

Grizzly Peak

Steam Train

CEDAR STREET

North Berkeley (BART) ★

HEARST AVENUE

UNIVERSITY AVENUE

Berkeley (BART)

YMCA ■ ❾

BANCROFT WAY

DWIGHT WAY

**②**

OXFORD STREET

SHATTUCK AVENUE

Hearst Mining Building

**The Campanile**

◆◆

Student Union ■

SPROUL PLAZA

**❺**

People's Park

Greek Theatre

University of California

Lawrence Hall of Science

CENTENNIAL ROAD

Botanical Gardens

GRIZZLY PEAK BLVD

**❻** University Art Museum

Christian Science Church

**❹ ❶**

Judah L Magnes Museum

RUSSELL ST

ASHBY AVENUE

Berkeley Open Space

The Berkeley Hills

Claremont Hotel

CLAREMONT AVE

N

ASHBY AVENUE

Ashby (BART) ★

MARTIN LUTHER KING JR HWY

TELEGRAPH AVENUE

COLLEGE AVENUE

CLAREMONT AVENUE

TUNNEL ROAD

Hwy 24

Contra Costa County

**ACCOMMODATION**

1 Elmwood House
2 French Hotel
3 Golden Bear Motel
4 Gramma's
5 Haste-Channing Summer Visitor Housing
6 Hotel Durant
7 Marriot Hotel
8 Ramada Inn
9 Shattuck Hotel

CHABOT ROAD

Rockridge (BART) ★

0    yds    400

Lake Temescal

▽ Mountain View Cemetery          ▽ East Oakland

small bookstores and regular political demonstrations, if not on the agenda of the city council.

The **University of California**, right in the centre of town, completely dominates Berkeley and makes a logical starting point for a visit. Its many grand buildings and 30,000 students give off a definite energy that spills down the raucous stretch of **Telegraph Avenue** which runs south from the campus and holds most of the studenty hangouts, including a dozen or so lively cafés, as well as a number of fine bookstores. Older students, and a good percentage of the faculty, congregate in the **Northside** area, popping down from their woodsy hillside homes to partake of goodies from the "Gourmet Ghetto," a stretch of Shattuck Avenue that collects many of Berkeley's internationally renowned restaurants, delis, and bakeries. Of quite distinct character are the flatlands that spread through **West Berkeley** down to the bay, a poorer but increasingly gentrified district that mixes old Victorian houses with builder's yards and light industrial premises. Along the bay itself is the **Berkeley Marina**, where you can rent sailboards and sailboats or just watch the sun set behind the Golden Gate.

## The University of California

Caught up in the frantic crush of students who pack the **University of California** campus during the semesters, it's nearly impossible to imagine the bucolic learning environment envisaged by its high-minded founders. When the Reverend Henry Durant and other East Coast academics decided to set up shop here in the 1860s, these rolling foothills were still largely given over to dairy herds and wheatfields, the last remnants of the Peralta family's Spanish land-grant rancho which once stretched over most of the East Bay. Construction work on the two campus buildings – imaginatively named North Hall and South Hall – was still going on when the first 200 students, including 22 women, moved here from Oakland in 1873. Since then an increasing number of buildings have been squeezed into the half-mile-square main campus, and the state-funded university has become one of America's most highly respected, with so many Nobel laureates on the faculty that it's said you have to win one just to get a parking permit. Overcrowding aside, the beautifully landscaped campus, stepping down from the eucalyptus-covered Berkeley Hills toward the Golden Gate, is eminently strollable. With maps posted everywhere, you'd have to try hard to get lost – though enthusiastic students will show you around on a free two-hour tour (Mon, Wed & Fri 10am & 1pm; ☎642-5215).

A number of footpaths climb the hill from the Berkeley *BART* station on Shattuck Avenue, but the best way to get a feel for the place is to follow Strawberry Creek from the top of Center Street across the southeast corner of the campus, emerging from the groves of redwood and eucalyptus trees at **Sproul Plaza**. It's the newest and largest public space on campus, enlivened by street musicians playing for quarters on the steps of the **Student Union** building and conga drummers pounding away in the echoing courtyard below. **Sather Gate**, which bridges Strawberry Creek at the north end of Sproul Plaza, marks the entrance to the older part of the campus. Up the hill, past the imposing facade of Wheeler Hall, the 1914 landmark **Campanile** is modelled after the one in the Piazza San Marco in Venice; take an elevator to the top for a great view of the campus and the entire Bay Area (daily 10am–4pm; 25¢). At the foot of the tower stands red-brick **South Hall**, the sole survivor of the original pair of buildings.

Inside the plain white building next door, the **Bancroft Library** (Mon–Sat 10am–5pm) displays odds and ends from its exhaustive accumulation of artefacts and documents tracing the history of California, including a faked brass plaque supposedly left by Sir Francis Drake when he claimed all of the West Coast for Queen Elizabeth I. It also contains an internationally important collection of manuscripts and rare books, from Mark Twain to James Joyce – though to see any of these you have to show some academic credentials. Around the corner and down the hill, just inside the arched main entrance to Doe Library, you'll find the **Morrison Reading Room**, a great place to sit for a while and read foreign magazines and newspapers, listen to a CD, or just ease down into one of the many comfy overstuffed chairs and unwind.

Also worth a look if you've got time to kill is the **Museum of Paleontology** in the nearby Earth Sciences Building, which details evolutionary concepts with hundreds of fossils, skeletons, and geological maps displayed along the corridors on the lower floors. From here it's a quick walk to the collection of cafés and restaurants lining Euclid Avenue and Hearst Avenue, and the beginning of Berkeley's Northside (see p.433).

The Hearst family name appears with disturbing regularity around the Berkeley campus, though in most instances this is due not to the notorious newspaper baron William Randolph but to his altruistic mother, Phoebe Apperson Hearst. Besides inviting the entire senior class to her home every spring for a giant picnic, she sponsored the architectural competition that came up with the original campus plan, and donated a good number of the campus buildings, including many that have since been destroyed. One of the finest survivors, the 1907 **Hearst Mining Building** (daily 8am–5pm) on the northeast edge of the campus conceals a delicate metalwork lobby topped by three glass domes, above ageing exhibits on geology and mining – which is how the Hearst family fortune was originally made, long before scion W R took up publishing. Another Hearst legacy is the **Greek Theater**, an open-air amphitheatre cut into the Berkeley Hills east of the campus, which hosts a summer season of rock concerts.

Higher up in the hills, above the 80,000-seat Memorial Stadium, the lushly landscaped **Botanical Garden** (daily 9am–5pm; free) defeats on-campus claustrophobia with its thirty acres of plants and cacti. Near the crest, with great views out over the bay, a full-size fibreglass sculpture of a sei whale stretches out in front of the space-age **Lawrence Hall of Science** (daily 10am–4.30pm; $5), an excellent museum and learning centre that features earthquake simulations, model dinosaurs and a planetarium, plus hands-on exhibits for kids in the Wizard's Lab. Both the gardens and the Lawrence Hall of Science are accessible on weekdays via the free UC Berkeley Shuttle bus from the campus or the Berkeley *BART* station.

In the southeast corner of the campus, the **Hearst Museum of Anthropology** in Kroeber Hall (daily except Wed 10am–4pm; $2, free Thurs) holds a variety of changing exhibits as well as an intriguing display of artefacts made by Ishi, the last surviving Yahi Indian who was found near Mount Lassen in Northern California in 1911. Anthropologist (and father of writer Ursula Le Guin) Alfred Kroeber brought Ishi to the museum (then located on the UC San Francisco campus), where he lived under the scrutiny of scientists and journalists – in effect, in a state of captivity – until his death from tuberculosis a few years later.

The brutally modern, angular concrete of the **University Art Museum** across Bancroft Way (Wed–Sun 11am–5pm; $5, free Thurs 11am–noon) is in stark contrast to

## BERKELEY'S BOOKSTORES

Berkeley's **bookstores** are as exhaustive as they are exhausting – not surprising for a university town. Perfect for browsing and taking your time, you won't be made to feel guilty or obliged to buy a book you've been poring over for ages.

**Black Oak Books**, 1491 Shattuck Ave (☎486-0698). Huge selection of second-hand and new books for every interest; also holds regular evening readings by internationally acclaimed authors.

**Cody's Books**, 2454 Telegraph Ave (☎845-7852). The flagship of Berkeley booksellers, with an excellent selection of fiction, poetry and literary criticism.

**Comics and Comix**, 2502 Telegraph Ave (☎845-4091). Great selection of comic books, both current and classic.

**Easy Going**, 1385 Shattuck Ave (☎843-3533). The essential bookstore for every traveller. Packed with printed travel paraphernalia, it offers a wide selection of guidebooks and maps for local, country-wide and worldwide exploration.

**Moe's Books**, 2476 Telegraph Ave (☎849-2087). An enormous selection of new and used books on four floors with esoteric surprises in every field of study; for academics, book-collectors and browsers. There's also an excellent art section on the top floor.

**Serendipity Books**, 1201 University Ave (☎841-7455). Damp and disorganized, but with an incredible selection of first edition and out-of-print books. A must for collectors of first editions and obscure fiction and poetry.

**Shakespeare and Company**, 2499 Telegraph Ave (☎841-8916). Crammed with quality secondhand books at reasonable prices. The best place to linger and scour the shelves for finds.

**Shambala Booksellers**, 2482 Telegraph Ave (☎848-8443). Have a transcendental out-of-body experience where eastern and western religious traditions meet in this cosy store near campus.

the campus' older buildings. Its skylit, open-plan galleries hold works by Picasso, Cézanne, Rubens and other notables, but the star of the show is the collection of Fifties American painter Hans Hofmann's energetic and colourful abstract paintings on the top floor. The museum is renowned for its cutting-edge, changing exhibitions: the main space hosts a range of major shows – such as Robert Mapplethorpe's controversial photographs – while the Matrix Gallery focuses on lesser known, generally local artists. Works on paper are shown downstairs outside the **Pacific Film Archive**, which shares the building, showing new films from around the world that you won't see elsewhere, as well as revivals from its extensive library (see "Nightlife" for details).

## Telegraph Avenue and South Berkeley

Downtown Berkeley – basically two department stores, a few banks, a post office, and the City Hall building – lies west of the university campus around the Berkeley *BART* station on Shattuck Avenue, but the real activity centres on **Telegraph Avenue**, which runs south of the university from Sproul Plaza. This thoroughfare saw some of the worst of the Sixties riots and is still a frenetic bustle, especially the four short blocks closest to the university, which are packed to the gills with cafés and secondhand book-stores. Sidewalk vendors hawk handmade jewellery and brilliantly coloured T-shirts, while down-and-outs hustle for spare change and spout psychotic poetry.

**People's Park**, now a seedy and overgrown plot of land half a block up from Telegraph between Haste Street and Dwight Way, was another battleground in the late Sixties when organized and spirited resistance to the university's plans to develop the site into dormitories brought out the troops, who shot dead an onlooker by mistake. To many, the fact that the park is still a community-controlled open space (and outdoor dosshouse for Berkeley's homeless legions) symbolizes a small victory in the battle against the Establishment, though it's not a pleasant or even very safe place to hang about, especially after dark. A mural along Haste Street remembers some of the reasons why the battles were fought, in the words of student leader Mario Savio: "There's a time when the operation of the machine becomes so odious, makes you so sick at heart, that you can't take part, you can't even tacitly take part. And you've got to put your bodies upon the gears and upon the wheels, upon the levers, upon all the apparatus, and you've got to make it stop" – ideals that can't help but be undermined by the state of the place these days. Recent efforts by the University to reclaim the space with volleyball and basketball courts were met with short-lived but violent protests: riot-ers thrashed Telegraph Avenue storefronts, and a nineteen-year-old woman was shot dead by police while trying to assassinate the Chancellor.

Directly across Bowditch Street from People's Park stands one of the finest buildings in the Bay Area, Bernard Maybeck's **Christian Science Church**. Built in 1910, it's an eclectic but thoroughly modern structure, laid out in a simple Greek Cross floor plan and spanned by a massive redwood truss with carved Gothic tracery and Byzantine painted decoration. The interior is only open on Sundays for worship and for tours at 11am, but the outside is worth lingering over, its cascade of many gently pitched roofs and porti-coes carrying the eye from one handcrafted detail to another. It's a clever building in many ways: while the overall image is one of tradition and craftsmanship, Maybeck also succeeded in inconspicuously incorporating such materials as industrial metal windows, concrete walls and asbestos tiles into the structure – thereby cutting costs.

## North Berkeley

**North Berkeley**, also called "Northside," is a subdued neighbourhood of professors and postgraduate students, its steep, twisting streets climbing up the lushly overgrown hills north of the campus. At the foot of the hills, some of the Bay Area's finest restau-rants and delis – most famously *Chez Panisse*, started and run by Alice Waters, the acclaimed inventor of California cuisine – have sprung up along Shattuck Avenue to form the so-called "Gourmet Ghetto", a great place to pick up the makings of a tasty al fresco lunch.

Above the Gourmet Ghetto on Euclid Avenue (if you want to avoid the fairly steep walk, take bus #65 from Shattuck Avenue), there are few more pleasant places for a picnic than the **Berkeley Rose Garden** (daily dawn–dusk; free), a terraced amphitheatre filled with some three thousand varietal roses and looking out across the bay to San Francisco. Built as part of a WPA job-creation scheme during the Depression, a wooden pergola rings the top, stepping down to a small spring.

Along the crest of the Berkeley Hills a number of enticing parks give great views over the bay. The largest and highest of them, **Tilden Park**, spreads along the crest of the hills, encompassing some 2065 acres of near wilderness. You can get there from downtown Berkeley via *AC Transit* #65 or #67 bus. Kids can enjoy a ride on the carved wooden horses or a mini-steam train through the redwood trees. In the warm months, don't miss a swim in Lake Anza (lifeguard on duty May–Oct daily 11am–6pm; $2).

Nearer to town at the north end of Shattuck Avenue and close by the shops and cafés along Solano Avenue, the grey basalt knob of **Indian Rock** stands out from the foot of the hills, challenging rock-climbers who hone their skills on its forty-foot vertical faces. (Those who just want to appreciate the extraordinary view can take the steps around its back.) Carved into similarly hard volcanic stone across the street are the mortar holes used by the Olhone to grind acorns into flour. In between, and in stark contrast, stands the rusting hulk of a Cold War-era air-raid siren.

### West Berkeley and the waterfront

From downtown Berkeley and the UC campus, **University Avenue** runs downhill toward the bay, lined by increasingly shabby frontages of motels and massage parlours. The liveliest part of this **West Berkeley** area is around the intersection of University and San Pablo Avenues – the pre-freeway main highway north – where a community of recent immigrants from India and Pakistan have set up shops and restaurants that serve some of the best of the Bay Area's rare curries.

The area between San Pablo Avenue and the bay is the oldest part of Berkeley, and a handful of hundred-year-old houses and churches – such as the two white-spired Gothic Revival structures on Hearst Avenue – survive from the time when this district was a separate city, known as Ocean View. The neighbourhood also holds remnants of Berkeley's industrial past, and many of the old warehouses and factory premises have been converted into living and working spaces for artists, craftspeople and computer software companies. Along similar lines are the cafés, workshops and galleries built in the late 1970s along **Fourth Street** north of University Avenue, somewhat yuppified now, but still good places to root out handicrafts and household gadgets.

The I-80 freeway, and the still-used rail tracks that run alongside it, pretty well manage to cut Berkeley off from its waterfront. The best way to get there is to take *AC Transit* bus #51M, which runs regularly down University Avenue. Once a major hub for the transbay ferry services – to shorten journey times, a three-mile-long pier was constructed, much of which still sticks out into the bay – the **Berkeley Marina** is now one of the prime spots on the bay for leisure activities, especially windsurfing.

## The North Bay and inland valleys

Compared to the urbanized bayfront cities of Oakland and Berkeley, the rest of the East Bay is sparsely populated, and places of interest are few and far between. The **North Bay** is home to some of the Bay Area's heaviest industry – oil refineries and chemical plants dominate the landscape – but also holds a few remarkably unchanged waterfront towns that merit a side trip if you're passing by. Away from the bay, the

**inland valleys** are a whole other world of dry rolling hills dominated by the towering peak of **Mount Diablo**. Dozens of tract house developments have made commuter suburbs out of what were once cattle ranches and farms, but so far the region has been able to absorb the numbers and still feels rural, despite having doubled in population in the past twenty years.

## The North Bay

North of Berkeley there's not a whole lot to see or do. In **ALBANY**, *Golden Gate Fields* has horse-racing from October to June, and El Cerrito's main contribution to world culture was the band Creedence Clearwater Revival, who staged most of their *Born on the Bayou* publicity photographs in the wilds of Tilden Park in the hills above; El Cerrito is still home to one of the best record stores in California, *Down Home Music*, at 10341 San Pablo Ave. **RICHMOND**, at the top of the bay, was once a boomtown, building ships during World War II at the Kaiser Shipyards, which employed 100,000 workers between 1940 and its closure in 1945. Now it's the proud home of the gigantic Standard Oil refinery, the centre of which you drive through before crossing the **Richmond–San Rafael Bridge** ($1) to Marin County. About the only reason to stop in Richmond is that it marks the north end of the *BART* line, and the adjacent Amtrak station is a better terminal for journeys to and from San Francisco than the end of the line in West Oakland.

Though not really worth a trip in itself, if you're heading from the East Bay to Marin County, **Point Richmond** merits a look. A cosy little town tucked away at the foot of the bridge between the refinery and the bay, its many Victorian houses are rapidly becoming commuter territory for upwardly mobile professionals from San Francisco. Through the narrow tunnel that cuts under the hill stands the most obvious sign of this potential gentrification: "Brickyard Landing," an East Bay docklands development with modern bay-view condos, a private yacht harbour, and a token gesture to the area's industrial past – disused brick kilns, hulking next to the tennis courts on the front lawn. The rest of the waterfront is taken up by the broad and usually deserted strand of **Keller Beach**, which stretches for half a mile along the sometimes windy shoreline.

## The Carquinez Straits

At the top of the bay some 25 miles north of Oakland, the land along the Carquinez Straits is a bit off the beaten track, but it's an area of some natural beauty and much historic interest. The still-small towns along the waterfront seem worlds away from the bustle of the rest of the Bay Area, but how long they'll be able to resist the pressure of the expanding commuter belt is anybody's guess. *AC Transit* bus #74 runs every hour from Richmond *BART* north to **CROCKETT** at the west end of the narrow straits – a tiny town cut into the steep hillsides above the water that seems entirely dependent upon the massive *C&H Sugar* factory at its foot, whose giant neon sign lights up the town and the adjacent Carquinez Bridge.

From Crockett the narrow Carquinez Straits Scenic Drive, an excellent cycling route, heads east along the Sacramento river. A turn two miles along drops down to **PORT COSTA**, a small town that was dependent upon ferry traffic across the straits to Benicia until it lost its livelihood when the bridge was built at Crockett. It's still a nice enough place to watch the huge ships pass by on their way to and from the inland ports of Sacramento and Stockton. If you don't have a bike (or a car) you can enjoy the view from the window of an Amtrak train which runs alongside the water from Oakland and Richmond, not stopping until Martinez at the eastern end of the straits, two miles north of the John Muir house (see p.437).

## Benicia

On the north side of the Straits, and hard to get to without a car (see "Getting around", p.422), **BENICIA** is the most substantial of the historic waterfront towns, but one that has definitely seen better days. Founded in 1847, it initially rivalled San Francisco as the major Bay Area port and was even the state capital for a time; but despite Benicia's better weather and fine deep-water harbour, San Francisco eventually became the main transport point for the fortunes of the Gold Rush, and the town very nearly faded away altogether. Examples of Benicia's efforts to become a major city stand poignantly around the very compact downtown area, most conspicuously the 1852 Greek Revival structure that was used as the **first State Capitol** for just thirteen months. The building has been restored as a museum (Thurs–Mon 10am–5pm; $2), furnished in the legislative style of the time, complete with top hats on the tables and shining spitoons every few feet.

A walking-tour map of Benicia's many intact Victorian houses and churches is available from the **tourist office**, on 601 First St (☎707/745-2120), including on its itinerary the steeply pitched roofs and gingerbread eaves of the **Frisbie-Walsh house** at 235 East L St – a prefabricated Gothic Revival building that was shipped here in pieces from Boston in 1849 (an identical house was put up by General Vallejo as his residence in Sonoma; see p.512). Across the City Hall park, the arched ceiling beams of **St Paul's Episcopal Church** look like an upturned ship's hull; it was built by shipwrights from the Pacific Mail Steamship Company, one of Benicia's many successful nineteenth-century shipyards. Half a dozen former brothels and saloons stand in various stages of decay and restoration along First Street down near the waterfront, from where the world's largest train ferries used to ply the waters between Benicia and Port Costa until 1930.

In recent years Benicia has attracted a number of artists and craftspeople, and you can watch glass-blowers and furniture-makers at work in the **Yuba Complex** at 670 East H St (Mon–Fri 10am–4pm). Judy Chicago is among those who have worked in the converted studios and modern light industrial parks around the sprawling fortifications of the old **Benicia Arsenal** east of the downtown area, whose thickly walled sandstone buildings formed the main Army storage facility for weapons and ammunition from 1851 up to and including the Korean War. One of the oddest parts of the complex is the **Camel Barn** (summer Fri, Sat & Sun 1–4pm; rest of year Sat & Sun 1–4pm; free), now a museum of local history, but formerly used to house camels that the Army imported in 1856 to transport supplies across the deserts of the Southwestern US. The experiment failed, and the camels were kept here until they were sold off in 1864.

## Vallejo and Marine World/Africa USA

Across the Carquinez Bridge from Crockett, the biggest and dullest of the North Bay towns – **VALLEJO** – was, like Benicia, an early capital of California, though it now lacks any sign of its historical significance. In contrast to most of the other Gold Rush-era towns that line the Straits, Vallejo remained economically vital, largely because of the massive military presence here at the **Mare Island Naval Shipyard**, a sprawling, relentlessly grey complex that covers an area twice the size of Golden Gate Park. Slated for closure in the next few years, Mare Island is Vallejo's largest employer, and its less than glamorous history – the yard builds and maintains supply ships and submarines, not carriers or battleships – is recounted in a small museum in the old city hall building at 734 Mare St (Tues–Fri 10am–4.30pm; $1), where the highlight is a working periscope that looks out across the bay. Though no great thrill, it's worth a quick stop, sited in the centre of town right on Hwy-29, the main route from the East Bay to the Wine Country.

The best reason to come to Vallejo, however, is **Marine World/Africa USA** (daily 9.30am–6pm; $25.95), five miles north of Vallejo off I-80 at the Marine World Parkway (Hwy-37) exit. Operated by a nonprofit educational group, it offers a well above average range of performing sea lions, dolphins, and killer whales kept in approximations of their natural habitats, as well as water-ski stunt shows and the like. It can be a fun day out, especially for children, and it's not bad as these things go: the animals seem very well cared for, their quarters are clean and spacious, and the shows are fun for all but the most jaded. The shark exhibit lets you walk through a transparent tunnel alongside twenty-foot Great Whites, and the tropical butterfly aviary is truly amazing. The best way to get here from San Francisco is on the *Red and White Fleet* catamaran ferry boat from Fisherman's Wharf, which takes an hour each way and adds another $13 onto the admission price (☎546-2805 for details).

## The inland valleys

Most of the inland East Bay area is made up of rolling hills covered by grasslands, slowly yielding to suburban housing developments and office complexes as more and more businesses abandon the pricey real estate of San Francisco. The great peak of **Mount Diablo** that dominates the region is twice as high as any other Bay Area summit, and surrounded by acres of campgrounds and hiking trails; other attractions include two historic homes that serve as memorials to their literate and influential ex-residents, John Muir and Eugene O'Neill.

*BART* tunnels from Oakland through the Berkeley Hills to the leafy-green stock-broker settlement of **ORINDA**, continuing east through the increasingly hot and dry landscape to the end of the line at **CONCORD**, site of a controversial nuclear weapons depot. A few years ago, a peaceful, civilly disobedient blockade here ended in protester Brian Willson losing his legs under the wheels of a slow-moving munitions train. The event raised public awareness – before it happened few people knew of the depot's existence – but otherwise it's still business as usual.

From Pleasant Hill *BART*, one stop before the end of the line, Contra Costa County Connection buses leave every thirty minutes for **MARTINEZ**, the seat of county government, passing the preserved home of naturalist **John Muir** (daily 10am–4.30pm; $1), just off Hwy-4 two miles south of Martinez. Muir, an articulate, persuasive Scot whose writings and political activism were of vital importance in the preservation of America's wilderness, spent much of his life exploring and writing about the majestic Sierra Nevada mountains, particularly Yosemite. He was also one of the founders of the **Sierra Club** – a wilderness lobby and education organization still active today (see p.296 for more). Anyone familiar with the image of this thin, bearded man wandering the mountains with his knapsack, notebook and packet of tea might be surprised to see his very conventional, upper-class Victorian home, now restored to its appearance when Muir died in 1914. Built by Muir's father-in-law, only those parts of the house Muir added himself reflect much of the personality of the man, not least the massive, rustic fireplace he had built in the East Parlor so he could have a "real mountain camp-fire." The bulk of Muir's personal belongings and artefacts are displayed in his study on the upper floor, and in the adjacent room an exhibition documents the history of the Sierra Club and Muir's battles to protect America's wilderness.

Behind the bell-towered main house is a large, still productive orchard where Muir cultivated grapes, pears and cherries to earn the money to finance his explorations (you can sample the fruits free of charge, pre-picked by staff gardeners). Beyond the orchard, it's worth a look at the 1849 **Martinez Adobe**, homestead of the original Spanish land-grant settlers and now a small **museum** of Mexican colonial culture. The contrast between Mexican and American cultures in early California is fascinating; as a bonus, the building's two-foot-thick walls keep it refreshingly cool on a typically hot summer day.

At the foot of Mount Diablo, fifteen miles south, playwright **Eugene O'Neill** used the money he got for winning the Nobel Prize for Literature in 1936 to build a home and sanctuary for himself, which he named **Tao House**. It was here, before 1944 when he was struck down with Parkinson's Disease, that he wrote many of his best-known plays: *The Iceman Cometh*, *A Moon for the Misbegotten* and *Long Day's Journey into*

*Night*. Readings and performances of his works are sometimes given in the house, which is open to visitors, though you must reserve a place on one of the free guided tours (Wed–Sun 10am & 12.30pm; ☎838-0249). There's no parking on site, so the tours pick you up in the town of **Danville**.

As for **Mount Diablo** itself, it rises up from the rolling ranchlands at its foot to a height of nearly four thousand feet, its summit and flanks preserved within **Mount Diablo State Park** (daily 8am–sunset; parking $5). The main road through the park (there's no public transport, though the Sierra Club sometimes organizes day trips: see *Basics*) reaches within three hundred feet of the top, so it's a popular place for an outing and you're unlikely to be alone to enjoy the marvellous view: on a clear day you can see over two hundred miles in every direction.

Two main entrances lead into the park, both well marked off I-680. The one from the southwest by way of Danville passes by the **ranger station**, where you can pick up a trail map ($1) which lists the best day-hikes. The other runs from the northwest by way of Walnut Creek, and the routes join together five miles from the summit. March and April, when the wild flowers are out, are the best times to come, and since mornings are ideal for getting the clearest view, you should drive to the top first and then head back down to a trailhead for a hike, or to one of the many picnic spots for a leisurely lunch. In summer it can get desperately hot and dry, and parts of the park are closed because of fire danger.

### Livermore and Altamont

Fifteen miles southeast of Mount Diablo on the main road out of the Bay Area (I-580), the rolling hills around sleepy **LIVERMORE** are covered with thousands of shining, spinning, high-tech **windmills**, placed here by a private power company to take advantage of the nearly constant winds. The largest wind farm in the world, you'll probably have seen it used in a number of TV ads as a space-age backdrop to hype flashy new cars or sexy perfumes. Though the federal government provides no funding for this nonpolluting, renewable source of energy, it spends billions of dollars every year designing and building nuclear weapons and other sinister applications of modern technology at the nearby **Lawrence Livermore Laboratories**, where most of the research and development of the nuclear arsenal takes place. A small **visitor center** holds hands-on exhibits showing off various scientific phenomena and devices, two miles south of I-580 on Greenville Rd (Mon–Fri 9am–4.30pm, Sat & Sun noon–5pm; free).

Up and over the hills to the east, where I-580 joins I-5 for the four-hundred-mile route south through the Central Valley to Los Angeles, stand the remains of **Altamont Speedway**, site of the nightmarish Rolling Stones concert in December 1969. The free concert, which was captured in the film *Gimme Shelter*, was intended to be a sort of second Woodstock, staged in order to counter allegations that the Stones had ripped off their fans during a long US tour. In the event it was a complete disaster: three people died, one of whom was kicked and stabbed to death by the Hell's Angels "security guards" – in full view of the cameras – after pointing a gun at Mick Jagger while he sang *Sympathy for the Devil*. Needless to say, no historical plaque marks the site.

## East Bay eating

Official home of **California cuisine** and with some of the best restaurants in the state, Berkeley is an upmarket diner's paradise. But it's also a college town, and you can eat cheaply and well, especially around the southern end of the campus, along and around Telegraph Avenue. The rest of the East Bay is less remarkable, except for when it comes to **plain American** food such as barbecued ribs, grilled steaks or deli sandwiches, for which it's unbeatable.

## Budget Food: Diners and Delis

**Bette's Ocean View Diner**, 1807 Fourth St, Berkeley (☎548-9494). Named after the neighbourhood, not after the vista, but serving up some of the Bay Area's best breakfasts and lunches. Very popular at weekends, when you may have to wait an hour for a table, so come during the week if possible.

**Brick Hut Café**, 2510 San Pablo Ave, Berkeley (☎486-1124). All appetites satisfied for breakfast and lunch in this welcoming women-owned and operated diner. Large portions with small prices.

**Flint's Barbecue**, 3314 San Pablo Ave, Oakland (☎658-9912). Open until the early hours of the morning for some of the best ribs and link sausages west of Chicago.

**Holy Land Kosher Food**, 677 Rand Ave, Oakland (☎272-0535). Casual diner-style restaurant near the lake serving Israeli food, including excellent falafel, to those who can find it.

**Homemade Café**, 2454 Sacramento St, Berkeley (☎845-1940). Non-traditional Californian-style Mexican and Jewish food served for breakfast and lunch at shared tables when crowded.

**Lois the Pie Queen**, 851 60th St at Adeline, Oakland (☎658-5616). Famous around the bay for its Southern-style sweet potato and fresh fruit pies, this cosy diner also serves massive, down-home breakfasts and Sunday dinners.

**Saul's Deli**, 1475 Shattuck Ave, Berkeley (☎848-DELI). For pastrami, corned beef, kreplach or knishes, this is the place. Great sandwiches and picnic fixings to take away, plus a full range of sit-down evening meals.

**Time to Eat**, 325 Franklin St, in Oakland's Produce Market (☎835-4455). A Chinese bar and café that serves breakfasts from 5am. Cheap beer, plus a pool table at 25¢ per game.

**Top Dog**, 2534 Durant Ave, Berkeley (☎843-7250). Not just a hot dog stand, it stays open late for such assorted goodies as bockwurst, bratwurst, kielbasas, Louisiana Hot Sausages and veggie dogs.

**Tropix**, 3814 Piedmont Ave, Oakland (☎653-2444). Large portions of fruity Jamaican delicacies at reasonable prices with plenty of authentic jerk sauce and thirst-quenching mango juice.

## American

**Bay Wolf Café**, 3853 Piedmont Ave, Oakland (☎655-6004). Comfortable restaurant serving grilled meat and fish dishes on an ever-changing, moderately expensive menu.

**Chez Panisse**, 1517 Shattuck Ave, North Berkeley (☎548-5525). The first and still the best of the California Cuisineries – although at $45, $55 and $65 a head prix-fixe (plus wine) on Mon, Tues–Thurs and Fri respectively, you may prefer to try the comparatively inexpensive cafe upstairs, especially if you don't have the obligatory three-months-in-advance reservation.

**Gulf Coast Oyster Bar & Specialty Co**, 736 Washington St, Oakland (☎836-3663). Popular and reasonably priced Cajun-flavoured seafood restaurant.

**Spenger's**, 1919 Fourth St, West Berkeley (☎845-7771). About as far as you can get from the subtle charms of Berkeley's high-style restaurants, this is nonetheless a local institution. As the largest restaurant in the whole Bay Area, *Spenger's* serve up literally tons of seafood to thousands of customers every day.

## Asian and African

**The Blue Nile**, 2525 Telegraph Ave, Berkeley (☎540-6777). Come with a group to share the giant platters of Ethiopian stewed meats and veggies, eaten by hand with pancake-like injera bread.

**Cha-Am**, 1543 Shattuck Ave, Berkeley (☎/848-9664). Climb the stairs to this unlikely-looking, always crowded small restaurant, for deliciously spicy Thai food at bargain prices.

**Jade Villa**, 800 Broadway, downtown Oakland (☎839-1688). For endless dim sum lunches or traditional Cantonese meals, this is one of the best places in Oakland's thriving Chinatown.

**Maharani**, 1025 University Ave, West Berkeley (☎848-7777). One of the best of the handful of restaurants that have sprung up here in Little India, and certainly the least expensive, with $6 lunch-time buffets on weekdays.

**O Chame**, 1830 Fourth St, West Berkeley (☎841-8783). One of the very best Japanese restaurants in the US, with beautifully prepared sashimi and sushi as well as a full range of authentic Japanese specialities. A treat.

**Sala Thai**, 807 First St, Benicia (☎707/745-4331). Small-town Thai food can be just as delicious here as in any big city. Check out the enormous fish tank as your feet dangle in foot caves under the tables.

**Steve's Barbeque**, in the *Durant Center*, 2521 Durant Ave, Berkeley (☎848-6166). Excellent, low-priced Korean food (*kim chee* to die for); other cafés in the centre sell Mexican food, healthy sandwiches, deep-fried doughnuts and slices of pizza – not to mention bargain pitchers of beer.

## Mexican and South American

**Alvita's Restaurant**, 3522 Foothill Blvd, East Oakland (☎536-7880). Arguably the best Mexican restaurant in the Bay Area, with great chiles rellenos, carnitas and a range of seafood dishes.

**Café de la Paz**, 1600 Shattuck Ave, Berkeley (☎843-0662). Located upstairs inside a complex of boutiques, Latin American entrées and tapas are served fresh and sometimes spicy. Don't miss the Brazilian seafood stew.

**Café Oliveto**, 5655 College Ave, Rockridge (☎547-5356). Popular sidewalk tapas bar, where good-sized portions cost around $4 per plate. Upstairs is a pricey Italian restaurant where you can watch the chef and the cooking team in action.

**Juan's Place**, 941 Carleton St, West Berkeley (☎845-6904). The original Berkeley Mexican restaurant, with great food (tons of it) and an interesting mix of people.

**Mario's La Fiesta**, 2444 Telegraph Ave at Haste, Berkeley (☎540-9123). Always crowded with students and other budget-minded souls who flock here for the heaped portions of good, inexpensive Mexican food.

**Picante**, 1328 Sixth St at Gilman, West Berkeley (☎525-3121). Good, inexpensive tacos with fresh salsa, plus live jazz at weekends.

**Taqueria Morelia**, 4481 E 14th St, East Oakland (☎535-6030). Excellent burritos and the more unusual but authentic tortas.

## Italian and pizza

**Blondie's Pizza**, 2340 Telegraph Ave, Berkeley (☎548-1129). Takeout New York-style pizza by the slice ($1.50, plus topping) or by the pie; stays open until late (2am), and always crowded.

**Cheese Board Pizza**, 1512 Shattuck Ave, Berkeley (☎549-3055). Tiny storefront selling some of the world's best "designer pizza" at very reasonable prices: $1.75 a slice, with a different topping every day. Worth searching out, but keeps irregular hours; usually Tues–Sat 11.30am–2pm & 4.30–7pm.

**Gio's Trattoria**, 2220 First St, Livermore (☎606-6644). Offers outstanding Italian food in an elegant atmosphere.

**Pizza Rustica**, 5422 College Ave, Oakland (☎654-1601). Intimate adobe-style, upscale eatery for designer pizza with a pesto and sun-dried tomatoes motif. If it's too expensive, try the tapas bar upstairs.

**Zachary's Pizza**, 5801 College Ave, Rockridge (☎655-6385). Also at 1853 Solano Ave, North Berkeley (☎525-5950). Good salads, and arguably the best pizzas in the East Bay.

## Ice cream and desserts

**Dreyers Grand Ice Cream Parlor**, 5925 College Ave, Oakland (☎658-0502). Oakland's own rich ice cream, which is distributed through California, is served at this small, slightly dull Rockridge café.

**Fenton's Creamery**, 4226 Piedmont Ave, N Oakland (☎658-4949). A brightly lit 1950s ice cream and sandwich shop, open until 11pm on weeknights, midnight at weekends.

**Yogurt Park**, 2433A Durant Ave, Berkeley (☎549-0570). Frozen yoghurt a speciality, open until midnight for the student throngs.

## Speciality shops and markets

**Acme Bread**, 1601 San Pablo Ave, West Berkeley (☎524-1327). Small bakery that supplies most of Berkeley's better restaurants; the house speciality is delicious sourdough baguettes.

**Berkeley Bowl**, 2777 Shattuck Ave, Berkeley (☎841-6346). A converted bowling alley which is now an enormous produce, bulk and healthfood market. The least expensive grocery in town, with the largest selection of fresh food.

**Cheese Board**, 1504 Shattuck Ave, North Berkeley (☎549-3183). Collectively owned and operated since 1967, this was one of the first outposts in Berkeley's Gourmet Ghetto and is still going strong, offering over 200 varieties of cheese and a range of delicious breads. Great pizzas a few doors down, too; see above.

**Genova Delicatessen and Ravioli Factory**, 5th and Telegraph, Oakland (☎652-7401). Tiny traditional deli, with myriad hanging sausages and enormous, inexpensive sandwiches.

**La Farine**, 6323 College Ave, Rockridge (☎654-0338). Small but highly rated French-style bakery, with excellent pain au chocolat.

**Monterey Foods**, 1550 Hopkins St, North Berkeley (☎526-6042). The main supplier of exotic produce to Berkeley's gourmet restaurants, this boisterous market also has the highest quality fresh fruit and vegetables available.

## East Bay drinking: cafés and bars

One of the best things about visiting the East Bay is the opportunity to enjoy its many **cafés**. Concentrated most densely around the UC Berkeley campus, they're on a par with the best of San Francisco's North Beach for bohemian atmosphere – heady with the smell of coffee, and from dawn to near midnight full of earnest characters wearing their intellects on their sleeves. If you're not after a caffeine fix, you can generally also get a glass of beer, wine, or fresh fruit juice, though for serious drinking you'll be better off in one of the many **bars**, particularly in rough-hewn Oakland. Grittier versions of what you'd find in San Francisco, they're mostly blue-collar, convivial, and almost always cheaper. Not surprisingly, Berkeley's bars are brimming with students, academics, and those who don't mind mixing with them.

### Cafés

**Café Mediterraneum**, 2475 Telegraph Ave, Berkeley (☎841-5634). Berkeley's oldest café, straight out of the Beat archives: beards and berets optional, battered paperbacks *de rigeur*.

**Café Milano**, 2522 Bancroft Way, Berkeley (☎644-3100). Airy, arty café across from UC Berkeley.

**Café Strada**, 2300 College Ave, Berkeley (☎843-5282). Upmarket, open-air café where art and architecture students cross paths with would-be lawyers and chess wizards.

**Coffee Mill**, 3393 Grand Ave, Oakland (☎465-4224). Spacious room that doubles as an art gallery, and often hosts poetry readings.

**In the Company of Wolves**, 737 First St, Benicia (☎707/746-0572). Progressive coffee house, with sketch pads on the tables for caffeine-induced doodles.

**Mama Bear's**, 6536 Telegraph Ave, N Oakland (☎428-9684). Mainly a women's bookstore, it doubles as a café and meeting place and has regular readings, often for women only, by lesbian and feminist writers. Open daily 10.30am–7pm, later for readings.

**Peet's Coffee and Tea**, 2124 Vine St, Berkeley (☎841-0564), 3258 Lakeshore Ave, Oakland (☎832-6761), and numerous branches throughout the Bay Area. Originating in Berkeley, *Peet's* has grown from a dedicated cult following to a local market leader, with many charming outlets. Widely considered as the standard of extra-strong coffee.

### Bars

**Bison Brewing Company**, 2598 Telegraph Ave, Berkeley (☎841-7734). Eat and drink on the terrace, at great prices, where some of the best Bay Area beers are brewed. Honey Basil ale is highly recommended. Noisy bands at the weekend.

**Brennan's**, Third St and University, Berkeley (☎841-0960). Solidly blue-collar hang-out that's a great place for drinking inexpensive beers, watching a game on TV.

**Chalkers Billiard Club**, 5900 Hollis St, Emeryville (☎658-5821). The antithesis of a pool hall dive, this posh hall has the best tables and equipment around. Pay by the hour, which is not cheap. Drinks served to tables.

**Eline Ale House**, 5612 College Ave, Oakland (☎5547-8786). Large selection of microbrewed beer from around the US and excellent food of mixed origins.

**Heinhold's First and Last Chance Saloon**, 56 Jack London Square, Oakland (☎839-6761). Authentic waterfront bar that's hardly changed since the turn of the century, when Jack London was a regular.

**The Kingfish**, 5227 Claremont Ave, Oakland (☎655-7373). More like a tumbledown shed than a bar, selling low-priced pitchers of cold beer to UC Berkeley rugby players and other headbangers.

**Rickey's Sports Lounge**, 15028 Hesperian Blvd, San Leandro, near Bayfair *BART* (☎352-0200). With seven giant-screen TVs and 35 others spread around the cavernous room, this bar-cum-restaurant is the place to go to watch sports.

**Triple Rock Brewery**, 1920 Shattuck Ave, Berkeley (☎843-2739). Buzzing, all-American beer bar: the decor is Edward Hopper-era retro, and the beers (brewed on the premises) are highly carbonated to suit the soda-pop palates of the studenty crowd, but it's still fun.

**The White Horse**, 6560 Telegraph Ave at 66th St, Oakland (☎652-3820). Oakland's oldest gay bar – a smallish, friendly place, with mixed nightly dancing for men and women.

# Nightlife

**Nightlife** is where the East Bay really comes into its own. Even more than in San Francisco, dancing to canned music and paying high prices for flashy decor is not the done thing, which means that discos are virtually non-existent. Instead there are dozens of **live music** venues, covering a range of musical tastes and styles – from small, unpretentious jazz clubs to buzzing r'n'b venues – of which Oakland's hot spots are unsurpassed. Berkeley's clubs tend more towards folk and "world" music, with occasional bouts of hardcore thrash, and the university itself holds two of the best medium-sized venues in the entire Bay Area, both of which attract touring big-name stars. **Tickets** for most venues are available at their box office or, for a $3 service charge, through BASS (☎762-2277).

Though not bad by US standards, the East Bay theatre scene isn't exactly thriving, and shows tend to be politically worthy rather than dramatically innovative. By contrast, the range of **films** is first class, with a dozen movie theatres showing new releases and Berkeley's Pacific Film Archive, one of the world's finest film libraries, filling its screens with obscure but brilliant art flicks.

Check the free *East Bay Express* or the *SF Weekly* for details of who and **what's on** where in the entire East Bay region.

## The large performance venues

**Berkeley Community Theater**, 1930 Allston Way, Berkeley (☎845-2308). Jimi Hendrix played here, and the 3500-seat theatre still hosts major rock concerts and community events.

**Center for Contemporary Music**, Mills College, 5000 MacArthur Bvld, Oakland (☎430-2191). One of the prime centres in the world for experimental music.

**Oakland Coliseum Complex**, Coliseum *BART*, near the airport (☎639-7700). Mostly stadium shows, inside the 18,000-seat Arena or outdoors in the adjacent 55,000-seat Coliseum.

**Paramount Theater**, 2025 Broadway, downtown Oakland (☎465-6400). Beautifully restored Art Deco masterpiece, hosting classical concerts, big-name crooners, ballets and operas. Tickets $6–20. Friday nights they play old Hollywood classics for $5.

**Zellerbach Hall** and the outdoor **Greek Theater** on the UC Berkeley campus (☎642-9988). Two of the prime spots for catching touring big names in the Bay Area. Tickets cost $15–25.

## Live music venues

**Ashkenaz**, 1317 San Pablo Ave, Berkeley (☎525-5054). World music and dance café. Acts range from modern Afro-beat to the best of the Balkans. Kids and under-21s welcome. Cover $5–8.

**Caribee Dance Center**, 1408 Webster St, Oakland (☎835-4006). For reggae, rockers, calypso, soca, dub, salsa or lambada, this place is hard to beat. Cover $3–8.

**Eli's Mile High Club**, 3629 Martin Luther King Jr Way, North Oakland (☎655-6661). The best of the Bay Area blues clubs. Waitresses balance pitchers of beer on their heads to facilitate a safer passage through the rocking crowds. Cover $5–8.

**Freight and Salvage**, 1111 Addison St, W Berkeley (☎548-1761). Singer-songwriters in a coffee house setting. Cover $6–12.

**Gilman Street Project**, 924 Gilman St, W Berkeley (☎525-9926). On the outer edge of the hardcore punk scene. Cover $3–6.

**Kimball's East**, 4800 Shellmound St, Emeryville (☎658-2555). Fairly slick, high-style jazz and dancing venue. Cover $10–25.

**Koncepts Cultural Gallery**, Oakland (☎763-0682). Excellent, ground-breaking jazz organization, hosting a wide variety of different acts at venues around Oakland. Cover $8–25.

**La Peña Cultural Center**, 3105 Shattuck Ave, Berkeley near Ashby *BART* (☎849-2568). More folk than rock, often politically charged. Cover $3–6.

**tork Club**, 380 12th St, Oakland (☎444-6147). Local alternative bands and experimental musicians play at this downtown Oakland bar with pool table. Doubles as a country and western bar during the day.

## Cinemas

**Act One and Act Two**, 2128 Center St, Berkeley (☎548-7200). Foreign films and non-mainstream American ones.

**Grand Lake Theater**, 3200 Grand Ave (☎452-3556). The grand dame of East Bay picture palaces, right on Lake Merritt, showing the best of the current major releases.

**Pacific Film Archive**, 2621 Durant Ave, Berkeley, in the University Art Museum (☎642-1124). For the serious film fan, this is perhaps the best cinema in all California, with seasons of contemporary works from around the world, plus revivals of otherwise forgotten favourites. Two films a night; tickets $5.50 each, $7 for both.

**UC Theater**, 2036 University Ave, Berkeley, just below Shattuck Ave (☎843-6267). Popular revival house, with a huge auditorium and a daily double feature. Tickets $5.

## Theatre

**Berkeley Repertory Theater**, 2025 Addison St, Berkeley (☎845-4700). One of the West Coast's most highly respected theatre companies, presenting updated classics and contemporary plays in an intimate modern theatre. Tickets $6–25.

**Black Repertory Group**, 3201 Adeline St, Berkeley near Ashby *BART* (☎652-2120). After years of struggling, this politically conscious company moved into its own specially built home in 1987, since when they've encouraged new talent with great success. Tickets $5–15.

**California Shakespeare Festival**, Siesta Valley, Orinda (☎548-3422). After 15 seasons in a North Berkeley park, this summer-long outdoor festival was forced to move to a larger home in the East Bay Hills. Tickets $8–30.

**Julia Morgan Theater**, 2640 College Ave (☎845-8542). A variety of touring shows stop off in this cunningly converted old church. Tickets $8–20.

# The Peninsula

The city of San Francisco sits at the tip of a five-mile-wide **Peninsula**. Home of old money and new technology, this stretches south from San Francisco along the bay for fifty miles of relentless suburbia, past the wealthy enclaves of Hillsborough and Atherton, to wind up in the futuristic roadside landscape of the **"Silicon Valley"** near **San Jose** – though your only glimpse of the area may be on the trip between San Francisco and the airport. There was a time when the region was covered with orange groves and fig trees, but the concentration of academic interest around Stanford University in Palo Alto and the continuing boom in computers – since the 1970s the biggest local industry – has buried any chances of it hanging on to its agricultural past.

Surprisingly, most of the land along the **coast** (separated from the bayfront sprawl by a ridge of redwood-covered peaks) remains rural and undeveloped; it also contains some of the best **beaches** in the Bay Area and a couple of affably down-to-earth farming communities, all well served by public transport.

The telephone **area code** for the peninsula is ☎415; for San Jose it's ☎408.

## Getting around and information

*BART* only travels down the Peninsula as far as **Daly City**, from where you can catch *SamTrans* (☎1-800/660-4287) buses south to Palo Alto or along the coast to Half Moon Bay. For longer distances, *SamTrans* runs the *Caltrain* rail service from its terminal at Fourth and Townsend in downtown San Francisco, stopping at most bayside towns between the city and San Jose, for $1–5; *Greyhound* runs buses along US-101 to and from its San Jose terminal at 70 S Almaden, on the corner of Santa Clara Street. *Santa Clara County Transit* (*SCCT*) (☎408/321-2300) runs buses and modern trolleys around metropolitan San Jose. If you're going to spend most of your time down here, you could fly direct into **San Jose International Airport** (SJO), surprisingly (perhaps dangerously) close to downtown San Jose.

### Information

The **Palo Alto Chamber of Commerce**, 325 Forest Ave (Mon–Fri 9am–noon & 1–5pm; ☎324-3121), has lists of local restaurants and cycle routes; for information on nearby Stanford University phone ☎723-2560. To find out what's on and where, pick up a free copy of the *Palo Alto Weekly*, available at most local shops. At the southern end of the bay, the **San Jose CVB**, 333 W San Carlos Street, Suite 1000 (Mon–Sat 9am–5pm; ☎408/295-9600 or 1-800/SAN-JOSE), is the best bet for tourist information; for local news and events pick up a copy of the excellent *San Jose Mercury* newspaper or the free weekly *Metro*. Along the coast, the **Half Moon Bay Chamber of Commerce**, 520 Kelly Ave (☎726-5202), gives out walking tour maps and information on accommodation.

## Peninsula accommodation

Many visitors to San Francisco choose to **stay on the Peninsula** rather than in the city. Dozens of $60-a-night motels line Hwy-82 – "El Camino Real", the old main highway – and, with a bit of advance planning (and a car), sleeping here can save a lot of money. Also, if you're **arriving late** or departing on an early flight from SFO you might want to avail yourself of one of the many airport hotels listed on p.366. Perhaps the best reason to spend the night down on the Peninsula is its many low-priced, pleasant **hostels**, two of which are housed in old lighthouses bang on the Pacific coast. San Jose offers little in the way of an overnight stay.

### Hostels

**HI-Hidden Villa**, 26807 Moody Rd, Los Altos Hills (☎941-6407). Located on an 1800-acre ranch in the foothills above the Silicon Valley; closed June–Sept. $11 a night, $13 non-*HI* members. ①.

**HI-Pigeon Point Lighthouse**, Hwy-1, south of Pescadero, 50 miles south of San Francisco (☎879-0633). Worth planning a couple days around, this beautifully sited hostel is ideal for exploring the redwoods in the hills above or watching the wildlife in nearby Año Nuevo State Reserve. $11 *HI* members; $13 others. ①.

**HI-Point Montara Lighthouse**, Hwy-1, Montara, 25 miles south of San Francisco (☎728-7177). Dorm rooms in a converted 1875 lighthouse, accessible from the city via *SamTrans* bus #1A. $11 a night *HI* members; $13 others. ①.

**HI-Sanborn Park Hostel**, 15808 Sanborne Rd, Saratoga (☎741-0166). Comfortable rooms in a wooded area fifteen minutes outside San Jose. $7.50 members, $9.50 non-members. ①.

### Motels and hotels

**Best Western Inn**, 455 S Second St, San Jose (☎298-3500). Right in downtown San Jose, with pool and sauna. ④.

**Best Western Stanford Park Hotel**, 100 El Camino Real, Menlo Park (☎322-1234). Very pleasant hotel near Stanford University. ⑤.

**Hotel De Anza**, 233 W Santa Clara St, downtown San Jose (☎286-1000). Marvellously restored 1930s hotel, richly packed with Moorish and Mission-style Art Deco trappings. ⑤.

**Old Thyme Inn**, 779 Main St, Half Moon Bay (☎726-1616). Half a dozen incredibly quaint rooms, each with private bath, in lovely Victorian house surrounded by luxuriant herb and flower gardens. ⑤.

**San Benito House**, 356 Main St, Half Moon Bay (☎726-3425). Twelve restful B&B rooms in a 100-year-old building, just a mile from the beach. Excellent restaurant downstairs. ⑤.

**Valley Inn**, 2155 The Alameda, San Jose (☎241-8500). Standard motel not far from the Rosicrucian Museum. ③.

## Campgrounds

**Butano State Park**, Pescadero (☎879-0173). RV and tent spaces in a beautiful redwood forest.

**Half Moon Bay State Beach**, Half Moon Bay (☎726-6238). Sleep out (illegally but safely) along the beach for free, or in the campground for $14.

# South along the Bay

US-101 runs **south** from San Francisco along the bay through over fifty miles of unmitigated sprawl to San Jose, lined by light industrial estates and shopping malls. The only place worth stopping at is the **Coyote Point Museum** (Wed–Fri 9am–5pm, Sat & Sun 1–5pm; free), four miles south of the airport off Poplar Avenue in a large bayfront park, where examples of the natural life of the San Francisco Bay – from tidal insects to birds of prey – are exhibited in engaging and informative displays, enhanced by interactive computers and documentary films.

A more pleasant drive is via **I-280**, the newest and most expensive interstate highway in California, which runs parallel to US-101 but avoids the worst of the bayside mess by cutting through wooded valleys down the centre of the Peninsula. Just beyond the San Francisco city limit the road passes through **COLMA**, a unique place made up entirely of cemeteries, which are prohibited within San Francisco. Beside the expected roll call of famous San Franciscans are a few surprises, such as Wild West marshal Wyatt Earp.

Beyond Colma the scenery improves quickly as I-280 continues past the **Crystal Springs Reservoir**, an artificial lake that holds the water supply for San Francisco – pumped here all the way from Yosemite. Surrounded by twenty square miles of parkland, hiking trails lead up to the ridge from which San Francisco Bay was first spotted by eighteenth-century Spanish explorers; it now overlooks the airport to the east, but there are good views out over the Pacific coast, two miles distant.

At the south end of the reservoir, just off I-280 on Canada Road in the well-heeled town of **WOODSIDE**, luscious gardens surround the palatial **Filoli Estate** (tours Tues–Sat 10.30am & 1pm; $8; reservations required on ☎364-2880). The 45-room mansion, designed in 1915 in neo-Palladian style by architect Willis Polk, may look familiar – it was used in the TV series *Dynasty* as the Denver home of the Carrington clan. It's the only one of the many huge houses around here that you can actually visit, although the gardens are what make it worth a look, especially in the spring when everything's in bloom.

## Palo Alto and Stanford University

**PALO ALTO**, just south and three miles east of Woodside between I-280 and US-101, is a small, leafy community with all the contrived atmosphere you'd expect to find in a college town but little of the vigour of its northern counterpart, Berkeley. Though it doesn't merit an overnight stay, you could spend a lazy day in the bookstores and cafés that line University Avenue, the town's main drag. Or, if you're feeling energetic, try cycling around the town's many well-marked bike routes; a range of bikes is available for $12–25 a day from *Action Sports Limited* at 401 High St (☎328-3180), near the

*Caltrain* station a block west of University Avenue. Be aware, however, that **East Palo Alto**, on the bay side of US-101, has a well-deserved reputation for gang and drug-related violence, with one of the highest per capita murder rates of any US city. Founded in the 1920s as the utopian Runnymeade colony, an agricultural, poultry-raising cooperative – the local historical society (☎329-0294) can point out the surviving sites – East Palo Alto is an anomaly on the otherwise wealthy Peninsula, and about as far as you can get off the San Francisco tourist trail.

**Stanford University**, spreading out from the west end of University Avenue, is by contrast one of the tamest places you could hope for. The university is one of the best – and most expensive – in California, though when it opened in 1891, founded by rail magnate Leland Stanford in memory of his dead son, it offered free tuition. Ridiculed by East Coast academics, who felt that there was as much need for a second West Coast university (after UC Berkeley) as there was for "an asylum for decayed sea captains in Switzerland," Stanford was defiantly built anyway, in a hybrid of Mission and Romanesque buildings on a huge campus that covers an area larger than the whole of downtown San Francisco.

Stanford, whose reputation as an arch-conservative think-tank was enhanced by Ronald Reagan's offer to donate his video library to the school (Stanford politely declined), hasn't always been an entirely boring place, though you wouldn't know it to walk among the preppy future-lawyers-of-America that seem to comprise ninety percent of the student body. Ken Kesey came here from Oregon in 1958 on a writing fellowship, working nights as an orderly on the psychiatric ward of one local hospital, and getting paid $75 a day to test experimental drugs (LSD among them) in another. Drawing on both experiences, Kesey wrote *One Flew Over the Cuckoo's Nest* in 1960 and quickly became a counterculture hero.

Approaching from the Palo Alto *Caltrain* and *SamTrans* bus station, which acts as a buffer between the town and the university, you enter the campus via a half-mile-long, palm-tree-lined boulevard which deposits you at its heart, the **Quadrangle**, bordered by the phallic **Hoover Tower** and the colourful, gold-leaf mosaics of the **Memorial Church**. Free hour-long walking tours of the campus leave from here daily at 11am and 2pm, though it's fairly big and is best seen by car or bike.

The **Stanford Museum of Art**, between "the Quad" and the town, was damaged by the 1989 earthquake and is scheduled to reopen in 1998. Until then, the best reason to come here is to have a look at the distinguished collection of **Rodin sculpture**, including a a *Gates of Hell* flanked by a shamed *Adam and Eve*, displayed in an attractive outdoor setting on the museum's south side. Also, if you keep up on the latest trends in subatomic behaviour, you won't want to miss the **Stanford Linear Accelerator** (Mon–Fri by appointment only; ☎926-3300), a mile west of the central campus on Sand Hill Road, where infinitesimally small particles are crashed into one another at very high speeds to see what happens.

# San Jose

Despite the Burt Bacharach song, **SAN JOSE**, the fastest-growing major city in California, is not strong on identity, though in area and population it's close to twice the size of San Francisco. Sitting at the southern end of the Peninsula, located almost exactly in the centre of the state, its abundance of cheap land brought developers and businessmen into the area in the 1960s, hoping to draw from the concentration of talent in the commerce-oriented halls of Stanford University. Fuelled by the success of computer firms such as Apple, Intel and Hewlett-Packard, in the past 25 years San Jose has emerged as the civic heart of **Silicon Valley**, surrounded by miles of faceless high-tech industrial parks where the next generations of computers are designed and crafted. None of these is open to the public, and about the only place to key in on the emerging cyberworld is at the **Tech Museum of Innovation** (Tues–Sun 10am–5pm; $6), right downtown at 145 W San Carlos St, with hands-on displays of high-tech engineering.

Ironically enough, San Jose is one of the oldest settlements in California, though the only sign of it is at the late eighteenth-century **Mission Santa Clara de Asis**, on the grounds of the Jesuit-run University of Santa Clara, walkably close to the Santa Clara *Caltrain* station. Next to the mission, the **de Saisset Museum** (Tues–Fri 10am–5pm, Sat & Sun 1–5pm; $1) holds a permanent display of objects from the Mission era along with changing shows of contemporary art. Otherwise there are only a couple of good reasons to subject yourself to San Jose's relentlessly boring cityscape. The main attraction is the **Rosicrucian Museum**, 1342 Naglee Ave (daily 9am–5pm; $4). Languishing in the suburbs, this grand structure contains a brilliant collection of Assyrian and Babylonian artefacts, with displays of mummies, amulets, a replica of a tomb, and ancient jewellery.

You could also stop off at the **Winchester Mystery House**, 525 S Winchester Blvd, just off I-280 near Hwy-17 (daily 9.30am–4.30pm; $12.50). Sarah Winchester, heir to the Winchester rifle fortune, was convinced by an occultist upon her husband's death that he had been taken by the spirits of men killed with Winchester rifles. She was told that unless a room was built for each of the spirits and the sound of hammers never ceased, the same fate would befall her. Work on the mansion went on 24 hours per day for the next thirty years, with results that need to be seen to be believed – stairs lead nowhere, windows open on to solid brick, and so on. It is however a shameless tourist trap, and you have to run a gauntlet of ghastly gift shops and soda stands to get in or out.

One other Peninsula place might exercise a certain attraction, particularly to those fond of roller coasters, log rides, and all-American family fun: **Great America** (summer daily 10am–10pm; rest of year Sat & Sun only; $27.95). This huge hundred-acre amusement park on the edge of San Francisco Bay, just off US-101 north of San Jose, is not in the same league as Disneyland, but doesn't suffer from the same crowds and lengthy queues, and the range of high-speed thrills and chills – from the loop-the-looping "Demon" to "The Edge," where you free-fall in a steel cage for over a hundred feet – is well worth the entry fee, especially on weekdays when you may well have the place to yourself. The whole park is laid out into such heritage-themed areas as "Hometown Square," "Yankee Harbor," or "County Fair," each filled with all sorts of sideshow attractions and funfair games.

## The coast

The **coastline** of the Peninsula south from San Francisco is more appealing than inland – relatively undeveloped, with very few buildings, let alone towns, along the 75 miles of coves and beaches that extend down to the resort city of Santa Cruz. Bluffs protect the many nudist beaches from prying eyes and make a popular launching pad for hang-glider pilots, particularly at **Burton Beach** and **Fort Funston**, a mile south of the San Francisco Zoo – also the point where the earthquake-causing San Andreas Fault enters the sea, not to surface again until Point Reyes. Skyline Boulevard follows the coast from here past the repetitious tracts of proverbial ticky-tacky houses that make up Daly City, where it is joined by Hwy-1 for the rest of the journey.

**San Pedro Point**, a popular surfing beach fifteen miles south of the city proper, marks the southern extent of San Francisco's suburban sprawl. The old **Ocean Shore Railroad Depot** here, now a private residence, is one of the few surviving remnants of an ill-advised train line between San Francisco and Santa Cruz. Wiped out during the 1906 earthquake, the line was in any case never more than a third complete. Its few patrons had to transfer back and forth by ferry to connect the stretches of track that were built, the traces of which you can still see scarring the face of the bluffs. The continually eroding cliffs don't take very well to building work, as evidenced a mile south by the **Devil's Slide**, where the highway is washed away with some regularity in winter storms. The slide area was also a popular dumping spot for corpses of those who'd fallen foul of rum-runners during Prohibition, and features under various names in many of Dashiell Hammett's detective stories.

Just south of the Devil's Slide, the sands of **Gray Whale Cove State Beach** (daily dawn–dusk; $5 parking) are clothing-optional. Despite the name it's not an especially great place to look for migrating gray whales, but it is nevertheless a fine beach, accessible by a stairway from the bus stop. Two miles south, the red-roofed buildings of the Montara Lighthouse, set among the windswept Monterey pines at the top of a steep cliff, have been converted into a youth hostel (see p.444). There are a few good places to stop for a drink or a bite to eat in the town of **MOSS BEACH**, across Hwy-1.

South of the lighthouse, the **James Fitzgerald Marine Reserve** strings along the shore, a two-mile shelf of flat, slippery rocks that make excellent tidal pools. The ranger often gives guided interpretive walks through the reserve at low tide, the best time to explore. At the south end of the reserve, **Pillar Point** juts out into the Pacific; just to the east, along Hwy-1, fishing boats dock at **Pillar Point Harbor**. In the faintly touristy, ramshackle town adjacent to the waterfront – **PRINCETON-BY-THE-SEA** – a couple of bay-view restaurants sell fish (sometimes freshly caught) and chips.

## Half Moon Bay

**HALF MOON BAY**, twenty miles south of the city and the only town of any size between San Francisco and Santa Cruz, takes its name from the crescent-shaped bay formed by Pillar Point. Lined by miles of sandy beaches, the town is surprisingly rural considering its proximity to San Francisco and Silicon Valley, and sports a number of ornate Victorian wooden houses around its centre. The oldest of these is at the north end of Main Street: built in 1849, it's just across a little stone bridge over Pillarcitos Creek. The **Chamber of Commerce** (see p.444 for details) on Hwy-1 has free walking tour maps of the town and information on the two annual festivals for which the place is well known. These are the **Holy Ghost and Pentecost Festival**, a parade and barbe-cue held on the sixth Sunday after Easter, and the **Pumpkin Festival**, celebrating the harvest of the area's many pumpkin farms, just in time for Halloween when the fields around town are full of families searching for the perfect jack-o'-lantern to greet the hordes of trick-or-treaters. Free, primitive campgrounds line the coast in **Half Moon Bay State Park**, half a mile west of the town.

**San Gregorio State Beach**, ten miles south of Half Moon Bay, is at its best in the spring, after the winter storms, when flotsam architects construct a range of driftwood shelters along the wide beach south of the parking area. In summer the beach is packed with well-oiled bodies; the sands around the bluffs to the north are quieter.

## The Butano redwoods and the Año Nuevo State Reserve

If you've got a car and it's not a great day for the beach, head up into the hills above, where the thousands of acres of the **Butano redwood forest** feel at their most ancient and primeval in the greyest, gloomiest weather. About half the land between San Jose and the coast is protected from development in a variety of state and county parks, all of which are virtually deserted despite being within a half-hour's drive of the Silicon Valley sprawl. Any one of a dozen roads heads through endless stands of untouched forest, and even the briefest of walks will take you seemingly miles from any sign of civilization. Hwy-84 climbs up from San Gregorio through the Sam McDonald County Park to the hamlet of **LA HONDA**, from where you can continue on to Palo Alto, or, better, loop back to the coast via Pescadero Road. A mile before you reach the quaint town of **PESCADERO**, Cloverdale Road heads south to **Butano State Park**, where you can hike and camp overlooking the Pacific. Tiny Pescadero itself has one of the best places to eat on the Peninsula – *Duarte's* (see opposite).

Back on Hwy-1, five miles south of Pescadero you can stay the night in the old lighthouse keeper's quarters and soak your bones in a marvellous hot tub at the **Pigeon Point Lighthouse Hostel** (see p.444). If you're here in December or January, continue south another five miles to the **Año Nuevo State Reserve** for a chance to see one of nature's most bizarre spectacles – the mating rituals of the northern elephant seal. These massive, ungainly creatures, fifteen feet long and weighing up to three tons, were once found all along the coast, though they were nearly hunted to extinction by whalers in the last century. During the mating season the beach is literally a seething mass of blubbery bodies, with the trunk-nosed males fighting it out for the right to sire as many as fifty pups in a season. At any time of the year you're likely to see a half dozen or so dozing in the sands. The reserve is also good for bird-watching, and in March you might even catch sight of migrating gray whales.

The slowly resurgent Año Nuevo seal population is still carefully protected, and during the breeding season the obligatory guided tours – designed to protect spectators as much as to give the seals some privacy – are often oversubscribed (hourly 8am–4pm; ☎879-2025). Otherwise tickets are usually made available to people staying at the *Pigeon Point Hostel*, and *SamTrans* (☎348-SEAL) sometimes runs charter bus tours from the town of **San Mateo** on the bay side of the Peninsula. (See "The Central Coast" for an account of the area from Año Nuevo south to Santa Cruz and Monterey.)

## Peninsula eating and drinking

Though the **restaurants and bars** of the Peninsula hardly compete with those of San Francisco, the pace is more relaxed down here, and you may even get more for your dollar. Most of the restaurants are good spots for a drink and vice versa, so we've listed them all together, concentrating primarily on establishments centrally located in the downtown areas of the various Peninsula cities, and a few others that are worth almost any effort to get to. For late-night partying, check out the clubs described under "Nightlife"; all serve drinks until the early hours.

**Barbara's Fish Trap**, 281 Capistrano Rd, off Hwy-1, Princeton-by-the-Sea (☎728-7049). Oceanfront seafood restaurant with good-value fish dinnners and an unbeatable view.

**Barrio Fiesta**, 909 Antoinette Lane, off El Camino Real, S San Francisco (☎871-8703). Hard to find amid the shopping sprawl of South City, but well worth it for the huge portions of beautifully presented, delicious Filipino dishes, especially seafood. Full meals cost around $25, but you can snack for a lot less.

**Chateau de Flores**, 532 Church St, Half Moon Bay (☎712-8837). A small, pricey French restaurant fronted by an exquisite flower garden

**Duarte's**, 202 Stage Rd, Pescadero (☎879-0464). Traditional American food, especially fish, for around $10 in a downhome find connected to a bar full of locals in cowboy hats.

**Fresco**, 3398 El Camino Real, Palo Alto (☎493-3470). A wide range of pastas, pizzas and salads with palpably fresh ingredients in unusual combinations. Opens early.

**Lytton Street Roasting Company**, 401 Lytton St, Palo Alto (☎324-4320). Sit among large cloth bags of coffee beans in this small cafe a few blocks off the hustle of University Avenue.

**Original Joe's**, 301 S First St, San Jose (☎292-7030). Grab a stool at the counter or settle into one of the comfy booths and enjoy a burger and fries or a plate of pasta at this San Jose institution, where $10 goes a long way.

**The Peninsula Creamery**, 566 Emerson St, Palo Alto (☎323-3175). Nearly authentic 1950s American diner serving notable ice cream, milk shakes, and hearty burgers.

**Thep Thai**, 23 N Market St, San Jose (☎408/292-7515). Delicious, zestily spiced Thai food, with excellent satay and a broad range of tofu and chicken dishes.

**Vicolo Pizzeria**, 473 University Ave, Palo Alto (☎324-4877). Café serving a variety of tasty, affordable gourmet pizza.

## Peninsula nightlife

Many San Franciscans would deny it and think you were crazy even to suggest the possibility, but there's a surprisingly good **nightlife** scene on the Peninsula, particularly in San Jose, but also in the studenty environs of Palo Alto.

**Cactus Club**, 417 S First St, San Jose (☎491-9300). One of two very good clubs near each other in downtown San Jose, hosting some of the better up-and-coming bands with music ranging from roots reggae to hardcore thrash. Cover $4–8.

**The Edge**, 260 California Ave, Palo Alto (☎324-EDGE). Cheap drinks and low (or no) cover charge make this dance club a lively option. Good live bands some nights, when tickets cost $5–7.

**FX: The Club**, 400 S First St, San Jose (☎298-9796). The other good San Jose club, more jazz/hip-hoppy, great for drinking and dancing; 21 and over only. Closed Mon and Tues; free before 10pm, $6 after.

# Marin County

Across the Golden Gate from San Francisco, Marin County (pronounced *Ma-RINN*) is an unabashed introduction to Californian self-indulgence: an elitist pleasure zone of conspicuous luxury and abundant natural beauty, with sunshine, sandy beaches, high mountains, and thick redwood forests. Often ranked as the wealthiest county in the US, Marin has attracted a sizeable contingent of northern California's wealthiest young professionals, many of whom grew up during the Flower Power years of the 1960s and lend the place its New Age feel and reputation. Though many of the cocaine-and-hot-tub devotees who seemed to populate the swanky waterside towns in the 1970s have traded in their drug habits for mountain bikes, life in Marin still centres around personal pleasure, and the throngs you see hiking and cycling at weekends, not to mention the hundreds of esoteric self-help practitioners – Rolfing, Re-Birthing, and soul-travel therapists fill up the classified ads of the local papers – prove that Marinites work hard to maintain their easy air of physical and mental wellbeing.

Flashy modern ferry boats, appointed with fully stocked bars, sail across the bay from San Francisco and give a good initial view of the county; heading past desolate Alcatraz Island, curvaceous **Mount Tamalpais** looms larger until you land at its foot in one of the chic bayside settlements of **Sausalito** or **Tiburon**. **Angel Island**, in the middle of the bay but accessible most easily from Tiburon, provides relief from the excessive style-consciousness of both towns, retaining a wild untouched feeling among the eerie ruins of derelict military fortifications.

Sausalito and Tiburon, and the lifestyles that go with them, are only a small part of Marin. The bulk of the county rests on the slopes of the ridge of peaks that divides the peninsula down the middle, separating the sophisticated harbourside towns in the east from the untrammelled wilderness of the Pacific coast to the west. The **Marin Headlands**, just across the Golden Gate Bridge, hold time-warped old battlements and gun emplacements that once protected San Francisco's harbour from would-be invaders, and now overlook surfers and backpackers enjoying the acres of open space. Along the coastline that stretches north, the broad shore of **Stinson Beach** is the Bay Area's finest and widest stretch of sand, beyond which Hwy-1 clings to the coast past the rural village of **Bolinas** to the seascapes of **Point Reyes**, where in 1579 Sir Francis Drake landed and claimed all of California for England.

Inland, the heights of Mount Tamalpais – and specifically **Muir Woods** – are a magnet to sightseers and nature-lovers, who come to wander through one of the few surviving stands of the native coastal redwood trees that once covered most of Marin. The trees were chopped down to build and rebuild the dainty wooden houses of San Francisco, and the long-vanished lumber mills of the rustic town of **Mill Valley** over-

The telephone **area code** for Marin County is ☎415.

looking the bay from the slopes of Mount Tam, as it's locally known, bear the guilt for much of this destruction; the oldest town in Marin County is now home to an eclectic bunch of art galleries and cafés. Further north, Marin's largest town, **San Rafael**, is best left alone, though its outskirts contain two of the most unusual places in the county: **Frank Lloyd Wright**'s peculiar Civic Center complex and the preserved remnants of an old Chinese fishing village in **China Camp State Park**. The northern reaches of Marin County border the bountiful wine-growing regions of the Sonoma and Napa valleys, detailed in Northern California.

## Arrival and getting around

Just getting to Marin County can be a great start to a day out from San Francisco. *Golden Gate Transit* **ferries** (☎923-3000) leave from the Ferry Building on the Embarcadero, crossing the bay past Alcatraz Island to **Sausalito** and **Larkspur**; they run from 5.30am until 8pm, approximately every thirty minutes during the rush hour, less often the rest of the day, and every two hours at weekends and holidays. Tickets cost $4.25 one-way to Sausalito, $2.50 to Larkspur, and refreshments (including a well-stocked bar) are served on board. The *Red and White Fleet* ferries ($6.50 each way; ☎546-2805) sail from Pier 43$^1$/$_2$ at Fisherman's Wharf to **Sausalito** and to **Tiburon** – from where the *Angel Island Ferry* ($5 round-trip, plus $1 per bicycle; ☎435-2131) nips back and forth to **Angel Island State Park** daily in summer, weekends only in the winter.

*Golden Gate Transit* also runs a comprehensive **bus service** around Marin County and across the Golden Gate Bridge from the Transbay Terminal in San Francisco (from Marin County, phone ☎453-2100), and publishes a helpful and free system map and timetable, including all ferry services. Bus fares range from $1 to $3, depending on

### SAN FRANCISCO–MARIN COUNTY FERRIES

Note: the ferry **schedules** change four times per year, when new timetables are issued at the terminals. The changes are not drastic, therefore the following schedules give a close estimation of arrival and departure times.

*GOLDEN GATE TRANSIT* FERRIES (☎923-3000)

**San Francisco–Sausalito**: depart at 7.40am, 10.25am, 11.45am, 1.10pm, 2.35pm, 4.10pm, 5.30pm, 6.40pm & 8pm.

**Sausalito–San Francisco**: depart at 7.05am, 8.15 am, 11.05am, 12.25pm, 1.55pm, 3.20pm, 4.45pm, 6.05pm & 7.20pm.

**San Francisco–Larkspur**: depart at 6.50am, 7.50am, 8.50am, 10.45am, 12.45pm, 2.45pm, 3.35pm, 4.15pm, 4.50pm, 5.20pm, 6pm, 6.45pm & 8.25pm.

**Larkspur–San Francisco**: depart at 6am, 7am, 7.30am, 8am, 8.40am, 9.45am, 11.45am, 1.45pm, 3.45pm, 4.25pm, 5.05pm, 5.40pm & 7.35pm.

*RED AND WHITE FLEET* FERRIES (☎546-2805)

**San Francisco–Sausalito**: depart at 11am, 12.15pm, 1.35pm, 3pm & 4.50pm.

**Sausalito–San Francisco**: depart at 11.50am, 1.05pm, 2.20pm, 3.30pm, 5,45pm & 8pm.

**San Francisco–Tiburon**: depart at 11am, 12.45pm, 1.35pm, 3pm, 4.05pm & 4.50pm.

**Tiburon–San Francisco**: depart at 11.25am, 12.40pm, 1.55pm, 3.20pm, 5.25 & 7.45pm.

## MARIN COUNTY BUS SERVICES

**#10**: San Francisco–Sausalito–Marin City–Mill Valley–Tiburon

**#20**: San Francisco–Marin City–Larkspur–San Anselmo–San Rafael

**#24**: San Francisco–San Anselmo–Fairfax–Point Reyes Station; once a day at 5.40pm, weekdays only.

**#50**: San Francisco–Sausalito–Marin City–San Rafael

**#63**: Marin City–Stinson Beach; Sat, Sun & holidays only 8.45am, 9.45am & 10.45am.

**#65**: San Rafael–Point Reyes; Sat & Sun only 9am & 4pm.

the distance travelled. Basic *GGT* bus routes run every half hour throughout the day, and once an hour late at night. *GGT* commuter services, which run only during the morning and evening rush hours, can be the only way to get to some places. Also, San Francisco's *Muni* bus #76 runs hourly from San Francisco direct to the Marin Headlands on Sundays only.

If you'd rather avoid the hassle of bus connections, San Francisco *Gray Line* offers four-hour **guided bus tours** (daily 9am, 11am & 1.30pm; $37.50; ☎558-9400), taking in Sausalito and Muir Woods; the *Red and White* ferry fleet also has a boat-and-bus trip ($24) to Muir Woods, via Tiburon.

One of the best ways to get around Marin is by **bike**, particularly by mountain bike, cruising along the many trails that crisscross the county. If you want to ride on the road, **Sir Francis Drake Highway** – from Larkspur to Point Reyes – makes a good route, though it's best avoided at weekends when the roads can get clogged up with cars. All ferry services (except Alcatraz) allow bicycles.

## Information

Three main on-the-spot sources give further information regarding Marin County: the **Marin CVB**, 30 N San Pedro Rd, San Rafael (Mon–Fri 9am–5pm; ☎472-7470); the **Sausalito Chamber of Commerce**, 333 Caledonia St (Mon–Fri 9am–5pm; ☎332-0505); and the **Mill Valley Chamber of Commerce**, 85 Throckmorton Ave (Mon–Fri 9.30am–4pm; ☎388-9700), in the centre of town.

For information on **hiking** and **camping** in the wilderness and beach areas, depending on where you're heading, contact the **Golden Gate National Recreation Area**, Building 201, Fort Mason Center (daily 9am–4pm; ☎556-0560), **Mount Tamalpais State Park**, 801 Panoramic Highway, Mill Valley (daily 9am–5pm; ☎388-2070), or the **Point Reyes National Seashore**, Bear Valley, Point Reyes (daily 9am–5pm; ☎663-1092). Information on **what's on** in Marin can be found in the widely available local freesheets, such as the down-to-earth *Coastal Post* or the New-Agey *Pacific Sun*.

## Across the Golden Gate: Marin Headlands and Sausalito

The headlands across the Golden Gate from San Francisco afford some of the most impressive views of the bridge and the city behind. Take the first turn past the bridge, and follow the road up the hill into the **Marin Headlands** section of the Golden Gate National Recreation Area – largely undeveloped land, except for the concrete remains of old forts and gun emplacements standing guard over the entrance to the bay. The coastline here is much more rugged than it is on the San Francisco side, and though it makes a great place for an aimless clifftop scramble or a walk along the beach, it's impossible not to be at least a little sobered by the presence of so many military relics – even if none was ever fired in a war. The oldest of these artillery batteries dates from the Civil War, while the newest was built to protect against a Japanese invasion during

World War II, but even though the huge guns have been replaced by picnic tables and brass plaques – one of the concrete bunkers has even been painted to make a *trompe-l'oeil* Greek temple – you can't overlook their violent intent. **Battery Wallace**, the largest and most impressive of the artillery sites, is cut through a hillside above the southwestern tip, and the clean-cut military geometry survives to frame views of the Pacific Ocean and the Golden Gate Bridge. If you're interested in such things, come along on the first Sunday of the month and take a guided tour of an abandoned 1950s ballistic missile launchpad, complete with disarmed nuclear missiles. The one non-military sight, the **Point Bonita Lighthouse**, stands at the very end of the Headlands, where it's open for tours at weekends, except during the winter.

Most of what there is to do out here is concentrated half a mile to the north, around the rocky cliffs and islets of the point. At the end of the *Muni* bus #76 route from San Francisco (Sun and holidays only), a wide sandy beach fronts the chilly ocean and marshy warm water of **Rodeo Lagoon**, where swimming is prohibited to protect the nesting seabirds. Next to the centre, the **Marine Mammal Center** rescues and rehabilitates injured and orphaned sea creatures, which you can visit while they recover; there's also a series of displays on the marine ecosystem and a bookstore selling T-shirts and posters. The largest of the old army officers' quarters in the adjacent **Fort Barry**, half a mile to the east, has been converted into the spacious and cosy **Marin Headlands Youth Hostel** (see p.459), a good base for exploring the inland ridges and valleys.

## Sausalito

**SAUSALITO**, along the bay below US-101, is a pretty, smug little town of exclusive restaurants and pricey boutiques lining a picturesque waterfront promenade. Expensive, quirkily designed houses climb the overgrown cliffs above **Bridgeway Avenue**, the main road and bus route through town. This used to be a fairly gritty community of fishermen and sea traders, full of bars and bordellos, and despite its upscale modern face it still makes a fun day out from San Francisco by ferry, the boats arriving next to the Sausalito Yacht Club in the centre of town. Hang out in one of the waterfront bars and watch the crowds strolling along the esplanade, or climb the stairways above Bridgeway and amble around the leafy hills. If you have sailing experience, split the $85 daily rental fee of a four- to six-person sailing boat at *Cass's Marine*, 1792 Bridgeway Ave (☎332-6789).

The old working wharves and warehouses that made Sausalito a haven for smugglers and Prohibition-era rum-runners are long gone; most have been taken over by dull steakhouses such as the *Charthouse* – fifty years ago one of the settings for Orson Welles' waterfront murder-mystery, *The Lady from Shanghai*. Half a mile north of the town centre along Bridgeway Avenue, an ad hoc community of exotic barges and houseboats, some of which have been moored here since the 1950s, is being threatened with eviction to make room for yet another luxury marina and bay-view offices. But for now many of the **boats** – one looks like a South Pacific island, another like the Taj Mahal – can be viewed from the marina behind the large shed that houses the Army Corps of Engineers **museum** (Mon–Sat 9am–4pm; free). Don't overlook the museum, either, which features a massive working model of the San Francisco Bay, simulating changing tides and powerful currents.

## The Marin County Coast to Bolinas

The **Shoreline Highway**, Hwy-1, cuts off west from US-101 just north of Sausalito, following the old main highway towards Mill Valley (see p.455). The first turn on the left, Tennessee Valley Road, leads up to the less-visited northern expanses of the Golden Gate National Recreation Area. You can make a beautiful three-mile hike from the parking lot at the end of the road, heading down along the secluded and lushly green **Tennessee Valley** to a small beach along a rocky cove; or take a guided tour on horseback from *Miwok Livery* ($25 per hour; ☎383-8048).

Hwy-1 twists up the canyon to a crest, where **Panoramic Highway** spears off to the right, following the ridge north to Muir Woods and Mount Tamalpais (see opposite); *Golden Gate Transit* bus #63 to Stinson Beach follows this route every hour on weekends and holidays only. Two miles down from the crest, a small unpaved road cuts off to the left, dropping down to the bottom of the broad canyon to the **Green Gulch Farm and Zen Center** (☎383-3134), an organic farm and Buddhist retreat, with an authentic Japanese tea house and a simple but refined prayer hall. On Sunday mornings the centre is opened for a public meditation period and an informal discussion of Zen Buddhism, after which you can stroll down to Muir Beach. If you already have some experience of Zen, enquire about the centre's Guest Student Program, which enables initiates to stay from three days to several weeks at a time (it costs about $10 a night). If you just want a weekend's retreat, you can also stay overnight in the attached *Lindisfarne Guest House* (⑨), whose rates include meals, and take part as you choose in the communal life. Residents rise well before dawn for meditation and prayer, then work much of the day in the gardens, tending the vegetables that are eventually served in many of the Bay Area's finest restaurants (notably *Green's* in San Francisco – see p.397).

Beyond the Zen Center, the road down from Muir Woods rejoins Hwy-1 at **Muir Beach**, surprisingly dark and usually uncrowded, stretched around a semicircular cove. Three miles north, **Steep Ravine** drops sharply down the cliffs to a small beach, past very rustic $30-a-night cabins and a $9-a-night campground, bookable through Mount Tamalpais State Park (see under "Information", p.452). A mile further on is the small and lovely **Red Rocks** nudist beach, down a steep trail from a parking area along the highway. **Stinson Beach**, which is bigger, and more popular despite the rather cold water (it's packed at weekends in summer, when the traffic can be nightmarish), is a mile farther. You can rent boogie boards and wetsuits from the *Livewater Surf Shop* (☎868-0333), 3448 Shoreline Hwy, or kayaks ($35–$50 per day) a bit further down the road at the *Stinson Beach Health Club*, no. 3605 (☎868-2739).

## Bolinas and southern Point Reyes

At the tip of the headland, due west from Stinson Beach, is the village of **BOLINAS**, though you may have a hard time finding it – road signs marking the turnoff from Hwy-1 are removed as soon as they're put up by locals hoping to keep their place all to themselves. The campaign may have backfired, though, since press coverage of the "sign war" has done more to publicize the town than any road sign ever did; to get there, take the first left beyond the estuary and follow the road to the end. Bolinas is completely surrounded by Federal property: the Golden Gate National Recreation Area and Point Reyes National Seashore. Even the lagoon was recently declared a national bird sanctuary. The village itself is a small colony of artists and writers (the late trout-fishing author Richard Brautigan and basketball diarist Jim Carroll among them), and there's not a lot to see – though you can get a feel for the place (and pick up a tasty sandwich and bags of fresh fruit and vegetables) at the *Bolinas People's Store* in the block-long village centre.

Beyond Bolinas there's a rocky beach at the end of Wharf Road west of the village; and at low tide the **Duxbury Reef Nature Reserve**, half a mile west at the end of Elm Road, is well worth a look for its rock pools, full of starfish, crabs, and sea anemones. Otherwise, Mesa Road heads north from Bolinas past the **Point Reyes Bird Observatory** (☎868-0655) – open for informal tours all day, though best visited in the morning. The first bird observatory in the US, this is still an important research and study centre: if you time it right you may be able to watch, or even help, the staff as they put coloured bands on the birds to keep track of them. Beyond here, an unpaved road leads on to the **Palomarin Trailhead**, the southern access to the Point Reyes National Seashore (see p.458). The best of many beautiful hikes around the area leads past a number of small lakes and meadows for three miles to **Alamere Falls**, which throughout the winter and spring cascade down the cliffs onto Wildcat Beach.

## Mount Tamalpais and Muir Woods

**Mount Tamalpais** dominates the skyline of the Marin peninsula, hulking over the cool canyons of the rest of the county in a crisp yet voluptuous silhouette and dividing the county into two distinct parts: the wild western slopes above the Pacific coast and the increasingly suburban communities along the calmer bay frontage. Panoramic Highway branches off from Hwy-1 along the crest through the centre of **Mount Tamalpais State Park**, which has some thirty miles of hiking trails and many campgrounds, though most of the redwood trees which once covered its slopes have long since been chopped down to form the posts and beams of San Francisco's Victorian houses. One grove of these towering trees does remain, however, protected as the **Muir Woods National Monument** (daily 8am–sunset; free), a mile down Muir Woods Road from Panoramic Highway. It's a tranquil and majestic spot, with sunlight filtering through the three-hundred-foot trees down to the laurel- and fern-covered canyon below. The canyon's steep sides are what saved it from Mill Valley's lumbermen, and today it's one of the few first-growth redwood groves between San Francisco and the fantastic forests of Redwood National Park, up the coast near the Oregon border (see p.526).

Its proximity to San Francisco makes Muir Woods a popular target, and the paved trails nearest the parking lot are often packed with bus-tour hordes. However, if you come during the week, or outside midsummer, it's easy enough to leave the crowds behind, especially if you're willing to head off up the steep trails that climb the canyon sides. Winter is a particularly good time to come, as the streams are gurgling – the main creek flows down to Muir Beach, and salmon have been known to spawn in it – and the forest creatures, including the colonies of ladybugs that spend their winter huddling in the rich undergrowth, are more likely to be seen going about their business. Keep an eye out for the various species of salamanders and newts that thrive in this damp environment; be warned, though, that some are poisonous and will bite if harassed.

One way to avoid the crowds, and the only way to get here on public transport, is to enter the woods from the top by way of a two-mile hike from the **Pan Toll Ranger Station** (☎388-2070) on Panoramic Highway – on the *Golden Gate Transit* #63 bus route. As the state park headquarters, the station has maps and information on hiking and camping and rangers can suggest hikes to suit your mood and interests. From here the **Pan Toll Road** turns off to the right along the ridge to within a hundred yards of the 2571-foot summit of Mount Tamalpais, from where you'll get breathtaking views of the distant Sierra Nevada and close-ups of red-necked turkey vultures, listlessly circling the peak.

## Mill Valley

From the East Peak of Mount Tamalpais, a quick two-mile hike downhill follows the **Temelpa Trail** through velvety shrubs of chaparral to **MILL VALLEY**, the oldest and most enticing of Marin County's inland towns – also accessible every half hour by Golden Gate Transit bus #10 from San Francisco and Sausalito. Originally a logging centre, it was from here that the destruction of the surrounding redwoods was organized, though for many years the town has made a healthy living out of tourism. The **Mill Valley and Mount Tamalpais Scenic Railroad** – according to the blurb, "the crookedest railroad in the world" – was cut into the slopes above the town in 1896, twisting up through nearly three hundred tight curves in under eight miles. The trip proved so popular with tourists that the line was extended down into Muir Woods in 1907, though road-building and fire combined to put an end to the railroad by 1930. You can, however, follow its old route from the end of Summit Avenue in Mill Valley, a popular trip with daredevils on all-terrain bikes, which were, incidentally, invented here.

Though much of Mill Valley's attraction lies in its easy access to hiking and mountain bike trails up Mount Tam, its compact yet relaxed centre also boasts a number of cafés and some surprisingly good shops and galleries. The *Book Depot and Café* is an especially popular bookstore, café and meeting place on Throckmorton and Miller (daily 7am–10pm). Next door, the **Chamber of Commerce** (Mon–Sat 9am–5pm; ☎1-800/388-9701) has maps and restaurant listings, as well as information on the wide range of local entertainments, including summer plays in the outdoor *Mountain Theater* and a world-class **film festival** in October.

## Tiburon and Angel Island

**TIBURON**, at the tip of a narrow peninsula three miles east of US-101, is, like Sausalito, a ritzy harbourside village to which hundreds of people come each weekend, many of them via direct *Red and White Fleet* **ferries** from Pier 43½ in San Francisco's Fisherman's Wharf. It's a relaxed place, less touristy than Sausalito, and if you're in the mood to take it easy and watch the boats sail across the bay, sitting out on the sunny deck of one of many cafés and bars can be idyllic. There are few specific sights as such, but it's pleasant enough simply to wander around, popping into the odd gallery or antique shop. The best of these are grouped together in **Ark Row**, at the west end of Main Street: the quirky buildings are actually old houseboats that were beached here early in the century. On a hill above the town stands **Old St Hilary's Church** (tours Wed & Sun 4–6pm), a Carpenter Gothic beauty that is best seen in the spring, when the surrounding fields are covered with multicoloured buckwheat, flax, and paintbrush.

If you're feeling energetic, rent a bicycle from *Bike Sport*, 1701 Tiburon Blvd (☎435-5064), and cruise around the many plush houses of **Belvedere Island**, just across the Beach Road Bridge from the west end of Main Street, enjoying the fine views of the bay and Golden Gate Bridge. More ambitious cyclists can continue along the waterfront bike path, which winds from the bijou shops and galleries three miles west along undeveloped Richardson Bay frontage to a bird sanctuary at **Greenwood Cove**. The pristine Victorian house here is now the western headquarters of the National Audubon Society and open for tours on Sundays (10am–4pm); a small interpretive centre has displays on local and migratory birds and wildlife.

### Angel Island

However appealing, Tiburon is soon exhausted, and you'd be well advised to take the hourly *Angel Island Ferry* a mile offshore ($5 round-trip, plus $1 per bicycle; ☎435-2131) to the largest island in the San Francisco Bay, ten times the size of Alcatraz. **Angel Island** is now officially a state park, but over the years it's served a variety of purposes, everything from a home for Miwok Native Americans to a World War II prisoner-of-war camp. It's full of ghostly ruins of old military installations, and with oak and eucalyptus trees and sagebrush covering the hills above rocky coves and sandy beaches, feels quite apart from the mainland. The island offers some pleasant biking opportunities: a five-mile road rings the island, and an unpaved track (and a number of hiking trails) leads up to the eight-hundred-foot hump of **Mount Livermore**, which gives a panoramic view of the Bay Area.

The ferry arrives at **Ayala Cove**, where a small snack bar selling hot dogs and cold drinks provides the only sustenance available on the island – bring a picnic if you plan to spend the day here. The nearby **visitor center** (daily 9am–4pm; ☎435-1915), in an old building that was built as a quarantine facility for soldiers returning from the Philippines after the Spanish-American War, has displays on the island's history. Around the point on the northwest corner of the island the **North Garrison**, built in 1905, was the site of a prisoner-of-war camp during World War II, while the larger **East Garrison**, on the bay a half mile beyond, was the major transfer point for soldiers bound for the South Pacific.

**Quarry Beach** around the point is the best on the island, a clean sandy shore that's protected from the winds blowing in through the Golden Gate; it's also a popular landing spot for kayakers and canoeists who paddle across the Bay from Berkeley.

## Sir Francis Drake Boulevard and Central Marin County

The quickest route to the wilds of the Point Reyes National Seashore, and the only way to get there on public transport, is by way of **Sir Francis Drake Boulevard**, which cuts across central Marin County through the inland towns of **San Anselmo** and **Fairfax**, reaching the coast thirty miles west at a crescent-shaped bay where, in 1579, Drake landed and claimed all of what he called Nova Albion for England. The route makes an excellent day-long cycling tour, with the reward of good beaches, a youth hostel, and some tasty restaurants at the end of the road.

The Larkspur *Golden Gate Transit* **ferry**, which leaves from the Ferry Building in San Francisco, is the longest and, surprisingly, least expensive of the bay crossings. Primarily a commuter route, it docks at the modern space-frame terminal at Larkspur Landing. The monolithic, red-tile-roofed complex you see on the bayfront a mile east is the maximum-security **San Quentin State Prison**, which houses the state's most violent and notorious criminals, and of which Johnny Cash sang so resonantly "I hate every stone of you". If you arrive by car over the Richmond-San Rafael Bridge, follow road signs off Hwy-101 for the prison **museum**, Building 106, Dolores Way (Mon, Wed & Fri 11am–3pm, Sat 10am–3pm; $3).

### San Anselmo, Fairfax and Point Reyes Station

**SAN ANSELMO**, set in a broad valley two miles north of Mount Tam, calls itself "the antiques capital of Northern California" and sports a tiny centre of speciality shops, furniture stores and cafés that draws out many San Francisco shoppers at weekends. The ivy-covered **San Francisco Theological Seminary**, off Bolinas Avenue, dominates the town from the hill above, and the very green and leafy **Creek Park** follows the creek that winds through the town centre, but otherwise there's not a lot to do but eat and drink – or browse through fine bookstores such as *Oliver's Books* at 645 San Anselmo Ave.

Center Boulevard follows the tree-lined creek west for a mile to **FAIRFAX**, a town that, much less ostentatiously hedonistic than the harborside towns, in many ways still typifies Marin lifestyles, with an array of wholefood stores and bookstores geared to a thoughtfully mellow crowd. From Fairfax, the narrow Bolinas Road twists up and over the mountains to the coast at Stinson Beach, while Sir Francis Drake Boulevard winds through a pastoral landscape of ranch houses hidden away up oak-covered valleys.

Ten miles west of Fairfax along Sir Francis Drake Boulevard, **Samuel Taylor State Park** has excellent camping (see p.460 for details); five miles more brings you to the coastal Hwy-1 and the town of Olema, a mile north of which sits the town of **POINT REYES STATION**, a good place to stop off for a bite to eat or to pick up picnic supplies before heading off to enjoy the wide-open spaces of the **Point Reyes National Seashore** just beyond. *Trailhead Rentals*, a half-mile from the Point Reyes visitor center (see below) along Bear Valley Road (☎663-1768), rents mountain bikes – a great way to get around.

## The Point Reyes National Seashore

From Point Reyes Station, Sir Francis Drake Boulevard heads out to the westernmost tip of Marin County at Point Reyes through the **Point Reyes National Seashore**, a near-island of wilderness surrounded on three sides by more than fifty miles of isolated coastline – pine forests and sunny meadows bordered by rocky cliffs and sandy, wind-swept beaches. This wing-shaped landmass, something of an aberration along the generally straight coastline north of San Francisco, is in fact a rogue piece of the earth's crust that has been drifting slowly and steadily northward along the San Andreas Fault, having started some six million years ago as a suburb of Los Angeles. When the great earthquake of 1906 shattered San Francisco, the land here – the epicentre – shifted over sixteen feet in an instant, though damage was confined to a few skewed cattle fences.

The park's **visitor center** (daily 9am–5pm; ☎663-1092), two miles southwest of Point Reyes Station near Olema, just off Hwy-1 on Bear Valley Road, holds engaging displays on the geology and natural history of the region. Rangers will suggest good places to hike or cycle to and have up-to-date information on the weather, which can change quickly and be cold and windy along the coast even when it's hot and sunny here, three miles inland. They also handle permits and reservations for the various **campgrounds** within the park. Nearby, a replica of a native Miwok village has an authentic religious **roundhouse**, and a popular hike follows the Bear Valley Trail along Coast Creek four miles to **Arch Rock**, a large tunnel in the seaside cliffs that you can walk through at low tide.

North of the visitor center, Limantour Road heads west six miles to the **HI-Point Reyes Hostel** (see p.460), continuing on another two miles to the coast at **Limantour Beach**, one of the best swimming beaches and a good place to watch the seabirds in the adjacent estuary. Bear Valley Road rejoins Sir Francis Drake Boulevard just past Limantour Road, leading north along the Tomales Bay through the village of **Inverness**, so-named because the landscape reminded an early settler of his home in the Scottish Highlands. Eight miles west of Inverness, a turn leads down past **Johnson's Oyster Farm** (Tues–Sun 8am–4pm; ☎669-1149) – which sells bivalves for around $5 a dozen, less than half the price you'd pay in town – to **Drake's Beach**, the presumed landing spot of Sir Francis in 1579. Appropriately, the coastline here resembles the southern coast of England, often cold, wet and windy, with chalk-white cliffs rising above the wide sandy beach. The main road continues west another four miles to the tip of Point Reyes, where a precariously sited lighthouse stands firm against the literally crashing surf. The **lighthouse**, which you can't tour, is reached via a tiring three hundred steps down the steep cliffs, but even without making the trek all the way, the bluffs along here are excellent places to look out for sea lions and, in winter, migrating gray whales.

The northern tip of the Point Reyes seashore, **Tomales Point**, is accessible by the Pierce Point Road, which turns off Sir Francis Drake Boulevard two miles north of Inverness. Jutting out into Tomales Bay, it's the least-visited section of the park and a refuge for hefty **tule elk**; it's also a great place for admiring the lupines, poppies and other wild flowers that appear in the spring. The best swimming (at least the warmest water) is at **Heart's Desire Beach**, a little way before the end of the road; also down the bluffs from where the road comes to a dead end, there are excellent tidal pools at rocky **McClure's Beach**. North of Point Reyes Station, Hwy-1 continues along the coast, through Bodega Bay up to Mendocino and the Northern California coast.

## San Rafael and Northern Marin County

You may pass through **SAN RAFAEL** on your way north from San Francisco, but there's little worth stopping for. The county seat and the only big city in Marin County, it has none of the woodsy qualities that make the other towns special, though you'll come across a couple of good restaurants and bars along Fourth Street, the main drag. Its one attraction is an old **Franciscan Mission** (daily 11am–4pm; free), in fact a 1949 replica that was built near the site of the 1817 original on Fifth Ave at A Street. The real points of interest, however, are well on the outskirts: the Marin County Civic Center to the north and the little-known China Camp State Park along the bay to the east.

The **Marin County Civic Center** (Mon–Fri 9am–5pm; free; ☎472-3500), spanning the hills just east of US-101 a mile north of central San Rafael, is a strange, otherworldly complex of administrative offices, plus an excellent performance space that resembles a giant viaduct capped by a bright blue-tiled roof. These buildings were architect **Frank Lloyd Wright**'s one and only government project, and although the huge circus tents and amusement park at the core of the designer's conception were never built, it does have some interesting touches, among them the atrium lobbies that open directly to the outdoors.

From the Civic Center, North San Pedro Road loops around the headlands through **China Camp State Park** (☎456-0766), an expansive area of pastures and open spaces that's hard to reach without your own transport. It takes its name from the intact but long-abandoned Chinese shrimp-fishing village at the far eastern tip of the park, the sole survivor of the many small Chinese communities that once dotted the California coast. The ramshackle buildings, small wooden pier and old boats lying on the sand are pure John Steinbeck; the only recent addition a chain-link fence to protect the site from vandals. At the weekend you can get beer and sandwiches from the old shack at the foot of the pier, but the atmosphere is best during the week at sunset, when there's often no one around at all.

Six miles north of San Rafael, the **Lucas Valley Road** turns off west, twisting across Marin to Point Reyes. Although he lives and works here, it was not named after Star Wars film-maker George Lucas, whose sprawling **Skywalker Ranch** studios are well hidden off the road. Hwy-37 cuts off east, eight miles north of San Rafael, heading around the top of the bay into the Wine Country of the Sonoma and Napa valleys (see p.504).

## Accommodation

You might prefer simply to dip into Marin County using San Francisco as a base, and if you've got a car or manage to time the bus connections right it's certainly possible, at least for the southernmost parts of the county. However, it can be nicer to take a more leisurely look at Marin, staying over for a couple of nights in some well-chosen spots. Sadly there are few hotels, and those that there are often charge in excess of $100 a night; motels tend to be the same as anywhere, though there are a couple of attractively faded ones along the coast. If you want to stay in a B&B, contact the **Bed and Breakfast Exchange**, 45 Entrata Drive, San Anselmo (☎485-1971), which can fix you up with rooms in comfortable private homes all over Marin County from $50 a night for two, ranging from courtyard hideaways on the beach in Tiburon to houseboats in Sausalito. The best bet for budget accommodation is a dorm bed in one of the beautifully situated **hostels** along the western beaches.

### Hostels

**HI-Marin Headlands**, Building 941, Fort Barry, Marin Headlands (closed 9.30am–4.30pm; ☎331-2777). Hard to get to unless you're driving – it's near Rodeo Lagoon just off Bunker Road, five miles west of Sausalito – but worth the effort for its setting, in cosy old army barracks just across the Golden Gate Bridge. On Sundays and holidays only, *Muni* bus #76 from San Francisco stops right outside. Dorm beds $11 a night. ①.

**HI-Point Reyes**, in the Point Reyes National Seashore (closed 9.30am–4.30pm; ☎663-8811). Also hard to reach without your own transport: just off Limantour Road six miles west of the visitor center and two miles from the beach, it's located in an old ranch house and surrounded by meadows and forests. Dorm beds $16 a night. ①.

## Motels and hotels

**Casa Madrona**, 801 Bridgeway, Sausalito (☎332-0502). Deluxe hideaway tucked into the hills above the bay. ⑧.

**Grand Hotel**, 15 Brighton Ave, Bolinas (☎868-1757). Basic rooms in downtown Bolinas. ②.

**Ocean Court Motel**, 18 Arenel St, Stinson Beach (☎868-0212). Just a block from the beach, west of Hwy-1. Large rooms with kitchens. ④.

**San Rafael Inn**, 865 E Francisco Blvd, San Rafael (☎454-9470). Large roadside motel, just off US-101. ③.

**Stinson Beach Motel**, 3416 Shoreline Hwy, Stinson Beach (☎868-1712). Basic roadside motel right on Hwy-1, ten minutes' walk from the beach. ③.

## Bed and Breakfast

**The Blue Heron Inn**, 11 Wharf Rd, Bolinas (☎868-1102). Lovely double rooms in an unbeatable locale. Breakfast is served at the owner's cosy restaurant, *The Shop Café* at 46 Wharf Rd, which also serves lunch and dinner. ⑤.

**Lindisfarne Guest House**, part of the *Green Gulch Zen Center*, Muir Beach (☎383-3036). Restful rooms in a meditation retreat set in a secluded valley above Muir Beach. Rate includes three excellent vegetarian meals. ⑤.

**Mountain Home Inn**, 810 Panoramic Hwy, Mill Valley (☎381-9000). Romantically located on Mount Tamalpais' crest, this B&B offers great views and endless hiking. Some rooms with hot tubs. ⑥.

**Pelican Inn**, 10 Pacific Way, Muir Beach (☎383-6000). Very comfortable rooms in a pseudo-English country inn, with good bar and restaurant downstairs, ten minutes from beautiful Muir Beach. ⑦.

**Ten Inverness Way**, 10 Inverness Way, Inverness (☎669-1648). Quiet and restful, with a hot tub, in a small village of good restaurants and bakeries on the fringes of Point Reyes. ⑥.

## Campgrounds

**China Camp State Park**, off N San Pedro Rd, north of San Rafael (☎456-0766). Walk-in plots (just 600 ft from the parking lot) overlooking a lovely meadow. First-come, first-camped for $12 a night.

**Marin Headlands**, just across the Golden Gate Bridge (☎331-1540). The best of four campgrounds here is at Kirby Cove (open summer only, and very popular), at the northern foot of the Golden Gate Bridge. Free.

**Mount Tamalpais State Park**, above Mill Valley (☎388-2070). Free plots for backpackers on the slopes of the mountain, and a few rustic cabins ($25 a night), along the coast at Steep Ravine.

**Point Reyes National Seashore**, 40 miles northwest of San Francisco (☎663-1092). A wide range of sites for backpackers, near the beach or in the forest.

**Samuel Taylor State Park**, on Sir Francis Drake Blvd, 15 miles west of San Rafael (☎488-9897). Deluxe, car-accessible plots with hot showers, spread along a river for $14 a night. Don't miss the swimming hole or bat caves. In summer, reserve a place through *MISTIX* (☎1-800/445-7275).

# Eating

For all its healthy and wealthy prosperity, Marin County's **eating** options aren't really among the Bay Area's best. However, there are some good places well worth searching out if you're in the area, as well as a couple whose top-rate food or gorgeous settings – on the waterfront or high up in the hills – make them quite special indeed.

**The Cantina**, 651 E Blithedale Rd at Camino Alto, Mill Valley (☎381-1070). Usually packed, as it offers some of the best Mexican food in Marin, with the hottest salsa for miles.

**Casa Madrona**, 805 Bridgeway, Sausalito (☎332-0502). Mediterranean staples meet California cuisine in this delectable hotel-restaurant that does excellent fresh seafood. Great view of the harbour, and relaxed service. Get a window seat for the ocean view.

**Dipsea Café**, 1 El Paseo, Mill Valley (☎381-0298). Hearty diner food, especially good for breakfast before a day out hiking on Mount Tamalpais.

**Fairfix Café**, 33 Broadway, Fairfax (☎459-6404). Excellent Mediterranean food with occasional evening poetry readings.

**Greater Gatsby's**, 39 Caledonia St, Sausalito (☎332-4500). Handy, inexpensive pizza parlour a block from the waterfront on the north side of town.

**Hilda's**, 639 San Anselmo Ave, San Anselmo (☎457-9266). Great breakfasts and lunches in this downhome, cosy café.

**Lark Creek Inn**, 234 Magnolia Ave, Larkspur (☎924-7766). One of the Bay Area's most popular and highly rated restaurants, with wildly eclectic California cuisine served up in a comfortable waterfront garden. Expensive, but worth it.

**Milly's**, 1613 Fourth St, San Rafael (☎459-1601). Extremely healthy, wide-ranging vegetarian dishes such as Thai vegetable curries and jalapeño ravioli. Evenings only.

**Mountain Home Inn**, 810 Panoramic Hwy, above Mill Valley (☎381-9000). Another place that's as good for the atmosphere as for the food, with a range of broiled meats and fish dishes served up in a rustic lodge on the slopes of Mount Tam.

**New Morning Café**, 1696 Tiburon Blvd, Tiburon (☎435-4315). Lots of healthy wholegrain sand-wiches, plus salads and omelettes.

**Piazza D'Angelo**, 22 Miller Ave, Mill Valley (☎388-2000). Delicious salads and large portions of tasty Italian dishes, especially pasta, for around $18 a plate. Almost like eating in Rome.

**Rice Table**, 1617 Fourth St, San Rafael (☎456-1808). From the shrimp chips through the crab pancakes and noodles on to the fried plantain desserts, these fragrant and spicy Indonesian dishes are worth planning a day around. Dinners only, but excellent value at $5–8 a plate.

**Sam's Anchor Café**, 27 Main St, Tiburon (☎435-4527). This rough-hewn, amiable waterfront café has been around for over 75 years. Good burgers, soups and sandwiches, plus Sunday brunches.

**Station House Café**, Main St at Third, Point Reyes Station (☎663-1515). Open for breakfast, lunch, and dinner every day but Tues, this friendly local favourite brings people from miles around.

## Drinking and nightlife

While the Marin County nightlife is never as charged as it gets in San Francisco, almost every town has at least a couple of **cafés** that are open long hours for a jolt of caffeine, and any number of saloon-like **bars** where you'll feel at home immediately. In addition, since most of the honchos of the Bay Area music scene and dozens of lesser-known but no less brilliant session musicians and songwriters live here, Marin's night-clubs are unsurpassed for catching big names in intimate locales.

### Cafés

**Book Depot and Café**, 87 Throckmorton Ave, Mill Valley (☎383-2665). Lively café housed in an old train station, which it shares with a bookstore and newsstand.

**Café Trieste**, 1000 Bridgeway, Sausalito (☎332-7770). This distant relative of San Francisco's North Beach institution serves good coffee, a wide menu of pastas and salads, and great gelati.

**Caffe Nuvo**, 556 San Anselmo Ave, San Anselmo (☎454-4530). Great coffee and pastries, with a large balcony overhanging a creek, plus poetry readings and live music most nights.

**Patrick's Bookshop and Café**, 9 Bolinas Rd, Fairfax (☎454-2428). Coffees and teas, and tasty soups and sandwiches, in this low-key hippy hangout; good selection of books and mags, too.

**Sweden House**, 35 Main St, Tiburon (☎435-9767). Great coffee and marvellous pastries on a jetty overlooking the yacht harbour, all for surprisingly reasonable prices.

### Bars

**Marin Brewing Company**, 1809 Larkspur Landing, Larkspur (☎461-4677). Lively pub opposite the Larkspur ferry terminal, with half a dozen tasty ales – try the malty Albion Amber or the creamy St Brendan's Irish Red – all brewed on the premises.

**no name bar**, 757 Bridgeway, Sausalito (☎332-1392). A thriving ex-haunt of the Beats that still hosts poetry readings and evening jam sessions.

**Pelican Inn**, Hwy-1, Muir Beach (☎383-6000). Fair selection of traditional English and modern Californian ales, plus fish and chips (and rooms to rent in case you overdo it).

**Sweetwater**, 153 Throckmorton Ave, Mill Valley (☎388-3820). Large open room full of beer-drinking locals that after dark evolves into Marin's prime live music venue (see below).

## Nightlife

**Fourth Street Tavern**, 711 Fourth St, San Rafael (☎ 454-4044). Gutsy, no-frills beer bar with free, bluesy music most nights.

**New George's**, 842 Fourth St, San Rafael (☎457-1515). Large dance floor and wide range of music in a friendly, good-time place that doubles as a charcoal grill restaurant. Performers range from local cover bands to Leon Redbone to Robyn Hitchcock, and cover varies from nothing to $15.

**Sweetwater**, 153 Throckmorton Ave, Mill Valley (☎388-3820). Small, comfortable saloon that brings in some of the biggest names in music, from jazz and blues all-stars to Jefferson Airplane survivors.

## travel details

### Trains

An *Amtrak* shuttle bus departs from Transbay Terminal to Oakland depot, from where there is a daily service east to Sacramento and south to Los Angeles and San Diego.

### Buses

*Greyhound*

**San Francisco to**: Los Angeles (11 daily; 8hr; or 3 Green Tortoise weekly; 11hr); Redding (4 daily; 7hr 30min); Reno (6 daily; 5hr); San Diego (11 daily; 10hr 30min); Sacramento (4 daily; 2hr); San Jose (6 daily; 1hr).

# CHAPTER EIGHT

# THE GOLD COUNTRY AND LAKE TAHOE

The single most enduring image of California, after surfers and movie stars, is that of the rough and ready 49ers. Not the Steve Young/Joe Montana football-playing variety, but the Argonauts of the Gold Rush of 1849, who came from all over the world to get rich quick in the goldfields of the Sierra Nevada foothills, 150 miles east of San Francisco. The first prospectors on the scene sometimes found large nuggets of solid gold sitting along the river banks. Most, however, worked long hours in the hot sun, wading through fast-flowing, ice-cold rivers to recover trace amounts of the precious metal that had been eroded out of the hard-rock veins of the **Mother Lode**, the name given by miners to the rich source of gold which underlies the heart of the mining district.

The **Gold Country** ranges from the foothills near Yosemite National Park to the deep gorge of the Yuba River two hundred miles north. The heart of the Mother Lode, where gold was first discovered in 1848, is Sutter's Mill in Coloma, forty miles east of **Sacramento**. The largest city in the Gold Country – now the state capital and much the best jumping-off point for the area as a whole – Sacramento was a tiny military outpost and farming community that boomed as a supply town for miners. The mining areas spread to the north and south of Sacramento and preserve distinct identities. The **northern mines** around the twin towns of **Grass Valley** and **Nevada City** were the richest fields, and today retain most of their Gold Rush buildings, although there's been practically no development in the intervening years in a beautiful, near-alpine setting halfway up the towering peaks of the Sierra Nevada mountains. The hot and dusty **southern mines**, on the other hand, became depopulated fast: they were the rowdiest and wildest of all the mines, and it's not too hard to imagine that many of the abandoned towns sprinkled over the area once supported upwards of fifty saloons and gambling parlours, each with its own cast of card sharks and thieves, as immortalized by writers like Bret Harte and Mark Twain.

## RIVER RAFTING IN THE GOLD COUNTRY

Although plenty of people come through the area to see the Gold Rush sights, at least as many come to enjoy the thrills and spills of **white-water rafting** and kayaking on the various forks of the American, Stanislaus, Tuolumne and Merced rivers, which wind down through the region from the Sierra crest towards Sacramento. Whether you just want to float in a leisurely manner downstream, or fancy careering through five-foot walls of water, contact one of the many river trip operators, among them *Ahwahnee* (☎1-800/359-9790), *CBOC Whitewater Raft Adventures* (☎1-800/356-2262), *Mother Lode River Trips* (☎1-800/427-2387), *Oars Inc* (☎1-800/346-6277), or *Tributary Whitewater Tours* (☎916/346-6812).

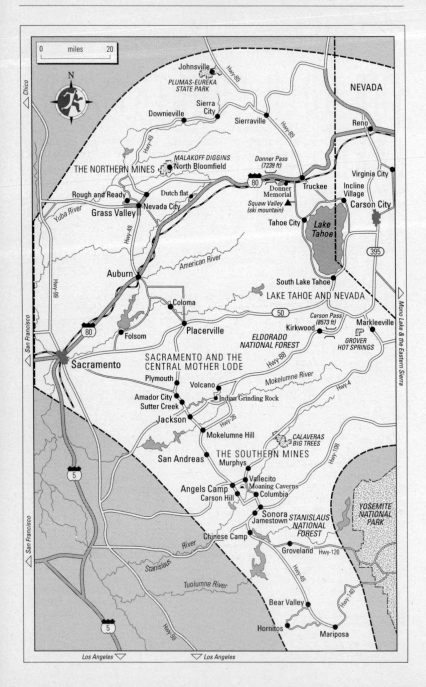

> The telephone **area code** for Sacramento and the
> northern half of the Gold Country is ☎916.

Most of the mountainous forest along the Sierra crest is preserved as near-pristine wilderness, with excellent hiking, camping and backpacking. There's great skiing in winter around the mountainous rim of **Lake Tahoe** – "Lake of the Sky" to the native Washoe – on the border between California and Nevada, aglow under the bright lights of the nightclubs and casinos that line its southeastern shore. East of the mountains, in the dry Nevada desert, sit the highway towns of **Reno**, famed for low-budget weddings and speedy divorces, and **Carson City**, the Nevada state capital and one-time boom-town of the Comstock silver mines.

### Getting around

Hwy-49 runs north to south, linking most of the sights of the Gold Country; two main highways, US-50 and I-80, along with the transcontinental railroad, cross the Sierra Nevada through the heart of the region, and there are frequent *Greyhound* bus services to most of the major towns. To get a real feel for the Gold Country, however, and to reach the most evocative ghost towns, you'll need a **car**. Also, though it's all very pretty, the region is far too hilly and the roads too narrow to be much good for **cycling**.

# SACRAMENTO AND THE
# CENTRAL MOTHER LODE

Before gold was discovered in 1848, the area around what's now the state capital at Sacramento belonged entirely to one man, John Sutter. He came here from Switzerland in 1839 to farm the flat, marshy lands at the foot of the Sierra Nevada mountains, and the prosperous community he founded became a main stopping place for the few trappers and travellers who made their way inland or across the range of peaks. But it was after the discovery of flakes of gold in the foothills forty miles east that things really took off. Although Sutter tried to keep it a secret, word got out and thousands soon flocked here from all over the world to mine the rich deposits of the Mother Lode.

This area is still very much the centre of the Gold Country, though it's rather richer in history than specific attractions. **Sacramento**, roughly midway between San Francisco and the crest of the Sierra Nevada mountains and well connected by *Greyhound* and *Amtrak* and the arterial I-5 highway, is likely to be your first stop, a green open city of wide tree-lined streets centring on grandiose state government buildings and a waterfront quarter restored from the days of the Pony Express. From Sacramento two main routes climb east through the gentle foothills of the Mother Lode: US-50 passes through the old supply town of **Placerville** on its way to Lake Tahoe, and I-80 zooms by **Auburn** over the Donner Pass into Nevada. Both towns have retained enough of their Gold Rush past to merit at least a brief look if you're passing through, and Auburn in particular makes a good base for the more picturesque towns of the northern mines.

# Sacramento

California's state capital, **SACRAMENTO**, is not at the top of most travellers' itineraries; indeed, until recently, it had the reputation of being decidedly dull, a suburban enclave of politicians and bureaucrats surrounded by miles of marshes and farmland. However, in the 1990s the town has been undergoing something of a transformation. Flashy office towers and hotel complexes, catering to the promoters and lobbyists, have sprung up out of the faceless streetscape, enlivening the grid of leafy, tree-lined blocks; and multi-million-dollar redevelopment efforts have gone some way toward resurrecting the rowdy, free-for-all spirit of the city's Gold Rush past.

Set at the confluence of the Sacramento and American rivers in the flatlands of the northern Central Valley, Sacramento was founded in 1839 by a Swiss immigrant, **John Sutter**, on fifty thousand acres granted to him by the Mexican government. Sutter was a determined settler, and for ten years worked hard to build the colony into a busy trading centre and cattle ranch, only to be thwarted by the discovery of gold at a nearby sawmill. Instead of making his fortune, the gold left Sutter a broken man. His workers quit their jobs to go prospecting, and many thousands more flocked to the goldfields without any respect for Sutter's claims to the land. The small colony was soon overrun: since the ships of the day could sail upriver from the San Francisco Bay, Sacramento quickly became the main supply point for miners bound for the isolated camps in the foothills above. The city prospered, and in 1854 Sacramento was chosen to be the sixth capital of the young state of California, equidistant to the gold mines, the rich farmlands of the Central Valley and the financial centre of San Francisco. As the Gold Rush faded, Sacramento remained important as a transport centre, first as the western terminus of the Pony Express and later as the western headquarters of the transcontinental railroad.

# Arrival, information and city transport

At the intersection of the I-5, I-80, US-50 and Hwy-99 freeways, Sacramento is the hub of all the long-distance transport networks. Sacramento Metro **airport** (☎929-5411), twelve miles northwest of downtown, is served by most major domestic airlines, including *America West, American, Delta, Southwest* and *USAir*. *Air Commuter* vans ($10; ☎424-9640) will take you from the terminals to downtown. **Trains** from Los Angeles, San Francisco and Chicago stop at the station at Fourth and I streets, near Old Sacramento, with good *Thruway* bus links to the main Gold Country towns and the Lake Tahoe area. An almost continuous stream of *Greyhound* **buses** pull into the station at Seventh and L streets, a block from the K Street Mall.

The **tourist office** at 1421 K St (Mon–Fri 8am–5pm; ☎264-7777) has the *Sacramento Visitors' Guide* with maps and listings of accommodation and places to eat and drink, while the **Division of Tourism** at 801 K St (Mon–Fri 8am–5pm; ☎322-2882 or 1-800/ 862-2543) holds tons of background and practical information on the rest of California. For the latest on events and entertainment in Sacramento, pick up the free *Sacramento News & Review*, read *Ticket*, the weekend supplement of the *Sacramento Bee* newspaper, or browse the less useful but entertaining and hard-hitting music and style reviews in *Citi:Zen*. The *KVMR* 993FM non-commercial community radio station is also useful.

The entire city is compact, deadly flat and entirely **walkable**, though many locals get around (especially along the 25-mile cycle path along the American River to Folsom Lake) by **bike** – rentable from *Cycle Depot* at 918 Second St in Old Sacramento ($16 a day; ☎441-4143). You're unlikely to need it, but there is also a combined **bus and light-rail** transport system; pick up timetables and route maps from the office at 907 J St (Mon–Fri 9.30am–1.45pm & 3–4.30pm; ☎321-2877). One of the best ways to see the town is on a **river-boat tour**: the paddle-wheel steamboats *Matthew McKinley* and *Spirit of Sacramento* both depart from the L Street landing in Old Sacramento for varied trips along the Sacramento River ($10–25; ☎552-2932 or 1-800/433-0263).

Should you need to rent a **car**, *Enterprise*, 1401 16th at P (☎444-7600) will provide one for under $40 a day, $7 more if you're between 21 and 25.

---

**ACCOMMODATION PRICES**

All accommodation prices in this book have been coded using the symbols below. Note that prices are for the least expensive double rooms in each establishment. For a full explanation see p.33 in *Basics*.

① up to $30    ② $30–45    ③ $45–60    ④ $60–80    ⑤ $80–100

⑥ $100–130    ⑦ $130–175    ⑧ $175–250    ⑨ $250+

Bear in mind that in Sacramento all quoted room rates are subject to a **room tax** – currently 12 percent on top of your total bill.

---

## Accommodation

Sacramento has plenty of reasonably priced places to stay, all within easy walking distance of the centre. A number of **motels** cluster around the old Governor's Mansion on the north side of town around 16th and H streets, and dozens more line the highways on the outskirts, particularly Richards Boulevard, just off I–5. **Downtown**, there are a few rather down-at-heel 1930s hotels and flashy new ones springing up every year. There's no good **camping** anywhere within easy reach of Sacramento, though *KOA* runs the RV-heavy *Sacramento Metro* site, 3951 Lake Rd (☎371-6771 or 1-800/5454-5267), four miles west of the centre.

**Abigail's**, 2120 G St (☎441-5007 or 1-800/858 1568). Luxurious bed and breakfast in a quiet and appealingly furnished 1912 home. There's a hot tub out in the secluded gardens. ⑥.

**Americana Lodge**, 818 15th St (☎444-3980). The pick of the low-priced motels near the old Governor's Mansion, equipped with a pool. ②.

**Central**, 818 16th St (☎446-6006). Another central motel, not as good as the nearby *Americana Lodge*, but a shade cheaper. ②.

**Clarion**, 700 16th St at H (☎444-8000 or 1-800/443-0880). Better than you might expect for a large chain motel, centrally located with excellent facilities and lower weekend rates if you book ahead. ⑤.

**Delta King Hotel**, 1000 Front St (☎444-KING or 1-800/825-5464). A 1926 paddle-wheel river boat now permanently moored on the water beside Old Sacramento. The rooms fail to justify their "stateroom" description, but nonetheless the vessel makes an enjoyably unusual place to stay. The price rises at weekends. ⑤.

**HI-Sacramento**, 900 H St (☎443-1691). Brand-new hostel in a superb and rambling 1885 mansion right in the centre of town. All the usual facilities plus free bike hire, but there's a daytime lockout and 11pm curfew. $10 for members, $13 for others. ①.

**Hyatt Regency**, 12th and L streets (☎443-1234 or 1-800/233-1234). Very flashy, perfect for an expense account stay. Lower prices at weekends. ⑤.

**Vagabond Inn**, 909 Third St (☎446-1481 or 1-800/522-1555). Modern place near the river and Old Sacramento, with a swimming pool and continental breakfast. ④.

## The Town

Everything you'd want to see in Sacramento is downtown, divided by the I-5 highway into touristy **Old Sacramento** along the river, and the commercial city centre along the **K Street Mall**.

### The riverfront: Old Sacramento

Sacramento grew up along the riverfront, where the wharves, warehouses, saloons and stores of the city's historic core have been restored and converted into the novelty shops and theme restaurants of **Old Sacramento**, inevitably a major tourist trap but not entirely without appeal. Most of the buildings are original, though some were moved here from nearby in the Sixties to make way for the massive I-5 highway that cuts between the river and the rest of Sacramento, and the area, small though it is, has

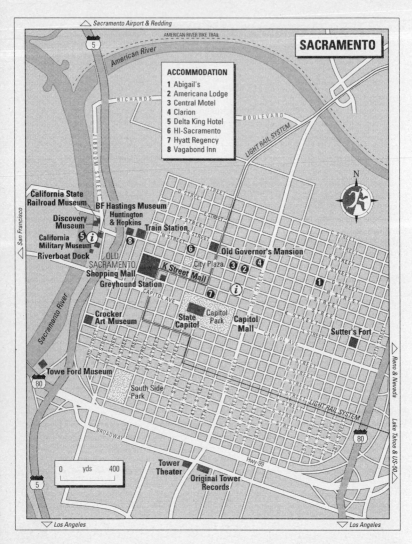

a period aspect not completely sanitized out of all recognition. The **Information Center** at 1104 Front St (daily 9am–5pm; ☎442-7644) has walking tour maps and historical information.

On I Street, between First and Second, is the *Huntington & Hopkins* hardware store where the **Big Four** – Leland Stanford, Mark Hopkins, Collis P Huntington and Charles Crocker – first got together to mastermind the *Central Pacific* and later *Southern Pacific* railroads (see box below). It's now a **museum** (daily 10am–5pm; free), highlighting the humble beginnings of the men who became some of the richest in the country, with a collection of old woodworking and blacksmith's tools; upstairs there's a low-key homage to the men, with a re-creation of their boardroom and an archive of rail history.

The **Discovery Museum of History, Science and Technology**, 101 I St (June–Sept Tues–Sun 10am–5pm; Oct–May Wed–Fri noon–5pm, Sat & Sun 10am–5pm; $3.50), a few steps away, neatly fills in the gaps in California's development before and after the Big Four, though it fails to be as stimulating as the adjacent **California State Railroad Museum** (daily 10am–5pm; $5), which brings together a range of lavishly restored 1860s locomotives with "cow-catcher" front grilles and huge bulbous smokestacks. A number of opulently decked-out passenger cars include the 1929 *St Hyacinthe Pullman* sleeper car, which simulates movement with flashing lights, clanging bells and a gentle rhythmic swaying. The old passenger station and freight depot a block south have also been restored as part of the museum; on summer weekends a refurbished **steam train** (10am–5pm; $4) makes a seven-mile, 45-minute round trip beside the river.

Two smaller museums are really only worth a look if you're desparate to escape the souvenir shops. The **California Military Museum**, 1119 Second St (Tues–Sun 10am–5pm; $2.25) provides an uninspiring chronicle – with documents, weaponry and uniforms – of California's involvement in armed struggles from pre-statehood days to the present day. The **B F Hastings Museum**, at Second and J streets (daily 10am–5pm; free), is an even less compelling stock of early communications equipment used by companies such as Pony Express and Wells Fargo. Most people only pass through to use the ATMs located inside this 1853 bank building, which also held the first State Supreme Court, the unassuming old chambers of which are sometimes open for public view on the top floor.

There's another museum two blocks south across I-5, at Third and O: the **Crocker Art Museum** (Wed–Sun 10am–5pm, Thurs until 9pm; $4.50), which exhibits European paintings collected by Supreme Court judge Edwin Crocker, brother of railroad baron Charles, in an odd complex of Renaissance Revival and modern buildings. More appropriate to its Sacramento setting, however, in the shadow of the massive I-5 and I-80 interchange along the river and two blocks south, is the **Towe Ford Museum** (daily 10am–6pm; $5) – the world's most complete collection of antique Ford cars and trucks, from Model Ts and As to classic '57 T-birds and the "woody" station wagons beloved of the Beach Boys.

## K Street: the modern centre

Running east from the riverfront and the Old Sacramento development, past the *Greyhound* and *Amtrak* stations, the **K Street Mall** is the commercial heart of

---

### THE BIG FOUR AND CALIFORNIA'S EARLY RAILROADS

For over twenty years from 1861, the Central Pacific and Southern Pacific Railroads monopolized transport and dominated the economy and politics of California and the western US. These companies were the creation of just four men – Leland Stanford, Mark Hopkins, Collis P Huntington and Charles Crocker – known as the **Big Four**.

For an initial investment of $15,000, the four financiers, along with the railroad designer and engineer Theodore Judah who died before its completion, received federal subsidies of $50,000 per mile of track laid – twice what it actually cost. On top of this, they were granted half the land in a forty-mile strip bordering the railroad: as the network expanded, the Southern Pacific became the largest landowner in the state, owning over twenty percent of California. An unregulated monopoly – caricatured in the liberal press as a grasping octopus – the railroad had the power to make or break farmers and manufacturers dependent upon it for the transport of goods. In the cities, particularly Oakland and Los Angeles, it was able to demand massive concessions from local government as an inducement for rail connections, and by the end of the 1800s the Big Four had extracted and extorted a fortune worth over $200 million each.

Sacramento, with the downtown end of the modern suburban tramway running through the centre of a pedestrianized shopping precinct, amid a growing forest of new office blocks and hotels that tower over Art Deco movie theatres and neon-signed storefronts.

Two blocks north of the mall, at 16th and H, the old **Governor's Mansion** (tours on the hour 10am–4pm; $2) was the elaborate Victorian home of all California governors up to Ronald Reagan; when this white 1874 structure was condemned as a firetrap, he abandoned these high ceilings and narrow staircases in favour of a ranch-style house on the outskirts of town.

The noble dome of the **State Capitol** stands proudly in the middle of a spacious green park two blocks south of the mall, at the geographical centre of Sacramento. Restored in the 1970s to its original nineteenth-century elegance, and still the seat of state government, the luxurious building brims over with finely crafted details. Although you're free to walk around, you'll see a lot more if you take one of the free **tours** (daily 9am–5pm) that leave hourly from room B-27 on the lower ground floor, passing through the old legislative chambers decked out in turn-of-the-century furnishings and fixtures.

**Sutter's Fort** (daily 10am–5pm; $2), on the east side of town at 27th and L, is a recreation of Sacramento's original settlement. An adobe house displays relics from the Gold Rush, and on summer weekends local volunteers dress up and pretend they're living in the 1850s. The adjacent **Indian Museum** (daily 10am–5pm; $2) on K Street displays tools, handicrafts and ceremonial objects of the Native Americans of the Central Valley and the Sierra Nevada mountains.

## Eating, drinking and entertainment

Dozens of fast-food stands and pricey Western-themed **restaurants** fill Old Sacramento, but you'd do better to steer clear of these and search out the places we've listed below – at least four of them are clustered near the junction of Capitol and 20th, where you'll also find the odd good **bar**. The best venue for slightly off-beat **live music** is the *Cattle Club*, 7041 Folsom Blvd (☎386-0390), while major touring bands usually play at the newly refurbished *Crest Theater*, 1013 K St (☎44-CREST). Arthouse **movies** are shown at *Tower Theater* at Broadway and 16th (☎443-1982).

**Annabelle's**, 200 J St (☎448-6239). Bustling Old Sacramento Italian joint with all-you-can-eat lunchtime buffets for under $4.

**Beatnik's Acoustic Café**, 1216 20th St at Capitol (☎443-9520). A juice bar and vegetarian café with live music on the menu most nights.

**Greta's Café**, 1831 Capitol Ave at 19th (☎442-7382). Quality salads, sandwiches, baked goods and fine vegetarian dishes at prices sure to please. Only open during the day in winter, but until 9 or 10pm Thurs–Sat in summer.

**New Helvetia Roasters & Bakers**, 1215 19th St at Capitol (☎441-1106). An old firehouse that's one of the best of the cafés in town, boasting home-roasted coffee, good cakes and pastries and communal tables inside and out. Open until 11pm most nights, with a mixed clientele but popular with gay men.

**Megami Bento-Ya**, 1010 10th at J St (☎448-4512). A functional, bargain Japanese restaurant with lunch mains and combination sushi plates for under $5. Try the sesame chicken.

**Paragary's**, 1401 28th St at N St (☎457-5737). A broad range of tastes catered for, with good giant-size portions of pasta, and tasty, brick-oven pizzas with unusual toppings. Moderate prices.

**Rubicon Brewing Company**, 2004 Capitol Ave (☎448-7032). One of the more enjoyable haunts in town, serving the flavourful house-brewed *Amber Ale* and the wonderfully hoppy *India Pale Ale*.

**The Tower Café**, 1518 Broadway at 16th (☎441-0222). Nineties version of a Fifties diner, good for burgers, veggie burgers, and late-night caffeine fixes.

**Weatherstone Coffee & Trading Co**, 812 21st St at H (☎443-6340). Sacramento's oldest coffee house with garden seating and cool brick interior. A favourite with locals both for its bulging sandwiches and many coffee concoctions. Open until 11pm or later.

# The Central Mother Lode

From Sacramento, US-50 and I-80 head east through the heart of the Gold Country, up and over the mountains past Lake Tahoe and into the state of Nevada. The roads closely follow the old stagecoach routes over the Donner Pass, and in the mid-1860s local citizens, seeking to improve dwindling fortunes after the Gold Rush subsided, joined forces with railroad engineer Theodore Judah to finance and build the first railroad crossing of the Sierra Nevada over much the same route – even along much of the same track – as that used by *Amtrak* today. However, while the area holds much historic interest, its towns aren't nearly as nice as those elsewhere in the Gold Country. Neither Placerville nor Auburn is worth much more than a quick look, though Coloma and Folsom, in between the two highways, have slightly more to offer.

## Folsom

In 1995, just as the **FOLSOM** powerhouse was gearing up for the centennial celebration of its pioneering efforts in long-distance electricity transmission, one of the sluice gates on the Folsom Dam gave way, sending millions of gallons of water down the American River towards Sacramento, twenty miles downstream. The levees held but Folsom Lake had to be almost completely drained before repairs could be undertaken. The event sent shockwaves through California's extensive hydro-electric industry and brought a fame to Folsom unknown since Johnny Cash sang of being "stuck in Folsom Prison" after having "shot a man in Reno, just to watch him die". The stone-faced **Folsom State Prison**, two miles north of town on Green Valley Road, has an arts-and-crafts gallery (daily 7.20am–5.30pm) selling works by prisoners, who get the proceeds when released. Across the road, a small **museum** (daily 10am–5pm; $1) is filled with grisly photographs and the medical records of murderers and thieves who were hanged for their crimes.

Folsom itself is attractive enough, with a single main street of restored homes and buildings that date from the days of the Pony Express. A reconstruction of the 1860 Wells Fargo office makes an imposing setting for the **Folsom History Museum**, 823 Sutter St (Wed–Sun 11am–4pm; free), whose prized possessions include a working scale model of a steam-powered gold dredge, artefacts from the Chinese community that settled here in the 1850s, and a huge mural depicting the area's main Native American people, the Maidu.

## Placerville

**PLACERVILLE**, forty miles east of Sacramento, takes a perverse delight in having been known originally as *Hangtown* for its habit of lynching alleged criminals in pairs and stringing them up from a tree in the centre of town. Despite these gruesome beginnings, Placerville has always been more of a market than a mining town, and is now a major crossroads, halfway between Sacramento and Lake Tahoe at the junction of US-50 and Hwy-49. For a time it was the third-largest city in California, and many of the men who went on to become the most powerful in the state got their start here: railroad magnates Mark Hopkins and Collis P Huntington were local merchants, while car mogul John Studebaker made wheelbarrows for the miners.

The modern town spreads out along the highways in a string of fast-food restaurants, gas stations and motels. The old Main Street, running parallel to US-50, retains some of the Gold Rush architecture, with an effigy dangling by the neck in front of the *Hangman's Tree* bar; you'll also see many fine old houses scattered among the pine trees in the steep valleys to the north and south of the centre. Nearby, one of the best of the Gold Country museums is located in the sprawling El

## EL DORADO WINE COUNTRY

Back in the 1860s, when the now-famous Napa and Sonoma valleys were growing potatoes, **vineyards** flourished in El Dorado county. However, the fields were neglected after the Gold Rush and killed off by phylloxera, only being re-established in 1972. Since then, however, the wineries in El Dorado county, around Placerville, have rapidly gained a reputation which belies their diminutive size. Most are low-key affairs where no charge is made for tasting or tours, and you're encouraged to enjoy a bottle out on the verandah. At quiet times you may even be shown around by the winemaker, a far cry from the organized tours and rampant commercialism of Napa and Sonoma.

The differences in altitude and soil types throughout the region lend themselves to a broad range of grape varieties, and the producers here are often criticized as being unfocused. Nonetheless, the wines have notched up a string of gold medals in recent years. Zinfandel and Sauvignon Blanc are big, but it is the Syrah/Merlot blends which attract the attention, and the Barbera (from a Piedmontese grape) is said to be the best in the world.

If you're out for a relaxed day's tasting, avoid the **Passport Weekend**, usually the last weekend in March or the first in April and booked out months in advance (☎446-6562 or 1-800/306-3956), when the purchase of said passport entitles you to all manner of foodie extravagances to complement the tastings. Better to pick up the *El Dorado Wine Country Tour* leaflet from the Chamber of Commerce and make your way to *Boeger*, 1790 Carson Rd (daily 10am–5pm; ☎622-8094), less than a mile from the *Greyhound* stop (see below), where you can sit under an arbour of apples and pears, or *Lava Cap*, 2221 Fruitridge Rd (daily 11am–5pm; ☎621-0175), which in recent years have produced some excellent Chardonnay and Muscat Canelli.

The quality of the local produce – not only grapes, but also apples, pears, peaches, cherries and more – is widely celebrated around the district, especially so during the **Apple Hill Festival** in October when a shuttle bus runs from Placerville to the majority of the orchards and wineries. At other times, you'll have to make your own way – it's not inconceivable to visit a couple of places on foot, given most of the day: the roads are generally quiet and the scenery pleasant.

Dorado County Fairgrounds, just north of US-50. This, the **El Dorado County Historical Museum** (Wed–Sat 10am–4pm; free), gives a broad historical overview of the county from the Miwok to the modern day, including logging trains and a mock-up of a general store. For more on the days of the Argonauts, head across US-50 to the **Gold Bug Mine Park**, Bedford Ave (May to mid-Sept daily 10am–4pm; mid-March to April & mid-Sept to Oct Sat & Sun only; $1) for a self-guided tour of a typical Mother Lode mine.

### Practicalities

*Amtrak Thruway* **buses** pull up twice daily outside *Buttercup Pantry*, 222 Main St; while *Greyhound* buses on their way to South Lake Tahoe stop three times a day at 1750 Broadway, a mile and a half east of town and linked with the centre by *Eldorado Transit* buses. Near the *Greyhound* stop are a number of **motels**, such as the *Hangtown Motel*, 1676 Broadway (☎622-0637; ②), and the nicer but slightly pricier *National 9 Inn*, 1500 Broadway (☎622-3884; ②). With more money, you're far better off at the *Chichester-McKee House*, 800 Spring St (☎626-1882 or 1-800/831-4008; ⑤), a very comfortable and welcoming **B&B** reached by turning north off US-50 onto Hwy-49 at the traffic lights in town.

The El Dorado County **Chamber of Commerce** office at 542 Main St (late May to early Sept Mon–Fri 9am–5pm, Sat 10.30am–3.30pm; rest of year closed Sat; ☎621-5885 or 1-800/457-6279) has local information, and can help set up **river rafting** trips in Coloma (see below).

For **eating**, try the local concoction, "Hangtown Fry" (included in the *Penguin Book of American Cookery*), an omelette-like mix-up of bacon, eggs and breaded oysters that you can taste at *The Bell Tower Café*, 423 Main St (☎626-3483), or *Powell Bros Steamers Co*, 425 Main St (☎626-1091). Not to be missed if you've got a car is *Poor Red's Barbeque*, housed in the old *Adams and Co* stagecoach office in El Dorado on Hwy-49 three miles south of Placerville, which serves the Gold Country's best barbecued dinners for under $6, with $1 beers and two-fisted margaritas. If none of these appeal, *Lil Mama D Carlos*, 482 Main St (☎626-1612), serves up fine, affordable Italian food.

## Coloma

Sights along Hwy-49 north of Placerville are few and far between, but it was here that gold fever began, when on January 24, 1848 James Marshall discovered flakes of gold in the tailrace of a mill he was building for John Sutter along the south fork of the American River at **COLOMA**. By the summer of that year thousands had flocked to the area, and by the following year Coloma was a town of ten thousand – though most left quickly following news of richer strikes elsewhere in the region, and the town all but disappeared within a few years. The few surviving buildings, including the cabin where Marshall lived, have been preserved as the **Marshall Gold Discovery State Historic Park** (daily 10am–dusk; $5 per car).

A reconstruction of **Sutter's Mill** stands along the river, and working demonstrations are often held at weekends at 10am and 1pm, and in 1998 – the sesquicentennial of the original discovery – the World Gold Panning Championships will take place here. There's a small historical museum across the road, and on a hill overlooking the town a statue marks the spot where Marshall is buried. Marshall never profited from his discovery, in fact it came to haunt him. At first he tried to charge miners for access to what he said was his land along the river (it wasn't), and he spent most of his later years in poverty, claiming supernatural powers had helped him to find gold.

Other supernatural forces are at work in the *Vineyard House Inn* (Tues–Sun; ☎622-2217; ⑤), adjacent to the state park on Cold Springs Road, where the ghost of a man tormented by his wife is said to haunt the cellar – now a popular **bar**, with music on weekend nights. If you want to sleep off a night's revelry, **bed and breakfast** is also available.

## Auburn and Dutch Flat

If you're heading for the northern mines you might stop off at **AUBURN**, eighteen miles northwest of Coloma at the junction of I-80 and Hwy-49; *Greyhound* **buses** from Sacramento to Reno stop at 246 Palm Ave and *Amtrak Thruway* stop outisde *Foster's Freeze* on Hwy-49 at Elm Avenue. The outskirts are sprawling and modern, but the Old Town district just off Hwy-49 has been preserved: a cluster of antique stores and saloons around California's oldest post office and the unmissable red-and-white tower of the 1891 **firehouse**. For a free map stop by the **Chamber of Commerce** in Auburn's old railroad station (Mon–Fri 9am–5pm Sat 10am–2pm; ☎887-2111 or 1-800/427-6463). South of the Old Town, the **Placer County Historical Museum** (Tues–Sun 10am–4pm; $1) has the standard displays of guns and mining equipment.

The twenty or so miles of Hwy-49 north of Auburn are a dull but fast stretch of freeway to one of the best parts of the Gold Country – the twin cities of Grass Valley and Nevada City. For an interesting side trip on the way there, or if you're heading for Lake Tahoe, take I-80 from Auburn 27 miles east to the small town of **DUTCH FLAT**, where old tin-roofed cottages are sprinkled among the pine and aspen-covered slopes. Miners here used the profitable but very destructive method of hydraulic mining (see p.480) to get at the gold buried under the surface – with highly visible consequences.

# THE NORTHERN MINES

The northern section of the Gold Country includes some of the most spectacularly beautiful scenery in California. Fast-flowing rivers cascade along the bottom of steeply walled canyons, whose slopes in fall are covered in the flaming reds and golds of poplars and sugar maples highlighted against an evergreen background of pine and fir trees. Unlike the freelance placer mines of the south, where wandering prospectors picked nuggets of gold out of the streams and rivers, the gold here was (and is) buried deep underground, and had to be pounded out of hard-rock ore. In spite of that, the northern mines were the most profitable of the Mother Lode – more than half the gold that came out of California came from the mines of **Nevada County**, and most of that from **Grass Valley**'s Empire Mine, now preserved as one of the region's many excellent museums. Just north, the pretty Victorian houses of **Nevada City** make it perhaps the most attractive of all the Gold Rush towns.

A few miles away, at the end of a steep and twisting back road, the scarred land-forms of the **Malakoff Diggins** stand as an exotic reminder of the destruction wrought by overzealous miners, who, as gold became harder to find, washed away entire hillsides to get at the precious metal. Hwy-49 winds up further into the mountains from Nevada City, along the Yuba River to the High Sierra hamlet of **Downieville**, at the foot of the towering Sierra Buttes. From here you're within striking distance of the northernmost Gold Rush ghost town of **Johnsville**, which stands in an evocative state of arrested decay in the middle of the forests of **Plumas-Eureka State Park**, on the crest of the Sierra Nevada.

You'll need a **car** to get to any of the outlying sights, but there is public transport to Grass Valley and Nevada City in the form of four daily *Amtrak Thruway* buses. Though there are no youth hostels, you'll find a few inexpensive motels and a handful of B&Bs; **camping** is an option too, often in unspoilt sites in gorgeous mountain scenery.

## Grass Valley and Nevada City

Twenty-five miles north of Auburn and I-80, the neighbouring towns of **GRASS VALLEY** and **NEVADA CITY** were the most prosperous and substantial of the gold-mining towns and are still thriving communities, four miles apart in beautiful surroundings high up in the Sierra Nevada mountains. Together they make one of the better Gold Country destinations, with museums and many balconied, elaborately detailed buildings, staggering up hills and hanging out over steep gorges.

Gold was the lifeblood of the area as recently as the mid-1950s, and although both towns look largely unchanged since the Gold Rush days, they're by no means stuck in the past: the engineering expertise that enabled miners to extract millions of dollars' worth of gold from deep subterranean veins is now being put to work to make electronic equipment for TV studios and freeze-dried food for backpackers. Also, since the 1960s, a number of artists and craftspeople have settled in the old houses in the hills around the towns, lending a vaguely alternative feel that's reflected in the *Community Endeavor* newspaper, the *KVMR* 89.5FM non-commercial community radio station, and in the friendly throngs that turn out for the annual Bluegrass Festival in the middle of June. Alternative lifestyles don't always accord with more hard-headed businessfolk in the twin towns and there is an understated but distinct tension between the two factions.

**Getting around** is relatively easy: both towns are very compact, and connected every thirty minutes by the *Gold Country Stage* minibus (Mon–Fri 8am–5pm, Sat 9.15am–5.30pm; $1 a trip, $2 for a day pass; ☎477-0103).

**CAMPING IN NEVADA COUNTY**

One of the best ways to get a feel for the day-to-day life of the miners is to "rough it" your-self, camping out in one of the many easily accessible **campgrounds** in the surrounding hills, all of which you can only reach by car. On Hwy-20 five miles east of Nevada City towards I-80, *Scott's Flat Lake* (☎265-5302) is privately operated, has the best facilities and charges $16 a night; seven miles on, *White Cloud* costs $10 a night; much further out, 24 miles east of Nevada City and four north of Hwy-20, *Fuller Lake Campground* is free but has no running water. Along Hwy-49 north of Nevada City there are half a dozen more campgrounds, the most attractive of which, the *Sierra* campground ($10) seven miles beyond Sierra City and *Chapman Creek* ($10) another mile upstream, lie along the Yuba River. For details contact the **ranger station** (☎265-4531) in Nevada City on Coyote Street, a quarter of a mile past the tourist office.

## Grass Valley and Nevada City accommodation

Places to stay don't come cheap, but if you can afford to splash out on a **bed and breakfast**, Nevada City in particular has some excellent options. Otherwise there are a couple of revamped old **Gold Rush hotels**, and a scattering of motels, though be warned that these may be booked up weeks in advance.

**Airway Motel**, 575 E Broad St, Nevada City (☎265-2233). Quiet, 1940s motel with swimming pool, a 10-min walk from the centre of town. Credit cards are not accepted. ②.

**Annie Horan's**, 415 W Main St, Grass Valley (☎272-2418 or 1-800/273-7390). Sumptuous small home with antiques galore. ④.

**Downey House**, 517 W Broad St, Nevada City (☎265-2815). Pretty 1870s Victorian home at the top of Broad Street, looking out over the town and surrounding forest. Simple decor and original artwork makes a welcome change from the over-fancy B&B norm. Rates include wine on arrival and full breakfast. ④–⑤.

**Flume's End**, 317 South Pine St, Nevada City (☎265-9665). Across the Pine Creek bridge from the centre of town, this small inn overlooks a pretty waterfall and features lovely gardens ranged along Deer Creek. ⑤–⑥.

**Holbrooke Hotel**, 212 W Main St, Grass Valley (☎273-1353 or 1-800/933-7077). Recently renovated and right in the centre of town, this historic hotel, where Mark Twain once stayed, has great rooms and an opulent bar. ④–⑥.

**Northern Queen Inn**, 400 Railroad Ave, Nevada City (☎265-5824). Good-value hotel with a heated pool. Attractive woodland cottages and chalets and simpler rooms. ④/⑤.

**Shady Rest Motel**, 10845 Rough and Ready Hwy, Grass Valley (☎273-4232). A little way out of town, but a pleasant walk; good-value weekly rates available. ②.

**Sierra Motel**, 816 W Main St, Grass Valley (☎273-8133). Central, but a bit run-down. ②.

**Swan-Levine House**, 328 S Church St, Grass Valley (☎272-1873). Accommodation with the artist in mind; the friendly owners also give instruction in printmaking. Attractively decorated, sunny rooms in an old Victorian hospital. ④.

## Grass Valley

Jonathan Richman wasn't the first performer to settle in **GRASS VALLEY**: Lola Montez, an Irish dancer and entertainer who had been the mistress of Ludwig of Bavaria and a friend of Victor Hugo and Franz Liszt, embarked on a highly successful tour of America, playing to packed houses from New York to San Francisco. Her provocative "Spider Dance", in which she wriggled about the stage shaking cork spiders out of her dress, didn't much impress the miners, but she liked the wild life-style of the town, gave up dancing and retired to Grass Valley with her pet grizzly bear, which she kept tied up in the front yard.

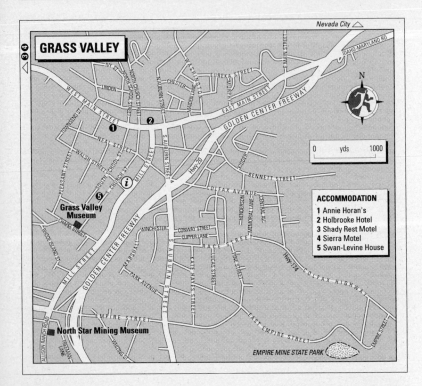

A few mementoes of Lola's life are displayed in the **Grass Valley Museum**, in the Old St Mary's Academy at the corner of Church and Chapel streets (June–Oct Tues–Fri 10am–3pm, Sat & Sun noon–3pm; Nov–May closed Sat & Sun; donation). The town's **tourist office** (Mon–Sat 10am–5pm; ☎273-4667 or 1-800/655-4667) is housed in a replica of her home, on the south side of town at 248 Mill St. It also has reams of historical information, lists of accommodation, and a walking tour **map** of the town, pointing out the oldest hardware store in California (which, sadly, closed in 1990 and has been converted into a tacky art gallery) among the wooden awnings and store-fronts of the gas-lighted business district.

## The North Star Mining Museum

Two intriguing museums illustrate the days when Grass Valley was the richest and most important of all the California mining towns. The **North Star Mining Museum** at the south end of Mill Street (May–Sept daily 10am–4pm; Oct–April irregular hours; donation) is far and away the best of all the Gold Country museums, both for the quality of the exhibits and the knowledge and enthusiasm of the guides. Housed in what used to be the power station for the North Star Mine, the featured exhibit is the giant **Pelton wheel**. Resembling nothing so much as a thirty-foot-diameter bicycle wheel, this was patented in 1878 and became one of the most important inventions to come out of the Gold Country. A hundred or so small iron buckets, each divided into bowl-like scoops, are fixed to the rim of the wheel; a jet of water shot into the centre of the buckets is turned around to create a secondary jet, spinning the wheel at a speed of over seventy miles per hour. Many Pelton wheels were used to generate electricity, though the one here drove an air compressor to power the drills and hoists of the mine.

A series of dioramas in the museum describe the day-to-day working life of the miners, three-quarters of whom had emigrated here from the depressed tin mines of Cornwall in England. Besides their expertise at working deep underground, the "Cousin Jacks", as they were called by the non-Cornish miners, introduced the Cornish pump (not to mention the Cornish pastie, a traditional pastry pie) to the mines. Some of these pumps had rods over a mile long, made of lengths of wood spliced together with iron plates – you can see a mock-up of one of these mammoth beasts here, as well as a replica of the old surface mechanism.

The great machines are now at peace, but when they were in action the racket could be heard for miles around. The noisiest offenders were the thundering **stamp mills**, a scaled-down version of which is operated upon request. In a full-size stamp mill, banks of from ten to eighty huge pistons, each weighing upwards of 1500 pounds, mashed and pulverized the gold-bearing quartz ore, freeing up the gold which was then separated from the gravel and dust by a variety of chemical amalgamation processes.

### The Empire Mine State Park

The largest and richest gold mine in the state, and also the last to shut down, was the **Empire Mine**, now preserved as a state park a mile southeast of Grass Valley, just off Hwy-174 at the top of Empire Street. The 800-acre park (June to early Sept daily 9am–6pm; early Sept to April daily 10am–5pm; May daily 9am-5pm; $2) is surrounded by pines amongst which are vast quantities of mining equipment and machinery, much of it only recently re-instated here after having been sold off for scrap after the mine closed in 1956. But in recent years a fair quantity has been bought back or replaced and it is now easy to imagine the din that shook the ground 24 hours a day, or the cages of fifty men descending the now-desolate shaft into the 350 miles of underground tunnels. After more than six million ounces of gold had been recovered, the cost of getting the gold out of the ground exceeded $35 an ounce – the government-controlled price at the time – and production ceased. Most of the mine has been dismantled, but there's a small, very informative **museum** at the entrance with a superb model of the whole underground system, built secretly to help predict the location of lucrative veins of gold. You can get some sense of the mine's prosperity by visiting the owner's house, the **Empire Cottage** at the north end of the park – a stone and brick, vaguely English manor house with a glowing, redwood-panelled interior overlooking a formal garden.

## Nevada City

**NEVADA CITY**, four miles north, may have less to see than Grass Valley, but it's smaller and prettier, with dozens of elaborate Victorian homes set on the winding, narrow, maple tree-lined streets that rise up from Hwy-49. It's the least changed of all the Gold Country towns, and a gem for aimless wandering or following the many steep streets up into the surrounding forest.

A good first stop is at the **tourist office** (Mon–Fri 9am–5pm Sat 11am–4pm; ☎265-2692) at 132 Main St, a block north of Hwy-49, where you can pick up a free walking-tour **map** of the town. It's hard to select specific highlights, but one place to start is the newly restored, lacy-balconied and bell-towered **Old Firehouse**, 214 Main St, next to the tourist office, which houses a small **museum** (May–Sept daily 11am–4pm; Oct–April daily except Wed 11.30am–4pm; donation) describing the social history of the region. The heart of town is Broad Street, which climbs up from the highway past the 1852 *National Hotel* and a number of antique shops and restaurants, all decked out in

Gold Country balconies and wooden awnings. Almost the only exception to the rule of picturesque nostalgia is the Art Deco 1937 **City Hall**, near the top of Broad Street.

The **Miner's Foundry Cultural Center** (daily 9am–5pm; free), perched precariously above the Deer Creek canyon at 325 Spring St, is an old tool foundry converted into a multi-use cultural centre, art gallery, performance space and *KVMR* radio studios. Immediately next door stands the **Nevada City Winery**, 321 Spring St (noon–5pm; ☎265-9463), where you can taste the produce of one of the state's oldest vineyards.

Above the town at the top of Pine Street a small plaque marks **Indian Medicine Rock**, a granite boulder with sunbeds worn into the hollows of the rock by Native Americans who valued the healing power of sunshine. Broad Street intersects Hwy-49

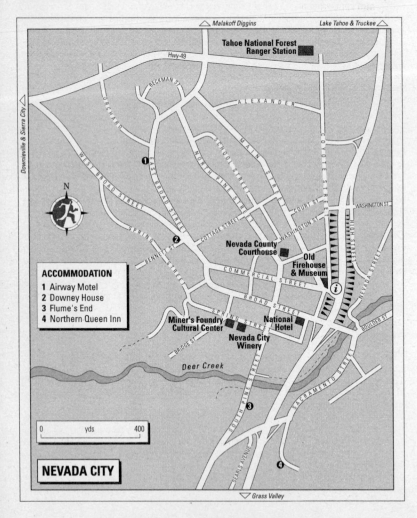

ACCOMMODATION
1 Airway Motel
2 Downey House
3 Flume's End
4 Northern Queen Inn

NEVADA CITY

a block further on, and continues up into the mountains as the North Bloomfield Road, which twists up the hills to the Malakoff Diggins (see overleaf).

## Eating and drinking

Both Grass Valley and Nevada City have some good places to **eat and drink**, including a few **cafés** that are open only for breakfast and lunch. After dark head to one of the many **bars and saloons**, where you'll often be treated to free live music. Look out for pasties, brought to the Gold Country by Cornish miners, and crisp-tasting *Nevada City* beer, brewed locally and available at better establishments.

### Cafés and restaurants

**Cirino's**, 309 Broad St, Nevada City (☎265-2246). Good deli sandwiches for lunch and Italian specialities at dinner, plus a full bar.

**Café Mekka**, 237 Commercial St, Nevada City (☎478-1517). Relaxed, fabulously decorated coffee shop – from exposed piping to *trompe l'oeil* wallpaper – popular with teenagers, trendies and ex-hippies. Open 8am–11pm weekdays, and until 1.30am at weekends.

**Earth Song**, 135A Argall Way, about a mile southwest of Nevada City, following S Pine St (☎265-8025). Excellent gourmet vegetarian café and wholefood supermarket. The café closes for an hour or two in the afternoon.

**Main Street Café**, 213 W Main St, Grass Valley (☎477-6000). The best bet for a really good meal, this casual but refined restaurant has an eclectic range of dishes – from pastas to cajun specialities – as well as good grilled meats and fresh fish, all at moderate prices.

**Marshall's Pasties**, 203 Mill St, Grass Valley (☎272-2844). Mind-boggling array of fresh filled pasties.

**Moore's Café**, 216 Broad St, Nevada City (☎265-1959). Plain-looking, all-American diner for breakfast and burgers during the day and a broader menu in the evening (until 11pm) when it's known as *Chuck's Tonight*. Closed Mon.

**Railroad Café**, 111 W Main St, Grass Valley. Decent diner food accompanied by the clatter of a model railroad continuously operating overhead.

### Saloons, bars and clubs

**Friar Tuck's**, 111 N Pine St, Nevada City (☎265-9093). Somewhat kitsch wine bar, with occasional live folk and jazz music.

**Gold Exchange Saloon**, 158 Mill St, Grass Valley (☎272-5509). Lively, unpretentious and unthreatening beer bar and saloon, great for quenching a thirst after a day's hiking, biking or prospecting.

**Mad Dogs and Englishmen**, 211 Spring St, Nevada City (☎265-8173). Pub-like bar with darts, good beer and regular live, danceable blues and rock music.

**Main Street Café**, 215 W Main St, Grass Valley (☎477-6000). Wine and cocktail bar next to restaurant, with live music most weekends.

**Wiley's**, 235 Commercial St, Nevada City (☎265-0116). Popular live music venue with a changing programme of mainly local acts.

# Nevada County and the Malakoff Diggins

Grass Valley, Nevada City and the foothills of **Nevada County** yielded more than half the gold that came out of California. Before the deep, hard-rock mines were established in the late 1860s, there were mining camps spread all over the northern Gold Country with evocative names like "Red Dog" and "You Bet", that disappeared as soon as the easily recovered surface deposits gave out. **ROUGH AND READY**, five miles west of Grass Valley, survives on the tourist trade alone, its visitors coming to take a look at the only mining town ever to secede from the United States, which Rough and Ready did in 1850. The band of veterans who founded the town, fresh from the

Mexican-American War, opted to quit the Union in protest against unfair taxation by the federal government, and although they declared their renewed allegiance in time for that summer's Fourth of July celebrations, the conflict was not officially resolved until 1948. Now the place isn't worth visiting; little more than a handful of ramshackle buildings, including a gas station and a general store.

Six miles northwest of Rough and Ready, off the winding Bitney Springs Road, is the **Bridgeport covered bridge**, the largest in the US, spanning the Yuba River: splintery wood shingles disguise the hefty trussed arch structure that's clearly visible from the inside if you walk the 250 feet across. The swimming area underneath offers some relief from a hot summer's day, but don't jump from the bridge – it's further than it looks.

## Malakoff Diggins State Park

The waters of the Yuba River are now crisp and clear, but when the bridge was completed in 1862 they were being choked with mud and residue from the many hydraulic mining or **hydraulicking** operations upstream. Hydraulic mining was used here in the late 1850s to get at the trace deposits of gold which were not worth recovering by orthodox methods. It was an unsophisticated way of retrieving the precious metal: giant nozzles or monitors sprayed powerful jets of water against the gold-bearing hillsides, washing away tons of gravel, mud and trees just to recover a few ounces of gold. It also required an elaborate system of flumes and canals to collect the water, which was sprayed at a rate of over thirty thousand gallons a minute. Some of these canals are still used to supply water to local communities. Worst of all, apart from the obvious destruction of the landscape, was the waste it caused, silting up rivers, causing floods, impairing navigation and eventually turning San Francisco Bay muddy brown.

The worst offender, whose excesses caused hydraulic mining to be outlawed in 1884, was the **Malakoff Diggins**, sixteen miles up steep and winding North Bloomfield Road from Nevada City (or reachable via the sixteen-mile Tyler Foote Road, which turns off Hwy-49 twelve miles northwest of Nevada City), where a canyon more than a mile long, half a mile wide and over six hundred feet deep was carved out of the red and gold earthen slopes. Natural erosion has softened the scars somewhat, sculpting pinnacles and towers into a miniature Grand Canyon now preserved as a 3000-acre **state park** (summer daily 9am–4.30pm; rest of year Sat & Sun only; $5 per car). Inside the park, old buildings from ghost towns around the Gold Country are being moved to the restored town of **NORTH BLOOMFIELD**, where a small **museum** (June–Aug daily 10am–5pm, May & Sept Sat & Sun only, call ☎265-2740 for winter hours) shows a twenty-minute film on hydraulicking, and there's a $14-a-night **campground** near the eerie cliffs.

# Downieville and the High Sierra towns

From Nevada City, Hwy-49 climbs up along the Yuba River gorge into some of the highest and most marvellous scenery in the Gold Country, where waterfalls tumble over sharp, black rocks bordered by tall pines and maple trees. In the middle of this wilderness, an hour's drive from Nevada City, **DOWNIEVILLE**, the most evocatively sited of the Gold Rush towns, spreads out along both banks of the river, crisscrossed by an assortment of narrow bridges. Hwy-49 runs right through the centre of town, slowing to a near-stop to negotiate tight curves that have not been widened since the stagecoaches passed through. Thick stone buildings, some enhanced with delicate wooden balconies and porches, others with heavy iron doors and shutters, face on to raised wooden sidewalks, their backs dangling precipitously over the steep banks of the river.

For what is now a peaceful and quiet little hamlet of three hundred people, Downieville seems strangely proud of its fairly nasty history. It has the distinction of being the only mining camp ever to have hanged a woman, Juanita, "a fiery Mexican dancehall girl", who stabbed a miner in self-defence. A restored wooden gallows, last used in 1885, still stands next to the County Jail on the south bank of the river, to mark the ghastly heritage. Across the river and two blocks north, at the end of a row of 1850s storefronts, the **Downieville Museum** (April–Oct daily 10am–5pm; Nov–March Sat & Sun only; 50¢) is packed full of odd bits and historical artefacts, including a set of snow-shoes for horses and a scaled-down model of a stamp mill, "made by the boys of the shop classes 1947–8". Pick up a walking tour map of the town from the **tourist office** kiosk (☎386-3122), next to the firebell tower in the centre of town. It can also help out with **accommodation**, which is provided by *Riverside Motel* (☎289-3574; ②) and *Robinson's Motel* (☎289-3573; ②), both centrally located on Hwy-49 alongside the Yuba River; and the wonderfully sited *Sierra Shangri-La* (☎289-3455; ③–④), four miles further east, which has B&B rooms and fully-fixtured cottages, the latter available weekly in high summer. **Eat and drink** at *The Forks Restaurant & Bar*, 20 Main St (☎289-3479).

The full-size original of the county museum stamp mill is maintained in working order at the **Kentucky Mine Museum** (summer Wed–Sun 10am–5pm; winter Sat & Sun only; $1), a mile east of **SIERRA CITY** further up Hwy-49, where a guided tour (11am, 1pm & 3pm; $4) takes you inside a reconstructed miner's cabin, down a mine shaft and gives you a look at various other pieces of equipment used for retrieving the gold-bearing ore. Until the mine was shut down during World War II, the ore was dug out from tunnels under the massive **Sierra Buttes**, the craggy granite peaks that dominate the surrounding landscape.

Sierra City is full of rustic charm, and can be a useful base for visiting the surrounding area, staying at the *Busch & Heringlake Inn* B&B (☎862-1501; ④), the *Sierra Chalet Motel* (☎862-1110; ②), or, best of the lot, *Buttes Resort*, Hwy-49 (☎862-1170; ③), which has self-contained units and suites. There's a **campground** ($10) half a mile to the east.

Hwy-49 continues east, passing **SIERRAVILLE** after twenty miles, where you'll find basic facilities, and **Bassetts Junction** where Hwy-89 heads north to Johnsville, ending near US-395, and south to Truckee and the Lake Tahoe area.

## Johnsville

**JOHNSVILLE**, 25 miles north of Bassett Junction, is after Bodie (see p.268) the best-preserved and most isolated old mining town in California. Surrounded by over seven thousand acres of pine forest and magnificent alpine scenery, it lies at the centre of the **Plumas-Eureka** state park – which has $14 **camping** (reserve through *MISTIX*) and miles of hiking trails. Johnsville's huge stamp mill and mine buildings are being restored, and in the meantime a small **museum** (daily 9am–5pm; $2) describes the difficult task of digging for gold in the High Sierra winters.

# THE SOUTHERN MINES

Though never as rich or successful as the diggings further north, the camps of the **southern mines** had a reputation for being the liveliest and most uproarious of all the Gold Rush settlements, and inspired most of the popular images of the era: Wild West towns full of gambling halls, saloons and gunfights in the streets. The mining methods here were quite different from those used further north. Instead of digging out gold-bearing ore from deep underground, claims here were more often worked by itinerant, roving prospectors searching for bits of gold washed out of rocks by rivers and streams, known as **placer** gold (from the Spanish word meaning both "sand bar", where much of the gold was found, and, appropriately, "pleasure"). Nuggets were sometimes found sitting on the river banks, though most of the gold had to be labori-ously separated from mud and gravel using handheld pans or larger sluices. It wasn't a

The telephone **area code** for the southern mines is ☎209.

particularly lucrative existence: freelance miners roamed the countryside until they found a likely spot, and if and when they struck it rich quickly spent most of the earnings, either in celebration or buying the expensive supplies needed to carry on digging.

The boom towns that sprung up around the richest deposits were abandoned as soon as the gold ran out, but a few slowly decaying ghost towns have managed to survive more or less intact to the present day, hidden among the forests and rolling ranchland. Other sites were buried under the many **reservoirs** – built in the 1960s to provide a stable source of water for the agricultural Central Valley – that cover much of the lower elevations.

During spring the hillsides are covered in fresh green grasses and brightly coloured wildflowers, though by the end of summer the hot sun has baked everything a dusty golden brown. Higher up, the free-flowing rivers rush through steep canyons lined by oak trees and cottonwoods, and the ten-thousand-foot granite peaks in the Sierra Nevada mountains above offer excellent skiing in winter, and hiking and camping in the pine and redwood forests all year round. South from Placerville, Hwy-49 passes through **Jackson**, which makes a good base for exploring the many dainty villages scattered around the wine-growing countryside of **Amador County**, continuing on through the mining towns of **Calaveras County**. The centre of the southern mining district, then as now, is **Sonora**, a small, prosperous town of ornate Victorian houses set on ridges above steep gorges. Once an arch rival but now a ghost town, neighbouring **Columbia** has a carefully restored Main Street that gives an excellent – if slightly contrived – idea of what Gold Rush life might have been like. The gold-mining district actually extended as far south as **Mariposa**, but the mines here were comparatively worthless and little remains to make it worth the trip, except perhaps as a quick stop on the way to Yosemite National Park (see p.294).

You'll need your own **transport** to see much of the southern Gold Country. Trains steer well clear of the hill terrain and buses only pass through Mariposa on their way from Fresno and Merced to Yosemite.

# Amador County

South from Placerville and US-50, the old mining landscape of **Amador County** has been given over to the vineyards of one of California's up-and-coming **wine-growing** regions, best known for its robust *Zinfandel*, a full-flavoured vintage that thrives in the sun-baked soil. Most of the wineries are located above Hwy-49 in the Shenandoah Valley, near Plymouth on the north edge of the county.

### Amador City and Sutter Creek

About thirty miles east of Sacramento, Hwy-16 joins Hwy-49 at **AMADOR CITY,** whose short strip of false-fronted antique shops give it a distinctive, Old West look. The landmark *Imperial Hotel* at the northern edge dominates the town, its four-foot-thick brick walls standing at a sharp bend in Hwy-49. The hotel has just been done up, with sunny double **rooms** (☎267-9172; ⑤), and the **restaurant** on the ground floor is one of the more sophisticated in the Mother Lode, but otherwise there isn't much to the place.

The real appeal of **SUTTER CREEK**, a much larger town two miles south of Amador City, is at first obscured behind the tidy facades of the cloying touristy restaurants and antique shops that line up along Hwy-49 through town. Though there are a number of surprisingly large Victorian wooden houses – many styled after Puritan New

England farmhouses – the town lacks the dishevelled spontaneity that animates many of the other Gold Rush towns, perhaps because its livelihood was based not on independent prospectors panning for *placer* gold but on hired hands working underground in the more organized and capital-intensive hard-rock mines. It was a lucrative business for the mine-owners: the Eureka Mine, owned by Hetty Green, at one time the richest woman in the world, operated until 1958; while the Lincoln Mine made enough money for owner Leland Stanford to become a railroad magnate and Governor of California. One unusual place that's worth a look – especially for closet Luddites and fans of Dickensian technology – is three blocks up Eureka Street from Hwy-49, where the cavernous and dimly lit **Knight's Foundry** (daily 9am–4pm; self-guided tour $2.50) still operates, using flapping belts, line shafts and wooden pulleys driven by a water-powered mill to make the moulds for cast-metal gears and machine parts. Believed to be the last water-powered foundry still operating in the US, it is also the town's main source of **visitor information**.

Sutter Creek also holds the bulk of Amador County's **accommodation** and **eating** places, with two central and very comfortable B&Bs: *The Foxes*, 77 Main St (☎267-5882; ⑤), with well-appointed rooms and claw-foot baths; and the larger, more communally minded *Sutter Creek Inn*, 75 Main St (☎267-5606; ④), with no TVs, no phones and no fake Victoriana, but a nice garden with hammocks and a welcoming atmosphere. The *Bellotti Inn*, 53 Main St (☎267-5211; ②), has the cheapest accommodation in town and a decent restaurant serving full meals for $15 and pasta dishes for $7. The *Eureka Street Courtyard*, a half-block east of Hwy-49, has a handful of eating places around a shaded gazebo and, across the street, the *Sutter Creek Coffee Roasting Co.* serves the best coffee in town.

## Jackson

After Sutter Creek, the town of **JACKSON**, four miles south, can seem distinctly blue-collar, mainly because of the huge *Georgia Pacific* lumber mill that serves as its northern gateway. Despite this first impression, Jackson makes a more affordable base for exploring the surrounding countryside. Its well-preserved centre of photogenic brick facades makes a fine frame for the beautiful, but architecturally inappropriate 1939 Art Deco front of the **County Courthouse** at the top of the hill, and further along the crest, the **Amador County Museum** at 225 Church St (Wed–Sun 10am–4pm; $1) has displays of all the usual Gold Rush artefacts, but is worth a look most of all for its detailed models of the local hard-rock mines that were in use up until World War II, with shafts over a mile deep. The headframes and some of the mining machinery are still standing a mile north of the museum on Jackson Gate Road, where two sixty-foot diameter **tailing wheels** (8am–dusk; free), which carried away the waste from the Kennedy Mine, are accessible by way of short trails that lead up from a well-signposted parking area. The headframe of the six-thousand-foot shaft), the deepest in North America, stands out at the top of the slope, along Hwy-49. The other major mine in Jackson, the **Argonaut Mine**, (of which nothing remains), was the scene of a tragedy in 1922, when 47 men were killed in an underground fire.

The **Amador County Chamber of Commerce** (daily 9am–5pm; ☎223-0350 or 1-800/649-4988), at the junction of Hwy-49 and Hwy-88, gives away an excellent *Visitors Guide to Amador County*, full of maps and interesting local anecdotes, at its office on Hwy-49 behind Main Street. The best **place to stay** is the down-to-earth, friendly *National Hotel*, 77 Main St (☎223-0500 or 1-800/894-3446; ③), an 1860s hotel with individually decorated rooms, such as the "Bordello Room" with flock wallpaper, a four-poster bed and a claw-foot bath. On Saturday night the price jumps by $30 but includes a wonderful meal in the hotel restaurant. If the *National* is full, try the *Amador Motel* (☎223-0970; ②) on Hwy-49 north of town, or nearby, the *Jackson Holiday Lodge* (☎223-0486; ③). *Mel's Diner* (☎223-0835), on Hwy-49 near the town centre, is open all day for

**breakfasts and burgers**, while *Café Max Swiss Bakery*, 140 Main St (☎223-0174), serves pastries and a mean cup of coffee. For **drinking**, the *Pioneer Rex Pool Hall and Card Room*, 28 Main St (☎223-3859), is the modern equivalent of a Wild West saloon, with cheap beers and all-night poker games behind swinging louvre doors.

## Indian Grinding Rock and Volcano

Hwy-88 heads east from Jackson up the Sierra Crest through hills that contain one of the most fitting memorials to the Native Americans who lived here for thousands of years before the Gold Rush all but wiped them out. Nine miles from Jackson, off Hwy-88, a side road passes by the restored remains of an old Miwok settlement at **Indian Grinding Rock State Historic Park** (daily dawn–dusk; $5 per car), where eleven hundred small cups – *Chaw'Se* in Miwok – were carved into the limestone boulders to be used as mortars for grinding acorns into flour. If you look closely from the small elevated plaform next to the biggest of the flat rocks, you can just detect the faint outline of some of the 360 petroglyphs. The state has developed the site into an interpretive centre and has constructed replicas of Miwok dwellings and religious buildings – interesting, even if they haven't managed to disguise the nails. Descendants of the Miwok gather here during the third week in July for "Big Time", a celebration of the survival of their culture with traditional arts and crafts, and to play a spirited game a bit like soccer. At the entrance to the site, the **Chaw'Se Regional Indian Museum** (Mon–Fri 11am–3pm, Sat & Sun 10am–4pm; free) explores the past and present state of the ten Sierra Nevada Native groups in a building said to simulate a Miwok roundhouse. The full process of producing acorn flour is covered, but modern Miwok life is given scant regard. A **campground** in the surrounding woods costs $14 a pitch and can be booked through *MISTIX*.

Named after the crater-like bowl in which it sits, **VOLCANO**, a tiny village a mile and a half north, once boasted over thirty saloons and dance halls – though the town is now little more than a shadow of its Gold Rush self. The densely forested countryside around, however, makes it well worth a visit, especially during spring (particularly mid-March to mid-April) when **Daffodil Hill** (free), three miles north of Volcano, is carpeted with more than 300,000 of the bobbing heads. Signs directing you there are only displayed when the daffs are in bloom. The sole accommodation in the immediate area is the *St George Hotel*, Main St (☎296-4458; mid-Feb to Dec only; ④), offering bed and breakfast without the comforts of televisions, phones or private bathrooms. Guests congregate in the bar, whose ceiling is covered in dollar bills and whose walls are decked with every office poster and wisecrack bumper sticker imaginable. This is the only place to **eat** in town, too, but it's excellent. From here, a narrow, scenic road follows Sutter Creek twelve miles down a wooded canyon back to the eponymous town.

## Highway 88

Hwy-88 heads east beyond the Volcano turn-off to Pioneer where it meets Hwy-26 from Mokelumne Hill (see below). Three miles east, the **Amador Eldorado Forest Ranger Station** (June to early Sept Mon–Sat 8am–4.30pm; early Sept to May Mon–Fri 8am–4.30pm; ☎295-4251) supplies wilderness permits for overnighting in the **Mokelumne Wilderness**, a segment of the Stanislaus and Toiabe national forests south of Hwy-88 which closely follows the route of many early settlers. The ranger station also has details of camping and hiking in the **Eldorado National Forest**, beautiful in the fall, just before the winter snows turn the Sierra Nevada mountains around the 8500-foot Carson Pass into one of California's best cross-country ski resorts.

The few hotels along Hwy-88 cater almost exclusively to cross-country skiers, leaving summer visitors with little to choose from except the **campsites** dotted along the highway. Most are RV-friendly and cost at least $10, but some are free.

Beyond Carson Pass and the mountain meadows around **Lake Kirkwood**, close to the Nevada border, Hwy-88 joins Hwy-89, from where it is a short drive south to **MARKLEEVILLE**, a town of two hundred people on the Sierra Crest. The major attraction here is the **Grover Hot Springs State Park**, four miles west (May–Sept daily 9am–9pm, reduced hours through winter, closed last two weeks in Sept; $4; call ☎916/694-2248 for off-season hours), with its two concrete tubs – one hot, one tepid – in which the water appears yellow-green due to mineral deposits on the pool bottom. There's a $14-a-night **campground** (reserve through *MISTIX*) on site, or you can stay back in Markleeville at the motel-style *J Marklee Toll Station* (☎916/694-2244; ②).

# Calaveras County

**Calaveras County** lies across the Mokelumne River, eight miles south of Jackson. You'll find a few good swimming and hiking spots on the north side of the river, along Electra Road; or you can push straight over the bridge, where a barely marked "Historic 49" turn-off loops around through the centre of **MOKELUMNE HILL**, perhaps the most evocative – and least touristed – town in the southern Gold Country. Moke Hill, as it's called, was as action-packed in its time as any of the southern Gold Rush towns, but tourism has been slower to take hold here and the town today remains an intriguing concoction of ruined and half-restored buildings. It also has a couple of good **bars**, one on the south side of town in the lobby of the old *Hotel Léger*, 8305 Main St (☎286-1401; ④), and another inside the three-storey **Odd Fellows Hall** at the north end of Main Street, where the *Adams and Co* saloon – and ad-hoc museum – is one of the few places in the region to retain much of the rowdy spirit of the pioneer years. On a more sober note, the range of names and languages on the headstones of the **Protestant Cemetery**, on a hill a hundred yards west of town, gives a good idea of the mix of people who came from all over the world to the California mines.

### San Andreas

After the haunting decay of Moke Hill, **SAN ANDREAS**, eight miles south, hardly seems to warrant a second look: the biggest town for miles, it's now the Calaveras County seat, and has sacrificed historic character for commercial sprawl. What remains of old San Andreas survives along Main Street, on a steep hill just east of the highway, where the 1893 granite and brick County Courthouse has been restored and now houses an interesting collection of Gold Rush memorabilia in the **Calaveras County Museum**, 30 N Main St (daily 10am–4pm; 50¢). Local **nightlife** revolves around the *Black Bart Inn*, 55 St. Charles St (☎754-3808; ③) across the street, which hosts bands on weekends. It is named after the gentleman stagecoach robber, **Black Bart**, who was captured and convicted here. Black Bart led a double life: in San Francisco he was a prominent citizen named Charles Bolton, who claimed to be a wealthy mining engineer; in the mining camps he made his name by committing thirty robberies between 1877 and 1883, always addressing his victims as "Sir" and "Madam" and sometimes reciting bits of poetry before escaping with the loot. He was finally discovered after dropping a handkerchief at the scene of a hold-up; police got him by tracing the laundry mark. He spent four years of a six-year sentence in San Quentin, and after his release disappeared without trace.

### Angels Camp and Carson Hill

The mining camps of southern Calaveras County were some of the richest in the Gold Country, both for the size of their nuggets and for the imaginations of their residents. The author Bret Harte spent an unhappy few years teaching in and around the mines in the mid-1850s and based his short story, *The Luck of the Roaring Camp*, on his stay in

### LIMESTONE CAVERNS IN THE GOLD COUNTRY

Limestone caverns abound in the southern Gold Country. Three have been developed for the public, and any one of them can provide, at the very least, a cool and constant 55°F relief from the sometimes baking-hot summer days. At Vallecito, just south of Hwy-4 and five miles east of Angels Camp on Parrot's Ferry Road, the **Moaning Cavern** (daily 10am–4pm; $5.75) is the largest in California, filled with strange rock formations, 150ft below ground; the human remains on display here greeted gold-seekers who found the cave in 1851. The natural acoustics of the cavern, which caused the low moaning sounds after which it is named, were destroyed by the insertion of the spiral staircase that takes visitors down into its depths (although for $25 you can abseil the 180 feet). **Mercer Caverns** (late May to Sept daily 9am–5pm; Oct to late May Sat & Sun 11am–4pm; $5), a mile north of Murphys on Sheep Ranch Road, focus on an 800-foot-long gallery of sculpted limestone, which takes the shape of angel's wings and giant flowers; the third cave system, **California Caverns** (mid-May to Oct daily 10am–5pm; Nov Sat & Sun 10am–4pm; $5.75), six miles east of San Andreas then two miles south from Mountain Ranch, offers a Wild Cave Expedition ($59): call ☎736-2708 for details and times.

**ANGELS CAMP**, thirty miles south of Jackson. There isn't much to see here these days, except for the saloon in the _Angels Hotel_ on Main Street, where the 29-year-old **Mark Twain** was told a tale that inspired him to write his first published short story, the _Celebrated Jumping Frog of Calaveras County_. The unfortunate legacy of the story is the **Jumping Frog Jubilee** held on the third weekend in May each year and attended by thousands of people.

On the north side of town, the **Angels Camp Museum**, 753 Main St (March–Nov daily 10am–3pm; Dec–Feb Wed–Sun 10am–3pm; $1) presents a cornucopia of gold panning equipment, though this isn't a match for the hangar full of carriages behind the museum.

**CARSON HILL**, now a ghost town along Hwy-49 four miles south of Angels Camp, boasted the largest single nugget ever unearthed in California: 195 pounds of solid gold that was fifteen inches long and six inches thick, worth $43,000 then and well over a million dollars today.

## Murphys

Nine miles east of Angels Camp, up the fairly steep Hwy-4, **MURPHYS'** one and only street is shaded by locust trees and graced by rows of decaying monumental buildings. One of the Gold Country's few surviving wooden water flumes still stands on Murphys' northern edge, while the oldest structure in town now houses the **Oldtimer's Museum** (Fri–Sun 11am–4pm; donation), a small gathering of documents and a wall-full of rifles. If you want to **stay**, head across the street to the old _Murphys Hotel_, 475 Main St (☎728-3454 or 1-800/532-7684; ④), which hosted some of the leading lights of the boom days in its rustic double rooms. The **Big Trees of Calaveras** state park, fifteen miles east ($5 per car), covers six thousand acres of gigantic Sequoia trees, threaded with trails. It makes for fine ski touring in winter, with hiking and **camping** ($14; reserve mid-summer through _MISTIX_) the rest of the year.

# Sonora, Columbia and Jamestown

**SONORA**, fifteen miles southeast of Angels Camp, is the centre of the southern mining district. Now a logging town, set on steep ravines, the town makes a good base for exploring the southern region, with a thriving commercial centre that manages to avoid tourist overkill. There's little to see beyond the false-fronted buildings and Victorian houses on the main **Washington Street** and the Gothic **St James**

**Episcopal Church** at its far end, but it's a friendly, animated place, which warrants an afternoon's amble. You can pick up architectural and historical walking-tour **maps** (25¢) from the tourist office desk inside the small **Tuolumne County Museum**, in the old County Jail at 158 W Bradford Ave (summer daily 10am–3.30pm; winter Mon–Sat 10am–3.30pm; free), which is worth a look for the restored cell block, if not for the collection of old clothes and photographs.

Walking-tour maps are also available from the **Tuolumne County Visitors Bureau**, 55 W Stockton St (June–Aug Mon–Fri 9am–7pm, Sat 10am–6pm, Sun 10am–5pm; Sept–May Mon–Sat 9am–5pm; ☎533-4420 or 1-800/446-1333), a block from Washington Street, and the best source of **information** on the area; for specific details on camping, backpacking or outdoor recreation head for the *Sierra Nevada Adventure Co.* at 173 S Washington St (☎532-5621).

The best **place to stay** in Sonora is the *Ryan House*, 153 S Shepherd St (☎533-3445; ④), a comfortable and welcoming old home set in lovely rose gardens two blocks east of the town centre. Other options include the old adobe *Gunn House* at 286 S Washington St (☎532-3421; ③), or the good-value *Miner's Motel* (☎532-7850; ③) on Hwy-108 half way to Jamestown. For **lunch** try the gourmet health foods at *Good Heavens*, 49 N Washington St (☎532-3663); after dark make for *Alfredo's*, 123 S Washington St (☎532-8332), widely regarded as the best reasonably priced Mexican restaurant in these parts. Of several **bars** along S Washington Street, *The Brass Rail* at no. 131, and the *Horseshoe Club* at no. 97, are the places to go for a real Wild West atmosphere around the pool and poker tables.

## Columbia

Perhaps the most striking introduction to the southern Gold Rush towns is **COLUMBIA**, four miles north of Sonora on Parrots Ferry Road. Now a ghost town, it experienced a brief burst of riches after a Dr Thaddeus Hildreth and his party picked up thirty pounds of gold in just two days in March 1850. Within a month over five thousand miners were working claims limited by local law to ten square feet, and by 1854 Columbia was California's second largest city, with fifteen thousand inhabitants supporting some forty saloons, eight hotels and one school. The town missed becoming the state capital by two votes – just as well, since by 1870 the gold had run out and the town was abandoned, after over two and a half million ounces of gold (worth nearly a billion dollars at today's prices) had been taken out of the surrounding area.

Columbia is preserved as a state historic park, but there is no main gate or entrance fee: the dusty streets and wooden boardwalks are open all the time. Most of the buildings that survive date from the late 1850s, built in brick after fire destroyed the town for a second time. Roughly half of them house historical exhibits – including a dramatized visit to the frontier dentist's office, complete with a two-hundred-proof anaesthetic and tape-recorded screams. The rest have been converted into shops and restaurants, where you can sip a sarsaparilla or eat a Gold Rush hot dog. There's even a **stagecoach ride** ($3) along the old mining trails around the town, which leaves from in front of the Wells Fargo Building. Needless to say it's all a bit contrived, and summer weekends can be nightmarishly crowded, especially on Living History Days when volunteers dress up and act out scenes from the old days. But most of the year the tree-lined streets are empty, and the place as a whole makes for a reasonably effective evocation of Gold Rush life. If you want to **stay**, the *Royal Hotel*, 18239 Main St (☎984-5271; ④), is luxurious and central, while a mile south of town the *Columbia Gem Motel*, 22131 Parrots Ferry Rd (☎532-4508; ②), offers basic accommodation in rustic cabins.

## Jamestown

Three miles south of Sonora on Hwy-49 lies **JAMESTOWN**, a saccharine-sweet little village that serves as the southern gateway to the Gold Country for drivers coming on

Hwy-120 from the San Francisco Bay Area. Before 1966, when much of Jamestown burned down in a fire, it was used as location for many well-known Westerns – most famously for the filming of *High Noon*. The train from that movie is now the biggest attraction of **Railtown 1897 State Historic Park**, four blocks east of Main Street – a collection of old steam trains that's open year round, on summer weekends offering trips on restored local railroads ($9). Along with its train collection, Jamestown is one of the few Gold Country towns that still has a working mine – the huge open-pit Sonora Mining Corp operation west of town on Hwy-49 – and a number of outfits take visitors on gold-mining expeditions. Among them, *Gold Prospecting Expeditions* ($35; ☎984-4653) gives brief instruction in the arts of panning, sluicing and sniping, kits you out and allows you two hours to pan what you can from its local stream. Main Street is the town's main drag, lined with old balconied Gold Rush **hotels** such as the *National* (☎984-3446; ③) and the *Royal* (☎984-5271; ③), and with a few good **places to eat**. The *Mother Lode Coffee Shop* (☎984-3386) is popular with locals, while the more touristy *Smoke Café* (☎984-3733) has fairly tame Mexican food and huge margaritas, and across the street *Michelangelo* (☎984-4830) serves excellent pastas and pizzas in a stylish setting.

# Mariposa County and south to Yosemite

Hwy-49 winds south from Sonora through some sixty miles of the sparsely populated, rolling foothills of **Mariposa County**, passing near the remains of the town of **CHINESE CAMP**. It was here that the worst of the Tong Wars between rival factions of Chinese miners took place in 1856, after the Chinese had been excluded from other mining camps in the area by white miners. Racism was rampant in the southern Gold Rush camps, something which also accounts for its most enduring legend, the story of the so-called Robin Hood of the Mother Lode, **Joaquin Murieta**. Very little is actually known of the truth behind the stories of this figure, yet virtually every southern Gold Rush town has some tale to tell of him. A romantic hero, rather than a real one, Murieta was probably a composite of many characters, mostly dispossessed Mexican miners driven to banditry by violent racist abuse at the hands of newly arrived white Americans. In May 1853, the State Legislature hired a man named Harry Love to capture any one of five men named "Joaquin" wanted for cattle theft. Love soon returned with the head of a man pickled in a glass jar, and collected the reward. A year later J R Ridge wrote a story called *The Life and Times of Joaquin Murieta, the Celebrated California Bandit*, mixing together flights of fancy with a few well-placed facts – including the pickled head – and the legend was born.

Hwy-49 continues south right on the fringes of the Gold Country. Branching off it, Hwy-120 passes **Groveland**, a way-station on the San Francisco to Yosemite run. The ranger station (☎586-3234) has information on hiking and camping in the nearby Stanislaus National Forest.

## Hornitos

The town with the most likely claim to Murieta's patronage is **HORNITOS**, twenty miles west of Bear Valley on the southern edge of the Gold Country. Hornitos, which is Spanish for "little ovens", was named after the oven-shaped tombs in the cemetery at the edge of town and was once a quiet little Mexican pueblo, one of the few in the area founded before the Gold Rush. The population swelled to over fifteen thousand when Mexican miners were exiled from nearby mining camps by white miners who didn't feel like sharing the wealth, and the town became notorious for its saloons, opium dens and gambling halls, a favourite haunt of many an outlaw like Murieta – who, it's claimed, had his own secret escape route out of town via an underground tunnel. Today Hornitos is a heap of substantial ruins grouped around a central plaza.

**Mariposa**

Hwy-49 continues south to **MARIPOSA**, the county seat and the last major supply stop before Yosemite. The **Mariposa Museum and History Center** (summer daily 10am–4.30pm; rest of year Sat & Sun only, closed Jan; donation), behind the *Bank of America* off Hwy-49 at the north end of town, has a little bit of everything to do with the Gold Rush – from miners' letters home to ancient bottles of *E & J Burke's Guinness Stout* – and is well worth a look if you're passing through. From Mariposa Hwy-140 heads east along the Merced River into Yosemite National Park (see p.294). Along its length, the *Meadows Ranch Café* at no. 5029 serves good all-day café **food**.

# LAKE TAHOE, RENO AND CARSON CITY

High above the Gold Country, just east of the Sierra ridge, **Lake Tahoe** sits placidly in a dramatic alpine bowl, surrounded by high granite peaks and miles of thickly wooded forest. It's a heavily touristed area; the sandy beaches attract thousands of families throughout the summer, and in winter the snow-covered slopes of the nearby peaks are packed with skiers. The eastern third of the lake lies in Nevada, and gleams with the neon signs of flashy casinos.

    **Truckee**, 25 miles north of Lake Tahoe, ranges along the Truckee River, which flows out of Lake Tahoe down into the desert of Nevada's Great Basin. It's a main stop on *Greyhound* and *Amtrak* cross-country routes, but is otherwise little visited, life revolving around the lumber mill that dominates its old centre. **Donner Pass**, just west of town, was named in memory of the pioneer Donner family, many of whom lost their lives when trapped here by heavy winter snows.

    Across the border in Nevada, **Reno**, at the eastern foot of the Sierra Nevada, is a downmarket version of Las Vegas, popular with slot-machine junkies and elderly gamblers; others come to take advantage of Nevada's lax marriage and divorce laws. Though far smaller than Reno, **Carson City**, thirty miles south, is the Nevada state capital, with some engaging museums recounting the town's frontier history. Heading deeper into Nevada in the arid mountains further east, the silver mines of the Comstock Lode, whose wealth paid for the building of much of San Francisco, are buried deep below the tourist centre of **Virginia City**.

    The two main trans-Sierra highways, I-80 and US-50, head east from Sacramento and are kept open all year round, regardless of snowfall, passing by Truckee and Lake Tahoe respectively. Both places are served by *Greyhound*, and there are also services from the Nevada cities to the Tahoe casinos, though there's no public transport between Truckee and the lake.

# Lake Tahoe

Fault-formed **LAKE TAHOE** is one of the highest, largest, deepest, cleanest, coldest and most beautiful lakes in the world. More than sixteen hundred feet deep, it is so cold – or so the story goes – that at its depths cowboys who drowned over a century ago have been recovered in perfectly preserved condition, gun holsters and all. It's a place for all seasons, thronged with jet-skiers, boaters and anglers in summer, and

The telephone **area code** for the Californian section of the Lake Tahoe region is ☎916.

equally packed with snowboarders and skiers in winter. When the snows melt, the wilderness areas all around the lake offer excellent hiking.

Its position, straddling the border between California and Nevada lends the lake a schizophrenic air, the dichotomy most evident at **South Lake Tahoe**, the lakeside's largest community, where ranks of restaurants, modest motels and pine-bound cottages stand cheek by jowl with the highrise gambling dens of **Stateline** a street away. Among the smattering of small and mostly missable settlements around the lake, the only other town of any appreciable size is **Tahoe City** on the north shore, a relaxed and likeable place in a dull kind of way.

## Arrival, information and getting around

One hundred miles east of Sacramento on US-50, Lake Tahoe is well served by *Greyhound* **buses** and a number of coach tours, mainly catering to weekend gamblers. The five daily *Greyhound* buses from San Francisco and Sacramento use *Harrah's* casinos in South Lake Tahoe as a terminus: *Amtrak Thruway* buses stop twice daily on their Sacramento to Carson City run. *Tahoe Casino Express* buses ($15 one-way; ☎702/785-2424 or 1-800/446-6128) run half-hourly from 9am to 5pm between Reno airport and the Stateline casinos, and *Gray Line* (☎702/331-1147) has daily tours from Reno around the lake, stopping off at Virginia City; for "gambler's special" coach tours from San Francisco. If you're **driving**, expect to get here in a little over three hours from San Franciso unless you join the Friday night exodus in which case you can add an hour or two, more in winter when you'll need to carry chains.

There are booths claiming to be visitor centers all over South Lake Tahoe, but most are just advertising outlets for the casinos or fronts for timeshare agents. Instead, get useful **information**, maps and help with finding a place to stay at the **South Lake Tahoe Chamber of Commerce**, 3066 US-50 (Mon–Fri 8.30am–5pm Sat 9am–4pm; ☎541-5255) just west of El Dorado beach. The **North Lake Tahoe Chamber of Commerce**, 245 North Lake Boulevard opposite the Tahoe City "Y" crossroads (Mon–Sat 9am–5pm; ☎581-6900) is the best bet for information on the north lake region.

### Getting around

*STAGE* buses (☎541-6328) run 24 hours a day all over the South Lake Tahoe area, and will take you anywhere within a ten-mile radius for a flat $1.25 fare. *Tahoe Casino Express* (☎1-800/446-6128) runs northeast from South Lake Tahoe to Glenbrook then east to Carson City; and, in the north, *TART* (6am to 6pm; $1 flat fare, $2.50 for an all-day pass; ☎581-6365) runs between Truckee, Tahoe City, Sugar Pine Point State Park and Incline Village. There is no transport going right around the lake. **Car rental**, at about $30 a day, is available through the South Lake Tahoe outlets of all the national chains: *Avis* (☎542-5638 or 1-800/831-2847); *Enterprise* (☎544-7788); and *Hertz* (☎544-2327 or 1-800/654-3131) – as well as slightly cheaper local firms such as *Tahoe Rent-a-car* (☎544-4500). You could also **rent a bicycle** for around $20 a day from any of over a dozen lakeside shops, among them *Anderson Bike Rental*, 645 Emerald Bay Rd (☎541-0500).

## Lake Tahoe accommodation

Most of the hundred or so **motels** that circle the lake are collected together along US-50 in South Lake Tahoe. During the week, except in summer (the peak season), many have bargain rates, from around $30 for a double; however, these rates can easily double at weekends, so be sure to confirm all prices. If you get stuck for a room, the **South Lake Tahoe Visitors' Authority**, 1156 Ski Run Boulevard (☎583-3494 & 1-800/

AT-TAHOE) runs a free **reservation service**. **Tahoe City** lacks the range and competition of its southerly neighbour, so you can expect to pay a little more for a room there. Unlike Las Vegas or Reno, the **casinos** rarely offer good-value accommodation. **Camping** (see box on p.493) is only an option during summer (Tahoe gets upwards of 20ft of snow every winter).

### The south shore

**Caesars Tahoe Resort/Casino**, US-50, Stateline, Nevada (☎702/588-3515 or 1-800/648-3353). Deluxe resort and upmarket casino; the best rooms overlook the lake. ⑥.

**Doug's Mellow Mountain Retreat**, 3787 Forest Ave, S Lake Tahoe (☎544-8065). Essentially Doug's home operating as a relaxed, if cramped, hostel with cooking facilities, cheap bike rental and occasional barbecues. Beds are $13 a night and double rooms are available. A mile from the *Greyhound* stop but Doug will pick you up. ①.

**Inn by the Lake**, 3300 Lake Tahoe Blvd, S Lake Tahoe (☎542-0330 or 1-800/877-1466). Nicely furnished rooms, a heated swimming pool and Jacuzzi, free breakfast and use of bicycles make this relaxing spot good value for money. Free shuttle bus to the casinos. ⑤.

**Lamplighter Motel**, 4143 Cedar Ave, S Lake Tahoe (☎544-2936). Just off US-50, near the casinos and the lakeshore. It has a hot tub with views of the skifield behind. ②.

**Motel 6**, 2375 Lake Tahoe Blvd, S Lake Tahoe (☎542-1400). Huge, and one of the better bets for budget accommodation. It's filled during the ski season and in summer, so book early. ③.

**Seven Seas**, 4145 Manzanita Ave, S Lake Tahoe (☎544-7031). One of the south shore's countless small motels, offering clean, simple rooms and a hot tub. ②.

### The north shore

**Falcon Motor Lodge**, Hwy-28, Kings Beach (☎546-2583). Ordinary but dependable budget accommodation. ②.

**Lake of the Sky Motor Inn**, 955 N Lake Blvd, Tahoe City (☎583-3305). Justifiably a little more expensive than the *Tahoe City Inn*.. ④.

**Tahoe City Inn**, 790 N Lake Blvd, Tahoe City (☎581-3333 or 1-800/800-TAHO). This place can cost as little as $45 midweek off-season. ③.

## South Lake Tahoe and Stateline

Almost all of Tahoe's lakeshore is developed in some way or other, but nowhere is it as concentrated as at the contiguous settlements of **SOUTH LAKE TAHOE** and **STATELINE**. The latter is compact, a clutch of gambling houses huddled, as you might expect, along the Nevada–California border, the half-dozen-or-so casinos competing for the attentions of the punters who almost all base themselves in the much larger South Lake Tahoe on the Californian side. At some time during their stay, almost everyone chances their arm at the tables and slot machines, but few come for that purpose alone. Lake Tahoe is primarily an outdoors attraction, as the numerous lakefront sporting paraphernalia outlets will attest.

Though many stretches of Lake Tahoe are breathtakingly beautiful, the 75-mile **drive** around the lake can be a bit of a disappointment. A better way to see the lake is to take one of two **paddle-wheel boat** cruises: the *Tahoe Queen*, a restored Mississippi riverboat, sets sail from the end of Ski Run Boulevard in South Lake Tahoe (daily 11am, 1.30pm & 3.55pm; $14; ☎541-3364 or 1-800/23-TAHOE); and the *MS Dixie II*, a modern replica, leaves from Zephyr Cove, three miles north of Stateline in Nevada, for a two-hour cruise to Emerald Bay (daily 11am, 2pm & 5pm; $14; ☎702/588-3508).

Perhaps most impressive is the view of the lake from above, either skiing in winter or hiking along the many trails that rim the lake basin (see "Hiking"box on p.493). The lazy way to get up is on the **Heavenly Valley Tram** (summer daily 10am–9pm; winter times vary depending on ski conditions; $10.50), a ski lift that shifts tourists up the 8200-foot mountain from South Lake Tahoe to the south lake's largest ski resort.

## West around the lake

In summer, many enjoyable music and arts events take place at the **Tallac Historic Site** (April–Oct daily 10am–6pm; free), beside Hwy-89 on the western side of the lake two miles northwest of the South Lake Tahoe "Y". Even when there's nothing special going on, the historic site's sumptuous wood-built homes – built by wealthy San Franciscans as lakeside vacation bases from the late 1800s – are well worth a look. You can also see the remains of the lavish casino-hotel erected by Elias "Lucky" Baldwin, which brought the rich and famous to Lake Tahoe's shores until it was destroyed by fire in 1914. Inside the former Baldwin house, the **Tallac Museum** (daily 11am–3pm; free) records the family's impact on the region.

The prettiest part of the lake, however, is along the southwest shore, where **Emerald Bay State Park**, ten miles from South Lake Tahoe (daily dawn–dusk; $5 per vehicle), surrounds a narrow, rock-strewn inlet and the lake's one island, Fanette Island, topped by a small and unused teahouse. In the park, at the end of a mile-long trail from the parking lot is **Vikingsholm**, an authentic reproduction of a Viking castle, believe it or not, built as a summer home in 1929. It is open for **tours** (every 30min summer daily 10am–4pm; $2). From Vikingsholm, the **Rubicon Trail** runs two miles north along the lakeside to **Rubicon Bay**, flanked by other grand old mansions, dating from the days when Lake Tahoe was accessible only to the most well heeled of travellers. You can also drive here on Hwy-89 and enter through the **D L Bliss State Park** (extremely limited parking $5). The 15,000-square-foot **Ehrman Mansion** here (guided tours daily 10am–4pm on the hour; free), decorated in a happy blend of 1930s opulence and backcountry rustic, and surrounded by extensive lakefront grounds which were used as a location for the movie *Godfather II*.

## Tahoe City and around

**TAHOE CITY** feels very different to South Lake Tahoe; it's compact – you can easily walk around it in half an hour – active and youthful in feel. That's not to say it is entirely alien to an older set; the resorts and campsites all along the north shore are geared towards families.

At the western end of town, Hwy-89 meets Hwy-28 at what is known as the Tahoe City "Y". Immediately south, Hwy-89 crosses Lake Tahoe's outlet, the Truckee River, its flow controlled by sluice gates immediately upstream. These are remotely controlled from Reno, but were once operated by a gatekeeper who lived in what is now the **Gatekeeper's Museum** (mid-June to early Sept daily 11am–5pm; May to mid-June & early to late Sept Wed–Sun only 11am–5pm; free), a well-presented hodge-podge of artefacts from the last century, and a good collection of native basketware. Nearby, the **Truckee River Bike Trail** begins its three-mile waterside meander to Midway Bridge.

However, time is better spent five miles north off Hwy-89 at **Squaw Valley**, the site of the 1960 Winter Olympics. The original facilities (except the flame and the Olympic rings) are now swamped by the rampant development which has made this California's largest ski resort, able to cater for 49,000 skiers an hour. Lift tickets are $41 a day, or it's $8 for night skiing on the three-and-a-half-mile Mountain Run, the longest floodlit run in the country. You can also go bungee jumping (☎583-4000), or there's ice skating for $7, an artificial climbing wall and even swimming 8200ft up in the new *High Camp Bath and Tennis Club*.

East from Tahoe City are unremarkable settlements, among them Incline Village, a short distance from the eminently missable **Ponderosa Ranch** (April–Oct daily 9.30am–5pm; $8.50) where *Bonanza* was filmed. The best single destination on the

## HIKING AND CAMPING AROUND LAKE TAHOE

Of the many wonderful hikes in the Lake Tahoe area, only one – the 150-mile **Tahoe Rim Trail** – makes the circuit of the lake, some of it on the Pacific Crest National Scenic Trail which follows the Sierra ridge from Canada to the Mexican border. Most people tackle only a tiny section of it, such as **Kingsbury Grade to Big Meadows** (22 miles) starting off Hwy-207 northwest of South Lake Tahoe and finishing on Hwy-50, south of Lake Tahoe. Many other sections are equally spectacular: ask at the **US Forest Service visitor center,** 870 Emerald Bay Rd (summer Mon–Thurs & Sat–Sun 8am–5.30pm, Fri 8am–7pm; ☎573-2674), three miles northwest of the South Lake Tahoe "Y", for recommendations, free maps and brochures.

There are also many **mountain biking** trails around the lake: **Meiss Country,** between Luther Pass and Carson Pass twenty miles south of South Lake Tahoe is one favoured area. The three-mile loop of the **Pope-Baldwin Trail** near the south shore is another winner, as is the popular **Marlett Lake/Flume Trail** in the Nevada State Park.

### CAMPING

Lake Tahoe's best **campsite** is *Campground by the Lake*, on the lakeshore three miles west of Stateline (☎542-6096; $16). Other south shore sites include *Nevada Beach* (☎544-5994 reserve through *Biospherics*; $16) a mile east of Stateline, and there are any number of backcountry sites in the surrounding forest. The **north** has several sites within striking distance of Tahoe City, including *Tahoe State Recreation Area* (☎583-3074; $14) right in the centre and as crowded as you would expect. A mile and a half east, *Lake Forest* (☎583-3796; $10) is cheaper though a way from the beach; and two miles southwest along Hwy-89, there's the large *William Kent* site (☎*MISTIX*; $12).

Along the western side of the lake, the Tahoe Rim Trail follows the Pacific Crest Trail through the glaciated valleys and granite peaks of the **Desolation Wilderness.** Here, **wilderness permits** are required by all users, though for day users these are self-issued. For overnighters, a quota system operates in summer: fifty percent of these are first-come-first-served on the day of entry from the Forest Service visitor center, the remainder are reservable up to ninety days in advance (☎644-6048). Primitive sites include *Bayview* (☎544-6096; free). The other wilderness areas around the lake – Granite Chief to the northwest and Mount Rose to the northeast – are used much less and consequently no wilderness permits are needed, though campfire permits are.

west side of the lake is the **Lake Tahoe Nevada State Park** at Sand Harbour, which has a great beach – though the water is always prohibitively cold – and trails winding up through the backcountry to the Tahoe Rim Trail.

## Lake Tahoe eating and drinking

Lake Tahoe has very few exceptional **restaurants**, but dozens of burger and steak places, rustic in decor with raging fireplaces standard. Far better are the **buffets** at the Nevada **casinos:** *Harrah's*, for example, serves a wonderful spread, with good all-you-can-eat food for low rates. The casinos are also good places to **drink** – roving barmaids bring free cocktails to gamblers – and hold most of the region's entertainment options as well: crooners and comedians mostly, plus small-scale versions of Las Vegas revues. For its size, Tahoe City has a very good range of inexpensive places to eat, all within easy walking distance of each other.

### South shore

**Carlos Murphy's,** 3678 US-50, S Lake Tahoe (☎542-1741). Pseudo-Mexican cantina, serving up large platefuls of anodyne Tex-Mex food; come early in the evening for free Happy Hour nachos, cheap margaritas and $1 shots of *Jose Cuervo*.

**Nephele's**, 1169 Ski Run Blvd, S Lake Tahoe (☎544-8130). Longstanding restaurant at the foot of Heavenly Valley ski resort, with a great selection of moderate to expensive California cuisine: grilled meat, fish and pasta dishes.

**Red Hut Waffle Shop**, 2479 US-50, S Lake Tahoe (☎541-9024). Ever-popular coffee shop, justifiably crowded early winter mornings with carbo-loading skiers.

**Sprouts**, 3123 US-50, S Lake Tahoe (☎541-6969). Almost, but not completely vegetarian, with good organic sandwiches, burritos and smoothies.

**Steamers Bar and Grill**, 2236 US-50 (☎541-8818). Fairly cruisey après-ski hangout that gets especially lively when there's a game on the big-screen TV; the bar food is good value.

### North shore

**Bobby's Brockway Café**, Hwy-267 at Hwy-28, King's Beach (☎546-2329). An excellent and inexpensive North Shore diner, with good breakfasts and Tahoe's best barbecued ribs.

**Bluewater Brewing Company**, Lighthouse Centre (☎581-BLUE), Tahoe City. Fine microbrews and live music.

**Bridgetender**, 30 Emerald Bay Rd, Tahoe City (☎583-3342). For burgers, sandwiches or just a beer by the rushing Truckee River, make for this wonderfully sited place with heavy wooden tables outdoors and a rustic log-cabin feel inside. The food is better than average and well priced, but the styrofoam beakers aren't pleasant.

**Coyote's Mexican Grill**, 521 N Lake Blvd, Tahoe City (☎583-6653). Great-value burritos and enchiladas in a lively atmosphere.

**The Eggschange**, 120 Grove St, Tahoe City (☎583-2225). Predominantly a breakfast place open until 2pm, with beautiful lake views.

**Lakehouse**, downstairs from _The Eggschange_, 120 Grove St, Tahoe City (☎583-2222). A good place for pizza and a popular spot for cocktails at sundown.

# Truckee and Donner Lake

Just off I-80, along the main transcontinental _Amtrak_ train route, **TRUCKEE**, 25 miles north of Lake Tahoe, makes a refreshing change from the tourist-dependent towns around the lake. A small town, lined up along the north bank of the Truckee River, it retains a fair amount of its late nineteenth-century wooden architecture along the main street, Commercial Row – some of which appeared in Charlie Chaplin's _The Gold Rush_ – but is nevertheless more of a stop-off than a destination in its own right, with a livelihood dependent on the forestry industry and the railroad. The town's rough, lively edge, however, makes it as good a base as any from which to see the Lake Tahoe area, a fact which hasn't escaped the businesses beginning to exploit the commercial opportunities. There's even public transport between the two (see below).

### Practicalities

_Greyhound_ buses from San Francisco stop in Truckee five times a day and are met by _TART_ buses to Tahoe City (daily 6.30am–6.30pm; $1; ☎581-6365). One _Amtrak_ train and two _Thruway_ buses a day in each direction stop at the station on Commercial Row in the middle of town. A selection of visitor information is available in the lobby, but the **visitor center**, a couple of miles west at 12036 Donner Pass Rd (Mon–Sat 9am–6pm; ☎587-2757 or 1-800/548-8388), is better. Where Hwy-89 branches north off I-80, a **Forest Service Ranger Station** (Mon–Thurs & Sat Sat 8am–5pm, Fri 8am–6pm; ☎587-3558) has details of camping and hiking in the surrounding countryside.

To get around, rent a **mountain bike** from _Truckee Bike Works_, 11400 Donner Pass Rd ($25 a day; ☎587-7711); or a **car** from _Rent-a-Dent_ ($25 a day; ☎587-6711).

Truckee's cheapest **place to stay** is the _Cottage Hotel_, 10178 Donner Pass Rd (☎587-3108; ②), central but a bit shabby. Much nicer is the _Truckee Hotel_, 10007

Bridge St almost opposite the station (☎587-4444 or 1-800/659-6921; ④), once decorated in the grand old railroad tradition, now decked out in Victorian B&B style, but with some of the best rooms in town. A number of low-priced **campgrounds** line the Truckee River between the town and Lake Tahoe, off Hwy-89: the closest and largest is *Granite Flat*, a mile and a half from Truckee; others are *Goose Meadows* and *Silver Creek*, four and six miles south respectively (you can contact all three campgrounds on ☎587-3558).

Commercial Row has several good **places to eat**, especially the diner-style *Coffee And* at no. 10106 (☎587-3123), the more expensive, French-style *The Left Bank* at no. 10096 (☎587-4694), and *Cafe Meridian* at no. 10118, a refreshingly modern place with a rooftop terrace, good light food, coffee and drinks. Though the old *Bucket of Blood* saloons of frontier-lore are long gone, there are a few good places to stop for a **drink**, including the *Bar of America* (☎587-3110), or *The Passage* (☎587-7619)at the east end of Commercial Row – both featuring free **live music** most nights.

## Donner Lake

Two miles west of Truckee, surrounded by alpine cliffs of silver-grey granite, **Donner Lake** was the site of one of the most gruesome and notorious tragedies of early California, when pioneers trapped by winter snows were forced to eat the bodies of their dead companions (see box).

The horrific tale of the Donner party is recounted in some detail in the small **Emigrant Trail Museum** (summer daily 10am–5pm; rest of year daily 10am–4pm; $2) – just off Donner Pass Road, three miles west of Truckee in **Donner Memorial State Park** – which shows slides and a dramatized video of the events. Outside, the **Pioneer Monument** stands on a plinth as high as the snow was deep that fateful winter – 22 feet. From the museum an easy nature trail winds through the forest past a memorial plaque marking the site where the majority of the Donner Party built their simple cabins. Nearby, on the southeast shore of the lake, there's a $14-a-night **campground** (reserve through *MISTIX*).

Above Donner Lake the Southern Pacific railroad tracks climb west over the **Donner Pass** through tunnels built by Chinese labourers during the nineteenth century – still one of the main rail routes across the Sierra Nevada. For much of the way the tracks are protected from the usually heavy winter snow by a series of wooden sheds, which you can see from across the valley, where Donner Pass Road snakes up

---

### THE DONNER PARTY

The **Donner Party**, named after two of the pioneer families among the group of 91 travellers, set off for California in April 1846 from Illinois across the Great Plains, following a short cut recommended by the first traveller's guide to the West Coast (the 1845 *Emigrant's Guide to California and Oregon*) that actually took three weeks longer than the established route. By October they had reached what is now Reno, and decided to rest a week to regain their strength for the arduous crossing of the Sierra Nevada mountains – a delay that proved fatal. When at last they set off, early snowfall blocked their route beyond Donner Lake, and the group were forced to stop and build crude shelters, hoping that the snow would melt and allow them to complete their crossing; it didn't, and they were stuck.

Within a month the pioneers were running out of provisions, and a party of fifteen set out across the mountains to try and reach Sutter's Fort in Sacramento. They struggled through yet another storm, and a month later, two men and five women stumbled into the fort, having survived by eating the bodies of the men who had died. A rescue party set off from Sutter's Fort immediately, only to find more of the same: thirty or so half-crazed survivors, living off the meat of their fellow travellers.

the steep cliffs. Rock-climbers from the nearby *Alpine Skills Institute* can often be seen honing their talents on the 200-foot granite faces; the institute offers a variety of climbing and mountaineering courses and trips. At the crest the road passes the *Soda Springs*, *Sugar Bowl* and *Royal Gorge* ski areas before rejoining I-80, which runs east from Donner Pass to Reno, Nevada, and west to Sacramento.

# Into Nevada: Reno and around

If you don't make it to Las Vegas (see p.229), you can get a feel for the nonstop, neon-lit gambler's lifestyle by stopping in **RENO, Nevada**: "the biggest little city in the world", as it likes to call itself. It's a downmarket version of Vegas, with miles of gleaming slot machines and poker tables, surrounded by kitsch wedding chapels and quickie divorce courts.

On I-80 at the foot of the Sierra Nevada, thirty miles east of Truckee, Reno is quick and easy to reach, with plenty of places to stay and eat, making it a good – and unique – stop-off. The town itself may not be much to look at – apart from the stream of blazing neon – but its setting is magnificent, with the Truckee River winding through and the snowcapped Sierra peaks as a distant backdrop. When the gambling begins to pall, you can still pass a pleasant afternoon here ambling in the dry desert heat or visiting one of the mildly diverting museums.

Reno is also another good place from which to visit Lake Tahoe (see p.490).

> The telephone **area code** for Reno, Carson City and Virginia City is ☎702

## Arrival and information

Reno's Cannon International **airport** is served by most major domestic carriers – including *American*, *Delta*, *United*, *Southwestern* and *RenoAir*. Local bus #24 makes the twenty-minute journey from the terminals to the casinos in Reno's town centre. *Greyhound* **buses** from San Francisco via Sacramento and Truckee, and from LA via the Owens Valley, use the terminal at 155 Stevenson St also used by *KT Services* (☎945-2282) which operate a daily bus to Las Vegas and Phoenix. The *Amtrak* California Zephyr **train** from Chicago stops in the centre of town on Second Street. To **rent a car**, try *Avis* (☎785-2727 or 1-800/831-2837) or *Thrifty* (☎329-0096 or 1-800/367-2277), both at the airport.

The **visitor center** (daily 9am–5pm; ☎1-800/FOR-RENO) is inside the National Bowling Centre at 300 N Centre St near the main casinos, identified by the silver geodesic dome. It has maps of the fairly extensive **local bus** services run by *RTC/Citifare* whose main depot is across the road.

## Accommodation

Inexpensive **places to stay** are plentiful, though if you arrive at a weekend you should book ahead and be prepared for rates to all but double. All the **casinos** offer accommodation, often with discounted rates that are advertised on hard-to-miss billboards.

**Camping** is an RV experience in Reno; for tent sites head west to the numerous campgrounds around Lake Tahoe (see p.493).

**Circus Circus**, 500 N Sierra St (☎329-0711 or 1-800/648-5010). Generally the cheapest and definitely the largest of the casinos with over 1600 rooms. ③.

**Crest Inn**, 525 W Fourth St (☎329-0808 or 1-800/FOR-RENO). Simple motel with few trimmings but low prices. ②.

**Eldorado**, 345 N Virginia St (☎786-5700 or 1-800/648-5966). The nicer rooms are on the upper floors, those lower down are cheaper. ③–⑤.

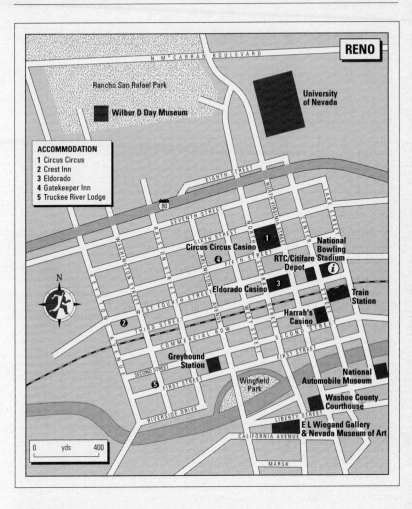

**Gatekeeper Inn**, 221 W Fifth St (☎786-3500 or 1-800/822-3504). Mainstream motel with cable TV and prices which don't double at weekends. ②

**Truckee River Lodge**, 501 W First St (☎786-8888 or 1-800/635-8950). Non-smoking hotel with an emphasis on recreation. It has a fitness centre and rents bikes from $20 a day. ②

## The casinos

It may lack the glitz and the glamour (and the unrepentant kitsch) that helps make Vegas a global draw, but Reno is unchallenged as northern Nevada's number one **gambling** spot. Almost all of its dozen or so casinos are located within a few minutes' walk of each other downtown and all of them offer a 24-hour diet of slot machines, blackjack (most have daily and weekly competitions), craps, keno, roulette and many more ways to win and lose a fortune.

### GETTING MARRIED (AND DIVORCED) IN RENO

If you've come to Reno to get **married**, you and your intended must: be at least eighteen years old and able to prove it; swear that you're not already married; and appear before a judge at the **Washoe County Court**, south of the main casino district at S Virginia and Court streets (daily 8am–midnight; ☎328-3275), to obtain a **marriage licence** ($35). There is no waiting period or blood test required. Civil services are performed for an additional $25 – at the **Commissioner for Civil Marriages**, behind the Courthouse at 195 S Sierra St (☎328-3461). If you want something a bit more special, however, wedding chapels all around the city will help you tie the knot; across the street from the court- house, the *Starlight Chapel*, 62 Court St (☎786-6882) – "No Waiting, Just Drive In" – does the job for around $80, providing a pink chintz parlour full of plastic flowers. Fork out more cash and you get the tux and frock and can invite a few guests. Other chapels include the *Park Wedding Chapel*, 136 S Virginia St (☎323-1770), and *Silver Bells Wedding Chapel*, 628 N Virginia St (☎322-0420 or 1-800/221-9336). If it doesn't work out, you'll have to stay in Nevada for another six weeks before you can get a **divorce**.

*Harold's Club*, 250 N Virginia St, founded in 1935, was among the first of Nevada's casinos to make gambling a socially acceptable pastime, earning a reputation for giving punters a (comparatively) fair shake. Reno's newest casino, *Silver Legacy*, 407 N Virginia St, is also its first "themed attraction", with over 1700 rooms and a planetar- ium-style dome under which a 120-foot mining derrick, appearing to draw raw silver ore out of the ground, spilling cascades of coins – presumably an inducement for you to continue feeding the machines in the hope of a similar deluge.

To gain a modest inkling into the intricacies of the casinos, join the free ninety- minute **Casino Tour**, which leaves from the Town Center Mall, 100 N Sierra St (every half hour Mon–Fri 9am–1pm, Sat 9am–noon; proof of hotel or motel registration neces- sary), and takes you behind the scenes at several of the town's biggest gambling dens. The tour includes food, drink and gambling credits. If you miss the tour, most of the casinos run teaching sessions at quieter times.

### Reno's museums

A number of museums struggle to lure visitors away from Reno's casinos and wedding chapels. Largest among them is the **National Automobile Museum**, at Mill and Lake streets (daily 9.30am–5.30pm; $7.50), which holds an excellent collection of several hundred vintage and classic cars, some of them artfully arranged along re-created city streets of bygone decades. Art buffs should take a look at the inventive contemporary exhibitions at the **E L Weigand Gallery and Nevada Museum of Art**, 160 W Liberty St (Tues–Sat 10am–4pm, Sun noon–4pm; $3). You'll find Reno's most curious trove, however, at the **Wilbur D May Museum** (summer Tues–Sun 10am–5pm; rest of year Wed–Sun 10am–5pm; around $2 depending on temporary exhibits), which sits on the edge of Rancho San Rafael Park, a mile north of downtown Reno off North Sierra Street. Already heir to the May department store fortunes, Wilbur May made even more money through a stroke of luck just prior to the Depression and later distin- guished himself as a traveller, hunter, military aviator and cattle-breeder. The museum outlines his eventful life with several rooms of furnishings, mounted animal heads and plunder from his trips to Africa and South America.

On the the other side of US-395 the University of Nevada campus hosts the **Nevada Historical Society Museum**, 1650 N Virginia St (Mon–Sat 10am–5pm; $2), full of items of local interest, especially Native American artefacts; and, next door, the **Fleischmann Planetarium** (Mon–Fri 8am–10pm Sat & Sun 11am–10pm; $5) where, amongst the telescopes and solar system galleries, OMNIMAX style films (2–4 shows daily;☎784-4811) are projected onto a huge dome.

## Eating and nightlife

**All-you-can-eat-buffets** are the order of the day in Reno. Everyone goes out and stuffs themselves to bursting whenever they can drag themselves from the tables. They can be fun, if a little bland, and we list the best of them below along with alternatives.

**The Blue Heron**, 1091 S Virginia St (☎786-4110). Great vegetarian restaurant much favoured by locals of all persuasions. Soy burgers and falafel are the staples but there's a wide range, and nightly specials for around $6, posted up to a month ahead on the window.

**Café Royale**, 236 California Ave (☎322-3939). Daytime and evening café with seats outside and a wide range of light snacks and pastries to accompany good coffee.

**Circus Circus**, 500 Sierra St. The place to go for a buffet meal if your budget is of greater concern than your stomach, with all-you-can-eat lunches for under $4.

**Eldorado Casino**, Fourth and Virginia. The best of Reno's buffets, serving breakfast, lunch and dinner for a dollar or two more than its counterparts. $5–6 for an excellent lunch.

**La Vecchia Varese**, 130 West St. Unfussy decor and an excellent, moderately priced selection of gourmet Italian dishes, with several vegetarian choices.

**Java Jungle**, 246 W First St (☎324-5282). Some of the best coffee in town with *biscotti* and magazines to boot, just a couple of blocks from the casinos. Daily until 6pm.

# Around Reno: Carson City

US-395 heads south from Reno along the jagged spires of the High Sierra past Mono Lake, Mount Whitney and Death Valley. Just thirty miles south of Reno it briefly becomes Carson Street as it passes through **CARSON CITY**, the state capital of Nevada. It is small compared to Reno but has a number of elegant buildings, excellent historical museums and three world-weary casinos, populated mainly by old ladies armed with buckets of nickels which they pour ceaselessly into the "one-arm bandits".

Named, somewhat indirectly, after frontier explorer Kit Carson in 1858, Carson City is still redolent with Wild West history: you'll get a good introduction at the **Nevada State Museum** at 600 N Carson St (daily 8.30am–4.30pm; $3). Housed in a sandstone structure built during the Civil War as the Carson Mint, the museum's exhibits deal with the geology and natural history of the Great Basin desert region, from prehistoric days up through the heyday of the 1860s, when the silver mines of the nearby Comstock Lode were at their peak. Amid the many guns and artefacts, the two best features of the museum are the reconstructed **Ghost Town**, from which a tunnel allows entry down into a full-scale model of an **underground mine**, giving some sense of the cramped and constricted conditions in which miners worked.

Four blocks from the museum on the other side of Carson Street, the impressively restored **State Capitol** (daily 9am–5pm; free), dating from 1875, merits a look for its stylish architecture and the commendable stock of artefacts relating to Nevada's past housed in an upper floor room.

A visit to the visitor center (see below) leaves you just a stone's throw from the **Nevada State Railway Museum**, 2180 S Carson St (Wed–Sun 8.30am–4.30pm; $2), displaying carefully restored locos and carriages, several of them from the long since defunct but fondly remembered *Virginia & Truckee Railroad*, founded in the nineteenth century.

Further south from Carson City's diminutive centre, the **Stewert Indian Culture Center**, 5366 Snyder Ave (daily 9am–4pm; free), occupies one of the eye-catching stone buildings which, until 1980, formed the campus of a Native American boarding school. The first intake of 37 students was enrolled in 1890, part of a federal plan to provide Nevada's Native Americans with a basic education and work skills. The museum actually reveals comparatively little about the school – save for a roomful of trophies won by its numerous victorious sports teams – but has many fine examples of basketry and other crafts.

## Practicalities

*Greyhound* buses stop once a day in each direction between Reno and Los Angeles outside the *Frontier Motel* on N Carson Street. *KT Services* (☎945-2282) also stop by here on their daily journey between Reno and Las Vegas. The twice daily *Amtrak Thruway* services from Sacramento and South Lake Tahoe stop outside the Nugget casino at the junction of Robinson and Carson streets.

There are a number of reasonably priced **motels** in town, among them the *Westerner* at 555 N Stewart St (☎883-6565; ②), behind the *Nugget* casino and the more characterful *St Charles Hotel*, 310 S Carson St (☎882-1887; ③) almost opposite the State Capitol. The **visitor center**, on the south side of town at 1900 S Carson St (Mon–Sat 9am–5pm; ☎882-1565 or 1-800/NEVADA-1), can help with practical details, and give you the *Kit Carson Trail Map*, a leaflet detailing a **walking tour** of the town, taking in the main museums, the state capitol and many of the fine 1870s Victorian wooden houses and churches on the west side. If exploring Carson City gives you an appetite, you could try the generous **breakfasts and lunches** served at *Heidi's Dutch Mill*, 1020 N Carson St (☎882-0486).

# Virginia City

Much of the wealth on which Carson City – and indeed San Francisco – was built came from the silver mines of the Comstock Lode, a solid seam of pure silver discovered underneath Mount Hamilton, fourteen miles east of Carson City off US-50, in 1859. Raucous **VIRGINIA CITY** grew up on the steep slopes above the mines, and very soon a young writer named Samuel Clemens made his way west with his older brother, who'd been appointed acting Secretary to the Governor of the Nevada Territory, to see what all the fuss was about. His descriptions of the wild life of the mining camp, and of the desperately hard work men put in to get at the valuable ore, were published years later under his adopted pseudonym, **Mark Twain**. Though Twain also spent some time in the Gold Rush towns of California's Mother Lode on the other side of the Sierra – which by then were all but abandoned – his accounts of Virginia City life, collected in *Roughing It*, give a hilarious, eyewitness account of the hard-drinking life of the frontier miners.

The miners left, but Virginia City still exploits a rich vein, one which runs through the pocketbooks of tour parties bussed up here from Reno. Day trips seem to consist of a cursory look at the clutch of museums (anyone who has more than two artefacts over fifty years old seems to open a museum), half an hour of camera toting amid the reconstructed Wild West shopfronts, and an afternoon tucked away in ersatz honky-tonk bars and Olde-Style gambling halls.

# travel details

## Trains

**Oakland to**: Reno (1 daily; 7hr 30min); Sacramento (5 daily; 2hr).

**Reno to**: Sacramento (1 daily; 5hr); Oakland for San Francisco (1 daily; 7hr 30min); Truckee (1 daily; 55min).

**Sacramento to**: Reno (1 daily; 5hr); Truckee (1 daily; 4hr).

## Buses

*All buses are Greyhound unless otherwise stated*

**Reno to**: Las Vegas (1 *KT Services* daily; 12hr); Los Angeles (1 daily; 12hr); San Francisco (4–5 daily & *Amtrak Thruway* 2 daily; 5hr);

**Reno airport to**: Carson City (6 daily *No Stress Express*; 40min); Stateline (14 daily *Tahoe Casino Express*; 1hr ).

**Sacramento to**: Auburn (8 daily; 1hr); Truckee (5 daily; 2hr); Placerville (3 daily; 1hr 30min); Reno (4–5 daily & *Amtrak Thruway* 2 daily; 3hr 30min); South Lake Tahoe (5 daily; 4hr).

**San Francisco to**: Auburn (4 daily; 3hr 30min); Reno (4 daily & *Amtrak Thruway* 2 daily; 5hr); Sacramento (23 daily; 2hr); South Lake Tahoe (11 daily; 6hr); Truckee (3 daily; 4hr 30min).

**San Francisco, Pleasant Hill *BART* to**: Sonora (3 *Calaveras Transit* daily).

**South Lake Tahoe to**: Placerville (3 Greyhounds daily & 2 Amtrak Thruways daily; 1hr 30min); Sacramento (3 Greyhounds daily & 2 Amtrak Thruways daily; 2hr 10min).

**Stockton to**: Sonora (3 *Calaveras Transit* daily; 2hr)

# CHAPTER NINE

# NORTHERN CALIFORNIA

C alifornia's **northern coast and interior** covers around a third of the entire state, a huge area (four hundred miles long and over half as wide) of sparsely populated, densely wooded and almost entirely unspoilt terrain. A massive and eerily silent land of volcanic proclivity, this is California at its most deeply rural, and much of the region has more in common with the states of Oregon and Washington further north than with the built-up areas that make up much of Southern California. Commerce is thin on the ground, and most settlements are small towns populated by a mixture of die-hard locals, most involved in logging, fishing and farming activities, and ageing hippies who have moved north from San Francisco to work on the marijuana farms of the so-called "Emerald Triangle". For both groups, the uniting factor is the land – and a deep-rooted suspicion of the big cities to the south.

As with elsewhere in California, the first inhabitants of the north were Native Americans, whose past has all but been erased, leaving only the odd reservation or crafts museum. Much later, the Russians figured briefly in the region's history when they had a modest nineteenth-century settlement at Fort Ross on the coast, ostensibly to protect their interests in otter hunting and fur trading though more likely to promote territorial claims. Mexican explorers and maintenance costs that exceeded revenues prevented them extending their hunting activities further south, and in the 1840s they sold the fort to the Americans. It was the discovery of gold in 1848 that really put the north on the map, and much of the countryside bears the marks of this time, dotted with abandoned mining towns, deserted since the gold ran out. Not a lot has happened since, although in the 1980s New Ageism triggered a kind of future for the region, with low prices drawing more and more devotees up here to sample the delights of a landscape they see as rich with rural symbolism. More realistically, however, it will probably be the upsurge in weekend homes for the wealthy that will save the region's bacon.

Immediately north of the Bay Area, the **Wine Country** might be your first – indeed your only – taste of Northern California, though it's by no means typical. The two valleys of Napa and Sonoma unfold in around thirty miles of rolling hills and premium real estate, home to the Californian wine barons and San Franciscan weekenders wanting to rough it in comfort. The third, though less significant wine-growing area, **Lake County**, lies to the north of its prosperous counterparts on the other side of Mount St Helena, a mountain that deters most visitors, leaving it blissfully empty and easily affordable. Most people see the Wine Country on a day trip from San Francisco; it is also feasible to take the area in before encountering the grittier territory further north, hooking up to the coast by bus from Santa Rosa.

It's the **coast** which provides the most appealing route through the region, beginning just north of Marin County and continuing for four hundred miles of rugged bluffs and forests as far as the Oregon border. The landscape varies little at first, but given time reveals tangible shifts, from the cutesy seaside homes of **Sonoma** to the coastal elegance of **Mendocino** and the big logging country further north in **Humboldt**. Trees are the big attraction up here: some thousands of years old and hundreds of feet

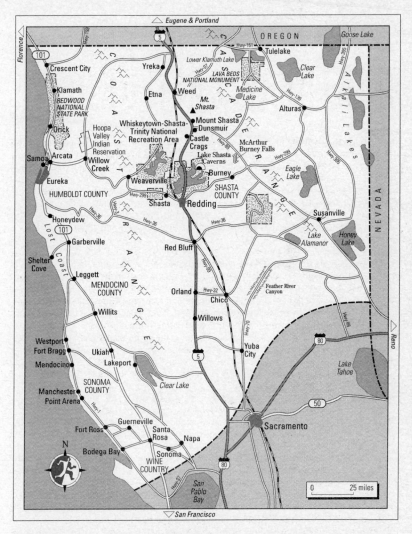

high, dominating a very sparsely populated landscape swathed in swirling mists. In summer, areas like the **Redwood National Park**, stretching into the most northerly **Del Norte** county, teem with campers and hikers, but out of season it can be idyllic. Even if things are rarely exactly swinging, towns like **Eureka** and **Arcata** at the top end of the northern coast make a lively refuge when the great outdoors begins to pall.

The **interior** is more remote still, an enchanting land whose mystery and sheer physical enormity can't help but leave a lasting impression. I-5 neatly divides the region, cutting through the forgettable Sacramento Valley northeast to the **Shasta Cascade**, a mountainous area of isolated towns, massive lakes and a forbidding

---

**ACCOMMODATION PRICES**

All accommodation prices in this book have been coded using the symbols below. Note that prices are for the least expensive double rooms in each establishment. For a full explanation see p.33 in *Basics*.

| ① up to $30 | ② $30–45 | ③ $45–60 | ④ $60–80 | ⑤ $80–100 |
| ⑥ $100–130 | ⑦ $130–175 | ⑧ $175–250 | ⑨ $250+ | |

---

climate. In winter much of this corner of the state is completely impassable and the region's commercial activities are centred around the lower, warmer climes of the largest town and transport hub of **Redding**. Redding is not an especially inviting place – too big to retain any vestige of small-town cordiality, too small to have many of the social amenities of a city – but it is, however, the only feasible base for exploring the outlying regions of the **Whiskeytown-Shasta-Trinity National Recreation Area** and the **Lassen Volcanic National Park**, both massive slabs of wilderness set aside for public use. During the summer months you'll find them packed with camper vans, windsurfers and hikers, but again, outside of peak season you're on your own.

### Getting around

**Public transport** is sparse all over Northern California, and to enjoy the region you'll need to be independently mobile. Infrequent *Greyhound* buses run from San Francisco and Sacramento up and down I-5, calling at Chico, Redding and Mount Shasta, and Hwy-101, calling at Garberville, Eureka, Arcata and Crescent City – though this does not solve the problem of actually getting around once you've arrived. Frankly, your best bet is a **driving tour**, fixing on a few points. Only the largest of Northern California's towns have any local bus service and for some of the remoter spots you could, perhaps, consider an organized trip, notably *Green Tortoise*'s one-week tours – see *Basics* for details.

---

# THE WINE COUNTRY

San Francisco during the summer can be a shock – persistent fog and cool temperatures dog the city from May to September – but you only need to travel an hour north to find a warm and sunny climate among the rolling hills of the Napa and Sonoma valleys, known jointly as the **Wine Country**. With its cool, oak-tree shaded ravines climbing up along creeks and mineral springs to chapparal-covered ridges, it would be a lovely place to visit even without the vineyards, but as it is, the "wine country" tag dominates almost everything here, including many often overlooked points of historical and literary interest. The Wine Country area doesn't actually yield all that much wine – production is something like five percent of the California total, most of which is of the Gallo and Paul Masson jug-wine variety and comes from the Central Valley – but what it produces is by far the best in the country. The region has been producing wines since the days of the Spanish missions, and though most of the vines withered during Prohibition, the growers these days manage to turn out premium vintages that satisfy wine snobs around the world. It's a wealthy region, and a smug one, thriving as much on its role as a vacation land for upper-crust San Franciscans as on the wine trade: designer restaurants (all with massive wine lists) and luxury inns line the narrow roads that, on summer weekends especially, are bumper-to-bumper with wine-tasting tourists.

By and large the **Napa Valley** is home to the larger concerns, but even here the emphasis is on quality rather than quantity, and the highbrow tones of the winery tour guides-cum-sales reps can get maddeningly pretentious. However, wineries are everywhere, and while the sprawling town of **Napa** is quickly done with, the many small towns further up the valley, particularly **St Helena**, have retained enough of their turn-of-the-century-homestead character to be a welcome relief. **Calistoga**, at the top of the valley, offers the best range of non-wine-related distractions – mostly involving tubfuls of hot spring water.

On the western side of the dividing Mayacamas Mountains, the small back-road wineries of the **Sonoma Valley** reflect the more down-to-earth nature of the place, which is both more beautiful and less crowded than its neighbour to the east. The town of **Sonoma** itself is by far the most attractive of the Wine Country communities, retaining a number of fine Mission-era structures around its gracious central plaza. **Santa Rosa**, at the north end of the valley, is the region's sole urban centre, handy for budget lodgings but otherwise unremarkable.

The telephone **area code** for the Wine Country is ☎707.

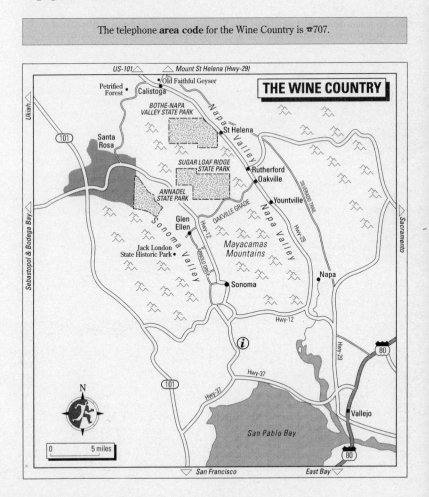

# Arrival and getting around

The Wine Country region spreads north from the top of San Francisco Bay in two parallel, thirty-mile-long valleys, **Napa** and **Sonoma**, divided by the Mayacamas Mountains. As long as you avoid the rush-hour traffic, it's about an hour's drive from the city along either of two main routes: from Marin County via the Golden Gate Bridge and US-101, or from the East Bay via the Bay Bridge and I-80.

As the regions's attractions are spread over a fairly broad area, a **car** is pretty much essential. However, its main towns at least are well served by **buses** from San Francisco and the Bay Area – *Greyhound* links the city and Sonoma (1 daily), Napa (1 daily) and Santa Rosa (2 daily), while *Amtrak Thruway* runs five daily buses from Martinez, calling at Vallejo, Napa, Yountville, St Helena and Calistoga. *Golden Gate Transit* ($4.50 one way; ☎415/923-2000) runs commuter buses all day between San Francisco and Santa Rosa, from where *Sonoma County Transit* (☎576-RIDE) buses serve the Sonoma Valley. Another possibility is the *Sonoma Airporter* (6 daily; 1hr 30min; $20; ☎938-4246) from San Francisco airport to Sonoma City Hall.

The **ferry** from Pier 39 in San Francisco to Vallejo (4 daily; $10 round trip) is met by hourly *Napa Valley Transit* buses (☎1-800/696-6443) to Napa, some of which continue to Calistoga – there is no Sunday service. *VINE* buses (☎1-800/696-6443) serve only the immediate Napa area.

The much-hyped **Wine Train** (☎253-2111 or 1-800/427-4124) runs from Napa up the valley to St Helena, but is more a wining and dining experience (tours from $60) than a means of transport.

### Cycling in the Wine Country

If you don't want to drive all day, **cycling** is a great way to get around. You can bring your own bike on *Greyhound* (though it costs $10, and the bike must be in a box), or rent one locally for around $25 a day from such outlets as *St Helena Cyclery*, 1156 Main St, St Helena (☎963-7736); *Sonoma Valley Cyclery*, 20079 Broadway, Sonoma (☎935-3377); and *Getaway Bike Tours*, 1117 Lincoln Ave, Calistoga (☎942-0332).

Both valleys are generally flat, although the peaks in between are steep enough to challenge the hardiest of hill-climbers. If the main roads through the valleys are packed out, as they are most summer weekends, try the smaller parallel routes: the **Silverado Trail** in Napa Valley and pretty **Arnold Drive** in Sonoma Valley. For would-be Kings of the Mountains, the **Oakville Grade** between Oakville in the Napa Valley and Glen Ellen in the Sonoma Valley has tested the world's finest riders. Alternatively, plot your own route with the *Bicycle Rider Directory* (see "Books" in *Contexts*).

A few local firms organize **tours**, providing bikes, helmets, food and sag wagons in case you get worn out. *Rob Mondavi's Napa Valley Biking Picnics* (☎252-1067) sets up leisurely four-hour tours – highlighted by gourmet lunches – all over the Napa area for $50 a person. More ambitious (and quite expensive) overnight tours are run most weekends by *Backroads Bicycle Tours*, 1516 Fifth St, Berkeley (☎510/527-1555) and *Getaway Bike Tours* (see above).

### Ballooning in the Wine Country

The most exciting way to see the region is on one of the widely touted **hot-air balloon rides** over the Napa Valley. These usually lift off at dawn (hot air rises more strongly in the cold morning air) and last ninety magical minutes, winding up with a champagne brunch. The first and still the best of the operators is *Napa Valley Balloons* (☎944-0228 or 1-800/253-2224), which flies out of Yountville. Others include *Balloons Above The Valley* (☎253-2222 or 1-800/464-6824), *Once in a Lifetime* (☎578-0580 or 1-800/799-9133) and *Sonoma Thunder* (☎LETS-FLY or 1-800/759-5638). The crunch comes with the price – around $170 a head.

# Information

Not surprisingly for such a tourist-dependent area, the Wine Country has a well-developed network of **tourist information** outlets, though the rivalry between the two valleys makes it next to impossible to find out anything about Sonoma when you're in Napa, and vice versa. Some common ground is covered at the **Wine Country Visitor Center**, 25200 Arnold Drive, six miles south of Sonoma on Hwy-121 (daily 9am–5pm; ☎935-4747), but the **Napa Valley Visitors Bureau** in downtown Napa (daily 9am–5pm; ☎226-7459), and the **Sonoma Valley Visitors Bureau** in Sonoma's central plaza (June–Aug daily 9am–7pm; Sept–May daily 9am–5pm; ☎996-1090) are your best bets for specifics in each area.

If you're keen on **touring the wineries**, buy the widely available *Gousha*'s "Napa-Sonoma Wine Country" map ($2.25) – much better than anything you'll get at a visitor center.

# Accommodation

Most people are content to visit the Wine Country as a day trip from San Francisco, visiting a few of the wineries and maybe having a picnic or a meal before heading back to the city. This is fine if you have a car and are happy to spend most of the day on the road, but if you really want to absorb properly what the region has to offer plan to spend at least one night here, pampering yourself in one of the many (generally pricey) **hotels** and **B&Bs** that provide the bulk of the area's accommodation options. At peak times rooms of all descriptions get snapped up – don't even *think* of spending a summer Saturday night in either valley unless you have reserved accommodation way in advance. Various **accommodation services** try to help out: try the *Sonoma County Reservation Service* (☎1-800/5-SONOMA), *B&B Inns of Sonoma* (☎996-INNS or 1-800/284-6675), *B&B Association of Sonoma Valley* (☎938-9513 or 1-800/969-4667) or the *Napa Valley Reservations Unlimited* (☎252-1985 or 1-800/251-NAPA).

**Campers** can find a pitch eight miles north of Sonoma at the *Sugar Loaf Ridge State Park*, 2605 Adobe Canyon Rd ($14; ☎833-5712); or outside Santa Rosa at the *Spring Lake Regional Park*, Summerfield Drive ($12; ☎539-8092).

## Hotels and motels

**Calistoga Inn**, 1250 Lincoln Ave, Calistoga (☎942-4101). Comfortable rooms, most with private bath, in a landmark building with its own restaurant and micro-brewery. ③/④. See "Eating".

**The Chablis Lodge**, 3360 Solano Ave, Napa (☎257-1944). The cheapest place in the valley with reasonable rooms, a pool and hot tub. ②.

**Comfort Inn**, 1865 Lincoln Ave, Calistoga (☎942-9400). Quiet, modern motel on the edge of town with heated mineral pool, steam room and sauna. ③.

**El Bonita Motel**, 195 Main St, St Helena (☎963-3216). Old roadside motel recently done up in Art Deco style, with a pool and Jacuzzi. ④.

**El Pueblo Motel**, 896 W Napa St, Sonoma (☎996-3651). Basic highway motel. ③.

**Hillside Inn**, 2901 Fourth St, Santa Rosa (☎546-9353). Clean, attractive motel with a pool. ③.

**Hotel St Helena**, 1309 Main St, St Helena (☎963-4388). Opulently redecorated 1881 inn. ⑤.

**Jack London Lodge**, 13740 Arnold Drive, Glen Ellen (☎938-8510). Modern motel near the Jack London State Park, with a good restaurant and pool. ④.

**Magliulo's Pensione**, 691 Broadway, Sonoma (☎996-1031). Cosy accommodation with an excellent Italian restaurant attached. ⑤.

**Motel 6**, 2760 Cleveland Ave, Santa Rosa (☎546-1500). A little distant from the main wine areas, but good and cheap. ②

**Mount View Hotel**, 1457 Lincoln Ave, Calistoga (☎942-6877). Lively historic hotel with a first-rate restaurant. ⑤.

**Sonoma Hotel**, 110 W Spain St, Sonoma (☎996-2996 & 1-800/468-6016). Antique-filled rooms in an 1870 hotel just off Sonoma Plaza. Has its own saloon (see "Bars"). ④.

**Vintage Inn**, 6541 Washington St, Yountville (☎944-1112 & 1-800/351-1133). Huge luxury rooms – all with fireplaces – plus swimming pool and free bike rental. Handy for Yountville's many fine restaurants, and great for romantic getaways. ⑦.

**White Sulphur Springs**, 3100 White Sulphur Springs Rd, west of St Helena (☎963-8588). A relaxing retreat from the hyper-tourism of the Napa Valley – unpretentious rooms in a ramshackle 300-acre hillside resort, surrounded by hiking trails, with an outdoor sulphur pool and bike rental. ④.

### Bed and breakfast

**Beazley House**, 1910 First St, Napa (☎257-1649). Napa's first B&B and still one of the best, in a 1902 mansion an easy stroll from downtown. Beautifully furnished rooms, some with hot tubs, surround a shaded garden. The breakfasts are excellent. ⑥.

**Calistoga Wine Way Inn**, 1019 Foothill Blvd, Calistoga (☎942-0680 or 1-800/572-0679). Small and friendly B&B with lovely garden and antique-filled rooms, a short walk from the centre of town. ⑤–⑥.

**Gaige House Inn**, 13540 Arnold Drive, Glen Ellen (☎935-0237). Restored Queen Anne Victorian farmhouse in country setting. No children under 14 permitted. ⑥–⑧.

**Thistle Dew Inn**, 171 W Spain St, Sonoma (☎938-2909 & 1-800/382-7895). Newly and elegantly restored antique-filled rooms near Sonoma plaza, plus one of the best full breakfasts around and free bike rental. Some rooms with private hot tub. ⑥.

# The Napa Valley

A thirty-mile strip of gently landscaped corridors and lush hillsides, the **Napa Valley** looks more like southern France than a near-neighbour of the Pacific Ocean. In spring the valley floor is covered with brilliant wild flowers which mellow into autumnal shades by grape-harvest time. Local Native Americans named the fish-rich river which flows through the valley "Napa", meaning "plenty"; the name was adopted by Spanish missionaries in the early 1800s, but the natives themselves were soon wiped out. The few ranches the Spanish and Mexicans managed to establish were in turn taken over by Yankee traders, and by the 1850s, with California part of the US, the town of Napa had become a thriving river port, sending agricultural goods to San Francisco and serving as a supply point for farmers and ranchers. Before long Napa was bypassed by the railroads and unable to compete with other, deep-water Bay Area ports, but the area's fine climate saved it from oblivion, encouraging a variety of crops including the grape, which spawned the now super-lucrative wine industry.

### Napa, Yountville and Oakville

**NAPA** itself, at the southern end of the valley, is still the local economic linchpin, and the highway sprawl that greets travellers is fair warning of what the rest of the town has to offer. But for a proud courthouse and some intriguingly decrepit old warehouses (ripe for gentrification), there's not much to see, though it's not bad for food, and the **visitor bureau** is the most helpful in the whole valley.

**YOUNTVILLE**, the next town north, has similarly little to see, though it boasts the highest proportion of **places to eat** in the whole region. There's little reason to stop in **OAKVILLE** further north along Hwy-29 except for the wonderful **Oakville Grocery**, an unmissable deli packed with the finest local and imported foods.

### St Helena

The first town worth a stop – and it's not really much more than a large village – is pretty **ST HELENA**, 22 miles north of Napa. Its main street, Hwy-29, is lined by some of the Wine Country's finest old buildings, most of which have been restored to – or maintained in – prime condition. The town is also at the heart of the greatest concentration of wineries, as well as boasting some unlikely literary attractions.

The **Silverado Museum** (Tues–Sun noon–4pm; free), housed in St Helena's former Public Library building signposted off Main Street in the centre of town, has a collection of over eight thousand articles relating to Robert Louis Stevenson, who spent just under a year in the area, honeymooning and recovering from an illness (see below). It's claimed to be the second most extensive collection of Stevenson artefacts in the US, though the only thing of interest to any but the most obsessed fan is a scribbled-on manuscript of *Dr Jekyll and Mr Hyde*. The other half of the building is taken up by the **Napa Valley Wine Library** (same hours), a briefly entertaining barrage of photos and clippings relating to the development of local viniculture. Another more bizarre collection is on display on the north side of town at 1515 Main St, where the **Ambrose Bierce House** bed-and-breakfast inn is packed with memorabilia of the misanthropic ghost-story writer, who lived here for some fifteen years before heading off to die for Pancho Villa in the Mexican Revolution.

## Calistoga

Beyond St Helena, towards the far northern end of the valley, the wineries become prettier and the traffic a little thinner. At the very tip of the valley, nestling at the foot of Mount St Helena, **CALISTOGA** is by far and away the most enjoyable of the Napa towns, with a few good wineries but really better known for its mud baths and hot springs – and the mineral water that adorns every Californian supermarket shelf. Sam Brannan, the young Mormon entrepreneur who made a mint out of the Gold Rush, established a resort community here in 1860. In his groundbreaking speech he attempted to assert his desire to create the "Saratoga of California", modelled upon the Adirondack gem, but in the event got tongue-tied and coined the town's unique name.

Calistoga's main attraction, then as now, has nothing to do with wines, but rather with another pleasurable activity: soaking in the soothingly hot water that bubbles up here from deep inside the earth. It's a cosy, health-conscious kind of place, with many spas and volcanic mud baths to draw jaded city-dwellers for the weekend. The extravagant might enjoy **Dr Wilkinson's Hot Springs**, 1507 Lincoln Avenue (☎942-4102; rooms and treatment from $100): a legendary health spa and hotel whose heated mineral water and volcanic ash tension-relieving treatments have been featured on TV's *Lifestyles of the Rich and Famous*. If swaddled luxury is not what you're after, a number of more down-to-earth establishments spread along the mile-long main drag, Lincoln Avenue. **Nance's Hot Springs**, 1614 Lincoln Ave (☎942-6211), for example, offers a full mineral rubdown, blanket sweat, steam bath and massage for around $50.

Another sign of Calistoga's lively underground activity is the **Old Faithful Geyser** (summer daily 9am–6pm; rest of year daily 9am–5pm; $3), two miles north of town on Tubbs Lane, off Hwy-128, which spurts boiling water sixty feet into the air at fifty-minute intervals. The water source was discovered while drilling for oil here in the 1920s, when search equipment struck a force estimated to be up to a thousand pounds per square foot; the equipment was blown away and despite heroic efforts to control it, the geyser has continued to go off like clockwork ever since. Landowners finally realized that they'd never tame it and turned it into a high-yield tourist attraction.

A further local tourist trap is the **Petrified Forest**, five miles west of Calistoga on the steep road over the hills to Santa Rosa (summer daily 10am–6pm; rest of year daily 10am–5pm; $5) – a forest that was toppled during an eruption of Mount St Helena some three million years ago. The entire redwood grove was petrified by the action of the silica-laden volcanic ash as it gradually seeped into the decomposing fibres of the uprooted trees.

## Mount St Helena

The clearest sign of the local volcanic unrest is the massive conical mountain that marks the north end of the Napa Valley, **Mount St Helena**, some eight miles north of Calistoga. The 4343-foot summit is worth a climb for its great views – on a very clear day you can see Point Reyes and the Pacific coast to the west, San Francisco to the south, the towering Sierra Nevada to the east and impressive Mount Shasta to the

### NAPA VALLEY WINERIES

Almost all of the Napa Valley's hundred-plus **wineries** offer tastings, though comparatively few have tours. Since all produce wines of a very high standard, it's entirely a question of taste which ones you choose to visit, though many attempt to distinguish themselves with fine art collections or distinctive architecture. The following selections are some long-standing favourites, plus a few lesser-known hopefuls. Keep in mind that the intention is for you to get a sense of a winery's product, and perhaps buy some, rather than get drunk on the stuff, so don't expect more than a sip or two of any one sort – though some wineries do sell wines by the glass. If you want to buy a bottle, particularly from the larger producers, you can usually get it cheaper in supermarkets than at the wineries themselves or from independent shops such as *Napa Wine Merchants*, 1146 First St, Napa (Tues–Sat 10am–6pm; ☎1-800/901-7434).
The wineries are listed from south to north.

**Codorniu Napa**, 1345 Henry Rd, Napa (☎224-1668). Owned by a noted Spanish winemaking family and designed by Catalan architect Domingo Triay, this looks like nothing so much as an unexcavated Zapotec pyramid. Inside, the beautifully executed reception area leads to entirely modern workings. Though the building is undoubtedly the star, it doesn't entirely overshadow the excellent *brut méthode champenoise*. Free tours and $4 tastings Mon–Thurs 10am–5pm, Fri–Sun 10am–3pm.

**Stag's Leap**, 5766 Silverado Trail, east of Yountville (☎944-2020). The winery that put Napa Valley on the international map by beating a bottle of Château Lafitte-Rothschild at a Paris tasting way back in 1976. Still quite highly rated. Tasting daily 10am–4.30pm; tours by appointment.

**Robert Mondavi**, 7801 St Helena Hwy, Oakville (☎963-9611). Long the standard-bearer for Napa Valley wines, with the most informative and least hard-sell tours. Free tours and tasting daily 10am–5pm, with free half-day tours available Sun & Mon; book ahead in summer.

**Beringer Brothers**, 2000 Main St, St Helena (☎963-4812). Napa Valley's most famous piece of architecture, the "Rhine House", modelled on an ancestral German Gothic mansion, graces the cover of many a wine magazine. Expansive lawns and a grand reserve-wine tasting room, heavy on dark wood, make for a regal experience. Free historical tours and tasting daily 9.30am–5pm. Reserve tasting $2–3.

**Christian Brothers**, 2555 Main St, St Helena (☎963-0765). This was the world's largest winery when erected in 1889, but was a bit of a white elephant that kept changing hands until its present owners – oddly enough a Catholic education order – bought it in 1950, and it now turns out extremely popular sparkling wines. Tours and tasting Sat & Sun 10am–4.30pm.

**Conn Creek Winery**, 8711 Silverado Trail, St Helena (☎963-9100). A truly modern organization whose lightweight stone and steel building is worlds away from the cutesy old-stone image that's the norm in the rest of the valley. Free tasting 10am–4pm daily; tours by appointment.

**Clos Pegase**, 1060 Dunaweal Lane, Calistoga (☎942-4981). A flamboyant upstart at the north end of the valley, this high-profile winery emphasizes the links between fine wine and fine art, with a sculpture garden around buildings designed by post-modern architect Michael Graves. Tours daily 11am & 2pm; tastings daily 10.30am–5pm ($2.50 for four, $3 for three reserve wines).

north. It is, however, a long hot climb (five steep miles each way) and you need to set off early in the morning to enjoy it – take plenty of water (and maybe a bottle of wine).

The mountain and most of the surrounding land is protected and preserved as the **Robert Louis Stevenson State Park** (daily 8am–sunset; $2), though the connection with him is fairly weak: Stevenson spent his honeymoon here in 1880 in a bunkhouse with Fanny Osborne, recuperating from tuberculosis and exploring the valley – a plaque marks the spot where his bunkhouse once stood. Little else about the park's winding roads and dense shrub growth evokes its former notoriety, though it's a pretty enough place to take a break from the wineries and have a picnic. In Stevenson's novel, *Silverado Squatters*, he describes the highlight of the honeymoon as the day he managed to taste eighteen of local wine baron Jacob Schram's champagnes in one sitting. Quite an extravagance, especially when you consider that Schramsberg champagne is held in such high esteem that Richard Nixon took a few bottles with him when he went to visit Chairman Mao.

# The Sonoma Valley

On looks alone the crescent-shaped **Sonoma Valley** beats Napa hands down. This smaller and altogether more rustic valley curves between oak-covered mountain ranges from Spanish colonial **Sonoma** a few miles north along Hwy-12 to **Glen Ellen**, to end up at the region's main city, **Santa Rosa**. The Sonoma Valley is also known as the "Valley of the Moon", after a Native American legend popularized by long-time resident Jack London that tells how, as you move through the valley, the moon seems to rise several times from behind the various peaks. Far smaller than Napa, most of the Sonoma Valley's wineries are informal, family-run businesses, many within walking distance of Sonoma itself, and with far fewer visitors, making it very much the stress-free alternative to the busy Napa Valley.

### Sonoma

Behind a layer of somewhat touristy stores and restaurants, the small town of **SONOMA** retains a good deal of its Spanish and Mexican architecture. Set around a spacious plaza, the town has a welcoming feel that's refreshing after brash Napa, although as a popular retirement spot with a median age of about fifty and a matching pace, it's not exactly bubbling with action. The **visitors bureau** (see p.507), in the middle of the leafy central plaza, has walking-tour plans of the town and excellent free maps and guides to the wineries. What there is to see in the town itself will take no more than an hour: Sonoma is a place better known for its history than its sights.

It's hard to believe now that Sonoma was the site of a key event in West Coast history, but the so-called **Bear Flag Revolt** of 1846 was just that – at least as far as the flag-waving Fourth of July crowds who take over the central square are concerned. In this much-romanticized episode, American settlers in the region, who had long lived in uneasy peace under the Spanish and, later, Mexican rulers, were threatened with expulsion from California along with all other non-Mexican immigrants. In response, a band of thirty armed settlers – some of whom came from as far away as Sacramento – descended upon the disused and unguarded presidio at Sonoma, taking the retired and much-respected commander, Colonel Guadalupe Vallejo, as their prisoner. Ironically, Vallejo had long advocated the American annexation of California and supported the aims of his rebel captors, but he was nonetheless bundled off to Sutter's Fort in Sacramento and held there for the next two months while the militant settlers declared California an independent republic. The Bear Flag, which served as the model for the current state flag, was raised on Sonoma Plaza. A month later the US declared war on Mexico, and without firing a shot took possession of the entire Pacific coast.

## SONOMA WINERIES

Fine **wineries** are scattered all over the Sonoma Valley, but there's a good concentration in a well-signposted group a mile east of Sonoma Plaza, down East Napa Street. Some are within walking distance, but often along quirky back roads, so take a winery map from the tourist office and follow the signs closely. If you don't want to chase around, Sonoma also has the handy *Wine Exchange of Sonoma*, 452 First St E (☎1-800/938-1794), a commercial tasting room where for a small fee – usually waived with a purchase – you can sample the best wines from all over the state.

**Bartholomew Park**, 1000 Vineyard Lane (☎935-9511). A lavish Spanish colonialist building, with some great topiary in the gardens and extensive vineyards. The wines are relatively inexpensive, middle-of-the-range vintages that appeal to the pocket and palate alike; if you're looking to buy a case, this one's a safe bet. There's a good little museum, too. Self-guided tours and free tastings daily 10am–4.30pm.

**Buena Vista Winery**, 18000 Old Winery Rd (☎938-1266). Oldest and grandest of the wineries, although the wine itself has a reputation for being pretty mediocre. The century-old stone champagne cellars – the best thing about the place – were damaged in the 1989 earthquake but can still be seen on the mainly historical tour. Free tasting daily 10am–4.30pm; tours Mon–Fri 2pm, Sat–Sun 11.30am & 2pm.

**Gundlach-Bundschu**, 2000 Denmark St (☎938-5277). Set back about a mile away from the main cluster, this is highly regarded for its wine, having stealthily crept up from the lower ranks of the wine league to the point where it now regularly steals from the big names. The plain, functional building is deceptive – this is premium stuff and not to be overlooked. Self-guided tours and free tasting daily 11am–4.30pm.

**Sebastiani Vineyards**, 389 Fourth St E, Sonoma (☎938-5532 or 1-800-888-5532). Only four blocks from central Sonoma. Free tasting daily 10am–5pm.

In memory of this, there's a monument to the Bear Flag revolutionaries in the middle of the plaza, and across the street to the north, a number of historic buildings in the sprawling **Sonoma State Historic Park** ($2 combined entry to all sites; all daily 10am–5pm), as well as some rusty old cannons, the spooky-looking remains of the old Mexican presidio and a replica of the ragged flag. The restored **Mission San Francisco Solano de Sonoma** here was the northernmost and last of the California missions, and the only one established while California was under Mexican rule. A mile west is the **General Vallejo Home**, the leader's ornate former residence, dominated by decorated filigreed eaves and slender Gothic-revival arched windows. The chalet-style storehouse next door has been turned into a **museum** of artefacts from the general's reign.

To see Sonoma at its unspoilt best, get out of the car and ride across the Valley of the Moon on **horseback**. *The Sonoma Cattle Co* (☎996-8566) offers daily tours, weather permitting, starting at $25.

### Glen Ellen and Jack London State Park

While the drive up the valley can be soothing, there's really very little to see north of Sonoma apart from a few small villages and the **Jack London State Park** (daily 8am to an hour before dusk; $5 per car) – just ten minutes from Sonoma on the London Ranch Road that curves sharply off Hwy-12 close to tiny **GLEN ELLEN** village. Jack London lived here with his wife for the last years of his short, unsettled life, on a 140-acre ranch in the hills above what he described as the "most beautiful, primitive land in California". A series of paths and walking trails leads through densely wooded groves to the lava-stone remains of the **Wolf House**, built for the Londons in 1913 but burned to the ground in an arson attack before they even moved in. London died three years later and is buried on a hill above. After his death, his widow Charmian built the more formal House of Happy Walls, not far from the main parking lot, which today serves as a small **museum** (daily 10am–5pm; free). Photographs and artefacts – including the desk where London cranked out his thousand words a day – enliven the otherwise dry details of the writer's life and work.

## Santa Rosa

Sixty miles due north of San Francisco on US-101, and about twenty miles from Sonoma, **SANTA ROSA**, the largest town in Sonoma County, sits at the top end of the Sonoma Valley and is more or less the hub of this part of the Wine Country. It's a very different world from the indulgence of other Wine Country towns, however; much of it given over to shopping centres and roadside malls, with signs downtown banning teenagers from cruising the rarely packed but confusing system of one-way streets.

Probably the most interesting thing about Santa Rosa is that it was the home town of Raymond Chandler's fictional private eye Philip Marlowe; after that it's all downhill. You can kill an hour or two at the **Luther Burbank Home and Gardens**, at the junction of Santa Rosa and Sonoma avenues (April–Sept Wed–Sun 10am–3.30pm; $1): California's best-known turn-of-the-century horticulturalist is remembered here in the house where he lived and in the splendid gardens where he created some of his most unusual hybrids. If you're not into gardening, nip across the street to the **Ripley Museum**, 492 Sonoma Ave (March–Oct Wed–Sun 11am–4pm; $1.50), one of the cartoonist Ripley's "Believe It or Not" chain of museums – Santa Rosa was Ripley's home town.

# Wine Country eating and drinking

Opportunities for **consuming** are everywhere in the Wine Country, and standards (and prices) are as high as anywhere in San Francisco, sometimes higher. California cuisine has caught on in a big way here, and freshness and innovative presentation are very much the order of the day. **Yountville**, in particular, is little more than a string of high-style restaurants, any of which is up there with the best San Francisco has to offer, with prices to match; and **Calistoga**, though more low-key, is a gourmet paradise. **Sonoma**, too, has its share and is strong on Italian food. **Bars** are rarer, thanks perhaps to the free booze on offer from the various wineries. There are a couple worth a look, though most are decidedly locals' hang-outs.

## Budget food: cafés and takeouts

**La Casa**, 121 E Spain St, Sonoma (☎996-3406). Friendly, festive and inexpensive Mexican restaurant just across from Sonoma Mission. Excellent salsa – buy some to take out.

**Checkers Pizza**, 1414 Lincoln Ave, Calistoga (☎942-9300). Soups, salads, and sandwiches, plus adventurous pizzas and good pasta dishes. Open daily until 10pm.

**The Diner**, 6476 Washington St, Yountville (☎944-2626). Start the day's wine-touring off with good strong coffee and brilliant breakfasts. Open Tues–Fri until 3pm, Sat & Sun until 10pm for flavoursome Mexican dinners.

**Juanita Juanita**, 19114 Arnold Drive, Glen Ellen (☎935-3981). A basic Mexican diner offering at least 20 salsas to accompany the sizeable burritos and tostadas.

**PJ's Café**, 1001 Second St, Napa (☎224-0607). A Napa institution, open daily 11am–10pm for pasta, unusual pizzas, sandwiches and a good range of speciality beers.

## Restaurants

**All Seasons**, 1400 Lincoln Ave, Calistoga (☎942-9111). This friendly bistro, serving up good-sized portions of California cuisine, is probably best known locally for its massive wine list, many of which are available by the glass. Main dishes cost between $13 and $20.

**La Boucane**, 1778 Second St, Napa (☎253-1177). Mouthwatering chunks of tender meat prepared in traditional but imaginative sauces, plus perfect fish (especially shellfish) and vegetables. Very expensive, dinner only.

**Calistoga Inn**, 1250 Lincoln Ave, Calistoga (☎942-4101). Very good seafood – spicy Cajun prawns, or crispy crab cakes – plus a wide range of wines, micro-brewed beers, excellent desserts and occasional live music. See also "Accommodation".

**Downtown Joe's**, 902 Main St at Second, Napa (☎258-2377). One of Napa's most popular and lively spots for sandwiches, ribs and pasta, with beer brewed on the premises. Open until midnight with outdoor dining by the river.

**Foothills Café**, 2766 Old Sonoma Rd, Napa (☎252-6178). Outwardly unprepossesing, tucked away in a suburban shopping mall, this big local favourite offers casual ambience, very reasonably priced oak-smoked chicken and wonderful lamb.

**Grist Mill Restaurant**, 14301 Arnold Drive, Glen Ellen (☎996-3077). Creekside dining in a spacious converted mill. A large menu plus an extensive list of local wines. Dinner only.

**Mustards**, 7399 St Helena Highway (Hwy-29), Yountville (☎944-2424). Credited with starting the late 1980s trend toward "grazing" food, emphasizing tapas-like titbits rather than main meals. Reckon on spending $15–20 a head, and waiting for a table if you come on a weekend.

**Tra Vigne**, 1050 Charter Oak Ave, St Helena (☎963-4444). Just north of town, but it feels as if you've been transported to Tuscany. Excellent food and fine wines, served up in a lovely vine-covered courtyard. They also have a small deli, where you can pick up picnic goodies.

**Ristorante Piatti**, 405 First St W, Sonoma (☎996-2351) and 6480 Washington St, Yountville (☎944-2070). Prices are high and portions are tiny, but otherwise this top-rate Italian restaurant can't be faulted. A good range of vegetarian plates and an impressive selection of wines by the glass. Dinner costs $35–50 with wine.

## Bars

**Ana's Cantina**, 1205 Main St, St Helena (☎963-4921). Long-standing, down-to-earth saloon and Mexican restaurant with billiards and darts tournaments, and open-mike nights.

**Babette's Restaurant & Wine Bar**, 464 First St E, Sonoma (☎939-8921). The place to see and be seen in Sonoma. Closed Sun & Mon.

**Joe Frogger's**, 527 Fourth Ave, Santa Rosa (☎526-0539). Lively bar with free live music most nights.

**Murphy's Irish Pub**, 464 First St E, Sonoma (☎935-0660). One of Sonoma's more rocking joints, with lagers, ales and stout on tap, pub food and occasional live music.

**Red Moon Saloon**, 110 W Spain St, Sonoma (☎996-2996). Funky century-old saloon in the *Sonoma Hotel* that's still going strong; the adjoining dining room is big on local cheeses and baked goods.

# THE NORTHERN COAST

Rugged in the extreme, often foggy, always dangerous and thunderously dramatic, the **Northern Coast** is leagues away from the gentle, sun-drenched beaches of Southern California. The climate, at best moderate, rules out both sunbathing and swimming; sudden ground swells and a strong undertow make even surf play risky, and there is no lifeguard service along any of the beaches. Instead, this is an area to don hiking boots, wrap up warm and explore the enormous forests with their plentiful camping facilities.

The only way to see the coast properly is on the painfully slow but scenically magnificent Hwy-1, which hugs the coast for two hundred miles through the wild counties of **Sonoma** and **Mendocino** before turning sharply inland at Legget to join Hwy-101 and **Humboldt County**. The shore it misses has become known, appropriately, as the **Lost Coast**, the hundred miles of coastline never reached by California's coastal highway. North of here, **redwood forests** swathe the landscape as far as the Oregon border, doubling as raw material for the huge logging industries (the prime source of employment in the area) and the region's prime tourist attraction, most notably in the **Redwood National Park**. **Eureka** and **Arcata** are the main towns here, both easily reached on public transport, and the principal centres of nightlife and action for the coast as a whole.

You'll need to be fairly independent to **get around** this region: one *Amtrak Thruway* and two *Greyhound* buses a day travel the length of US-101, which parallels the coastal highway, but don't link up with the coast until Eureka, far to the north.

# The Sonoma Coast and Russian River Valley

Proximity to San Francisco means the **Sonoma Coast** and **Russian River Valley** areas have never been short on weekend visitors. But tourist activity is confined to a few narrow corridors at the height of summer, leaving behind a network of north coast villages and backwater wineries that for most of the year are all but asleep. The coast is colder and lonelier than the villages along the valley, and at some point most people head inland for a change of scene and a break from the pervasive fog. What both areas have in common, however, is a reluctance to change. As wealthy San Franciscans cast their eyes coastwards for potential second-home sites, the California Coastal Commission endeavours to keep the architects at bay, keenly maintaining beach access for all, and most farmers have so far managed to resist the considerable sums offered for their grazing land. For the time being the Sonoma coastal area remains relatively undeveloped, the majority of it state beach, with good access to hiking trails and views.

## The Sonoma Coast

**BODEGA BAY**, about fifty miles north of San Francisco, is the first Sonoma village you reach on Hwy-1. Originally discovered by the Spanish in 1755, this is where Hitchcock filmed the waterside scenes for *The Birds* – an unsettling number of them are still squawking down by the harbour. Not so long ago, a depleted fishing industry, a couple of restaurants and some twee seaside cottages were all there was to Bodega Bay, but in recent years San Franciscans have got wind of its appeal and holiday homes and modern retail developments now crowd the waterside.

If you're travelling the whole coast, Bodega Bay makes a tolerable first stop, especially if you're in the mood for long moody walks and early nights. Of several **places to stay**, the *Bodega Harbor Inn*, 1345 Bodega Ave (☎875-3594; ③), is the only one with (a few) low-cost rooms, while the extremely comfortable *Holiday Inn Bodega Bay*, 521 Hwy-1 (☎874-1311 or 1-800/346-6999;⑤–⑥), has lovely rooms with fireplaces. Reservations are pretty much essential in summer and at weekends throughout the year. There's **camping** at the *Bodega Dunes Campground* (☎875-3382), two miles north of the village on Hwy-1 at the base of a windy peninsula known as **Bodega Head**; laid out across sand dunes that end in coastal cliffs behind the beach, it has places for $14 a night. There are hiking and horse-riding trails around the dunes behind the beach – though in summer these tend to be packed with picnicking families, and for less crowded routes you should head up the coast.

### North of Bodega Bay

North of Bodega Bay, along the **Sonoma Coast State Beach** (actually a series of beaches separated by rocky bluffs) the coastline coarsens and the trails become more dramatic. It's a wonderful stretch to hike – quite possible in a day for an experienced hiker – although the shale formations are often unstable and you must stick to the trails, which at best are demanding. Of Sonoma's thirteen miles of beaches, the finest are **Salmon Creek Beach**, a couple of miles north of Bodega Bay and site of the park headquarters and **Goat Rock Beach**, at the top of the coast.

Campsites are dotted along the coast, but the best **places to stay** are in the tiny village of **JENNER**, which marks the turn-off for the Russian River Valley. Choose between the salubrious cabins and cottages of *Murphy's Jenner Inn*, 10400 Hwy-1 (☎865-2377 or 1-800/732-2377; ⑧), the comfortable *River's End Resort* (☎865-2484; ⑤) or the inexpensive *Lazy River Motel* (☎865-2409; ②). The Russian River joins the ocean here, and a massive sand spit at its mouth provides a breeding ground for harbour seals from March to June.

### Fort Ross

North of Jenner, the population evaporates and Hwy-1 turns into a slalom course of hairpin bends and steep inclines for twelve miles as far as **Fort Ross State Historic Park** (daily 10am–4.30pm; $5). At the start of the nineteenth century, San Francisco was still the northernmost limit of Spanish occupation in Alta California, and from 1812 to 1841 Russian fur traders quietly settled this part of the coast, clubbing the Californian Sea Otter almost to extinction, building a fort to use as a trading outpost, and growing crops for the Russian stations in Alaska. Officially they posed no territorial claims, but by the time the Spanish had gauged the extent of the settlement, the fort was heavily armed and vigilantly manned with a view to continued eastward expansion. The Russians traded here for thirty years until over-hunting and the failure of their shipbuilding efforts led them to pull out of the region. They sold the fort and chattels to one John Sutter in 1841, who moved them to his holdings in the Sacramento Valley, so all you see is an accomplished reconstruction built using the original techniques.

Among the empty bunkers and storage halls, the most interesting buildings are the Russian Orthodox Chapel and the Commandant's house, with its fine library and wine cellar. At the entrance, a potting shed, which labours under the delusion that it is a **museum**, provides cursory details on the history of the fort, with a few maps and diagrams. You'll be better informed using one of the walkie-talkie-like wands, or catching one of the twice-daily **talks** at noon and 2pm.

Fort Ross has a small beach and picnicking facilities. You can **camp** here ($10; ☎847-3286) or in **Salt Point State Park** ($9–12; ☎884-3723), six miles north on Hwy-1. Just north of Salt Point, the **Kruse Rhododendron State Reserve** is a sanctuary for twenty-foot-high rhododendrons, indigenous to this part of the coast and at their best in early summer. You can drive through, or walk along a short trail. The beaches on this last stretch of the Sonoma coastline are usually deserted, save a few abalone fishermen, driftwood and the seal pups who rest here. Again, they're good for hiking and beachcombing, but stick to the trails.

## The Russian River Valley

Hwy-116 begins at Jenner (see above) and turns sharply inland, leaving behind the cool fogs of the coast and marking the beginning of a relatively warm and pastoral area known as the **Russian River Valley**. The tree-lined highway follows the river's course through twenty miles of what appear to be lazy, backwater resorts but in fact are the major stomping grounds for partying weekenders from San Francisco. The fortunes of the valley have come full circle; back in the Twenties and Thirties it was a recreational resort for well-to-do city folk who abandoned the area when newly constructed roads took them elsewhere. Drawn by low rents, city-saturated hippies started arriving in the late Sixties, and the Russian River took on a non-conformist flavour that lingers today. More recently, an injection of affluent Bay Area property seekers, many of them gay, has sustained the region's economy, and the funky mix of loggers, sheep farmers and wealthy weekenders gives it an offbeat cachet that has restored its former popularity.

The road that snakes through the valley is dotted with campgrounds every few miles, most with sites for the asking, although during the second weekend of September when the region hosts the **Russian River Jazz Festival** (☎869-3940), things can get a bit tight. The jazz festival is something of a wild weekend around here and a good time to come: bands set up on Johnson's Beach by the river and in the woods for impromptu jamming sessions as well as regular scheduled events. The new mid-June **Russian River Blues Festival** looks set to prove equally popular (call Guerneville's Chamber of Commerce for details).

*Sonoma County Transit* (☎576-7433) runs a fairly good weekday bus service (though patchy at weekends) between the Russian River resorts and Santa Rosa in the Wine Country (see p.513), although, to see much of the valley, you really need a **car** or a **bike** from *Mike's Bike Rental*, 16442 Hwy-116, Guerneville ($25 a day; ☎869-1106).

## Guerneville

The main town of the Russian River valley, **GUERNEVILLE**, has finally come out. No longer disguised by the tourist office as a place where "a mixture of people respect each other's lifestyles", it's quite clearly a **gay resort** and has been for the last fifteen years: a lively retreat popular with tired city-dwellers who come here to unwind. Gay men predominate, except during two **Women's Weekends** (☎869-4522) – in June and September – when many of the hotels take only women.

If you don't fancy venturing along the valley, there's plenty to keep you busy without leaving town. Weekend visitors flock here for the canoeing, swimming and sunbathing that comprise the bulk of local activities: **Johnson's Beach**, on a placid stretch of the river in the centre of town, is the prime spot, with canoes ($12 a day), pedal boats ($5 an hour) and tubes ($3 a day). But Guerneville's biggest natural asset is the magnificent **Armstrong Redwoods State Reserve**, two miles north at the top of Armstrong Woods Road ($5 parking) – 750 acres of massive redwood trees, hiking and riding trails and primitive camping sites. Take food and water and don't stray off the trails: the densely forested central grove is quite forbidding and very easy to get lost in. One of the best ways to see it is on horseback; the *Armstrong Woods Pack Station* (☎887-2939) offers guided horseback tours that range from a half-day trail ride for $35 to a three-day pack trip for $350. A natural amphitheatre provides the setting for the **Redwood Forest Theater** which stages dramatic and musical productions during the summer.

The **Chamber of Commerce**, 16200 First St (Mon–Fri 9am–5pm; 24hr info line ☎869-3533), has good free maps of the area, and **accommodation** listings. As with most of the valley, B&Bs are the staple; two luxurious choices are the comfortable *Fern Grove Inn*, 16650 River Rd (☎869-9083 or 1-800/347-9083; ⑤), and *Applewood: an Estate Inn*, 13555 Hwy-116 (☎869-9093; ⑦), where the price includes a full dinner. *Fife's*, 16467 River Rd (☎869-0656 or 1-800/7-FIFES-1; ⑥), is the original gay resort right by the river, while *Willow's*, 15905 River Rd (☎869-2824; ③) is more modest (pricewise anyway). A dearth of cheap motels (unless you head east to Hwy-101 or the one place in Monte Rio) makes **camping** the economical answer: *Austin Creek State Recreation Area*, Armstrong Woods Road ($10; ☎865-2391), is guaranteed RV-free, while *Johnson's Resort*, on First Street, also has cabins and rooms available ($10; ☎869-2022; ②). There are a couple of free primitive sites, and $7 walk-in sites, in the state reserve.

Guerneville has a good selection of reasonably priced, reliable **restaurants**, among them the mainly meaty *Breeze Inn Bar-B-Q*, 15640 River Rd (☎969-9208). *Brew Moon*, 16248 Main St (☎869-0201) is the top spot for dessert and coffee. Really, though, it's the **nightlife** that makes Guerneville a worthwhile stop. *Molly's Country Club*, 14120 Old Cazadero Rd (☎869-0511), is good for dining, dancing and ballyhoo in the company of cowboys and girls, and offers line dancing at the weekends. In a funkier vein, *The Jungle*, 16135 Main St (☎869-1400), is a happening Thursday to Sunday dance club with the occasional live act.

### RUSSIAN RIVER VALLEY WINERIES

The Guerneville Chamber of Commerce (see p.517) issues an excellent *Russian River Wine Road* map, which lists all the **wineries** that spread along the entire course of the Russian River. Unlike their counterparts in Napa and Sonoma, the wineries here neither organize guided tours nor charge for wine-tasting. You can wander around at ease, guzzling as many and as much of the wines as you please. Some of the wines (the *Cabernet Sauvignon*s and *Merlot*s in particular) are of remarkably good quality, if not as well known as their Wine Country rivals. By car, you could easily travel up from the Sonoma Coast and check out a couple of Russian River wineries in a day, although the infectiously slow pace may well detain you longer.

**Topolos at Russian River Vineyards**, 5700 Gravenstein Hwy, Forestville, five miles from Guerneville along Hwy-116 (daily 10am–5pm; ☎887-1575 or 1-800/TOP-OLOS). One of the Russian River Valley's most accessible wineries.

**Hop Kiln**, 6050 Westside Rd, Healdsburg (☎433-8281). Recently established rustic winery with a traditional atmosphere but not a snobbish attitude. Tastings 10am–6pm.

**Korbel Champagne Cellars**, 13250 River Rd, two miles east of Guerneville (☎887-2294). Even if you're not "doing" the wineries, you shouldn't miss this place. The bubbly itself – America's best-selling premium champagne – isn't anything you couldn't find in any supermarket, but the wine and brandy are sold only from the cellars, and are of such notable quality that you'd be crazy not to swing by for a snifter. The estate where they are produced is lovely, surrounded by hillside gardens covered in blossoming violets, coral bells and hundreds of varieties of roses – perfect for quiet picnics.

## Monte Rio

The small town of **MONTE RIO**, three miles west along the river from Guerneville, is definitely worth a look: a lovely, crumbling old resort town with big Victorian houses in stages of graceful dilapidation. For years it has been the entrance to the 2500-acre **Bohemian Grove**, a private park that plays host to the San Francisco-based *Bohemian Club*. A grown-up summer camp, its membership includes the very rich and very powerful male elite – ex-Presidents, financiers, politicians and the like. Every year in July they descend for "Bohemian Week" – the greatest men's party on earth, noted for its high jinks and high-priced hookers, away from prying cameras in the seclusion of the woods.

The best of Monte Rio's pricey **places to stay** are the lovely *Rio Villa Beach Resort*, 20292 Hwy-116 (☎865-1143; ③/④) in a beautiful spot on the banks of the Russian River, and the *Highland Dell Inn*, 21050 River Blvd (☎865-1759 or 1-800/767-1759; ⑤). You can sleep more cheaply at the *Village Inn* on River Boulevard (☎865-2304 or 1-800/303-2303; ②), with substantial reductions for three-day stays.

If you're touring the area by car, the lonely, narrow **Cazadero Highway** just to the west makes a nice drive from here, curving north through the wooded valley and leading back to Fort Ross on the coast.

# The Mendocino coast

The coast of Mendocino County, 150 miles north of San Francisco, is a dramatic extension of the Sonoma coastline – the headlands a bit sharper, the surf a bit rougher, but otherwise more of the same. Despite the best efforts of the local chambers of commerce, this remains a remote area, its small former lumbering towns served by limited public transport. It does thrive, however, as a location spot for the movie industry, having featured in such illustrious titles as *East of Eden*, *Frenchman's Creek*, and more recently, *The Fog*.

This is the place for a quiet get away weekend – join all the other couples avoiding the crowds in the pricey bed and breakfasts. Inland, there's little to see beyond the small contingent of wineries – stick to the coast where there is at least some sign of life, and content yourself with brisk walks and brooding scenery.

Only Willits, forty miles inland, is served by *Greyhound* and *Amtrak Thruway*. From here, the Skunk Trains (see next page) provide the sole **public transport** to the main towns of **Mendocino** and **Fort Bragg**, linked to each other by *Mendocino Stage and Transit Authority* (☎964-0167) buses, which continue south to the small villages of Navarro and Gualala.

# Mendocino

Fifty miles along the coast from the Sonoma border at Gualala, **MENDOCINO** sits on a broad-shouldered bluff with waves crashing on three sides. The coast's first viable stop, it's a weathered, quaint, New England kind of town that errs on the dangerous side of cute. Its appearance on the National Register of Historic Places and reputation as something of an artists' colony draw the curious up the coastal highway, and while people here make a big thing out of loathing tourists, they've also established a fairly extensive network of bed and breakfasts, craft shops, restaurants and bars.

## The Town

Like other small settlements along the coast, Mendocino was originally a lumber port, founded in the late nineteenth century by merchants from Maine who thought the proximity to the redwoods and exposed location made it a good site for sawmilling operations. The industry has now vanished, but a large community of artists gives the place a low-key, raffish charm and has spawned craftsy commerce in the form of art galleries, gift shops and boutique delicatessens.

The **visitor center**, 735 Main St (Mon–Sat 11am–4pm Sun noon–4pm; ☎937-5397), is housed in **Ford House**, one of many mansions built by the Maine lumbermen in the style of their home state. The **Kelley House Museum**, 45007 Albion St (daily 1–4pm), has exhibits detailing the town's role as a centre for shipping redwood lumber to the miners during the Gold Rush, and conducts **walking tours** of the town on Saturday mornings at 11am – though you could do it yourself in under an hour, collecting souvenirs from the galleries as you go. Among them, the **Mendocino Arts Center**, 45200 Little Lake St (daily 10am–5pm; free), gives classes and has a gallery showing some good works (if a little heavy on the seascapes) of mainly Mendocino-based artists.

Otherwise there's plenty to occupy you around the town: **hiking** and **cycling** are popular, with bikes available for around $25 a day from *Catch a Canoe & Bicycles, Too* (☎937-0273 or 1-800/320-2453), just south of Mendocino at the corner of Hwy-1 and Compche-Ukiah Road. The **Russian Gulch State Park** (☎937-5804; $5), two miles north of town, has bike trails, beautiful fern glens and waterfalls; just south of town, hiking and cycling trails weave through the unusual **Van Damme State Park** (☎937-5804; $5), which has a **Pygmy Forest** of ancient trees, stunted to waist-height because of poor drainage and soil chemicals. A walk along the **Mendocino Headlands**, a bracing beach area of cliffs and rocks at the end of Main Street, is good for appetite-building.

The best thing to do in Mendocino, however, is to pamper yourself. **Hot tubs** and **saunas** are a big thing here, and as the main tourist attraction they're pricey. **Sweetwater Gardens**, 955 Ukiah St (☎937-4140 or 1-800/300-4140), offer the usual hot tub, steam and sauna at reasonable prices, though often it's crowded and the waiting time irksome.

## Accommodation

**Room rates** in Mendocino are generally high, but provided you stay away from the chintzy hotels on the waterfront, it is possible to find adequate, reasonably priced hotels on the streets behind. The *Seagull Inn*, 44594 Albion St (☎937-5204; ③), is the best of the affordable options right in the centre, though the antique-filled rooms at *The Mendocino Hotel*, 45080 Main St (☎937-0511; ④–⑤), are more luxurious. Probably the most romantic place to stay in the whole region is at **ALBION**, a small fishing village ten miles south of Mendocino; the *Albion River Inn*, 3790 N Hwy-1 (☎937-1919; ⑦), on Hwy-1 just beyond the junction with Hwy-128, perches on the edge of a cliff, and all the rooms except one have ocean views. The inn also has a first-class restaurant, serving pricey, wonderful food.

There's $14 **camping** at Russian Gulch State Park (reserve through *MISTIX*), and Van Damme State Park; the latter has $3 hiker/biker sites.

### Eating, drinking and nightlife

Of Mendocino's **restaurants**, one of the best is *Café Beaujolais*, 961 Ukiah St (☎937-5614), which specializes in vegetarian California cuisine. The *Mendocino Bakery and Café*, 10485 Lansing St (☎937-0836; daily to 8pm), produce delicious breads, pastries and pizza.

In mid-July the town hosts the two-week **Mendocino Music Festival**, bringing in blues and jazz bands from all over the state, although the emphasis is largely on classical and opera. For an earthier experience (and cheaper beer), *Dick's Place*, on Main Street, is Mendocino's oldest **bar**, with all the robust conviviality you'd expect from a spit-and-sawdust saloon. The best bar in the area, however, is the *Caspar Inn* (☎964-5565) at **CASPAR**, three miles north, which features live rock, jazz and rhythm and blues from Thursday to Sunday.

## Fort Bragg, Willits and Leggett

**FORT BRAGG** is very much the blue-collar flipside to its comfortable neighbour. Where Mendocino exists on wholefood and art, Fort Bragg brings you the rib-shack and lumberjack, and sits beneath a perpetual cloud of steam choked out from the lumbermills of the massive Georgia Pacific Corporation, which monopolizes California's logging industry and to which Fort Bragg owes its existence. There was once a fort here, but it was only used for ten years until the 1860s when it was abandoned and the land sold off cheap. The otherwise attractive **Noyo Harbor** (south of town on Hwy-1) has been crammed full of commercial fishing craft, and the billowing smog does little to add to the charm. Nevertheless, its proximity to the more isolated reaches of the Mendocino Coast, an abundance of budget accommodation and no-nonsense restaurants make it a good alternative to Mendocino.

As for things to do, or even just a convenient way of getting to or from the coast, you can amuse yourself on the **Skunk Trains** operated by the *Californian Western Railroad* ($21 one-way, $26 roundtrip; ☎964-6371), which run twice daily from the terminus on Laurel Street forty miles inland to US-101 and the town of Willits. Taking their name from the days when they were powered by gas engines and could be smelt before they were seen, piled up with timber from the redwood forests, the trains now operate almost exclusively for the benefit of tourists – it's good fun to ride in the open observation car as it tunnels through mountains and rumbles across the thirty-odd high bridges on its route through the towering redwoods. **WILLITS**, where the trains end up, is the official county seat thanks only to its location in the centre of Mendocino, and is no different from other strip-development, mid-sized American towns – disembark only to get a drink, if at all.

A short drive or bus ride south of Fort Bragg will take you to the **Mendocino Coast Botanical Gardens** (daily 9am–5pm; $5), where you can see more or less every wild flower under the sun spread across seventeen acres of prime coastal territory. The coast here is also reputed to be one of California's best areas for **whale-watching**: if you're visiting in November when they pass on their way south to Baja to breed or, better still, in March when they're on their way back to the Arctic, a few patient hours spent on the beach may be rewarded by the sighting of a gray whale.

Hwy-1 continues north for another twenty miles of slow road and windswept beach before leaving Mendocino county and the coastline to turn inland and meet Hwy-101 at **LEGGETT**. Redwood country begins in earnest here: there's even a tree you can drive through for $3, though you'd do better to stay on course for the best forests further north.

## Practicalities

Fort Bragg's **Chamber of Commerce** (☎961-6300) is almost directly across the street from the train station at 332 N Main St. Most of the **motels** cluster along Hwy-1 in the centre of town, the lowest priced of which is the *Fort Bragg Motel*, 763 N Main St (☎964-4787 or 1-800/253-9972; ②). Other good options include the family-run *Old Coast Hotel*, 101 N Franklin St (☎964-6443; ②), which offers meals and comfortable rooms; the *Surf Motel*, 1220 S Main St (☎964-5361; ③) approaching town from the south; or the excellent *Grey Whale Inn B&B*, 615 N Main St (☎964-9800 or 1-800/382-7244; ⑤), which has great views from the rooms. But arguably the best place in the region is three miles north of Leggett: *Eel River Redwoods Hostel and Bell Glen B&B*, 70400 US-101 (☎925-6425; ①/⑤), boasting luxurious woodland cabins, $12 dorm beds, a sauna, open-air Jacuzzi and bar.

Finally, there's **camping** among coastal pines at **MacKerricher State Park** ($14 or $3 hiker/biker sites; reserve through *MISTIX*), three miles north of Fort Bragg, with a ranch that offers horse rides along the secluded stretch of beach.

**Restaurants** in Fort Bragg (of which there are plenty) tend to cater for the ravenous carnivore. Both *Jenny's Giant Burger*, 940 N Main St (☎964-2235), and the *Redwood Cookhouse*, 118 E Redwood Ave (☎964-1517), serve huge tree-felling dinners of steaks, ribs and burgers, and are usually full of men from the mills. Otherwise, *The Restaurant*, at 418 Main St (☎964-9800), has great Cajun and Creole fish dishes for around $6; *David's Restaurant & Deli*, 450 S Franklin St (☎964-1964), does great lunchtime sandwiches; and vegetarians can take refuge in the hearty Italian offerings at *Headlands Coffee*, 120 East Laurel St (☎77-964-1987). For big breakfasts, try *Egghead Omelettes of Oz* at 326 N Main St (daily 7am–2pm).

# The Humboldt Coast

Of the coastal counties, **Humboldt** is by far the most beautiful – overwhelmingly peaceful in places, in others plain eerie. The coastal highway doesn't get to its southern reaches, guaranteeing isolation and lending the region the name of the "Lost Coast". Humboldt is perhaps most renowned for its "Emerald Triangle", as it's known, which produces the majority of California's largest cash crop, **marijuana**. As the Humboldt Coast's fishing and logging industries slide, more and more people have been turning to growing the stuff to make ends meet. In the 1980s the Bush administration took steps to crack down on the business with CAMP (Campaign against Marijuana Planting), sporadically sending out spotter planes to pinpoint the main growing areas. Aggressive law enforcement and a steady stream of crop-poaching has been met with a defiant, booby-trapped and frequently armed protection of crops, and production goes on – the camouflage netting and irrigation pipes you find on sale in most stores clearly do their job.

Apart from considerable areas of clandestine agriculture, the county is almost entirely forestland, vast areas of which are protected in national parks. The highway rejoins the coast at **Eureka** and **Arcata**, Humboldt's two major towns and both spirited jumping-off points for the **redwoods**, which stretch up the coast with a vengeance to the north of here. These prehistoric giants are the real crowd-pullers in this part of the state, at their best in the **Redwood National Park**, which covers some 58,000 acres of skyscraping forest. Again, **getting around** is going to be your biggest problem. Although *Greyhound* and *Amtrak Thruway* buses run the length of the county along US-101, they're hardly a satisfactory way to see the trees, and you'll need a car to make the trip worthwhile. For information on **what's on** in Humboldt, two excellent, free county newspapers, *The Activist* and *North Coast View*, detail the local scene and people, and where to go and what to do in the area. Look out, too, for the campaigning Arcata-based *Econews*, which highlights the ecological plight of northern California's wild country.

## Southern Humboldt: Garberville and the "Lost Coast"

The inaccessibility of the Humboldt Coast in the south is ensured by the **Kings Range**, an area of impassable cliffs that shoots up several thousand feet from the ocean, so that even a road as sinuous as Hwy-1 can't negotiate a passage through. To get there you have to travel US-101 through deepest redwood territory as far as **GARBERVILLE**, a one-street town with a few good bars that is the centre of the cannabis industry and a lively alternative to the wholesome, happy-family nature of much of this part of California. Each week, the local paper runs a "bust-barometer" which charts the week's pot raids; and, every August, the town hosts the massive two-day **Reggae on the River** festival. Tickets cost around $75; reserve them on ☎923-3368 by early May.

### Garberville practicalities

*Amtrak Thruway* **buses** stop twice daily outside the *Waterwheel Restaurant* on Redwood Drive, Garberville's main street, while the two daily *Greyhound* services connecting north to Eureka and south to San Francisco pull in around the corner on Church Street. Sadly, most of the town's **accommodation** is overpriced. Of a couple you might try, the *Benbow Inn*, 445 Lake Benbow Drive (☎923-2124; ⑤), is a flash place for such a rural location (former guests include Eleanor Roosevelt and Herbert Hoover); the *Sherwood Forest Motel*, 814 Redwood Drive (☎923-27221; ③), is pleasant with a nice pool; and the *Lone Pine Motel*, 912 Redwood Drive (☎923-50532; ②) is more affordable, if a lot scruffier. The closest **campground** is three miles south at **Benbow Lake** ($14 or $3 for hiker/biker sites; reserve through *MISTIX*); if you're independently mobile you can head five miles further south on US-101 to the **Richardson Grove State Park** ($14; reserve through *MISTIX*).

Even if you don't intend to stay in Garberville, at least stop off to sample some of the town's **restaurants** and **bars**, which turn out some of the best live bluegrass you're likely to hear in the state. Redwood Drive is lined with bars, cafés and restaurants: the *Eel River Café* at no. 801 (☎923-3783) is a good bet for breakfast, while the *Wildrose Café* at no. 911 (☎923-3191) serves organic food in diner-style surroundings, and the *Mateel Café* at no. 478 (☎923-2030) serves gourmet dishes and coffee on the terrace. You're spoilt for choice when it comes to drinking. All the bars tend to whoop it up in the evening; the noisiest of the lot is probably *The Cellar*, at 728 Redwood Drive, with a small cover for its nightly live music.

### Shelter Cove and the Humboldt Redwoods State Park

From Garberville, via the adjoining village of **Redway**, the Briceland-Whitehorn road winds 23 miles through territory populated by old hippies and New Agers beetling around in battered vehicles, to the **Lost Coast** at **SHELTER COVE**, set in a tiny bay neatly folded between sea cliffs and headlands. First settled in the 1850s when gold was struck inland, its isolated position at the far end of the Kings Range kept the village small until recent years. Now, thanks to a new airstrip, weekenders arrive in their hordes and modern houses are indiscriminately dotted across the headland. Unfortunately, it's the closest real settlement to the **hiking** and **wildlife** explorations of the surrounding wilderness, which remains inhabited only by deer, river otter, mink, black bear, bald eagles and falcons, so you might find yourself using the *Marina Motel*, 461 Machi Rd (☎986-7595; ④), as a base. The **Lost Coast Trail** runs along clifftops dotted with primitive **campgrounds** ($9), all near streams and with access to black-sand beaches.

The heart of redwood country begins in earnest a few miles north of Garberville along US-101, when you enter the **Humboldt Redwoods State Park** (unrestricted entry): over 50,000 acres of predominantly virgin timber, protected from lumber companies, make this the largest of the redwood parks. The serpentine **Avenue of the Giants** weaves for 33 miles through trees which block all but a few strands of sunlight. This is the habitat of *sequoia sempervirens*, the coast redwood with ancestors dating back to the days of the dinosaur (see p.563). John Steinbeck described them as "ambassadors from another time" – and indisputably they're big, some over 350 feet tall, evoking a potent sense of solitude that makes a day of stopping off along the highway time well spent. Small stalls selling lumber products and refreshments dot the course of the highway, chief among them the **Chimney Tree** (daily 9am–5pm; free), a wonderfully corny gift shop built into the burnt-out base of a still-living redwood. There are three **campgrounds** ($14; reserve through *MISTIX*) within the park.

The Avenue follows the south fork of the Eel River, eventually rejoining US-101 at **Pepperwood**. Ten miles before this junction, the turn-off to **HONEYDEW** provides a possible respite from the trees in a region thin on even small settlements. A good base from which to explore the northerly Lost Coast, Honeydew is a postage-stamp town popular with marijuana growers who appreciate its remote location – and the two hundred inches of annual rain that sustains the crops.

Any visitors awed by the majesty of the redwood forests can soon be brought back down to earth a few miles north at **SCOTIA**, a one-industry town if ever there was one. In this case it is timber: the Pacific Lumber Company has been here since 1869, but with the decline in the industry and the rise in environmetal objections to clear-felling of native forests, the company is throwing itself at the tourist market. Boasting of being "The World's Largest Redwood Mill", it uses half-truths and stretched facts to win you over to the loggers' cause on self-guided **plant tours** (Mon–Fri 7.30am–2pm; free), starting at the **Scotia Museum** on Main Street.

## Eureka

Near the top of the north coast of California between the Arcata and Humboldt Bays, **EUREKA**, the largest coastal settlement north of San Francisco, is – despite some rather attractive Victorian mansions – an industrial, gritty and often foggy lumbermill town. It's not, as its name might suggest, a place that will make you think you've struck pay dirt, but it does make a useful stopover with its proximity to the largest groves of old-growth redwood trees in the world.

Downtown Eureka is fairly short on charm, lit by the neon of motels and pizza parlours, and surrounded by rail and shipyards, but the so-called **Old Town**, bounded by C, G, First and Third Streets, at the edge of the bay, is in the process of smartening up. For the moment, though, the peeling Victorian buildings and poky bars of the old sailors' district are pretty much rundown – though they do have a certain seedy appeal, along with a handful of lively, mostly Italian restaurants. What few sights there are include the **Carson Mansion**, 143 M St at Second, an opulent Gothic pile built in the 1880s by one William Carson, who made and lost fortunes in both timber and oil. It now operates as a private gentleman's club behind its gingerbread facade. Nearby, at

1410 Second St, the one-room **Maritime Museum** (daily 11am–4pm; $1) is chock-full of photos, maps and relics from the days when Eureka was a whaling port.

The collection of Native American applied art at the **Clarke Memorial Museum**, Third and E (Tues–Sat 10am–4pm; donation), can't hold a candle to the stuff at the **Indian Art Gallery**, 241 F St (Mon–Sat 10am–4.30pm; free), a rare opportunity for Native American artists to show and market their works in a gallery setting, and an even rarer opportunity to get your hands on some incredibly good, inexpensive silver jewellery. If dragging yourself around town for these low-key sights doesn't appeal, you might prefer the **Eureka Health and Spa**, 601 Fifth St (☎445-2992), with its salt-rubs, tranquillity tanks and saunas.

A few minutes by car from Eureka across the Samoa bridge, squashed against the Louisiana-Pacific plywood mill, the tiny community of **SAMOA** is a company town that is the site of the last remaining cookhouse in the west. **The Samoa Cookhouse** (Mon–Sat 6am–3.30pm & 5–10pm, Sun 6am–10pm; ☎442-1659) was where the lumbermen would come to eat gargantuan meals after a day of felling redwoods, and although the oilskin tablecloths and burly workers have gone, the lumbercamp style remains, with long tables, the most basic of furnishings, and massive portions of red meat.

### Practicalities

An abundance of affordable **motels** around the Broadway area at the northern (and noisy) end of town make Eureka bearable for a night or two. Try the *Matador Motel*, 129 Fourth St at C (☎443-9751; ②), or the *Downtowner*, 424 Eighth St at E (☎443-5061; ③); if you want more than just a bed and a shower, head for *An Elegant Victorian Mansion B&B*, 1406 C St at 14th St (☎443-6512; ⑤), which, as the name suggests, recalls the opulence and splendour of a bygone era and offers an architectural tour of the town in a Model "A" Ford. **Campgrounds** line US-101 between Eureka and Arcata; the best is the *KOA* (☎822-4243), a large site with copious amenities five miles north of town.

**Transport links** are good: *Greyhound*, 1603 Fourth St, connects Eureka to San Francisco in the south and Portland in the north twice daily, *Amtrak Thruway* goes from outside *Stanton's Coffee Shop* on Fifth and L streets. For getting around town and up the coast as far as Trinidad, *Humboldt Transit*, 133 V St (☎443-0826), has a weekday service. The Eureka **Chamber of Commerce** is at 2112 Broadway (June–Sept Mon–Fri 9am–7pm, Sat & Sun 10am–4pm; Oct–May Mon–Fri 9am–5pm, Sat & Sun 10am–4pm; ☎442-3738 or 1-800/356-6381).

In addition to the *Samoa Cookhouse* (see above), **eating** possibilities include most of the Italian restaurants of the Old Town, notably *Roy's*, 218 D St (☎442-4574), where complete meals cost under $15. The *Lost Coast Brewery and Café*, 617 Fourth St at F St (☎445-4480), serves large, hearty dishes to a rumbustious crowd of micro-brew drinkers and baseball watchers, while the *Humboldt Bay Coffee Company*, 211 F St (☎444-3961), is a quieter spot with good coffee, open until around 8pm. For the best (or at least the biggest) breakfasts in town, *Deb's*, Fifth and N, serve up tasty variations on the theme of bacon and eggs. For food with **entertainment**, the *Old Town Bar & Grill*, on Second and E, serves quality Italian/American dishes to a backdrop of serenades by the Humboldt Blues Society.

## Arcata and around

**ARCATA**, twelve miles up the coast from Eureka, is by far the more appealing of the two places, a small college town with a large community of rat-race refugees and Sixties throwbacks whose presence is manifest in some raunchy bars and an earthy, mellow pace. The beaches north of town are some of the best on the north coast, white-sanded and windswept, and known for their easy hikeability and random parties.

Arcata itself is centred on a main square of shops and bars, with everything you're likely to want to see and do within easy walking distance. In the middle of the square the statue of President McKinley, originally intended for nearby McKinleyville, fell off the train on the way and stayed put in Arcata.

At the foot of I Street, the **Arcata Marsh and Wildlife Sanctuary**, a restored former dump on 175 acres of wetland, is a peaceful place where you can lie on the boardwalk in the sun and listen to the birds. The **Interpretive Center** at the foot of South G Street (Mon–Fri 1–5pm, Sat & Sun 10am–4pm; ☎826-2359) runs **guided wildlife walks** (Sat at 2pm), as does the Audubon Society, which meets at the very end of I St at 8.30am every Saturday morning. For those who don't have time to explore the Redwood National Park, Arcata's own second-growth **community forest**, at 11th and 14th, makes a good alternative – a small, beautiful spot with manageable trails and ideal picnic areas.

If you're around over Memorial Day weekend, don't miss the three-day **World Championship Cross Country Kinetic Sculpture Race**, a spectacular event in which competitors use human-powered contraptions of their own devising to propel themselves over land, water, dunes and marsh from Aracata to Ferndale.

## Practicalities

*Greyhound* and *Amtrak Thruway* **buses** pull into the station at 925 E St between Ninth and Tenth, connecting with the Eureka services going north and south; there's also a weekday *Humboldt Transit* link with Eureka. The small but helpful **Chamber of Commerce**, 1062 G St (Mon–Fri 10am–4pm, Sat 9am–3pm; ☎822-3619), has free maps and lists of **accommodation**.

Motels just out of town on US-101 are lower-priced than the increasingly popular bed and breakfasts, if a little less inviting, and can usually be found for under $55 per night. Three blocks from the bus station, the *Arcata Youth Hostel*, 1390 I St (late June–late Aug only; ☎822-9995; ①), is easily the best deal in town with beds for $10 a night. You can get reasonable rooms at the *Fairwinds Motel*, 1674 G St (☎822-4824; ②), though if you've a bit more money the *Hotel Arcata*, 708 Ninth St (☎826-0217 or 1-800/344-1221; ④/⑤), on the town's main square, is a very stylish way to get rid of it. Of the B&Bs, try *The Lady Anne*, 902 14th St (☎822-2797) ④–⑥. There are several **campgrounds** north of Arcata along the coast, but none within easy reach of town unless you've got a car. *Big Lagoon County Park* (☎445-7650), fifteen miles north on Hwy-1, has spaces for $15, as does the nearby *Clam Beach County Park* (☎445-7650), four miles north of town on US-101.

Dotted around the plaza and tangential streets, Arcata's **bars** set the town apart. The best of the bunch, the *Jambalaya* at 915 H St, draws a long-haired crowd for its nightly diet of r'n'b, jazz and rock bands. *The Humboldt Brewery*, 856 Tenth St (☎826-2739), is a working beer factory with its own bar and low-priced restaurant, where you can sample the preferred stronger, darker brews of Northern California. There's also the café at the *Finnish County Sauna and Tubs*, on the corner of Fifth and J streets, with live acoustic sets at the weekend, chess on Tuesdays, and tubs in the garden for $12 an hour. Good **restaurants** are in shorter supply, though *Wildflower Café and Bakery*, 1604 G St (☎822-0360), turns out good, cheap organic meals, and *Abruzzi*, 791 Eighth St (☎826-2345), serves top-quality Italian food at moderate prices.

## Around Arcata

If you've got a car, take time to explore the coastline just north of north of Arcata along Hwy-101. **Moonstone Beach**, about ten miles north of town, is a vast, sandy strip that, save the odd beachcomber, remains empty during the day, and by night hots up with guitar-strumming student parties that rage for as long as the bracing climate allows. **Trinidad Harbor**, a few miles further on, is a good stop for a drink, to nose around the small shops or just sit down by the sea wall and watch the fishing boats being tossed about beyond the harbour. **Patricks Point State Park,** five miles further north, offers reasonably secluded **camping** for $14 and $3 hiker/biker sites (reserve through *MISTIX*).

A more adventurous – some would say insane – destination is **Hoopa Valley Indian Reservation,** sixty miles inland. In past years the site of often violent confrontation between Native Americans and whites over fishing territory, Hoopa is now seen by some as the badlands of Humboldt and few take the time to check out the valley. There's a dead, lawless feel about the place, the locals hanging around listlessly outside their caravans or roaring up and down the dirt tracks on their Harley-Davidsons. Even the bar and bingo hall, once the lifeblood of the community, have been closed down as a result of alcohol-induced violence. The nervous will want to move on quickly, but if you're here in the last week in July you should make an effort to catch the All Indian Rodeo, which is held southwest of the village. Otherwise it is enough to visit the **Hoopa Tribal Museum** (Mon–Fri 8am–5pm, Sat 10am–4pm; donation) – full of crafts, baskets and jewellery of the Natinixwe (aka Hupa) and Yurok tribes.

To get to the reservation, take Hwy-299 west out of Arcata for forty miles until you hit **WILLOW CREEK** – self-proclaimed gateway to "Bigfoot Country". Reports of giant 350 to 800-pound humanoids wandering the forests of northwestern California have circulated since the late nineteenth century, fuelled by long-established Indian legends, though they weren't taken seriously until 1958, when a road maintenance crew found giant footprints in a remote area near Willow Creek. Photos were taken and the Bigfoot story went worldwide, since when there have been more than forty separate sightings of Bigfoot prints. At the crossroads in Willow Creek stands a huge wooden replica of the prehistoric-looking apeman, with its slanted forehead, flared nostrils and short ears, an identikit of the creature who in recent years has added kidnapping to his list of alleged activites. Beside the statue, a small **Chamber of Commerce** (summer daily 9am–4pm; rest of year irregular hours; ☎629 2693) has details of Bigfoot's escapades, and information on the **whitewater rafting** that is done on the Smith, Klamath and Trinity rivers near here. Among the numerous rafting companies in the area, two are based in Willow Creek – *Aurora River Adventures* (☎629-3843 or 1-800/562-8475) and *Bigfoot Rafting Company* (☎629-2263 or 1-800/722-2223), both offering trips from $40. Otherwise, the town comprises a handful of grocery stores, diners and motels such as the *Willow Creek Motel,* Hwy-96 (☎629-2115; ②). Just north of town, the **Lower Trinity Ranger Station** (summer Mon–Sat 8am–4.30pm; rest of year Mon–Fri 8am–4.30pm; ☎629-2118) handles camping and wilderness permits for the immediate surroundings.

# The Redwood National and State Parks

Some thirty miles north of Arcata, the small town of **Orick** marks the southernmost end of a contiguous strip of forest jointly managed as the **REDWOOD NATIONAL AND STATE PARKS** (unrestricted access; free), a massive area that stretches up into Del Norte County at the very northernmost point of California, ending at the dull town of **Crescent City**. The fragmented Redwoods National Park and the three state parks which plug the gaps – Prairie Creek Redwoods, Del Norte Coast Redwoods and Jediah Smith Redwoods – together contain the world's first, third and sixth highest trees; the pride of California's forestland, especially between June and September when every school in the state seems to organize its summer camp here. Increasingly, and despite being designated as a World Heritage Site by UNESCO, it's also becoming a controversial area – campers awake to the sound of chainsaws and huge lumber trucks ploughing up and down the highway. Despite this, locals are still dissatisfied and claim that they've lost much of the prime timber they relied on before the days of the parks to make their living.

One word of warning: **bears** and **mountain lions** inhabit this area, and you should heed the warnings in *Basics* on p.44.

## Practicalities

The parks' 58,000 acres divide into distinct areas: the southern entrance and **Orick Area**; the **Prairie Creek Redwoods State Park**, past the riverside town of **Klamath**; and the area in the far north around the **Del Norte** and **Jedediah Smith State Parks**, in the environs of Crescent City in Del Norte County. The park headquarters are in Crescent City, at 1111 Second St (daily 8am–5pm; ☎464-6101 or 1-800/423-6101), but the **visitor centers** and **ranger stations** throughout the parks are far better for maps and information. Most useful is the **Redwood National Park Information Center** (daily 9am–6pm; ☎488-3461), right by the southern entrance.

The one daily *Amtrak Thruway* and two *Greyhound* **buses** that run along US-101 to Crescent City will, if asked, stop (and if you're lucky can be flagged down) along forested stretches of the highway, and there's a twice-a-day *Redwood Coast Transit* service looping out from Crescent City and back, but unless you want to single out a specific area and stay there (not the best way to see the parks), you'll be stuck without a **car**.

As for accommodation, **camping** is your best bet. You can stay at the many primitive and free campgrounds all over the parks; for more comfort, head for the sites we've mentioned in the text below (all $14, with $3 hiker/biker sites), along with a hostel and a couple of motel recommendations. If you're really desperate, get onto US-101 and look for **motels** around Crescent City.

## Orick and Tall Trees Grove

As the southernmost, and therefore most used, entrance to the Redwood National Park, the **Orick** area is always busy. Its major attraction is **Tall Trees Grove**, home of the world's tallest tree – a mightily impressive specimen that stands at some 367 feet. The easiest way to get there, avoiding too much picking amongst the lush undergrowth, is the **shuttle bus** ($7) which runs twice daily from the Redwood Information Center (see above), although many choose to hike the **Tall Trees Trail** (3 miles round trip; 700ft ascent on way back). Some people prefer to hike the 8.5 mile **Redwood Creek Trail** (permit needed) from near Orick: take a right off US-101 onto Bald Hills Road, then, 600 yards along, fork off to the picnic area where the trail starts. The bridge, 1.5 miles away, is passable in summer only. If you can make it from here, a bit further east another trail turns north off Bald Hills Road and winds for half a mile to **Lady Bird Johnson Grove** – a collection of trees dedicated to the former US President LBJ's wife, Lady "Bird" Johnson, a big lover, apparently, of flora and fauna. A mile-long self-guided trail winds through the grove of these giant patriarchs. **Permits** are available from the Information Center.

In **ORICK** itself (actually two miles north of the entrance and ranger station), *Lane's Pack Station* (☎488-5225) offers **horseback trips** through the forests and along the coast. Trips vary from two-hour rides along coastal trails to full weekends in the forest. Several **stores and cafés** string north along US-101, where you can pick up supplies and have a sit-down meal. Of several places, the *Elkhorn Saloon*, midway between Orick and Prairie Creek, is your best bet for avoiding the crowds.

Three miles north of Orick, the narrow Davison Road turns coastwards for five miles to **Gold Bluffs Beach** (dawn–dusk) where you can camp. The $5 per vehicle fee also covers **Fern Canyon**, visited on an easy three-quarter-mile trail, its 45-foot walls slippery with mosses, fern and lichen.

## Prairie Creek State Park and Klamath

Of the three state parks within the Redwood National Park area, **PRAIRIE CREEK** is the most varied and popular, and while bear and elk roam across all three, it's only here that you can be taken around by the rangers for a **tour** of the wild and damp profusion of a solidly populated redwood forest. Whether you choose to go independently, or opt for an organized tour, main features include the meadows of **Elk Prairie** in front of the **ranger station** (summer daily 8am–6pm; rest of year daily 8am–5pm; ☎488-2171), where herds of Roosevelt Elk, massive beasts weighing up to four hundred pounds, roam freely, protected from poachers. Day use is $5 per vehicle but you can park beside the road and wander at will. There's a **campsite** on the edge of Elk Prairie, and at the hub of a network of trails.

A mile north of the ranger station the magnificent **Big Tree Wayside** redwood, more than three hundred feet tall and, at over 21ft in diameter, the fattest of the coastal redwoods, overlooks the road.

Prairie Creek also has the main concentration of **restaurants** on the southern approach on US-101. All do a good line in wild boar roasts, elk steaks and the like, as well as a more traditional menu of burgers and breakfasts: *Rolf's Park Café* (☎488-3841), just by the Fern Canyon turn off US-101 is one of the best with outdoor seating and a handful of German offerings.

### Klamath Area

**KLAMATH** isn't technically part of the Redwood area nor, by most definitions, does it qualify as a town as most of the buildings were washed away when the nearby Klamath River flooded in 1964. Nonetheless, there are spectacular coastal views from trails where the Klamath River meets the ocean, a few decent accommodation options and, for a bit of fun, the **Trees of Mystery** (daily 8am–6pm; $6) on US-101, where you'll notice two huge wooden sculptures of Paul Bunyan and Babe, his blue ox. You can drive through, jump over and scoot under the trees – with the exception of the most impressive specimen of all, the **Cathedral Tree**, where nine trees have grown from one root structure to form a spooky circle. Never slow to cash in, enterprising Californians hold wedding services here throughout the year. The most spectacular scenery in Klamath, however, is not the trees, but the ocean: take Requa Road about three quarters of a mile down to the estuary, to a point known as the **Klamath Overlook**, from where, once the fog has burnt off, there is an awe-inspiring view of the sea and coast. From here, a coastal trail begins and leads for ten miles along some of California's most remote beach, ending at Endert's Beach in Crescent City.

The *Requa Inn*, 451 Requa Rd (☎482-8205; ④) offers some of the best **accommodation** around. There are the simple cabins at *Woodland Villa*, a mile and a half north of Requa (☎482-2081; ②), and the *HI-Redwood National Park Hostel* three miles further along US-101(☎482-8265; ①) has dorm beds for $10 whether you are a member or not. A couple of miles yet further north is the free, primitive *DeMartin* **campsite**.

## Crescent City and around

The northernmost outpost of the national park, the Del Norte and Jedediah Smith state parks sit either side of **CRESCENT CITY**, a woebegone place with little to recommend it other than its proximity to the parks. However, if you've come this far, and are tired of camping and inadequate food supplies, it could save you from despair.

*Greyhound* **buses** stop at 1125 Northcrest Drive, *Amtrak Thruway* outside *Denny's* on Fifth Street. The helpful **visitor center** is at 1001 Front St (Mon–Fri 8am–7pm, Sat & Sun 9am–5pm; ☎464-3174 or 1-800/343-8300).

Of several good **motels** on US-101, try *Curly Redwood Lodge*, 701 US-101 S (☎464-2137; ②), the *Ocean Way Motel* (☎464-9845; ①) further south at no. 1875; or the *Royal Inn*, Front and L streets (☎464-4113; ③). To **eat**, try the moderately priced *Da Lucianna Ristorante*, 105 N St (☎465-6566), or the seafood and steaks at *the Harbor View Grotto*, 155 Citizens Dock Rd (☎464-3815). Considerably cheaper is *Los Compadres*, a Mexican diner on US-101 opposite the marina.

While here, take an hour to visit the **Battery Point Lighthouse** (usually Wed–Sun 10am–4pm, tours Sat 10am–12.30pm & Sun 10am–1pm; $2) reached by a causeway from the western end of town. The oldest working lighthouse on the west coast, it houses a collection of artefacts from the *Brother Jonathan*, wrecked off Point St George in the 1870s. Because of this loss, the **St George Lighthouse**, the tallest and most expensive in the US, was built six miles north of Crescent City.

### Del Norte and Jedediah Smith State Parks

**Del Norte Park**, seven miles south of Crescent City, is worth visiting less for its redwood forests (you've probably had enough of them by now anyway), than its fantastic beach area and hiking trails, most of which are an easy two miles or so along the coastal ridge where the redwoods meet the sea. From May to July, wild rhododendrons and azaleas shoot up everywhere, laying a floral blanket across the park's floor. **Jedediah Smith Park,** nine miles east of Crescent City, is named after the European explorer who was the first white man to trek overland from the Mississippi to the Pacific in 1828, before being killed by Comanche tribes in 1831. Not surprisingly, his name is everywhere and no less than eighteen separate redwood groves are dedicated to his memory. Sitting squatly on the south fork of the Smith River, the park attracts many people to canoe downstream or, more quietly, sit on the riverbank and fish. Of the hiking trails, the **Stout Grove Trail** is the most popular, leading down to a most imposing goliath – a twenty-foot diameter redwood.

If you're heading further east and can't face more highway, you could opt for the painfully slow, but scenic, route that follows Howland Hill Road from Crescent City through the forest to the **Hiouchi Information Center** (May–Oct 9am–5pm) on Hwy-199, about five miles away. Branching off this are several blissfully short and easy trails (roughly half a mile) which are quieter than the routes through the major parts of the park. You'll also find the *Jedediah Smith Redwoods* **campground** (reserve through *MISTIX*), and **picnicking** facilities at the end of the Howland Hill Road.

# THE NORTHERN INTERIOR

As big as Ohio, yet with a population of only 250,000, the **northern interior** of California is about as remote as the state gets. Cut off from the coast by the **Shasta Cascade** range, it's a region dominated by forests, lakes, some fair-sized mountains – and two thirds of the state's precipitation. It's largely uninhabited too, and, for the most part, infrequently visited. This is, of course, the greater part of its appeal, and while it doesn't have the biggest waterfalls, the bluest lakes or the highest mountains, it lacks the congestion that marks many of California's better-known areas. Those who do come stick to a few easily accessible locations, leaving vast miles of the state for the more adventurous to explore.

I-5 leads through the very middle of this near wilderness, forging straight up the **Sacramento Valley** through acres of unspectacular farmland to **Redding**: neatly placed for the best of the northern interior's natural phenomena. Redding isn't much of a place in itself, but makes a useful base from where you can venture out on loop trips a day or so at a time. Most accessible, immediately west and north of Redding, the **Whiskeytown-Shasta-Trinity National Recreation Area** is a series of three lakes and forests set aside for what can be heavily subscribed public use, especially in summer when it's hard to move for camper vans, windsurfers, jet-skiers and packs of happy holidaymakers. East of here the **Lassen National Volcanic Park** enjoys its biggest crowds in winter, when the volcanic summits and slopes make for some increasingly fashionable cross-country skiing territory – come the summer thaw it returns to a much emptier panorama. The **Plumas National Forest**, which spreads southeast as far as the borders of Nevada and the Gold Country, will hold no surprises: another mountainous cloak of forestland with almost repetitive appeal.

By far the most interesting town in the region is the schizophrenic **Mount Shasta**, in the shadow of the 14,000-foot volcano of the same name. Mountaineers and anglers flock here in the summer and co-exist with a hardcore community of alternative lifestylers. When this palls, and you have a yen for the boonies, make for the very northeastern tip of the state and the loneliest of all California's verdant landscapes, the **Modoc National Forest**. Isolation makes the volcanic **Lava Beds National Monument** one of the least visited in the state, all the more reason to come and explore the hollow lava tubes and unearthly, arid landscapes.

It's the usual story with **public transport**: reasonably frequent *Greyhound* and *Amtrak Thruway* buses connect San Francisco and Sacramento to Portland via I-5, stopping off at the Sacramento Valley towns and Redding on the way, and trains from Oakland call at Redding and Chico. But neither route provides anything like comprehensive access to the area, and if you're going to come here at all it should be in a **car**. Anything worth seeing lies at least five miles from the nearest bus stop. The area is too big and the towns too far apart to make travelling by bus even faintly enjoyable.

> The telephone **area code** for the Northern Interior is ☎916.

# The Sacramento Valley

The **Sacramento Valley** lays fair claim to being California's most uninteresting region; a flat, largely agricultural corridor of small, sleepy towns and endless vistas of dull arable land. By far the best thing to do is pass straight through on I-5 – the half-empty, speedy freeway cuts an almost two-hundred mile-long swathe through the region, and you could forge right ahead to the more enticing far north quite painlessly in half a day.

## Chico

**CHICO**, about midway between Sacramento and Redding and some thirty miles east of I-5, might be a good stop-off if you don't want to attempt to cover the whole valley from top to bottom in one day, or if you're here to visit Lassen Volcanic Park and need somewhere to stay. A typical small American college town, its low-key charm lies in its cosy suburban appeal rather than anything you can see or do when you get here.

### Arrival, information and getting around

Chico is right on Hwy-99. **Trains** (and *Amtrak Thruway* buses) stop at the unattended station at Fifth and Orange; while *Greyhound* buses pull into the depot at 717 Wall St, between Seventh and Eighth.

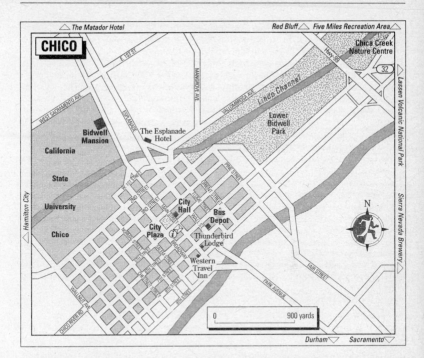

On the south side of the central Downtown Park Plaza, the **Chamber of Commerce**, 500 Main St at Fifth (June–Aug Mon–Fri 9am–5.30pm, Sat 10am–3pm: Sept–May Mon–Fri 9am–5.30pm; ☎891-5556 or 1-800/852-8570), can supply you with a poor free map and a detailed street plan ($1) as well as comprehensive lists of accommodation and eating options. To find out **what's on**, consult the free Chico *News & Review*, published every Thursday and available all over town; or tune in to *KCHO*, the charmingly slapdash local community radio on 88.9 FM.

The majority of places you are likely to want to visit are within walking distance of the town centre, although you can **rent a bike** from *Campus Bicycles* right by the plaza at 501 Main St (☎345-2081).

## The Town
Short on sights as Chico is, you might try the three-storey **Bidwell Mansion** at 525 The Esplanade, the continuation of Main Street (daily, tours on the hour 10am–4pm; $2). Built in 1868 by the town's founder, General Bidwell, it's an attractive enough Victorian building, filled with family paraphernalia visited on 45-minute anecdotal tours. It's reasonably interesting, but **Bidwell Park** (most sections open daylight hours; free) is a more pleasurable place to spend your time. Extending from the centre of the town for ten miles to the northeast, this is a tongue of semi-wilderness and oak parkland where, incidentally, the first *Robin Hood* film, starring Errol Flynn, was made. No road runs right through the park, and it is too large to cover on foot, so cycling (see bike rental below) is by far the best way to explore. The most heavily used areas are around the recreation areas at One-mile Dam and Five-mile Dam, both reached off Vallombrosa Avenue, and Cedar Grove, reached off E Eighth Street, but a half-hour stroll into Upper Park will leave most of the regulars behind.

Back in town, vintage American car fans will enjoy **Cruces Classic Auto Sales**, downtown on 720 Main St, a commercial showroom with a walk-through museum showing some of the really rare models that are brought here to be restored. Or visit the **Sierra Nevada Brewing Company**, 1075 E 20th St (☎893-3520), which gives free and fairly cursory twenty-minute tours of the plant (Tues–Fri 2.30pm, Saturday noon–3pm) and the chance to sample each of the ten or so brews on tap for under $5.

## Accommodation

Chico has much more in the way of **accommodation** than it does in sights, though for camping you'll need to head to the Plumas National Forest to the east or Lassen Volcanic National Park. Motels are everywhere in town, particularly in the Main Street and Broadway area, and there are a couple of good B&Bs.

**The Esplanade**, 620 The Esplanade (☎345-8084). A particularly good value B&B right across from the Bidwell Mansion. The beds are so high you almost need to pole-vault onto them, and tasty breakfasts are served on the back verandah. ③.

**The Matador**, 1934 The Esplanade (☎342-7543). A pretty Spanish Revival building ten blocks north of the Plaza, with tasteful rooms each featuring individual tiling. Set out around a courtyard with palms shading one of Chico's largest pools, this is one of the town's best deals. ②.

**O'Flaherty House Bed and Breakfast**, 1462 Arcadian Ave (☎893-5494). Sumptuous bedrooms in a comfortable house. ④.

**Thunderbird Lodge**, 715 Main St (☎343-7911). Decent and low-cost motel two blocks from the Plaza, with a new large pool, indoor Jacuzzi and exercise room. Some rooms have refrigerators and coffee-makers. ②.

**Western Travel Inn**, 740 Broadway (☎343-3286). About the cheapest downtown motel just two blocks south of the Plaza, with refrigerators in rooms and a pool. ②.

## Eating and entertainment

Chico also does itself proud when it comes to **food**. Being a California State University town, there are many excellent places aimed at the younger (and poorer) customer, as well as a handful of lively **bars** to while away your evenings. It's noticeably quieter when school's out, but on summer Friday evenings, **free concerts** by talented locals draw the crowds to the Downtown Park Plaza.

**Café Sandino**, 817 Main St (☎894-6515). Small, rather plain Mexican and vegetarian café with plenty of low-fat and vegan dishes, and good tamales for under $5. Open until 9pm, closed Sun.

**Caffe Siena**, 128 Broadway (☎345-7745). Relaxed java joint with light meals served during the day, and a lively beer garden in the evenings, open until 11pm or midnight. The refreshing mocha shakes are highly recommended.

**La Comida**, 954 Mangrove Ave (☎345-2254). One of the cheapest Mexican places in town, serving very good food daily until 9pm.

**The Graduate**, 344 W Eighth St (☎343-2790). Massive hall with long tables at which students enjoy hamburgers, steaks and salads. Good value, if you can put up with the video screens that glare at you from every available patch of wall space. Daily until 9pm or 10pm.

**Jack's Family Restaurant**, 540 Main St (☎343-8383). 24-hour diner, a bit on the greasy side, but good for breakfasts and late-night filling up.

**Juanita's**, 126 W Second St (☎893-4215). Though it serves reasonable American-Mexican food, the main draws are the almost nightly live bands (small cover) and the 4–7pm happy hour.

**Madison Bear Garden**, 316 W Second St (☎891-1639). As the name suggests, a place for swigging beer with students from the nearby campus. Burgers, buffalo wings and the like are also served.

**The Reddengray Pub**, 912 W First St (☎343-6848). Large, pub-like place with draught beers from around the world and live music at weekends. "British" pub food served daily until 8pm.

**Sierra Nevada Brewing Company**, 1075 E 20th St (☎893-3520). The bar food is unexceptional , but the pale ale, porter, stout and seasonal brews are a strong draw. There's usually jazz on Mondays and good local bands some weekends.

**Thai Chada**, downstairs at 117b W Second St (☎342-7121). Authentic, and predominantly vegetarian, Thai cuisine at very reasonable prices, especially at lunchtime. Closed Sun.

## Red Bluff

Strung along the Sacramento around 45 miles north from Chico up Hwy-99, **RED BLUFF** is not a particularly exciting place, and has long since outgrown the small-town friendliness exuded by Chico. Still, it's the one point at which you can pick up **public transport** heading towards Lassen National Volcanic Park (see p.535), so you may find yourself staying over. There's a reasonable selection of $30-a-night motels along Main Street – among them the *Crystal Motel*, 333 S Main St (☎527-1021; ①) – and a handful of diners and burger joints in town. You may consider visiting the **Kelly-Grigs House Museum**, 311 Washington St (Thurs–Sun 1–4pm; donation), where there's an exhibit on Ishi, "the last wild Indian", who appeared out of what is now the Ishi Wilderness in 1911 and was feted until his death in 1916. Pick up more information from the **Chamber of Commerce**, 100 Main St (Mon–Thurs 8.30am–5pm; Fri 8.30am–4.30pm; ☎527-6220).

# Redding and around

After the high-flown descriptions of Northern California's isolated beauty and charm, **REDDING**'s sprawl of franchise motels and fast-food chains comes as something of a shock to most visitors, and the town doesn't improve with longer acquaintance. But Redding's position, close to both the Whiskeytown-Shasta-Trinity National Recreation Area to the west and the Lassen Volcanic National Park to the east, makes it a premium transit point and the major source of accommodation for those wanting to sample the best of this part of the state without being forced under canvas. It's a railroad centre basically, a characterless assembly of cheap lodgings and little else whose streets only really brighten during midsummer when the tourists hit town.

If conditions don't suit hiking, there's not a lot to do here, other than visit **Shasta** on the outskirts (see below). You could kill thirty minutes at the **Redding Museum of Art & History** in Caldwell Park on the banks of the Sacramento (Tues–Sun 10am–5pm; $1), which has a permanent display of Native American artefacts, and rotating contemporary and historical art exhibits. The neighbouring **Carter House Natural Science Museum** (Tue–Sun 10am–5pm; $1) is aimed at kids, with hands-on exhibits and a self-guided nature walk through an arboretum. The river bank here forms part of the **Sacramento River Trail**, a pleasant, six-mile loop designed for walkers and cyclists.

## Practicalities

Considering its position at the crossroads of northern California, **public transport** in Redding is woefully inadequate, though the new **Intermodal Transportation Facility**, the terminus for *Greyhound*, *Amtrak*, *Amtrak Thruway* and the local *RABA* bus system (☎241-2877), at least provides a central focus for what there is. As ever, you're not going to get to see much without a car. If you are driving, check ahead for weather conditions, and if necessary, make extra provisions (de-icer, tyre chains, etc) in case of snowstorms. Though fiercely hot in summer, the temperature drops forbiddingly in some of the surrounding areas in winter, and what looks like a mild day in Redding could turn out to be blizzard conditions a few miles up the road (and several thousand feet up a mountainside).

The **Redding CVB**, 777 Auditorium Drive (Mon–Fri 8am–5pm; ☎225-4100 or 1-800/874-7562), can give advice on accommodation in Redding, information on camping in the outlying areas and details on where to rent camping equipment. For information more specifically on the surrounding area the **Shasta Cascade Wonderland**

△ Mount Shasta

Redding
Shopping
Center

Burney ▷ / Lava Beds National Monument

Hwy-229

Redding Museum
of Art and History

Carter House Natural
Science Museum ❶

❸

*Sacramento River*

❷

Shasta & Weaverville ◁

Thunderbird
Lodge

ℹ️ Hwy-299

❹

Lassen Volcanic National Park

Hwy-299

Intermodal
Transportation
Facility

Downtown
Redding Mall

Hwy-44

*Sacramento River*

**ACCOMMODATION**

1 Budget Lodge
2 Palisades Paradise
3 Redding Lodge
4 River Inn

**REDDING**

0 _____ 1 mile

Sacramento ▽

**Association**, on Wonderland Boulevard, six miles north of town off I-5 (Mon–Fri 8.30am–5pm; ☎275-5555 or 1-800/474-2782), has a more detailed collection of maps and information, and is staffed by helpful outdoor experts. As a general rule, Lassen National Volcanic Park is for the hardier and more experienced hikers, and novices are pointed in the direction of the Whiskeytown-Shasta Trinity National Recreation Area, where there are warmer climes and easier trails.

**Motels** are concentrated along Redding's main strip, Market Street (Hwy-273), and Pine Street. *Budget Lodge*, 1055 Market St (☎243-4231; ②), is a good budget option, while the *Redding Lodge*, 1135 Market St (☎243-5141; ②), is slightly more luxurious. For something grander still, try either *River Inn*, close to the river at 1835 Park Marina Drive (☎241-9500 or 1-800/995-4341; ③), or *Palisades Paradise*, 1200 Palisades Ave (☎-800/382-4649; ③–④), an upscale B&B with a fabulous view of the Trinity mountains to the west.

**Restaurants** are as ubiquitous as motels, many of them 24-hour, most of them unappealing. Exceptions include *Jack's Grill*, 1743 California St (☎241-9705; closed Sun) with fine grilled steak and shrimp and chicken dishes for $10–15. You'll probably have to wait for a table, but you can always go across the road to *Downtown Espresso*, 1545 Placer St at California (☎243-4548), attached to the *Redding Bookstore* and the only place in town where you can get a decent coffee in the evening. In the mornings, good coffee and healthy breakfasts are served at *Hill o' Beans*, 1804 Park Marina Drive (☎246-8852). *The Hatchcover*, 202 Hemsted Drive (☎223-5606), serves tasty steak and seafood from its riverside terrace.

## Shasta

Huddling four miles west of Redding, the ghost town of **SHASTA** – not to be confused with Mount Shasta, see p.540 – is altogether more appealing as a destination. A booming gold-mining town when Redding was an insignificant dot on the map, Shasta's fortunes changed when the railroad tracks were laid to Redding. Abandoned since then, it remains today a row of half-ruined brick buildings that were once part of a runaway prosperity, and literally the end of the road for prospectors. All roads from San Francisco, Sacramento and other southerly points terminated at Shasta; beyond, rough and poorly marked trails made it almost impossible to find gold diggings along the Trinity, Salmon and Upper Sacramento Rivers, and diggers contented themselves with the rich pickings in the surrounding area, pushing out the local Native Americans in a brutal territorial quest for good mining land. The **Courthouse**, on the east side of Main Street, has been turned into a museum (Thurs–Mon 10am–5pm; $2), full of mining paraphernalia and paintings of past heroes, though best are the gallows at the back and the prison cells below – a grim reminder of the daily executions that went on here. The miners were largely an unruly lot, and in the main room of the Courthouse a charter lays down some basic rules of conduct:

> *IV Thou shalt neither remember what thy friends do at home on the sabbath day, lest the remembrance may not compare favourably with what thou doest here.*
>
> *VII Thou shalt not kill the body by working in the rain, even though thou shallt make enough money to buy psychic attendance. Neither shalt thou destroy thyself by "tight" nor "slewed" nor "high" nor "corned" nor "three sheets to the wind", by drinking smoothly down brandy slings, gin cocktails, whiskey punches, rum toddies and egg nogs.*

From the Miners' Ten Commandments

The **Shasta State Historic Park** (unrestricted entry) straddles Main Street, and is less grand than it sounds. Indistinguishable ruins of brick buildings are identified by plaques as shops and hotels, and the central area, not much bigger than the average garden really, features miscellaneous mining machinery and a picnic area.

# Lassen National Volcanic Park

Around forty miles directly east from Redding, the 106,000 acres that make up the pine forests, crystal-green lakes and boiling thermal pools of the **LASSEN NATIONAL VOLCANIC PARK** are one of the most unearthly parts of California. A forbidding climate, which brings up to fifty feet of snowfall each year, keeps the area pretty much uninhabited, with the roads all blocked by snow and (apart from a brief June to October season) completely deserted. It lies at the southerly limit of the Cascades, a low, broad range which stretches six hundred miles north to Mount Garibaldi in British Colombia and is characterized by high volcanoes forming part of the Pacific Circle of Fire. Dominating the park at over 10,000ft is a fine example, **Mount Lassen** itself, which – although quiet in recent years – erupted in 1914, beginning a cycle of outbursts which climaxed in 1915 when the peak blew an enormous mushroom cloud some seven miles skyward, tearing the summit into chunks that landed as far away as Reno. Although eighty years of geothermal inactivity have since made the mountain a safe and fascinating place, scientists predict that of all the Californian volcanoes, Lassen is the likeliest to blow again.

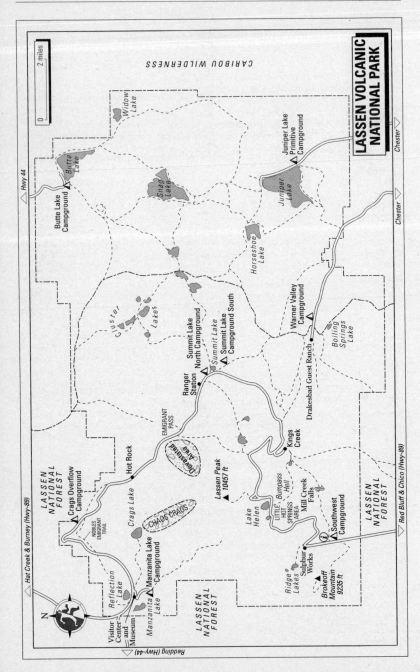

LASSEN VOLCANIC NATIONAL PARK

CARIBOU WILDERNESS

Hwy 44

Chester

Chester

Red Bluff & Chico (Hwy-89)

Hat Creek & Burney (Hwy-89)

LASSEN NATIONAL FOREST

Redding (Hwy-44)

LASSEN NATIONAL FOREST

LASSEN NATIONAL FOREST

N

0    2 miles

Widow Lake

Butte Lake

Butte Lake Campground

Shag Lake

Juniper Lake

Juniper Lake Primitive Campground

Horseshoe Lake

Cluster Lakes

Summit Lake North Campground

Summit Lake

Summit Lake Campground South

Warner Valley Campground

Boiling Springs Lake

Ranger Station

Drakesbad Guest Ranch

EMIGRANT PASS

Kings Creek

Hot Rock

Devastated Area

Crags Overflow Campground

Crags Lake

NOBLES EMIGRANT TRAIL

CHAOS CRAGS

Lassen Peak 10457 ft

Lake Helen

LITTLE HOT SPRINGS AREA

Bumpass Hell

Mill Creek Falls

Southwest Campground

Manzanita Lake Campground

Sulphur Works

Ridge Lakes

Brokeoff Mountain 9235 ft

Reflection Lake

Manzanita Lake

Visitor Center and Museum

## Arrival and information

Lassen is always open ( $5 per vehicle for seven days, $3 per hiker or biker), but you'll have a job getting in or around without a car. The only **public transport** that even approaches the park is provided by *Mount Lassen Motor Transit* (Mon–Sat from 8am; ☎529-2722) from **Red Bluff**, in the Sacramento Valley (see p.533), but even this only reaches **MINERAL**, some eight miles short of the park's southwestern entrance. From Mineral, Hwy-89 leads through Lassen to the northern entrance at the junction of Hwy-44 and Hwy-89 near Manzanita Lake.

The Park Service has its **headquarters** in Mineral (summer daily 8am–4.30pm; PO Box 100, Mineral, CA 96063; ☎595-4444), where you can get free maps and information (there's a box outside when it's closed), including the *Lassen Park Guide*. The main **visitor center** (summer daily 9am–5pm; ☎335-7575) is at Manzanita Lake, just inside the northern entrance, and occupies the same building as the Loomis Museum (see below).

## Accommodation and eating

The only way to **stay** inside the Lassen park is to camp (see box), but even in August night temperatures hover around freezing, and many people prefer to stay in one of the resorts and lodges that pepper the surrounding forest. To be sure of a room in the popular summer months, it pays to book well ahead. For **food**, you don't have an awful lot to choose from. There's a reasonable general store at Manzanita Lake campsite (see box), and Lassen Chalet has a surprisingly good café (daily 9am–6pm), but beyond that you'll have to go outside the park.

---

### CAMPING IN AND AROUND LASSEN

During the few months of the year when conditions are suitable for camping, this is by far the best option. All **developed campsites** in the park are listed below and operate on a first-come first-served basis; not a problem except on midsummer weekends.

**Primitive camping** requires a free **wilderness permit** obtainable in advance from the park headquarters in Mineral (see above), or in person from the visitor centers and entrance stations. There is no self-registration and chosen sites must be a mile from developed campgrounds and a quarter of a mile from most specific sites of interest. In the surrounding **Lassen National Forest**, camping is permitted anywhere, though you'll need a free permit to operate a cooking stove or to light a fire; these are sometimes refused in the dry summer months. In addition there are a couple of dozen developed sites strung along the highways within thirty miles of Lassen, most charging between $5 and $11.

**Juniper Lake** ($6; 6800ft). In the far southeastern corner of the park, with good hiking trails nearby and swimming in the lake. Drinking water must be boiled or treated.

**Manzanita Lake** ($10; 5900ft). By far the largest of the Lassen campsites and the only one with a camp store (8am–8pm), firewood for sale ($6), 24-hour showers (50¢ for 4 minutes), and a laundromat. Rangers run interpretive programmes from here.

**Southwest** ($8; 6700ft). Small tent-only campground by the southwest entrance on Hwy-89 with walk-in sites, water and fire rings.

**Summit Lake** ($8/10; 6700ft). The pick of the Hwy-89 campgrounds, right in the centre of the park and at the hub of numerous hiking trails. It's divided into two sections, the northern half equipped with flush toilets, the southern half only vaults. There's swimming in the lake for the brave.

**Warner Valley** ($8; 5700ft). Off Hwy-89 in the south of the park, this is a beautiful site, but its distance from the road makes it only worth heading for if you're planning extended hiking in the region.

**Hat Creek Resort**, Hwy-89, Old Station, eleven miles northwest of the northern entrance (☎335-7121). A complex of motel units and fancier cabins with kitchens (two-day minimum stay). ③.

**Lassen Mineral Lodge**, Hwy-36, Mineral (☎595-4422). Unspectacular base-rate rooms and considerably more comfortable family ones for just $5 extra. There's a pool, general store, restaurant and bar on site. ③.

**Mill Creek Park**, Mill Creek Road, off Hwy-44, 14 miles east of the northern entrance (☎474-5384). Set amid pines and cedars, simple cabins with cold-water kitchenettes cost $30, those with hot water and bath are $10 more, and space at the campsite is $9. ②.

**Padilla's Rim Rock Ranch Resort**, 13275 Hwy-89, Old Station (☎335-7114). A collection of cabins of varying standards, the best sleeping up to six, dotted around a meadow. ②–④.

**Weston House**, Red Rock Rd, Shingletown, a few miles east of Mineral (☎474-3738). One of the nicest B&Bs in all of California, with four elegant rooms beautifully sited on a volcanic ridge with pool and deck, overlooking the Ishi National Wilderness Area. ⑤.

## The park

Unlike most other wilderness areas, you don't actually need to get out of the car to appreciate Lassen, as some of the best features are visible from the paved Hwy-89 that traverses the park. A thorough tour should take no more than a few hours. Pick up a copy of the *Road Guide: Lassen Volcanic National Park* ($3.50) in the visitor center.

Starting from the northern entrance, the first points of interest along Hwy-89 are **Manzanita Lake** and the **Loomis museum** (summer daily 9am–5pm; free), a memorial to Benjamin Loomis whose documentary photos of the 1914 eruption form the centrepiece of an exhibition strong on local geology – plug domes, composite cones and cinder cones – and flora. An easy trail circles the lake, but so do many of the campers from the nearby campground: an early start is needed for any serious wildlife spotting.

---

### HIKING IN LASSEN PARK

For a volcanic landscape, a surprisingly large proportion of the walking trails in the park are predominantly flat, and the heavily glaciated terrain to the east of the main volcanic massif is pleasingly gentle. Rangers will point you toward the hiking routes best suited to your ability – the park's generally high elevations will leave all but the most experienced walker short of breath, and you should stick to the shorter trails at least until you're acclimatized. For anything but the most tentative explorations, you should pick up a copy of *Lassen Trails* ($2.50) or the better, colour *Hiking Trails of Lasssen* ($10.95), which describe the most popular hikes.

**Chaos Crags Lake** (3.5 miles round trip; 2–3hr; 800ft ascent). From the *Manzanita Lake* campground access road, the path leads gently up through pine and fir forest to the peaceful lake. An adventurous extension climbs a ridge of loose rock to the top of Chaos Crags, affording a view of the whole park.

**Lassen Peak** (5 miles round trip; 4hr; 2000ft ascent). A fairly strenuous hike from road marker 22 to the highest point in the park. Be prepared with water and warm clothing.

**Manzanita Lake** (1.5 miles; 1hr; flat). Easy trails on level ground make this one of the most popular short walks in the park.

**Nobles Emigrant Trail** (2.5 miles; 1–2hr; 200ft ascent). The most accessible and one of the more interesting sections of a trail forged in 1850 starts opposite the Manzanita Lake entrance station and meets Hwy-89 at marker 60. It isn't maintained, but is heavily compacted and easy going.

**Paradise Meadows** (3 miles round trip; 3hr; 800ft ascent). Starting either at the Hat Creek parking area (marker 42) or marker 27, and passing Terrace Lake on the way, this hike winds up at Paradise Meadows, ablaze with wildflowers in the summer and a marvellous spot to pass an afternoon.

At the halfway point you'll come to **Summit Lake**, a busy camping area set around a beautiful icy lake, from where you can start on the park's most manageable hiking trails. Press on further to the **Devastated Area**, where, in 1914, molten lava from Lassen poured down the valley, denuding the landscape as it went, ripping out every tree and patch of grass. Slowly the earth is recovering its green mantle, but the most vivid impression is one of complete destruction.

Further south along Hwy-89, you reach the parking area (8000ft up) where the steep five-mile ascent to Lassen Peak begins. Wilderness seekers will have a better time pushing east to the **Juniper Lake** area.

Continuing south, Lassen's indisputable show-stealers are **Bumpass Hell** and **Emerald Lake**, the former – named after a man who lost a leg trying to cross it – a steaming valley of active pools and vents that bubble away at a low rumble all around. It looks dangerous, but the trails are sturdy and easy to manage. Be warned, though, that the crusts over the thermal features are often brittle, and breaking through them could literally land you in very hot water – *never* venture off the trails. The paths around Emerald Lake are spectacular too, in a much quieter fashion; the lake itself resembles a sheet of icy-green glass, perfectly still and clear but for the snow-covered rock mound which rises from its centre. Only during summer does the lake approach swimmable temperatures, and if you're visiting outside of July or August you'll have to content yourself with gazing at its mirror-like surface.

Before leaving the park at Mineral, you'll notice the rising steam and acrid smell of **Sulphur Works**, a boiling cauldron of fumaroles and mud pots visible from the road and reached on a 200-yard boardwalk. The far south of the park also contains **Lassen Chalet**, site of some limited skiing facilities.

# Whiskeytown-Shasta-Trinity National Recreation Area

Travelling west from Redding through the ghost town of Shasta (see p.535), Hwy-299 is a deserted, often precipitous but enjoyable road that leads after ten miles into the western portion of the **Whiskeytown-Shasta-Trinity National Recreation Area**. Assuming the road's open – it's often blocked off due to bad weather – this huge chunk of land is open for public use daily, year-round. Its series of three impounded lakes – Trinity, Whiskeytown and Shasta – have artificial beaches, forests and camping facilities designed to meet the needs of anyone who has ever fancied themselves as a water-skier, sailor or wilderness hiker. Sadly, during summer it's completely congested, as windsurfers, motorboats, jet skis and recreational vehicles block the narrow routes which serve the lakes. But in the winter when the tourists have all gone, it can be supremely untouched, at least on the surface. In fact there's an extensive system of tunnels, dams and aqueducts directing the plentiful waters of the Sacramento River to California's Central Valley to irrigate cash crops for the huge agribusinesses. The lakes are pretty enough, but residents complain they're not a patch on the wild waters that used to flow from the mountains before the Central Valley Project came along in the 1960s.

Of the three lakes, **Whiskeytown**, just beyond Shasta, is the smallest, easiest to get to, and inevitably the most popular. Ideal for watersports, it hums with the sound of jet skis and powerboats ripping across the still waters. Those who don't spend their holiday in a wet suit can usually be found four-wheel driving and pulling action-man stunts on the primitive roads all around. The best place for **camping** and **hiking** is in the **Brandy Creek** area – a hairy five-mile drive along the narrow J F Kennedy Memorial Drive from the main entrance and **Whiskeytown Visitor Information Center** on

Hwy-299 (daily 9am–6pm; ☎246-1225). There's a small store at the water's edge in Brandy Creek and three campgrounds (mostly $11–14 sites) about a mile behind in the woods.

Northeast on Hwy-3 (off Hwy-299 40 miles west of Whiskeytown), **Trinity Lake** (officially called Clair Engle Lake, but not locally referred to as such) is much quieter, rarely used in summer and in winter primarily a picturesque stop-off for skiers on their way to the **Salmon-Trinity Alps** area beyond, part of the extensive **Salmon Mountains** range. It's very remote round here, and most people only venture this far west to visit the small Gold Rush town of **WEAVERVILLE**, a few miles west along Hwy-299. The distinctive brick buildings, fitted with exterior spiral staircases, were built to withstand fires – indeed, the fire station itself is particularly noteworthy. The main draw, though, is the **Joss House** on Main Street (Thurs–Mon 10am–5pm; $2), a small Taoist temple built in 1874 by indentured mineworkers. A beautiful shrine, still in use today, it features a three-thousand-year-old altar and can be visited on a poor guided tour.

You can **stay** at the *Weaverville Hotel*, 205 Main St (☎623-3121; ②) a century-old, gracefully dilapidated place with large characterful rooms and no phones or TV – register in *Brady's* sports store next door. Alternatives include the *49er Motel*, 718 Main St (☎623-49ER; ②). You can **eat** healthy breakfasts and lunches at *The Mustard Seed Café* at the junction of highways 299 and 3 (☎623-2922), or knock back local microbrews over a hearty meal at the eclectically decorated *Pacific Brewery Restaurant & Bar*, 401 S Main St (☎623-3000). For more information, consult the **Chamber of Commerce**, 317 S Main St (summer daily 9am–5pm; rest of year Mon–Fri 9am–5pm; ☎623-6101 or 1-800/421-7259).

East of the other two, eight miles north of Redding, is **Shasta Lake**. The biggest of the three lakes – larger than the San Francisco Bay – it's marred by the unsightly and enormous **Shasta Dam**, 465ft high and over half a mile long, bang in the middle. Built between 1938 and 1945 as part of the enormous Central Valley irrigation project, the dam backs up the Sacramento, McCloud and Pit rivers to form the lake, the project's northern outpost. The best views are from marked vista points along the approach road (US-151, off I-5), but a more vivid way to experience the sheer enormity of the thing is to drive down to the powerhouse (daily 9am–4pm) and take the **free tour** of the dam and ancillary structures, feeling the power of millions of gallons of water gushing beneath you.

On the north side of the lake, the massive limestone formations of the **Shasta Caverns** (daily 10am–3pm; $12) are the largest in California, jutting above ground and clearly visible from the freeway. The interior, however, is something of a letdown: a fairly standard series of caves and tunnels in which stalactite and stalagmite formations are studded with crystals, flow-stone deposits and miniature waterfalls. The admission price covers the short ferry journey from the ticket booth across an arm of Shasta Lake. From Lake Shasta, I-5 races up towards Mount Shasta, an impressive drive against a staggering backdrop of mountains and lakes.

# Mt Shasta ... and Mount Shasta

*Lonely as God and as white as a winter moon.*

Joaquin Miller, about Mt Shasta

The lone peak of the 14,162-foot **Mt Shasta** dominates the landscape for a hundred miles all around, almost permanently snow-covered, hypnotically beautiful but menacing in its potential for destruction: it last erupted over two hundred years ago, but is still considered an active volcano. Hard under the enormous bulk of the mountain, the town of **MOUNT SHASTA** has a compact and pleasing centre free from the worst excesses of urban sprawl. This, and the energy channels which are said to converge on the mountain, have combined over the last decade to make it California's ascendant hotbed of spiritual activity, a fact not lost on those who prey on the centred, but barely grounded, individuals who flock here, exploiting every weakness in their holistic armour through expensive courses and retreats.

## Arrival and information

Merely getting to Mount Shasta is a rewarding journey, easily accomplished on *Greyhound* **buses** which connect the town with Redding to the south and stop on Commercial Way, a couple of blocks from the very helpful **Visitors' Bureau**, 300 Pine St (Mon–Sat 9am–5pm, Sun 9am–3pm; ☎926-4865 or 1-800/926-4865). *Amtrak* trains stop in Dunsmuir, six miles south, in the middle of the night; from there, six daily *STAGE* buses (☎842-8295 or 1-800/24-STAGE) connect with town.

## Accommodation

Mount Shasta has no shortage of **accommodation**, and reservations should only be necessary at weekends in the height of summer. **Campgrounds** abound in the surrounding area, but few have full amenities (hot showers are vital when the mercury drops).

### Hotels, motels and B&Bs

**Alpenrose Cottage Hostel**, 204 E Hinkley St (☎926-6724). A top-quality independent hostel with a relaxed atmosphere and a great deck for watching the sunset over Mt Shasta immediately behind. There's a fully equipped kitchen, a double room for those who don't fancy the small dorms, and showers which are available to non-guests for $2. Rates are $13 a night, less by the week, and you may even be able to work for your board. Follow N Mount Shasta Blvd north for a mile and follow the *KOA* signs. ①.

**McCloud Guest House**, 606 W Colombero Drive, McCloud (☎964-3160). Though inconveniently sited twelve miles away in McCloud, you can't go far wrong in this plush B&B set in the former logging company headquarters. Excellent breakfasts, and dinners served too. ④.

**Dream Inn**, 326 Chestnut St (☎926-1536). Very central B&B, a block east of Mount Shasta Blvd, in a Victorian house with all the usual trappings. ④.

**Evergreen Lodge**, 1312 S Mount Shasta Blvd (☎926-2143). Bargain motel a mile south of town with basic rooms (and more expensive ones with kitchenettes), a pool and hot tub. ②.

**Mount Shasta Cabins & Cottages**, 500 S Mount Shasta Blvd (☎926-5396). This organization acts as an agency for a wide range of cabins and houses in and around Mount Shasta, rented by the night but particularly suited for longer stays. Most have kitchenettes, TVs and wood stoves and drop their rates substantially outside the summer season. ③.

**Mount Shasta Ranch B&B**, 1008 W A Barr Rd (☎926-4029). A stylish ranch house with spacious rooms and a great view of Mt Shasta. ⑤.

**Travel Inn**, 504 S Mount Shasta Blvd (☎9264617). A decent, clean motel with basic rooms. ②

## Camping

The most picturesque campground in the area is the woodland *Lake Siskiyou Campground* ($18; ☎926-2618), four miles west of town on a lake of the same name, where you can picnic, bathe and go boating. More **primitive sites** tend to be free if there is no piped drinking water, though creek water is often available. The most useful of these is the walk-in *Panther Meadows* (7400ft), high up on the mountain at the end of the Everitt Memorial Highway, though *McBride Springs* ($6; 6000ft) being lower down the same road tends to be open for longer. The fully equipped *KOA*, 900 N Mt Shasta Blvd (☎926-4029), two blocks from downtown, charges $15 per site.

## The town and around

Quite rightly, few people come to Mount Shasta for its museums, but given bad weather and a full stomach you might visit the otherwise missable **Sisson Museum**, 1 N Old Stage Rd (June–Aug daily 10am–5pm; Sept–May Mon–Sat noon–4pm, Sun 1–4pm; donation), with a few examples of Native basketware, a fair bit on pioneering life in the region, and some more diverting material on the mountain itself. The brown, rainbow and eastern brook trout in the **fish hatchery** outside (daily 8am–4pm; free) can be fed on food from a vending machine.

A couple of New-Age **bookshops** along N Mount Shasta Boulevard provide the key to some of the town's more off-beat activities: *Golden Bough Books* at no. 219 (☎926-

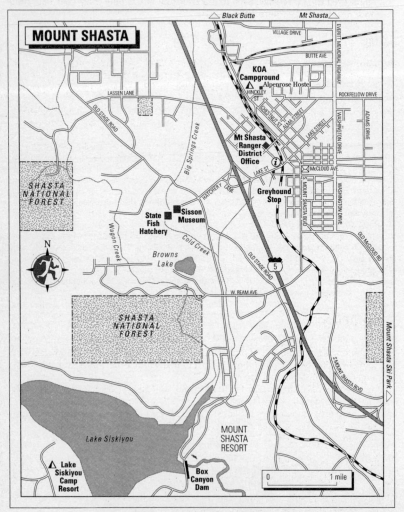

3228 or 1-800/343-8888), and *Wings Bookstore* at no. 226 (☎926-3041 or 1-800/70-WINGS), have active bulletin boards and stacks of publications exhorting you to visit a sweatlodge or discover your inner goddess.

Mainly, though, Mount Shasta is full of outfits hoping to help you into the **outdoors**. Competition keeps prices reasonable and the options wide open. Obviously, there are a thousand ways to climb Mt Shasta, and these are covered in the box below. Otherwise, *Shasta Mountain Guides*, 1938 Hill Rd (☎926-3117), arranges jeep trips up the mountain and conducts rock- and ice-climbing courses for all levels from $65. For real thrills, **white-water rafting trips** on the churning Upper Sacramento are offered by *Turtle River Rafting* (☎926-3223) and *River Dancers* (☎926-3517), both starting at $80 a day. You might even try a three-day, $400 **llama trek** (the beasts only carry your bags, not you) with *Rainbow Ridge Ranch* (☎926-5794).

## Eating

Aside from a rash of fast food outlets towards I-5, Mount Shasta's **eating** options are largely health-conscious, with vegetarian dishes featured on almost every menu. Hardy mountain types are amply catered for, too, with plenty of opportunities to stoke up on hearty fare before hitting the mountain heights.

**The Bagel Café and Natural Bakery**, 105 E Alma St (☎926-1414). A favourite with Mount Shasta's spiritual community, serving moderately priced soups, sandwiches, great huevos rancheros and, of course, bagels.

**Lily's**, 1013 S Mount Shasta Blvd (☎926-3372). Moderately priced and consistently good restaurant serving California cuisine, vegetarian and Mexican dishes. Mains cost $12–15, sandwiches around $6.

**Mike and Tony's**, 501 S Mount Shasta Blvd (☎926-4792). An excellent Italian restaurant with some good wines. Dinner only. Closed Wed.

**Serge's**, 531 Chestnut St (☎926-1276). Moderately priced and informal French dining at lunchtime and evenings. Several vegetarian plates are featured, and the Sunday brunch is something of a local tradition.

**Simply Vegetarian**, at the *Stoney Brook Inn*, 309 W Colombero Drive, McCloud (☎964-2300). The only fully vegetarian place around, twelve miles away in McCloud. There's a lunchtime soup and organic salad bar, and $8 full dinners, most of them vegan, in the evening.

**Willy's Bavarian Kitchen**, 107 Chestnut St (☎926-3636). The pick of the town's restaurants, serving sauerbraten and wiener schnitzel alongside tasty vegetarian dishes inside or on the deck. Wash your dinner down with German beer, local micro-brews or fabulous fruit shakes.

## Around Mt. Shasta

Five miles north of town, the treeless cone of **Black Butte** (2.5 miles; 2–3hr; 1800ft ascent), offers a more modest alternative to climbing Mount Shasta. The switchback trail to this 6325ft volcanic plug dome is hard to find without the leaflet available from the ranger station or Visitors' Bureau.

The decade-old **Mt Shasta Ski Park**, near McCloud on Hwy-89, has yet to establish itself on the ski circuit, so its rental charges ($17) and tow tickets ($26) are quite uniquely attractive. In summer, it transforms into some of the best **mountain biking** territory in the region, with marked trails following the ski runs. A pass is $16, and bikes can be rented for $8 a day. There's also an artificial tower for climbing ($8 an hour).

After a day or two trudging around or up Mt Shasta, **Stewart Mineral Springs** (Sun–Thurs 10am–6pm, Fri & Sat 10am–8pm; ☎938-2222 or 1-800/322-9223; ①–③) at 4617 Stewart Springs Rd off I-5 just north of Weed provides welcome relief. Individual bathing rooms in a cedar and pine forest glade soothe your aches away for $15, less if you stay in the cabins, dorm units, teepees or campsite here.

## Yreka

There's little to justify more than an hour or two in quiet, leafy **YREKA** (pronounced *Why-reeka*), fifteen-odd miles north of Weed, but it makes a pleasant break. Most people come here to ride the Yreka Western Railroad, better known as the **Blue Goose** (mid-June to Aug Wed–Sun; late May to mid-June & Sept–Oct Sat & Sun only; ☎842-4146), a 1915 Baldwin steam engine pulling attractive carriages to and from the nearby historic town of **Montague**; the three-hour excursion costs $9 and includes an hour in Montague – all very agreeable. The **Siskiyou County Museum**, 910 S Main St (summer Tues–Fri 9am–8pm, Sat 9am–5pm; rest of year Tues–Sat 9am–5pm; $1) deserves some attention, particularly the outdoor section (closes 4pm) with its historic buildings – church, houses and shops – transported here from around the county. Finally, there's a paltry collection of gold nuggets in the **County Courthouse**, 311 Fourth St (Mon–Fri 8am–5pm; free).

The **Chamber of Commerce**, 117 W Main St (summer Mon 9am–5pm, Tues–Fri 9am–7.30pm, Sat 10am–6.30pm, rest of year Mon–Fri 9am–5pm; ☎842-1649), issue maps for a self-guided **Historic Walking Tour** around Yreka's numerous Victorian homes. It can also help you find **somewhere to stay**, not difficult with dozens of chain motels and the *Thunderbird Lodge*, 526 S Main St (☎842-4404 or 1-800/554-4339; ②). **Eating** is best done along the street at *Nature's Kitchen*, 412 S Main St (☎842-1136; closed Sun), not at the cutesy *Grandma's Restaurant* which has an unfathomable, state-

---

### CLIMBING MT SHASTA

Even if you are only passing through the region, you'll be tempted to tackle Mt Shasta. Ambling among the pines of the lower slopes is rewarding enough, but the assault on the summit is the main challenge – and it can be done in a day with basic equipment.

Every year several deaths occur and numerous injuries are sustained through inexperience and over-ambition. The wise will stick to the routes prescribed by the **Mt Shasta Ranger District Office**, 204 W Alma St (summer daily 8am–4.30pm; rest of year Mon–Fri 8am–4.30pm; ☎926-4511), who will insist that you obtain a **wilderness permit** (also self-issued outside the office when closed and at the trailhead) and enter your name in the **voluntary climbers' register** before and after your ascent.

The mountain's isolation creates its own weather, which can change with alarming rapidity. In early summer, when most novice attempts are made, the snow cover is complete and crampons get a good grip; later during the season, as the snow melts, patches of loose ash and cinder appear, making the going more difficult and the chance of rockfall greater. Only at the end of summer,with most of the snow melted, is there a chance of climbing safely without crampons and axe. There are countless equipment rental agencies in town, such as *Fifth Season*, 300 N Mount Shasta Blvd (☎926-3606), which can fit you out with boots ($16), crampons and ice axe ($12) and camping gear ($12 a day); and provide a mountain weather forecast on ☎926-5555. *House of Ski*, 1208 Everitt Hwy (☎926-2359), offers much the same at very competitive rates.

Even for fit, acclimatized climbers **the ascent**, from 7000ft to over 14,000ft, will take eight to ten utterly exhausting hours. The easiest, safest and most popular way up is via **Avalanche Gulch** – just follow the footprints of the person in front of you. Drive up the mountain on the Everitt Memorial Highway to the Bunny Flat trailhead at 7000ft. A gentle hour's walk brings you to **Horse Camp**, a good place to acclimatize and spend the night before your ascent. The return trip is done in two to four hours, depending on the recklessness of your descent: Mt Shasta is a renowned spot for **glissading** – careering down the slopes on a jacket or strong plastic sheet – a sport best left to those proficient in ice-axe arrests, but wonderfully exhilarating nonetheless.

On the lower slopes, keep your eyes skinned for the inedible **watermelon snow**, its bright red appearance caused by a microbe which flourishes here.

wide appeal to elderly Americans whose RVs fill the car park. Yreka can be reached by *STAGE* **bus** (☎842-8295 or 1-800/24-STAGE) from Mount Shasta and Dunsmuir.

If you're here on a Saturday, fancy a drink and don't mind backtracking a little, head twenty miles south of Yreka along Hwy-3 to charming, turn-of-the-century **ETNA**, home to the *Etna Brewery*, 131 Callahan St (Sat 1–5pm; ☎467-5277), a tiny microbrewery producing just 300 barrels a year for local distribution. There are usually four or five of the malty real ales and other beers available to taste, each and every one a beer drinker's dream. While here, check out the Fifties soda fountain in the *Scott Valley Drugstore* at the top of Main Street. And if you're really struck by the place, you can **camp** for free in the town park on Diggles Street.

# Lava Beds National Monument and around

After seeing Mount Shasta you could push on to the **Lava Beds National Monument** in the far northeastern corner of the state. Carved out of the huge **Modoc National Forest**, it's actually a series of volcanic caves and huge black lava flows with a history as violent as the natural forces that created it.

Lava Beds is the most remote and forgotten of California's parks in the heart of Modoc country, a desolate outback where cowboys still ride the range, and where, as the territory of one of the last major battles with the Native Americans, there is still a suspicious relationship between the settlers and the native peoples. Until the 1850s Gold Rush it was home to the Modoc tribe, but after their repeated and bloody confrontations with the miners, the government ordered them into a reservation with the Klamath, their traditional enemy. After only a few months, the Modoc drifted back to their homeland in the lava beds, and in 1872 the army was sent in to return them by force to the reservation. It was driven back by 52 Modoc warriors under the leadership of one Kientpoos, better known as "Captain Jack", who held back an army of US regulars and volunteers twenty times the size of his for five months, from a stronghold at the northern tip of the park (see below).

Eventually Captain Jack was captured and hanged and what was left of the tribe sent off to a reservation in Oklahoma, where most of them died of malaria. Today the lava beds region is inhabited only by the wild deer and three million migrating ducks who attract the trickle of tourists that make it this far.

Yet further north, the **Klamath Basin National Wildlife Refuge** spreads over the border into Oregon, seemingly choked with birdlife and a good side trip.

## Practicalities

Lava Beds National Monument ($4 per vehicle for 7 days; $2 for hikers and bikers) is 160 miles northeast of Redding, and inaccessible without a **car**. It's a conceivable daytrip from Mount Shasta, two and a half hours away, but is far more rewarding as an overnight, or even two-night, trip. The most tortuous route follows Hwy-89 to Bartle, then passing Medicine Lake (see p.547); the approach via Hwy-139 is easier, but the fastest is from the north, off US-97, and through the Klamath Basin National Wildlife Refuge (see p.548).

Pick up an excellent map of the monument from the **visitor center**, just inside the southwestern entrance (summer daily 8am–6pm; rest of year Sat & Sun 8am–5pm and sporadic weekdays; ☎667-2283). Close by, at Indian Wells, is the park's one **campground** ($10 in summer; $6 in winter). All **wilderness camping** throughout the monument is free and no permits are neccessary, but campers must pitch at least a mile from any road, trail or camping area, and fifty yards from any cave. Be warned,

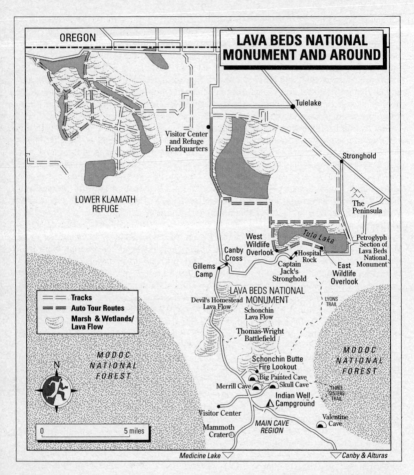

though, that elevation throughout the park ranges from 4000 to 5700 feet and there's snow and freezing nights for most of the year, which can make camping uncomfortable.

The only **accommodation** centre in the area, and the one place to pick up supplies (the monument can only muster a soda machine), is **TULELAKE**, 25 miles north. The near-deserted main street (Hwy-139) holds the *Park Motel* (☎667-2913; ②) and the *Ellis Motel* (☎667-5242; ②) and a few restaurants. Nearby is the **Modoc Ranger Station** (Mon–Fri 8am–4.30pm; ☎667-2248) with general information on the Modoc National Forest.

## The monument

A day spent in the **Lava Beds** is akin to exploring the innards of a volcano, scampering down hollow tubes through which molten lava once coursed. The youngest of them were formed 30,000 years ago when volcanic upwellings sent molten, basaltic magma careering across the Modoc Plateau. As the magma came into contact with cool air, it solidified, leaving a flowing molten core feeding the expanding lava field downhill. In time, the magma flow stopped and the molten lava drained out, leaving the world's largest concentration of such hollow tubes. Most remain unexplored, but where the casing has collapsed, access is possible and you are free to scramble through. Some of the caves are so small that you have to crawl along on all fours, while others are an enormous 75 feet in diameter. Some contain Native American petroglyphs – not to be confused with the names painted on the cave walls by J D Howard, one of the first white men to explore and name the caves.

After being guided, herded, molly-coddled and generally treated as a child in any number of Californian attractions it comes as a surprise to find that at Lava Beds you are free to explore at will. Initially, though, entering the darkness alone can be an unnerving experience, so most people prefer to take the **free guided ranger walks** (daily early June to early Sept). Two-to-three-hour morning walks (9am) leave from the visitor center and explore little-known sections of the monument; afternoon tours (2pm) concentrate on guided cave trips of up to an hour and a half, and in the evening (9pm) rangers lead hour-long campfire talks and slide shows.

If you insist on being butch and eschewing ranger guidance, you must abide by a few rules. Don't go alone, wear decent shoes, and take two flashlights each. These are available for loan (free) from the visitor center but – to ensure no-one remains underground – they must be returned by closing time. For night explorations (the caves remain open) you'll need your own light source. Hard hats are strongly advised and available for $3.50 at the visitor center.

A car is vital if you're planning to tackle the northern reaches of the park around **Captain Jack's Stronghold**, a natural fortress of craggy lava flows and shallow caves on the shores of the Old Tule Lake. When you get here you'll see how the Modoc managed to hide and move around through the passageways of the hill (which from the outside looks like nothing special). Two **self-guided trails** (one half a mile, the other 1.5 miles) will take you through the fort, pointing out significant spots along the way. Two miles west, the shallow lava bowl of **Hospital Rock** marks the point where one Lt Sherwood, wounded by the Modoc, was unsuccessfully tended in a makeshift field hospital towards the end of the siege on the stronghold.

## Around the monument

Small volcanic craters, buttes, spatter cones and chimneys dot Lava Beds, but the flows which produced most of the lava tubes came from **Mammoth Crater** on the southern perimeter of the monument, where a short path leads to a viewpoint overlooking the deep conical crater.

Underlying the most recent of Lava Beds' fabulous creations is a bed of basalt, the product of a huge shield volcano with a profile so flat it is barely noticeable. Its core is now filled by the sub-alpine **Medicine Lake**, ten miles southwest of Mammoth Crater. Formerly a Modoc healing centre, the only therapies on offer today are fishing and swimming from the $7 **campsites** along the north shore.

More volcanic spectacle lies just west at **Glass Mountain**, made almost entirely of glassy, black obsidian – source of Modoc arrowheads – but covered in fluffy, white pumice quarried for stonewashing jeans. A short and fairly easy trail leads in from the road. Just beyond the monument's northeast corner, a small outlier known as the **Petroglyph Section** contains **Petroglyph Point**, a three-hundred-yard-long cliff face made of "tuff", volcanic rock formed when lava flows hit Old Tule Lake. The soft rock offers some fine, but cryptic, examples of ancient art: shields, female figures and a series of small circles thought to represent travel. Pick up an interpretive leaflet at the visitor center.

### EXPLORING THE LAVA TUBES

Most of the interest in Lava Beds lies around the visitor center, where the largest concentration of caves can be visited on the short **Cave Loop** access road. For a confidence-building handle on your location in the twenty-five "developed" caves – less than a tenth of the known total – get the *Lava Caves Map* ($5) from the visitor center. New ones are discovered all the time, so the possibilities are almost endless, but for the moment, the tried and tested caves below should be enough to be going on with.

**Catacomb Cave** At over a mile long, this is the longest open tube in the monument, though you need perseverance, a slim body and a cool head to get anywhere near the end. The profusion of interconnecting passageways make it one of the most confusing; keep track of whether you are heading up or downhill.

**Fern Cave** Full of ferns growing in patches of light where the roof has fallen in, with Native pictographs on the walls.

**Labyrinth** Striking geological features – lava pillars and lavacicles – and evidence of Native American habitation.

**Mushpot Cave** Right by the visitor center, this is the most developed of the miand provides a good introduction, lit during center opening hours, and with interpretive panels highlighting key features.

**Skull Cave** Named for Bighorn skulls found when the cave was discovered by early explorer E L Hopkins, this has the largest entrance of any of the lava tubes and contains ice all year round.

**Symbol Bridge** and **Big Painted Cave** (1.5 miles round trip; almost flat). Two very worthwhile cavesadjacent to each other on a trail north of the visitor center. No flashlight is needed though one could come in handy. Some of the best examples of pictographs in the Monument – tentatively dated between 1000AD and 1500AD – show up as different angles of sunlight catch the rocks beside the entrance. Respecting Modoc sensibilities, make two clockwise turns before descending into a large cave, open at both ends (hence the "bridge" name), in which zigzags, squiggles, sunbursts and human figures are picked out in grease and charcoal on pumice-washed background. Make a single anti-clockwise turn on departure for Big Painted Cave, where the pictographs are less impressive. In the mid 1920s J D Howard excavated a small tunnel at the very back of the cave to reveal an ice flow in a cavity fifteen feet down: with a flashlight you can scramble down there.

East of the Petroglyphs Section, the road continues to Hwy-139 and the town of **NEWELL**, site of the **Tule Lake Camp**, where 110,000 people of Japanese descent, many of them American citizens, were interned without charge or trial between 1942 and 1946. Many of the camp buildings have been sold off to local farmers, but the wooden-sided police and military barracks remain.

Perhaps the most rewarding excursion from the monument, though, is to the **Klamath Basin National Wildlife Refuge** (open daylight hours), just to the north and spreading into Oregon. One of the last wetlands in California, with swathes of open water and emerging vegetation on the shoreline, it attracts an estimated eighty percent of birds following the Pacific Flyway, the major migration routes from Alaska and northern Canada to Baja California in Mexico. In spring and fall, almost a hundred species are present and the population tops a million. The most accessible reaches are the **Lower Klamath Refuge** and **Tule Lake**, an open body of water surrounded by reeds ("Tule" in Modoc). At the northwestern corner of the latter, the **visitor center** (Mon–Fri 8am–4.30pm, Sat & Sun 10am–4pm; ☎667-2231) issues free permits for the birdwatching blinds: call ahead to be sure of getting one. Surprisingly, the best way of spotting the wildlife is by driving along designated routes: getting out of the car and walking scares the birds off.

## travel details

### Trains
**Oakland** to: Chico (1 daily; 4hr 30min); Redding (1 daily; 5hr 44min).

### Buses
*Combined Greyhound and Amtrak Thruway schedules*
**Arcata to**: Crescent City (3 daily; 1hr 30min); Garberville (4 daily; 1hr 30min).
**Chico to**: Redding (5 daily; 1hr 30min).
**Eureka to**: Crescent City (3 daily; 1hr 50min); Garberville (4 daily; 1hr 10min).

**Mount Shasta to**: Yreka (2 daily; 1hr).

**Redding to**: Chico (5 daily; 1hr 30min); Mount Shasta (2 daily; 1hr 30min); Sacramento (8 daily; 3hr 30min); Yreka (3 daily; 3hr).

**San Francisco to**: Chico (5 daily; 3hr 30min); Redding (3 daily; 5hr); Santa Rosa (5 daily; 1hr 30min).

**Santa Rosa to**: Arcata (4 daily; 5hr); Crescent City (2 daily; 6hr 30min); Eureka (4 daily; 4hr 40min); Garberville (4 daily; 3hr 30min); Leggett (4 daily; 3hr); Willits (4 daily; 2hr).

# PART THREE

# THE
# CONTEXTS

# THE HISTORICAL FRAMEWORK

To many people, California seems one of the least historic places on the planet. Unburdened by the past, it's a land where anything seems possible, whose inhabitants live carefree lives, wholly in and for the present moment. Its very name, appropriately for all its idealized images, is a work of fiction, free from any historical significance. The word first appeared as the name of an island, located "very near to the terrestrial paradise" and inhabited entirely by Amazons "without any men among them", in a popular Spanish picaresque novel of the early 1500s, *Las Sergas de Esplandián* by García de Montalvo.

## NATIVE PEOPLES

For thousands of years prior to the arrival of Europeans, the aboriginal peoples of California flourished in the naturally abundant land, living fairly peacefully in tribes along the coast and in the deserts and the forested mountains. Anthropologists estimate that nearly half the native population then living within the boundaries of the present-day US were spread throughout what's now California, in small, tribal villages of a few hundred people, each with a clearly defined territory and often its

own distinct language. Since there was no political or social organization beyond the immediate level of the tribe, it was not difficult for the colonizing Spaniards to divide and conquer, effectively wiping them out – though admittedly more died through epidemics of disease than outright genocide.

Very little remains to mark the existence of the Californian Native Americans: they had no form of written language, relatively undeveloped craft skills, and built next to nothing that would last beyond the change of seasons. About the only surviving signs of the coastal tribes are the piles of seashells and discarded arrowheads that have been found, from which anthropologists have deduced a bit about their cultures. Also, a few examples of **rock art** survive, as at the Chumash Painted Cave, near Santa Barbara on the Central Coast. Similar sorts of petroglyph figures were drawn by the Paiute Native Americans, who lived in the deserts near Death Valley, and by the Miwok from the Sierra Nevada foothills.

## DISCOVERY AND EARLY EXPLORATION

The first Europeans to set foot in California were Spanish explorers, intent on extending their colony of New Spain, which under the 1494 Treaty of Tordesillas included all the New World lands west of Brazil and all of North America west of the Rocky Mountains. In 1535, **Hernán Cortéz**, fresh from decimating the Aztecs, headed westward in search of a short cut to Asia, which he believed to be adjacent to Mexico. Though he never reached what's now California, he set up a small colony at the southern tip of the Baja (lower) California peninsula. He thought it was an island, and named it Santa Cruz, writing in his journals that he soon expected to find the imagined island of the Amazons.

The first explorer to use the name California, and to reach what's now the US state, was **Juan Cabrillo**, who sighted San Diego harbour in 1542, and continued north along the coast to the Channel Islands off Santa Barbara. He died there six months later, persistent headwinds having made it impossible to sail any further north. His crew later made it as far north as what is now the state of Oregon, but were unable to find any safe anchorage and returned home starved and half-dead from scurvy. It was fifty years before another Spaniard braved the difficult journey: **Juan de Fuca**'s 1592 voyage caused great excitement when he claimed to have discovered the Northwest Passage, a potentially lucrative trade route across North America. It has long since turned out that there is no such thing as the Northwest Passage (de Fuca may have discovered the Puget Sound, outside Seattle), but Europeans continued to search for it for the next two hundred years.

The British explorer **Sir Francis Drake** arrived in the *Golden Hind* in 1579, taking a break from his piracy of Spanish vessels in order to make repairs. His landing spot, now called Drake's Bay, near Point Reyes north of San Francisco, had "white bancks and cliffes" that reminded him of Dover. Upon landing, he was met by a band of native Miwoks, who feted him with food and drink and placed a feathered crown upon his head; in return, he claimed all of their lands – which he called Nova Albion (New England) – for Queen Elizabeth, supposedly leaving behind a brass plaque that's now on display in the Bancroft Library at the University of California.

Setting sail from Acapulco in 1602, **Sebastián Vizcaíno**, a Portuguese explorer under contract to Spain, made a more lasting impact than his predecessors, undertaking the most extensive exploration of the coast, and bestowing most of the place names that survive. In order to impress his superiors he exaggerated the value of his discoveries, describing a perfect, sheltered harbour which he named **Monterey** in honour of his patron back in Mexico. Subsequent colonizers based their efforts, 150 years later, upon these fraudulent claims (the windy bay did not live up to Vizcaíno's estimation), and the headquarters of the missions and military and administrative centre of the Spanish government remained at Monterey, 100 miles south of San Francisco, for the next 75 years.

## COLONIZATION: THE SPANISH AND THE BRITISH

The Spanish occupation of California began in earnest in 1769 as a combination of military expediency (to prevent other powers from gaining a foothold) and Catholic missionary zeal (to convert the heathen Native Americans). Father **Junipero Serra** and a company of three hundred soldiers and clergy set off from Mexico for Monterey, half of them by ship, the other half overland. After establishing a small mission and *presidio* (fort) at San Diego, in June 1770 the expedition arrived at Monterey, where another mission and small *presidio* were constructed.

The Spanish continued to build missions all along the coast, ostensibly to Catholicize the Native Americans, which they did with Inquisitional obsession. The mission complexes were broadly similar, with a church and cloistered residential structure surrounded by irrigated fields, vineyards, and more extensive ranchlands. The labour of the Native American converts was co-opted: they were put to work making soap and candles, were often beaten and never educated. Objective accounts of the missionaries' treatment of the indigenous peoples are rare, though mission registries record twice as many deaths as they do births, and their cemeteries are packed with Native American dead. Not all of the Native Americans gave up without a fight: many missions suffered from raids, and the now ubiquitous red-tiled roofs were originally a replacement for the earlier thatch to better resist arson attacks.

Most of the mission structures that survive today were built to the designs of Serra's successor, Father **Férmin de Lasuén**, who was in charge of the missions during the period of their greatest growth. By the time of his death in 1804, a chain of twenty one missions, each a long day's walk from its neighbours and linked by the dirt path of *El Camino Real* (The Royal Road), ran from San Diego to San Francisco.

During this time the first towns, called **pueblos**, were established in order to attract settlers to what was still a distant and undesirable territory. The first was laid out in 1777 at San Jose, south of the new mission at San Francisco. Los Angeles, the second *pueblo*, was established in 1781, though neither had more than a hundred inhabitants until well into the 1800s.

One reason for Spain's military presence in California – which all told consisted of four *presidios*, with twelve cannons and only two hundred soldiers – was to prevent the expansion of the small **Russian** colony based in Alaska, mostly trappers collecting beaver and otter pelts in the Northwestern states of Washington and Oregon. The two countries were at peace and relations friendly, and in any case the Spanish *presidios* were in no position to enforce their territorial claims. In fact, they were so short of supplies and ammunition that they had to borrow the gunpowder to fire welcoming salutes whenever the two forces came into contact. Well aware of the Spanish weakness, in 1812 the Russians established an outpost, called **Fort Ross**, sixty miles north of San Francisco. This further undermined Spanish sovereignty over the region, though the Russians abandoned the fort in 1841, selling it to John Sutter (who features prominently in later California history).

## THE MEXICAN ERA

While Spain, France and England were engaged in the bitter struggles of the Napoleonic Wars, the colonies of New Spain rebelled against imperial neglect, with Mexico finally gaining independence in 1821. The Mexican Republic, or the United States of Mexico as the new country called itself, governed California as a territory, though none of the fifteen distinct administrations it set up – lacking the money to pay for improvements and the soldiers needed to enforce the laws – was ever able to exercise any degree of authority.

The most important effect of the Mexican era was the final **secularization** in 1834, after years of gradual diminution, of the Franciscan missions. As most of the missionaries were Spanish, under Mexican rule they had seen their position steadily eroded by the increasingly wealthy, close-knit families of the *Californios* – Mexican immigrants who'd been granted vast tracts of ranchland. The government's intention was that half of the missions' extensive lands should go to the Indian converts; however, this was never carried out, and the few powerful families divided most of it up among themselves.

In many ways this was the most lawless and wantonly wasteful period of California's history, an era described by **Richard Henry Dana** – scion of a distinguished Boston family, who dropped out of Harvard to sail to California – in his 1840 book *Two Years Before the Mast*. Most of the agriculture and cottage industries that had developed under the missionaries disappeared, and it was a point of pride amongst the *Californios* not to do any work that couldn't be done from horseback. Dana's Puritan values led him to heap scorn upon the "idle and thriftless people" who made nothing for themselves. For example, the large herds of cattle that lived on the mission lands were slaughtered for their hides and sold to Yankee traders, who turned the hides into leather which they sold back to the *Californios* at a tidy profit. "In the hands of an enterprising people", he wrote, "what a country this might be."

## THE FIRST AMERICANS

Throughout the Mexican and Spanish eras, foreigners were legally banned from settling, and the few who showed up, mostly sick or injured sailors dropped off to regain their health, were often jailed until they proved themselves useful, either as craftsmen or as traders able to supply needed goods. In the late 1820s the first **Americans**, males without exception, began to make their way to California. They tended to fit in with the existing Mexican culture, often marrying into established families and converting to the Catholic faith. The American presence grew slowly but surely as more and more people emigrated, still mostly by way of a three-month sea voyage around Cape Horn. Among these was **Thomas Larkin**, a New England merchant who, in 1832, set up shop in Monterey, and later was instrumental in pointing the disgruntled *Californios* towards the more accommodating US; Larkin's wife Rachel was the first American woman on the West Coast.

The first people to make the four-month journey to California overland – in a covered wagon like in so many Hollywood Westerns – arrived in 1841, having forged a trail over the Sierra Nevada mountains via Truckee Pass, just north of Lake Tahoe. Soon after, hundreds of people each year were following in their tracks. In 1846, however, forty migrants, collectively known as the **Donner Party**, died when they were trapped in the mountains by early winter snowfall. The immense difficulties involved in reaching California, over land and by sea, kept population levels at a minimum, and by 1846 just seven thousand people, not counting Native Americans but including all the Spanish and Mexicans, lived in the entire region.

## THE MEXICAN-AMERICAN WAR

From the 1830s on – inspired by **Manifest Destiny**, the popular, almost religious belief that the United States was meant to cover the continent from coast to coast – US government policy regarding California was to buy all of Mexico's land north of the Rio Grande, the river that now divides the US and Mexico. President Andrew Jackson was highly suspicious of British designs on the West Coast – he himself had been held as a (14-year-old) prisoner of war during the Revolutionary War of 1776 – and various diplomatic overtures were made to the Mexican Republic, all of which backfired. In April 1846 Jackson's protégé, President James Polk, offered forty million dollars for all of New Mexico and the California territory, but his simultaneous annexation of the newly indpendent Republic of Texas – which Mexico still claimed – resulted in the outbreak of war.

Almost all the fighting of the **Mexican-American War** took place in Texas; only one real battle was ever fought on Californian soil, at San Pasqual, northeast of San Diego, where a roving US battalion was surprised by a band of pro-Mexican *Californios*, who killed 22 soldiers and wounded another 15 before withdrawing south into Mexico. Monterey, still the territorial capital, was captured by the US Navy without a shot being fired, and in January 1847, when the rebel *Californios* surrendered to the US forces at Cahuenga, near Los Angeles, the Americans controlled the entire West Coast.

Just before the war began California had made a brief foray into the field of self-government: the short-lived **Bear Flag Republic**, whose only lasting effect was to create what's still the state flag, a prowling grizzly bear with the words "California Republic" written below. In June 1846, American settlers in the Sonoma Valley took over the local *presidio* – long abandoned by the Mexicans – and declared California independent, which lasted for all of three weeks until the US forces took command.

## THE GOLD RUSH

As part of the Treaty of Guadalupe Hidalgo, which fomally ended the war in 1848, Mexico ceded all of the *Alta California* territory to the US. Nine days before the signing of the accord, in the distant foothills of the Sierra Nevada mountains, flakes of **gold** were discovered by workmen building a sawmill along the American River at Coloma, though it was months before this momentous conjunction of events became known.

At the time, California's non-Native American population was mostly concentrated in the few small towns along the coastal strip. Early rumours of gold attracted a trickle of prospectors, and, following news of their subsequent success, by the middle of 1849 – eighteen months after the initial find – men were flooding into California from all over, in the most madcap migration in world history. **Sutter's Fort**, a small agricultural community, trading post and stage stop which had been established six years earlier by John Sutter on the banks of the American River, was overrun by miners, who headed up into the nearby foothills to make their fortune. Some did, most didn't; but in any case, within fifteen years most of the gold had been picked clean. The miners moved on or went home and their camps vanished, prompting Mark Twain to write that "in no other land, in modern times, have towns so absolutely died and disappeared as in the old mining regions of California".

## STATEHOOD

Following the US takeover after the defeat of Mexico, a **Constitutional Convention** was held at Monterey in the autumn of 1849. The men who attended were not the miners – most of whom were more interested in searching for gold – but those who had been in California for some time (about three years on average). At the time, the Territory of California extended all the way east to Utah, so the main topic of discussion was where to draw the eastern boundary of the intended state. The drawing up of a state constitution was also important, since it was the basis on which California applied for admission to the US. In it were a couple of noteworthy inclusions. To protect the dignity of the manually labouring miners, **slavery** was prohibited; and to attract well-heeled **women** from the East Coast, California was the first state to recognize in legal terms the separate property of a married woman. In 1850, California was admitted to the US as the 31st State.

## THE INDIAN WARS

Though the US Civil War had little effect on California, many bloody battles were fought throughout the 1850s and 1860s by white settlers and US troops against the various Native American tribes whose lands the immigrants wanted. At first the government tried to move willing tribes to fairly large reservations, but as more settlers moved in the tribes were pushed onto smaller and smaller tracts. The most powerful resistance to the well-armed invaders came in the mountainous northeast of California, where a band of **Modoc** fought a long-running guerrilla war, using their superior knowledge of the terrain to evade the US troops.

Due to a combination of disease and lack of food, as well as deliberate acts of violence, the Native American population was drastically reduced, and by 1870 almost ninety percent had been wiped out. The survivors were concentrated onto small, relatively valueless reservations, where their descendants still live: the Cahuila near Palm Springs, the Paiute/Shoshone in the Owens Valley, and the Hupa on the northwest coast continue to reside near their ancestral homelands, and are quite naturally defensive of their privacy.

## THE BOOM YEARS: 1870–1900

After the Gold Rush, **San Francisco** boomed into a boisterous frontier town, exploding in population from 500 to 50,000 within five years. Though far removed from the mines themselves, the city was the main landing spot for shipborne argonauts (as the prospectors were called), and the main supply town. Moreover, it was the place where successful miners went to blow their hard-earned cash on the whisky and women of the **Barbary Coast**, then the raunchiest waterfront in the world, full of brothels, saloons and opium dens. Ten years later, San Francisco enjoyed an even bigger boom as a result of the silver mines of the Comstock Lode, in Nevada but owned in the main by San Franciscans, who displayed their wealth by building grand palaces and mansions on Nob Hill – still the city's most exclusive address.

The completion in 1869 of the **transcontinental railroad**, built using imported Chinese labourers, was a major turning point in the settlement of California. Whereas the trip across the country by stagecoach took at least a month, and was subject to scorching hot weather and attacks by hostile natives, the crossing could now be completed in just five days.

In 1875, when the Santa Fe railroad reached Los Angeles (the railroad company having extracted huge bribes from local officials to ensure the budding city wasn't bypassed), there were just ten thousand people living in the whole of **Southern California**, divided equally between San Diego and Los Angeles. A rate war developed between the two rival railroads, and ticket costs dropped to as little as $1 for a one-way ticket from New York. Land speculators placed advertisements in East Coast and European papers, offering cheap land for homesteaders in towns and suburbs all over the West Coast that as often as not existed only on paper. By the end of the nineteenth century, thousands of people, ranging from Midwestern farmers to the East Coast elite, had moved to California to take advantage of the fertile land and mild climate.

## MODERN TIMES

The greatest boost to California's fortunes was, of course, the **film industry**, which moved here from the East Coast in 1911, attracted by the temperate climate that enabled films to be shot outdoors year-round, and by the incredibly cheap land that allowed large indoor studios to be built at comparatively little cost. Within three years movies like D W Griffith's *Birth of a Nation* – most of which was filmed along the dry banks of the Los Angeles River – were being cranked out by the hundred.

**Hollywood**, a suburb of Los Angeles that was the site of many of the early studios – and ever since the buzzword for the entire entertainment industry – has done more to promote the mystique of California as a pleasure garden landscape than any other medium, disseminating images of its glamorous lifestyles around the globe. Los Angeles still dominates the world film industry, and, increasingly, is an international centre for the music business as well.

This widespread, idealized image had a magnetic effect during the **Great Depression** of the 1930s, when thousands of people from all over the country descended upon California, which was perceived to be – and for the most part was – immune from the economic downturn which crippled the rest of the US. From the Dust Bowl Midwest, entire families, who came to be known as **Okies**, packed up everything they owned and set off for the farms of the Central Valley, an epic journey captured by John Steinbeck's bestselling novel *The Grapes* *of Wrath*, in the photographs of Dorothea Lange, and in the baleful tunes of folk singer Woody Guthrie. Some Californians who feared losing their jobs to the incoming Okies formed vigilante groups and, with the complicity of local and state police, set up roadblocks along the main highways to prevent unemployed outsiders from entering the state.

One Depression-era initiative to alleviate the poverty, and to get the economy moving again, were the US government-sponsored **Works Progress Administration (WPA)** construction projects, ranging from restoring the California missions to building trails and park facilities, and commissioning art works like the marvellous Social Realist murals in San Francisco's Coit Tower.

Things turned around when **World War II** brought heavy industry to California, as ship-yards and aeroplane factories sprang up, provid-ing well-paid employment in wartime factories. After the war, most stayed on, and still today California companies — McDonnell Douglas, Lockheed, Rockwell and General Dynamics, for example — make up the roll call of suppliers to the US military and space programmes. More recently, the "Silicon Valley" area south of San Francisco has been at the forefront of hi-tech developments in the computer industry.

After the war many of the soldiers who'd passed through on their way to the battle-grounds of the South Pacific came back to California and decided to stay on. There was plenty of well-paid work, the US government subsidized house purchases for war veterans and, most importantly, constructed the **free-ways** and Interstate highways that enabled land speculators to build new commuter suburbs on land that up until then had been used for farms and citrus orchards.

The **1950s** brought prosperity to the bulk of middle-class America (typified by President Eisenhower's goal of "two cars in every garage and a chicken in every pot"), and California, particularly San Francisco, became a nexus for alternative artists and writers, spurring an immigration of intellectuals that by the end of the decade had become manifest as the **Beat Generation**, pegged "Beatniks", in honour of Sputnik, the Soviet space satellite, by San Francisco columnist Herb Caen.

California remained at the forefront of youth and social upheavals into and throughout the **1960s**. In a series of drug tests carried out at Stanford University — paid for by the CIA, who were interested in developing a "truth drug" for interrogation purposes — unwitting students were dosed with LSD. One of the guinea pigs was the writer Ken Kesey, who had just published the highly acclaimed novel *One Flew Over the Cuckoo's Nest*. Kesey quite liked the experience and soon secured a personal supply of the drug (which was as yet still legal) and toured the West Coast to spread the word of "**Acid**". In and around San Francisco Kesey and his crew, the Merry Pranksters, turned on huge crowds at Electric Kool-Aid Acid Tests — in which LSD was diluted into bowls of the soft drink Kool-Aid — complete with psychedelic light shows and music by the Grateful Dead. The Acid craze reached its height during the **Summer of Love** in 1967, when the entire Haight-Ashbury district of San Francisco seemed populated by barefoot and drugged Flower Children.

Within a year the superficial peace of Flower Power was shattered, as protests mounted against US involvement in the **Vietnam War**; Martin Luther King and Bobby Kennedy, heroes of left-leaning youth, were both gunned down — Kennedy in Los Angeles after winning the California Primary of the 1968 Presidential elec-tion. By the end of the 1960s the "system", in California especially, seemed to be at breaking point. The militant **Black Panthers**, a violent group of black radicals based in Oakland, terror-ized a white population that had earlier been enthusiastic supporters of the Civil Rights Movement, and the atrocities committed by **Charles Manson** and his "Family" proved what the rest of the US had known all along: that California was full of madmen and murderers.

The antiwar protests, concentrated at the University of California campus in Berkeley, continued through the early **1970s**. Emerging from the milieu of revolutionary and radical groups, the Symbionese Liberation Army, a small, well-armed and stridently revolutionary group, set about the overthrow of the US, attract-ing media (and FBI) attention by murdering civil servants, robbing banks and, most famously, kidnapping nineteen-year-old heiress **Patty Hearst**. Amid much media attention Hearst converted to the SLA's cause, changing her name to Tanya and for the next two years — until her capture in 1977 — went underground, provoking national debate about her motives and beliefs.

After the unrest of the previous decade, the **late 1970s** were decidedly dull. The one interesting phenomenon was the rise of **cults**, among them LA's Scientology Church, megalomaniac L Ron Hubbard's personality-testing sect; the Moonies, who pestered people at airports and public places all over the coast; and San Francisco's People's Temple, of which over a thousand members died when their leader, Jim Jones, dosed them with cyanide in a religious service held at their commune in Guyana. The most public and visible of the lot were the followers of the **Bhagwan Shree Rajshneesh**, clothed entirely in shades of red.

Californian **politics**, after Watergate and the end of American involvement in Vietnam, seemed to lose whatever idealistic fervour they might once have had, and popular culture withdrew into self-satisfaction, typified by the smug harmonies of musicians like the Eagles and Jackson Browne. While the Sixties upheavals were overseen by California Governor Ronald Reagan, who was ready and willing to fight the long-haired hippies, the 1970s saw the reign of "Governor Moonbeam" Jerry Brown, under whose leadership California enacted some of the most stringent **anti-pollution** measures in the world – one of which pays environmental activists to expose corporate polluters, offering a 25 percent commission on the multi-million-dollar fines imposed by the courts. The state also actively encouraged the development of renewable forms of energy such as solar and wind power, and protected the entire coastline from despoilation and development. California also decriminalized the possession of under an ounce of marijuana (though it remains an offence to grow or sell it), and the harvesting of **marijuana** in both states continues to account for over $1 billion each year, making it the number-one cash crop in the number-one agricultural region in the US.

The easy-money **Eighties** crash-landed in a tangled mess, with LA junk-bond king Michael Milkin convicted of multi-billion-dollar fraud and the S&L banking scandals enmeshing such high-ranking politicos as California Senator Alan Cranston, and the **Nineties** kicked off with a stagnant property market, rising unemployment and no sign of hope on the horizon.

In the cities the picture is especially bleak. In **Los Angeles**, the videotaped beating of black motorist Rodney King by uniformed officers of the LA Police Department, and the subsequent acquittal of those officers by the jurors of conservative Simi Valley, sparked off destructive **rioting** in April 1992. State and federal authorities, forced into taking notice of LA's endemic poverty and violence, promised all sorts of new initiatives – with, as yet, few concrete results. The race issue also dominated the year-long trial of black former football star **O J Simpson** – accused and finally acquitted of murdering his ex-wife and a male friend – splitting public opinion into directly opposed camps of black and white. The result, when it came, prompted jubilation and disbelief in equal measure.

Such events, coupled with a chain of natural disasters – the wildfires of 1993, followed by the devastating 6.8-scale earthquake (see p.128 for more details) and mud slides of January 1994 – have so eroded local morale that for the first time in history a majority of residents would like to move *away from* LA – if they could. Many of those with the means have upped sticks to Oregon, Washington or the desert states to the east. Those who remain fence themselves off from the lawless streets in exclusive, security-patrolled compounds, and the 1994 passage of Proposition 187, a state law denying access to health and education services to illegal immigrants, has only served to widen the chasm between rich and poor.

San Francisco, too, has been hit hard: on top of AIDS-related illnesses stretching health services to breaking point (more than one in every hundred residents has already died from it), the area has been hit by a series of natural disasters. An **earthquake** in October 1989 devastated much of the San Francisco Bay Area, followed two years later by a massive **fire** in the Oakland Hills which burned over two thousand homes and killed two dozen people – the third worst fire in US history.

Somehow, despite all this, California still clings on to its aura as something of a promised land, and, barring its complete destruction by the **Big One** – the earthquake that's destined one day to drop half of the state into the Pacific and wipe out the rest under massive tidal waves – the state seems set to continue much as it is: source (and home) of so much of the nation's wealth, yet displaying the starkest examples of some of its most pressing social problems.

# CALIFORNIA WILDLIFE

Though popularly imagined as little more than palm trees and golden sand beaches, for sheer range of landscape, California is hard to beat: with glaciated alpine peaks and meadows, desolate desert sand dunes and flat, fertile agricultural plains, it's no wonder Hollywood film-makers have so often and successfully used California locations to simulate so many distant and exotic scenes. These diverse landscapes also support an immense variety of plant and animal life, much of which – due to the protection offered by the various state and national parks, forests and wilderness areas – is both easily accessible and unspoiled by encroaching civilization.

## BACKGROUND: LANDSCAPES, GEOLOGY & EARTHQUAKES

California's landscape has been formed over millions of years through the interaction of all the main geological processes: Ice Age glaciation, erosion, earthquakes and volcanic eruptions. The most impressive results can be seen in **Yosemite National Park**, east of San Francisco, where solid walls of granite have been sliced and shaped into unforgettable cliffs and chasms. In contrast, the sand dunes of **Death Valley** are being constantly shaped and reshaped by the dry desert winds, surrounded by foothills tinted by oxidized mineral deposits into every colour of the spectrum.

**Earthquakes** – which earned Los Angeles the truck driver's nickname "Shakeytown" – are the most powerful expression of the volatile unrest underlying the placid surface. California sits on the Pacific "Ring of Fire", at the junction of two tectonic plates slowly drifting deep within the earth. Besides the occasional earthquake – like the 1906 quake which flattened San Francisco, or the 1994 tremor which collapsed many of LA's freeways – this instability is also the cause of California's many **volcanoes**. Distinguished by their symmetrical, conical shape, almost all of them are now dormant, though Mount Lassen, in Northern California, did erupt in 1914 and 1915, destroying much of the surrounding forest. Along with the boiling mud pools that accompany even the dormant volcanoes, the most attractive features of volcanic regions are the bubbling **hot springs** – pools of water that flow up from deep underground, heated to a sybaritically soothing temperature. Hot springs occur naturally all over the state, and though some have now been developed into luxurious health spas, most remain in their natural condition, where you can soak your bones *au naturel* surrounded by mountain meadows or wide-open deserts. The best of these are listed throughout the *Guide*.

Of the **wildlife**, though some of the most fantastic creatures, like the grizzly bear – a ten-foot-tall, two-ton giant that still adorns the state flag of California – and the California condor – one of the world's largest birds, with a wingspan of over eight feet – are now extinct in their natural habitats, plenty more are still alive and thriving, like the otters, elephant seals and gray whales seen all along the coast, and the chubby marmots – shy mammals often found sunning themselves on rocks in higher reaches of the mountains. Plant life is equally varied, from the brilliant but short-lived desert wild flowers to the timeless Bristlecone pine trees, which live for thousands of years on the arid peaks of the Great Basin desert.

Below you will find details of the major **ecosystems** of California. They are inevitably brief: the area encompasses almost 320,000 square miles, ranging from moist coastal forests and snowcapped Sierra Nevada peaks to Death Valley, 276 feet below sea level with an annual rainfall of two inches, and is inhabited by multitudes of species. Native to

California are 54 species of cactus, 123 species of amphibians and reptiles, 260 species of birds, and between 27,000–28,000 species of insects. See "Books" for recommendations of more specific habitat guides. Bear in mind, also, that museums all over the state examine and exhibit the natural world in depth, notably Monterey's superb Aquarium – see the *Guide* for details.

## THE OCEAN

The Pacific Ocean determines California's climate, keeping the coastal temperatures moderate all year round. During the spring and summer, cold nutrient-rich waters rise or well up to produce cooling banks of fog and abundant crops of phytoplankton (microscopic algae). The algae nourishes creatures such as krill (small shrimps), which in their turn provide baby food for juvenile fish. This food chain provides fodder for millions of nesting seabirds, as well as harbour and elephant seals, California sea lions and whales. **Gray whales**, the most common species spotted from land, were once almost hunted to the point of extinction, but have returned to the coast in large numbers. During their southward migration to their breeding grounds off Mexico, from December to January, it is easy to spot them from prominent headlands all along the coast, and most harbours have charter services offering whale-watching tours. On their way back to the Arctic Sea, in February and March, the newborn whale pups can sometimes be seen playfully leaping out of the water, or "breaching". Look for the whale's white-plumed spout – once at the surface, it will usually blow several times in succession.

### TIDEPOOLS

California's shoreline is composed of three primary ecosystems: tidepools, sandy beach and estuary. To explore the **tidepools**, first consult a local newspaper to see when the low tides (two daily) will occur. Be careful of waves, don't be out too far from the shore when the tide returns, and also watch your step – there are many small lives underfoot. There are miles of beaches with tidepools, some of the best at Pacific Grove near Monterey. Here you will find sea anemones (they look like green zinnias), hermit crabs, purple and green shore crabs, red

sponges, purple sea urchins, starfish ranging from the size of a dime to the size of a hub cap, mussels, abalone and chinese-hat limpets – to name a few. You may also see black oyster-catchers, their squawking easily heard over the surf, foraging for an unwary, lips-agape mussel. Gulls and black turnstones are also common, and during summer brown pelicans dive for fish just offshore.

The life of the tidepool party is the **hermit crab**, who protects its soft and vulnerable hindquarters with scavenged shells, usually those of the aptly named black turban snail. Hermit crabs scurry busily around in search of a detritus snack, or scuffle with other hermit crabs over the proprietorship of vacant snail shells.

Pacific Grove is also home to large populations of **sea otters**. Unlike most marine mammals, sea otters keep themselves warm with a thick soft coat rather than blubber. The trade in sea otter pelts brought entrepreneurial Russian and British fur-hunters to the West Coast, and by the mid-nineteenth century the otters were virtually extinct. In 1938, a small population was discovered near Big Sur, and with careful protection otters have re-established themselves in the southern part of their range.

Sea otters are charming creatures with big rubbery noses and Groucho Marx moustaches. With binoculars, it's easy to spot them amongst the bobbing kelp, where they lie on their backs opening sea urchins with a rock, or sleep entwined within a seat belt of kelp which keeps them from floating away. The bulk of the population resides between Monterey Bay and the Channel Islands, but – aside from Pacific Grove – the best places to see them are Point Lobos State Park, the 17-Mile Drive and the Monterey Wharf, where, along with sea lions, they often come to beg for fish.

Many of the **seaweeds** you see growing from the rocks are edible. As one would expect from a Pacific beachfront, there are also **palms** – sea palms, with four-inch-long rubbery stems and flagella-like fronds. Their thick root-like holdfasts provide shelter for small crabs. You will also find giant **kelp** washed up on shore – harvested commercially for use in thickening ice cream.

### SANDY BEACHES

The long, golden **sandy beaches** for which California is so famous, may look sterile from a distance. However, observe the margin of sand exposed as a gentle wave recedes, and you will see jetstreams of small bubbles emerge from numerous clams and mole crabs. Small shore birds called sanderlings race amongst the waves in search of these morsels, and sand dollars are often easy to find along the high tide line.

The most unusual sandy-shore bathing beauties are the **northern elephant seals**, which will tolerate rocky beaches but favour soft sand mattresses for their rotund torsos. The males, or bulls, can reach lengths of over six metres and weigh upwards of four tons; the females, or cows, are petite by comparison – four metres long, and averaging a mere two thousand pounds in weight. They have large eyes, adapted for spotting fish in deep or murky waters; indeed, elephant seals are the deepest diving mammals, capable of staying underwater for twenty minutes at a time, reaching depths of over four thousand feet, where the pressure is over a hundred times that at the surface. They have to dive so deeply in order to avoid the attentions of the great white sharks who lurk offshore, for whom they are a favourite meal.

Like otters, elephant seals were decimated by commercial whalers in the mid-nineteenth century for their blubber and hides. By the turn of the century less than a hundred remained, but careful protection has partially restored the California population, which is concentrated on the Channel and Farallon Islands and at Año Nuevo State Park.

Elephant seals only emerge from the ocean to breed or moult; their name comes from the male's long trunk-like proboscis, through which it produces a resonant pinging sound that biologists call "trumpeting", which is how it attracts a mate. The Año Nuevo beach is the best place to observe this ritual. In December and January, the bulls haul themselves out of the water and battle for dominance. The predominant, or alpha, male will do most of the mating, siring as many as fifty young pups, one per mating, in a season. Other males fight it out at the fringes, each managing one or two couplings with the hapless, defenceless females. During this time, the beach is a seething mass of ton upon ton of blubbery seals – flopping sand over their back to keep cool, squabbling with their neighbours while making

rude snoring and belching sounds. The adults depart in March but the weaned pups hang around until May.

Different age groups of elephant seals continue to use the beach at different times throughout the summer for moulting. Elephant seals are completely unafraid of people, but are huge enough to hurt or even kill you if you get in their way, though you're allowed to get close, except during mating season, when entry into the park is restricted to ranger-guided tours. See the *Guide* for more details.

## ESTUARIES

Throughout California, many **estuarine or rivermouth habitats** have been filled, diked, drained, "improved" with marinas or contaminated by pollutants. Those that survive intact consist of a mixture of mud flats, exposed only at low tide, and salt marsh, together forming a critical wildlife area that provides nurseries for many kinds of invertebrates and fish, and nesting and wintering grounds for many birds. Cord grass, a dominant wetlands plant, produces five to ten times as much oxygen and nutrients per acre as does wheat.

Many interesting creatures live in the thick organic ooze, including the fat Innkeeper, a revolting-looking pink hot dog of a worm that sociably shares its burrow with a small crab and a fish, polychaete worms, clams and other goodies. Most prominent of estuary birds are the great blue herons and great egrets. Estuaries are the best place to see wintering shore birds such as dunlin, dowitchers, east and western sandpipers and yellowlegs. Peregrine falcons and osprey are also found here.

Important Californian estuaries include Elkhorn Slough, near Monterey, San Francisco Bay and Bolinas Lagoon.

## COASTAL BLUFFS

Along the shore, coastal meadows are bright with pink and yellow sand verbena, lupines, sea rocket, sea fig and the bright orange California poppy, the state flower. Slightly inland, hills are covered with coastal scrub, which consists largely of coyote brush. Coastal canyons contain broadleaf trees such as California laurel, alder, buckeye and oaks – and a tangle of sword ferns, horsetail and cow parsnip.

Common rainy-season canyon inhabitants include four-inch-long banana slugs and rough-skinned newts. In winter, orange and black **Monarch butterflies** inhabit large roosts in a few discreet locales, such as Bolinas, Monterey and Pacific Grove. Coastal thickets also provide homes to weasels, bobcats, grey fox, racoons, black-tailed deer, California quail and garter snakes. Tule elk, a once common member of the deer family, have also been reintroduced to the wild; a good place to view them is on Tomales Point at the Point Reyes National Seashore.

## RIVER VALLEYS

Like most fertile **river valleys**, the Sacramento and Central (San Joaquin) valleys have both been greatly affected by agriculture. Riparian (streamside) vegetation has been logged, wetlands drained and streams contaminated by agricultural runoff. Despite this, the riparian habitat that does remain is a prime wildlife habitat. Wood ducks, kingfishers, swallows and warblers are common, as are grey fox, racoon and striped skunks. The Sacramento National Wildlife Refuge has one of the world's largest concentrations of snow geese during winter months. Other common winter migrants include Canada geese, green-winged and cinnamon teals, pintail, shovelers and wigeon. These refuges are well worth a visit, but don't be alarmed by large numbers of duck-hunters – the term "refuge" is a misnomer. However, most have tour routes where hunting is prohibited.

Vernal pools are a valley community unique to California. Here, hardpan soils prevent the infiltration of winter rains, creating seasonal ponds. As these ponds slowly evaporate in April and May, sharply defined concentric floral rings come into bloom. The white is meadow-foam, the blue is the violet-like downingia, and the yellow is goldfields. Swallows, meadow-larks, yellowlegs and stilts can also be found. Jepson Prairie Nature Conservancy Reserve is the easiest to visit, south of Sacramento near the small town of Rio Vista.

## FORESTS

Perhaps the most notable indigenous features of Californian forests are the wide expanses of **redwood and sequoia trees**. It's easy to confuse the coastal species, *Sequoia sempervi-*

*rens*, or redwood, with the *Sequoiadendron giganteum*, or giant sequoia (pronounced *suk-oy-ah*), as both have the same fibrous reddish-brown bark. Redwoods are the world's tallest trees, sequoias have the greatest base circumference and are the largest single organisms on earth. Both species can live for over two thousand years, and recent research now indicates a maximum age of 3500 years for the Sequoia. Their longevity is partially due to their bark: rich in tannin, it protects the tree from fungal and insect attack and inhibits fire damage. In fact fire is beneficial to these trees and necessary for their germination; indeed, prescribed fires are set and controlled around them. The wood of these great trees is much sought after both for its beauty – near any forest you'll see signs advertising redwood burl furniture – and its resistance to decay (the bark continues to protect the tree for several hundred years after felling).

They are the only surviving members of a family of perhaps forty species of trees which, fossil records show, grew worldwide 175 million years ago. Now just a few pockets remain, and a tremendous battle between environmentalists and loggers is being waged over the remaining acres. These virgin forests provide homes to unique creatures such as the spotted owl and marbled murrelet.

**Redwoods** are a relict species, which means that they flourished in a moister climate during the Arcto-Tertiary (just after the golden age of the dinosaurs), and now occupy a much-reduced range. As the weather patterns changed, redwoods slowly retreated to their current near-coastal haunts. Today, they are found from the border with Oregon to just south of Monterey.

The floor of the redwood forest is a hushed place with little sunlight, the air suffused with a rufous glow from the bark, which gives the trees its name. One of the commonest ground covers in the redwood forest is the redwood sorrel, or oxalis. It has shamrock leaves and tubular pink flowers. Ferns are also numerous. Birds are usually high in the canopy and hard to see, but you might hear the double-whistled song of the varied thrush, or the "chickadee" call from the bird of that name. Roosevelt elk, larger than the tule elk, also inhabit the humid northwest forests. Prairie Creek Redwoods State Park, near the border with Oregon, has a large herd.

**Sequoias** are found on the western slopes of the Sierra Nevada, most notably in Yosemite and Kings Canyon National Parks – though saplings given as state gifts can be found growing to more modest dimensions all over the world.

The sequoia forest tends to be slightly more open than the redwood forest. Juvenile sequoias – say up to a thousand years old – exhibit a slender conical shape which, as the lower branches fall away, ages to the classical heavy-crowned shape with its columnar trunk. For its bulk, its cones are astonishingly small, no bigger than a hen's egg, but they live on the tree for up to thirty years before falling.

## THE SIERRA NEVADA

In the late nineteenth century, the environmental movement was founded when John Muir fell in love with the **Sierra Nevada** mountains, which he called the Range of Light. Muir fought a losing battle to save Hetch Hetchy, a valley said to be more beautiful than Yosemite, but in the process the Sierra Club was born and the move to save America's remaining wilderness began.

The Sierra mountains, which run almost the entire length of the state, have a sharp, craggy, freshly glaciated look. Many of the same conifers can be found as in the forests further west, but ponderosa and lodge-pole pines are two of the dominants, and the forests tend to be drier and more open. Lower elevation forests contain incense cedar, sugar pine (which has the longest pine cones – over eighteen inches – in the world) and black oak. The oaks, along with dogwood and willows, produce spectacular autumnal colour. The east side is drier and has large groves of aspen, a beautiful white-barked tree with small round leaves that tremble in the wind. **Wildflowers** flourish for a few short months – shooting star, elephant's head and wild onions in early spring, asters and yarrow later in the season.

The dominant campground scoundrels are two sorts of noisy, squawking bird: Steller's jays and Clark's nutcrackers. Black bears, who may make a raid on your campground, pose more danger to iceboxes than humans, but nonetheless you should treat them with caution. The friendly twenty-pound pot-bellied rodents that lounge around at the fringes of your encampment are **marmots**, who probably do more damage than bears; some specialize in chewing on radiator hoses of parked cars.

Other common birds include mountain chickadees, yellow-rumped warblers, white-crowned sparrows and juncos. Deer, golden-mantled ground squirrels and chipmunks are also plentiful.

## THE GREAT BASIN

The little-known **Great Basin** stretches from the northernmost section of the state down almost to Death Valley, encompassing all of Nevada and parts of all the other bordering states. It's a land of many shrubs and few streams, and what streams do exist drain into saline lakes rather than the ocean.

**Mono Lake**, reflecting the 13,000-foot peaks of Yosemite National Park, is a spectacular example. Its salty waters support no fish but lots of algae, brine shrimp and brine flies, the latter two providing a smorgasbord for nesting gulls (the term "seagull" isn't strictly correct – many gulls nest inland) and migrating phalaropes and grebes. Like many Great Basin lakes, Mono Lake faces destruction through diversion of its freshwater feeder streams to provide water for the city of Los Angeles.

Great Basin plants tolerate hot summers, cold winters and little rain. The dominant Great Basin plant is sagebrush. Its dusky green leaves are very aromatic, especially after a summer thunderstorm. Other common plants include bitterbrush, desert peach, junipers and piñon pines. Piñon cones contain tasty nuts that were a mainstay of the Paiute diet.

The **sage grouse** is one of the most distinctive Great Basin birds. These turkey-like birds feed on sage during the winter and depend on it for nesting and courtship habitat. In March and April, males gather at dancing grounds called leks, where they puff out small pink balloons on their necks, make soft drumbanging calls, and in general succeed in looking and sounding rather silly. The hens coyly scout out the talent by feigning greater interest in imaginary seeds.

**Pronghorns** are beautiful Africanesque tawny-gold antelope seen in many places in the Great Basin. Watch for their twinkling white rumps as you drive.

Other Great Basin denizens include golden eagles, pinyon jays, black-billed magpies, coyotes, feral horses and burros, black-tailed jackrabbits and western rattlesnakes. Large concentrations of waterfowl gather at Tule Lake in northeastern California, where hundreds of wintering **bald eagles** gather in November before the cold really sets in.

## THE MOJAVE DESERT

The **Mojave Desert** lies in the southeast corner of the state, near Death Valley. Like the Great Basin, the vegetation here consists primarily of drought-adapted shrubs, one of the commonest of which is Creosote, with its olive-green leaves and puffy yellow flowers. Death Valley is renowned for its early spring wild-flower shows. The alluvial fans are covered with desert trumpet, gravel ghost and pebble pincushion. Quantity and timing of rainfall determines when the floral display peaks, but it's usually some time between mid-February and mid-April in the lower elevations, late April to early June higher up.

Besides shrubs, the Mojave has many interesting kinds of cactus. These include barrel, cottontop, cholla and beavertail cactus, and many members of the yucca family. Yuccas have stiff, lance-like leaves with sharp tips; a conspicuous representative is the **Joshua Tree**, whose twisting arm-like branches are covered with shaggy upward-pointing leaf fronds, which can reach to thirty feet high.

Many Mojave desert animals conserve body moisture by foraging at night, including the kit fox, wood rat and various kinds of mice. The **kangaroo rat**, an appealing animal that hops rather than runs, has specially adapted kidneys that enable it to survive without drinking water. Other desert animals include mammals such as the Mojave ground squirrel, bighorn and coyote; birds like the roadrunner, ash-throated flycatcher, ladder-backed woodpecker, verdin and Lucy's warbler; and reptiles like the Mojave rattlesnake, sidewinder and chuckwalla.

# CALIFORNIA ON FILM

California is probably the nearest America has come to providing itself with the proverbial land of milk and honey. It's also the home of the world's film industry: film-makers shifted to Hollywood as far back as the 1910s, drawn here by the climate and low rents and the rich array of natural landscapes, and as such the state has figured regularly in countless movies, either as itself or masquerading as somewhere else in the world.

Where appropriate we've mentioned a number of films in the *Guide*. What follows is a selection that runs a gamut from the obvious to what are hopefully a few surprises. It's a wide and disparate list, but if there is a factor which links the movies it's perhaps California's obsession with itself – and just how much mileage an almost auto-erotic navel-gazing and starry-eyed Hollywood has got out of zealously pulling skeletons from its own luxurious closet.

**Alex in Wonderland** (Paul Mazursky 1970). Hollywood satire given a Fellini slant, as first-time director Donald Sutherland frets and fantasizes over his next picture. Plenty of late-1960s Hollywood ambience.

**American Gigolo** (Paul Schrader 1980). Arty, muted, pulp thriller about hunky male prostitute

Richard Gere framed for political murder. High-sheen view of LA life and mores: very 1980s.

**American Graffiti** (George Lucas 1973). Remarkable cast in enormously popular, influential small-town teen rites of passage movie, based on Lucas's hometown of Modesto.

**The Bad and the Beautiful** (Vincente Minnelli 1952). Overwrought Hollywood self-analysis at its best, with Kirk Douglas as a ruthless movie producer trying to reclaim those he launched and subsequently lost.

**Bad Day at Black Rock** (John Sturges 1954). Creepy Cinemascope exposé of the racial tension that arises in a small Mojave Desert town over the covered-up murder of a Japanese farmer. Spencer Tracy stars as the one-armed stranger out to set things right.

**Bagdad Café** (Percy Adlon 1988). Lovable, inspiring fable about a bunch of ill-matched drifters thrown together in the Mojave Desert, the US debut of German director Adlon.

**Barfly** (Barbet Schroeder 1987). Entertaining self-indulgence, penned by low-life specialist Charles Bukowski and featuring an admirably scatty, brave performance from Mickey Rourke as a drunken writer.

**Beverly Hills Cop** (Martin Brest 1984). Street-smart Detroit cop Eddie Murphy is let loose in LA's ritziest environs in this phenomenally successful crime comedy.

**The Big Sleep** (Howard Hawks 1946). Detective classic, starring Humphrey Bogart as Chandler's moral shamus Philip Marlowe and ripe with the corrupt atmosphere of nocturnal, studio-bound LA.

**Big Wednesday** (John Milius 1978). Highly admired in some quarters, this is a California surfing movie of epic intentions, following the lives of three beach buddies during the 1960s.

**A Bigger Splash** (Jack Hazan 1974). Meandering, semi-documentary cult film about the California influence on David Hockney's paintings.

**Bird Man of Alcatraz** (John Frankenheimer 1962). Earnest but over-long study of real-life convicted killer Robert Stroud (Burt Lancaster) who becomes an authority on birds while in prison.

**The Birds** (Alfred Hitchcock 1963). Some brilliant set pieces in this allegory about our hostile feathered friends, set on the Northern California coast.

**Bob and Carol and Ted and Alice** (Paul Mazursky 1969). Still funny hit film about Southern California attitudes and values, contrasting the sexual hang-ups and experimentations of two married couples.

**Boyz n the Hood** (John Singleton 1991). Singleton's debut film, a sober portrayal of life in South Central LA, highlights the odds against success in a community riddled with drugs, poverty and violence.

**Bullitt** (Peter Yates 1968). Steve McQueen gives an assured central performance in this overpraised but entertaining cop thriller, which contains the definitive San Francisco car chase.

**California** (John Farrow 1946). Mia's dad directed Barbara Stanwyck and Ray Milland in an elaborate Western about the founding of the state.

**California Suite** (Herbert Ross 1978). Maggie Smith and Jane Fonda shine in two episodes of gagmeister Neil Simon's four-part omnibus script, set in the *Beverly Hills Hotel*. The tone ranges from low-grade slapstick to bittersweet sentimentality.

**Car Wash** (Michael Schultz 1976). Crude, cool microcosmic black American comedy recording a day in the life of an LA car wash. A big hit.

**Chan Is Missing** (Wayne Wang 1982). Low-budget sleeper hangs a thoroughly impressive, unpredictable study of San Francisco's Chinatown and the Chinese-American experience on a mystery-suspense peg. Often satirical, it shows a Chinatown tourists don't usually see.

**Chinatown** (Roman Polanski 1974). Superlative detective thriller, with Jack Nicholson sleuthing in a 1930s LA crawling with corruption. Faye Dunaway and John Huston co-star in Robert Towne's intricately structured, Oscar-winning script.

**Citizen Kane** (Orson Welles 1941). Some call it the greatest film ever made, relevant for its depiction of Xanadu, which was more than loosely based on William Randolph Hearst's San Simeon – where the aging tycoon Kane (Welles) holes up in massively empty luxury with his no-talent mistress (Dorothy Comingore).

**Clueless** (Amy Heckerling 1995). A fitfully amusing foray into the empty heads of shop-ping-obsessed Beverly Hills High schoolgirls, its script peppered with contemporary rich-kid lingo.

**Colors** (Dennis Hopper 1988). Gritty location shooting enhances this violent, controversial LA gang warfare drama, with Robert Duvall and Sean Penn turning in resourceful performances as a veteran cop and his young firebrand sidekick.

**Coming Home** (Hal Ashby 1978). Award-winning drama, as politically naive volunteer-nurse Jane Fonda falls in love with paraplegic Jon Voight while her husband Bruce Dern is off fighting the Vietnam War. It reeks of soft-centred, California liberal attitudes circa 1968.

**The Conversation** (Francis Ford Coppola 1974). This chilling character study of San Francisco surveillance expert Harry Caul (Gene Hackman at his finest) is one of the best films of the Watergate era. The key, titular sequence is set in Union Square, San Francisco.

**Cutter's Way** (Ivan Passer 1981). Cult film teaming beach bum Jeff Bridges with crippled Vietnam vet John Heard in investigating upper-echelon homicide in soured California paradise. Santa Barbara is the main setting.

**The Day of the Locust** (John Schlesinger 1975). Overdone treatment of Nathanael West's famous novel that brings the apocalypse to Hollywood.

**Devil in a Blue Dress** (Carl Franklin 1995). "Easy" Rawlins, the 1940s black PI of Walter Mosely's books, hits the big screen in the form of Denzel Washington. A fairly stylish interpretation.

**Dim Sum** (Wayne Wang 1985). Appealing little film about a more-or-less westernized Chinese family in San Francisco. A treat.

**Dirty Harry** (Don Siegel 1971). Sleek and exciting sequel-spawning thriller casts Clint Eastwood in epitomical role as neo-fascist San Francisco cop. Morally debatable, technically dynamic.

**D.O.A.** (Rudolph Mate 1949). Surprisingly involving suspense in which Edmond O'Brien tries to discover who poisoned him before he dies. Excellent use of LA and SF locales.

**Double Indemnity** (Billy Wilder 1944). Sensational *film noir* has femme fatale Barbara Stanwyck duping LA insurance salesman Fred MacMurray into murdering her husband.

**Down and Out in Beverly Hills** (Paul Mazursky 1986). Upwardly mobile hobo Nick Nolte works wonders on the neurotic family of Richard Dreyfuss and Bette Midler, in this satire of filthily nouveau riche Californians.

**Earthquake** (Mark Robson 1974). Topnotch special effects saddled with stock B-movie characterizations, as LA topples into the ground. Starring square-jawed Charlton Heston.

**Escape from Alcatraz** (Don Siegel 1979). Tense, well-crafted picture, based on a true story about an escape from the famous prison.

**Experiment in Terror** (Blake Edwards 1962). The inspiration for David Lynch's *Twin Peaks*, this entertaining Cold War period piece has dozens of FBI agents trying to track down an obscene phone caller in San Francisco's Twin Peaks neighbourhood.

**Falling Down** (Joel Schumacher 1993). Unable to tolerate the height-of-summer LA traffic jam in which he finds himself, Michael Douglas abandons his car to trawl around some of the city's less lovely neighbourhoods, wreaking havoc with every step.

**Family Plot** (Alfred Hitchcock 1976). The master's last film is a lark about stolen jewels, kidnapping and psychic sleuthing in and around San Francisco.

**Faster, Pussycat! Kill! Kill!** (Russ Meyer 1965). Meyer's wonderfully lurid action flick unleashes a trio of depraved go-go girls upon an unsuspecting California desert. One of a kind.

**Fat City** (John Huston 1972). Superb cast in a beautifully directed portrait of barflies, has-beens and no-hopes on Stockton's small-time boxing circuit.

**Fearless** (Peter Weir 1993). Jeff Bridges survives a plane crash and tries to make sense of his life while stumbling through San Francisco.

**52 Pick-up** (John Frankenheimer 1986). Blackmailed businessman Roy Schneider is up against three of the slimiest LA extortionists imaginable in this well-crafted adaptation of Elmore Leonard's novel.

**Forty Pounds of Trouble** (Norman Jewison 1962). Tony Curtis comedy about an orphan who enters the life of a casino manager; some neat character acting and a climactic visit to Disneyland.

**Foxes** (Adrian Lyne 1980). Underrated if sometimes slick study of four troubled teenage girls in the San Fernando Valley.

**Gates of Heaven** (Errol Morris 1978). Cult documentary about California pet cemeteries (particularly the Bubbling Well Pet Memorial Park in Napa) that's oddly humorous and touching in its revelations about the human condition.

**The Graduate** (Mike Nichols 1967). Dustin Hoffman in his breakthrough role as the college grad whose attentions shift from mother Anne Bancroft to daughter Katharine Ross. Dated, but understandably a huge hit. UCLA doubles for Berkeley campus.

**Grand Canyon** (Lawrence Kasdan 1992). Danny Glover, Kevin Kline and Steve Martin cross LA's many racial and class barriers in this black, symbol-laden buddy movie that expresses the everyday horrors of living in the city in the 1990s.

**The Grapes of Wrath** (John Ford 1940). California is a dubious Promised Land in this tremendous adaptation of Steinbeck's novel about uprooted Depression-era sharecroppers.

**Greed** (Erich von Stroheim 1924). Legendary, lengthy silent masterpiece about the squalid, ultimately tragic marriage of a blunt ex-miner with a dental practice on San Francisco's Polk Street, and a simple girl from nearby Oakland. Unforgettable, especially the classic finale in Death Valley.

**Harper** (Jack Smight 1966). High-powered cast, led by gumshoe Paul Newman, in flat-footed but popular attempt to recreate the spirit of the old Bogart private eye films set in typically overripe Southern California.

**Heat** (Michael Mann 1995). Much-hyped meeting of the Method masters – De Niro and Pacino – in a disappointingly downbeat thriller, with some gorgeous, stylized LA vistas.

**Hicky and Boggs** (Robert Culp 1972). Down-at-heel detectives Culp and Bill Cosby trail stolen money and a black power group through an LA of deserted public areas: parks, beaches and the Coliseum.

**Hollywood Cowboy** (Howard Zieff 1975). Engaging low-key comedy set in 1930s Hollywood, as naive pulp Western writer Jeff Bridges trades life in Iowa for a stint as an extra in low-budget westerns.

**Hollywood Hotel** (Busby Berkeley 1937). The title says it all – an amiable flick full of guests and music. Songs include "Hooray for Hollywood".

**Hollywood on Trial** (David Helpern Jr 1976). Valuable documentary about the Hollywood Ten, a group of screenwriters and producers persecuted for their possible Communist leanings. Includes footage of the HUAC hearings, plus contemporary interviews.

**Hollywood Shuffle** (Robert Townsend 1987). Townsend wrote, directed and stars in this sharp send-up of racial stereotyping in the movie industry. Very entertaining, despite its minuscule budget and shaky narrative.

**In a Lonely Place** (Nicholas Ray 1950). Curiously compelling psychological melodrama about the ill-fated romance between Gloria Grahame (Ray's soon-to-be ex-wife) and dangerously temperamental screenwriter Humphrey Bogart.

**Inside Daisy Clover** (Robert Mulligan 1965). Natalie Wood as a brassy young Hollywood discovery who refuses to be eaten up by the movie industry.

**Invasion of the Body Snatchers** (Don Siegel 1956). Low-budget sci-fi horror classics don't come much better than this taut, allegorical tale about the takeover of Santa Mira, California by emotionless pod people.

**Joy Luck Club** (Wayne Wang 1993). Amy Tan's best-selling novel faithfully translated to the screen with mixed results. Moving, excellent performances in all roles.

**The Killer Elite** (Sam Peckinpah 1975). Familiar themes of betrayal and trust in this mostly straightforward action flick, built around the internal politics of an underground San Francisco company and a wounded agent (James Caan) who seeks revenge. Excellent set pieces include a Chinatown shoot-out and dockland siege.

**LA Story** (Steve Martin 1991). Martin stars in sentimental, only-in-LA love story, laced with in-jokes and visual homages.

**The Last Tycoon** (Elia Kazan 1976). Harold Pinter's version of F Scott Fitzgerald's unfinished Hollywood novel is all prestige and pedigree, with a star-filled cast but little energy or invention.

**The Long Goodbye** (Robert Altman 1973). Raymond Chandler's private eye Philip Marlowe confronts 1970s me-generation LA in terrific update starring Elliot Gould. Funny and serious, the film superbly evokes the city's sick, sun-drenched, shadowy soul.

**The Loved One** (Tony Richardson 1965). Perverse fun in this three-ring circus adaptation of Evelyn Waugh's satirical novella, inspired by Forest Lawn Memorial Park. Robert Morse and Rod Steiger head a diverse cast.

**The Maltese Falcon** (John Huston 1941). Humphrey Bogart is San Franciscan Sam Spade in this candidate for best detective movie ever made. Diamond-hard and near perfection.

**Monterey Pop** (D A Pennebaker 1969). The first major rock concert movie includes turns by Jimi Hendrix, Otis Redding, Janis Joplin, the Who, Simon and Garfunkel, and many others.

**Murder, My Sweet** (Edward Dymytryk 1944). Former crooner Dick Powell changed his lightweight image to play LA detective Philip Marlowe in the character's first screen appearance. Exudes a splendidly seedy atmosphere.

**The Onion Field** (Harold Becker 1979). Grim crime thriller based on Joseph Wambaugh's best-selling account of a real-life 1963 cop-killing near Bakersfield.

**The Outside Man** (Jacques Deray 1972). Undeservedly little-known crime picture; French hit-man-on-the-run Jean-Louis Trintignant meets LA cocktail waitress Ann-Margret. Good location shooting, and much violence.

**Petulia** (Richard Lester 1968). San Francisco surgeon George C Scott takes up with unhappily married kook Julie Christie in richly detailed, deliberately fragmentary comedy-drama set in a messy, decadent society.

**Play It Again, Sam** (Herbert Ross 1972). Woody Allen as a (what else?) neurotic San Francisco film critic who has an affair with his best friend's wife, Diane Keaton.

**Play It as It Lays** (Frank Perry 1972). Tuesday Weld wanders around in numb anguish in this movie version of Joan Didion's novel that presents Hollywood as a stylized hell.

**Play Misty for Me** (Clint Eastwood 1971). Eastwood's directorial debut, about the consequences of a DJ's affair with a psychotic fan (the topnotch Jessica Walter). Genuinely scary, and much of it shot on big Clint's own two hundred acres of Monterey coastland.

**The Player** (Robert Altman 1992). Tim Robbins is perfect as an egocentric studio executive caught up in a farcical murder cover-up. Altman's usual all-star cast make cameo appearances, mostly as themselves, and the movie is packed with cinematic in-jokes. The perfect screen version of Robert Tolkin's book, a cruelly accurate depiction of Hollywood attitudes and aspirations.

**Point Blank** (John Boorman 1967). Virtuoso brutality around LA and at Alcatraz, as vengeance-seeking hood (the excellently malevolent Lee Marvin) goes after some underworld bosses. One of Hollywood's definitive 1960s art movies.

**Rebel Without a Cause** (Nicholas Ray 1955). The iconographic James Dean in seminal youth flick set in Hollywood High School.

**Remember My Name** (Alan Rudolph 1978). Geraldine Chaplin is the spidery habitual criminal who comes back to avenge herself on remarried ex-husband Anthony Perkins in laidback Southern California.

**Repo Man** (Alex Cox 1984). Clever cult comedy, set in a wonderfully sleazy LA, about a young punk (Emilio Estevez) who accidentally lands a job repossessing cars.

**San Francisco** (W S Van Dyke 1936). Elaborate, entertaining hokum about a Barbary Coast love triangle circa 1906. The script is upstaged by the climactic earthquake sequence.

**The Sandpiper** (Vincente Minnelli 1965). Camp classic of awfulness, as clergyman Richard Burton has an affair with bounteous beatnik Elizabeth Taylor on the beaches of Big Sur.

**Seconds** (John Frankenheimer 1966). Superb sci-fi thriller in which a bored, middle-aged businessman pays a secret organization to give him a new body and identity in bohemian, beachside California.

**Shadow of a Doubt** (Alfred Hitchcock 1943). A sterling comedy-drama from Thornton Wilder's script, set in well-scrubbed Santa Rosa.

**Shampoo** (Hal Ashby 1975). Great cast in a spot-on adult comedy, which sees LA as a big bed on the eve of the 1968 American Presidential Election. Co-writer Warren Beatty has one of his best roles as an inarticulate, confused, priapic Beverly Hills hairdresser.

**Short Cuts** (Robert Altman 1993). Freely adapted from Raymond Carver's short stories, and featuring turns by a gaggle of Hollywood stars, including Tim Robbins, Lily Tomlin, Lyle Lovett and Tom Waits. A dysfunctional and depressing look at the suburban underbelly of contemporary LA.

**Singin' in the Rain** (Stanley Donen/Gene Kelly 1952). Everybody's favourite movie musical is a lovingly made satire of the transition from silents to talkies. Great songs and perceptive gags; the pinnacle of pure pleasure.

**Speed** (Jan De Bont 1994). Keanu Reeves with a brutal haircut is the LA cop/bomb specialist on board a bus set to blow up if it drops below 50mph. In a city whose traffic is bumper-to-bumper, the idea of getting anywhere fast on an LA freeway is pure Hollywood fantasy.

**Stand and Deliver** (Ramon Menendez 1988). Fine ensemble playing lifts this inspirational low-budget drama, based on a true story about a middle-aged computer programmer who quits his high-paying job to teach remedial maths at East LA's notoriously tough Garfield High School.

**A Star is Born** (William Wellman 1937). Janet Gaynor and Fredric March in the first version of inside-Hollywood weepie about a couple: her career goes up while his plunges down. The Judy Garland/James Mason (1954) remake is much better – the later Streisand version definitely isn't.

**The State of Things** (Wim Wenders 1982). Avant-garde European film-maker runs out of money and winds up doing deals in his Hollywood mobile home. Excellent soundtrack, with songs by the band X.

**Sunset Boulevard** (Billy Wilder 1950). Screenwriter William Holden in the clutches of half-mad ex-silent film star Gloria Swanson in this bitter satirical drama. A classic.

**The Terminator** (James Cameron 1984). Terrifically paced action flick starring Arnold Schwarzenegger as roving robot from a gladiatorial LA of the future.

**Terminator 2** (James Cameron 1989). Uneasily reflecting a more caring, sharing 1990s stance, this effects-filled replay has Arnie on the side of the good guys, all paternal and only using his gun to shoot people in the knee caps, rather than to kill.

**Three Women** (Robert Altman 1977). Fascinating, hard-to-categorize film about identity exchange set in and around a geriatric centre in Desert Springs, California. Brilliant, until it gets stuck in its own mysticism. With Shelley Duvall and Sissy Spacek.

**The Times of Harvey Milk** (Robert Epstein 1984). Exemplary feature-length documentary about America's first "out" gay politician chronicles his career in San Francisco and the aftermath of his 1978 assassination.

**To Live and Die in LA** (William Friedkin 1986). Successful flick that's as cynical and brutal about LA crime as "The French Connection" was about New York.

**True Confessions** (Ulu Grosbard 1981). 1940s LA corruption is vividly depicted in this nonetheless muffed and emotionally muffled crime drama linking brothers Robert de Niro (a Monsignor) and Robert Duvall (a cop).

**Vertigo** (Alfred Hitchcock 1958). A tragedy of obsession, stunningly set in San Francisco, in which detective James Stewart tracks down two Kim Novaks.

**Whatever Happened to Baby Jane** (Robert Aldrich 1962). No-holds-barred performance from Bette Davis, co-starring with real-life rival Joan Crawford, as ageing sisters and ex-child stars, living horrifically in a rotting Malibu house.

**What Price Hollywood** (George Cukor 1932). Aspiring actress Constance Bennett, a waitress at the Brown Derby restaurant, is befriended by alcoholic director Lowell Sherman. His career hits the skids as her star rises.

**What's Up Doc?** (Peter Bogdanovich 1972). Some people went bananas over this screwball comedy pastiche, set in San Francisco and starring Barbra Streisand and Ryan O'Neal as a cook and a naive professor.

**Who Framed Roger Rabbit?** (Robert Zemeckis/Richard Williams 1988). Dazzling, groundbreaking, wildly popular fusion of live-action and animation, as private eye Bob Hoskins investigates dirty doings in Toontown, Hollywood's cartoon ghetto, circa 1947.

**The Wild Angels** (Roger Corman 1966). Members of the Venice branch of the Hell's Angels motorcycle gang appear in this seminal exploitation flick starring Peter Fonda.

**The Wild One** (Laslo Benedek 1954). Marlon Brando is the magnetic antihero of this prototypical motorcycle film, based on events in 1947 when 4000 leather-clad bikers terrorized the town of Hollister, California. Not as good as legend would have it, but Brando is ace.

**The Wild Party** (James Ivory 1975). James Coco and Raquel Welch star in drama based on the 1920s sex scandal involving silent screen clown Fatty Arbuckle.

**Zabriskie Point** (Michelangelo Antonioni 1970). Visually gorgeous though thematically pretentious outsider's view of disaffected youth and the American system, shot in LA and Death Valley.

# BOOKS

While California may be mythologized as the ultimate stimulant for the imagination, it has, oddly enough, inspired comparatively few travel books. In contrast, floods of fiction have poured out of the state, in particular Los Angeles, over the last few decades, not only shaping perceptions of the region, but often redefining the whole course of contemporary American writing.

In the following listing, wherever a book is in print, the publisher's name is given in parentheses after the title: the UK publisher first, separated, where applicable, from the US publisher by an oblique slash. Where books are published in only one of these countries, we have specified which one; when the same company publishes the book in both, it appears just once.

## TRAVEL AND IMPRESSIONS

**Tim Cahill** *Jaguars Ripped My Flesh* (UK Fourth Estate). Adventure travel through California and the world, including skin diving with hungry sharks off LA and getting lost and found in Death Valley. Thoughtful and sensitive yet still a thrill a minute.

**Jan Morris** *Destinations* (OUP). Of the essay on LA in this fine collection of essays written for *Rolling Stone* magazine, Joan Didion said, "A lot of people come here and don't get it. She got it."

**Peter Theroux** *Translating LA* (Norton). East Coaster-gone-West Theroux tours some of the more interesting neighbourhoods which make up his new home. Part history, part observation and part anecdote, it digs deeper than some, but ultimately fails to spark.

**Mark Twain** *Roughing It* (Penguin). Vivid tales of frontier California, particularly evocative of life in the silver mines of the 1860s Comstock Lode, where Twain got his start as a journalist and storyteller.

**John Waters** *Crackpot* (Fourth Estate/Random House). Odds and ends from the Pope of Trash, the mind behind cult film *Pink Flamingos*, including a personalized tour of LA.

**Edmund White** *States of Desire* (Picador/NAL-Dutton). Part of a cross-country sojourn that includes a rather superficial account of the gay scene in 1970s LA.

**Tom Wolfe** *The Electric Kool-Aid Acid Test* (Black Swan/Bantam). Take a trip with the Grateful Dead and the Hell's Angels on the magic bus of Ken Kesey and the Merry Pranksters as they travel through the early days of the psychedelic 1960s, on a mission to turn California youth onto LSD.

## HISTORY

**Walton Bean** *California: An Interpretive History* (UK McGraw-Hill). Blow-by-blow account of the history of California, including all the shady deals and back-room politicking, presented in accessible, anecdotal form.

**Daniel Boorstin** *The Americas 2:The National Experience* (US Vintage). Heavy going because of the glut of detail, but otherwise an energetic appraisal of the social forces that shaped the modern US, with several chapters on the settlement of the West.

**Carey McWilliams** *Southern California: An Island on the Land* (US Gibbs Smith). The bible of Southern Californian histories, focusing on the key years between the two world wars. Evocatively written and richly detailed.

**Kevin Starr** *Inventing the Dream* (OUP). One of a series of captivating books — the other two are *Material Dreams* (OUP) and *Americans and the Californian Dream* (US OUP) studying the phenomenon known as California. Cultural histories written with a novelist's flair.

## POLITICAL, SOCIAL AND ETHNIC

**Jean Baudrillard** *America* (Verso/Routledge Chapman & Hall). Scattered thoughts of the trendy French philosopher, whose (very) occasionally brilliant but often overreaching exegesis of American Pop Culture, especially in LA, is undermined by typos and factual inaccuracies.

**Mike Davis** *City of Quartz: Excavating the Future in Los Angeles* (Vintage/Routledge Chapman & Hall). The best modern history of LA bar none, with a wealth of factual and anecdotal info painting a clear picture of a city on the edge of apocalypse.

**Joan Didion** *Slouching Towards Bethlehem* (UK Flamingo). Selected essays from one of California's best journalists, taking a critical look at 1960s California, from the acid culture of San Francisco to a profile of American hero John Wayne. In a similar style, *The White Album* (UK Farrar Straus & Giroux) traces the West Coast characters and events that shaped the Sixties and Seventies, including The Doors, Charlie Manson, and the Black Panthers.

**Frances Fitzgerald** *Cities on a Hill* (US Simon & Schuster). Intelligent and sympathetic exploration of four of the odder corners of American culture, including San Francisco's gay Castro district.

**Lynell George** *No Crystal Stair* (Verso/Doubleday). A perceptive account of life in LA's black community from one of the city's most respected African-American journalists; particularly welcome in the wake of the Rodney King riots.

**Russel Miller** *Barefaced Messiah* (US Holt). An eye-opening study of the rise and rise of L Ron Hubbard and his Scientology cult, who have their world HQ in LA and their devotees lurking everywhere.

**Jay Stevens** *Storming Heaven: LSD and the American Dream* (Grafton/Harper Collins). An engaging account of psychedelic drugs and their relationship with American society through the Sixties, with an epilogue to bring things up to date with "designer drugs" – Venus, Ecstasy, Vitamin K and others – and the inner space they apparently help some modern Californians chart.

**Danny Sugarman** *Wonderland Avenue* (Sphere/Little, Brown). Publicist for The Doors and other seminal US rock bands from the late Sixties on, Sugarman delivers a raunchy autobiographical account of sex, drugs, and LA rock 'n' roll.

## ARCHITECTURE

**Reyner Banham** *Los Angeles: The Architecture of Four Ecologies* (UK Penguin).

The most lucid account of how LA's history has shaped its present form – the author's enthusiasms are infectious.

**Philip Jodidio** *Contemporary Californian Architects* (Taschen). This glossy trilingual (English, French and German) book argues that the public and private buildings of Frank Gehry, Eric Owen Moss, Frank Israel and Michael Routundi, among others, are strongly influenced by the state itself. The gorgeous photographs strengthen the case.

**Sam Hall Kaplan** *LA Lost and Found: An Architectural History of Los Angeles* (US Crown). The text is informative but dull, though the outstanding photos vividly portray the city's growth and the trends in its design.

**Charles Moore** *The City Observed: Los Angeles* (US Random House). The best book to guide you around the diffuse buildings and settings of LA, loaded with maps, illustrations and historical anecdotes.

## HOLLYWOOD/THE MOVIES

**Kenneth Anger** *Hollywood Babylon* (Arrow/Dell). A vicious yet high-spirited romp through Tinseltown's greatest scandals, although the facts are bent rather too often. A rarer second volume covers more recent times, but was hurriedly put together and shoddily researched.

**David Bordwell, Janet Staiger & Kirstin Thompson** *The Classical Hollywood Cinema* (Routledge/Colorado Univ Press). Academic handbook aimed at the serious student but still a generally interesting account of the techniques used in the best-known Hollywood movies up to 1960.

**Bruce Crowther** *Film Noir: Reflections in a Dark Mirror* (Columbus/Burning Deck). A welcome down-to-earth description of the background and realization of the American *film noir* genre.

**Clayton R Koppes & Gregory D Black** *Hollywood Goes to War* (I B Tauris/UC Press). Masterly examination of the influence of World War II on the film industry – and vice versa.

**Michael Munn** *The Hollywood Murder Casebook* (Robson Books/St Martin's Press). The tragic, seamy side of fame and fortune in Tinseltown is revealed in these case studies of murders of actors and actresses.

**Barry Norman** *Talking Pictures: The Story of Hollywood* (UK Arrow). The most accessible mainstream outline of the growth of movies in Hollywood, informative and pleasantly irreverent in tone.

**Julia Phillips** *You'll Never Eat Lunch in This Town Again* (Mandarin/NAL-Dutton). From the woman who became a Hollywood somebody by co-producing *The Sting*; a diary of drug abuse, spouse abuse and film-business bitching.

## SPECIFIC GUIDES

**Bicycle Rider Directory** (US Cycle America). Low-cost guide to do-it-yourself bicycle touring around the Bay Area and Napa and Sonoma valleys, with good fold-out route maps.

**Tom Steinstra and Michael Hodson** *California Hiking: The Complete Guide* (US Foghorn Press). Dense 800-page tome detailing over 1000 hikes, from hour-long strolls to the 1700 Californian miles of the Pacific Crest Trail. Unfortunately, the trail notes and maps are limited, and the text is hardly inspirational.

**Jack Erickson** *Brewery Adventures in the Wild West* (RedBrick Press). A comprehensive list of over 100 beer-bars and breweries.

**Tom Kirkendall & Vicky Spring** *Bicycling the Pacific Coast* (Mountaineers Books). Detailed guide to the bike routes all the way along the coast from Mexico up to Canada.

**National Audobon Society Nature Guides:** *Western Forests*; *Deserts*; *Pacific Coast*; *Wetlands* and others (US Knopf). California has six of the world's seven major ecosystem types, and between them, these immaculately researched and beautifully photographed field guides, though not specific to California, cover the lot. At $20 each, you might want to pick the one most relevant to the area you're visiting.

**National Geographic Society** *A Field Guide to the Birds of North America* (National Geographic). Self-explanatory – and thoroughly useful.

**Peterson Series Field Guides:** *A Field Guide to Western Reptiles and Amphibians*; *A Field Guide to the Insects of America North of Mexico*; *A Field Guide to Pacific State Wildflowers* (Houghton Mifflin). Excellent general field guides to the flora and fauna of California and the West Coast.

**Schaffer** *The Pacific Crest Trail (California)* (Wilderness Press). A guide to the southern

For guidebooks of specific relevance to **travellers with disabilities**, see p.48 in *Basics*.

section of the trail that leads all the way from Mexico to Canada through the Sierra Nevada range.

**David & Kay Scott** *Traveling and Camping in the National Park Areas: the Western States* (Globe Pequot). How to get around and camp in the West's national parks, including Yosemite, Kings Canyon, etc.

**Walking the West Series:** *Walking Southern California*; *Walking the California Coast*; *Walking California's State Parks* and others (Harper San Francisco). Well written and produced paperbacks each covering over a hundred excellent day walks from two to twenty miles. They're strong on practical details (maps, route decriptions etc) and walking ethics, and boast inspiring prose and historical background. Recommended.

## CALIFORNIA IN FICTION

**James P Blaylock** *Land of Dreams* (US Morrow). A fantastic tale spun out as the twelve-year Solstice comes to a Northern Californian coastal town.

**Ray Bradbury** *The Martian Chronicles* (Flamingo/Bantam). Brilliant, lyrical study of colonization, of new worlds and new lands – it's very easy to read the Martian setting as a Californian one. Bradbury's first, and still best, book.

**Scott Bradfield** *What's Wrong With America* (Picador/St Martin's Press). Humour and idiosyncratic absurdity combine as Bradfield explores America's malaise through an elderly woman's slide towards mental breakdown. Southern California provides the backdrop and its people the caricatured bit players.

**Charles Bukowski** *Post Office*; *Women* (both Virgin/Black Sparrow). Three hundred-hangovers-a-year Henry Chinaski (the author, thinly veiled) drinks and screws his way around downbeat LA, firstly as a misfit mailman, then as a moderately successful writer with his own tab at the local liquor store and an endless supply of willing female fans. Savage and quite unique. See also *Factotum* (Virgin/Black Sparrow), which recounts Chinaski's early days.

**James M Cain** *The Five Great Novels of James M Cain* (UK Pan); *Double Indemnity; The Postman Always Rings Twice; The Butterfly; Mildred Pierce; Love's Lovely Counterfeit* (US all Vintage). Haunting stories of smouldering passion told with clipped prose and terse dialogue.

**Raymond Carver** *What We Talk About When We Talk About Love* (US Random House); *Where I'm Calling From: New and Selected Stories* (Harvill/Random House). Set mostly in the Northwest and Northern California, Carver's deceptively simple eye-level pictures of plain-dealing Americans, concise and sharply observed, are difficult to forget.

**Raymond Chandler** *Three Novels* (Penguin/ Random House); *The Raymond Chandler Omnibus* (US Random House). Essential reading, some of the toughest and greatest LA crime fiction of the Thirties and Forties — including *The Big Sleep, The Lady in the Lake,* and *Farewell My Lovely,* to name only the best.

**Susan Compo** *Life After Death and Other Stories* (Faber). Strange and zany romp through the clubs, clothes and characters of LA's goth scene; completely original in style and scope, and very believable.

**Philip K Dick** *A Scanner Darkly* (Panther/ Random House). Of all Dick's erratic but frequently brilliant books, this is the best evocation of California. Set in the mid-1990s, when society is split between the Straights, the Dopers and the Narks, it's a dizzying study of individual identity, authority and drugs. Among the pick of the rest of Dick's vast legacy is *Blade Runner/Do Androids Dream of Electric Sheep?* (Panther/Ballantine), set (unlike the movie) in San Francisco.

**Joan Didion** *Run, River* (US Random House. Focuses on the Sacramento Valley of the author's childhood and follows its change from agriculture into a highly charged consumer society. In contrast, but just as successfully done, *Play It As It Lays* (Flamingo/Farrar Straus & Giroux) is an electrifying dash through the pills, booze, and self-destruction linked with the LA film world.

**Bret Easton Ellis** *Less Than Zero* (Picador/ Penguin). Numbing but readable tale of wealthy LA teen life. A classic brat-pack tome, with influence and fame far in excess of its worth.

**James Ellroy** *White Jazz* (Arrow/Fawcett). The final instalment of Ellroy's quartet of LA books exploring, in nail-biting noir style, the mind-set of corrupt LA cops and psychotic criminals over three decades. The series began with *The Black Dahlia* and continued with *The Big Nowhere* and *LA Confidential* (all Arrow/Warner).

**Robert Ferringo** *The Horse Latitudes* (US Avon). Drug-dealer turned lecturer on Mayan civilization returns to his Newport Beach house after a midnight swim to find his wife has run off — leaving behind a corpse.

**David Freeman** *A Hollywood Education* (Sceptre/Carroll & Graf). Cumulatively powerful collection of short stories concerning a writer's lot in Hollywood.

**Ursula le Guin** *Always Coming Home* (UK Harper Collins). Impressive "archeology of the future," describing the lifestyles and culture of a mysterious race living in Northern California many years from now.

**Dashiell Hammett** *The Four Great Novels* (UK Picador); *The Maltese Falcon* (US Random House). The former is a volume of seminal detective novels starring Sam Spade, the private investigator working out of San Francisco; the latter is probably Hammett's best-known work. See also the absorbing biography of Hammett: Diane Johnson's *Dashiell Hammett: A Life* (Picador/Fawcett).

**Joseph Hansen** *The Dave Brandsetter Omnibus* (UK No Exit Press); *Death Claims* (US Holt); *Gravedigger* (Peter Owen/Holt); *Skinflick* (US Holt); *Troublemaker* (US Holt ). Entertaining tales of Dave Brandstetter, a gay insurance claims investigator, set against a vivid Southern California backdrop.

**Aldous Huxley** *Ape and Essence* (Flamingo/I R Dee); *After Many a Summer Dies the Swan* (Panther/I R Dee). Huxley spent his last twenty years earning a crust as a Hollywood screenwriter, and both these novels are a product of that time. The first chronicles moral degeneracy and Satanic rituals in post-apocalyptic Southern California; the latter, based on William Randolph Hearst, concerns a rich, pampered figure who surrounds himself with art treasures and dwells on the meaning of life.

**Jack Kerouac** *Desolation Angels* (Paladin/ Riverhead Books); *The Dharma Bums* (Paladin/ Penguin).The most influential of the Beat writers on the rampage in California. See also his first novel *On The Road* (Penguin), which has a little of San Francisco and a lot of the rest of the US.

**David Lodge** *Changing Places* (Penguin). Thinly disguised autobiographical tale of an English academic who spends a year teaching at UC Berkeley and finds himself bang in the middle of the late 1960s student upheaval.

**Jack London** *The Call of the Wild* (UK Penguin); *White Fang and Other Stories* (UK Penguin); *Martin Eden* (Penguin); *The Iron Heel* (Wordsworth Editions/Star Rover). *The Call of the Wild*, a short story about a tame dog discovering the ways of the wilderness while forced to labour pulling sleds across the snow and ice of Alaska's Klondike, made London into the world's best-selling author almost overnight. Afterwards, frustrated by the emptiness of his easy fame and success, the young, self-taught author wrote the semi-autobiographical *Martin Eden*, in which he rails against the cultured veil of polite society. Besides his prolific fiction, London also wrote a number of somewhat sophomoric political essays and socialist tracts; the most effective was *The Iron Heel*, presaging the rise of Fascism.

**Ross MacDonald** *Black Money* (Allison & Busby/Random House); *The Blue Hammer* (Allison & Busby/Amereon); *The Zebra-Striped Hearse* ( Allison & Busby/Knopf); *The Doomsters*; *The Instant Enemy* (both US Knopf). Following in the footsteps of Sam Spade and Philip Marlowe, private detective Lew Archer looks behind the glitzy masks of Southern California life to reveal the underlying nastiness of creepy sexuality and manipulation. All captivating reads.

**Armistead Maupin** *Tales of the City; Further Tales of the City* (both Black Swan/Harper Collins); *More Tales of the City* (Corgi/Harper Collins). Lively and witty soap operas detailing the sexual antics of a select group of archetypal San Francisco characters of the late 1970s/early 1980s. See also *Babycakes* (Corgi/Harper Collins) and *Significant Others*, which continue the story, though in more depth, and *Sure of You* (last two Black Swan/Harper Collins) – set several years later and more downbeat, though no less brilliant.

**Brian Moore** *The Great Victorian Collection* (UK Grafton). A professor dreams up a parking lot full of Victoriana, which becomes the biggest tourist attraction of Carmel, California.

**Walter Mosely** *Devil in a Blue Dress* (Pan/Pocket Books). The book that introduced Easy Rawlins, a black private detective in late-1940s South Central LA, the central character in an excellent portrayal of time and place. Easy gets further into his stride in the subsequent *A Red Death* and *White Butterfly* (both Pan/Pocket Books).

**Thomas Pynchon** *The Crying of Lot 49* (Vintage/Harper Collins). Follows the hilarious adventures of techno-freaks and potheads of 1960s California, and reveals the sexy side of stamp-collecting.

**Richard Rayner** *Los Angeles without a Map* (UK Paladin). An English non-driving journalist goes to LA on a romantic whim and lives out movie fantasies made even more fantastic by the city itself.

**Danny Santiago** *Famous All over Town* (US NAL-Dutton). Coming-of-age novel set among the street gangs of East LA, giving a vivid depiction of life in the Hispanic community.

**Vikram Seth** *The Golden Gate* (Faber/Random House). A novel in verse which traces the complex social lives of a group of San Francisco yuppies.

**Mona Simpson** *Anywhere But Here* (Abacus/Random House). Bizarre and unforgettable saga of a young girl and her ambitious mother as they pursue LA stardom for the daughter.

**John Steinbeck** *The Grapes of Wrath* (Mandarin/Penguin). The classic account of a migrant family forsaking the Midwest for the Promised Land. For more localized fare, read the light-hearted but crisply observed novella, *Cannery Row*, capturing daily life on the prewar Monterey waterfront, or the epic *East of Eden* (both Mandarin/Penguin) which updates and resets the Bible in the Salinas Valley and details three generations of familial feuding.

**Michael Tolkin** *The Player* (Faber/Random House). Convincing, multilayered story of a movie executive using his power and contacts to skirt justice after committing murder.

**Nathanael West** *Complete Works* (UK Picador). Includes *The Day of the Locust*, an insightful and caustic tale that is *the* classic satire of early Hollywood.

**Rudolph Wurlitzer** *Quake* (Midnight Classics). Long out of print, this recently republished 1972 cult novel follows its nihilistic narrator's passage through LA's western suburbs on the day the Big One struck. A product of its time, more intriguing than it is entertaining.

# USEFUL MEXICAN-SPANISH TERMS FOR CALIFORNIA

California is bound to its Spanish colonial and Mexican past; a fact manifest in the profusion of Spanish place names, particularly in the south of the state. Today large numbers of people living in California speak Spanish as their first language, and though you will seldom find yourself in need of speaking the lingo, it can be useful to know a few terms. Note that the double-L is pronounced like a "Y" and an "Ñ" sounds like an N and a Y run together.

| | | | |
|---|---|---|---|
| **ABIERTO** | open | **MAR** | sea |
| **AGUA** | water | **MESA** | high plateau, |
| **ALTA, ALTO** | high | | literally 'table' |
| **ANGELES** | angels | **MONTE** | mount(ain) |
| **ARROYO** | canyon or gully | **NEVADA** | snowy |
| **AVENIDA** | avenue | **NORTE** | north |
| **BUENA, BUENO** | good | **OBISPO** | bishop |
| **CALIENTE** | hot | **ORO** | gold |
| **CALLE** | street, pronounced | **PARQUE** | park |
| | "ka-ye" | **PESCADERO** | fisherman |
| **CERRADO** | closed | **PLAYA** | beach |
| **COSTA** | coast | **REY** | king |
| **CRUZ** | cross | **RIO** | river |
| **DE** | of | **SAN, SANTA, SANTO** | saint |
| **DEL** | of the | **SIERRA** | mountain range |
| **DORADO** | golden | **SOL** | sun |
| **EL** | the | **SUR** | south |
| **ESCONDIDO** | hidden | **TAQUERIA** | taco stall or shop |
| **GRANDE** | big | **TIENDA** | shop |
| **HERMOSA** | beautiful | **TIERRA** | land |
| **JOLLA** | jewel, pronounced 'hoya' | **TRES** | three |
| **LAS, LOS** | the (plural) | **VERDE** | green |

For the basics, the most useful Language book on the market is *Mexican Spanish: A Rough Guide Phrasebook* (Rough Guides); £3.50/$5, which covers the essential phrases and expressions, as well as dipping into grammar and providing a fuller vocabulary in dictionary format.

# INDEX

### HELP US UPDATE

We've gone to a lot of effort to ensure that this edition of *The Rough Guide to California* is accurate and up-to-date. However, things do change – places get "discovered," opening hours are notoriously fickle, restaurants and rooms raise prices or lower standards. If you feel we've got it wrong or left something out, we'd like to know, and if you can remember the address, the price, the time, the phone number, so much the better.

We'll credit all contributions, and send a copy of the next edition (or any other Rough Guide if you prefer) for the best letters. Please mark all letters "Rough Guide California Update" and send to:

Rough Guides, 1 Mercer Street, London WC2H 9QJ or,
Rough Guides, 375 Hudson Street, 9th Floor, New York NY10014

# DIRECT ORDERS IN THE UK

| Title | ISBN | Price |
|---|---|---|
| Amsterdam | 1858280869 | £7.99 |
| Andalucia | 185828094X | £8.99 |
| Australia | 1858281415 | £12.99 |
| Bali | 1858281342 | £8.99 |
| Barcelona & Catalunya | 1858281067 | £8.99 |
| Berlin | 1858281296 | £8.99 |
| Big Island of Hawaii | 185828158X | £8.99 |
| Brazil | 1858281024 | £9.99 |
| Brittany & Normandy | 1858281261 | £8.99 |
| Bulgaria | 1858280478 | £8.99 |
| California | 1858280907 | £9.99 |
| Canada | 185828130X | £10.99 |
| Classical Music on CD | 185828113X | £12.99 |
| Corsica | 1858280893 | £8.99 |
| Costa Rica | 1858281369 | £9.99 |
| Crete | 1858281326 | £8.99 |
| Cyprus | 185828032X | £8.99 |
| Czech & Slovak Republics | 1858281210 | £9.99 |
| Egypt | 1858280753 | £10.99 |
| England | 1858281601 | £10.99 |
| Europe | 1858281598 | £14.99 |
| Florida | 1858280109 | £8.99 |
| France | 1858281245 | £10.99 |
| Germany | 1858281288 | £11.99 |
| Goa | 1858281563 | £8.99 |
| Greece | 1858281318 | £9.99 |
| Greek Islands | 1858281636 | £8.99 |
| Guatemala & Belize | 1858280451 | £9.99 |
| Holland, Belgium & Luxembourg | 1858280877 | £9.99 |
| Hong Kong & Macau | 1858280664 | £8.99 |
| Hungary | 1858281237 | £8.99 |
| India | 1858281040 | £13.99 |
| Ireland | 1858280958 | £9.99 |
| Italy | 1858280311 | £12.99 |
| Jazz | 1858281377 | £16.99 |
| Kenya | 1858280435 | £9.99 |
| London | 1858291172 | £8.99 |
| Malaysia, Singapore & Brunei | 1858281032 | £9.99 |
| Mexico | 1858280443 | £10.99 |
| Morocco | 1858280400 | £9.99 |
| Moscow | 185828118 0 | £8.99 |
| Nepal | 185828046X | £8.99 |
| New York | 1858280583 | £8.99 |
| Nothing Ventured | 0747102082 | £7.99 |
| Pacific Northwest | 1858280923 | £9.99 |
| Paris | 1858281253 | £7.99 |
| Poland | 1858280346 | £9.99 |
| Portugal | 1858280842 | £9.99 |
| Prague | 185828015X | £7.99 |
| Provence & the Côte d'Azur | 1858280230 | £8.99 |
| Pyrenees | 1858280931 | £8.99 |
| Romania | 1858280974 | £9.99 |
| St Petersburg | 1858281334 | £8.99 |
| San Francisco | 1858280826 | £8.99 |
| Scandinavia | 1858280397 | £10.99 |
| Scotland | 1858281660 | £9.99 |
| Sicily | 1858281784 | £9.99 |
| Singapore | 1858281350 | £8.99 |
| Spain | 1858280818 | £9.99 |
| Thailand | 1858281407 | £10.99 |
| Tunisia | 1858280656 | £8.99 |
| Turkey | 1858280885 | £9.99 |
| Tuscany & Umbria | 1858280915 | £8.99 |
| USA | 185828161X | £14.99 |
| Venice | 1858281709 | £8.99 |
| Wales | 1858280966 | £8.99 |
| West Africa | 1858280141 | £12.99 |
| More Women Travel | 1858280982 | £9.99 |
| World Music | 1858280176 | £14.99 |
| Zimbabwe & Botswana | 1858280419 | £10.99 |

## Rough Guide Phrasebooks

| | | |
|---|---|---|
| Czech | 1858281482 | £3.50 |
| French | 185828144X | £3.50 |
| German | 1858281466 | £3.50 |
| Greek | 1858281458 | £3.50 |
| Italian | 1858281431 | £3.50 |
| Spanish | 1858281474 | £3.50 |

Rough Guides can be obtained directly in the UK* from Penguin by contacting: Penguin Direct, Penguin Books Ltd, Bath Road, Harmondsworth, West Drayton, Middlesex UB7 0DA; or telephone our credit line on 0181-899 4036 (9am–5pm) and ask for Penguin Direct. Visa, Access and Amex accepted. Delivery will normally be within 14 working days. Penguin Direct ordering facilities are only available in the UK.

The availability and published prices quoted are correct at the time of going to press but are subject to alteration without prior notice.

# DIRECT ORDERS IN THE USA

| Title | ISBN | Price |
|---|---|---|
| Amsterdam | 1858280869 | $13.59 |
| Andalucia | 185828094X | $14.95 |
| Australia | 1858281415 | $19.95 |
| Barcelona & Catalunya | 1858281067 | $17.99 |
| Bali | 1858281342 | $14.95 |
| Berlin | 1858281296 | $14.95 |
| Big Island of Hawaii | 185828158X | $12.95 |
| Brazil | 1858281024 | $15.95 |
| Brittany & Normandy | 1858281261 | $14.95 |
| Bulgaria | 1858280478 | $14.99 |
| California | 1858280907 | $14.95 |
| Canada | 185828130X | $14.95 |
| Classical Music on CD | 185828113X | $19.95 |
| Corsica | 1858280893 | $14.95 |
| Costa Rica | 1858281369 | $15.95 |
| Crete | 1858281326 | $14.95 |
| Cyprus | 185828032X | $13.99 |
| Czech & Slovak Republics | 1858281210 | $16.95 |
| Egypt | 1858280753 | $17.95 |
| England | 1858281601 | $17.95 |
| Europe | 1858281598 | $19.95 |
| First Time Europe | 1858282101 | $9.95 |
| Florida | 1858280109 | $14.95 |
| France | 1858281245 | $16.95 |
| Germany | 1858281288 | $17.95 |
| Goa | 1858281563 | $14.95 |
| Greece | 1858281318 | $16.95 |
| Greek Islands | 1858281636 | $14.95 |
| Guatemala & Belize | 1858280451 | $14.95 |
| Holland, Belgium & Luxembourg | 1858280877 | $15.95 |
| Hong Kong & Macau | 1858280664 | $13.95 |
| Hungary | 1858281237 | $14.95 |
| India | 1858281040 | $22.95 |
| Ireland | 1858280958 | $16.95 |
| Italy | 1858280311 | $17.95 |
| Jazz | 1858281377 | $24.95 |
| Kenya | 1858280435 | $15.95 |
| London | 1858291172 | $12.95 |
| Malaysia, Singapore & Brunei | 1858281032 | $16.95 |
| Mexico | 1858280443 | $16.95 |
| Morocco | 1858280400 | $16.95 |
| Moscow | 1858281180 | $14.95 |
| Nepal | 185828046X | $13.95 |
| New York | 1858280583 | $13.95 |
| Nothing Ventured | 0747102082 | $19.95 |
| Pacific Northwest | 1858280923 | $14.95 |
| Paris | 1858281253 | $12.95 |
| Poland | 1858280346 | $16.95 |
| Portugal | 1858280842 | $15.95 |
| Prague | 1858281229 | $14.95 |
| Provence & the Côte d'Azur | 1858280230 | $14.95 |
| Pyrenees | 1858280931 | $15.95 |
| Romania | 1858280974 | $15.95 |
| St Petersburg | 1858281334 | $14.95 |
| San Francisco | 1858280826 | $13.95 |
| Scandinavia | 1858280397 | $16.99 |
| Scotland | 1858281660 | $16.95 |
| Sicily | 1858281784 | $16.95 |
| Singapore | 1858281350 | $14.95 |
| Spain | 1858280818 | $16.95 |
| Thailand | 1858281407 | $17.95 |
| Tunisia | 1858280656 | $15.95 |
| Turkey | 1858280885 | $16.95 |
| Tuscany & Umbria | 1858280915 | $15.95 |
| USA | 185828161X | $19.95 |
| Venice | 1858281709 | $14.95 |
| Wales | 1858280966 | $14.95 |
| West Africa | 1858280141 | $24.95 |
| More Women Travel | 1858280982 | $14.95 |
| World Music | 1858280176 | $19.95 |
| Zimbabwe & Botswana | 1858280419 | $16.95 |

## Rough Guide Phrasebooks

| | | |
|---|---|---|
| Czech | 1858281482 | $5.00 |
| French | 185828144X | $5.00 |
| German | 1858281466 | $5.00 |
| Greek | 1858281458 | $5.00 |
| Italian | 1858281431 | $5.00 |
| Spanish | 1858281474 | $5.00 |

In the USA charge your order by Master Card or Visa ($15.00 minimum order): call 1-800-253-6476;
or send orders, with name, address and zip code, plus list price, plus $2.00 shipping and handling pe
order to: Consumer Sales, Penguin USA, PO Box 999 – Dept #17109, Bergenfield, NJ 07621. No
COD. Prepay foreign orders by international money order, a cheque drawn
on a US bank, or US currency. No postage stamps are accepted. All orders
are subject to stock availability at the time they are processed. Refunds will
be made for books not available at that time. Please allow a minimum of
four weeks for delivery.

The availability and published prices quoted are correct at the time
of going to press but are subject to alteration without prior notice.

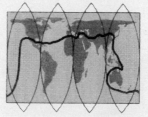

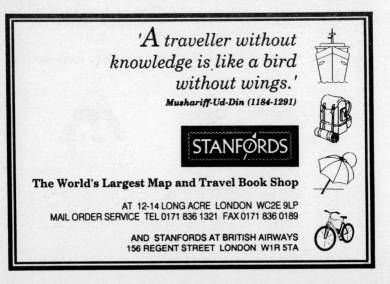